THE MAKING
OF MODERN MAN

THE MAKING OF MODERN MAN

From the Renaissance to the Present

BY LOUIS L. SNYDER

THE CITY COLLEGE OF THE CITY UNIVERSITY OF NEW YORK

D. VAN NOSTRAND COMPANY, INC.

PRINCETON, NEW JERSEY

TORONTO   LONDON   MELBOURNE

VAN NOSTRAND REGIONAL OFFICES: *New York, Chicago, San Francisco*

D. VAN NOSTRAND COMPANY, LTD., *London*

D. VAN NOSTRAND COMPANY, (Canada), LTD., *Toronto*

D. VAN NOSTRAND AUSTRALIA PTY. LTD., *Melbourne*

First Printing, March 1967
Second Printing, August 1967
Third Printing, November 1968

PRINTED IN THE UNITED STATES OF AMERICA

To

IDA MAE SNYDER

My lifelong companion

Preface

This book seeks to find a balance between the presentation and interpretation of facts. This, of course, should be the aim of all textbooks in history. However, there is always the danger that the student may accept the author's interpretation merely because it appears in print, as a kind of unchallenged voice—"This must be true because it is in the book." There is the further danger that, in later study, the student may compound a particular author's prejudices and biases. Yet, there are varying interpretations of almost every major movement in modern times. It is for this reason that, as a mark of respect for the student and for historical scholarship, almost every chapter of this book has a subsection on "Historical Controversy." These are necessarily brief, but they at least alert the student to widely differing opinions. They can also serve as departure points for more intensive discussion of opposing points of view. Students are urged to devote further attention to the dynamics of controversy itself, although they should be aware that historical differences are seldom resolved.

During the past decade there has been a growing trend toward the use of documents in the study of history. Ideally, a book of this kind might well be composed of half narrative text and half illustrative documents but, because of space limitation, this is impossible here. The one key document included near the end of each chapter is designed to supplement and lend additional clarification to the material treated in the text.

At the close of each chapter is a brief treatment of the subject matter by an outstanding historian in the field. From these excerpts the student can obtain a taste of historiography which might well arouse his interest in further reading among the great historians. Some of these selections present a traditional point of view, others are highly controversial. Introductory notes place these interpretations in historical context.

At the end of each of the forty-three chapters is a list of Ten Basic Books on the subject treated in the chapter. These lists will be of value to those who wish to do further reading in the field and, in effect, they represent a selected bibliography presented in a manner intended to make the references readily accessible to the student. The books selected are basic in the sense that they represent, in the author's estimation, indispensable writing.

There is always the possibility that a special view of influences, interactions, and developments in history may place too much emphasis upon one monistic factor within a multiplicity of trends, such as was the case with political motivations in the nineteenth century and economic motivations in the twentieth century. An attempt to find a balance has been made in the consideration of economic, political, social, cultural, religious, and psychological factors affecting the course of history. Because there is little doubt that the historiography of the next fifty years will be increasingly concerned with psychological motivations, more than passing attention should be given to these factors. A presidential address delivered before the annual meeting of the American Historical

Association in 1957 by the Harvard historian William L. Langer stressed just this theme; and such far-sighted historians as David Donald and others have contributed much light to this approach. Thus far, the results of scholarly efforts in this direction have been probing but tentative. For that reason the presentation of psychological motives in this book is on a relatively small scale.

The illustrations have been taken as far as possible from contemporary sources and are designed as an integral part of the text. Union of text and pictures is stressed in the captions. The selection and design of the maps for this volume are based upon the particular focus of the text they accompany; it is intended that they should complement as well as lend clarity and emphasis to the subjects under discussion.

It is with pleasure that I express my warmest thanks to Richard M. Brace, series editor, for his expert, efficient, and conscientious assistance in the production of this book. I am also indebted to Professor Wilbur Gaffney, of the University of Nebraska, for the many hours he devoted to the manuscript.

I am most grateful to my wife, Ida Mae Snyder, who, increasingly over the years, has become not only my treasured collaborator but more precisely co-author in every sense of the word. In long and laborious sessions she has proven to be the ideal research scholar who has rescued this volume from slips, omissions, inaccuracies, and its one-time oversupply of clichés.

L. L. S.

Contents

List of Maps

THE MAKING
OF MODERN MAN

Introduction

THE PAST is intelligible to us only in the light of the present; and we can fully understand the present only in the light of the past. To enable man to understand the society of the past and to increase his mastery over the society of the present is the dual function of history.

—EDWARD HALLETT CARR

1. The Meaning of History

What Is History? History, said Jakob Burckhardt, is "the record of what one age finds worthy of note in another." It is the story of the development of man. The historical picture is one preselected and predetermined by men who, consciously or unconsciously, hold special views and preserve the facts which help to preserve those views. It is fair to say that the history we read, although certainly based on facts, is in reality not factual at all, but a series of accepted judgments. We must select from the vast wealth of material those developments which have significance beyond the mere fact that they occurred.

The Search for Meaning. From the time of primitive man to the present, one of the dominant urges of the human being has been a need to comprehend the riddle of the universe, to know the significance of man's existence, and to learn the meaning of his aspirations. Man seeks for a purpose in events. At no time since the ancient Greek historian Herodotus has he relaxed his efforts to understand the nature and significance of his history and to establish satisfactory principles and methods for the study of his past. Yet the power of synthesis of the human mind is not sufficiently well developed to give a definitive answer to the enigmas of history. The real problem is too immense to allow perfect understanding. There is little proof that the meaning of the universe must be revealed through human history. Historians often are bemused by a teleological approach, that is, that history is directed toward an end or shaped to a purpose. The course of history has too often been accidental, highly casual, complex, and seemingly confused.

The study of history has long occupied the attention of scholars. Herodotus and Thucydides of Greece, writing in the fifth century B.C., and the Roman Livy (59 B.C.–A.D. 17) gave it an early stimulus. History, as a branch of knowledge, made its greatest progress after eighteenth-century rationalism had aroused an interest in the natural and social sciences. In the nineteenth century, questions of definition, interpretation, philosophy, purpose, methods, and instruments were raised.

Interpretation of History. Scholars have seen history in varied lights. Many interpretations have been made; each has its virtues and its faults. All philosophies of history are open to challenge. They may be divided into three groups: first, the theological interpretation, which explains the course of history by the intelligence and will of a Divine Being, who created the earth and man, and who always directs humanity onward and upward; secondly, the humanistic concept, which looks upon history as motivated by the thinking and actions of man himself; and thirdly, the naturalistic–materialistic interpretation, which regards history as determined not by God or by man but by what are called decisive environmental factors. All three interpretations are based upon the assumption that history is governed by a law, but no final proof has yet been given that such a law of history exists.

The theological interpretation was set by

the early Christian philosopher St. Augustine (354–430) in his *The City of God,* to which theologians to this day turn as a guide. St. Augustine conceived of two kingdoms, one divine and the other earthly, the first for believers and the second for the lost souls of heretics and unbelievers. The humanistic interpretation, which regards history as the work of man, is best exemplified by the works of the German philosopher Georg Wilhelm Friedrich Hegel (1770–1831). According to Hegel, the "perpetual law of thought" is a doctrine of thesis, antithesis, and synthesis—the belief that progress comes through the clash of an idea (thesis) and its opposite (antithesis); the resulting idea (synthesis) in turn becomes a new thesis. Karl Marx (1818–1883) saw history as determined basically by economic factors. According to Marx, history in all its phases has been influenced by economic conditions. Whatever changes take place in the development of institutions, he said, are due chiefly to changes in the methods of producing and exchanging goods.

There are many variations of these themes. In his voluminous work *The Decline of the West,* Oswald Spengler (1880–1936) repudiated the theory of progress and revived older notions of cyclical change. All civilizations, he said, have a limited amount of vital energy and all pass through the four stages of spring, summer, fall, and winter; they are destined by their nature to go into old age and death and eventually perish. Each civilization came to separate life, independent of any other, achieved its climax, declined, fell, and died in a cycle identical with those of other civilizations. Arnold Toynbee (1889–   ), in *A Study of History,* attributed the growth of civilization primarily to a condition of "challenge and response," and the decline of civilization to such factors as militarism, war, barbarization from within, and the rise of an "internal proletariat."

These and other philosophers of history conceived of uniform patterns at work. They have aroused interest and wonder. But none has given us the definitive meaning of history.

Why Study History? What is the purpose of the study of history? First, it enables us to see our own time in perspective. We learn from the pages of history how the people who preceded us on this planet faced all sorts of crises and how they successfully surmounted such crises. We learn that peoples in all the periods of history feared the "end of the world" and "the end of civilization." History teaches us how to understand social change, the evolution of institutions and ideas, the shaping of varied societies. It shows us how to judge situations and how to act in accordance with our judgment. By examining issues and problems critically, by verifying facts, by checking sources, we can obtain clues on how to act and live in our own day. A knowledge of what has happened in the past may well give us at least an inkling as to what is likely to occur in the future. In history we have an indispensable key to an understanding of the past as well as an appreciation of those magnificent works of man's mind which form a precious legacy.

The Time Element. It is traditional to divide the study of history into Ancient History (5000 B.C. to A.D. 500), Medieval History (A.D. 500 to 1500), and Modern History (A.D. 1500 to the present). Strictly speaking, there is no such thing as "modern" history, any more than there is "ancient" or "medieval" history. The most important characteristic of historical development is its continuous nature; the past merges almost imperceptibly into the present, and the present into the future. Any historical epoch or period nearly always retains elements of past eras, and contains within itself the roots of future ages. In history there are no abrupt dividing lines—no catastrophic ends and no completely new beginnings.

Yet it would be impossible to make sense of so complex a development as the history of European civilization, unless some arbitrary lines of division were adopted. Because the period from about A.D. 1500 onward is marked by certain characteristic factors, it is generally called Modern History.

Concepts differ as to when the medieval period ended and modern times began. Some historians begin modern times with the fall of Constantinople in 1453, some with the discovery of America by Columbus in 1492, or with the subsequent era of European expansion.

Others accept the date 1520, when the attention of Western Europe was concentrated upon the quarrel between Luther and the papacy. Still others select 1789, the date of the outbreak of the French Revolution, in which feudalism received its death blow, and Church–State relations were severed. Some recent historians begin the modern period as early as the thirteenth century, when the papacy began to lose prestige and power, when town life was revived, royal power was strengthened, and national states were being formed. These differences are unimportant. Because there can be no scientifically verifiable division points in history, we use dividing lines merely as a convenience.

Theme of This Volume. The final key to the riddle of history cannot be found in a monistic or single interpretation, or in any one of the auxiliary fields of history—geography, philology, diplomacy, paleography, archaeology, ethnology, and anthropology. The historian looks at the broad, complex pattern with the field glass of his special interest, but in doing so he is apt to miss fundamental factors that do not always come under that localized scrutiny. Moreover, it is not always possible to weigh with accuracy all the elements of historical development and to give to each element its true value. Within limits, however, one can study certain factors that seem basic. In this volume, economic developments will be emphasized. This direction by no means presupposes that political, social, cultural, psychological, and religious factors are negligible. The interpretation here will stress the environment of modern man as crucial, but the narrative will not be limited by this one factor. The aim is to find a medium between economic factors, political narrative, institutional forms, and cultural developments.

2. The Course of Ancient History

The Ancient Near Orient. Man learned to control nature in the two cradlelands of Western civilization—the fertile river-valleys of the Nile and the Tigris-Euphrates. There he learned to use metals while the greater part of Europe remained in the Stone Age.

There he built his first cities, constructed his first houses of worship, and set up his first advanced social order.

Bounded on the north by the Mediterranean and on the south by natural barriers, Egypt lay between two deserts. "Egypt," said Herodotus, "is the gift of the Nile." Rising in equatorial Africa, the Nile River overflowed its banks once a year, bringing down from the vegetation of the tropics sufficient alluvial soil to open the region for farming. Near the end of the Predynastic period (*c.* 4000–3200 B.C.) two kingdoms emerged: Lower Egypt, including Memphis and the Nile Delta, and Upper Egypt, extending as far as Aswan. The two kingdoms were joined about 3200 B.C. and a single capital city was established. The first six dynasties ruled during the Old Kingdom (2780–2280 B.C.). Political disintegration came under the Middle Kingdom (2133–1786 B.C.) when local governors paid only nominal tribute to the royal house. The New Kingdom (1574–1085 B.C.) saw a reunification of the country. Then followed an era of decadence which led to Persian rule (525 B.C.) and two centuries later to conquest by the Greeks under Alexander the Great.

The Egyptians left a great heritage to Western civilization. They initiated not only organized government but also agricultural progress (irrigation, diversity of crops), the oldest form of writing (hieroglyphics), and the solar calendar. They gave us our earliest systems of jurisprudence and political theory. They were the first to mold a national religion.

The second cradleland of Western civilization, Mesopotamia, lay in the southern portion of the Fertile Crescent between the rivers Tigris and Euphrates. A series of independent states appeared. With no natural defenses (such as those of Egypt), Mesopotamia was invaded time and time again. There were no homogeneous civilizations in this area. The early Sumerians contributed advances in mathematics, surveying, astronomy, the lunar calendar, and cuneiform (wedge-shaped) writing. Conquering the Sumerians in 1800 B.C., the early Babylonians gave the world the sexagesimal system, the arch, and methods of trading and banking. Hammurabi, who united all Mesopotamia under his rule in 1760 B.C., contributed his famous Code, which marked the transition from tribal to king's law.

Successive peoples invaded the Mesopotamian area, established their own societies, and made their own gifts to Western civilization. Among these were the Kassites (*c.* 1600 B.C.), who introduced the use of the horse; the Assyrians (722–612 B.C.), who devoted their attention to empire-building; the Chaldeans (612–539 B.C.), who laid the foundations for modern astronomy; and the Persians (559–330 B.C.), who set up a great military empire and originated the idea of conflict between Good and Evil (dualism).

While not equal to that of Egypt, the Mesopotamian legacy was not less significant. The Mesopotamians gave us the seven-day week, the 360-degree circle, arithmetical processes, and the signs of the zodiac. Other ancient peoples contributed additional elements. The Hittites (*c.* 2300–1200 B.C.) were the first to work iron. The Lydians (*c.* 660–546 B.C.) devised a system of weights and measures and were the first to use coined money. As missionaries of culture, the Phoenicians (1700–539 B.C.) devised the phonetic alphabet and, as innovators in navigation and colonization, carried the arts of the East to the western Mediterranean. The Hebrews (*c.* 2000 B.C.–A.D. 70) gave the world the idea of universal monotheism, a single spiritual God, the Old Testament, and the Ten Commandments.

Ascendancy of Greece. The stream of civilization which arose in the valleys of the Nile and the Tigris-Euphrates gradually flowed westward and touched the shores of the Aegean Sea. In Greece, within a brief three centuries, was added a new and significant chapter to the history of mankind. The Greeks were the first people to develop a sense of history, the first to realize that the problems of man must be solved not by supernatural forces but by man himself. Convinced that the state should be above religion, they evolved a new secularism. Advocates of the free mind, cleared of ignorance and superstition, the Greeks projected an ideal of human freedom replacing the despotism so popular in the ancient Near Orient.

From the *Iliad* and the *Odyssey* of the Homeric Age (*c.* 1200–800 B.C.) we learn of the early pattern of Greek life in which heroes lived on a plane with the gods. On the Greek mainland, a little peninsula jutting into the Mediterranean Sea, a society emerged centering around the *polis*, or city-state. Outstanding among these city-states were Sparta and Athens, the two most powerful and widely contrasting city-states of ancient Hellas. Sparta was the most striking example of the conquering type of city-state. Its government, resembling the modern elite dictatorship, was an oligarchy (rule by the few) or a timocracy (rule by fear). The state was dominated by a ruling class of some 30,000 persons, forming an exclusively warrior class called "Spartiates." The Spartan military system crushed intellectual life. It left few monuments to its existence.

The story of Athens was different. Here was the essence of the Greek spirit—a democracy of free citizens who emphasized human values and a rich, expanding culture. The earliest form of government in Athens was a limited monarchy, which was followed by a period of aristocratic rule. Then (*c.* 594 B.C.) came the reforms of the archon Solon, by which the poorer people of Athens were given a voice in government. About fifty years later the Athenian statesman Cleisthenes projected legislation which promoted the growth of democracy. The golden age of Athenian power and culture (480–430 B.C.) reached its highest point under Pericles (*c.* 490–429 B.C.). The creative impulse of the Greeks rose ever upward despite the Peloponnesian Wars (431–403 B.C.) and a period of civil war

Greek contributions to philosophy ranged from the early pre-Socratic cosmologists, who tried to clarify the origins and forms of the material world, to the skeptical Sophists, and to the big three—Socrates, Plato, and Aristotle. Among the triumphs of Greek art were the magnificent Parthenon constructed from 447 to 432 B.C., the perfect sculptures of Phidias and Praxiteles, and the graceful Doric, Ionic, and Corinthian columns. Added to these contributions were the poetic dramas of Aeschylus, Sophocles, and Euripides.

The prosperity of Athens began to decline

from the end of the Peloponnesian Wars in 403 B.C., when Sparta became the supreme state of Greece. But Athenian intellectual supremacy long outlived its temporal power. Later, in the Hellenistic Age, from 338 B.C., when Philip of Macedon conquered Greece, to 30 B.C., when Rome subdued Egypt, the Hellenic, or pure-Greek, culture mingled with the Oriental. The result was a cosmopolitan culture which helped diffuse Greek culture throughout the world. For a brief time Alexander the Great (356–323 B.C.) ruled as the Oriental despot of a great empire. In a historical fusion the East was Hellenized and the West was Orientalized. But this empire, like Alexander himself, was destined for only a short life.

The Hegemony of Rome. The whole field of human relationships has been influenced by the Greek experience. After the disruption of the Alexandrian empire, the heir of Greece, the unification of the Mediterranean region was achieved by a little city-state on the banks of the Tiber in the Italian peninsula. Long before the glory of Greece began to fade, Rome was already on her way to power. By 200 B.C. an expanding Rome held Sicily, Sardinia, Corsica, Spain, the Po Valley, and controlled the Mediterranean margins of Europe, Africa, and Asia. In a vast, unplanned growth Rome emerged as the seat of a great empire. From the Golden Age of Augustus (27 B.C.–A.D. 14) through the reign of Marcus Aurelius (A.D. 161–180), Rome gave the Western world an era of peace and prosperity, the *Pax Romana*.

Gradually, Roman government became democratized. In a conflict between the patricians, the upper class, and the plebeians, the lower class, the latter forced recognition of their rights as citizens. They also acquired a share of political power. But these gains were mostly illusory, for the plebeians never quite gained full control of political life.

"Captive Greece made captive her conqueror." The Romans, seldom a creative people, took much of their cultural life from the Greeks. Most Roman cultural contributions came during the years of the *Principate* from 27 B.C. to A.D. 200, when Roman philosophy became of age (Seneca, Epictetus, Marcus Aurelius, all apostles of Stoicism). Among the major Roman literary figures were Vergil, Livy, Juvenal, Tacitus, and Ovid. Roman architecture, monumentally designed to symbolize power and grandeur, lacked the simplicity and grace of Greek edifices. Roman contributions to science were negligible.

Important contributions to law as a living institution came from the Romans. In no other field were the Romans more independent of outside help than in law. Roman ideas—social contract, separation of powers, sovereignty of the people, the supremacy of the law—these had a vital influence on subsequent Western legal thought.

There were many reasons for the decline of the Roman civilizing force. On the borders of the Empire, Roman legions had long fought off barbarian invaders from beyond the Rhine and Danube. Rome was unable to adapt her dominantly agricultural economy to the demands of a world-empire. Nor did she ever solve the problems of land distribution and competition from the provinces. The moral fiber of the Romans was weakened by the loss of men in war. When the Germanic barbarians penetrated into the Roman world, they found the people already too weakened to resist them. Meanwhile, Christianity gave a new philosophy to a people degenerating in moral decay.

Even though they were synthesizers and imitators, the Romans gave to the world political theory, administration, and legal codes. Added to these were the legacies of the Latin language, the concept of a world-state, and the formative aspects of Christianity. Rome was a civilizing power. Any date for the so-called "Fall of Rome" is misleading, because this great society, though it weakened, never actually died.

3. Western Civilization in the Middle Ages

Transition: The Middle Ages. The term Middle Ages refers to a chronologically intermediate period between the culture of classical antiquity and the Renaissance. It was not a homogeneous era. Until the eleventh century, roughly from A.D. 500 to 1000, there was a formative period, sometimes described as the Dark Ages, but the term is inexact. Much of Roman civilization was lost under the surge of the Germanic invaders from Northern Europe. The times were not completely barbaric, although there was a relapse in trade and industry, cities vanished, and learning and education lost their vigor. One link with the past remained, a tradition of order in a time of disorganization and invasion. In Western Europe three cultures were in process of merging —the Roman, the Germanic, and the Christian. Christianity survived the Germanic invasions, to be adopted ultimately by the invaders themselves.

By the end of the eleventh century the political organization of Western Europe achieved a degree of stability sufficient to permit the growth of a civilization which may be called medieval. During this period, from roughly 1100 to 1500, generally called the Later Middle Ages, international trade was revived. Towns appeared once more, a merchant class emerged, and a cultural regeneration took place. The new institutions of modern times appeared.

The Byzantine Empire. This empire, often called the Greek Empire, Later Empire, Eastern Empire, or Eastern Roman Empire, came into existence with the founding of the city of Constantinople by the Roman emperor Constantine (c. 280–337). The empire was basically Roman and carried on many of the fundamental ideas of the Roman Empire. Here in the East the Byzantine Empire continued to exist, despite domestic strife and invasion, for a thousand years until the fall of Constantinople in 1453. While Western Europe sank to semi-barbarism, the Byzantine Empire preserved many qualities of Oriental and classical civilizations, fused with Christian morality and ethics.

The key to the strength of this society was Byzantium (Constantinople), which, impregnably fortified, remained a formidable barrier between the exhausted West and the aggressive East. Able to withstand the periodic waves of barbarian invaders and Muslim conquerors, it provided a refuge for the ancient civilizations. Constantinople gave the new ideals of the empire a permanent abode, and for centuries, even when the Byzantine Empire seemed to be at its weakest, it formed a Christian bulwark of resistance to the attacks by paganism as well as by other religions.

The reign of Justinian (A.D. 527–565) saw the Byzantine Empire at its most vigorous power. During his reign the Vandals fell before the onslaught of his general, Belisarius, the Ostrogoths were overcome, a large part of Italy restored, and part of Spain reconquered. It seemed for a time that the Roman Empire would be recreated again in all its glory. Byzantine prosperity was due in large part to state regulation of commerce. Ecclesiastical authority and imperial rule were combined in the state church. In law Justinian was famous; his *Corpus iuris civilis* was a remarkable codification. Byzantine artists drew inspiration from the ancient Greeks, to whose art forms they added a touch of Oriental color and a dash of Christian tradition.

The great work of reconstructing the Roman Empire begun by Justinian was soon undone by his successors. It became impossible for the empire to bear the expense of continued war and conquest.

The Muslims. While the Byzantine Empire sought to revive the glories of ancient Rome, a new religion emerged in the East. Islam, an Arabic word meaning to submit, to surrender, was the religion preached by Muhammad (c. A.D. 569–632), who was born in an impoverished family of the tribe Quraish in Mecca. Appearing as a prophet, he called men to worship one God and to flee from the wrath to come. The faith of Muhammad is summed up in the confession: "There is no god but God and Muhammad is His prophet." Muhammad did not claim to bring a new religion but instead to revive the faith which had been taught first to Adam and then to Abraham, was followed by Moses, Jesus, and other prophets, but then corrupted. It was said that the inspired word of God was communicated to

Muhammad *sura* (chapter) by *sura*, verse by verse, and word by word, by the Archangel Gabriel. This was the *Koran,* the sacred book of Islam.

The religion preached by Muhammad was assumed by the Arabs of Western Asia, heirs of the Hellenistic civilization. Gradually, the teachings of Muhammad spread westward across North Africa and into Spain, and eastward into China and India. Within a century, a huge Muslim empire ranged from the borders of India to the Atlantic Ocean, from the Caspian Sea to the Indian Ocean. In the eighth century the militant Muslims threatened to overwhelm all Christendom, but they were halted by the Franks led by Charles Martel at the Battle of Tours in 732. It was a narrow victory: the Muslim army was composed of mounted soldiery, while the Frankish force consisted mainly of foot soldiers. A strong Christian counterattack came with the Crusades, religious wars carried on by the European nations against Islam from 1096 to 1291. Originally devised to ensure the safety of pilgrims visiting the Holy Sepulcher and to set up Christian rule in Palestine, the Crusades eventually assumed political and economic overtones.

The Muslim culture was an advanced one, attaining high levels between 800 and 1300. Much of it seeped through to the West, to a large extent through the efforts of Spanish Muslims. But the Muslim Empire, after a century of splendor, was destined for decline. It was replaced by the Turks who, after taking Constantinople in 1453, laid siege to Vienna as late as 1683.

The Middle Ages witnessed several patterns of civilization in contact with each other—the cultures of Western Europe, the Byzantine Empire, and the Muslim state. At the end of the medieval era, the two latter societies seemed to be superior in political organization, commerce, and cultural activities. But Western Europe was to surge forward in modern times. Byzantines and Muslims declined from their earlier high levels.

Medieval Administrative System: Feudalism. A new government and a new economy had to be devised to replace centralized rule after Charlemagne (r. A.D. 768–814) failed to revive the Roman Empire under Germanic and Christian auspices. Europe dropped into political chaos. Feudalism appeared as a transitional stage, not really a substitute for strong centralized government but as a kind of stopgap government used until a more effective political system could be developed.

Feudalism originated out of both Roman and German practices. In essence it was based upon a reciprocal contract between lord (suzerain) and vassal, by which the former protected the vassal in return for various services. The powers of government were exercised by private lords over persons economically dependent upon them. Not always were the relations assumed freely nor was there always a mutually satisfactory agreement. Might was right in this society; the strong controlled the weak; power and authority alone were respected.

By the year 900, feudalism emerged as a governmental system in most of Western Europe. It was a crude substitute for centralized government. It was never a "system" in the real sense of the word. It managed to maintain some semblance of law and order on the local level. It varied from time to time and from place to place. In theory it was a vast hierarchy, with the emperor or king at the top, supposedly owning all the land, with nobles holding land as tenants-in-chief, and they in turn parceled out portions of their fiefs to lesser nobles. Lord and vassal were united by a personal bond.

The people of the day idealized feudalism because of its relationship with chivalry, which became a code of behavior for the nobility. Chivalry appeared during the eleventh century at a time when many unemployed knights had to find some new focus of attention. Despite the cruelty of feudalism, chivalry stressed honor, a gentler attitude to life, and generosity toward the Church and womanhood.

Economic Life in the Middle Ages: Manorialism. The feudal system was the means by which society obtained protection, while the manor was the agency which provided sustenance for the members of both feudal and manorial groups. The term "manorial system" refers to the type of economic or social life centered around the manor. The manor might consist of a few hundred or thousand acres of land, in one block or perhaps in several noncontiguous blocks of land. Self-sustaining, the manor generally included all the lands needed for a variety of crops and pastures.

Manorialism, like feudalism, seems to have had its origin in both Roman and Germanic institutions. In the late Roman Empire the taxes were so high that the small farmer often gave his land to nobles who assumed the tax burden for them. The German contribution, somewhat more difficult to trace, was a relationship of serf to master. In the medieval manor both Roman and German elements were blended.

Agriculture was the chief function of the manorial village. The land was divided into the lord's demesne (the best land), the lord's close (rented to tenant cultivators), villagers' strips, common meadow land, common wood land, waste land, and the domain of the village priest. The land was worked under the open-field, or three-field system. The arable land was divided into three sections—one for fall planting, one for spring planting, and the third left fallow. Farming techniques were inefficient and wasteful. However, the system represented a cooperative agricultural enterprise useful at the time. The life of the peasant was not easy in this system. He lived in a squalid home, his food was coarse and seldom plentiful, and he always took a subservient position to the nobility.

Feudalism and manorialism were bridges between the old authoritarian Roman government and the national states of modern Europe. Eventually these bridges began to decay. As long as government was decentralized and the economy agrarian, feudalism and manorialism survived. By the dawn of the modern era, however, they were well on the way to extinction. There were new factors: the revival of trade with the East, the growth of cities, the expansion of commerce and industry, introduction of new methods of warfare, the emergence of a middle class, and the rise of national monarchies. Feudalism and manorialism were crude responses to medieval needs, but they had brought some order out of the chaos into which Europe had been thrown. They provided for law and order, for some stability. And by maintaining a king at the head of the feudal order, at least in theory, they kept intact vestiges of monarchy which passed on into the modern period.

Spirit and Structure of the Medieval Church. Rome's political empire was eventually supplanted by a spiritual empire of the Christian faith. The Church was influential in preserving classical civilization and in converting the barbarian Germans to Christianity. Gradually, as the Church developed an organization, it grew in secular power. The Roman episcopate was transformed into the papacy, which claimed supremacy over the entire Christian Church. Papal persistence overcame local authority. The Church became an institution controlling not only the religious life of Western Europeans but also their political institutions. Pope Nicholas I, who held the papal office from A.D. 858 to 867, demanded strong temporal power, an idea to be achieved later.

By the end of the twelfth century the medieval Church became a great international and supranational empire under papal leadership. Its hierarchy of officials controlled the processes of salvation. The influence of the Church was felt by every inhabitant of every town and village in Western Europe. Meanwhile, a struggle arose for power between Church and State, between Pope and Holy Roman Emperor. This long battle was won by neither side. In the tenth century the Church began a reform movement at Cluny. In the Investiture Struggle between Pope Gregory VII (1073–1085) and Henry IV (1050–1106), German emperor, the latter was forced to submit to a humilating penance at Canossa (1077), which indicated the growing influence of the papacy in European temporal affairs. The Church bolstered its position by promoting a series of armed pilgrimages to the Holy Land in the Crusades (1096–1291) under papal auspices.

The Church reached the height of its power

with Pope Innocent III (1198–1216), who forced emperors and kings to accede to his demands. The Church thus maintained its power through centuries of political upheaval. In difficult times it possessed the only unified system of law and administration.

This militant drive to political hegemony could not be maintained. In the long run, it proved impossible for the papacy to retain its great power. In the thirteenth century the Church showed signs of being exhausted by its long struggles with temporal authorities. Weakened by internal schisms and the growth of heresy, it was unable to prevent the rise of national states and national sentiment. Church dominance depended upon continuance of the medieval world order, but new forces were at work which were changing the Western world. The universality of the Middle Ages was being shattered into fragments.

Nature of Medieval Thought and Culture. Western European culture sank to a level of darkness in the early Middle Ages. Latin, Christian, and Germanic elements slowly mingled. Education, literature, the arts, and the sciences entered an era of ignorance and superstition. But there were flashes of light in the gloom. The Celtic Christians in Scotland and Ireland produced a high culture in the seventh and eighth centuries. There was much of value in the Carolingian Renaissance (775–825) and in the Saxon Renaissance (875–950).

At the root of medieval culture were pagan learning, literature, and art. In Western Europe, culture was closely supervised by the Church. Elsewhere, in Eastern Europe the Byzantine culture, which attained its height from 850 to 1100, consisted of Greek, Roman, and Oriental influences. The scintillating Muslim culture, which reached its high point from 800 to 1300, was a blend of Greek, Arabic, and Oriental elements. In this dark time in Western Europe, both Muslims and Byzantines played an important role in maintaining the old learning.

The period from 1050 to 1200, the height of the Middle Ages, marked the true awakening of medieval culture. There was an exciting in-tellectual life, epitomized in the scholastic philosophy of Pierre Abélard (1079–1142), in the rise of the medieval universities (1150–1250), in the beginnings of Gothic art (1150–1200), and in the appearance of vernacular literatures (1100–1400). Between 1200 and 1300 the medieval synthesis was completed.

Although medieval culture on the whole lacked the quality of uniformity, it was not deficient in intellectual curiosity. Medieval man was aware of the problems of his time. He struggled with the implications of the new knowledge. He was much more successful in this task than is generally acknowledged. It is incorrect to use the term "medieval" as an expression of abuse. Medieval man gave us training in logic and analysis; he maintained for us the best of our ancient heritage; he made us the gift of vernacular languages; he sought to limit the power of his monarchs; and he taught us the nature of representative assemblies.

With town life revived, with the social order in ferment, a new social order, the middle class, emerged. Deriving its wealth and status from trade and industry instead of landholding and political exploitation, this class gave support to the Renaissance and generated the sixteenth- and seventeenth-century revival of science.

Transition: Economic Expansion and Territorial Consolidation. Medieval commerce was preserved, despite the manorial economy, by four sources: (1) the Muslims, who advanced along the North African coastline and linked the two ends of the Mediterranean; (2) the Byzantines with their great trading bazaars in Constantinople; (3) the Italian cities, such as Genoa and Venice, which promoted sea trade with the Near East and land trade with Northern Europe; and (4) the German Hanseatic cities which monopolized trade in the north. The Crusades, which in the public imagination were primarily religious in aspect, actually stimulated a reviving trade and commerce. The rise of the towns, evolutionary in process but revolutionary in results, came in the eleventh and twelfth centuries. Trade and industry were organized to satisfy new wants. Wealth and prosperity, discouraged under feudalism's violence, gradually increased. Towns, rebelling against their despots, won new charters of liberties. New town markets arose simultaneously with the end of serfdom, the drift of people from the manors to the towns, and the use of money. A commercial and financial revolution was under way.

As territories were consolidated, national states were fashioned. Both the Holy Roman Empire and the universal papacy were undermined and weakened in this new age. The monarchs of England, France, and Spain were already consolidating their countries at the expense of the feudal lords. Both monarchs and merchants wanted *national* laws, *national* culture, *national* control. The French national monarchy was fashioned by Philip Augustus (1180–1223), Louis IX (1226–1270), and Philip the Fair (1285–1314). It was helped by

the expulsion of the English from the Continent in the Hundred Years' War (1338–1453). In England national monarchy originated in the reign of William the Conqueror (r. 1066–1087). There were recurrent royal feuds and Tudor and Stuart despotisms, but England eventually produced representative institutions. In the Germanies and the Italies, however, the ideal of a universal empire survived; national monarchies in those lands did not appear until long after the end of the Middle Ages.

Instead of giving his loyalty to the international Church centered at Rome, man now reserved his attachment for his own country and monarch. It was a new age, with new institutions, new loyalties, new ways of thinking. The Middle Ages were ended. This was the beginning of the era of modern man.

Astronomer making astronomical calculations. Copper engraving by Stradanus.

PART I

THE OPENING ERA IN THE WEST

CONTINUITY: MEDIEVAL ELEMENTS IN OUR MODERN POLITICAL HERITAGE[1]

Charles Howard McIlwain

WE MUST always bear in mind the vast difference between the earlier and the later part of the long period to which we apply the word "medieval." As a whole, I suppose we might roughly describe the epoch generally as one in which rather primitive men gradually and progressively assimilated the more advanced institutions and ideas that antiquity had bequeathed them. It is amazing how long a period of contact is required for men at such a primitive state of culture to make their own the remains of a civilization so much higher than theirs. In western Europe one can hardly make this period of progressive assimilation shorter than seven or eight centuries. It was a long, gradual, progressive development, a slow evolution; and the term "medieval" is probably most fittingly applied to the culmination in its later centuries on Aristotle's general teleological principle that the nature of any developing thing is only fully knowable in the final outcome of that development.

One of the things, probably the most important of all the things in my own particular field, that we seem to owe in largest part to these developments of the Middle Ages, is the institution of limited government, which I take to be the synonym for constitutionalism.

This constitutionalism was, of course, no new thing when the medieval records of it first appear. It had been a characteristic of republican Rome, had never been wholly obliterated by the growing absolutism of the Empire, and it was enshrined in the Roman legal sources which ruder successors of the Romans inherited and gradually came in course of time to assimilate, understand, and apply to their own lives. . . .

The best way to learn most about an acorn is to look at an oak. It is thus, and thus only, that the present should influence our views of the past. But "Art is long and life is fleeting," and if we are to be good medievalists we must devote our main attention to the Middle Ages themselves and at the cost of some other periods.

Yet I submit that this must not lead to the narrow view that we should look at nothing else. The true nature of the Middle Ages cannot be fully understood except by some study of their outcome in the Renaissance and of their modern development. We can no more understand the true nature of this period in our history without consideration of its outcome than we could know all about a tadpole without studying the toad. As indicated above, in some things, particularly in the growth of the institutions and ideas with which I have been chiefly concerned, the so-called "Renaissance of the twelfth century" seems to me to be on the whole more significant on a perspective of the whole history, than the later

[1] Charles Howard McIlwain, "Medieval Institutions in the Modern World," in *Speculum*, XVI (1941), 277–283. By permission of the Medieval Academy of America.

development to which we usually attach the word "Renaissance." But this is in no way to belittle that later period whose influence is undeniable, and ought to be so to the medievalist above all others, because he, more clearly than any others, is able to see the utter falsity of the notion that then for the first time since the ancients men rediscovered both the world and man. He knows that the Renaissance is in many ways only an extension of the Middle Ages, and this knowledge ought to heighten, not to lessen, his interest in that later period, even though life is too short to study it in detail; for undoubtedly some of the best and most important elements of the culture of the Renaissance are a heritage from the period before. . . .

It is a commonplace of modern constitutional history that the power of the purse has been the principal means of securing and maintaining the liberties of the subject against the encroachment of the prince. Probably in no part of our constitutional history is the influence of the Middle Ages upon the modern world more obvious than here. For the constitutional principle just mentioned can be shown to be the outgrowth, the gradual and at times almost unperceived outgrowth, of the medieval principle that a feudal lord in most cases can extract no aid from his vassal save with the consent of all like vassals of the same fief. The whole principle contained in our maxim, "no taxation without representation," has this feudal practice as its origin.

This is probably so obvious and so generally admitted that it needs little proof or illustration. But one aspect of it we are likely to overlook. These rights of the vassal are proprietary rights, and we are likely to give them a definition as narrow as our own modern definition of proprietary rights. This, however, is to misinterpret the nature of these limitations and vastly to lessen the importance of the principle of consent in the Middle Ages. For these rights of vassals, though protected by what we should call the land-law, included almost all of those rights which today we term "personal," such as the right to office, the right to immunities, or, as they were usually called then, to "liberties" or franchises, and even to the right of one's security in his social and personal status. A serf, for example, was protected against the abuse by his lord of rights which we call "personal" by remedies which it is difficult to distinguish from those used for the protection of the seisin[2] of land. One might be truly said to have been "seized" of the rights securing his person as much as of those protecting his fief. It may be said of the Middle Ages generally, then, that private rights were immune from governmental encroachment under the political principles of the time. In this the Middle Ages shared the principles of Roman Law, and no doubt it was this common feature of both systems that enabled Glanvil and Bracton and all the jurists in the period between to liken the English Law in so many respects to the Roman.

If we are estimating the importance of the medieval in the modern in this field from which I have chosen to illustrate it, this constitutionalism, this limitation of governmental authority by private right, is the main tradition handed down by the Middle Ages to the modern world. It is the chief element in the political part of our medieval heritage. With the decay of feudal institutions, however, the sanctions by which these principles were

---

[2] Seisin: from the French *sesin*, a medieval feudal term denoting the possession of status with relation to land arising from completion of feudal investiture. In its modern sense, seisin means possession of a freehold estate in land by one having title thereto.

maintained in practice tended to be greatly weakened, and no doubt it is the lawlessness of this later period of weakness following the decay of the feudal and preceding the development of the national sanctions for law, which had led to the popular impression that the Middle Ages as a whole are nothing more than one long stretch of uncontrolled violence. No doubt the violence of this later period may also be considered to be the chief cause of the increasing power of monarchy and the almost unlimited theories of obedience which we find among the chief characteristics of the period of the Renaissance. As was said then, it is better to submit to one tyrant than to a thousand. And without doubt the weakness of these sanctions of law in the later Middle Ages is a prime cause of the strength of monarchy in the period immediately following. In the reaction and revolution which in time were provoked in the period of the Renaissance or afterward by the extension and abuse of these powers of government we may find the true causes of the modern sanctions for the subjects' rights. In the early stages at least of this revolution the precedents cited in favor of liberty are largely drawn from the Middle Ages.

The particular side of the Middle Ages with which we have been dealing certainly offers little proof of either of the extreme interpretations that we find in modern times. It was both a lawful and a lawless period. At no time was law more insisted upon, but at times few of these laws were observed. When we consider this period in comparison with periods following, the same discrimination is necessary. The political theory of that time included more limitations upon governmental power than many theories of a much later time. It may indeed be said that political absolutism, at least as a theory of government, is a modern and not a medieval notion. In fact, the great champions of liberty against oppression, if their own words are to be trusted, have fought for the maintenance of liberties inherited from the Middle Ages. In our own day such traditional conceptions of liberty appear less seldom perhaps, for many liberals, and certainly most extreme radicals, are now frequently struggling for rights for which the Middle Ages can furnish few precedents. But this should not blind us to the all-important fact that for a long period in this historic struggle, indeed for the whole of the early part of it, it was for their medieval inheritance that all opponents of oppression engaged.

The lesson of it all is discrimination. If some modern elements had not been added to our medieval inheritance, elements, non-existent before modern times, even that inheritance could scarcely have persisted; and yet the central principle for which free men have always fought, the sanctity of law against oppressive will, is a principle recognized by our medieval ancestors as fully as by ourselves, and more fully, apparently, than by their successors of the sixteenth century. We cannot, therefore, truly entertain notions of the Middle Ages which make it one long, dreary epoch of stagnation, of insecurity, of lawless violence; neither can we truly consider it the Golden Age that some have pictured. What we need above all is discrimination and yet more discrimination.

1

Transition in Economic Life: The Commercial Revolution

CHANGES ARE always going on, of course, in commerce as well as in social and political affairs; revolutions are perhaps as frequent in one as in another. But between 1400 and 1700 changes in methods of conducting business, in trading centers, in shipping, in the financial aspects of commerce and in the theories underlying practice were so numerous, so pronounced and so rapid that the total effect seems to have been revolutionary.

—LAURENCE B. PACKARD

1. Society Atomized: The Age of European Commercial Isolation

Economic Revolution. Concurrent with the expansion of Europe was a change in the economic life of the Continent. The closed medieval economy, largely agricultural and self-sustaining, with commerce restricted to localities, began to disintegrate. There were rapid and revolutionary changes in volume, range, commodities, and organization of commerce. Trade and industry changed from inter-municipal to worldwide as a greater variety of goods in greater volume was distributed over a larger part of the world's surface. The desire for new diets and new goods both stimulated and was stimulated by the flood of gold from America. New earth under men's feet helped to put new desires into their minds.

Along with the Commercial Revolution appeared a complex economic system called capitalism. A new economic principle, "mercantilism," was used to justify the theory and practice of the new commerce. In the nineteenth century, economic life was to move in the direction of free trade and an uncontrolled economy (*laissez-faire*), only to change in the twentieth century into a resurgent economic nationalism called neo-mercantilism.

Profound changes in the texture of society accompanied this economic revolution. Population grew rapidly. The accident of birth still counted, as the nobility retained its trappings and titles, but social fluidity increased as newly wealthy burghers began to climb the social ladder. The lower classes in this time of transition also made modest progress, but their gains were much smaller than those of the bourgeoisie. There was a new world, with a spirit of revolution in the air.

Cracks in the System. As feudal Europe lay in agricultural isolation, several forces kept alive the commercial legacy of the ancient world or contributed to the economic awakening of the later Middle Ages. Scandinavia gave northern Europe its most vigorous seamen and traders. The Eastern Byzantine Empire remained commercially active for a thousand years after the fall of Rome. The Muslim Empire of shopkeepers stretched from one end of the Mediterranean to the other. Commercial enterprise in the Italian cities never ceased entirely. In the north a group of German merchants, successors to the Northmen, organized an extensive network called the Hanseatic League and monopolized trade in that area.

In the fifteenth century came a series of polit-

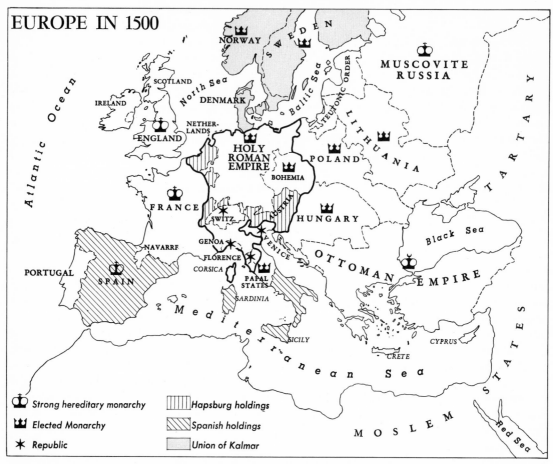

EUROPE IN 1500

NORWAY · SWEDEN · MUSCOVITE RUSSIA · SCOTLAND · North Sea · DENMARK · Baltic Sea · TEUTONIC ORDER · LITHUANIA · IRELAND · NETHER-LANDS · ENGLAND · HOLY ROMAN EMPIRE · POLAND · TARTARY · BOHEMIA · Atlantic Ocean · FRANCE · AUSTRIA · HUNGARY · SWITZ. · GENOA · VENICE · Black Sea · NAVARRE · FLORENCE · CORSICA · OTTOMAN · EMPIRE · PORTUGAL · SPAIN · PAPAL STATES · SARDINIA · Mediterranean Sea · SICILY · CYPRUS · CRETE · MOSLEM STATES · Red Sea

♔ Strong hereditary monarchy   ‖‖‖ Hapsburg holdings
♕ Elected Monarchy   ⧄ Spanish holdings
✳ Republic   ░ Union of Kalmar

ical innovations which helped break down the closed system of medieval commercial control. In England, France, Spain, and the Low Countries, feudalism as an administrative and governmental system was disintegrating. The age of chivalry, when knighthood was in flower, started to fade away. Strong central governments appeared. Powerful kings and princes began to dominate the weaker feudal lords.

2. From Man to Money: The Commercial Revolution

Meaning. The economic transformation to European life which took place from 1400 to 1700 we call the "Commercial Revolution." The changes in business, industry, finance, production, distribution, and regulation were numerous and rapid. With the discovery of the world's sea lanes and the beginnings of the colonial system, commerce escaped from guild

control and was organized on a worldwide basis. Goods of many kinds were sent in great quantities over a larger area of the world's surface. The changes took place at different times and in varying degrees in different places. No two regions of Europe developed along identical economic lines.

Characteristics of the Commercial Revolution. It was an age of rapid movement in the economic sphere, marked by the breakup of medieval society and the reconstruction of economic organization. Changes occurred not only in the volume of trade, but even more in the introduction of different methods of commercial practice. The new society gradually overcame medieval obstacles, broke down commercial restrictions, swept away local exclusiveness, and developed large economic areas. Uniform laws, weights, measures, and currencies were introduced, customs barriers were lifted, and local privileges and protection were eliminated.

These economic developments went hand-in-hand with political, social, cultural, and religious factors. As civic gave way to national economic life, the policy of the town was submerged into that of the state. Powerful states pursued strong national policies, and their rulers regulated all economic life—trade, industry, finance, shipping, and agriculture.

3. The Growth of Capitalism

Nature of Capitalism. Capitalism is a distinctive type of economic system in the modern era. J. A. Hobson defined it as "the organization of business upon a large scale by an employer or company of employers possessing an accumulated stock of wealth wherewith to acquire raw materials and tools, and hire labor, so as to produce an increased quantity of wealth which shall constitute profit." Werner Sombart stated that capitalism, like all other economic systems, can be understood best by probing separately its spirit, form, and technology. According to Sombart, the spirit of capitalism is characterized by three ideas. (1) *Acquisition* of money or possessions is the basic goal of economic activity. Modern man under the capitalist economy is motivated by the urge to increase the sum of money on hand and to augment his stock of material things. In short, his aim is to acquire profit. This is the exact opposite of the precapitalist feudal-handicraft economy, in which man's own interests as a producer or a consumer determined the organization of economic life. (2) *Competition,* the attitude displayed in the process of acquisition, rests upon freedom from regulation for the individual in his struggle for profit. (3) *Rationality* holds that capitalism invariably adopts those modes of behavior which seem most rational, systematic, and best adapted to the production of constantly increasing profits.

The form of capitalism is characterized by (1) economic freedom from all restrictions except those which affect the most marginal of activities; (2) typically private enterprise or undertaking, with the capitalist assuming full risk of failure or an unrestricted chance of success; (3) an aristocratic structure, in which the number of economic agents is small as compared with the large number engaged in business; (4) a highly developed division of labor, depending always upon the profits to be brought to the entrepreneur; and (5) a business exchange basis, by which all production enters into commercial traffic, with price regulating the quantity and character of output. The large-scale entrepreneur dominates the organization of production, although the small-scale capitalist also has a place in the system.

The technology of capitalism must satisfy two conditions: (1) it must insure a high degree of production, which cannot be allowed to fall below a certain minimum; and (2) it must also lend itself readily to the improvement and perfection of production as well as to the reduction of costs.

Every economic system first appears within the framework of another. The capitalist system developed through several centuries. There were symptoms of an incipient capitalism in the ancient world, but neither the spirit, form, nor techniques of capitalism as we understand them today existed then. During the Middle Ages, the manorial-handicraft system, with its emphasis upon men instead of money and upon the "just price" instead of profit, precluded the existence of large-scale capitalism. Capitalist principles were first applied to finance in the later Middle Ages, then to commerce in the early modern period (during the Commercial Revolution), and later to industry (the Industrial Revolution).

Financial Capitalism. In late medieval Europe the organization of commerce and industry under the corporate guild system, the limitations of business activity by the interests of the whole community, the lack of extensive commerce, and the restrictions on prices and interest, prevented the acquisition of capital and the growth of capitalism. Nevertheless, with increasing amounts of money in circulation, a few wealthy families began to accumulate surplus capital with the intention of investing it for profit whenever the opportunity appeared. Among these families of merchant princes who were successful in speculative trading and banking all over Europe were the Florentine Medici in the fifteenth century and the Fuggers of Augsburg in the fifteenth and sixteenth centuries. Their most important clients were European rulers and princes who required large sums of money for mercenary armies or to meet the expenses of a centralized administration and an extravagant court. But the lending of large sums of money to royalty

Jakob Fugger died in 1525, leaving no children to take his place in the gigantic Fugger enterprises. His nephew, Anton, succeeded him and reaped the benefits of Jakob's commercial wisdom. This reproduction from the Fugger books gives an idea of the vastness of the Fugger firm. The balance of 2,132,791.18 gulden in 1527 was equivalent to more than 50 million dollars.

was a risky business; family banking houses often collapsed when princely borrowers neglected or refused to repay loans. On the whole, however, these precapitalistic ventures were small and limited when compared with

the extent of modern financial enterprise. Interest rates were erratic, there was relatively little capital available, and much moneylending was for unproductive purposes.

Commercial Capitalism. During the sixteenth century, most of the old legal and religious restrictions upon trade were removed. The new economic system was free from any restraints which in any way might have hindered the working of the forces of supply and demand. It was strongly supported by the new Protestantism, which regarded thrift and industry as virtues and profit-taking as blessed. The idea that competition and profits were honorable contradicted the medieval attitude, but it took deep root and has persisted to the present day. By the dawn of the modern period, man had discovered the potentialities of capital, insisted upon introducing it into commerce and industry, and sought to accumulate profits instead of a mere living.

4. The New Finance: Combination of Resources

New Methods of Finance. In the Middle Ages the merchant and craft guilds monopolized production and prevented the emergence of large-scale commerce. Trade was carried on by individuals, and there was almost nothing of what we would now call "wholesale trading." Merchants were either peddlers or retailers and were rarely able to accumulate enough money for investment. Toward the end of the Middle Ages came a vigorous development of a partnership form of enterprise, at first on a small scale and for limited undertakings. In order to lessen the risk, two merchants often shared the expenses of an explorer to the New World, with the understanding that they would divide alike all booty, loot, and plunder. Sometimes the partnership was formed to finance only one trip; on other occasions it lasted for several years.

New Opportunities in Trade. It now became obvious that the limited partnership was an unsatisfactory means of satisfying the requirements of a growing trade. When the gigantic size of America and the vastness of its natural resources were perceived, and when the tremendous possibilities of trade with the Orient became apparent, a large-scale organization of finance became imperative. The risks in foreign trade were great, but the profits to be made were enormous. The new, oceangoing trade, the use of more expensive equipment, and the mounting costs of acquiring large quantities of goods to meet the growing demand, required far more money or capital than the average merchant possessed. There now developed a system of combining resources in the form of companies. At first there was no established system of credit. People gingerly entrusted their money to others with the earnest hope that it would come back to them with a handsome profit. "Goodwill" and "prestige" are relatively recent developments in finance.

Regulated Companies. The regulated, or open, company was the first type of business organization constructed specifically to meet the needs of an expanding commerce. A group of individuals, feeling the need of protection and common support, joined together with the aim of obtaining a monopoly of trade in a certain area. Each merchant traded in the area of his company, but carried on his activities with his own resources, in competition with his fellow members. All agreed to abide by definite regulations laid down by the group for the protection of common interests. All paid assessments to a central treasury for the maintenance of a common protecting force, for the expenses of ambassadors, and for charitable aid to members. All worked in common to prevent the competition of interlopers, those traders who did not belong to the company. In essence, the idea of the regulated company was the extension of the old merchant guild idea into the international field.

Joint-Stock Companies. The regulated company did not bring any far-reaching change in the method of trading; it represented no genuine combination of capital or resources. The more important innovation, and the real forerunner of our modern corporation, was the joint-stock company, so called because it was a genuine joint or sharing undertaking. A company or group of persons joined together to provide a fund with which they could undertake a common business enterprise. Each person put some money into the company and received a proportionate share of the stock, thus sharing in the risks, losses, and gains. He contributed to the common fund, but did not necessarily engage in trade. Whereas the regulated company was an association of *men,* the joint-stock company was an association of *capital.* The joint-stock company could be organized for either a temporary or a permanent undertaking. In the "temporary" form, at the end of a definite period the investor received the amount of his original investment plus a share of profits, or if the enterprise was unsuccessful, he shared in the loss. In the "permanent" company, the investor received dividends at certain intervals, as is the practice among modern corporations. In fact, in almost every respect the joint-stock company was similar to the modern corporation, with its thousands of investors and its professional direction.

Chartered Companies. In addition to the regulated and joint-stock companies there was another innovation—the chartering by government of commercial enterprises. The practice of granting charters, giving privileges or rights, had been developed during the later Middle Ages, when towns sought to obtain immunity from feudal dues or from the exactions of feudal lords. The kings graciously granted such charters because they helped enhance the royal power at the expense of the nobility. The idea carried over into the Commercial Revolution. Monarchs anxious to increase their own power granted loyal merchants a monopoly of trade in a particular colony, as well as the right to establish all settlements there. In 1600 a charter was granted to "the Governor and Company of Merchants of London trading into the East Indies," the English East India Company, which became a model for many other chartered companies. Holding exclusive rights to trade in the Indian and Pacific oceans, it assumed military and treaty-making rights and bought land in unlimited quantities. Char-

:ered companies transformed the economic organization of Europe in the sixteenth and seventeenth centuries by providing markets for manufacture, by furnishing new areas for investment of capital, and by importing new products.

Development of Banking. Commercial banking in its modern sense, the utilization of the machinery of deposits, clearance, and short-term loans, is a product of the nineteenth century. In the Middle Ages there was some banking, consisting of the acceptance of deposits and the lending of money, with the accent primarily upon moneylending. Of great

The importance of the art of coinage in the sixteenth century is indicated in this illustration from a 1520 translation of a Latin work on the institutions and administration of political affairs.

importance was the specialized business of money changing, a necessity at a time when there was a progressive debasement of coinage in both weight and quality, as well as a multiplicity of inefficient monetary systems almost completely useless for the purposes of trade. Toward the end of the Middle Ages a rapidly

growing credit business developed to meet the increased scale of business operations. Merchants became more and more accustomed to depositing their money in banks for safekeeping, and these funds on hand were used as the basis for a system of credit. Banks began to issue bills of exchange, by which a bank having branches in several cities could receive money in one locality and issue a bill of exchange redeemable in another city, thus obviating the necessity for transporting large sums of money from one city to another. Originally a currency instrument, the letter of exchange was soon transformed into a credit instrument.

5. The Price Revolution and Inflation

American Treasure. The importation of bullion from America had an electrifying effect on the European economy. After a short period of disappointment, Spanish explorers in America uncovered those precious metals and rare stones which Marco Polo had led them to expect if they reached Cathay. In 1503 came the first trickle of American gold from the West Indies. In the 1520's and 1530's the *conquistadores* appropriated huge treasures in precious metals from the Aztecs in Mexico and the Incas of Peru. When they discovered a decade later that the treasure above ground was infinitesimal compared to that available underground, the Spaniards began to work the mines of Peru, Bolivia, and Mexico. Between 1521 and 1660, some 18,000 tons of silver and approximately 200 tons of gold passed from America to Spain, a large percentage of which went into circulation as coins. Gathered by private enterprise, the bullion was delivered to royal assay offices in Seville, where it was cast into bars, plates, or coins, with a quint (one-fifth) taken by the state as royalty, and the rest sent on to other sections of Western Europe. Spain had the lead in the race for American bullion, but her advantage was offset to some extent by British acumen and zeal. English adventurers pounced on gold-laden ships in Spanish harbors, removing the treasure and then burning the ships "to singe the beard of the king of Spain." All the while, despite severe penalties, there was a continuous smuggling of precious metals. Large amounts of gold and silver reached other European countries without going through the Spanish bottleneck.

Rise in Price Level. The influx of treasure from America led to a rise in the price level. It was not immediately apparent, since all the European countries, possessing manorial and other nonmonetary wealth, could absorb for the time being large quantities of gold and silver imported from the New World. As the precious metals became more common, their purchasing power fell: the prices of other commodities rose in exchange for gold and silver. Spanish prices about 1600 were three times as high as those in 1500. Eggs sold at 14¢ a dozen in 1500 in England, but in 1570 were quoted at 75¢ and $1.00. Although this general rise in the price level was due primarily to the increase of precious metals, there were other contributory factors, notably repeated debasement of the currency in many European countries, introduction of a new system of credit, existence of vast business monopolies, desire of merchants and governments to keep prices high, long and costly national wars, and extravagant rulers. All these, however, were contingent upon the flow of gold and silver from the New World.

The Long Inflation. The inflation which followed the influx of precious transatlantic metals into Europe worked hardship upon those whose wages did not rise with prices. As his real wages fell, the worker was unable to keep pace with the high cost of living. Journeymen, especially, found themselves unable to subsist upon wages fixed by the guilds, which strongly resisted wage increases. Another group which suffered were those landlords who lived largely on fixed rents, the amount of which had been regulated for many years past and in some cases for generations ahead. On the other hand, some elements in the European population benefited from the long inflation. Landlords who received their rents in kind instead of in cash were not deeply affected, nor were those who worked their own farms and brought their produce to the markets. Those who had long-term leases profited at the expense of the landlords. Small

craftsmen met the rising prices by the simple expedient of raising the price of their own goods or services. The real gainers from the price revolution were the middle-class merchants who siphoned off the new supply of precious metals and used it to their own advantage.

New Articles of Commerce. The price revolution was closely tied up with the introduction of new commodities and the transformation of European tastes. A variety of foodstuffs now appeared in the European markets in quantity: tea, coffee, chocolate, molasses, tomatoes, tapioca, lima beans, yams, coconuts, peanuts, bananas, lemons, corn (maize), oil, and rice. The potato was brought to Europe from Peru by Pizarro, but it did not enjoy great popularity until the nineteenth century. Sugar, imported from the West Indies, became increasingly popular as a substitute for honey to sweeten coffee, tea, and cocoa. Turkeys were brought in from Mexico, but were given an Oriental name because anything of unusual appearance was commonly attributed to the East. Tobacco, introduced from the New World, immediately caught the popular fancy, and an enormous habit of smoking and snufftaking arose. The already varied alcoholic drinks of Europe were supplemented by wines and rum from the New World. New drugs were imported from America to ease the suffering of the European sick. All these goods drew the attention of European merchants who saw the possibilities of profit in a seller's market.

6. *The Putting-Out, or Domestic, System*

Revolution in Production. Medieval production was defined and limited by the guild system, which emphasized the social ideals of subsistence, security, and equality of opportunity. During the thirteenth and fourteenth centuries, in the heyday of the Italian and German monopolies, the function of the merchant in commercial life was considerably enhanced. The development of luxury trades and the changing of demand called for a transformation of production. A system of production was needed which would (1) stress initiative, risk-taking, and profit-taking; (2) substitute wage payments to home-workers instead of price to handicraftsmen; and (3) be used in suitable industries without upsetting the established order. The term now used by economic historians to designate the new form of economic organization designed to meet these needs is the "putting-out system," commonly known as the domestic system (*Hausindustrie* in German, *industrie à domicile* in French). Under this system, the entrepreneur, or organizer of industrial enterprise, gave out orders and "put out" material to be manufactured into the finished article by craftsmen. The self-directing worker agreed to do, or to have done by other hired craftsmen, work assigned under contract. This distinguished the worker from a handicraftsman who made a product for sale or to order for a consumer.

Characteristics. The main characteristic of the putting-out system was production to order. The entrepreneur, motivated by a spirit of independence and a desire for profit, placed his capital in industry in order to obtain the kind of goods he wanted. To meet the demands of both local consumers and the outside market, he supplied materials under contract to craftsmen who worked it with their own equipment, or he contributed both materials and equipment. He would sell the material to the craftsmen, under the condition that they sell the finished product exclusively to him at a price specified in advance. The means of production, maintained at the worker's home, were operated by hand. The worker, who made the complete product, was independent and self-directing. Ordinarily, he owned the means of production or equipment himself, although in some cases he obtained them from the entrepreneur. Production costs were high as compared with costs under the subsequent factory system.

The Entrepreneur. The putting-out system relieved the entrepreneur of the expense of maintaining a large shop or factory, as well as the trouble of carefully watching the production stages of his goods. If the workman-

ship were not acceptable, he simply refused to accept the finished product, or he made certain to place his orders elsewhere the next time. The system was especially attractive to entrepreneurs of small means, for they did not need a large investment to realize a profit. Against these advantages there were some disadvantages. Precious time was lost in carting materials back and forth through successive stages of manufacture. Moreover, the lack of supervision, made it difficult for the entrepreneur to maintain high and uniform standards of quality.

The Worker. For the worker, the era of the putting-out system brought no golden age. True, he was self-directing and free to work in his own home when and how he pleased, and he was free to shift from employer to employer, conditions highly regarded by workers in a time of growing individualism. He generally had the assistance of members of his family to meet the date of delivery. He was not at first subjected to the evils of unemployment, and he could easily find work as long as there was a demand for products. He had a chance to earn extra income at harvest time. If dissatisfied with his lot he could move to better-paid or more inviting regions. But counteracting these advantages were a number of disadvantages, most of which appeared as the system developed. In the early days of the putting-out system, the worker supplied his own equipment, but with increased production he found himself increasingly bound to the entrepreneur by rented tools and equipment. The rising competition for work, resulting from the steady increase in the number of available workers, eventually led to the misery of unemployment. With lower prices paid for finished goods, the laborer had to spend more and more time at his grinding work. To make a living, many laborers found it necessary to use the services of wife and children, all working long hours at low wages.

7. The New Regulation: Mercantilism

Meaning. Mercantilism may be defined as the means used by European statesmen from 1500 to 1750 to create powerful commercial and industrial states. It was the economic counterpart of political unification. A form of national economic control superseding the weakened regulation of the guilds, it was the result of an alliance between kings and commercial groups in an age of expanding economic frontiers. It was never a system, or a philosophy, or a specific school of economic thought, but rather a tendency.

Aims. The first aim of mercantilism as it developed in England, France, and Spain was concentration of economic life in the interests of a strong national state. Mercantilist policy held that the State must make its authority in the economic sphere as decisive as in political life, and that economic unity went along with political unity. The second aim of mercantilism was to strengthen the State against all other states. In an age of rising national feeling, every state was presumed to be the natural commercial rival or at least a potential enemy of every other state. It must increase its own prosperity as much as possible and at the same time restrict the commerce of its rivals.

Principles. The basic principles of mercantilism can be stated as follows: (1) The power of a state, the happiness of its subjects, and the extent of its trade and industry depend upon its supply of precious metals. According to this principle, often called the *bullionist theory,* the possession of bullion or gold and silver, instead of commodities, was the basis of economic prosperity. As a result, the great nations of Western Europe joined in a scramble for the precious metals of the New World. (2) Those states which had no external sources of precious metals could attract treasure by manufacturing as much goods as possible to sell abroad. This principle, called the *merchandising theory,* was designed by English, French, and Dutch mercantilists, who at first had no access to sources of precious metals but who refused to resign their countries to weakness while the Spanish became rich and powerful. (3) As a means of discouraging the drain of bullion out of a country, mercantilists advocated placing of customs duties, or tariffs, on all imported goods. The tariffs would raise the prices of certain goods to so high a point that people would naturally prefer to buy similar goods manufactured in their own country. This principle, termed the *protectionist theory,* was supposed not only to encourage home production and keep bullion in the country, but also to furnish surplus goods for sale abroad and hence attract additional money into the country. (4) The state would know whether it was gaining or losing trade by maintaining a *balance of trade.* The objective was the establishment of a favorable balance of trade, by which a state exported more goods than it imported, the difference flowing into the country in the form of gold. Thus additional bullion was attracted to the state to make its people prosperous, strong, and happy.

Methods. Mercantilists offered several suggestions for the important business of maintaining a favorable balance of trade. First was positive aid and encouragement given to industry and commerce. All manufacturing, particularly that which was not required to use imported raw materials, was favored by laws designed to protect the home product. The government granted bounties, subsidies, and bonuses to infant industries; it assisted in the establishment of new manufacturing undertakings by providing some of the capital; it exempted some industries from taxation or guild restraints; to others it granted monopoly rights to make certain commodities, or exclusive trading rights in certain areas; it protected the home markets by erecting high tariff barriers or by prohibiting imports; it encouraged the importation of raw materials but forbade the export of such materials to competing countries; and it stimulated the consumption of homemade products. In addition, mercantilists believed that it was to the advantage of the state to take adequate measures to ensure a large supply of industrial workers; hence, they encouraged marriage and urged that skilled foreign workers be welcomed as immigrants and that the emigration of artisans be forbidden. They strongly favored such national improvements as the construction of bridges, canals, roads, and harbors, on the ground that whatever helped trade and industry always furthered the prosperity of the state. They supported a strong navy on the assumption that protective convoys were necessary for merchant shipping.

Aware that even a few inferior or defective articles might ruin a nation's commercial reputation abroad, mercantilists brought all production under systematic regulations, not

The East India wharf. Painting by Peter Monarny.

dissimilar to the restrictions of the old craft guilds.

Place of Colonies in the System. Mercantilists regarded colonies as an indispensable cog in the machinery of a successful state. Colonies existed primarily to be monopolized and exploited. They received protection from the mother country, but they in turn were expected to supply raw materials for home industries, buy products of the mother state,

and in general supplement the needs of the mother country. Furthermore, to make the colonial market as large as possible, the colonies were forbidden to manufacture anything the mother country had for sale, lest they exhaust their own raw materials and refrain from buying Europe-made goods. The mother country made certain to exclude all foreign traders from the colonial markets. Most European states which possessed colonies maintained the practice of colonial regulation, usually issuing Navigation Acts which required all goods imported to be brought in ships owned and operated by the mother country.

Mercantilist Fallacies. Mercantilism was of greater interest for what it attempted than for what it achieved. Although the pattern was a popular one, many of its assumptions were erroneous, particularly the premise that bullion is the most important measure of national prosperity and that a favorable balance of trade necessarily means an increase in the supply of precious metals. Moreover, mercantilists assumed that the amount of possible trade in the world was static, so that what one state gained in commerce, another lost. They did not understand that trade, far from being static, is susceptible to expansion. They did not realize that new trade could be created by the expedient of fashioning new tastes and desires through advertising and promotion.

Ebb of Mercantilism. Mercantilism flourished in the sixteenth and reached its peak in the seventeenth century. Under the combination of the Grand Monarch, Louis XIV, and his great minister, Colbert (1619–1683), mercantilism was more completely and vigorously applied than at any other time. Colbert utilized every conceivable phase of mercantilist policy. It did not succeed in its aims. Nevertheless, the idea of mercantilism revealed few signs of disintegration and the states of Europe showed no intention of abandoning it completely. By the end of the eighteenth century, it had passed its peak. The conditions which had brought it into being no longer existed; the great economic changes were now to be industrial and agricultural, and nations which had once sought merely to acquire bullion now became more and more interested in finding markets for expanding industries.

8. Modern Man and the New Economy

Europe's Common Man. There were striking changes as Europe burst its economic bonds. Out of the redirection of social energies that marked the Commercial Revolution came new economic ideas which became foundations for ensuing thought and action. At first only a very small class—the bourgeoisie—benefited as commerce shifted from the town to the State and as the scale of commercial operations was enlarged and deepened. This class remained comparatively small from the fifteenth to the eighteenth centuries. Allied with the willing kings, it utilized the rapidly growing national feelings to triumph over the feudal landlords and then went on to push both clergy and nobility to a position of minor importance in society.

But what about the common man, the average man, the man on the farm and the man on the street? Although he knew little about the revolutionary changes that were taking place unseen in his economic life, he was nevertheless affected by them. An anonymous unit in the vast mass of peasants, artisans, and small shopkeepers, he was reduced to a worse state than before, through misfortune, through blind adherence to old ideals and methods, or as a result of the commercial and industrial practices of the energetic middle class. Without actually knowing it, he was guided firmly by the impelling hand of the commercially powerful, who fostered and carefully watched all his interests, whether economic, political, religious, or cultural. He was engulfed in the great wave of national spirit which swept away the old feudal loyalty and established in its place a greater loyalty to king and country. He shared some of the successes of the middle class, yet despite the rise of wealth and the standard of living, he received but a small and disproportionate share of the fruits of trade.

Economic Transformation. What, in summary, were the changes that distinguished the economic life of early modern man from that of his predecessor, the medieval man?

(1) *From Agrarianism to Urbanization:* For nearly a thousand years the economic foundations of European life had been agrarian. Medieval man, always living on the margin of subsistence, toiled unremittingly on the land to sustain life for himself and his family. He

performed his allotted or inherited tasks without question, because there was no room for economic innovation in a society in which individuals necessarily depended upon one another's efforts. Modern man, on the other hand, was impelled by circumstance to shift his

interest from an agrarian to an urban economy, from village to town, and then from town to State. True, millions still lived in hamlets which dotted the countryside, but most men were part of, or were influenced by, the new urbanized, cosmopolitan civilization.

Shops under a covered market (goldsmith, dealer in stuffs, and shoemaker). From a miniature in Aristotle's *Ethics and Politics,* translated by Nicholas Oresme. Manuscript of the fifteenth century, Library of Rouen.

(2) *From Sustenance to Exchange:* Bound in the framework of self-sustaining economic units insulated from the rest of the world, medieval man had no incentive to improve his lot. By custom he was interested only in a bare subsistence, just enough to maintain life without luxury or refinements. In a changing world which brought new commercial techniques, a quickening of trade, an enlargement of markets, and improvements in transportation and communication, modern man quite naturally deserted the old sustenance economy and concentrated upon the exchange of goods. A surplus economy was the new ideal of men motivated by the desire for profits.

(3) *From Communalism to Individualism:* Although there were some notoriously individualistic aspects in his society, medieval man was absorbed in the communal life of manorialism and the guild system. With the rise of capitalism the medieval spirit of communalism gave way to individualism. Modern man was imbued with the spirit of individual gain as well as individualism in thought.

(4) *From Frugality to Riches:* Whereas medieval man was interested in his frugal comfort and was undisturbed by visions of great profits and riches, modern man became increasingly devoted to the acquisition of money. He once thought in terms of goods and services as the main components of his

economic life, but now he regarded money and profit as the most attractive goals of his stay on earth. Money was universally accepted as the new instrument of wealth. It bought not merely subsistence but power. It was the solvent which transformed the manorial regime into the capitalist economy.

(5) *From Restriction to Freedom:* Medieval man was restricted and regulated in his eco-nomic life; modern man broke the bonds of restraint and demanded more and more free-dom. He wanted no obstacles in the path of commercial or industrial enterprise. At first guild restrictions were replaced by state regu-lations, but eventually the bourgeoisie—key class in the new society—was to demand and obtain *laissez-faire,* or freedom from economic interference.

⊰[KEY READING]⊱

THOMAS MUN ON THE DOCTRINE OF MERCANTILISM

Thomas Mun, *England's Treasure by Foreign Trade* (Oxford, 1933), pp. 5–13. By per-mission of Basil Blackwell, Publisher.

ABOUT 1630 THOMAS MUN (1571–1641), a wealthy London merchant and a director of the East India Company, wrote *England's Treasure by Foreign Trade,* a statement of the mercantilist doctrine of economic self-sufficiency by the creation of a favorable trade balance. The ordinary means, he said, to increase England's wealth and treasure was by foreign trade, but always observing the rule: to sell more to strangers yearly than we consume of theirs in value. The following excerpts from Mun's book in sum-mary form illustrate how mercantilists of his day regarded the nature and sources of a state's prosperity.

The revenue or stock of a kingdom by which it is provided of foreign wares is either natural or artificial. The natural wealth is so much only as can be spared from our own use and necessities to be exported unto strangers. The artificial con-sists in our manufactures and industrious trad-ing with foreign commodities, concerning which I will set down such particulars as may serve for the cause we have in hand.

1. First, although this realm be already ex-ceeding rich by nature, yet might it be much increased by laying the waste grounds (which are infinite) into such employments as should no way hinder the present revenues of other ma-nured lands, but hereby to supply ourselves and prevent the importations of hemp, flax, cordage, tobacco, and divers other things which now we fetch from strangers to our great impoverishing.

2. We may likewise diminish our importa-tions, if we would soberly refrain from excessive consumption of foreign wares in our diet and raiment.

3. In our exportations we must not only re-gard our own superfluities, but also we must consider our neighbors' necessities, that so upon the wares which they cannot want, nor yet be furnished thereof elsewhere, we may (besides the sale of the materials) gain so much of the manufacture as we can, and also endeavor to sell them dear, so far forth as the high price cause not a less sale in the quantity. . . .

4. The value of our exportations likewise may be much advanced when we perform it ourselves in our own ships, for then we get not only the price of our wares as they are worth here, but also the merchants' gains, the charges of in-surance and freight to carry them beyond the seas. . . .

5. The frugal expending likewise of our own natural wealth might advance much yearly to be exported unto strangers; and if in our rai-ment we will be prodigal, yet let this be done with our own materials and manufactures, as cloth, lace, embroideries, cutworks, and the like,

where the excess of the rich may be the employment of the poor, whose labors notwithstanding of this kind, would be more profitable for the commonwealth, if they were done to the use of strangers.

6. The fishing in His Majesty's seas of England, Scotland, and Ireland is our natural wealth, and would cost nothing but labor, which the Dutch bestow willingly, and thereby draw yearly a very great profit to themselves by serving many places of Christendom with our fish, for which they return and supply their wants both of foreign wares and money. . . .

7. A staple or magazine for foreign corn, indigo, spices, raw-silks, cotton, wool, or any other commodity whatsoever, to be imported will increase shipping, trade, treasure, and the King's customs, by exporting them again where need shall require. . . .

8. Also we ought to esteem and cherish those trades which we have in remote or far countries, for besides the increase of shipping and mariners thereby, the wares also sent thither and received from thence are far more profitable unto the kingdom than by our trades near at hand. . . .

9. It would be very beneficial to export money as well as wares, being done in trade only, it would increase our treasure; but of this I write more largely in the next chapter to prove it plainly.

10. It were policy and profit for the state to suffer manufactures made of foreign materials to be exported custom-free, as velvets and all other wrought silks, fustians, thrown silks and the like, it would employ very many poor people, and much increase the value of our stock yearly issued into other countries, and it would (for this purpose) cause the more foreign materials to be brought in, to the improvement of His Majesty's customs. But if any man allege the Dutch proverb, Live and let others live; I answer, that the Dutchmen notwithstanding their own proverb do not only in these kingdoms, encroach upon our livings, but also in other foreign parts of our trade (where they have power) they do hinder and destroy us in our lawful course of living, hereby taking the bread out of our mouth, which we shall never prevent by plucking the pot from their nose, as of late years too many of us do practise to the great hurt and dishonor of this famous nation. . . .

11. It is needful also not to charge the native commodities with too great customs, lest by endearing them to the stranger's use, it hinder their sale. . . .

12. Lastly, in all things we must endeavor to make the most we can of our own, whether it be natural or artificial. And forasmuch as the people which live by the arts are far more in number than they who are masters of the fruits, we ought the more carefully to maintain those endeavors of the multitude, in whom doth consist the greatest strength and riches both of King and Kingdom; for where the people are many, and the arts good, there the traffic must be great, and the country rich.

ꕤ HISTORICAL INTERPRETATION ꕤ

JEAN BODIN ON THE CAUSE OF RISING PRICE LEVELS, 1568

Condensed from Jean Bodin, *Concerning the Dearness of All Things* (1568), as quoted in Arthur Eli Monroe, ed., *Early Economic Thought: Selections from Economic Literature Prior to Adam Smith* (Boston, 1924), pp. 127–132, *passim*. By permission of Harvard University Press.

JEAN BODIN (1530–1596), French philosopher and economist, was interested primarily in creating a system of political science but he also turned his attention to economic matters. In 1568 he wrote an explanation of the rapid increase of prices during his day in an effort to correct what he believed to be false impressions.

I find that the high prices we see today are due to some four or five causes. The principal and almost the only one (which no one has referred to until now) is the abundance of gold and silver, which is today much greater in this Kingdom than it was four hundred years ago, to go no further back. The second reason for the high prices arises in part from monopolies. The third is scarcity, caused partly by export and partly by waste. The fourth is the pleasure of kings and great lords, who raise the price of the things they like. The fifth has to do with the price of money, debased from its former standard.

The principal reason which raises the price of everything, wherever one may be, is the abundance of that which governs the appraisal and price of things. Now it was not the scarcity of lands, which can neither increase nor diminish, or monopoly, which cannot exist in such a case: but it was the abundance of gold and silver which causes the depreciation of these and the dearness of the things.

It is therefore necessary to demonstrate that there was not as much gold and silver in this Kingdom three hundred years ago as there is now: which is evident at a glance. For if there is money in a country, it cannot be so well hidden that Princes will not find it, when they are in straits. Now the fact is that King John was unable to obtain a loan of sixty thousand francs (let us call them *escus*) in his extreme need.

Now if we come down to our own times, we shall find that in six months the King obtained in Paris, without going outside, more than three million four hundred thousand livres, besides the household charges, which were also obtained in Paris, as well as the subsidies and domainal revenues.

The fact is that the Spaniard, who gets his subsistence only from France, being compelled by unavoidable necessity to come here for wheat, cloths, stuffs, dye-stuffs, paper, books, even joinery and all handicraft products, goes to the ends of the earth to seek gold and silver and spices to pay us with.

On the other hand, the English, the Scotch, and all the people of Norway, Sweden, Denmark, and the Baltic coast, who have an infinity of mines, dig the metals out of the center of the earth to buy our wines, our saffron, our prunes, our dye, and especially our salt, which is a manna that God gives us as a special favor, with little labor. The other cause of the great amount of wealth that has come to us in the last hundred and twenty or thirty years is the huge population which has grown up in this Kingdom, since the civil wars between the houses of Orleans and Bourgogne were ended.

Another cause of the riches of France is the trade with the Levant, which was opened to us as a result of the friendship between the house of France and the house of the Ottomans in the time of King Francis the first; so that French merchants since that time have done business in Alexandria, in Cairo, in Beirut, in Tripoli, as well as the Venetians and Genoese; and have as good standing at Fez and at Morocco as the Spaniard.

Another cause of the abundance of gold and silver has been the bank of Lyons, which was opened, to tell the truth, by King Francis the First, who began to borrow money at the twelfth penny, and his successor at the tenth, then the sixth, and up to the fifth in emergencies.

These, Sir, are the means which have brought us gold and silver in abundance in the last two hundred years. There is much more in Spain and Italy than in France, owing to the fact that in Italy even the nobility engage in trade, and the people of Spain have no other occupation; and so everything is dearer in Spain than in Italy. It is the abundance of gold and silver which causes, in part, the high prices of things.

❧ TEN BASIC BOOKS ❧

TRANSITION IN ECONOMIC LIFE: THE COMMERCIAL REVOLUTION

1. Cole, Charles, *French Mercantilist Doctrines Before Colbert* (New York, 1931).
2. Gras, Norman, *A History of Agriculture in Europe and America,* 2nd ed. (New York, 1940).

3. Heaton, Herbert, *Economic History of Europe,* rev. ed. (New York, 1948).

4. Heckscher, Eli, *Mercantilism,* 2 vols., rev. 2nd ed. (New York, 1955).

5. Ogg, Frederick A., and W. R. Sharp, *Economic Development of Modern Europe* (New York, 1929).

6. Packard, Laurence B., *The Commercial Revolution* (New York, 1927).

7. Pares, Richard, *War and Trade in the West Indies, 1739–1763* (New York, 1963).

8. Sée, Henri, *Modern Capitalism: Its Origins and Evolution* (London, 1928).

9. Sombart, Werner, *The Quintessence of Capitalism: A Study of the History and Psychology of the Modern Businessman* (London, 1915).

10. Tawney, Richard H., *Religion and the Rise of Capitalism* (New York, 1926).†

† In the selected bibliographies which follow each chapter, a dagger is used to indicate that a paperback edition is now available.

2

The Expansion of Europe

ALTHOUGH the discoveries actually accomplished appear great and surprising, yet I should have effected much more had I been furnished with a proper fleet. Nevertheless the great success of this enterprise is not to be ascribed to my own merits, but to the holy Catholic faith and the piety of our Sovereigns, the Lord often granting to men what they never imagine themselves capable of effecting, as He is accustomed to hear the prayers of His servants and those who love His commandments, even in that which appears impossible; in this manner has it happened to me who have succeeded in an undertaking never before accomplished by man. For although some persons have written or spoken of the existence of these islands, they have all rested their assertions upon conjecture, no one having ever affirmed that he saw them, on which account their existence has been deemed fabulous.

And now ought the King, Queen, Princes, and all their dominions, as well as the whole of Christendom, to give thanks to our Saviour Jesus Christ who has granted us such a victory and great success. Let processions be ordered, let solemn festivals be celebrated, let the temples be filled with boughs and flowers. Let Christ rejoice upon earth as He does in heaven, to witness the coming salvation of so many people, heretofore given over to perdition. Let us rejoice for the exaltation of our faith, as well as for the augmentation of our temporal prosperity, in which not only in Spain but all Christendom shall participate.
—CHRISTOPHER COLUMBUS to Rafael Sanchez, March 1493

1. El Dorado: Discovery of the World's Highway

Age of European Dominance. The period between 1500 and the present may be called the Age of European Dominance. From the relatively small European continent flowed the language, art, laws, religion, inventions, and ideas that largely shaped the modern world. At the same time there was a reverse effect as the non-European world came to play an increasingly important role in commerce, diplomacy, and war.

When the New World was discovered, European civilization began to expand. Stimulated by the success of Prince Henry the Navigator, mariners began to compete for new routes to the rich lands of the East. Explorers reached areas of the globe never before touched by Europeans. As commerce and exploration increased, the flags of territorial claimants appeared in many new lands.

It was an epic age of remarkable exploits, of raw courage under great difficulties, of energy and determination. In turn, Portuguese, Dutch, Spanish, and French colonial empires rose and declined, eventually leaving England as the dominant imperial–colonial power. European civilization, European ideas, European attitudes, European culture, all were spread out upon an expanded horizon. In contrast to this dynamism, the older civilizations of China and India lived on placidly in cultural and religious isolation.

The New Navigation. The discovery of the world's highway was due in part to a series of inventions in the art of navigation and improvements in maritime architecture. The magnetic compass was now in general use among Mediterranean mariners. Latitude could be determined by use of the cross staff and the astrolabe, but it was not until the eighteenth century that an instrument was devised for calculating longitude, the distance east or west of a given point. Sixteenth-century mariners, with stronger ships, compass charts of the coasts, and a growing knowledge of winds,

Spanish caravel in which Columbus discovered America. From a drawing attributed to Columbus and placed in the *Epistola Christofori Columbi,* undated edition (1494?).

currents, and astronomy, ventured farther and farther from land and groped their way to distant places. Navigation instruments were steadily improved. With the aid of the compass, the astrolabe, the quadrant, the sextant (*c.* 1731), the marine chronometer (1735),

and telescopes, mariners sailed with more and more confidence over the oceans. They were aided by improvements in marine architecture. A new type of ship, the caravel—light, short, with a square poop—was more fitted for the hazardous open seas than anything that had been used earlier for ocean transport. With the construction of lighthouses, the clearing of harbors, and the inauguration of pilot service, maritime activity increased still further.

All-water Route to the Orient. The search for an all-water route to the Orient resulted from the commercial conditions of the day. The Crusades had stimulated trade in various Eastern products, which many Europeans now regarded as necessities rather than as luxuries. In 1453 the Ottoman Turks captured Constantinople, the emporium of trade on the Black Sea and key to the best land route between Europe and Asia. At one time it was the fashion among historians to attribute the shift in the world's commerce from the Mediterranean to the Atlantic to the fact that when the Turks threatened the old trade routes, Europeans were forced to find a new route to India and Cathay. Europeans were supposed to be starved for spices and doomed either to eat flavorless food or to pay outrageous prices, unless they could find a way to circumvent the Turks. Besides, to those nineteenth-century historians who stressed the fall of Constantinople the Turk was an "unspeakable fanatic" whose main pursuit was trade and whose hobby was the persecution or slaughter of Christians. This is an interesting thesis, but it is untrue. The Turks, like their Muslim predecessors, maintained commercial relations with Western Europeans. There was no drying-up of commerce with the Orient, nor was there any scarcity of Oriental goods, which never ceased to be available during the fifteenth century. The price of pepper actually declined during the decades before the outburst of great discoveries. There is no evidence in the narratives of the explorers to indicate that their maritime adventures were forced upon them by the Turks. The expansion of European commerce would have taken place even if Constantinople had not fallen. The

Mediterranean had simply outlived its usefulness as the main artery of commerce.

Motives for Expansion: Gold, Glory, Gospel. Among the complex motives which stimulated men, monarchs, and nations in the new era was the inspiration of the three G's: Gold, Glory, Gospel. Desire for gold was a factor of prime importance. The discovery of gold in the New World aroused intense interest among Europeans. The possibility of acquiring bullion attracted both individuals and nations. The discovery came with incredible timeliness, since the exhaustion of European mines, especially in the Rhineland, had led to a shortage of the precious metal. The New World also offered adventurous Europeans the opportunity for personal glory as well as riches. Men who desired to play the hero were fascinated by stories of tremendous fortunes in gold and silver to be acquired in the New World without trouble once the ferocious savages who stood in the way were eliminated. Added to these motives was a desire to spread the Gospel. Faced with internal difficulties, the growth of heresy, and the rise of national states, the Roman Catholic Church sought to revive its waning influence in Europe and also to acquire a foothold in the New World. There were millions of people outside Europe waiting to be converted. Explorers, adventurers, and missionaries gladly undertook the task. Many were attracted by the prospect of eternal salvation awarded to servants of the Church who planted the Cross in foreign lands.

Historical Controversy: Gold or Missionary Zeal? At one time it was believed that the expansion of Europe from the end of the fifteenth century to the eighteenth century was merely a political reflection of the power struggles of the great European states. In the triple aim of "Gold, Glory, and Gospel," it was assumed that political glory was the dominating factor in the great expansion of European arms, commerce, and culture. Gradually, however, scholars turned their attention to economic, social, and religious factors in overseas expansion.

In his *American Treasure and the Price Revolution in Spain* (1934), Earl J. Hamilton saw the leading motive as the hope of material gain, especially hope of profit from the spice trade. A monopoly on colonial trade was connected contractually with European expansion into the West, as the kings of England and France promised exclusive trading privileges in their early patents for discovery and colonization. Similarly, the monopoly on trade gave the Dutch, English, and French East India Companies an incentive to commerce and empire in the East.

On the other hand, J. H. Parry, in his *Europe and a Wider World* (1949), while accepting the thesis of the profit motive, placed much greater emphasis upon the rule of missionary zeal, which he tied up with the Crusades. Admitting that no nation undertakes the labor and expense of colonial expansion without hope of profit, he held that throughout the whole story of European expansion there was an imperialism which accepted duties as well as profits. The continuous missionary tradition running back to the thirteenth century, he said, was vitally important in the Europeanization of the world. Parry envisaged the Spanish conquest of America as a "genuine crusade," appealing at the same time to the missionary's zeal for souls and to the professional soldier's desire for military glory and for plunder.

2. *Portuguese Activity*

Portugal. Medieval Portugal had been merely an obscure border section of Spain, whose history it shared. By the end of the Middle Ages, however, she was one of the most unified nations in Europe. While others were preoccupied with Mediterranean trade, the Portuguese looked toward the west. Using excellent harbors on the western seaboard of Europe, they had already developed a maritime trade in wine, fruit, and oil with France and England by hugging the coasts and venturing northward. When the impulse came for opening the world's highway, the Portuguese were ready. Between 1440 and 1580 they constructed the first colonial empire of modern times, reaching from Brazil to the East Indies.

Prince Henry the Navigator. The emergence of Portugal as a prosperous maritime power was due in large part to the brilliant planning of Prince Henry, surnamed the Navigator (1394–1460). During his early manhood, Henry had taken part in a series of crusades against the Moors and led expeditionary campaigns along the African coastline. Throughout his life he was intrigued by the possibility of establishing contact with a legendary

Christian ruler, Prester John, who was said to have established a Christian kingdom in the East. The possibility of trade was a byproduct of his crusading zeal. In 1419 he settled in Sagres, on the southwest tip of Portugal, where he established a kind of research institute, complete with shipyards, observatory, and classrooms. Here he trained pilots, navigators, captains, astronomers, and cartographers. His captains set out southward and westward on a series of island-hops, reaching the Madeiras, the Cape Verde Islands, and the Azores.

The Portuguese Empire. Shortly after Prince Henry's death in 1460, Portuguese captains

attempted the circumnavigation of Africa, a venture completed in 1486 by Bartholomeu Díaz. Late in 1497 Vasco da Gama rounded the Cape of Good Hope and struck boldly across the Indian Ocean, reaching Calicut on the western coast of India the following spring. Soon other Portuguese explorers swarmed into the Sahara hinterland, the interior of Africa, the Far East, and the New World. In 1500 King Emanuel of Portugal assumed the designation of "Lord of the Conquest, Navigation, and Commerce of India, Ethiopia, Arabia, and Persia," a high-sounding title confirmed by the papacy two years later.

As Mediterranean trade decayed and the Italian cities lost their importance, Portugal constructed a huge commercial empire. Lisbon became the center of trade in bullion, slaves, and ivory. Portuguese merchants established a string of settlements between the homeland and the Orient. They sent out a great fleet of merchant ships, manned by energetic and courageous sailors. The idea was to circumvent the African middleman by gaining direct access to sources of gold and slaves. The trade in slaves was justified on the ground that it was necessary to save the souls of unfortunate black men.

For a brief century the Portuguese in the Far East and the Spanish in America shared the fruits of a comprehensive trade monopoly. In 1580, however, Spain invaded Portugal and held her throne in captivity for sixty years. This, added to several other factors, brought a decline of Portuguese commercial life. The Portuguese fleet was spread so thinly that it could not possibly serve the needs of an expanded commerce. Moreover, Portugal had a manpower problem. A small nation with fewer than two million people, she found it impossible to meet the demands of worldwide trade. For a time she sought to impress convicts, criminals, and young boys to provide the lifeblood for empire, but these devices were no more successful than the expedient of encouraging alliances between Portuguese men and local women in the colonies. Portuguese capitalists, caught short on funds, found themselves in the grip of German and Italian financiers. Moreover, Portuguese colonial administration was weakened by inefficiency and corruption. By the time her dynasty was restored in 1640, Portugal had to face the competition of the Dutch, French, and English, all of whom had access to virtually unlimited supplies of capital and manpower.

3. The Role of Spain

Spain. While Portugal painstakingly planned the way for empire, Spain's rewards fell to her accidentally, unexpectedly, and without much effort on her part. By the end of the fifteenth century the long crusade against Muslim power had come to an end. Unity was foreshadowed by the marriage of Ferdinand of Aragon and Isabella of Castile, which joined the central pastoral kingdom with the eastern agricultural and commercial areas. The accidental discovery of America enabled the Spanish to construct a colonial empire in the New World and to emerge as the most powerful European nation of the sixteenth century. Once set on the road to international supremacy, they drove ahead with tremendous energy.

Christopher Columbus. Of Christopher Columbus (*c.* 1451–1506), who discovered America for Spain, less is known than of Shakespeare. Born in the neighborhood of Genoa, he went to sea at the age of fourteen, settled at Lisbon, married the daughter of one of Prince Henry's captains, and served for some years under the Portuguese crown. It is not certain whether his purpose was to reach the East Indies and Cathay by sailing west, or whether he wanted to discover new islands in the Atlantic for his sponsors. At any rate, he appealed for financial backing to several persons, all of whom rejected his proposals as fantastic. Finally, on April 17, 1492, he was commissioned by Ferdinand and Isabella to test his theory that he could reach the fabulous wealth of Asia by sailing westward. In four voyages Columbus opened the New World to Spanish enterprise. At first his fruitless search for wealth disappointed his sponsors, but if Spain did not immediately obtain access to the enormous riches of the Orient, she later became incredibly rich from resources in the New World.

Columbus died in the belief that he had reached the outskirts of China and India. Amerigo Vespucci (1451-1512), a Florentine navigator who reached the northern coast of South America in 1499, gave publicity to the idea that a new world had been discovered; ironically, it was his name, rather than that of Columbus, which became that of the new continents.

Spain Versus Portugal. The voyages of Columbus and the beginnings of Spanish exploration in the New World alarmed the Portuguese. In 1493 Spain requested Pope Alexander VI to settle the rivalry. A papal Bull of Demarcation assigned to Spain all the land west of a line from the Arctic Pole to the Antarctic at a point "a hundred leagues towards the west and south of the Azores and Cape Verde Islands." Portugal was to have all lands discovered east of this line. In 1494, the line was moved westward 370 leagues by the Treaty of Tordesillas between the two powers. England and France, whose claims were excluded, paid no attention to this agreement.

Spanish Enterprise. During the half-century after the first voyage of Columbus, Spanish navigators, explorers, and *conquistadores* (conquerors) set out on enthusiastic expeditions to the New World to stake their claims. Attracted originally by the hope of acquiring prized commodities in the Far East, the Spaniards quickly shifted their field of vision when they heard reports of fabulous wealth in the New World. It was a movement of discovery, conquest, and colonization. In 1513 Ponce de León landed in Florida near the site of the present city of St. Augustine in search of a legendary fountain of perpetual youth. He was doomed to disappointment, for he found neither youth nor gold. In the same year Vasco Núñez de Balboa crossed Central America and became the first European to behold the waters of the Pacific from its eastern shore. Intoxicated by a report of the existence of gold, Hernando Cortés led an army into Mexico, where, between 1519 and 1521, he conquered the Aztec government. In the meantime, starting in 1519, the expedition of

Cortés scuttles his ships, thereby cutting off all chances of his discontented followers abandoning the enterprise. Lithograph after painting by O. Graeff.

Ferdinand Magellan, a Portuguese mariner in the service of Spain, completed the first circumnavigation of the globe. Between 1531 and 1535, Francisco Pizarro subjugated the rich Inca empire centering in Peru. In 1540 Francisco Vasquez de Coronado set out to explore the western area of North America, and the next year Fernando de Soto discovered the Mississippi River.

The Spanish Colonial Empire. The construction of the Spanish empire was a story of conquest in the grand manner, colored by avarice and bigotry. The deeds of Spanish explorers inflamed the imaginations of others, who flocked to the New World in search of gold and glory. Missionaries accompanied the soldiers and settlers to convert the natives to Christianity. The *conquistadores* became rich beyond their dreams. These men on horseback struck down the prosperous Aztec and Inca civilizations, which now lay prostrate at their feet. They received *encomiendas*—the right to

extract service and tribute, in return for which they agreed to civilize the backward tribes. In effect, this meant the transplanting of European feudalism and the European labor system to the new continents. In her Golden Century, Spain acquired a colonial empire, which included Central and South America (excluding Portuguese Brazil), the West Indies, Florida, California, and Mexico—one of the most extensive empires which the world had ever known.

Paralyzing absolutism and economic deficits soon shattered the fruits of Spanish imperialism. The empire disintegrated because of a combination of unfavorable political and economic factors. Politically, the Spanish colonial system was an appendage of royal absolutism. The Spanish dynasty was attempting a tremendous task and one with which it simply could not cope; it dissipated its energies as it sought to preserve its control in Europe, run the Netherlands, extirpate Protestantism, combat Turkish power, and at the same time construct a strong empire in the New World. From Madrid a centralized bureaucracy supervised and directed the experiment in colonialism. It was a hard task to subdue, convert, and administer the indigenous peoples of the New World in view of the distances, the difficulties of transportation and communication, and the dogged resistance of the natives.

From the beginning the *conquistadores* were obsessed by the lust for precious metal. The attempts to build industrial and commercial enterprises in Spain failed dismally, as Spanish merchants and capitalists sent their gold supply to other countries to buy products instead of using it to build a healthy economy in Spain itself. The motherland became exhausted by the burden of exploration and colonial government, while the Spanish people were oppressed by taxation and inflation. With business initiative stifled, tax evasion rampant, bribery considered normal in official circles, trade and industry scorned, Spain was unable to meet the competition of the Netherlands, France, and England. The final blow came in 1588, when Spain's proud "Invincible Armada" was annihilated by a combination of British seamanship and unfriendly nature. The empire declined shortly after this decisive defeat, although the Spanish cultural-religious heritage in the New World remained durable.

4. The Dutch, French, and English

Dutch Commercial Supremacy. With a favorable geographical position but with limited soil, the Dutch turned to maritime enterprise. In the late sixteenth and early seventeenth centuries, Dutch merchants broke into the Oriental trade at the expense of Portugal, acquiring Ceylon, Sumatra, the Spice Islands, and Java. Other explorers and merchant adventurers penetrated into South Africa, Brazil, the West Indies, and established a settlement at New Amsterdam, now New York. By the seventeenth century the Dutch, supplanting the Portuguese and the Spanish, had become the commercial masters of Europe. Like bees, they gathered honey from every land: Norway was their forest; the banks of the Rhine and the Garonne their vineyards,

the Germanies, Spain, and Ireland their sheep pastures; Poland and Prussia their grain fields; and India and Arabia their spice gardens. Amsterdam became the financial center of Europe and the world. But this great prosperity did not survive the seventeenth century. Dutch commerce succumbed to the aggressive rivalry of the French and English.

French Colonialism. Stimulated by discovery of the New World, France began to construct a colonial empire in the familiar fashion by sending out explorers and adventurers to gain a foothold on the North American continent. In 1524 Francis I sent out an expedition under command of Giovanni da Verrazano, a Florentine, who explored the American coast from Cape Fear southward, and then northward to Newfoundland. A decade later the king sent Jacques Cartier to find a westward passage to China; although Cartier failed in the mission, he did discover the Saint Lawrence River. In 1608 Samuel de Champlain founded Quebec, one of the first French settlements in America. In the late 1670's and early 1680's, René Robert Cavelier Sieur de La Salle explored the Mississippi River and claimed the entire valley for Louis XIV, calling it Louisiana. On the trail of these explorers came traders and trappers (Louis Joliet) and Jesuit missionaries (Jacques Marquette). The French carved out an inland empire in America, and in addition established colonies and trading posts in Africa and Asia. By the late seventeenth century, the French and English had supplanted the Portuguese, the Spanish, and the Dutch as the dominant colonial powers. A gigantic struggle between the French and English for world colonial power took place in the late eighteenth century.

English Initiative. With characteristic zeal the English entered the race for empire. In the search for a northeastern or northwestern passage to the riches of the Far East, John Cabot (1497) and his son Sebastian (1499), Venetians in the service of Henry VII, reached and laid claim to the northeastern coasts of North America. In 1576 Martin Frobisher reached what is now Baffin Land, and in 1585 John Davis discovered Davis Straits, between Greenland and Baffin Land. In 1609 Henry Hudson discovered the Hudson River, Hudson Strait, and Hudson Bay. All these expeditions —and others—failed to reach the Far East. During the reign of Elizabeth (1558–1603), gentleman adventurers, financed by English merchants and encouraged by the English government, began to prey on Spanish commerce. English sea dogs, including John

Sir Francis Drake (*c.* 1545–1596). Sailor and navigator, Drake played an important part in founding the English naval supremacy which was to last for centuries after his death. More than any other seaman, he epitomized the spirit of the Elizabethan age.

Hawkins and Francis Drake, preferred the lucrative business of privateering to the more difficult process of extracting treasure from America. The defeat of the Spanish Armada in 1588 and the foundation of the English East India Company in 1600 helped the formation of a commercial empire.

James I, called "the wisest fool in Christendom," becoming vexed with the Puritans among his subjects, decided to "harry them out of the land, or else do worse." The subsequent exodus of Puritans from England stimu-

lated the colonization of North America. The settlement of Plymouth in 1620 was followed by the rapid growth of sturdy young communities along the Atlantic seaboard. British companies chartered for trade in America became colonizing agencies, whose colonial planting gave England a firm foothold in the New World. Whereas New France was a commercial empire sparsely populated and closely regulated by the mother country, New England had many settlements and a large, rapidly increasing population. English colonists came to America impelled by political opposition to the government at home, religious dissent, or economic pressure, or a combination of two or three of these motives. The home government placed no obstacles in the way of emigration. Thus the American colonies in their early days had a class of solid British yeomen, who wanted land, security, religious freedom, and the right to govern themselves. On the whole, the English avoided the mistakes of the Spanish and French by taking care to refrain from dictatorial or despotic control. Their colonies were modeled on familiar British lines, with considerable local autonomy except in commercial affairs. British parliamentarianism and constitutionalism proved to be more durable than Spanish bureaucracy and absolutism.

In 1651 the English Parliament passed a Navigation Act making it illegal for any products to be imported into England except in British ships. Designed to wrest control of trade from the Dutch, the act led to a series of wars between the English and the Dutch (1652–1654, 1664–1666, and 1672–1674), as a result of which the English seized the Dutch colonies in America and smothered Dutch imperialism. Another conflict was inevitable in North America when the English began to expand westward into French spheres of influence. The Seven Years' War (1756–1763) between the English and French in America, and their struggle for the mastery of India (1751–1761) were phases in a worldwide test of strength. England, emerging as the victor, went on to build the greatest empire in world history.

⌈ KEY DOCUMENT ⌉

MAXIMILIANUS TRANSYLVANUS DESCRIBES THE FIRST
VOYAGE AROUND THE WORLD, 1519–1522

The First Voyage Round the World by Magellan, A Letter from Maximilianus Transylvanus to the Most Reverend Cardinal of Salzberg, trans. by Lord Stanley of Alderley for the Hakluyt Society (London, 1874), pp. 191–195.

FERDINAND MAGELLAN (Portuguese: Fernão de Magálhães) (1480–1521), the celebrated navigator, set off in five vessels on September 20, 1519, under the sponsorship of Charles V to discover a west route to the East Indies. Three years later a lone vessel of his fleet returned, the first ship to circumnavigate the globe. Magellan himself was killed in the Philippines in 1521. In the following selection Maximilianus Transylvanus, undersecretary of Charles V, describes how Magellan's small fleet passed the straits which bear his name.

Though Magellan perceived that any longer stay there was useless, yet, as the sea for several days was stormy and the sky threatening, and the land stretched continuously southwards, so that the farther they went the colder they would find that region, his departure was necessarily put off from day to day, till the month of May was close upon them, from which time the winter there begins to be most severe, so that it became necessary to winter at the very time when we have our summer. Magellan foreseeing that the voyage would be a long one, ordered provisions to be served out more sparingly among his crews, so that the stock might last longer. When the Spaniards had borne this patiently for some days, fearing the severity of the winter and the barrenness of the country, they at last petitioned their admiral, Magellan, that as he saw that the land stretched uninterruptedly to the south, and that no hope remained of its terminating or of the discovery of a strait through it, and that a severe winter was imminent, and that many of them were dead of starvation and hardships; and declared that they could no longer bear the rule which he had made about the allowance of provisions (*lex sumptuaria*), and begged that he would increase the allowance of provisions, and think about going home; that Caesar never intended that they should too obstinately attempt what nature itself and other obstacles opposed; that their exertions were already sufficiently known and approved of—for they had gone farther than either the boldness

or rashness of mortals had ever dared to go as yet; and that they could easily reach some milder shore, if they were to sail south [north?] for a few days, a south wind being then blowing. But in reply, Magellan, who had already made up his mind either to die or to complete his enterprise, said that his course had been laid down for him by Caesar himself, and that he neither could nor would depart from it in any degree, and that he would in consequence sail till he found either the end of the land or some strait.

That though they could not at present succeed whilst winter was against them, yet that it would be easy in the summer of that region. But that, if they would continue towards the Antarctic portion of this country, the whole of its summer would be one perpetual day. . . . He had certainly made up his mind to endure the worst rather than return ignominiously to Spain, and he trusted that all his comrades, or at least those in whom the noble Spanish spirit was not yet dead, would be of the same mind.

He advised them to bear at least the remainder of the winter patiently, and said that their rewards would be the more abundant the more difficulties and dangers they had endured in opening to Caesar a new unknown world, rich in spices and gold. Magellan thought that the minds of his crews were soothed and cheered by this harangue, but within a few days was harassed by a shameful and foul conspiracy. For talking began amongst the crews about the old eternal hatred between the Portuguese and the

Spaniards, and about Magellan's being a Portuguese. He, they said, could do nothing more glorious for his own country than to cast away this fleet, with so many men. Nor was it credible that he should wish to discover the Moluccas, even if he were able; but he would think it sufficient if he could lure Caesar on for some years with a vain hope, and meanwhile something new would turn up, by which the Spaniards would for the future be diverted from the search for spices. Nor even had their course begun to turn towards those happy Moluccas, but rather to distant snows and ice, and to perpetual storms.

Magellan, very much enraged by these sayings, punished the men, but rather more harshly than was proper for a foreigner, especially when commanding in a distant country. So, having planned a conspiracy, they seized upon a ship, and made ready to return to Spain. But he, with the rest whom he had still obedient to his commands, attacked that ship, and put to death the head man and the other ringleaders, those even who could not lawfully be so treated sharing the same fate. For these were certain servants of the king, upon whom no one but Caesar and his Council could lawfully pronounce a sentence of death. Nevertheless, no one from the time dared to disparage the power of the commander. Still,

there were not wanting some who whispered that Magellan would, in the same manner, murder all the Spaniards to the last man, until he, having got rid of them all, might return with a few Portuguese with the fleet to his own country. And so this hatred settled more deeply in the hearts of the Spaniards.

As soon as ever Magellan saw the storminess of the sea and the rigour of the winter mitigated, he set sail from the Gulf of St. Julian on the 24th of August. And, as before, he followed the course of the coast southwards for many days. A promontory was at last sighted, which they called Santa Cruz, when a severe storm, springing from the east, suddenly caught them, and one of the five ships was cast on shore, the men being all saved, with the merchandise and equipment, except one Ethiopian slave who was caught and drowned by the waves. After this the land seemed to bear a little east and south, and this they began to coast along as usual, and on the 26th of November certain inlets of the sea were discovered, which had the appearance of a strait. Magellan entered them forthwith with the whole fleet, and when he saw other and again other bays, he gave orders that they should be all carefully examined from the ships, to see if anywhere a passage might be discovered.

❧ HISTORICAL INTERPRETATION ❧

CHARLES E. NOWELL ON THE ROLE OF MERCANTILISM IN COLONIAL EXPANSION

Charles E. Nowell, *The Great Discoveries and the First Colonial Empires* (Ithaca, N.Y., 1954), pp. 137–139. Copyright 1954 by Cornell University. By permission of Cornell University Press.

THERE WERE many motives for the expansion of Europe. Individuals went to the New World to seek gold, adventure, freedom from tyranny, or escape from injustice. They went to spread what they believed to be the true faith, or merely to farm free land and grow rich. The role of mercantilism as a causative factor was summarized by Charles E. Nowell in this passage.

The rulers and governments that fostered and regulated all these efforts were motivated largely by a hope of profits, a hope conceived in mercantilistic theories and developed along mercantilistic lines. The different European powers formed their companies and built their empires

in different ways, but across the gap of several hundred years it is the similarities in their methods that now stand out most clearly.

European governments felt always more interest in the quick profits promised by trade or treasure troves than in the more solid investment of colonies. For this same reason they liked to avoid the burden of colonization wherever possible. Taking a page from the feudal past, they often escaped the expense of colonies by throwing the responsibility of pioneering and development upon private individuals. The Portuguese called these entrepreneurs *donataries,* the Spaniards called them *adelantados* or *encomenderos.* To the French they were seigneurs, to the Dutch patroons, and to the English proprietors. These territorial lords at times stimulated colonization, yet often blocked it either by failing to understand the needs of the colonists or by insisting on terms that prospective colonists were unable to meet. One after another, with very few exceptions, these proprietarial dignitaries were removed by their governments and were replaced by varying combinations of local and royal administrators.

The early empires failed strikingly to live up to the economic hopes and visions that had presided over their founding. Although their impact upon the economy and culture of Europe was tremendous, the impact came in ways not foreseen or planned. The empires had all been started on the mercantile theory, in the expectation that they would enrich the mother countries by causing gold and silver to pour in. Gold and silver did of course enter Europe through Spain from Spanish America, but this could not make mercantilism a sound doctrine. Since real wealth consists of goods, and since silver and gold are but convenient measuring sticks for determining value, the arrival of all this bullion created no wealth but merely brought a rise in prices and a dislocation of European economy. Yet for centuries the governments of Europe stuck to mercantilism; each one trying, by colonial trade monopolies, to restrict commerce so as to pour cash into its own treasury and cut competitors out. The result was to keep trade from flourishing as it might have flourished and to force it

into restricted, artificial channels. Europe, to be sure, was enormously richer by 1700 than in 1500, and the overseas world had contributed greatly to the increased prosperity. This, however, was in spite of mercantilism, not because of it. The true wealth consisted of the goods the outside world had sent to Europe, a flow that no mercantilistic regulations could altogether stop. Mercantilism had slowed the process of trade and wealth production; it could not stifle it entirely.

The colonists, in the meantime, failed to play passively the cut-and-dried role assigned to them. They were expected to buy the products of the mother country, to produce nothing that competed with those products, and to ship home raw stuffs priced much lower than the European goods they imported. The balance they were supposed to make up in cash. Insofar as they were able, the colonists declined to do as they were told. When opportunity offered they bought goods, from whatever source, at the lowest price. Likewise, they sold when they could in the best market, wherever it might be. This uncontrollable tendency on the part of their colonial subjects added to the mercantilists' difficulties by making law enforcement very costly, since it required fleets of ships patrolling the seas, revenue cutters patrolling the shores, and many vigilant officials on land. In the contest between the law and the law evader, colonial public opinions tended to be with the evader, and rightly. The smuggler who brought cheap goods into a colony and the local merchant who dealt *sub rosa* with him were unintentionally greater fomenters of world prosperity than were the sage European statesmen who spent their time planning ways and means of enforcing the laws.

Before the end of the eighteenth century Europeans were realizing, even without Adam Smith, that mercantilism somehow did not pay. This realization came at about the time the old colonial empires were starting to disintegrate.

❧ TEN BASIC BOOKS ❧

THE EXPANSION OF EUROPE

1. Abbott, Wilbur C., *The Expansion of Europe, 1415–1815,* 2 vols. (New York, 1938).

2. Baker, John N. L., *A History of Geographical Discovery and Exploration,* rev. ed. (New York, 1963).

3. Beazley, Charles R., *The Dawn of Modern Geography: A History of Exploration and Geographical Science,* 3 vols. (London and Oxford, 1897–1906).

4. Brebner, John, *The Explorers of North America* (New York, 1933).†

5. Haring, Clarence H., *The Spanish Empire in America* (New York, 1947, R.* 1963).†

6. Means, Philip A., *Fall of the Inca Empire and the Spanish Rule in Peru, 1530–1780* (New York, 1932).

7. Nowell, Charles E., *The Great Discoveries and the First Colonial Empires* (Ithaca, N. Y., 1954).†

8. Penrose, Boies, *Travel and Discovery in the Renaissance, 1420–1620,* 2nd ed. (Cambridge, Mass., 1952, R. 1962).†

9. Prestage, Edgar, *The Portuguese Pioneers* (London, 1933).

10. Sykes, Percy M., *A History of Exploration,* 3rd ed. (London, 1950).†

---

* Throughout the lists of basic books the letter "R" followed by a date is used to indicate a re-issue or more recent printing, sometimes involving revision.

3

Cultural Rebirth: The Age of the Renaissance in Italy

THE MAN of the Renaissance lived, as it were, between two worlds. The Christian world of the Middle Ages, in which the significance of every phenomenon was ultimately determined through uniform points of view, no longer existed for him. On the other hand, he had not yet found in a system of scientific concepts and social principles stability and security for his life.

—B. GROETHUYSEN

1. The Secularization of Culture

Age of Transition. Every age is in some sense one of transition. The opening era of modern history saw three revolutionary movements taking place at one time: the rise of capitalism, the emergence of the bourgeoisie, and the Renaissance. All three, interacting with each other, were also the consequences, in varying fields, of changes in the circumstances of man's life.

In the two centuries intervening between the last of the Crusades and the beginning of the Reformation there was a rebirth of Greek and Latin thought, resuscitated into vigorous life by that revival we call the Renaissance. The great capacity of the classical mind, once restored to the civilized world, became a part of the higher life of modern times. Shaking himself free from the bondage of medieval corporate society, the man of the Renaissance awoke to a new appreciation of his world. He took advantage of new possibilities for wealth and power, for esthetic and intellectual satisfaction. There were profound changes in his interests, ideals, and attitudes, all of which resulted in the creation of truly great esthetic forms of expression.

Although the Renaissance looked back to the pristine glory of Athens and Rome, at the same time it provided a beacon for the future. Its roots were fixed in the Middle Ages; much in it was still medieval, parts were modern in character, and much also was peculiar to the movement itself. It was a bridge between past and future, an age of transition. But even this great age, filled though it was with the stimulating spirit of human individuality, was not completely mature. While aware of the problems of existence, it made no really serious attempts to discover a rational solution. The issue was evaded by shifting the bases of authority: in the South from Christian to pagan sources, in the North from medieval Christian to early Christian fountainheads.

Historical Controversy: Revival or Reunion? Few periods of history have stimulated as much historical controversy as the Renaissance. On one side, exemplified in the work of the French historian Jules Michelet (1798–1874), it was held that medieval civilization witnessed the destruction of freedom and the debasement of the human spirit, while the Renaissance, a distinct epoch, saw the "discovery of man," the "discovery of the world," and the rebirth of the magnificent art of ancient Greece and Rome. The second and basically more traditional view was projected by Jakob Burckhardt (1818–1897), Swiss historian and art critic, who asserted that Renaissance Italy was the prototype of the modern world. On the Italian peninsula, Burkhardt pointed out, the old feudal order—based on land and a rigid political hierarchy structured by hereditary right and Church sanction—gave way to the independent city-state, or commune, in which power could be seized by any man with the strength and wit to do so. This sociopolitical structure produced an elite of merchant rulers as in Florence and Venice, tyrannical independent princes as in Milan and Ferrara, and an urbanized nobility as in Naples. The new elite, established through the skilled use of money resources, efficient administration, and military prowess, saw the state as a "work of art" and responded as patrons to the revival of learning and the arts. Exuberant individuality and uninhibited creativity were predominant characteristics of this new, more mobile society. Thus, the Renaissance in Burckhardt's view "was not the revival of antiquity alone, but its union with the genius of the Italian people, which achieved the conquest of the Western world."

The validity of Burckhardt's thesis, defended by a long line of able scholars, was widely accepted despite its neglect of intellectual, social, and economic phases. At the same time, however, it was challenged and attacked at many different points. Some denied the existence of the "so-called Renaissance" and emphasized the unbroken continuity of medieval forms and interests. The constitutionalism of the modern world owes much to the twelfth and thirteenth centuries (C. H. McIlwain); the thirteenth and fourteenth centuries were very active in penetrating natural science (Lynn Thorndike); the late medieval commercial revolution made more effective progress than the Renaissance which really had no dynamic economic expansion (R. S. Lopez). Others accepted Burckhardt's designation of Renaissance Italy as the model of the modern world, but at the same time tended to regard the age as one of transition from medieval to modern civilization, a period showing a clearly defined shift from one type of civilization to another.

A recent trend in scholarship on the Renais-

sance stresses what is called a synthetic interpretation. This view holds that it is incorrect to regard the Renaissance as strictly a cultural movement, and that it cannot be understood completely without consideration of contemporaneous changes in economic activity, political institutions, and social configurations. It is just as important, say these scholars, that attention be paid not only to *what* occurred but also to *why* it may have occurred. The word Renaissance, they continue, should be applied generally to the entire civilization of the age, not merely to its literary and artistic achievements. Supporters of Burckhardt deny that this new scholarship has produced any "synthesis" or reinterpretation more valuable than Burckhardt's original thesis. Burckhardt, they say, by focusing his attention on the fourteenth and fifteenth centuries, "saw the source of greatness as well as the guilt of the age," and in this way succeeded in creating a new vista. The word-battle still goes on.

2. Background: The Mind of Medieval Man

The Age of Faith. The mind of medieval man was molded in an age of faith. Where the Greeks had looked for salvation through intelligence or knowledge, medieval man forbad inquiry and substituted faith in its place. All things were carefully explained for him in a rigid and completely ordered universe, and he believed exactly what he was told. The universe was like a giant clock; the earth was the center of the universe; man was the most important object on earth. Though but worm of the dust, still he was the central life-force in the whole universe. Lord of creation, he was the very image of God.

Credulity, then, was the basic characteristic of the medieval mind. Added to this was a complete reliance upon authority. The man of the Middle Ages felt, and was taught, that it was not given to mortal reason to decipher the universe in detail; this was to be reserved for more learned minds and official philosophers. The Church, the real successor to the Roman Empire, was one, holy, apostolic, and all-embracing. To doubt its teachings was treason to God, the greatest of all crimes. The main sources of authority were the Bible, the writings of the Church Fathers, the works of Aristotle, and Roman and canon law, and few men dared to stride beyond these limits.

Along with his credulity and belief in supernaturalism and the after life, medieval man regarded the world as sinful and himself as permeated with sin. Man had originally been created in a state of perfection along with the sun, moon, and stars, but the first pair of human beings, Adam and Eve, had yielded to temptation, defied God, and as a result had been driven from the Garden of Eden. Thus, sin came into the world to taint every man.

These characteristics of the medieval mind were accentuated by a narrow provincialism. The manorial serf rarely saw the world outside his native village, nor did he particularly care what was going on in that outer world. Similarly, the town dweller of the later Middle Ages knew little about the world beyond his cramped home within the crowded, unsanitary town. This type of provincialism was not conducive to a free spirit and an open mind. Only gradually did audacious individual thinkers escape this environment.

From the twelfth century onward, conditions began to be more favorable for the revival of forgotten knowledge. Professors in the new universities established an impressive intellectual structure known as scholasticism. The aim of the scholastics, or schoolmen, was to explain the existence of God and the laws of the Church with the the aid of logic. In the late thirteenth and in the fourteenth centuries, scholasticism declined concurrently along with the papacy and the Church. Renaissance men turned against what they called scholastic hairsplitting.

3. Dignity of the Natural Man: Characteristics of the Renaissance

The Age of Awakening. Renaissance man rose above the narrow spirit of the Middle Ages. The rebirth meant a transition from a relatively rigid to a dynamic culture, Medieval scholasticism, authority, and asceticism were rejected, although not entirely, in favor of secularism and the dignity of the natural man. Man could now find inspiration in his own past achievement and learn from earlier epochs and cultures. He looked backward across the Middle Ages to antiquity, but at the same time he laid the broad foundations of our modern civilization, with its emphasis upon science, skepticism, and individualism. His was an age of expanding horizons, of new intellectual frontiers.

There was a close connection between the Renaissance and the great increase of wealth which came with the revival of commerce. With the introduction of a money economy and the increase in the volume of business, medieval institutions began to crumble and a new type of society arose to shape European civilization. The vigorous, independent, highly individualistic middle class at first sought to adjust itself to medieval ways, but soon gave up the task and began to fashion its own corporate organization in the form of capitalism. The magic wand of this new society was money.

Characteristic of the Renaissance, with its violent contrasts of emotion and conduct, was an insistence upon individuality. We must be careful not to overemphasize the concept of individuality, although it is true that there was in this transitional age a growing awareness of personality and individual autonomy that had not been possible in the climate of the Middle Ages. It was this spirit which caused Western man to question authority. He rejected old conventional standards and developed his own personality. Freed from traditional restraints, he became an exuberant being, joyously interested in his earthly life and in the world around him, fascinated by youth and beauty, proud of his own achievements. He dared to be himself without regard for what any person or institution thought of him.

The soaring spirit of the Renaissance was caught by the architect Leon Battista Alberti, whose maxim was: "Men can do all things if they will." The age of self-expression called into play the varied potentialities of each individual. Not content to specialize in one art form, the man of the Renaissance, urged on by boundless curiosity and his earnest search for the ideal and the marvelous, tried his hand in many mediums. During the Middle Ages, there were indeed men of encyclopedic knowledge in many countries, but they were confined within narrow limits. In the Renaissance we find versatile men who are still the wonder of today, men who created new and perfect works of art and at the same time were masters of many interests. It was an age of varied self-expression—in paint, stone, letters, and deeds.

4. Italian Origins

Crossroad of Civilization. The Renaissance, a Europe-wide phenomenon, received its earliest and most characteristic expression in the Italian peninsula. The northern Italian cities had been the centers of medieval commerce as well as of culture. Strategically located near the Mediterranean, still the main highway of trade in the early fifteenth century, they had felt the civilizing influence of the Roman, Byzantine, and Muslim cultures. Venice and Genoa, enjoying a brisk trade with the Near East, grew rich by commerce. Among the more important communes was the Tuscan city-state of Florence, situated on both banks of the Arno river. With prosperous trade and industry, large banking interests with branches all over Europe, and a remarkable intellectual and artistic life, Florence became the cradle of the Renaissance.

Patrons of the Arts. During the fourteenth and fifteenth centuries, the Italian communes were plagued by political struggle and internal strife. A strong civic pride resisted both pope and emperor. Unscrupulous individuals often formed private armies, usurped political authority, and seized power for themselves. But these despotic adventurers were anxious to prove to one and all that their despotism was tinged with benevolence, their dictatorship mellowed by culture. Since their continued lease on political life depended largely upon the support of the wealthy burghers, they made certain to ally themselves with the giants of commerce. Each side of the alliance saw a community of interest in the fact that both—

despots and burghers—had risen in the social scale by their own initiative and individuality. As they accumulated wealth, both the ruling despots and the great merchants became the patrons of artists, scholars, and scientists, who in their own way exemplified the triumph of individual talents. Competition for the services of artists was intense: rulers, merchants, and papacy vied with one another in sponsoring the creation of works of art or in collecting classical manuscripts.

5. Classicism Revived: Humanism

Meaning and Goals of Humanism. Standing midway between medieval scholasticism and eighteenth-century rationalism, humanism represented a rebirth of interest in the Greek and Latin classics and, with that interest, an increased concern with the secular activities of the everyday world. Classical literature had been used throughout the Middle Ages, chiefly because it provided excellent logic to support faith. But because it was basically pagan in outlook, it had been fused with Christian symbolism, mysticism, and allegory. The humanists, on the other hand, were attracted not only by the boundless variety of content and the logical form of the classics, but also by their expression of freedom of thought. It became popular to read Greek and Latin literature for meaning as well as for logic. Thus, the newly awakened intellectuals, freed from inhibiting doctrine, regarded the ancient writers as kindred spirits. Men now studied the classics with a new appreciation for their beauty and variety. Scholars whose familiarity with classical Greek literature was based on texts which had often gone through several translations—from Greek to Arabic to Latin—now eagerly studied the works in their original language.

The classical manuscript became the Renaissance pot of gold. Seldom in history has there been so sustained and feverish a hunt for anything of value as the humanistic search for ancient manuscripts. The list of known classical writers was expanded to include many additional names. Agents of the papacy and rival patrons went on treasure hunts in old monasteries and libraries in the hope of unearthing precious manuscripts of the Roman world. The accumulation of Greek classics followed as a matter of course. Peregrinating Italian booksellers journeyed enthusiastically to Constantinople and Alexandria and triumphantly brought home the works of Greek authors. These were copied and recopied, edited, criticized, translated into Latin and Italian, and eventually printed. Humanist scholars who rediscovered the works of Aristotle in the original Greek took delight in demonstrating how the texts had been misconstrued by scholastics who had been concerned with justifying faith by Aristotelian logic. A cult dedicated to the "dialectical, logical, and rationalistic Plato" appeared in Florence. Italian humanists extended an invitation to the renowned Byzantine scholar, Manuel Chrysoloras, who came to lecture at Florence and who gave Western scholars a workable grammar of the Greek language.

Between the accumulators of Latin literature and the advocates of Greek philosophy there arose a healthy rivalry, with each school insisting that its own field provided the most fertile source of classical learning. Teachers, students, writers, and officials joined this cultural battle between Hellenists and Latinists, which ended in a happy truce. One of the most celebrated patrons of the Renaissance, Cosimo de' Medici, assembled a great library at Florence, and Pope Nicholas V spent large sums to augment the papal collection. The competition extended even to the field of commerce: Venetian and Genoese merchants, when traveling in the Near East, sought to acquire ancient manuscripts as a kind of business sideline.

Humanism did not limit itself merely to Italian and Latin poetry. Humanist writers, interested in every subject, produced a variety of poems, letters, orations, literary essays, histories, biographies, and editions of the classics. They were inspired by the earnest faith that they were restoring its birthright to humanity "after the expiration of ten centuries." An audience of humanist scholars could be moved to tears by eloquent orations in Latin, but it would just as quickly ridicule a speaker who made a mistake in grammar or rhetoric. The new spirit of humanism was especially effective in education, where the former grammar, rhe-

toric, dialectic, and all-pervading religious ideals gave way to Greek and Latin grammar, literature, philology, poetry, and history. The Renaissance belief that classical studies provided the best foundations for an active and well-rounded life was little questioned until the rise of science and technology in the nineteenth century.

Humanists made important contributions to the objective study of history. Medieval historians saw the world as a divinely ordained universal empire which began with the Christian story of man's creation. Actual fact was interwoven with myth and legend. Humanist scholars threw out the religious and mythical aspects, and with a growing comprehension of development and change occurring throughout the passage of time, began to distinguish one historical period from another. The past became the past *per se*. The Renaissance historian was thus freed from the necessity of making his history fit into the universal empire concept and could focus his attention on just one era or geographical area.

Most humanists were uninterested in theological matters; some were critical of the Church. Some were themselves ecclesiastics. Lorenzo Valla, a papal secretary, published in 1440 his famous exposure of the spurious *Donation of Constantine*, which since the ninth century had been used as a legal document to justify ecclesiastical domination over Rome, the Italian peninsula, and "the provinces, places, and *civitates* of the Western regions." By analysis of linguistic and historical content of the document, Valla presented definite proof that it could not have been written until several hundred years after the death of Constantine. The science of critical philology was founded by Valla and other humanists as they worked to determine the authenticity of ancient manuscripts by careful study of style, grammatical form, and content.

Petrarch. From admiration of the classics to imitation and creation was but a step. One of the earliest and greatest of the humanists was Francesco Petrarch (1304–1374), who has been variously called "the intellectual arbiter of Europe," "the first modern scholar," and even "the first modern man." The son of a notary, he rebelled against his father's ambition to have him study law, and turned for consolation to the study of the classics. There is a story that Petrarch the elder one day threw his son's books of poetry and rhetoric into the fire, but at Francesco's passionate entreaties rescued Vergil and Cicero half-burned from the flames. In 1327, the young poet met Laura for the first time, and inspired by deep love, composed a number of exquisite love lyrics in pure Tuscan Italian. Soon his fame increased until he became a European celebrity, with enthusiastic followers everywhere. Petrarch was the first important spokesman for humanism. His teaching was revolutionary: the classics were living creations, beautiful, elegant, magnificent. Standing within the late Middle Ages, he surveyed the kingdom of the modern literary world and opened for Europe a new sphere of intellectual activity. He was the first enthusiastic student of classical archaeology, the first collector of manuscripts and coins, the first champion of Latin and Greek writers as "living men."

Boccaccio. Another great Florentine humanist was Giovanni Boccaccio (1313–1375) who, with Petrarch, gave fresh impetus to the study of classical literature. As a young man, Boccaccio turned with distaste from commerce and law and finally devoted himself to the pursuit of learning. For a lady love he composed the romances *Il Filocolo* and *L'Amorosa Visione*, which contain passages of grace and vivacity. Like Petrarch, Boccaccio was a collector of ancient manuscripts; both were travelers who employed much of their time and money in rescuing precious memorials of antiquity from destruction. Although Boccaccio wrote numerous works in both Italian and Latin, and in both prose and poetry, his great fame rests upon the *Decameron,* or *Ten Days' Entertainment*. This collection of a hundred tales was supposed to have been told by a party of ladies and gentlemen at a villa near Florence in 1348 while the Black Death was raging in that city. The *Decameron* was notable for a passionate love of mankind and a tolerant understanding. Marking a break from medieval asceticism and with a secular approach to man's problems, it became an inspiration for many of the great figures of Western literature. The general form of the *Canterbury Tales* suggests that Chaucer was acquainted with the *Decameron,* and Shakespeare also availed himself of Boccaccio's masterpiece in *Cymbeline* and *All's Well That Ends Well.*

Shortcomings of Humanism. Despite its dazzling accomplishments, humanism had some serious limitations, which eventually led to its decadence. Humanist scholars were so deeply intrigued by Greek and Latin forms and styles that they tended to degenerate into pedantic imitators. The immediate successors of the intellectual giants who had set the standards of humanist scholarship were too often mere copyists, who thus temporarily rendered the name of humanism ridiculous. So intent were some humanists on reviving the literary spirit of Rome that they ignored the best of medieval literature and looked backward beyond all contemporary literature. Others refused to welcome the invention of printing, which came when the movement was at its height, and insisted that the new method threatened the time-honored hand copying of manuscripts. Unfortunately, humanism also often reserved its benefits for princes, diplomats, courtiers, and others of noble birth. In all humanistic pursuits there was an aristocratic tendency which placed them well beyond the range of the common man. Humanists as a group were also inclined to scoff at scientific studies simply because their intellectual heroes, the Greeks and Romans, had disdained scientific experiment. On science the humanistic impulse was negligible, for it consisted mainly of ideas and superstitions taken from the *cabala* (Hebrew cosmogony and magic), Pythagorean number-lore, Babylonian myths, and Neo-Platonic mysticism.

6. *The Artistic Renaissance: Revival of Painting*

The Revolution in Color. The medieval painter was a guildsman who was restricted by rules and tradition of his craft. His work, highly formalized in technique, reflected the point of view of a predominantly ecclesiastical society. His human figures were unrealistic and forced into awkward and unnatural attitudes; he used color lavishly but with little sense of harmony; his landscapes were drab and lacking in perspective. He had but little incentive to break away from the conventional methods of his fellow artists. The theological subjects which he could paint were limited, and he always executed them in the same way, with little imagination and little attempt to capture the spirit of pure beauty.

This way of painting was in direct contrast to the development of art in the Renaissance. Of all the major arts, painting was most characteristic of the period, and it was developed to a high degree of perfection. The Renaissance artist studied nature and gave his attention to color, perspective, foreshortening, drapery, and anatomy. He rejected the formalized figures of medieval painting and instead turned to naturalism; he depicted the human body as contoured rather than flat; and he seriously studied the blending of colors and the use of light and shadow. He still used religious subjects, but he gave his Madonnas and prophets the appearance of everyday people. He dedicated his work to man and his environment. He took great pride in his own production.

Transitional Phase. In the opening years of the fourteenth century, Giotto di Bondone (c. 1276–1337), a Florentine, turned from the conventionalized spirit of religious painting to a greater naturalism. Illustrating the life and works of St. Francis of Assisi, he depicted human emotions and expressions in ways far removed from the usual medieval techniques. It was a powerful impulse, for during the rest of the century his successors moved in a new direction. For the first time portrait painting became fashionable, as wealthy patrons engaged artists to catch their likenesses for the benefit of posterity. The transition from medieval anonymity to individualism was marked by the new tendency of painters to place their names on their work as identification.

One of the most brilliant geniuses of the age of transition was Masaccio ("shiftless"), nickname of Tommaso di Giovanni de Guidi (1401–c. 1428), a precocious young artist who achieved remarkable effects through color and tone instead of draughtsmanship. An advocate of dramatic realism, he set a high standard of technical perfection for those who came after him. Among the great painters of this period were Fra Angelico (1387–1455), "The Blessed Brother John the Angelic of Fiesole," artist of delicate religious sincerity whose spirit remained essentially medieval, and Fra Filippo Lippi (c. 1406–1469), a worldly friar who executed portraits of his friends in gracious religious works. Sandro Botticelli (c. 1445–1510), a pupil of Fra Filippo Lippi, showed sensitive and lyrical draughtsmanship in introspective paintings inspired by classical paganism. The famous *Primavera* gave testimony of his classical learning, characteristic of the thought and art of the age.

The Grand Masters. The Golden Age of Renaissance painting came with the work of three great Florentine masters, Michelangelo, Raphael, and Leonardo da Vinci, a trio of artistic geniuses such as the world has seldom, if ever, seen. Michelangelo Buonarroti (1475–1564), a vital figure in a tumultuous age, turned from sculpture to painting at the behest of Julius II, most persistent of the pontifical patrons of Renaissance art. In 1508, the pope commissioned Michelangelo to decorate the ceiling of the Sistine Chapel. This series of frescoes of several hundred figures, architecturally designed, has been extravagantly but perhaps accurately described as the most overwhelming and mightiest single pictorial creation in the history of art. It is an allegory of the life of man, an outline of the early chapters of Genesis "with a new Michelangelesque race of human beings."

The second of the great Florentine trio, Raphael Santi (1483–1520), was a master of composition, form and design, and color purity. Although his work was neither so intellectually inspiring as that of Leonardo nor so emotionally overwhelming as that of Michelangelo, it possesses a unique gentleness and tender grace which makes him one of the most appeal-

Detail of Botticelli's *Primavera*.

ing religious painters. At a time when his older colleague, Michelangelo, worked next door in the Vatican, Raphael completed his own fresco masterpiece, the *School of Athens*, a representation of the philosophers, poets, and scientists of the Golden Age of Greece. His famous easel-picture, the *Sistine Madonna*, a triumph of color and form, is considered one of the world's great paintings.

Man of the Renaissance. Towering above the many-sided men of this remarkable era

was the great Florentine, Leonardo da Vinci (1452–1519), sculptor, painter, architect, musician, inventor, goldsmith, engineer, and natural philosopher. History tells of no man more gifted than Leonardo in both art and science; he was, in truth, *the* man of the Renaissance. He was born at the Vinci palace, a *castello* or fortified hill village in the Florentine territory, the natural son of a lawyer. From his youth he was remarkable for his handsome and noble presence, charming manners and tact, and an inexhaustible intellectual energy and aptitude in almost all branches of art and science. He speedily excelled his teacher, Andrea del Verrocchio, as goldsmith, sculptor, and painter. From the beginning of his artistic career he was a keen student of nature.

Here was the great world-genius, whose art opened new depths of truthfulness and rendered the human body in forms of intrinsic dignity and lofty graciousness. Leonardo was at once inheritor and perfector. His work passed onward the best that had been done in the past, and at the same time it was distinct creation. His anticipations of the great discoveries in astronomy, geology, and other sciences were astonishing, given the state of scientific knowledge at that time. His artistic creations and his scientific research were but partial expressions of an insatiable curiosity and astounding insight. His work gave to his contemporaries as well as those who came after him a new revelation of the power of art.

The Venetian School: Titian. The two dominant schools of Italian painting were the Florentine, concerned mostly with composition, and the Venetian, which stressed color. The first masters of Venetian art were the Bellini family, consisting of Jacopo (*c.* 1400–1470) and his two sons, Gentile (*c.* 1429–1507) and Giovanni (*c.* 1430–1516). Giovanni, the most talented, worked in oils, introducing a lyrical style distinguished by warm coloring. His pupils, Giorgione (1477–1511) and especially Tiziano Vecellio, or Titian (1477–1576), became the greatest of Venetian artists. Titian stands alone as the master colorist of the Renaissance; as a portrait painter he ranks with the first of any age. Not a universal genius like Leonardo or Michelangelo, his one supreme achievement was in the art of painting. His remarkable handling of light and color to differentiate and contrast textures foreshadowed the realism of Velásquez and Rembrandt. Michelangelo's verdict on Titian was "That man would have had no equal if art had done as much for him as nature." The Florentine master was thinking mainly of draughtsmanship, for he added: "Pity that in Venice they don't learn how to draw well."

7. Rhythm in Stone: Development of Sculpture

Break with Medieval Formalism. The development of Renaissance sculpture was in many respects similar to that of painting, in that it bridged the medieval centuries by reverting to Greek and Roman naturalism. Some classical techniques and styles had never been completely extinguished, especially a sense of reality which carried over in Romanesque sculpture and architecture. Many medieval sculptors were exceedingly skillful artists, gifted in carving leaves, flowers, and fruit for decorative purposes. But here again, as in painting, they worked almost exclusively on ecclesiastical subjects, carving thin and gaunt figures, emaciated faces, and angular gestures. Renaissance sculptors, on the other hand, rejected medieval formalism in favor of classical freedom of expression.

The first break with medieval tradition was the work of Niccolò Pisano (*c.* 1220–*c.* 1283), whose pulpit in the baptistery of the Cathedral of Pisa is a synthesis of medieval subject matter and Greek sense of the dignity of the human form. His son, Giovanni Pisano (*c.* 1250–*c.* 1328), as well as other thirteenth century pioneers, helped to break the bonds of medieval conventionalism, and evolved a style daring in innovation, full of movement, and realistic in its copying of nature. In sculpture, as in painting, the fifteenth century was a period of experiment and technical progress. Two great sculptors in this era were Lorenzo Ghiberti (1378–1455) and Dontao de Nicolo di Betto Bardi, known as Donatello (*c.* 1386–1466). Trained as a goldsmith, Ghiberti created the massive pair of bronze doors for the baptistery of the Cathedral of Florence. This is an extraordinary *tour de force*, consisting of twenty-eight small panels illustrating, directly and incisively, stories from the Bible. The arrangements of the figures to give the illusion of perspective, the skillful use of many planes, the rich architectural background, and the adaptation of antique forms of drapery combine to make these doors an artistic triumph. Michelangelo declared them "worthy to be the gates of Paradise." While Ghiberti devoted a lifetime to this single great creation of religious art, another Florentine, Donatello, contributed a new secular type of sculpture. His celebrated bronze statue of *Gattamelata* the *condottiere* (professional soldier), the first equestrian statue since that of the Emperor Marcus Aurelius, is distinguished by the sculp-

Verrocchio's *Colleone*. One of the earliest successful equestrian statues.

tor's knowledge of anatomy; at the same time, it is an accurate representation of the spirit of the age. Another celebrated equestrian portrait, that of the *condottiere* Colleone, was the work of Andrea del Verrocchio (1435–1488), teacher of Leonardo da Vinci. Verrocchio's horse has one leg unsupported, a real achievement, considering the casting difficulties of the time.

The Golden Age. The Golden Age of Renaissance sculpture coincided with that of paint-

ing. Here again the genius of Michelangelo towered above his contemporaries. The sculptors of the Middle Ages had regarded nudity as indecent, but Michelangelo glorified it. So remarkable was his knowledge of anatomy and so great his skill that he made no elaborate preparation preceding his work in marble but instead "literally tore the figure out of the block." He absorbed much from his study of classical style, but added to it that stamp of individuality so highly prized in his own day. Few sculptors in the history of art have attained such perfection as that displayed by Michelangelo in his statue of David, the adolescent shepherd boy upon the threshold of manhood, in the deeply religious *Pietà* depicting Mary with the body of Christ, and in the Medici tombs of Giuliano, son of Lorenzo the Magnificent, and of Lorenzo, grandson of the Magnifico. In Michelangelo's hands the human form became a kind of musical instrument through which he could express his own deep emotion.

8. *The Language of Architecture*

Renaissance Revival. There were two basic forms of medieval art: the Romanesque, which took from the Romans the basilica plan and Roman vaulting, and the Gothic, which introduced the pointed arch, slender window, flying buttress, delicate pinnacle, and towering spire. Whereas classical architecture had embodied the secular life, the Gothic form usually expressed an ecclesiastical civilization. Medieval Gothic cathedrals, creations of grandeur and harmony, sought to voice the religious aspirations of the human soul. Yet much of the classical spirit survived throughout the Middle Ages.

The architecture of the Renaissance evolved slowly in an ensemble of styles. There was no abrupt departure from medieval forms. What was needed was a style which could adapt the ancient Roman and the medieval Gothic to contemporary ideas and at the same time express the originality which was so much a part of the general Renaissance movement. Turning back to classical ideals for inspiration, Renais-

The *Pietà* by Michelangelo.

sance artists began to study the ruined arches and broken columns of Roman architecture at their very doorsteps, and soon progressed from the borrowing of decorative designs to the use of classical planning. To the Greek simplicity of line and form, perspective, proportion, and balance, they added a new quality of individualism; the resulting product was highly original. Some of the early Renaissance architects designed secular buildings, such as the palace (*palazzo*), refining their rugged buildings by using dressed stone in the upper stories, enlarging the windows, and adding decorative cornices. Several palaces in Florence, used successively as fortress, dwelling, and art gallery, are good examples of this secular form of art.

Brunelleschi. Filippo Brunelleschi (1379–1446), a Florentine, was the first Renaissance architect to influence the direction of his art toward the antique. Dissatisfied with the confusing forms of existing architecture, the young

Cathedral of Florence. The apse and dome from the southeast.

artist, with his faithful friend Donatello, journeyed to Rome to study the construction of the classic buildings. So assiduously did they dig among the ruins that they were regarded as seekers of hidden treasure—which, in fact, they were. Returning to Florence, Brunelleschi

was commissioned to complete the dome of the Cathedral of Florence, a task which had baffled architects for a century. He erected a magnificent dome 120 feet high and 140 feet in diameter, one of the architectural triumphs of the world. This famous sharply pitched dome became the prototype for those at St. Peter's in Rome, St. Paul's in London, the Pantheon in Paris, and the Capitol in Washington.

From Florence to Rome. When the Tuscan city of Florence lost its artistic ascendancy in the sixteenth century, Rome became the center of Italian architecture. Here Renaissance architecture reached its greatest height, with the papacy as its outstanding patron. Most eminent of the architects of the Roman school was Donato d'Agnolo Bramante (*c.* 1444–1514), master of an architectural style distinguished by mass, breadth, and classic perfection. Com-

missioned by Pope Julius II as the architect for the new St. Peter's, Bramante visualized an enormous edifice in the form of a Greek cross executed in classical design. "I want to raise the Roman Pantheon on the vaults of the Temple of Peace," he said. But Bramante died before the church could be completed. In 1546 Pope Paul III gave supervision of the work to Michelangelo, then seventy-one years old. The latter devoted his remaining years to the undertaking. He was responsible for the great dome, based upon Brunelleschi's dome at Florence, and for the structural soundness of the huge building.

⤜ KEY DOCUMENT ⤚

VASARI ON LEONARDO DA VINCI

Giorgio Vasari, *Lives of the Most Eminent Painters, Sculptors, and Architects,* ed. by E. H. and E. W. Blashfield and A. A. Hopkins (New York, 1896), IV, 370–376. Courtesy of Charles Scribner's Sons.

GIORGIO VASARI (1511–1574), Italian historian of art, was born at Arezzo. He achieved some fame as painter and architect, but it is now conceded that his paintings lacked inspiration. Noted as an unbiased art historian, Vasari wrote his *Lives of the Most Eminent Painters, Sculptors, and Architects* in 1550, and rewrote and enlarged it in 1568. Dedicated to Cosimo de' Medici, this book became a most important source of information on the artists of his day. Following is Vasari's tribute to Leonardo da Vinci.

The richest gifts are occasionally seen to be showered, as by celestial influence, on certain human beings, nay, they sometimes supernaturally and marvellously congregate in one sole person; beauty, grace, and talent being united in such a manner, that to whatever the man thus favoured may turn himself, his every action is so divine as to leave all other men far behind him, and manifestly to prove that he has been specially endowed by the hand of God Himself, and has not obtained his pre-eminence by human teaching, or the power of man. This was seen and acknowledged by all men in the case of Leonardo da Vinci, in whom, to say nothing of his beauty of person, which yet was such that it has never been sufficiently extolled, there was a grace beyond expression which was rendered manifest without thought or effort in every act and deed, and who had besides so rare a gift of

talent and ability, that to whatever subject he turned his attention, however difficult, he presently made himself absolute master of it. Extraordinary power was in his case conjoined with remarkable facility, a mind of regal boldness and magnanimous daring; his gifts were such that the celebrity of his name extended most widely, and he was held in the highest estimation, not in his own time only, but also, and even to a greater extent, after his death, nay, this he has continued, and will continue to be by all succeeding ages.

Truly admirable, indeed, and divinely endowed was Leonardo da Vinci; this artist was the son of Ser Piero da Vinci; he would without doubt have made great progress in learning and knowledge of the sciences, had he not been so versatile and changeful, but the instability of his character caused him to undertake many things which having commenced he afterwards abandoned. . . .

But, though dividing his attention among pursuits so varied, he never abandoned his drawing, and employed himself much in works of relief, that being the occupation which attracted him more than any other. His father, Ser Piero, observing this, and considering the extraordinary character of his son's genius, one day took some of his drawings and showed them to Andrea del Verrocchio, who was a very intimate friend of his, begging him earnestly to tell him whether he thought that Leonardo would be likely to secure success if he devoted himself to the arts of design. Andrea Verrocchio was amazed as he beheld the remarkable commencement made by Leonardo, and advised Ser Piero to see that he attached himself to that calling, whereupon the latter took his measures according, and sent Leonardo to study in the bottega, or workshop, of Andrea. Thither the boy resorted therefore, with the utmost readiness, and not only gave his attention to one branch of art, but to all the others, of which design made a portion. Endowed with such admirable intelligence, and being also an excellent geometrician, Leonardo not only worked in sculpture (having executed certain heads in terra-cotta, of women smiling, even in his first youth, which are now reproduced in gypsum, and also others of children which might be supposed to have proceeded from the hand of a master); but in architecture likewise he prepared various designs for ground-plans, though still but a youth, first suggested the formation of a canal from Pisa to Florence, by means of certain changes to be effected on the river Arno. Leonardo likewise made designs for mills, fulling machines, and other engines which were to be acted on by means of water; but as he had resolved to make painting his profession, he gave the larger portion of time to drawing from nature. . . . He drew on paper also with so much care and so perfectly, that no one has ever equalled him in this respect. I have a head by him in chiaro-scuro, which is incomparably beautiful. Leonardo was indeed so imbued with power and grace by the hand of God, and was endowed with so marvellous a facility in reproducing his conceptions; his memory also was always so ready and so efficient in the service

of his intellect, that in discourse he won all men by his reasonings, and confounded every antagonist, however powerful, by the force of his arguments.

This master was also frequently occupied with the construction of models and the preparation of designs for the removal or the perforation of mountains, to the end that they might thus be easily passed from one plain to another. By means of levers, cranes, and screws, he likewise showed how great weights might be raised or drawn; in what manner ports and havens might be cleansed and kept in order, and how water might be obtained from the lowest deeps. From speculations of this kind he never gave himself rest and of the results of these labours and meditations there are numberless examples in drawings, etc., dispersed among those who practice our arts: I have myself seen very many of them. . . . In conversation Leonardo was indeed so pleasing that he won the hearts of all hearers, and though possessing so small a patrimony only that it might almost be called nothing, while he yet worked very little, he still constantly kept many servants and horses, taking extraordinary delight in the latter: he was indeed fond of all animals, ever treating them with infinite kindness and consideration; as a proof of this it is related, that when he passed places where birds were sold, he would frequently take them from their cages, and having paid the price demanded for them by the sellers, would then let them fly into the air, thus restoring to them the liberty they had lost. Leonardo was in all things so highly favoured by nature, that to whatever he turned his thoughts, mind, and spirit, he gave proof in all of such admirable power and perfection, that whatever he did bore an impress of harmony, truthfulness, goodness, sweetness, and grace, wherein no other man could ever equal him.

Leonardo, with his profound intelligence of art, commenced various undertakings, many of which he never completed, because it appeared to him that the hand could never give its due perfection to the object or purpose which he had in his thoughts, or beheld in his imagination; seeing that in his mind he frequently formed the idea of some difficult enterprise, so subtle and so wonderful that, by means of hands, however excellent or able, the full reality could never be worthily executed and entirely realized. His conceptions were varied to infinity; philosophizing over natural objects; among others, he set himself to investigate the properties of plants, to make observations on the heavenly bodies, to follow the movements of the planets, the variations of the moon, and the course of the sun.

❧ HISTORICAL INTERPRETATION ❧

JAKOB BURCKHARDT ON THE NATURE OF THE RENAISSANCE IN ITALY

Jakob Burckhardt, *The Civilization of the Period of the Renaissance in Italy*, trans. by S. G. C. Middlemore (London, 1892), pp. 172–175. Courtesy of Swan, Sonnenschein and Co.

JAKOB BURCKHARDT (1818–1897), Swiss historian, wrote the first comprehensive survey of the Italian Renaissance. His thesis was that it was not the revival of antiquity alone, but its union with the genius of the Italian people, which achieved the cultural conquest of the Western world. Other historians attacked Burckhardt's interpretation from every conceivable angle: he was a "dilettante in history"; his research was unscientific; his use of sources was one-sided; he neglected intellectual, social, and economic phases. Despite criticisms, Burckhardt's book went through scores of editions. Following is an excerpt giving Burckhardt's general view of the revival of antiquity.

The civilization of Greece and Rome, which, ever since the fourteenth century, obtained so powerful a hold on Italian life, as the source and basis of culture, as the object and ideal of existence, partly also as an avowed reaction against preceding tendencies—this civilization had long been exerting a partial influence on medieval Europe, even beyond the boundaries of Italy. The culture of which Charles the Great was a representative was, in face of the barbarism of the seventh and eighth centuries, essentially a Renaissance, and could appear under no other form. Just as in the Romanesque architecture of the North, beside the general outlines inherited from antiquity, remarkable direct imitations of the antique also occur, so too monastic scholarship had not only gradually absorbed an immense mass of materials from Roman writers, but the style of it, from the days of Eginhard onwards, shows traces of conscious imitations.

But the resuscitation of antiquity took a different form in Italy from that which it assumed in the North. The wave of barbarism had scarcely gone by before the people, in whom the former life was but half effaced, showed a consciousness of its past and a wish to reproduce it. Elsewhere in Europe men deliberately and with reflection borrowed this or the other element of classical civilization; in Italy the sympathies both of the learned and of the people were naturally engaged on the side of antiquity as a whole, which stood to them as a symbol of past greatness. The Latin language, too, was easy to an Italian, and the numerous monuments and documents in which the country abounded facilitated a return to the past. With this tendency other elements—the popular character, which time had now greatly modified, the political institutions imported by the Lombards from Germany, chivalry and other Northern forms of civilization, and the influence of religion and the Church—combined to produce the modern Italian spirit, which was destined to serve as the model and ideal for the whole Western world.

How antiquity began to work in plastic art, as soon as the flood of barbarism had subsided, is clearly shown in the Tuscan buildings of the twelfth and in the sculptures of the thirteenth centuries. In poetry, too, there will appear no want of similar analogies to those who hold that the greatest Latin poet of the twelfth century, the writer who struck the keynote of a whole class of

Latin poems, was an Italian. We mean the author of the best pieces in the so-called *Carmina Burana*. A frank enjoyment of life and its pleasures, as whose patrons the gods of heathendom are invoked, while Catos and Scipios hold the place of the saints and heroes of Christianity, flows in full current through the rhymed verses. Reading them through at a stretch, we can scarcely help coming to the conclusion that an Italian, probably a Lombard, is speaking; in fact, there are positive grounds for thinking so. To a certain degree these Latin poems of the *Clerici vagantes* of the twelfth century, with all their remarkable frivolity, are, doubtless, a product in which the whole of Europe had a share; but the writer of the song *De Phyllide et Flora* and the *Aestuans Interius* can have been a Northerner as little as the polished Epicurean observer to whom we owe *Dum Dianae vitrea sero lampas oritur*. Here, in truth, is a reproduction of the whole ancient view of life, which is all the more striking from the medieval form of the verse in which it is set forth. . . .

But the great and general enthusiasm of the Italians for classical antiquity did not display itself before the fourteenth century. For this a development of civic life was required, which took place only in Italy, and there not till then. It was needful that noble and burgher should first learn to dwell together on equal terms, and that a social world should rise which felt the want of culture, and had the leisure and the means to obtain it. But culture, as soon as it freed itself from the fantastic bonds of the Middle Ages, could not at once and without help find its way to the understanding of the physical and intellectual world. It needed a guide, and found one in the ancient civilization, with its wealth of truth and knowledge in every spiritual interest. Both the form and the substance of this civilization were adopted with admiring gratitude; it became the chief part of the culture of the age. The general condition of the country was favourable to this transformation. The medieval empire, since the fall of the Hohenstaufen, had either renounced, or was unable to make good, its claims on Italy. The Popes had migrated to Avignon. Most of the political Powers actually in existence owed their origin to violent and illegitimate means. The spirit of the people, now awakened to self-consciousness, sought for some new and stable ideal on which to rest.

❧ TEN BASIC BOOKS ❧

CULTURAL REBIRTH: THE AGE OF THE RENAISSANCE IN ITALY

1. Berenson, Bernard, *The Italian Painters of the Renaissance*, trans. by S. G. C. Middlemore (Oxford, 1930, R. 1957).†

2. Burckhardt, Jakob, *The Civilization of the Period of the Renaissance in Italy* (London, 1892, R. 1958).†

3. Ferguson, Wallace K., *Europe in Transition; 1300–1520* (Boston, 1962).

4. Ferguson, Wallace K., *The Renaissance in Historical Thought: Five Centuries of Interpretation* (Boston, 1948).

5. Huizinga, Johan, *The Waning of the Middle Ages* (London, 1924, 1950).†

6. Kristeller, Paul Oskar, *The Classics and Renaissance Thought* (Cambridge, Mass., 1955).†

7. Thomson, S. Harrison, *Europe in Renaissance and Reformation* (New York, 1963).

8. Thorndike, Lynn, *Science and Thought in the Fifteenth Century* (New York, 1929).

9. Vasari, Giorgio, *Lives of the Most Eminent Painters, Sculptors, and Architects*, 4 vols. (New York, 1896).†

10. Young, George F., *The Medici* (New York, 1933).

4

The Renaissance North of the Alps

THE IMPORTANCE of printing cannot be overestimated. There are few events like it in the history of the world. The whole gigantic swing of modern democracy and of the scientific spirit was released by it. The veil of the temple of religion and of knowledge was rent in twain, and the arcana of the priest and clerk became exposed to the gaze of the people. The reading public became the supreme court before whom, from this time, all cases must be argued. The conflict of opinions and parties, of privileges and freedom, of science and obscurantism, was transferred from the secret chamber of a small, privileged, professional, and sacerdotal coterie to the arena of the reading public.

—PRESERVED SMITH

1. The Renaissance in Transalpine Europe

Spread of the Renaissance. The Italian peninsula was the fountainhead of the Renaissance: from it flowed the appeal to antiquity, the challenge to authority, the zeal for the New Learning, the glorification of man, and the tempestuous spirit of reborn art forms. Hundreds of students from northern and western Europe crossed the Alps in search of wider knowledge and returned home as missionaries of classical learning. Once again, even as in ancient times, the currents of esthetic revolt swept slowly along the channels of commercial expansion. The Renaissance, instead of remaining exclusively Italian, became a movement of European-wide proportions, with some variations in each country where it appeared.

The Italians expressed the exuberance of their own personalities in artistic and literary production. Italian humanists either disregarded ecclesiastical authority, or accepted the Church as they found it. Northern humanists and artists, on the other hand, were more conservative in intellectual and artistic pursuits. Although they turned for guidance to classical antiquity, they subordinated the secular themes and, instead, studied the writings of the Church Fathers and the Bible as a means of reviving the doctrines and practices of early Christianity. They read Greek not merely as a beautiful classical language but to discover new meaning in the Greek New Testament. Italian humanists showed little zeal for religious reform, but the northern humanists thought of their work as stimulating a religious and social movement. In criticisms of the Church and especially in appeals to the sources of Christian faith and practice, the northern humanists, perhaps unconsciously, helped prepare the way for the Reformation. These differences in humanistic development also existed in art forms. Italian artists tended to abandon themselves to sensual enjoyment of life; the more serious northern artists adopted a humble and more mystical attitude.

Development of Printing. Probably the most important factor in the spread of the literary Renaissance was the invention of printing, about the middle of the fifteenth century. This ranks with firemaking, the wheel, the bow, and the plow as one of the giant strides in civilization. Several elements were necessary for the use of printing—paper, ink, and movable type. Egyptians, Greeks, and Romans had used papyrus, a cultivated reed, for official and ordinary correspondence, accounts, and contracts. In the Middle Ages almost the only material employed for writing purposes was parchment, prepared from the dressed skins of sheep, calves, and goats. Both processes, however, were slow and costly. In the eighth century, the Muslims learned from the Chinese how to make paper of cotton fiber and introduced it into Spain on their journeys of conquest. By the thirteenth century, paper was made from flax and rags to produce a linen texture. It was this kind of paper which became the medium for printing. Although the manufacture of ink had reached a high degree of perfection in the Middle Ages, that used by the first printers was an oily pigment attributed to the Van Eyck brothers, Flemish painters.

As late as the middle of the fourteenth century, virtually all books used in Western Europe were copied by hand, many of them in the *scriptorium* (writing-room of the medieval monasteries). Shortly afterward, the practice of printing from engraved blocks, which had been used by the Chinese as early as the sixth century, was introduced into Western Europe. Although printing from crude blocks

Facsimile of the Bible of 1455 (I Samuel xix, 1–5), printed at Mainz by Gutenberg. Over 50,000 such lines required 641 double-column leaves that were divided into two, or three, or even four volumes.

represented an advance over hand-copying, still it was expensive, and moreover, the wooden blocks wore out quickly. A revolutionary improvement was needed to produce more books more cheaply. This came with the invention of printing from movable type, which allowed separate types to be cast in quantity.

Some mystery has surrounded the epoch-making "invention," but primacy is usually claimed for Johann Gutenberg (*c.* 1398–1468) of Mainz, who introduced the new method to Europeans some time in the decade after 1440. Whether or not he actually invented printing, he certainly was the first to convert it into an important industry. Casting separate types for each letter of the alphabet, he assembled words, set pages, printed copies, then removed the type from the forms, and reset it. The earliest dated documents printed by Gutenberg were two indulgences printed in 1454. The publication (1452–1455) of the famous forty-two-line Latin Bible, known as the Gutenberg Bible, marked the completion of the experimental stage of printing. Clear-cut and legible, this book demonstrated the success of the new art.

Within a few decades, printing from movable type spread widely throughout Europe, bypassing only a few backward countries. By 1500 more than a thousand printers earned their living in the new industry, and there were some 30,000 editions of different works. It has been estimated that by 1500 there were about 9,000,000 books in Europe, as contrasted with the few-score thousand manuscripts that only a few years before had held the knowledge and wisdom of all time. Printing reached the Italies in 1465, but Italian humanists, far from being pleased with it, at first were hostile, maintaining that the copying by hand of ancient manuscripts was the proper occupation for a scholar. Vespasiano da Bisticci (died 1498), an Italian humanist, wrote that one of his patrons, the Duke of Urbino, would have been ashamed to own a printed book. This attitude, however, was revised in the light of experience, and within a short time at least seventy-three Italian cities had printing presses, which produced many editions, chiefly of the classics.

The invention of printing was of great significance for the diffusion of humanism as well as a stimulus for the growth of literacy. At almost a single stroke many works of great literature became available to those who had never before had access to them. Communication of ideas on a wide scale was now possible, for texts could be duplicated inexpensively. The printing of cheap pamphlets enabled intellectual leaders of the Renaissance and the Reformation to extend their influence among groups previously unconcerned with ecclesiastical problems. Thus a relatively simple device revolutionized the intellectual history of Western Europe as well as the world, opening new vistas to the mind of man.

2. Northern Humanism

German Humanism. Northern humanism, distinctly middle class in character, was centered in the towns and the universities. German cities, sitting astride the lanes of commerce and open to cosmopolitan influences, became strongholds of humanism. Some of the older universities, notably Prague (1348), Vienna (1364), Heidelberg (1386), Cologne (1388), and Leipzig (1409), retained the spirit of scholasticism, still militant and arrogant in mood, while the newer universities, especially Freiburg (1460), Tübingen (1477), Mainz (1477), and Wittenberg (1502), stressed the rising humanism. There were frequent struggles between the two schools of thought. In contrast to Italian humanism, which lasted for two centuries, the German movement was comparatively short-lived, covering roughly the last half of the fifteenth century and the first quarter of the sixteenth. It was finally absorbed in the Reformation.

German and Dutch scholars, attracted by Italian humanism, journeyed south to study the meaning of the new doctrines at first hand. Returning to their homelands, they became the traveling salesmen of humanism, wandering restlessly from place to place, disputing with scholastics, and sowing the seeds of the fresh learning. Some settled down to become schoolmasters, and organized Latin schools known as *Gymnasia*. The most important

cradle of early northern humanism was the Rhineland, and the most influential of the Rhenish humanists was Rodolphus Agricola (1443–1485), a Dutchman. Educated at Louvain, Paris, and Ferrara, Agricola eventually accepted a professorship at Heidelberg, where he lectured on Greek and Roman literature. Under his enthusiastic teaching, Heidelberg became the center of humanism in the Germanies. "He was the first," Erasmus said, "to bring a breath of higher culture from Italy."

Sebastian Brant, Schoolmaster Humanist. A leading schoolmaster humanist who sought reform inside the Church was Sebastian Brant (1457–1521), a native of Strasbourg, who for some time held a professorship of jurisprudence at Basle. He achieved worldwide fame for his pungent satire *The Ship of Fools* (1494), an allegory telling the story of a ship, laden with and steered by fools, sent to sail the seas of life to the fool's paradise of Narragonia. With a hundred and ten passengers aboard—including the book-fool, the miser-fool, and fashion-fool, and the fool of useless studies—the ship sails a perilous course past the land of idlers to its destination. Under this convenient cloak Brant vigorously lashed the weaknesses and vices of his time, especially the immorality and ignorance of some of the clergy. The most celebrated German poem of its time, *The Ship of Fools*, despite its coarse satire, appealed to popular taste. It was supposed to have given Erasmus the idea for his *Praise of Folly*. It helped prepare the way for the Reformation.

Johann Reuchlin, Rational Humanist. German humanists, unlike the Italian, refused to abandon themselves to a secular enjoyment of life and, instead, placed the Church Fathers and the Bible on an equal plane with classical writers. Where the older and more conservative humanists merely hinted at reform of ecclesiastical abuses, the younger, vigorous crowd of "rational humanists" were more eager for conflict. Johann Reuchlin (1455–1522), although he never left the Catholic Church, denounced scholastic theologians and led the struggle of the humanists against scholasticism.

A distinguished Hellenist and Latinist, he was, at the same time, a devoted student of Hebrew, which he regarded as a holy language. He found himself the center of a stormy controversy when Johann Pfefferkorn, a converted Jew, accused him of being inclined secretly to Judaism. A furious literary battle ensued between the Reuchlinites (humanists) on the one side, and Pfefferkorn and his followers (called "obscurantists" by their opponents) on the other. Since he was no intellectual match for Reuchlin, Pfefferkorn joined forces with Jakob van Hoogstraten, dean of the Dominicans at Cologne and chief papal inquisitor.

"The Letters of Obscure Men." In the midst of this violent literary feud, a group of humanists, led by Crotus Rubianus of Erfurt, attacked the theological party by issuing anonymously between 1515 and 1517 a series of epistles called *The Letters of Obscure Men* ("obscure" at that time meaning "ignorant" or "illiberal"). Written purposely in bad Latin and signed with absurdly fictitious names, the letters asked the most ridiculous questions and disclosed the most astonishing ignorance. Yet so clever was the satire that the epistles of the "obscurantists" were accepted, at first, as genuine. The dramatic publication added fuel to the controversy. Finally, Pope Leo X imposed silence upon both sides, after which the quarrel was forgotten in the agitation aroused by Luther's attacks on the Church. In the meantime, classical literature and the Hebrew language were studied everywhere in the Germanies.

Erasmus, Prince of Humanists. Most influential of northern humanists was Desiderius Erasmus, who was born at Rotterdam in 1466 and died at Basle in 1536. Entering the priesthood in 1492, he pursued his studies in Paris, London, and Rome, and soon became acknowledged as the greatest humanist of the day. He was so renowned a scholar that he was received with distinction not only by universities but by kings and princes. Impelled by a restless temperament to wander from one country to another, he associated with the most distinguished scholars of his day. The wandering Dutchman became Europe's most cosmopolitan scholar. He possessed a pungent wit, a prodigious knowledge, and a flowing, eloquent, classical style of writing. The ideal humanist, he epitomized both its virtues and its faults.

The eminent Desiderius Erasmus of Rotterdam, adaptor of humanism to religious needs, portrayed in an engraving by Albrecht Dürer in 1526.

Thoroughly at home in the polished circles of Cicero and Horace, he found the society of Rotterdam or London intellectually stagnant. Convinced that man is a rational animal, Erasmus turned to classical society for the inspiration he failed to find in his own age. At the same time, his narrow interests reflected the limitations of humanism: he was uninterested in the magnificent art of his own age and was even hostile to science.

Erasmus exposed the inconsistencies of unimaginative scholastic theologians and ridiculed their pedantic hairsplitting. He found much to criticize in the ecclesiasticism of the day: the follies of the monks, the superstition of the common people, the blind reliance on authority, and the excesses of ceremonial formalism. Although he unconsciously prepared the mind of Europe for religious reformation, he was not himself one of the leaders of the Protestant Revolt nor did he question the essential doctrines of the Roman Catholic Church. Luther, at first his warm friend and admirer, later found that Erasmus was not ready to adopt the extreme tenets of the reformers. The German monk first expostulated, then ridiculed, and finally denounced his former friend as a coward and as a foe of "the true religion." On his own part, Erasmus found many of Luther's ideas excellent, but objected to his "intolerable faults." What Erasmus wanted to do was to humanize Christianity and to wean men away from the formalism which he felt had been superimposed on the enlightened moral philosophy of Christ.

The work which won for Erasmus a high place in contemporary letters, as well as enduring fame, was his *Praise of Folly*, written at the house of Sir Thomas More, illustrated by Holbein, and published in 1509. The purpose of this inimitable satire was to cover every species of foolish men and women with ridicule; yet through all the biting sarcasm runs an unbroken vein of religious seriousness. More than any other man of his age, Erasmus made people conscious of their follies and superstitions.

Humanism in France. In France the progress of humanism was halted temporarily by scholars of the University of Paris, noted as a stronghold of scholasticism. The real beginning of the French Renaissance was the Italian expedition in 1494 of Charles VIII, which was instrumental in bringing many humanistic ideas from the south into France. The leading French humanist of his time was Guillaume Budé (1467–1540), who was said to have been the equal of Erasmus in Greek scholarship and knowledge of Latin. Among his achievements was a treatise on Roman laws and coinage, the first serious work on that subject. He was held in high esteem by Francis I, for whom he acted as an agent in founding the *Collège de France*. Francis I (1494–1547), "pre-eminently the king of the Renaissance," adopted a policy of encouraging art and literature. A man of high intelligence and a sincere lover of letters, he invited men of learning to

France, and even installed such artists as Leonardo da Vinci and Benvenuto Cellini at his court. At the urging of Budé he instituted in 1530 the *Lecteurs royaux*, who, in spite of the opposition of the Sorbonne, were granted full liberty to teach Greek, Latin, and Hebrew.

Rabelais, Multitudinous Monk. The central figure of French humanism, the Franciscan monk François Rabelais (*c.* 1495–1553), lived exactly as a monk should not live. He was charged with heresy. It is not at all improbable that this accusation contributed to the vagabond character of his life. He was a veritable incarnation of humanistic spirit, as revealed in his love for the classics, his contempt for the mysticism and conventional scholasticism of the theologians, and his bursting joy in the secular life. He was a firm believer in freedom of thought; human nature was to him a manifestation of God's will, and the less restricted and bound by tradition it was, the better. Impatient of hypocrisy and deceitfulness, he refused to recognize accepted standards of conduct, with the result that he was continually involved in fierce quarrels and battles of invective. Whether he be termed "the great jester of France," or "a comic Homer," or "an obscene fool," he nevertheless epitomized the spirit of humanism. Erasmus recognized his stature by labeling him "the wonder of France."

Rabelaisian gusto in life was demonstrated by the romantic tales of Gargantua and Pantagruel in *The Great and Inestimable Chronicles of the Enormous Giant Gargantua,* and its sequel, *Pantagruel.* In the coarse tradition of French buffoonery, Rabelais described the adventures of Gargantua, a giant of French folklore, of tremendous size and appetite, and his son Pantagruel. In the course of his story, Rabelais delivered a withering attack on the people, opinions, and follies of his age. He took special delight in heaping ridicule on scholastics, pedants, monks, priests, despots, doctors, Catholics, and Calvinists alike. The literary device was a convenient cloak for a serious purpose; his life would have been considerably shortened had he openly attacked the objects of his venom. A deliberate vulgarizer, he wrote in the French vernacular, which delighted those Frenchmen attracted by his broad burlesque and hidden seriousness.

Montaigne. When Rabelais died in 1553, his position as France's leading humanist was taken over by Michel Eyquem Seigneur de Montaigne (1533–1592), one of the masters of the essay. A lover of the classics, a thoroughgoing individualist, and a profound student of man, Montaigne represented the best of Renaissance humanism. His *Essays,* consisting of ninety-three sketches of diverse character, represented a lifetime of study and observation. "My sole object is to leave for my friends and my relations a mental portrait of myself, defects and all; I care neither for utility nor for fame." There is a rich mine of scholarly wit and worldly wisdom in this collection of moral adages, provincial sayings, quotations, esthetic treatises, and observations on classical and current scholarship.

Spanish Humanism. Spanish humanists, like their German, English, and French counterparts, went to the Italian states for inspiration and returned with new enthusiasm for classical antiquity. Others were strongly influenced by the work of Erasmus. Eventually, the Iberian movement lapsed into silence under the onslaught of the Inquisition; but during its heyday there were two outstanding figures: Juan Luis Vives (1492–1540) and Miguel de Cervantes (1547–1616). Probably the most influential Spanish schoolmaster of his time, Vives, a native of Valencia, studied at Paris, Louvain, and Oxford. Called Doctor Mellifluous by his students at Oxford, he wrote numerous works attacking scholasticism and the authority of Aristotle. Erasmus, who was his teacher, said that no man was better fitted than Vives "to overwhelm the battalions of the dialecticians." Emphasizing induction as the best method of philosophical and psychological discovery, Vives preceded Descartes and Francis Bacon as a psychological theorist.

According to Victor Hugo, Miguel de Cervantes was the deep poetic spirit of the Renaissance. Cervantes' masterpiece, *Don Quixote,* a novel of adventure and manners, satirized the outworn customs of Spanish chivalry. One of the most appealing characters in literature, Don Quixote was a brave, humane, and courteous, if somewhat eccentric, hero, who was accompanied on his travels by a shrewd, selfish, and much less gallant servant, Sancho Panza. Tilting at windmills, mistaking serving-maids for noble ladies, and lamenting the invention of gunpowder as a catastrophe for all good knights, Don Quixote goes blithely through life holding firmly to the decadent spirit of medievalism. Many have seen in *Don Quixote* a profound political satire, but Cervantes himself insisted that it was a burlesque upon the romances of chivalry. It presents a magnificent panorama of Spanish life with a host of colorful characters: nobles and knights, priests and innkeepers, hidalgos and beggars, scullions and convicts.

English Humanism: Chaucer. The secular spirit of humanism was already evident in England in the work of Geoffrey Chaucer (1340–1400). Writing in the vernacular Middle English, Chaucer endowed his stories with a humanity, grace, and strength which place them among the world's greatest narratives. Chaucer, a "well of English undefiled" gave supreme expression to a broad and delicate wit, piercing pathos with immortal beauty, and a keen sense of the realities of life. His boldness of speech and ribaldry exemplified the Renaissance spirit of freedom of expression.

The New Learning. English humanism lay relatively dormant as the country was kept in turmoil by the Wars of the Roses and persecution of the Lollards. Not until Henry VII (r. 1485–1509) restored some semblance of order did conditions favor the spread of humanism. In England, as in other European countries, the movement acquired distinguishing characteristics. The English form early developed a practical tendency. English scholars journeyed to the Italian peninsula to learn about the "humanities," and on their return, introduced new studies and methods into English schools. These humanists laid the basis for the famous English school and university systems.

The interest in classical learning was quickened by a group known as the Oxford Reformers, of whom Grocyn, Linacre, and Colet were the outstanding leaders. William Grocyn (c. 1446–1519), who studied Greek and Latin in Florence, Rome, and Padua, returned to lecture at Oxford on classical learning. "He was a friend and preceptor of us all," Erasmus wrote in 1514. Thomas Linacre (c. 1460–1524), physician to Henry VIII, was another of the brilliant Oxford group who, having studied at the fountainhead in Italy, returned to spread the new learning in England. Among his pupils was Erasmus. The foundation by royal charter of the College of Physicians in London was mainly due to Linacre, who also established readerships in medicine at Oxford and Cambridge. A third member of the Oxford humanists was John Colet (c. 1467–1519), who completed his formal education at Oxford and later visited France and Italy to study canon and civil law, patristics, and Greek. For six years he lectured at Oxford on the personality and times of St. Paul, introducing a new critical approach to Biblical subjects. Called as dean of St. Paul's Cathedral, he refounded at his own expense St. Paul's Grammar School, the first example of nonclerical management in education, where a young man could obtain a Christian education tempered by Greek and Ciceronian Latin. As the first English school devoted to humanistic learning, St. Paul's became a model for the reorganized English school system. Henry VIII encouraged the work of Colet and his colleagues.

Sir Thomas More. The outstanding figure of English humanism was Sir Thomas More (1478–1535), a pupil of Grocyn and Linacre and an intimate friend of Dean Colet and Erasmus. Cardinal Morton, who was the young man's guardian in 1495, predicted that "whoever shall live to see it, this child will prove a marvelous rare man." The prophecy was accurate; Sir Thomas became one of the most illustrious classical scholars of his time. Drawn into public life by Henry VIII, he became lord chancellor after the fall of Wolsey, resigned

Lawyer, statesman, and author, Sir Thomas More would not give way on the matter of Henry VIII's royal divorce. In 1534 he refused to take the oath of supremacy, whereupon he was indicted for high treason and beheaded. He was canonized in 1935. The portrait is by Hans Holbein the Younger.

later on a point of conscience, and was finally beheaded on a charge of treason for refusing to acknowledge the secular supremacy over the Church. More's *Utopia,* which appeared in Latin in 1516, was the first important book since Plato's *Republic* to project an ideal commonwealth, or a paradise here on earth. One of the world's great classics, *Utopia* was a biting satire on the England of More's day—its low morals, cruel laws, wretched poverty and gross luxury, abuse of power, and interminable warfare.

Sixteenth-Century English Poetry. Although the humanist movement on the Continent was eventually to be engulfed by the Reformation, in England it continued to exert a profound influence on the development of literature. A popular form of lyric verse was used by the poets Sir Philip Sidney (1554–1586), Christopher Marlowe (1564–1593), Edmund Spenser (1552–1599), William Shakespeare (1564–1616), and Ben Jonson (1573–1637). Sir Thomas Wyatt (1503–1542) and the Earl of Surrey (*c.* 1518–1547) imported and adapted the Petrarchan sonnet, a form also used by Shakespeare and Spenser, and later by John Milton (1608–1674).

Greatest of all literary forms was the flowering of poetic drama in Elizabethan England. Accent on the drama was indeed an all-European phenomenon, but no country surpassed England in the number and excellence of her great dramatists. The brilliant but erratic Christopher Marlowe was born at Canterbury in 1564, the year of Shakespeare's birth. After taking his degree at Cambridge in 1583, the young poet went to London where he spent a decade in riotous living but at the same time composed works pregnant with promise. At the age of twenty-five he produced the *The Tragical History of Dr. Faustus*, an interpretation of the Faust legend. At twenty-nine his career was terminated in a tavern brawl, which cost the world a priceless literary heritage.

Apotheosis: William Shakespeare. Some of literature's most shining lights—Homer, Langland, Shakespeare—are almost legendary figures. We know little with certainty about William Shakespeare. He was born at Stratford-on-Avon in 1564, married and raised a family there, then went to London, where he acted, wrote plays, and composed poems. He returned to Stratford, where he made his will, died, and was buried. Yet this mysterious poet has been acclaimed as the last and most wondrous voice of the Renaissance in England and as the supreme poet and interpreter of human character in all literature. Shakespeare took over Marlowe's blank-verse line, appropriated and developed the themes and plots of a number of predecessors, and then left us a cycle of thirty-seven plays which have become universally known as one of the great treasures of literature. His dramatic power lay not in

his plots, which for the most part were not original, but in unsurpassed delineation of character. It was always character—the development of spiritual and psychological conflicts in the individual—that interested him; and it was by his prolific and inspired creation, not of stage copies, but of real men and women, that he established his position as the foremost literary artist in history. Moved by the spirit of the Renaissance, he glorified the individual and his struggles with himself.

3. Art in Northern Europe

Italian Impetus. Just as Italian humanism gradually penetrated into other areas of Europe, so did the art of the southern peninsula move beyond the Alps into the Low Countries, the Germanies, France, England, and Spain. Northern European artists learned much from the creative genius of Italian masters, and worked to emulate their remarkable skill in handling color, portraying harmonious action, and infusing subjects with life and emotion. There were also valuable local contributions, which deserve to be ranked with those of the Italian masters, in design, color, and interpretation.

Flemish and Dutch Art. The first of the northern peoples to develop the art of painting were the Flemings. The Early Flemish School, founded by Hubert van Eyck (*c.* 1366–1426), Jan van Eyck (*c.* 1385–1441), and Margaret van Eyck (*c.* 1377–1431), brothers and sister, is credited with the invention of painting in oils, and with perfecting methods of mixing colors. Their work was still mainly medieval in conception, although they showed a tendency toward naturalism and secularism in portraying Flemish types of people and their dress. In the sixteenth century, Flemish artists began to visit Italy and returned home to "Italianize" their style of painting by greater emphasis upon the interpretation of character, closer attention to depicting the beauties of the human body, and improved composition. One Flemish painter, however, Pieter Brueghel (1525–1569), nicknamed "Peasant Brueghel," was not influenced

The Marriage of Giovanni Arnolfini and Giovanna Cenami, 1434. Jan van Eyck, early Flemish painter, was a great master of portraiture and detail. His technical brilliance is clearly revealed in this masterpiece.

by southern artistic ideas even though he studied in Italy; his paintings of Flemish peasant scenes, executed with abundant spirit and comic power, were masterpieces of realism. He painted religious scenes, too, but always interpreted them in terms of everyday Flemish life. His landscapes are among the finest in European art.

The Flemish School lost much of its individuality and creativeness when it fell under the influence of the Italian masters, but later in the post-Renaissance period it regained its vigor with the surpassing work of Peter Paul Rubens (1577–1640), one of the most talented of European painters. Rubens' trio of religious paintings, including the famous *Descent from the Cross* (now in the Cathedral of Antwerp), are works of consummate genius. An incredibly active artist, he completed, with the help of his pupils, some 2,200 paintings of all kinds, including religious and mythological subjects, historic scenes, landscapes, portraits, and animals. In each of these forms he exhibited a remarkable sense of pictorial perception, drawing, composition, and coloring.

Dutch painting was similar to the Flemish in both subjects and techniques, but there was less emphasis upon religious themes. The complacent, prosperous Dutch burghers, patrons of the arts, wanted a thoroughly secular form of art, and preferred small paintings which would fit into their homes. Their tastes ran to *genre* paintings—portrayal of scenes of ordinary life, and portraits. The Dutch artists depicted tavern scenes, village festivals, life at the marketplace, fishing scenes, and seascapes, all done with quiet simplicity and beautiful coloring.

⌐{ KEY DOCUMENT }⌐

"THE LETTERS OF OBSCURE MEN," 1515–1517

Ulrichi Hutteni equitis operum supplementum, Epistolae obscurorum virorum (Leipzig, 1864), I, 226 ff.

"THE LETTERS OF OBSCURE MEN," written anonymously between 1515 and 1517 by Ulrich von Hutten and several others, were addressed to one of Reuchlin's opponents, presumably from his admirers. Written deliberately in bad Latin, they were designed to satirize the ignorance and stupidity of the obscure priests and monks who sought to defend tradition. Following is an example of one of the letters.

Henricus Schaffsmulius to Master Ortuin Gratius, Many Salutations:

You informed me that I should write to you often when I first went to the Curia, and to address any theological problems to you, as you desired to answer them in a more satisfactory fashion than could those at the papal court at Rome. Therefore, I now desire to ask your opinion in the matter of whether one should on Friday, the sixth day, or on any other day of fasting, eat an egg in which there is a chick. We were recently dining in an inn in the Campo Fiore, and we were eating eggs. Opening my egg, I found that there was a chick within. Upon showing it to my colleague, I was urged to swallow it immediately before the host saw me; otherwise I should have to pay a Carolinus or a Julius for a chicken, for it is the custom here to pay for everything the host places on the table and nothing will be taken back. If he saw that there was a chick in the egg, he would demand payment for the chick—and he would charge as much for a little one as for a big one.

I, therefore, immediately swallowed the egg and the chick at the same time. Afterwards I realized that it was Friday. I then said to my colleague: "You have made me commit a mortal sin by eating meat on Friday."

But he replied that it was not a sin, not even a venial sin, since a chick cannot be considered as anything else but an egg until it is born. He also remarked that it is just the same in the case of cheese in which there are worms, as well as worms in cherries, peas, and beans. They, however, are eaten on the sixth day, and even during the vigils of the apostles. But the proprietors of inns are such rascals that they, on occasion, label these things as meat in order to gain thereby.

I went out and thought about this matter. By Heaven, Master Ortuin, I am most disturbed. I do not know what I ought to do about it. I know that I might seek counsel with the papal court, but those men have bad consciences. As to my own feelings, it seems to me that the chicks in the egg are meat, since the body is already formed and shaped, and it has animal life. Quite the contrary with the matter of worms in cheese and in other foods, for worms are said to be

fish, as I have learned from a physician, who is also a very capable scientist.

I earnestly beg you to answer my question. If you hold it to be a mortal sin, I must seek absolution before I go to Germany. You may know that our lord, Jakob van Hoogstraten, borrowed a thousand florins from the bank; he may want to make something out of the case. May the devil take Johann Reuchlin and those other poets and lawyers, who are attempting to fight the Church of God—or, rather, the theologians who are the real backbone of the Church; as Christ said, "Thou art Peter, and upon this rock I will build my Church."

May the Lord God preserve you. Farewell. Written in the city of Rome.

⌇ HISTORICAL INTERPRETATION ⌇

PRESERVED SMITH ON THE GENIUS OF ERASMUS

Preserved Smith, *Erasmus, A Study of His Life, Ideals, and Place in History* (New York, 1923), pp. 440–441. By permission of Harper and Brothers.

PRESERVED SMITH (1880–1941), late Professor of History at Cornell University, wrote a sympathetic appreciation of the great Dutch reformer Desiderius Erasmus (1466–1536), with special attention to his relations with humanism. Smith presented the personality of Erasmus not only as a product of the Renaissance in the North but also as typical of a turbulent period in European history.

Physically a small man, thin, slight, and pale, everything about his form and chiseled features indicated delicacy, refinement, exquisite temper. If Luther was a Richard Coeur de Lion whose sword could cleave a bar of iron, Erasmus was a Saladin, whose blade could sever a pillow without knocking it down. His tastes were fastidious and shrinking, as if—one may repeat the epigram once more—he had been descended from a long line of maiden aunts. His eyelids, veiling his eyes demurely, do not keep him from keen vision, but only from fierce glances; his mouth is curved in kindly irony, which is perhaps the ripest of all moods in which poor humanity can look at itself.

Purely intellectual as he was, he could not be a partisan, not because of timidity, but because he saw the good and the bad of all sides. He would not follow Luther, because he had

mixed some evil with his good; he could not wish him utterly crushed, because of the Pharisees in the Catholic Church. He was always making exceptions, discovering distinctions, and toning down an otherwise too glaring statement. He could hardly write anything without some hedging, some slight doubt as to the unqualified validity of what he said. He, almost alone in his age, knew that truth had many facets, that no rule can be without exceptions, and that no position is unassailable.

If his life did not furnish another example of supreme self-sacrifice and heroism, still less did it have in it anything vulgar, or angry, or ugly. As I compare his portrait with that of Sir Thomas More, I find that More's face is the one on which I love to look for occasional inspiration, but Erasmus's is the face of the man I should prefer to live with. More would die for his faith, and would have you punished for yours; Erasmus would be companionable and chatty and courteous and tolerant even to an infidel. What anecdotes the man could tell, what pictures he could call up, what wit he could scintillate! And, above all, how much one might have learned from him, both in matters of mere erudition and in the conduct of life!

As the broadest scholar and as the most polished wit of his generation Erasmus is sure of a lasting place in the history of literature and of learning. As that actor in the great contemporary revolution who typified the contact of Renaissance and Reformation, who felt most deeply their common spirit and most delicately their various contrasts, his biography is worthy of close study. Most of all does he deserve to be remembered for the rare spirit which combined the ethical and the rational; for the common sense really so uncommon, and for the humanity so called, one might think, like *lucus a non lucendo*, from its conspicuous absence in many human breasts. That he saw through the accretions of superstition, dogma, and ritual to the "philosophy of Christ"; that he let his mind play freely on the sacred arcana of the traditional faith; that he recognized reason as the final arbiter in these matters as well as in social and political affairs—all this is the noble genius of Erasmus.

❧ TEN BASIC BOOKS ☙

THE RENAISSANCE NORTH OF THE ALPS

1. Allen, Percy S., *The Age of Erasmus* (Oxford, 1914, R. 1963).
2. Benesch, Otto, *The Art of the Renaissance in Northern Europe* (Cambridge, Mass., 1945, R. 1965).
3. Friedlander, Max J., *From Van Eyck to Bruegel*, 2nd ed. (Greenwich, Conn., 1965).
4. Gilmore, Myron P., *The World of Humanism, 1453–1517* (New York, 1952).†
5. Huizinga, Johan, *The Waning of the Middle Ages* (London, 1924, 1950).†
6. Mather, Frank J., *Western European Painting of the Renaissance* (New York, 1939, R. 1966).
7. Panofsky, Erwin, *The Life and Art of Albrecht Dürer* (Princeton, N. J., 1955).
8. Sichel, Edith, *Michel de Montaigne* (London, 1916).
9. Smith, Preserved, *Erasmus, A Study of His Life, Ideals, and Place in History* (New York, 1923).†
10. Weiss, Roberto, *Humanism in England During the Fifteenth Century*, 2nd ed. (Oxford, 1957).

5

The Great Religious Secession: The Reformation

THE REFORMATION was one of the most remarkable episodes in world history, whether we regard it in bulk or in detail. It is rich in' striking incidents and in display of human character, both on the Catholic and on the Protestant side: we may find here the loftiest heroism and the lowest depths of turpitude. It exemplifies all the problems of daily life, magnified in proportion to the greatness of the issues here involved. And from the heat of this conflict between two irreconcilable ideals one principle has slowly emerged, theoretically repudiated by one side and too often violated by the other in practice, yet finally victorious through the mere force of circumstances: the principle of religious toleration.

—GEORGE GORDON COULTON

1. The Split in Christianity

From Reform to Revolution. The Reformation, or Protestant Revolt, which ran its course from 1517 to 1648, commenced as a reform movement within the Roman Catholic Church but ended in revolution and secession. The product of highly complex forces, the Reformation was not exclusively religious. Spiritually, the new Protestant theologies challenged the Catholic Church's claim to be the only instrument of salvation. From the material point of view, it involved a struggle between the all-embracing international medieval Church and the rising national states. It was, in effect, a rebellion against the political and economic privileges of the Church.

At the beginning of the fifteenth century it appeared that many of the common abuses of the clergy might be eliminated, and that the unity and cohesion of the Church could thereby be preserved. By the opening of the sixteenth century this was no longer possible, because the powerful forces of reform and rebellion against established ecclesiastical authority had combined to bring about a climax. The result was a series of national, or quasi-national, revolts against a religious system that was considered inappropriate to the new economic, political, social, and intellectual temper of the day.

The Reformation meant the nationalization of organized religion. A number of European states seceded from the Catholic Church and adopted some form of Protestantism. In the Germanies, the revolt under the leadership of Martin Luther led to the formation of a new religious confession, and to state control of religion. In Switzerland, the Zwinglian movement and the influence of Calvin resulted in the extension of the revolution and the foundation of Calvinism. In England, which had long enjoyed a position of semi-independence from papal authority, the national interest was preeminent. The Catholic Reformation, or Counter-Reformation, an integral part of the whole movement, was a housecleaning by the Church itself to sweep away the abuses which had weakened it and left it open to attack.

Economically, the Reformation went hand-in-hand with the Commercial Revolution, and the two movements acted upon each other. Socially, the bourgeoisie, which proved particularly susceptible to Protestant dogma and practice, formed the backbone of the new churches. Politically, the man of the Reformation shifted his loyalty from the *international* Church to the *national* State, from support of the papacy to support of the national monarchy.

It was in the cultural field (including both religious and intellectual factors) that the Reformation had its most important influence on the making of modern man:

(1) *Individualism:* Cracks appeared in the rigid system of medieval belief, and the struggle of the individual's right to make up his own mind began. It was a revolutionary change when intellectual authority was transferred from the Church to the individual.

(2) *Dogmatism:* Modern man at first, no matter what his religion, persisted in regarding his own religious beliefs as the only possible truth and tried hard to suppress dissenters.

(3) *Toleration:* Despite bitter fratricidal strife, European man slowly learned the fundamental truth that intolerance breeds intolerance.

(4) *Education:* Although the Reformation contributed little to the content of education, it was nevertheless responsible for its spread.

The story of this revolt, in which Christian was pitted against Christian, is an unhappy one. It includes such unattractive phases as the debasement of religious ideals, the slaughter of the innocent, the existence of intolerance and bigotry, and various other excesses.

Historical Controversy: Modern or Medieval? According to the historian Wilhelm Dilthey, both the Reformation and the Renaissance had their origins in the struggle for intellectual liberty, impelled by the growth of industry and commerce, the rise of towns, and the emergence of national states. The Reformation, he stated, represented a deep opposition to the ecclesiastical domination of the Middle Ages and hence opened the way to the modern world.

This point of view was attacked by the theologian Ernst Troeltsch, who insisted that the Reformation was in all its essential characteristics basically medieval, because it raised medieval questions and solved them by medieval methods. The Reformation, in Troeltsch's view, was a religious movement in opposition to the secular interests of the Renaissance. Therefore, even if the Reformation contributed to the emergence of modern freedom and tolerance, modern history did not begin until the eighteenth-century Age of Reason.

Articulate exponents of both these views have appeared in each new generation. Some follow the lead of Dilthey in describing the Reformation as essentially a modern movement and devote relatively little attention to theological problems. Others support Troeltsch in contending that theological problems of the Reformation deserve major attention and that the movement must be considered a part or extension of the medieval world.

Historical Controversy: Catholic Versus Protestant Views. There has been much scholarly work on the Reformation. Historians treat its political, social, and economic aspects, but a comprehensive analysis involves theological as well as historical judgments. Scholars trained in theology have devoted long and detailed study to the origins and meaning of the Reformation. The conclusions of these scholars run parallel to their own religious convictions.

Reverend Philip Hughes, a leading Roman Catholic Church historian, considers the Reformation as catastrophic. The whole fabric of organized Christianity—the Church, the pope, cardinals, bishops, priests, sacraments, ritual, canon law, asceticism, prayer, penance, —all this, he says, is considered by Protestantism a "vast irrelevancy," "even a hindrance to man's salvation." In his view, therefore, the Reformation was "an immensely harmful achievement," "a revolt of clerics against clerics."

A diametrically opposed view is taken by Ernest G. Schweibert, a Protestant historian, who sees the movement not as a revolt but as a much-needed reform. Together with Luther he looks upon the "real Christian Church" as a communion of true believers, which had existed from the first and which still exists in spite of the many human encrustations clinging to it. Others before Luther, says Schweibert, had arrived at the same conclusion. Some, like Erasmus, lacked the courage of their convictions. Others, like John Huss, died for their beliefs "because the world was not ready." In Martin Luther "the propitious moment and qualities of leadership combined to produce the much-needed Reformation."

Here again we see how opposite conclusions can be reached from the same set of facts. Controversies evolve from fundamental differences in the philosophy of history, sometimes from differences in method. The student should listen to both sides, sift the arguments, and then reach a judgment of his own.

2. Cracks in the Medieval Structure

Rise of New Forces. In the early thirteenth century the Church seemed to be unassailable in prestige and power. The pontificate of Innocent III (1198–1216) marked the zenith of its authority. Under this vigorous rule the temporal power—the Holy Roman Empire—was enfeebled, and the Church emerged as the triumphant authority. But throughout the remainder of the thirteenth, and through the fourteenth century, the Church progressively declined in strength and power. New forces were arising in Europe, with which the Church found it difficult to cope. Heresy increased as individuals and groups wandered outside the limits set by authority. The papacy became involved in a prolonged struggle with the princes over taxation of the clergy. The rise of a prosperous urban middle class gave the Church another opponent which fought stubbornly against ecclesiastical interference in temporal affairs. The growing sense of nationality among the peoples of Europe became a force opposing international ecclesiastical control.

By the middle of the fifteenth century the great institution was tottering. Neither excommunication nor interdict, neither Inquisition nor reform, could check the disintegration. By the opening of the sixteenth century, the Church, with its authority challenged and its prestige waning, could no longer withstand the blows of revolt.

Early Critics and Heresy. Group opposition to the Church appeared in southern France as early as the twelfth century. The Waldensians, a Christian denomination founded by Peter Waldo, a wealthy merchant of Lyons, claimed that the Church had lost its apostolical purity and had become beset by corruption, indolence, and immorality. In the early thirteenth century another French sect, the Albigensians, struck at the very foundations of Catholic Christianity by rejecting its fundamental doctrines, and maintaining that life on earth is a punishment and the only hell that exists. They were crushed by Innocent III in a war of extermination. An English master at Oxford, John Wycliffe (c. 1320–1384), maintained that the Church should be subordinated to the state, that salvation was primarily an individual matter between man and God, that the doctrine of transubstantiation was false, and that the veneration of saints was idolatrous. Insisting that the Scriptures were the only law of Christianity, Wycliffe assisted in their translation from Latin into the English vernacular. His teaching made a profound impression upon Bohemian students who heard him at Oxford.

John Huss (c. 1373–1415), a Bohemian patriot, taught his followers that Christ, not the pope, was the true head of the Church, and that the individual could read and interpret the Bible for himself. Ordered to appear before the Council of Constance to clear themselves of charges of heresy, Huss and his colleague, Jerome of Prague, courageously defended their views. Although granted safe-conduct, the two reformers were condemned and burned at the stake in 1415. In the same year the remains of Wycliffe were disinterred and burned as a symbol of heresy.

Decline in Prestige. In the meantime the Church continued to lose prestige. Boniface VIII, like his predecessor Innocent III, sought to compel France and England to bow before his commands, but where Innocent had been successful Boniface came out second best. In an involved conflict with Philip IV of France and Edward I of England, concerning the right of the monarchs to tax the Church for the war which they were about to wage with one another, the embattled pope was beaten. His famous bull, *Clerics laicos* (1296), which forbade the kings to tax the clergy without papal consent, was simply disregarded. His bull, *Unam sanctum*, which restated the old papal claims to supremacy, was likewise ignored. The triumph of the monarchs was a powerful blow to the temporal claims of the papacy. The papal hope of universal temporal leadership was dashed by rising national sentiment.

A further blow was the papacy's enforced residence at Avignon in southern France from 1309 to 1378 (since called the Babylonian Captivity of the Church). The Great Schism which followed (1378–1417), when two popes claimed universal sovereignty, each excommunicating the other as anti-Christ and each presiding over his own College of Cardinals, caused a still further decline in prestige. After 1409 there were three popes, each claiming sole power. A series of general Church Councils (Conciliar Movement) finally managed to end the Great Schism but failed to rescue the Church from its precarious state. The movement neither altered the fundamental character of the papacy nor brought about those reforms which might have arrested the steady weakening of the centuries-old ecclesiastical authority.

By the sixteenth century the papacy once more succeeded in establishing itself firmly at Rome, which became a center of Renaissance learning and art. The popes still claimed the enormous powers of their predecessors. But it was too late now to avoid a major split.

3. Mainsprings of Revolt

Moral Causes: Ecclesiastical Abuses. The Church had a long record of service and achievements. It had converted the barbarian Germanic hordes which had invaded the Roman Empire and had given them the elements of Western civilization. At a time when but few persons enjoyed the benefits of literacy, the Church maintained an educated class and kept alive the light of classical culture until its rebirth in the Renaissance. It officially opposed war and violence. It inculcated the principle of charity among its followers. But much of this was overshadowed by the fact that the ecclesiastical hierarchy from top to bottom was weakened by a human interest in material things.

The papacy of this period was brought to its lowest level by Alexander VI (pontificate 1492–1503). Siring a family, he endowed his relatives at the expense of the Church. The disorganization of the papal curia under his pontificate was appalling; the sale of offices, especially, was a scandal. He confiscated the wealth of cardinals, noblemen, and officials, and cast them into prison while he spent their money.

The clergy below the papacy had been weakened by greed and carelessness. The problem of clerical celibacy was one with which conscientious ecclesiastical authorities found it difficult to cope. The Oxford chancellor Gascoigne, a strong anti-Lollard, wrote in 1450 that the bishop of St. Asaph was earning the equivalent of to-day's $20,000 a year from the licenses for concubinage that he sold to his priests. The figure may possibly be exaggerated, but it does suggest the extent of an evil which kindled popular resentment. There was additional ground for criticism in the multiplicity of holy days, the traffic in holy relics, and the extent to which clerical immunities encouraged disrespect for law and order.

The clergy on the whole reflected the general moral tenor of the day, but the fact that it was unable to rise much above the crassness of the times lowered it in popular estimation. Throughout the Middle Ages distinguished churchmen, well aware of such moral lapses, urged reforms. That the discipline so often demanded was never realized left the Church open to attack all along the line.

Doctrinal Causes: Man's Relation to God. The Church had long held the position that the individual must prepare for salvation through justification by faith *and* good works (the sacramental system). Dissenters now proposed that it was possible to obtain salvation by faith *alone*. This idea was not altogether new, for Wycliffe and Huss a century earlier had preached the priesthood of all believers. But these earlier reform movements had failed partly because the people felt the need for services which only the clergy could perform. In the meantime, new conditions, especially the rise of a spirit of individualism, had created a greater tendency toward rebellion against the orthodox doctrines of the Church. The prosperous self-reliant middle class resented the necessity for communing with God through the medium of the priesthood. What it wanted was an emphasis upon salvation as a direct and immediate relation between the soul of the individual and God. It called for an inner and deeply personal religion, a simplification of the body of Christian belief, and the reform of the sacramental system and its attendant hierarchy of priests. Their spokesmen, the reformers, dreamed of a return to the golden age of the Church as it was supposed to have existed before the days of Constantine.

Economic Causes: Financial Abuses. The Reformation was conditioned by new forces which ushered in the modern system of capitalism. The expansion of commerce was remaking Europe. As the European economy shifted from a landed to a money basis, the Church had to accumulate wealth to maintain its position. During the later centuries of the Middle Ages, it had owned from one-fifth to one-third of all the landed property in Western Europe, yet it claimed exemption from taxation by secular governments. National monarchs, great bankers, and merchants, all alike intent upon augmenting their own capital, power, and privileges, found themselves in increasing conflict with ecclesiastical authority.

The most common financial abuse within the Church involved the sale of offices, or simony (so-called from Simon the Magician, who was said to have offered Saint Peter money for the power to confer the Holy Spirit). Ecclesiastical positions which carried with them large revenues were sought by young noblemen who were more interested in material income than in spiritual grace. Justice was on occasion sold in Church courts, whose officials sometimes derived much of their income from bribes. The practice of pluralities, or the holding of more than one ecclesiastical office, made it possible for high officials to acquire enormous revenues. Sometimes a churchman would leave an office unfilled at the death of its occupant but would continue to collect its stipend. Some highly placed clerics practiced nepotism, a form of favoritism by which relatives were given lucrative posts.

Vast sums of money were drawn to Rome from all parts of Western Europe. The papacy took from each bishop a part of his income in the form of annates, and proportionately from the abbots of the great monasteries. The tithe (one-tenth of an individual's income) and Peter's Pence (a tax paid by every household in Christendom) helped swell the papal coffers. It has been estimated that at the beginning of the Reformation the income of the Holy See was greater than the combined revenues of all the kings of Western Europe.

Social Causes: Role of the Middle Class. The Reformation recruited many of its adherents from the middle class, while the priesthood and the nobility supported the ecclesiastical status quo. With the rise of urban life in the later Middle Ages, the middle class, numerically small but politically ambitious, invariably joined with the territorial rulers in their opposition to the Church. This social alignment showed a cleavage between the conservative aristocracy of wealth, clergy, and nobility, on the one side, and the territorial rulers plus the aspiring middle class on the other. The middle class opposed the older order at every turn. It resented the fact that enormous wealth was tied up in Church lands, and it demanded that national wealth be used for supporting commerce and industry at home. In an age of business enterprise, it could not accept ecclesiastical opposition to profit-making, and it was sensitive to the fact that the Church, which preached poverty as a saintly virtue, had amasssed colossal wealth.

Political Causes: Rise of National Spirit. As long as temporal power in Western Europe was weakened by the decentralized conditions of feudalism, the papacy could enforce its claim to moral dictatorship and political dominion. But now there were new and formidable rivals—national monarchs, national armies, national laws, national courts, national currencies. As the territorial rulers began to concentrate wealth and power into their own hands, they resolved that the Church must not interfere in their internal affairs. Accordingly, they demanded (1) that the Church limit its interests to matters of faith and morals; (2) that the wide jurisdiction of the ecclesiastical courts be revoked in favor of national justice; (3) that control of ecclesiastical patronage, the right to appoint clergymen to office, be placed in the hands of the state; and (4) that the right to tax property be reserved for the monarch.

To discourage the forces for division within the Church, the popes of the fifteenth century made concordats with various national monarchs. The object was to safeguard the papal power, but in practice the concordats served to bring ecclesiastical institutions under national control. The monarchs assumed more and more control over churches in their realms, imposed taxes, nominated clergymen, and in general established the framework of purely national churches. Even before the outbreak of the Reformation, temporal rulers were beginning to contest papal power. The era of the international Church was passing.

Intellectual Causes: Role of Humanism. Renaissance humanists had a marked influence on the ideology and development of the Reformation, although we must be careful not to overemphasize their contribution. Seeking to recapture the spirit of pagan antiquity, they attempted to restore man to a more central place in the universe, in short, to "humanize" him. Although they stressed the study of classical Latin and Greek, they found their authority in "true early Christianity." They ridiculed the "barren" scholasticism of clerical philosophers and criticized the attempt to justify faith by reason. They belittled allegory, symbolism, and mysticism, spoke contemptu-

ously of monastic discipline, and criticized the temporal pretensions of the papacy. Dissatisfied with the abuses which they claimed were corrupting the ecclesiastical system, they sought to lead men back to the sources of Christian faith and practice.

When put to the test, however, most humanists declined to become Protestants. Quick to criticize but cautious in action, they remained loyal to the Church, making it plain that they merely wished to see an end to ecclesiastical abuses. "It is not everyone who has strength for martyrdom," wrote Erasmus. At first an enthusiastic supporter of Luther in his demand for reform, Erasmus was later repelled by the German monk's violent tactics and denial of Church doctrine. "May I be lost," he announced, "if in all of Luther's works there is a single syllable of mine." Yet, by encouraging skepticism and a disrespect for authority, Erasmus and the humanists helped undermine the prestige of the papacy and unwittingly assisted in preparing the way for the revolt.

Historical Controversy: Protestantism and Capitalism. In the early twentieth century, Max Weber, a German sociologist, projected the idea that two seemingly diverse phenomena, Protestantism and capitalism, were closely related. The Protestant Reformation, he said, especially the Calvinist or Puritan phase, had an important influence on the development of modern capitalism. Accepting the thesis of the economic historian Werner Sombart that the "spirit of capitalism" was vital in the development of the new economy, Weber went on to describe this special "spirit" as an offshoot of Calvinism. He noted two essential points: (1) Calvinism was the first Christian denomination which considered the accumulation of wealth as a sign of God's favor, rather than a detriment to salvation; but (2) although the accumulation of wealth was sanctioned, its enjoyment was not. The Calvinist was expected to lead a simple, thrifty life. Because he could not spend his riches on luxurious living, he kept his surplus money in circulation by the continuing processs of investment, gain, and reinvestment which is a characteristic of capitalism. There was, Weber said, a close connection of the spirit or "ethos" of modern economic life with the rational ethics of ascetic Protestantism.

Both Catholic and Protestant theologians attacked the Weber thesis for the role which he assigned to Protestantism. Some argued that capitalism was actually much older than Protestantism and that other impelling motives were much stronger in the development of modern capitalism. Even Sombart joined the attacks on Weber by pointing out that the evolution of capitalism had begun much earlier than the great religious secession. Sombart suggested that the spirit of capitalism could be traced more accurately to the social attitudes and economic practices of early Judaism. Meanwhile, the great Protestant theologian, Ernst Troeltsch, accepted Weber's view of the relationship between Protestantism and Calvinism.

In 1926 R. H. Tawney's study, *Religion and the Rise of Capitalism,* made a distinction between early Calvinism and later Calvinism, thereby correcting Weber's pioneer work. To explain capitalism Tawney placed much more emphasis on the role of the entire Protestant movement as well as the general political, social, and economic conditions in sixteenth- and seventeenth-century Europe.

The debate on the Weber Protestant Ethic continues, with new works published on both sides. Weber's defenders attack critics because of their religious affiliation; critics of Weber point to the economic orientation of the defenders. Defenders say that Protestantism and capitalism cannot be separated as joint forces shaping modern civilization. Critics insist that Protestantism was in no way progressive in its economic interests and, therefore, could not possibly have had any effect on the development of capitalism. For the student attempting to resolve this scholarly struggle, the debate on the Weber thesis stands out as a sure indication that in the study of history there are few final truths of interpretation.

4. God's Angry Monk: The Lutheran Rebellion

Ground for Revolt: The Germanies. The historian—wise after the event—now knows that it was not merely the excellence of Luther's theology, but the more material economic, social, and political conditions present in the Germanies which made the revolt—at least in part—a successful movement. At the close of the fifteenth century, there was no state called Germany, but rather a geographical expression—the Germanies, consisting of hundreds of large and petty sovereignties under the nominal rule of the Holy Roman Emperor. With no strong centralized government, the German people found it impossible to obtain concessions from the Church, and there was no convenient and practical way to impose restrictions upon papal authority. The German princes and the middle class, both becoming more and more nationally conscious, resented the payment of taxes to Rome and the interference of the papacy in their affairs. The invention of printing had stimulated critical reading as well as scholarship. Several editions of the vernacular Bible had been published as well as many religious books and pamphlets. The Germanies seemed to be well prepared for the coming break.

Role of Martin Luther. The spark which kindled this mass of flammable material was Martin Luther, who unwittingly harnessed the historical forces and gave them direction. Here was the leader, the epitome of German national consciousness, who evolved from a loyal son of the Church into a violent rebel. Fascinated, the German people followed his personal struggle, publicized through the printing press as effectively as a modern streamlined advertising and promotional campaign, until he emerged as the founder of a national religious system and as a great German hero.

Martin Luther was born on November 10, 1483, in the Saxon village of Eisleben, the son of a prosperous peasant miner. As a child he was often beaten by his teachers, sometimes as many as fifteen times a day, all for trivial offenses. This severity may have left its mark on his character: he was always melancholy and distrustful and suffered from a strained nervous system. At the age of eighteen, he entered the University of Erfurt, where he became a master of arts. On the threshold of a brilliant legal career, he suddenly decided to

Ain Sermõ.von dem
vnrechten Mammon Luce am XVI.
D.M.Luther.Anno M.D.XXij.

ÆTERNA IPSA SVÆ MENTIS SIMVLACHRA LVTHER
EXPRIMIT AT VVLTVS CERA LVCÆ OCCIDVOS.
M. D XXI.

Martin Luther. Facsimile of a portrait by Cranach
(1520). It was published in the fly-leaf of a sermon
preached by Luther against the authority of the
Roman Church (in octavo, Wittenberg, 1522), when
he threw off his garb of an Augustine monk.

enter the Church. One account explains that
on July 2, 1505, as he was returning from a
visit to his parents at Magdeburg, a violent
storm overtook him near Erfurt. A bolt of
lightning struck in his immediate vicinity and
laid him prostrate on the ground. He cried in
terror: "Help me! Help me! If thou helpest
me, St. Anne, I shall become a monk!" In the
monastery of the Augustinian friars at Erfurt,
the young man fasted, prayed, and scourged
himself in the approved medieval fashion as
a means of storing up a supply of merits for
the Last Judgment Day. Although desperately
anxious to win favor in the eyes of God, he
found no comfort or peace of soul in asceticism.

In 1508 Luther was called to the University
of Wittenberg, newly founded by Frederick
the Wise of Saxony, where he taught philosophy and lectured on the Bible. In 1511 he
interrupted his teaching to journey to Rome
on business for his order. He was shocked
by the abuses he observed in the holy city,
but for the moment he dismissed them from
his mind. In 1515 he was appointed district
vicar with eleven monasteries under his control. He was still plagued by doubts. "Physically I am fairly well, but I suffer in spirit,"
he confessed. "For more than the whole of
last week I was tossed about in death and
hell, so that I still tremble all over my body
and am exhausted. Billows and tempests of
despair and blasphemy assailed me, and I had
lost Christ almost entirely."

Then came a discovery which changed his
life. In preparing a lecture he read a verse in
St. Paul's Epistle to the Romans: "For therein
is the righteousness of God revealed from
faith to faith: as it is written, *the just shall
live by faith.*" For him, this bolt of spiritual
lightning cleansed the atmosphere. Obviously,
a sinner could never hope, no matter how hard
he tried, to obtain a sufficient store of merits
to save his soul. Only the blood of Christ could
wash away sin. Therefore, a sinner could be
saved only *by faith alone* in the atoning blood
of Christ. This disclosure became the central
fact of Protestantism.

**Historical Controversy: The Personality of
Luther.** Few men in history have influenced
their age as much as Luther, and few have
aroused such contradictory estimates of character. His defenders insist that he was a God-
inspired teacher, a man of amiability, kindliness,
and goodness. They accept the judgment of
Luther given by Philip Melanchthon, a close
associate and disciple, in his funeral oration:
"His heart was true and without falseness, his
utterance friendly and kindly." He was "a man
of rare intellectual acumen who hated intrigue
and cunning," and he was "worthy to stand
beside Isaiah, Paul, and Augustine."

To this the critics of Luther reply that he
was a man of violent contradictions, unstable,
emotional, neurotic. He suffered from "de-

lirious hallucinations" (Funck-Brentano), "religious melancholia" (A. Hausrath), or "a neuropathic disorder" (J. Maritain).

The truth lies somewhere near the middle of these extreme views. Luther was neither saint nor devil. He was, indeed, a man of remarkable energy and courage, motivated by deep piety, and possessing great talents. He was sharp and bitter in denunciation of his enemies, hard and rough in his controversial writings. He was capable of arousing loyalty in his friends and hatred among his enemies. A man of violent temper and passions, he never hesitated to attack what he believed to be wrong and anti-Christian. He gave us a clue to his character when he described himself as "rough, boisterous, stormy, and altogether warlike, born to fight innumerable monsters, to remove stumps and stones, to cut down thistles and thorns, and to clear the wild woods."

Psychological Approach to Luther. More books and articles have been written on Luther than on most other individuals in European history. In recent years there have been attempts to understand Luther through the application of psychological and psychoanalytical methods. This is in line with the presidential address to the American Historical Association of William L. Langer, who in December 1957 spoke of "the next assignment" for young historians as investigation-in-depth in the fields of psychology and psychoanalysis. An example is the penetrating book by an American psychiatrist, Erik H. Erikson, entitled *Young Man Luther: A Study in Psychoanalysis and History* (New York, 1958). The author attempted to give a deeper insight into the life of the reformer by analyzing as objectively as possible what Luther wrote about himself, about his own anxieties, fears, temptations, and drives. Some historians regard this analysis, as well as similar treatments of Napoleon, Bismarck, and others, as important in that it stimulates interest in and understanding of the lives and works of great men. Others, however, say that it is impossible for the psychoanalyst or historian to have his subject lie on the couch, and that psychoanalysis

of dead historical figures is plainly impossible. To indict Luther as a manic-depressive on the basis of his writings, as did the Danish Catholic psychiatrist Paul J. Reiter, in 1937, seems to be most questionable. Yet it is clear that, in the case of Luther as well as others, future historians will devote more and more attention to psychological motivations.

Traffic in Indulgences. Luther's first epoch-making challenge to the Church was his criticism of the abuse of indulgences. The indulgence, which grew out of the penitential system of the Church, was a remission, or pardon, either plenary (full) or partial, granted by Church authority, of the punishment due for sins. The earnest Christian was much concerned by the possible length of his stay in purgatory—a place or state after death in which his soul was to be purified before being eligible for heaven. Originally, an indulgence was granted in exchange for the performance of some simple act of piety. But in the course of time it became customary to permit the sinner to make restitution, at least in part, with a money payment.

During the later Middle Ages, the income from indulgences was used for such religious purposes as the Crusades. Those who went on armed pilgrimages to the Holy Land or who contributed to the movement were granted relaxation of penance for their sins, or even full remission. By the fifteenth century many persons began to conceive of the indulgence as a cash transaction, by which they could buy remission of punishment for sins and thereby lessen their stay in purgatory. Some people began to look upon the indulgence as a ticket to heaven. Selling grace and remission became a business. To raise money, the papacy would arrange with a financial house to sell an issue of indulgences. The financial house, in turn, would send out agents who peddled the pardons on a commission basis to local bishops and clergy, who, in their turn, would receive a portion of the profits. Only 30 to 45 per cent of the gross receipts arrived at the papal treasury.

Pope Leo X issued the Indulgence of 1515–1517 professedly for the purpose of completing a magnificent new cathedral at St. Peter's in Rome. In reality, however, the object was to give the youthful Albrecht of Brandenburg, the newly appointed Archbishop of Mainz, a monopoly on the sale of indulgences, so that he could repay the large sum he had borrowed from the Augsburg banking house of Fugger to buy his ecclesiastical post, and at the same time keep a substantial profit for himself. Among the agents whom the archbishop entrusted with the business of distributing the indulgences was John Tetzel, an eloquent Dominican preacher. Tetzel was doing a brisk trade when he suddenly ran head-on into the criticisms of Martin Luther.

The 95 Theses. Angered by Tetzel's activity as a peddler of indulgences, Luther took what he considered to be a reasonable way of attracting theological attention.

—From a desire to elicit the truth, the following theses will be maintained at Wittenberg under the presidency of the reverend father Martin Luther, master of arts, master and lecturer in theology, who asks such as are not able to dispute verbally with him, will do so in writing. In the name of our Lord Jesus Christ. Amen.

Thus began the 95 Theses, which Luther nailed to the door of the Castle Church in Wittenburg on October 31 (the Eve of All Saints' Day), 1517. Such a posting on the bulletin board was a customary procedure when a professor wished to challenge others to a debate. Luther did not understand at the time that what he had to say was opposed to the teachings of the Church. Yet he was in effect challenging not only the abuse but the entire procedure of indulgences:

21. Those preachers of the indulgences err who say that a papal pardon frees a man from all penalty and assures his salvation. . . .
28. It is certain that avarice is fostered by the money clinking in the chest, but to answer the prayers of the Church is in the power of God alone. . . .

86. Why does not the pope, whose riches are at this day more ample than those of Croesus, build the basilica of St. Peter with his own money rather than with that of poor believers? . . .

Luther wrote his theses in Latin, but enterprising publishers, sensing their importance, had them translated into German, and scattered them throughout Europe. Almost overnight the obscure monk of Wittenberg became the hero of reform-minded critics everywhere. According to one observer, "The bottom fell out of the indulgence market."

Luther–Eck Debate: Leipzig, 1519. At this point Luther considered himself merely a moderate critic and reformer, but the logic of events drove him into an increasingly radical position. Pope Leo X sought unsuccessfully to restrain him, but Luther reiterated his criticism of indulgences. At Leipzig, in June 1519, Luther was challenged to debate by Dr. Johann Eck, a renowned theologian, on the question: "Is the papacy a divine or a human institution?" Skilled in dialectics, Eck made Luther admit publicly that the papacy was a man-made institution and that Wycliffe and Huss had been unjustly condemned by the Council of Constance. Eck cited the Church Fathers: "Though I quoted to him Augustine, Jerome, Ambrose, Gregory . . . , he [Luther] contradicted them all without a blush; and said that he would stand alone against a thousand, though supported by no other, because Christ only is the foundation of the Church, for other foundations can no man lay."

Luther's Three Treatises of 1520. Luther was aware by now that the curia in Rome was preparing a papal edict for his condemnation. His sense of depression disappeared, to be supplanted by "the rage which acts as a stimulant for my whole being." From this time on there flowed from his pen a stream of invectives. In 1520 he composed three pamphlets which made his condemnation as a heretic inevitable. (*See page 90 ff.*)

The Diet of Worms. In the meantime, on

June 15, 1520, a papal bull, *Exsurge Domine,* condemned forty-one errors in Luther's teaching and gave him just sixty days to cease his "heretical course." Otherwise, he was to be cut off from the Church and handed over to the temporal authorities for punishment. On December 10, 1520, a crowd of professors, students, and burghers in Wittenberg applauded while Luther consigned the papal bull to the flames. Pope Leo X was appalled by this defiance of his authority, all the more since a little more than a year before the "squabbling monk of Wittenberg" had sent him an almost apologetic letter: "Ah, Holy Father, before God, before the whole creation, I affirm that I have never once had it in my thought to weaken or shake the authority of the Holy See." The appearance of Luther's pamphlets settled the issue: the pope decreed a bull of excommunication against him and called on the emperor, Charles V, to execute it.

Instead of complying, Charles V, a devout son of the Church, invited Luther to the Diet of Worms for a hearing. Armed with a safe-conduct, Luther appeared before the assembly. His words were clear: "Since then your imperial majesty and your highnesses demand a simple answer, I will give you one, brief and simple, but deprived neither of its teeth nor its horns. Unless I am convicted of error by the testimony of Scripture, or by evident reason, . . . I cannot and will not retract, for we must never act contrary to our conscience. Such is my profession of faith, and expect none other from me. I have done: God help me! Amen!"

On the next day the twenty-year-old emperor denounced Luther: "A single monk, led astray by private judgment, has set himself against the faith held by all Christians for a thousand years or more, and impudently concludes that all Christians till now have erred."

At the close of the session, the emperor formally signed the Edict of Worms, which placed Luther and his adherents under the ban of the Empire: "Since Martin Luther still persists obstinately and perversely in maintaining his heretical opinions, and consequently all pious and God-fearing persons abominate and abhor him as one mad or possessed by a demon, we have declared and made known that the said Martin Luther shall hereafter be esteemed by each and all of us as a limb cut off from the Church of God, an obstinate schemer and manifest heretic."

Luther at the Wartburg. On his way home from the diet, Luther was spirited away by friends of Frederick the Wise, Elector of Saxony, to the Wartburg Castle in the Thuringian forest. Under the pseudonym of "Knight George," he spent nearly ten months of work and study at the castle. Musically inclined, he composed hymns, including "A Mighty Fortress is Our God!", which Heine called the *Marseillaise* of the Protestant Reformation. He also held nightly wrestling bouts with his old enemy, the Devil, whom he invariably trapped in a corner. Most important of the tasks he accomplished in exile was his translation into German of the Greek New Testament. "I sweat blood and water in my efforts to render the prophets into the vulgar tongue. Good God! What work it is!" But what emerged was a monument to Luther's linguistic ability. The modern German language owes its origin to Luther's translation of the Bible.

Revolt in Flux. Excommunicated by the Church and outlawed by the Empire, Luther now set to work to establish a national church separated from Rome and based upon individual interpretation of the Scriptures. This difficult task was performed in the midst of a mass of conflicting sociopolitical and economic crosscurrents. All the malcontents in the Germanies had rallied to Luther's banner in his struggle with the Church: ecclesiastical radicals, Anabaptists, humanists, knights, peasants, princes, and the middle class. Luther himself had always been a combination of the revolutionary and the conservative, but his conservatism now became more evident. The result was that one by one most of his supporters dropped away. He arraigned the reformers of Wittenberg, notably Carlstadt, on the ground that they were attempting to put his ideas into practice through force and violence. He excoriated the Anabaptists, who denied the validity of infant baptism and who administered the rite only to adults, because their theological ideals drifted far from his own. He forfeited the support of the humanists, who had backed him at first but who now objected to his dogmatism and intolerance. He condemned the imperial knights, penniless but arrogant, who looked upon the religious revolt as a means of exalting their class at the expense of both clerics and princes. Within five years he had lost most of his supporters except the princes and the bourgeoisie.

The Peasants' War. Luther's revolt against the Catholic Church, his passionate appeals for the rights of the individual man, and his concept of the spiritual priesthood of all believers contained egalitarian implications which the peasants, especially, quickly translated into a social as well as a religious reformation. Luther had attracted peasant support by denouncing the German feudal lords, among whom were many of his most zealous supporters, as "rascals, hangmen, rogues, and swindlers." Ground down by taxation and unbearable living conditions, the peasants expressed their demands in the *Twelve Articles,* a moderate, dignified petition asking for popular election of pastors; reform in the payment of tithes; hunting, fishing, and wood-cutting rights; elimination of excessive services; readjustment of rents; the right to use common land; and abolition of the heriot (an inheritance tax).

The demands were reasonable enough, but it was still to be three centuries before they were granted. When princes and lords paid no attention to this appeal, the peasants, in union with equally miserable town workers, took up arms and attempted to enforce their program of social reform. This was, in reality, a proletarian revolution, but without direction or leadership. The rebels burned castles and monasteries, and proposed to slaughter the "godless" priests and nobles. Alarmed by these events, Luther issued an appeal for a war of extermination: *Against the Murderous and Thieving Peasant Bands.* He advised the princes: "Whosoever can, should smite, strangle, and stab, secretly or publicly, and should remember that there is nothing more poisonous, pernicious, and devilish than a rebellious

man. Just as one must slay a mad dog, so, if you do not fight the rebels, they will fight you, and the whole country with you." To Luther, law and order were of far greater importance than social reform. The princes and lords took savage retribution in putting down the revolt.

The Protestants Get Their Name. In 1526 the Diet of Speyer decided upon compromise in the matter of Catholics versus Lutherans: each of the German states was at liberty to order its religious affairs as it saw fit. In 1529 another Diet of Speyer, composed of a compact Catholic majority and a weak Lutheran minority, altered this tolerant decree, restored the Catholic worship everywhere, and placed Lutherans under the ban. Thereupon the Lutheran members issued a remonstrance: "We hereby protest that we know not how to, cannot, and may not, concur therein, but hold your resolution null and not binding." The action of this minority group, consisting of six princes and the representatives of fourteen free imperial cities, gave to the party the name of "Protestant," later applied to all those who had withdrawn from the Catholic Church.

Official Creed: The Augsburg Confession, 1530. For the Diet of Augsburg in 1530, Philip Melanchthon drafted the Augsburg Confession, one of the major Protestant statements of belief drawn up during the Reformation and the official creed of the Lutheran churches. Presented in Latin and German to the Emperor Charles V, who was determined to reconcile the two faiths, the document was conciliatory in tone. It maintained that its signatories were still faithful to the "ancient Catholic Church." The first part attempted to prove that nothing in Lutheran doctrines was at variance with those of the universal Church "so far as that Church is known in the writings of the Fathers." The second part condemned "abuses in the Church," such as monastic vows, celibacy, compulsory confession, festivals, and fasts. Charles V, dissatisfied with the document, ordered the Protestants to return immediately to the old Church.

Schmalkaldic War. When Charles V threatened force, Lutheran princes and burghers joined together in 1531 in the Schmalkaldic League, "solely for the sake of our defense and deliverance." At this time Charles was concerned that Sultan Suleiman the Magnificent, with a large Turkish army, might march on Vienna. Busy with this and other equally pressing affairs, he agreed to a truce with the German princes. In the meantime, the Schmalkaldic League was gradually enlarged to the position of a great European power. Luther died in 1546, but his passing seems to have had but little effect on the subsequent course of the Reformation in the Germanies. Shortly afterward, Charles V declared war .on the Protestants and defeated them in several battles. In the long run, however, his efforts to drive Lutheranism from the Germanies were unsuccessful, and he abandoned the attempt.

Religious Peace of Augsburg, 1555. The war was ended in 1555 by the Religious Peace of Augsburg, which was a compromise. Its main provisions were (1) Lutheranism was recognized as a separate and independent creed. (2) Each prince was himself to choose between Catholicism and Lutheranism. There was, however, no provision made for any other sect: "All such as do not belong to the two above-mentioned religions shall not be included in the present peace but totally excluded from it." (3) Church property seized by the Lutherans before 1552 was to be retained by them. (4) If an ecclesiastical prince should become a Lutheran, he was to resign and surrender his territories.

By this compromise Protestantism was legalized for about half the population of the Germanies, a proportion maintained thereafter without much alteration. Charles V avoided the humiliating task of signing the peace by abdicating. He died in 1558 in the cell of a Spanish monastery, complaining in his last days that he had made a serious error by not burning Luther at Worms in 1521.

Spread of Lutheranism. As a new and dynamic religious faith, Lutheranism showed itself to be contagious. Outside the Germanies its strongest foothold was gained in Denmark, Norway, and Sweden, as well as among the German populations of Hungary, Transylvania, the German towns along the Baltic, and Poland. It had many followers in Bohemia, but proportionately fewer in France and England, where it was overshadowed by other movements.

5. Thrift, Prosperity, and Morals by Statute: Calvinism

The Swiss Confederation. A mountainous region situated in the heart of Europe, Switzerland was surrounded by great neighbors— France on the west, the Italies on the south, and the Germanies on the east and north. At the opening of the sixteenth century, the Swiss Confederation consisted of thirteen small, independent, self-governing communities called cantons, differing from each other in character and government. The original forest cantons, rural communities engaged in agriculture, were pure democracies. Others, such as Zürich, Berne and Basle, were urban, with aristocratic governments. Swiss foot soldiers fought as mercenaries in French and Italian armies, which prized their services and often attracted them by bribes and pensions. Ensconced in almost inaccessible villages. the independent-minded Swiss were not strongly bound by episcopal government.

Huldreich Zwingli. The first of the great Swiss reformers, Huldreich Zwingli (1484–1531), was born in the northern urban area, where Christian humanism had taken deep root. Of a well-to-do burgher family, he was educated at Berne and Basle in a stimulating intellectual atmosphere, and after studying philosophy at Vienna, he became a master of arts and a teacher. Ordained at the age of twenty-two, he entered the priesthood, probably because the career offered him leisure and opportunity to pursue humanistic studies. He learned Greek as a means of absorbing "the teaching of Christ from the original sources," read the writings of the Church Fathers, and studied some Hebrew. As a humanist, he was inspired by Erasmus' dictum that Christian ethics should be renovated on the basis of the Sermon on the Mount. Soon

Zwingli progressed from mild criticism to outright denunciation of prevalent religious practices, such as the traffic in indulgences, the machinery of salvation, and certain aspects of monasticism. In 1519 he was transferred to Zürich. A reading of Luther's early pamphlets convinced him that mere intellectual and moral reform of ecclesiastical abuses was no longer a satisfactory solution.

In Zürich, Zwingli began to preach vigorous sermons, in which he demanded doctrinal reform and urged the Swiss to show their resentment of Roman domination. He gradually won over the city council and a majority of the people. Soon several cantons declared themselves for Zwingli's cause, but others, especially the five forest cantons, opposed him and remained loyal to Rome. The Protestant movement in Switzerland then broke into two contending factions. Eventually there was a civil war. On October 10, 1531, a battle disastrous to the Protestant cause was fought at Kappel. Accompanying the army as a chaplain, Zwingli was badly wounded and later was killed. His corpse was quartered and burned with dung. For the moment the Protestant movement in Switzerland was left leaderless.

John Calvin. Deprived of Zwingli by a stroke of fate, Swiss Protestants found a new leader in a young Frenchman. Born in Picardy, John Calvin (1509–1564) was the son of a secretary of the Noyon bishopric. Embarking upon a theological career, he studied philosophy and theology, but obediently took up the study of law when his father decided that law offered better prospects. This legal training was later to prove of some importance, for Calvin's religious ideas during the rest of his life retained a strongly legalistic cast. Familiar with the ideas and writings of Luther and a convincing speaker, he soon became well known in France. He appealed to Francis I to reform the Church and to restore the simple religious ideals of the apostolic age, insisting at the same time that his only aim was to purify the Church of the abuses that had corrupted it. For his pains he was driven from France in 1534. He hastened to Basle, where he was welcomed by a band of like-minded scholars. By this time he

Luther   *Pabst*   *Calvinus.*

The struggle between two Protestant leaders is satirized in a contemporary cartoon.

was openly in sympathy with the Reformation.

Differences between Lutheranism and Calvinism were due in part to the variations in character between the founders of the two faiths, but also to the politico-economic and religious developments which brought the Reformation into being. Luther was the man of action—loud, bombastic, and positive—while Calvin was the scholar—quiet, introspective, and scrupulously just. Luther was violent in temper and language; Calvin spoke simply and directly, but effectively. Where Luther was mystical, Calvin was coldly rational. According to Luther, "reason is the Devil's harlot, which can only blaspheme and dishonor everything God has said or done." Calvin, the classical scholar and lawyer, placed his trust in logic and reason and sought to construct a rational system in harmony with the Scriptures.

In 1536, at the age of twenty-six, Calvin published *The Institutes of the Christian Religion* as a statement of faith for the Protestants and as a brief manual of Christian doctrine. The first edition consisted of only six chapters: (1) The Law; (2) Faith; (3) Prayer; (4) The Sacraments; (5) False Sacraments; and (6)

Christian Liberty, Ecclesiastical Power, and Civil Administration. The original edition contained the germs of the complete Calvinist theological system, but from time to time Calvin issued revised and more elaborate versions. This textbook, which heavily influenced contemporary theologians and for several centuries enjoyed unrivaled authority in France, Scotland, England, and America, gave Calvin front rank among the reformers.

Calvinism. The central dogma of Calvinism, which distinguished it from all other forms of Protestantism, was the doctrine of predestination, or election. Because of Adam's fall in the Garden of Eden, depravity and corruption attach to all men. Some, however, have been chosen (predestined) by God to be saved. It is God's purpose to select some for eternal life and some for eternal death. The number is unalterable and cannot be changed. Those who are not chosen are left to suffer the penalty which they deserve because of their sins. Calvin made this clear in the *Institutes:* "Predestination we call the eternal decree of God, whereby He has determined with Himself what He wills to become of every man. For all are not created to like estate; but to some eternal life and to some eternal damnation is foreordained. Therefore, as every man is created to the one or the other end, so we say that he is predestinated either to life or to death."

It became the obligation of the elect not only to fulfill the moral laws of the Bible, but also to make other men moral. The "divine mission" of the Calvinist to join an international crusade to reform society and to establish the "City of God" on earth gave to Calvinism a militant, aggressive character. "The doctrine of predestination, the consciousness of being chosen soldiers of Christ, inspired those Puritans who founded the commonwealths of England, of Holland, and of America with a contempt of toil, danger, and death, which enabled them to accomplish things almost supernatural" (John Lothrop Motley).

Calvin made the city of Geneva the laboratory of his system. Here he established a "model Christian community after God's will."

At the head was Calvin himself, who ruled firmly with the assistance of an autocratic consistory composed of six (later twelve) clergymen and twelve elders. Calvin considered it his duty to supervise the morals of the Genevese and to enforce the will of God. He introduced an inflexible system of laws, based upon the Bible. He regulated the life of every citizen down to the finest detail. He demanded sobriety, regular church attendance, frugality, industry, and the faithful pursuit of a trade. He forbade idleness, gaiety, dancing, card playing, wearing of exaggerated hats, frivolous pastimes, and marriage to Catholics.

To Calvin, Geneva was a City of God, the most moral city in Europe, but to his critics it was merely a place where sin had been driven beneath the surface. Punishments for lawbreaking were of Draconian severity. A child who struck his parents was formally placed on trial, condemned to death, and executed. Michael Servetus (1511–1553), a Spaniard who had practiced medicine in southern France and had written a book assailing the doctrine of the Trinity, made the error of coming to Geneva to pursue an argument with Calvin. The Genevan reformer ordered his arrest, relentlessly prosecuted the case against him, and finally had him condemned to death by fire.

Calvinism and Capitalism. Calvinism was the first of the Reformation movements to recognize the existence of the commercial bourgeoisie and to give a theological and philosophical justification for its economic pursuits. In many ways it was a fitting religious system for the age of world markets, of national monarchies, of competitive rivalries between merchants and between nations. Wherever Calvin's reforms spread, society was being reshaped to promote business and industrial enterprise. The conditions of the time which called Calvinism into being were in themselves reasons for its wide acceptance. Calvin's teachings explain his popularity among the bourgeoisie. He removed all stigma from personal enrichment through business activity by glorifying trade and dignifying ordinary economic activities as "callings," or tasks set directly by God. He believed that worldly success was obviously a token of grace and a sign of God's favor. Industry, discipline, honesty—the moral virtues—entitled a man to material reward, while slothfulness was the deadliest of sins, and poverty was an evidence of sin and moral weakness. In this respect Calvin accepted the Old Testament concept of prosperity as a reward for virtue, and poverty as a probable badge of vice. In justifying the taking of interest, which medieval moralists had roundly condemned, he showed that he understood the nature of early modern capitalism.

Diffusion of Calvinism. Calvinism spread from Switzerland to other countries, particularly to those which Lutheranism had by-passed. It was widely accepted in southern Germany and in Bohemia. Despite obstacles, it made rapid headway by 1559 in France, where Calvin founded the French Reformed Church and where his followers were called Huguenots. It was adopted in the northern area of the Netherlands, where it became the Dutch Reformed Church. In Scotland, where Calvinism came under John Knox's vigorous leadership, it was known as the Presbyterian Church, with complete control vested in representative councils (presbyteries), composed of ministers and elders (presbyters). Early in the seventeenth century, the Puritans carried the Calvinist faith to New England, where it left an indelible impression on early American civilization. The Pilgrim Fathers, the Dutch burghers, the Scotch Presbyterians, and the French Huguenots all brought the Calvinistic creed to the New World.

6. Henry VIII Breaks with Rome

The English Reformation. The idea that the Reformation in England was the result of a whim of Henry VIII (r. 1509–1547) is historically inaccurate. In England, as well as on the Continent, the currents of Protestantism were deep. The breakdown in England of the medieval alliance between Church and State was caused by multiple factors, primarily politico-economic and nationalistic. There was in six-

teenth-century England a rising feeling of national pride. The growth of royal power had been accompanied by sharp clashes between English national interests and papal authority. The monarch, anxious to inaugurate a program of political absolutism, was attracted by the wealth of the Church. The ambitious commercial class resented and opposed any papal interference in English affairs, especially in such all-important matters as taxation and the conflict between English common law and Church canon law. The peasants were antagonistic to their landlords, among whom were churchmen. Earlier critics of the Church, such as John Wycliffe in the fourteenth century, had not been entirely suppressed, nor were groups like Wycliffe's followers, the Lollards, extinct. Although English Renaissance humanists wanted reform rather than revolution, they nevertheless helped undermine the old fabric by arousing popular impatience of ecclesiastical abuses.

All these different streams merged in a current of revolt against Rome. It was certain that in any quarrel between Crown and Church, almost all Englishmen would unite to support the Crown. An observant ambassador then in London wrote in 1515: "Nearly all the people here hate the priests."

"Defender of the Faith." "His Majesty is twenty-six years old and extremely handsomer than any other sovereign in Christendom. He is very accomplished, a fine jouster, speaks good French, Latin, and Spanish. He is very religious—hears three masses daily when he hunts, and sometimes five on other days." In these friendly words, the Venetian envoy, Giustiniani, described Henry VIII in 1519.

The young English king impressed others as a very religious man. When Luther in 1520 issued his *On the Babylonian Captivity of the Church*, attacking the Catholic sacramental system, Henry wrote a blistering reply in a Latin treatise: *In Defense of the Seven Sacraments Against Luther*. For this counterattack Pope Leo X awarded Henry, as a loyal son of the Church, the title of *Fidei Defensor*, "Defender of the Faith," a title which British monarchs have retained to the present day. That Henry VIII's religious temperament was genuine, however, is open to some doubt. While he clung outwardly to the old religious forms and faith, inwardly he was the most secular-minded of European rulers. A man with an insatiable lust for power and unscrupulous in political as well as in personal life, he was the incarnation of Machiavelli's *The Prince*. His love life was notorious. Six women fell prey to this affable egotist; their fate may be summarized briefly in the aphorism: "divorced; beheaded; died; divorced; beheaded; survived."

Need for a Male Heir. Shortly after ascending the throne in 1509, Henry VIII married his brother's widow, Catherine of Aragon. High churchmen expressed some doubt concerning the validity of this marriage arranged by Catherine's father, Ferdinand. "She is thirty-five years old and not handsome, although she has a beautiful complexion. She is religious, and as virtuous as words can express." Thus wrote the same Giustiniani who had been attracted by Henry's charm. Catherine presented her husband with six children, all of whom died in infancy, except one, Mary, who later became queen. Henry was disgruntled by the lack of a male heir, which he deemed politically necessary to insure the continuance of the Tudor dynasty. His counselors warned him that a female' ruler or a disputed succession might mean disaster for the kingdom. With unreasonable ardor, Henry blamed his aging wife for the situation. The matter was complicated by Henry's passion for Anne Boleyn, pretty, vivacious, unscrupulous, and twenty years younger than the queen.

These two issues—(1) the need for a male

The divorce trial of Catherine of Aragon and Henry VIII at Blackfriars, 1529.

heir, and (2) the desire of the love-smitten king—combined to provide the immediate occasion for the split with Rome, though the fundamental causes had long been generating. It seems probable that Henry was motivated more by the national issue than by sensuality, for there was nothing to prevent him from keeping a harem, if he so desired. Pope Clement VII actually advised him in 1530 to settle the difficulty by taking two wives at once. Henry for a time seriously considered the proposal, which was said to have Old Testament precedents, but he finally rejected it.

Divorce to Order. Technically, a divorce was impossible in the Catholic Church, but a decree of nullity, or annulment, was accessible in Henry's case. The Church in principle opposed a man's marrying the widow of his brother, since there was a clear-cut sentence in the Bible (*Leviticus 20:21*) which read: "And if a man shall take his brother's wife, it is an unclean thing." Henry ordered his minister Thomas Wolsey (*c.* 1475–1530), to obtain an annulment from the papacy on the ground that the dispensation for his marriage to Catherine had been invalid. Wolsey induced the pope to send a legate to England to hold court and determine the issues. At this trial Catherine knelt dramatically before her husband and said: "Sire, in what have I offended you? Or what occasion of displeasure have I given you, intending thus to put me from you? I take God to be my judge, I have been to you a true and humble wife."

Henry's abrupt demand placed Pope Clement VII in a difficult position. Catherine was aunt to the most powerful sovereign in Europe, Charles V, from whom the pope had much to fear. The pontiff dared not offend his protector by granting Henry's request, yet at the same time he realized that a refusal would compromise his position in England. With great caution he temporized, hoping that something would turn up to relieve him of the necessity of offending either emperor or king. Wolsey failed to carry the negotiations with Rome to a successful conclusion, whereupon he was dismissed in disgrace and obliged to retire. Only his death saved him from a trial for treason.

Exasperated, Henry finally took matters into his own hands, divorced Catherine, married Anne Boleyn, cut off the flow of funds from England to Rome, and in 1534 commanded Parliament to name him head of the Church of England.

Act of Supremacy, 1534. The Parliament which met in 1529, the so-called Reformation Parliament, sat in successive sessions for seven years, during which it curtailed the pope's authority over England. It abolished annates, one of the most lucrative sources of papal revenue, and forbade any appeals from English courts to Rome. The separation of the English Church from the Roman was completed by the Act of Supremacy (November 1534), which repudiated all papal authority: "Albeit the King's Majesty justly and rightfully is and ought to be the Supreme Head of the Church of England, and so is recognized by the clergy of this realm in their Convocations; yet nevertheless for corroboration and confirmation thereof, and for increase of virtue in Christ's religion within this realm of England, and to repress and extirpate all errors, heresies, and other enormities and abuses heretofore used in the same, Be it enacted by authority of this present Parliament that the King, our Sovereign Lord, his heirs and successors, kings of this realm, shall be taken, accepted, and reputed the only Supreme Head in earth of the Church of England, called *Anglicana Ecclesia.*"

Thus the English Church became a national church, neither Lutheran nor Calvinist, under the control of the king. A new Treason Act forbade anyone, on penalty of death, to refer to the king as "heretic, tyrant, infidel, or usurper."

Suppression of the Monasteries. For Henry VIII the idea of "the papacy without the pope" had been an obsession. Now he had achieved his aim. The rest of his reign has been described succinctly as "spent in ruthless warfare against those who believed in medieval Catholicism less than he, or against others who believed more than he." Those who opposed him did so at the peril of their lives.

When Sir Thomas More and Bishop Fisher refused to recognize the Act of Supremacy, they were tried, condemned, and beheaded. Henry now turned to the important business of confiscating the wealth of the monasteries. Using the excuse that the monasteries were centers of pro-papal influences, he ordered Thomas Cromwell, vicar-general of the Church, to dissolve them and confiscate their holdings for the Crown. Cromwell chose willing and able agents. Thousands of monks and nuns were forced into a world which they had renounced. Monasteries and their vast holdings were distributed among various beneficiaries: the king appropriated a large part for himself, while other shares went to the commercial class, the aristocracy, and to such public institutions as the navy, the coastal defense, and the schools.

The Six Articles, 1539. Although papal jurisdiction had been abolished and the monasteries suppressed, Henry VIII and the English people did not regard themselves as any less Catholic. The Six Articles, passed in 1539 at Henry's request, reaffirmed nearly all the main points of medieval doctrine and practice, such as transubstantiation, clerical celibacy, the vow of chastity, private masses, auricular confession, and communion. Strict obedience to this law was required, and no deviation from the faith was permitted upon pain of death. Those who wandered from Catholic doctrine were subject to trial for heresy, while those who refused to recognize the supremacy of Crown over Church could be accused of treason.

Doctrinal Change: Edward VI. Henry VIII had been responsible for the definite rupture with Rome. Under his successor, Edward VI (r. 1547–1553), religious changes came more rapidly. Before his death, Henry appointed a regency to serve during the minority of his invalid son, then only ten years old. It became the task of these advisers to decide upon the doctrines of the Church. They abolished such Catholic ceremonies as the use of candles, palms, and holy water. Some extremists destroyed images and whitewashed Church murals. In the meantime, steps were taken to prepare an English liturgy. The first Book of Common Prayer, written by Archbishop Thomas Cranmer (1489–1556), was made the only legal service book in England by the Act of Uniformity in 1549. In 1552 it was revised in order to be more acceptable to extreme Protestants by repudiating such Catholic doctrines as clerical celibacy and transubstantiation and by renouncing the medieval pomp of public worship. In 1553, the last year of Edward's reign, the Six Articles were replaced by the definitely Protestant Forty-Two Articles of Faith.

Mary Tudor and Catholic Reaction. Upon the premature death of Edward in 1553, Mary Tudor (r. 1553–1558), daughter of Catherine and Henry VIII, ascended the throne. As devout as her mother and as obstinate as her father, Mary quickly made it clear that she proposed to adhere to the religion that she had professed since her youth. An eyewitness described her as "rash, disdainful, and parsimonious, endowed with great humility and patience, but withal high-spirited, courageous, and resolute." She had never forgotten that the reformers who had been responsible for the disgrace of her mother had thereby placed the brand of illegitimacy upon her. Winning the promise of Parliament that it would not oppose a return to Catholicism, she effected the repeal of the ecclesiastical legislation of Edward's reign as well as the antipapal legislation passed during the reign of Henry VIII. The pope was once more recognized as head of the Church of England.

Then Mary became violently obsessed with the desire to root out Protestantism from England, a task which won the approval of her husband, Philip II of Spain. Nearly 300 Protestants were executed during the last three years of Mary's reign, and the rate was rising at her death. To the hostile public the word "Catholic" became synonymous with "foreigner" and the word "Protestant" with "English." Mary's plan did not work. She died in 1558, deserted by her husband and detested by her people.

Reformation Settlement. Queen Elizabeth (r. 1558–1603), daughter of Anne Boleyn and last of the Tudor line, and her ministers achieved a successful compromise in the Reformation settlement. Although she had no strong religious faith, she realized that intolerance would react to the disadvantage of both Catholics and Protestants among her subjects. Her goal was a national church which would claim the allegiance of the majority of her people. When Parliament met in 1559 it repealed the reactionary laws which had been enacted during the reign of Mary. A new Act of Supremacy (1559) declared the Crown to be "supreme in all causes ecclesiastical as well as civil." Elizabeth declined to accept the title "Supreme Head of the Church," however, on the ground that it might offend her subjects, and instead declared that this title belonged to Christ alone. Parliament also passed the Act of Uniformity (1559), which declared the Prayer Book, only slightly changed from the Second Prayer Book of Edward VI (1552), to be the only legal form of common worship. The Church of England as it exists today was established, with the English monarch as its head, with English as its language of worship, and with a clergy which is allowed to marry. The national religion quickly gained popularity.

ⸯ{ KEY DOCUMENT }ⸯ
LUTHER'S THREE TREATISES OF 1520

MARTIN LUTHER was led step by step, against his original intention, to a complete repudiation of the system in which he had been educated. In 1520 he published three popular pamphlets as a means of stating his case before the country. The first, entitled *Address to the Christian Nobility of the German Nation,* called upon the princes of the Germanies to unite and destroy the power of the papacy. Sometimes called the political and social manifesto of the Lutheran Reformation, this treatise was, in effect, a declaration of independence from the papacy.

Luther's second pamphlet, *The Babylonian Captivity of the Church,* subjected the entire system of the Seven Sacraments to attack. He rejected all the sacraments except two, Baptism and the Lord's Supper, though he granted that Penance might have some value.

The third tract, *On Christian Liberty,* was devoted to a simple exposition of Luther's proposition that every man is his own priest. A Christian, in Luther's eyes, was a free lord over all things, and subject to no man. The soul, he said, needs only the Holy Gospel, the Word of God preached by Christ. Faith alone, without works, makes righteous, and through faith all believers are priests.

Though many details were added later to the Lutheran system, the broad outlines were expounded in these three treatises.

I. *Address to the Christian Nobility of the German Nation Respecting the Reformation of the Christian Estate*[1]

The time for silence is gone, and the time to speak has come, as we read in *Ecclesiastes (3:7).*

[1] *Luthers Werke* (Erlangen, 1828–1870), translated and edited by H. Wace and C. A. Buckheim in *First Principles of the Reformation* (Philadelphia, 1885), p. 159 ff, *passim.*

I have, in conformity with our resolve, put together some few points concerning the reformation of the Christian estate, with the intent of placing the same before the Christian nobility of the German nation, in case it may please God to help His Church by means of the laity, inasmuch as the clergy, whom this task rather befitted, have become quite careless. . . .

It is not out of mere arrogance and perversity

that I, an individual poor man, have taken upon me to address your lordships. The distress and misery that oppress all the Christian estates, more especially in Germany, have led not only myself, but every one else, to cry aloud and to ask for help, and now forced me too to cry out and to ask if God would give His Spirit to any one to reach a hand to His wretched people. Councils have often put forward some remedy, but it has adroitly been frustrated, and the evils have become worse, through the cunning of certain men. Their malice and wickedness I will now, by the help of God, expose, so that, being known, they may henceforth cease to be so obstructive and injurious. . . .

The Romanists have, with great adroitness, drawn three walls round themselves, with which they have hitherto protected themselves, so that no one could reform them, whereby all Christendom has fallen terribly.

Firstly, if pressed by the temporal power, they have affirmed and maintained that the temporal power has no jurisdiction over them, but on the contrary, that the spiritual power is above the temporal.

Secondly, if it were proposed to admonish them with the Scriptures, they objected that no one may interpret the Scriptures but the pope.

Thirdly, if they are threatened with a council, they pretend that no one may call a council but the pope. . . .

Now may God help us, and give us one of those trumpets that overthrew the walls of Jericho, so that we may blow down these walls of straw and paper, and that we may set free our Christian rods for the chastisement of sin, and expose the craft and deceit of the devil, so that we may amend ourselves by punishment and again obtain God's favor. . . .

Let us now consider the matters which should be treated in the councils, and with which popes, cardinals, bishops, and all learned men should occupy themselves day and night, if they love Christ and His Church. . . .

1. It is a distressing and terrible thing to see that the head of Christendom, who boasts of being the vicar of Christ and the successor of Saint Peter, lives in a worldly pomp that no king or emperor can equal. . . .

2. What is the use in Christendom of the people called "cardinals"? I will tell you. In Italy and Germany there are many rich convents, endowments, fiefs, and benefices, and as the best way of getting these into the hands of Rome, they created cardinals, and gave them the sees, convents, and prelacies, and thus destroyed the service of God. That is why Italy is almost a desert now. . . .

II. *The Babylonian Captivity of the Church*[2]

To begin. I must deny that there are seven sacraments, and must lay it down, for the time being, that there are only three, Baptism, Penance, and the Bread, and that by the Court of Rome all these have been brought into miserable bondage, and the Church despoiled of all her liberty. And yet, if I were to speak according to the usage of Scripture, I should hold that there was only one sacrament, and three sacramental signs. . . .

It has seemed best, however, to consider as sacraments, properly so called, those promises which have signs annexed to them. The rest, as they are not attached to signs, are simple promises. It follows that, if we speak with perfect accuracy, there are only two sacraments in the Church of God, Baptism and the Bread; since it is in these alone that we see both a sign divinely instituted and a promise of remission of sins. The sacrament of Penance, which I have reckoned along with these two, is without any visible and divinely appointed sign; and is nothing else, as I have said, than a way and means of return to Baptism. Not even the Schoolmen can say that Penitence agrees with their definition; since they themselves ascribe to every sacrament a visible sign, which enables the senses to apprehend the form of that effect which the sacrament works invisibly. Now Penitence or Absolution has no such sign; and therefore they will be compelled by their own definition either to say that Penitence is not one of the sacraments, and thus to diminish their number, or else to bring forward another definition of a sacrament.

Baptism, however, which we have assigned to the whole of life, will properly suffice for all the sacraments which we are to use in life;

[2] Wace and Buckheim, *op.cit.*, pp. 147, 243–244.

while the Bread is truly the sacrament of the dying and departing, since in it we commemorate the departure of Christ from this world, that we may imitate Him. Let us then so distribute these two sacraments that Baptism may be allotted to the beginning and to the whole course of life, and the Bread to its end and to death; and let the Christian, while in this vile body, exercise himself in both, until, being fully baptized and strengthened, he shall pass out of this world, as one born into a new and eternal life, and destined to eat with Christ in the kingdom of His Father, as He promised at the Last Supper, saying: "I say unto you, I will not drink of the fruit of the vine until the kingdom of God shall come" (*Luke 22:18*). Thus it is evident that Christ instituted the sacrament of the Bread that we might receive the life which is to come; and then, when the purpose of each sacrament shall have been fulfilled, both Baptism and the Bread will cease.

III. *On Christian Liberty*[3]

. . . That I may open, then, an easier way for the ignorant—for these alone I am trying to serve—I first lay down these two propositions, concerning spiritual liberty and servitude.

A Christian man is the most free lord of all, and subject to none; a Christian man is the most dutiful servant of all, and subject to everyone.

Although these statements appear contradictory, yet when they are found to agree together, they will be highly serviceable to my purpose. They are both the statements of Paul himself, who says: "Though I be free from all *men*, yet have I made myself servant unto all" (*I Cor. 9:19*), and: "Owe no man anything, but to love one another" (*Rom. 13:8*). Now love is by its own nature dutiful and obedient to the beloved object. Thus even Christ, though Lord of all things, was yet made of a woman; made under the law; as once free and a servant; at once in the form of God and in the form of a servant. . . .

And it will profit nothing that the body should be adorned with sacred vestments, or dwell in holy places, or be occupied in sacred offices, or

[3] Wace and Buckheim, *op.cit.*, pp. 104–125, *passim*.

pray, fast, and abstain from certain meats, or do whatever works can be done through the body and in the body. Something widely different will be necessary for the justification and liberty of the soul, since the things I have spoken of can be done by any impious person, and only hypocrites are produced by devotion to these things. . . .

The first care of every Christian ought to be, to lay aside all reliance on works, and strengthen his faith alone more and more, and by it grow in the knowledge, not of works, but of Christ Jesus, who has suffered and risen again for him; as Peter teaches, when he makes no other work to be a Christian one. Thus Christ, when the Jews asked Him what they should do that they might work the works of God, rejected the multitude of works, with which He saw that they were puffed up, and commanded them one thing only, saying, "This is the work of God, that ye believe on him whom He hath sent, for him hath God the Father sealed" (*John 6:27, 29*). . . .

But you ask how it can be the fact that faith alone justifies, and affords without works so great a treasure of good things, when so many works, ceremonies, and laws are prescribed to us in the Scriptures. I answer: Before all things bear in mind what I have said, that faith alone without works justifies, sets free, and saves. . . .

True are these two sayings: Good works do not make a good man, but a good man does good works. Bad works do not make a bad man, but a bad man does bad works. Thus it is always necessary that the substance or person should be good before any good works can be done, and that good works should follow and proceed from a good person. As Christ says: "A good tree cannot bring forth evil fruit, neither *can* a corrupt tree bring forth good fruit" (*Matt. 7:18*). Now it is clear that the fruit does not bear the tree, nor does the tree grow on the fruit; but, on the contrary, the trees bear the fruit and the fruit grows on the trees. . . .

Here is the truly Christian life; here is faith really working by love; when a man applies himself with joy and love to the works of that freest servitude, in which he serves others voluntarily and for naught; himself abundantly satisfied in the fullness and riches of his own faith.

{ HISTORICAL INTERPRETATION }

ROLAND H. BAINTON ON THE SOCIOLOGICAL BACKGROUND OF THE REFORMATION

Roland H. Bainton, *The Age of the Reformation*, Anvil Book No. 13 (Princeton, N. J. 1956), pp. 17–19.

WHILE HE PAID due attention to the moral and doctrinal causes of the Reformation, the distinguished theologian, Roland H. Bainton, Titus Street Professor Emeritus of Ecclesiastical History at Yale University, also called attention to the sociological interpretation. He, too, saw the Reformation as a transition from a predominantly feudal ecclesiastical manifestation to a commercial and industrial society in which a simple money economy evolved into capitalism.

The attempt of the Church to adjust to the new urban economy based on coin rather than on kind gave rise to financial abuses, and conflicts with the national states over money entailed political changes. The immediate produce of the land had been the basis of the Church's financial structure in the early Middle Ages. The Church could scarcely have operated otherwise in a landed society, but the consequence was entanglement in the feudal system with the danger of dependence on lay lords. The new economy offered a way to obviate this by drawing revenues not directly from lands often in lay hands but through levies on the local churches to be paid in coin. To this, however, the rising national monarchies objected, and in the first instance France. The papacy, depleted of resources, succumbed to France, and the residence of the popes was transferred to Avignon for a period called the Babylonian Captivity because it was roughly seventy years in duration (1309–1378).

During that period the attempt continued unabated to centralize the wealth of the Church by levies on the local sees. Pope John XXII, in particular, exploited and devised such expedients as annates, reservations, expectations, commutations and others, and the French crown objected little, inasmuch as the money was not to cross the Alps. The subjection of the papacy to France, however, occasioned such disaffection in other lands that the secession manifest in the Protestant Reformation was in danger of anticipation by some 200 years. To avert this the pope returned to Rome. The Cardinals, however, remained in France and elected another pope. There followed the Papal Schism lasting until 1417. Attempts were made to end the scandal by the summoning of councils, and they in turn undertook the reform of the Church, but every effort proved abortive. Conciliarism was impotent because the conflict with the rising, consolidated, national monarchies required an increasingly centralized government on the side of the Church. In the end the papacy overcame conciliarism, but only at the price of recognizing the sovereignty of the national states. Conceding this, the popes then made separate bargains (called concordats) with the nations.

All of this involved a great recession from the universal claim and the universal jurisdiction which the Church had once exercised at the peak of the feudal period. By way of compensation the Church in the Renaissance entrenched itself in Italy. The papacy became one of the Italian powers, and the popes behaved like the despots of the city-states, cunning in diplomacy, ruthless in war, magnificent in the arts and literature, unscrupulous and unbridled in morals. The reform movements were set over against a thoroughgoing secularization of the papacy itself. The pope who dealt with Martin Luther, Leo X, was an elegant dilettante, a patron of artists, a gambler, hunter, and composer of elegant, impromptu Latin orations, a man who, according to a modern Catholic historian, would not have been deemed fit to be a doorkeeper in the house of the Lord had he lived in the days of the apostles.

In the social changes, some would see the

basic ground of the Reformation, involving on the Catholic side a grudging relinquishment of medieval claims, a recognition of nationalism, and even a nationalizing of the Church, which in France and Spain fell under the control of the Crown.

Protestantism took on the complexion of the land in which it chanced to be. With complete opportunism, alliances were made with whatever power offered protection to the Word of God. This might mean Tudor absolutism, German particularism, Polish feudalism, or even extra-Europeanism under the suzerainty of the infidel Turks. The Protestants were politically conservative and only slowly and reluctantly resisted the political regimes of their particular countries. As for the control of the Church over the civil structure of society, Luther renounced all this, but Calvin struck out in the direction of a new type of theocracy.

The changes taking place in the society can-not be gainsaid and, unquestionably, the Church did have to come to terms with urbanization, commercialization, nationalism, and the emergence of a lay and secular culture, but the Reformation, whether Catholic or Protestant, is not to be equated with the accommodation which, in many instances, was grudging and, when cordial, was transforming. Consider the case of lay culture, which the Catholic Reformation naturally did not foster. Instead it enhanced sacerdotalism. Protestantism did contribute to laicism but not to secularism. The priesthood of all believers was designed not to make all priests into laymen, but all laymen into priests. The net result, of course, was to demote the clerical caste, but not to diminish the religious orientation. The Protestants desired that every member of the congregation should be as spiritual and, in so far as might be possible, as instructed in matters religious as the ministers. The Jesuits undertook the education of the Catholic masses that the laity might be religiously literate.

⟨ TEN BASIC BOOKS ⟩

THE GREAT RELIGIOUS SECESSION: THE REFORMATION

1. Bainton, Roland H., *Here I Stand: A Life of Martin Luther*, (New York and Nashville, Tenn., 1951).†
2. Bainton, Roland H., *The Age of the Reformation*, Anvil Book No. 13 (Princeton, N. J., 1956).†
3. Grimm, Harold, *The Reformation Era* (New York, 1954, R. 1966).
4. Hughes, Philip, *A Popular History of the Reformation* (New York, 1957).†
5. Mackinnon, James, *The Origins of the Reformation* (New York, 1939).
6. Murray, Robert H., *Political Consequences of the Reformation* (London, 1926, R. 1961).
7. Palm, Franklin C., *Calvinism and the Religious Wars* (New York, 1932).
8. Powicke, Frederick Maurice, *The Reformation in England* (New York, 1941).†
9. Smith, Preserved, *The Age of the Reformation* (New York, 1920, 1936).†
10. Taylor, Henry O., *Thought and Expression in the 16th Century*, 2 vols. (New York, 1930, R. 1959).

6

The Catholic Counter-Reformation

A REFORM of clerical morality and a revival of piety within the Church, a true Catholic reformation, would undoubtedly have taken place without the stimulus of the Protestant Reformation. But, lacking the stimulus, the Catholic Reformation would have followed a very different course from that which it actually took. As the Protestant menace increased, the efforts of the Catholic reformers were turned more and more toward the combating of heresy, so that in its mature form the Catholic Reformation was in very large part a counter-reform. The activity of the Council of Trent, the repressive measures of the Inquisition and the Index, and the work of the Jesuits, which were the chief agencies of the Reformation, were directed principally to the defense of the Church against heresy and to the recovery of those who were lost to it.
—WALLACE K. FERGUSON

1. The Catholic Reaction

The Reform Movement. For a full fifty years after Luther nailed his Ninety-five Theses on the church door at Wittenberg, the tide of Protestantism rose until it threatened to engulf the Western world. For a time it appeared that the Roman Catholic Church was destined for disintegration. Then came a dramatic reversal. Under the stimulus of the great religious secession, the Catholic Church began a drastic reform movement, since called the Catholic Reformation, or Counter-Reformation. It was both defensive and aggressive. Catholicism on the defensive sought to achieve reform without sacrificing doctrinal orthodoxy and to infuse the cadre of the old Church with new spiritual life. Catholicism on the aggressive sought to repress heresy and to recover the territory lost to the Protestants. The defensive phase was worked out at the Council of Trent, while Catholicism on the offensive utilized the work of the Jesuits and the repressive measures of the Inquisition and the Index. During the latter half of the sixteenth century, this double-barreled movement achieved a large measure of success.

The Council of Trent, 1545–1563. Since the beginning of the great secession, there had been a demand for the convocation of a general council to rescue the Church from its critical position. When, at last, after many delays, the Council of Trent was convened in December 1545, the time for healing the schism had long since passed. Three separate sessions of the council took place over a period of nineteen years. During the early meetings, the Protestants were invited to attend, with right of discussion but no vote. The invitation was rejected.

Decrees of the council revived and reaffirmed the ancient dogma of the Church. It was agreed that the Catholic traditions were as binding as the Bible. The Catholic doctrine of justification by faith and good works was declared to be correct, as opposed to the Protestant concept of justification by faith alone. The right of interpreting the Scriptures was reserved for the Church, as opposed to the Protestant conception that every man could be his own priest. It was agreed that the Seven Sacraments were the necessary machinery of salvation. The doctrines of purgatory, indulgences, and veneration of relics and images were maintained. In basic theological doctrine the Council of Trent refused to retreat from the long-established dogma. The line of demarcation with Protestantism was sharply drawn.

On the other hand, the Council recommended a number of reforms designed to eliminate the worst abuses which had left the Church open to attack. It decreed a thoroughgoing reform of the monastic life; denounced the appointment of unworthy men to high ecclesiastical office and the buying and selling of Church positions (simony); forbade the holding of more than one ecclesiastical office (pluralities); condemned family favoritism (nepotism); banned money payments for indulgences; and provided for the establishment of theological seminaries to train clerical leaders of good reputation and education. The Council was not timid in its decrees: "If

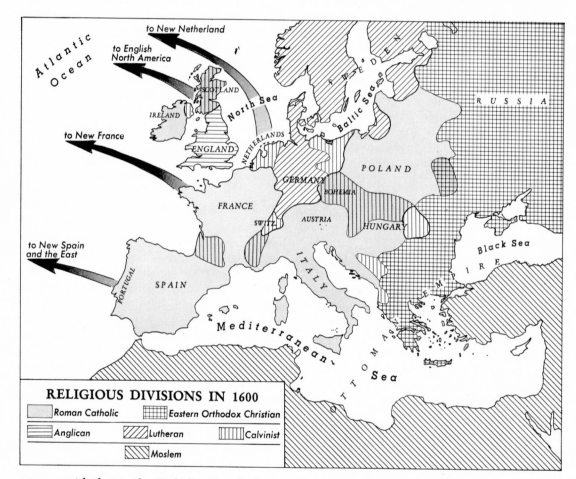

RELIGIOUS DIVISIONS IN 1600

- Roman Catholic
- Eastern Orthodox Christian
- Anglican
- Lutheran
- Calvinist
- Moslem

anyone saith that in the Catholic Church there is not a hierarchy instituted by divine ordination, consisting of bishops, priests, and ministers, let him be anathema."

The Council adjourned in 1563 on a note of confidence: "This is the faith of the blessed Peter and of the Apostles. This is the faith of the Fathers. This is the faith of the Orthodox. Anathema to all heretics!" The outcome was a militant Church, appreciably reformed but more strongly centralized than ever before. The pope, maintained in his position as God's vice-regent on earth, was given the task of reconquering the lost spiritual and geographical ground. By its agreement on a series of doctrinal points until then undecided, the Council had elaborated the Catholic creed and made reconciliation with Protestants unlikely. With its vigorous presentation of orthodox faith, it gave its members spiritual food for resistance to the inroads of Protestantism. From now on, the Catholic Church, restored and reinforced, could present a united front to its opponents.

Ignatius Loyola. Catholicism on the offensive sought to retain the loyalty of those who remained among its members and to win back those who had deserted it. For this purpose several religious orders had been founded in the sixteenth century. By far the most effective and the most powerful missionary organization in history was founded by a young Spanish nobleman, Don Iñigo de Oñez y Loyola, known as Ignatius Loyola (1491–1556). Pursuing a career in arms, he had fought against the French in the war between Charles V and Francis I. The turning point in his life came in 1521, when his right leg was smashed by a cannon ball. Later he described how one night as he lay awake reading a life of Christ, he suddenly saw a likeness of the Blessed Virgin with her divine Son, whereupon he was seized by a loathing for his former way of life. Deciding to emulate the deeds of the saints, he gave his rich clothes to a beggar and went to live in a cave. Here he spent seven hours a day in prayer and three times daily scourged his emaciated body. After a long test, he abandoned the extravagant self-denials of asceticism and turned his attention to the task of helping his fellow man attain salvation. Aware of his lack of knowledge, he went to the University of Paris, where for seven years he studied theology and Latin.

Loyola's treatise, the *Spiritual Exercises,* has been described as one of the world-moving books. It was dedicated to "the true Spouse of Christ, and our holy Mother, which is the Orthodox, Catholic, and Hierarchical Church." An account of his own spiritual struggle in the early days of his conversion, it sought to show the reader how he could achieve the same practical results as the author's conversion. The reader was to undergo four series of "meditations" technically called "weeks," each of which might be as long as was considered necessary. During the first week the reader ponders on man, sin, death, judgment, and hell. In the second week he is asked to medi-tate upon the life of Christ and the kingdom of God; during the third week, upon Christ's suffering and death; and during the fourth week, upon the Resurrection. It is made clear throughout the book that between the soul and God there is a director, to whom unquestioned obedience is essential.

Society of Jesus. In 1534 Loyola discussed his idea for a society, "organized to fight against spiritual foes," with a small set of followers at Paris, including Francis Xavier, a Basque nobleman who later became the most famous of the Jesuit missionaries. In 1540 the group obtained official sanction from Pope Paul III for the Society of Jesus, despite the opposition of higher clerics who objected to the formation of another religious order. The Society of Jesus, or more properly, the Company of Jesus, was to be a military order composed of spiritual soldiers fighting under the banner of Christ. Its purpose: "He who desires to fight for God under the banner of the cross in our society, after a solemn vow of perpetual chastity, shall set this thought before his mind, that he is part of a society founded for the special purpose of providing for the advancement of souls in Christian life and doctrine and for the propagation of the faith through public preaching and the ministry of the word of God, spiritual exercises and deeds of charity, and in particular through the training of the young and ignorant in Christianity."

Members of the Society of Jesus were not shut up in monasteries, but were sent out into the world for spiritual conquest. All owed implicit obedience to the head of the society and special loyalty to the pope. In addition, cardinal principles were discipline, efficiency, and education. Novices were carefully chosen, put through a long and trying period of spiritual training, and then assigned to special work wherever they were needed. All took the customary vows of poverty, chastity, and obedience, but they were freed from such monastic disciplines as asceticism and regular hours, so that they could continue their work as missionaries and teachers.

The Society of Jesus increased in size until at the time of its founder's death it had more than a thousand members scattered through a hundred communities. The Jesuits infused a new spiritual vitality into the Catholic Church. They were to a great extent responsible for the retention of Catholicism in such doubtful countries as Poland, Hungary, and Bohemia, and they obtained additional recruits by missionary work in North and South America, China, India, the East Indies, and Africa.

The Index. As one of its agencies for reform, the Council of Trent charged the papacy with the task of preparing a list of works which Roman Catholics could not read or possess upon doctrinal or moral grounds. The idea was not new: since the early days of the Church various books had been condemned as suspect, pernicious, or heretical. The presumed need for supervision became even more urgent after the invention of printing, which had led to the cheap diffusion of all sorts of books. The *Index librorum prohibitorum* was a catalog of books censured by the supreme authority of the Catholic Church as prejudicial to faith and good morals. Until 1917 the Index was published by the Congregation of the Index, composed of cardinals designated by the pope, with a secretary who was a Dominican monk, and a body of examining theologians.

The Revived Inquisition. A second agency of reform was the revived inquisition (Latin *inquisitio*, an inquiry), originally organized in the Middle Ages, but now renewed and strengthened to meet the challenge of Protestantism. The purpose was to detect and punish not only all heretics but also those guilty of any offense against Catholic orthodoxy. The tribunal sought to extract confessions by the use of psychological questioning and, as a final resort, by torture. Sentences passed by the Inquisitional court were read in a ceremonial *auto-da-fé* (act of faith). The revived Inquisition was successful mainly in the Italies, where it suppressed Protestantism. In Spain it was used to wipe out "the national scourge of heresy." Despite many legends, few of those convicted of heresy at this time were formally handed over to the state authorities

for execution. The vigilance of the Inquisition gradually relaxed as religious passions died down.

2. Bloody Battleground: Europe, 1562–1648

Fratricidal Conflict. Although Protestantism had been established in its characteristic forms, and Catholicism had already begun its own Reformation, the grave issues arising out of the cleavage were to be decided on the battlefield. Ironically, the two religions, each accepting and supporting the principle of peace on earth to men of good will, attempted to exterminate the other by fire and sword. The struggle for mastery involved an almost century-long series of intricate civil and foreign conflicts, begun sometimes with, and sometimes without, declarations of war.

The Huguenot Wars, 1562–1598. By the middle of the sixteenth century, the Protestants, or Huguenots, had become more and more influential in French affairs. French monarchs sought to suppress Calvinist "heretics," but they were unsuccessful. A complex political and religious situation came to a head in 1562 when the Catholic Guise family, pledged to extirpation of Protestantism, led an attack on a congregation of Huguenots assembled for worship in a barn. Eight distinct conflicts occurred, in which the countryside of France was devastated and its population materially reduced. On August 24, 1572, St. Bartholomew's Day, several thousand Huguenots were massacred in one of the most hideous blood-baths of modern times. This senseless crime was typical of the bitterness engendered by religious wars. In 1598 the civil wars were brought to an end by the Edict of Nantes, which granted the Huguenots political and religious toleration.

The Revolt of the Netherlands. In the second theater of religious wars, the Netherlands, the Spanish king and Holy Roman emperor, Charles V, sought to defend the old religion against the Protestantism sweeping in from the Germanies and France. His successor,

Philip II, a fervent Catholic, sent the narrow-minded Duke of Alva to stamp out heresy in the Netherlands. The king's agent inaugurated a campaign of terror, until "the whole land ran with blood." Instead of extirpating Protestantism, this blind policy aroused the populace to revolt. Under the leadership of William the Silent of Orange, the small Dutch state single-handedly waged war against Spain, the mightiest power in Christendom. Later, this revolt, which had important economic and political as well as religious aspects, was merged into the Thirty Years' War, and the Dutch were no longer without friends. In the long run, the Spanish fury failed to hold the northern provinces for Spain, although the southern provinces (now Belgium) were restored to Catholicism.

The Thirty Years' War 1618–1648. The last and most destructive of the religious wars growing out of the Protestant Reformation was the Thirty Years' War which, though it involved almost every important nation in Europe, was fought mostly on German soil. The Treaty of Augsburg (1555) was supposed to have settled the issues between Catholicism and Protestantism; but it contained defects which were certain to make trouble. The Protestants weakened themselves in mutual recriminations on points of doctrine; the Catholic Church, purged now of abuses, experienced a revival of energy. Moreover, the Hapsburg dynasty, having so far failed to pacify the Germanies, decided upon further intervention. These developments were complicated by rivalries among the Catholic, Lutheran, and Calvinist princes in the Germanies, who agreed only in their opposition to imperial authority.

The war broke out first in Bohemia, when in 1618 the Bohemian Protestants refused to accept Ferdinand II as their king. Supported by the German Protestants of the Palatinate, Bohemian nobles captured two of the emperor's envoys and threw them out of the window of the royal castle in Prague (since called the "defenestration"). Spanish troops then invaded the Palatinate, and in 1620 Bohemia was overwhelmed. With the collapse

of the revolt, the country was brought back to Catholicism.

Fearing further aggression upon the part of the victorious Catholics, Protestant princes to the north of the Palatinate began to arm in self-defense. In 1625 Christian IV, king of Denmark, went to battle to aid his German Protestant co-religionists. The emperor's army, under the command of Count Tilly, moved north. Tilly was assisted by Albrecht von Wallenstein, a soldier of fortune, who had recruited an army of irregulars, peasants, and adventurers. The Catholic forces inflicted several severe defeats on the Protestants. The victorious emperor Ferdinand II then issued the Edict of Restitution (1629) restoring to the Catholic Church all the land and property it had lost since the Peace of Augsburg.

The next year, Gustavus Adolphus, the Lutheran king of Sweden, came to the aid of the embattled Protestants. Invading Pomerania in 1630, he won an important victory at Leipzig in 1631, and then pushed on to Bavaria and Bohemia. Gustavus Adolphus and Wallenstein met in 1632 at Lützen, where the Swedes were again victorious, though Gustavus Adolphus lost his life. Wallenstein, detested by his patron the emperor, and by Catholics and Protestants alike, was assassinated in 1634 by his own officers.

The entrance of France into the Thirty Years' War was due to Cardinal Richelieu's desire to humiliate the Hapsburg family and to extend the boundaries of France to the Rhine, the Alps, and the Pyrenees. The fact that the French cardinal had no scruples about joining the Protestant cause against the Catholic emperor symbolized the triumph of state policy over religious conviction. The war now resolved itself into a phase of the dynastic conflict between the Bourbons and the Hapsburgs for European supremacy. The power of Spain was finally broken, at the expense of the devastated Germanies.

The Peace of Westphalia, 1648. The Peace of Westphalia, signed in 1648, placed Calvinism on an equal footing with Lutheranism and Catholicism. Protestant princes were permitted to retain all lands in their possession in the year 1624. Catholics and Protestants were to share in administration, and the restoration of Catholicism in Austria, Bohemia, and Bavaria was confirmed. In the political settlement, the small princes triumphed, receiving international status. An important result of the war was the virtual dissolution of the Holy Roman Empire, which was a mere shell in the succeeding centuries.

The Peace of Westphalia ended the long period of religious wars. Both papacy and empire emerged from the struggle with greatly reduced powers. France now became the leading power on the Continent, while Sweden gained supremacy in the north. The real losers were the German states, oppressed by ruin, suffering, and misery. Whole villages were destroyed; the population was drastically reduced; trade, industry, and agriculture suffered heavily; and the general level of culture sank.

HAPSBURG HOLDINGS IN 1648

Austrian Hapsburgs [||||||]   Spanish Hapsburgs [\\\\\]

German political unification and economic recovery were delayed for more than two centuries. Promoters of German nationalism never allowed the German people to forget the devastation caused by the Thirty Years' War and its blow to German unity.

Historical Controversy: Traditionalism Versus Revisionism. The traditional view of the Thirty Years' War describes it as a dominantly religious conflict generated by the Reformation and Counter-Reformation, as one of the worst catastrophes in history, and as a period of great national tragedy for Germany. In recent years all three of these assumptions have been challenged by revisionist historians. In 1894 Franz Mehring, a Marxist historian, pointed to economic factors as dominant in the era, that "religion was as little the final cause . . . as any ideology, because only in the field of economics can these causes be sought." This materialist conception of motivation was accepted not only by Marxists but also in part by other historians who tended in their accounts to give less attention to religious causation.

Revisionist opinion also attacked the traditional thesis that the war was a social catastrophe of enormous significance. In a detailed study Robert R. Ergang demonstrated that the extent of devastation was not as great as described in almost all accounts of the conflict. Other scholars joined in concluding that the destruction was not as great as claimed and that the ruinous effects of the war years have been exaggerated. The British historian S. H. Steinberg referred to the "legend of cultural exhaustion and desolation," and maintained that the war itself had little and certainly no detrimental influence upon the cultural life of Germany. To these revisionist historians war itself is by nature destructive and the Thirty Years' War was no exception, but the campaigns were short and the armies small. Many areas of Germany were hardly affected at all. "On the whole, the national income, productive power and standard of living were higher in 1650 than they had been fifty years earlier."

The third traditional view, holding that the bloody catastrophe was due to a conflict between the interests of the house of Hapsburg and of the German nation, is denounced by revisionists as an incorrect insular view. In popular German literature the war was interpreted as resulting in the decimation of the Germanies as well as the destruction of the power of the Hapsburg emperor. To the revisionists this is a simplistic picture which distorts what was, they say, actually a European-wide conflict. Not only Germans but French, Dutch, Spaniards, Swedes, and Czechs were involved.

The change in attitude toward the Thirty Years' War is seen most clearly in the interesting treatment by an English historian, C. V. Wedgwood. Describing it as "an unmitigated catastrophe," Miss Wedgwood paid relatively little attention to religious causation as compelling the conflict. She was convinced that the war need not have happened and that it settled nothing worth settling. "Morally subversive, economically destructive, socially degrading, confused in its causes, devious in its course, futile in its result, it is the outstanding example in European history of meaningless conflict."

3. Modern Man and the Reformation Era

Significance of the Epoch. The era of the Reformation and the Counter-Reformation had profound effects on the history of modern man. Considered as a unit the movement was comparable in scope and importance with the French Revolution of 1789 or the Industrial Revolution commencing in the middle of the eighteenth century. It helped shape the transition from the medieval to the modern world. It stimulated nationalism and capitalism. Although most results are associated primarily with the Protestant phase of the movement, the Catholic Counter-Reformation had similar influences. Both Protestant and Catholic reformers held the same point of view regarding absolutism in both Church and state. Both supported despotic rule in countries where they had the majority of the population, and both opposed absolutism in countries where they formed a minority.

Both Reformation and Counter-Reformation aimed at restoring the golden days of the past when decency, good will, and justice prevailed over greed, dishonesty, and injustice. The leaders of the Counter-Reformation looked with longing back to the thirteenth century when both Christian religion and leadership were at their best. But, unfortunately, both Catholic and Protestant reformers became embroiled in inconsequential controversies of dogma, which embittered both sides and prevented a major liberation of the mind of modern man.

Individualism: Private Judgment. All through the great Protestant secession and the Catholic reaction the question of private judgment—in effect, individualism in religious doctrine—was the real issue. Reformers agreed on the necessity for saving souls, but they differed on whether the Bible was to be interpreted *by* the individual himself (Protestants) or *for* the individual through the medium of the priesthood (Catholics). This conflict between authority and private judgment was now resolved in favor of the latter in the sense that the Protestant formula was now supported by a large portion of the Christian population of Europe. The man of the sixteenth century broke restrictive bonds and began the process of a long struggle for liberty of conscience and for the right to his own private judgment.

Dogmatism. At first the Protestant Reformation seemed to spell the death of toleration, because both the ancient Catholic Church and the new Protestant sects matched one another in enforcing uniformity of belief. Protestant reformers demanded the right of individual judgment for themselves as a criticism of Catholicism, yet they denied it to their followers. For example, in his pamphlet *The Freedom of a Christian Man,* Luther wrote a ringing appeal for ecclesiastical liberty, but soon denied it to others, such as Anabaptists and Catholics. His followers even introduced an inquisition in Saxony. Calvin revolted against Catholicism, yet established a kind of medieval theocracy at Geneva and forbade even slight deviations from his own formula for salvation. Anyone rash enough to challenge the Calvinist doctrine in Geneva stood a good chance of conviction for heresy. Henry VIII to his dying day considered himself a "good Catholic," yet anyone who believed in Catholicism any more or less than he, was in peril of his life.

Growth of Toleration. Despite the rigid dogmatism, modern man's conception of toleration sprang from the Reformation epoch. The reasons were complex:

(1) *Trial by fire:* The nightmare of the Thirty Years' War revealed the futility of religious intolerance. The Germans paid a high price for this ferocious contest.

(2) *Seeds of growth:* The theory of toleration was gradually built up by minority sects, one after the other. The Anabaptists, who were driven from place to place by persecution, the

Catholics and Puritans in England, and the Huguenots in France, all became devoted proponents of the idea of liberty of conscience, at first in self-preservation and later as a matter of policy.

(3) *Politico-economic necessity:* With the growth of trade and the concurrent enlargement of dynastic power, religious issues receded and the existence of absolute conformity of conscience no longer seemed to be as important as it once was. Theological authority was weakened as the way opened for increasing secularization of government. Such monarchs as Elizabeth of England and Henry IV of France saw the political and economic advantages of granting toleration and protection to all.

(4) *Religious quid pro quo:* Through experience it became obvious to even the most obtuse that one's own religion deserved tolerance only if he, in turn, was tolerant of all others. It was a painful truth that both sides learned toleration only under outside pressure.

(5) *Role of intellectuals:* In the midst of conflict and slaughter, influential men of learning pointed to the absurdity of religious fanaticism and intolerance. This was a sphere, they maintained, in which persuasion was of more value than force. Since men were willing to die for what they believed to be true, the idea was to convince them by reason and not by threats of death. Religion, they said, was a matter of personal conviction, not governmental pressure, which in the end would defeat itself.

Political Considerations. The impact of the Reformation era helped transfer the loyalty of modern man from international Church to national state. He now owed his allegiance not to the papacy at Rome but to the monarch at home. The native of France no longer regarded himself as a Roman Catholic who happened to live in France, but as a Frenchman who happened to be Catholic by religion. Protestantism became closely identified with the national, political, and governmental interests of the state. This idea was the direct opposite of the medieval theory that the Church was supreme. From now on the dominating idea was the supremacy of the state over the Church and particularly the separation of the two. At first the new Protestant religions supported the absolutism of the national monarchs, but later they inclined in the direction of constitutionalism and representative government, thus opening the way to the principle of individualism in politics as well as in religion.

Change in Economic Concepts. The attitude of the medieval man toward trade and industry was conditioned by the teachings of the Church. His concept of business was a carry-over from the time of the Greeks and Romans, both of whom looked down upon trade as unworthy of people who really mattered. He was taught, and he firmly believed, that the profit motive was undesirable, and that the taking of interest was morally reprehensible because it took advantage of human needs. If he were a member of a merchant guild, he was forbidden to monopolize material or products, to corner the market, or even to sell at higher than a regulated profit. If he were a master craftsman, he was required to accept a "just price" for his work. All these economic ideas were rationalized by official Church philosophy.

The Reformation era effected profound economic changes by destroying these medieval doctrines and establishing in their place what have since been recognized as sound economic practices. All stigma was removed from business enterprise. Modern man has a high regard for business success. He considers it ethical to buy at a low price and sell at as high a price as the traffic will bear. He regards interest-taking as justifiable and fair. He looks upon trade and industry as indispensable activities of the social order and, instead of damning the acquisitive instinct, he blesses it as a natural right. In short, he expresses in the economic sphere the same individualism he had earlier shown in his religious and intellectual pursuits. Calvinism, especially, which originated in the urban areas of Switzerland and which spread particularly among the bourgeoisie of France and the Netherlands, stressed material gain as a sign of God's favor, thrift as commendable, and reinvestment of profits as desirable. By removing all the restrictions of the older Church from business enterprise, Calvinism echoed the spirit of the new age.

❧ KEY DOCUMENT ❧

CANONS OF THE COUNCIL OF TRENT, 1545–1563

University of Pennsylvania, *Translations and Reprints* (Philadelphia, 1897), vol. II, pp. 28–29.

THE LAST of the great Church councils, before the nineteenth century, was held at Trent in the Italian Tyrol from 1545 to 1563. Its aim was not to overthrow Protestantism, but rather to consolidate what was left of the prestige of the Church, to eliminate abuses, and restate its doctrines. A series of canons was drawn up in which those holding special opinions were declared anathematized. The following examples give the central ecclesiastical dogmas of the Roman Catholic Church and declared accursed those who refused to accept these holdings.

Thirteenth Session, Chapter IV.—Since Christ our Redeemer declared that it was truly His body which He offered up in the form [*sub specie*] of bread, and since the Church has moreover always accepted this belief, this Holy Council declares once more that by the consecration of the bread and the wine the whole substance of the bread is converted into the substance of the body of Christ our Lord, and the whole substance of the wine into the substance of His blood, which change is aptly and properly termed trans-substantiation by the Catholic Church.

Thirteenth Session, Canon I.—If any one shall deny that the body and blood of our Lord Jesus Christ together with His spirit and divinity, to-wit, Christ all in all, are not truly, really and materially contained in the holy sacrament of the Eucharist, and shall assert that the Eucharist is but a symbol or figure, let him be anathema.

Thirteenth Session, Canon VI.—If any one shall say that Christ, the only-begotten son of God, is not to be worshipped with the highest form of adoration (*Latriae*) including external worship, in the holy sacrament of the Eucharist, or that the Eucharist should not be celebrated by a special festival, nor borne solemnly about in procession according to the praiseworthy and universal rite and custom of the Holy Church, nor held up publicly for the veneration of the people and that those who adore it are idolators, let him be anathema.

Twenty-second Session, Canon I.—If any one shall say that a real and fitting sacrifice is not offered to God in the mass, or that nothing is offered except that Christ is given us to eat, let him be anathema.

Twenty-second Session, Canon II.—If any one shall say that by the words, "This do in remembrance of Me," Christ did not institute the apostles as priests, or did not ordain that they themselves and their successors should offer up His body and blood, let him be anathema.

Twenty-second Session, Canon III.—If any one shall say that the sacrifice of the mass is only a praiseworthy deed or act of edification, or that it is simply in commemoration of the sacrifice on the cross and is not in the nature of a propitiation; or that it can benefit only him who receives it and ought not to be offered for the living and the dead, for sins, punishment, atonement and other necessary things, let him be anathema.

❧ HISTORICAL INTERPRETATION ☙

LEOPOLD VON RANKE ON THE RESOURCES OF THE PAPACY FOR ACTIVE CONFLICT

Leopold von Ranke, *The History of the Popes*, 3 vols. (London, 1847), I, 406–409.

AT THE TIME of his death, Leopold von Ranke (1795–1886) was regarded as one of the greatest of modern historians. Few scholars had so great an influence on German academic life. Casting aside all theories and prejudices, he sought to find out "exactly what happened" (*"wie es eigentlich gewesen ist"*). His *History of the Popes,* from which the following excerpt on the Counter-Reformation is taken, is considered to be his masterpiece.

The papacy and Catholicism had long maintained themselves against these advances of their enemy, in an attitude of defence it is true, but passive only; upon the whole they were compelled to endure them.

Affairs now assumed a different aspect. . . .

It may be affirmed generally that a vital and active force was again manifested, that the Church had regenerated her creed in the spirit of the age, and had established reforms in accordance with the demands of the times. The religious tendencies which had appeared in southern Europe, were not suffered to become hostile to herself, she adopted them, and gained the mastery of their movements; thus she re-newed her powers, and infused fresh vigor into her system. The Protestant spirit alone had hitherto filled the theatre of the world with results that held the minds of men enthralled; another spirit, equally deserving of esteem perhaps, if regarded from an elevated point of view, though of decidedly opposite character, now entered the lists, displaying similar power to make the minds of men its own, and to kindle them into activity.

The influence of the restored Catholic system was first established in the two southern peninsulas, but this was not accomplished without extreme severities. The Spanish Inquisition received the aid of that lately revived in Rome;

every movement of Protestantism was violently suppressed. But at the same time those tendencies of the inward life, which renovated Catholicism claimed and enchained as her own, were peculiarly powerful in those countries. The sovereigns also attached themselves to the interests of the Church. . . .

Now the papacy resumed a [new] position. . . . Although it had experienced great changes, it still possessed the inestimable advantages of having all the externals of the past and the habit of obedience on its side. In the council so prosperously concluded, the popes had even gained an accession of that authority which it had been the purpose of the temporal powers to restrict; and had strengthened their influence over the national churches; they had moreover abandoned that temporal policy by which they had formerly involved Italy and all Europe in confusion. They attached themselves to Spain with perfect confidence and without any reservations, fully returning to the devotion evinced by that kingdom to the Roman Church. The Italian principality, the enlarged dominions of the pontiff, contributed eminently to the success of his ecclesiastical enterprises; while the interests of the universal Catholic Church were for some time essentially promoted by the overplus of its revenues.

Thus strengthened internally, thus supported by powerful adherents, and by the idea of which they were the representatives, the popes exchanged the defensive position, with which they had hitherto been forced to content themselves, for that of assailants.

❧ TEN BASIC BOOKS ❧

THE CATHOLIC COUNTER-REFORMATION

1. Boehmer, Heinrich, *The Jesuits* (Philadelphia, 1928).
2. Corbett, James A., *The Papacy,* Anvil Book No. 12 (Princeton, N. J., 1956).†
3. Daniel-Rops, Henri, *The Catholic Reformation,* trans. from the French by John Warrington (New York, 1962).†
4. Hughes, Philip, *The Church in Crisis: A History of the General Councils, 325–1870* (Garden City, N. Y., 1961).†
5. Janelle, Pierre, *The Catholic Reformation* (Milwaukee, Wisc., 1963).†
6. Kidd, Beresford, *The Counter-Reformation, 1550–1600* (London, 1937).
7. Lea, Henry C., *A History of the Inquisition of Spain,* 4 vols. (New York and London, 1906–1907).
8. Roth, Cecil, *The Spanish Inquisition* (London, 1938, R. 1964).†
9. Sedgwick, Henry D. *Ignatius Loyola* (New York, 1923).
10. Van Dyke, Paul, *Ignatius Loyola, the Founder of the Jesuits* (New York, 1926).

7

The Social Structure in Flux

JUST AS the nobles were wearing away in civil strife and were seeing their castles shot to pieces by cannon, just as the clergy were wasting in supine indolence and were riddled by the mockery of humanists, there arose a new class, eager and able to take the helm of civilization, the moneyed men of city and trade. *Nouveaux riches* as they were, they had an appetite for pleasure and for ostentation unsurpassed by any, a love for the world and an impatience of the meek and lowly Church, with her ideal of poverty and of chastity. In their luxurious and leisured homes they sheltered the arts that made life richer and the philosophy, or religion, that gave them a good conscience in the work they loved.

—PRESERVED SMITH

1. The Transformation of Modern Society

Revolutionary Social Change. Economic life underwent a revolutionary change in the opening centuries of the modern era. Concurrent with the Commercial Revolution came social changes which reshaped European society. In reality, the two revolutions are part of the same development. There were realignments in class structure. The word "class," from the Latin *classis,* a division of the Roman people, may be defined as a group of individuals who —through common descent, similarity of occupation, wealth, and education—have a similar mode of life, an analogous stock of ideas, feelings, attitudes, and forms of behavior, and who regard themselves as belonging to one group. In ancient times social differentiation was not of "class" but of *status* or *rank:* a man was born to a certain station in life as determined by law and custom; he was rarely able to rise above his rank, and he died within it. This concept carried over into the medieval period and continued to shape the social order. Two types of social organization, status and class, existed side by side and often overlapped.

Somewhere along the line there was a transformation from status into class, when an individual found it easily possible to transfer from one social group to another. The important thing was the development of the individual's consciousness of belonging to a class.

The lines of demarcation between classes are not always sharp. Often class mingles with class through marriage or other social means, or through economic opportunity. A social class such as the bourgeoisie has within itself gradations of rank, differences of position, variations of attitudes. Little about it is static, and it is always in flux. Its blurred edges merge imperceptibly into other classes. It undergoes changes in personnel and policies. But what distinguishes it from other classes is the *common economic interests* of its members. Here its aims appear in sharp outline.

In the Middle Ages *power* was based upon inherited position, whereas *wealth* was measured in land, or in the control of hereditary contracts, or in the ability to command services, or in all three. In the early modern period, with the rise of capitalism, wealth was often reckoned in terms of money, which in itself created power to control the services of men. Society assumed the form and structure it was to maintain until the French Revolution. Gradually, as a concomitant of changing economic conditions, a new and wealthy class—the bourgeoisie—emerged to dominate the rest of society. This new and vigorous class was well aware of what it wanted—political and social power commensurate with its economic power. At first the bourgeoisie allied itself with the monarchy, and for a time it was content to consider its own interests as synony-

Allegorical representation of the discord which exists between the various classes of society. After a miniature of "The Tree of Battles" in a manuscript of the fifteenth century.

mous with those of the monarch. Pressed to the wall by this powerful combination, the old feudal nobility and the aristocratic clergy lost their privileged position in society. They still retained rank and prestige, pride of class, and their old manners, but they no longer dominated European society politically. Once certain of its victory, the bourgeoisie turned on

the monarch and either stripped him of his sovereign powers or discarded him altogether.

In the meantime, the great class of industrial workers, the proletariat, was subjugated. No longer considered within the category of the bourgeoisie, the proletariat as a class did not rise with it to power. The new use of capital drove a wedge between the controllers of capital on the one hand and the wage-earners on the other. Originally unorganized and lacking in class-consciousness, the proletariat only slowly became aware of its strength. During the nineteenth century and to a greater extent during the twentieth, there was a gradual quickening of conflict between bourgeoisie and proletariat, as the former strengthened its position in society and as the latter became aware of its potentialities.

Historical Controversy: Social Conflict. The first modern emphasis on group or class struggle as a historic factor came in the early 1830's when such historians as de Tocqueville, Mignet, Thiers, and Macaulay began to rewrite history in terms of social conflict. This tendency was accelerated with the writings of Louis Blanc and the Saint Simonists. After these forerunners came the specific doctrine of the class struggle formulated by Karl Marx and Friedrich Engels in the *Communist Manifesto* (1848). Marx later elaborated the theory and applied it to interpreting the revolutions of 1848 and the Paris Commune of 1870–1871. The theory held that members of society are segregated into classes which hold different positions in the social organization. There is an antagonism of interests between these classes, and the class struggle has persisted. The history of mankind therefore has been a continuous struggle of classes. In Marx's view, the class struggle was not only a theory but also a principle of action through which economic exploitation could be ended only by establishment of a socialist society based on collective ownership.

Marx's emphasis on social conflict was accepted by many historians as a needed corrective for that overemphasis in the past on political and religious factors in historical development. But in the twentieth century virtually all nonsocialist historians pointed to its limitations in the light of the more dominating struggle between national and racial groups. Moreover, the theory was attacked because it set up definite and permanent boundary lines between the classes, whereas in fact there were indistinct lines at which the classes merged into one another. In addition, it was said, there are periods when antagonisms between classes are obscure, or completely concealed, or even of a minor character. Inside the socialist movement itself, the Fabians in England, the revisionists in Germany, and the syndicalists in France all pointed out that the trends in the class struggle which Marx had predicted had failed to materialize and that the assumption of revolutionary change had not been realized.

The controversy has been prolonged, embittered, and filled with polemical overtones. Those who support the Marxian dogma in its rigid sense reject all other approaches to the study of history as incorrect and inconsequential. Those who see the potency of nationalist feelings and ideals as overshadowing the class struggle, regard the Marxian analysis as a closed-mind approach to the study of history.

2. The Man of the Middle Ages

Life on the Manor. European society disintegrated and centralized government virtually disappeared in the Middle Ages. The flow of trade diminished to a mere trickle. Cities lay devastated. The ordinary man lived on the manor, center of his little world. His main aim in life was to keep alive. He was born, he lived, and he died in his hamlet. He preserved himself from starvation only by hard, backbreaking labor. In a conservative and severely restricted society he accepted his destiny without question. The Church taught him, and he firmly believed, that he was permanently ensconced in that station of life to which it had pleased God to assign him. He no more nourished a desire to rise above his own station than to cut his own throat: any such thoughts he considered to be a dangerous defiance of the will of God. Since all life was based on in-

terdependence, any change was regarded as a break in the foundations of an ordered world.

Medieval Nobility. For a thousand years the agrarian aristocrat had maintained a secure seat in medieval society. His place was cemented by special advantages or privileges in both military and civil spheres. His most precious possession was land—the only source and measure of wealth. When not engaged in private warfare, his most enjoyable pursuit, he lived in a condition of rough and uncouth plenty. He had few of the advantages of modern man: he slept on a hard bed in drafty castles or manor houses, ate very little, and bathed only when it could no longer be avoided. He rode, hunted, hawked, and drank to excess. As a member of the military aristocracy he fought in chivalrous combat against other lords with the almost certain assurance that he would survive. In intervals between fighting he played at warfare in tournaments and jousting bouts while his lady-fair on the sidelines admired his grace and courage. He was a privileged character in a society where accident of birth was the all-important determinant.

Added to the great nobility were the knights, or chevaliers, who possessed just enough land to support with full equipment the needs of a horseman. The knight was literally lifted above the common man by his horse. In theory, he was one of a brotherhood of arms in which all were equal. He was first, last, and always a warrior, whose strongest asset was personal valor.

Medieval Clergy. Alongside the privileged nobility on the topmost rung of the social ladder were the upper clergy, who exercised a powerful influence over the lives of ordinary men. The great ecclesiastics controlled religious life, education, charity, and public welfare. Where the regular clergy (monks and nuns) resided in religious houses and ordered their lives according to an established set of rules (*regula*), the secular clergy (archbishops, bishops, and parish priests) lived in the world (*saecula*) and came into contact with everyday life. The clergy claimed exemption from taxation as a privilege, on the ground that their wealth was "dedicated to God and his service."

While the upper clergy lived like secular lords, the lower clergy (the *curés*) eked out, much like their poor parishioners, a mere existence under miserable conditions. Humble, with little education and without polished manners, the parish priests were, nevertheless, loyal and devoted sons of the Church and shepherds of their flocks. With the quickening of class rivalries in the eighteenth century, the lower clergy cast its lot with the unprivileged commoners, but the higher clergy rallied to the side of the nobility.

Medieval Peasant. For centuries a large part of the peasant population of most European countries remained unfree, economically tied down by heavy obligations, politically without influence, and socially at the bottom rung of the ladder. Chained to the land, the medieval peasant never left his native village except on some fighting expedition with his lord. He was caught in a network of social convention, which made him deeply sensitive to evil omens, monsters, spirits, and the ways and practices of witchcraft. He could neither read nor write. He ate a limited and monotonous diet, he nearly froze in winter, and he hungered in time of famine. The privileged classes regarded him as a kind of animal, with no human dignity or sensitivity. To them he was merely "an ugly, boorish, brutish fellow, with a skull like an ape, a loud prater, a ribald jester." But upon his work-hardened back rested the thin superstructure of the leisured class, which profited from his toil.

Exploited by the landowner, hungry, dissatisfied, and desperate, the peasant sometimes burst from his bonds into open revolt. Because, however, he lacked discipline and leadership, he was invariably beaten into submission, or hanged, or massacred. Only when stirred beyond human capacity to endure did he attempt any concerted action; but always he was struck down by powers which he understood only vaguely.

The ravages of the Black Death (1347–1351), which spread throughout Europe leaving death and devastation in its wake, plus the misery and anarchy of the Hundred Years' War (1338–1453), resulted in one peasant rebellion after another. In France in 1358 a motley army of peasants, called Jacquerie (after Jacques, a common name for a peasant), expressed their resentment blindly in a series of plundering expeditions. Savagely suppressed by the nobility, the French peasantry did not entirely free itself from feudal dues and services until the French Revolution. In 1351 the English Parliament passed the Statute of Labourers, designed to force both peasants and workers to work at wages prevalent before the era of the great plague. The subsequent revolt which broke out in 1381 quickly collapsed after an attack on London under the leadership of Wat Tyler, Jack Straw, and John Ball. The fourteenth-century Flemish revolt, the fifteenth-century Bohemian rebellion, and the sixteenth-century German revolts all were phases of the same movement—the peasants' demand for social and economic equality. All these outbursts were mercilessly crushed.

Medieval Worker. The medieval manor contained butchers and bakers and various types of artisans and craftsmen who manufactured armor, furniture, and a hundred other articles in the village workshops. These men were workers, but in the dominantly agrarian manorial economy their status was hardly distinguishable from that of the peasants. With the rise of a money economy, with the commutation of personal services into money payments, the rise of the local grain markets, agricultural specialization, and the emergence of towns, trade, and industry, there appeared an urban working class whose activities centered about the guilds. In the craft-guild hierarchy—apprentice, journeyman, and master—the middle group, the journeymen, began to find it increasingly difficult to become masters, and hence organized associations of their own. The great majority, however, joined the urban proletariat, now in process of formation.

Ill-clad, ill-housed and ill-fed, the city workers and wage earners became the urban counterpart of the peasants. If anything, their existence was even more precarious than that of the farm laborers. Like the peasants, they were occasionally driven to desperation. Violent revolts in the late fourteenth century at Florence, Cologne, Paris, and Lyon were ruthlessly suppressed—as usual because the rebels had no common program, no effective organization, and no efficient leaders.

3. Transition: Medieval into Modern

Society in Flux. In the transition of European society from its medieval into its modern form, conditions differed among various nations, but there is enough consistency to trace a pattern. The fifteenth and sixteenth centuries saw a fascinating panorama of social life. The

A lady of Nuremberg, about 1508.

landed nobleman, the aristocrat, dressed in colorful and costly garments and guided in every move by an elaborate code of manners, held tenaciously to old privileges. The new bourgeois merchant, literate, enterprising, ag-

gressive, and wealthy, enjoyed the fruits of prosperity, living in a comfortable home, distinguished externally by beautifully colored windowpanes and inside by luxurious feather beds and hallmarked silverware. The merchant's wife measured her social status by the height and elaborateness of her hairdress and hats. The small educated class consisted for the most part of the clergy, who—like the teachers—were poorly paid. The peasant, perennial man of toil, worked in the fields from sunrise to sunset to provide food for a society dependent upon him and to obtain a mere existence for himself and his family.

The status of society during the transitional period between the medieval and modern eras may be summarized as follows:

(1) There was a steady growth in the population of Europe.

(2) People were on the move from one area of Europe to another, as well as to the New World.

(3) The nobility, socially preeminent and politically privileged for many centuries, began to decline in wealth and prestige.

(4) As society became more and more secular-minded, the upper clergy, like the nobility, began to lose many traditional privileges.

(5) The bourgeoisie, between the older, privileged aristocracy on the one hand and the unprivileged peasants and workers on the other, was successful in its drive to monopolize economic power and emerged as the dominant social class.

(6) In the midst of great economic and social changes, the great mass of workers was shaped into a class which began to express itself as an independent historical force.

Population Growth. At its height the great Roman Empire had a population of more than 40,000,000 people, but in its decline this was substantially reduced by war, disease, and famine. Little is known of the population trends of Europe before modern times, but there is no reason to assume that the population in 1600 was much larger than in 1300. It is probable that throughout the Middle Ages there was but little increase because of such factors as an inadequate food supply, primitive sanitation facilities, and a high death rate. Beginning in the late seventeenth century, there was an accelerating momentum, as indicated by the following approximate figures:

ESTIMATED POPULATION (*Millions*)

Europe		England & Wales		France	
1650	100	1066	1.5	1500	12
1800	186	1415	3	1700	19
1850	226	1600	5	1800	27
1900	400	1700	6	1900	39
1914	462	1800	9	1914	40
1920	455	1900	32	1920	38
1930	505	1914	36	1930	41
1938	570	1931	39	1942	39
1960	641	1960	45	1960	45
1966	668 (with USSR)	1966	49	1966	48

The increase in the population of Europe was due in part to improvements in agricultural production, as well as to the greater food supply because of commodities introduced from the New World. Added to these factors was the development of medical knowledge and practice.

Most progress in the extension of life has been achieved in very recent times, yet there is some evidence to show that the trend began earlier in the modern period. Herbert Heaton points out that in England the death rate began to fall about 1730 and dropped rapidly after about 1780, thanks to improved sanitation, the establishment of dispensaries and hospitals, better medical knowledge and practice, obstetrical developments, and the decline in fever, scurvy, and smallpox, as well as a general decline in gin-drinking.

Increased Mobility of Peoples. During the opening years of the modern era there began an extensive movement of people both inside Europe and to overseas areas. Such persecuted sects as the Puritans and Huguenots, roughly treated in their native lands, sailed for the New World in search of religious toleration. Others were attracted by stories of golden treasures said to be readily available in America. Still others were drawn by the lure of adventure and by vivid tales of strange lands and peoples. Added to these were the convicted criminals and indentured servants sent under coercion to work out their freedom in the new

lands. This steady movement of European peoples continued in succeeding centuries.

4. The Flower of Privilege Fades

Decline of the Nobility. As economic power gradually passed from the manor to the city, as the money economy extended itself throughout Western Europe, and as commerce was organized for world trade, the feudal nobility stood firmly aloof and jealously adhered to its old personal privileges. This was an unwise attitude to take in a changing world, particularly at a time when the power of both the purse and the sword was shifting to the bourgeoisie. The feudal aristocracy had always repudiated money as a standard and continued to express contempt for it, although money was rapidly replacing land as a measure of wealth. The flood of silver and gold from America led to a rise in prices as well as to higher standards of living, but the income of the nobility, based on hereditary rights and customs, remained relatively unchanged. Men of noble birth refused to lose caste by engaging in commerce and industry. This loss of economic power was matched by a decline in military power.

All through the Middle Ages the political independence of the nobility and its high status in society depended largely upon its monopoly of the arts of warfare. Now with money at their disposal, the kings could raise and maintain armies against which the old nobility was helpless. This became evident as early as the first phase of the Hundred Years' War, when Edward III in 1346 transported an army to France and met the warriors of the French nobility. The battle of Crécy demonstrated the superiority of a disciplined army over a disorganized feudal host, of hired soldiers over knights, and of the longbow over the lance, sword, and crossbow. The introduction of gun-powder about the middle of the fourteenth century was a crowning blow to the type of chivalrous warfare preferred by the aristocracy.

The Nobility in France. Although the status of the nobility differed in some respects in various European countries, its decline in France was typical of a trend. Here the old aristocracy, the "nobility of the sword," hung grimly on to feudal rights, exacted dues and services from the peasants, and by bribing or intimidating the collectors managed to escape payment of taxes. The right of freedom from taxation was based on a loudly professed willingness to "shed blood for king and country." About a thousand favorites of the king—the court nobility—relinquished their feudal rights to the monarch, in return for which they received government sinecures, commissions in the royal army, or pensions. Their daily life consisted of a constant and inelegant scramble for favors at the royal hand.

A far larger number of the nobility—provincial nobles—perhaps a hundred thousand, who possessed impressive ancient ancestries but no money, were forced to live unrewarding, parsimonious lives. Although these aristocrats were out of place in an era of a money economy and national armies, they nevertheless persisted in retaining their old customs. Each provincial noble maintained his traditional pigeon house, from which birds swooped down on the peasants' fields to gorge themselves on precious grain. The unfortunate peasant was not permitted to kill the flying marauders, though he was given the privilege of trying to frighten them away with rattle or drum. Not until the French Revolution, when his century-old resentment reached the boiling point, did the bewildered peasant attempt to kill both pigeons and nobles.

The French kings, as a reward for services, created a new *noblesse de la robe,* a nobility of the robe, from among the middle-class servants of the Crown. Many high judicial and financial officials, intendants, and administrative leaders, who were not blood heirs of feudal families, began to assume positions in a class which was gradually losing its privileged status. Despite being wealthy, enlightened, and enterprising, the nobility of the robe failed to reinvigorate a class that was fast losing its contest with the bourgeoisie for socioeconomic power and political hegemony.

Decline of the Clergy. There was a parallel decline in the fortunes of the upper clergy.

As society became more and more secular-minded and more subject to bourgeois control, the clergy came to be regarded as a stone of reaction "blocking the road of progress." The rise of commerce and industry and the introduction of a money economy affected the clergy fully as much as the nobility. The attack on the clergy was bitter but calculated, with emphasis directed at its "vested interests." It was a harsh struggle for economic power. On occasion, the offensive went so far as to accuse the clergy of being "deliberate purveyors of superstition and ignorance."

It was no accident that in the nationalization of religion which accompanied the Protestant Reformation the bourgeoisie turned to those sects which justified profit-taking, interest, and the aims and ideals of the middle class. In general, the Protestant clergy did not enjoy large incomes, and an ecclesiastical career lost most of its attractions for the higher classes. The historian Macaulay describes the poverty of the parish priest of the Anglican Church under the later Stuarts: "As children multiplied and grew, the household of the priest became more and more beggarly. Holes appeared more and more plainly in the thatch of his parsonage and in his single cassock. Often it was only by toiling on his glebe [the land belonging to the parish church], by feeding swine, and by loading dung-carts that he could obtain daily bread; nor did his utmost exertions always prevent the bailiffs from taking his concordance and his inkstand in execution. It was a white day on which he was admitted into the kitchen of a great house, and regaled by the servants with cold meat and ale. His children were brought up like the children of the neighboring peasantry. His boys followed the plough, and his girls went out to service." Members of the upper clergy still lived in palaces and served in the House of Lords, but they enjoyed none of the wealth, pomp, and circumstance that had distinguished the ecclesiastical life of Cardinal Wolsey.

5. Power to the Bourgeoisie

Meaning. The term "bourgeoisie," originating in France, at first denoted the freemen of the medieval borough. A product of the concentration of commercial and industrial enterprise in the urban centers during the later Middle Ages, the bourgeoisie was held together at first by a common desire to obtain and solidify legal rights and privileges. It was interested in putting an end to the restrictions placed on the towns by the feudal landowners, and it was this common aim which first gave it a sense of social cohesion. Later on, the term "bourgeoisie" was extended to mean the whole class between the nobility and the worker. Since the bourgeoisie holds an intermediate status between the older privileged nobility and clergy on the one hand and the peasants and workers on the other, between the disappearing nobility and the proletariat of the industrial system, it is also called the "middle class." The words "bourgeoisie" and "middle class" are now used as synonymous terms.

As the industrial organization of Europe was transformed from a guild basis to capitalism, and as the differences between the powerful bourgeoisie and the new class-conscious proletariat became sharper and sharper, the term "bourgeoisie" lost its original good-humored implications and took on a kind of insulting and vindictive meaning. Critical socialist writers in the nineteenth and twentieth centuries denounced the bourgeoisie as a reactionary class and called for its overthrow. Marxian socialist theory has its own definition of the bourgeoisie, which it regards as a privileged minority of capitalists who feed on surplus value and state favoritism and who inevitably drive their victims—the petty bourgeoisie—down into the ranks of the proletariat.

Divisions. The bourgeoisie was not a fixed and unchanging entity. Its character, like that of all great social groupings, was always in flux. In the modern period, succeeding waves of middle-class groups rose from the ranks of the peasants and workers through the position of merchants and manufacturers to the wealthy landowning aristocracy. The upper and lower boundaries of the bourgeoisie were not rigid walls. However, for the sake of convenience we can divide the bourgeoisie into two recognizable groups, the *petty bourgeoisie*, sometimes called the lower middle class, and the

great bourgeoisie, ordinarily called the upper middle class.

The petty bourgeoisie, the largest single group, which originally developed from the transformation of the lowly but thrifty artisan or peasant into the capitalist class, included the entrepreneur who conducted a small-scale business or a shop, the simple producer of goods (such as the small craftsman), the government official, the banker, the tax collector, and the salaried employee. An offshoot of this group was the professional branch of moderately wealthy lawyers, magistrates, physicians, university professors, clerks, bookkeepers, functionaries, auditors, and business agents, most of whom would today be placed in the white-collar category.

The upper ranks, the great bourgeoisie, grew out of the transformation of the small capitalist into the "captain of industry." In its early stages this subdivision included such diverse elements as the wealthy merchant capitalist whose principal aim was monopoly and concessions, proprietors, financiers, colonial entrepreneurs, manufacturers of luxuries, slave-traders, and munitions-makers. It also counted in its ranks such professionals as wealthy lawyers and physicians.

Bourgeois Characteristics. The history of modern man is to some extent a record of the growth of bourgeois power. His destinies were shaped and determined by the bourgeoisie, more than by any other class. This was the class which successfully drove to economic power as the capitalist system unfolded, and in the process transformed the medieval into the modern economy. It enriched itself by control of banking, commerce, and industry, by speculation, and by monopolizing foreign trade. Its most successful members were cold, calculating realists who measured values in terms of hard cash and whose philosophy always boiled down eventually to the commonplace maxim: "Money talks!" Those who made large profits in business and industry were proud of it and were inclined to look with amusement and even contempt upon people who persisted in retaining the medieval concept that the urge to acquire wealth represented a "fall from grace."

Once it began to match the nobility in wealth, the bourgeoisie established a plutocracy, based on material goods rather than on hereditary privilege. As for social prestige, that could be achieved through the purchase of great landed estates and made-to-order coats-of-arms. Some of the great bourgeoisie became landowners by marriage, by making gifts to the king, or by less legitimate means. Others, unimpressed by the trappings of nobility, kept their attention riveted upon account books, profit and loss, supply and demand, and whatever material matters might pay for a superior standard of living.

There were conflicts between bourgeoisie and nobility, and between bourgeoisie and proletariat. To the nobility the bourgeoisie were upstarts, *nouveaux riches,* who were seeking to smash the ancient privileges of the well-born. To the proletariat the bourgeoisie was the dominant class which reaped profits from the toil of the worker and gave in return only a subsistence wage.

Bourgeois Development. The development of the bourgeoisie may be divided into two periods of roughly equal length. From approximately 1500 to 1700 it favored the mercantilist policy of a strong state and the regulation of commerce and industry. To achieve these ends, it allied itself with the monarchy during the Age of Absolutism. All mercantilist policies were designed to increase the effectiveness of this alliance. The following excerpts from a letter of Louis XIV addressed to the town officers and people of Marseilles in 1664 indicate the favorable attitude of the king toward "our merchants":

> We are setting apart, in the expense of the State, a million *livres* each year, for the encouragement of manufactures and the increase of navigation. . . .

> We shall assist by money from our royal treasury all those who wish to re-establish old manufactures or to undertake new ones. . . .

> We are giving orders to all our ambassadors to make, in our name, all proper efforts to assure for our merchants commercial freedom.

During the first half of the modern era, the bourgeoisie was unable to govern directly, for the landed aristocracy still controlled the legislative institutions. Deprived of political power, the bourgeoisie therefore adopted any and all means to protect and promote its own interests, including smuggling, bribery, and corruption. The generally low business ethics of the day may be attributed in part to bourgeois resentment of its lack of political power.

In the second period of its development, beginning about 1700, the bourgeoisie found the alliance with the monarchy too hampering. It began to shake off restraints, and worked for the development of representative institutions which would give it more political control. It insisted that now the state should be limited to the function of protecting life and property, and it demanded freedom for itself in socio-economic and political life. In England it steadily increased its capacity for resistance to the royal will. In the French Revolution it entered into an alliance with the loosely organized proletariat to combat the combination of king, nobility, and clergy. The nineteenth century was the century of bourgeois dominance. In the meantime, its youthful rival, the industrial proletariat, began to build up its power, and think and act in terms of social challenge.

6. Emergence of the Proletariat

Meaning. The term "proletariat" designates the class of industrial workers who sell their labor power for wages to a capitalist entrepreneur for a definite period of time. The word is derived from the Latin *proletarius,* a citizen of the lowest class, who was useful to the state by producing children (from *proles,* offspring). The modern proletariat possessses legal freedom, which distinguishes it from slaves or serfs. As a class it includes skilled, semi-skilled, and unskilled workers in capitalist enterprise, with the exception of technical or executive employees. The term "working class" is a bit broader, including not only the proletariat but also such groups as servants, domestic workers, and other semi-proletarians who receive low wages. Both proletariat and working class should be distinguished from the word "masses," which cuts across class lines, and includes proletarians, semi-proletarians, and others—in other words, working-class, petty-bourgeois, and agrarian elements.

Rise of the Proletariat. The rise of the proletariat in modern times is closely linked with the development of capitalism. Industrial capitalism could function only if it possessed a large free-labor market. As the precapitalist medieval order of society declined, there arose a large army of individuals without roots and socially shipwrecked, beggars, vagabonds, and adventurers, men who were eventually absorbed into the proletariat along with the urban workers. In the meantime, business and industrial entrepreneurs complained that they could not obtain a sufficient supply of labor. The most important factor in the emergence of the proletariat was the expropriation of peasant land under the enclosure system, which forced the peasants into the towns, where they became the first generation of this new class. Added to this was the gradual disintegration of the guild system, as the journeymen broke away from the masters and became members of either the bourgeoisie or the proletariat. Other contributing factors were the dissolution of the monasteries, the ruin caused by constant wars, and the effects of oppressive taxation.

Development of the Proletariat. Slowly but surely the proletariat developed a consciousness and a movement of its own. In the words of Alfred Meusel: "The early proletariat in the period of its emergence was not a conscious, independent historical force. It had no rights, neither suffrage nor freedom of combination, the absence of which in turn expressed the lack of an independent proletarian will. . . . By reason of the tension between the passivity of the proletariat and its wretched condition, urgently demanding relief, the workers directed their hopes beyond their own class. They looked for a god or a king made omnipotent by divine grace, for a savior who would relieve them of the burden of independent activity and responsibility."

Thrown together in large numbers in slum areas, having nothing to sell but their labor, subjected to abuses both by their employers and an unkind fate, the urban workers led a miserable life. They were always threatened by the evil of unemployment—the scourge of proletarian life. It was in this atmosphere that the proletariat eventually fashioned a unanimity of opinion and molded its class aspirations. By the nineteenth century it had increased in numbers and possessed a new social consciousness. It began to gird itself for a decisive contest with the bourgeoisie for political, social, and economic power. Its leaders proclaimed that just as it was the historical task of the bourgeoisie to replace the feudal and guild systems by capitalism, so was it the mission of the proletariat to substitute common ownership of the means of production for private ownership.

7. The Peasant Bypassed

The Peasant and the Good Earth. The status of the European peasant changed little in the opening centuries of the modern era. Technically a free man, he was still in practice bound to the soil. For a thousand years it had been the same: toiling and weather-worn, he had worked in the fields from dawn to dusk. For him the meaning of life lay in his relationship to the land. Badly clothed, wretchedly fed, ill-housed, he lived in ignorance, squalor, and misery. His economic status did not improve in proportion to that of other classes. The bourgeois merchant could not picture the toiling brute beneath him as a man like himself, with inalienable human dignities and rights. If evicted from his land, the peasant joined the swelling ranks of the agricultural wage-earners, or if he deserted the countryside for the towns he found himself sinking into a new type of bondage in the slums. The emergence of the proletariat as a class meant nothing to him. It was not until the late nineteenth and early twentieth centuries that the peasant had any inkling of any community of his own interests with those of the urban worker.

Peasantry in France. In seventeenth-century France, nine-tenths of the Third Estate was composed of peasants who eked out a miserable existence just as they had done for centuries. The great majority, some 16 millions, were free from the restrictions of serfdom; they could go and come as they pleased,

A peasant delivers dues to feudal lord.

marry, buy and sell property. But very few held full ownership rights. Some two-fifths of the land in France was in the hands of peasant copyholders, while the clergy, the nobility, and the Crown each controlled one-fifth. The lot of the sharecroppers (*métayers*), those who did not own land, was miserable indeed, for few were ever out of debt. The farm laborers worked only during the busy season, and for the remainder of the year subsisted as well

as they could. Despite the fertility of the soil, the peasant population remained in constant fear of famine. Above all, the peasant wanted some measure of relief from the vexatious manorial dues and the government's system of both direct and indirect taxation.

Peasantry in England. As the old system of agriculture in England began to break down during the sixteenth century, the rural landlords, finding sheep-raising more profitable than grain-growing, enclosed their lands and converted them into sheep pastures. This was one method of responding to the demands of an expanding commerce. The process of enclosure brought ruin to thousands of peasants. Laws pushed through Parliament demanded that the peasants show legal title to their property, which for most of them was simply impossible. Most had accepted it as a matter of course that the land belonged to the family and that it was passed down from father to son.

By this "legal" chicanery the large landowners in effect expropriated the property. The result was a transformation of rural society. Country squires began to rent land in lots of 50, 100, or 200 acres to tenant farmers and then hired agricultural laborers to cultivate what remained. Here and there especially vigorous yeomen, or freeholders, managed to hold onto small estates. Those who remained in the country areas had to work as agricultural laborers, while others who drifted into the towns took their place in the urban working class. The distressing results were described by Oliver Goldsmith in *The Deserted Village:*

Ill fares the land, to hastening ills a prey,
Where wealth accumulates, and men decay;
Princes and lord may flourish, or may fade;
A breath can make them, as a breath has
　　made;
But a bold peasantry, their country's pride,
When once destroyed, can ever be supplied.

Peasants' Revolts. The condition of the French and English peasants was bad in the opening centuries of the modern era, but it was better than that of the German, Italian, Russian, Polish, or Spanish peasants. There was intense dissatisfaction. The peasants were not yet conscious of the reasons for their suffering. The pattern of peasants' revolts, which had taken place sporadically throughout the Middle Ages, continued on through the early modern period. The classic examples of this type of rebellion and its suppression were the revolts which took place in the Germanies, beginning in 1524. Oppressed by taxation and unbearable living conditions, the German peasants found in Martin Luther's preaching of "Christian liberty" a justification for a general social change. The bitterness engendered by centuries of misery broke into revolt. Beginning in southwestern Germany, the movement spread rapidly. Enraged peasants destroyed monasteries and castles and proposed to slaughter all the "godless priests and nobles."

Michael Eisenhart, a citizen of Rothenburg-ob-der-Tauber, witnessed the revolt and kept a running account of the events in his diary:

March 21. On Tuesday, thirty or forty peasants got together in a mob at Rothenburg, purchased a kettledrum, and marched about the town. They got together again on Thursday and on Friday, as many as four hundred.

March 26. On Tuesday eight hundred peasants came together. Those who would not join them willingly they forced to do so or took their property, as happened to a peasant at Wettring. . . .

April 30. The monastery at Anhausen was plundered and burned in the night. The peasants also attacked the monastery at Schwarzach, and the castle of Reichelsberg was burned.

May 15. The peasants attack the castle at Würzburg and scale the walls, but all are killed. The peasants attempt to get possession of Rothenburg by conspiracy, but are ejected without bloodshed.

May 21. Certain Hohenlohe peasant burn their lord's castle. On the next Monday, Margrave Casimir proceeds with his forces to subdue and punish the peasants. Hans Krelein the Older, priest at Wernitz, was beheaded, with four peasants, at Leuterschausen. Seven have their fingers cut off. At Kitzingen fifty-eight have their eyes put out and are forbidden to enter the town again.

On Friday before Whitsuntide the forces of the Swabian League slay four thousand peasants at Königshofen.

On Monday after Whitsunday eight thousand peasants are slaughtered by the troops of the League near Buttart. In all these battles the League lost not over one hundred and fifty men.

Alarmed by the extent of the rebellion, Luther called for counter-measures: "It is right and lawful to slay at the first opportunity a rebellious person." He was taken at his word. The nobles savagely put down the revolt, and the peasants once more sank into hopeless misery.

⤏{ KEY READING }⤎

EUROPEAN POPULATION DISTRIBUTION IN THE SEVENTEENTH CENTURY

George N. Clark, *The Seventeenth Century* (Oxford, 1931), pp. 1 ff., *passim.* By permission of the Clarendon Press.

IN THE FOLLOWING passage, George N. Clark, an English historian, discusses the population of seventeenth-century Europe. Today we have fairly accurate statistics on population, but in the seventeenth century there were scarcely any statistics to be had, and those which existed were seldom used. No European country had a regular national census before the French Revolution. Historians depend upon elaborate guesswork to judge the size of the European population before the eighteenth century.

There is, indeed, no doubt at all that the population of Europe, taken all together, and of almost every part of it, as long as the unit taken is not so small as a single town or village, was very much smaller than it is now. There are villages and towns which have shrunk since then; there are even a few fair-sized districts, such as the Scottish Highlands, which have become less populous because their industries have decayed; but these are exceptions. No place in Europe is far from some countryside which is much more thickly inhabited than it was then. Roughly speaking, this change has been brought about in the last century and a half. It is connected with the great modern changes in sanitation, and in the technique and organization of industry and commerce. It has been greatest in those countries which have been most completely "industrialized," though exactly how or why it came about we do not yet understand. . . .

The next question which suggests itself is how population was distributed about the Continent, and this has two sides: one economic and the other political. About the economic question, however, the question of how the denser aggregations of people were caused by their economic activities, little need be said. Where certain trades or manufactures flourished, towns grew up and increased. Although some of the great towns of former days, Lisbon, Antwerp, Milan, Venice, were dwindling, others such as London, Paris, Vienna, Amsterdam, and many lesser places multiplied exceedingly. Where towns prosper the country is apt to prosper and employ more hands. The population of Europe was still predominantly rural, and although the growth of towns was a characteristic of the period, this balance was nowhere seriously disturbed. But it is unlikely that we shall ever be able to estimate at all closely the density of population except in a few particular cases, or to decide how it was affected by differences of geography, social custom, and law, and how districts became congested or relieved themselves of an excessive population. The estimates that exist of the density of population in different regions follow in the main political boundaries. They show a great variation from Italy, which besides its great cities had rich country resources, to the bare north of Sweden, Norway, and Finland.

The order given by Dr. Beloch is this (the numbers standing for souls to the square kilometre): Italy, 44; Netherlands, 40; France, 34; England and Wales, 30; Germany, 28; Spain and Portugal, 17; Denmark (with its frontiers of 1918), 15; Poland with Prussia, 14; Scotland and Ireland, 12½; Sweden, Norway, and Finland, 1.3; the average for all these countries being less than 20.

These regions mostly correspond to political units or groups of units, and a comparison of their population is, of course, a good starting-point for a study of their political relations. Here not only the density is interesting, but also the total number, which is a matter of density multiplied by area, so that the order is not at all the same. Germany comes first with about 20 millions, but Germany, by which the Empire is here meant, is rather an aggregate than a single unit. Its strongest unit during most of the century was the Habsburg power, and this appears to have had in the middle of the sixteenth century about 5½ millions, 2 millions in the "old" dominions (Austria, Styria, Carinthia, Carniola, and the Tyrol), the rest in Bohemia, Moravia, Silesia. Switzerland, still nominally a part of the Empire, though not reckoned in with it here, had about a third of a million. After the Empire in population came France, with 16 millions. Spain and Portugal together had about 10, perhaps 8 or more of these being in Spain. England and Wales had about 4½, Scotland and Ireland 2 millions between them, or perhaps a million each. The Dutch Republic was well under 3 millions. Poland, with Prussia, which was still nominally under its suzerainty, had in all its enormous area perhaps 11 million people: as late as 1713 East Prussia had still less than half a million. In 1600 Sweden, Norway, and Finland together had less than a million and a half; Denmark, as its frontiers were before 1919, about 600,000. Politically divided as they were in 1600 these countries had, Sweden about 1½ millions, Denmark rather more than a million. No less than 13 million people, more than there were in any unitary state except France, were divided among the petty principalities and republics of Italy. Venice had nearer two millions than one, Milan more than one, Florence more than three-quarters of a million, Naples nearly as much; but the main point about them is that they were all comparatively small, so that the history of Italy in this century is passive rather than active, and yet that altogether they formed a considerable part of Europe, and therefore made a very tempting bait for invaders who wanted money and men. For Russia and Turkey no plausible estimate is possible.

⸻ HISTORICAL INTERPRETATION ⸻

JEROME BLUM ON REVOLTS OF THE EUROPEAN PEASANTRY

Jerome Blum, *The European Peasantry from the Thirteenth to the Nineteenth Century*, Publication No. 33, Service Center for Teachers of History, The American Historical Association (Washington, D. C., 1960), pp. 18–20. By permission of The American Historical Association.

IN 1800 THE PEASANTS who lived on the land made up 90 per cent or more of the population of nearly every European country. Europe's economy and its social organization rested predominantly on the utilization of the soil. How the peasants reacted against oppressive conditions was described in this passage by Jerome Blum.

Unlike the variations in legal status, there was near unanimity throughout Europe so far as the political position of the peasantry was concerned. With the exception of only a few countries, the peasants, whether free, half free, or serfs, had no voice in their governments. No matter what the form of government was, nor how enlightened its policies may have been, most peasants had no formal, organized way of expressing their political, social, and economic interests and demands, or of influencing the decisions of their rulers at the national or provincial level. . . .

Most peasants, most of the time, accepted without protest their exclusion from participation in their governments. To their minds, national assemblies and lawmaking and statecraft were matters for kings, and churchmen, and nobles, and city people. They grumbled about the legal and economic powers their lord had over them, the taxes they had to pay the state and the church, the laws that forbade them to hunt and fish and cut wood wherever they wanted, the costs of quartering soldiers in their homes, the maintenance work they had to do on the roads and bridges, and so on. They tried—as men have ever since organized society began—to evade their obligations, and they paid up peacefully enough when they were caught.

But every once in a while they would suddenly decide that they had had enough, and that they must fight back against the domination and exactions of those who called themselves their betters. Often only a single village would rise; at other times whole regions would be convulsed by mass discontent and disturbances. Most of their protests were of a passive nature, such as the concerted refusal to render certain obligations to their lords or to the state, flight to some new frontier, or to the cities. But sometimes they seized up their scythes and pitchforks and axes, and, driven by some blind fury, poured out of their villages to beat or murder the lords and officials who ruled over them, and to pillage the homes and burn the records of their oppressors.

Every land of Europe, from England across to Russia, experienced these troubles, though in some countries they were far less frequent than in others. Many of these disturbances, whether passive or violent, seemed to have no immediate cause. Peasants who for years and generations had been meeting the same obligations and living under the same conditions with no sign of discontent, without warning would resort to disobedience or violence. Often, though, some new or increased exaction, so some change in economic or religious conditions, provided the spark. Sometimes they were led by one of their fellow villagers, and sometimes by a peasant or an adventurer from outside. Still other risings seemed to have been entirely leaderless. A rumor might sweep through the countryside, carried perhaps by peddlers or vagabonds, or villagers back from the market town, or priests, and as if by magic the peasants would decide that they must right old standing wrongs.

Nearly all the disturbances burned themselves out in a short time. The odds were all against the peasants. They lack the organization, weapons, and most important, the leadership, needed to triumph over their opponents. Most of their risings gained them nothing beyond the momentary exhilaration that their acts of violence must have brought. But not all of them were without effect. In certain lands peasant unrest and violence played an important part in convincing governments that changes had to be made.

❧ [TEN BASIC BOOKS] ☙

THE SOCIAL STRUCTURE IN FLUX

1. Clark, George N., *The Seventeenth Century*, 2nd ed. (New York, 1947).†
2. Goodwin, Albert, ed., *The European Nobility in the Eighteenth Century* (London, 1953).
3. Hazard, Paul, *The European Mind: The Critical Years, 1680–1715* (New Haven, Conn., 1953).†
4. Larkin, Paschal, *Property in the Eighteenth Century* (Dublin, 1930).
5. Laski, Harold J., *The Rise of European Liberalism* (London, 1936, R. 1963).†
6. Ogg, David, *Europe in the Seventeenth Century*, 8th ed. (New York, 1960).†
7. Smith, Preserved, *A History of Modern Culture*, 2 vols. (New York, 1930–1934).†
8. Turberville, Arthur S., *Commonwealth and Restoration* (London, 1936).
9. Willey, Basil, *The Eighteenth Century Background* (New York, 1941).†
10. Wingfield-Stratford, Esmé C., *The Squire and His Relations* (London, 1956).

PART II

"L'ÉTAT, C'EST MOI!"

THE AGE OF ABSOLUTISM

1485–1789

THE DIVINE RIGHT OF KINGS[1]
Jacques Bossuet, Bishop of Meaux,
1670

IT APPEARS from all this that the person of the king is sacred, and that to attack him in any way is sacrilege. God has the kings anointed by his prophets with the holy unction in like manner as he has bishops and altars anointed. But even without the external application in thus being anointed, they are by their very office the representatives of the divine majesty deputed by Providence for the execution of His purposes. . . .

There is something religious in the respect accorded to a prince. The service of God and the respect for kings are bound together. St. Peter unites these two duties when he says, "Fear God. Honor the king." . . .

But kings, although their power comes from on high, as has been said, should not regard themselves as masters of that power to use it at their pleasure. . . . They must employ it with fear and self-restraint, as a thing coming from God, and of which God will demand an account. . . .

Kings should tremble then as they use the power God has granted them; and let them think how horrible is the sacrilege if they use for evil a power which comes from God. We behold kings seated upon the throne of the Lord, bearing in their hand the sword which God Himself has given them. . . .

The royal power is absolute. With the aim of making this truth hateful and insufferable, many writers have tried to confound absolute government with the arbitrary government. But no two things could be more unlike, as we shall show when we come to speak of justice.

The prince need render account of his acts to no one. "I counsel thee to keep the king's commandment, and that in regard of the oath of God. Be not hasty to go out of His sight: stand not on an evil thing for He doeth whatsoever pleaseth Him. Where the word of a king is, there is power: and who may say unto him, What doest thou? Whoso keepeth the commandment shall feel no evil thing." Without this absolute authority the king could neither do good nor repress evil. . . .

I do not call majesty that pomp which surrounds kings or that exterior magnificence which dazzles the vulgar. That is but the reflection of majesty and not majesty itself. Majesty is the image of the grandeur of God in the prince.

God is infinite, God is all. The prince, as prince, is not regarded as a private person: he is a public personage, all the state is in him; the will of all the people is included in his.

---

[1] Jacques-Bénigne Bossuet, *Oeuvres Complètes*, ed. by F. Lachat (Paris, 1862–1866), XXIII, 533 ff., 558 ff., 642 ff. Trans. in J. H. Robinson, *Readings in European History* (New York, 1934), II, 274–277. By permission of Ginn and Company.

As all perfection and all strength are united in God, so all the power of individuals is united in the person of the prince. What grandeur that a single man should embody so much!

The power of God makes itself felt in a moment from one extremity of the earth to another. Royal power works at the same time throughout all the realm. It holds all the realm in position, as God holds the earth. Should God withdraw His hand, the earth would fall to pieces; should the king's authority cease in the realm, all would be in confusion.

Look at the prince in his cabinet. Thence go out the orders which cause the magistrates and the captains, the citizens and the soldiers, the provinces and the armies on land and on sea, to work in concert. He is the image of God, who, seated on His throne high in the heavens, makes all nature move. . . .

Finally, let us put together the things so great and so august which we have said about royal authority. Behold an immense people united in a single person; behold this holy power, paternal and absolute; behold the secret cause which governs the whole body of the state, contained in a single head: you see the image of God in the king, and you have the idea of royal majesty. God is holiness itself, goodness itself, and power itself. In the image of these things lies the majesty of the prince.

So great is this majesty that it cannot reside in the prince as in its source; it is borrowed from God, who gives it to him for the good of the people, for whom it is good to be checked by a superior force. Something of divinity itself is attached to princes and inspires fear in the people. The king should not forget this. "I have said,"—it is God who speaks—"I have said, Ye are gods; and all of you are children of the Most High. But ye shall die like men, and fall like one of the princes." "I have said, Ye are gods"; that is to say, you have in your authority, and you bear on your forehead, a divine imprint. "You are the children of the Most High"; it is he who has established your power for the good of mankind. But, O gods of flesh and blood, gods of clay and dust, "ye shall die like men, and fall like princes." Grandeur separates men for a little time, but a common fall makes them all equal at the end.

O kings, exercise your power then boldly, for it is divine and salutary for human kind, but exercise it with humility. You are endowed with it from without. At bottom it leaves you feeble, it leaves you mortal, it leaves you sinners, and charges you before God with a heavy account.

8

Greatness and Decay: Absolute Monarchy in Spain

THE FALL of Spain from its high position in Europe was gradual, but the causes of its decay were financial. It had to pay for the great plans of Charles V and Philip II, and it received no national advantage to recompense it for the injurious results of their failure. Philip II left to his successor a high position, an impoverished exchequer, and a ruinous system of government. It required only a few years for the last two legacies to destroy the first.

—MANDELL CREIGHTON

1. The Empire of Charles V

Background of Hapsburg Power. As the unity of the Holy Roman Empire disintegrated and fragments were welded into national states, monarchs enlarged their personal holdings and assumed governmental functions that formerly had been the province of their vassals. They now controlled rights of taxation, administration of justice, regulation of trade, and military leadership. Their position took on authority and glamor.

The growth of absolute monarchy in Spain was comparatively rapid. In the thirteenth century what is today Spain was divided into four Christian kingdoms in the north of the peninsula— Aragon, Castile, León, and Navarre —and the large southern half of the peninsula in possession of the Muslims. In 1469 the marriage of Ferdinand of Aragon and Isabella of Castile united the two strongest Christian kingdoms in Spain. With the capture of Granada in 1492, eight centuries of Muslim rule came to an end. Ferdinand and Isabella expelled both Muslims and Jews from the country. The Spanish monarchy, through war, diplomatic negotiation, and marriage, became for a time the most powerful in the world.

At the beginning of the sixteenth century,

Spain together with France moved into the disunited Italies. By 1504 the Spaniards had defeated the French, annexed Naples, and assumed control of the Italian peninsula. Ferdinand then arranged a series of marriages to strengthen his dynasty. He married one daughter, Catherine, to the English heir, soon to become Henry VIII, and another to Philip of Hapsburg, son of the Holy Roman Emperor, Maximilian I. The offspring of this latter union, Charles V, inherited a huge domain: the Hapsburg possessions in Austria, the Germanies, and the Netherlands; the Burgundian lands (through the marriage of Maxmilian with Mary of Burgundy); and Spain and her possessions in the Italian peninsula and in the New World.

Charles V Ascends the Throne. When his grandfather Ferdinand died in 1516, Charles V became king of the Spanish dominions. On the death of his grandfather Maximilian in 1519 he succeeded to the Hapsburg possessions as Holy Roman Emperor. His accession may be attributed to the long-established tradition (since 1273) of electing Hapsburgs to the post. Some energetic bribery also helped him to the title. With his imposing array of possessions, Charles seemed to be the most

Charles V, Holy Roman Emperor. Painting by Titian.

Charles V in Spain. Although born and reared in the Netherlands, Charles found his home in Spain. In time he became a thorough-going Spaniard, winning the loyalty of his people there after convincing them that Spain was the center of his empire and that their interests were his own. Although he allowed no encroachments on his absolutism, he showed his respect for constitutional rights by summoning regular meetings of the Castilian and Aragonese parliaments. He made no serious attempts to lessen the power of the Spanish feudal nobility. Rigidly orthodox, he was determined to destroy the Muslim population of the southern provinces, thereby diminishing Spain's most industrious class. Although he encouraged Spanish colonization in the New World, he regarded America merely as a source of gold and silver, ignoring its potentialities for commerce and industry. This policy, also pursued by the Spanish aristocracy and Charles' own successors, helps explain in part why Spain's colonial empire disintegrated.

Charles V versus Francis I: Hapsburg versus Valois. The rivalry between Charles V and Francis I became one of the determining factors in European history. France was surrounded by Hapsburg territory, reason enough for Francis, for self-preservation, to seek to break the Hapsburg power. Both Charles and Francis laid claim to the territory throughout Europe—Burgundy, the Netherlands provinces of Flanders and Artois, Navarre, the duchy of Milan, and the kingdom of Naples. Added to these grounds for war was the fact that Francis was a candidate for the imperial title, which led to a strong sense of rivalry between the two young monarchs.

The war began in 1521 after Charles had obtained Henry VIII and Pope Leo X as allies. It was waged in three areas—in the Netherlands, in Navarre, and in the Italies, with the fighting concentrated in the Italies. The French were driven from the Duchy of Milan, and out of the Italies altogether in 1522. Francis invaded the peninsula again in the spring of 1525. Success this time seemed certain. But in the bloody battle of Pavia, the imperial troops of Charles V destroyed the French army and

powerful monarch in Europe, but appearances were deceiving. His states were so scattered and so diverse in nationality, language, economic interests, and culture, that he could never apply any consistent policy to all of them. It was not enough to think in terms merely of Hapsburg aggrandizement.

The nineteen-year-old Charles V was a young man of common sense, patience, and determination, but he had some powerful competition in Europe. In 1519 almost all of Western Europe owed allegiance to three young and ambitious monarchs, of whom Charles was one. Francis I of France, a little older than Charles, had already distinguished himself by the conquest of Milan. Vain, selfish, and frivolous, he ruled less territory than Charles, but his domain was one compact national state and he held absolute control of it. The Tudor king, Henry VIII of England, was pleased by the rivalry between Charles of Hapsburg and Francis of Valois. His goal was to keep the two so well-balanced that England, relatively weak, might profit and become the determining factor in European affairs.

captured Francis. The latter was forced to sign the Treaty of Madrid (1526), by which he renounced his pretensions to Italian territory. When Francis threatened war again, Charles V, in 1542, allied with Henry VIII, marched into France and forced the French monarch to sign a humiliating treaty. With the death of Francis in 1547 came a truce, but Francis's son, Henry II (r. 1547–1559), carried on the feud. In 1556, when Charles V voluntarily laid down his scepter, the strife was not yet ended.

Charles V and the Germanies. Charles V was unfortunate in his relationship with the Germanies. Although this area was the ancestral home of the Hapsburg dynasty, Charles made it a point to spend as little time there as possible. He was never able fully to control the complex forces at work there: the insistence of the princes upon territorial sovereignty; the demands of the free cities for independence; the rivalries between social classes; and the difficult religious differences. No centralized force was strong enough to overcome the forces which made for disunity in the Germanies.

In 1521 Charles called a great Imperial Diet to deal with the heresy of Luther and to introduce reforms in the imperial government. He was unsuccessful in both attempts. The Lutherans went ahead and organized their church despite his opposition. To reform the imperial government, Charles appointed a council of regency which was to rule during his absence. But, without military or financial means, the council found itself powerless. It could not suppress the rebellion of Franz von Sickingen and the Rhineland knights in 1522 or the Peasants' Revolt which came a few years later. Unable to give his full attention to the area because he was busy fighting the Turks, Charles V found that he could not solve the irritating German problems.

Further Problems: The Turkish Menace. Charles V's difficulties in the Germanies were aggravated by the periodic attempts of the Ottoman Turks to invade Europe. In 1453 the Turks had captured Constantinople. In 1526

they defeated the king of Hungary, and in 1529 Suleiman II, the Magnificent (1494–1566) very nearly captured Vienna. Alarmed by Turkish persistence in storming the citadels of Europe, Charles marched against them, and forced them back to the Danube (1532). His earnest hope of reconquering Hungary for Christendom was frustrated. In 1547 he bought off the Turks with a promise of annual tribute. It was a precarious peace, attained partly by recognizing the right of the Turks to the greater part of Hungary. Charles V now turned his attention to the fermenting rebellion in the Germanies.

Religious War in the Germanies. While Charles V was away campaigning against the Turks, Protestantism advanced rapidly in the Germanies. In the early 1530's the chief Protestant states, convinced that Charles would one day return to his Hapsburg lands to deal with them, organized the League of Schmalkalden for mutual defense. Charles was engaged meanwhile in campaigns against the Turks and French, and was faced with rebellion in the Netherlands. By the time he was ready to deal with it, the Schmalkaldic League included half of the Germanies.

Charles opened his war against the League in 1546, entrusting his campaign to the energetic Duke of Alva (1508–1583). Taking advantage of the lack of unity among the League members, Alva turned on the Protestant princes one at a time and administered one crushing defeat after another. But it was much like trying to stamp out quicksilver. Although the princes were defeated, it was far too late to eliminate Protestant Lutheranism among the people. Eventually, Charles was forced to sue for peace. The Peace of Augsburg (1555) established Protestantism over a great part of the Germanies (see page 83), and eliminated further religious war for more than half a century. The conflict was to break out again in 1618 in the Thirty Years' War.

Abdication of Charles V, 1556. Charles V failed to halt the advance of Protestantism because he had challenged an enemy far too powerful for his armies or for his Diets. Interested not merely in the destiny of Spain but also in the welfare of the Church and the European situation in general, he had two basic aims: (1) to restore the religious unity of Christendom, and (2) to refashion the Holy Roman Empire into a pillar of power. He failed in these larger objectives, even if he did hold his broken realm together by defeating the French in the Italies and by frustrating the Turks in their desire to overrun Europe. In the long run he mistook for a purely theological dispute what was fundamentally a politico-economic struggle for the mastery of Europe. Eventually, he saw the unity of the Holy Roman Empire, long a shadowy pretense anyhow, destroyed in a conflict of irreconcilable national interests. In 1556, at the age of fifty-six, ill, disillusioned, discouraged, and disappointed in his ambitions, he abdicated and retired into a monastery. There, at Yuste in the valley of Estremadura, he spent the three remaining years of his life. He left a legacy of troublesome difficulties to his successor.

2. The Reign of Philip II, 1556–1598

Philip II (1527–1598). Philip II came to the throne in 1556 while Spain was still at the height of her glory, still retaining her position as the greatest power in Europe. After the untimely death of his first wife, Philip in 1554 married Mary Tudor, daughter of Henry VIII and the Catholic English queen, Catherine of Aragon. When the unattractive Mary, older than Philip, failed to produce an heir, the marriage foundered.

Philip II more of a Spaniard than his father, inherited—in addition to Spain—the Netherlands, Naples, and Spanish America. With a powerful army and navy, he seemed to be in an advantageous position; but he was faced with an impossible burden in administering both Spain and the overseas possessions. The government was supposed to function through councils of ministers who were to advise the monarch, but in practice the burden of administration fell upon Philip. Unfortunately, he was pursued by the same ill-fortune that had plagued his father.

Domestic Policies. In a country broken up by the separatist spirit, Philip sought to assert absolute authority. He made it clear to the nobility and to the Cortes that he would tolerate no disobedience. He tried to centralize the administration without disturbing the rights of the old kingdoms, but he invariably showed preference for Castile at the expense of Aragon.

From his father, Philip inherited an empty treasury. Although gold and silver poured into Spain from the American mines, they could not satisfy the demands of domestic life and foreign wars. Throughout his reign Philip II found himself, despite the apparently inexhaustible wealth from Mexico and Peru, overburdened with debt. Both Church and aristocracy were careful to avoid contributing revenue to the state in proportion to their wealth. Philip had to resort to such money-raising schemes as a crippling sales tax (the *alcabala*) and the sale of governmental offices. Industry and agriculture were both hampered by heavy taxation.

Among the more pressing problems was that of the Moriscos, the "converted" Moors living in the southern and eastern provinces of Spain. Still strongly attached to their former religion, the Moriscos grudgingly observed the outward forms of Christian practice, but retained many Moorish customs. Spanish Christians demanded that Philip "Hispaniolize the Moriscos." In 1566 he issued a ban on Moorish customs and gave the Moriscos three years in which to learn Castilian Spanish. In 1569 the Moriscos rose in rebellion, only to be crushed by Philip's army. The next year Philip decreed the exile of all Moriscos from Andalusia, a southern province. The expulsion was accomplished with great brutality. The Moriscos were finally expelled from Spain in 1609 by Philip's successor.

A fervent Catholic, Philip II made it a goal of his life to extirpate Protestantism in Spain and her possessions. To achieve this end he gave a free hand to the Inquisition, which had been revived by Ferdinand and Isabella as early as 1480. Under the impulse of the Inquisition, Protestant heretics were burned to death in a mass ceremony called *auto-da-fé* ("act of faith"). Great crowds flocked to these

An *auto-da-fé* procession in Spain. Facsimile of a large copper engraving in a work of 1692 entitled *Historia Inquisitionis.*

morbid rites. While the Inquisition may well have cleared Spanish soil of Protestantism, its intolerant spirit helped divorce Spain from the mainstream of European thought.

Foreign Policy of Philip II. During the opening years of his reign, Philip II resumed warfare with Henry II of France in the seemingly interminable Hapsburg-Valois conflicts. With English assistance, Philip won several notable victories. But both monarchs sought peace when it became obvious that Protestantism was spreading rapidly in their realms. By the Treaty of Cateau-Cambrésis (1559), Spain and France agreed (1) to relinquish lands captured from each other since 1551; (2) to recognize Spanish claims to Franche-Comté and Spain's Italian holdings; (3) to recognize

French claims to the strategic bishoprics of Metz, Toul, and Verdun; and (4) to arrange a marriage between Philip II and Elizabeth of Valois, daughter of Henry II. This was the first of a series of great European settlements which preceded the Peace of Westphalia in 1648. Philip's marriage to Elizabeth of Valois encouraged him to interfere in French affairs, and this led to a decade of war with Henry of Navarre, from 1589 to 1598. Defeated in this conflict, Philip was forced by the Treaty of Vervins to restore his conquests to France. The peace merely reaffirmed the Treaty of Cateau-Cambrésis. Philip's meddling in French affairs thus brought him nothing but further strain on an already overstrained treasury.

Philip II Checks the Turks. From his father,

Philip II inherited the necessity of holding the Mediterranean front against the Turks. Charles V had temporarily checked the Ottoman menace to Western Europe by bribing the Turks to remain outside his territories. Early in the reign of Philip II, the Turks under Selim II, son of Suleiman the Magnificent, began to ravage Christian lands, pillaging and burning cities and carrying Christians into captivity. At the instigation of the pope, a Holy League was formed, uniting the Papal States, Spain, Venice, Genoa, and the Knights of Malta in a coalition under the military leadership of Don John of Austria, Philip II's half brother. On October 7, 1571, the coalition engaged a great Turkish fleet in the Gulf of Corinth, off Lepanto. The Turks lost 20,000 men and most of their 273 warships. The victors freed 15,000 Christians from slavery at the oars of Turkish men-of-war. The victory at Lepanto, one of the great naval battles of history, marked the turning point in the struggle to rid Western Europe of the Turkish invaders. It was hailed with jubilation throughout Christendom. But dissension between Spaniards and Venetians worked against adequate exploitation of the triumph: Turkish power in the Mediterranean remained strong and formidable.

The Spanish Armada, 1588. Angered by English adventurers who were aiding the Dutch and preying on Spanish commerce, and unable to humble England by indirect means, Philip II in 1588 sent his "Invincible Armada" with 27,000 men to destroy Queen Elizabeth's navy. It was an unfortunate enterprise, which foundered on the rocks of British patriotism and seamanship, and some disastrous weather. The maneuverable English fleet easily dispersed the Spanish fleet into the violent waters of the North Sea where, buffeted by storms, the Spanish Armada perished. (*See page 160.*) The destruction of the Armada cost Spain her supremacy on the seas and opened the way for British colonization of America. Spain never recovered from this disaster. The greatness and glory of Spain were nearing an end.

Spain Overseas. During the reign of Philip II the Spanish empire overseas was expanded.

Royal appointees went to the New World to represent the crown and to drain its riches back to the homeland. All economic life in the colonies was regulated in favor of the mother country. A convoy system was organized to protect Spanish ships from both pirates and British sea dogs. But the great Spanish empire in the New World was destined for an ignominious end. Unable to compete with either the British or the French, Spain gradually lost her hold. She left behind, however, a residue of Spanish culture which has persisted to the present day.

Historical Controversy: Philip II, Saint or Sinner? Radically conflicting assessments of Philip II's character show how difficult it is for the historian to remain objective when he makes moral judgments. The Spanish king remains the classic case of how an individual may be judged from exactly opposite points of view. On the one side, he is described by his Spanish Catholic contemporary, Luis Cabrera de Córdoba (1559–1623), as a prince of many virtues, a wise, just monarch, a devoted father, a pious Christian. "He was strong in adversity, restrained in prosperity. . . . Experience, the guide to understanding, ruled his will and made him the soul of prudence." To his subjects he was Philip the Prudent, greathearted, devoted to Spain, a saintly symbol of the Catholic Counter-Reformation.

The other side, represented by the American historian John Lothrop Motley, depicted Philip II as the incarnation of evil, a royal criminal, a man who believed himself not a king but a god, a murderously cruel fanatic, an administrator of perfect despotism. (*See page 133.*) To this stern Protestant-moralist view others added the labels of "Devil of the South," "The Spider King," "Escorial's Father of Lies," a bigot bent on conquering Europe for the Spanish empire.

In the nineteenth century the German historian Leopold von Ranke (1795–1886), who pleaded for objective history based on the sources, took a midway view between panegyricists and polemicists. To Ranke, Philip II was neither saint nor sinner, but simply a human being, a sincere patriot, a defender of the Church, who reflected the strength and weaknesses of the Spanish people.

3. Checkmate: Revolt in the Netherlands

Background. The seventeen provinces of the Netherlands, which today comprise Holland and Belgium, were united in a loose confederation under the protection of the Holy Roman Empire. The northern provinces were Germanic and Dutch-speaking, while the southern were almost French in tradition and language. During the Middle Ages, they were ruled by feudal lords. At the end of the medieval era they were consolidated under the house of Burgundy. When the Burgundian, Charles the Bold, was slain on the battlefield of Nancy in 1477, the dynasty was left without a male heir. His daughter, Mary, married Maximilian of Hapsburg, thereby bringing the Netherlands into the domain of the Hapsburgs. The Holy Roman emperor, Charles V, was the grandson of Mary of Burgundy and Maximilian of Hapsburg.

Charles V strove energetically to defend the old religion in the Netherlands against the Protestantism seeping in from the Germanies and France. Although he issued nine edicts for its suppression, he was careful not to allow the religious issue to disturb the prosperity of the Netherlands. Proud of his wealthy inheritance, he was anxious to retain the support of the merchants, manufacturers, and financiers in Haarlem, Amsterdam, and Rotterdam in the north, and Ghent, Bruges, Brussels, and Antwerp in the south.

Philip II and the Netherlands. The accession of Philip II in 1556 to the Hapsburg throne had immediate repercussions in the Netherlands. Completely Spanish in his views, a fervent believer in authoritarianism, and a religious bigot, Philip had no use for Protestantism. His aim was to stamp out heresy wherever he found it, whether in Spain, England, France, the Germanies, or the Netherlands. It was said, perhaps without justification, that he preferred to lose his empire rather than surrender to religious freedom.

Although Philip II began his reign in the Netherlands, he returned in 1559 to Spain, where he felt more at home and where he spent the remainder of his life. Ruling from a distance, he sought to eliminate heresy in the Netherlands by strengthening the Inquisition there. He centralized the administration, but paid no attention to local customs and traditions and sought no help from local officials. The Dutch population, finding that their petitions for redress of grievances were useless, finally resorted to mob action and attacked Catholic Church property in several cities.

Philip II countered by appointing the narrow-minded, bigoted Duke of Alva (1508–1583) as administrator of the Netherlands. Alva entered Brussels at the head of 10,000 Spanish troops, nicknamed "blackbeards" by the Netherlanders. He began a campaign of terror, confiscating property and performing wholesale executions until "the whole land ran red with blood." To intimidate the population, Alva's Council of Blood would place several scores of prisoners on trial at the same time. In addition, the Spanish administrator, to meet the heavy costs of his regime, imposed a tax of 1 per cent on all property and a 10 per cent sales tax. Dutch commerce was stifled.

William the Silent. Instead of extirpating Protestantism, the ferocious Duke of Alva, by his blind and remorseless cruelty, aroused the Dutch to revolt. They found a leader in William of Orange, called William the Silent (1533–1584), a man of remarkable patience, perseverance, and skill. During the early days of Alva's administration, William the Silent emigrated to the Germanies, there to plan resistance against the invaders of his homeland. Philip II was forced to recall the Duke of Alva in 1573 after it became obvious that his policies had failed in the Netherlands. In 1579 the Union of Utrecht was formed, uniting the Protestants of the seven northern provinces. Two years later, in 1581, representatives of the seven provinces announced their independence.

Spain Loses the Netherlands. The small Dutch state now waged war against Spain, the mightiest power in Christendom. Though William the Silent was assassinated in 1584, the Dutch persisted in their struggle. Spain's hope of reconquering the rebellious provinces was stifled by events: the destruction of the Spanish Armada (1588); the accession of Henry IV to the throne of France (1589); and the death of Philip II (1598). In 1609 Philip III arranged a twelve-year armistice. Before this truce expired, the great powers were busily engaged in the Thirty Years' War in the Germanies. The hard-pressed Dutch were no longer without friends. The independence of the seven provinces was formally recognized by Spain in the peace settlement of Westphalia (1648), which formally ended hostilities between Spain and the United Provinces of the Netherlands. The "Spanish fury" was over. The Dutch Republic now came into existence. Philip II's reign of terror had failed to hold the Netherlands for Spain.

4. Decline of the Hapsburgs

The Decay of Spain. During the century after the death of Philip II, Spain sank to the status of a second-rate power. After the destruction of her Armada, she never again played a dominant role in European affairs, although she continued to furnish financial aid to the Catholic powers in the Thirty Years' War. The expulsion of the Jews and Moors from Spain, her failure to develop industry, the deterioration of agriculture, the ruinous expense of long and costly wars, the crushing of her naval power by England and Holland, her internal political decadence, and the decline of population, all contributed to the deterioration.

The decline of Spain was due in part to the fact that she did not have the resources to maintain the wars of Charles V and Philip II. She tried to live on unearned increment stolen from the New World. It could not work. Bullion brought in from America paid only a part of the enormous expenses of the wars, and the mines were gradually exhausted. Added to this was the inability of the authorities to check piracy. Under the regime of Philip III (r. 1598–1621) an attempt was made to increase purchasing power by debasing the coinage. Good gold and silver coins were driven out of circulation; copper replaced gold and silver as a medium of exchange. This suicidal policy,

plus shortsighted taxation, resulted in economic chaos. By the seventeenth century Spain's industry, commerce, and agriculture had fallen into a recession from which they never recovered. It was an unbearable economic combination: monetary anarchy, unintelligent taxation, inadequate investment, and inability to meet foreign competition. The social order was in ruins: a dictatorial dynasty; lazy, wasteful, arrogant nobility; a middle class with its roots destroyed; and a peasantry and a laboring class kept in ignorance and poverty. Not even an overseas empire could rescue Spain from this morass.

Historical Controversy: The Decline of Spain. The rapid decline of Spain from the most prosperous power in Europe in the sixteenth century to the role of a second-rate power in the seventeenth century was almost unique as a historical phenomenon. Historians, fascinated by this development, have reached varying conclusions on the reasons for this precipitous decline. Some attribute it mainly to a weakening of the Spanish national character, particularly a rising contempt for manual labor as well as an aversion to commerce, expressed in the term "hidalgoism." The Spanish temperament, it is said, led to increasing debauchery and a withering of national morale which weakened the foundations of the state and led to its virtual collapse. Added to this was a series of inept rulers and advisors who let the country drift into decline.

Against this politico-psychological interpretation is the view held by other historians that economic factors were of major importance. Spain was weakened by the crushing burden of taxation resulting from costly wars, the extravagance of the royal household, the inefficiency of tax farmers and collectors, the expulsion of the Moors and Jews from the country, and monetary chaos. A loss of economic strength was more largely a cause than a result of the political decline. With state intervention and paternalism prevailing in Spain, the economic decline was hastened by progressively inferior administration. Also decisive were the numerous and sharp fluctuations in the price structure, which impeded business and led to economic havoc.

❧ KEY READING ❧

THE SPANISH INQUISITION IN ACTION DURING THE REIGN OF PHILIP II

Henry Charles Lea, *A History of the Inquisition of Spain*, 4 vols. (New York and London, 1906–1907), III, 437–442.

THE INQUISITION reinvigorated during the reign of Ferdinand and Isabella was designed to stamp out all heresies and discourage the growth of Protestantism in Spain. Early in his reign (1556–1598) Philip II discovered two groups of Protestants, one at Seville and one at Valladolid. How Philip used the fires of the *auto-da-fé*, the terrible ceremony in which heretics were burned to death, was described in this passage by Henry Charles Lea.

Nothing was spared to enhance the effect of the *auto-da-fé* of Trinity Sunday, May 21, 1559, in which the first portion of the Valladolid prisoners were to suffer. It was solemnly proclaimed fifteen days in advance, during which the buildings of the Inquisition were incessantly patrolled, day and night, by a hundred armed men, and guards were stationed at the stagings in the Plaza Mayor, for there were rumors that the prison was to be blown up and that the stagings were to be fired. Along the line of the procession palings were set in the middle of the street, forming an unobstructed path for three to march abreast. . . .

The procession was headed by the effigy of Leonor de Vivero, who had died during trial, clad in widow's weeds and bearing a mitre with flames and appropriate inscriptions, and followed by a coffin containing her remains to be duly burnt. Those who were to be relaxed in person numbered fourteen, of whom one, Gonzalo Baez, was a Portuguese convicted of Judaism. Those admitted to reconciliation, with penance more or less severe, were sixteen in number, including an Englishman variously styled Anthony Graso or Bagor—probably Baker— punished for Protestantism, like all the rest, excepting Baez. When the procession reached the plaza, Agustin Cozalla was placed in the highest seat, as the conspicuous chief of the heresy, and next to him his brother, Francisco de Vivero. Melchor Cano at once commenced the sermon, which occupied an hour, and then Valdés and the bishops approached the Princess Juana and Prince Carlos, who were present, and administered to them the oath to protect and aid the Inquisition, to which the multitude responded in a mighty roar, "To the death!" Cozalla, his brother and Alonso Pérez who were in orders, were duly degraded from the priesthood, the sentences were read, those admitted to reconciliation made the necessary adjurations and those condemned to relaxation were handed over to the secular arm. Mounted on asses, they were carried to the Plaza de la Puerta de Campo, where the requisite stakes had been erected, and there they met their end. . . .

Herrezuelo, the only martyr in the group . . . avowed his faith and resolutely adhered to it, in spite of all effort to convert him and of the dreadful fate in store for him. On their way to the brasero, Cozalla wasted on him all his eloquence. He was gagged and could not reply, but his stoical endurance showed his unyielding pertinacity. When chained to the stake, a stone thrown at him struck him in the forehead, covering his face with blood, but, as we are told, it did him no good. Then he was thrust through the belly by a pious halberdier, but this moved him not and, when the fire was set, he bore his agony without flinching and, to the general surprise, he thus ended diabolically. Illescas, who stood so near that he could watch every expression, reports that he seemed as impassive as flint but, though he uttered no complaint and manifested no regret, yet he died with the strangest sadness in his face, so that it was dreadful to look upon him as on one who in a brief moment would be in hell with his comrade and master, Luther. . . .

The remainder of the Valladolid reformers were reserved for another celebration, October

8th, honored with the presence of Philip II, who obediently took the customary oath, with bared head and ungloved hand. It was, if possible, an occasion of greater solemnity than the previous one. A Flemish official, who was present, estimates the number of spectators at 200,000 and, though he must have been hardened to such scenes at home, he could not repress an expression of sympathy with the sufferers. Besides a Morisco who was relaxed, a Judaizer reconciled and two penitents for other offences, there were twenty-six Protestants. The lesson was the same as in the previous *auto*, that few had the ardor of martyrdom. . . .

There never was the slightest real danger that Protestantism could make such permanent impression on the profound and unreasoning religious convictions of Spain in the sixteenth century, as to cause disturbance in the body politic; and the excitement created in Valladolid and Seville, in 1558 and 1559, was a mere passing episode leaving no trace in popular beliefs. Yet, coming when it did, it exercised an enduring influence on the fortunes of the Inquisition, and on the development of the nation. At the moment, the career of the Holy Office might almost seem to be drawing to a close, for it had nearly succeeded in extirpating Judaism from Spain.

❦ HISTORICAL INTERPRETATION ❦

JOHN LOTHROP MOTLEY ON PHILIP II AS A ROYAL CRIMINAL

John Lothrop Motley, *History of the United Netherlands*, 4 vols. (New York, 1867), III, 538–543. Courtesy of Harper and Brothers.

JOHN LOTHROP MOTLEY (1814–1877), American historian, was graduated from Harvard University and then went to Europe, studying at Göttingen and Berlin. His historical work on the Netherlands was received with praise by such able critics as Froude and Prescott. A vivid and dramatic manner revealed the influence of Carlyle. A stern Protestant moralist, Motley viewed Philip II in terms of his own Protestantism. He regarded Philip as the incarnation of evils, as one of the most reprehensible figures in all human history. Following is an excerpt from Motley's condemnation of Philip II.

As for the royal criminal called Philip II, his life is his arraignment, and these volumes will have been written in vain if a specification is now required.

Homicide such as was hardly ever compassed before by one human being was committed by Philip when in the famous edict of 1568 he sentenced every man, woman, and child in the Netherlands to death. That the whole of this population, three millions or more, were not positively destroyed was because no human energy could suffice to execute the diabolical decree. But Alva, toiling hard, accomplished much of this murderous work. By the aid of the "Council of Blood," and of the sheriffs and executioners of the Holy Inquisition, he was able sometimes to put 800 human beings to death in a single week for the crimes of Protestantism or of opulence, and at the end of half a dozen years he could

boast of having strangled, drowned, burned, or beheaded somewhat more than 18,000 of his fellow-creatures. These were some of the non-combatant victims; for of the tens of thousands who perished during his administration alone, in siege and battle, no statistical record has been preserved.

In face of such wholesale crimes, of these forty years of bloodshed, it is superfluous to refer to such isolated misdeeds as his repeated attempts to procure the assassination of the Prince of Orange, crowned at last by the success of Balthazar Gerard, nor to his persistent efforts to poison the Queen of England; for the enunciation of all these murders or attempts at murder would require a repetition of the story which it has been one of the main purposes of these volumes to recite.

For indeed it seems like mere railing to specify

his crimes. Their very magnitude and unbroken continuity, together with their impunity, give them almost the appearance of inevitable phenomena. The horrible monotony of his career stupefies the mind until it is ready to accept the principle of evil as the fundamental law of the world.

His robberies, like his murders, were colossal. The vast system of confiscation set up in the Netherlands was sufficient to reduce unnumbered innocent families to beggary, although powerless to break the spirit of civil and religious liberty or to pay the expenses of subjugating a people. . . . He . . . was accustomed to consider himself the first statesman in the world.

His reign was a thorough and disgraceful failure. . . . He had spent his life in fighting with the spirit of the age—that invincible power of which he had not the faintest conception—while the utter want of adaptation of his means to his ends often bordered, not on the ludicrous, but the insane.

He attempted to reduce the free Netherlands to slavery and to papacy. Before his death they had expanded into an independent republic, with a policy founded upon religious toleration and the rights of man. . . . He had sought to invade and to conquer England, and to dethrone and assassinate its queen. But the queen outwitted, outgeneralled, and outlived him; English soldiers and sailors, assisted by their Dutch comrades in arms, accomplished on the shores of Spain what the Invincible Armada had in vain essayed against England and Holland; while England, following thenceforth the opposite system to that of absolutism and the Inquisition, became, after centuries of struggles towards the right, the most powerful, prosperous, and enlightened kingdom in the world.

His exchequer, so full when he ascended the throne as to excite the awe of contemporary financiers, was reduced before his death to a net income of some four millions of dollars. His armies, which had been the wonder of the age in the earlier period of his reign for discipline, courage, and every quality on which military efficiency depends, were in his later years a horde of starving, rebellious brigands, more formidable to their commanders than to the foe. Mutiny was the only organized military institution that was left in his dominions, while the Spanish Inquisition, which it was the fell purpose of his life from youth upwards to establish over the world, became a loathsome and impossible nuisance everywhere but in its natal soil.

If there be such a thing as historical evidence, then is Philip II convicted before the tribunal of impartial posterity of every crime charged in his indictment. He lived seventy-one years and three months, he reigned forty-three years. He endured the martyrdom of his last illness with the heroism of a saint, and died in the certainty of immortal bliss as the reward of his life of evil.

❧ TEN BASIC BOOKS ❧

GREATNESS AND DECAY: ABSOLUTE MONARCHY IN SPAIN

1. Geyl, Pieter, *The Revolt of the Netherlands, 1555–1609*, 2nd ed. (New York, 1958).†

2. Hamilton, Earl J., *American Treasure and the Price Revolution in Spain, 1501–1650* (Cambridge, Mass., 1934, R. 1965).

3. Hume, Martin A. S., *Court of Philip IV: Spain in Decadence* (New York, 1907).

4. Klein, Julius, *The Mesta: A Study in Spanish Economic History, 1273–1836* (Cambridge, Mass., 1920, R. 1963).

5. Lea, Henry C., *A History of the Inquisition of Spain*, 4 vols. (New York and London, (1906–1907).

6. Livermore, Harold V., *A History of Spain* (London, 1958).

7. Motley, John Lothrop, *History of the United Netherlands,* 4 vols. (New York, 1867).

8. Seaver, Henry Latimer, *The Great Revolt in Castile; A Study of the Comunero Movement of 1520–1521* (Boston, 1928, R. 1966).

9. Walsh, William, *Philip II* (New York, 1953).

10. Wedgwood, Cicely V., *William the Silent, William of Nassau, Prince of Orange, 1533–1584* (New Haven, Conn., 1944).

9

Prelude to Upheaval: The Ascendancy of France

FOR NEARLY thirty years, your principal Ministers have destroyed and reversed all the ancient maxims of the state in order to raise your authority to its highest pitch, an authority which has become theirs because they have it in their own hands. They no longer speak of the state and of its constitution; they only speak of the King and of his royal pleasure. They have pushed your revenues and your expenses to unprecedented heights. They have raised you up to the sky in order, they say, to outshine the grandeur of all your predecessors. . . .

Meanwhile, your people, whom you should love as your children, and who until now have been so eager to support you, die of hunger. The cultivation of the soil is almost abandoned; the towns and the countryside are depopulated; all business enterprise is stagnant, and no longer offers employment to workingmen. All commerce is destroyed. As a result, you have ruined half of the real forces within your state in order to make and defend vain conquests outside. Instead of taking money from these poor people, one should give them alms and feed them. All France is nothing more than a great poorhouse, desolate and without provisions. . . .

There, Sire, is the state of things. You live as one whose eyes are fatally blinded.

—FÉNELON (François de Salignac de La Mothe, Archbishop of Cambrai),
in "Remonstrances" (c. 1694), an anonymous letter to Louis XIV

1. France at the Dawn of the Modern Age

Origin of the French National State. What we know today as France first appeared as a separate nation under the terms of the Treaty of Verdun (843), by which the lands comprising roughly what became France, Germany, and Italy were awarded to the three grandsons of Charlemagne. In 987, Hugh Capet mounted the French throne, beginning the Capetian dynasty which was to rule continuously until 1328. The story of the Capetian dynasty is one of gradual extension of royal domains by con- quest, purchase, marriage, and inheritance. All the Capetian kings, including Louis VI (r. 1108–1137), Philip II, Augustus (r. 1180–1223), Louis IX (r. 1226–1270), and Philip IV (r. 1285–1314), worked to enhance the royal authority at the expense of the petty feudal lords. Philip IV broke the influence of the papacy in France when he defeated Pope Boniface VII in a struggle for temporal power.

The French monarchy emerged triumphant from the Hundred Years' War with England (1338–1453). Charles VII (r. 1422–1461) saved his country from disintegration, drove out the English, and laid the groundwork upon which his Valois and Bourbon successors later built the structure of absolute monarchy. Although the long war left France weakened, it gave her a growing sense of national unity. There still remained a hard core of selfish nobles who controlled their own fiefs. The commercial and industrial middle class, as well as the people generally, desired a strong monarchy, but before that centralized authority could be achieved, the fiercely independent nobility had to be subjugated. Charles VII began the task.

Consolidation and Centralization. Louis XI (r. 1461–1483), obtaining the support of the middle class and the gentry, also centralized the administration at the expense of the nobility. His most stubborn enemy was Charles the Bold, Duke of Burgundy (1433–1477), whose house, descended from the French royal family, had acquired extensive territories outside of France. Already in possession of Burgundy, Franche-Comté, Luxemburg, and the Netherlands, Charles the Bold added Alsace and Lorraine to his holdings. The clash with Louis XI was inevitable. The Swiss entered the war against Charles the Bold, and helped bring about his defeat and death. His daughter Mary, assisted by her husband, Maximilian of Hapsburg, carried on the war against France until she died in 1482. The final result was that Louis XI acquired Burgundy. Meanwhile, he put unceasing pressure on the remaining feudal lords. By the time of his death in 1483 he had taken a giant step toward uniting France by adding to the royal domain virtually all the huge fiefs except for Brittany. The feudal lords had lost their independence, but they intended to regain it at the first opportunity.

Charles VIII (r. 1483–1498) carried the unification a step further by acquiring Brittany through marriage to Anne, Duchess of Brittany, in 1491. This meant the consolidation of France as a national state. As in Spain, power was now centralized in the hands of an absolute monarch. The Estates-General was deprived of strength, and the nobility lost its position of political preeminence. To maintain its power and prestige, the Crown gave the nobility certain compensations for their loss of

independence. For example, they were allowed to retain those social rights which they had long held as members of a feudal hierarchy. Economically, they were permitted to hold the old immunities from taxation. Many entered military service in the new standing army of the Crown, or became courtiers tied to the royal family. All these developments favored the status of the king as the rallying point of the nation.

2. The Wars of Religion in France

The Course of French Protestantism. The Reformation in France began independently, in the sense that French humanists had helped prepare the way. When it came in full force, however, it was imported from the Germanies and Switzerland. At first Francis I (r. 1515–1547) was tolerant of Protestantism, but as it gained strength, he sought to persecute it out of existence. Henry II (r. 1547–1559) was even more anxious to extirpate it. Neither king was successful. In bitter conflicts with Spain for control of the Italian peninsula, they were unable to prevent the rapid spread of the new religion in France. The stimulus came from John Calvin, himself a Frenchman and organizer of the Protestant French communities. Calvinist ideals and organization spread rapidly. By the middle of the sixteenth century, French Protestant Huguenots numbered from 300,000 to 400,000. Drawn chiefly from the nobility, gentry, and burghers (the lower class, unlike that in the Germanies, remained loyal to Catholicism), the Huguenots became more and more influential in French affairs.

Before Henry II could take up arms against the Huguenots, he was killed in an accident (1559). That year marked the end of the persistent French wars against the Hapsburgs and the interminable quarrels for domination of the Italies. For the next several decades France was to shift from foreign wars to civil wars of religion.

Huguenots Versus Guises. The French nobility split into two opposing camps. On one side, the Bourbon family, closely related to the royal house, turned to Protestantism and supported the Huguenots. Its cause was supported by two Princes of the Blood, Anthony of Bourbon, King of Navarre by his marriage to Jeanne d'Albert, and his brother, Prince Louis of Condé (1530–1569). Joined with them by marriage was Admiral Gaspard de Coligny (1519–1572), deeply religious leader of the Protestant party. For support the Bourbon-Coligny group relied upon dissatisfied nobles and the Huguenot middle class.

On the other side was the Catholic Guise family, allied with the Catholic nobility which was pledged to the extermination of Protestantism. Related by marriage to the royal families of both France and Scotland, the Guises were headed by Duke Francis, a popular military figure in the recent wars with Spain. The Guise faction held the loyalty of the majority of the population.

Catherine de' Medici. Henry II had gravely underestimated the strength of French Protestantism. His three sons, Francis II (r. 1559–1560), Charles IX (r. 1560–1574), and Henry III (r. 1574–1589) were only nominal rulers of France. Since Francis II was too young at his ascendancy, the government came into the hands of the queen's uncles, the brothers Guise. Persecution of the Bourbon-Huguenot faction began in earnest. The prisons were filled. Many Huguenots were executed. In self-defense the Protestant party began to organize along politico-military lines to defend itself against extinction.

Francis II died after a reign of only one year. The crown passed to Charles IX, also still a child, whereupon his mother, Catherine de' Medici, seized control of the government. Until this moment the daughter of the famed Florentine family had played a minor role as the wife of Henry II and the mother of Francis II. But for the next quarter of a century, this shrewd and cunning woman dominated her remaining weak sons. Her aims were clearcut and consistent: she would maintain the royal power against the Bourbon pretenders; she would preserve the territories of France; she would establish the supremacy of Catholicism. Though suspicious of political alliances,

she accepted the support of the Catholic Guises and the Catholic nobility, but she was not above playing Guise against Bourbon, or Catholic against Huguenot.

Catherine at first issued an edict granting limited freedom of worship to the Protestants and halting the persecutions. However, her hopes of satisfying the Huguenots were quickly blasted. The Protestants, though only a small portion—about 10 per cent—of the population, had no intention of settling for anything less than full freedom of worship and religious equality. They refused to accept Catherine's moderate edict.

The Wars of Religion Begin, 1562. In 1562 the Duke of Guise forced Catherine to recall the edict of toleration. He attacked a congregation of Huguenots assembled for worship in a barn. Now the Huguenots took up arms in earnest. Eight distinct conflicts occurred in the French Wars of Religion. For more than three decades the countryside was ravaged by marauding armies; towns, villages, roads, and bridges were destroyed; robbers terrorized the people; trade and industry were dislocated. Within a few years the original leaders of both Bourbons and Guises fell in battle, leaving Admiral Coligny the outstanding figure in France.

The Massacre of St. Bartholomew's Day, 1572. At this time there occurred a radical change in Catherine's attitude toward Admiral Coligny. Annoyed by his popularity with the people, and fearful of his influence on the king, Charles IX, now of age, she was even more angered when he suggested that she declare war on Philip II of Spain. She decided to throw in her lot again with the Guises, but this time in a final way. Asserting that the Huguenots were conspiring to overthrow the dynasty, she persuaded her son to order a purge of all Protestants, including the admiral and the principal Huguenot leaders as obstacles to peace. The signal was given in the early morning of Sunday, August 24, 1572, the day of the festival of St. Bartholomew. One of the first victims was Coligny, who was murdered in his home. At least 2,000 Hugue-

The massacre of St. Bartholomew's Day.

nots were killed in Paris. Some 8,000 others were slaughtered in the provinces.

Despite the loss of their leaders, the Huguenots fought on. The religious wars broke out again with even greater fury. Within a few years, however, it became apparent that the Protestant forces could not win. Cut down by war and massacre, they retained vestiges of power only in the west and south of France. The Guises, with support from Philip II, continued to suppress the Protestants. The *Politiques,* moderate Catholic Frenchmen who placed national loyalty above religious conviction, were alienated by this alliance with the Spanish king and feared his further influence.

The War of the Three Henrys. During the reign of the last Valois, Henry III (r. 1574–1589), Henry, Duke of Guise, head of the reactionary Catholics, and Henry of Navarre, leader of the Huguenots, engaged in a dynastic contest called the War of the Three Henrys. Henry III, leader of the *Politiques,* was in feeble health and had no sons. The death of Catherine de' Medici's fourth son, the Duke of Alençon, last possible heir of the Valois line, brought the issue to a head. Henry III was caught between Henry of Navarre, the closest heir to the throne, and the Catholic faction led by Henry of Guise. At first he submitted to the Catholic group, but in a moment of frustration he arranged for the elimination of Henry, Duke of Guise. The murder took place on December 23, 1588. The next year the house of Guise had its revenge when, on August 1, 1589, Henry III fell victim to an assassin. Meanwhile, the queen-mother, Catherine de' Medici, had died on January 5, 1589. The beneficiary was Henry of Navarre, left with a clear title to the throne of a sadly attenuated kingdom.

3. Reconstruction of France Under Henry IV

The Edict of Nantes, 1598. The assassination of Henry III did not mean the end of the Huguenot wars, for it was necessary that his successor deal with the Catholic League as well as with Philip II. After four more years of fighting, Henry IV (r. 1589–1610) embraced Catholicism on the ground that "Paris is worth a mass." This conversion took care of his difficulties inside France. But he had to carry on the war with Spain, which he brought to a conclusion in 1598.

In that same year, 1598, Henry IV issued the Edict of Nantes. By its terms the Huguenots were granted equality with the Catholics, including eligibility to all public offices. They could now reside anywhere in France without molestation; they were given the right to worship in designated towns and castles, though not at the king's court or within five leagues of Paris; they could hold certain fortified towns; they were given amnesty for past offenses; and they could establish new churches and universities. Technically, the Edict of Nantes was a grant of specified rights, but in reality it was a treaty of peace between the Catholic monarchy of France and the Huguenots.

Thus ended the French wars of religion. At long last Protestantism obtained a legal status in France. It had not succeeded, however, in displacing Catholicism, and during the next century it was to become progressively weaker.

The Task of Henry IV. With the restoration of peace the new king faced the task of reconstructing France, restoring the power of the monarchy, and uplifting French prestige in Europe. The government was close to bankruptcy and its finances were in chaotic shape. Henry IV's first aim was to reestablish his own position as monarch by conquering the whole of France. Tenacious, courageous, quick-witted, he went to work zealously. He forced the weaker nobles to submit to his authority, and bribed the stronger ones to go along with

him. Maintaining that he ruled by divine right, he ignored the Estates-General, though he made a pretense of listening to the Assembly of Notables, but only "with a sword in his hand." Addressing the provincial estates in Burgundy, Henry said coldly: "Your most precious possessions are the favors bestowed on you by the king." He appointed a working council of five loyal followers who, under his guidance, suppressed brigandage by steady use of the gallows. He kept a careful eye on the mushrooming conspiracies of embittered nobles plotting to regain their lost power.

Henry and Sully. Henry IV was fortunate to obtain the services of Maximilien de Béthune Sully (1560–1641), a most important figure in French administration after 1594. A wise and able statesman, Henry IV realized that he was not an expert administrator and that he needed a firm hand at the helm. He found an ideal assistant in Sully, whose intelligence and imagination he utilized for the benefit of France. "A madman for work but of a cross-grained honesty," Sully became the king's good right arm. The two worked as a team. Sully remained a zealous Calvinist and never hesitated to criticize his master for what he regarded as a foolish financial edict or some unwise romantic affair. Together they achieved what amounted to a political, social, and economic revolution.

Rehabilitation of Finances. Henry IV's immediate problem was to lift the government from threatened bankruptcy. He ordered a complete overhauling of the national finances. Sully complied by reforming the system of taxation, introducing careful accounting methods, and insisting upon rigid honesty in all governmental financial dealings. He recovered royal domains for the Crown; collected feudal dues; eliminated thousands of useless middlemen in the tax system; removed sources of abuse and corruption; and devised new methods of raising revenue, such as reviving the old custom of having the clergy give "free gifts" to the king. Sully was brilliantly successful as financial watchdog. Just as the English Henry VII, a century earlier, had begun his reign with an empty treasury after the Wars of the Roses, so Henry IV had started his rule with empty coffers after the religious wars. At the end of Henry IV's reign, Sully had balanced the budget, paid off or canceled a great part of the national debt, relieved the people of illegal taxation, and filled the coffers in the cellars of the Bastille with a great treasure of gold and silver.

Agriculture, Industry, and Commerce. Henry IV and Sully agreed that "husbandry and pasture are the two breasts of France." French prosperity, they reasoned, depended to a large extent on a healthy agricultural system. Sully reduced the taxes on the peasants; forbade the practice of seizing farm tools for debts; restricted the right of nobles to ride over peasants' crops and vineyards in search of game; drained the marshes; and permitted the exportation of grain from France, thereby giving the peasants a larger market in years of good harvest. The ideal was that every peasant family "have a fowl in its pot on Sunday" (*poule au pot*). These measures brought improvements, though the peasants continued to live on manors and worked the land under the old, traditional, wasteful three-field system.

Complementing Sully's efforts in agriculture, Henry IV turned to trade and industry, his fields of special interest. He was anxious to have the surplus products of French industry sold abroad for precious metals, thereby increasing the wealth of France. He granted greater liberties to the city artisans; encouraged silk-weaving, carpet-making, and the manufacture of leather goods; decreed tariffs for competing foreign products; granted subsidies and bounties to businessmen; constructed new roads, bridges, and canals; built up a merchant marine; sent explorers and colonists to the New World; and chartered companies for trade with India. In general, he applied all the principles of mercantilism to breathe life into the French economy.

Domestic and Foreign Policies. Henry IV followed the example of Henry VIII of England by forming an alliance with the businessmen. He won their loyalty by encouraging the rise of a judicial and administrative caste, the "nobility of the robe," designed to act as a counterweight to the "nobility of the sword." Restive nobles quickly felt the weight of Henry's power. Among the malcontents was the Catholic Duke of Biron, who had dreams of reviving the Catholic League and renewing the wars of religion. Henry had him arrested, tried, and beheaded. The Protestant Duke of Bouillon demanded the whole of Southern France for the exclusive use of the Huguenots. He escaped Henry's vengeance only by fleeing to the Germanies. From then on the French nobility discreetly avoided any moves against Henry's government.

Henry IV inherited his foreign policy from his predecessors. The two branches of the Hapsburg family held France in a vise: it was the task of his life to free France from this encirclement by weakening Spain and Austria in any way he could. The Hapsburgs were entrenched in areas inside France's geographical barriers, such as the Pyrenees and Alps. He would try to break their power.

The opportunity for war came with the death in 1609 of the Duke of Cleves, Jülich, and Berg, three tiny but strategically important states on the lower Rhine near the borders of France. When the Hapsburg Emperor Rudolf sent an Austrian army to occupy the duchies until the succession was arranged, Henry denounced the move as hostile to France. Mobilizing his army, and fortified by Protestant allies in the Germanies and Holland, he set out for a general war against the Hapsburgs. Before he could leave with his army, however, Henry was struck down by the dagger of François Ravaillac, a religious fanatic, who believed that the king's conversion to Catholicism was not sincere. The death of Henry IV brought the projected war to a quick conclusion. France was paralyzed and the coalition against the Hapsburgs quickly evaporated.

4. Crystallization of Absolute Monarchy Under Richelieu and Mazarin

Interlude: Marie de' Medici. Much of the constructive work accomplished by Henry IV vanished after his death. During the interlude from Sully to Richelieu, France was plagued by maladministration, waste, extravagance, and weak foreign policy. Henry's widow, Marie de' Medici (regent, 1610–1624), foolish and irresponsible, quickly drained the treasury by gifts to her Italian favorites and by bribes to recalcitrant nobles. Completely misunderstanding her husband's policies, she reversed them one by one. The financial situation worsened so rapidly that she was forced to call the Estates-General in 1614 to search for a remedy (this was the last time this body was to be summoned until 1789, at the outbreak of the French Revolution). Hours of debate led to nothing. The queen dispersed the assembly and ordered her advisers to obtain more money somewhere. Reversing her husband's anti-Spanish policy, she sought an alliance with the Hapsburgs and had her son married off to the Spanish infanta.

Louis XIII (r. 1610–1643) was a child of nine when the queen-mother took over the regency. Brought up in an atmosphere of court intrigue and general insecurity, he was disregarded by his mother and her favorite, the Italian adventurer Concini, whom she had made chief minister of the kingdom. When Louis was sixteen, Concini was killed and the queen-mother banished from the court. The young king then took over the reins of government with almost disastrous results. The turning point came in 1624 when Louis handed control of administration to Cardinal Richelieu, who remained his chief minister almost to the end of his reign.

Ministerial Power: Cardinal Richelieu. By education and temperament a priest, Cardinal Richelieu (1585–1642) was a great master of the art of diplomacy. Cold, calculating, subtle, he dominated every side of the government. Though an earnest Catholic, he was guided by political rather than religious considerations. There were two major goals which he always kept in mind: (1) he would make the royal power supreme in France; and (2) he would make France supreme in Europe. Henry IV had similar aims, but Richelieu devoted himself to these goals with fanatical energy and in large part succeeded. Louis XIII, aware of Richelieu's great unpopularity at the royal court, nevertheless recognized him as the most

capable administrator in France and gave him full support.

Richelieu's Domestic Policies. Backed by the taciturn young king, Richelieu turned his attention to the destruction of the nobility's power. The great nobles, encouraged by the weakness and inefficiency of the government under Marie de' Medici and the young king, had resumed their arrogant drive for political domination. But this time they met an immovable object. Richelieu crushed them without mercy. He sent his spies everywhere throughout France to seek out traitorous nobles; those who were found, he consigned to execution no matter what their title.

Richelieu expanded the system of *intendants* instituted by Henry IV, entrusting local government to loyal citizens and bureaucrats. He sent out these royal officials to take over the duties of noble governors in the provinces. Later, the system of *intendants* formed the base of a governmental bureaucracy.

Richelieu was equally determined to destroy any political power retained by the Huguenots. Angered because the Edict of Nantes had left them in possession of a number of fortified towns, he bided his time. When they rebelled early in his administration, he made peace. But in 1627 he opened a two-year war with the Huguenots. The conflict centered around the seaport of La Rochelle, which fell to government forces in 1629. Richelieu imposed the Edict of Alais on the Huguenots, forcing them to give up the remainder of their fortified strongholds and to relinquish all special military and political privileges. Henceforth, the Huguenots ceased to form a separate body within the state. Having achieved this aim, Richelieu, with great wisdom, ceased any further religious persecution.

Richelieu's Foreign Policy. Richelieu's true greatness was manifested in his foreign policy. With the object of raising the name of the French king "to its rightful place," he entered the Thirty Years' War in its final phase (1635–1648). He maintained that this was a simple policy of self-preservation, for with the Austrian and Spanish Hapsburgs in alliance,

France was in great danger of being crushed between them. After settling the domestic problem of the Huguenots, Richelieu began to stir up opposition to the Holy Roman emperor, against whom he eventually waged war. The Hapsburg danger was finally eliminated by Spain's failure to subdue Holland, and by the success of the French armies against Austria. Richelieu died in 1642, before he could witness the triumph of his policies. Louis XIII followed him to the grave within six months.

Richelieu himself saw the meaning of his own life in these terms: "I employed all my

Portrait of Cardinal Richelieu by P. de Champagne.

energy to ruin the Huguenot faction, to humble the pride of the nobles, to reduce all subjects to their duty, and to exalt France to its proper position among foreign nations." The great cardinal accomplished what he had set out to do. The power of the monarchy was enhanced inside France, and the prestige of France was raised abroad. But all this had

been bought at fearful cost. The people had been ground down to pay for Richelieu's foreign wars. Agriculture, trade, and industry were seriously weakened. Worst of all, the state was again drifting toward bankruptcy. Richelieu had fashioned a magnificent police system, but he knew little about justice. He did not reform, he shattered. He left France outwardly resplendent, inwardly languishing.

Cardinal Mazarin. Once again the crown fell to a child, this time Louis XIV, only four years old. Anne of Austria, the widow of Louis XIII and mother of Louis XIV, became regent. Several years before his death, Richelieu had brought into his service an Italian-born papal delegate, Jules Mazarin. Like his teacher a cardinal of the Church, Mazarin became chief minister in 1643. He carried on the work designed by Richelieu.

Domestic Policies: The *Fronde* (1648–1653). During the long minority of Louis XIV, Mazarin faced a serious domestic situation. Nobles, gentry, the middle class, all suffering under the taxation imposed by Richelieu and Mazarin, united in rebellion. A series of civil wars followed, in which all people hostile to "the foreigner" took part in an anarchic upheaval. The uprising, called the *Fronde* (a sling), was named after a street game of Parisian urchins because the Paris mob pelted the windows of Mazarin's home with stones. Included among the rebels was the *parlement* of Paris, the ancient judicial body which tried to establish some popular control over the king's decisions. It hoped to substitute government by law for government by royal will. Though all classes took part in this "crazy farce," the real leaders were the nobles, who were making their last attempt to thwart the royal power.

The *Fronde* failed, and with it the last chance of an upper-class rebellion against the Crown. The failure also shook the power of the *parlement* of Paris. From now on, for nearly a century and a half, the nobility would be subordinate to the royal power. The monarchy was stronger than ever. The administration of France became more and more centralized.

Mazarin's Foreign Policy. Mazarin's foreign policy closely followed that of Richelieu: he would break the Hapsburg power that encircled France from the Germanies to Spain. His generals brought the Thirty Years' War to a successful conclusion. By the terms of the Treaty of Westphalia (1648), France emerged as the leading Continental power, and the Hapsburg dream of a united Catholic-German empire was destroyed. In 1659 Mazarin concluded peace with Spain by the Treaty of the Pyrenees, which supplemented the Peace of Westphalia in helping to destroy the Catholic empire of Philip II. By the terms of this treaty youthful Louis XIV was married to Maria Theresa, the daughter of the Spanish monarch. The marriage was not followed by a political alliance, but it did prepare the way for France to claim the throne of Spain in 1700.

5. Absolutism at Its Zenith: Louis XIV

Louis XIV Begins His Reign. Richelieu and Mazarin had done their work well. The feudal nobility was reduced to impotence; the Huguenots lost their lands and political independence; the religious wars were ended. France emerged from the Thirty Years' War with acquisitions which broke Spain's solid line on the eastern borders of France. Mazarin had brought the seemingly interminable war against the Spanish Hapsburgs to a successful conclusion.

On the death of Mazarin in 1661, Louis XIV, then twenty-three years old, took complete control. He was to rule France as absolute monarch for fifty-four years until his death in 1715. Under the new king, absolutism reached its height. Louis became the unchallenged autocrat of France and the cultural leader of Western society.

The Absolutism of Louis XIV. The theoretical basis for Louis XIV's absolutism was proclaimed by the theologian Jacques Bossuet of Meaux who sought to prove by Holy Scripture that Louis XIV was divinely ordained. (*See page 122.*) This philosophical reflection assumed a practical form with Louis XIV.

Though he did not originate the phrase, "*L'État, c'est moi!*" ("I am the State!"), all his actions reflected that famous saying. His subjects, Louis was fond of saying, were "born to obey without question," and from them he demanded a blind obedience. He arrogated unlimited powers to himself, although he set up a system of assistants: ministers whom he appointed; a Council of State to discuss matters of peace and war; a Council of Dispatches to handle internal affairs; and a Council of Finance to take care of money matters. He did not convene the Estates-General once during the long years of his reign. He took over the old system of intendancies which had been improved by Richelieu. He enlarged the number of *intendants* to thirty-four, choosing them carefully from the body of middle-class lawyers and businessmen. He sent to prison any of his subjects who dared challenge his authority, utilizing for this procedure an ingenious system of *lettres de cachet*, documents containing charges, signed with the king's seal and countersigned by secretaries. He destroyed any possible challenge to his own authority. It was said that in 1661 the queen mother, Anne of Austria, who thought him incompetent, had laughed aloud at the idea of her son as the ruler of France. Louis demonstrated that she was mistaken.

Historical Controversy. All historians agree that the reign of Louis XIV was of great importance in the history of early modern times, not only for France but for all Western Europe. Certainly the Grand Monarch was the apotheosis of absolutism at a time when it was the prevalent form of government throughout continental Europe. But at the same time there is a wide difference of opinion concerning the greatness of Louis XIV himself as monarch of the most powerful nation in Europe. On the one side there is the extravagant view that Louis XIV was a great leader of men, a master of administration, a wise and benevolent monarch whose absolutism was a matter of historical necessity, a ruler who revealed consistent unity in his policies (Voltaire, Lord Acton). On the other side, there are the charges that he was an opportunist, a man of incredible vanity, a monstrous, selfish, and misguided man who was the ruination of France. This view holds that he left his country crushed by war, its treasury empty, its entire body strained by violence and tension (Fénelon, Saint-Simon).

Here again is an example of the historical problem of the man and the times. What is the significance of the "great" man in history? How much can man control his own destiny and his life on earth? What about the concept of determinism, which holds that man is relatively helpless in the face of vital economic, social, and psychological forces which largely determine what happens in history? The case of Louis XIV, like those of Napoleon and others, reflects this problem of the "hero" in history. Today most historians hold to the idea that history is the sum total of man *and* his times—that men at least partially explain the trend of historical development. In this compromise view, Louis XIV, despite his obvious faults, objectively deserves the mantle of greatness. (*See page 151.*)

Psychology of Absolutism. The absolutism represented by Louis XIV was a form of government designed to satisfy two deeply intrenched psychological needs, one individual, one social. Louis XIV apparently felt that God had chosen him as His lieutenant on earth. "Jehovah hath chosen Solomon my son to sit upon the throne of the kingdom of Jehovah over Israel" (*I Chronicles 28:5*). And again: "Fear God. Honor the King" (*I Peter 2:17*). God, who had created all men from the same earth and equally placed His image and likeness in their souls, had chosen a single man to hold sacred, paternal, and final power. This concept justified the exercise of absolute power and simultaneously protected the person of the king from envious individuals who might refuse to accept his primacy.

At the same time the idea of absolutism satisfied the social need of the vast masses of people for security. In a dangerous age the monarchy represented a pillar of strength. Under the wise prince at Versailles, wars were

successful, peace was established, justice reigned and laws governed, commerce enriched the land. The king was absolute but not arbitrary, and it was arbitrary government that was barbarous and odious. The people accepted absolutism because they preferred it to anarchy, which would have destroyed all their legitimate rights. They accepted Louis XIV because he was the symbol of order and justice in the realm. They would demand freedom from absolutism only when a concatenation of circumstances drove them in 1793 to regicide as a means of assuring the security they sought in "Liberty, Equality, Fraternity."

The Aides of Louis XIV. Louis XIV chose a series of competent aides. At the beginning of his personal rule he inherited from Mazarin an able staff of assistants, which he strengthened during his reign. This was especially true in the military; France soon had the finest army in Europe. In François Michel Le Tellier, Marquis de Louvois (1641–1691), his minister of war, he found a competent organizer of armies. With the advice of Louvois, Louis introduced such improvements as severe discipline, the abolition of fraudulent contracts, uniforms to distinguish different regiments, the gradation of officers, the use of bayonets and other arms, new military maneuvers, and marching in step. In Viscount Henri de Turenne (1611–1675) and the Prince de Condé, Louis II of Bourbon (1621–1686), Louvois' best generals, the king had the services of the finest contemporary masters of strategy. Sebastien le Prestre de Vauban (1633–1707), a great military engineer, gave France a series of fortresses which made her impregnable from the east. The competence of Louis XIV's military aides accounted in large part for the brilliant successes of his reign.

Colbert, Superintendent of Finance. Of equal significance in Louis XIV's reign was Jean-Baptiste Colbert (1619–1683), minister of finance for twenty-two years. As soon as he was appointed to his office in 1661, Colbert, like Sully, Henry IV's financial minister, began to reform the national system of finance. He (1) prosecuted plunderers of public funds; (2) saw to it that tax evaders paid their just taxes; (3) cut down the cost of collecting taxes; (4) introduced efficient bookkeeping; (5) renegotiated contracts with tax collectors; and (6) repudiated the loans that had been contracted by Richelieu and Mazarin at the ruinous interest of 25 per cent. Although the landowning nobility still managed to maintain its tax exemptions, Colbert succeeeded in replenishing the coffers of state. Within a few years the treasury showed a healthy surplus—soon to be transformed into a deficit when Louis XIV embarked on his series of wars.

As a further means of increasing national revenues, Colbert reformed French industry, commerce, and agriculture. The complete mercantilist, he put into effect all the principles of mercantilism. He sought to obtain a steady flow of gold into France by encouraging exports over imports. He established *la grande industrie,* the artificial development of manufacturing in the premechanical factory system. He began a system of bounties, subsidies, tariffs, and monopolies to aid and protect infant industries. Like Henry IV, he built new bridges, roads, and canals, including the Toulouse waterway, connecting the Atlantic with the Mediterranean through the Garonne River. He launched France upon a vigorous program of colonial expansion by sending expeditions and colonists to America, Africa, and India. He constructed a navy which rivaled Britain's and which was used to protect the colonies. He reorganized the law courts, the police system, and local administration. He became a patron of arts, letters, and science. France for him was a well-oiled machine of which he was the engineer and Louis XIV the owner. It is fair to say that in no small measure the leadership of France in Western civilization during the late seventeenth and eighteenth centuries was due to the genius of Colbert.

The Wars of Louis XIV. Colbert's plans for a prosperous and financially secure France were frustrated by the wars of Louis XIV. With the waning of Hapsburg strength in Spain and in the Holy Roman Empire, the Grand Monarch dreamed of acquiring a realm greater than that of Charles V. He would fulfill the destiny of France by extending her borders to their "natural limits"—to the Rhine, the Alps, the Mediterranean, and the Pyrenees. When diplomacy failed, he turned to war. In four major wars, he squandered the manpower and resources of France, leaving her with little glory and a staggering debt.

The War of Devolution, 1667–1668. Louis XIV first tested the strength of Spain in the Netherlands. In 1665, on the death of the Spanish king, Louis claimed the Netherlands in his wife's name. He was entitled to inherit them, he said, on the principle of devolution, the custom by which the property of a man married more than once went to children of the first marriage. The marriage contract with his wife, Maria Theresa, eldest daughter of Philip IV of Spain, was null and void, he said, because his wife's dowry had not been paid. This was only a pretext, for Louis knew that the principle of devolution concerned only private property and certainly not the right of political succession.

When verbal arguments failed, Louis XIV, with the finest army in Europe, in 1667 marched on the Netherlands, there he encountered little resistance. The next year he invaded Franche-Comté. The other European powers, fearing French expansion, organized to hinder it. England, Sweden, and the United Provinces formed a Triple Alliance to retain the balance of power in Europe. With opposition stronger than he had expected, Louis accepted the compromise Treaty of Aix-la-Chapelle (1668), by the terms of which he returned Franche-Comté to Spain although he retained nearly a dozen small border towns in Flanders. He resolved to settle accounts later with the presumptuous little Dutch Republic, whose United Provinces had frustrated his first great war.

The Dutch War, 1672–1678. To punish the Calvinist Dutch, Louis XIV first detached England and Sweden from the Triple Alliance by a series of diplomatic bribes. The Dutch, finally isolated from foreign help, were grievously divided internally between the Orange faction, which wanted a monarchy, and the De Witt faction, which desired a republic. Louis attacked along the Rhine with overwhelming force in 1672. The Dutch, led by William of Orange, great-grandson of William the Silent, resisted doggedly, cutting their dikes and watching the waters of the North Sea overwhelm the invaders. Amsterdam was saved and the French advance momentarily checked. Meanwhile, fear of Louis XIV and sympathy for the hard-pressed Dutch led to the formation of another Grand Alliance including Spain, Austria, Denmark, Brandenburg, and England. Once again Louis hastened to make peace. By the Treaties of Njmwegen (1678–1679), he gained several border towns in Flanders, as well as Franche-Comté from Spain. But the Dutch Republic, despite military reverses, managed to retain its territorial integrity.

The War of the League of Augsburg, 1688–1697. For the next decade Louis XIV maintained an armed but uneasy peace in Europe. He had fought two expensive wars with but little to show for them. He would now try to absorb territory in less costly fashion. He discovered "legitimate claims" in the German Palatinate. His French courts of inquiry, called "chambers of reunion," sought land titles for hundreds of small areas along the Rhine frontier. Soon Louis was claiming Alsace, Luxemburg, and scores of other areas in order to enlarge his claims to additional territory. In 1686 Emperor Leopold I, angered by this practice, organized the League of Augsburg, another Grand Coalition composed of himself, the princes of North Germany, the rulers of Spain, Sweden, and the Dutch United Provinces.

In 1689 William of Orange, Louis XIV's implacable enemy, and his wife, Mary, replaced James II on the English throne. England immediately joined the coalition against France. Louis XIV responded by attacking the Netherlands, sending his armies to destroy land and property along the Rhine. The war raged on

for nearly a decade, spreading to the Italies and even to America, where French and English colonists and their Indian allies fought in what was called King William's War.

After early French victories, the war degenerated into a stalemate, with the French unable to win and the League too weak to invade France. This was the beginning of the final conflict between France and England for control of the seas and the New World. By the Peace of Ryswick (1697) Louis XIV was forced to surrender most of the territory he had gained since the Treaty of Nijmegen with the exception of Strasbourg. The boundaries of France were set back to their position at the beginning of the war. Louis agreed to recognize William III of Orange as king of England, and he was required to sign a favorable commercial treaty with the Dutch. But the Ryswick settlement failed to change colonial boundaries in the New World.

The War of the Spanish Succession, 1701–1714. The War of the Spanish Succession was less destructive than the Thirty Years' War. Fought by professional armies, rather than whole peoples, it spared the civilian population. It was the first great war of Louis XIV in which religion counted for little.

The struggle revolved around the succession to the throne of Spain. The two main aspirants for the Spanish inheritance—which included, in addition to Spain, some twenty-two crowns—were Louis XIV and the Holy Roman Emperor, Leopold I (r. 1658–1705). Both had married Spanish infantas, sisters of the old, sickly, and childless Charles II (r. 1665–1700), who was close to death. Louis XIV hoped to place a younger member of his family on the throne of Spain at the death of Charles II. But when Charles II died in 1700, it was found that his will left all his Spanish territory to the Duke of Anjou, second son of the dauphin of France and, therefore, Louis XIV's grandson. If Louis XIV refused to accept in the name of his grandson, then the inheritance would pass to the son of the Hapsburg emperor in Vienna. Louis XIV decided to accept. He sent his grandson to Spain, and announced to the world: "The Pyrenees no longer exist."

Once again the nations of Europe combined to maintain the balance of power. William III formed a new Grand Alliance consisting of the Dutch Netherlands, England, and Austria, and supported by Brandenburg-Prussia and later by Portugal and the Italian Duchy of Savoy. Louis XIV was allied with Spain and Bavaria, the latter because of its rivalry with Austria.

The long war was fought on the Continent, in Asia, and in America (where it was known as Queen Anne's War). The British sent troops to the Continent under the leadership of a great commander, John Churchill, Duke of Marlborough (1650–1722). Together with Austrian troops under the command of Prince Eugène of Savoy, the Allies won a series of battles at Blenheim in Bavaria (1704), and at Ramillies (1706), Oudenarde (1708), and Malplaquet (1709). Defeated, Louis XIV requested peace, but was reluctant to sign a treaty because of the enormous Allied demands. He fought on to control the crown of Spain. His Spanish ally remained loyal, especially when it saw the British move in at Gibraltar and make a treaty with Portugal. Meanwhile, the Austrians landed at Barcelona and invaded Catalonia, which rebelled and recognized the Austrian claimant to the throne.

The actual issues went far beyond the claim to the Spanish throne. In this complex cacophony of intersecting ambitions, Louis XIV fought to maintain his preeminent position as the Sun King. The British were anxious to keep the Catholic Stuarts (supported by the French) out of England, and to expel French merchants from Spanish America. The Dutch wanted freedom from French aggression. The Austrians fought to keep Spain for the Hapsburgs, to expand in the Italies, and to smash the Bavarians, their ancient enemies.

The War of the Spanish Succession was finally ended by the Treaty of Utrecht (1713) and the Treaty of Rastadt (1714), which partitioned the domains of Spain. Spain was deprived of her European possessions. The grandson of Louis XIV was confirmed as King Philip V of Spain on the condition that Spain and

France never be united under the same monarch. The Bourbons were to reign in Spain (with a few interruptions) from the accession of Philip V to the republican revolution in 1931. Austria received the Spanish Netherlands (from now on called the Austrian Netherlands), Milan, Naples, and Sardinia (soon exchanged for Sicily). The British remained at Gibraltar, to the profound annoyance of the Spaniards, and also annexed the island of Minorca, thereby gaining control of the western Mediterranean. In the New World the British acquired Newfoundland, Nova Scotia, and the Hudson Bay region—the gates of Canada. Spain also gave to England the *asiento*, or monopoly contract for thirty years of supplying the Spanish colonies with African slaves. Each principal victor, with the exception of the Dutch, who received guarantees of their security, shared in the division of the Spanish empire. And French hegemony in Europe was at an end.

Revocation of the Edict of Nantes, 1685. In the midst of his wars, Louis XIV in 1685 revoked the Edict of Nantes, taking from the Huguenots their freedom of worship and their civil political rights. Persecuting the Protestants relentlessly, he drove thousands to the Netherlands, Belgium, or England. They took with them important secrets of French manufacture as well as an undying hatred for the French monarch. Though numbering only about a million among the fifteen million people of France, the Huguenots had been a valuable element in the nation. Louis XIV's senseless intolerance resulted in lasting economic injury to his own country. It was a serious error, for although the Huguenots were decimated in France, Protestantism was by no means destroyed.

The Sun King. The magnificence of Louis XIV's court at Versailles excited the envy of every monarch in Europe. The palace of Versailles, with its innumerable halls and apartments, its luxurious and costly decorations, and its gardens and outlying buildings, cost the people of France at least 100 million dollars. The life of the court was on an extravagant scale. Thousands of retainers tried to keep out of each other's way in the business of serving the king and his court. The nobility vied with one another for the privilege of handing the king his shirt, or of hearing his words of wisdom uttered while he bathed; they had in mind, of course, the possibility of receiving favors, offices, or pensions. An elab-

Cavalier of the Court of Louis XIV, about 1706.

orate etiquette was prescribed for every ceremony.

The king's munificence attracted to his court not only polished courtiers and glamorous ladies, but also savants and scholars of wit and learning. The age of Louis XIV was the most brilliant in the history of French literature: Corneille (1606–1684), Racine (1639–1699), Molière (1622–1673), Pascal (1623–1662), Chapelain (1595–1674), La Fontaine (1621–1695), and a long list of poets, dramatists, philosophers, scientists, and orators were encouraged and rewarded with pensions.

Versailles inspired every little princeling in Europe. The result was disastrous when some impecunious prince in Bavaria attempted to build a castle resembling Versailles, and sought to imitate the court life and etiquette of the Grand Monarch. There was also an ugly side to the grand picture: Versailles was constructed on a base of moral corruption and misery. If France was for some generations distinguished for the splendor of her courts, she was notable also for the terrible reaction against greed and exploitation which she later had to endure. Behind the luxurious halls of Versailles was the specter of rebellion, which was to strip the gilded coating from an antiquated society.

At the death of Louis XIV in 1715, France was staggering under an enormous public debt. Merchants, artisans, and peasants, backbone of the economy, were crushed by taxation. The Sun King, with his repetitive wars, had run the country into the ground. When the old king's body was borne through the streets of Paris to his grave, he was openly cursed by the people to whom his wars and extravagances had brought only misery and hunger.

The Idea of International Law. The Thirty Years' War and Louis XIV's wars awakened reasonable men to the necessity for some means of governing international relations. The catastrophic Thirty Years' War moved Hugo Grotius, a Dutch publicist and statesman, to write his famous treatise *On the Law of War and Peace* (1625). Grotius warned the new national states of Europe against completely irresponsible individualism. He asserted that there was an international law based on reason and on man's nature as a social being. He recommended that war be waged only for just causes; that no greater injury be inflicted upon the enemy than was absolutely necessary; that the rights of ambassadors and neutrals be carefully respected; and that treaties be observed. These proposals were amplified by Samuel Pufendorf, a German jurist, who declared in his *On the Law of Nature and of Nations* (1672) that international law was not restricted to Christendom, but bound together all the nations.

⤵{ KEY DOCUMENT }⤴

LOUIS XIV'S DECREE REVOKING THE EDICT OF NANTES, 1685

Emil Reich, ed., *Select Documents Illustrating Medieval and Modern History* (London, 1915), pp. 381–386.

LOUIS XIV's revocation of Henry IV's Edict of Nantes (1598) granting toleration to the Huguenots was preceded by a long campaign of conversion. In 1685, on the assumption that few Huguenots were left, he was persuaded to revoke the edict. The result was the exodus of many thousands of oppressed Huguenots, who escaped to the Netherlands, England, Prussia, and America. In Catholic countries, the decree revoking the Edict of Nantes was hailed as the most statesmanlike and glorious act of Louis XIV's reign.

King Henry the Great, our grandfather of glorious memory, being desirous that the peace which he had procured for his subjects after the great losses they had suffered on account of civil and foreign wars, should not be troubled on account of the *Religion Prétendue Reformée* [the religion which pretended to be reformed], as had happened in the reigns of his predecessors, by his edict, granted at Nantes in the month of April, 1598, regulated the procedure to be adopted with regard to those of the said religion . . . to be in a better position to work, as he had resolved to do, for the reunion to the Church of those who had so lightly withdrawn from it. . . .

We now see, with thankful recognition of our debt to God, that our endeavors have attained their proposed end, inasmuch as the better and the greater part of our subjects of the said *Religion Prétendue Reformée* have embraced the Catholic faith. And since by this fact the execution of the Edict of Nantes and of all that has ever been ordained in favor of the said *Religion Prétendue Reformée* has become useless, we have determined that we can do nothing better . . . than entirely to revoke the said Edict of Nantes. . . .

ARTICLE I. Be it known that . . . we have, by this present perpetual and irrevocable edict, suppressed and revoked, and do suppress and revoke, the edict of our said grandfather given at Nantes in April, 1598 . . . and the edict given at Nîmes in July, 1629. We declare them null and void. . . . It is our pleasure, that all the temples of those of the said *Religion Prétendue Reformée* situated in our kingdom, countries, territories,

and the lordships under our crown, shall be demolished without delay.

ARTICLE II. We forbid our subjects of the *Religion Prétendue Reformée* further to assemble in any place or private house for the exercise of the said religion. . . .

ARTICLE III. We likewise forbid all noblemen, of what condition soever, to hold such religious exercises in their houses or fiefs. . . .

ARTICLE IV. We enjoin all ministers of the said *Religion Prétendue Reformée*, who do not desire to become converts and to embrace the Catholic, Apostolic, and Roman religion to leave our kingdom and the territories subject to us within fifteen days of the publication of our present edict, without leave to reside therein beyond that period, or, during the said fifteen days, to engage in any preaching, exhortation, or any other function. . . .

ARTICLE VII. We forbid private schools for the instruction of children of the said *Religion Prétendue Reformée*, and in general all things whatever that can be held as a concession of any kind in favor of the said religion. . . .

ARTICLE IX. And to extend our clemency towards those of our subjects of the said *Religion Prétendue Reformée* who, before the publication of our present edict, have emigrated from our kingdom, lands, and territories subject to us, it is our will and pleasure that in case they return within four months from the day of the said publication, it shall be lawful for them and they may take possession again of their property. . . .

ARTICLE X. We repeat our most express prohibition to all our subjects of the said *Religion Prétendue Reformée,* together with their wives and children, against leaving our kingdom, lands, and territories subject to us, or transporting their goods and effects therefrom under penalty, as respects the men, of being sent to the galleys, and as respects the women, of imprisonment and confiscation of their goods.

⟅ HISTORICAL INTERPRETATION ⟆

FRANÇOIS GUIZOT ON THE HISTORICAL SIGNIFICANCE OF LOUIS XIV

François Pierre Guillaume Guizot, *The History of Civilization in Europe,* trans. by William Hazlitt (New York, 1900), pp. 208–216, *passim.* Courtesy of the Colonial Press.

FRANÇOIS PIERRE GUILLUAME GUIZOT (1787–1874), French historian and statesman, wrote *The History of Civilization in Europe,* in which he described Louis XIV as the great perfector of the French monarchy and the architect of modern France. But at the same time he charged that the Grand Monarch brought about a rigid absolutism which could not easily be adapted to new conditions and which had but little support from the French people. This view has been popular in historical scholarship since Guizot first presented it.

When we occupy ourselves with the government of Louis XIV, when we endeavor to appreciate the causes of his power and influence in Europe, we scarcely think of anything but his renown, his conquests, his magnificence, and the literary glory of his time. It is to external causes that we apply ourselves, and attribute the European preponderance of the French government. But I conceive that this preponderance had deeper and more serious foundations. We must not believe that it was simply by means of victories, *fêtes,* or even master-works of genius, that Louis XIV and his government, at this epoch, played the part which it is impossible to deny them. . . .

Recall to your memory the state into which France was fallen after the government of Cardinal Richelieu, and during the minority of Louis XIV: the Spanish armies always on the frontiers, sometimes in the interior; continual danger of an invasion; internal dissensions urged to extremity, civil war, the government weak and discredited at home and abroad. Society was perhaps in a less violent, but still sufficiently analogous state to ours, prior to the eighteenth *Brumaire* [November 9, 1799, the day Napoleon took power]. It was from this state that the government of Louis XIV extricated France. His first victories had the effect of the victory of Marengo: they secured the country, and retrieved the national honor. . . .

First of all let us speak of the wars of Louis XIV. The wars of Europe have originated, as you know, and as I have often taken occasion to remind you, in great popular movements. Urged by necessity, caprice, or any other cause, entire populations, sometimes numerous, sometimes in simple bands, have transported themselves from one territory to another. This was the general character of European wars until after the crusades, at the end of the thirteenth century.

At that time began a species of wars scarcely less different from modern wars than the above. These were the distant wars, undertaken no longer by the people, but by governments, which went at the head of their armies to seek states and adventures afar off. They quitted their countries, abandoned their own territories, and plunged, some into Germany, others into Italy, and others into Africa, with no other motives than personal caprice. Almost all the wars of the fifteenth and even a part of the sixteenth century were of this description. . . . The wars of Louis XIV had no such character; they were the wars of a regular government, fixed in the centre of its states, and laboring to make conquests around it, to extend or consolidate its territory; in a word, they were political wars.

They may have been just or unjust; they may have cost France too dearly; there are a thousand reasons which might be adduced against their morality and their excess; but they bear a character incomparably more rational than the antecedent wars: they were no longer undertaken for whim or adventure; they were dictated by some serious motive; it was some natural limit that it seemed desirable to attain; some population speaking the same language that they aimed at annexing; some point of defence against a neighboring power, which it was thought necessary to acquire. No doubt personal ambition had a share in these wars; but examine one after another of the wars of Louis XIV, particularly those of the first part of his reign, and you will find that they had truly political motives; and that they were conceived for the interest of France, for obtaining power, and for the country's safety. . . .

Let us now consider the interior of France, the administration and legislation of Louis XIV; we shall there discern new explanations of the power and splendor of his government. . . .

Up to this time, there had been nothing so difficult, in France as in the rest of Europe, as to effect the penetration of the action of the central power into all parts of society, and to gather into the bosom of the central power the means of force existing in society. To this end Louis XIV labored, and succeeded, up to a certain point; incomparably better, at least, than preceding governments had done. I cannot enter into details: just run over, in thought, all kinds of public services, taxes, roads, industry, military administration, all the establishments which belong to whatsoever branch of administration; there is scarcely one of which you do not find either the origin, development, or great amelioration under Louis XIV. It was as administrators that the greatest men of his time, Colbert and Louvois, displayed their genius and exercised their ministry. It was by the excellence of its administration that his government acquired a generality, decision, and consistency which were wanting to all the European governments around him. . . . The ordinances of Louis XIV, so very superior to anything preceding them, powerfully contributed to advance French society in the career of civilization.

You see that under whatever point of view we regard this government, we very soon discover the source of its power and influence. It was the first government that presented itself to the eyes of Europe as a power sure of its position, which had not to dispute its existence with internal enemies—tranquil as to its dominions and the people, and intent only on governing. Up to that time, all European governments had been unceasingly thrown into wars, which deprived them of security as well as leisure, or had been so beset with parties and internal enemies that they were compelled to spend their time in fighting for their lives. The government of Louis XIV appeared as the first which applied itself solely to the conduct of affairs, as a power at once definitive and progressive; which was not afraid of innovating, because it could count upon the future. . . .

And now we inquire—and it is impossible to help doing so—how it happened that a power, thus brilliant, and, judging from the facts which I have placed before you, thus well established, so rapidly fell into decline? How, after having played such a part in Europe, it became, in the next century, so inconsistent, weak, and inconsiderable? The fact is incontestable. In the seventeenth century the French government was at the head of European civilization; in the eighteenth century it disappeared; and it was French society, separated from its government, often even opposed to it, that now preceded and guided the European world in its progress.

It is here that we discover the incorrigible evil and the infallible effect of absolute power. . . . By the very fact that this government had no other principle than absolute power, and reposed upon no other base than this, its decline became sudden and well merited. What France, under Louis XIV, essentially wanted, was political institutions and forces, independent, subsisting of themselves, and, in a word, capable of spontaneous action and resistance. The ancient French institutions, if they merited that name, no longer existed: Louis XIV completed their ruin. He took no care to endeavor to replace them by new institutions; they would have cramped him, and he did not choose to be cramped. All that appeared conspicuous at that period was will, and the action of central power. The government of Louis XIV was a great fact, a fact powerful and splendid, but without roots. . . .

❧ TEN BASIC BOOKS ❧

PRELUDE TO UPHEAVAL: THE ASCENDANCY OF FRANCE

1. Belloc, Hilaire, *Richelieu, 1585–1642* (London, 1930).
2. Cole, Charles W., *Colbert and a Century of French Mercantilism,* 2 vols. (New York, 1939).
3. Doolin, Paul R., *The Fronde* (Cambridge, Mass., 1935).
4. England, Sylvia L., *The Massacre of St. Bartholomew* (London, 1938).
5. Federn, Carl, *Mazarin, 1602–1661* (Paris, 1934).
6. Grant, Arthur, *The Huguenots* (London, 1934).
7. Ogg, David, *Louis XIV* (New York, 1933).
8. Packard, Laurence B., *The Age of Louis XIV* (New York, 1929).
9. Usher, Abbott, *The History of the Grain Trade in France, 1400–1700* (Cambridge, Mass., 1950).
10. Wedgwood, Cicely V., *Richelieu and the French Monarchy* (New York, 1950).†

10

The Tudor Monarchy in England: From Henry VII to Elizabeth

A TYPICAL Englishman . . . is descended in four different lines from Irish
kinglets; he is descended in as many lines from Scottish and Pictish kings.
He has Manx blood. He claims descent from at least three lines from Alfred
the Great, and so links up with Anglo-Saxon blood, but he links up also in
several lines with Charlemagne and the Carlovingians. He sprang also from
the Saxon emperors of Germany, as well as from Barbarossa and the Hohenstaufens. He has Norwegian blood and much Norman blood. He has descent
from the Duke of Bavaria, of Saxony, of Flanders, the Prince cf Savoy, and
the Kings of Italy. He has the blood in his veins of Franks, Alamans, Mero-
vingians, Burgundians, and Langobards. He sprang in direct descent from
the Hun rulers of Hungary and the Greek emperors of Constantinople. If
I recollect rightly, Ivan the Terrible provides a Russian link. There is probably
not one of the races of Europe concerned in folk-wanderings which has not
had a share in [his] ancestry.

—KARL PEARSON

1. Beginnings of the English National State

Development of National Unity. English
history starts with the departure of the Romans in the early fifth century A.D. In 449,
Teutonic tribes—Angles, Saxons, and Jutes—
began to arrive, and gradually pushed the
Britons westward. At the end of the eighth
century a new set of invaders, the Northmen
or Danes, overran about half of Britain, and
settled in the Danelaw, or eastern district.
Alfred the Great (r. 871–899) halted the
ravages of the Northmen. The Treaty of Wed-
more (878) put a limit to their advance,
thereby setting the foundation for a national
monarchy. Alfred's Saxon successors gradually
recovered all England. William the Conqueror
(r. 1066–1087) invaded England in 1066, defeated King Harold at the Battle of Hastings
and ended Saxon supremacy.

William was careful to avoid those disruptive
tendencies which had divided the Continent
into so many petty principalities. By the Oath
of Salisbury he required his vassals to swear
allegiance to him directly instead of to their
immediate overlords, thus strengthening the
Crown. Never having been a part of the Holy
Roman Empire, England was not subjected to
those feudal rivalries which had caused fragmentation on the Continent.

The process of national consolidation was
carried on steadily by William's successors. In
the Hundred Years' War (1338–1453), a conflict growing out of dynastic and economic
rivalries, England lost all her possessions in
France, with the exception of Calais. Driven
from France, England suffered war between
the house of York and the house of Lancaster,
rival claimants to the throne. In the struggles
known as the Wars of the Roses (1455–1485)
from the badges of the two houses, the white

rose of York and the red rose of Lancaster, the feudal nobility nearly succeeded in destroying itself. Richard III (r. 1483–1485) lost his life at the battle of Bosworth (1485), at which point the senseless slaughter came to an end. So great was the national disgust with these wars in which rival claimants fought to exhaustion that most Englishmen welcomed the resulting absolutism as an alternative preferable to anarchy. The middle class, unable to function in the chaos, yearned for the protection of a strong, centralized monarchy. By the fifteenth century England was further advanced than France or Spain on the way to national unity and a national government. National feeling was to consolidate around the house of Tudor.

The term "Tudor absolutism" is utilized to describe the type of strong royal government which characterized this English dynasty. However, it is important to remember that this was absolutism of a very special nature, certainly not to be confused with that totalitarian absolutism of the twentieth century. At the height of Tudor absolutism, every institution and every individual in England was under the sovereignty of the monarch, but the Tudors never claimed completely unrestricted powers. Major policy changes were ratified by acts of Parliament. The Tudors, cognizant of the needs and wishes of their subjects, and skilled in statecraft, were careful to seek a constitutional basis for their government.

2. The Reign of Henry VII

Henry VII Subjects the Feudal Nobility. Henry Tudor, Earl of Richmond, victor over Richard III at Bosworth Field, was hailed as king on the field of battle. He was publicly crowned at Westminster as Henry VII (r. 1485–1509). Only remotely descended from the House of Lancaster, and ignoring heirs of the Yorkist line with superior claims, Henry nevertheless announced that he had come to the throne "by the just title of inheritance and by the judgment of God who gave him victory." He further consolidated his position by marrying Elizabeth, heiress of the house of York,

thereby uniting the claims of the rival houses. Conscientious, systematic, able, he was well fitted for the task of leading England from feudalism to national unity. He faced a difficult situation. The government was demoralized by dynastic quarrels; the treasury was empty; trade and industry were at a standstill; laws were flouted by wealthy nobles and outlaws alike. Henry VII offered his people a strong hand to end these chaotic conditions and restore order. They, in turn, were quite willing to overlook Henry's weak claim to the throne in return for peace, order, and security.

Henry VII's first step was to subjugate the feudal nobility. In this aim he was supported by the lesser nobility, who had not taken part in the civil strife, and the middle class, which needed peace and order for the effective pursuit of business. The surviving great nobles still controlled large bands of armed followers who wore the livery (badge, collar, or other insignia) of their lords, and who were "maintained" in lawsuits in the courts by their lords. Ready to fight on command, these bands, if organized into larger armies, could have become a definite threat to the royal power. Henry VII suppressed these intractable nobles and forbade all liveries, except for lowly domestics (Statute of Livery and Maintenance). He harshly put down the rebellions of Lambert Simnel (1477–1534) and Perkin Warbeck (c. 1474–1499).

The Court of Star Chamber. In 1487 Henry VII set up a new court, known later as the Court of Star Chamber (it met in a room decorated with stars, hence its name). Consisting of a committee of his loyal ministers, councilors, and judges, this extraordinary court was used to try powerful noble offenders who might have overawed the ordinary tribunals. Not bound by ordinary court procedures, it could act swiftly against those who would have bribed their way out of the lower courts. Acting upon Roman principles, it used Roman rules of evidence, and dispensed with a jury. The Star Chamber punished those lords guilty of interfering with the course of justice or of encroaching on the rights of poor neighbors. The lower courts were thus left free to handle lesser crimes. During Henry VII's reign the Star Chamber was an effective instrument for correcting injustice because it was speedy and certain. (Later, under the Stuarts, it aroused hostility as an instrument of royal tyranny and was abolished in 1641.)

Henry VII Encourages Trade and Industry. While thus restraining and subjugating the nobility, Henry VII also began to promote the interests of the commercial class. There was method in his encouragement of trade and industry: customs duties provided an important source of royal revenue. In 1496 he signed an agreement, later known as the *Intercursus Magnus,* which obtained for English wool merchants favorable conditions in trade with the Netherlands, the chief market for English wool and cloth. He also negotiated trade pacts with the Scandinavian countries, Spain, and Italian cities, notably Venice. To protect the position of English shipping on the high seas, he instituted the first navigation laws, which provided that certain types of goods could be imported into England only in English ships manned by English sailors. He promoted such mercantilistic policies as acquisition of bullion, protective tariffs, favorable balance of trade, expansion of the navy and merchant marine, and chartering of monopolies.

Henry VII was not quite so successful in agriculture. The demand for wool led many landlords to turn to sheep-farming as a more profitable venture than working the soil. To gain more land for pasture the landlords began to evict their tenants or appropriate their common lands. This practice, called enclosure, ultimately contributed to the prosperity of the country, but it was resented by the peasants who were evicted or forced to sell their land. Parliament tried without success to limit the practice of enclosures. Distressed and resentful, the peasants broke into a series of rebellions, all of which were harshly suppressed.

The Royal Treasury. Throughout his reign Henry VII devoted himself to the task of filling the royal treasury. During the Middle Ages, English kings, always in need of funds, had begun the practice of calling upon Parliament for additional money. Henry was determined to avoid this procedure, which he regarded as a serious error, since it gave Parliament a "power of the purse" to curtail his authority. He called for strict economy in all public expenditures. Anxious to obtain popular support for his regime, he placed a heavier tax burden on the nobility and the wealthy merchants. He required those who could afford it to hand over "benevolences," or forced loans, on the ground that if they appeared prosperous they must have an excess of money, or if they looked poverty-stricken, they must be hiding their wealth. He confiscated the land and property of disloyal nobles. Regularly exploiting the law courts for additional revenue, he obtained vast sums from fines levied by the Court of Star Chamber. He also pocketed surpluses from funds extracted from Parliament to carry on his wars. As a condition of peace, he demanded and got indemnities from his foreign enemies. All these steps together resulted in an overflowing treasury. No previous king of England had accumulated as much wealth as Henry VII held at the time of his death. Although his subjects were displeased by his hoarding and avarice, they were thankful that he had delivered them from political anarchy.

Foreign Policy of Henry VII. Henry VII's shrewd foreign policy was based on the assumption that conquest by marriage was by far cheaper than conquest by war. Two of his marriage alliances were important for the future history of England. In 1501 he concluded a marriage treaty with Spain by awarding the hand of Catherine of Aragon to his eldest son, Arthur, thus joining the Tudor dynasty with the royal house of Spain. When Arthur died within six months. Catherine was then given to the king's second son, Henry (later Henry VIII). Henry VII was eager to keep Catherine in the family, despite her lack of beauty. He then negotiated several commercial treaties with Spain. He gave the hand of his daughter, Margaret, to James IV of Scotland, thereby gaining ten years of peace on the

English-Scottish frontier. This marriage resulted, about a hundred years later, in 1603, in the personal union of England and Scotland and later in the parliamentary union of England and Scotland in 1707.

The Tudor Dynasty Firmly Established. Henry VII, worn out by toil and worry, died in 1509 at the age of fifty-two. He left England in better condition than it had been at his accession. He had brought an end to a century of strife. He had led his country from feudal turmoil to peace and prosperity. His King's Peace prepared England for her glorious days of commercial supremacy. The people preferred his form of benevolent absolutism to the frustrating civil wars of the old days. The framework of Tudor despotism was established—a strong hand at the helm, a full treasury, an undisputed succession.

Historical Controversy: Nature of the New Monarchy. In 1907 the Oxford historian Alfred F. Pollard projected the "New Monarchy" thesis, which pointed to the Tudor kings as embodying national aspirations and voicing the national will. England in the sixteenth century put its trust in its princes far more than in its Parliaments. The Tudors themselves crystallized this feeling into a practical weapon of absolute government. "This is the real tyranny of Tudor times; individual life, liberty, and conscience were as nothing compared with national interests. . . . The New Monarchy . . . had a great and indispensable part to play in the making of modern England; it was strong, unprincipled, and efficient."

This point of view was attacked by, among others, the Cambridge historian, Geoffrey Rudolf Elton, who in 1953 warned against its acceptance. While admitting the growing power of the national state, he insisted that it was less autocratic and self-consciously innovatory than is commonly supposed. "It will not do . . . to regard the Tudor state as a purely personal monarchy. . . . The most powerful dynasty ever to sit on England's throne was powerful only as long as it did not go outside the limits laid down by a nation fully conscious of its nationhood."

Here, once again, we see the same set of facts interpreted from diametrically opposed points of view. The student should always be on guard and understand that almost all historical movements are explained in varying conclusions by competent historians.

3. Henry VIII Strengthens the Monarchy

Accession of Henry VIII. Henry VIII (r. 1509–1547), second son of Henry VII and Elizabeth of York, united in his person the blood of the rival houses of Lancaster and York, a good omen for both the nobility and the common people. Young, handsome, and athletic, he was intelligent, fascinated by the New Learning, and on good terms with his subjects. Though he had hardly completed his eighteenth year when he ascended the throne, he gave great cause for rejoicing. The people placed much faith in his ability and leadership.

Domestic Affairs. At first Henry VIII paid little attention to the affairs of government. For nearly two decades he left both domestic and foreign affairs in the capable hands of Thomas Wolsey (c. 1475–1530), appointed chancellor of England in 1515 and raised to the rank of cardinal by the pope in the same year. (Wolsey thus held the highest temporal and ecclesiastical offices open to a subject in England.) It was said that Wolsey "ruled both king and kingdom," but actually Henry's will was always paramount.

In the beginning of his reign, Henry VIII enhanced his popularity with the people by checking the nobles' practice of extortion on the pretext of enforcing forgotten laws. He also brought his father's financial ministers to trial on charges of treason. But he soon abandoned this liberal attitude and reverted to all the policies which his father had recommended as necessary for Crown and State. He continued to suppress the feudal nobility; he chose his advisers from among the dependable gentry; he maintained an alliance with the com-

Henry VIII and his wives. Clockwise from the bottom they are Catherine of Aragon, Catherine Parr, Jane Seymour, Anne of Cleves, Catherine Howard, and Anne Boleyn.

mercial middle class; he nurtured trade and industry; he watched the administration of justice. Laboring incessantly to advance the prestige of the Crown, he broke with the papacy at Rome and destroyed the power of the Catholic Church in England. (*See page 86 ff.*)

Henry VIII, in common with other members of the Tudor dynasty, considered his absolutism far removed from that of the princes of the Italian Renaissance. He scrupulously preserved a constitutional course by seeing to it that all repressive measures were ratified by Parliament. He allowed that body to retain its traditional authority of making laws and controlling taxation. He was careful to register with Parliament his break with Rome and his dissolution of the monasteries. He never ig-

nored popular sentiment. His despotism was thus a sort of dictatorship by popular consent.

Henry VIII's Foreign Policy. Both Henry VIII and Cardinal Wolsey wanted to win for England a position of equality with France and Spain, at that time the dominant Continental powers. Both king and minister hoped to profit from the lifelong rivalry between Francis I of France and the Emperor Charles V. England would be the arbiter between them, thus enhancing her own prestige. Both Francis I and Charles V sought Henry's favor. Unlike his cautious, thrifty father, Henry was drawn into adventures on the Continent. His first venture made it clear to him that France was now too strong to be overrun in the old fashion. Landing with 25,000 men at Calais in 1513, with the intention of joining Ferdinand of Spain in a war against France, Henry believed that he could recover the duchy of Aquitaine. When he discovered that Ferdinand's assistance was ephemeral, he made peace quickly. While Henry was thus contained in France, the Scots, as a matter of tradition, attacked England, only to be beaten back by the Earl of Surrey at the Battle of Flodden Field (1513).

During the next few years the great monarchs of Europe died one by one—Louis XII of France (1515), Ferdinand of Aragon (1516), and Maximilian I, Holy Roman Emperor (1519). Francis I succeeded Louis XII, while Charles I took over control of Spain and the Netherlands in 1516 and of the Empire (1519). Valois and Hapsburgs now engaged in a series of wars. Henry VIII, pleased by the rivalry and anxious to prevent victory by either side, magnanimously promised help to both houses. He reasoned that if either side won a complete victory, England would be reduced to a second-rate power. In the long run Henry VIII's extravagant policy was doomed to failure. The House of Commons, appalled by the cost of Continental commitments, in 1523 rebelled by granting only half the subsidies requested, and warned the king that the treasury could not sustain any further foreign adventures. The king, blaming Wolsey, turned his attention to the task of building up the royal navy.

Estimate of Henry VIII. Henry VIII ended his reign with the reputation of a tyrant. A great eater, he grew fat and lazy, his body attacked by debilitating disease. He died on January 29, 1547, at the age of fifty-six, after a reign of some thirty-eight years. His personality and achievements have caused controversy to the present day. Crafty, hypocritical, and selfish, he was morally a weakling. Although he labored mightily to make England great, it was not because of overwhelming love for his people but because of his own egoism. He strengthened the power of the Crown by his ecclesiastical policies. Despite his personal idiosyncrasies it is fair to say that he was one of the most successful rulers in British history.

4. Culmination of Tudor Sovereignty: Reign of Queen Elizabeth

Elizabeth. There were important doctrinal and liturgical changes during the reign of Edward VI (1547–1553). During the reign of Mary (1553–1558) the English people were alienated from the Roman Catholic Church. Protestantism in England was assured. Childless, deserted by her husband failing to reestablish the Catholic faith, Mary died on November 17, 1558. In the reign of Elizabeth (1558–1603) a national religion was established as a compromise between the extremes of Catholicism and Protestantism. The settlement was peaceful and permanent. (*See page 89 ff.*)

Elizabeth, daughter of Henry VIII and Anne Boleyn, spent her early years in obscurity and disgrace. Well educated, she became increasingly vain as she grew older. She came to the throne at the age of twenty-five. She acted shrewdly and ruthlessly when it became necessary. Living simply, working hard, she governed her realm with rigid economy. Throughout her forty-five-year reign she was constantly in danger of either overthrow or assassination, but she lived to give England one of the most brilliant periods of her history.

The Dynastic Problem. "More than a man, and sometimes less than a woman," Elizabeth never married. Apparently, she had an unconquerable distaste for marriage. She was called the Virgin Queen. Childless, she was annoyed by the very existence of Mary Stuart, known as Mary, Queen of Scots (1542–1587), daughter of James V of Scotland and Mary of Lorraine and the nearest heir to the English throne. Mary had become queen of Scotland when an infant. Educated in France with the royal children, she was married in 1558 to the sickly French dauphin. When Mary of England died in 1558, the Scottish Mary formally laid claim to the throne of England on the ground that she had the most legitimate claim. Elizabeth, she asserted, was not only an illegitimate daughter of Henry VIII but also "usurper" of the throne. The issue was complicated by religious difficulties, for Mary of Scotland was a devout Catholic while Elizabeth was inclined toward Protestantism.

Mary returned to Scotland in 1560 on the death of her French husband. A product of her times, she surrendered wholeheartedly to the tradition of conspiracy. With no control over her heart, she became involved in one romantic episode after another, including the death of her Italian favorite, David Rizzio, at Holyrood Palace in 1566; the murder of her consort Darnley in 1567; her marriage to the murderer, Bothwell; her escape from the Protestant Scottish nobles; and her flight to England to place herself under the protection of Elizabeth.

Elizabeth's position was difficult. She could not let Mary of Scotland, her greatest rival for the throne, escape her now. While Mary lived, even though a Catholic, she remained a barrier between Elizabeth and the other more dangerous claimant to the throne, Philip II of Spain. For nineteen years Elizabeth, biding her time, held Mary prisoner. After 1586 it became clear that a head-on collision with Spain was inevitable anyway. As the principal Catholic contender to the throne, and as one increasingly dependent upon Spanish help, Mary of Scotland became more dangerous than useful. She was therefore sentenced to death. If Mary did not know how to live, she knew at least how to die, for she met her death with dignity and courage. Elizabeth denied responsibility for the execution. But the threat to the throne was removed.

Domestic Policies: Commercial Prosperity. During the reign of Elizabeth there was a rapid growth of commercial prosperity. The queen, careful to follow the pattern set by earlier Tudors, encouraged a sound fiscal policy. She utilized all the mercantilist policies used by her predecessors, such as acquisition of bullion, a favorable balance of trade, and tariffs, bounties, and subsidies. While promoting business and industry, Elizabeth inherited the agricultural problem of enclosures, which remained unremedied during her reign. The amount of available farmland was diminished as the small independent landowning farmers were frozen out. This process continued unabated, with disastrous effects upon British agriculture. Elizabeth was unable to protect the farmers against eviction. They went to the cities where they became lost in the changing labor market.

Elizabeth encouraged her hardy sea captains to ply the high seas in search of business and loot. They sailed to all portions of the globe, searching for new trade routes, raw materials, and new markets. These "gentlemen adventurers" preyed on Spanish and Portuguese commerce. Privateering—individual enterprise on the high seas—became a kind of patriotic duty. English sea dogs such as Drake and Hawkins sailed the Spanish main or assaulted Spain's commercial monopoly in America. Englishmen followed Drake's lead into the Pacific; sought for northeast or northwest passages to the Far East; hunted for slaves in Africa; ran chartered commercial companies such as the Moscovy (1555), the Levant (1581), and East India (1600) companies; and laid the foundations for the colonies of Virginia and Newfoundland. The result was a period of prosperity such as England had never known.

Foreign Policy: Anglo-Spanish Rivalry. Elizabeth was as adept in the arts of double-dealing as any of her predecessors. Her foreign policy hinged on the traditional Tudor scheme of playing one power against the other so that no one power could dominate Europe. Exploiting her maidenhood, she allowed several high-placed suitors to get to the point of asking her hand in marriage, only to retreat when the issue became heated.

Anglo-Spanish rivalry became more aggravated during Elizabeth's reign. Philip II of Spain could not reconcile himself to the rise of Protestantism in England and to the loss of Spanish influence there. The increase in English commerce and industry, plus the profitable English trade with the Spanish colonists in the New World, was galling to proud Spaniards. When Mary, Queen of Scots, was executed in 1587, Philip decided that he would crush the island-kingdom which had become the chief obstacle to the well-being of Spain and to the restoration of Catholicism in Europe. To him the issues were simple: Catholicism versus Protestantism, and Spanish aggrandizement versus English expansion. No longer would he seek to regain his ascendancy over England, which he had lost at the death of Mary of England, by marrying Elizabeth. He obtained an edict from Pope Sixtus V anathematizing Elizabeth and proclaiming a crusade against her. He would destroy both Elizabeth and English power by force of arms.

The Blunder of the Spanish Armada. Philip II strained his treasury to produce a tremendous fleet designed to smash the English navy and transport his armies to English soil. Unfortunately, he listened to the advice of inexperienced landlubbers who had no understanding of the nature of sea power. The entire expedition of the armada turned out to be a grotesque failure from beginning to end. In May 1588 the fleet, which the Spaniards named the Invincible Armada, sailed from Tagus. The great flotilla of 132 ships carried 8,000 seamen and 19,000 soldiers. Philip would sail to the English Channel, establish contact with his Dutch allies, and then invade the British Isles. The danger of invasion drew all Englishmen together. Everyone, Catholics as well as Protestants, united in an outburst of patriotic fervor. The naval heroes Hawkins, Howard, Frobisher, and Drake were assigned to command a total of 180 ships to defend the country, while on land two armies numbering 60,000 men lay in wait for the Spanish.

In July 1588 the two great fleets met in the English Channel near the British coast. The historian John R. Green describes how the Spanish ships broke under the fury of the northern seas. Fifty reached Corunna, bearing 10,000 men stricken with pestilence and death. Of the rest, some were sunk, some dashed to pieces against the Irish cliffs. "The wreckers of the Orkneys and the Faroes, the clansmen of the Scottish Isles, the kernes of Donegal and Galway, all had their part in the work of murder and robbery. Eight thousand Spaniards perished between the Giant's Causeway and the Blaskets. On a strand near Sligo an English captain numbered 1,100 corpses which had been cast up by the sea."

It was a crushing defeat, compounded of English mastery, Spanish weakness, and the winds and waters of the English Channel. The myth of Spanish invincibility was shattered. England no longer feared invasion. From that time on English sea dogs raided Spanish commerce with even greater zest. Although the war with Spain was renewed spasmodically through the rest of Elizabeth's reign, the English were able to retain their advantage in war and trade.

Last Years of Elizabeth. The defeat of the Spanish Armada was the climax of Elizabeth's reign. In the remaining fifteen years of her life she began to lose touch with her subjects. Parliament became increasingly nettled by Tudor despotism, a sentiment that was to merge into a struggle between Crown and Parliament with the accession of the Stuarts. Lonely, without husband or children, the elderly Virgin Queen pined away. A tragic fate deepened the gloom of her last years. Her one favorite, Robert Devereux, Earl of Essex, lost his head on the block after an unsuccessful revolt in London. The desolate, despairing queen did not even try to save his life. Two years later, on March 24, 1603, the last of the Tudors died. Elizabeth left a nation triumphant

in its chief foreign war, convincedly Protestant, economically prosperous, and politically self-confident. Her last address to Parliament revealed her greatness as a ruler: "This I count the chief glory of my crown, that I have reigned with your love."

Elizabethan Culture. There are others who would say that the chief glory of Elizabeth's reign was either the exploits of Elizabethan seamen or the works of Elizabethan writers. Elizabethan literature marked the height of the Renaissance in England. The awakening of national culture, and the increase of wealth, with the consequent increase of leisure and refinement, combined to produce a brilliant literary revival. The production of literary masterpieces reflected a new national sense of security, energy, and power. Of the large number of literary figures only a token trio can be mentioned here.

Edmund Spenser (c. 1552–1599) dedicated his epic *The Faerie Queen* to "the magnificent Empress, renowned for Pietie, Vertue, and all Gratious Government." A poet of exceptional charm, Spenser was an enthusiastic cultivator of the New Learning. His great imagination, his power of language, rhyme, and rhythm, gained him the title of the "Poet's Poet." Shakespeare, Milton, Dryden, and Pope all owed debts to this master of English literature.

William Shakespeare (1564–1616), supreme poet and interpreter of human character and emotions, was one of the most renowned dramatists in history. A versatile genius, Shakespeare gave us some of the best tragedies as well as the most delightful comedies in theatrical history. Superlatives seem inadequate to describe this greatest of all English writers. In the words of Dryden: "He was the man who of all modern, and perhaps ancient poets, had the largest and most comprehensive soul. All the images of nature were still present to him, and he drew them not laboriously, but luckily; when he describes any thing, you more than see it, you feel it, too." Dr. Johnson, ordinarily a harsh critic, spoke of him in reverent tones: "The stream of time, which is continually washing the dissoluble fabrics of other poets, passes without injury by the adamant of Shakespeare." His great gift was an ability to draw character, an art so perfect that his creations seem more real than one's own living acquaintances. At the age of forty-five, Shakespeare retired to his native Stratford-on-Avon to spend the rest of his days in ease, leaving to others the task of carrying on the course of English literature. Shakespeare reflected the Elizabethan age in all its glory.

A third major figure was Francis Bacon (1561–1626), lawyer, statesman, scientist, and man of letters, who sought to revolutionize philosophy by placing the emphasis on experimental science instead of speculative meta-physics. "I have vast contemplative ends as I have moderate civil ends, for I have taken all knowledge to be my province." Today Francis Bacon is regarded as the father of modern scientific research. By abandoning deductive reasoning based on traditional arbitrary premises, and substituting the principle of inductive reasoning, he formulated a new system for interpreting nature and presaged the coming of the Enlightenment. In Macaulay's words: "The art which Bacon taught was the art of inventing arts. The knowledge in which Bacon excelled all men was a knowledge of the mutual relations of all departments of knowledge."

◄ KEY DOCUMENT ►

THE SIX ARTICLES ACT, 1539:
HENRY VIII FORBIDS DOCTRINAL INNOVATIONS

Henry Gee and William John Hardy, eds. *Documents Illustrative of English Church History* (New York, 1896), pp. 305–306.

HENRY VIII dissolved the monasteries as a means of nationalizing the English Church and maintaining his strong Tudor monarchy. He was content to retain the doctrines of the Catholic Church, as indicated by the Six Articles Act passed in 1539 by Parliament. This statute required uniformity in doctrine and practices, reasserted fundamental Catholic beliefs, and called for the death penalty for nonconformity. There was strong Protestant opposition in Parliament—("The Reformation goes backwards in England!")—but it was ineffective.

First, that in the most blessed Sacrament of the altar, by the strength and efficacy of Christ's mighty word (it being spoken by the priest), is present really, under the form of bread and wine, the natural body and blood of our Saviour Jesus Christ, conceived of the Virgin Mary; and that after the consecration there remaineth no substance of bread or wine, nor any other substance, but the substance of Christ, God and man.

Secondly, that communion in both kinds is not necessary *ad salutem*, by the law of God, to all persons; and that it is to be believed, and not doubted of, but that in the flesh, under the form of bread, is the very blood; and with the blood, under the form of wine, is the very flesh; as well apart, as though they were both together.

Thirdly, that priests after the order of priest-hood received, as afore, may not marry, by the law of God.

Fourthly, that vows of chastity or widowhood, by man or woman made to God advisedly, ought to be observed by the law of God; and that it exempts them from other liberties of Christian people which without that they might enjoy.

Fifthly, that it is meet and necessary that private masses be continued and admitted in this the king's English Church and congregation, as whereby good Christian people, ordering themselves accordingly, do receive both godly and goodly consolations and benefits; and it is agreeable also to God's law.

Sixthly, that auricular confession is expedient and necessary to be retained and continued, used and frequented in the Church of God.

❧ HISTORICAL INTERPRETATION ❧

JAMES ANTHONY FROUDE ON ENGLAND IN THE SIXTEENTH CENTURY

James Anthony Froude, *History of England from the Fall of Wolsey to the Defeat of the Spanish Armada*, 12 vols. (London, 1858), I, pp. 86–88. Courtesy of John W. Parker and Son.

JAMES ANTHONY FROUDE (1818–1894), English historian, saw history as a drama and therefore gave prominence to the personal element. The theme of his *History of England* is in the assertion that "the Reformation was the root and source of the expansive force which has spread the Anglo-Saxon race over the globe." He was influenced by Carlyle, especially in his admiration for strong rulers and strong government and in his high praise of Henry VIII. In the following excerpt Froude reviews the system under which England was governed in the sixteenth century. Note his statement that "Of liberty . . . there was no idea."

The state of the country was critical; and the danger from questionable persons traversing it unexamined and uncontrolled was greater than at ordinary times. But in point of justice as well as of prudence, it harmonized with the iron temper of the age, and it answered well for the government of a fierce and powerful people, in whose hearts lay an intense hatred of rascality, and among whom no one need have lapsed into evil courses except by deliberate preference for them. The moral substance of the English must have been strong indeed when it admitted of such stringent treatment; but, on the whole, they [the people] were ruled as they preferred to be ruled; and if wisdom may be tested by success, the manner in which they passed the great crisis of the Reformation is the best justification of their princes. The era was great throughout Europe. The Italians of the age of Michael Angelo; the Spaniards who were the contemporaries of Cortez; the Germans who shook off the pope at the call of Luther; and the splendid chivalry of Francis I, of France, were no common men. But they were all brought face to face with the same trials, and none met them as the English met them. The English alone never lost their self-possession; and if they owed something to fortune in their escape from anarchy, they owed more to the strong hand and steady purpose of their rulers.

In . . . the system under which England was governed, we have . . . a state of things in which the principles of political economy were, consciously or unconsciously, contradicted; where an attempt, more or less successful, was made to bring the production and distribution of wealth under the moral rule of right and wrong; and where those laws of supply and demand, which we are now taught to regard as immutable ordinances of nature, were absorbed or superseded by a higher code. It is necessary for me to repeat that I am not holding up the sixteenth century as a model which the nineteenth might safely follow. The population has become too large, and employment too complicated and fluctuating, to admit of such control; while, in default of control, the relapse upon self-interest as the one motive principle is certain to ensue, and when it ensues is absolute in its operations. But as, even with us, these so-called ordinances of nature in time of war consent to be suspended, and duty to his country becomes with every good citizen a higher motive of action than the advantages which he may gain in an enemy's market; so it is not uncheering to look back upon a time when the nation was in a normal condition of militancy against social injustice; when the government was enabled by happy circumstances to pursue into detail a single and serious aim at the well-being—well-being in its widest sense—of all members of the commonwealth. There were difficulties and drawbacks at that time as well as this. Of liberty, in the modern sense of the word, of the supposed right of every man "to do what he will with his own" or with himself, there was no idea. To the question, if ever it was asked, May I not do what I will with my own? there was the brief answer, No man may do what is wrong, either with that which is his own or with that which is another's. Workmen were not allowed to take advantage of the scantiness of the labour market to exact extravagant wages. Capitalists were not allowed to drive the labourers from their holdings, and destroy their healthy independence. The antagonism of interests was absorbed into a relation of which equity was something more than the theoretic principle, and employers and employed were alike amenable to a law which both were compelled to obey. The working-man of modern times has bought the extension of his liberty at the price of his material comfort. The higher classes have gained in luxury what they have lost in power. It is not for the historian to balance advantages. His duty is with the facts.

❧ TEN BASIC BOOKS ☙

THE TUDOR MONARCHY IN ENGLAND: FROM HENRY VII TO ELIZABETH

1. Bindoff, S. T., *Tudor England* (London, 1950).†
2. Black, John B., *The Reign of Elizabeth, 1558–1603*, 2nd ed. (New York, 1959).
3. Cheyney, Edward P., *History of England from the Defeat of the Spanish Armada to the Death of Elizabeth*, 2 vols. (New York, 1914–1926).
4. Feiling, Keith G., *England under the Tudors and Stuarts* (London, 1935).
5. Froude, James Anthony, *A History of England from the Fall of Wolsey to the Defeat of the Spanish Armada*, 12 vols. (London, 1858).
6. Mattingly, Garrett, *The Armada* (New York, 1959).†
7. Pollard, Albert F., *Henry VIII* (London, 1951).†
8. Read, Conyers, *The Tudors: Personalities and Practical Politics in Sixteenth-Century England* (New York, 1936).
9. Rowse, Alfred L., *The Elizabethan Age*, 2 vols. (London, 1950–1955).
10. Strachey, Giles Lytton, *Elizabeth and Essex: A Tragic History* (New York, 1934).

11

The Germanies: The Rise of Prussia

THE SOVEREIGN represents the State; he and his people form but one body, which can only be happy as far as united by concord. The prince is to the nation he governs what the head is to the man; it is his duty to see, think, and act for the whole community, that he may procure it every advantage of which it is capable. If it be intended that a monarchical should excel a republican government, sentence is pronounced on the sovereign. He must be active, possess integrity, and collect his whole powers, that he may be able to run the career he has commenced.

—FREDERICK THE GREAT

1. Background: Early German History

Early History of the Germanies. The history of Germany begins with the division of the Carolingian Empire among the grandsons of Charlemagne by the Treaty of Verdun (843). Louis the German was unable to fashion an ordered society in the East Frankish (German) kingdom after the destruction caused by the new barbarian invasions of Moravians and Hungarians. When, in 911, the East Frankish line of the Carolingian dynasty died out, there came a struggle for political control as the dukes of Bavaria, Swabia, Franconia, and Lorraine, as well as hundreds of lesser lords of the stem-duchies, resisted any attempts to infringe upon their independence. Any bearer of the German crown was confronted with the double hostility of regionalism and tribalism.

The Early Dynasties. This urge to centralization persisted in the medieval Germanies, because of the efforts of a series of dynasties—the Ottonians, the Franconians, the Hohenstaufens, and the Hapsburgs—to bring about some kind of unity. Otto I (r. 936–973), belonging to the Ottonian (Saxon) dynasty, was able to make the Germanies one of the foremost powers in Europe. Crowned at Rome in 962 by Pope John XII as Holy Roman Emperor, Otto sought to make himself the successor of Augustus, Constantine, and Charlemagne. Thus the attempt was made to re-create the Roman Empire under Germanic auspices. Subsequent German kings also tried to forge unity among the particularistic German duchies and at the same time to control the Italian peninsula and the papacy, but none was successful. Each time a German king embarked on a campaign in the Italies, he had to fight his way through northern Italy and then seek to smash his way back home. Lombardy is filled with the bones of Germans slain in these ineffectual operations.

The central authority remained vague and undefined. Otto's successor, Otto II (r. 973–983), finding the difficulties of his position unsurmountable, was unable to conquer southern Italy. Otto III (r. 983–1002) likewise attempted to expand the German state, but his ambitions brought him into direct conflict with the German princes and the papacy. Henry 11 (r. 1002–1024) contented himself with governing the Germanies.

The Franconian dynasty ruled the Germanies for more than a century. Since there was no direct heir upon the death of Henry II in 1024, Conrad of Franconia was elected by the princes. Conrad II (r. 1024–1039) suppressed rebellions in the Italies and annexed Burgundy (1033). His son Henry III (r. 1039–1056) extended German influence over Slavic areas and Hungary and preserved domestic peace by maintaining the royal authority over both nobility and clergy. The youthful Henry IV, who ascended the throne in 1056, was unable to maintain authority over the papacy and yielded important prerogatives to Pope Gregory VII in the Investiture Struggle.

The Hohenstaufens. The attempt of the Hohenstaufen dynasty—"the most brilliant failures of the Middle Ages"—to consolidate the strength of the empire at the expense of the papacy was likewise unsuccessful. Conrad III (r. 1138–1152), the first of the Hohenstaufens, and Frederick I, known as Barbarossa (r. 1152–1190), were unable to subdue the rebellious northern Italian city-states, nor did the later Hohenstaufens—Henry VI (r. 1190–1197), and Frederick II (r. 1212–1250)—succeed in their goal of breaking the temporal power of the papacy. Despite its failure, the reign of the Hohenstaufen dynasty is regarded by Germans as one of the most glorious periods of their history. The Hohenstaufens, termed by the papacy a "viper brood," did not achieve unity, but they at least promoted German expansion, increased colonization in the northeast, and encouraged the development of urban life.

The Hapsburgs. After the death of the last Hohenstaufen in 1254, there was a period of chaos, the Great Interregnum, lasting until 1273. With the decline of the central power, such strong independent houses as the Luxemburgs, Hapsburgs, and Hohenzollerns each sought to consolidate its position as the leading power in the Germanies. In this period of disunity, the Age of *Faustrecht* (fist law), each local district depended for security upon its own strength. In 1273 Rudolf of Hapsburg was elected to the imperial dignity. Rudolf vigorously suppressed the feuds between local barons and knights and established a semblance of royal authority. He abandoned the Italian peninsula and sought to consolidate his German realm. Freed from the necessity

of sending a constant stream of men and supplies to the south to maintain a shadowy imperial pretense, he was able to strengthen his position in the Germanies.

The breakdown in imperial authority was legally recognized in the next century by an important constitutional document. The independent princes, the great ecclesiastics, and the league of German cities all resisted any increase in royal authority. From Charles IV of Luxemburg (r. 1347–1378), the princes and ecclesiastics were successsful in extracting a document, the Golden Bull (1356), which defined and increased the powers of the prince electors and which, in effect, became the constitution of the medieval Empire. This instrument provided that the Holy Roman Emperor was to be chosen by seven electors: four lay princes (the King of Bohemia, the Duke of Saxony, the Count Palatine of the Rhine, and the Margrave of Brandenburg) and three ecclesiastics (the archbishops of Mayence, Cologne, and Trier). The election was to take place at Frankfort-on-Main and the coronation was to be held at Aix-la-Chapelle (Aachen). There was to be no papal interference in the elections. This epoch-making imperial law effectively froze the sovereign position of the electors and perpetuated the internal divisions of the Germanies.

Broken again into small, independent states, the Germanies degenerated once more into feudal chaos. A compact German Empire, extending to the waters of the Dnieper and the Gulf of Bothnia, might have been fashioned early in German history; instead, the German monarchs squandered their energies in relentless and unsuccessful pursuit of a vague, shadowy ideal.

From the thirteenth century down to the Napoleonic era there was no Germany in a political sense, but only a great number of virtually independent states, some large, some small. The most important Hapsburg leaders, Maximilian I (r. 1493–1519) and Charles V (r. 1520–1555) still pursued the dream of acquiring control over the Italies; they were unsuccessful either because their main interests were elsewhere or because the local German princes were too powerful. While English and French monarchs were consolidating strong national unions, the Germanies remained an aggregation of weak, squabbling states.

The Reformation. At this time Austria was the nominal head of the Holy Roman Empire, which had at best no more than a theoretical unity. The disruptive force of the Reformation weakened the control of the Catholic emperors over the Protestant German states. The revolt against Rome in the Germanies sprang from resentment against the papacy which, as a tried and fixed policy, always supported the particularistic lords against the German emperor as a means of preventing national German unity. Luther gave the Germans a consciousness of national existence, but at the same time contributed heavily to the dualism of German history. He broke with the medieval dream of universalism, only to lead the German people once more into the quagmire of particularism. Lutheranism began by eliminating papal influence in the north of Germany, but leadership promptly fell into the hands of the princes. Lutheran Protestantism, accepted by only half the German population, made its way among the princes of the North Sea and Baltic area, while in Bavaria, in the southwest, and in the Rhineland the princes and people remained loyal to Rome. It was a permanent split.

In the Thirty Years' War (1618–1648) the German princes, helped by Denmark, Sweden, and France, successfully resisted the imperial power. The Treaty of Westphalia (1648), depriving the Holy Roman Emperor of his powers over the German principalities, marked the end of imperial efforts to unify the Germanies. Freed from centralized control, the petty princes were left again to their own devices. By the late eighteenth century the Germanies took on the quality of a geographical expression, consisting of 314 states and 1,475 estates, a total of 1,789 independent sovereign powers. Many kings, dukes, and margraves attempted, despite limited budgets, to create their courts on the majestic model of Louis XIV's Versailles. The development of a normal, healthy nationalism out of this crazy-quilt pattern was, perhaps, too much to expect. Although feudalism was broken in other Western European countries, it lingered on for several additional centuries in the conglomerate Germanies.

2. The Emergence of Prussia

The Nuclei of Prussia. Three small separated territories in northern Germany were eventually joined together to form the nucleus of the Brandenburg-Prussian state: Brandenburg in the center, between the Elbe and the Oder; Prussia in the east, along the Baltic; and the Cleves-Mark inheritance on the Lower Rhine. During the latter part of the reign of Otto the Great in the tenth century, border provinces, or marks, had been established along the whole eastern frontier of the Holy Roman Empire as bulwarks against the Slavs. One of these marks, Brandenburg, a remote frontier state of sandy wastes, had been carved out as a feudal domain by the crusading Teutonic knights, who had either exterminated or converted the local Slavs. The margrave of Brandenburg was the least important of the Seven Electors who traditionally elected the Holy Roman Emperor and whose positions were legalized by the Golden Bull of 1356.

After some five centuries of separate existence, Brandenburg, Prussia, and Cleves-Mark were united in a personal union under John Sigismund, Elector of Brandenburg (r. 1608–1619). Together with fresh territory, these three lands emerged to form the Frederician state and the basis of the Bismarckian empire. There was no "growth" of Prussia in the accepted sense, for she represented no popular force, and she scarcely belonged to Germany, either geographically or culturally. Her lone, and decisive, asset was a sense of ruthless power acquired in the long process of dominating the Slavic peoples. But it was Prussia that impressed upon the remainder of the Germanies a pattern of traditions and ideals that came to be recognized as universally German.

Historical Controversy: The Role of Prussia. There is a difference of opinion among historians on the role of Prussia in German history. Inside nineteenth-century Germany the three great masters of the nationalist Prussian school of historiography, Johann Gustav Droysen, Heinrich von Sybel, and Heinrich von Treitschke, lauded Prussia as the repository of efficiency, progress, and reform, as the embodiment of German might, and praised the Hohenzollerns as destined to revive the glory of the old imperial Germany. To these professor–prophets, who tried to work politically through history *("durch die Geschichte politisch zu wirken")*, Prussia was the real State-forming source in German history. This "weapon-proud eagle land of the North," said Treitschke, gave Germany its national genius and character.

Quite different points of view were taken by twentieth-century historians outside Germany, notably Lewis B. Namier and A. J. P. Taylor in England, Edmond Vermeil in France, and Koppel S. Pinson in the United States. These historians saw the emergence of Prussia as impressing upon the rest of Germany a set of values, traditions, and ideals (obedience, discipline, thoroughness, respect for leadership, love for order, worship of the state, belief that might makes right), which came to be accepted as German. The supremacy of the military over the civil, the special position of the army in German life, these features of later Germany bore witness to the triumph of the Prussian spirit. It was this touchy, sensitive Prussian attitude which gave content to German national character and to German aggressive nationalism. It was fundamentally different from the spirit of Western Europe.

The Hohenzollern Dynasty. The ancestral home of the Zollerns was a Swabian castle near the Danube and the Neckar, just north of Switzerland. In 1170 Conrad of Hohenzollern left his home to seek his fortune by serving under Frederick Barbarossa. Two centuries later, one of Conrad's descendants was invested with the sovereignty of Brandenburg. Displaying its symbolic emblem—"From the Mountains to the Sea"—the Hohenzollern family began to play in northern Germany a role

comparable to that of the Hapsburgs in the south. To consolidate and increase their territories by acquiring intermediate lands became their steady goal. In the religious wars following the Reformation, Brandenburg emerged as an important Protestant state. During the seventeenth century the Hohenzollerns became wealthy by confiscating Catholic properties.

The Junkers. The emergence of Prussia was an outgrowth of a union of the Hohenzollern dynasty and a noble squirearchy of bellicose Junkers. Brandenburg, an area of savagery and conquest, had been dominated by a ruthless, arrogant, ignorant nobility, many of whom were of Slavic origin. These Junkers— the name is derived from *junc herre* (young lord)—were great landed nobles who understood the arts of war and efficient administration. From their ranks came many of the generals, statesmen, and businessmen who played an important part in later German development. The Prussian Junkers have been aptly described as barbarians who had learned to handle a rifle and, still more, bookkeeping by double entry. Politically, they remained in a primitive stage, but economically and administratively they foreshadowed the era of the Industrial Revolution.

From the political, social, and economic disturbances that accompanied the making of modern Germany, the Junkers emerged as the dominant, governing social class. They learned, as Frederick William I had hoped, "to recognize no leaders other than God and the King of Prussia." Combining physical courage with worship of the sword, political knowledge with cruelty and brutality, tenacity with arrogance, the Junkers exhibited a capacity to endure under any circumstances. Always mercenary and selfish, they identified the national interests of Germany with their own. When the new industrial and financial aristocracy of western and southern Germany attained a position of power, it soon became amalgamated with the Junkers. In the process the Junkers were able to smooth off some of the rough edges of their eastern heritage.

Allied with three Hohenzollern rulers, the

Junkers fashioned absolutism and militarism into a social system that made them its chief beneficiaries. They took advantage of every historical movement—nationalism, liberalism, imperialism, capitalism, and even socialism—all of which they used shrewdly to make their own position in the social order more secure and more dominant. Although they declined somewhat in economic importance during the nineteenth and twentieth centuries, the Junkers were able to weather every political, military, and economic storm—the War of Liberation in 1806–1807, the crises of 1848–1849, 1862–1866, 1870–1871, and 1878–1879, the collapse of 1918, the Weimar Republic, and even the Nazi regime. Again and again they outwitted their rivals, and emerged from each struggle rejuvenated and intact as a governing class and as a political power. History has seldom shown a better example of how one vital caste can profoundly influence the entire social order of a nation. The Junker

ideals of *Realpolitik,* military power, patriotism, materialism, respect for order, and public service were impressed indelibly on the German mind.

3. *The Early Hohenzollerns*

The Great Elector, Frederick William (r. 1640–1688). One of the Seven Electors who chose the Holy Roman Emperor, the Great Elector, Frederick William, worked for nearly half a century to link his scattered domains. While increasing the area of his lands (Eastern Pomerania in 1648 as a reward for his part in the Thirty Years' War, the renunciation of Polish sovereignty over East Prussia in 1660, and definite establishment of his title to Cleves and Ravensburg in 1666), at the same time he showed remarkable administrative skill. As a youth he spent four years at the University of Leyden in the Netherlands, where he imbibed Western ideas. A tireless worker, he

The Great Elector in the Battle of Fehrbellin, 1675. Frederick William founded the Prussian state and established what became known as the Hohenzollern tradition.

centralized the administration of Brandenburg, organized a Council of State, revised the
financial system, encouraged commerce, industry, and agriculture, constructed the Frederick
William Canal (which joined the Oder to a
branch of the Elbe and thus created an outlet
to the North Sea), augmented educational
facilities, and replaced his once inefficient
troops with a strong and disciplined national
force. He knew well that the chaotic condition
of the Germanies made a strong army indispensable.

The beginning of Brandenburg-Prussia as a
great power came with the victory of Frederick William over the Swedes at the Battle
of Fehrbellin on June 28, 1675. He drove the
Swedes out of his country and occupied nearly
all of the Swedish continental territory.
Thenceforth he was called the "Great Elector."
This epoch-making victory actually hastened
a Swedish retreat that had already begun.
When it was demonstrated that the Swedes
could be defeated, a coalition against them
was immediately organized, as a result of
which their empire in the Germanies was
overrun. In his own account of the battle,
the Great Elector complained that the enemy
withdrew too quickly for him to achieve an
annihilating victory. He castigated those in
his cavalry "who did not do their duty." But,
he continued, "by God's grace I have kept
the battlefield, even though it has cost me
many officers and men."

After Louis XIV's revocation of the Edict
of Nantes in 1685, Frederick William welcomed to his country more than 20,000 French
Huguenots. The Great Elector established a
French commissariat to bring in and settle the
industrially valuable refugees. He sent them
guides and traveling money, gave them land
and building materials, and granted them
exemption from taxes for six years. At one
time, the Huguenots formed a sixth of the
population of Berlin. (At the Great Elector's
accession there were 8,000 people in Berlin; at
his death the population had risen to 20,000.)
The skill and industry of the Huguenot new-
comers contributed much to the welfare
and prosperity of their adopted homeland.
(Among other things, they popularized the

eating in German homes of lettuce, cauliflower,
asparagus, and artichokes.) From their ranks
eventually came many leading Prussian officers.

The services of Frederick William can be
appreciated by comparing the condition of
his country at the beginning of his reign and
at its end (1688). At his accession, he found
a country virtually buried in ruins—its villages
deserted, its agriculture at a standstill, its
landowners and peasants impoverished, its
industry and commerce ruined, its wealth exhausted, and its intellectual life demoralized.
At his death, the state was enjoying relative
prosperity. Frederick the Great gave him a
fitting eulogy: *"Messieurs, celui-ci a fait des
grandes choses."*

In matters of government, the Great Elector,
like his contemporary Louis XIV, was a convinced believer in monarchical absolutism.
Frederick William regarded absolute rule as
the best guarantee for the internal and external welfare of his people. He believed that,
though liberties were sacrificed, the nation
would be compensated by a large measure of
unity, strength, and order. The system of rule
which he established became later the basis
for the most highly centralized government
in Europe.

Frederick I (r. 1688–1713). The son of the
Great Elector lacked many of the qualities of
his father. "Great in small things, and small
in great things," he allowed some of the work
accomplished by his father to be undone.
Disturbed by the fact that he possessed no
royal title, Frederick III, Elector of Brandenburg and Duke of Prussia, was determined to
obtain one. It was said that he had been
deeply humiliated when in an interview with
William III of England he was obliged to sit
in a chair without arms while the British
monarch was comfortably seated in a magnificent armchair. Tradition demanded the
consent of his liege lord, the Holy Roman
Emperor, Leopold I, for a royal title. An
opportunity came in 1700, just before the
War of the Spanish Succession, when the
emperor required Frederick's support. In 1701
Leopold granted him the coveted dignity, but

made the title read Frederick I, King *in* Prussia, thus sparing the feelings of the king of Poland, who still ruled West Prussia, and at the same time making it clear that Prussia lay outside the boundaries of the Holy Roman Empire. Subsequent Prussian kings changed the title to King *of* Prussia.

Frederick William I (r. 1713–1740). The next Prussian monarch, Frederick William I, grandson of the Great Elector and very much like him, inaugurated the policy of building an efficient army and a subservient bureaucracy. A man of phenomenal energy and violent temper, a gruff disciplinarian, Frederick William annexed Swedish Pomerania from Sweden, consolidated and centralized his government, practiced rigid economy, and encouraged the development of commerce and industry. His ideal of kingship was paternal despotism. Absolutism was for him the only kind of government for his scattered dominions. Although he had little education himself, he nevertheless felt its importance and founded several hundred elementary schools.

Although the history of militarism in modern Prussia began with the Great Elector's organization of a standing army, it was Frederick William I who was the real father of Prussian militarism. Though miserly in other respects, Frederick William never hesitated to spend state funds lavishly for military purposes. He increased the Prussian army from 38,000 to 80,000 men. His chief pride and his one extravagance was an almost pathological love for tall soldiers, the only luxury which the parsimonious monarch allowed himself. This passion involved him in international squabbles and made him the jest of the civilized world. His agents combed every corner of Prussia to find tall recruits, who were either persuaded or forced into service. He even attempted by forced marriages to influence the biological character of the next generation, commanding tall men and women to marry one another. "The tallest of the tall men his agents collected," wrote Robert R. Ergang, "or that he received as gifts, Frederick William added to the Potsdam Giant Regiment. It was a collection of giants such as the world

Frederick William I drilling his giant guards.

had not seen before; nor has there been any similar collection since. Composed at first of two battalions of 600 men each, the regiment grew until it reached a maximum of almost 3,000. No man was admitted to the regiment unless he was over six feet tall, some of the tallest members being nearly eight feet."

4. The Reign of Frederick the Great

Frederick the Great (r. 1740–1786). Frederick II as crown prince was an effeminate young man who detested the endless drills and monotonous service to which he was subjected. In 1721, when the boy was nine, his father drew up a set of instructions for his son's tutor, for which every minute of the day was accounted. When Frederick was sixteen, he complained to his father in a pitiful message. The king replied in a coarse and brutal letter which undoubtedly left its mark on the young man. Modern psychoanalysis would attribute Frederick's hard and scornful attitude during his mature years to this stern and degrading background.

Young Frederick was unhappy and embittered. Detesting military pursuits, he showed a preference for gay clothes, French verse, extravagant entertainment, and friends of questionable morals. He hated his father's hard tyranny, religious zeal, and stinginess. He felt his own position to be so intolerable that he attempted to escape to England. For this he was imprisoned in the fortress of Küstrin, where he was forced to witness the execution of one of his friends. From this education the young Frederick emerged sobered and cured of his follies, but hardened and skeptical. To the surprise of many who had known him in his youth, Frederick developed into a powerful warlord and a master of statecraft. He became one of the outstanding enlightened despots of Europe, elevating Prussia, once backward and unimportant, to a position of equality with Austria, France, and Spain in the Continental councils.

The War of the Austrian Succession. In 1740, exactly a hundred years after the Great Elector had started his reign, his great-grandson, aged twenty-eight, ascended the throne as Frederick II. In that same year the Hapsburg emperor, Charles VI, died without a male heir. Charles hoped that his daughter, Maria Theresa, would inherit the Hapsburg lands intact, and through the last years of his reign he worked to assure her succession by means of the Pragmatic Sanction, which he urged or bribed the European powers to accept. Frederick II took advantage of the situation with his small but efficient army of 80,000 men. He was determined to claim from the Empress of Austria the four Silesian duchies which had been lost in the Thirty Years' War. The empress, a woman "with the heart of a king," refused. Without a declaration of war, without any moral or legal right for his action, Frederick invaded and annexed the Austrian province of Silesia.

Emboldened by Frederick's coup, Bavaria, supported by France, Spain, and Saxony, began the War of the Austrian Succession (1740–1748). Frederick entered and withdrew from the struggle several times. By 1748 all parties were thoroughly weary of the war. According to the Peace of Aix-la-Chapelle, Maria Theresa was recognized as ruler of all the Hapsburg lands, thus emerging from the contest with her empire almost intact. Frederick, however,

by the Treaty of Dresden (1745), retained possession of Silesia.

The Seven Years' War, 1756–1763. During eight years of uneasy peace there was a diplomatic revolution, designed to throttle the Prussian king. Austria and France, convinced now that Frederick was a menace, signed a secret treaty, to which Russia, Poland, Sweden, and Saxony also subscribed, agreeing to divide Prussia among them. England, whose interests in North America were threatened by French trade and colonization, promised to help Prussia. The resulting Seven Years' War (1756–1763) was worldwide. Hostilities between England and France began in India (1751) and in North America (1754).

Faced with an overwhelming coalition and almost assured destruction, but certain that his best defense lay in striking swiftly, Frederick began the war in Europe in 1756, winning two brilliant victories at Rossbach and Leuthen (1757). Next came the Russians, who were bloodily defeated at Zorndorf (1758). These astonishing victories were achieved despite odds of two to one against the Prussian warrior-king. He was hailed as one of the greatest military geniuses in history. The city of London was illuminated in his honor, and the English Parliament voted him $3,500,000 a year (which it discontinued a few years later).

Then followed a long series of disasters as Frederick sought to drag the war along, to exhaust and separate his opponents. In 1759 he suffered a stunning defeat by the Russians and Austrians at Kunersdorf, where he had overreached himself. In 1760 Frederick was trapped with 200,000 bayonets goading him from all sides. He was rescued from this predicament by what he later called a miracle—the death of his relentless enemy, the Czarina Elizabeth, in January 1762. Her erratic successor, Peter III, a warm admirer of Frederick, not only made peace with him but sent an army to help him. The enemy coalition evaporated.

The Peace of Hubertusburg (1763) required Frederick to evacuate occupied Saxony, but he was permitted to retain Silesia. By the separate Treaty of Paris of the same year, England took the greater part of the French colonial empire. Although Prussia had gained no new territory, she was now hailed as a Great Power in the Germanies and Eastern Europe.

Frederick the Great as Enlightened Despot. Frederick II returned from the Seven Years' War an old man but still buoyant in spirit. Prussia having been wasted and weakened by the long struggle, Frederick now set about the task of repairing the damage. Since many of his hardiest soldiers had fallen in the war, he induced tens of thousands of colonists to settle in his dominions and founded some 500 villages. He put cavalry horses to the plow. He reduced the taxes on free farmers, though he did not abolish serfdom. He allowed the nobles to retain their large holdings, but required them to rebuild thousands of ruined farmhouses. He reclaimed vast areas of farm lands by draining swamps and building levees. He introduced the cultivation of the potato as a cheap article of food, despite riots arising from the legend that potatoes caused leprosy and fevers. Pursuing a mercantilist policy, he en-

couraged commerce and industry, helped backward industries, prevented the flow of money from Prussia, levied duties on foreign imports, and nourished home industries. To make Prussia economically strong, he imported silkworms (together with mulberry trees for them to grow on) despite the unsuitable Prussian climate. He tried to discourage his people from drinking coffee because it could not be grown at home. He constructed roads and waterways, including a canal connecting a tributary of the Oder with the Vistula River.

An enlightened despot, nourished by his faith in God and Voltaire, Frederick II regarded himself as the first servant of the state. "The people," he said, "are not here for the sake of the rulers, but the rulers for the sake of the people." He regulated every conceivable administrative matter in the most minute detail, and filled the public positions with faithful servants, all inspired by his dictum that idleness was akin to death. He helped the Academy of Sciences, promoted elementary education, remodeled the judicial system, and granted toleration to both Catholics and

Frederick the Great gives a chamber concert at Sans Souci, his new palace at Potsdam. Music was another of this monarch's varied interests, and it is quite possible that he is playing one of his own compositions for the flute. From the drawing by Adolph Menzel.

Protestants. Eighteenth-century rationalists regarded him as a kind of political demigod.

The Dazzling Success of Frederick II. Frederick the Great died on August 17, 1786, at the age of seventy-four. The outstanding monarch of his time, brilliant in statecraft as well as in war, he won for himself a reputation as one of the great men of history. His reign marked the culmination of the development of Brandenburg-Prussia from a weak electorate to one of the strongest military states in Europe. The following figures show the extraordinary progress of the state from the end of the Thirty Years' War to the death of Frederick the Great:

	1648	1740	1786
Population	750,000	2,500,000	5,000,000
Army	8,000	83,000	200,000
Annual revenue, in *thalers*	?	7,000,000	19,000,000
Stored treasure, in *thalers*	0	8,000,000	51,000,000

"But Prussia," Sidney B. Fay reminds us, "still remained a despotic state, such as was characteristic of the eighteenth century. Un-fortunately Frederick's genius as an Enlightened Despot was not a heritable quality to be transmitted to his immediate successors. It required the shock of the Napoleonic conquest and the genius of Freiherr vom Stein to bring about a new creative period of institutional changes which were to regenerate and further strengthen Prussia in the nineteenth century."

Building on the foundations laid by his predecessors, he raised his small and comparatively poor kingdom to a position of first-rate military importance. He asserted his equality with the emperor, made Prussia the one important rival of Austria in the Germanies, and virtually forced his nation into the ranks of the Great Powers. He made Prussia great, although in the process he further assured German disunity. "By his cult of military force and by his own example of military success," says Koppel S. Pinson, "he implanted in Prussia, and through Prussia in Germany, that inordinate reliance on military strength which both the Germany of Bismarck and the Germany of Hitler were to follow. He became the supreme example of the amoral national hero who hovered over and above the everyday concepts of good and evil."

╡ KEY DOCUMENT ╞

FREDERICK THE GREAT'S ADDRESS TO HIS GENERALS BEFORE THE VICTORY OF LEUTHEN, DECEMBER 5, 1757

M. Schilling, *Quellenbuch zur Geschichte der Neuzeit*, 2nd ed., (Berlin, 1890), p. 274. Translated by the editor.

THE SEVEN YEARS' WAR (1756–1763) arose from the formation of a coalition between Austria, France, Russia, Sweden, and Saxony, with the aim of destroying or crippling the power of Frederick the Great. Despite Prussia's military superiority, she would probably have been defeated ultimately had she not received British support. At the Battle of Leuthen, December 5, 1757, Frederick inflicted a disastrous defeat on the Austrians, who lost 37 per cent of their 72,000 men and some 20,000 prisoners to the brilliant Prussian. Frederick's address to his generals before the great battle is reprinted here.

Gentlemen,

You are aware that Prince Karl of Lorraine has succeeded in taking Schweidnitz, defeating the Duke of Bevern and making himself master of Breslau. This was done while I was engaged in halting the advance of the French and the imperial forces. A part of Silesia, my capital, and all the military supplies it contained, are lost. I should feel myself in a most difficult position, indeed, were it not for my unlimited confidence in your courage, your constancy, and your love for the Fatherland, all of which you have proved to me on many occasions in the past. Your services to me and to the Fatherland have touched the deepest fibers of my heart. There is hardly one of you who has not distinguished himself by some outstanding deed of courage; hence, I flatter myself that in the approaching opportunity you will not fail in any sacrifice that your country may demand of you.

This opportunity is now close at hand, I feel that I have accomplished nothing if Austria retains Silesia. I tell you now that I propose to attack wherever I find the army of Prince Karl, three times as large as ours, in defiance of all the rules of the art of war. There is no question of the numerical superiority of the enemy or the importance of the positions they have gained. I hope to overcome all this by the devotion of my troops and by the careful implementation of my plans. I must take this step, else all will be lost. We must defeat the enemy, or we shall all lie buried under his batteries. This I believe. So shall I act.

Pass on my decision to all officers of the army.

Prepare the troops for the trials that are to come. Tell them that I expect blind obedience. Always remember that you are Prussians and that you cannot fail to show yourself worthy of that distinction. If there be any one among you who fears to share with me any and all danger, he shall be given his discharge immediately without any reproaches from me. [*Pause.*]

I was convinced that not one of you would desire to leave me. I count, then, absolutely, on your faithful assistance and on certain victory. If I do not return to reward you for your devotion, the Fatherland itself must do it. Return now and repeat to your troops what you have heard from me. . . .

If any regiment of cavalry does not attack the enemy immediately upon given orders, it will be unmounted at once after the battle and made a garrison regiment. Any infantry battalion that hesitates, no matter what the danger may be, shall lose its colors and swords and shall have the gold lace stripped from its uniforms.

And now, Gentlemen, farewell. Before long we shall either have defeated the enemy or we shall see each other no more.

❧[HISTORICAL INTERPRETATION]❧

THOMAS CARLYLE ON THE PERSONALITY OF FREDERICK THE GREAT

Thomas Carlyle, *History of Friedrich II of Prussia, called Frederick the Great*, 10 vols. (New York, 1872), I, pp. 1–3. Courtesy of Scribner, Welford and Company.

THOMAS CARLYLE (1795–1881), British essayist, historian, and philosopher, was a leading exponent of the "great man" theory of history, i.e., that outstanding leaders give direction and content to historical development. We see this view in his masterpiece, his biography of Frederick the Great, the first two volumes of which appeared in 1852, and the succeeding eight volumes in 1862, 1864, and 1865. Emerson declared this work to be the wittiest ever written. The value of his *Frederick* was acknowledged in Germany by the award of the Prussian Order of Merit in 1874. But historians criticized Carlyle severely for his over-romantic attitude toward history, his reduction of complicated history to simple situations, his "poor jargon . . . a mere veil to hide from Carlyle himself the essential poverty of his thoughts." Following is Carlyle's tribute to Frederick.

PROEM: FRIEDRICH'S HISTORY FROM THE DISTANCE WE ARE AT.

About fourscore years ago, there used to be seen sauntering on the terraces of Sans Souci, for a short time in the afternoon, or you might have met him elsewhere at an earlier hour, riding or driving in a rapid business manner on the open roads or through the scraggy woods and avenues of that intricate amphibious Potsdam region, a highly interesting lean little old man, of alert though slightly stooping figure; whose name among strangers was King *Friedrich the Second*, or Frederick the Great of Prussia, and at home among the common people, who much loved and esteemed him, was *Vater Fritz*, Father Fred,—a name of familiarity which had not bred contempt in that instance. He is a King every inch of him, though without the trappings of a King. Presents himself in a Spartan simplicity of vesture: no crown but an old military cocked-hat,—generally old, or trampled and kneaded into absolute *softness*, if new;—no sceptre but one like Agamemnon's, a walking-stick cut from the woods, which serves also as a riding-stick (with which he "hits the horse between the ears," say authors);—and for royal robes, a mere soldier's blue coat with red facings, coat likely to be old, and sure to have a good deal of Spanish snuff on the breast of it; rest of the apparel dim, unobtrusive in colour or cut, ending in high over-knee military boots, which may be brushed (and, I hope, kept soft with an underhand suspicion of oil), but are not permitted to be blackened or varnished; Day and Martin with their soot-pots forbidden to approach.

The man is not of godlike physiognomy, any more than of imposing stature or costume: close-shut mouth with thin lips, prominent jaws and nose, receding brow, by no means of Olympian height; head, however, is of long form, and has superlative gray eyes in it. Not what is called a beautiful man; nor yet, by all appearance, what is called a happy one. On the contrary, the face bears evidence of many sorrows, as they are termed, of much hand labour done in this world; and seems to anticipate nothing but more still coming. Quiet stoicism, capable enough of what joys there were, but not expecting any worth mention; great unconscious and some conscious pride, well tempered with a cheery mockery of humor,—are written on that old face; which carries its chin well forward, in spite of the slight stoop about the neck; snuffy nose rather flung into the air, under its old cocked-hat,—like an old snuffy lion on the watch; and such a pair of eyes as no man or lion or lynx of that Century bore elsewhere, according to all the testimony we have. "Those eyes," says Mirabeau, "which, at the bidding of his great soul, fascinated you with seduction or with terror (*portaient, au gré de son âme héroïque, la séduction ou la ter-*

reur)!" Most excellent potent brilliant eyes, swift-darting as the stars, steadfast as the sun; gray, we said, of the azure-gray colour; large enough, not of glaring size; the habitual expression of them vigilance and penetrating sense, rapidity resting on depth. Which is an excellent combination; and gives us the notion of a lambent outer radiance sprung from some great inner sea of light and fire in the man. The voice, if he speak to you, is of similar physiognomy: clear, melodious, and sonorous; all tones are in it, from that of ingenuous inquiry, graceful sociality, light-flowing banter (rather prickly for most part), up to definite word of command, up to desolating word of rebuke and reprobation; a voice the clearest and most "agreeable in conversation I ever heard," says witty Dr. Moore. "He speaks a great deal," continues the doctor; "yet those who hear him, regret that he does not speak a good deal more. His observations are always lively, very often just; and few men possess the talent of repartee in greater perfection."

Just about threescore and ten years ago, his speakings and his workings came to finis in this World of Time; and he vanished from all eyes into other worlds, leaving much inquiry about him in the minds of men;—which, as my readers and I may feel too well, is yet by no means satisfied. As to his speech, indeed, though it had the worth just ascribed to it and more, and though masses of it were deliberately put on paper by himself, in prose and verse, and continue to be printed and kept legible, what he spoke has pretty much vanished into the inane; and except as record or document of what he did, hardly now concerns mankind. But the things he did were extremely remarkable; and cannot be forgotten by mankind. Indeed, they bear such fruit to the present hour as all the Newspapers are obliged to be taking note of, sometimes to an unpleasant degree. Editors vaguely account this man the "'Creator of the Prussian Monarchy," which has since grown so large in the world and troublesome to the Editorial mind in this and other countries. He was indeed the first who, in a highly public manner, notified creation; announced to all men that it was, in very deed, created; standing on its feet there, and would go a great way, on the impulse it had got from him and others. As it has accordingly done;

and may still keep doing to lengths little dreamt of by the British Editor in our time; whose prophesyings upon Prussia, and insights into Prussia, in its past, or present or future, are truly as yet inconsiderable, in proportion to the noise he makes with them! The more is the pity for him,—and for myself too in the Enterprise now on hand.

❧ TEN BASIC BOOKS ❧

THE GERMANIES: THE RISE OF PRUSSIA

1. Bruford, Walter H., *Germany in the Eighteenth Century* (Cambridge, 1935).†
2. Carlyle, Thomas, *History of Friedrich II of Prussia, Called Frederick the Great,* 10 vols. (New York, 1872).
3. Dill, Marshall, Jr., *Germany: A Modern History* (Ann Arbor, Mich., 1961).
4. Dorwart, Reinhold A., *The Administrative Reforms of Frederick William I of Prussia* (Cambridge, Mass., 1953).
5. Ergang, Robert R., *The Potsdam Führer, Frederick William I* (New York, 1941).
6. Fay, Sidney B., *The Rise of Brandenburg-Prussia to 1786,* 2nd rev. ed. (New York, 1964).†
7. Flenley, Ralph, *Modern German History* (London, 1953).
8. Gooch, George P., *Frederick the Great: The Ruler, the Writer, the Man* (London and New York, 1947).
9. Schevill, Ferdinand, *The Great Elector* (Chicago, 1947).
10. Valentin, Veit, *The German People: Their History and Civilization* (New York, 1946).

12

Expansion: The Rise and Westernization of Russia

IF I SHOULD die in Tsarkoe Selo, I wish to be buried in the Sophien town cemetery. . . .

The coffin should be carried by Chevalier Guards and nobody else.

My body should be dressed in white and a golden crown bearing my name should be placed on my head.

The mourning to last six months, not more and even better if less.

After the first six weeks all public entertainments to be resumed.

Marriages and music to be allowed immediately after the burial. . . .

For the good of the Russian and Greek Empires I advise that the Princes of Württemberg should be banished from the affairs of these Empires and have as little to do with them as possible; I also advise avoiding consulting all Germans of both sexes.

—THE WILL OF CATHERINE THE GREAT, 1792

1. The Foundations of Russia

The Land and People. The vast area of Russia extends from the Black Sea to the Arctic Ocean, from the Baltic to the North Pacific. The surface of European Russia, with the exception of the Caucasus, is a vast, monotonous plain, broken by low plateau country in the west, by the Urals in the east, and by the Crimean or Yaila range in the south. In the north are marshy tablelands and impenetrable forests, in the south the steppe region, a gentle, undulating plain covered with a layer of bare, uncultivated black earth. Before the sixteenth century this area was peopled by many ethnic groups: Great Russians, who lived in the central plain; Little Russians, or Ukrainians, in the southwestern plain; White Russians in Lithuania; and a conglomeration of Poles, Letts, Finns, Swedes, Lithuanians, Jews, Mol-davians, Georgians, Armenians, Tartars, Mongolians, and others.

The people who lived in this rude, backward area had long been subjected to internal tribal quarrels, to raids by the Scandinavians from the west, and to Mongol conquest from the east and south. In the middle of the ninth century, three Scandinavian brothers, Rurik, Sineus, and Truvor, organized feuding tribes into a loose confederation, and founded Novgorod (New Town). In 879 Rurik's successors transferred the capital to Kiev on the Dnieper River. About this time the word *Russian* came into being: the Finnish word *Ruotsi,* meaning seafarers or vikings, was used to describe the Scandinavians in Kiev; *Ruotsi* developed into Rous, or Russ.

Led by Genghis Khan (1162–1227), a horde of Asiatic Mongol-Tartars descended on southern Russia and swept through the entire country. In 1241 the invaders disastrously defeated a combined army of Poles and Germans at Liegnitz. For more than two centuries the Golden Horde of Mongol-Tartars held Russia in subjugation. They left internal conditions undisturbed, and made no attempts to change the language, literature, and institutions of the Russians, preferring instead to extract periodic tributes.

2. The Rise of Muscovy

End of Mongol Domination. Moscow, founded in 1147, grew in size and prestige during the era of Mongolian overlordship. Its favorable location in the middle of the central plain—at the junction of trade routes connecting north and south—made Moscow the natural nucleus of the future empire. Muscovite grand dukes organized powerful armies, demanded the loyalty of the boyars (the aristocracy), encouraged the prosperous middle class, and supported the Orthodox Church. The first of the energetic, ruthless Muscovite rulers was Ivan III, known as "Ivan the Great" (r. 1462–1505), of Scandinavian origin, who regarded it as his task to smash Mongolian power, and fashion a strong national monarchy. He was highly successful. He cast off the Mongolian yoke, united the numerous petty tribal states, and extended boundaries northward to the Arctic and westward to the Baltic. He was unable, however, to subjugate Poland and Lithuania.

Because Constantinople had fallen to the Ottoman sultan in 1453, Ivan III pronounced Moscow its heir and made it the capital of the Orthodox Church, the "Third Rome." He married the ambitious Sophia Paleologue, niece and nearest in blood relationship to Constantine XI, last of the Byzantine emperors, who had died when the Turks took Constantinople. Through her influence Ivan tried to make himself known as successor of the Graeco-Roman emperors. He required the court at Moscow to adopt the ceremonials of Constantinople, took the double-headed Byzantine eagle for his coat of arms, and assumed the title of Tsar, equivalent to the Latin Caesar. Until this time the Russian rulers

had been called *veliki kniaz,* roughly Grand Duke. Ivan III, as unchallenged autocrat, set the foundation for Russian absolutism.

Ivan the Terrible. Ivan IV, called "Ivan the Terrible" (r. 1533–1584), the grandson of Ivan III, took the title of Tsar and Autocrat of All the Russias. Consumed with hatred for the boyars who had maltreated him in his youth, Ivan IV struck back at them as soon as he ascended the throne. He executed boyar after boyar by throwing their bodies to the dogs. His record was stained with senseless crimes: he strangled clerics who refused to bless him; he sacked Novgorod, the most prosperous city in his kingdom, because he suspected it of harboring traitors; and in 1580, in a paroxysm of rage, struck down and killed Ivan, his eldest surviving son, whom he had loved passionately. He was a merciless, brutal autocrat, burdened with an ungovernable temper, infuriated against God and man by the death of his wife and son.

Ivan IV continued his predecessor's policy of territorial consolidation. He conquered the Volga Basin and annexed Siberia. He profited from the growing weakness of Poland and

Ivan the Terrible. Sculpture by Antokolsky.

Sweden, but his attempt to obtain an outlet to the Baltic did not succeed. He established closer trade relations with Western Europe by negotiating commercial treaties with the English, Dutch, and Swedes thus anticipating the policy of Westernization later favored by Peter the Great.

On the domestic scene, Ivan IV pursued a simple but omnipresent goal: he would increase the power of the Crown. Depriving the boyars of their territorial possessions, he made them subservient to Moscow. He divided all Russia into two parts—one his own private property, and the other a "land" under control of a loyal follower. Imitating Byzantine models, he reorganized the system of taxation; centralized the treasury, separating this income from his own; encouraged the merchant class; reformed the army; and revised the entire system of administration. For territorial expansion, he used in the vanguard a peculiar class of fierce warriors from the Don region known as Cossacks. Like the American frontiersmen, the Cossacks lived an adventurous life in which they mingled agricultural and pastoral pursuits with hunting and fighting. Ivan IV carefully vitiated the strength of the boyars by sending them on campaigns against his enemies with the hope that many would die in battle.

The Time of Troubles (1584–1613). At the end of the sixteenth century, the direct line of Ivan IV died out. There followed three decades of civil war, known as the Time of Troubles. Ivan IV's son, Feodor I, was almost an imbecile; his father called him more fitted to be a bell-ringer in a convent than a Russian tsar. Power was soon assumed by Ivan's brother-in-law, Boris Godunov (r. 1598–1605), a boyar of Tartar descent. In 1598, at the death of Feodor, Boris prevailed upon the boyars to elect him tsar. Some resentful boyars promptly revolted. The consequent anarchy invited foreign intervention. The Poles swarmed into the country and for a time occupied the Kremlin, the citadel of Moscow. The Swedes pushed to the eastern shore of the Baltic and seized the vital trading center of Novgorod. In the south the Ottoman Turks attacked the Cos-

sacks and strengthened their hold on the Crimean area. Boris died in 1605 in the midst of the Time of Troubles.

The Romanovs. Under such discouraging circumstances, a national assembly of Russian nobles and representatives of the cities convened in Moscow in 1613 to elect a tsar. The choice fell on Michael Romanov, a young boyar of royal blood. Michael's accession brought the end of civil war. The Time of Troubles was over. The crown was awarded to a new dynasty that was to rule almost without interruption until it was overthrown in the March Revolution of 1917.

Russia remained a backward country. Her commercial contacts with the Western world were few and infrequent. She was untouched by the great cultural explosions of the West: the religious upheavals, the New Learning, the scientific revolution, and the rising capitalism. It was not until the eighteenth century that Russia entered the European family of nations and began to play an important role in international affairs. Meanwhile, the Russian peoples started a process of expansion along the river courses and over the broad plains, pushing westward to Europe and eastward until by the end of the seventeenth century they looked upon the Pacific. Wherever the Russians went, they retained their language and national customs as well as their loyalty to Russian Orthodox Christianity. By military and ecclesiastical means the tsars began to attain control over ever-greater territories.

Internally, Russia remained characteristically Asian for several reasons. First, she was a strict autocracy, with powerful landlords ruling over a huge peasant class sinking gradually into serfdom. Secondly, the Mongol-Tartars had done well their work of saturating the Russian mind with Oriental customs and habits. Thirdly, the topography of Russia tended to favor agriculture and to discourage industry and commerce, and also stimulated expansion toward the east. Finally, with Sweden and Poland barring access to the Baltic Sea in the north, and the Ottoman Empire blocking off entrance to the Black Sea in the south, Russia had no ports which could enable her to compete on an equal scale with Western commerce.

3. The Career of Peter the Great

The Early Years. The grandson of Michael Romanov became Peter I, the Great (r. 1682–1725), called the father of modern Russia. When his half-brother, Feodor III died in 1682 without children, the leading boyars and the Patriarch of Moscow decided that Peter should be tsar instead of his older but half-witted half-brother Ivan. The latter's sister, Sophia, organized a coup which led to the coronation of Ivan and Peter as joint tsars and Sophia as regent. Peter spent the next seven years in a villa near Moscow with his mother. His education was neglected in favor of war games. Early in life he acquired an enthusiasm for the arts and sciences of Western Europe, particularly for its armies and fleets. He picked up a mass of technical skills from foreigners in Russian service who lived in a nearby suburb.

In 1689, at the age of seventeen, Peter received news of a plot by Sophia against him. He struck suddenly, forced her to resign, and banished her to a convent, where she died in 1704. Peter from this moment on ruled the country himself. Six feet eight inches tall, endowed with a powerful physique, extremely dark, "as if he had been born in Africa," Peter was admired by his Russian people as a giant in body and mentality. He was a strange mixture of cruelty and clear intellect, of savagery and administrative genius. He could not endure restraint of any kind. He dressed carelessly, selecting garbs of the most grotesque description. Driven by a feverish love of movement, he awakened his servants by blows, falling on them with sticks and not infrequently with axes. His moods were unaccountable: he changed from gaiety to ill-humor instantaneously.

Peter became sole tsar in 1696 at the age of twenty-four. Almost immediately he went to war against the Turks, and soon captured the valuable port of Azov. It was of little use, however, as long as the sultan held the Dardanelles. Gaining no other success in the Turkish war, he came to the conclusion that he had to learn more of western technical methods before he could realize the Russian dream of wresting the Baltic coast from Sweden and the Black Sea from the Turks.

Journey to the West. To obtain practical experience in the ways of the West, Peter sent a mission, a Grand Embassy, to Europe (1697–1698), to which he attached himself as "Peter Mikhailov," a volunteer sailor. The aim of the mission was to obtain help against the Turks, but in this it failed, primarily because the European states, concerned with their own dynastic problems, were on the verge of the War of the Spanish Succession. But Peter learned much. He studied shipbuilding in Holland. He learned about gunnery and military science in Prussia. He visited England, where he observed the House of Commons. With insatiable curiosity he inspected factories and museums, collected instruments and models, and studied such subjects as anatomy (at Leyden) and engraving (at Amsterdam). He engaged artists, engineers, and technicians to return with him to Russia, promising them enormous salaries (which proved to be illusory). He returned home with respect for the efficiency of the Prussian army, the effectiveness of the English and Dutch navies, and the centralized administration of Western governments.

Revolt of the *Streltsy*. While on his way from Vienna to Venice, Peter received news about a formidable revolt of the *Streltsy*, the Moscovite army. The soldiery had taken advantage of his absence of a year and a half from Moscow to break into mutiny. Enraged, Peter hurried home only to find that the rebellion had already been crushed. But he took terrible vengeance. (*See page 189.*)

Autocracy in Government. Peter's observation of the government of Louis XIV convinced him that monarchical absolutism, called autocracy in Russia, was necessary for the well-being of his state. After the subjugation of the *Streltsy*, he created a strong, dependable army to maintain his power in domestic affairs and to extend it abroad. He recruited troops from the Russian masses and had them led and disciplined by foreigners loyal to the Crown. He divided the country into individual governments (*Gubernya*), each province controlled by an army officer whose job it was to extort money enough to maintain his specified number of troops.

Administrative and Educational Reform. Issuing *ukases* or decrees for administrative reform, all designed to bolster the position of the throne, Peter centralized the government by introducing the Swedish system of *collegia,* or administrative colleges, to manage foreign affairs, the army and navy, finance, commerce, manufacturing, and agriculture. He broke the power of the nobility, the priesthood, and the army officers. He surrounded himself with trusted foreign advisers, and formed his men of service into a unified class of *Dvorianstvo,* or gentry, who were required to spend a certain number of years in service to the state. He virtually abolished the medieval assembly, or *Duma,* of great nobles, which had formerly exercised legislative powers.

Peter failed in his efforts to introduce educational reforms. Although he established some forty schools, he had to resort to force to obtain pupils for them. He introduced the present Russian alphabet and ordered the publication of many books, most of which were unread. The Russian masses remained illiterate.

Economic Conditions. Peter had grandiose plans to improve economic conditions in Russia, but he was far too occupied with military matters to do much about Russia's torpid economy. He molded the servile land laborers into a unified class and subjected them to taxes. Aware that Russia lacked a healthy middle class, he tried to create one by advocating mercantilist doctrines and encouraging trade and industry. He failed in his attempts to establish the German system of merchant guilds in the cities and to introduce municipal self-government. Under Peter and his successors the Russian economy lagged far behind Western Europe.

Control of the Orthodox Church. Aware of the great influence of the Russian Orthodox Church over his people, Peter took steps to make it subservient to the throne. Professing a deep loyalty to the Orthodox faith, he attempted to root out heretics and dissenters. But, at the same time, he placed the Church under his thumb by abolishing the patriarchate (1700) and appointing a new Holy Synod, presided over by an appointed lay official, the Procurator. No appointment could be made to ecclesiastical office without the approval of the Holy Synod; no books could be published and no sermons preached without its approval. The Orthodox Church became the right arm of the monarchy.

Westernization of Russia. Peter was adamant in his desire to make the Russian people look like Europeans. After returning from his European journey, he began with externals by summoning the chief boyars and, without warning, shocking them by cutting off their beards. From that time on, Oriental beards became a symbol of conservatism, worn only on condition of the payment of a tax graduated in proportion to the length of the beards. Peter also issued a series of *ukases* designed to eliminate other ancient and cherished customs. He encouraged ballroom dancing, which he had learned in the West. He advocated the use of tobacco. He forbade the wearing of long Oriental robes, and prescribed instead Saxon or Magyar jackets and French or German hose. He ordered women to cast aside their veils and emerge from seclusion. The aristocracy complied with these radical innovations, although the masses resented those decrees which struck at old traditions. Peter had begun a process of Westernization which was to have significant results in the future.

4. The Wars of Peter the Great

The Great Northern War, 1700–1721. The keynote of Peter the Great's foreign policy was acquisition for Russia of warm-water ports which would enable the Russians to reach the rest of the world during the entire year. To obtain an outlet to the Baltic, a window to the

West, he knew that he would have to wage war on Sweden, at this time a great power holding Finland, Estonia, Livonia, Karelia, and West Pomerania. A favorable opportunity presented itself in 1697 with the death of the Swedish King Charles XI and the accession of his son, Charles XII, a presumably weak and incompetent fifteen-year-old boy. Peter first organized a coalition against Sweden, consisting of himself, Augustus II, Elector of Saxony and King of Poland, and the king of Denmark (1699). He then made temporary peace with the Turks, thus guarding his southern flank. Because Western Europe was involved in the struggle for the Spanish inheritance, he expected a quick and easy victory.

The allies, however, had underestimated the character and ability of the youthful Swedish ruler. Charles XII unexpectedly struck at Denmark and forced her to sue for peace. In November 1700, with an army of 8,000 men, he met Peter's 40,000 troops and inflicted a shattering defeat. The young king then carried the war into the heart of Poland, obliging the Poles to dethrone Augustus II of Saxony and accept Charles's choice, Stanislaus Leszczynski, as king (1704). His pride swollen by these successes, Charles XII ordered his troops in Denmark, Poland, and Russia to "slay, burn, and destroy." "Better that the innocent should suffer," he said, "than the guilty be allowed to escape." The boy-king of Sweden soon won the title of "Madman of the North."

Neither Peter the Great nor his ally the Elector Augustus II of Saxony, could afford to abandon the struggle. While Charles XII was busy in Poland, Peter conquered the Swedish provinces around the Gulf of Finland. In 1703 he built his new capital, St. Petersburg, among the marshes along the mouth of the river Neva. He now had his desired "window to the West." Charles XII, however, confidently pressed his war against the Russians. Unable to take Moscow, he turned south to effect a junction with rebellious Cossacks. He was soon cut off from reinforcements and supplies. At Poltava, on July 8, 1709, he was totally routed, but he escaped and took refuge with the Turks. When Peter bought off the Turks, the disappointed Charles returned to

Peter the Great.

his homeland, where he found his territories gone and Swedish power plunged to its nadir. He tried to regain what he had lost, only to fall in battle in 1718 at the age of thirty-six while directing an invasion of Norway.

The Great Northern War came to its close with the death of Charles XII. By the Treaty of Stockholm (1719–1720) Sweden lost all her German territory except a small area of West Pomerania. Denmark obtained Holstein and an indemnity. Prussia got the bulk of Swedish West Pomerania, including the important city of Stettin. Augustus II of Saxony was restored to his Polish throne, though he gained no territory. Great Britain, Prussia, and Denmark inherited Sweden's commerce.

The Treaty of Nystadt (1721) awarded Ingria, Estonia, and Livonia, as well as parts of Carelia and Finland, including the fortress of Viborg, to Russia. According to Peter, this was "the most profitable peace Russia ever concluded." Sweden surrendered her hegemony in the north to Russia and plummeted to the position of a second-rate power, to be succeeded by Russia as the most powerful nation in the north. In 1721 Peter proclaimed himself "Emperor of All the Russias." He promulgated a new law of succession enjoining that each monarch should nominate his own successor.

Peter and the Ottoman Empire. Despite his recurrent wars with the Turks, Peter made no permanent advances in the south, where Russia remained cut off from the Mediterranean by Ottoman control of Constantinople. He never obtained a Russian port on the Black Sea. Although he had captured and held Azov for a time, he was forced to relinquish it as a means of preventing the Turks from joining Charles XII.

When Peter the Great died in 1725 he left a compact empire, an efficient army, and a highly dissatisfied peasantry. True, he had awakened Russia from centuries of slumber and had turned her face westward. But, while changing the form of the government, he was not successful in transforming the nation's character. Russia remained basically Eastern, her heritage traced to Mongolian and Byzantine sources. Though personally cruel and barbaric, Peter was a man of dominant will who literally forced Russia into the concert of the great European nations.

Historical Controversy: Benevolent Despot or Autocrat? Both inside and outside of Russia Peter the Great has been described in different terms varying from "the greatest of historical leaders" all the way to "bloody tyrant." The nineteenth-century Russian historian, Sergei M. Soloviev who, like Carlyle, saw history as the work of great men, regarded Peter as the "epic hero" who was responsible for the emergence of Russia as a great nation. "Peter was not an egotistic conquerer. . . . [His] genius

manifested itself in a clear understanding of his people, and of himself as its leader. . . . We know of no historical leader whose area of action was as comprehensive as Peter's."

Other Russians made a cult of worshipping the great king, "Father of the Fatherland." He was praised for defending the country while at the same time returning to it lands that had been wrested away. He was the wise Solomon who brought reason and wisdom with his rule, the distinguished man who had shaped Russia and "made her lovable to good men," the talented genius of Russian history.

This view was rejected by Georgii V. Plekhanov, theoretician of Russian Marxism, who, while admitting that Peter did much to westernize Russia, still never ceased to think in Eastern terms as an Oriental despot. Was it not true that the Oriental despot always had the right to dispose of the property of his subjects in any manner he chose? And was it not further true that the benevolent despots of Western Europe could do so only within the limits set by custom and law? Peter's work, said Plekhanov, was the very antithesis of the democratic system.

5. Reign of Catherine the Great, 1762–1796

The Successors of Peter the Great. Peter the Great gave himself the right to designate his successor, but ironically, he failed to do so before his death. Married twice, he had descendants from both marriages. Until the accession of Catherine the Great in 1762 there were palace revolutions and struggles between native Russians and foreign favorites. Peter's wife, Catherine I (r. 1725–1727), and his two grandsons, Peter II (r. 1727–1730) and Peter III (r. 1762), were weak and ineffectual. His niece Anna (r. 1730–1740) and his daughter Elizabeth (r. 1741–1762) were stronger, more dominant monarchs.

During this era there arose a conflict between the old and new forces in Russia. The conservative pro-Russian party believed that Russia had a distinct culture of her own which could not be mingled with that of the West. It resented especially the elevation of foreigners to high positions in the government. The pro-European party held that Russia's salvation lay in keeping open her window to the West. The conflict continued during the reign of Elizabeth, during which foreign influences, especially French, gained headway. Although a woman of loose morals and ugly disposition, Elizabeth encouraged the arts and sciences, and supported national poetry, a Russian theatre, and the first Russian university. She did what she could to lessen the horrors of Russia's ferocious penal code. In a conflict with the weakened Swedish state, she managed to acquire some territory in Finland (1743) and joined France and Austria against England and Prussia in the Seven Years' War (1756–1763).

The Accession of Catherine. The childless Empress Elizabeth hoped to obtain the succession for her nephew Peter. In 1745 the Tsarevitch Peter, at the age of sixteen, was married to Sophia Augusta Frederica, the daughter of a minor German prince, Christian Augustus of Anhalt-Zerbst. The German princess, shamelessly neglected by her weakling husband, consoled herself with learning the language and customs of her adopted country. A drunken, lascivious lout, who played with dolls, Peter lost the sympathy of his people by open hostility to everything Russian. Meanwhile Sophia, who took the Russian name Catherine, steadily made herself more popular. Obtaining the support of guard officers and other favorites, she successfully managed a court revolution. Her half-insane husband was forced to abdicate in her favor. Peter III died under questionable circumstances a few weeks later; whether or not he was murdered remains a mystery.

For thirty-four years Catherine was Tsarina of Russia. Her rule was harsh and strict. Consummating the reforms begun by Peter the Great, she encouraged Westernization of her country, and extended its boundaries in all directions. Dissolute in her love affairs, and Machiavellian in her politics, she nevertheless took a leading part in the affairs of Europe. In foreign affairs she proved herself to be the able executor of Peter the Great's policies.

Catherine as Enlightened Despot. Catherine was a despot, though she wished her people to regard her as enlightened. She chose men of ability for important posts in her government, and rewarded them for loyal service. At all times she showed herself deeply devoted to her adopted country. A prolific letter-writer, she maintained a correspondence with such *philosophes* as Voltaire, d'Alembert, and Diderot, and with her fellow sovereigns, Frederick II of Prussia and Joseph II of Austria. She regarded herself as a liberal, although at the same time she maintained her position of autocrat on the ground that the Russian people were not yet ready for the heady wine of self-government. To the Governor of Moscow she wrote prophetically: "When the day comes when our peasants wish to become enlightened, both you and I will lose our places."

The Reforms of Catherine the Great. In 1767, the early part of her reign, Catherine compiled from Montesquieu's *Spirit of Laws* (1748) and Cesare Beccaria's *On Crime and Punishment* (1764) a set of *Instructions (Nakaz)* to be used as a basis for a new legal code. To revise and codify the Russian laws she summouned to Moscow a grand commission chosen from all classes except the peasants. The *Instructions,* consisting of 654 paragraphs, promised more than they could perform. The conservative gentry, alienated by Catherine's intention of limiting its power over the serfs, threatened rebellion. Catherine yielded, and in appeasement distributed some of the Crown estates among the gentry. This stimulated the growing dissatisfaction among the unprivileged. The peasants revolted several times, only to be mercilessly put down. The Pugachev Rebellion (1773–1775), led by Cossacks of the Volga region, was crushed, and its leaders were tried and beheaded in Moscow. The knout, the heavy whip, remained the royal language for the peasants.

Administratively, Catherine divided Russia into fifty provinces. She announced that each province was to control its own affairs, but in practice, she kept power in her own hands.

Economically, in line with the policy of Peter the Great, Catherine encouraged Russian manufacturers, established new industries, and fostered a series of commercial treaties with other countries. To prepare her people for the responsibilities of citizenship, she established schools and academies. However, most of her educational efforts were limited to the upper class. She encouraged the nobility to use French as the language of

Catherine the Great, Empress of Russia, promoted two successful wars with Turkey, a war with Sweden, and played a role in the three partitions of Poland by which Russia made large territorial gains. Portrait by G. B. Lampl.

polite society; she sent Russian princes to England to observe the latest experiments in agriculture; she assisted artists and writers and even countenanced radical books which had been condemned in France as dangerous and revolutionary; she founded hospitals and orphanages.

Despite this long series of reforms, Catherine left the vast masses of Russia illiterate and ignorant. As a young woman she had been distinguished by modest, conventional behavior. Later her private life became the talk of Europe, as she lavished funds of state on a long line of favorites who flattered her in middle and old age. The mind was calculating and shrewd, the heart was kind but weak.

Foreign Policy of Catherine the Great. This scandalously immoral woman pursued a strong, aggressive foreign policy, and one that was eminently successful. Her aim was simply to obtain as much territory as possible. Sweden, which had blocked Russian expansion, had been humbled and shorn of her Baltic provinces by Peter the Great. Now there remained Poland and the Ottoman Empire.

Catherine began by cultivating a close friendship with Prussia. She assisted Frederick the Great in the final stage of his conflict with Austria, and worked with him in the first partition of Poland. The death of Augustus III, Elector of Saxony and King of Poland (r. 1733–1763), gave her the opportunity of intervening in Poland and setting up a puppet government at Warsaw. One of her own favorites, Stanislas Poniatowski, became Stanislaus II of Poland in 1764. The dominance of Russia in Polish affairs was now established. Whenever dissident Poles objected, Russia and Prussia joined to thwart them.

With Prussia on her side and Austria against her in the First Turkish War (1768–1772), Catherine got free access to the Black Sea, and the right to protect Turkish Christians. With Austria on her side and Prussia against her in the Second Turkish War (1787–1792), she annexed additional territory along the Black Sea. As a result of her campaigns against the Turks, Russia acquired a natural boundary in southern Europe and became the major power on the Black Sea. Catherine and Russia now had a second window to the West. In addition, the Russians were now regarded everywhere as the natural allies of the oppressed Christians inside the Ottoman Empire. Finally, the wars revealed that the power of the Ottoman Empire was waning with increasing rapidity. Russia was the favorite in the race for Turkish spoils.

Catherine the Great died in 1796 of an apoplectic fit. She had done much for her country. No other Russian sovereign, with the exception of Ivan the Terrible, had conquered so much territory, even though the annexed areas remained thereafter sources of friction. The success of Catherine's brilliant foreign policy was in direct contrast to the meager results of her domestic policy. The peasants, backbone of Russia, had little for which they could thank her. Her Russia remained substantially the same as that of Peter the Great, with the same autocratic monarch, the same privileged nobility, and the same oppressed, ignorant peasantry. One day, crown and nobility would pay dearly for their unwillingness to better the conditions of the unprivileged in Russia.

6. The Partitions of Poland

Decline of Poland. The name of Poland first appears in history as the designation of a tribe, the Polani, who lived between the Oder and the Vistula. The history of Poland before the middle of the tenth century is so intermixed with fables as to be untrustworthy. Mieszko I (c. 963–992), the first ruler to be converted to Christianity, induced his subjects to accept the new religion. With him Poland took her place as one of the political powers of Europe. In 1241 the invading Mongols defeated the Poles at Liegnitz, whereupon Poland began to decline. In 1386, because of fear of the Teutonic Order, Poland and Lithuania were combined under the rule of Vladislav V, once Grand Prince of Lithuania. In 1466, after a decade of war, a peace treaty was signed at Thorn between Casimir IV (1424–1492) and the Teutonic Knights. Thereafter, until the eighteenth century, the history of Poland is a story of continuous decline, attributable to a succession of ineffectual rulers, a privileged nobility, an oppressed peasantry, a weak constitution, and religious conflicts. The government was a kind of legalized anarchy.

The major weakness of eighteenth-century Poland lay in a privileged nobility which placed its own well-being far ahead of that of the state. The monarchy was elective, and the nobles were opposed to any ruler who might call them to account for their misrule. They would on occasion choose as ruler a French, Swedish, or Saxon prince unfamiliar with Polish affairs who would let them alone and do nothing to curb their political and economic power. The nobles controlled the Diet, and had absolute power in matters of war and peace, legislation, and the imposition of taxes. Any member, by the principle of *liberum veto,* had the right to block a bill or dissolve the chamber. Under this extraordinary arrangement one million nobles mercilessly exploited thirteen million serfs. The peasantry was the most miserable in Europe. Added to these adverse conditions were religious conflicts among a conglomerate people: Catholics in Poland, Greek Orthodox in Lithuania, Protestants in the area near Prussia. With a weak Crown, a selfish nobility, an ineffective Diet, permanently quarreling national groups, and religious differences, eighteenth-century Poland was a prime target for greedy neighbors.

First Partition, 1772. The rulers of Russia, Prussia, and Austria were all eager to carve slices of territory from weaker states in their vicinity. Poland, falling victim, was destroyed

PARTITIONS OF POLAND

1772
1793
1795

RUSSIAN EMPIRE

Baltic Sea

Riga

Danzig 1793

PRUSSIA

EAST PRUSSIA

Warsaw

PRUSSIA

TO RUSSIA

Kiev

AUSTRIA

TO AUSTRIA

DOMINIO:

OTTOMAN EMPIRE

in three successive partitions. In 1772 Frederick the Great of Prussia, Maria Theresa of Austria, and Catherine II of Russia, asserting piously that an anarchic Poland was a perpetual menace to her neighbors, came to an

understanding that each should annex a share of the weakened kingdom.

After being urged on by Joseph II, Maria Theresa abandoned whatever moral scruples she had and reluctantly accepted the treaty of partition. Frederick the Great acquired the palatinates of Marienburg, Pomorska, Warmia, Kulm, and a part of Great Poland, but he failed to obtain Danzig, for which he had hoped. By the annexation of West Prussia he was able to link up East (or Ducal) Prussia with the core of his dominions in Brandenburg. Maria Theresa acquired Galicia, and parts of Podolia and Little Poland. Catherine took White Russia and the area beyond the Dnieper. The First Partition undoubtedly strengthened Prussia more than Russia or Austria. Russia gained the least, because in agreeing to a partition she lost the opportunity of maintaining Poland as an undivided satellite.

Second Partition, 1793. Sobered by this "national crime" and fully aware of the danger, the Polish magnates began to realize the necessity of achieving reform to strengthen the country. In this they were encouraged by Prussia, whose new king, Frederick William II, gave his word that he would defend them against Russia. The Polish Diet enacted a series of sweeping reforms: it amended the constitution, abolished the *liberum veto,* made the monarchy hereditary, and sought to improve the condition of both burghers and peasants. Some nobles, enraged by these reforms, plotted with agents of Russia and Prussia to overthrow the new government.

In the meantime occurred the deaths of Maria Theresa (1780) and Frederick the Great (1786), but their successors were quite willing to cooperate with Catherine II in her determination to destroy Poland. Prussia turned on Poland, whereupon foreign troops once again moved into the country, despite fruitless resistance led by Thaddeus Kosciuszko (1746–1817), a Polish patriot who had fought with George Washington in the American Revolution. The King of Poland lost his nerve and joined the Polish conservatives backed by Russia. This was appeasement, and it failed. In the second division of Poland

(1793), Prussia took the remainder of Great Poland, while the Russian boundary was advanced to the central part of Lithuania. Austria, at this time busy with war against revolutionary France, got nothing.

Third Partition, 1795. In 1794 Kosciuszko made a final effort to free his country from invasion on all sides. Desperately hoping for help from the French revolutionaries, he appealed to burghers and townsmen for aid. He marched on Warsaw, forced the Russians to raise the siege, and held both Warsaw and Vilna for six months. But his defense against the veteran allies was in vain. "Freedom shrieked when Kosciuszko fell." Taken prisoner, he was released two years later.

In 1795 Poland was partitioned for the third time. This time Prussia acquired the capital and territory as far as the Niemen; Austria took Cracow, with the area bounded by the Pilica, the Vistula, and the Bug; Russia annexed what was left. Poland ceased to exist as an independent state. Two years later the allies agreed in secret never again to use the name Poland. King Stanislaus II abdicated and went to St. Petersburg, where he died in 1798.

Revolutionary France had given the Poles no help. Indeed, the sacrifice of Poland probably saved France by distracting the great powers which were at war with her. In a sense, the partitions of Poland preserved the balance of power among Austria, Prussia, and Russia, which thus replaced Sweden, Turkey, and Poland as the three great powers of East Central Europe. Russia, long buried in the East, now took a place as a disturbing member of the European family of nations.

To such a pass had the selfish Polish nobility brought their country. But each of their new masters was to find the Poles an unassimilable element. True, Poland had disappeared from the map, but not the Poles. The stage was set for nationalistic uprisings in the nineteenth century, to be followed in 1919 by the revival of Poland as a national state.

⤛ KEY READING ⤜

KAZIMIERZ WALISZEWSKI: THE REVOLT OF THE *STRELTSY*, 1698

Kazimierz Waliszewski, *Peter the Great*, trans. from *Pierre le Grand* (New York, 1897), pp. 397–405. Courtesy of D. Appleton and Company.

KAZIMIERZ WALISZEWSKI, a Pole long resident in France, wrote a series of ten monographs covering nearly three centuries of Russian history from Ivan the Terrible to the end of the nineteenth century. Based on extensive research, the books make excellent reading. The following extract from his *Peter the Great* gives vivid details of Peter's terrible repression of the dissident *Streltsy* on his return from Western Europe.

When the young Tsar returned from his first European journey, he appeared before his subjects in the cast-off garments of Augustus of Poland—a Western costume, which, hitherto, he had never worn in their sight. A few hours later, at a banquet given by General Sheïn, he laid hands on a pair of scissors, and began to clip the guests' beards. His jester, Tourguénief, followed his example. The witnesses of this scene may have thought it a mere despot's whim. Peter himself was naturally hairless, his beard was sparse, and his moustache grew thinly. He had been drinking freely, and his behaviour may have been taken for a mere outburst of gaiety. But no! A few days later, the clipping was sanctioned by a ukase. A huge reform, moral, intellectual, and economic, had been initiated by an absurd festive incident, which took place between the drinking of two glasses of wine. . . .

Close upon this came the suppression of the *Streltsy*. . . . A body of *Streltsy*, numbering some 2000 men, was detached from the Azof garrison, and sent to Viélikié-Louki to guard the Polish frontier. The men were furious at being separated from their comrades, and forced to march from one end of the Empire to the other. The *Streltsy* had always been left at home in time of peace. They mutinied, and marched on Moscow. General Sheïn marched against them with superior forces and artillery, met them on the 17th of June, within sight of the Monastery of the Resurrection, killed some, took the rest, hung several of his prisoners, after having put them to the question,—and the incident appeared closed.

But it was far from being closed. Peter, when he learnt the news, hastened his return, resolved to take advantage of the circumstances, and strike a decisive blow. Ever since his childhood, the *Streltsy* had stood in his way. They had put his relations and friends to the sword; they had supported a usurper's power against his own, and on this last occasion, when parleying with Sheïn, before the skirmish in which they were routed, they had used the most violent language with respect to Lefort, and the other foreigners who surrounded him. He was weary of it all; he was determined to make an end, to clear his native soil of these seeds of perpetual revolt, and drown the visions which had haunted him, from his cradle, in a sea of blood. A few blows with the knout, and half a dozen executions, would not suffice him; the work, this time, was to be done on a large scale, and satisfy him wholly. . . .

The investigation proved nothing, but it exasperated the young Tsar's instinctive violence, and hardened him yet more. He was present at the examinations, and in the torture-chambers. Is it true, as some writers have declared, that he enjoyed it,—delighting in the sight of the panting bodies, the long-drawn anguish, and all the bitter incidents of suffering and death? I cannot believe it. He may have watched it all, I will admit, with curiosity,—with the zest of a man thirsting for new sensations, and inexorably resolved to see and touch everything himself,—his heart growing yet more hard, and his imagination running wild, amidst the bloody orgy of sovereign justice. When the trial was over, nothing would suffice him but wholesale executions, heads falling in heaps under the executioner's axe, forests of gallows, hecatombs of human life.

On the 30th of September 1698, the first procession, numbering 200 condemned men, took its way to the spot chosen for the final scene. Five of these were beheaded on the road, in front of the Tsar's house at Préobajenskoïé, and Peter himself was their executioner. This fact is attested by numerous witnesses, adopted by contemporary opinion, and accepted by the majority of historians. Leibnitz himself, in spite of his weakness for the Reforming Sovereign, expresses horror and indignation at the incident. And Peter was not content with wielding the axe himself, he insisted that those about him should follow his example. Galitzin bungled at the work, and caused his victims terrible suffering. Menshikof and Romodanovski were more skilful. Two foreigners only, Lefort and Blomberg, Colonel of the Préobajenskoïé regiment, refused to perform their abominable task. When the doomed men reached the Square at Moscow, whither they were taken in sledges, two in each, holding lighted tapers in their hands, they were placed in rows of 50 along a tree trunk which served for a block.

There were 144 fresh executions on the 11th October, 205 on the 12th, 141 on the 13th, 109 on the 17th, 65 on the 18th, and 106 on the 19th. Two hundred *Streltsy*, three of them holding copies of a petition to the Tsarevna, were hung before the windows of Sophia's apartments in the *Novodiévitchyï Monastery*. She herself escaped pretty easily. She lost the rank which she had hitherto retained, was confined in a narrow cell, and thenceforth was only known as the Nun Susanna. Her sister Marfa was condemned to the same fate, in the Convent of the Assumption (*Ouspienski*), in the present Government of Vladimir, where she took the name of Margaret. Both sisters died in their cloisters, the elder in 1704, and the younger in 1707.

Other inquiries, followed by wholesale executions, took place at Azof, and in various parts of the Empire. The unhappy *Streltsy* were hunted hither and thither. It was a war of extermination. At Moscow, in January 1699, there were more inquiries and more executions. Peter's absence, during November and December, at Voronèje, had necessitated a pause of some weeks. The corpses which strewed the Square, were carried off in thousands, and thrown on to the neighbouring fields, where they rotted unburied,—and still the axe worked busily. . . .

Thus the executioner's tools, and his victims' corpses, and all the hideous paraphernalia of criminal punishment, did not here produce the impression which would elsewhere have made them objects of horror and repugnance. For they were associated with the most august incidents in the public life, and when Peter appeared on the scaffold, axe in hand, he neither derogated from his high dignity, nor made himself odious in the eyes of his subjects. All he did was to carry out his functions as their supreme judge. Any man,

at that period, might turn executioner, if the occasion arose. When the work was heavy, supplementary assistance in the bloody business was sought for in the open streets, and the supply never failed. Peter, without ceasing to be Tsar, could still be the Tsar's headsman, just as he had been his drummer and his sailor. He turned his hand to the executioner's duty, just as he had previously turned it to the rigging of his ships. No one was shocked by his action nor blamed him for it. He was much more likely to be praised!

⤳ HISTORICAL INTERPRETATION ⤶

ANATOLE G. MAZOUR ON PETER THE GREAT'S REORGANIZATION OF GOVERNMENT

Anatole G. Mazour, *Russia: Past and Present* (Princeton, N. J., 1955), pp. 87–90.

THE ABSOLUTISM of Ivan IV was carried by Peter the Great to its logical conclusion. Peter removed any shadows of representative government that might have had a restraining effect on autocracy. How Peter reorganized the government to fit in with his own conception of absolutism was shown by Anatole G. Mazour, professor emeritus of history at Stanford University, in this passage.

Central authority underwent a complete overhauling under the reign of Peter. In place of the *Boyar* Council he formed a smaller body of loyal members sympathetic with his program. This body was entitled the "Intimate Chancellory," renamed "the Senate" in 1711, and was under Peter's own strict supervision. For all practical purposes the Senate was a mere executive office with administrative and clerical functions. Since Peter was rarely in the capital but was constantly roaming the country or fighting on the battlefield, the Senate eventually assumed considerable authority, though its judgments represented those of the Emperor. Always preoccupied and always in haste, Peter authorized the Senate to draft laws, giving its members only the essence of the projected bills, and ordering that body to enforce the adopted laws. In this manner the Senate acquired the power of judicial interpretation of the laws as well as serving as a final court of appeal, although the will of the Emperor remained supreme.

The organization of the Cabinet was a different story. The old Muscovite regime had a number of Departments or *Prikazy*. These were created at various times, when the need called for them; their status was often undetermined, their functions vague and sometimes conflicting. Upon consulting several authorities abroad Peter accepted the scheme suggested by Baron Fick, a scheme which followed the Swedish system of ministerial *Collegia* or Councils. These were Ministries headed not by individual administrators, but by collective groups carrying the responsibility for their representative departments or *Collegia*. . . .

Realizing the magnitude of the task he had undertaken, Peter sensed that some degree of self-government would have to be allowed. Again he copied what he had witnessed abroad, chiefly in Germany. He granted municipal governments to various towns, with city assemblies enjoying minor local administrative and judicial powers. But if the towns and cities received a small degree of self-government, the old provincial units were deprived of it altogether. In 1710 the country was divided into eight provinces or *Gubernia*, increased to eleven in 1719, each of them tied to central authority; each *Gubernia* was subdivided into smaller units of *provintsii*. A governor appointed from the national capital headed each *Gubernia*.

The most drastic reforms were carried out in the realm of ecclesiastical affairs, and the future of the Church . . . was profoundly affected. The Greek Orthodox Church of Russia was independent from the Mother Church and its Patriarch residing at Constantinople. The head of the Russian Church, the Patriarch, became independent of the other sister Churches in the Near East. He assumed not only an ecclesiastical power but, on frequent occasions, served as beneficial counselor to the Tsar. But many leading churchmen, not excepting the Patriarch himself, objected to Peter's radical reforms. The bitterest opponents were, of course, the Old Believers; but even the members of the official church looked upon the reforms as sheer heresy and considered Peter the Anti-Christ. . . .

Adrian, the Patriarch of Russia and a strong opponent of the reforms, died in 1700, at the insistence of Peter the election of a successor was indefinitely postponed. Hence, the Patriarchal office remained vacant until 1721, when, by law of that date, the Emperor, under the influence of Protestantism, instituted a new form of administration which abolished the office altogether. . . .

The date 1721 is thus an important one: it transformed the Church into a secular department and a bureaucratic agency, with unhealthy effects upon the spirituality of ecclesiastical affairs. But if the Church lost, the State gained by demobilizing the most potent critic of the government. Whether it gained permanently is another question, but temporarily it was strength-ened. The Church was now a tool of the government; it persecuted, condemned, or excommunicated not only religious but political heresy. Spirituality left the halls of the Synod for the huts of the masses.

To finance the stupendous projects undertaken by Peter, everything was sacrificed on the altar of the State. Peasants were tied to their soil and dominated by landlords as never before. Every conceivable object, from land to stovepipes, became taxable. Old social distinction was virtually wiped out by the new gentry, most of whom were social climbers and were conveniently servile to Peter. In reality the backbone of the Church was broken by its complete secularization and the abolition of the Patriarchate. The process of Westernization was accelerated during the reign of Peter, but it touched only the social surface; beneath lay an impenetrable and resentful mass —the people of Russia. On the banks of the Neva had risen a new capital—St. Petersburg. Here on the marshy land rose the new government buildings, the characteristic brick and stucco with granite revetments along the river where a new bureaucracy and Western absolutism came to rule the nation for nearly two centuries. "O Russia, seeing what a great man has left you, see also how great he has left you," chanted Prokopovich in his funeral sermon on Peter. But that greatness was in many respects illusory or superficial. Peter forced Russia to change from a medieval into a modern state and ordered the people to face westward. This might have been an historical necessity, but it imposed crucial readjustments and an unbearable price for the privilege of joining the western European family of nations.

❧ TEN BASIC BOOKS ❧

EXPANSION: THE RISE AND WESTERNIZATION OF RUSSIA

1. Eckhardt, Hans von, *Ivan the Terrible* (New York, 1949).
2. Florinsky, Michael T., *Russia: A History and an Interpretation,* 2 vols. (New York, 1953).
3. Halecki, Oscar, *Borderlands of Western Civilization: A History of East-Central Europe* (New York, 1952).
4. Kaplan, Herbert H., *The First Partition of Poland* (New York, 1962).

5. Kliuchevskii, Vasilii O., *A History of Russia,* 4 vols. (New York, 1911–1926).

6. Lamb, Harold, *The March of Muscovy: Ivan the Terrible and the Growth of the Russian Empire, 1400–1648* (New York, 1948).

7. Mazour, Anatole G., *Russia: Tsarist and Communist,* rev. ed. (Princeton, N. J., 1962).

8. Pares, Sir Bernard, *A History of Russia,* rev. ed. (London, 1953).†

9. Sumner, Benedict H., *Peter the Great and the Emergence of Russia* (New York, 1951).†

10. Vernadsky, George, and Michael Karpovich, *A History of Russia,* 3 vols. (New Haven, Conn., 1943–1953).

PART III
THE AGE OF REVOLUTIONS

THE ANATOMY OF REVOLUTION[1]

Crane Brinton

WE MUST be very tentative about the prodromal symptoms of revolution. Even retro-spectively . . . there is little ground for belief that anyone today has enough knowledge and skill to apply formal methods of diagnosis to a contemporary society and say, in this case revolution will or will not occur shortly. But some uniformities do emerge from a study of the old regimes in England, America, France, and Russia.

First, these were all societies on the whole on the upgrade economically before the revo-lution came, and the revolutionary movements seem to originate in the discontents of not unprosperous people who feel restraint, cramp, annoyance, rather than downright crushing oppression. Certainly these revolutions are not started by down-and-outers, by starving, miserable people. These revolutionists are not worms turning, not children of despair. These revolutions are born of hope, and their philosophies are formally optimistic.

Second, we find in our prerevolutionary society definite and indeed very bitter class antagonisms, though these antagonisms seem rather more complicated than the cruder Marxists will allow. It was not a case of feudal nobility against bourgeoisie in 1640, 1776, and 1789, or of bourgeoisie against proletariat in 1917. The strongest feelings seem gen-erated in the bosoms of men—and women—who have made money, or at least who have enough to live on, and who contemplate bitterly the imperfections of a socially privileged aristocracy. Revolutions seem more likely when social classes are fairly close together than when they are far apart. "Untouchables" very rarely revolt against a God-given aristocracy, and Haiti gives one of the few examples of successful slave revolutions. But rich merchants whose daughters can marry aristocrats are likely to feel that God is at least as interested in merchants as in aristocrats. It is difficult to say why the bitterness of feeling between classes *almost* equal socially seems so much stronger in some societies than others—why, for instance, a Marie Antoinette should be so much more hated in eighteenth-century France than a rich, idle, much publicized heiress in contemporary America; but at any rate the existence of such bitterness can be observed in our prerevolutionary societies, which is, clinically speaking, enough for the moment.

Third, there is what we have called the desertion of the intellectuals. This is in some respects the most reliable of the symptoms we are likely to meet. Here again we need not try to explain all the hows and whys, need not try to tie up the desertion of the intellectuals with a grand and complete sociology of revolutions. We need state simply that it can be observed in all four of our societies.

Fourth, the governmental machinery is clearly inefficient, partly through neglect, through a failure to make changes in old institutions, partly because of new conditions . . . condi-

[1] Crane Brinton, *The Anatomy of Revolution*, rev. ed. (New York, 1952), pp. 278–283, *passim*. By permission of Prentice-Hall.

tions attendant on economic expansion and the growth of new monied classes, new ways of transportation, new business methods—these new conditions laid an intolerable strain on governmental machinery adapted to simpler, more primitive conditions.

Fifth, the old ruling class—or rather, many individuals of the old ruling class—come to distrust themselves, or lose faith in the traditions and habits of their class, grow intellectual, humanitarian, or go over to the attacking groups. Perhaps a larger number of them than usual lead lives we shall have to call immoral, dissolute, though one cannot by any means be as sure about this as a symptom as about the loss of habits and traditions of command effective among a ruling class. At any rate, the ruling class becomes politically inept.

The dramatic events that start things moving, that bring on the fever of revolution, are in three of our four revolutions intimately connected with the financial administration of the state. In the fourth, Russia, the breakdown of administration under the burdens of an unsuccessful war is only in part financial. But in all our societies the inefficiency and inadequacy of the governmental structure of the society come out clearly in the very first stages of the revolution. There is a time—the first few weeks or months—when it looks as if a determined use of force on the part of the government might prevent the mounting excitement from culminating in an overthrow of the government. These governments attempted such a use of force in all four instances, and in all four their attempt was a failure. This failure indeed proved a turning point during the first stages, and set up the revolutions in power. . . .

The extremists are helped to power no doubt by the existence of a powerful pressure toward centralized strong government, something which in general the moderates are not capable of providing, while the extremists, with their discipline, their contempt for half measures, their willingness to make firm decisions, their freedom from libertarian qualms, are quite able and willing to centralize. Especially in France and Russia, where powerful foreign enemies threatened the very existence of the nation, the machinery of government during the crisis period was in part constructed to serve as a government of national defense. Yet though modern wars . . . demand a centralization of authority, war alone does not seem to account for all that happened in the crisis period in those countries.

What does happen may be a bit oversimply summarized as follows: emergency centralization of power in an administration, usually a council or commission, and more or less dominated by a "strong man"—Cromwell, Robespierre, Lenin; government without any effective protection for the normal civil rights of the individual—or if this sounds unrealistic, especially for Russia, let us say the normal private life of the individual; setting up of extraordinary courts and a special revolutionary police to carry out the decrees of the government and to suppress all dissenting individuals or groups; all this machinery ultimately built up from a relatively small group—Independents, Jacobins, Bolsheviks—which has a monopoly on all governmental action. Finally, governmental action becomes a much greater part of all human action than in these societies in their normal condition: this apparatus of government is set to work indifferently on the mountains and molehills of human life—it is used to pry and poke about corners normally reserved for priest or physician, or friend, and it is used to regulate, control, plan, the production and distribution of economic wealth on a national scale.

13

The Great Rebellion in England: The Commonwealth

FOR THE people. And truly I desire their liberty and freedom as much as anybody whomsoever. But I must tell you that their liberty and freedom consists in having of government, those laws by which their life and their goods may be most their own. It is not for having share in government, Sir, that is nothing pertaining to them. A subject and a sovereign are clean different things, and, therefore, until they do that, I mean, that you do put the people in that liberty as I say, certainly they will never enjoy themselves. . . . If I would have given way to an arbitrary way, for to have all laws changed according to the power of the sword, I needed not to have come here. And, therefore, I tell you, and I pray God it be not laid to your charge, that I am the martyr of the people.

—CHARLES I on the scaffold

1. Conflicts Between King and Parliament, 1603–1642

Legacy of the Tudors. The Tudor period came to an end with the death of Queen Elizabeth in 1603. The Crown passed to the house of Stuart, but with an important legacy —a tradition of strong government. For nearly a half-century after the death of Elizabeth the Stuarts tried to maintain Tudor despotism, only to fail in the task. The Stuart kings, usually ignoring the popular demand for increased political rights, found their royal authority under assault. When that crucial half-century was over, absolute monarchy was broken, never to be restored in England. This was in contrast to concurrent developments in France, where Louis XIV was perfecting his own special brand of absolutism.

While the Tudors had ruled despotically, they were careful to make use of constitutional forms: at all times they sought harmony with the desires of the powerful middle class. Both Henry VIII and Elizabeth were experts in the art of convincing Parliament that what the Crown wanted coincided beautifully with the interests of the people. They kept alive a subservient Parliament to give legal sanction to royal acts. The Tudors bequeathed to the Stuarts a constitutional body which one day would assert its rights against the throne. When absolutism succumbed in England, it was succeeded by a parliamentary system in continuing evolution.

The Absolutism of James I, 1603–1625. The heir to the Tudor legacy was a cousin of Elizabeth, James Stuart, who had been James VI of Scotland, only son of the unhappy Mary, Queen of Scots, and her second husband, Henry, Lord Darnley. James endured a precarious and abnormal childhood. His education was weighted with rigid Presbyterian and Calvinist political doctrine, against which the quick-witted, sensitive lad reacted violently. He was to turn for his political philosophy to the theory of the divine right of kings.

Acceding to the English throne in 1603,

James I of England brought with him to London some greedy Scottish favorites who immediately incurred great popular scorn and dislike. Ironically dubbed "the wisest fool in Christendom," James misunderstood the temper of his times. He failed to understand that the English people had tolerated the Tudors' benevolent absolutism only because they were beset by a host of troubles—oppression by the feudal nobility, religious dissension, and danger from foreign enemies—and needed a strong royal power to meet these problems. The situation had changed, but James was not aware of it. The feudal nobility had been subjugated, the danger of foreign invasion had disappeared with the destruction of the Spanish Armada in 1588, and the execution of Mary, Queen of Scots, had removed the last center of intrigue against the Crown.

To James all this meant nothing. He stayed solidly with the old line: "As it is atheism and blasphemy in a creature to dispute what God can do, so is it presumptuous and high contempt in a subject to question what a king can do." Nevertheless, James possessed a kind of shrewdness and discretion which his son Charles I lacked: he was always ready to give way, even on the divine-right principle, whenever it became politically expedient.

Religious Policy of James I. James I's religious policy was straightforward: the supremacy of the Crown in religious matters, and intolerance of any religious force opposed to it. In achieving this goal he succeeded in alienating both Puritans and Catholics. One of his first actions was directed against the Puritans—those extreme Protestants, essentially Calvinist in theology, who desired to "purify" the church of remnants of Catholic ritual. The name Puritan was given probably in derision because of the purity of doctrine or discipline which the more rigid reformers claimed as their own. They were certain that they alone followed the word of God as opposed to all "human inventions," which they believed had been retained by the Church of England despite its "alleged reformation." They hoped to find a champion in the new king, but in this they were frustrated.

The Puritans in 1604 presented to the king a Millenary Petition requesting slight changes in church procedure, such as the abolition of the ring in marriage ceremonies. James I, who believed himself an ecclesiastical authority, considered this petition ground for debate, and hence summoned a conference of Puritans and Anglican officials. At first James argued with the Puritans, then lost his temper with the famous epigram: "No Bishop, no King." By this he meant that the absence of bishops in Puritan Church organization made it impossible for the king to exercise proper control. After hearing Puritan arguments, James replied with a final: "If this be all they have to say, I shall make them conform themselves, or I shall harry them out of the land, or else do worse." Such was the defective wisdom of an overconfident monarch.

In that same year, 1604, James issued a decree depriving of their livelihood all clergymen who refused to recognize the authority of the Anglican Prayer Book. Many outraged but courageous Puritans, holding it impossible to live any longer in England, emigrated to the Netherlands, and in 1620 founded the Plymouth colony in Massachusetts. Those Puritans who remained in England worked in Parliament to protest the king's policies.

While antagonizing the radical wing of Protestants, James I also managed to alienate the Catholics. The Catholics had deplored both the change in the state religion and the Elizabethan Compromise. At first James was disposed to conciliate them because he wanted to win favor with Catholic Spain, with whom he desired an alliance. When embittered Catholics began to plot against the throne, James in 1604 issued an edict banishing priests and restoring the old penal laws against Catholics. A group of fanatics, disgruntled by these measures, organized a conspiracy to blow up the palace of Westminster on November 5, 1605, at a time when the king, his council, and Parliament would be assembled. They rented a cellar under the palace and placed thirty-six barrels of gunpowder there. Shortly before Parliament met, a letter writer who wished to spare the Catholics present unwittingly exposed the conspiracy. The Gunpowder Plot was discovered, and its leader, Guy Fawkes, and his fellow conspirators were executed. The result was a renewal for English Protestants of the old, long-lasting hatred and fear of Catholicism. Discovery of the conspiracy gave the king a temporary popularity which was soon to be dissipated.

James I's one great accomplishment in religious matters was granting one of the requests made by the Puritans in the Millenary Petition—a demand for a new translation of the Bible. In 1611, at his instigation and after eight years of work by forty-seven scholars, appeared the authorized King James Version of the Bible, based on the Hebrew and Greek texts of the Old and New Testaments. One of the most magnificent works in all literature, the King James Bible had a vital influence on the subsequent development of the English language.

Foreign Policy of James I. About all that James I accomplished in his foreign policy was to exasperate an already dissatisfied populace. His aims were (1) a *rapprochement* with Spain, and (2) a general peace, with England as the arbiter of Europe. These goals were dictated largely by personal vanity and his desire to avoid a drain on the nation's finances. He wanted no dependence on Parliament for fiscal help. His foreign policy failed, resulting in a loss of national confidence and prestige, later to react disastrously on his son. James concluded a peace treaty with Spain (1604) to the dismay of the commercial bourgeoisie in Parliament, who had derived considerable profit from raids on Spanish shipping and from illicit trade with the Spanish colonies.

Opposition of the anti-Catholic Parliament to James's treaty with Spain was as nothing compared to its fury at his plan for promoting Anglo-Spanish friendship by a marriage between his son Charles and the daughter of the king of Spain. Parliament was appalled by the possibility of England later getting a half-Spanish and a Catholic king. The Spanish infanta refused the marriage proposal, threatening to enter a convent rather than marry the English "heretic." To the relief of his countrymen, young Charles, angered and

resentful, returned from Spain still a bachelor and still a Protestant. A more lasting monument to James I's foreign policy was his marrying off his daughter, Elizabeth, to the Elector-Palatinate, a leader of the German Protestants. This was to result in an eventuality which James could not possibly have foreseen: the Hanoverian succession to the British throne.

James I and Parliament. Parliament had long been under control of the Tudors, but now, with an unpopular ruler, it was no longer content to remain subservient. It was filled with members who opposed James on religious, commercial, and national grounds. The Puritans denounced his religious views. The merchants disliked his commercial policies, and for national reasons opposed his attempts to promote friendship with Spain. Some members issued a stirring protest, insisting that "the liberties, privileges, and jurisdiction of Parliament are the ancient and undoubted birthright of the subjects of England, and that the arduous and urgent affairs concerning the King, the State, the Church, and defense of the realm, making and maintenance of laws, and the redress of grievances, which happen daily within the realm, are proper subjects for debate in Parliament; and that in the handling and proceedings of those businesses, every member of the Commons . . . has freedom of speech . . . to bring to conclusion the same." James had the authors of this protest thrown into prison.

James's tactlessness was enough to alienate Parliament, but he further annoyed it by his extravagances. Always in need of money, without the right of arbitrary taxation, he found the old feudal dues insufficient to cover governmental expenses. Forced to ask a stubborn Parliament, which traditionally held the purse strings, for subsidies or new taxes, he was infuriated when it usually refused his request unless he agreed to adjust some grievance. He sought to increase revenues by raising the rates on tonnage and poundage (taxes on imported merchandise, granted to English sovereigns for life). He also imposed duties on articles which hitherto had been exempted. He tried to obtain additional funds by selling titles, a practice which aroused widespread resentment. King and Parliament remained at odds on the problems of money, absolutism, freedom of speech, and the Spanish question. The struggle was in full blast when James I died in 1625.

Accession of Charles I. It was not yet too late to heal the breach between Crown and Parliament, but Charles I (r. 1625–1649) did little to remedy the situation. If anything, more self-willed and dogmatic than his father, Charles adhered unflinchingly to the divine-right theory, continued governing through favorites, and carried on what amounted to a war against the Puritans. In the opening years of his reign he was in constant struggle with Parliament, which stubbornly opposed his religious and fiscal policies. He quarreled with his first Parliament in 1625 and dismissed it. Brooding about his unsuccessful mission to obtain the hand of the Spanish infanta, he embarked on war against Spain. His fleet was defeated at Cadiz. Parliament, convoked again in 1626, refused any additional funds, and threatened to impeach his favorite adviser, the brilliant but unstable Duke of Buckingham. Charles replied by dissolving Parliament again. Buckingham, the power behind the throne, was assassinated in 1628.

To obtain needed funds for his war, Charles I was forced to try the expedient of raising money by exacting benevolences, or forced loans. Poor freeholders who refused to pay these thinly disguised taxes ran the risk of being impressed into military or naval service. Meanwhile, Charles, as a means of saving money, quartered soldiers in the homes of citizens, a practice which aroused widespread resentment. Both rich and poor protested against forced loans, and many of them, including seventy of the gentry, died in the king's dungeons. In 1628, after having exhausted all means of raising additional revenue, Charles convoked his third Parliament.

Petition of Right, 1628. As the price of its cooperation in raising taxes, Parliament insisted upon redress of grievances. The Petition of Right, presented to Charles in 1628, is one of the cornerstones of British freedom. After an account of the Crown's violation of certain ancient statutes, the document forbade the king (1) to impose any loans, gifts, benevolences, or taxes without the consent of Parliament; (2) to imprison anyone without due process of law; (3) to billet any soldiers or sailors in private houses; or (4) to declare martial law in time of peace. (*See page 209.*)

Charles I signed the Petition of Right under pressure, but probably never considered it binding because, in his view, it conflicted with his idea of the divine right of kings. Yet all its provisions weakened the royal power to rule without Parliament. It was at this stage that Parliament ceased to defend its established rights, and instead, initiated the constitutional struggle.

Personal Government of Charles I, 1629–1640. Although Charles had signed the Petition of Right, he promptly violated its provisions by levying customs at the ports. Parliament, protesting again, passed a resolution condemning him. He dissolved Parliament and for eleven years, from 1629 to 1640, ruled without it. He made many attempts to raise money for his immediate needs. He continued the old customs duties of tonnage and poundage. In 1634 he made the first levy of ship-money, which formerly had been a tax on port-cities to provide ships in times of national danger and which he now converted into a direct general tax payable even in inland counties. In 1637 came the John Hampden case, when a country gentleman was brought to trial for refusal to pay ship-money. Hampden was found guilty. Charles's right to levy ship-money was acknowledged by the courts, but the king resented the fact that the courts had even questioned his "divine right" to tax.

To political and economic oppression the blustering Charles added religious trespass. Working closely with the king was William Laud, Archbishop of Canterbury, who favored the High Church party, tolerated the Catholics, and persecuted the Puritans. In response to Laud's repression, many Puritans made their way to America. Matters were precipitated to a crisis by Charles's Scottish policy.

To attain uniformity of religious practice, the king and Laud tried to force the Anglican service upon the Scottish Presbyterian Kirk. In 1636 he introduced into Scotland a prayer book closely resembling that of the Anglican Church. This led to a riot the next year in St. Giles's Cathedral in Edinburgh. The Lowland Scots rose in rebellion and prepared to make war on Charles.

Charles I's administrative adviser, Thomas Wentworth, Earl of Strafford, advised the king to call Parliament to authorize a punitive force against Scotland. Both the king and Strafford believed that the Scottish war would galvanize Parliament into voting supplies, but they were mistaken. The Short Parliament, meeting in 1640, immediately began to discuss grievances and protested against unfair taxation, whereupon it was dissolved within three weeks. Charles went north with a meager army to attack the Scots, who had sworn to defend their religion to the death.

Long Parliament, 1640–1660. Charles I grudgingly made peace with the Scots practically on their own terms. His finances exhausted again, he was forced in November 1640 to summon what later was called the Long Parliament. The first aim of the new Parliament was to bring Strafford, responsible for many repressive measures, to account by an act of attainder (a legislative act which extinguishes the civil rights of a person on sentence of death). The wavering Charles signed Strafford's death warrant, thus sacrificing his most loyal and capable servant (1641). Led by the Puritan, John Pym, Parliament imprisoned Archbishop Laud and four years later had him executed.

Parliament, not yet satisfied, forced Charles to give concession after concession. For example, Parliament could not be dissolved or prorogued (adjourned) without its own consent. The Triennial Act required the king to summon Parliament at least once every three years. The Court of Star Chamber and the Court of High Commission were abolished. Ship-money and various other taxes were declared illegal. Within a few months this

avenging Parliament destroyed absolutism in England.

Grand Remonstrance, 1641. Charles I needed money again, this time to suppress a rebellion in Ireland. Leaders of Parliament introduced a statement called the Grand Remonstrance (1641), which narrated in a series of clauses all the alleged unconstitutional acts of the king, both in Church and State matters, since the beginning of his reign. The resolution demanded that the government be placed in the hands of ministers responsible to Parliament; otherwise no funds would be voted. After a vigorous debate, the Grand Remonstrance was carried by eleven votes and ordered to be printed as an appeal to the nation. The king refused to honor the petition. On January 4, 1642, he attempted to arrest the Five Members—leaders of Parliament John Pym, Denzil Holles, Sir Arthur Haselrig, William Strode, and John Hampden—on a charge of treason. This act brought the conflict between king and Parliament to a head. It was one of the incidents which touched off the Civil War.

2. Revolution and Civil Wars, 1642–1648

Emergence of Cromwell. Gradually, two opposing political factions crystallized. To the king's standard rallied most of the nobles, the gentry, and the Catholics, the royal party who took the name Cavaliers. In opposition were the Parliamentarians, consisting of several great earls and most of the Puritan middle class—traders, manufacturers, shopkeepers, and the yeomanry (gentleman farmers, or freeholders, who possessed small estates). The close-cropped hair of these commoners won them the derisive nickname of Roundheads. The Cavaliers wore their hair in long curls, court-fashion. The king's party had its greatest strength in the north and west, while the Roundheads were centered mostly in London and the south and east of England.

The conflict brought a hitherto unknown Englishman named Oliver Cromwell (1599–

1658) to the foreground. A man of ponderous earnestness and sincerity, Cromwell had been a member of both the Short and Long Parliaments, 1639 and 1640, but at first played a relatively insignificant role in parliamentary

Oliver Cromwell who, after leading the Parliamentarians to victory, was pronounced Lord Protector of England, Ireland, and Scotland. After a contemporary painting by Van der Faes.

battles. An unbending, God-fearing Puritan, Cromwell decided that Parliament needed a powerful force to oppose the royal army. He discovered his answer in the stern piety of the yeoman farmers of eastern England. Raising in his own district a troop of "godly men," later called "Ironsides," he trained them himself as an effective military force, the "New Model Army." For them Protestant exaltation was the basis of morale; they were to go into battle with old Hebraic war psalms on their lips. As honest, sober Christians, they were fined twelve pence if they swore. They killed with a pious prayer on their lips. These fanatically loyal troops were to become the champions of advanced democratic ideas in England.

Religious Issues. There were serious differences among English Protestants. The Episcopal, or Anglican Church, the Church of England, was governed by bishops, who were regarded as the successors in office, in a long, unbroken continuity, of the Twelve Apostles of Christ. Like Roman Catholics, the Episcopalians recognized a hierarchy, an organized, graded clergy. Anglican bishops possessed chief ecclesiastical authority within a defined district or diocese. Because they were

unpopular everywhere, they had few followers.

The Presbyterians, predominant in Parliament, formed the middle group of Protestants, who were midway between reforming Episcopalians and radical Independents. The Presbyterians called for a State Church governed by councils of elders, or presbyters. They recognized no priest but Christ, their ministers enjoyed no priestly privileges, and they observed only two sacraments: baptism and the Lord's Supper. They sought the abolition of the episcopal office and of the Prayer Book, and called for the introduction of the Scottish system of democratic local organization.

Cromwell and his army, objecting to both Anglicanism and Presbyterianism, preferred to call themselves Independents. Opposed to ecclesiastical organization of any kind, they demanded a purely congregational system, as well as freedom of worship and conscience.

Civil War. In August 1642 Charles I raised his standard at Nottingham. The early stages of the war were well in his favor, but, because of Cromwell's Ironsides, victory after victory fell to the Parliamentarians. At Marston Moor (1644) the Ironsides, in alliance with the Scots, turned defeat into victory. The royal power was ended in the north. The Presbyterian majority in Parliament immediately abolished the office of the bishops and sought to make peace with the king.

Meanwhile, the Puritan army was growing ever more restive. It had proved itself so efficient that the whole parliamentary army was revised to meet its standards. Cromwell's men went into action against the royalists and defeated them at Naseby (1645) in the most decisive battle of the entire campaign.

In May 1646 Charles surrendered to the Scots who handed him over to the English parliamentary forces. Parliament demanded punishment of the king's supporters, control of the army, and the establishment of Presbyterianism. The king refused. He then tried to ally himself with the Scots and obtain their aid to fight against England. But Cromwell, now recognized as the greatest soldier in England, quickly routed Charles's royalists and the Scots.

Cromwell and his army soon turned on the Presbyterian majority in Parliament, which was ready to restore Charles to the throne. Mistrusting Cromwell, Parliament called for an end to his military force and began to pass measures directed against the Independent radical Puritans. One of Cromwell's officers, a certain Colonel Pride, was stationed with a body of his troops at the door of the House of Commons with orders to "purge" the house. The Long Parliament had started on December 6, 1640, with about five hundred members. On December 6, 1648, Pride arrested forty-seven members of Parliament, turned back about ninety-six, and left some sixty Inde-

pendent members, a minority, to deliberate on the nation's business. The House was thus purged "in the name of the people."

The Rump, sixty members, the only part of the house that remained sitting, declared itself the only body truly representing the people. It appointed a High Court of Justice to try the king on a charge of treason. When the House of Lords objected, the Commons passed the bill a second time, declaring that assent of the Lords was unnecessary. Cromwell now became convinced that the execution of Charles was not only politically expedient but also divinely predestined. The king refused to recognize the jurisdiction of the court. Throughout the trial he behaved with dignity and self-possession, claiming in private that he desired

Charles I insulted by Cromwell's guards.

the freedom of his people as much as any Englishman. He was not allowed to make any answer to the charges against him. The death warrant, signed by Cromwell and forty-nine others, called for "Charles Stuart, King of England . . . to be put to death by the severing

of his head from his body . . . in the open street before Whitehall upon the morrow."

On January 30, 1649, Charles I met his death with calm dignity and pious resignation. His body was exposed for several days "so that all men would know that he was not alive." An autopsy showed that "no man ever had his vital parts so perfect and unhurt." The irregularities of his trial and the manner of his death made him appear a martyr to many Englishmen, and eventually produced a popular reaction in his favor. Though in later years assailed by doubt, Cromwell seemed not to have been conscience-stricken by the death of the king.

Historical Controversy. Few subjects have been as exhaustively studied by scholars as the origins of the English Civil War, and there are few on which scholars have differed so widely. The war was a complex phenomenon composed of many strands, but historians have persisted in stressing one side of a many-faceted situation.

The political or Whig interpretation depends primarily on the argument that Charles I was a despot who aimed consciously at the subversion of established institutions and violated the English "constitution." Other English kings had occasionally committed unconstitutional acts, but few before Charles had ever tried systematically to make themselves despots. By attempting to arrest five members of Parliament, Charles made inevitable a war to limit the royal prerogative. This point of view, expressed in the first chapter of Volume I of Thomas Babington Macaulay's *The History of England from the Accession to James II* (1848–1861), placed the origins of the Civil War squarely on the political basis of despotism versus liberty.

The religious interpretation emphasizes Puritan resentment against the Church of England, with its formal liturgy, ornamentation, and ceremonial practices by bishops. William Haller describes Puritanism as a noble movement dedicated to active service, a movement proud of representing the elect who were inherently superior to others in the world. This view holds that religious differences were interwoven with the social order because the Church of England held property and jurisdictional rights.

In the early twentieth century, historians began to seek the origins of the English Civil War in economic factors. Thus, according to

Christopher Hill, the causes should be sought not in the conspiracy of individuals, nor in the political demands of Parliament, nor in the crusade of Puritanism against the Church of England, but in society—in the class struggle. A victory for Charles I would have meant the economic stagnation of England, and the stabilization of a backward feudal society in a commercial age. Hence, the English Civil War was a "bourgeois revolution," the political act by which English capitalism overthrew feudalism.

There are other variant economic interpretations. According to the economic historian, Richard H. Tawney, the English Civil War was called into being by the gentry, that farming class between the nobility and yeomanry, who took advantage of the economic squeeze on the old aristocracy to bring their political influence into line with their new economic power. Other historians (such as J. H. Hexter) deny that the gentry and aristocracy were distinct economic groups.

As on most historical problems, scholars are still working on the origins of the English Civil War, studying such component parts as Church and State, Parliament and law, and Crown and property rights. But here, as elsewhere, we must examine the historical problem by considering pluralistic factors and not by settling for a monistic interpretation, no matter how attractive. In history there are no easy or final answers.

3. Military Dictatorship of Cromwell

The Commonwealth, 1649–1653. The Rump Parliament abolished the monarchy, and England became a Commonwealth with neither king nor House of Lords. Executive power, hitherto vested in the king, was lodged in a Council of State composed of forty-one members, of whom thirty were in the House of Commons. Cromwell, as head of the army, was the real ruler. England became a military dictatorship, a radical Puritan oligarchy, without free elections, popular representation, and with curtailed civil rights.

There was strong opposition from the beginning. The people had been opposed to the

This Great Seal of England, issued in 1651, reveals that Cromwell was not unversed in the art of propaganda: the legend reads, "In the third yeare of freedome by Gods blessing restored."

garrisons and other Irish Catholics at Drogheda and Waterford. "I am persuaded," he said, "that this is a righteous judgment of God upon those barbarous wretches who have imbrued their hands in so much innocent blood, and that it will tend to prevent effusion of blood for the future." He was certain that the Lord was exclusively on his side. Many of the unfortunate Irish were shipped to Barbados as slaves.

Returning to England in 1650, Cromwell put an end to the Scottish alliance with Charles II by annihilating their scattered forces at Dunbar (1650) and Worcester (1651). Prince Charles, who had obtained the support of the Scots by agreeing to be a "Presbyterian king" upon his accession to the throne, was forced into exile in France. It seemed that the Stuarts were gone from England forever.

misgovernment of Charles I, but they were shocked and angered by his death at the hands of the army and a small group of extremists. The royalists hated the Commonwealth and vowed its destruction. Englishmen in general resented Cromwell's rule by the sword, his excessive taxation, and his pious suppression of popular amusements. In Scotland, angry Presbyterians joined with Anglicans to support Charles's son, whom they proclaimed Charles II. In Ireland, the Catholic population rose in open rebellion against the Commonwealth regime.

Suppression of the Opposition. To face this dangerous opposition Cromwell relied on his fanatically disciplined army. He crossed to Ireland at the head of his troops to crush Royalist resistance and to stifle plots to proclaim the son of Charles I as king. Impelled by the belief that he was a servant of the Lord sent to purify the people and root out "papistry and episcopacy" by any and all means necessary, he savagely butchered Irish Royalist

Cromwell and Parliament. Meanwhile, Cromwell began to have difficulties with his Rump Parliament. It had disregarded the demands of that army which had ensured its supreme position, and it seemed to be on the verge of transforming itself into a permanent oligarchy. There were rumors that its members were accepting bribes and placing relatives in positions of responsibility. Cromwell upbraided the body and charged it with self-interest, drunkenness, and impiety. On behalf of the army, Cromwell forcibly dissolved the Rump of the Long Parliament in April 1653. "Your hour is come," he said; "the Lord hath done with you!"

Cromwell and his Council of State then broke with tradition entirely by selecting one hundred forty members (one hundred twenty-nine English, six Irish, and 5 Scottish), all pious Puritan notables, on the recommendation of Independent ministers of the three kingdoms. This body was speedily styled the Little Parliament or Barebones Parliament after an obscure member, a rich leather merchant of London with the descriptive Puritan name of Praisegod Barebone or Barbon.

Foreign Policy. Cromwell early sought to increase the popularity of his regime by directing legislation against the Dutch, at that time England's most dangerous commercial rival. In 1651 the Rump passed the first Navigation Act, which required that all goods brought from America, Asia, and Africa to England be carried only in English ships or in vessels belonging to the country which produced the goods. Obviously, the aim was to exclude Dutch vessels from trading between England and other countries. This act provoked a war with the Dutch (1652–1654), the first of several which hastened the decline of Dutch sea power and commerce and at the same time increased the prestige of Britain. Cromwell then negotiated commercial treaties with Denmark, Sweden, and Portugal. He was quite prepared, in working for the goal of British and Protestant commercial supremacy, to ally himself with Catholic France against Catholic Spain. Together with his admiral, Robert Blake (1599–1657), author of *Instructions for the Better Ordering of the Fleet in Fighting*, he made the English navy a powerful striking force and laid the foundations for its later greatness.

England Under the Commonwealth. Cromwell, the supreme military and religious dictator of England, Scotland, and Wales, presided over a state which sought to imitate the moral standards of Calvinist Geneva. He denied freedom of speech, press, and assembly to critics. He closed theaters as "dens of iniquity." Although he himself often took "a cup of wine too much," and shocked his fellow Puritans by his taste in nude statuary, he was careful to guard the morals of his fellow citizens. His Barebones Parliament equalized taxes, reduced public spending, and initiated plans for the compilation of a new legal code. Its proposal to abolish tithes shocked the landowners who accused it of confiscation, and its plan for civil marriage angered the clergy. Cromwell himself desired general religious toleration, but he was unable to moderate the intolerance of his fellow Puritans. Catholics were not granted official toleration, although few attempts were made to prevent private worship. Cromwell allowed the Jews, who had been driven out by Edward I in 1290, to return to England.

The acts of the Barebones Parliament were ideal in theory but unworkable in practice. Its ardor for reform unhappily outran its ability for constructive thought. It soon became more unpopular than the Rump. In 1653 it was induced to "deliver up into the Lord-General Cromwell the powers we received from him." A minority of its members, meeting without a general announcement, declared the Parliament dissolved. It departed, unhonored, unsung, and unregretted.

The Protectorate, 1653—1660. With the collapse of the unruly and incapable Barebones Parliament, the leaders of the army prepared an "Instrument of Government," or constitution, declaring Cromwell Lord Protector of England, Ireland, and Scotland for life. Though the Instrument gave the Protector vast executive powers, it did provide for an elected Parliament of one chamber (four hundred English members and thirty each from Scotland and Ireland). A safeguarding clause barred former or prospective opponents of the administration from membership. The Instrument of Government was one of the first written constitutions of modern times, in contrast to the later unwritten English constitution. England became a constitutional monarchy in all but name. Parliament was to meet every three years to make laws and levy taxes. Cromwell had the right to delay, but not to veto, legislation. Puritan Congregationalism became the state religion.

Failure of the Protectorate. Cromwell's first Parliament (1654–1655) insisted upon full power to revise the Instrument of Government and to debate the advisability of government "by a single person." This effort to limit the Protector's power infuriated Cromwell, and he dissolved it as soon as he could. For the next eighteen months he governed as a military dictator with the country in the hands of twelve major-generals, each of whom governed one district. This was the period for which Cromwell is best remembered. There was relative tolerance of all Protestants—who were not in favor of episcopacy. The Royalists suffered most severely. More Calvinist practices were introduced; cock-fighting, horse-racing, and Sunday sports were suppressed. To maintain constitutional forms, Cromwell in 1656 suspended the unpopular major-generals and called another Parliament, from which he excluded at least one hundred of its elected members.

In May 1657, by a majority vote of two to one, Parliament passed the Humble Petition and Advice, which offered Cromwell the Crown and asked for a second chamber. Cromwell accepted this latter suggestion, but flatly rejected the proffered kingship, probably because he expected objections from the army. This made little difference to him, for after the dissolution of Parliament in January 1658, Cromwell was king in all but name. In practice, his government since 1653 had been almost free of parliamentary restraints; the only curb on his rule was the powerful clique of army officers.

Worn out by his labors, Cromwell died in September 1658. Almost immediately, his government began to crumble, an indication that it was based in the long run on his personal rule. The army was left without a master and the country without a government. Cromwell's son, Richard, sought for a time to fill his father's place, but he soon lost control of the army and abdicated. The great experiment in republicanism failed miserably in the hands of its friends. There were too many forces opposed to Cromwell and his army. Aligned against him were Royalists, who demanded the restoration of the Stuarts; Anglicans offended by loss of their estates and intent upon regaining their former positions of authority; Catholics dissatisfied with their religious status; and Levelers, or radical reformers, who resented authoritarianism and called for representative government, civil liberties, and suffrage reforms. The average Englishman resented Cromwell's puritanical rule, his reliance on the sword, and especially, his excessive taxation. A satisfactory constitutional government in the midst of these conflicting currents of opinion seemed to be impossible.

Historical Controversy. As with all great men of action, historical judgments on Cromwell's personality and achievements vary considerably. On the one side, he is portrayed as merely one more ruthless dictator, a man of violent temper who misunderstood the nature of English society and sought to impose on it a harsh tyranny for which it had no desire. His savage treatment of the Irish is projected as an indication of a fanatical quality which characterized his every movement. He was overcome by the belief that he was performing God's work.

On the other side, Cromwell is described as a capable and honest man elevated to power by the pressure of events. He was a reluctant but efficient despot, the beloved leader of an army respected for its discipline and feared for its prowess. His encouragement of commerce and industry was responsible for the revival of England's prosperity. His conduct of foreign affairs was said to be profitable to England. "That he was in himself a good man is shown in this: that, although highly tried as a revolutionary leader, he has few crimes to his score; he was not greedy, or lustful, or cruel, or unmerciful—save only, as in Ireland, where his fanatic zeal overmastered his human qualities" (Stanley M. Leathes).

The truth, as usual in historical controversy, lies somewhere between polemics and panegyrics. Cromwell's progress to supreme power was not accomplished without sincere attempts to find some workable alternatives. His career displays the same kind of contradictions present in most human beings. There was a conflict between Cromwell the political theorist and Cromwell the Puritan idealist. There was another between Cromwell the man of order and Cromwell the fighting man. There was still another between Cromwell the violent Puritan and Cromwell the man of toleration. Disregarding the attacks and the praise, it is most probable that Cromwell in the long run achieved the defeat of monarchical absolutism as well as the survival of English parliamentary institutions. Part of his success was due, as Clarendon states, to the fact that "he possessed a wonderful understanding about the natures and humors of men."

⊰{ KEY DOCUMENT }⊱

THE PETITION OF RIGHT, 1628

Samuel R. Gardiner, *The Constitutional Documents of the Puritan Revolution, 1625–1660*,
3rd revised ed. (Oxford, 1906), pp. 66–70.

THE PETITION OF RIGHT was a document embodying Parliament's demands and presented to Charles I on June 7, 1628, by the House of Commons. By appealing to the Magna Carta and by asserting the rights of the people against royal prerogative, the Petition of Right was an important boundary mark in the history of English constitutionalism.

To THE KING'S MOST EXCELLENT MAJESTY

Humbly show unto our Sovereign Lord the King, the Lords Spiritual and Temporal, and Commons in Parliament assembled, that whereas it is declared and enacted by the statute made in the time of the reign of King Edward the First, commonly called *Statutum de Tallagio non concedendo*, that no tallage or aid shall be laid or levied by the King or his heirs in this realm, without the goodwill and assent of the Archbishops, Bishops, Earls, Barons, Knights, Burgesses, and other freemen of the commonalty of this realm: and by authority of Parliament holden in the five and twentieth year of the reign of King Edward the Third, it is declared and enacted, that from thenceforth no person shall be compelled to make any loans to the King against his will, because such loans were against reason and the franchise of the land; . . . it . . . [seems that] your subjects have inherited this freedom, that they should not be compelled to contribute to any tax, tallage, aid, or other like charge, not set by common consent in Parliament:

Yet, nevertheless, of late divers commissions directed to sundry Commissioners in several countries with instructions have issued, by means whereof your people have been in divers places assembled, and required to lend certain sums of money unto your Majesty, and many of them upon their refusal so to do . . . have been therefore imprisoned, confined, and sundry other ways molested and disquieted. . . .

And where also by the statute called, "The Great Charter of the Liberties of England," it is declared and enacted, that no freeman may be taken or imprisoned or be disseized of his freeholds or liberties, or his free customs, or be outlawed or exiled; or in any manner destroyed, but by the lawful judgement of his peers, or by the law of the land:

And in the eight and twentieth year of the reign of King Edward the Third, it was declared and enacted by authority of Parliament, that no man of what estate or condition that he be, should be put out of his lands or tenements, nor taken, nor imprisoned, nor disinherited, nor put to death, without being brought to answer by due process of law:

Nevertheless, against the tenor of the said statutes, and other the good laws and statutes of your realm, to that end provided, divers of your subjects have of late been imprisoned without any cause showed. . . .

And whereas of late great companies of soldiers and mariners have been dispersed into divers counties of the realm, and the inhabitants against their wills have been compelled to receive them into their houses, and there to suffer them to sojourn, against the laws and customs of this realm, and to the great grievance and vexation of the people. . . .

They [Parliament] do therefore humbly pray your Most Excellent Majesty, that no man hereafter be compelled to make or yield any gift, loan, benevolence, tax, or such like charge, without common consent by Act of Parliament; and that none be called to make answer or take such oath, or to give attendance, or be confined, or otherwise molested or disquieted concerning the same, or for refusal thereof; and that no freeman, in any such manner as is before-mentioned, be imprisoned or detained; and that your Majesty will be pleased to remove the said soldiers and mariners, and that your people may not be so burdened in time to come. . . .

All which they most humbly pray of your most Excellent Majesty, as their rights and liberties according to the laws and statutes of this realm.

❧ HISTORICAL INTERPRETATION ❧

GEORGE MACAULAY TREVELYAN ON THE ACHIEVEMENTS OF OLIVER CROMWELL

George Macaulay Trevelyan, *England Under the Stuarts* (original ed. 1904, 14th ed. London, 1928), pp. 327–328. By permission of Methuen and Company, Ltd.

GEORGE MACAULAY TREVELYAN (1876–1962), Regius Professor of Modern History at Cambridge, took a neutral view in judging the achievements and character of Oliver Cromwell. Where others either praised or condemned Cromwell, Trevelyan presented the following balanced view in his *England Under the Stuarts.*

On the 3rd of September, 1658, the anniversary of Dunbar and of Worcester, Oliver went to his rest. "Let us all," he had once said, "be not careful what men will make of these actings. They, will they, nill they, shall fulfil the good pleasure of God, and we shall serve our generations. Our rest we expect elsewhere: that will be durable."

The trust in God that had been his strength had also been his bane. In all that he did of good and of evil in the three kingdoms, it was too much his way to trust that the Lord would support him in everything that he undertook. What he judged to be necessary for the present, that he thought to be predestined for the future. His victories seemed to him, not the result of the means which he employed, but proofs that his policy was also the will of Heaven. It was from Ireland that he wrote to the Speaker—

Sir, what can be said of these things? Is it the arm of the flesh that hath done these things? Is it the wisdom and counsel, or strength of men? It is the Lord only. God will curse that man and his house that dares to think otherwise. Sir, you see the work is done by a Divine leading. God gets into the hearts of men, and persuades them to come under you.

Hence, it was easy for him to think that the Irish themselves would be converted by "assiduous preaching," when their priests had been removed to penal settlements. In England and Scotland he made, though in a less degree, the same mistake of trusting God to reconcile public opinion.

Yet in England and Scotland, at least, he had no obvious alternative. Early in his political career, he had striven hard for conciliation and consent. But he soon found that there was no general consent to be had in England to any plan, either Royalist, Presbyterian or Independent. There was no active agreement of public opinion between 1641 and 1660; and no human being who ever lived could have made a permanent settlement out of the situation left by King and Parliament in 1648. In that general wreck of powers and parties, Oliver saved the British Empire from partition, the civil liberties of England from Royalist reconquest, the Free Churches and free-thinkers from destruction by those of the narrow way. Those deeds outlived him, and the lovers of England, of civil liberty, and of free-thought will for ever be grateful for such benefits, though all else for which he fought perished with him.

But to value men solely by uncertain calculations of their achievement, is to disinherit the human race. If some who have done great things were only men with better opportunities or more of common talent than the rest, others, like Cromwell as his comrades knew him and as modern learning has let us know him again, show to what height the plant Man can sometimes grow. In the agony of war, in the interminable crisis of revolutionary state-craft, he kept his noblest qualities of mind untired. He was always fresh from nature, open to new spiritual desires and human joys. In the hardest years of his last solitary struggle against unyielding destiny, a meeting with George Fox could move him first to tears, and on another occasion very seasonably to laughter. He sought always, and often with deep questioning, what was right and noble in every choice of action. He could not bear the stiff and dry: in all human relations, his tenderness, his humour, his fellowship were always striving to burst through. For while he aspired to heaven, he had his roots deep in earth.

❧ TEN BASIC BOOKS ❧

THE GREAT REBELLION IN ENGLAND: THE COMMONWEALTH

1. Abbott, Wilbur, ed., *The Writings and Speeches of Oliver Cromwell,* 4 vols. (Cambridge, Mass., 1937–1947).
2. Davies, Godfrey, *The Early Stuarts, 1603–1660,* 2nd ed. (Oxford, 1959).
3. Gardiner, Samuel R., *History of England from the Accession of James I to the Outbreak of the Civil War, 1603–1642,* 10 vols. (London, 1884–1886).
4. Hexter, J. H., *The Reign of King Pym* (Cambridge, Mass., 1941).
5. Notestein, Wallace, *The English People on the Eve of Colonization, 1603–1630* (New York, 1954, R. 1962).†
6. Tanner, Joseph R., *English Constitutional Conflicts of the Seventeenth Century, 1603–1689,* 2 vols. (Cambridge, 1928, R. 1960).†
7. Trevelyan, George M., *England Under the Stuarts,* 14th ed. (London, 1928, R. 1957).†
8. Trevor-Roper, Hugh, *Archbishop Laud, 1573–1645,* 2nd ed. (New York, 1962).
9. Wedgwood, Cicely V., *The King's Peace, 1637–1641* (New York, 1959).
10. Wingfield-Stratford, Esmé C., *Charles, King of England, 1600–1637* (London, 1949).

14

Triumph of Parliamentary Government in England

ORDERED BY the Lords and Commons assembled in Parliament, that the carcasses of Oliver Cromwell, Henry Ireton, John Bradshaw, Thomas Pride, whether buried in Westminster Abbey or elsewhere, be with all expedition taken up, and drawn upon a hurdle to Tyburn, and there hanged up in their coffins for some time, and after that buried under the said gallows; and that James Norfolk, esquire, sergeant-at-arms attending the House of Commons, do take care that this order be put in effectual execution by the common executioner for the county of Middlesex and all such others to whom it shall respectively appertain, who are required in their several places to conform to and observe this order with effect; and the sheriff of Middlesex is to give his assistance herein as there shall be occasion. And the dean of Westminster is desired to give directions to his officers of the Abbey to be assistant in the execution of this order.

—ORDER OF THE HOUSE OF LORDS AND THE HOUSE OF COMMONS,
December 10, 1660

1. Foundations of English Parliamentarianism

Early History. An English national assembly of sorts can be traced back to Saxon times. The Anglo-Saxon *Folk-moot,* or tribal assembly, although a popular body which declared the laws or customs of the land, was a localized institution which did not debate such matters as war and peace. More important was the *Witenagemot,* an aristocratic gathering of the great landlords, nobles, and clergymen, which advised the king about matters on which he asked their opinion. The people probably attended on such occasions as the election of a new king. With the Norman Conquest of 1066 the *Witenagemot* became the Great Council (*Magnum Concilium*), composed of the king's trusted noble and clerical followers. The Great Council, forerunner of the House of Lords, eventually developed into the bicameral Parliament. When King John (r. 1199–1216) sought to assert absolute royal authority, his recalcitrant nobles assembled at Runnymede in 1215 and forced him to accept the Magna Carta, a document designed to protect their feudal rights. The assembly at Runnymede is sometimes regarded as the lineal progenitor of the House of Commons.

Development of Parliament. For some time the Great Council remained but a single chamber. In 1265 Simon de Montfort, Earl of Leicester, and leader of the opposition to Henry III, called a national assembly to which he invited not only the knights of the shires (the lesser landowners), but also the representatives of the cities and boroughs (citizens and burgesses). There were to be not only two knights from each shire, but also two citizens from each city and two burgesses from each borough. Until this time the people had been taxed without their assent by juries of their neighbors; now the national assembly advanced a claim to the exclusive right of taxation. Montfort may be called the creator of the House of Commons, which from its earliest days demanded the critical right of taxation. The Model Parliament, summoned by Edward I in 1295, was supposed to include all classes.

The authority of Parliament was established during the reign of Edward II (r. 1307–1327). When Edward tried to impose illegal taxes with consent of Parliament, he was opposed by all the groups, who united and forced him to confirm the Magna Carta. In 1322 Parliament passed a statute defining its right to redress grievances and to make national liberties secure. It even felt strong enough to declare the succession of Edward III in 1327.

Separation of the Two Houses. The reign of Edward III (r. 1327–1377) saw the consolidation of the House of Commons. The burgesses had long been ignored in legislative matters, but the fact that they were summoned regularly gave them political status. At first knights and burgesses voted apart (the former considered themselves socially superior), but gradually the two began to join in petitions to the government. At length the knights broke away from the greater barons and turned to the House of Commons as their appropriate body. Some of the upper clergy, desiring to remain independent of lay control, ceased to attend Parliament. The Commons now became much bolder, insisting upon the right to veto legislation affecting the people and declaring to the king that they "refused to be bound by any of his statutes or ordinances unless made with their assent." Parliament succeeded in placing important restrictions on the royal power by such acts as asserting its control of customs as tonnage and poundage. The House of Commons was separated from the House of Lords; the latter limited its membership to the greater barons and high-ranking churchmen.

Parliamentary Power. Until the Revolution of 1688 the history of the English Parliament reflected the struggles between king, nobility, and people. After 1688 it became the story of struggle for franchise reform, ministerial responsibility, and the political party system. Before that revolution, king and people were allied against the tyranny of the feudal barons; later there evolved a combination of nobility and people against royal absolutism. By the Tudor period, the middle class was strong enough to be taken into account by the king. By the Stuart era, Parliament, dominated by merchants, bankers, and country squires, was able to limit royal prerogatives.

2. The Stuart Restoration, 1660

The Accession of Charles II, 1660. It was said that none cried but the dogs when Cromwell died. The people of England were tired of both Commonwealth and Protectorate and sick of Puritanism and military despotism. They were very nearly unanimous in the opinion that the Stuarts, in the person of Charles II, should be restored to the throne. That decision was helped along by General George Monck, first Duke of Albemarle (1608–1670), commander of Cromwell's army in Scotland, who marched on London, and recalled all members of the Long Parliament who had been expelled by Pride in 1648. Parliament, thus restored, voted its own dissolution. The new Convention Parliament (so-named because it was not called by a king), largely Presbyterian and almost wholly royalist, welcomed a messenger from the Stuart house.

Meanwhile, Prince Charles, son of Charles I, issued from Holland the Declaration of Breda, in which he promised to grant a general amnesty, liberty of conscience within the laws enacted by Parliament, the right of Parliament to settle property disputes, and full payment of back salary to the troops. This recognition of its rights pleased the new Parliament, which then invited Charles to return as Charles II. The Stuart heir was welcomed home with delirious demonstrations of joy. The streets were strewn with flowers, the bells rang, the fountains ran with wine. Charles, although bewildered by the acclaim of the people, was delighted. England had a king again, Charles II (r. 1660–1685), but neither he nor any of

The Restoration. Charles II, summoned back to England, is welcomed by his Court.

his successors would ever again successfully revive the absolutist theories of their predecessors. England's experiment with a republic, religious extremism, and civil war had come to an end.

The Restoration Settlement. The Convention Parliament, loyal to king and Church, raised funds to pay the arrears due the army and fleet, but disbanded Cromwell's troops because they were no longer needed. Cromwell's rule had convinced the English that a standing army was incompatible with freedom.

Charles II, however, was allowed to maintain for his own protection several regiments which became the nucleus for the later standing army. Parliament restored to the original owners, whether Crown, Church, or private individuals, many of the lands that had been confiscated during the revolution. An act of indemnity pardoned all who had opposed the king during the Civil War, with the exception of those who had been involved in the execution of Charles I. Thirteen persons were executed for regicide. Samuel Pepys recorded in his diary (October 13, 1660): "I went out to Charing Cross to see Major-General Harrison hanged, drawn, and quartered, which was done there, he looking as cheerful as any man could do in that condition. He was presently cut down and his heart shown to the people, at which there were great shouts of joy. . . . Thus it was my chance to see the king beheaded at Whitehall, and to see the first blood shed in revenge for the king at Charing Cross."

After these executions Charles II wrote to his chancellor: "I must confess I am weary of hanging—let it sleep." But Cromwell's remains were taken from Westminster, hanged from the gallows at Tyburn, and then buried along with the bones of common criminals.

Charles II and the "Cavalier" Parliament. Charles II, who came to the throne at the age of thirty, was undoubtedly the most capable of the English Stuarts, though his witty, affable exterior concealed indolence and a weakness for extravagant living. Reluctant to "resume his travels," he wanted to stay in England and maintain his position as king. Gifted with a shrewd feeling for politics, he had the ability to sense the moment when ruthless action was safe or when compromise was necessary. In exile in France he had absorbed both absolutism and Catholicism. Restricted by a Parliament jealous of its rights, he wished throughout his reign to attain absolute power, which he nearly won at the moment of his death. He was a Catholic in his secret conviction, which could hardly be reconciled with the religious temper of the England of his day.

Cautiously and shrewdly, Charles played one political faction against another with the aim of making himself master of all. These factions included the Anglicans, dedicated to the Church of England; the squirearchy, composed of country landlords and gentry who had opposed not only early Stuart absolutism but also the Puritan Commonwealth; the merchants and traders who wanted to control Parliament because of their sensitivity to taxation; the Dissenters, those Puritans who refused to accept Anglican teachings and were, therefore, denied civil and military office; and the remaining Catholics, especially in Ireland, who continued to exist despite periodic persecutions. In 1662 Charles married the Portuguese Infanta Catherine of Braganza; his wife brought to England not only a dowry of half a million pounds but also the North African port of Tangier and Bombay in India.

The first seven years of Charles II's reign were passed under the tutelage of Edward Hyde, first Earl of Clarendon (1609–1674), statesman and historian, who had shared his exile in France. The Convention Parliament was dissolved in December 1660, and a new assembly, the "Cavalier" Parliament, was convened in May 1661. The new Parliament, dominated by the squirearchy and supporters of Anglicanism, was ardently royalist, but at the same time it insisted that its rights be recognized. The gentry was anxious to have any remaining feudal dues on their lands lifted. Charles was careful to avoid friction with his headstrong Parliament, and allowed it to impose taxes, to regulate ecclesiastical affairs, and even to direct foreign policy. He was annoyed when Parliament fixed his income at a figure scarcely large enough to pay his expenses, but there was little he could do about it.

The Anglicans in the Cavalier Parliament, intent upon restoring the Church of England to its full privileges and to punish recalcitrants, enacted a series of measures directed against dissenters. The Corporation Act (1661) required all municipal officeholders to receive Holy Communion in the Church of England, thereby barring all non-Anglicans from municipal government. The Act of Uniformity (1662) required all clergymen, college fellows, and schoolmasters to accept the Anglican Prayer Book, whereupon 2,000 Puritan ministers who refused to adopt it verbatim were expelled from their pulpits. The Conventicle Act (1664) forbade the holding of nonconforming religious meetings by more than five persons, except in a private household, and condemned to imprisonment or transportation those who did so. The Five-Mile Act (1665) made it illegal for any dissenting minister to come within five miles of any town or village in which he had formerly preached.

Many of those hit by these statutes emigrated from England. Although Charles II had little to do with this persecution, he thought it best for the time being to defer to the wishes of his determined Parliament. Secretly, he may have desired the triumph of Catholicism instead of Anglicanism, but he had no intention of endangering his throne by battling with Parliament over religious issues.

Foreign Policy of Charles II. The foreign policy of Charles II was precisely the same as that of Cromwell and his Tudor predecessors: he would make England a great commercial and imperial power. The Navigation Acts of 1660, 1663, and 1673 carried on Cromwell's attempt to destroy the Dutch, England's most persistent rival. A conflict with the Dutch had taken place in 1652–1654. Charles had his first encounter with them in 1664–1667. In 1664 the Dutch sailed up the Thames as far as Chatham and destroyed British shipping there. The English seized the Dutch colony of New Amsterdam and renamed it New York, thus putting an end to Dutch colonial ventures on the North American mainland. Then, without consulting his advisers, Charles II entered into such close relations with Louis XIV of France that he became almost a pensioner. In 1670, Charles signed the secret Treaty of Dover, in which he pledged to support Louis in his wars against the Netherlands and Spain, and to become openly a Roman Catholic as soon as it was feasible. In return Louis promised Charles £200,000 a year for as long as the war continued, and the help of 6000 men in the event of an uprising among Charles' subjects. Thus, Charles II hoped to avoid becoming a financial prisoner of Parliament. His promise to become a Catholic was not restricted to a special date (in fact, Charles did not do so until he was on his deathbed). The funds he obtained from Louis XIV he spent on his extravagant court, a new mistress, Louise de Kéroualle, and on the organization of a standing army.

The Plague and Fire of London. The somber and sternly pious Puritan spirit gave way during the Restoration to an era of lighthearted immorality and licentiousness. The king's court reflected this new spirit as the Cavaliers gave free rein to desires long held in leash by austere Puritanism. Court literature, especially the drama, grew increasingly indecent.

During Charles II's first Dutch War occurred two great disasters which shook London. In the autumn of 1664 a few isolated cases of what was probably bubonic plague were noted in London, but they were not taken seriously because the disease had recurred frequently throughout Europe in the preceding three centuries. But the mortality rose rapidly from forty-three cases in May 1665 to 31,159 cases in August, after which it began to decline. Filthy conditions in London

helped the scourge. In the middle of the night, carts made their rounds in the city to collect corpses; bells were rung to signal the people to bring out the dead bodies. Each house visited by the plague was marked with a red cross and the legend: "Lord have mercy on us!" According to some authorities, the plague was imported from the Netherlands in bales of merchandise originally from the Levant. Others say the disease was brought in by Dutch prisoners of war. From London it spread throughout England. Daniel Defoe's *A Journal of the Plague Year* (1722) described the event in all its shocking details, though he called on his gifted imagination to assist in the documentation.

Contributing to the end of the plague in London was a devastating fire which started on September 2, 1666, in a bakery in Pudding Lane. In seven days the conflagration consumed 13,200 houses, most of wooden construction, 89 parish churches, St. Paul's Cathedral, the Guildhall, and other public buildings. There were few deaths, but at least 200,000 people were made homeless. A Frenchman who confessed that he had started the fire as part of a Roman Catholic plot was executed even though judge and jury believed him to be innocent. In his *Diary*, Samuel Pepys gave an absorbing description of the fire as he viewed it from the top of Barking Steeple. After five days the king ordered several rows of houses to be blown up to make a gap across which the fire could not pass.

Both plague and fire were crippling blows to the country still at war. They were regarded by the Puritans as visitations of the Divine Power, angered by the immoralities of the court of Charles II as well as by Parliament's impositions on the Puritans. Rebuilt London was graced by the magnificent structures of Sir Christopher Wren.

The "Popish Plot," 1678. Charles II, anxious to increase religious toleration, issued a Declaration of Indulgence in 1672 which suspended all penal laws directed against Catholics and Dissenting Protestants. He based this action on what he called his "power of dispensation," the king's right to suspend any laws of which he did not approve. To his dismay there was immediate protest. Parliament pronounced the Declaration illegal, and within a year (1673) passed the Test Act, by which all officeholders of the Crown, both civil and military, were obliged within six months after appointment to make a declaration against transubstantiation, take the Anglican sacrament, and subscribe to the oath of supremacy. By this act both Catholics and Protestant Dissenters were excluded from public office.

Some rumors began to spread about a "Popish Plot" to restore state Catholicism by force. The matter revolved around the person of the king's brother, James, Duke of York, who, confessing himself a Catholic, aroused the hopes of that party. In 1678 an adventurer named Titus Oates announced that he had discovered a conspiracy to murder Charles and, with the help of the French, to place James on the throne. The English people nearly went wild with fear. Barricades were set up in London, and armed bands made ready to "repel invasion." Oates, a confirmed liar, probably knew nothing about such a plot, but his testimony was enough to send thirty-five innocent Catholics to their death. He was rewarded with a pension for his work in "rescuing England from the domination of Rome." The king cagily turned the incident to his own advantage and, although he did not believe one word of what Oates said, signed the death warrants.

Rise of Political Parties. Again the shadow of Civil War hung over England. In the uproar political leaders ranged themselves more definitely into two opposing parties. On the one side were the Tories, or conservatives, who supported the Crown, the principle of divine right of kings, the right of hereditary succession, and the Church of England. The term was borrowed from the Irish, whose outlaws had been known as Tories. The second faction, the Whigs, opposed a despotic Crown, favored a constitutional monarchy, and demanded religious toleration for Protestant Dissenters. The Whigs took their name from the Scottish *wiggamores*, or horse drovers. Both words, Tories and Whigs, were originally applied as

terms of contempt, but eventually they were assumed as honored party designations. The names survived until well into the nineteenth century, when they were changed to Conservative and Liberal.

The Exclusion Bill, 1679. The Whigs won the election of 1679, thereby ending the eighteen-year session of the Cavalier Parliament. The new Parliament pressed for the exclusion of James, Duke of York, from the throne because he was a Catholic. Charles II, insisting that he would never consent to the Exclusion Bill, nevertheless sent James out of the country for a short time and announced his pleasure at the attempts to convert James to Protestantism. Still, he dissolved Parliament. The new Whig Parliament passed the bill again (1680), but it was vetoed by the House of Lords. A third Parliament, meeting at Oxford, went too far in asserting the claims of James, Duke of Monmouth, illegitimate son of the king. Charles II dissolved the unruly body again and appealed to the nation to support him against the extremists. The people agreed. In a country already weakened by civil war, there was little taste for further domestic conflict. They preferred Charles's easygoing despotism to further chaos.

Habeas Corpus Act, 1679. The only point the Whigs won in their struggle to limit the king's power was the passage of the Habeas Corpus Act. Previously, many persons had been imprisoned and, without any legal proceedings, conveyed in custody to places outside of England. The Habeas Corpus Act ([that] "you have the body") established the principle that no subject accused of a crime could be held in prison at the king's pleasure. The statute made it necessary for a judge or a court of justice to issue a writ commanding the person to whom it was directed to bring the body of the accused to a court or to an authorized official, and to give a written statement explaining the grounds for detention. This was to be done immediately, or on the day appointed in the writ. If no valid cause for detaining the prisoner were given, he was to be discharged absolutely, or, in doubtful cases, freed on bail. This act, which in substance expanded a clause in the Magna Carta, was a safeguard against arbitrary arrest. It is one of the cornerstones to British justice.

Charles II: Masked Despot. For the rest of his reign Charles II, ruling alone, was supreme. His position was strengthened by the standing army which he had refrained from disbanding and which was now under his control. His popularity among the people was great. Left without constitutional recourse, a small group of desperate Whig leaders plotted to assassinate the king and bring the Duke of Monmouth to the throne. The king's life was saved by discovery of the Rye House Plot (1683). William, Lord Russell, Algernon Sidney, and the Earl of Essex were arrested and confined to the Tower, where Essex committed suicide. The other two were executed, though the evidence against them was hardly conclusive.

Charles II decided to pay the price for Tory support: he dropped his efforts to reestablish Catholicism. He had finally found a way to rule without Parliament. His triumph was cut short in February 1685, when he was stricken with apoplexy. "I am afraid, gentlemen," he told those at his bedside, "that I am an unconscionable time a-dying." He was mourned by the people and by his many mistresses, who left him numerous progeny.

James II: Despot in Trouble. Upon the death of Charles II, his illegitimate son, the Protestant Duke of Monmouth, organized a revolt in both England and Scotland, but it was promptly crushed. There followed the "Bloody Assizes," in which at least a thousand followers of Monmouth were condemned to death or transportation. The Catholic Duke of York, the second surviving son of Charles I, ascended the throne as James II (r. 1685–1688) at the age of fifty-two. During the agitation caused by the Popish Plot, he had been driven to the Continent. The Whigs unsuccessfully sought to exclude him from the throne. He returned to England. On becoming king in 1685, he promised to defend the Church of England. At first he was popular,

but within a short time he succeeded in alienating all parties. The Tories, ordinarily loyal to royalty, were shocked by his sudden actions on the religious issue. With no idea of the strength of Protestant opinion in England, he violated the Test Act by appointing Catholics to the army, civil service, and universities. In 1687 and 1688 he issued two Declarations of Indulgence which exempted both Catholics and Protestant Dissenters from punishment for infractions of laws which Parliament had enacted. When seven Anglican bishops refused to endorse the 1688 Declaration, they were tried for libel and sedition. They were acquitted amidst applause of the nation.

In dispensing with and suspending the laws of England, and in showing favor to Catholics, James II also incurred the hostility of the Whigs. Misunderstanding the temper of the times, he ignored the Magna Carta, the Petition of Right, and the Habeas Corpus Act. By failing to heed the law courts, by arbitrarily increasing the standing army, and by dismissing Parliament, he stirred up bitter opposition on all sides.

Problem of Succession. Both Tories and Whigs were content to endure James II's despotism so long as they could look forward to the accession of his Protestant daughters Mary and Anne. However, the birth of a son to James and his Catholic second wife in June 1688 destroyed hopes for a Protestant succession, for the king made it clear that his son was to be educated as a Catholic. The rumor spread throughout England that the young prince was not in reality the son of James II and his queen. A group of nobles of both principal political factions, some of whom had previously supported James, began to look elsewhere for a successor to the throne. The next in line of succession after the infant prince was Mary, the elder of James's two daughters, the wife of William III of Orange, and above all, an Anglican.

Tory and Whig leaders then dispatched an invitation to William of Orange to come and claim the English throne. William, intent upon defending his Dutch republic against Louis XIV, reasoned that as King of England he could combine both English and Dutch forces against France. Bringing with him a fleet of warships and transports, he led an invasion of England on November 5, 1688. Despite repeated warnings, James II appeared to be unconscious of what was happening. His generals deserted him one by one.

The English turned to William as a deliverer from tyranny. James fled to France, where Louis XIV gave him a palace at St. Germain and a pension of £40,000. William then summoned a Convention Parliament, which decided that James had abdicated, that England would not be ruled by a "Popish Prince," and that William and Mary should ascend the throne as joint sovereigns. Parliament delivered the final blow at the theory of divine right of kings. Thus was accomplished the Glorious Revolution, without bloodshed although with a maximum of duplicity.

3. The Glorious Revolution of 1688

Political Settlement: Bill of Rights, 1689. The Convention Parliament's offer of the crown to William and Mary was on condition that they recognize the Magna Carta of 1215, the Petition of Right of 1628, and a number of principles stated in another document, the Bill of Rights, which ranks with the other two as landmarks of English constitutional history. Parliament, having no intention of giving itself into the hands of another despot, drew up a settlement which included the following principles: (1) It is illegal for the king to suspend or dispense with the laws of England, levy taxes, or maintain a standing army without consent of Parliament. (2) Members of Parliament are to be freely elected, have freedom of debate, and should meet frequently. (3) It is the right of subjects to petition the king, and those charged with crimes should not be refused jury trial or be exposed to cruel and unusual punishments. (*See page 225.*)

This celebrated declaration of the rights and liberties of the English people, expressed in thirteen provisions, firmly established the supremacy of Parliament over the throne after several centuries of struggle.

Religious Settlement: Toleration Act, 1689. The Bill of Rights was supplemented by the Toleration Act, which granted a limited degree of toleration to Protestant Dissenters but not to Catholics, Unitarians, or Jews. The Anglican Church still remained the State Church; Catholics and Protestant Dissenters were still barred from civil and military office. Nevertheless, the act marked a long step toward religious toleration, for persecution, imprisonment, and transportation of people on religious grounds subsided after 1689.

There were also other strides in the direction of free government. The first Mutiny Act, passed in 1689, placed the army under special laws and tribunals. Originally enacted for a period of six months, the Mutiny Act was later made annual. The Triennial Act (1694) limited the life of Parliament to three years.

Historical Controversy: Glorious Whig Revolution, or Royal Conquest by Power? The events of 1688 have been interpreted in two diametrically opposite ways by historians. One point of view, held by the mid-nineteenth-century Whig historian, Thomas Babington Macaulay, and seconded by the twentieth-century scholar, George Macaulay Trevelyan, saw the Glorious Revolution as the final end of tyranny in England and the beginning of Parliament's supremacy. It was a revolutionary but bloodless event, they said, which meant the triumph of that type of free representative government which England projected as an example for the entire world. Before 1688 class was divided against class in a rigid structure; after 1688 there emerged one national consciousness—the voice of Parliament. Thus, the revolution was a vital landmark in the history and development of modern democracy.

In the other view, epitomized in the work of the nineteenth-century political writer, Walter Bagehot, 1688 was not a true revolution at all but more accurately a change in dynasty. Far from being the critical turning point in the triumph of Parliament, it was a carefully engineered capture of England's throne by a strong-willed pretender who knew exactly what he wanted and how to get it. The "Revolution Settlement," in Bagehot's view, consisted of acts passed by Parliament *after* William became king. The end of absolutism and the emergence of the limited monarchy, he said, were merely accidental factors which accompanied a palace revolution.

The Irish Problem. Because of the moderation shown in its political and religious settlements, the Revolution of 1688 is often referred to as the Glorious Revolution. In its far-reaching effects there was, indeed, a contrast

The armor worn by James II at the Boyne, 1690. This battle was the culmination of James' unsuccessful attempt to regain the throne from William III.

between this revolution and the Puritan Revolution. But this moderation was not to be applied to Ireland. Cromwell had reduced the Irish to virtual bondage by distributing their land to Protestant landholders. In 1689 the Irish broke into rebellion against their Protestant overlords. The next year, 1690, James II came to Ireland from France with the aim of leading a combined French-Irish army against William III. After the French fleet inflicted a defeat on the English and Dutch at Beachy Head (June 1690), the invaders prepared to attack England proper. But William III, with his new throne in danger, defeated James II at the Battle of the Boyne (July 1, 1690). For Louis XIV this was an opening loss in the War of the League of Augsburg. Once again the Irish settled into apathy as wards of the English.

Act of Settlement, 1701. To regulate the royal succession it was decided that if William and Mary died without issue, the throne would pass to Mary's sister, Anne, and her descendants. Mary's death in 1694, and the death of the last surviving child of Anne in 1701, brought the matter to a head. By the Act of Settlement (1701), the succession was decreed for the next Protestant heir, the Electress Sophia of Hanover, granddaughter of James I, and her descendants. There were better claims to the throne, but all were Catholics and hence eliminated by Parliament. Additional clauses restricted the power of the Crown by providing: (1) that every future sovereign must join in communion with the Church of England, thereby excluding any Roman Catholic from the throne; (2) that in the event the Crown came to any person not a native of England, the nation would not be obliged to engage in war for territories not belonging to England without the consent of Parliament; and (3) the judiciary be independent of the Crown and responsible to Parliament.

Accession of Queen Anne. William III survived the Act of Settlement only a short time, dying on March 8, 1702, at the age of fifty-two, after being thrown from his horse in Hampton Court Park. The English were not too much grieved by the loss of the taciturn Dutchman. But he had rendered a service in preparing the way for liberal constitutional government. Queen Anne, like her brother-in-law William III, was not a legitimate hereditary monarch. Educated as an Anglican, her religion was the one subject on which she held consistent views. In 1683 she married Prince George of Denmark, who showed more interest in marital than state affairs—the couple produced seventeen children, of whom only one survived infancy, and he died at the age of eleven. Fat, aged thirty-seven, suffering from convulsions and gout, worn out by childbearing when she came to the throne, Anne governed through her ministers. She vetoed acts of Parliament (she was the last English ruler to attempt this), and toward the close of her reign chose a Tory cabinet despite a parliamentary Whig majority.

The Act of Union, 1707. When William and Mary ascended the throne, it seemed that England and Scotland would drift apart. The Scots distrusted their neighbor to the south, and the English were concerned that Scotland might take France's side in the interminable disputes between the Channel nations. In Anne's reign, however, the Act of Union (1707) united the two kingdoms of England and Scotland as Great Britain. From now on Great Britain's national flag became what was called the Union Jack, which at first combined the crosses of St. George and St. Andrew. The Scots sent forty-five representatives to the House of Commons and sixteen to the House of Lords. Presbyterianism was recognized as the established religion in Scotland.

Reign of Queen Anne, 1702–1714. Queen Anne's reign saw the participation of England in the War of the Spanish Succession (1701–1714), known in North America as Queen Anne's War. It was also notable for British military victories won in Europe by the Duke of Marlborough. On August 13, 1704, at Blenheim (German *Blindheim*), a Bavarian village on the left bank of the Danube, Marlborough, allied with the Austrians, won a great victory over the French and Bavarians. British arms gained additional victories at Ramillies (1706), Oudenarde (1708), and Malplaquet (1709).

While the personal conduct of the queen was exemplary, her reign marked a low point in political and private morality. Anne always worried about the problem of succession. Because of family loyalty she was convinced that the kingship should revert to the son of her father's second marriage. On her death she was entombed in Westminster Abbey and the throne passed by the Act of Settlement of 1701 to her cousin, the German Elector of Hanover, George I.

4. The House of Hanover: Limited Monarchy and Parliamentary Control

George I, First Hanoverian, r. 1714–1727. George I, aged fifty-four at his accession, knew no English and even less about the English way of thinking. Absolute ruler of Hanover, he preferred his German homeland, from which he obtained inspiration, favorites, and mistresses. Critics said that George's main interest was to fill his pockets and those of his German followers with British gold. To the British he remained a foreigner who was allowed to rule only because he represented the Protestant royal succession. He was more acceptable to the Whigs than the Roman Catholic son of James II. His succession may be regarded as the final step in the Protestant revolution in England. Since George I did not understand English and his ministers did not understand German, the new ruler sensibly refrained from attending cabinet meetings, supported the Whigs against the Tories, and accepted every act of Parliament without exercising the royal veto. This situation helped immeasurably in the freezing of parliamentary and cabinet power.

George II, r. 1727–1760. George I had been on bad terms with his son, who regularly plotted with the opposition against his father. A coarse, drill-sergeant type of man, the younger George was known both for his niggardliness and his prodigious memory. Like his father, George II regarded Hanover as the more desirable of his possessions. He was careful, however, to nurture his English throne, and for the better part of his reign he was content to play the part of a constitutional monarch. In 1745 an extreme group of Tories took part in an uprising in Scotland led by the dashing Prince Charlie, grandson of James II. The rebellion revealed that personal loyalty to Hanoverian kings was not yet an overriding sentiment among Englishmen, but the uprising was decisively beaten. This was the final Stuart effort.

Rise of Cabinet Government. William III began the practice of selecting his chief ministers from the Whig party when it enjoyed a majority in the House of Commons, and from the Tory party when it obtained most seats. This precedent made the ministry an established part of the British constitution. With the consolidation of parliamentarianism in the eighteenth century, cabinet government, in which the executive power was exercised by ministers responsible to the House of Commons, was established.

During the period of Whig ascendancy the office of prime minister came into existence. Both the Puritan and Glorious Revolutions had established the supremacy of Parliament over the king, but they had not provided any governmental machinery to implement the change. The office of prime minister—prime in importance, prime in power—was set up precisely for this purpose, to act as liaison between king and Parliament. The process was a long one. Gradually, it became traditional under the British constitution that the Crown appoint the leader of the majority party in Parliament as prime minister and as head of the cabinet. All other cabinet ministers were appointed by the Crown upon nomination by the prime minister.

Walpole, Apostle of Peace and Prosperity. Superimposed on the reigns of the first two Georges of the Hanoverian line was the ministry of the Whig, Sir Robert Walpole, First Earl of Orford (1676–1745). In 1708 he became secretary for war, but, accused by the Tories in 1712 of embezzling public moneys,

he was dismissed and sent to the Tower. He was restored to favor during the Protestant succession and in 1715 became chancellor of the Exchequer. His first and major problem was to reconcile a recalcitrant nation to the new Hanoverian dynasty; this task he accomplished well. He maintained his own position by holding the confidence of the monarch and by controlling parliamentary elections and the votes of members. He was certain that the final goal of statesmanship was prosperity: that as British merchants prospered, all Britain would prosper. He supported mercantilist policies by removing duties on imports and exports and enlarging the merchant marine. Although not a great financial minister, Walpole had ideas of sound financing which strengthened the government. Britain thrived under his ministry.

Walpole opposed foreign entanglements and war because they might lessen national prosperity. Both Tories and Whigs denounced his pacifism as shameful. Toward the end of his ministry he was driven into the War of Jenkins' Ear against Spain (1739). Considering his well-known pacifism, he should have resigned, but he clung to office until his majority had dwindled to two.

Walpole's championing of the doctrine of ministerial cohesion is enough to justify his reputation as the first effective English prime minister. W. E. H. Lecky says that Walpole found England with a disputed succession to the throne, an unpopular monarch, a corrupt Parliament, and a dissatisfied people. He gave it two decades of peace and prosperity, an established dynasty, a House of Commons as the real political center of gravity, an effective cabinet, and an improved party system.

The Era of William Pitt. In the period from Walpole's resignation in 1742 to the outbreak of the Seven Years' War in 1756, the glory of Britain had been dimmed by disaster. The War of the Austrian Succession (1740–1748) had been indecisive. A series of second-rate prime ministers had done little to prepare the nation for the gigantic colonial struggle with France. Into this era stepped William Pitt, First Earl of Chatham (1708–1778), parliamentarian, politician, orator, and promoter of British militarism and imperialism. Quickly gaining a reputation in the House of Commons, Pitt had to struggle for some time against the king's dislike, which blocked his political progress. In 1756 he became leader of the House of Commons and then prime minister in 1757. Presiding over the cabinet during the Seven Years' War, he transformed a conflict that had begun disastrously for the English into a brilliant success. Directing British conquest in America and India, he insured British supremacy on the high seas. The "Great Commoner" was one of England's finest statesmen, a man distinguished by integrity of character in an age of selfish politicians.

Reign of George III, 1760–1820. George III, in contrast to the first two Georges, was thoroughly English and gloried in the name of Briton. Born and reared in England, he took seriously the business of kingship. A hard worker, patriotic, popular, he hoped to strengthen the position of the monarchy; but at the same time, he had no intention of undoing the accomplishments of the Glorious Revolution of 1688. He preferred Tories to Whigs, and got rid of Whig ministers in favor of his own Tory followers (the King's Friends) in Parliament. In 1761 he promoted William Pitt to the House of Lords, thereby depriving England of a superbly effective prime minister.

The sixty years of George III's reign saw many momentous events. America won her independence from England by the Peace of Versailles in 1783. But George III (the Americans called him "that royal British brute") fought to the end in what he regarded as a justifiable war. Neither he nor the British nation as a whole could understand why Americans would not contribute to the cost of a war being fought in their defense, or why it was unconstitutional to levy taxes on the American colonies. During George III's reign the Pacific area was brought into European range by the explorations of the celebrated navigator, Captain James Cook; England's energies were taxed in the struggle with Napoleon (1798–1815); revolution and civil war broke out in Ireland; England's economy was transformed by the Industrial Revolution; and parliamentary government was reconstructed. George III, long troubled by instability, increasingly suffered from attacks of insanity. His reason failed him in 1811, but he lived on, blind and insane, for another nine years.

5. Social Life in Eighteenth-Century England

The Social Order. The tone of one of England's most successful centuries was set by the oligarchy, the ruling few. At the top of the ruling class were the magnates, holders of noble titles, who owned much of the land, filled high offices, controlled the House of Lords, held seats in the House of Commons, and influenced the king. They were skeptical in matters of religion, proponents of a vigorous foreign policy, and imperial in their interests. They allied themselves with the great merchants and bankers who supplied them with money for personal and political needs. They dressed in powdered wigs, velvet coats with laced sleeves, knee breeches, and silk stockings. They were elegant and artificial in their everyday pursuits, slaves of a severely prescribed etiquette.

Slightly lower in the social hierarchy of the ruling class were the smaller landowners—the squires, or country gentlemen. They were conservative, devoted to Church and Crown. They exercised local power as justices of the peace and made up the local courts. They usually gave their political support to the Tories. The spiritual needs of the aristocracy were served by the officials of the Church of England. Anglican bishops, many the sons of nobility, sat in the House of Lords. Highly secular in their outlook, they deemed it an important part of their duties to train the poor in loyalty to Crown and constitution.

Below the aristocracy in the social scale were the affluent merchants and bankers, the middle class, which had already begun to assert its power in Parliament and which wanted political power commensurate with its prosperity and prestige. Because of the fluid mobility of English society, movement up and down the social ladder, merchants and bankers of sufficient wealth could well become gentle-men or peers and be welcomed in highest society. There were many marriages between rich burgesses and impecunious noble ladies.

At the lower level were the artisans and small independent farmers, and below them the peasants and city workers. Most of these did not share in the good fortune of a prosperous England. The miserable workers, especially, were chained to the machines of industry.

The parliamentary system was a compro-mise: it retained the monarchy but at the same time denied any real share in govern-ment to the masses. The government remained in the hands of the magnates and merchants, who took their responsibilities seriously and guaranteed fundamental liberties against arbi-trary rule to everyone. Represented in the House of Commons were two major areas: the counties, or country areas, and the boroughs, or towns. The country members were elected by those who owned land with an appraised value of forty shillings, but in practice many were virtually appointed by the aristocrats. The burgesses, chosen by the towns, persis-tently sought to improve their political position against the landowners.

The Nature of Eighteenth-Century English Life. Everyday English life reflected political and social controls. During the Puritan era, austerity and curbs upon human appetites were imposed by the authorities. The Restora-tion period saw a violent reaction against the piety and restraints of Puritanism. In eigh-teenth-century England, life was convivial, colorful, and seldom dull. Aristocrats, impelled by form, placed greater stress on manners than on morals. Ladies and gentlemen danced the stately minuet and on occasion paid little attention to marriage vows. The poorer classes found life much more complicated. The death penalty could be imposed for dozens of crimes, even including theft of a horse or of as little

In this scene (Bedlam) from William Hogarth's famous series, *The Rake's Progress*, an unusu-ally wide variety of human pursuits are depicted—or satirized.

money as five shillings. Bankrupts and debtors were consigned to filthy prisons, where they died by the thousands. There was danger everywhere: in London bands of hooligans patrolled the streets, in the open country footpads practiced their nefarious skills.

Alcoholism, increasing at an appalling rate, affected all classes. Aristocrats became addicted to port, imported from Portugal, which helped contribute to gout, the painful disease of gluttonous nobility. The lower classes steeped themselves in beer and gin, the poor man's drinks. The drawings of Thomas Rowlandson and William Hogarth depict satirically this extraordinary addiction to alcohol. The consumption of gin, at first encouraged, reached such proportions in mid-century that Parliament was forced to step in and limit its use by law.

Added to alcoholism as an English habit was the interest shown by all English classes, rich and poor, in gambling and sports, from tennis to angling to football and horse-racing. Noble gentlemen considered it quite the normal thing to avenge any real or imaginary insult by challenging an offender to a duel. These ghastly, immature battles on the "field of honor" were common.

Eighteenth-century rationalism had some influence on this variegated English life. Social idealists called for reform of criminal codes to diminish the long list of capital crimes, to relieve debtors from imprisonment, and to end once and for all time the blight of slavery. Other rationalists, in an aura of optimism, proposed plans for eternal peace. Protests against prevalent evils eventually were directed toward better conditions for the lower classes. An impelling motive here was political, because the politically-conscious middle class needed the support of both the city workers and the peasants in their drive to cut down the power of the aristocracy. Thomas Paine expressed this new attitude in a famous aphorism: that a single honest plowman is worth more than all the crowned ruffians who ever lived.

⊰{ KEY DOCUMENT }⊱

THE BILL OF RIGHTS, 1689

Printed in Edward P. Cheyney, *Readings in English History* (New York, 1922), pp. 545–547. By permission of Ginn and Company.

AFTER ENUMERATING the illegal acts of James II, and declaring his abdication legal, the Bill of Rights enacted in detail the celebrated declaration of the rights and liberties of the English people. This was the third great step, after the Magna Carta and the Petition of Right, in the development of the structure of constitutional monarchy in England. It introduced no new principle into the English constitution but rather declared the law as it stood. Since 1689, all rulers of England have been pronounced eligible to the throne only by act of Parliament. The supremacy of Parliament over the throne was thus firmly established; the struggle of more than four centuries between Crown and Parliament was finally resolved in favor of Parliament.

Whereas the said late King James II having abdicated the government, and the throne being thereby vacant, his Highness the prince of Orange (whom it hath pleased Almighty God to make the glorious instrument of delivering this kingdom from popery and arbitrary power) did (by the advice of the lords spiritual and temporal, and diverse principal persons of the Commons) cause letters to be written to the lords spiritual and temporal, being Protestants, and other letters to the several counties, cities, universities, boroughs, and Cinque Ports, for the choosing of such persons to represent them, as were of right to be sent to parliament, to meet and sit at Westminster upon the two-and-twentieth day of January, in this year 1689, in order to such an establishment as that their religion, laws, and liberties might not again be in danger of being subverted; upon which letters elections have been accordingly made.

And thereupon the said lords spiritual and temporal and Commons, pursuant to their respective letters and elections, being now assembled in a full and free representation of this nation, taking into their most serious consideration the best means for attaining the ends aforesaid, do in the first place (as their ancestors in like case have usually done), for the vindication and assertion of their ancient rights and liberties, declare:

1. That the pretended power of suspending laws, or the execution of laws, by regal authority, without consent of parliament, is illegal.

2. That the pretended power of dispensing with laws, or the execution of laws, by regal authority, as it hath been assumed and exercised of late, is illegal.

3. That the commission for erecting the late court of commissioners for ecclesiastical causes, and all other commissions and courts of like nature, are illegal and pernicious.

4. That levying money for or to the use of the Crown by pretense of prerogative, without grant of parliament, for longer time or in other manner than the same is or shall be granted, is illegal.

5. That it is the right of the subjects to petition the king, and all commitments and prosecutions for such petitioning are illegal.

6. That the raising or keeping a standing army within the kingdom in time of peace, unless it be with consent of parliament, is against law.

7. That the subjects which are Protestants may have arms for their defense suitable to their conditions, and as allowed by law.

8. That election of members of parliament ought to be free.

9. That the freedom of speech, and debates or proceedings in parliament, ought not to be impeached or questioned in any court or place out of parliament.

10. That excessive bail ought not to be required, nor excessive fines imposed nor cruel and unusual punishments inflicted.

11. That jurors ought to be duly impaneled and returned. and jurors which pass upon men in trials for high treason ought to be freeholders.

12. That all grants and promises of fines and forfeitures of particular persons before conviction are illegal and void.

13. And that for redress of all grievances, and for the amending, strengthening, and preserving of the laws, parliament ought to be held frequently. . . .

The said lords spiritual and temporal, and commons, assembled at Westminster, do resolve that William and Mary, prince and princess of Orange, be, and be declared, king and queen of England, France, and Ireland, and the dominions thereunto belonging, to hold the crown and royal dignity of the said kingdoms and dominions to them the said prince and princess during their lives. . . .

Upon which their said Majesties did accept the crown and royal dignity of the kingdoms of England, France, and Ireland, and the dominions thereunto belonging, according to the resolution and desire of the said lords and commons contained in the said declaration.

❧ HISTORICAL INTERPRETATION ❧

THOMAS BABINGTON MACAULAY ON THE REVOLUTION OF 1688

Thomas Babington Macaulay, *The History of England from the Accession of James the Second* (London, 1914) III, 1304–1308, 1310–1311. Courtesy of Macmillan and Company, Ltd.

IN HIS *History of England,* Thomas Babington Macaulay (1800–1859) intended to cover the period from 1685 to 1820, but he never got beyond 1702. The section reprinted here—written in 1847 at a time when most of Continental Europe was about to be engulfed in revolution—praised the 1688 Revolution in England as heralding the end of tyranny and the beginning of the supremacy of Parliament.

Thus was consummated the English Revolution. When we compare it with those revolutions which have, during the last sixty years, overthrown so many ancient governments, we cannot but be struck by its peculiar character. Why that character was so peculiar is sufficiently obvious, and yet seems not to have been always understood either by eulogists or by censors.

The Continental revolutions of the eighteenth and nineteenth centuries took place in countries where all trace of the limited monarchy of the Middle Ages had long been effaced. The right of the prince to make laws and to levy money had, during many generations, been undisputed. His throne was guarded by a great regular army. His administration could not, without extreme peril, be blamed even in the mildest terms. His subjects held their personal liberty by no other tenure than his pleasure. Not a single institution was left which had, within the memory of the oldest man, afforded efficient protection to the subject against the utmost excess of tyranny. Those great councils which had once curbed the regal power had sunk into oblivion. Their composition and their privileges were known only to antiquaries.

We cannot wonder, therefore, that, when men who had been thus ruled succeeded in wresting supreme power from a government which they had long in secret hated, they should have been impatient to demolish. . . . As little can we wonder that the violent action of the revolutionary spirit should have been followed by reaction equally violent, and that confusion should speedily have engendered despotism sterner than that from which it had sprung.

Had we been in the same situation; had Strafford succeeded in his favourite scheme of Thorough; had he formed an army as numerous and as well disciplined as that which, a few years later, was formed by Cromwell; had a series of judicial decisions, similar to that which was pronounced by the Exchequer Chamber in the case of ship-money, transferred to the Crown the right of taxing the people; had the Star Chamber and the High Commission continued to fine, mutilate, and imprison every man who dared to raise his voice against the government; had the press been as completely enslaved here as at Vienna or at Naples; had our Kings gradually drawn to themselves the whole legislative power; had six generations of Englishmen passed away without a single session of Parliament; and had we then at length risen up in some moment of wild excitement against our masters, what an outbreak would that have been!

With what a crash, heard and felt to the farthest ends of the world, would the whole vast fabric of society have fallen! How many thousands of exiles, once the most prosperous and the most refined members of this great community, would have begged their bread in Continental cities, or have sheltered their heads under huts of bark in the uncleared forests of America! How often should we have seen the pavement of London piled up in barricades, the houses dinted with bullets, the gutters foaming with blood! How many times should we have rushed wildly from extreme to extreme, sought refuge from anarchy in despotism, and been again driven by despotism into anarchy! How many years of blood and confusion would it have cost us to learn the very rudiments of political science! How many childish theories would have duped us! How many rude and ill poised constitutions should we have set up, only to see them tumble down! Happy would it have been for us if a sharp discipline of half a century had sufficed to educate us into a capacity of enjoying true freedom.

These calamities our Revolution averted. It was a revolution strictly defensive, and had prescription and legitimacy on its side. Here, and here only, a limited monarchy of the thirteenth century had come down unimpaired to the seventeenth century. Our parliamentary institutions were in full vigour. The main principles of our government were excellent. They were not, indeed, formally and exactly set forth in a single written instrument; but they were to be found scattered over our ancient and noble statutes; and, what was of far greater moment, they had been engraven on the hearts of Englishmen during 400 years. That, without the consent of the representatives of the nation, no legislative act could be passed, no tax imposed, no regular soldiery kept up; that no man could be imprisoned, even for a day, by the arbitrary will of the sovereign; that no tool of power could plead the royal command as a justification for violating any right of the humblest subject, were held, both by Whigs and Tories, to be fundamental laws of the realm. A realm of which these were the fundamental laws stood in no need of a new constitution.

But, though a new constitution was not needed, it was plain that changes were required. The misgovernment of the Stuarts, and the troubles which that misgovernment had produced, sufficiently proved that there was somewhere a defect in our polity; and that defect it was the duty of the Convention to discover and to supply. . . .

And yet this revolution, of all revolutions the least violent, has been of all revolutions the most beneficient. It finally decided the great question whether the popular element which had, ever since the age of Fitzwalter and De Montfort, been found in the English polity, should be destroyed by the monarchical element, or should

be suffered to develope itself freely, and to become dominant. The strife between the two principles had been long, fierce, and doubtful. It had lasted through four reigns. It had produced seditions, impeachments, rebellions, battles, sieges, proscriptions, judicial massacres. Sometimes liberty, sometimes royalty, had seemed to be on the point of perishing. . . .

The highest eulogy which can be pronounced on the revolution of 1688 is this, that it was our last revolution. Several generations have now passed away since any wise and patriotic Englishman has meditated resistance to the established government. In all honest and reflecting minds there is a conviction, daily strengthened by experience, that the means of effecting every improvement which the constitution requires may be found within the constitution itself.

❧[TEN BASIC BOOKS]❧

TRIUMPH OF PARLIAMENTARY GOVERNMENT IN ENGLAND

1. Bahlman, Dudley W., *The Moral Revolution of 1688* (New Haven, Conn., 1957).
2. Bell, Walter, *The Great Fire of London in 1666* (London, 1923).
3. Clark, George, *The Later Stuarts, 1660–1714,* 2nd ed. (Oxford, 1955).
4. Feiling, Keith G., *A History of the Tory Party, 1640–1714* (Oxford, 1924).
5. Holdsworth, William S., *A History of English Law,* Vol. VI (London, 1924).
6. Laski, Harold J., *Political Thought in England from Locke to Bentham* (London, 1955).
7. Ogg, David, *England in the Reigns of James II and William III* (Oxford, 1955).
8. Pinkham, Lucile, *William III and the Respectable Revolution* (Cambridge, 1954).
9. Straka, Gerald M., *Anglican Reaction to the Revolution of 1688* (Madison, Wisc., 1962).
10. Trevelyan, George Macaulay, *The English Revolution, 1688–1689,* 2nd ed. (London, 1946).†

15

Revolution of the Mind: The Age of Reason, 1650-1800

LAW IN general is human reason, inasmuch as it governs all the inhabitants of the earth: the political and civil laws of each nation ought to be only the particular cases in which human reason is applied. They should be adapted in such a manner to the people for whom they are framed that it should be a great chance if those of one nation suit another. They should be in relation to the nature and principle of each government: whether they form it, as may be said of politic laws; or whether they support it, as in the case of civil institutions. They should be in relation to the climate of each country, to the quality of its soil, to its situation and extent, to the principal occupation of the natives, whether husbandmen, huntsmen, or shepherds: they should have relation to the degree of liberty which the constitution will bear; to the religion of the inhabitants, to their inclinations, riches, numbers, commerce, manners, and customs. In fine, they have relations to each other, as also to their origin, to the intent of the legislator, and to the order of things on which they are established; in all of which they ought to be considered.
—MONTESQUIEU, *The Spirit of the Laws* (1748)

1. Meaning and General Characteristics

The Era of Enlightenment. The Age of Reason—known to German observers as the *Aufklärung*, to British historians as the "Illumination," to French scholars as *la lumière* and now generally termed the "Enlightenment"—was a great intellectual revolution which gave the modern mind its temper and spirit. Rejecting medieval theology as the final authority, Western man now sought to interpret the universe, the world, and himself in terms of reason or logical analysis. In contrast both to Renaissance humanism and to the Reformation, the Age of Reason was an intellectual, rational movement, which substituted for the medieval Age of Faith, an Age of Faith in science. Thinkers began to attack all sorts of problems with fewer preconceived notions and inhibitions based upon doctrine or dogma.

The rationalism emerging in the sixteenth century was considered in the eighteenth century to be the final key to the problems of mankind. During these two centuries the rationalists, finding in mathematics what they believed to be an infallible method, accepted a mechanical interpretation and constructed a "world-machine" to explain the secrets of nature. Remarkable advances in science and technology, resulting from the spirit of inquiry and encouraged by the opportunities of an expanding commerce, confirmed the rationalists in their faith. In the nineteenth and twentieth centuries, however, a reaction against rationalism set in, with the argument that the Enlightenment did not offer an ultimate and exclusive answer to the meaning of life.

Various characteristic strains may be observed in the pattern of the Age of Reason:

1. *Secularization of Learning:* Whereas medieval philosophers and theologians interpreted the universe and man in terms of the Scriptures, rationalists tended to avoid ecclesiastical authority and turned more and more toward the secularization of knowledge. The door to understanding, they said, was not revelation but mathematics, reason, and logic.

2. *Faith in Reason:* The Age of Reason was an age of faith in the rational behavior of nature and in immutable scientific laws. Reason, said the rationalists, was the omnipotent arbiter of all things, a powerful and beneficial guide which was superior to all traditional authority. Therefore man was destined to use his intellect in solving the manifold mysteries of nature and his own mind.

3. *Utilitarianism:* The spirit of the Age of Reason was utilitarian and practical. Human beings must promote their own happiness and welfare by remaking their lives and institutions on this earth. That which was useful was good. And men deserved the blessings of life, liberty, and property.

4. *Optimism and Self-Confidence:* The rationalists were supremely confident and optimistic men, fully convinced of their ability to discover natural laws and to perfect the world and life in accordance with them. They were, perhaps, overconfident and too certain of their intellectual power. Science was still in its early stages and there was much to be learned, but these self-assured men were exalted by their discovery of a new gospel for mankind.

Transition from Medieval to Modern Mind. In the Middle Ages the world was regarded simply as a portion of the Kingdom of God. All phenomena were believed to have been caused by God's will, acting sometimes by obvious and sometimes by inscrutable means. It was not deemed either necessary or wise to investigate further into the causes of natural phenomena. Interest in nature lay primarily in its meaning in terms of God's purpose. Omniscient and omnipotent God had created the world in six days. Man himself had been created by God in perfect form, but because of his disobedience in the Garden of Eden, he had fallen

from grace and was condemned to everlasting damnation. Man had been redeemed by the sacrifice of God's only son. Life on earth was merely a temporary test for the human being. Eventually, the earth would be destroyed by a great catastrophe. A final separation would take place between good and evil men, the latter being sent to Hell for eternal punishment and the good men transported to Heaven where they would dwell forever in happiness. This was the drama of human history. In the medieval climate of opinion, man was expected to recognize his role in this great drama and, above all, make no unnecessary attempt to alter it.

The change from this medieval conception of nature was hastened by the needs and discoveries of an expanding commerce and by the intellectual milieu resulting from them. New institutions arose—the sovereign national state, absolute monarchy, representative government, diverse Christian sects, commercial capitalism, and a politically conscious bourgeoisie. Along with these came a distinct cultural transformation which reflected the age in all its variegated designs.

Where the medieval thinker had turned to theology for answers to the problems of the universe and life, the rationalists preferred to rely on scientific investigation. While medieval scholars, dismayed by the multiplicity of things and events that seemed to defy logical interpretation, took refuge in broad theological concepts, the rationalists had confidence in their ability to ascertain truth by logic. Where medieval scholars had been motivated by ideas, concepts, and forms, the rationalists turned to the consideration of laws and functions. The rationalists, dissatisfied with medieval hairsplitting, looked forward, not backward.

Contrast with Other Revolutions. The Age of Reason differed in character from all previous and subsequent intellectual revolutions. The Greek philosophers often descended into skepticism, whereas the rationalists, considered as a group, optimistically saw no limit to their ability to ascertain the truth. The humanists of the Renaissance, although influenced by classical freedom of inquiry, were more interested in man himself than in nature. They attacked the old barren scholasticism because of its continued emphasis upon theology, but they paid only passing attention to the natural laws which attracted the interest of the rationalists. During the Reformation, the reformers of the various Protestant sects substituted for medieval orthodoxy their own national types of dogma and sought for absolute, revealed truth in the Bible. The rationalists, on the other hand, turned away from revelation and attempted deliberately to change existing institutions, traditions, and standards.

Search for an Infallible Method. During the course of the Age of Reason, European intellectuals cast off their narrow provincialism in favor of cosmopolitanism and humanitarianism. What was the key to the secrets of the universe? What was the infallible method for solving the persistent problems of mankind? The early rationalists, seeking for natural laws, discovered the magic key in mathematics. Then came an intensive effort to "mathematicize the universe." Subsequently, other rationalists applied the methods of rationalism to religion, society, and government, on the assumption that human behavior could be explained on the basis of universal principles.

Historical Controversy. Historians differ on interpretation of the Age of Reason. Some see it as a definite break with the past, others place it within a framework of continuity. This latter point of view holds that, despite the seemingly radical break with the past, the rationalists were nearer the Middle Ages and less emancipated than they thought. Carl Becker, in his *The Heavenly City of the Eighteenth-Century Philosophers*, added a word of caution: "If we examine the foundations of their faith, we find that at every turn the *Philosophes* betray their debt to medieval thought without being aware of it."

Other historians see the Age of Reason as one of the few movements in history that resulted in a fresh outlook upon existence and that laid the foundation for untried ways in the future. Granted that the rationalists could not purge themselves altogether of the old provincial outlook upon life, they did succeed in opening a dynamic world perspective. They were responsible for the formation of an attitude which would challenge, both orally and by the written word, the accepted systems of belief and conduct.

2. From Rigid Cosmos to Universe Without Limit

The Ptolemaic System. Astronomy, the science of celestial bodies, first took shape in Babylonia where, in the third millenium B.C., initial measurements were made of the heavens and many constellations were named. Greek and Roman philosophers fashioned astronomy into a coherent science. From their point of view, the earth was located at the center of a number of transparent spheres, on which were fixed planets and stars, some turning clockwise, others counterclockwise, These early efforts culminated in the work of Claudius Ptolemy, a celebrated Alexandrian mathematician and astronomer, who lived in Egypt in the second century A.D. In his *Almagest,* Ptolemy projected the geocentric theory, holding that the earth is an immovable sphere, fixed in the center of the universe. The sphere of the heavens revolves around the earth from east to west, carrying all celestial objects with it, once in every twenty-four hours.

Although they regarded the Ptolemaic System as a pagan theory, theologians of the Middle Ages accepted it because it harmonized with appearances and seemed correct to the senses. Obviously, the earth had to be the center of the universe, since it had to be important enough to serve as an abode for the people of God before they left it for the next world.

The Revolutionary Copernican Thesis. The man who proved the solar system to be heliocentric (sun-centered) was a Polish astronomer, Nicholas Copernicus, (1473–1543), who projected an entirely new system of astronomy. In 1507 he began work on a great astronomical treatise, *De revolutionibus orbium coelestium,* which he completed in 1530. The Copernican thesis exchanged the positions of the sun and the earth in the scheme of fixed crystalline spheres. According to Copernicus, the sun remains stationary, while the planets, including the earth, revolve around it. This was a daring revolt against the long and accepted dictatorship of Ptolemy. Copernicus relied in part upon ancient Greek astronomical knowledge and in part on discoveries made in the fourteenth and fifteenth centuries, but he was the first modern astronomer to give scientific expression to the heliocentric theory. Astronomy was now recast on an inverted design. The first powerful argument was given for the existence of a harmonious order of the universe.

The Copernican proposition, one of the great achievements of human thought, was only slowly accepted as truth. It resulted in a revolutionary change of man's attitude toward the whole universe and even toward himself. It swept him from his position as the central figure in the universe and made of him "a tiny speck on a third-rate planet revolving around a tenth-rate sun drifting in an endless cosmic ocean." In denying that the earth was the center of the universe, the Copernican theory contradicted the doctrine that the earth as well as the universe were created solely to serve the needs of man.

Both Catholic and Protestant theologians condemned the Copernican theory as absurd. The Vatican officially pronounced it to be "false and altogether opposed to Holy Scripture." From 1616 to 1757 the *De revolutionibus* was listed on the Index as being subversive of truth. Not until 1822 was this ban lifted and the sun given formal sanction to become the center of the planetary system. Despite the unfavorable circumstances surrounding its appearance, the Copernican theory gradually won its way to acceptance.

Pre-Telescopic Observation. The Copernican theory was elaborated and popularized by an Italian philosopher, Giordano Bruno (*c.* 1548–1600). Despite his magnificent achievement, Copernicus understood little about astrophysical relativity and the plurality of worlds and universes. Some important gaps in the Copernican system were filled in by

Bruno on the basis of "brilliant intuitions," later confirmed: (1) There is neither a center nor a limit to the universe, since everything is relative to the point of observation; (2) there are other universes besides our own; and (3) there are no fixed starry spheres, since the heavenly bodies move freely in space. These conclusions are all the more remarkable when it is considered that they were made before the invention of the telescope.

A disdainful, boastful, arrogant individualist, Bruno had little patience with those who dared to disagree with him. His attempts to popularize the Copernican theory and his scoffing attitude toward Aristotelian astronomy drew upon him the wrath of the Church. He

The huge arc of Tycho's quadrant was fixed in a western wall of his observatory, and had as its center an open window high up in the southern wall. The area above the instrument was decorated with a painting depicting the astronomer and his dog, student-assistants, and many of the observatory's main instruments. This engraving is after a sketch in Tycho's own book.

was arrested in 1593 by emissaries of the Inquisition, brought to Rome, and imprisoned for seven years. Finally, he was excommunicated and burned at the stake in 1600. The first person to sense the infinity of the universe, Bruno became the initial martyr of the new science.

The Copernican system was simpler than the Ptolemaic. It soon became obvious, however, that there could be no decisive test between the two theories until observations of greater accuracy could be recorded. This was accomplished by a Danish scholar, Tycho Brahe (1546–1601), who, although not altogether convinced of the validity of the Copernican theory, nevertheless contributed to its final acceptance. Constructing one of the best astronomical observatories of his time, the Castle of Heaven, on an island between Denmark and Sweden, Tycho Brahe located scores of fixed stars, prepared the most useful stellar charts of his day, and, in general, perfected the art of pre-telescopic observation.

Kepler and Planetary Motion. Tycho Brahe's brilliant young German assistant, Johann Kepler (1571–1630), a youth of unlimited imagination, was not content with his duties of observation and record-keeping. He became familiar with the body of material gathered in Tycho's observatory. Patient and untiring, he evaluated, compared, and calculated the data at his disposal. By applying to his work a great theoretical talent, as well as a mastery of mathematics, he effected such a major revolution that it is reasonable to call him the founder of modern physical astronomy. Although a convinced Copernican, he was nevertheless destined to destroy a part of the Copernican order, namely, the system of fixed crystalline spheres which were supposed to control the motion of the heavenly bodies. Originally, he had accepted the traditional belief that all celestial revolutions must be performed in fixed circles, but after laborious computations he came to the conclusion that the planets traveled freely in space around elliptical orbits. This was the basis for a new cosmic system, which Kepler expressed in three laws of planetary motion:

1. The radius vector drawn from the sun to the planet describes equal areas in equal times (i.e., the planet moves fastest when nearest the sun).
2. The planet describes an ellipse around the sun in one focus.
3. The squares of the periodic times (i.e., their times of revolution) of the several planets are proportional to the cubes of their respective mean distances from the sun.

These laws were described by Kepler in an extraordinary book, *De harmonice mundi (On the Harmony of the World)*, which appeared in 1619. Kepler recounted his intense belief in the idea of an underlying harmony in nature, and gave an extensive mathematical analysis to prove it. His discoveries resulted in the perfection of a mathematical plan of the solar system as well as an enhancement of the predicting powers of astronomy.

Galileo and Dynamic Mechanics. Mathematics as the key to knowledge was the paramount discovery of the sixteenth century, but it remained for an Italian astronomer and experimental physicist, Galileo Galilei (1564–1642), to give it practical and convincing application. Galileo was a mathematical and mechanical genius. Born in Pisa, the son of a well-known mathematician, he constructed mechanical toys while still a child. As a student at the University of Pisa, he made one of his most important discoveries—the law of vibrations or swings of a pendulum. He also invented the hydrostatic balance as a means of ascertaining the specific gravity of solid bodies. In 1588 he became a professor at the University of Pisa, where he propounded the theorem that all falling bodies descend with equal velocity. According to legend, he is said to have proved his point by several experiments conducted from the famous Leaning Tower. Driven from Pisa in 1591 by the Aristotelians, whose enmity he had incurred by his experiments, he went to the University of Padua, where he attracted students from all over Europe.

By far the most important of Galileo's improvements was his telescope, which enabled him to make many significant advances in astronomy. In 1610 he discovered four of Jupiter's satellites, which revolve around that planet as the moon revolves around the earth. He demonstrated the uneven configurations on the surface of the moon, and calculated the height of its mountains. He contemptuously dismissed the prevalent notion that the spots on the moon were "the stains of Adam's sins," and instead, stated that they were simply valleys. He described the Milky Way as a great collection of stars, and he detected sunspots, from which he inferred the rotation of the sun.

Galileo's experimental confirmation of the Copernican theory on the construction of the universe and his sarcastic attacks upon those who persisted in their reverence for Aristotle led him into difficulties with the Church. His work was found to be at odds with passages from the Scriptures. He replied with an exposition of a formal theory on the relation of physical science to Holy Writ, embodied in his book, *The Authority of Scripture* (1614). As a sincere Catholic, Galileo was genuinely interested in reconciling Copernican theory with orthodoxy: "It is surely harmful to souls," he wrote, "to make it a heresy to believe what is proved. The prohibition of astronomy would be an open contempt of a hundred texts of the Holy Scriptures, which teach us that the glory and the greatness of Almighty God are admirably discerned in all His works, and divinely read in the open book of the universe."

Ecclesiastical authorities felt otherwise. Galileo was warned by the Inquisition against holding, teaching, or defending the subversive theories of Copernicus. The position of the Church was stated flatly: "The doctrine that the sun is the center of the world is false and absurd, formally heretical and contrary to Scripture, whereas the doctrine that the earth is not the center of the world but moves, and has further a daily motion, is philosophically false and absurd and theologically at least erroneous."

Although he promised to obey this injunction, Galileo in 1632, ignoring his pledge, published his *Dialogue on the Ptolemaic and Copernican Systems,* which gave the Ptolemaic theory its deathblow. He continued his at-

tacks on the Aristotelians: "The number of thick skulls is infinite, and we need neither record their follies nor endeavor to interest them in subtle and sublime ideas. No demonstrations can enlighten stupid brains." Galileo was again summoned before the Inquisition. After a long and wearisome trial, he was sentenced to incarceration at the pleasure of the court, condemned to abjure by oath on his knees the truth of his scientific beliefs, and enjoined to recite penitential psalms once a week for three years.

Early in his career Galileo had accepted the traditional cosmology, but reading Kepler persuaded him to join the ranks of the Copernicans. His discoveries eventually confirmed and gave tangible expression to the Copernican theory. He made his work easily intelligible to the general public, thus popularizing a theory which until his time had made an impression only upon a relatively small group of scholars. It was most unfortunate that Galileo and Kepler ignored each other's work in the field of planetary motion. Had they been able to work together it is possible that Galileo's practical dynamic mechanics and Kepler's generalizations would have resulted in an earlier discovery of the force of gravitation. Yet it is fair to say that both these brilliant intellects prepared the way for the Newtonian synthesis.

Francis Bacon: Scientific Methodology. Among the apostles of the inductive, experimental method, none was more influential than the illustrious Francis Bacon (1561–1626), philosopher, lawyer, essayist, and Lord Chancellor of England. During an active public career, Bacon never lost sight of a dominant passion—to revolutionize philosophy by turning its material from speculative metaphysics to experimental science. In three remarkable books, *Novum Organum, The Advancement of Learning,* and *The New Atlantis,* he astutely attacked the deductive method of scholasticism and with great eloquence supported the new scientific methodology. An enthusiastic herald of modern science, he repudiated traditional authority in favor of experimentation. He warned that the man of science must center his interest on the laboratory, not the cathedral. In widening the intellectual breach which separated the men of his day from the Middle Ages, he helped formulate a fresh concept of the universe and contributed much to the triumph of the mechanical interpretation of nature.

Descartes: Language of Mathematics. While Galileo confined himself to the study of mathematical and astronomical phenomena, his contemporary, René Descartes (1596–1650), French philosopher and mathematician, began to describe in clear-cut terms the full outline of the new universe discovered by the rationalists. His first published work, *Discourse on Method,* accompanied by three scientific treatises on geometry, optics, and general physics, appeared in 1637. In this work he projected four major principles which he believed should be followed for best results in philosophic and scientific method:

1. Never accept anything as true when it is recognized not to be so, that is to say, carefully avoid precipitancy and prejudice, but include in one's opinions nothing beyond that which should present itself so clearly and distinctly to the mind that there will be an occasion to doubt it.

2. Divide up the difficulties to be examined into as many parts as possible, and as should be required for their better solution.

3. Conduct one's thoughts in order, by beginning with the most simple objects and those most easy to know, and then mount little by little, by stages, to the most complex knowledge.

4. Everywhere make enumerations so complete, and surveys so wide, that one can be sure of omitting nothing.

Descartes was one of history's great pioneers in the discipline of mathematics. Speculating on mechanical problems, he came to the conclusion that the source of all true science lies in a combination of geometrical analysis and algebra. He was the founder of analytical geometry—the application of algebra to geometry. So certain was he of finding an explanation for all things in purely mechanical terms that he boasted: "Give me extension and motion, and I will construct the universe!" He

went on to invent a system of notation, the classification of curves, and the treatment of negative roots, all of which have survived to the present day.

In recognizing that mathematics constituted the fundamental basis of physical science, Descartes laid the groundwork for that exactness of observation and calculation which was to become the outstanding characteristic of modern science. His work is considered of such importance that it is generally recognized by the term "the Cartesian Revolution." The old Aristotelian idea that nature consists of a variety of unrelated objects, each of which seeks to fulfill its aim in its own way, was now superseded by the Cartesian principle that nothing in nature is accidental or arbitrary, but that everything is governed by universal mathematical laws. Cartesianism became the official beacon of the new science, even if its explanations were as yet a little too simple and not always demonstrable by experimentation. Most important of all, it prepared the way for the great synthesis of Newton, the greatest of Cartesians.

Newtonian Synthesis: The triumph of the mechanical interpretation of nature may be attributed to Isaac Newton (1642–1727), English natural philosopher. Recognizing the validity of Galileo's law of falling bodies and Kepler's three laws of planetary motion, Newton synthesized and combined these into his own law of universal gravitation. He described his great discovery in his *Philosophiae naturalis principia mathematica,* published as a whole in 1687. The planets revolve around the sun in harmony with Galileo's law of falling bodies. From one of Kepler's laws, namely, the proportionality of the areas to the times of their description, Newton inferred that the force which retained the planet in its orbit was always directed to the sun. From another one of Kepler's laws, namely, that every planet describes an ellipse around the sun in one focus, Newton drew the more general inference that the force by which the planet moves around the focus varies inversely as the square of the distance therefrom. He demonstrated that a planet acted upon by such a force could

PHILOSOPHIÆ

NATURALIS

PRINCIPIA

MATHEMATICA·

Autore *JS. NEWTON,* *Trin. Coll. Cantab. Soc.* Matheſeos
Profeſſore *Lucaſiano,* & Societatis Regalis Sodali.

IMPRIMATUR

S. PEPYS, *Reg. Soc.* PRÆSES.
Julii 5. *1686.*

LONDINI,

Juſſu *Societatis Regiæ* ac Typis *Joſephi* Streater. Proſtant Vena-
les apud *Sam. Smith* ad inſignia Principis *Walliæ* in Cœmiterio
D. *Pauli,* alioſq; nonnullos Bibliopolas. *Anno* MDCLXXXVII.

The title page of Newton's *Principia* shows that it was
published with the official sanction (*Imprimatur*) of
the Royal Society which was then under the presidency of Samuel Pepys.

not move in any other curve than a conic section. Moreover, this force of attraction existed
even in the smallest particle of matter. From
all this he outlined the universal law of gravitation—"*Every particle of matter is attracted
by or gravitates to every other particle of matter with a force inversely proportional to the
squares of their distances.*"

The crowning achievement of seventeenth-
century science, Newton's law of gravitation
was another gigantic stride forward. "If I have
seen farther than Descartes," said Newton
modestly, "it is by standing on the shoulders
of giants." Newton's achievement was the construction of a world-machine. Instead of a
series of planets, each going its own way independent of all others, the universe now
appeared as a well-ordered, mechanical whole,
held together by gravity.

Newton's law of gravitation marked the

closing of one epoch in the history of human
thought and the beginning of another. The
theories of the cosmos as propounded by Aristotle, Ptolemy, and the medieval astrologers
were completely overthrown and placed in
the category of outmoded knowledge. In their
place appeared a cosmic theory of infinite
scope and complexity.

The orderliness of the universe was the
supreme discovery of science in the Age of
Reason. Painstaking observations and calculations had proved that celestial phenomena
occur at regular intervals, often complex, but
always systematic and invariable. The running
of no clock ever approaches in precision the
motions of the heavenly bodies. To this day,
clocks are corrected and regulated by comparing them with the diurnal motion of the
planets.

**Historical Controversy: The Scientific Revo-
lution.** Herbert Butterfield, in his book, *The
Origins of Modern Science* (1949), presented
the view that the scientific revolution of the
sixteenth and seventeenth centuries "outshines
everything since the rise of Christianity and
reduces the Renaissance and the Reformation
to mere episodes, mere internal displacements,
within the system of medieval Christendom."
According to the Butterfield theory, it cannot
be said that essentially new ingredients were
introduced at the time of the Renaissance.
The secularization of thought which was locally achieved in certain circles at that time
was not unprecedented: it was a "hot-house
growth," soon to be overwhelmed by the fanaticism of the Reformation and the Counter-
Reformation. The scientific revolution, on the
other hand, was the real origin of the modern
world and the modern mentality. Thus Butterfield rejects the traditional periodization of
modern history, customarily begun at 1500, as
incorrect and invalid. Modern history, he feels,
should begin later with the outburst of scientific discoveries and inventions.

In contrast to the Butterfield thesis, other
scholars call attention to the Italian humanists
as beginning the scientific revolution. Paul
Oskar Kristeller states that by popularizing the
works of classical antiquity, the fifteenth-cen-

tury humanists made an important, though indirect, contribution to the development of science, and that this contribution bore fruit in the work of scientists in the following century. Leonardo Olschki points out that the scientific education of Copernicus was "Italian and humanistic." These scholars see crucial intellectual and scientific changes at the time of the Renaissance which transformed the character and structure of civilization.

3. From Revelation Through Deism to Materialism

Revelation Versus Natural Religion. The unity of the medieval Church had been broken by the Protestant Revolt and the Catholic Counter-Reformation, together with the accompanying religious wars. Religious thought, however, had changed but little during these upheavals. Theological disputes remained strongly emotional in character. The rationalists now began to apply the findings of their intellect to religion. They became convinced that it was not only practical but also desirable to consider religion from points of view similar to those which they had used in constructing a mechanical universe. As this rationalistic pattern of thought crystallized, there emerged the framework for a theory of "natural religion."

Traditional Christianity had been grounded on revelation—the disclosure or communication of truth to man by God himself or by his authorized agents, the prophets and apostles. According to the new lines of thought, the basis of religion was to be found not in revelation but in the very nature of man himself. Man's religion, the rationalists insisted, was planted in him by his own nature. Natural religion had always existed as a perfect thing, and revelation could add nothing to it. Miracles, prophecy, and all religious rites, they said, are mere superstitions. These views meant, in effect, that for the first time since the triumph of Christianity in the Western world, there was a definite break with the theological tradition. An impassioned struggle ensued between the believers in revelation and the proponents of natural religion.

Dualism and Pantheism. Among the first to apply the idea of natural law to religion was Descartes. Conservative in his approach, he sought to harmonize medieval thought with science by projecting a mechanistic universe in which everything could be explained by mathematics. From this mechanistic explanation he exempted two things—God and the soul of man, both of which he described as beyond and above science. He advocated a kind of philosophic dualism, by which God (or mind) and man (or nature) are distinct from one another.

Baruch Spinoza (1632–1677), born in Amsterdam of Portuguese-Jewish parents, was excommunicated by his synagogue for heretical views He was influenced by Descartes but was unwilling to accept his dualistic concept. In an era of voluptuous epicureanism, this "pious, virtuous, God-intoxicated man" lived the simple life of a lens polisher. Few human beings have ever been more maligned on the one hand and more venerated on the other than was this genius. Scrupulously following the methods outlined by Descartes, Spinoza tried to create a mechanico-naturalistic philosophy of the universe. But he rejected Cartesian dualism and substituted for it the idea that God and the universe are one (pantheism). Spinoza saw God as the supreme and only real substance in the universe, the only object of true knowledge, an absolute and infinite Being. In Spinoza's view, God as substance consists of infinite attributes, each expressing eternal and definite essence.

Contemporary Jews and Christians attacked Spinoza as an atheist and condemned his view of an all-embracing naturalistic God as impossible and heretical. The philosopher died a persecuted man. Today there is more inclination to recognize as a brilliant philosophic system his ingenious attempt to combine devout mysticism and scientific axioms.

Scientific Scholasticism: Leibnitz. Another attempt to reconcile religion and science was made by Gottfried Wilhelm Freiherr von Leibnitz (1646–1716), German philosopher, mathematician, and versatile man of affairs. Descartes had separated things into two substances connected by the omnipotence of God, and Spinoza had absorbed both into one divine substance; Leibnitz rejected both because, in his view, they were wrong in their understanding of substance. Substance, the ultimate reality, said Leibnitz, can be conceived of only as a force. The universe is made up of an infinite number of individual centers of force, or *monads*. "The monads," he said, "are the very atoms of nature—in a word, the elements of things, but as centers of force, they have neither parts, extension, or figure."

Leibnitz was a firm believer in God. To substantiate his belief, he borrowed available scholastic proofs of the existence of God and, in effect, restated the old Augustinian philosophy in terms of mathematics and physics. He formulated a new scholasticism in terms of science. Medieval theologians had drawn their data from religious texts, but Leibnitz turned to the impressive mathematical and scientific discoveries of his own century. His primary aim was to throw the light of reason on old theological concepts.

Deism: Religion of Reason. Another group of rationalists, the Deists, refused to compromise with the old mysticism, and established a new religion of reason. According to the Deists, God is an impersonal force, the custodian of the world-machine and the clock-winder of the universe. The God who fashioned the Newtonian world-machine, they said, would never "reveal" anything to man unless it were simple, clear-cut, and logical. Admittedly, God had created the universe, but once the work was done, immutable laws came into existence. It was useless and presumptuous to attempt to change these laws by prayer or by any other human means. The Deists accepted the ethical teachings of Christ, but they refused to recognize the tenets of orthodox Christianity because these formed a mysterious and incomprehensible body of revelation. They urged all creeds to follow four precepts of natural religion: (1) God is to be regarded as the master of the universe; (2) He asks only the good of man, human perfection, and happiness; (3) the aim of all religion is virtue or decent living; and (4) men must rely upon reason to solve their problems.

In England a long line of Deists attacked, some calmly and moderately, some vigorously, all that distinguished Christianity from natural religion. Lord Herbert of Cherbury (1583–1648) announced his belief in the existence of God and in immortality, but rejected "all superstitious rites and doctrines." Charles Blount (1654–1693), the first popularizer of Deism in England, attacked miracles as fabrications, and ridiculed the sacramental system as a shameless money-grubbing scheme. Matthew Tindal (c. 1656–1733) excoriated religious rites: "To imagine that God can command anything inconsistent with this universal benevolence is highly to dishonor Him; 'tis to destroy His impartial goodness, and make His power and wisdom degenerate into cruelty and craft." Thomas Morgan, who called himself a Christian Deist, maintained in his *Moral Philosopher* (1737) that Christianity was a revival of the religion of nature. Thomas Chubb (1679–1746) sought to make Deism palatable by contending that Christ was a true Deist. Anthony Collins (1676–1729) claimed that the fulfillment of prophecy by events in Christ's life was all "secondary, secret, allegorical, and mystical." Thomas Woolston (1670–1733) made a withering attack on the miracles recorded in the New Testament, calling them "foolish, trivial, contradictory, absurd, unworthy of a divinely commissioned teacher, and characteristic only of a sorcerer and wizard." For his pains he was imprisoned for blasphemy and died in captivity.

The Deists' attacks on revelation and on Christianity in general had been calm and moderate in England, but in France they were bitter and impassioned. French *philosophes* considered themselves to be students of society whose task it was to enlighten mankind, sweep away the cobwebs of ancient superstitions, and let in the light of reason. The foremost propagandist of French Deism was François-Marie Arouet, known as Voltaire (1694–1778). Witty, erudite, and irascible, he ridiculed Christianity, attacking it as a system of absurdities. In his estimation, Christ was a religious fanatic, the Bible was the work of ignorant men, and miracles should be dismissed as simple falsehoods.

Voltaire's consummate controversial skill won him a reputation far beyond the borders of France. In his native land his chief rival was not to be found among his many imitators and followers, but in a famous set of books, the *Encyclopedia*. Like Voltaire, Denis Diderot (1713–1784), the leading French encyclopedist, satirized the obscurity of Christian doctrine, poked fun at the petty squabbles of priests and clergymen, and ridiculed the numerous sects of Christianity.

Jean-Jacques Rousseau (1712–1778) was more moderate in his religious views. Voltaire rejected both Christianity and Christ; Rousseau accepted both. He recommended that "one should regard in silence what cannot be disproved or comprehended, and one should humble one's self before the Supreme Being who alone knows the truth." Rousseau proposed, nevertheless, to establish Deism as the national civil religion.

The attacks of the French Deists on Christianity presaged the intense anticlericalism of the French Revolution. But although Deism may be accounted as a revolutionary movement in France, it took root only among a small group of German and American intellectuals. Two of the leading German Deists were Hermann Samuel Reimarus (1694–1768), who denied the validity of miracles and maintained that natural religion was the absolute antithesis of revelation, and Gotthold Lessing (1729–1781), who, although he praised "true Christianity," published extracts of Reimarus' works and thereby exposed himself to much petty persecution. The classic German expression of Deism is to be found in the work of Immanuel Kant (1724–1804), who supported the deistic tenets of God, freedom, and immortality while defending religion unsupported by revelation.

Deism was transferred along with rationalistic political ideas to the American states, where Thomas Jefferson, John Adams, and Benjamin Franklin, among others, supported reason as the key to religion. The various threads of deistic arguments were synthesized by Thomas Paine (1737–1809), propagandist for Enlightenment and an important figure in both the American and French Revolutions. "I believe in one God and no more," Paine stated in *The Age of Reason* (1796), "and I hope for happiness beyond this life. I believe in the equality of man, and I believe that religious duties consist in doing justice, loving mercy and endeavoring to make our fellow-creatures happy. . . . I do not believe in the creed professed by the Jewish Church, by the Roman Church, by the Greek Church, by the Turkish Church, by the Protestant Church, nor by any Church that I know of. My own mind is my Church."

Defense of Christianity. The deistic attacks upon religion stimulated a spirited defense of Christianity. The argument took the form of questioning the validity of natural religion William Law (1686–1761), an English mystic, insisted that religion need not submit itself to any test of reason. "A course of plain undeniable miracles attesting the truth of revelation," he said, "is highest and utmost evidence of its coming from God, and not to be tried by our judgments about the reasonableness or necessity of its doctrines." In his *The Case of Reason, or Natural Religion Fairly Stated* (1732), Law claimed that revealed religion is as worthy of belief as natural religion. One must either abandon religion or abandon reason. In this case, Law, said, the latter must be rejected.

A strong attack upon Deism was made by Bishop Joseph Butler (1692–1752) in his *The Analogy of Religion, Natural and Revealed* (1737). Seeking to meet the Deists on their own ground, Butler claimed that revealed religion, as well as natural religion, could meet the tests of reason. Revelation, he said, supplemented and did not contradict reason, though he admitted that its content could be comprehended only obscurely. He warned that it was impossible for true revelation to oppose the dictates of conscience, for both come from God. Using the analogy of a two-edged sword, Butler maintained that both natural and revealed religion form a unit and cannot be separated. The course of nature, with all its mysteries, inconsistencies, and contradictions is just as incomprehensible to human reason as the so-called mysteries and injustices of the Scriptures.

Deism Evaluated. Deism as a religious movement was far too radical and unyielding for the Christian and, at the same time, too conservative and compromising for the religious radical. It left a permanent residue in nineteenth- and twentieth-century thought, particularly because of its emphasis upon religious toleration, its high regard for ethics, its attempts to harmonize religion with science, and its insistence upon regarding religion in the light of current intellectual and moral needs. Those who defended Deism praised it as a liberating influence in the emancipation of man from superstitition and supernaturalism. Critics continued to regard it as a destructive force which attacked traditional beliefs and offered nothing of value in their place.

Rise of Skepticism. The Skeptics denounced Deism as too restrained and timid and said that, like Christianity, it was beset by fallacies and inconsistencies. They were unwilling to acknowledge the existence of God, the truth of any religion, the divine origin of Christianity, and the validity of revelation. Thomas Hobbes (1588–1679) proclaimed to the heavens that he was a good Christian, and then proceeded to denounce religion as "accepted superstition," miracles as impossibilities, immortality as wishful thinking, and theological argumentation as "noise." "Religious and theological writings," he said, "fill our libraries and the world with their noise and uproar, but wherefrom the last thing we may expect is conviction."

Hume's Attack on Miracles. David Hume (1711–1776), Scottish philosopher and historian, ridiculed revelation and, at the same time, attacked natural religion. A confirmed agnostic, holding that God is unknowable, Hume said that the mind cannot comprehend God, because Absolute God cannot come into intimacy nor make Himself known to the finite mind. He rejected the idea that miracles provided the supreme proof for Christianity. In his *Essay on Miracles* (1748), he stated flatly that no testimony is sufficient to establish a miracle, unless the testimony be of such a kind

that its falsehood would be more miraculous than the fact which it endeavors to establish. "When anyone tells me," Hume wrote, "that he saw a dead man restored to life, I immediately consider with myself, whether it be more probable, that this person should either deceive or be deceived, or that the fact which he relates should have happened. I weigh the one miracle against the other; and according to the superiority, which I discover, I pronounce my decision, and always reject the greater miracle." Hume denounced miracles as violations of the laws of nature. He claimed that, since a firm and unalterable experience has established those laws, the proof against a miracle, from the very nature of the fact, is as entire as any argument from experience can possibly be imagined. He pointed out that the many instances of forged miracles, prophecies, and supernatural events, which, in all ages, have either been detected by contrary evidence, or which detect themselves by their absurdity, prove sufficiently the strong propensity of mankind to believe in the extraordinary and the marvelous.

Attacks on miracles were recurrent in rationalistic thought. For those who accepted the Newtonian concept of the universe, there could be no violation of nature's laws. Whatever the cause of miracles (and Hume did not deny that they could take place), the clue was to be sought in natural law and not in revelation.

Kant's Critique of Pure Reason. Kant's *Critique of Pure Reason* (1781) is probably the most celebrated defense of agnosticism ever written. Kant felt that all arguments to prove the existence of God, in order to be valid theoretically, must start from specifically and exclusively sensible or phenomenal data, must employ only the conceptions of pure science, and must end with demonstrating in sensible experience congruous with, or corresponding to, the idea of God. But this requirement cannot be met, for scientifically speaking, the existence of an absolutely necessary God cannot be either proved or disproved. Kant thus rejected entirely the old rational cosmology, theology, and philosophy, all of which, he said, profess to attain a knowledge of superphenomenal realities. He rejected rational theology, but in its place he tried to gain a more real and accessible faith which springs from man's consciousness. While God cannot be known as First Cause and Architect of the Universe, we can and must believe in him as a *moral* Governor. Man must seek, Kant advised, a high and austere morality, the true and basic function of religion.

Mechanistic Materialism: Atheism. The atheists denied the existence of God. Holding that a completely mechanistic interpretation of man and the universe offered a correct explanation, they claimed that no further additions were necessary. They denounced religion as useful only to priests and politicians and insisted that it is unnecessary as a means of improving man's moral and ethical conduct. Baron Paul Heinrich Dietrich d'Holbach (1723–1789), a French chemist and philosopher, of German origin, who settled in Paris, delivered powerful attacks on Christianity in his *System of Nature* (1770) and *Common Sense* (1772). There is nothing in the universe, he said, except matter in spontaneous movement. Holbach regarded religious feeling as a combination of superstitious fear and the desire to change unfavor-

able circumstances. Hence, he said, man believed in miracles and in the power of God to change the order of events to do man a favor—e.g., during droughts, men pray for rain. Holbach described God as naught but an exaggerated man, later spiritualized to absurdity. In ridiculing his fellow-men for their religious beliefs, Holbach was seeking a simple solution for all the ills of mankind. With gusto and conviction, he presented his views in black and white—there was knowledge (science, evidence) and there was ignorance (religion). Reject religion, he said, and the mind of man would soar; substitute knowledge for ignorance, and the millennium would arrive.

4. Natural Law and Society: The Science of Man

The Social Sciences. Although Newtonian scientific method tended to have a destructive effect upon religious traditions, it was responsible constructively for the creation of the modern social sciences. Distinct from such physical sciences as astronomy, physics, and chemistry, the social sciences may be defined as the mental or cultural disciplines devoted to the study of human relationships. The Greeks, the first secular-minded people to become in-

During the period of the Enlightenment, numerous societies were formed and met regularly for discussion and the exchange of ideas. Less formal, but perhaps even more frequent and spontaneous, were the gatherings of active minds—social philosophers, scientists, writers—in English coffee houses, French cafés, and drawing rooms on both sides of the Atlantic.

terested in man as man, had made many valuable contributions to the understanding of social relationships, but they had too little scientific knowledge to establish a solid structure of the social sciences. Until the Age of Reason, the ideas of political philosophy projected by Aristotle embraced all the social sciences. During the Middle Ages the social sciences were superseded by theology, which regarded man's functioning in the group as important only so far as it affected salvation in the world to come. The rationalists broke political philosophy down into its component elements. This, they believed, was their crowning glory. They sought for demonstrable laws to explain human institutions and behavior. They were certain that natural law could be applied to man and society as well as nature.

Scientific Materialism: Hobbes. Influenced by rapid advances in the mathematical and physical sciences, Thomas Hobbes (1588–1679) attempted to construct a universal system of human knowledge which would explain man and society in the same manner as it explained natural phenomena. He accepted Newton's concept of a world in mechanical harmony and he used the language of mathematics projected by Descartes. He would apply the new principles of mathematics and mechanics to mind as well as matter. Man, in both body and soul, said Hobbes, is an integral part of the natural order. The soul of man is not a spiritual substance distinct from matter, but is the result of the organization of matter in the body. It is possible to construct a science of human nature in the sense of a human physics. All that is needed is to observe and analyze the processes of thought in one's own mind; from these we can learn to know what the thoughts of other men are on like occasions.

Hobbes reasoned that man, in common with the rest of the universe, was fashioned like a machine and functioned like one. He projected a theory of sensationalism, according to which the fundamental element of human life is to be found in matter in motion—the only reality in the world outside of man's mind. "All that exists is body (matter); all that occurs is motion." When this motion comes into contact with man's sense organs, certain sensations take place. All knowledge is derived from these sensations. It follows that all positive knowledge is the direct result of the impact of bodily particles on sense organs.

Empiricism: Locke. John Locke (1632–1704), English philosopher, scientist, and physician, is generally regarded as the founder of the school of empiricism, which believes that knowledge comes only from sensory experience. In his *Essay Concerning Human Understanding* (1690), Locke popularized Hobbes' theory of sensationalism. The effect of this work may be judged by the fact that it went through twenty editions within ten years. According to Locke, the mind at birth is a *tabula rasa*, a blank tablet, upon which all sensations, and ultimately all thoughts, are written. The materials of reason and knowledge spring from experience, upon which all knowledge is founded and from which it ultimately derives itself. Our observation either of external objects or about the operations of our minds, perceived and reflected on by ourselves, is that which supplies our understanding with all the materials of thinking. These are the fountains of knowledge whence spring all the ideas we have, or can naturally have. Here is the chain which explains how the human mind becomes stocked with ideas: All knowledge begins with the reception of sensations from without; these sensations become images; these images, in turn, are elaborated in a chain; and the chain becomes intelligible thought. Once the understanding is stored with simple ideas, it has the power to repeat, compare, and unite them even to an almost infinite variety, and so we can make, at will, complex new ideas.

Locke, in effect, was attacking Plato's doctrine of innate ideas, that is, that ideas are inherent in the mind at birth. The struggle between those who advocate heredity and those who emphasize environment as decisive for the human mind is one which has persisted among scientists to the present day. The importance of Locke in intellectual history is that, in demonstrating that knowledge should be based upon experience and reason, he literally created a new science of the human mind.

Equality: Helvétius. From the generalizations on sensationalism by Hobbes and Locke to the concept of the democratic ideal was but a short step. Claude Adrien Helvétius (1715–1771), French reformer and idealist, believed that since all human beings at birth have exactly the same mind, and since all knowledge they acquire is the result of environmental influences, it must follow logically that all men must be equal at birth. He rejected the idea that the masses are mentally inferior, arguing that they are mentally just as capable as the upper classes, but simply lack opportunity. He believed that educational opportunities for all classes are essential and reasonable. He described the art of education as placing young people in a set of circumstances fitted to develop in them the germs of intelligence and virtue. There would be a better society, he argued, if reforming monarchs would recognize the equality of all men and grant them equal rights.

Idea of Social Progress. Helvétius was among the first rationalists to express the opinion that social progress was both possible and desirable. The medieval emphasis upon the future world and its insistence that the present world was an inferior and sinful place left little ground for the fullness of joy on earth. The rationalists were more optimistic about the possibility of social progress. They felt that, although there had been but little biological change in man since ancient times, there had been remarkable progress in human learning. Each generation, they said, inherits the intellectual possessions of its predecessors and adds its own achievements. The future of man lies in his own hands. He can use his brain to strive for perfection or he can work for his own destruction.

This concept of social progress was an impelling element in the work of Giovanni Battista Vico (1668–1744), Italian jurist and philosopher, who utilized it in constructing his version of the story of civilization. Vico saw in the development of man the motivating power of a law of cycles—divine, heroic, and human, each successive stage higher than the preceding one. He described the history of humanity as a process of development from "poetic wisdom," the impersonal, instinctive ideas of primitive society, to "occult wisdom," which turns divinely implanted ideas into conscious philosophical wisdom.

The most elaborate exposition of the idea of social progress was that made by the Marquis de Condorcet (1743–1794), French philosopher, mathematician, and freethinker. In his *Outline of an Historical Picture of the Progress of the Human Mind* (1795), Condorcet theorized that the human race was continually advancing toward perfection. He divided the history of mankind into nine epochs: (1) hunters and fishermen; (2) shepherds; (3) tillers of the soil; (4) commerce, science, and philosophy in Greece; (5) science and philosophy from Alexander to the decline of the Roman Empire; (6) the decadence of science to the Crusades; (7) from the Crusades to the invention of printing; (8) from the invention of printing to the philosophical revolution effected by Descartes; and (9) from Descartes to the Revolution of 1789, including the discoveries of Locke, Newton, and Rousseau, when reason, tolerance, and humanitarianism became the watchwords of man. In the tenth epoch—that of the future—man will progress to the point at which all inequalities of opportunity will be destroyed, and individual human nature will be perfected. The key factor in this progress will be popular education.

The New Political Economy. The application of natural law to economics brought the emergence of a system of political economy, with its own theories and symbols. The rising middle class, driving for political and economic power, began to see economics, like the universe, religion, and man, as subject to natural law. It judged the mercantile system outmoded. Mercantilism had been developed in Europe as the medieval and manorial systems decayed; its policies were to obtain a favorable balance of trade, to develop agriculture and manufactures, to create a merchant marine, to establish foreign trade monopolies, and above all, to keep commercial enterprises under state control. By the middle of the eighteenth century, the merchant and manufacturing classes had become so powerful that they began to resent state interference in their affairs and called for freedom of action. The middle class wanted protection for its rights of property and contract, but at the same time, it insisted upon freedom from interference. The idea of natural law provided a perfect outlet for the demands of the manufacturing and business entrepreneurs. A body of doctrine was devised to assist the attack on mercantilism and to prove that capitalism and natural law were in complete harmony. Nature, it was said, meant the businessman to be entirely free in his aim to obtain profits. Any attempt to destroy that freedom was a violation of the laws of nature.

Economic Liberalism. Economic liberalism, which extolled capitalism, individual liberty, and natural law, was closely identified with the principle of *laissez-faire* ("Let Alone," or "Hands Off!"). The *laissez-faire* school was founded by a group of French physiocrats, who received their name from a book written in 1767 by Pierre Du Pont de Nemours, *Physiocracy, or The Natural Constitution of That Form of Government Most Advantageous to the Human Race.* All human institutions—economic, social, and political—said the physiocrats, are governed by natural law. They can be perfected only if they are made to conform to the natural order. Any legislative attempts to curb economic processes will violate natural law and lead to much unhappiness and misery. The government, in the physiocrats' view, should limit itself to the protection of life and property and to the promotion of public works and education. Private property, especially land, must be placed above everything else. Commerce and industry are of great utility to society, but they must be made subservient to agriculture. It was to the interest of all that restrictions on agriculture be removed, that there be complete freedom of cultivation, and that each individual be permitted to engage in free competition—"the mainspring of human perfectibility." Du Pont de Nemours (1739–1817), François Quesnay (1694–1774), and Jean Vincent, Sieur de Gournay (1712–1759) presented an elaborate structure of physiocratic reasoning, all of which was given a practical application by Baron de Turgot (1727–1781).

Adam Smith (1723–1790), a Scottish philosopher, published his great work, *An Inquiry into the Nature and Causes of the Wealth of Nations,* in 1776. Smith's doctrines were not completely new, in that he took a mass of fragmentary ideas and arranged them into an organized system of economics. Instead of drawing conclusions from abstract principles, he observed the socioeconomic facts around him and then sought to elicit their significance. He concluded that economic life is ordered by laws of nature. Mercantilism, he believed, had arisen from the mistaken theory that wealth consists in money. Once this theory had been established in general belief, it became the great object of political economy to diminish as much as possible the importation of foreign goods for home consumption and to increase as much as possible the exportation of domestic products. This, according to Smith, was fallacious and evil.

The policy of economic freedom was beneficial when applied to business, but its effects on the workers were quite the opposite. Increasing industrialization led to widespread unemployment, poverty, and disease. Could it possibly be that there were immutable natural laws which made these conditions inevitable? Answers were given by Malthus and Ricardo, who have been called the creators of the "dismal science" of *laissez-faire* economics.

Law of Populations: Malthus. In 1798 Thomas Robert Malthus (1766–1834), an English clergyman and social philosopher, published anonymously the first edition of *An Essay on the Principles of Population.* This original edition, written largely from memory and without substantiating material, aroused a storm of controversy. Malthus later published a second version full of detail and abundantly documented. According to Malthus, population, when unchecked, increases in geometrical ratio (1, 2, 4, 8, 16, 32 . . .), while subsistence increases only in arithmetical ratio (1, 2, 3, 4, 5 . . .). Population always increases up to the limit of the means of subsistence. It is prevented from going beyond this limit by the positive checks of war, famine, and pestilence, as well as by misery and vice. Whereas population is capable of doubling itself at least once in every twenty-five years, and because the supply of food can increase only in arithmetical ratio, it follows that the increase of population must always be checked by the lack of food. But, except in case of famine, this check is never operative.

In spite of the checks of moral restraint, vice, and misery, Malthus went on, there is a constant tendency for population to increase beyond the means of subsistence. Such an increase is followed by lower wages, higher prices, and a lower marriage and birth rate. The lower classes, in turn, induce more agricultural enterprise, whereby the means of subsistence become more abundant again. Cheaper and more ample food then promotes marriage and increases the population, until again there is a shortage of food. This oscillation, although somewhat irregular, will always be found, and there will always be a tendency for the population to fluctuate around the food limit. Malthus saw no way in which man could escape from the weight of this law "which pervades all animated nature." He was profoundly pessimistic about the possibilities for future progress of mankind.

Iron Law of Wages: Ricardo. David Ricardo (1772–1823), English economist, pamphleteer, banker, and member of Parliament, had little sympathy for the working class, which he regarded as an instrument in the hands of successful entrepreneurs. He believed the misery of the workers to be inevitable and permanent, a result of the unchangeable natural laws governing human nature. There was an irreconcilable antagonism, he said, among the three groups of the community—landowners, capitalists, and wage-earners. In his subsistence theory of wages, also called the "iron law of wages," Ricardo asserted that wages for the worker always decline to a point at which they provide him only with the means of keeping body and soul together. "The natural price of labor is that price which is necessary to enable the laborers one with another to subsist and to perpetuate their race without either increase or diminution." Since there is only a definite amount of wages for the worker, if one gets more than his share the rest will suffer. "The only solution is to render less frequent among them early and improvident marriages."

Malthus was a benevolent clergyman and Ricardo was considered an upright businessman, but both came to exceedingly pessimistic conclusions. They were convinced that poverty and misery were a part of God's natural order and were as certain as the rising of the sun. Critics denounced both Malthusian and Ricardoan doctrines because of their "incomplete data, defective methods, and misleading conclusions." But contemporaries of the two believed in their ideas and used them to resist any change. This was the tightly held dogma of the bourgeois entrepreneurs—if there were to be any adjustment of the miserable conditions of the workingman, it could occur only as a consequence of the natural order. Man himself could do nothing.

5. From Absolutism to Popular Sovereignty: Natural Law and Government

Theory of Natural Rights. In politics, rationalists constructed a body of theory which, together with the profound socioeconomic changes taking place in the eighteenth century, helped bring about the French Revolution and its effects upon the whole of Europe. Efforts to rationalize political life on the basis of universal principles took two main directions. One school of thought, originating in the seventeenth century and continuing in the eighteenth, wished to justify absolutism in government as consonant with the laws of nature. The second, and by far the more important school, used scientific arguments to support democracy and constitutionalism, tolerance and popular sovereignty. From this school emerged the theory of natural rights of man.

Four Theories of Government. Four trends may be noted in eighteenth-century political science:

1. *Scientific argument in support of absolutism:* the idea of a scientific and enlightened despotism, which had strong roots in all Western Europe, with the exception of England, until the French Revolution.

2. *Scientific argument in support of constitutionalism:* the English idea of constitutionalism based on natural rights, popularized by the Frenchman, Montesquieu.

3. *Scientific argument in support of democracy:* the idea that democracy is by far the best of all possible political systems, since it is based on natural rights. This view was projected and popularized by Rousseau.

4. *Development of utilitarianism:* a rationalized exposition of sociopolitical problems, judging any scheme of society by its usefulness, founded by Jeremy Bentham.

Benevolent Absolutism. The idea of an enlightened, scientific despotism was promoted by a group of intellectuals who had little or no faith in the common man, but a fervent belief in the sacred economic laws of property and security. Opposed to *absolute* monarchy, which they regarded as an outworn vestige of earlier societies, they agreed to accept the political leadership of a monarch, provided that he showed due respect for the natural rights of man, such as political, social, economic, and religious freedom. They were willing to tolerate such enlightened despots as Frederick the Great, Catherine II, and Joseph II, so long as these monarchs enforced the natural rights of the bourgeoisie. Thomas Hobbes approved the idea of absolute monarchy and believed that the sovereign's formal judgment was the law of God and Nature. This point of view was of little interest to the rising middle class, which saw ultimate sovereignty in itself and not in the person of the monarch. What the bourgeoisie wanted was a system of government which would protect it simultaneously against the envy of the masses and the dominance of a powerful monarch.

Literary Weapon: The *Encyclopedia.* Among the most enthusiastic proponents of enlightened despotism were the Encyclopedists. Diderot and Jean d'Alembert, perpetual secretary of the French Academy of Sciences, visualized the *Encyclopedia*—to which Voltaire, Montesquieu, Buffon, Quesnay, Rousseau, d'Holbach, and others contributed—as the first important attempt to create a positive synthesis of human knowledge. Its aim, according to Diderot, was "to gather together the knowledge scattered over the face of the earth, to set forth its general plan to the men with whom we live, and to transmit it to the men who will come after us." More precisely, its goal was to combat the older systems of thought based on tradition and authority and substitute for them an edifice of knowledge based on science and reason. Perhaps no encyclopedia has ever been of such great political importance, for it attempted not only to inform but to guide opinion. The organ of the most advanced and revolutionary opinions of the time, it became an intellectual weapon and a proselytizing agent for freethinking rationalists. Its execution was unequal, with excellent contributions mingled among loosely written articles. Much of its material was verbose, dogmatic, and inaccurate. It was denounced by governmental and ecclesiastical authorities as "the work of an organized band of conspirators against society," and was ridiculed as "chaos, nothingness, the Tower of Babel, a work of disorder and destruction, the gospel of Satan." But it was a mighty instrument in unifying the scattered ideas of the *philosophes* and in spreading their beliefs. Thousands of sets were published in France and translations were issued throughout Europe.

Anti-Despotism: Montesquieu. The leading theorist of anti-despotism was Charles Louis de Secondat, Baron de la Brède et de Montesquieu (1689–1755). Born near Bordeaux, Montesquieu was president of the Bordeaux court of justice for ten years. Interested in the philosophy of law, rather than in administration, he traveled over Europe to study political and legal systems. For twenty years he worked on his book, *De l'Esprit des lois (The Spirit of Laws)*, which he published anonymously in 1748. In this book Montesquieu surveyed every political system, ancient and modern, examined the principles and defects of each one, and came to the conclusion that English constitutionalism should be the model for all countries. He postulated three types of government: republican, monarchical, and despotic. Under a republic, he said, the people, or a part of the people, have the sovereign power. Under a monarchy, one man alone rules, but by fixed and established laws. Under a despotism, a single man, without law or regulation, impels everything according to his will or caprice. Montesquieu indicated a strong distaste for the latter form. Its requisite, he said, was the prevalence of fear.

Montesquieu contrasted the despotic state with the popular state. In the latter the people are divided into certain classes. The way in which this division is carried out plays an important part in the duration of a democracy and its prosperity. Election by lot is the democratic method, which allows every citizen a reasonable hope of serving his country. In a democracy, everything depends upon the political virtues of the people. When a democracy loses its patriotism, its frugality, and its passion for equality, it is soon destroyed. The principle of democracy may grow corrupt, not only when a people loses its spirit of equality, but also when this spirit of equality becomes excessive, with each man desiring to be the equal of those whom he has chosen to rule over him.

Science of Society. More than any other writer of his century, Montesquieu was responsible for the development of a unified science of human society. Sensitive to the delicate complexity of social organisms, he realized that an enormous amount of investigation was essential before any improvements could be made in legislation and government. His life was devoted to the accumulation of facts, from which he inferred concrete recommendations. He strongly influenced his contemporaries by his championing of the right of remonstrance, his skillful thrusts at slavery, his denunciation of religious intolerance, his attack on primitive penal codes, and his eulogy of commerce as a stimulus to civilization. He prepared the foundations for nineteenth-century jurisprudence and sociology. His great and enduring book

not only stimulated the movement which culminated in the French Revolution, but it also induced those nations which sought for some golden mean between despotism and mob-rule to adopt the British parliamentary system.

The Idea of Tolerance. The principle of tolerance was one of the most persistent ideas of the Age of Reason. Rationalists argued that even error should be permitted to exist and must not be attacked except by reason. It was wrong, they said, to force any man to believe what his reason tells him is false. There is no truth sure enough to justify persecution. This point of view was expressed eloquently by England's great epic poet, John Milton (1608–1674). When the Long Parliament in 1643 published an order regulating the printing, circulation, and importation of books, Milton published his *Areopagitica*, a classic defense of freedom of conscience and speech. The central core of Milton's faith was liberty, the most powerful, beneficial, and sacred factor in human progress.

Nothing escaped the fearless, caustic, and irreverent pen of Voltaire, "that mere skeleton with a long nose and eyes of preternatural brilliancy peering out of his wig." In his prodigious literary production he attacked and lampooned royal absolutism, serfdom, slavery, war, ecclesiastical abuses, judicial incompetence, and ignorance. But the recurrent theme of his works was his fierce opposition to intolerance, bigotry, and superstition. Not only did Voltaire use his powerful pen in the struggle for liberty of conscience, but he also plunged into the battle by opposing intolerance wherever he saw it. (*See page 251 ff.*)

Social Contract. The idea of a social contract between people and ruler had been forecast by Plato and had been developed in Roman and medieval thought. With the revival of Roman law in the Middle Ages, the social-contract idea was taken over by the temporal authorities as a weapon against the supremacy of the Church. In its general sense, this theory held that authority, resting originally with the people, had been conferred by them on the ruler, so that he could perform the necessary functions of state. There were two possible interpretations: the theory could be used to assert the authority of the ruler, or it could be used to show the sovereignty of the people as the ultimate source of that authority. In the Age of Reason the idea of the social contract was revived as a doctrinal counterbalance to the theory of the divine right of kings. It could be employed as a weapon by which the subjects might justify their resistance to the acts of an unrestrained despot.

In his *Leviathan, or the Matter, Form, and Power of a Commonwealth* (1651), Thomas Hobbes conceived of the Commonwealth or State ("Leviathan") as an artificial man. "Nature," Hobbes wrote, "the art whereby God hath made and governs the world, is by the art of man so imitated that he can make an artificial animal. For by art is created the great leviathan called a Commonwealth, or state, which is but an artificial man; in which the sovereignty is an artificial soul, as giving life and motion; the magistrates and other officers the joints; reward and punishment the nerves; concord, health; discord, sickness; lastly, the pacts or covenants by which the parts were first set together resembles the 'fiat' of God at the Creation." Hobbes found the origin of sovereignty in an original compact, whereby man, weary of war—"the state of nature"— agrees to submit to the authority of an individual or a group strong enough to maintain order and security. Otherwise, the life of man must remain "solitary, poor, nasty, brutish, and short." The common power thus set up both restrains and protects every individual.

In Hobbes' view, the sovereignty may be in one man, or in a limited assembly, or in an assembly of all—monarchy, aristocracy, democracy; these three forms only, though when they are not liked they are called other names. In any case, the power of the sovereign is absolute, whether a monarchy or an assembly. It matters not who the sovereign power is, only that he be powerful. Hobbes himself favored absolute monarchy, which he regarded as a political necessity ("If two men ride upon a horse one must ride in front"), but he was dissatisfied with divine right as a basis for it. Repelled by the Great Rebellion of 1649,

Hobbes refused to sanction the right of revolution which the social contract implied.

Locke's Version. A different version of the social contract was projected by John Locke in his *Two Treatises of Government* (1690), which was written to justify the Glorious Revolution of 1688. Locke gave these stages in the formation of the social contract:

1. Men originally lived in a state of nature, without law, order, or government, but possessing certain natural rights, such as life, liberty, and property, all of which were inalienable, sacred, and inherent in nature.

2. This condition was inconvenient, dangerous, and unsatisfactory, because the strong oppressed the weak, and the life of man was poor and short.

3. The more rational members of society therefore agreed to institute a government to maintain order and to guarantee the enjoyment of man's natural rights. By common consent, rulers and ruled entered into an agreement, or social contract.

4. The contract, or constitution, defined the rights and powers of both rulers and ruled. The people—the ruled—gave up some of their rights to the government, but did not surrender their basic, natural rights.

5. The dissolution of the contract—revolution—is justifiable when the terms of the contract are violated by the rulers.

6. Thus, the people are the real rulers, and if a majority of them declares that the contract has been broken, they have the right to rebel and install a new government. Popular sovereignty, it follows, is a precious possession of the people.

Popular Sovereignty: Rousseau. The doctrine of the social contract took a revolutionary shape in the hands of Rousseau. His *Contrat social* (1762) attributed all government to the consent, direct or implied, of the governed. "Man is born free, and yet is everywhere in chains." Abandoning his originally free state, man had accepted the chains of government. All civil governments exist by virtue of the social contract or agreement, whereby each individual surrenders his rights to the central

This painting of a public book-burning in Geneva, 1763, depicts an attempt by the established government to stop the spread of "dangerous" ideas such as those put forth in Rousseau's *Contrat social* and *Émile.*

authority in accordance with the will of all members of the community. If a ruler rejects the sovereignty of the people, and therefore violates the agreement, he must recognize the fact that the people have a natural right to overthrow him. "The essence of the pact," Rousseau wrote, "is the total and unreserved alienation by each partner of all his rights to the community as a whole."

Rousseau thus converted Locke's dry-as-dust projection into a magnificent piece of popular political propaganda. There were fantastic arguments and gaping flaws in Rousseau's exposition of the social contract. Yet, curiously, its mixture of eloquence and logic was exactly the sort of approach which could set the minds of men on fire and carry the multitude with it. Rousseau's *Contrat social* became one of the most important inspirations for the tremendous events of the French Revolution. The watchwords "Liberty, Equality, and Fraternity" were taken directly from Rousseau's book. What Rousseau did was to place democracy squarely on the basis of natural rights, systematize it as a conception, and give it direction. He wanted man to return to the primitive way of life, which he felt to be a happy one, whereas civilization, with its knowledge, laws, and cosmopolitan institutions, had brought only wickedness and misery. Democracy was not only a natural right of man but was also best suited to his spiritual nature.

Historical Controversy: Liberty or Authority? The thinkers of the Age of Reason were involved in a great debate over the nature of man and the State. Historians concerned with the Enlightenment continue the discussion.

The problem is a complex one, and there are difficult questions. Were the rationalists trying to promote the freedom of the individual citizen, his right to do what he wanted subject to a minimum of restraint by the government; or were they, on the other hand, trying to impose on men, for their own good, a more enlightened and efficient government? Were the rationalists proponents of individual liberty or collective authority? Was the ideal society one that turned to the direction of anarchism, or one that preferred enlightened despotism, another way of saying authoritarianism? There are no easy answers: the debate still goes on.

In his *Contrat social* (1762), Rousseau stated his basic principle:

> Each of us puts his person and all his power in common under the supreme direction of the general will, and, in our corporate capacity, we receive each member as an indivisible part of the whole.

This was interpreted in two ways: some saw in it a defense of individual freedom: others said that it was plainly a defense of collective authority. Rousseau himself, with his somewhat nebulous views, gave no satisfactory solution. His ideas have been used to justify both democracy and dictatorship.

Utilitarianism: Bentham. To the Utilitarians it was unimportant whether any scheme of society was natural or divine. What counted was whether it was reasonable and socially useful. This point of view was expressed by Jeremy Bentham (1748–1832), an English philosopher and jurist, in his *Introduction to Principles of Morals and Legislation* (1789). Bentham defined utility as that property in any object whereby it tends to produce pleasure, good, or happiness, or to prevent the happening of mischief, evil, or unhappiness to the party whose interest is considered. "The principle of utility," he wrote, "makes utility the criterion for approval or disapproval of every kind of action. An act which conforms to this principle is one which ought to be done, or is not one which ought not to be done; is right, or, at least, not wrong. There is no other

criterion possible which cannot ultimately be reduced to the personal sentiment of the individual."

The idea of utilitarianism was not new, but Bentham cemented the alliance between utility and happiness, placed it on the plane of science, and made it into a faith. He shifted economics and politics to the serene, impersonal sphere of mathematics. Applied to the discipline of economics, utilitarianism called for free trade, low taxes, efficient government, abolition of monopoly, and unlimited competition. Applied to politics, it advocated a constitutional government enforcing security and justice, individual liberty, and civil liberties. All these were useful and hence desirable. These views were supported by James Mill (1773–1836) and his son, John Stuart Mill (1806–1873), both of whom sought to show the harmony of utilitarianism and economic liberalism.

6. Revolt Against the Enlightenment: Romanticism

Rise of a Counter-Movement. About the middle of the seventeenth century the term romantic began to be used as the rough equivalent of "freely imaginative," "visionary," or "extraordinary." Later, it became a revolt against the Enlightenment, distinguished by a reaction against the scientific method. It laid stress on emotion and individualism, and urged a return to the Middle Ages. Romantics stressed the claims of the imagination, of emotion and feeling, above all for a synthetic expression of the national genius in all its manifold aspects of literature, art, religion, and politics. Though at first little concerned with politics and the state, romanticism played an important role in the development of nationalism.

The first collective manifestation of romanticism appeared in the Germanies in the early 1770's, when youthful protagonists of the cult of genius rallied around the slogan of *Sturm und Drang* (Storm and Stress). The new doctrine emphasized intuition and mysticism, originality and power, a vindication of childhood as preached by Rousseau, and objections to French *Vernunftelei* (sterile rationalism). These young Germans glorified crime, as in Schiller's *Die Räuber,* and exalted suicide, as in Goethe's *Werther,* whose hero killed himself as a protest against the social hierarchy.

The classic expression of German romanticism appears in the work of the Grimm brothers, Jakob Ludwig Karl Grimm (1785–1863) and Wilhelm Karl Grimm (1786–1859), who devoted themselves to the scientific study of the German language and literature, and also produced the well-known fairy tales. In their philological investigations the Grimms sought to unlock the poetry and experiences of the German people which were encased in words and dramatic forms. They saw the organic conception of culture as an expression of the German national soul which had its beginnings in the heroic Middle Ages. They issued a plea for the claims of the imagination, of emotion and feeling, of individualism. "I strove to penetrate the wild forests of our ancestors," wrote Wilhelm Grimm, "listening to their whole language, and watching their pure customs."

In the Germanies as well as other European countries, romanticism attracted many shades of political opinion: humanitarians, esthetes, even champions of totalitarianism. Gradually, over the course of the nineteenth century, the literary expressions of romanticism were exhausted, while its philosophical and political implications began to receive more and more emphasis. By the twentieth century there emerged a movement called Fascism, a romantic synthesis composed of nationalism and socialism. The consciousness of national genius inevitably led to claims of the inequality of human races and the superiority of one people over another.

Historical Controversy: The Problem of Romanticism. Romanticism took a variety of forms because of the multiplicity of tendencies which went into its making. As it became an international movement, its original philosophic nucleus was engulfed in a mass of contradictions, from sentiment to restless fury to mystic symbolism. The problem is essentially one of definition. The main difficulty lies in this: if romanticism is a movement, then how can a unity be made out of its obvious diversity and contradictions? Jacques Barzun, intellectual historian and social critic, sought to resolve the difficulty by distinguishing between "historic romanticism," a group of men living as contemporaries between 1770 and 1850, and "intrinsic romanticism," an *attitude* which became noticeable and dominant in that period. He links all romanticists "on the double problem of making a new world and making it in the knowledge that man is creative and limited."

Some historians reject the idea of using such convenient signposts as the Renaissance, the Industrial Revolution, or the Enlightenment, and dismiss all such designations as figments of the imagination. Thus Arthur O. Lovejoy insisted that there is no such thing as romanticism. One could speak, he said, of several romantic movements, "but only confusion and error can result from the quest of some suppositious intrinsic nature of a hypostatized essence called 'romanticism.' " He admitted "a massive historical fact" of a large number of influential ideas in the 1780's and 1790's, which developed, ramified, and were diffused and which profoundly altered habitual preconceptions and valuations. But he protested the use of the word "romanticism" as a "ruling catchword" to describe this period.

ᕦ KEY DOCUMENT ᕤ

VOLTAIRE: PHILOSOPHICAL DICTIONARY

Voltaire, *Philosophical Dictionary* (Boston, 1856), II, pp. 132, 344, 356–357, 360 ff. Adapted.

FRANÇOIS-MARIE AROUET (1694–1778), known by his assumed name of Voltaire, was born in Paris the son of a well-to-do notary, and was educated by the Jesuits in the

Collège Louis-le-Grand. He never ceased speculating and satirizing, a tendency that led to his being twice exiled from Paris and twice imprisoned in the Bastille. Poet of a royal court, friend of princes and politicians, idol of beautful women, gambler and wit, this long-nosed, beady-eyed rebel lived a full life, dying at eighty-four from exhaustion after a party in his honor. His life span covered nearly the whole of the eighteenth century, of which he was the dominant literary symbol, producing masterpieces in every department of letters then in vogue. These extracts from his *Philosophical Dictionary* illustrate his biting satire and his conception of Deism (Theism). Note particularly his oft-quoted essay on tolerance. These extracts reveal several of the key ideas of the Age of Reason.

General Reflection on Man

It needs twenty years to lead man from the plant state in which he is within his mother's womb, and the pure animal state which is the lot of his early childhood, to the state at which the maturity of his reason begins to appear. It has taken some thirty centuries to learn a little about his structure. It would need an eternity to learn something about his soul. It takes but an instant to kill him.

Superstition

The superstitious man is to the rogue what the slave is to the tyrant. Further still, the superstitious man is governed by the fanatic and himself becomes fanatic. Born in paganism, superstition was adopted by Judaism, and infested the Christian Church from the earliest times. All the Fathers of the Church, without any exception, believed in the power of magic. The Church herself always condemned magic, but she nevertheless always believed in it. She did not excommunicate sorcerers as mistaken madmen, but as men who were in reality in communication with the devil.

Today a half of Europe thinks that the other half has long been and still is under the influence of superstition. The Protestants look upon relics, indulgences, mortifications, prayers for the dead, holy water, and all the rites of the Roman Church, as superstitious dementia. According to them, superstition consists in taking useless practices for necessary practices. Among the Roman Catholics there are some more enlightened than their ancestors, who have renounced many of the usages formerly regarded as sacred; they defend themselves against the others who have

retained them by saying: "They are indifferent, and what is merely indifferent cannot be classed as an evil." . . .

In Christian societies, therefore, no one agrees as to what superstition is. The sect which seems to be the least attacked by this malady of the intelligence is that which has the fewest rites. . . .

The less superstition, the less fanaticism; and the less fanaticism, the less misery.

Theist

The theist is a man firmly persuaded for the existence of a Supreme Being as good as He is powerful, who has formed all beings with extension, vegetating, sentient and reflecting, who perpetuates their species, who punishes crime without cruelty, and rewards virtuous actions with kindness.

The theist does not know how God punishes, how He protects, how He pardons, for he is not reckless enough to flatter himself that he knows how God acts, but he does know that God acts and that He is just. Difficulties against Providence do not shake him in his faith, because they remain merely great difficulties, and not proofs. He submits to this Providence, even though he perceives but a few effects and a few signs of this Providence, and, judging the things he does not see by the things which he does see, he considers that this Providence reaches all places and all centuries.

Reconciled with the rest of the universe by this principle, he does not embrace any of the sects, all of which contradict one another. His religion is really the oldest and most widespread, for the simple worship of God has come before all the systems of the world. . . .

Tolerance

What is tolerance? It is the consequence of humanity. All of us are formed of frailty and error. Let us mutually pardon each other's folly. That is the first law of nature.

It is quite clear that the individual who persecutes a man, his brother, because he is not of the same opinion, is nothing more than a monster. That admits of no difficulty. But the Government! The Magistrates! The Princes! How do they treat those who have different worships from theirs? . . .

Of all religions, the Christian is no doubt the one which should inspire tolerance most, although to this point in history the Christians have been the most intolerant of men. The Christian Church was divided in its cradle, and was divided even in the persecutions which under the first emperors it sometimes endured. Often the martyr was regarded as an apostate by his brethren, and the Carpocratian Christian expired beneath the sword of the Roman executioners, excommunicated by the Edionite Christian, which in its turn was anathema to the Sabellian.

This terrible discord, which has lasted for so many centuries, is a very striking lesson that we should pardon each other's errors. Discord is the great ill of mankind. Tolerance is the only remedy for it. . . .

Every sect, as one knows, is a ground of error; there are no sects of geometers, algebraists, arithmeticians, because all the propositions of geometry, algebra, and arithmetic are true. In every other science one may be deceived. What Thomist or Scotist theologian would dare say seriously that he is certain of his case?

If it were permitted to reason consistently in religious matters, it is clear that we all ought to become Jews, because Jesus Christ our Savior was born a Jew, lived a Jew, died a Jew, and because he said expressly that he was accomplishing and fulfilling the Jewish religion. But it is clearer still that we ought to be tolerant of one another, because we are all weak, inconsistent, liable to fickleness and error. Shall a reed laid low in the mud by the wind say to a fellow reed fallen in the opposite direction: "Crawl as I crawl, wretch, or I shall petition that you be torn up by the roots and burned!"

❦ HISTORICAL INTERPRETATION ❧

CARL L. BECKER ON THE TEMPER OF EIGHTEENTH-CENTURY THOUGHT

Carl L. Becker, *The Heavenly City of the Eighteenth-Century Philosophers* (New Haven, Conn., 1932), pp. 28–31. By permission of Yale University Press.

CORNELL UNIVERSITY's distinguished Carl L. Becker disclosed the fallacy of believing that the eighteenth century was completely modern in its temper. In a needed corrective, he showed that the Age of Reason was far from that. The *Philosophes,* he said, lived in a medieval world and "demolished the Heavenly City of St. Augustine only to rebuild it with more up-to-date materials." The underlying conceptions of the eighteenth century "were essentially the same as those of the thirteenth century."

If I could stand on high and pronounce judgment on [the *Philosophes*], estimate authoritatively the value of their philosophy, tell wherein it is true, wherein false—if I could only do all th's it would be grand. But this, unfortunately, is not possible. Living in the twentieth century, I am limited by the preconceptions of my age. It was therefore inevitable that I should approach the subject from the historical point of view; and if I have been at great pains to contrast the climate of opinion of Dante's time with that of our own, it is merely in order to provide the historical setting in which the ideas of the *Philosophes* may be placed. Before the historian can do anything with Newton and Voltaire, he has to make it clear that they came, historically speaking, after Dante and Thomas Aquinas and before Einstein and H. G. Wells. . . . The modern mind has a predilection for looking at men and things in this way; it finds a high degree of mental satisfaction in doing it. . . .

We are accustomed to think of the eighteenth century as essentially modern in its temper. Certainly, the *Philosophes* themselves made a great point of having renounced the superstition and hocus-pocus of medieval Christian thought, and we have usually been willing to take them at their word. Surely, we say, the eighteenth century was preeminently the age of reason, surely the *Philosophes* were a skeptical lot, atheists in effect if not by profession, addicted to science and the scientific method, always out to crush the infamous, valiant defenders of liberty, equality, fraternity, freedom of speech, and what you will. All very true. And yet I think the *Philosophes* were nearer the Middle Ages, less emancipated from the preconceptions of medieval Christian thought, than they quite realized or we have commonly supposed. If we have done them more (or is it less?) than justice in giving them a good modern character, the reason is that they speak a familiar language. We read Voltaire more readily than Dante, and follow an argument by Hume more easily than one by Thomas Aquinas. But I think our appreciation is of the surface more than of the fundamentals of their thought. We agree with them more readily when they are witty and cynical than when they are wholly serious. Their negations rather than their affirmations enable us to treat them as kindred spirits.

But, if we examine the foundations of their faith, we find that at every turn the *Philosophes* betray their debt to medieval thought without being aware of it. They denounced Christian philosophy, but rather too much, after the manner of those who are but half emancipated from the "superstitions" they scorn. They had put off the fear of God, but maintained a respectful attitude toward the Deity. They ridiculed the idea that the universe had been created in six days, but still believed it to be a beautifully articulated machine designed by the Supreme Being according to a rational plan as an abiding place for mankind. The Garden of Eden was for them a myth, no doubt, but they looked enviously back to the golden age of Roman virtue, or across the waters to the unspoiled innocence of an Arcadian civilization that flourished in Pennsylvania. They renounced the authority of Church and Bible, but exhibited a naïve faith in the authority of nature and reason. They scorned metaphysics, but were proud to be called philosophers. They dismantled heaven, somewhat prematurely it seems, since they retained their faith in the immortality of the soul. They courageously discussed atheism, but not before the servants. They defended toleration valiantly, but could with difficulty tolerate priests. They denied that miracles ever happened, but believed in the perfectibility of the human race. We feel that these philosophers were at once too credulous and too skeptical. They were the victims of common sense. In spite of their rationalism and their humane sympathies, in spite of their aversion to hocus-pocus and enthusiasm and dim perspectives, in spite of their eager skepticism, their engaging cynicism, their brave youthful blasphemies and talk of hanging the last king in the entrails of the last priest—in spite of all of it, there is more of Christian philosophy in the writings of the *Philosophes* than has yet been dreamt of in our histories.

❧ TEN BASIC BOOKS ❧

REVOLUTION OF THE MIND: THE AGE OF REASON, 1650–1800

1. Becker, Carl L., *The Heavenly City of the Eighteenth-Century Philosophers* (New Haven, Conn., 1932, R. 1959).†
2. Brinton, Crane, *Ideas and Men,* 2nd ed. (New York, 1963).
3. Cassirer, Ernst, *The Philosophy of the Enlightenment,* trans. by Fritz C. A. Koelin and James P. Pettegrove, 2nd ed. (Boston, 1955).†

4. Frankel, Charles, *The Faith of Reason* (New York, 1948).

5. Gierke, Otto F. von, *Natural Law and the Theory of Society, 1500 to 1800*, ed. and trans. by E. Barker, 2 vols. (Cambridge, 1934, R. 1955).†

6. Laski, Harold, *Political Thought in England from Locke to Bentham* (New York, 1920).

7. Lovejoy, A. O., *The Great Chain of Being* (Cambridge, Mass., 1942, R. 1960).†

8. Randall, J. H., Jr., *The Making of the Modern Mind* (Boston, 1940).

9. Snyder, Louis L., *The Age of Reason*, Anvil Book No. 6 (Princeton, N. J., 1955).†

10. Willey, Basil, *The Eighteenth-Century Background* (New York, 1941, R. 1961).†

16

The Dynamics of Industrialism

... IN ENGLAND the material condition of the criminal is better than that of the poor who are fed by the parish, and that of the honest man who works. Is this not monstrous? Well, it is necessary. England has workers, but fewer workers than inhabitants. But, because there is no middle way between feeding and killing the excess poor, English legislators have chosen to do the first. . . ! It remains to be seen if French legislators can look with unconcern upon the abominable consequences of the industrial regime which they have borrowed from England.

Competition produces misery. Statistics prove it.

Misery is horribly prolific. Statistics prove it.

The fecundity of the poor throws unfortunates into society who have need of work and who find no work. Statistics prove it.

At this point society has only the choice between killing the poor or feeding them gratuitously—atrocity or folly.

—LOUIS BLANC

1. Meaning of the Industrial Revolution

The Great Economic Transformation. About 1750 came a great change in the economic life of man. From the beginning of history the world's work had been done by hand tools, but now there was a shift to the use of power machinery. It was primarily a story of economic growth, by which Western society moved from a low subsistence living standard to a substantially higher level in a comparatively short period of time. The effects were striking: there was increased production; capital enhanced its power and resourcefulness; goods were moved more rapidly and in greater bulk over longer distances at lower cost; the middle class assumed socioeconomic power. All these developments, interacting one on the other, produced important results which together have come to be called the Industrial Revolution. A decisive force in the Industrial Revolution was an agrarian revolution (*see page 265*) which began in the middle of the seventeenth century.

The opening stage, the First Industrial Revolution (1750–1850), came in Britain and then spread to the Continent. The whole complexion of European life was changed: production shifted from home to factory; the old agricultural society was supplanted by an urban one; differences emerged and grew between capitalists, owners of the machines, and workers, who toiled in the factories. The entrepreneurs were strengthened in their beliefs by the creation of a "science of political economy," which stressed *laissez-faire*, or freedom to act, the basis of classical economics.

The Industrial Revolution was important in setting the pattern of nineteenth- and twentieth-century society. It stimulated a combination of historical circumstances, arousing demands for the extension of political democracy, encouraging social legislation to meet problems engendered by the machine, and, as class conflicts sharpened, encouraging revolutionary philosophies. Aggressive nationalism in the form of imperialism or neo-mercantilism arose to satisfy needs for raw materials, markets, and areas in which to invest excess capital. The proletariat, solidifying as a class, began to create its own social institutions, including trade unions, cooperatives, and fraternal organizations, as a means of bettering itself in a more prosperous society.

Historical Controversy: "Industrial Revolution" or Evolution? The great economic upheaval which replaced the Commercial Revolution with a dynamic capitalism is variously interpreted by historians. Here again is an example of sharply differing conclusions drawn from the same set of facts. The architect of the classic view of the era was Arnold Toynbee (1852–1883), whose *Lectures on the Industrial Revolution of the Eighteeenth Century*, given at Oxford University in 1880–1881, were published posthumously. Toynbee pointed out that during the period from 1750 to 1850 there occurred a rapid growth of population; modernization of the techniques and organization of farming; sudden changes in invention, especially in the textile industry; and appearance of powerful machines and their grouping into factories. All these events were revolutionary. Because of Toynbee's brilliant exposition, the term "Industrial Revolution" has been attributed to him, although it had been used previously by Friedrich Engels (1845), John Stuart Mill (1848), and Karl Marx (1867). This catastrophic or cataclysmic view—that the old quiet world was broken into pieces by the mighty blows of the steam engine and the power loom—was prevalent among historians until the early twentieth century.

Proponents of the continuity view (history is a continuous process) believe that the economic transformation was by no means sudden, that it did not break in on an almost unchanging world of small-scale non-capitalistic units, that the speed of transformation was far from rapid, and that the ground was emphatically not quickly captured. New research reveals that in both mechanical and agricultural changes there had been an almost unbroken continuity of development. In 1920 A. P. Usher criticized Toynbee for historical inaccuracies. Criticism mounted. Harry L. Beales termed the Industrial Revolution "an unhappily chosen epithet for a singularly constructive epoch" (1928); Herbert Heaton said: "As a label it is admittedly unsatisfactory" (1938); John U. Nef concluded: "There is scarcely a conception in economic history more misleading" (1943).

Often in the writing of history, new interpretations become outmoded almost as soon as they are accepted. Scholars became reconciled to the term Industrial Revolution. A. P. Usher later stated that "important aspects of the economic history of England . . . seem to warrant the qualified use of the term 'revolution'" (1937). Thomas S. Ashton published a new study titled simply *Industrial Revolution, 1760–1830* (1948). And Herbert Heaton, as recently as 1955, admitted that "*the* Industrial Revolution still stands provided you . . . develop a sense of . . . proportion."

The traditional label, the Industrial Revolution, will be used here for want of a better term. There was, indeed, continuity of development; but, at the same time, the period from 1750 to 1850 was distinguished by the cumulative effects of earlier, virtually unnoticed movements, in which older economic factors blended almost imperceptibly with the new. We must be careful also to extend this period both backward and forward in time.

Effects of the Commercial Revolution. The earlier Commercial Revolution rejected the semi-static economy of the Middle Ages and replaced it with a worldwide expansion of commerce. But this was not enough. There was even greater demand for more and more manufactured products to be exchanged for products from beyond the seas. By 1700 there had developed a crucial change in focus of economic development from the Levantine world to the fringes of the North Atlantic, a shift that gave impetus to the Industrial Revolution. Localism lessened, horizons were raised.

Increased industrial activity brought calls for more raw materials, more capital, more gold, newer business techniques. The new class of capitalists, enterprising and profit-hungry, had money available for the development of manufacturing. Attracted by the possibility of vast profits, they demanded an end to constricting guild regulations and called for better methods of production to produce more and cheaper goods. They were aware of an all-important social factor: with the rapid increase of the population of Western Europe came a parallel enlargement of the markets at home. For a time the established putting-out, or domestic, system seemed to fulfill the demand for broader markets, but the old handicraft methods of manufacturing were plainly unsatisfactory. Added to this was the stimulating factor of mercantilism, which had been designed to increase the quantity of manufactured goods and which still preached its basic gospel of growth.

Technological Improvements. Artists of the Renaissance, notably the versatile Leonardo da Vinci, had invented ingenious machines, mainly for the amusement of rich patrons. Isolated inventions of practical value appeared well before 1750; the machine age was by no means created by a sudden stroke of lightning from the heavens. There had long been an interest in mechanical innovations. During the early modern era there had been improvements in the spinning wheel and stocking frame, as well as in techniques of smelting ores, glass-blowing, and shipbuilding. Interest in mathematics by the men of the Enlightenment enabled the inventors of machines to achieve accuracy in their work. Steady improvements in technology were cumulative: they made necessary the use of factory methods. The demand for power-driven machinery did not yet exist on a large scale. When it arose, one invention after another appeared with astonishing rapidity. The cliché proved true—necessity became the mother of invention.

The need for mechanical improvements in certain fields of production became urgent.

Limited industrial production could be satisfied by man power, horse power, wind power, or water power. When these were not able to satisfy the demand, power-driven machinery appeared. Economic life ascended to a threshold where political, social, and economic conditions merged to unleash the great productive power of the machine.

Why the Industrial Revolution Began in Britain. Britain was destined to become the industrial leader of the world for more than a century after 1750. This resulted from a combination of fortunate circumstances:

1. *Effects of the Commercial Revolution:* Britain, more than any Continental nation, had profited from the Commercial Revolution. Because of the international situation, she was in an extremely favorable position for assuming industrial leadership. She had already acquired valuable colonies in America, and she was soon to assert her commercial supremacy by defeating the French in the Seven Years' War (1756–1763). Her triumphs in America and India assured her a steady supply of raw materials, and her busy merchants found ever-expanding markets for British goods.

2. *Domestic Political and Social Conditions:* Conditions inside Britain were favorable for industrial change. The advance of British parliamentarianism brought with it the concept that the state should not interfere with man's natural rights of liberty and property. Mercantilist restrictions on domestic business were gradually abolished. The nobility's distaste for business changed into a positive advocacy of what was now called the aristocracy of wealth.

3. *The Guild System:* The system of guilds, with its elaborate restrictions on and regulations of production, had never become firmly established in Britain. Thus British industry was more free to develop.

4. *Leading Capitalist Nation:* Britain's new class of merchant princes, her businessmen and landlords, had accumulated huge fortunes which they were eager to invest. Britain's monetary system was sound. The Bank of England, a private institution founded in 1694, was a stabilizing factor in public finance.

Britain's joint-stock companies were developed far beyond any similar organization on the Continent.

5. *Labor Supply:* In a spectacular increase, the population of England and Wales rose from seven millions to more than nine millions between 1750 and 1800. Along with the breaking down of rural isolation and the subsequent drift of farmers to the cities, this made available a virtually inexhaustible supply of cheap labor. Added to these workers were the thousands of commercially active Huguenots driven from France to England after the revocation of the Edict of Nantes (1685). In England it was said that a drop of Huguenot blood in the veins was worth a thousand pounds sterling.

6. *Essential Raw Materials and Climate:* Britain had abundant supplies of coal and iron, lying fairly near each other. She also had large quantities of domestic wool, a cotton supply from the colonies, and a great merchant marine to insure communications between colonies and mother country. Her damp climate was suitable for textile manufacturing.

7. *Markets:* Britain's growing population assured her manufacturers an ever-increasing domestic market. Her expanding factories produced great quantities of cheap goods. Moreover, Britain was triumphant in the competition for overseas markets.

8. *Pressure for Inventions:* All these factors combined to produce conditions favorable for invention. The British were, perhaps, no better inventors than Frenchmen or Italians. But when the demand for techniques became overriding, a line of ingenious innovators emerged in the island kingdom. So great was the need that the Royal Society of Arts offered premiums for the introduction of new machines. The inventors well served the economic needs of their time. Their greatest contribution was the "invention of invention."

2. Evolution of Textile Inventions

Men and Machines. The early stage of the Industrial Revolution saw a phenomenal change in the application of machinery to industry. The first branch of industry to be mechanized was the production of cotton cloth. For centuries the spinning of yarn and the weaving of cotton cloth had been a manual operation. In early eighteenth-century England, whole families worked in their homes, as women and children and heads of the family divided the labor. Fine yarns and fabrics were produced, but time was a serious problem and output was too meager to satisfy the demand. Then came a series of inventions which replaced old-fashioned methods of weaving and spinning. Inventions followed one another in logical order: as soon as a machine to increase the speed of spinning was introduced, another had to be devised to increase the speed of weaving. Technical improvement tended to break the common rhythm of the industry as a whole, thus calling for further changes to restore the balance of the system.

Kay's Fly-Shuttle, 1733. The old hand loom carried the woof (or weft, the cross-threads of the web) from one side of the warp (threads stretched lengthwise in the loom) to the other, the entire process moving slowly by hand. In 1733 John Kay, a Lancashire weaver, took out a patent for his fly-shuttle, (or flying-shuttle), which needed only one hand to throw the shuttle backward and forward. On each side of the loom, Kay placed hammers which were operated with strings, and which propelled the shuttle back and forth between the warp threads. While the worker used his right hand for this purpose, his left hand was free to operate the lathe to beat up the woof. Kay profited little from his invention: angered weavers, fearing that his fly-shuttle would throw them out of work, attacked his home and destroyed his machines. But this simple semiautomatic device which sped the weaving of cloth stimulated a whole series of similar textile inventions.

Hargreaves' Spinning Jenny, 1764. About 1764 James Hargreaves, who earned his living as a weaver and carpenter near Blackburn, Lancashire, noted a hand-operated, one-thread spinning machine overturned on the floor, with both the wheel and the spindle, the latter now upright, revolving. The thought flashed through his mind that if a number of spindles were placed upright, several threads might be spun at once with only one wheel. Patented in 1770, the spinning jenny, named after Hargreaves's wife, was a compound spinning wheel, capable of producing eight threads simultaneously (soon increased to 16, 20, 30, and 40). It was a simple machine: even a child could turn the crank. Hargreaves's worried fellow spinners mobbed him, destroyed his frames, and forced him to move to Nottingham.

Arkwright's Water-Frame, 1769. Now spinners could come closer to meeting the demand of weavers for thread. Unfortunately, the threads produced by the spinning jenny lacked the strength and firmness needed for the longitudinal fibers, or warp, of cotton cloth. In 1769 Richard Arkwright took out a patent for the water-frame, or spinning frame, which spun thread strong enough to be used as warp. Born in humble circumstances, the youngest of thirteen children, this young Lancashireman first became a barber and then began to study cotton machinery. His water-frame was so heavy and complicated that he had to house it in a special building where workers had to gather to perform their services. Arkwright thus became the innovator of factory administration. Angry workers wrecked his plant. Prying neighbors accused him of witchcraft; rival inventors infringed on his patents; the woolen interests kept him busy with lawsuits. But patience and common sense enabled him to amass a fortune from his improved machines. By 1790 he was employing 600 men at his mill in Manchester. The embattled inventor was eventually knighted by his king for services to industrial Britain.

Crompton's "Mule," 1779. Another Lancashireman, Samuel Crompton, a hard-working farmer and weaver, invented in 1779, after five years of toil, a machine which was to produce the finest yarn ever woven to his day. Combining Hargreaves's spinning jenny and Arkwright's water-frame, he constructed a hybrid

contraption which he called the spinning mule. Within two decades it could spin simultaneously 400 strands of excellent yarn. Although his invention became the most popular spinning machine on the market and was preferred over earlier machines, Crompton received little recognition for his work.

Cartwright's Power Loom, 1785. Edmund Cartwright, a mathematically inclined Kentish clergyman, visited Arkwright's cotton mills, where he was much impressed by improvements in spinning. If automatic machinery could be applied to spinning, he reasoned, why not to weaving? Since he knew nothing about mechanics, he hired a carpenter and a smith to help him. In 1785 he patented the power loom, which improved Kay's fly-shuttle. The new machine could weave cloth of any width, and several machines could be controlled by one operator. Cartwright set up power looms first at Doncaster and then at Manchester. He profited little from his invention. In 1809, however, a grateful government gave him a grant of £10,000.

Whitney's Cotton Gin, 1793. One of the most serious problems in the production of raw cotton was the separation of the seeds from the fiber. This was solved in 1793 by an ingenious Connecticut Yankee, Eli Whitney, who, after his graduation from Yale, went to Georgia and there devised the cotton gin. This was a spike-studded cylinder which rotated through a bed piece, containing spikes placed in rows. When cotton was fed into the cylinder, the seeds were separated mechanically to produce a cheap fiber. This simple comb-like device eliminated the necessity of picking seeds by hand, a tedious process that had been performed by Negro slaves. Whitney's neighbors stole his idea and forestalled his patent. He constructed a factory in Connecticut in 1798 only to see litigation swallow up its profits.

Significance of Textile Inventions. The great source of cotton supply for the English mills in Lancashire and Derbyshire had been the Southern states in America. The importation of raw cotton into England increased from 1½ million pounds in 1730 to more than 100 million in 1815. The full effects of the new inventions were felt at the opening of the nineteenth century. In 1811 there were 5,000,000 spindles at work, of which 310,500 employed the Arkwright principle, 4,600,000 that of Crompton's mule, and 156,000 that of Hargreaves' jenny spindle. Some 100,000 of Cartwright's power looms were constructed between 1822 and 1833. England, by 1835, was producing 63 per cent of the world's cotton cloth.

British mill owners manufactured cotton mostly for export. Other British industries soon followed cotton's lead. Wool continued to be produced for the domestic market. Soon power-driven machinery came to be used for the weaving of woolen goods. Then, to match these developments, the manufacture of silk was improved.

3. *The Steam Engine: Coal and Iron Metallurgy*

Newcomen's Atmospheric Engine, 1705. The problem of power was crucial. New techniques in the textile industry called for improvements in power sources. The first power loom invented by Cartwright was operated by a cow, and later ones were worked by horses, hardly a satisfactory method. It had been known for centuries that steam could be used for power: Hero of Alexandria, in the latter half of the first century A.D., demonstrated a simple toy steam engine used to open a temple door, and Leonardo da Vinci during the Renaissance described the steam engine. In 1698 Thomas Savery invented a steam engine, without pistons, which was used to pump water from mines, and raise water to supply houses and towns. But Savery's engine could be used only with lethal effect: the great heat and high pressures melted its joints and exploded its seams; moreover, it required an enormous amount of heat to operate it.

The first man to apply the power of steam for industrial purposes was Thomas Newcomen, a Dartmouth ironmonger. In 1705–1706, Newcomen, together with Savery and John Calley, took out a patent for a fire-engine notable for its safety and economy. Separating the boiler from the cylinder, and using artificial means to condense the steam, Newcomen used steam pressure not much greater than that of the atmosphere (hence the name

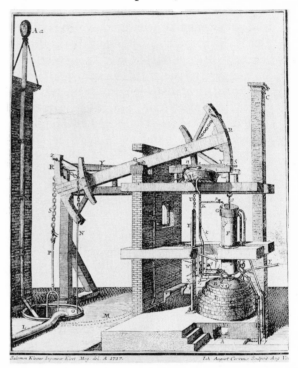

This atmospheric steam engine, invented by Thomas Newcomen, was used primarily for pumping water out of mines. Subsequently, James Watt's engine offered much greater efficiency through the introduction of a separate condenser.

of atmospheric engine). Within a few years the Newcomen engine was being used to pump water from British coal mines. It had serious faults: steam was wasted by the alternate heating and cooling of the vessel into which it was led; the engine, with a single action, exerted force only while the piston moved in one direction; it could produce only a dozen strokes a minute; it provided only 20 horsepower but consumed 13 tons of coal per day. These defects, wasting both fuel and power, prevented its wide use for industrial purposes.

James Watt's Improved Engine, 1769. In 1764, James Watt, a Scottish engineer and mathematical instrument maker for Glasgow University, while repairing a model of Newcomen's engine, discovered the cause of its power wastage. The next year Watt devised a separate condenser to remedy the defects. In 1769 he patented his steam engine, following it with such further improvements as sun-and-planet motion (continuous revolving motion); double action (applying the forces of steam and vacuum separately to opposite sides of the piston); and the expansive principle (stopping the admission of steam after the piston had made only part of its stroke, so that the stroke was completed by the steam already in the cylinder). A man of limited business ability, Watt fell into debt until he formed a partnership with Matthew Boulton of Soho near Birmingham. By 1800 the firm had sold 289 engines for use in factories and mines.

What Watt had done was to transform Newcomen's atmospheric engine into the modern steam engine. The final perfection of the steam engine did not come until the nineteenth century with the appearance of heavy-duty machine tools, but already it was of decisive influence in the industrial age. Few inventions have had so important an effect. Horse power was an undependable power source; wind power was too uncertain; manufacturers depending on water power were restricted by the number and location of waterfalls. But the steam engine gave abundant power at low cost. It could be moved wherever and whenever necessary; no longer was it vital to locate factories beside streams and rivers. The steam engine began to replace water power in the textile factories and increased its own fuel supply by freeing English mines of water.

The steam engine was not, as sometimes stated, the cause of the Industrial Revolution. It was in part an effect, which came simultaneously with the development of machines and techniques in the textile and metallurgical industries. Watt's improved engine was the response to a demand for a new source of power to work the heavy machines already invented. It accelerated the momentum of the revolution in manufacturing and transportation already under way. The first great source of artificial power, it supplied a motive force far beyond the wildest dreams of its inventors.

Extraction of Coal. Steam, coal, and iron formed the triple foundation of modern industry. Coal had been used as a fuel for a long time, but mining had been slow and dangerous. Miners who toiled with pick and shovel deep in the bowels of the earth always feared floods, cave-ins, and gas explosions. Forced to work in small areas, they could extract only limited quantities of coal. The increasing demand for coal was followed by improvements in mining techniques. Stronger supports were devised for the roofs and sides of mine tunnels. New methods were used for detecting the presence of fire damp, choke damp, carbon monoxide, and coal dust. Ventilation in the shafts was improved. Mining safety was increased by systems of siphoning and continuous pumping, designed to rid the mines of water. Improved methods were contrived to sink shafts to work the veins, and eliminate waste. In 1815 Sir Humphry Davy (1778–1829), a distinguished Cornwall chemist who had been investigating the causes of fire damp, invented the miners' safety lamp, which brought him numerous honors. Extraction of coal from English mines rose from 10,000,000 tons in 1800 to 57,000,000 tons in 1861.

Evolution of Iron Metallurgy. The improved steam engine gave a strong impetus to the manufacture of iron and iron products. In the early eighteenth century, iron ore was smelted (melted to extract the metal) with charcoal, for which large supplies of wood were necessary. As English forests became exhausted, charcoal and iron were imported from the Continent, scarcely a satisfactory procedure in a mercantilist society. Then, in 1709, Abraham Darby, an ironmaster, devised a method of smelting in which charcoal was replaced by coke, a by-product of coal. Coke produced a hotter fire than charcoal, but the resultant product, pig iron, was not sufficiently malleable and, moreover, had too high a carbon content.

In 1784 Henry Cort, an ironmaster and naval contractor, invented a process of purifying iron called "puddling." The puddling (or reverberatory) furnace maintained a temperature so low that the final product was a pasty solid instead of a liquid. When purified to the desired degree, the pasty mass was rolled into balls, removed from the furnace, and subjected to successive squeezing and rolling to eliminate the impurities, or slag. Carbon was burned out of the iron, and a purer material was produced in quantities. The process was facilitated by the invention of the steam hammer and the rolling mill. The resulting tough wrought iron revolutionized iron metallurgy. In the eighteen years from 1788 to 1806 the production of iron quadrupled, from 68,000 tons to 250,400 tons. The price dropped to a fraction of what it had been, thereby further stimulating manufacturing and transportation.

4. Revolution in Transportation

Roads and Canals. The problem of how to move the increasing quantities of factory-produced goods to distant places cheaply and quickly was solved by continuing improvements in transportation. The horse-drawn wagon and the sailing vessel were now outmoded. In England a new type of road called the "turnpike" was introduced. Turnpike acts passed after 1663 authorized individuals, corporations, and communities to construct highways as a business enterprise, with tolls as reimbursement. Thomas Telford (1757–1834), a British civil engineer, improved roads by using the Roman method of laying a foundation of heavy stones bound together with pitch and then covering this with smaller stones. John Loudon McAdam (1756–1836), a Scottish engineer, gave his name to the surfacing of roads with granite or other durable stone broken small enough to form a hard, smooth surface (macadamizing). After the middle of the eighteenth century, Parliament passed several hundred acts dealing with the construction of roads. By 1830 a network of 20,000 miles of new highways extended through the main industrial areas of England.

The necessity for better transportation led in 1761 to the completion of the first modern canal, from the coal mines of Worsley to Manchester, a distance of just seven miles. During the period between 1761 and 1830, the great era of canal-building, England was crisscrossed by artificial waterways connecting industrial areas. By the end of the eighteenth century, stimulated by Parliament's passing of many canal acts, Britain had nearly 3,000 miles of canals. A similar spurt in canal-building took place on the Continent. But about 1825, after the introduction of the railroad, canal-building went into decline.

The Steamboat: The *Clermont* and *Great Western*. The steam engine was put to many uses, not the least of which was the steamboat. Most eighteenth-century vessels were unwieldy and even unseaworthy. Dependent on wind power, they could not possibly handle the vastly enhanced output of the factories. There were pioneer attempts to construct steamboats, some of which were destroyed by workmen who feared that the new invention would throw them out of work.

The first man to make the steamboat pay was Robert Fulton (1765–1815), an American inventor and engineer, who in 1807 launched the *Clermont*, equipped with a Watt engine. Steaming up the Hudson River from New York to Albany, a distance of 154 miles, in 32 hours, the strange ship frightened the farmers by its noise and "seemed to them a monster moving upon the waters, defying wind and tide, and breathing smoke and flame." This epoch-making voyage inaugurated the era of steam navigation. In 1838 the first ocean greyhound, the *Great Western,* crossed the Atlantic in fifteen days using steam for the entire trip; it cut in half the previous time of the sailing packets. The earliest steamships were made of wood, but later models made of iron proved to be more buoyant and stronger than the wooden ones.

The Steam Locomotive. The steam engine became equally effective in land travel. Richard Trevithick (1771–1833), a native of Cornwall, experimented with model locomotives from 1796 on, and in 1801 completed the first steam carriage that drew passengers. In 1808 he built a new model which he operated on a circular track in London at speeds of 12 to 15 miles an hour.

An even more important pioneer of the locomotive was George Stephenson (1781–1848), an engineer at Killingworth colliery. In 1814 he designed a steam locomotive called "My Lord," which was successfully tried on the tramroads of the colliery. He subsequently improved this model. He insisted upon carefully prepared roadbeds, which became standard in railroad construction. Appointed engi-

The first successful locomotive, Stephenson's "Rocket," which made a trial trip at 32 miles per hour in 1830.

neer for a railroad between Manchester, center of the cotton industry, and Liverpool, the great seaport, he built a roadbed, completed in 1829, over graded surfaces and filled-in swamps. On this line his improved locomotive, the *Rocket,* made its famous trial trip in 1830, a train of cars covering the distance at the hitherto unheard-of speed of 32 miles an hour. This demonstration ended all doubts about the future of the railroad. The steam locomotive eventually freed industry from the limitations of the river systems. The age of the iron

horse was at hand. Soon all Europe would be covered by a network of rails.

5. *The Factory System*

Production Before the Industrial Revolution. Under the old putting-out system the means of production were at home and by hand. The worker received raw material from an entrepreneur, fashioned it into a finished product, and delivered it to the entrepreneur. He manufactured only enough to satisfy a limited demand. He made the product from beginning to end, and he took great pride in his product, which he regarded as a tribute to his skill. Under this system, the market was always local, limited, and certain.

Rise of the Factory System. The breakdown of the putting-out system was the result of cumulative forces: the expansion of industry, the increased demands of commerce, the urbanization of society, the increase of wealth, the rise in population, the revolution in the cotton textile industry, the advent of steam, and additional uses of coal and iron. The answer to these needs was the factory system. The outward, visible sign of the Industrial Revolution, the factory, displaced the shop. Its distinguishing features were the use of machinery, division of labor, and the organization of production under one roof. There had been factories in England long before the eighteenth century, but the factory system, dependent upon power machinery, was a distinct innovation.

The new power machines, too bulky and too expensive to be set up in individual homes, were housed in special buildings where they could be regulated and controlled. It would not pay to set up a costly steam engine unless its power could be transmitted to a number of machines. Factories tended to become concentrated in areas where water power or supplies of coal and iron were readily available. Machines were grouped together in factories, which were then collected into factory cities. To run the machines there had to be attendants working at regular hours. Thus, gradually, although hand workers were not entirely displaced, the putting-out system was doomed.

Work in the factories was broken down into many routine operations. Division of labor, quicker and cheaper, required each worker to specialize in the making of one part of the article and nothing else. The unskilled worker turned wheels, and pulled levers. He had no opportunity to express his own taste and character. He took little joy or pride in the final product of his labor. He lost that creative impulse which had distinguished the skilled craftsman. He was little more than a cog in a machine. No longer an independent artisan, he was now merely a hired hand who came to the factory to perform his allotted task at a fixed wage. He had to abide by definite rules for hourly work, for division of labor, and for behavior in the factory. Liable to fine or dismissal if he rested or slowed his pace, he worked furiously. Fatal accidents were frequent, and bodily injury was common. The relentless discipline was eased only when the machines broke down. Such regimentation was necessary to assure the smooth running of the system. Despite the toll it exacted from the worker, the factory system, in the eyes of the entrepreneurs, was the most efficient method of production ever devised.

The factory was used for mass production of standardized products. Articles made by machinery were exactly alike in size, texture, and quality. The machine simply duplicated an individual pattern many times. In this respect machine industry was markedly different from handicraft production. Machine-made products were often inferior in quality to hand-made goods, but there were more of them and they meant great profits.

6. *The Agrarian Revolution*

The Enclosure System. Between the midseventeenth and the late eighteenth century the entire English countryside was transformed. The widespread changes in industrialization were accompanied by parallel developments in agriculture. In an era of high prices, there were new opportunities for profit. A rapidly increasing population called for ever-greater quantities of food. The response to this need was the enclosure system. More and more landowners decided to "enclose" smaller plots, especially common lands, in order to raise crops and meat cattle on a larger scale. The unfortunate freeholder, thus deprived of the use of common lands and thrust aside by the process of consolidation, found independent farming more and more difficult and hence tended to disappear into the ranks of farm or city workers. The hiring of agricultural laborers to work on the larger estates became a general practice. The great estates were now used to produce one valuable crop to be sold as a commodity, instead of a variety of crops for home consumption.

The government, influenced by the agricultural landlords, cooperated by passing laws facilitating enclosures. From 1740 to 1788 at least 40,000 farms were enclosed by the landed proprietors. Common meadows and pasture lands were enclosed and redistributed as farms. Enclosure meant three things: (1) an increase in the supply of food; (2) the decline of subsistence farming; and (3) increased production for a much larger market.

The two revolutions were reciprocal in effects. The Industrial Revolution eventually gave to agriculture the mechanical devices necessary for increased production. The new agriculture, in turn, acted upon the Industrial Revolution by producing an ever-increasing supply of food and furnishing a class of uprooted peasants for the urban labor market. Agriculture was affected by the same forces as manufacturing and commerce. Industrialism, like so many other aspects of our culture, was born in the country and moved into the towns only when well advanced in years. Most people still lived off the soil and continued to do so long after the Industrial Revolution sparked the rise of urban communities.

Jethro Tull's Drill, 1701. English agriculture was influenced by the work of a small group of agrarian theorists and experimenters. The old method of sowing by hand was wasteful, since seeds were deposited unevenly over the ground; many failed to sprout because of insufficient moisture, and others were eaten by birds. In 1701 Jethro Tull (1674–1740), an agricultural writer, invented a drilling machine which deposited the seeds in the ground in parallel rows, thereby reducing the amount of seed required from ten pounds an acre to two pounds. In 1733 Tull published his major work, *Horse-Hoeing Husbandry*, in which he discussed his agricultural theories. Although some of Tull's ideas on soils and fertilizers were erroneous, his work in the "science of agriculture" stimulated imitators. It became fashionable among landlords to improve agri-

cultural methods as a sure means to greater profits.

Lord Townsend's Rotation of Crops. Among those influenced by Tull was Lord Charles Townsend (1674–1738), a statesman who in 1730 retired from politics to devote himself to agriculture. He encouraged turnip growing according to the methods prescribed by Tull, and thereby earned for himself the nickname of "Turnip" Townsend. He revived the old practice of marling, or using rich soil containing calcium carbonate as a fertilizer. He also initiated the so-called Norfolk Rotation by rotating the sowing of turnips, barley or oats, clover, and wheat successively. This simple improvement meant the end of the old medieval three-field system.

Robert Bakewell's Selective Breeding. One of the unsolved problems of the Middle Ages was the feeding of livestock during the winter. Cattle, sheep, and pigs were left to their own devices during the cold months; those who survived emerged as little more than skin and bones. The problem was partially met in the eighteenth century by the cultivation of turnips, clover, other root crops, and grasses. The outstanding pioneer in the improvement of livestock by selective breeding was Robert Bakewell (1725–1795), an agriculturalist of Leicester. Bakewell's new long-wool Leicester sheep and the Dishley longhorn cattle became famous all over the world. He also improved the breed of horses by producing a stronger animal than the large English draught horse. Between 1710 and 1795 the average weight of sheep in England rose from 28 to 80 pounds, and that of beef cattle from 370 to 800 pounds.

7. *The Industrial Revolution on the Continent*

France. In the early Industrial Revolution, Britain was the workshop of the world. Her potential was superior to that of any country on the Continent, primarily because her coal supply was decisive. The English Midlands and the Scottish Lowlands sent cotton goods and steam engines to all corners of the earth. When the economic revolution spread to the Continent, its pace was considerably less rapid than in Britain. France in the eighteenth century also had expanding domestic and foreign markets, but in virtually every aspect of economic change she failed to keep pace with Britain. What progress she did enjoy was halted by the outbreak of the French Revolution. The French overseas market was hit badly by the wars of the late eighteenth century and the Napoleonic campaigns of the early nineteenth. Napoleon tried to improve French industry and trade by giving subsidies and bounties to manufacturers. He rewarded inventors who adopted or copied British industrial inventions, or established technical schools. But by 1815, as a consequence of the Napoleonic era, France was economically exhausted, her foreign trade diminished, her capital almost run dry, her business and industry nearly in chaos. These conditions were remedied during the nineteenth century, when the Industrial Revolution came to France with full force.

Other Countries. The Industrial Revolution did not touch the Germanies until well after the middle of the nineteenth century, but then it came with an enormous impact. The Italies, poor in natural resources, without iron or coal, and like the Germanies, divided by internal dissension, did not take a major role in industrialization until later in the nineteenth and twentieth centuries. Russia remained isolated from the West in economic as well as in political, social, and cultural matters. Belgium, with large coal deposits and a class of energetic entrepreneurs, was the first to follow England's lead; her economic status far outweighed her small size. Holland, once one of the great colonial powers, had no natural resources with which to build a competitive industrial state.

The Continent as a whole failed in the eighteenth century to get very far on the road to industrialization. In most European countries, land instead of risk capital remained the basis for wealth. Although the Continent had vast supplies of raw materials or could obtain

them through overseas trade, most countries did not take advantage of these possibilities. This situation was remedied as the nineteenth century wore on and as the rewards of industrialization became apparent to those who remained behind in the race for economic gains.

The United States. In the United States, Yankee craftsmen and inventors soon mastered the techniques of mechanization. By the middle of the nineteenth century American machines and products began to find their way into European markets. By the end of the century American industrialization, with its key contribution—the mass production of standardized articles—jumped to a point where it was ready to take the lead in world production. The American contribution, however, belongs to the New Industrial Revolution, a later development.

8. *Economic and Social Problems Engendered by the Industrial Revolution*

Production Versus Consumption. Unfortunately, technological progress was not accompanied by a parallel development in economic planning, with the result that production leaped ahead of consumption. What was called overproduction was in reality underconsumption, the inability of great masses of people to buy the products of the machines. The adjustment of consuming to productive capacity remained an unsolved problem in the industrial age.

Unemployment. From the beginning of the Industrial Revolution one of its gravest problems was unemployment. The handiworker sensed an enemy in the machine: were not these mechanical monsters taking away his work? On more than one occasion angered workers smashed machines. But machines could be built faster than workers could destroy them, and the useless rebellions eventually ceased. The irritating problem of unemployment remained. In pre-factory days, mass unemployment was a rare and fleeting phenomenon. Although the fruits of labor might be meager, there was usually work to do. With the advent of the machine, the picture was changed. There was more work to do, but much of it was done by women and children while men were unable to find employment. As industry became more and more mechanized, the competition for jobs became more intense. With no jobs, and dependent upon private or public charity, the unemployed formed a hopeless, miserable element in society. Hard times were frequent, factories closed down for months at a time, workers were left without wages for food. There was always the nagging threat of unemployment, for a worker who displeased his boss could easily be replaced. There was also the ever-present threat that the labor market might be again depressed by further revolutionary advances in technology.

Economic Insecurity. As long as society was based on agriculture, and commerce was local, most people enjoyed a certain amount of security. Prices remained relatively stable, most people were employed, and there was only the fear of a poor harvest. With industrialism came insecurity, instability, uncertainty. The world market was more irregular than the old local markets: capital might be invested unwisely; the flow of raw materials might be impeded for one reason or another; new machinery changed the complexion of production. Worst of all was the business cycle, rhythmic variations in economic activity: expansion, boom, collapse, depression. There seemed to be a pattern. Business expanded and production increased. A boom period followed, distinguished by inflated currency and higher prices. Suddenly, an important business enterprise went bankrupt. Then came a general financial crisis, with banks closed, and a precipitous decline in values with severe losses to investors. The period of panic was followed by months or years of depression, or deflation, during which business was at a standstill, unemployment vastly increased, prices low, and production stifled. Eventually, a new period of expansion began, only to result in the same cyclical pattern.

Unequal Distribution of Wealth. Added to these economic obstacles was the problem of unequal distribution of wealth. The Industrial Revolution brought great material advantages to the peoples of Western Europe, supplying them with tremendous quantities of cheap goods, but not all classes shared these benefits. How to prevent poverty in the midst of multiplying wealth was an exasperating problem in the industrial age. Labor was regarded as a commodity purchased to serve the machine; it received for its efforts only a small income and a low standard of living. Wages remained at a subsistence level. The worker seldom earned enough to tide himself and his family over a period of enforced idleness. John Stuart Mill said in 1848 that it was questionable whether all the mechanical inventions made up to that time had lightened the day's toil of a single human being.

Yet, despite this bleak picture, the Industrial Revolution meant some progress for the lower classes. To the peasant who migrated to the cities, the factory gave an opportunity to work for regular wages. Rooted in the soil, he had made no progress; in the city he had freedom of movement. If conditions became too insecure, he might emigrate to the promised land of America.

Evil Factory Conditions. The Industrial Revolution compounded economic problems, but its greatest impact was on people. The early factories, crude structures designed specifically to house machines, were built with little, if any, consideration for the health and comfort of the workers. Without adequate ventilation, heating, or sanitary facilities, the factories were virtually prisons. The small windows were usually kept closed to preserve the moisture necessary for cotton manufacture. Safety devices were rare, and the wages of an injured worker ceased at the moment of the accident. During working hours the doors of the factory were locked to prevent laborers from deserting their posts. The normal working day ran from 6 A.M. to 8:30 P.M.; during the rush season, workers were often at their posts at 3:00 A.M. Keeping pace with the machine was deadly and monotonous. For workers in general, the factory weakened and virtually destroyed family solidarity, community feeling, and intellectual enthusiasm.

The Slums. The new industrial towns grew up rapidly and haphazardly. Workers were herded into hastily built tenement homes, often no more than dingy shacks or industrial barracks blackened with the soot of the coal age. In these wretchedly crowded quarters, great numbers of workers, victims of low wages and unemployment, lived on the edge of starvation. Gone were the days of living in picturesque cottages in the English countryside. Under such abominable conditions the sturdy yeoman of yesterday, the independent farmer class, was subjected to physical, mental, and nervous degeneration. Now he stooped because of long hours at the machine; the pallor in his cheeks meant indoor work. It was little wonder that many were driven to drunkenness and crime.

Female and Child Labor. Equally scandalous and depressing was the exploitation of women and children, hired largely because the role of human labor in machine production was so simple that they could easily do the work hitherto required of men. As many as three-fourths of the workers in the early cotton factories were either women or children. Boys and girls, working the same long hours as adults, were recalled to consciousness by the lash if they fell asleep at the machines. Pauper children were imported by cartloads from London to the cotton factories of Lancashire and Yorkshire. Because of the law forcing pauper children to work, thousands of these unfortunates were bought and sold in gangs. If they refused to work, they were chained to the machines and locked up at night in sleeping huts. Many died of overwork. Breathing the close air of the mills, children developed into sickly, deformed adults. The babies of factory women, receiv-

A factory supervisor whips a child worker in an English cotton factory.

ing inadequate care, died by the hundreds. In the words of one observer: "The children lived the life of a machine while working, and at other times that of a beast." (*See page 272.*)

Degradation of the Miners. Conditions in the mines were even worse than in the factories. Among the exhausted men chopping at the veins of coal were women crawling on all fours, tugging small coal carts, while six-year-old children, sitting in darkness, "trapped," or opened and closed the doors for passage of the coal carts. The work was back-breaking and the pay was low. Men who spent their days in the mines would seek some rest in the pubs instead of going to their wretched homes. Many, suffering from lung diseases, became tubercular skeletons in their twenties.

The Beginning of Reform. When the attention of factory owners was called to these shocking conditions, they replied that business would not show a profit if wages were raised or if the laborer worked fewer hours. Above all, they denied the right of government to interfere in the "natural law" which decreed a subsistence wage for the worker. Did not the cotton lords do the poor a favor by furnishing them with work and seeing to it that they worked diligently to produce goods, Britain's lifeblood? Poverty, said the industrialists, was always the result of laziness and incompetence. But later, impelled by Tory landowners, workers' revolts, and the necessity for increased efficiency, they agreed to some reforms. The English Health and Morals of Apprentices Act (1802), pushed through Parliament by the elder Robert Peel, a cotton magnate, limited to twelve hours daily the work of pauper children in the mills. The Factory Act of 1819 prohibited child labor under nine years of age. Acts of 1824–1825 partially recognized the right of workers to form labor unions. The Truck Act of 1831 compelled payment of wages in full. The Factory Act of 1833 limited the working hours of persons under eighteen in the textile mills and, for the first time, provided factory inspectors to enforce the act. The Mines Act of 1842 prohibited child labor under the age of ten. The Factory Act of 1844 provided for a twelve-hour working day for women. The Factory Act of 1847 reduced the working day of women and children in textile factories from twelve to ten hours.

With only token protection against notoriously evil conditions, workers continued to sink into poverty. It seemed that machines, far from being a boom for mankind, had become an instrument of bourgeois oppression. When, after the "hungry 1840's," there was some amelioration of the horrors of the "satanic mills and mines," the new social legislation and political reform may have been due in part to rising productivity as much as to humanitarian motives.

9. Results of the Industrial Revolution

Economic Effects. Direct results of the new mechanical inventions could be seen in the expansion of commerce and industry. The production of great quantities of goods made possible the sale at low prices of products once considered luxuries. Better communi-

cation between countries enabled them to specialize in particular products: Britain concentrated on cloth and cutlery, while depending on Canada and Russia for its wheat. Industry became more concentrated. With the gradual consolidation of industries, the number of firms decreased as smaller factories were absorbed by the larger. Whole industries were taken over by energetic entrepreneurs. The drive to capture foreign markets deepened national rivalries.

The multiplication of wealth was phenomenal. At first great wealth accumulated in the hands of relatively few men, but as time went by, surplus wealth became sufficient to give comforts and even a few luxuries to millions of people. In the nineteenth century, as the effects of the revolution became more apparent, the national income of Britain increased tenfold and its purchasing power doubled.

Capitalism came of age. The spirit or economic outlook of capitalism was distinguished by three ideas: *acquisition,* or the accumulation of profits; *competition,* or the efforts of individual entrepreneurs to obtain profits even though others were attempting the same task; and *rationality,* or the mode of economic behavior that seemed to be most rational, systematic, and adaptable. The form of capitalism was characteristically free: that is, the individual entrepreneur possessed freedom of economic action as long as he did not violate the laws of his country.

Early capitalism first appeared in the late stages of the Commercial Revolution; its practitioners were hard-working, thrifty men, who turned back into industry part of the wealth they had amassed. This form of capitalism was succeeded in the mid-eighteenth century by industrial capitalism. Wealthy factory owners, leaders of the bourgeoisie, regarded themselves as justly entitled to a large share of the rewards of production because the risk of failure had been great. Opportunities for profit were to be found in an expanding market, and fortunes were made by those able to buy machinery, build factories, and provide effective management. This early type of industrial capitalism was succeeded in the nineteenth century by the new forms of monopoly capitalism and finance capitalism.

The new order was defended, explained, and justified by a set of theories known as economic liberalism. It was believed that all institutions, including economic life, should conform to the laws of nature and should be allowed to develop without artificial restrictions. Natural law—this was the highest sanction of the time. The ideal was *laissez-faire* ("Let Alone"). Business should be permitted freedom of operation; markets should not be controlled by tariffs; relations between employers and employees, between buyers and sellers should not be restricted; extensive social legislation should not interfere with natural law; and the State must defend property.

Social Consequences. The growth of commerce and industry was accompanied by significant increases in population. During the nineteenth century the number of people in Europe rose from approximately 186,000,000 to some 400,000,000. This growth amounted to a trend in most European countries. Responsible for this phenomenal growth were such diverse factors as greater supplies of food brought about by improvements in agriculture and food preservation; more food available because of new means of transportation; and medical discoveries and improvements in sanitation, which led to a decline in the death rate (scurvy and cholera would soon be eliminated from Western Europe and America).

Closely related to the growth of population was increasing urbanization. People drifted to the cities because of the steady decline in the need for agricultural labor. The isolation of medieval life began to break down. In England in 1800 there were but a dozen cities with a population of over 20,000; by 1900 there were nearly two hundred. Population in the capitals of Europe multiplied: between 1800 and 1880 London grew from 850,000 to more than 4,700,000 people; Paris from 600,000 to over 2,700,000; Berlin from 172,000 to 1,-300,000. Previously, towns had been established to meet military, commercial, or political needs; now they grew up around industries.

The machines and factories helped crystallize the character of the bourgeoisie and the proletariat, bringing wealth and political influence to one, poverty and misery to the other. The industrial bourgeoisie, owners of factories, mines, and railroads, merged with the older middle class of merchants, bankers, and lawyers to become the ruling element in society. In England the capitalists and entrepreneurs—textile kings and merchant princes—purchased feudal castles and pushed the landed aristocracy into the background. On occasion they absorbed the older aristocracy by intermarriage, or by various means managed to obtain titles of nobility. They resisted government intervention and insisted that free enterprise was necessary for economic growth.

The proletariat, including all those dependent upon wages for their living, had existed throughout history. Before the Industrial Revolution, however, wage earners composed only a small portion of the working class; the majority of workers were engaged in agriculture. The Industrial Revolution concentrated wage earners in the cities where, subjected to common abuses, they developed a sense of solidarity. No longer did they live in relative security in a closed economy: their jobs, their manner of living, their very lives, depended upon unfamiliar and unseen economic forces. They were unable to share in the comforts and luxury they had helped to produce. Moreover, they were limited as an economic class by stringent legislation.

Political Connotations. Equally far-reaching were the political effects of the Industrial Revolution. The period of industrialization was marked not only by social but by political tension. For a time the political structure of Europe as well as its social fabric was threatened by unleashed technological forces. It was inevitable that the strengthened middle class should exercise a powerful influence upon politics. Merchants, bankers, and promoters, captains of industry, all considered themselves deserving of power and dignity in the government. As men of wealth they could afford to buy votes or seats in Parliament. They began a long struggle to break down the power of aristocracy and monarchy. For this purpose they advocated the idea of democracy, until this time merely a rallying cry of placid philosophers. As a matter of political strategy, they allied themselves with the proletariat in a common front against the conservative landed aristocracy. But this union lasted only as long as it was necessary to guarantee bourgeois triumph in the struggle.

Nationalism, impelled by the concentration of the economic interests of the nation, also received impetus from the Industrial Revolution. The older nations, England and France, relinquished their provincial differences in customs, laws, and speech. Both Germans and Italians, long divided, were stimulated by the new industrialism to seek national unity.

Cultural Manifestations. Although its progress nearly everywhere was slow, in general, the industrial era promoted a higher standard of living. The essential needs of men—food, clothing, and shelter—were better fulfilled, in both quality and quantity. As the social evils of early industrialization were overcome, there was more leisure time for recreation and self-improvement. There was an increased use of educational facilities, especially by the worker who at one time had regarded education for his children as the greatest and most impossible of luxuries. These benefits of leisure and education were not given freely to the masses; in many cases they were painfully won. The common man, once illiterate, superstitious, and ignorant, now had new interests and perspectives. For centuries adjusted to a simple, agrarian life, he now became a part of a complicated urban life on a higher plane. For the uncommon man—the artist, scientist, composer—there were the rich captains of industry to replace the earlier aristocratic patrons.

❧ KEY DOCUMENT ❧

EVIDENCE BEFORE LORD ASHLEY'S MINES COMMISSION, 1842

Parliamentary Papers (London, 1842), XV–XVII, Appendices 1, 2.

THE EARLY unregulated industrialism of the First Industrial Revolution had a severe effect on urban workers who bore the greatest weight of the machines. Economic changes were accompanied by human degradation and social antagonisms. Behind the facade of prosperity was the harassed industrial proletariat coping desperately with the problem of keeping alive. Evidence produced before parliamentary commissions of inquiry led to measures regulating conditions in the factories and mines and restricting the hours of work for women and children. Following are excerpts from testimony given before Lord Ashley's Mines Commission of 1842.

Sarah Gooder, aged 8 years

I'm a trapper in the Gawber pit. It does not tire me, but I have to trap without a light and I'm scared. I go at four and sometimes half past three in the morning, and come out at five and half past. I never go to sleep. Sometimes I sing when I've light, but not in the dark; I dare not sing then. I don't like being in the pit. I am very sleepy when I go sometimes in the morning. I go to Sunday-school and read *Reading Made Easy*. [She knows her letters and can read little words.] They teach me to pray. [She repeated the Lord's Prayer, not very perfectly, and ran on with the following addition:—"God bless my father and mother, and sister and brother, uncles and aunts and cousins, and everybody else, and God bless me and make me a good servant. Amen. I have heard tell of Jesus many a time. I don't know why he came on earth, I'm sure, and I don't know why he died, but he had stones for his head to rest on. I would like to be at school far better than in the pit."]

Thomas Wilson, Esq., of the Banks, Silkstone, owner of three collieries

The employment of females of any age in and about the mines is most objectionable, and I should rejoice to see it put an end to; but in the present feeling of the colliers, no individual would succeed in stopping it in a neighborhood where it prevailed. . . .

I object on general principles to government interference in the conduct of any trade, and I am satisfied that in mines it would be productive of the greatest injury and injustice. The art of mining is not so perfectly understood as to admit of the way in which a colliery shall be conducted being dictated by any person, however experienced, with such certainty as would warrant an interference with the management of private business. I should also most decidedly object to placing collieries under the present provisions of the Factory Act with respect to the education of children employed therein. First, because, if it is contended that coal-owners, as employers of children, are bound to attend to their education, this obligation extends equally to all other employers, and therefore it is unjust to single out one class only; secondly, because, if the legislature asserts a right to interfere to secure education, it is bound to make that interference general; and thirdly, because the mining population is in this neighborhood so intermixed with other classes, and is in such small bodies in any one place, that it would be impossible to provide separate schools for them.

Isabella Read, 12 years old, coal-bearer

[Works on mother's account, as father has been dead two years. Mother bides at home, she is troubled with bad breath, and is very weak in her body from early labor.] I am wrought with sister and brother; it is very sore work; cannot say how many rakes or journeys I make from pit's bottom to wall face and back, thinks about 30 or 25 on the average; the distance varies from 100 to 250 fathom.

I carry about 1 cwt. and a quarter on my back; have to stoop much and creep through water, which is frequently up to the calves of my legs. When first down, fell frequently asleep while waiting for coal from heat and fatigue.

I do not like the work, nor do the lassies, but they are made to like it. When the weather is warm there is difficulty in breathing, and frequently the lights go out.

Isabella Wilson, 38 years old, coal-putter

When women have children thick [fast] they are compelled to take them down early. I have been married 19 years and have had 10 bairns; seven are in life. When on Sir John's work was a carrier of coals, which caused me to miscarry five times from the strains, and was ill after each. Putting is not so oppressive; last child was born on Saturday morning, and I was at work on the Friday night.

Once met with an accident; a coal brake my cheek-bone, which kept me idle some weeks.

I have wrought below 30 years, and so has the guid man; he is getting touched in the breath now.

None of the children read; as the work is not regular. I did read once, but not able to attend to it now; when I go below lassie 10 years of age keeps house and makes the broth or stir-about. . . .

Patience Kershaw, aged 17

My father has been dead about a year; my mother is living and has ten children, five lads and five lassies; the oldest is about thirty, the youngest is four; three lassies, go to mill; all the lads are colliers, two getters and three hurriers; one lives at home and does nothing; mother does nought but look after home.

All my sisters have been hurriers, but three went to the mill. Alice went because her legs swelled from hurrying in cold water when she was hot. I never went to day-school; I go to Sunday-school, but I cannot read or write; I go to pit at five o'clock in the morning and come out at five in the evening. . . . The getters that I work for are naked except their caps; they pull off all their clothes; I see them at work when I go up; sometimes they beat me, if I am not quick enough, with their hands; they strike me upon my back; the boys take liberties with me; sometimes they pull me about; I am the only girl in the pit; there are about 20 boys and 15 men.

⸙{ HISTORICAL INTERPRETATION }⸙

ARNOLD TOYNBEE ON THE NATURE OF THE INDUSTRIAL REVOLUTION

Arnold Toynbee, *The Industrial Revolution of the 18th Century in England* (London, 1887; New York, 1916), pp. 69–73. Courtesy of Longman's Green & Co. Ltd.

ARNOLD TOYNBEE (1852–1883), economist and social reformer, died at the age of thirty-one. His only work, a volume of lectures published in 1884 after his death, presented a classic definition of the Industrial Revolution. In the section which follows Toynbee gives a summary of the changes taking place at the close of the eighteenth century when the domestic, or putting-out, system was being replaced by the factory system.

Passing to manufacturers, we find here the all-prominent fact to be the substitution of the factory for the domestic system, the consequence of the mechanical discoveries of the time. Four great inventions altered the character of the cotton manufacture; the spinning-jenny, patented by Hargreaves in 1770; the water-frame, invented by Arkwright the year before; Crompton's mule introduced in 1779 and the self-acting mule, first invented by Kelly in 1792, but not brought into use till Roberts improved it in 1825. None of these by themselves would have revolutionised the industry. But in 1769—the year in which Napoleon and Wellington were born—James Watt took out his patent for the steam-engine. Sixteen years later it was applied to the cotton manufacture. In 1785 Boulton and Watt made an engine for a cotton-mill at Papplewick in Notts, and in the same year Arkwright's patent expired. These two facts taken together mark the introduction of the factory system. But the most famous invention of all, and the most fatal to domestic industry, the power-loom, though also patented by Cartwright in 1785, did not come into use for several years, and till the power-loom was introduced the workman was hardly injured. At first, in fact, machinery raised the wages of spinners and weavers owing to the great prosperity it brought to the trade. In fifteen years the cotton trade trebled itself; from 1788 to 1803 has been called its "golden age"; for, before the power-loom but after the introduction of the mule and other mechanical improvements by which for the first time yarn sufficiently fine for muslin and a variety of other fabrics was spun, the demand became such that "old barns, cart-houses, out-buildings of all descriptions were repaired, windows broke through the old blank walls, and all fitted up for loom-shops; new weavers' cottages with loom-shops arose in every direction, every family bringing home weekly from 40 to 120 shillings per week." At a later date, the condition of the workman was very different. Meanwhile, the iron industry had been equally revolutionised by the invention of smelting by pit-coal brought into use between 1740 and 1750, and by the application in 1788 of the steam-engine to blast furnaces. In the eight years which followed this latter date, the amount of iron manufactured nearly doubled itself.

A further growth of the factory system took place independent of machinery, and owed its origin to the expansion of trade, an expansion which was itself due to the great advance made at this time in the means of communication. . . . Improved means of communication caused an extraordinary increase in commerce, and to secure a sufficient supply of goods it became the interest of the merchants to collect weavers around them in great numbers, to get looms together in a workshop, and to give out the warp themselves to the workpeople. To these latter this system meant a change from independence to dependence; at the beginning of the century the report of a committee asserts that the essential difference between the domestic and the factory system is, that in the latter the work is done "by persons who have no property in the goods they manufacture." Another direct consequence of this expansion of trade was the regular recurrence of periods of overproduction and of depression, a phenomenon quite unknown under the old system, and due to this new form of production on a large scale for a distant market.

These altered conditions in the production of wealth necessarily involved an equal revolution in its distribution. In agriculture the prominent fact is an enormous rise in rents. . . . Much of this rise, doubtless, was due to money invested in improvements—the first Lord Leicester is said to have expended £400,000 on his property—but it was far more largely the effect of the enclosure system, of the consolidation of farms, and of the high price of corn during the French war. Whatever may have been its causes, however, it represented a great social revolution, a change in the balance of political power and in the relative position of classes. The farmers shared in the prosperity of the landlords; for many of them held their farms under beneficial leases, and made large profits by them. In consequence, their character completely changed; they ceased to work and live with their labourers, and became a distinct class. The high prices of the war time thoroughly demoralised them, for their wealth then increased so fast, that they were at a loss what to do with it. Cobbett has described the change in their habits, the new food and furniture, the luxury and drinking, which were the consequences of more money coming into their hands than they knew how to spend. Meanwhile, the effect of all these agrarian changes upon the condition of the labourer was an exactly opposite and most disastrous one. He felt all the burden of high prices, while his wages were steadily falling, and he had lost his common-rights. It is from this period, *viz.*, the beginning of the present century, that the alienation between farmer and labourer may be dated.

Exactly analogous phenomena appeared in the manufacturing world. The new class of great capitalist employers made enormous fortunes, they took little or no part personally in the work of their factories, their hundreds of workmen were individually unknown to them; and as a consequence, the old relations between masters and men disappeared, and a "cash nexus" was substituted for the human tie. The workmen on their side resorted to combination, and Trades-Unions began a fight which looked as if it were between mortal enemies rather than joint producers. The misery which came upon large sections of the working people at this epoch was often, though not always, due to a fall in wages, for . . . in some industries they rose. But they suffered likewise from the conditions of labour under the factory system, from the rise of prices, especially from the high price of bread before the repeal of the corn-laws, and from those sudden fluctuations of trade, which, ever since production has been on a large scale, have exposed them to recurrent periods of bitter distress. The effects of the Industrial Revolution prove that free competition may produce wealth without producing well-being. We all know the horrors that ensued in England before it was restrained by legislation and combination.

❧ TEN BASIC BOOKS ❧

THE DYNAMICS OF INDUSTRIALISM

1. Ashton, Thomas S., *The Industrial Revolution, 1760–1830* (New York, 1948).†

2. Clapham, John, *An Economic History of Modern Britain, 1820–1929*, 2nd ed., 3 vols. (Cambridge, 1930–1938).

3. Clark, George N., *The Idea of the Industrial Revolution* (Glasgow, 1953).

4. Dietz, D. R., *The Industrial Revolution* (New York, 1927).

5. Ernle, Rowland E., *English Farming, Past and Present*, ed. by Sir Alfred D. Hall, new ed. (New York, 1936).

6. Gras, Norman S. B., *A History of Agriculture in Europe and America*, 2nd ed. (New York, 1940).

7. Henderson, William O., *Britain and Industrial Europe, 1750–1870,* 2nd ed. (New York, 1965).

8. Mantoux, Paul J., *The Industrial Revolution in the Eighteenth Century* (London, 1928).†

9. Toynbee, Arnold, *The Industrial Revolution of the 18th Century in England* (London, 1887; New York, 1916, R. 1959).†

10. Usher, Abbott, *A History of Mechanical Inventions,* rev. ed. (Cambridge, Mass., 1954, R. 1959).†

17

The American Revolution

> WHAT HEROES from the woodland sprung,
>   When, through the fresh-awakened land,
> The thrilling cry of freedom rung
> And to the work of warfare strung
>   The yeoman's iron hand! . . .
>
> As if the very earth again
>   Grew quick with God's creating breath.
> And, from the sods of grove and glen,
> Rose ranks of lion-hearted men
>   To battle to the death. . . .
>
> Already had the strife begun;
>   Already blood on Concord's plain,
> Along the springing grass had run,
> And blood had flowed at Lexington,
>   Like brooks of April rain.
>
> That death-stain on the vernal sward
>   Hallowed to freedom all the shore;
> In fragments fell the yoke abhorred—
> The footsteps of a foreign lord
>   Profaned the soil no more.

—WILLIAM CULLEN BRYANT, "Seventy-Six"

1. Background and Causes

Rise of a New Nation. The United States of America began its history as an appendage of Europe. The earliest inhabitants of the new nation, except for the indigenous Indians and the slaves brought over from Africa, were all Europeans, who spoke European languages and who brought with them European ideas, customs, and traditions.

The nation was born in the Age of Reason, with its accent upon liberty, equality, fraternity, constitutionalism, and parliamentarianism. It had little use for medieval feudal, manorial, or ecclesiastical strictures. Above all, it valued the concept of individual liberty—the inalien-able right of every individual to life, liberty, and the pursuit of happiness. The poorer classes of Europe, burdened by political and religious restraints, flocked to the New World. Here, infused with a spirit of individualism, they entered enthusiastically into frontier life. Similar to the simple, natural man praised by Rousseau, they abolished monarchy and aristocracy, separated Church and State, and forged a national union based on freedom.

The new nation was fortunate to be blessed with great leaders attracted by the idea of personal liberty. Early American statesmen demanded a clean break from the tangled threads of European politics. Like the *philosophes,* they were men of great optimism who delighted in projecting the vision of a wonderful future. Their view was presented by John Adams in a letter to Thomas Jefferson in 1813: "Our sure, virtuous, public-spirited federative republic will last forever, govern the globe, and introduce the perfection of man."

Historical Controversy: Political Differences —or Economic Conflict? What were the causes of the American Revolution or, as some historians prefer to call it, the War of Independence? Few questions in either American or world history have evoked so intensive a clash of conflicting opinion. On the one hand there is the simplistic view that the break was motivated by differences in political ideas between Englishmen and American colonists. On the other hand there is the equally monistic view that an irrepressible economic conflict between mother country and colonies was the cause of the Revolution.

The political view, expressed by Charles McLean Andrews, was long accepted as the traditional explanation of American colonial history. According to Andrews, the mother country and colonies had been growing apart psychologically and institutionally for 150 years. Old and well-settled England, with her ruling class possessing the citadels of privilege, was guided by "rigid and sinister ideas of power and government." The colonies were young, growing, democratically minded. Thus, conflict broke out between aristocracy and democracy, between British Parliament and colonial assemblies. The colonists hated tyranny and loved freedom; they resented "taxation without representation," and they demanded the right to govern themselves. Therefore, they rose in heroic rebellion to make of America an independent nation founded on the rationalist principles of liberty, equality, and property.

Against this view was that of another group of historians, for some time led by Charles Austin Beard. In two early monographs, *An Economic Interpretation of the Constitution* (1913) and *The Economic Origins of Jeffersonian Democracy* (1915), Beard presented the cause of the Revolution from the viewpoint of economic determinism. Conflicts between British and colonial mercantile and industrial interests led to the Revolutionary War. The struggle was not really over highsounding political and constitutional concepts such as social contract and sovereignty of the people, but simply and forcefully over colonial manufacturing, land, currency, tea, and furs. It meant either the survival or collapse of English capitalism inside the framework of the mercantilist system.

American historians, all seeking to unravel the "mystery" of the Revolution, gravitated to one side or the other. There are variations of argument: the Revolution was in essence a product of the world struggle for empire (Lawrence Henry Gipson); the political and constitutional views of the colonists can be understood only in the light of the social background and the class interests of the various segments of the American people (James Truslow Adams).

Multiplicity of Causes. It would seem once again that there is more meaning to that pluralistic approach which takes into consideration all the complex political, economic, cultural, and psychological factors. The political conflict was there: between a regime which refused to grant freedom, and growing demands for self-government. The economic conflict was there: underlying the resounding phrases was a ground swell of economic grievances. Social irritation was there: the clash between British and colonial capitalists, the discontent of frontiersmen, artisans, and other radicals. Psychological differences were there: the feelings and sentiments of an long-established, wealthy aristocracy opposed to the pioneer, freedom-loving colonists anxious to break away from maternal supervision and start a life of their own. The latter regarded America as a symbol of change and reform, a new land where experiments, considered too radical for Europe, could be attempted. Unmeasurable extraneous factors were there: the accidental or illogical meeting of men and events, the ambitions and prejudices of members of Parliament and revolutionary leaders.

The American Revolution does not conform to any one pattern. It did not array class against class in the Marxist manner. It was accomplished without extremists seizing power, without emergence of a dictator, without that violent reaction (Thermidor) which in France caused continuing bloodshed. But out of it came ideological and social forces of incalculable consequences for our time—the ideals of freedom, inalienable rights, equality, and government by consent. In a sense it was the delta of the stream of converging historical forces of Western civilization.

The American Revolution was unlike any revolutions that preceded it or followed it. It was not like the French Revolution, or the abortive nineteenth-century revolutions, or the Russian or Chinese revolutions of our own day. It was closest, perhaps, to the English Revolution of 1688, which marked the supremacy of Parliament, but to a greater extent than that English revolution it unleashed ideas and forces which the world still feels today.

Political Differences. The British failed to grant the measure of self-government which the Americans desired. At the base of the quarrel were conflicting ideas of representation and the sovereignty of Parliament. The British called for representation by class instead of by geographical area. Thus, all aristocrats, whether in Kent or South Carolina, were to be represented by the home-grown nobility, and all commoners, in either London or Boston, were to be represented by the members of the House of Commons. To this argument the colonists replied that a true representative must live in the district he represented.

Added to this difference of opinion was an equally conflicting attitude on the role of Parliament. After eliminating absolute monarchy, the British people substituted for it the legality of Parliament's absolute sovereignty. The Declaratory Act (1766) granted authority to Parliament to "make laws and statutes of sufficient force and validity to bind the colonies in all cases whatsoever." Colonial leaders, in common with European rationalists of the Enlightenment, were not inclined to accept absolute sovereignty of any kind, whether of monarchs, Parliament, or anyone else.

Englishmen came to the new frontier that was America "carrying their traditional rights and privileges on their backs." From the early years in the New World, the colonists organized legislative assemblies elected by a restrictive suffrage. Although procedures varied in the Thirteen Colonies, on the whole the state governments were democratic in character. Between royal governors and colonial assemblies there were occasional contests for control. The provincial assemblies held the power of the purse over the British governors. With Parliament several thousand miles away, and the British navy still inadequate to enforce acts of Parliament, the colonists became convinced that they could control their own affairs. By the middle of the eighteenth century the conflict between governors and assemblies, between royal authority and democratic representation, came to a head. The center of gravity of colonial administration shifted from London to the capitals of the American States.

Economic Conflict. There were also grating economic conflicts. Expressed simply, Britain included the American colonies in her system of mercantilism, while the colonists resisted the application of mercantilist theories to themselves. In London's view the colonies were to serve not merely as an outlet for surplus population, but as a source of raw materials and a market for English goods. Parliament passed a series of acts to regulate trade and raise revenue. By the Acts of Trade and Navigation (1651, 1660–1672) trade between Britain and the colonies had to be carried on in British-owned or British-built ships; certain colonial articles, such as tobacco, sugar, and cotton, could be sent only to Britain; and shippers were required to unload and reload in Britain all foreign goods which were on their way to the colonies. (*See page 215 ff.*)

Parliament, however, made no serious attempts to enforce the Navigation Acts. In direct defiance of British laws, smugglers enjoyed a brisk, profitable, almost respectable business. In 1764, as a means of bolstering the Navigation Acts, Parliament sought to tighten the system with an American revenue law popularly known as the Sugar Act. Designed to protect the British West Indian Trade from French, Dutch, and Spanish competition, the new act levied additional duties on sugar, wines, coffee, silks, and linens, and called for more stringent methods of customs collection. This infuriated New England merchants, who had enjoyed handsome profits from the importation of sugar and molasses made into rum.

Religious Motives. The New World had an understandable appeal for religious groups who found further residence in Europe undesirable. Dissenters from established religions in their homeland flocked to America. Puritans and Quakers, as well as Catholics, beset by religious restrictions in England, came to the New World as a land of promise. French Huguenots, subjected to harassment and persecution by Louis XIV and driven out of France, brought their commercial and industrial skills to the new frontier. German religious groups, including Mennonites, Moravian Brethren, and Pietists, found religious haven in America. But soon these religious goals were intermixed with economic advantages to be found in the fast-developing colonial society. Once established in their new homeland, religious dissenters tended to forget the ties that bound them to the old country. The homelands, in turn, were glad to be rid of their troublesome religious minorities.

Psychological Drives. The Thirteen Colonies slowly outgrew their status as appendages of England. There emerged a sentiment of independence, a feeling that the mother country had neglected her offspring. John Adams later said that the Revolution "was in the minds of the people, and in the union of the colonies, both of which were accomplished before hostilities commenced." This psychological motivation was closely bound to political and economic drives. Some who came to America were attracted by the possibility of reaping a quick fortune in gold and silver or tobacco and then returning to the homeland to live in luxury and ease. But for many others the New World was a symbol of change, a frontier which, despite hardships, promised a new and

better life for them and their children. This was a unique country, blessed with potential greatness. The idea of independence, at first vague and shadowy, gradually took form in the minds of a people drifting farther and farther from ties with the European homeland.

Intellectual Stimuli. From its beginnings the colonial cause enlisted much of America's intellectual leadership. Among the political leaders were men attracted by the ideas and ideals of the English rationalists and French *philosophes:* John Adams (1735–1826) in Massachusetts, John Jay (1745–1829) in New York, Benjamin Franklin (1706–1790) in Pennsylvania, and Thomas Jefferson (1743–1826) in Virginia. Added to these was Thomas Paine (1737–1809), an irrepressible pamphleteer who enunciated clearly and passionately the abstract rights of man. These intellectuals, in common with their colleagues abroad, insisted that every human being, no matter where he lived, had fundamental rights which were not to be abridged. They wrote learnedly about natural law, social contract, rights of man, sovereignty of the people, and need for revolution. At first they grounded their case on British traditions, but later turned to the higher law, that law of nature, which, as Crane Brinton remarked, "was as definite and explicit as God had once been, and as dialectical materialism was to be." They gave the American Revolution its ideological base.

2. The Crystallization of Opposition

The Stamp Act, 1765. The close of the French and Indian War in 1763 (the American phase of the Seven Year's War) left the British treasury exhausted. London made it clear to the colonists that, since they, too, would profit by exploitation of the new territories, they were expected to help relieve the burden of debt. Therefore, George Grenville, chancellor of the Exchequer, introduced into Parliament a number of colonial taxation measures planned to raise money. The Stamp Act of 1765, designed to help support a British standing army of 10,000 men in America, called for a tax from a half-penny to 20 shillings on newspapers, legal documents, commercial papers, pamphlets, licenses, ships' papers, even dice and playing cards. The Sugar Act of 1764 had alienated New England businessmen. But the Stamp Act, detested by all sections of the colonial population because it touched everyone's pocketbook, aroused virtually unanimous opposition.

Patterns of Resistance. Resistance took several forms. Colonial intellectual leaders embarked upon a pamphleteering war vesting the Patriot cause with moral and legal arguments against British dictation. Merchants, objecting to taxation without representation, protested by organizing a boycott of British goods. They were supported by the professional class of editors, bankers, and lawyers, all of whom demanded an end once and for all time of colonial subservience to British mercantilism. The boycott hurt British business; it caused a decline of some 20 per cent in British exports to the colonies and stimulated a rise of unployment in England.

Of equal importance was the role of the masses in the mounting opposition. Organizations known as the Sons of Liberty and the Sons of Neptune forced stamp agents to resign their posts and merchants to cancel orders for British goods. A mob surged through the streets of Boston and burned and sacked the residence of Lieutenant-Governor Thomas Hutchinson. Intimidated, every stamp agent resigned even before the effective date of the Stamp Act. The detested stamps were publicly burned.

British Interference in the West. Added to the compounding annoyance from London was British interference with colonists in the West. Prospective settlers, speculators in land, adventurers, all of whom had hoped to settle in the West, were outraged when the British closed the area to colonization. A Royal Proclamation of 1763 reserved all western territories between the Alleghenies and the Mississippi, and between the Floridas and Quebec, for the exclusive use of Indians. Colonists could not purchase any land or settle in that area. In 1774 Parliament passed the new Quebec Act which, though designed to correct certain errors in the earlier proclamation, made matters much worse by annexing all territory north of the Ohio River to the Province of Quebec. Colonists were infuriated by what they regarded as a deliberate attempt to hem them into a small area.

The Crises Resolved and Renewed. American objections to the Stamp Act were so strenuous that it was repealed on March 18, 1766. An additional factor leading to repeal was the support given to Americans by British businessmen for whom enforcement of the tax would have meant a continuing loss of profits. But on that same day came the Declaratory Act, a statement of Parliament's authority over America.

The quarrel between mother country and colonies was reopened in 1767 by three Townshend Acts, named for Charles Townshend, chancellor of the Exchequer. The most important of these Acts imposed duties on tea, glass, lead, paper, and painters' colors brought into the colonies. The Townshend Acts opened once more the question of Parliament's authority to raise revenue in America. The colonists reacted not only with arguments but with physical violence on customs officials. The measures were repealed in 1770, except the duty on tea, retained as evidence of Parliament's authority.

In the next three years occurred a series of British blunders. British regulars stationed in Boston to assist the customs commissioners were heartily disliked by the populace, especially because they engaged in off-duty employment in competition with civilian workmen. In March 1770, under provocation, the soldiers fired upon a crowd of civilians and killed several of them. Colonists were infuriated by this "Boston Massacre." Two years later a mob burned the *Gaspée*, a British revenue cutter that had run aground off Providence, Rhode Island. English authorities ordered a trial in England for the guilty persons, who were never found.

Tempest Over Tea. Matters were aggravated when the English East India Company sent several cargoes of dutiable tea to its own

A contemporary drawing portrays patriot reprisal on Johnny Malcolm, an agent for British customs. Johnny was first tarred and feathered with his clothes on. When he taunted Boston citizens for a bad job, he was stripped, refeathered, and made to toast in tea all eleven members of the royal family.

agents in America. In Boston the reaction was so angry that on December 16, 1773, a group of men disguised as Mohawk Indians boarded a British ship and, through the night, dumped the total tea cargo of 342 chests, worth £10,000, into the harbor. No other property aboard was touched. This open destruction shocked most of the people in Britain. In retaliation the British government closed the port of Boston until cost of the tea was paid, increased the power of British representatives in Massachusetts, ordered transportation of political offenders to England for trial, and gave colonial governors the right to requisition quarters for troops (regulations known in the colonies as "Coercive Measures" or "Intolerable Acts").

The First Continental Congress, 1774. On September 5, 1774, a total of fifty-six delegates from twelve colonies (Georgia blocked the naming of delegates to represent her) assembled in the First Continental Congress at Philadelphia. Stigmatized by Dr. Samuel Johnson as "zealots of anarchy," and "croakers of calamity," the Congress—which included among its delegates George Washington and Patrick Henry (Virginia), John and Samuel Adams (Massachusetts), and John Jay (New York)—petitioned and memorialized George III, Parliament, and the English people for redress of grievances. Although most of its decisions were moderate in tone, the Congress drafted strong resolutions relative to the controversy with England. Revolution was in the air.

The Second Continental Congress assembled at Philadelphia on May 10, 1775. This latter body was transformed by 1781 into the Confederation Congress which lasted until 1789.

3. Resort to Arms: The War of Independence

The War Begins. As early as November 1774, George III had stated plainly: "The New England governments are in a state of rebellion. Blows must decide whether they are to be subject to this country or independent." In the spring of 1775, General Thomas Gage, commander of the British garrison in Boston, received word that Massachusetts patriots were collecting munitions at Concord. On the evening of April 18 he sent a force of 700 troops toward the supply depot. Learning of their destination, the Boston Committee of Public Safety dispatched Paul Revere and William Dawes to alert the countryside. When the British arrived at Lexington the next morning, they found 70 armed Minute Men, a special force authorized by the Provincial Congress. Someone fired a shot, followed by a series of volleys. Eight Americans were killed, 10 wounded, and there was one British casualty.

The British redcoats marched on to Concord, but on their return they were attacked by Minute Men hidden behind stone walls,

An American call to arms.

trees, fences, and houses. When the battle was over, the British had lost 73 killed, 174 wounded, and 26 missing, the Americans 93 dead, wounded, or missing. The battles of Lexington and Concord, marking the beginning of the Revolution, proved that raw Amercian militiamen could stand up against experienced British troops.

At Lexington came the "shot heard around the world." For the next fourteen months the struggle was continued in a half-dozen military and naval campaigns. At Bunker Hill on June 17, 1775, a British force of 2,400 men led by Generals Sir William Howe, Sir Henry Clinton, and John Burgoyne routed 1,600 Americans with six cannon under the command of Colonel William Prescott. It was a Pyrrhic victory, however, for British casualties exceeded 1,000, three times those of the Patriots. Meanwhile, seven days before Bunker Hill, Ethan Allen stormed and captured Fort Ticonderoga on Lake Champlain, a strategic post rich in artillery and other military supplies. At the same time an American expedition marched on Quebec.

The Declaration of Independence. Not until the summer of 1776 did the Congress abandon all hope for reconciliation. Many persons in the colonies, including British officials, Anglican clergymen, lawyers, and businessmen, still opposed the idea of independence. But under the driving leadership of such Patriots as Samuel and John Adams, Patrick Henry, and Benjamin Franklin, the moderates, including George Washington, John Jay, and Robert Morris, were won over to the revolutionary movement.

The Declaration of Independence, drafted by a congressional committee headed by Thomas Jefferson, was approved by the Congress on July 4, 1776. The document reflected the tenets of middle-class revolutionary theory. The first part expressed a philosophy of government and society—the equality of men, the inalienability of such human rights as life, liberty, and the pursuit of happiness; the duty of the government to protect such rights; and, in the event of the government's failure to perform these duties, the right of the people to resort to revolution. The second part described

causes of the decision to separate from England. The third formally declared that "these United Colonies are, and of Right ought to be, Free and Independent States."

For more than a century of British connection the colonists had remained subservient to the Crown. For better or worse, they now felt that continued dominance from London would mean a diminution of the advantages which the founders had settled in the New World to obtain. The American argument had come a long way, from (1) denying direct imperial taxes, to (2) denial of the right of Parliament to tax without representation, and to (3) denial of George III's sovereignty. John Locke had stated the doctrine of the natural rights of man, including the right of revolution, in his *Second Treatise on Government*. Thomas Jefferson consciously or unconsciously adopted that idea when he wrote the Declaration. The weight of grievances already piled up, plus fear of what the future held, tipped the scales in favor of revolution. The issue boiled down to one simple fact: Americans were not willing to be subjected to that kind of oppression which the English had for so long clamped on Ireland.

Redcoats Versus Patriots. On July 4, 1776, the British seemed to be in an advantageous position in America. They had a well-trained, disciplined force larger than that of the Patriots, some foreign mercenaries, a navy to transport troops and guard supply lines, and an active fifth column in the States. Against these the Patriots had the advantages of campaigning on their own ground, military experience gained in the French and Indian Wars, and a distinguished military leader in George Washington. The Patriot army was a ragged one, but it was a fighting force. The British underrated the Americans. According to Lord Sandwich, head of the Admiralty: "They are raw, undisciplined, cowardly men." But the Continental army managed, nevertheless, to inflict a decisive defeat on British arms. The British lost the war because of weakness in strategy and tactics, unwillingness to seize the initiative, and failure to concentrate their overwhelming forces at any one point. Britain's efforts were further hampered by her total lack of European allies, while France (1778), Spain (1779), and the Netherlands (1780) entered the war on the side of the Americans.

The New York Campaign, 1776. There were four major military campaigns between 1776 and 1778: at New York, Trenton-Princeton, Saratoga, and Philadelphia. After being forced out of Boston, the British in the spring of 1776 moved to Halifax in Nova Scotia. In June they returned to New York to meet American forces under General George Washington, named commander-in-chief of the revolutionary army by the Second Continental Congress on June 15, 1775. In engagements which lasted from August to November 1776, Washington's forces yielded ground to the British. It was a low point of discouragement for the Patriot cause. "These are the times that try men's souls," wrote Thomas Paine.

Trenton-Princeton, 1776–1777. Washington was determined to choose his own time and place for a counterattack. It came during the Christmas season, 1776–1777. In a series of quick marches, aided by weather conditions and British blunders, the Continentals overwhelmed Britain's Hessian mercenaries at Trenton on December 26, 1776, and eight days later drove the British from Princeton. These victories restored Patriot morale.

The Philadelphia Campaign, 1777. The British, fearing that Washington might join forces with the northern army against Burgoyne, moved toward Philadelphia to keep the American commander-in-chief to the southward. The British General Howe attacked in the Battle of Brandywine, September 11, 1777, which nearly ended in complete disaster for the Americans. On September 26 Howe occupied Philadelphia. During that bitter winter, the British lived comfortably in Philadelphia while Washington's army nearly froze at Valley Forge.

Knockout Blow at Saratoga, October 17, 1777. In early 1777 the British had large forces in Canada as well as a strong army in New York under command of General Sir William Howe. If the British had concentrated these 25,000 well-equipped regulars against Washington's little army of 8,000 Continentals in New Jersey, they might have crushed the revolt without further difficulty. But General John Burgoyne unwisely chose to leave his forces divided. One army, under his leadership, would move from Canada southward upon Albany; Howe's forces would move up the Hudson to Albany; between them they would trap the Americans. Orders came from London to Canada to launch the northern half of the joint expedition. However, no definite instructions went to Howe, who moved on Philadelphia instead of Albany.

Burgoyne's troops moving south ran into a hornets' nest of New England yeomanry. The American rifle was pitted against the British smoothbore musket. The Continentals confronted Burgoyne's main force on the Upper Hudson. Lost in the wilderness, surrounded on all sides by forces triple their own, Burgoyne's troops, 5,700 of them, laid down their arms. By the terms of the surrender agreement, the Saratoga Convention (October 17, 1777), the British troops were to return to England and not participate any further in the war.

Burgoyne's defeat had far-reaching consequences. In England it led to a request by Prime Minister Lord North, who had allowed George III to induce him to carry on the American war against his will, that he be allowed to resign. The American victory brought France into the war. Until Saratoga, French enthusiasm for the Patriot cause was cool. On February 6, 1778, France and the United States signed a treaty of alliance which placed an entirely new aspect on the war. Already the Marquis de Lafayette (1757–1834), French officer and politician, had come to the United States to serve in any capacity and had been made a major general by Congress. The kings of France and Spain made secret loans to the Americans for arms and munitions. French troops and ships were soon on their way to the embattled colonists. French assistance, however, was rooted in anti-British rather than pro-American sentiment.

The War in the South, 1778–1781. Having

failed to win in the north, the British now turned to the south. They planned to capture Georgia and then move northward. On December 29, 1778, British forces took Savannah and in 1779 occupied much of Georgia and South Carolina. In May 1780 they stormed Charleston, and in one of the heaviest blows of the war, captured General Benjamin Lincoln and his 5,400 men. General Horatio Gates, the hero of Saratoga, sent south in June 1780 to halt the British, was crushed by General Cornwallis at Camden, South Carolina. The Americans lost 800 killed and 1,000 captured, after which Gates fled for 160 miles without stopping to make a report. This defeat was counterbalanced on October 7, 1780, at King's Mountain on the southern border of North Carolina, when a Patriot army defeated the British in one of the most ferocious battles of the war.

Yorktown, 1781. Late in the spring of 1781 General Cornwallis moved northward to join Benedict Arnold (called a turncoat by the angry Americans) in Virginia. Pursuing American forces under command of Lafayette, Cornwallis withdrew to Yorktown at the mouth of the York River. Brilliantly seizing the opportunity, Washington joined his 6,000 men near New York and Rochambeau's 5,000 at Newport, Rhode Island, and in a series of rapid marches moved his men on Yorktown. Here Cornwallis's 8,000 troops were cut off from escape by the French fleet. American artillery battered down the British fortifications. On October 19, 1781, Cornwallis sent his sword to Washington. The war was virtually over, although an angered George III stubbornly refused to admit defeat.

The Peace Treaty, 1783. The Treaty of Paris ended the war. Britain acknowledged the independence of the Thirteen Colonies. Boundaries were fixed for the new nation: Canada and the Great Lakes on the north; Florida on the south; and the Mississippi River on the west. Spain recovered Florida and Minorca. The French acquired several small islands off the coast of Canada and in the West Indies, and Senegal.

Britain emerged from the American Revolution with diminished prestige and shrunken possessions. This setback, however, was only temporary, for the British began to build an even greater and more prosperous empire. The French hope of smashing British imperial pretensions was never fully realized. For the French the American Revolution was costly in that it helped contribute to their financial ruin.

Freed of British restrictions, the United States advanced rapidly. Settlers streamed across the Alleghenies. The natural march of the republic was westward in a direction which eventually would induce the new nation to purchase the Louisiana Territory from France. The United States and Canada, side by side, were to expand to the Pacific.

4. Consequences: Emergence of a Lusty Republic

Political Upheaval. The Revolution unleashed generating forces that were to change the American way of life and provide a model for much of the world. The successful drive for independence, proving that the republican form of government could function effectively, at the same time delivered a blow to the monarchic system. The colonists created a new governmental structure, with a Constitution which set up a balance between federal authority and states rights. For the first time in history a large group of states formed their own governments under written constitutions, each providing for a strong bicameral legislative system, with weak executives (governors). Each state constitution had a Bill of Rights which later would be incorporated into the first ten amendments of the federal Constitution. Thomas Jefferson's "inalienable rights of man" became permanent features of the law of the land.

Socioeconomic Results. At long last, freed from the bonds of British mercantilism, Americans could now turn to the manufacture of goods previously imported from Britain. Royal restrictions on the acquisition of western lands were eliminated. The vast British Crown lands and huge Tory estates were now at the disposal of the state legislatures, which sold them at low prices or gave them as outright bounties to those who had seen military service during the Revolution. Quitrents, formerly paid by farmers to the Crown or to colonial proprietary farmers, were abolished, thus putting an end to a feudal relic in the colonies. Laws of entail (the rule by which lands were settled inalienably on a person and his descendants) and primogeniture (descent of real property to the eldest son) were abolished by state legislation. The British government, generous in reimbursing Loyalists who had lost their property in America, settled many of them in Canada, while others were brought home to England.

Religious Consequences. The Revolution did much to promote the movement for religious toleration in America. The tax-supported Anglican Church was disestablished during the early part of the war in New York, Maryland, North and South Carolina, Georgia, and a few years later in Virginia. Disestablishment was a slower process in three of the New England states in which the official church was Congregational; final separation took place in New Hampshire in 1817, Connecticut in 1818, and Massachusetts in 1833. These religious changes were accompanied by broad humanitarian reforms in penal codes, prison system, and education.

Psychological Connotations. The American Revolution was something more than a mere breaking away of colonies from the motherland. The ideals of liberty and equality—the egalitarian formula, which the Revolutionary generation had so nobly phrased—were present in the minds of Americans long before the War of Independence. This was a new way of life which was working. It was there for all the world to see. From the revolutionary era there emerged a psychology of freedom, an attitude holding that equality was something more than a philosophical discussion by starry-eyed rationalists. It was a heady wine which penetrated far beyond the boundaries of North America. Here was a successful precedent for political evolution elsewhere. Revolutionaries and liberals of nineteenth-century Europe were psychologically armed by the American experience.

⚬{ KEY DOCUMENT }⚬
THE AMERICAN BILL OF RIGHTS, 1791

WHEN THE Constitution was being considered by state ratifying conventions in 1787–1788, several amendments were proposed. Some states approved the Constitution with the understanding that the amendments would soon be adopted. A committee reported twelve amendments, of which ten were ratified and became a part of the Constitution in December 1791. The amendments collectively are called the "Federal Bill of Rights." They assert limitations on the federal government, not on the state governments. Today, the Fifth Amendment, which safeguards the citizen from testifying against himself in criminal cases, has been given wide publicity by the large numbers of Congressional committee witnesses who "take the Fifth" as a matter of self-protection.

ARTICLE I

Freedom of religion, speech, of the press, and right of petition.—Congress shall make no law respecting an establishment of religion, or prohibiting the free exercise thereof; or abridging the freedom of speech, or of the press; or the right of the people peaceably to assemble and to petition the Government for a redress of grievances.

ARTICLE II

Right of people to bear arms not to be infringed.—A well-regulated militia, being necessary to the security of a free State, the right of the people to keep and bear Arms, shall not be infringed.

ARTICLE III

Quartering of troops.—No soldier shall, in time of peace be quartered in any house, without the consent of the owner, nor in time of war but in a manner to be prescribed by law.

ARTICLE IV

Persons and houses to be secure from unreasonable searches and seizures.—The right of the people to be secure in their persons, houses, papers, and effects, against unreasonable searches and seizures, shall not be violated, and no warrants shall issue but upon probable cause, supported by oath or affirmation, and particularly describing the place to be searched, and the persons or things to be seized.

ARTICLE V

Trials for crimes; just compensation for private property taken for public use.—No person shall be held to answer for a capital or otherwise infamous crime unless on a presentment or indictment of a Grand Jury, except in cases arising in the land or naval forces, or in the militia, when in actual service in time of war or public danger; nor shall any person be subject for the same offense to be twice put in jeopardy of life or limb; nor shall be compelled in any criminal case to be a witness against himself, nor be deprived of life, liberty, or property, without due process of law; nor shall private property be taken for public use, without just compensation.

ARTICLE VI

Civil rights in trials for crimes enumerated.—
In all criminal prosecutions, the accused shall enjoy the right to a speedy and public trial, by an impartial jury of the State and district wherein the crime shall have been committed, which district shall have been previously ascertained by law, and to be informed of the nature and cause of the accusation; to be confronted with the witnesses against him; to have compulsory process for obtaining witnesses in his favor, and to have the Assistance of Counsel for his defense.

ARTICLE VII

Civil rights in civil suits.—In suits at common law, where the value in controversy shall exceed twenty dollars, the right of trial by jury shall be preserved, and no fact tried by a jury, shall be otherwise re-examined in any Court of the United States than according to the rules of the common law.

ARTICLE VIII

Excessive bail, fines and punishments prohibited.—Excessive bail shall not be required, nor excessive fines imposed, nor cruel and unusual punishments inflicted.

ARTICLE IX

Reserved rights of people.—The enumeration in the Constitution of certain rights shall not be construed to deny or disparage others retained by the people.

ARTICLE X

Powers not delegated, reserved to states and people respectively.—The powers not delegated to the United States by the Constitution, nor prohibited by it to the States, are reserved to the States respectively, or to the people.

❧ HISTORICAL INTERPRETATION ❧

CARL L. BECKER ON THE DECLARATION OF INDEPENDENCE

Carl L. Becker, *The Declaration of Independence: A Study in the History of Political Ideas* (New York, 1922), pp. 18–23, *passim*. By permission of Frederick D. Becker.

CARL LOTUS BECKER (1873–1945), professor of history at Cornell University, was attracted by both European and American history. A brilliantly incisive writer, he was known for his ability to cut straight through to the heart of a subject. In the following excerpt from his discussion of the Declaration of Independence he summarized what was in the minds of the colonists when they issued the document. He showed how Jefferson and his friends, honest and good men, were convinced that the Declaration was a true bill against George III and the unnamed Parliament.

Superficially, the Declaration seems chiefly concerned with the causes of the Revolution, with the specific grievances; but in reality it is chiefly, one might say solely, concerned with a theory of government—with a theory of government in general, and a theory of the British empire in particular. The theory of government in general is explicitly formulated, the theory of the British empire is not explicitly formulated but is implicitly taken for granted; and the second part of the Declaration was carefully phrased so that no assertion or implication might appear as a contradiction or a denial of the assumed theory.

The Declaration thus becomes interesting for what it omits as well as for what it includes. For example, it does not, in its final form, contain the word, "Parliament"—a most significant omission, considering that the controversy of the preceding decade was occasioned, not by the acts of the king, who plays the leading part in the Declaration, but by the acts of the British Parliament. In all the controversy leading up to the Revolution the thing chiefly debated was the authority of the British Parliament. What is the nature, and what precisely are the limits, of the authority of the British Parliament over the colonies? This question was in fact the central issue. Nevertheless, the Declaration does not mention the British Parliament.

So striking an omission must have been intentional. It was of course impossible to make out a list of grievances against Great Britain without referring to such acts as the Stamp Act, the Declaratory Act, the Boston Port Bill, and many other legislative measures, and the framers of the Declaration, when they brought these measures into the indictment, had accordingly to resort to circumlocution in order to avoid naming the Parliament that passed them. . . .

Another significant omission is the term "rights of British subjects." Throughout the controversy the colonists had commonly protested against parliamentary taxation precisely on the ground that they possessed the rights of British subjects. They said that the British Parliament could not constitutionally tax British subjects without their consent, and that British subjects in the colonies were not, and in the nature of the case could not well be, represented in the British Parliament. For ten years the colonists had made the "rights of British subjects" the very foundation of their case. Yet this is just what the framers of the Declaration carefully refrain from doing: the term "rights of the British people" does not appear in the Declaration. . . .

The framers of the Declaration refrained from mentioning Parliament and the "rights of British subjects" for the same reason that they charged all their grievances against the king alone. Being now committed to independence, the position of the colonies could not be simply or convincingly presented from the point of view of the rights of British subjects. To have said: "We hold this truth to be self-evident, that it is the right of British subjects not to be taxed except by their own consent," would have made no great appeal to mankind, since mankind in general could not be supposed to be vitally interested in the rights of British subjects, or much disposed to regard them as axioms in political speculation. Separation from Great Britain was therefore justified on more general grounds, on the ground of the natural rights of man; and in order to simplify the issue, in order to make it appear that the rights of man had been undeniably and flagrantly violated, it was expedient that these rights should seem to be as little as possible limited or obscured by the positive and legal obligations that were admittedly binding upon British subjects. . . .

The specific grievances enumerated in the Declaration were accordingly presented from the point of view of a carefully considered and resolutely held constitutional theory of the British empire. The essence of this theory, nowhere explicitly formulated in the Declaration, but throughout implicitly taken for granted, is that the colonies became parts of the empire by their own voluntary act, and remained parts of it solely by virtue of a compact subsisting between them and the king. Their rights were those of all men, of every free people; their obligations such as a free people might incur by professing alle-giance to the personal head of the empire. On this theory, both the Parliament and the rights of British subjects could be ignored as irrelevant to the issue.

❧ TEN BASIC BOOKS ❧

THE AMERICAN REVOLUTION

1. Andrews, Charles, *The Colonial Background of the American Revolution,* rev. ed. (New Haven, Conn., 1931).†

2. Becker, Carl L., *The Declaration of Independence: A Study in the History of Political Ideas* (New York, 1942).†

3 Briderbaugh, Carl, *Cities in Revolt: Urban Life in America, 1743-1776* (New York, 1955).†

4. Commager, Henry Steele, *The American Mind* (New Haven, Conn., 1959).†

5. Jensen, Merrill, *The Making of the American Constitution,* Anvil Book No. 75 (Princeton, N. J., 1964).

6. Miller, John C., *Origins of the American Revolution* (Stanford, Calif., 1959).†

7. Morison, Samuel, ed., *Sources and Documents Illustrating the American Revolution, 1764-1788, and the Formation of the Federal Constitution,* 2nd ed. (New York, 1965).†

8. Morris, Richard B., *The Peacemakers: The Great Powers and American Independence* (New York, 1965).

9. Rossiter, Clinton L., *Seedtime of the Republic* (New York, 1953).

10. Savelle, Max, *Seeds of Liberty: The Genesis of the American Mind* (New York, 1948).

PART IV

WATERSHED: THE FRENCH REVOLUTION AND NAPOLEON

1789–1815

SCOPE AND SIGNIFICANCE OF THE FRENCH REVOLUTION[1]

Leo Gershoy

THE FIRST accounts of the Revolution were written by participants before the great upheaval had spent its force. Heated in tone, often intemperate, they were partisan histories, of dubious value. The contemporaries who penned them sought less to explain than to praise or damn the epic disruption which was ripping apart the closely knit fibers of French life. Everywhere, in France and out, the Revolution had fervent defenders with eyes for the good that it was doing; everywhere, too, there were detractors not less vehement than the champions, aghast over its violence and its rejection of established ways.

Searching their minds for an explanation of what was happening, men whose lives the Revolution uprooted tended, while they vigorously denounced its frightfulness, to discover religious–historical causes for the evil it had wrought. Human frailty and wickedness, they agreed, played their part. But to find a fuller explanation of this cruel attack upon European civilization, writers who were hostile to the Revolution made much of three forces; the subversive ideas of the Enlightenment; the conspiracy of the *philosophes* and their organized followers; and the workings of providence.

That such explanations gave emotional satisfaction, as well as solace for material losses, to men whose deepest sentiments had been outraged, is apparent. As commentaries on the origins of the revolutionary movement and its significance, they had defects which the passage of time has not lessened. After a century and a half of intensive scholarly research this type of explanation, in an intellectually more sophisticated form, still has a few never-say-die exponents. One cannot take it seriously. Every facet of the Revolution has been examined in the light of the specialized interest of the investigators. As much as research is capable, it has made that extraordinary explosion of human energies intelligible. What historical investigation has made abundantly clear is that the Revolution was not a conspiracy organized and plotted by purveyors of subversive ideas.

To be sure, the hopes of the future revolutionaries were kindled by ideas. Many young men were under the sway of a kind of prerevolutionary mentality in the years immediately preceding 1789 and immediately following the successful revolutionary activities across the ocean in America. Those activities were widely reported and enthusiastically endorsed. In the broadest sense the ideas by which men were moved held forth the prospect not only of an orderly world, such as France already had, more or less, but also of a world where

[1] Leo Gershoy, *The Era of the French Revolution, 1789–1799*, Anvil Book No. 22 (Princeton, N. J., 1957), pp. 9–13.

order for all would be founded upon the liberty of the individual. Not liberty unrestrained and unconfined, but a tempered liberty operating within a newer and different community than the one in which they lived, in a community where there would be equality and rights for its members, where each would work together to advance the happiness and prosperity of all.

These ideas, critical, often mocking, occasionally original, and ever emphatic in stressing liberty of enterprise, of expression and conscience, defended the natural right of the individual together with his fellows to work out his own destiny. They were weapons against the old order, obviously. They did not, however, spring full-grown from the heads of isolated thinkers, linked to one another only by evil intentions; they were conceived in the womb of circumstance. They were the reflection and the products of the historical evolution of the past generations. They accompanied sustained economic changes which were bringing wealth and power to merchants, manufacturers, and financiers. They attested the expansion of knowledge which had steadily widened the horizon of Europeans, transforming their living habits and secularizing their values. They gave evidence of waning faith in revealed truth and of supreme confidence in science and reason to regenerate the institutions of man.

This pattern of thought and feeling had fashioned itself more markedly in France than anywhere else on the continent of Europe. For in France of the Old Regime, circumstances were most favorable to it. . . .

As new social groups entered in turn upon the stage, new emotions, new grievances and observations were released to mingle with and reenforce the first currents—or to run counter to them. Yet there lay, under the surface of disorder and violence, an inner rhythm of development. It is in war and inflation, class tensions, real and fancied, counter-revolutionary plots and Terror at home, and in a revolutionary crusade against kings and aristocracies abroad, that one must seek the causes of the successive shocks which troubled the decade.

In 1799 when Bonaparte seized power, the Revolution had sorely disappointed the expectations of many followers. Its heroic proportions, nevertheless, were patent. Whether to admire or lament it, everyone recognized that it had burned its way through the history of France. . . .

The Revolution outlasted the revolutionary decade. Its ideas and institutions, perpetuated and extended by Napoleon's conquering troops, penetrated deeply into European life. The Revolution as the fulfillment of liberty conquered and converted Europe. It lived on in the consciousness of the hopeful and the disaffected as a passing and unfulfilled promise of equality, as an unforgettable moment in the struggle of democracy against privilege.

18

Liberty, Equality, Fraternity: The French People Launch a Revolution

THE NATIONAL ASSEMBLY, considering that it has been summoned to establish the constitution of the kingdom, to effect the regeneration of public order, and to maintain the true principles of monarchy; that nothing can prevent it from continuing its deliberations in whatever place it may be forced to establish itself; and, finally, that wheresoever its members are assembled, *there* is the National Assembly;

Decrees that all members of this Assembly shall immediately take a solemn oath not to separate, and to reassemble wherever circumstances require, until the Constitution of the kingdom is established and consolidated upon firm foundations; and that, the said oath taken, all members and each one of them individually shall ratify this steadfast resolution by signature.

—THE TENNIS COURT OATH, June 20, 1789

1. France Moves to Revolution

An Age of Upheaval. The French Revolution was the dynamic materialization of a new concept of liberty which conflicted with the old principle of obedience to authority and tradition. With resistance and civil war inside France, and opposition from outside the country, the current of change became ever swifter and deeper, cutting its way into all facets of society.

Revolution was brought on by a multiplicity of circumstances—economic chaos, inefficient administration, social inequality, persistence of feudal practices, religious abuses, and widespread fear and hostility. The nobility and clergy, a tiny percentage of the population, retained social control over such unprivileged groups as the energetic bourgeoisie and the discontented peasantry and urban proletariat. French *philosophes,* intellectuals of the Enlightenment, called for a new society grounded on liberty, equality, and fraternity.

The roots of change lay deep in the past. Then, suddenly and with great violence, came the explosion. Old institutions were shattered by new forces. The Old Regime, with its autocratic monarch and privileged nobility, was repudiated, and the middle class emerged triumphant. The Revolution then took on missionary zeal as it disseminated to all corners of Europe the ideas that shaped the history of the nineteenth and twentieth centuries. Nationalism, democracy, and liberalism, all reflected the principles underlying the French Revolution.

Unlike the Russian Revolutions of 1917, the French Revolution took place in the most advanced country in Europe. France was the fulcrum of the Enlightenment; French was everywhere the language of intellect and aristocracy. The established classes of Europe, all of whom looked to Paris for inspiration, were horrified and bewildered by events in France.

The upheaval was something more than the irresponsible mischief of eighteenth-century *philosophes.* It was not produced by magic. A combination of economic, social, political, and psychological forces converged at a moment when the Old Regime was ready to succumb to dry rot. How to interpret these confusing issues has become one of the more important problems facing contemporary historians. There is controversy at nearly every turn.

Historical Controversy—Political: National Occidental Revolution? On the one hand, there is the contention, earlier projected by Alexis de Tocqueville, and exemplified in the work of Marcel Reinhard, professor of history at the Sorbonne in Paris, that during the eighteenth century France alone underwent a revolution in the fullest and most profound sense of the word. Only France, Reinhard said, by her own means and under her own power, carried out the transformation. The Revolution belonged to the French people because, despite its universal aspects, it was uniquely and especially French in origin and development. Its singularity was derived from the very essence of the French nation, from French public opinion, economy, and society. Even the aristocratic resistance to the revolutionary energy of the Third Estate was uniquely French. The argument went further: no people ever repeated the French Revolution or passed through the same sequences. The France of today can be understood only when portrayed against this special background.

Against this exclusively nationalist approach is the view held by, among others, Jacques Godechot and Robert R. Palmer, that it is necessary to go far beyond the usual national perspective. It is an error, they say, to seek all revolutionary ideas and practices in the last forty years of the eighteenth century in France alone. Actually, the French Revolution was part of a great movement toward self-government and to that freer society which was to come into existence in Western Europe and America by the mid-nineteenth century. The explosion in France was dramatic and influential but it was not the cause of the enormous evolution in Western ideals and practices.

There were outbursts elsewhere, in the American colonies, Switzerland, the Italies, the Netherlands, and Ireland. "I believe," wrote Godechot, "that the great movement which overthrew the social, economic, and political order of most of Europe and America between 1770 and 1849 should be described as 'Western' or 'Atlantic.' While France and the United States played an overwhelming role in this revolution, its scope was broader. This is corroborated by examining the counterrevolution, . . . which, like the revolution itself, was also international and Western." Contemporary scholars, drawing on the experiences of the twentieth-century world, in which international revolutions and supranational blocs have become common, tend to see the French Revolution in terms of a common Western or Atlantic civilization. In other words, the French Revolution was but one phase of an era of democratic revolutions in the West.

It becomes the task of historians today to disentangle the French experience from a great revolutionary era in European history. Starting from France, revolutionary principles circled the world. In the nineteenth century every nation, in its own way, either adopted or opposed the principles of 1789. Eventually, these principles ranged the globe, to Africa, Asia, and the Latin-American countries The basic questions remain: 1. Was the French Revolution a national democratic revolution which caused an enormous change everywhere in Western ideals and practices? 2. Was the French Revolution merely a link in a chain of revolutions in the eighteenth-century Occidental world? Historians have no common answers.

Historical Controversy II—Economic: Misery or Prosperity? How the same historical facts can be used to support opposing points of view is illustrated further by controversy surrounding the role of the peasantry and the urban proletariat in the outbreak of the French Revolution. Jules Michelet presented the traditional view that the French Revolution may be attributed in large part to the misery of the oppressed peasantry and urban workers. Driven to desperation by a greedy, corrupt, royal government and nobility, harassed by a ruinous fiscal policy, the masses revolted in the name of freedom against tyranny. Everyone, wrote Michelet, could see the crisis approaching. "The evil consists in this, that the nation, from the highest to the lowest, is organized to go on producing less and less, and paying more and more. She will go on declining, wasting away, giving, after her blood, her marrow; and there will be no end to it, till having reached the last gasp, and just expiring, the convulsion of the death-struggle arouses her once more and raises that pale feeble body on its legs."

Exactly the opposite point of view was presented by Alexis de Tocqueville, who, in his study of the Old Regime, came to the conclusion that the French peasant was in fact far better off than any other peasants in Europe. The French peasant's desire for ownership of land was nothing less than an obsession. By the late eighteenth century he had become a landowner and was at long last emancipated from the control of his lord. France was steadily increasing in wealth and prosperity despite the unremedied shortcomings of governmental administration, obstacles with which industry still had to contend (inequality of taxation, vagaries of local laws, and feudal rights). "It is a singular fact that this steadily increasing prosperity, far from tranquilizing the population, everywhere promoted a spirit of unrest. The general public became more and more hostile to every ancient institution, more and more discontented; indeed, it was increasingly obvious that the nation was heading for revolution."

A middle position was taken by a third French historian, Georges Lefebvre, who admitted the rising level of prosperity in France, but at the same time pointed to the poverty and discontent of the peasants. The peasants, he said, were hostile to the capitalistic order which had begun to be established. They were in an alliance, but a fragile one, with the bourgeois landowners against their common enemy, the nobility. Thus, the Revolution was the culmination of a long socioeconomic development which eventually made the bourgeoisie the masters of the world. At the same time, he said, it is too narrow an interpretation to attribute the explosion solely to the rise of the bourgeoisie. One must keep in mind such motivating factors as peasant-and-bourgeois hatred for the feudal regime; resistance of the privileged classes to the new economic order; and opposition of the least favored classes to the new capitalism. According to Lefebvre, the characteristic feature of the French Revolution was the concurrence of four revolutions at the same time: by the aristocracy, by the bourgeoisie, by the peasants, and by the urban masses. These dynamic forces in common led to the outburst of liberation with its accompanying crudeness and brutality.

Psychological Motivation: The Great Fear. The more one contemplates its dramatic events and tumultuous extravagances the more he is convinced of the important role which both rational and irrational fear played in the Revolution. All elements of the French population were gripped by this psychology of dread. Louis XVI and Marie Antoinette were afraid for their own lives and for their family. Hesitant and vacillating, they easily yielded on the spur of the moment, but neither felt it necessary to keep promises made under stress. After the fall of the Bastille, all France was seized by the Great Fear, the haunting anxiety of people living in terror. The aristocrats were frightened by the accumulated hatred of centuries directed against them. The alarmed commoners of Paris and the hinterland were gripped by irrational anxieties: "The brigands are coming!" This was the characteristic whisper of apprehension: a vague someone being sent from some place by aristocrats to butcher the people. Revolutionary leaders, in deadly fear for their own lives, agreed to send friends to the guillotine. The 361 deputies who voted for the execution of Louis XVI, branded for life as regicides, could never again for their own safety allow a restoration of the Bourbon monarchy in France. At every stage of the Revolution events were dictated not only by inexorable economic, political, and social drives but also by fear. Historians cannot measure this fear; they can only point to its existence.

2. *The Old Regime: Pre-Revolutionary France*

The Outworn Society. The essential fact about the Old Regime was that it was still legally aristocratic and feudal. In France, as in every other European country, relics of half-overthrown medievalism still survived. The France of the Old Regime was a class society distinguished by inequality of rights. Everyone belonged legally to an "Estate" or "order" of society. In 1789 the population of France numbered approximately 25,000,000 people, of whom 500,000 individuals—just two per cent, at most—made up the two upper estates. This privileged minority owned a disproportionate share of the soil, monopolized income, and was almost exempt from taxation. The First Estate comprised the clergy, the Second Estate the nobility, and the Third Estate included all others, from the wealthy businessmen and professionals to the poor peasantry and urban workers. Politically, the system was already obsolescent. But not since 1614 had the Estates-General met to represent the whole kingdom. Socially, too, it had outlived its usefulness, for no longer did the triple division correspond to the real distribution of class interests among the French people.

The First Estate: Privileged Clergy. Although the doctrines of the Church had been under attack by the *philosophes,* the clergy still possessed influence far beyond its numbers. The Church, virtually a state within the State, had its own officers of administration, its own courts of law, even a representative assembly to regulate relations with the monarchy. It controlled schools, hospitals, and charitable institutions. Immensely wealthy, it derived revenue from its vast landed property, from the tithe levied on all crops, and from gifts and fees. It was a conservative force, a pillar of the old society. The upper clergy, like the nobility, was exempted from taxation. It made periodic "free gifts" to the royal treasury, but though of substantial size, its contributions were less than could have been obtained by direct taxation. The clergy was deeply involved in the prevailing system and,

upholding the traditions and values of the Old Regime, it was to face opposition from the masses.

The Second Estate: Privileged Aristocracy. The second order of nobility in 1789 was composed of about 400,000 persons, including women and children. Unlike the clergy, the nobility was not corporatively organized. A legally distinct social group, it had its own rights and privileges, such as the right to be tried in separate courts, exemption from onerous taxes (especially the *taille,* most important direct tax on land), and a monopoly of the highest positions in the Church, civil administration, army, and navy. Its main source of power was wealth, reckoned primarily in land. There were variations in fortune and influence. Just as the higher clergy had little in common with the parish priests, so did the court nobility differ from the petty, or lesser, nobility. The courtiers—social parasites, and lovers of conspicuous extravagance—enjoyed a round of parties and gambling, and spent much of their time in seeking pensions and titles. Others of the older nobility, the country gentry or lesser nobility, barred from the luxuries of Versailles, lived in want on their impoverished country estates. A third group, the bureaucratic nobility, the *noblesse de la robe,* obtained noble status through purchase of patents of nobility or intermarriage. From its ranks came the *parlementaires,* tough-minded opponents of absolutism. Wealthy, cultivated, and arrogant, they sparked the resurgence of noble power in the eighteenth century.

The Third Estate: Unprivileged Peasantry and Urban Proletariat. The Third Estate included the overwhelming majority of the population. A legal catchall, it numbered among its millions all nonclerical, non-noble Frenchmen. More than four-fifths of the people were peasants who had an almost unique status in Europe. Nearly all were legally free and, although still burdened with manorial dues and services, could bequeath, inherit, and improve their land. The fact that the average plot was small forced the peasants to work a large part of the remaining cultivable soil owned by Church, king, lay aristocracy, or bourgeoisie. Though they formed the backbone of French society, the peasants regarded themselves as an exploited class. They were not hopelessly downtrodden, but many were well enough off to wish to better themselves. The landless peasants had to find work as farmhands or go to the cities to do piecework as spinners and weavers.

The lot of the unskilled urban workers was only slightly better. Working for low wages, trapped in crowded quarters, with minimum supplies of food, the city proletariat had no alternative to disaster. Both peasants and urban workingmen suffered from a series of trials. A harvest failure in 1788, followed by the grim winter of 1788–1789, the coldest in memory of living men, hit both rural and urban population. Bread prices soared, and landlords, to meet rising costs, raised rents. When the boom in industrial expansion burst, city workers began to riot for bread and work.

The Utilitarian Bourgeoisie. Comprising the most important section of the Third Estate was the middle class, or *bourgeoisie*, some ten or twelve per cent of the population. The bourgeoisie was itself divided into an upper bourgeoisie, the wealthy business elite and non-noble governmental officials; the middle bourgeoisie, prosperous merchants and traders, craftsmen and artisans, teachers, and lawyers; and the petty bourgeoisie, including small shopkeepers, tradesmen, and even some who were also in the working class proper, such as clerks and domestics. Unlike the English middle class, which included many yeomen and tenant farmers, the French bourgeoisie was an urban class. Amassing a large portion of the nation's working capital, it resented the old clerical and noble privileges, and demanded economic, social, and political prerogatives commensurate with its wealth.

The upper bourgeoisie had its own creed: it was rationalistic and utilitarian. Its spokesmen, the *philosophes*, brilliantly expounded these beliefs in a kind of secularized faith. They saw man as a rational human being who could change things for the better. That which was useful was good. They passionately condemned the abuses of the Old Regime and called for improvement. They demanded freedom and equality of opportunity. They heaped ridicule and scorn on clergy, nobility, royalty, on the old established order and traditions, on all medieval institutions. Their cry of "liberty, equality, fraternity" directly challenged the old principles of autocracy and obedience to authority. Their new gospel spread from the salons of Paris to the most modest cafés of the hinterland. These were enthusiastic, able men who understood everything except the feelings of the uneducated and propertyless. They were certain that what was good for the bourgeoisie was good for the nation and all the world.

Failure of Economic Reform. Attempts at both economic and political reform were unsuccessful. The crippled fiscal system remained unchanged in pattern. While the privileged classes enjoyed partial or total exemption from taxes, the peasantry was heavily overburdened by a variety of direct taxes. Although serfdom had been abolished, its most essential characteristic, the payment of manorial dues, persisted. The most irritating of the indirect taxes was the *gabelle*, which raised the price of salt to many times its true value. A precious commodity used for preserving meat, salt was a government monopoly and could be bought only from official agents. Every household was required to buy at least seven pounds a year for each member over eight years of age. Variations in price were outrageous. The tax was levied with no regard for uniformity: no district could ever be certain of its salt-tax rate. Sometimes the tax was "farmed" to collectors, who kept any surplus for themselves. Only a small portion of the money collected ever reached the national treasury. Those who refused to pay the tax were sent to prison, whipping post, or galleys. Smuggling of salt was rampant, and there was literally a war between government and smugglers. The unjust and hated *gabelle* was one of the more important causes for the creation of a revolutionary spirit.

Reformers not only called for an end to the *gabelle*, but also demanded free trade in grain inside France, agricultural improvements, and

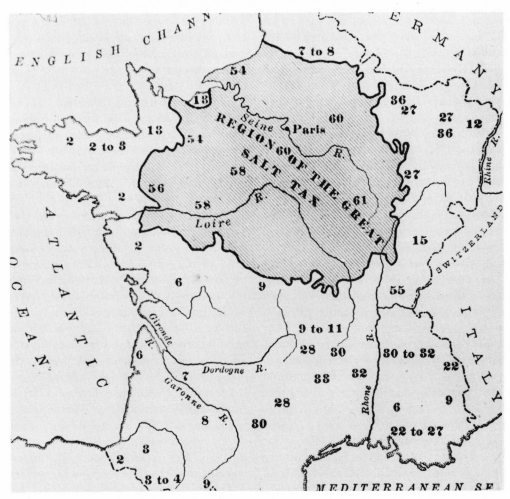

A major cause of France's critical economic condition in the years preceding the Revolution was the vexatious system of taxation. The figures in the map above indicate the inequity of salt prices in various regions subject to the *gabelle*.

release of industry from state controls and guild restrictions. As the country slid into economic chaos, nothing seemed to work.

Meanwhile, governmental deficits and the national debt grew larger and larger. By far the greater part was due to the high cost of war. The many wars which France pursued in the eighteenth century had been financed by borrowing; when the time came for payment there were no funds. As much as seventy-five per cent of the government's total expenditures went for military costs alone. There was need for more revenue, but there was a limit to money available.

Not the least influential factor in the plunge toward bankruptcy was the wastefulness and extravagance of court and nobility. The scale of living at Versailles was almost incredible, even though only five per cent of the national budget was used for the upkeep of the royal establishment. Marie Antoinette's private stables in 1780 housed nearly 100 vehicles and 330 horses. At Versailles there were 150 pages, 48 physicians and assistants, 128 musicians, 338 officers of the table, and 198 people whose only duty it was to wait upon the person of the king, including those whose high privilege it was to hold a towel for the king's bath.

The Administrative System Breaks Down. Louis XV (r. 1715–1774), great-grandson and successor to Louis XIV, was not without intelligence and ability. That he was aware of the impending storm was indicated in the expression attributed to him: *"Après moi, le déluge!"* The next Bourbon, Louis XVI (r. 1774–1793), grandson of Louis XV, was conscientious and well-intentioned, but lacked personality and initiative and suffered from the reflected unpopularity of his wife, the Austrian-born Marie Antoinette, daughter of Maria Theresa. Extravagant and indiscreet, the object of much scandal, she was detested by the people. The king often abandoned the advice of his ministers rather than face the scorn of the petticoat government of his queen.

Both Louis XV and Louis XVI functioned in a government which was in form and in fact an autocracy. They wielded absolute power on the assumption that their authority rested on the will of God. A Council of State, composed of royal favorites, enacted laws, fixed taxes, and raised funds for the military. A vast hierarchy of administrative officials in the centralized administration was responsible to the Crown. The country was divided into thirty-two intendancies or *généralités,* administered by *intendants,* or provisional governors, all subject to royal control. The superior courts were expected invariably to render judicial decisions favorable to the monarch. Letters bearing the royal seal, *lettres de cachet,* were often issued in blank and used by the privileged orders or petty officials to get their enemies imprisoned.

Governmental machinery, clumsy and inefficiently organized, was hampered by conflicts in authority, duplication of work, procedural confusion, and lack of uniform laws. Often the king interfered in affairs of state. If the *Parlement* of Paris refused to register a royal decree, the king himself might appear in person to order acceptance of the edict.

As early as 1715 the judicial aristocracy in the *parlements* used their right to make representations (*remonstrances*) to the Crown on proposed legislation. By 1766 it claimed the constitutional right to speak for the nation, thereby earning a scorching rebuke from Louis XV. In 1770 the *Parlement* of Paris was abolished, only to be restored in 1774 by Louis XVI on his accession. The demonstrations of joy all over France indicated that the prestige of the monarchy was declining, but Louis XVI was unaware of the quickening unpopularity of the throne.

The Financial Crisis Worsens, 1774–1789. Louis XVI saw the need for taxing the privileged classes. At the beginning of his reign he appointed Jacques Turgot (1727–1781), an experienced administrator, as comptroller-general of the treasury. With a policy of "no bankruptcy, no increase in taxes, no loans," Turgot attempted a series of reforms. He tried to make taxation more equitable, sought to relieve the burdens of the peasant class, and tried to remove the disabilities under which the townspeople suffered. He freed industry from restrictions by abolishing many powers of the guilds, cut expenses of the court, and curtailed the pension list. He was well on the way to accomplishing a peaceful revolution when he was suddenly dismissed. All the classes which in the past had been exempt from taxation combined against him. Marie Antoinette, convinced that Turgot was interfering in her pleasures, added her resistance. The king, too weak to resist, dismissed Turgot in 1776, and repealed most of the reform edicts. Unknowingly, he sealed his own doom.

The next finance minister, Jacques Necker (1732–1804), similarly attempted to promote economy and honesty in administration. Opposed to new taxes, he tried to make up the deficiency in income by economy and loans. When France in 1778 joined the American colonists in their war against England, Necker's fiscal problems were multiplied. In 1781, in a shrewd appeal to public opinion, he published the *Compte rendu présénte du roi*, which disclosed the state of the revenues and expenditures of France and listed the enormous amount spent on pensions. Angered by this alleged violation of their rights, the privileged nobility sought and won the king's agreement to dismiss Necker.

When a third finance minister, Charles Alexandre de Calonne (1734–1802), became comptroller-general, he found enormous debts but neither money nor credit. In an effort to remedy the critical fiscal situation, he persuaded

Louis XVI to call an Assembly of Notables (144 members) in 1787, to which he proposed that tax privileges be abolished. It was like talking to stones. He was told that "only the nation assembled in the Estates-General can give the consent necessary to the establishing of a permanent tax." This was obviously a scheme to play for time. The wheels of government ground to a halt. Unable to borrow money or collect taxes, the king was forced to a desperate solution. He saw that he would have to call the Estates-General, which had not been convened since 1614. On July 5, 1788, the king promised to summon the assembly the following May. All estates were invited to elect representatives and also to draw up lists of grievances.

3. From the Estates-General to the Bourgeois Revolution, 1789

Election to the Estates-General. It was becoming increasingly obvious that the aristocrats had overreached themselves. At one and the same time they had undermined the royal power on which they had depended for their privileges, and they had also aroused the bourgeois leaders, the "Nationals" or "Patriots." In the electoral campaign the "Patriots" aimed first of all to "double the Third"—in other words, to have the number of deputies of the Third Estate equal to the combined total of the deputies of the first two orders. In a famous pamphlet, the politically minded priest, Abbé Sieyès (1748–1836), a leader of the commoners, or Commons, asked:

What is the Third Estate? Everything!
What has it hitherto been in the political order? Nothing.
What does it ask? To become something!

This was a key issue. In previous meetings of the Estates-General there had been an equal number of representatives for each order— clergy, nobility, and commoners. Since each order voted as a unit, the vote of the two privileged classes always outnumbered that of the Third Estate by two to one. The clergy and nobility naturally insisted that voting

should be by orders; the commoners demanded a vote by head.

Millions went to the polls in early 1789. The electoral procedure for the first two orders was simple: they voted directly for their deputies. It was more complicated for the Third Estate, whose delegates were chosen by a complex system of electoral colleges. All men of the age of twenty-five or over whose names were inscribed on the tax rolls were privileged to cast ballots.

When finally chosen, the Estates-General consisted of 1,201 deputies (without counting alternates); 300 for the clergy, 291 for the nobility, and 610 for the commoners. Most representatives of the clergy were parish priests whose sympathies were with the commoners. Virtually all the noble deputies were conservative country landowners. Most deputies of the Third Estate came from the liberal professions, many of them lawyers in disproportionate numbers, including two young advocates, Maximilien Robespierre and Jacques Danton. Whereas the conservative nobility and clergy were opposed to change, the entire delegation of commoners was committed to constitutional reform.

Grievances in Writing: The *Cahiers*. According to tradition, the three Estates brought with them some 50,000 memorials or lists of grievances called *cahiers*, which had been drawn up in election meetings. But the composite final texts seldom included the wishes of the peasants and workers as recorded in the local or primary *cahiers*. There were areas of agreement in the general *cahiers*: they were composed in a respectful and "enlightened" tone; they professed devotion to the monarch and the Church; they called for the sacred right of private property. At the same time, they unanimously condemned autocracy in government, called for a written constitution, urged that the Estates-General be convoked regularly to vote taxes and pass laws, and requested fiscal reform.

There were also sharply divergent approaches in the *cahiers* of the various orders. The *cahiers* of the First and Second Estates opposed the idea of equal rights for all citizens, stressed their own feudal rights and honorific privileges, and insisted that voting in the Estates-General be by orders. The *cahiers* of the Commons denounced privilege and inequalities, called for an end to feudal practices, demanded abolition of the *lettres de cachet,* and petitioned for an end to censorship of the press. Many *cahiers* submitted from provincial districts bore the unmistakable stamp of Parisian dialects, indicating that the flood of grievances from the Commons was probably organized in Paris by bourgeois leaders who had a program. There were high hopes

that France would undergo a period of regeneration based on redress of these grievances.

The June Days. The Estates-General convened at Versailles on May 5, 1789. Louis XVI, speaking briefly and scarcely to the point, indicated that he was interested only in putting state finances in order. It was another way of saying that he wanted money. A crisis immediately came when the king commanded each order to verify its own credentials and to organize itself as a separate body. The Commons, aghast at this reception, insisted on voting by

Opening of the Estates-General in 1789.

head, but it was too loyal to defy the king openly. For five weeks, at a time when speedy action was imperative, the session was deadlocked on the voting issue. While hungry citizens, driven to desperation by crop failure, stood in line before the empty bakeshops, their representatives at Versailles were "deliberating" the manner of voting.

On June 10, on the assumption that the Third Estate was the nation, the Commons issued a "final" invitation to the two upper orders to certify credentials in common as representatives of the nation. The nobility ignored the invitation, although a minority of clergymen accepted. A week later, on June 17,

the Commons, on a motion by Abbé Sieyès and led by the Count Honoré Gabriel de Mirabeau (1749–1791), a bombastic nobleman, by a vote of 491 to 89 proclaimed themselves the National Assembly. Without royal assent and going far beyond their instructions, the deputies of the Third Estate assumed national sovereignty. A gathering of feudal estates was thus converted at one stroke into an assembly representing the people as a whole. This was the first act of the Revolution.

In response, the king gave orders to close the hall, the *Salle des Menus Plaisirs,* in which the Commons had been sitting, in order to make necessary alterations in seating capacity for all the deputies of the three estates. On June 20 the Commons, believing itself locked out, concluded that Louis was planning to dissolve the National Assembly. Accordingly, the commoners repaired to a large indoor tennis court nearby, which had been used by the aristocracy. There they took the celebrated Tennis Court Oath "not to separate . . . until the Constitution of the kingdom is established and consolidated upon firm foundations." Only one deputy refused to sign this act of defiance.

On June 23 the king summoned the three orders to consult with him. The Commons was in no mood for vacillation. The king issued a declaration "that the distinction between ancient Orders of the State be preserved in its entirety," and announced that the resolutions passed by the Commons on June 17 were null and void. When the king left, the deputies of the privileged orders followed him from the hall. The Commons remained. On the order of the king's officer to disperse, Mirabeau rose and cried: "Go tell your master that we are here by the will of the people, and nothing but the power of the bayonet will drive us away." The perplexed king, weary of the whole business, replied: "Well, then, damn it, let them stay!" The Commons then passed a decree declaring that the person of each of the deputies was inviolable, and that those who tried to arrest deputies "are infamous and traitors to the nation and guilty of capital crime."

Within the next few days deputies from the first two estates drifted over to the Commons. By June 27 there were 830 deputies attending the meetings of the National Assembly. When the king heard that 30,000 Parisians were ready to march on Versailles, he ordered the abstaining deputies to join the majority. But he also ordered French troops moved to Versailles and foreign mercenaries to take stations around Paris. It was the calm before the storm.

4. Reorganization of France, 1789–1791

Attack on the Bastille. The hungry Parisian masses, including workingmen, unemployed, and vagrants, were afraid that the troops would take vengeance on them for their agita- tion against high food prices. They felt instinctively that their interests were identical with those of the National Assembly. Businessmen organized their own guard (*milice bourgeoise*) to protect life and property against both foreign troops and the sullen mob. Intoxicated by the eloquent speeches of a young journalist, Camille Desmoulins, rioters broke into food stores and bakeries and pillaged the gunshops. On July 14, 1789, a milling crowd, composed mostly of workers and vagrants, reinforced by soldiers from the mutinous French Guards, surged to the east end of Paris to the royal fortress and prison of the Bastille. This symbol of Bourbon despotism housed only seven prisoners, of whom four were counterfeiters, two lunatics, and one of criminal bent. The mob decided to storm the prison and distribute its arms and ammunition for the defense of the National Assembly. The small garrison was quickly overcome, its governor, De Launay, was murdered, and the ancient prison razed to the ground.

The fall of the Bastille was a sign that the masses supported the Assembly and not the king. As the sensational news spread through Paris and France, the legend was born that a heroic people had risen to strike down despotism. Louis XVI was astonished. When a messenger, the Duke de Liancourt, came to the royal apartments to unfold the news, the king said: "Why, that is a revolt!" "Sire," answered Liancourt, "it is not a revolt—it is a revolution."

Uproar in the Provinces. Violence raged in the countryside. At first the peasants armed themselves against nonexistent brigands, but then turned their weapons against the bastilles of feudalism. They stormed the chateaux and castles of the hated lords and bailiffs and destroyed records of manorial dues. They drove out the *intendants* and their aides. Frightened, some nobles and their families fled from their homes and sought refuge elsewhere. Those who remained, unprotected by the police and gendarmerie, were left to face the pitchforks and scythes of the enraged peasants.

The fall of the Bastille and news of chaos throughout the country stirred the king to action. He withdrew the royal troops, removed Swiss and German troops from Paris, recognized the new government of Paris, recalled the popular finance minister, Necker, and confirmed the appointment of the liberal Lafayette as commander of the National Guard. He put on a red-white-and-blue cockade, combining the red and blue of Paris with the white of the Bourbons, to signify his acquiescence with the recent events. It was a nice gesture, but it was far too late.

Abolition of Privileges, August 4, 1789. When the news of revolt reached Versailles, some deputies of what was now called the National Constituent Assembly called for immediate and vigorous repression. In general, the bourgeois leaders were not averse to rebellion against the entrenched nobility, but the social upheaval had to be checked at a proper point. What they wanted was a middle-class rather than a working-class victory. Some of the more moderate deputies, seeking to salvage what they could from the debacle, called for abolition of peasant obligations as a means of ending the disorder. In the famous night session of August 4, 1789, held in an atmosphere of sacrificial enthusiasm, the Viscount de Noailles urged the nobles to surrender all feudal rights. One after another, deputies rose to their feet to call for abolition of special privileges. When the night ended, the Old Regime was legislated out of existence. Gone were the tithes of the clergy, hunting and fishing rights of the nobility, ancient prerogatives of the privileged orders. Within a week the various measures were incorporated into a decree "abolishing the feudal system," and Louis XVI signed it. What reformers had striven for years to achieve was thus accomplished at Versailles within a few days. The August days legalized the dissolution of the traditional class society of France.

Declaration of the Rights of Man and Citizen, August 27, 1789. On August 27, 1789, the National Constituent Assembly laid the foundation of the new regime by voting the Declaration of the Rights of Man and Citizen. Inspired by English and American ideas and

charters as well as by Rousseau's *Contrat social,* the Declaration proclaimed that men were born and remained free and equal in rights; that the source of all sovereignty was in the nation; that all citizens had the natural and inalienable right to share in formulating legislation; that all men possessed the right to religious freedom, and freedom of expression; that taxes should be equally apportioned among all citizens according to their means; and that the right of ownership was inviolable.

The Declaration, platform of the French Revolution, was designed specifically for French needs, even though its appeal was to be universal. The statement that property rights were sacred was not elaborated further. The charter did not include the rights of assembly, petition, and association, nor did it provide for the right to work. Freedom of thought was recognized, but along with it went responsibility for its abuse. In religious freedom the charter did not go beyond enjoining tolerance. Despite these omissions, the Declaration was a most important statement of public rights.

The National Constituent Assembly in Paris. France now began to settle down. The next crisis was precipitated by the vacillating king. Delaying his sanction of the decrees, he secretly gave orders for a detachment of foreign troops to be sent to Versailles. The Parisians, learning of an extravagantly loyal demonstration at a military banquet in Versailles, responded by forcing the king's hand. The "March of the Women to Versailles" began in innocuous fashion on the morning of October 5, 1789. A crowd of women assembled before the Hôtel de Ville to demand bread. There was no bread forthcoming. Someone shouted "To Versailles!" Along the way thousands joined the crowd. When the women arrived in Versailles, they surrounded the hall of the Assembly and sent in a deputation to demand that the price of bread be lowered. The Assembly appointed a delegation to go with the women to the king, who promised to provide Paris with bread. At midnight Lafayette arrived to restore order.

In the morning, after a scuffle at the queen's apartment, in which two members of the king's bodyguard were killed, the crowd forced the royal family to return to Paris. "We have the baker, and the baker's wife, and the baker's little boy! Now we shall have bread!" Neither Louis nor Marie Antoinette ever saw Versailles again. The National Constituent Assembly followed ten days later. Meanwhile, many nobles fled to foreign countries where they hoped to receive support against their own country.

Political Factions. Within the Assembly the revolutionists divided into a Right, Center, and Left, more or less similar to modern political groups. Sitting on the Right of the chairman were the "Blacks," the reactionary enemies of the Revolution who had contacts with counter-revolutionaries both inside and outside France. In the Center were the bourgeois Moderates, led by Mirabeau, Sieyès, and Lafayette, who would have been satisfied with a constitutional monarchy. On the Left, inspired by Rousseau and led by Robespierre, sat the Patriots, who demanded the establishment of a republic. Meetings were held in public; the galleries were opened to the disorderly Parisian mob, which packed the seats and hissed or cheered the speakers. In this tumultuous atmosphere, for a full two years, the Assembly gradually, section by section, framed a constitution.

Regulation of Public Finances. Confusion in financial matters, which had been the royal reason for summoning the Estate-General, became even more confounded as people failed to pay the old taxes, and bankers declined to make new loans. To save the nation from bankruptcy, the Assembly secularized Church lands, which covered about a fifth of the country, and declared them to be public property. Church lands, Crown lands, and confiscated estates of the *émigrés* were ordered sold, and pending their sale, were used to support the credit of the State. *Assignats,* negotiable paper money, redeemable in seized properties instead of cash, were issued as legal tender. As the treasury needed money, the government began to issue more and more *assignats* until they exceeded the security. By the end of 1791 some 2,000,000,000 livres in *assignats* were in circulation. By 1796 the paper money had

declined to worthlessness. Ultimately, the *assignats* were repudiated, and the seized lands passed into the hands of the peasantry and middle class. But the *assignats* had served their purpose. They had saved France from bankruptcy, and they had linked to the Revolution those who had bought Church lands.

Civil Constitution of the Clergy. On July 12, 1790, the Assembly enacted a Civil Constitution of the Clergy, by which all ecclesiastics, from parish priests to bishops, already reduced in numbers, were made a civil body. They were to be elected by the people and, like other civil servants, paid by the State. The number of bishoprics was reduced by more than one-third, from 139 to 83, one bishopric for each *département*. In December the Assembly forced the king to sign a decree requiring all the Catholic clergy in France to take an oath to support the Constitution, of which the Civil Constitution was to be a part. With these measures the Assembly subordinated the Gallic Church to the democratic state and loosened its bonds to the papacy.

Pope Pius VI, who had already protested against seizure of Church property and suppression of monasteries, condemned the Civil Constitution of the Clergy and forbade the French ecclesiastics to take the required oath. To the astonishment of the deputies, nearly all the bishops and at least half the parish priests refused to take the oath. Millions of Frenchmen continued to take the sacraments from the constitutional clergy, while other millions were loyal to the nonjuring or refractory clergy, henceforth included among opponents of the Revolution. France was split in half on the religious issue.

The Civil Constitution of the Clergy has been called the outstanding blunder of the Revolution. Its unfortunate outcome was the nineteenth-century quarrel between a now anti-democratic and anti-liberal Church on the one side and violently anticlerical democrats and liberals on the other. Traditionally, the Church in France had been proud of its "Gallican liberties" and also jealous of papal power. The Revolution threw the French Church into the arms of the papacy.

Limited Monarchy: Constitution of 1791.
Amidst these sweeping reforms the National
Constituent Assembly continued its work of
drafting a written constitution to define the
character and powers of the new government.
It was finally completed in September 1791
and signed by Louis XVI, who could do nothing else. By its provisions the power of the
king was deliberately restricted, while the

In this satirical cartoon, Marie Antoinette's brother
asks Louis XVI what he is doing in the cage. By
merely replying, "I am signing my name," the king
avoids directly admitting that he can do nothing more
than ratify the measures of the National Assembly.

powers of future assemblies were greatly extended, a transfer of authority which embittered the already angered king. This was the
first written constitution of any European
country; it was preceded by that of the United
States (drafted in 1787, put into effect in 1789).

The Constitution of 1791 made all Frenchmen equal before the law, denied special privileges to anyone, and guaranteed freedom of
religion and press, and trial by jury. Like the
American Constitution, it provided for a separation of powers and a system of checks and
balances between legislative, judicial, and executive departments, all springing from the
will of the people. France became a limited
monarchy with local self-government under

middle-class control. Because the *cahiers* had
complained about the crushing royal centralization, the reorganizers met the criticism by
decentralization of the government. The country was split into 83 *départements* (provinces)
of approximately equal size, which, in turn,
were divided into *arrondissements* (districts),
the districts into *cantons,* and the smallest
units into *communes.* The *communes* were left
unchanged (44,000). France was thereby pul-
verized into innumerable administrative atoms.
This urge to decentralize apparently went too
far, for within two years France was centralized again under the revolutionaries.

Executive power in the new limited monarchy was awarded to the king. Significantly,
his previous title, "Louis, by the grace of God,
King of France and Navarre," was changed
to "Louis, by the grace of God and the Constitution of the State, King of the French."
The king would exercise his powers through
agents subject to dismissal. The old all-powerful *intendants* were forced to give up their
offices. The king was given a two-year "suspensive veto" over laws. If any measure was
passed by three successive legislatures, it became a law without the assent of the monarch.
The king was deprived of any control over
local government, army and navy, and clergy.
In the years from 1789 to 1791 the royal power
had declined precipitously.

Legislative powers were to be exercised by
a single legislative assembly composed of 745
members chosen by electors for a term of two
years. This new Legislative Assembly could not
be dissolved by the king without its consent.

The Constitution of 1791 went a long way in
answering the criticism in the *cahiers* on legal
inequality. It abolished the medley of royal,
ecclesiastical, feudal, and manorial courts.
Magistrates who had hitherto bought their
positions were replaced by elected officials.
Judges for civil cases were to be named by
the same electorate which chose the deputies.
In criminal cases, one jury was to bring accusations, another to judge them. The entire
legal system, like the administration itself, was
made uniform for all France.

The contempt which the bourgeois framers
of the Constitution had for the lower classes

was revealed by their complicated system of indirect elections for the Legislative Assembly. The people voted for electors, who in turn chose the members of the Assembly. The distrust was further indicated by the basic conditions of the franchise. While the Constitution gave all French citizens political rights, it distinguished between "active" and "passive" citizens. The active citizens were those at least twenty-five years of age who paid direct taxes or owned property taxable to the amount of three days' labor annually. Tax and property qualifications barred about half the male population from voting. Thus, the bourgeois leaders, loyal to their class and traditions, exhibited their fear and contempt of the "ignorant citizens." It was clearly "All power to the bourgeoisie."

The Constitution of 1791 represented an attempt by the middle class to stabilize the revolution at a point consistent with its own needs. It was attacked from four directions. Louis XVI was not content with his role as a constitutional monarch. The Parisian people wanted to extend the revolution so that it would bring them equality as well as liberty. Counterrevolutionaries inside and outside France worked against the new government. And finally, a minority in the new Legislative Assembly was determined to smother the settlement in favor of a more radical solution.

The Flight to Varennes. Meanwhile, there was trouble from the royal family. Shorn of his powers and wounded in his conscience by the Civil Constitution of the Clergy, Louis XVI decided that he had had enough reform thrust upon him. On June 20, 1791, just as their labors were almost completed, the deputies of the National Constituent Assembly were shocked to learn that the king and his family, in disguise, had fled from Paris. The plan was to go to the French provinces in the north and east, win support there, and travel on to Austria, the queen's native land. The original plan of flight had been suggested by Mirabeau, but, worn out by his labors, he had died on April 2, 1791. The plot miscarried. The king and his family were recognized at Varennes, and within a few days returned to Paris as prisoners. Whatever remained of the king's

popularity vanished with this ill-starred flight. More than ever the Parisian populace detested the "Austrian woman," whom they suspected with good reason of being in touch with *émigrés*.

Massacre of the Champs-de-Mars. The deputies of the National Assembly were now in a dilemma. The new Constitution called for a king, but if they deposed Louis and set up a republic they might throw the fruits of the revolution from bourgeois to lower-class control. For the time being they hesitated and merely deprived the king of his functions. On July 17, 1791, a huge throng gathered on the Champs-de-Mars to sign a petition to dethrone the king. Lafayette and the National Guard, fearing that this meant a workers' revolution, dispersed the crowd with volleys of musket fire. The Assembly, its zest for change daily diminishing, decided that the king should be restored to his throne and that there should be no further changes in the Constitution for at least ten years. In mid-September the deputies voted a general amnesty, completed their last session, resigned their offices, and announced that the revolution was over. The critical problem now was whether or not the constitutional monarchy would work.

5. *The Legislative Assembly, 1791–1792*

The Legislative Assembly in Action. The retiring deputies of the National Constituent Assembly, on motion of the radical leader, Robespierre, decreed themselves ineligible for reelection to the new Legislative Assembly. The result was that the task of putting the Constitution into effect was left to 745 new deputies, most of them obscure provincials with little administrative or legislative training. The new Right, the Constitutionalists, with 264 deputies, supported a limited monarchy and suffrage reserved for property owners. In the Center was the Plain, with 345 members, not yet definitely republican, but advanced in that direction. On the extreme Left was the Mountain, 136 radicals sitting on elevated benches, who called for the end of the monarchy and for a new French Republic. Aggressively republican, the Mountain sought to lead the revolution to greater extremes.

Political Clubbism. The radical movement centering in Paris was supported by the formation of revolutionary clubs. Seats of political and social agitation, they originated in Versailles in 1789 in the form of "eating clubs" of deputies to the Estates-General who desired to take their meals together. By 1791 nearly every café in Paris had become a meeting place for politicians and patriots. Here members composed inflammatory articles, coarse pamphlets, and bitter speeches. There were some strictly constitutional and even reactionary clubs, such as the Feuillants, or Society of the Friends of the Constitution, called "cowardly moderates" by its enemies. Members included Lafayette, Sieyès, and Barère. Its object was to unite the old monarchy with the new constitution.

The Cordelier Society, middle-class in origin but radical in its aims and methods, enrolled among its members some of the leading revolutionaries, including Marat, Danton, Hébert, and Camille Desmoulins. It denounced all abuses and infractions of the Declaration of the Rights of Man and Citizen. Its badge was an open eye, a symbol of eternal watchfulness.

The Jacobin Club, which derived its name from a building belonging to the Dominican friars, then called Jacobins, was organized in 1789. Originally moderate in tone, it was transformed by Robespierre into a society even more radical than the Cordeliers. By 1790 it had 152 affiliated clubs in a network throughout France. Parisian Jacobins established regular correspondence with their branch units. Eventually, the term Jacobin became synonymous with the Parisian constituency from which it derived its power—the *sans-culottes* (without knee-breeches), lackeys, cosmopolitan tramps, and starving workers who crowded its tribune. It was this audience to whom the Jacobin orators addressed their appeal and which began to clamor for the blood of "traitors."

In the Assembly was a group of young deputies from the Department of the Gironde, at first called Brissotins, after the journalist Jean Pierre Brissot. Aggressive in tactics and republican in sentiment, romantic and idealistic, the Brissotins became better known as Girondins. Unlike the Jacobins, who called for government centralization, the Girondins, as anti-Paris provincials, demanded decentralization or states rights. Fastidious intellectuals, such as Vergniaud, Condorcet, and Madame Roland joined their ranks. Fanatically patriotic, the Girondins believed that foreign war would unmask traitors in their midst. The Girondins became the party of international revolution, declaring that the Revolution could never be secure in France until it had spread throughout the world.

Leadership Trio: Marat, Danton, Robespierre. The chief radical leaders, Marat, Danton, and Robespierre, although bourgeois by birth and training, became voices of the proletariat. They were all able, conscientious men, but they were unable to save the floundering monarchy. Jean Paul Marat, (1743–1793), a physician and scientist, took a leading part in the struggles between the Jacobins and Girondins. Tried and acquitted by the Girondist government, he became popular with the extremist Parisian mob. Implacable and vengeful, he demanded the execution of the king for the good of the people. Editor of a newspaper *L'Ami du Peuple (Friend of the People)* from 1789 to 1792, Marat attacked court, clergy, nobility, even the Assembly, with fierce invective. Hated by the authorities, he was venerated by the masses. On July 13, 1793, while seated in a warm bath to obtain relief from the painful skin disease he had acquired while hiding in the Parisian sewers, he was stabbed to death by Charlotte Corday, a fanatical Girondin.

Georges Jacques Danton (1759–1794), together with Marat and Desmoulins, founded the Cordelier Club in 1790, and later became its president through 1791 and 1792. In the latter year he was made minister of justice, and from then on he was one of the leading figures of the Revolution. It was Danton's eloquence which helped drive back the Prussians when they sought to restore the monarchy. "We must dare, and again dare, and forever dare!" Later, as leader of the radical Mountain (named from the high benches on which its members sat), he opposed the Girondin. When he tried to control the Terror, he found it impossible to halt the blood lust.

Maximilien Marie Isidore Robespierre (1758–1794) was one of the deputies of the Third Estate in the Estates-General of 1789. Fanatical, self-confident, and a remarkable orator, he established a secure position for himself among the extremist Jacobins. Calculating and shrewdly ambitious, he at first attached himself to the Marat-Danton group, used it to gain undisputed ascendancy, and then brought about its destruction. Thomas Carlyle called him the "sea-green Incorruptible" because of his conviction that only through him could the ideals of the Revolution be achieved. Robespierre was certain that the ideals of Rousseau would regenerate France as well as all mankind. A deadly serious orator, he would permit nothing and no one to stand in the way of what he deemed was best for France.

Era of Foreign War Opens, 1792. At first the reforms in France had been greeted by applause throughout Europe, but this attitude of tolerance changed under the impact of the Revolution. Every major European country at this time, with the exception of Great Britain, adhered to absolute monarchy. All over the Continent voices began to be raised against the events in France, where traditional society and civilization seemed to be under terrible assault. There was rising opposition from several sources. (1) The *émigrés* who had fled from France determinedly provoked opposition to the new French government. (2) Leopold II of Austria, brother of Marie Antoinette, was concerned with the fate of the royal family. (3) German landlords, deprived of feudal rights in Alsace, demanded compensation and called for overthrow of the French government. (4) The National Constituent Assembly, in 1790, had annexed Avignon, a part of the papal possessions, thereby alienating the papacy.

When the French government began missionary activities along the Belgian border, it was denounced as an aggressor by Leopold II of Austria and Frederick William II of Prussia. Leopold sent to the major sovereigns of Europe a circular note (Padua Letter) describing revolutionary France as a challenge to "the cause of kings." On August 27, 1791, the two monarchs issued the Declaration of Pillnitz, demanding the restoration of law and order in France.

To the Legislative Assembly the Declaration of Pillnitz was a provocative challenge. It quickly buried its factional differences in an outburst of patriotic fervor to defend itself against those who would liquidate the gains of the Revolution. The rightists welcomed war as a means of strengthening the king and the limited monarchy. The bourgeois Girondins favored immediate war with Austria. In April 1792 revolutionary France declared war on Austria, lightheartedly beginning a struggle that would last, with time out for recuperation, for some twenty-three years. Before it was over all the major capitals of the Continent were to see French armies passing through.

The war opened with a series of French reversals. Frederick William II was so preoccupied with the coming partition of Poland that he had to delay Prussia's active war effort, thereby giving a respite to French troops. Meanwhile, in Paris, Girondist orators accused the king of sympathizing with the enemy. There were rumors that Marie Antoinette was transmitting information about French plans to the Austrians. Louis XVI was astonished by the revolutionary fury directed by the people at enemies at home and the foe abroad. On June 20, 1792, on the anniversary of the Tennis Court Oath, a rowdy mob, terrified by Austrian and Prussian troops at the frontier, stormed into the Tuileries "to pay a visit to the king." Louis received them courageously and drank a toast to the Revolution. Impressed and embarrassed, the assembled market women, coal heavers, and hod carriers did nothing further.

Brunswick Manifesto. On July 25, 1792, the Duke of Brunswick, commander of the allied Prussian and Austrian forces, issued a bombastic proclamation calling for the restoration of peace and order and threatening to sack and burn Paris "if any outrage be offered to the royal family." Instead of intimidating the Parisians, this foolishly phrased manifesto only enraged them. They now were convinced that Louis was in collusion with the enemy. The Assembly announced that the king was no longer able to defend the nation from its foreign enemies. The fate of the French monarchy was sealed.

Fall of the Monarchy, 1792. Louis XVI disavowed the manifesto, but it was too late to save his throne. With deadly fury the insurrectionists struck first. On August 10, 1792, they took the royal palace by storm. Now they were fortified with Rouget de Lisle's revolutionary song, the *Marseillaise*. The municipality of Marseilles had sent a band of 500 men on a march to Paris singing verses of an intoxicating song which was to become the battle hymn of the French Republic. The king and queen fled to the hall of the Assembly for safety. When the rebels forced their way into the hall, they found that most of the delegates had already fled. The remainder, Jacobins and Girondins, deposed the king, sent him to prison, and called for election of a National Convention. The monarchy, the most ancient and venerable in Europe, had fallen. The experiment with constitutional monarchy had been a dismal failure.

Lynch Law: September Massacres. From the deposition of the king on August 10, 1792, to the assembling of the National Convention, France trembled in anarchy. As the allies advanced into France, fear merged into panic. Word reached Paris on August 29 that Longwy had surrendered to the invaders, and on September 2 that the frontier fortress of Verdun could hold out no longer. Danton, now virtual dictator, advised that the only way to stop the enemy was to terrify the royalists. Fearing that imprisoned aristocrats might escape, frenzied Parisian mobs attacked the prisons. For five days some 2,000 persons—men, women, children, priests, anyone suspected of royalist sympathies—were handed over to the "justice of the people." Executioners butchered unfor-

tunate victims in the prison yards. The Assembly was too terrified to halt the massacre, Danton was too busy recruiting troops to meet the enemy. It was popular violence at its worst.

Invasion of France Repelled. As Prussian and Austrian troops stood poised to strike, a great flame of enthusiasm arose for the threatened Republic. The youth of France poured into Danton's army. Soon the French troops were organized for war. On September 20, 1792, the allied armies were met at Valmy by raw but fanatically patriotic troops under General Charles François Dumouriez. The battle ended without a decision, but the Duke of Brunswick, dissatisfied with the strength of his forces, withdrew. On November 6, French troops, brandishing bayonets and chanting the *Marseillaise*, won the first real battle of the war at Jemmapes. The tide of French successes had begun.

The French Revolution and the Western World. News from France sped across frontiers on the European Continent and over the Atlantic to the United States. All Europe was split by a division that surged over frontiers. Everywhere there were hardened enemies of the French Revolution. In the areas nearest to France, such as the Netherlands, Switzerland, and northern Italy, the impact of the storm blown up in France was great. But elsewhere, especially in northern, southern, and eastern Europe, revolutionary ideas made little headway. In Russia, Scandinavia, southern Italy, Spain, and Portugal, predominantly rural states, royal and aristocratic control survived despite revolutionary threats. German intellectuals were at first delighted by the explosive news from Paris, but the rural German population remained buried in the feudal regime and the oppressed urban workers had no leaders to goad them into action.

The English, who had already had their own revolution, at first hailed the fall of the Bastille as the end of the feudal regime in France. But in 1790 Edmund Burke published his *Reflections on the Revolution in France*, a bitter attack on mob rule in Paris and a reasoned defense of conservative evolution instead of radical revolution. Despite refutation by Thomas Paine, there was a gradual change of opinion in England against the course of the French Revolution. British public opinion was alienated by news of the fall of the monarchy, the September massacres, and the advance of French armies into Belgium. The revolutionists across the Channel were now called atheists. Homes of French sympathizers in London were sacked. Paine was tried *in absentia* for seditious libel. The Revolution had gone too far too quickly for British sensitiveness.

In the United States the news from France was received with mixed emotions. The Federalists, led by Alexander Hamilton and favoring a strong government, saw their ideals menaced by a movement that challenged authority. The party of Thomas Jefferson, branded as Jacobin and pro-French, saw the future of America linked with the success of the French revolutionists. When word came in late 1792 that France had overthrown the monarchy and proclaimed a republic, there was widespread rejoicing in the United States. Many Americans were convinced that it was the example of the Thirteen Colonies that had fired the spark of revolution in France.

6. The First French Republic, 1792–1795

France, a Republic, 1792. Several key problems faced the National Convention, which held its first session on September 21, 1792, just as the news of Valmy reached Paris. (1) What was to be done about the deposed and imprisoned Louis XVI? (2) How would France be rescued from foreign invasion? (3) What would be the form of the new government? (4) How would insurrection be crushed inside France? (5) What could be done to complete and consolidate the earlier reforms?

The National Convention was not without experience, as most of its members had already sat in the National Constituent Assembly or in the Legislative Assembly. On the Right were the Girondins, advocates of bourgeois ideas of government. In the Center, the Plain or Marsh, were those irresolute bourgeois members not quite certain what they wanted,

but still attached to the principles of the Revolution. On the Left, the Mountain, were those radicals still playing to the Parisian mobs. At the opening session the members quickly proclaimed the abolition of royalty, and condemned all *émigrés* to perpetual banishment.

There was some enthusiasm, but many Frenchmen were troubled. Radicals had for

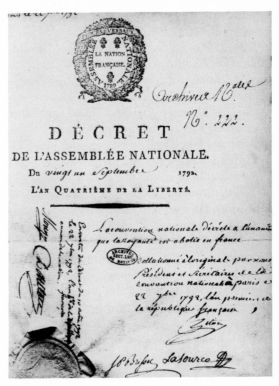

On September 21, 1792, the opening day of the National Convention, the Old Regime was ended with the issuance of the above decree abolishing royalty, and the First French Republic was officially proclaimed.

some time called for a republic, and intellectuals had often professed admiration for the city-republics of ancient times, but many bourgeois Frenchmen feared that the new republic would deliver the nation into the hands of the populace. The royal power had been discredited, but there was uncertainty as to what should take its place.

Louis XVI Guillotined. Louis XVI, now plain Louis Capet, was caught in the fierce, murderous struggle for political control between the

Girondins and the Mountaineers, mostly Jacobins. Both sides agreed that, in view of Louis' double dealings with foreign foes, he could not be set free, but they differed on the extent of his punishment. The Girondins favored exile, the Mountaineers demanded execution. In the stormy debate, Saint-Just declared that it was a crime merely to have been a king. Danton urged that the head of Louis be thrown at the feet of the allied invaders as a gauntlet of battle.

The trial began in early December. In mid-January 1793 the king was condemned to death. Voting for execution was the king's cousin, the Duke of Orléans, who had taken the title of Philippe Égalité. Those Girondins who called for submission of the vote to the people were howled down. On January 21, 1793, Louis XVI was beheaded near the overthrown statue of Louis XV in the Place de la Révolution, today renamed the Place de la Concorde. He met his death with dignity, his last words drowned in the roll of drums. A victim of events largely not of his own making, he sealed his own doom by incredible political obtuseness. It was announced that all true French patriots approved the punishment, but actually the people were gripped by fear.

First European Coalition Against France, 1793. Emboldened by victory, the Convention, on November 19, 1792, had proclaimed that France would propagate liberty and reform throughout Europe. On December 15, 1792, came an extraordinary decree:

The French nation declares that it will treat as enemies every people who, refusing liberty and equality or renouncing them, may wish to maintain, recall, or treat with a prince and the privileged classes; on the other hand, it engages not to subscribe to any treaty and not to lay down its arms until the sovereignty and independence of the people whose territory the troops of the republic shall have entered shall be established, and until the people shall have adopted the principles of equality and founded a free and democratic government.

Thus was inaugurated a French Peoples' Crusade against kings. Aghast, the royalists of Europe were driven into each other's arms. The British government, convinced that its national interests were in danger, swung into action. By the spring of 1793 Great Britain, Spain, Holland, Naples, Portugal, Austria, and Prussia had joined the First Coalition against France. Only Russia, busy in Poland, remained aloof. With Pitt as its paymaster, the First Coalition prepared to avenge the death of Louis XVI and destroy the revolutionary France which had killed him. With virtually all European governments lined up against France, the contest seemed one-sided, but it was less unequal than appeared on the surface. Oppressed classes in every country approved the French example. The French armies had the advantage of fighting enemy governments and not enemy peoples.

Overthrow of the Girondins. Meanwhile, Girondins and Jacobins were locked in quarrel in the Convention. The bourgeois Girondins, drawing support chiefly from the provinces, were opposed to the Parisian populace. The Jacobins, supported by fanatical Parisian *sans-culottes,* curried favor with the masses by advocating the confiscation of private wealth for the poor. Each side accused the other of treason. Girondins accused the Jacobins of being opportunists who used the masses for personal aggrandizement. Jacobins called their opponents "aristocratic republicans" and denounced their plans for decentralization as destructive for French unity. It was a struggle for control of the Revolution.

The Jacobins decided that the Revolution would be saved without the Girondins. From May 31 to June 2, 1793, a fresh insurrection by the Commune of Paris, supported by the National Guard, crushed the Girondins. Some 69 of the 83 departmental administrations protested in vain. The doom of the Girondins was sealed when Charlotte Corday murdered Marat, Jacobin leader who had been worshiped by the lower classes.

The triumphant Jacobins promulgated a popular constitution and submitted it to the voters. Although ratified by the French people, the Constitution of 1793 was never put into effect. It was laid aside on August 10, 1793, on the ground that because France was in danger from foreign war, her government must remain revolutionary until peace was assured. The Jacobins thus chose to regard the referendum as sufficient to justify their rule.

Nation in Arms. At first the allies threatened to overwhelm France. Their armies reoccupied Belgium and the Rhineland provinces and turned toward Paris. But the coalition, like most such combinations, was inept in concentrating its forces. Both Austria and Prussia were more interested in obtaining further spoils in Poland than in crushing recalcitrant France.

Under the leadership of Lazare Nicolas Marguerite Carnot (1753–1823), first "organizer of defense" and then "organizer of victory," the revolutionary army was reconstructed.

Infantry drill.

Carnot took the ill-disciplined and badly equipped French troops and transformed them into a powerful and efficient fighting force. He drafted men, silenced complaints, drilled the troops, and sent them to the front. By the end of 1793 he had some 770,000 fanatical men in the "nation in arms." France was able to meet the coalition with an eager citizen army, a *levée en masse,* instead of the old traditional,

easygoing professional army and its incompetent leaders. The revolutionary army turned the tide against the invaders. France was cleared of foreign enemies, and the Austrians and Prussians were thrown on the defensive. By 1794 Carnot's troops were pressing the war in the Netherlands, along the Rhine, and across the Pyrenees.

But military success was achieved at great cost. What had begun as a social revolution was deflected in aim to a Continental war. The Revolution was militarized. The national army, not the rectification of social injustice, became the chief concern of the revolutionaries.

Jacobin Dictatorship. In the spring of 1793 the National Convention entrusted supreme executive authority to a Committee of Public Safety composed originally of nine and later of twelve members. This small body included such Jacobin leaders as Danton, Robespierre, Saint-Just, and Carnot. At first the members were to hold office for only a month, but soon they continued on without the formality of elections. Transformed almost imperceptibly into dictatorship, the Committee directed military operations, administered finances, appointed and dismissed ministers, and suppressed all criticism. It sent representatives, "deputies on mission," to watch over the conduct of military leaders and to conduct negotiations with foreign powers. During its year of power, the Committee of Public Safety organized and equipped a dozen armies, and successfully expelled all foreign invaders from the soil of France. The French people submitted to this wartime dictatorship because they believed it to be, as they were told, a "bridge of bronze" between the decadent monarchy and the future glorious Republic.

"Despotism of Liberty": Reign of Terror. Just as it had accepted the necessity of Jacobin dictatorship in a critical war period, the French people tolerated the extraordinary steps taken against domestic enemies. The Committee of Public Safety, while repelling the foreign invaders, also crushed royalist and Girondist conspiracies at Lyons, Bordeaux, Marseilles, and Toulon. Two subsidiary bodies were given the task of eliminating domestic enemies. The Committee of General Security was given police power to sustain law and order throughout the country. The Revolutionary Tribunal was charged with trying and condemning any person—whether he be *émigré,* royalist, Girondin, or recalcitrant general—suspected of disloyalty to the Republic.

The Terror was on. Many thousands lost their lives in the blood purge. The total number of persons guillotined in France during the Terror is estimated as 16,594. To this figure must be added the thousands who died from disease and lack of food in congested prisons. At first prisoners were sent to the guillotine in small groups, but by the spring of 1794 the unfortunates were brought to the Place de la Révolution in batches of thirty to forty a day. Marie Antoinette, the Duke of Orléans, who had joined the revolutionaries, Madame Roland, and Madame du Barry, among others, perished on the guillotine. The Terror spread to the provinces, where many more thousands were sought out and condemned in an orgy of slaughter.

Struggle for Political Power. Concomitant with the execution of royalists and reactionaries was a continuing struggle for power among the various radicals. On the Left were the Hébertists, extreme republicans led by Jacques René Hébert (1757–1794), who advocated war against aristocrats at home and abroad. They were said to be responsible for the inhuman act at Nantes where 2,000 persons were loaded on barges and deliberately drowned. On the Right were the moderate Republicans, led by Danton, who called for an end to the bloodshed on the ground that the Revolution had already achieved its aims. He suggested a negotiated peace with the enemy. Followers of the austere Robespierre had no difficulty in convincing themselves that both sets of opponents were enemies of the nation and part of the foreign conspiracy which Pitt had financed to crush to Revolution.

The struggle for control ended in the spring of 1794. First, in March 1794 the Robespierrists, fortified with Dantonist assistance, seized the extremist Hébertist leaders, accused them of treason and atheism, and dispatched them to the guillotine. Then in April 1794 Robespierre turned on the moderates, arrested Danton and his adherents, accused them of conspiracy, and hurried Danton, Camille Desmoulins, and fourteen others to execution. The trials were legal parodies. Danton's last words, addressed to his executioner, were: "Show my head to the people; it is worth it!"

Republic of Virtue. Robespierre, the man who had destroyed his friends in the name of power, was now master of the Committee of Public Safety. A monomaniacal doctrinaire, he was one of those supreme egoists who, like Napoleon and Hitler, was convinced that he alone had been chosen by destiny to change the course of history. He would fashion a Utopian Republic in which all citizens would be distinguished by pure ideals, high morals, and selfless patriotism, a Republic of "good citizens and honest men." Recognizing the unifying moral force of religion, he inaugurated a Reign of Virtue on a religious basis. Although he rejected both Catholicism and atheism, he announced as the new religion an official cult of deism, which included "worship of a Supreme Being" and belief in the immortality of the soul. He decreed that every tenth day French citizens were to hold ceremonies in honor of the "benefactors of humanity" and of the revolutionary ideals of "liberty and equality."

Robespierre was determined to fulfill not only the political ideals of the rationalists but also their social and cultural aims. He inaugurated many changes in the everyday life of French citizens. They discarded names, clothing, fashions, and manners with the slightest royalist or clerical tinge, eliminated "Monsieur" and "Madame" in favor of "Citizen" and "Citizeness"; imitated the dress of ancient Greece and Rome; and substituted "liberty, equality, and fraternity" for the traditional jack, queen, and king on playing cards.

On September 22, 1792, the day after the abolition of the monarchy (coincidentally the day of the autumnal equinox), the deputies to the National Convention decreed the beginning of a new year, Year I of the Republic. Now Robespierre set up a new calendar consisting of twelve months of thirty days each, with five or six supplementary days at the end of the year; the months were divided into three ten-day periods instead of four weeks. To complete the break with old ways, the months were renamed: *Messidor* (harvest month), *Thermidor* (heat month), and *Fructidor* (fruit month) for summer; *Vendémiaire* (vintage month), *Brumaire* (fog month), and *Frimaire* (frost month) for autumn; *Nivôse* (snow month), *Pluviôse* (rain month), and *Ventôse* (wind month) for winter; and *Germinal* (budding month), *Floréal* (flower month), and *Prairial* (meadow month), for spring. The new calendar was devised as a substitute for the Gregorian calendar, with its many saints' days and religious holidays. Though never popular with the masses, it was used in France until January 1, 1806.

Unfortunately, Robespierre, motivated by the all-important necessity of remaining in power, adopted an economic policy satisfactory to no one. He estranged both his property-minded associates on the Committee, as well as landless peasants and city workers, by a series of decrees which disappointed those whom they were designed to help. The war made it imperative to nationalize a large part of the country's economy. This step alienated both the mercantile interests who wanted freedom of enterprise and the *sans-culottes* who wanted social justice.

Meanwhile, as the Terror reached its height, all France began to hate Robespierre and the Committee he dominated. In July 1794 Robespierre appealed to the Convention to support him in further purification of the government. But the country had had enough of the Jacobin terror. The members of the Convention, uncertain where the lightning would strike next, united to overthrow Robespierre before he became an unconquerable dictator. The plot was successful. Robespierre and his followers, thrown off balance, submitted meekly to arrest. Realizing that he no longer had majority support in the Convention, Robespierre predicted his own doom: "I am a lost man!" It was typical of the confusion that

some who voted against Robespierre were convinced that they were pushing the Revolution forward; others were just as certain that they were destroying a dictator and tyrant. Late on the night of July 27, 1794 (9 Thermidor), Robespierre tried to commit suicide, but he survived long enough to be brought to the guillotine the next day. The homicidal Republic of Virtue thus came to an abrupt end. Those who had once defended the Incorruptible now poured a torrent of abuse over his headless body.

Thermidorian Reaction, 1794–1795. The Thermidorian reaction, a great boundary mark of the Revolution, lasted fifteen months after the fall of Robespierre and the collapse of the Terror. In a major upheaval, both the men of the Terror and the Terror itself were thrown into the ash heap of history. The men who destroyed Robespierre were motivated by a desire to save their own necks; now they were greeted as heroes who had put an end to the Terror. There was an outburst of relief from the unbearable restraints of the puritanical Jacobins. France seemed to become delirious with joy. Thousands of persons suspected of treason were released from prisons.

Politically, the Thermidorian reaction marked a transition from republican democracy to rule by the propertied middle class. One by one the key changes of the revolutionary government were abolished. The dictatorial powers of the Committee of Public Safety were rescinded; the Revolutionary Tribunal was suppressed; the local revolutionary committees were abolished; the Jacobin clubs were closed down; and those responsible for the bloodletting were punished. Girondin deputies were readmitted to the Assembly. The Revolution was returning to its course of 1789.

In place of the Jacobin Terror a fanatical White Terror raged in southern and southwestern France. Gangs of *Jeunesse dorée* (gilded youth) waylaid the *sans-culottes* and Jacobins and killed former terrorists. But this White Terror also was crushed.

At last, giving up the attempt to establish democracy throughout Europe, apparently an impossible task, the Convention made treaties of peace with Prussia (March 5, 1795), with the Netherlands (May 16), and with Spain (June 22). But the war with Great Britain and Austria was continued.

Constitution of the Year III, 1795. After prohibiting use of the term "revolutionary," the Convention hastily drafted a new Constitution of the Year III to replace the stillborn Constitution of 1793. To forestall the rise of another Robespierre, a return of royal power, or a repetition of mob rule, executive power was entrusted to a Directory of five members named by the deputies. There would be a bicameral assembly, consisting of a 250-member upper house called the Council of the Ancients, and a lower chamber, the Council of Five Hundred. Suffrage was restricted to those who paid a land or property tax or had served in the army. The Constitution was promptly ratified in a popular referendum. But a rider attached to the plebiscite, providing that at least two-thirds of the 750 deputies of the new chambers had to be elected from the old delegates of the Convention, was rejected by the voters. The infuriated Parisian populace, spearheaded by royalists and conservatives, rebelled, but the revolt was quickly quelled by the army.

The final uprising against the Convention on October 5, 1795 (13 Vendémiaire), was easily ended by a "whiff of grapeshot" discharged by order of a youthful artillery officer named Napoleon Bonaparte. The young Corsican had already begun to sense that power was slipping into the hands of the army. The Convention now declared its work ended.

7. Achievements of the Revolution

Contrasting Effects. The French Revolution eliminated the Old Regime and laid the foundation of a modern, secular, urban society. Its ideas and ideals spread rapidly. Its lasting achievement was the introduction of new institutions. Its beneficial results became an enduring part of the nineteenth century world—the passion for liberty; the blow to absolute monarchy; the destruction of feudal practices; the separation of Church and State; educa-

tional reforms; and the codification of laws. Along with these came such dangerous developments as the emergence of fanatical nationalism; militarism; xenophobia—fear of and hatred of foreigners; and a cheapening of human life.

New Social Structure. The old medieval system, with its rigid class structure, its privileged clergy and nobility, was overthrown. Feudal rights were erased, the Church was stripped of its property, and the monarchy was abolished. The selfish aristocracy was succeeded in power by a vigorous bourgeoisie, sure of its rights and certain of its strength. But the new middle class had flouted the principle of equality by denying rights, privileges, and even the vote to the lower classes of peasants and workers. "The revolution is not finished," cried the Socialist leader, François Noël Babeuf, "for the rich monopolize all the wealth and govern exclusively, while the poor toil like slaves, languish in misery, and count for nothing."

Political Innovations. The fact that the French Revolution ended in a military dictatorship should not obscure the meaning of its political gains. Divine-right monarchy was repudiated and the principle of popular sovereignty was established in its place. The Declaration of the Rights of Man and Citizen challenged the idea that the people should have no voice in government, and affirmed the principle that supreme authority resides in the citizen. Freedom of speech, press, assembly, and worship, and security of property became watchwords which, though they were temporarily suppressed by Napoleon, were revived to become the directive slogans of the nineteenth century.

To the revolutionaries the words "Liberty, Equality, Fraternity" embodied the meaning of the Revolution. Not even Napoleon could erase them entirely. "Liberty" implied the political ideal of popular sovereignty and the rights of men. Freedom meant little on paper; it had to be anchored and maintained by justice under the law. "Equality" means the abolition of privilege, the destruction of serfdom, equality before the law, and equality of opportunity. "Fraternity" was the symbol of the new nationalism. The French nation, fused by revolution, sought to meet its destiny as a compact, aggressive state. This flaming national spirit, born in the French Revolution, was communicated to other countries and eventually emerged as the dominant political idea of Western society.

Economic Transformation. The revolutionary era ended by destroying the old feudal-manorial economy and abolishing the guild system and its monopoly of labor. The industrialism which had already begun in England was accelerated by the upheaval in France. The self-confident bourgeoisie encouraged commerce and industry as the lifeblood of society. The National Convention continued to print the inflated *assignats,* but they became worthless by the time of the Directory. Although inflation hurt the landowners, it was also responsible for the redistribution of large estates to the bourgeoisie and peasantry. The property of the Church and of noblemen, both regarded as enemies of the Republic, was placed on sale and bought by well-to-do farmers or townsmen. In the long run this was responsible for the emergence of a class of independent landowners, larger than in any other European country. Although the poorer peasants and city workers were excluded from this new bounty, the rich landowners were inclined to regard the Revolution as a boon and blessing.

Legal Reform. One of the main objectives of the eighteenth-century rationalists was legal reform. Accordingly, the various revolutionary assemblies introduced legislation to assure changes in laws. The Convention worked to prepare a single comprehensive code of laws and enact certain reforms eventually embodied in the *Code Napoléon.* Peasants were relieved of oppressive manorial dues and duties and artisans were freed from the old guild restrictions. Merchants and manufacturers were given legal freedom of business enterprise. Imprisonment for debt was abolished, and Negro slavery in the French colonies was prohibited. Women were given legal rights to property equal to those of men. Of great importance was the abolition of primogeniture: by allowing property to be distributed among all of a man's children, a long step was taken in the breaking up of large estates and permitting a wider distribution of property. The Convention also adopted the metric system of weights and measures.

Educational Reconstruction. On April 21 and 22, 1792, the Marquis de Condorcet (1743–1794), mathematician, philosopher, and revolutionary, presented a scheme for a system of State education that was ultimately adopted. In the chaos of the revolutionary era Condorcet, condemned and outlawed, died in prison, either of exhaustion or by poison. But his driving zeal to make the State responsible for the education of children caught on. From this time on, in France as well as in other countries, it became the great task of government to train children to become literate citizens. The Convention not only organized a system of public education but also established the Conservatory and the Institute.

◁{ KEY DOCUMENT }▷

DECLARATION OF THE RIGHTS OF MAN AND CITIZEN, AUGUST 26, 1789

Frank Maloy Anderson, ed., *The Constitutions and Other Select Documents Illustrative of the History of France, 1789–1907* (Minneapolis, Minn., 1908), pp. 59–61. Courtesy of the H. W. Wilson Company.

DURING THE weeks which followed the July insurrections, the National Assembly worked on a declaration of the rights of man which was to be a preamble for the new constitution. On August 26, 1789, that body agreed upon a table which listed the inalienable rights of free citizens. Historians believe that this Declaration derived its inspiration from both English charters, the American Declaration of Independence, and the democratic philosophy of Rousseau and other *philosophes*. The Declaration had an immense influence on nineteenth-century liberal thought.

The representatives of the French people, organized in National Assembly, considering that ignorance, forgetfulness or contempt of the rights of man are the sole causes of the public miseries and of the corruption of governments, have resolved to set forth in a solemn declaration the natural, inalienable, and sacred rights of man, in order that this declaration, being ever present to all the members of the social body, may unceasingly remind them of their rights and their duties: in order that the acts of the legislative power and those of the executive power may be each moment compared with the aim of every political institution and thereby may be more respected; and in order that the demands of the citizens, grounded henceforth upon simple and incontestable principles, may always take the direction of maintaining the constitution and the welfare of all.

In consequence, the National Assembly recognizes and declares, in the presence and under the auspices of the Supreme Being, the following rights of man and citizen:

1. Men are born and remain free and equal in rights. Social distinctions can be based only upon public utility.

2. The aim of every political association is the preservation of the natural and imprescriptible rights of man. These rights are liberty, property, security, and resistance to oppression.

3. The source of all sovereignty is essentially in the nation; no body, no individual can exercise authority that does not proceed from it in plain terms.

4. Liberty consists in the power to do anything that does not injure others; accordingly, the exercise of the natural rights of each man has no limits except those that secure to the other members of society the enjoyment of these same rights. These limits can be determined only by law.

5. The law has the right to forbid only such actions as are injurious to society. Nothing can be forbidden that is not interdicted by the law, and no one can be constrained to do that which it does not order.

6. Law is the expression of the general will. All citizens have the right to take part personally, or by their representatives, in its formation. It must be the same for all, whether it protests or punishes. All citizens being equal in its eyes, are equally eligible to all public dignities, places, and employments, according to their capacities, and without other distinction than that of their virtues and their talents.

7. No man can be accused, arrested, or detained except in the cases determined by the law and according to the forms that it has prescribed. Those who procure, expedite, execute, or cause to be executed arbitrary orders ought to be punished; but every citizen summoned or seized in virtue of the law ought to render instant obedience; he makes himself guilty by resistance.

8. The law ought to establish only penalties that are strictly and obviously necessary, and no one can be punished except in virtue of a law established and promulgated prior to the offense and legally applied.

9. Every man being presumed innocent until he has been pronounced guilty, if it is thought indispensable to arrest him, all severity that may not be necessary to secure his person ought to be strictly suppressed by law.

10. No one ought to be disturbed on account of his opinions, even religious, provided their manifestation does not derange the public order established by law.

11. The free communication of ideas and opinions is one of the most precious of the rights of man; every citizen then can freely speak, write, and print, subject to responsibility for the abuse of this freedom in the cases determined by law.

12. The guarantee of the rights of man and citizen requires a public force; this force then is instituted for the advantage of all and not for the personal benefit of those to whom it is entrusted.

13. For the maintenance of the public force and for the expenses of administration a general tax is indispensable; it ought to be equally apportioned among all the citizens according to their means.

14. All the citizens have the right to ascertain, by themselves or by their representatives, the necessity of the public tax, to consent to it freely, to follow the employment of it, and to determine the quota, the assessment, the collection, and the duration of it.

15. Society has the right to call for an account of his administration from every public agent.

16. Any society in which the guarantee of the rights is not secured, or the separation of powers not determined, has no constitution at all.

17. Property being a sacred and inviolable right, no one can be deprived of it unless a legally established public necessity evidently demands it, under the condition of a just and prior indemnity.

❧ HISTORICAL INTERPRETATION ❧

GEORGES LEFEBVRE ON THE PLACE OF THE FRENCH REVOLUTION IN WORLD HISTORY

Georges Lefebvre, "La Révolution française dans l'histoire du monde," *Annales—Économies, Sociétés, Civilisations,* III (1948), pp. 263–266. Trans. by the editor.

GEORGES LEFEBVRE (1874–1959), widely regarded as the outstanding French expert on revolutionary France, drew a careful distinction between the French Revolution, in which the bourgeoisie, opposed to a united front of king and nobility, was forced to adopt egalitarian ideas, and the Anglo-Saxon revolutions, in which nobility and bourgeoisie combined against royal absolutism. He made this point in several of his works, of which the following excerpt is an example.

The French Revolution holds a distinctive place in world history. While it appealed to natural law, as did the American Revolution, it left a universal imprint somewhat alien to the British concept of liberty. Its momentum was much greater. The French Revolution not only established a republic but it also advocated manhood suffrage. It was not enough merely to free the whites; the slaves, too, were freed. Not satisfied with words of toleration, it gave Protestants and Jews full citizenship, and by placing personal status on a secular basis, it recognized the right of the individual to hold any religious belief.

However, these contributions were secondary to the real mission of the revolution—the revolution of equality. Where in England and the United States the combination of nobility and upper bourgeoisie had negated a stress on civil equality, in France the middle class had been forced to emphasize it by the stiff attitude of the aristocracy. . . .

The French, by the act of gaining freedom and equality, became the Nation One and Indivisible. This novel interpretation of national sovereignty is a third leading characteristic of the revolution from which emerged the claim of France that nations, even as individuals, should be freed. Thus France claimed Alsace, Avignon, and Corsica by appealing to free consent instead of the traditional treaties between rulers. What was happening was that international law, as well as domestic civil law, was being revolutionized. In the early phase the revolution looked ahead to peace and cooperation among free nations united by a society of nations, even a universal Republic.

These characteristics do much to explain the impact of the French Revolution on the world as well as its long-range significance. Although these principles have since made gains, it would be erroneous to attribute their dissemination only to the Revolution. The examples of England and the United States had not been forgotten. It would be just as false—and this idea is widely held—to attribute this ideological expansion only to the magnetism of ideas. For example, in places near France, the Old Regime fell victim to the revolutionary armies led by Napoleon. Since then capitalism has become the main vehicle by which these new principles have conquered the world. These principles, as historians have pointed out during the last few decades, reflected the interests of the bourgeoisie who championed them. The bourgeoisie paved the way for capitalism by granting economic freedom, abolishing serfdom, putting an end to the system of tithes and manorial dues, and bringing Church property back into the springs of the economy. Wherever capitalism has penetrated, and, indeed, it has penetrated almost everywhere, similar transformations have taken place. . . .

Nevertheless, the French Revolution retains an emotional drawing power beyond any selfish interest. It is associated with popular uprising symbolized by the storming of the Bastille and the wars of liberation celebrated by the *Marseillaise*. This was produced by the men who died for the revolution. It would be bad history to ignore the influence of class interests and economics on the movement of ideas. One must not forget that the bourgeoisie was convinced that its rise was identified with justice and the welfare of all mankind. The fighters of July 14 and August 10, the soldiers of Valmy, Jemmapes, and Fleurus risked their lives not because of self-interest but because they zealously embraced what they regarded as a universal cause. . . .

Despite different approaches to history, the basic problem of our contemporary world appears to be the problem of equality within each nation and equality among nations. The historian is not supposed to prophesy how mankind will solve this problem, yet he can show that the French Revolution not only raised this issue but also pointed to the several directions in which a solution might be found. One can conclude, therefore, that, whether it be admired or hated, the name of the French Revolution will remain on men's lips for a long time.

❧ TEN BASIC BOOKS ❧

LIBERTY, EQUALITY, FRATERNITY:
THE FRENCH PEOPLE LAUNCH A REVOLUTION

1. Beik, Paul H., *The French Revolution Seen From the Right: Social Theories in Motion, 1789–1799* (Philadelphia, 1956).
2. Brinton, Crane, *A Decade of Revolution, 1789–1799* (New York, 1934).†
3. Gershoy, Leo, *The Era of the French Revolution, 1789–1799: Ten Years That Shook the World,* Anvil Book No. 22 (Princeton, N. J. 1957).†
4. Gottschalk, Louis, *The Era of the French Revolution (1715–1815)* (Boston, 1929).
5. Hyslop, Beatrice F., *A Guide to the General Cahiers of 1789* (New York, 1936, R. 1966).
6. Lefebvre, Georges, *The Coming of the French Revolution,* trans. by Robert R. Palmer (Princeton, N. J., 1947, R. 1957).†
7. Mathiez, Albert, *After Robespierre; the Thermidorian Reaction* (New York, 1931).†
8. Schapiro, J. Salwyn, *Condorcet and the Rise of Liberalism* (New York, 1934, R. 1963).
9. Stewart, John H., ed. *A Documentary Survey of the French Revolution* (New York, 1951).
10. Thompson, James, *The French Revolution,* 2nd ed. (New York, 1945).

19

Napoleon and the Grand Empire, 1795-1815

WHO COUNSELS peace at this momentous hour,
When God hath given deliverance to the oppress'd,
    And to the injured power?
Who counsels peace, when Vengeance like a flood
Rolls on, no longer now to be repress'd:
    When innocent blood
From the four corners of the world cries out
    For justice upon one accursed head;
When Freedom hath her holy banners spread
    Over all nations, now in one just cause
    United; when with one sublime accord
    Europe throws off the yoke abhorr'd,
And Loyalty and Faith and Ancient Laws
    Follow the avenging sword!

—ROBERT SOUTHEY, "Ode"

1. From Republic to Military Dictatorship

The Directory, 1795–1799. France was exhausted by six years of revolutionary upheaval and three years of war. The people were tired of bloodshed and turmoil, of casualty lists and lost sons and brothers, of political demagogues, speculators, and profiteers, of criminals and vagrants terrorizing the countryside. Tradesmen yearned for the restoration of normal business. Frenchmen had had enough of war talk and political slogans. They wanted peace, stability, quiet.

The executive power of the new bourgeois Republic was vested in a committee of five directors. The Directory promised the disillusioned people that it would "make concord reign." Lasting fewer than four years—from 1795 to 1799—it failed because of its own inefficiency and the rise of militarism. Unable to solve problems inherited from the Old Regime and the Revolution, the Republic slid almost imperceptibly into a military dictatorship which bled the nation to the point of death.

Internal Difficulties. The era of the Directory was a time of conspiracy and intrigue. The directors, far from being men of ability, turned out to be mediocrities, hard-working but possessing little talent. Outstanding among them was Comte Paul François de Barras (1755–1829), a dissolute, unscrupulous politician, member of the Jacobin Club from its beginning, and one of those who voted for the execution of Louis XVI. The leadership of the Directory reflected the increasing sordidness in national life as the Revolution lost its early idealistic impulse. Greedy politicians and profiteers who had amassed fortunes put their new wealth on display while the masses demanded bread.

The Directory sought to steer a middle course between vengeful royalists on the Right and irrepressible radicals on the Left. Reactionaries, who had been elected in considerable numbers to the legislature, plotted continuously to regain control of France. They were restrained only by force. On the other side, the Directory had to face the machinations of François Noël Babeuf (1760–1797), known as "Gracchus" Babeuf, editor of a paper called *Tribun du peuple*, uncompromisingly socialist in principle. Babeuf claimed that the bourgeoisie had elbowed the proletarians out of the way and had appropriated all the gains of the Revolution. Both royalties and Babeufists were crushed by the Directory. The royalist menace was disposed of by the expedient of depriving their deputies of their seats in the legislature. When Babeuf's followers plotted an insurrection against the Directory in 1796 (Conspiracy of the Equals), they were betrayed and arrested. Babeuf himself was tried and guillotined. His revolutionary socialist movement collapsed, but reasserted itself in 1848 and again under the Third Republic. Babeuf is often regarded as a forerunner of Karl Marx.

Not the least critical task facing the Directory was the salvaging of finances. The printing presses had been working overtime since the first *assignats* had been issued. In February 1796, when their value had declined to a point which made them worth less than the cost of printing, the Directory repudiated them and ordered the destruction of engraved plates and printing presses used to print them. It then issued a new currency in land notes *(mandats territoriaux)*, but it was unable to force their acceptance. After these depreciated, the Directory returned to a metallic currency.

Breaking the First Coalition. While the Directory was engulfed in political difficulties at home, it attained some success abroad. The army was functioning satisfactorily and on the whole the foreign war was going well. A triple assault on the First Coalition was planned. (1) The Army of the Sambre and Meuse, under Jourdan, would drive from the lower Rhine to Franconia. (2) The Army of the Rhine and the Moselle, under Moreau, would move from the upper Rhine into Bavaria. (3) The Army of Italy, under the youthful Napoleon Bonaparte, would be dispatched across the Alps to drive through northern Italy to Vienna.

The coalition against France was dissolving. Prussia, Holland, and Spain made peace in 1795. By the time the Directory was inaugurated, France was at war only with Austria, Sardinia, and Great Britain. The Directory intended to end the conflict as soon as possible, but it refused to conclude a peace that would restrict France to her old boundaries. Austria and Great Britain refused to guarantee France a natural frontier on the Rhine.

Early Life of Napoleon. Napoleon Bonaparte was born in Ajaccio, Corsica, in 1769, a year after the Italian island had been acquired by France. His father, poor but claiming noble lineage, obtained a scholarship for him at the French military school at Brienne. In his unhappy school days he showed little ability except a proficiency in mathematics. In 1784 he became a cadet at the *École Militaire* at Paris, where he studied with greater zest. On graduation he was commissioned a sublieutenant of artillery. Shy, uncouth, ashamed of his humble origin, he was treated as a social inferior by his fellow officers. He began to take prolonged absences without leave. He had intended to return to Corsica, but with the swift and dramatic development of the Revolution, his insular patriotism diminished and he resolved to seek his fortune in France. Since the revolutionary party could not afford to lose its trained officers, Napoleon was forgiven his repeated acts of insubordination. In 1793 he was sent as lieutenant-colonel of artillery to Toulon, which, supported by an English fleet under Admiral Hood, was holding out against the Convention. Here he laid the foundations of his military reputation by introducing new methods of artillery attack. Ultimately responsible for the withdrawal of the hostile fleet and for the recapture of the town, he was rewarded, at the age of twenty-four, by the rank of brigadier general. The next year he was sent to the Army of Italy, but he was recalled to Paris and arrested, and his name was struck off the army rolls. After the fashion of officers of that day, he began, as an adherent of Robespierre, to indulge in political schemes. He was soon released from prison; officers were too valuable to the Revolution.

In the summer of 1794 Napoleon was still unknown, a short, thin, badly dressed young officer suffering from an itch he had acquired on his campaigns. He was able to perform a valuable service in October 1795 when the angered Parisian masses tried to overthrow the Directory. Open to attack at any moment, the Directory entrusted its defense to Barras, who chose the recently disgraced Napoleon as one of his subordinates. The young officer collected several batteries of artillery and dispersed the insurgents. The name of Napoleon flashed through the entire country. The next year he married Josephine de Beauharnais, a

Young Napoleon's 1795 Parisian success at overcoming the insurgent threat to the Directory gained him great, if short-lasting, favor with the government and began his reputation as the man who saved the Republic.

light of Parisian society and the beautiful Creole widow of a general who had been guillotined during the Terror. Simultaneously, because he had saved the Republic, he was appointed by the Directory to his first command, that of the Army of Italy operating against the Austrians and their allies.

Italian Campaign, 1796–1797. The opening of the Italian campaign marked a new era in the history of the Republic. Until this time the French armies had fought in a frenzy of enthusiasm for the principles of the Revolution; now they were given some material incentive by the promise of spoil and plunder. Napoleon led 35,000 zealous French troops across the Alps. In a series of lightning moves, he separated the Austrian and Sardinian forces and then concentrated all his power on isolated detachments. It was dashing, brilliant strategy. Four times the Austrians sent armies, each larger than Napoleon's, into the Italies, but they never were able to match the daring maneuvers of the young general. The discomfited Austrians were driven back to within 80 miles of Vienna.

Threatened by a second French army in southern Germany, the Austrians hastened to make peace. Napoleon now turned diplomat. By the Treaty of Campo Formio (October 17, 1797), he persuaded Austria to give up Lombardy and the Austrian Netherlands (Belgium) and in exchange to accept Venetia as compensation. He joined Milan with lands taken from the papacy and Venetia to form the new Cisalpine Republic. He transformed the former city-state of Genoa into the Ligurian Republic. Both the Cisalpine and the Ligurian Republics were modeled on the French Republic. In the negotiations Napoleon acted without word from the Directory, on the ground that "the army has approved."

Napoleon posed before the Italians as a deliverer sweeping away Austrian despotism and the old feudalism. At the same time he strengthened his position at Paris by sending valuable plunder home as the natural spoils of the conqueror. Demanding enormous gifts from his vanquished enemies, he passed most of them along to his troops. This accounted in part for his magic influence on the morale of his soldiers.

Napoleon's Rising Star. All France was delighted with the twenty-eight-year-old Corsican who knew how to wage war and make peace. Paris hailed the little general as a conquering hero. Upon his return he was given a triumphal reception such as no other military leader had ever received from the Republic. The Directory was in a quandary. What could it do about the brilliant young officer whose spoils and booty might help in rescuing France from the threat of bankruptcy but who already was getting too popular? The best thing was to get him out of the way as soon as possible. The Directory at first placed him in command of an army originally intended to invade England. But Napoleon preferred to go to Egypt. It was an imaginative plan: he would strike at Egypt and then, in the footsteps of Alexander the Great, go farther and capture British outposts in India. "I saw myself," he said, "on the road to Asia, perched on an elephant, a turban on my head." The lawyers of the Directory, for whom Napoleon had only contempt, deemed it wise to fall in with his plans.

Egyptian Campaign, 1798–1799. In May 1798, Napoleon sailed from Toulon with an expedition of men-of-war, frigates, and transports conveying 35,000 picked troops. He took along a staff of experts to study the artistic and literary treasures of Egypt and Mesopotamia. Escaping a waiting British fleet in the Mediterranean, he captured the island of Malta from the Knights of St. John and proclaimed it a French possession. The expedition then headed for Alexandria, which it captured (July 2, 1798). Announcing himself the liberator of the Arabs, Napoleon pressed on and defeated the feudal Mamelukes within sight of the Pyramids. In three weeks he took Cairo and was master of Egypt.

Then came news of sea disaster. On August 1, 1798, British Admiral Horatio Nelson, who had sought Napoleon in vain, came upon the French fleet in Aboukir Bay, east of Alexandria, and won a crushing victory in the Battle of the Nile. Napoleon and his army were thereby cut off from the homeland. He turned to Syria, where his campaign was successful until he reached Acre. The British garrison there, assisted by Sir Sidney Smith of the British Navy, offered strong resistance.

Return to France. Disquieting news of the political situation in France impelled Napoleon to return home at once. The Egyptian campaign had failed. Little of it endured beyond Napoleon's cry: "Soldiers! From these pyramids forty centuries look down upon you!" The conqueror's dream of an Oriental empire vanished. Leaving his army in Egypt, where it was decimated by disease, he sailed secretly with a group of his most trustworthy soldiers. Narrowly escaping the British in the Mediterranean, he finally reached home in October 1799, after an exciting forty-seven-day voyage. When he sailed for Egypt, he had left France conscious of her strength and victorious in war. Now he found the country defeated and disgraced. The war in Europe was going badly. The Great Powers of Europe, encouraged by Nelson's victory, formed a Second Coalition (Great Britain, Russia, Austria, Naples, Portugal, and Turkey), and by mid-1799 had defeated France at almost every point. Napoleon's work in the Italies was undone. The internal situation was equally critical. The Directory, hewing to its shaky middle-of-the-road position between Bourbonists on the Right and Jacobins on the Left, was tottering to its fall. It alienated public opinion by arresting members of the legislative bodies, sending them without trial to penal colonies in South America, and declaring legal elections null and void.

Napoleon Seizes Power. Napoleon's hour had come. The French public, unaware of his defeats in the Middle East, welcomed him as a savior. Weary of war, they longed for a strong hand who could put an end to perpetual conflict abroad and anarchic conditions at home. They overwhelmed him as he journeyed in triumphal procession from the coast to Paris. Once back in Paris, Napoleon surveyed the situation and decided to organize a conspiracy to overthrow the Directory. Three of the five directors (Sieyès, Roger Ducos, and Barras) were favorably disposed, but the remaining two (Moulin and Gohier), enthusiastic Jacobins, wanted no "rescue" by Napoleon. The plot called for a triumvirate, Napoleon, Sieyès, and Roger Ducos, to take over executive power. Napoleon would furnish the support of the army, while Sieyès would organize the parliamentary side. A majority in the Council of Ancients was quickly won over, but approval by the lower body, the Council of Five Hundred, was debatable.

On 18–19 Brumaire (November 9–10, 1799), Napoleon surrounded the assemblies with a cordon of trustworthy troops. At his entrance to the Council of Five Hundred, he was greeted by cries from the Jacobins: "Down with the tyrant! Down with the dictator!" When several deputies rushed at him, Napoleon collapsed in a faint. For the moment all seemed lost. His brother Lucien, addressing the troops as president of the Five Hundred, saved the day when he declared dramatically that the right of free speech had been outraged and that his brother, who had been scratched in the excitement, had been wounded. With the hesitant soldiers won over, the plot succeeded. That evening Napoleon, Sieyès, and Roger Ducos were elected consuls by the Elders and some thirty members of the Five Hundred. With this *coup d'état* the Directory was overthrown, and the First French Republic ended in everything but name.

2. Prelude to Empire: Napoleon and the Consulate, 1799–1804

Constitution of the Year VIII. Napoleon's first task was to devise an instrument of government. Acting swiftly, he had the Constitution of the Year VIII ready just over a month after his *coup d'état*. Executive power was vested in a committee of three consuls. Napoleon was the First Consul; Jean Jacques Cambacérès, the minister of justice, the Second; and Charles François Lebrun, the Third. The First and Second Consuls were to serve for ten years, the Third for five years. The Consuls appointed a Senate, composed of about eighty members of forty years of age or more to serve for life. The Senate decided any constitutional question and selected, from lists chosen by popular voting, a Tribunate and a Legislative Chamber. The Tribunate, consisting of 100 members from the age of twenty-five upward, of whom one-fifth were to end their terms each year, discussed proposed legislation without voting on it. The Legislative Chamber, with 300 members of thirty years of age or over, renewable by fifths each year, voted without debate. This was democratic window dressing. By dividing the powers of the legislature, Napoleon destroyed its authority.

Actually, final authority was vested in the First Consul, who chose the members of the Council of State, initiated legislation, and appointed and dismissed most administrators, all military and naval officers, and all ambassadors. He could declare war and make peace, subject to ratification by the legislature. The Constitution was in fact an elaborate device for utilizing democratic sentiment on behalf of dictatorship. Submitted to the French people, it was accepted by an overwhelming vote of 3,011,107 to 1,567.

To keep the machinery of state under control, Napoleon devised the ingenious Notable system. In every commune all adult male tax-paying citizens were eligible to choose a tenth of their number to be Notables of the Commune. The latter, in like manner, chose a tenth of their number to be Notables of the *département*. These, in turn, selected a tenth of their number to be Notables of France. Napoleon chose all high public functionaries from this last group.

War Against the Second Coalition, 1801–1802. Napoleon's first task was to suppress brigandage inside France. By 1800 the military detachments he had sent out to deal summarily with lawbreakers wiped out all the bands that were terrorizing the countryside. With a combination of tough and conciliatory tactics, he ended the civil wars which had

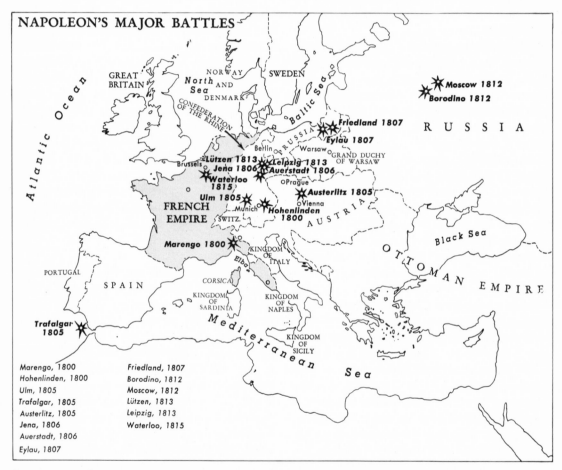

NAPOLEON'S MAJOR BATTLES

Marengo, 1800
Hohenlinden, 1800
Ulm, 1805
Trafalgar, 1805
Austerlitz, 1805
Jena, 1806
Auerstadt, 1806
Eylau, 1807

Friedland, 1807
Borodino, 1812
Moscow, 1812
Lützen, 1813
Leipzig, 1813
Waterloo, 1815

been raging for the last seven years. Frenchmen who put a premium on public order were impressed by the iron hand in Paris.

With his dictatorship consolidated, Napoleon now turned to the task of dissolving the Second Coalition. By flattery and diplomacy he succeeded in obtaining the withdrawal of Russia which, disgusted with Austria as an ally, retired from the alliance. Giving command of the Army of the Rhine to Moreau, he himself led another army of 40,000 men across the hazardous, rough, and icy Great St.

Bernard Pass into the Italies. He descended into the fertile valley of the Po, caught up with the retreating Austrians at Marengo on June 14, 1800, and inflicted an overwhelming defeat. The following December, when the Austrians were defeated by Moreau at Hohenlinden in southern Germany, they sued for peace. The Treaty of Lunéville (February 9, 1801) reaffirmed and strengthened the essential provisions of the Treaty of Campo Formio concluded in 1797. With these blows Napoleon extended France to the west bank of the

Rhine and once more forced recognition of the Cisalpine, Batavian, Helvetic, and Ligurian Republics.

What was to be done about Great Britain? The British controlled the seas, thanks to the exploits of Admiral Nelson, who had choked off the French expedition in the Battle of the Nile (August 1798) and who would later demonstrate his power by bombarding Copenhagen to break up the armed neutrality in the north (April 1801). Favorably impressed by Napoleon's destruction of the Jacobin democracy and his seemingly impregnable position on the Continent, the British government decided that it might be best to negotiate with him. Both sides chose peace in the Treaty of Amiens (March 27, 1802). Great Britain promised to relinquish all its recent colonial conquests with the exception of the islands of Dutch Ceylon and Spanish Trinidad. The French on their part promised to withdraw from southern Italy. Both agreed to restore Egypt to the Ottoman Empire and tacitly accepted the settlement made at Lunéville. This treaty between "the first two nations of the world," supposed to be permanent, turned out to be only a truce.

Thus far, the First Consul had brought domestic order to France and had virtually dictated peace to Europe, truly impressive accomplishments. In August 1802 the French people, by a vote of 3,568,885 to 8,374, elected Napoleon Consul for life. Until this time he had signed all official documents with his surname, Bonaparte. Now he began to use his given name, Napoleon. A legend was in the making.

Reorganization of France: Administrative Centralization. With swift comprehension, Napoleon mastered the problems of administration. The key question was centralization versus decentralization. The revolutionaries had decentralized the government, eliminating the old *intendants* and providing for the election of such local officials as civil servants and magistrates. Successive legislatures had made a partial return to the practice of appointing officials. Napoleon carried this practice to its logical end by centralizing the administration

even more intensively than it had been under the Old Regime. He transferred local governmen of *départements* as well as the small districts, or *arrondissements*, from elective officials to prefects and sub-prefects, who were directly responsible to him or his agents. Governmental offices were held by merit and no longer bought and sold. Many thousands of mayors were appointed either by the prefects or directly by the central government at Paris. An efficient civil service was created.

Although Napoleon's domestic reforms had a definite and lasting value, they were concurrent with a dangerous trend toward authoritarianism. Backed by the army, police force, and press censorship, there was a rigid despotism in France. The "son of the Revolution" and "the champion of liberty, equality, and fraternity" trimmed the Revolution by putting stress on equality rather than liberty, and emphasized fraternity in a national rather than an international sense. Almost imperceptibly the French people slid into the dungeon of another dictatorship.

Settlement of Religious Question: Concordat of 1801. Meanwhile, Napoleon worked to settle the religious conflict that had existed since the promulgation of the Civil Constitution of the Clergy in 1789. His own attitude was vaguely nonreligious. "I do not believe in religions. . . . It was by becoming a Mussulman that I managed to obtain a foothold in Egypt, by becoming an Ultramontane that I won the support of Italian priests; and if I were to govern a nation of Jews, I would rebuild Solomon's temple." Nevertheless, he thought it best to seek the support of French Catholics who had been alienated by the anticlerical measures of the revolutionaries.

After extensive and trying negotiations a settlement was negotiated between Pope Pius VII (elected 1800) and the French Republic whereby the Catholic Church was officially restored in France. Without jeopardizing toleration of other religions, the concordat stated that Roman Catholicism was the faith of a majority of Frenchmen. By abrogating stringent laws against the clergy, Napoleon won the support of French Catholics. But at the same time he tied the Catholic Church even more tightly to the state than it had been during the era of Louis XIV. In return for the Vatican's renunciation of claims to church property which had been seized during the Revolution, Napoleon agreed that the state would pay the salaries of the French clergy. New bishops were to be nominated by the First Consul and invested in office by the papacy; all the previous bishops were dismissed or forced to resign. The priests were to be chosen by the bishops with the consent of the government. This concordat was so advantageous to both sides that it lasted until 1905.

Economic Reforms. Restoration of order in national finances was a matter of critical importance. Napoleon consolidated the national debt by redeeming, at a portion of their nominal value, all outstanding securities. His new Bank of France, devised to serve the interests of the government and to stimulate commerce by granting loans at low interest rates, gradually became the most powerful financial institution in the country. He centralized the tax system by entrusting the collection of taxes to agents of his own choosing. He ordered strict economy in governmental expenditures. Frenchmen were delighted by the new stable coinage. Napoleon accomplished the almost miraculous feat of balancing the national budget during the year of 1801–1802.

Concurrent with these basic economic changes, Napoleon revealed himself as a benefactor of public works. With little cost to the treasury, he put prisoners to work constructing roads and canals, improving harbors, and draining marshes. He built new roads radiating from Paris to all parts of France. He extended waterways and enlarged and fortified such seaports as Cherbourg and Toulon. He widened the narrow streets of Paris into broad boulevards (with the further purpose of preventing barricades) and completed public gardens. In the Louvre he gathered great works of art acquired as fruits of victory in the Italies, Spain, and the Netherlands.

Social Reforms. To assure support for his regime Napoleon sought to improve the con-

dition of all levels of French society. He declared that all land obtained by the peasants during the course of the Revolution was to remain their property—a highly popular measure in the hinterlands. The city workers shared in the new prosperity through higher wages, but Napoleon was careful to strengthen legislation against unions and required every worker to obtain a *livret,* a passbook recording the nature of his employment and term of service, without which he was unable to work. Most fervent supporter of the regime was the bourgeoisie, who willingly accepted Napoleonic autocracy in exchange for freedom of enterprise and a stable, efficient administration. Thousands of nobles and clerics who had fled during the Terror, now promised security and employment, were welcomed back to France.

On May 19, 1802, Napoleon created the Legion of Honor, to be composed of citizens who had well served the state. It was a calculated move for popularity. All decorations and marks of distinction had been abolished during the Revolution, but Napoleon, who understood the psychological need for distinction, insisted that it was necessary to recognize civil merit. "Frenchmen have one feeling—honor. We must nourish that feeling." This aristocracy of merit was certain to be bound closely to his person. The Legion of Honor survived both Napoleon's fall and the revolutions of the nineteenth century.

Napoleon's Civil Code, 1804. Revolutionaries had already sought to clear up the frustrating complex of contradictory legal systems of the Old Regime. The Constitution of 1791 had promised reform, and the National Convention had started to sweep away many of the more antiquated laws. But real progress was made at last under the commanding personality of Napoleon. On August 12, 1800, he appointed a commission of four eminent jurists to codify the laws of France.

The *Code Napoléon,* later known as the Civil Code, issued in March 1804, preserved the basic revolutionary heritage concerning the rights of persons and property. Notable for its precision and clarity, it reduced the great mass of French laws to a simple and compact code. Essentially a new product based primarily on Roman law, it included also the best of Teutonic principles. There were additions later—the Code of Civil Procedure (1806), the Code of Commerce (1807), the Code of Criminal Procedure (1808), and the Penal Code (1810), the latter two begun during the Consulate and completed during the Empire. The simplicity of these codes attracted attention throughout Continental Europe. Napoleon himself, realizing the ephemeral nature of his battlefield victories, considered his Civil Code his chief claim to glory. At St. Helena, he said: "Waterloo will efface the memory of my victories. But that which nothing can efface, which will live forever, is my Civil Code."

National System of Education. The same motives that impelled Napoleon to codify the laws led him to inaugurate a national system of education. The function of the schools, from primary school to university, he believed, was to train citizens devoted to his person and to his state. "My aim in establishing a teaching body is to have a means of directing personal and moral opinions." Primary or elementary schools were to be maintained by each commune under supervision of prefects or subprefects. Secondary or grammar schools, designed to provide training in Latin, French, and science were also under governmental supervision. *Lycées* (high schools), technical schools, and military schools were all staffed by state-appointed teachers. The Imperial University, created in 1808, was a teaching corporation in charge of all French education. All its chief officials were appointed by the First Consul, and no one could teach who was not licensed by the University. The grand master, head of the Imperial University, was the forerunner of the later minister of national education. All education was expected to stress "the ethical principles of Christianity and loyalty to the head of the state."

Colonial Failures. Though successful in domestic reform, Napoleon was not able to restore the French colonial empire in the New World. In 1800 he did manage to obtain Louisiana, the large territory west of the Mississippi River, from Spain, but he failed to reassert French rule in Santo Domingo. In 1802 he sent 20,000 men under his brother-in-law, General Leclerc, to reestablish French rule by subjugating the Negro leader, Pierre Toussaint l'Ouverture, and restore the exiled whites. After several savage battles, Leclerc proposed a compromise, whereupon Toussaint laid down his arms. The Negro leader was seized and sent to France, where he died in prison. His outraged followers renewed the struggle. Despite their efforts in Santo Domingo, the French had little to comfort them. The expedition was hit by yellow fever which decimated its ranks to 8,000. When a threatening British fleet appeared, the French relinquished the island in late 1803.

Nor was Napoleon successful in his Louisiana venture. Resentful citizens in the United States called for war against "the French invader." With the prospect of war against both Great Britain and the United States, Napoleon sold the entire Louisiana territory to the United States for 80,000,000 francs (approximately $15,000,000). With this business deal the First Consul abandoned his scheme for a great colonial empire.

Crisis. Napoleon in 1803 was at the critical point of his career. He had pushed his way to ascendancy in Europe; he had extended the limits of France to her "natural" frontiers; and he had set up what many regarded as the most successful of modern states. He had obtained the support of the wealthy bourgeoisie; he had earned the devotion of the peasants; and he had obtained at least the tacit approval of the Church. At the end of his career, when in exile at St. Helena, he insisted that all along he had intended to win the rest of Europe to his side by moral persuasion rather than by force of arms. Britain, he charged, had driven him to war. But he failed to say, or to realize, that he himself was subjected to the dynamism released by the Revolution.

3. *The Napoleonic Empire, 1804–1814*

France an Empire, 1804. The First Consul's power was virtually absolute, but he was still not satisfied. From the beginning he intended to become another Caesar or Alexander the Great.

He wanted the pomp and trappings of a hereditary monarchy. Already popular because of his Italian victories, he achieved even greater status among the people by his shrewd reforms. Frenchmen now became as avid for authority as they had been for liberty. While the great masses revered the new national hero, he was hated by small cliques of royalists, disgruntled republicans, and salon revolutionaries. With the discovery of plots against his life, Napoleon saw an opportunity for change. Learning that royalists had conspired to assassinate him, he ordered the Duke of

Enghien, a young Bourbon prince, seized on the neutral soil of the duchy of Baden, court-martialed, and shot at Vincennes (March 21, 1804). There was a double reward for this deed: he had checked further royalist plots, and the republicans, convinced now that Napolean had broken with the older dynasty, rallied to his side.

The French people by plebiscite voted Napoleon the title of Emperor of the French. The vote was announced by Napoleon in slightly "corrected" figures as 3,572,329 to 2,569. He assumed the title on May 18, 1804,

The coronation of Napoleon and Josephine, December 2, 1804. This painting by Jacques Louis David portrays the event by which the Napoleonic Consulate was transformed into the First Empire.

and on December 2, in the cathedral of Notre Dame, he and Josephine were crowned in an amazing ceremony. To give religious significance to the coronation he invited Pope Pius VII. But remembering the experience of Charlemagne at Rome in 800, when the Frank-

ish king, without his previous knowledge, was suddenly crowned Emperor of the Romans by the pope, Napoleon snatched the imperial crown from the hands of Pius and placed it on his own head. There was symbolism here: Napoleon wanted the world to know that he had obtained the title only through his own efforts. "God gave this crown to me!" he cried. "Let him beware who touches it!" That challenge was quickly accepted.

Napoleon I, Emperor of the French. Wise in his understanding of French psychology, Napoleon was careful not to repudiate completely the gains of the Revolution. By submitting the key moves of his career to plebiscites he acknowledged the principle of popular sovereignty. He allowed continued use of the revolutionary motto: "Liberty, Equality, and Fraternity." He retained the tricolored national flag. Once ensconced in power, he catered to French susceptibility to pomp and ceremonies by restoring the trappings and grandeur of the monarchy. He appeased the revolutionary generals by making them "Marshals of the Empire." He employed "safe" aristocrats to teach his new nobility the fine points of etiquette. He replaced the title of "Citizen" with "Monsieur" and "Madame," and allowed the revolutionary calendar to lapse. He encouraged the members of his court to wear colorful aristocratic costumes, but for dramatic effect often appeared among them in ordinary uniform.

The five years of the Consulate had been marked by the domestic reconstruction of France and a policy of peace, but the ten years of the Empire were marred by incessant war. Napoleon had crushed all opposition inside France. Now, with the masses and a fanatically loyal army behind him, he could gratify his urge for glory. The man who had conquered France would conquer all Europe. He sensed that his type of dictatorship would wither away in peace. But he misjudged its stability and its need to be fed on more and more wars. At the same time the great Continental nations were appalled by Napoleon's increasingly powerful position in France and in Europe. Rumors spread that the French conquerer intended to fuse all nations into a single state. Had he not intimated that Europe could not be at rest except under a single ruler? More and more governments and peoples began to believe that there could be no lasting peace unless the presumptuous Corsican adventurer were overthrown.

War with Great Britain, 1803–1805. When Napoleon assumed the imperial mantle, the war between France and Great Britain, interrupted by the Treaty of Amiens, had already been resumed. The British had originally gone to war in 1793 in the belief that they were fighting against bloodthirsty revolutionists, but now the conflict assumed economic overtones. They had not forgotten French assistance to the American rebels, and they were determined that the new tyrant would not regain the colonial empire and the commercial power which France had enjoyed in the eighteenth century. Alarmed by his continual upsetting of the balance of power on the Continent, the British were even more angered by Napoleon's high protective tariff which virtually excluded British goods from France and countries dominated from Paris. As for Napoleon himself, he had never regarded the peace as anything more than a temporary respite in his efforts to destroy British commerce and the British colonial empire. He knew that unless he broke Great Britain all his designs for Continental hegemony were hopeless.

So intense was anti-French feeling that the British refused to carry out the provision of the Treaty of Amiens calling for the evacuation of Malta. Angered almost to the point of apoplexy, the Emperor denounced this as "a crime against Europe." Great Britain countered with a declaration of war. Napoleon welcomed it. Along the Channel coast he made elaborate preparations for an invasion of England. He established a naval camp at Boulogne, where he concentrated an army and collected transports, frigates, and flatboats. The British responded by taking every possible preparation against invasion, including fortification of the coast and concentration of their fleet in the Channel. For two years all Britain awaited the signal of invasion, which never came. Napoleon was never able to solve the problem of transporting troops across the Channel. Others said that the conqueror was afraid to risk seasickness.

In late October 1805 Napoleon received the depressing news that the British had inflicted a crushing defeat on the French and Spanish fleets off Cape Trafalgar, a low prom-

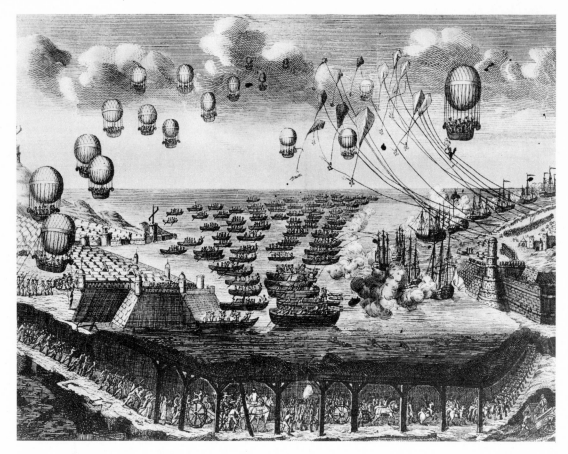

A plan for invasion of England, devised by Napoleon in 1804, provided for attack via channel tunnel, air armada, and invasion barges.

ontory on the southern coast of Spain. In the winter of 1804 Lord Nelson had kept a watch on Toulon harbor, where the French were preparing to embark a large body of troops for some unknown destination. To draw them out, Nelson sailed for Barcelona. Then came a cat-and-mouse game, with Nelson seeking to lure the French into battle. He got his opportunity on October 21, 1805. At the beginning of the battle, Nelson signaled the words: "England expects that every man will do his duty." The British captured 19 of the enemy's fleet of 33 sail-of-the-line and 7 frigates and blew one up. The prisoners numbered 12,000. Nelson himself was killed, and there were many other English casualties (450 killed and 1,250 wounded). The victory saved Great Britain from invasion and prepared the way for the ultimate overthrow of the French Empire.

War Against the Third Coalition. Meanwhile, William Pitt (1759–1806), second son of the elder Pitt, successfully organized the Third Coalition against France consisting of Great Britain, Austria, Russia, and Sweden. Characteristically, Napoleon decided to strike first, before the Austro-Russian armies could move westward to the frontiers of France. First he bought off the timid Prussian king, Frederick William III, by an offer of Hanover in exchange for neutrality. Then, abandoning the project for invasion of England, he shifted seven army corps from the Channel to the upper Danube. On October 17, 1805, his troops struck at the Austrians near Ulm in Württemberg, surrounded an army of 30,000 men, and forced it to surrender. After occupying Vienna, Napoleon turned on the combined Austro-Russian army in Moravia. Francis II and Alexander I, impatient of delay and unwilling to wait for reinforcements, were overwhelmed at Austerlitz ("battle of the three emperors"). It was December 2, 1805, Napoleon's lucky day, the anniversary of his coronation as Emperor. Austerlitz was probably the most celebrated of his many victories.

The immediate result of Ulm and Austerlitz was the withdrawal of Austria from the Third Coalition. Francis II, by the Treaty of Pressburg (December 26, 1805), ceded his Venetian territories, acquired in 1797, to Napoleon's kingdom of Italy, and relinquished the Tyrol to Bavaria and Hapsburg territory in western Germany to Württemberg. Both Bavaria and Württemberg were converted into kingdoms bound to Napoleon's France.

Conquest of Prussia, 1806–1807. Prussia, at peace with France for more than a decade, had declined to join the Third Coalition. But after Austerlitz it became clear that the French conqueror would not cease until he had controlled all of the Germanies. The war party in Prussia, led by the beautiful Queen Louisa, finally managed to convince Frederick William III to declare war on France. Without waiting for Russian assistance, the Prussian king sent 150,000 troops under the aged Duke of Brunswick against Napoleon's 200,000 willing veterans. It was a one-sided contest. In two terrible blows, at Jena and Auerstädt, both fought on the same day, October 14, 1806, Napoleon smashed the Prussians. With this disastrous defeat vanished that great military prestige acquired by the Prussians under Frederick the Great. Napoleon then unleashed his cavalry to range unopposed over north Germany. He captured Berlin and took possession of the greater part of Prussia. Frederick William III fled eastward to seek protection from Alexander I and the Russian army.

The Peace of Tilsit, 1807. Only the Russians now stood in the way of the terrible Corsican. Marching through Poland and into East Prussia, leading his troops across almost impassable roads and through forests, Napoleon met the Russians at Eylau on February 7–8, 1807, in

the midst of a hard winter. This battle, one of the most sanguinary of the Napoleonic wars, was inconclusive. On June 14, 1807, Napoleon inflicted on the Russians at the Battle of Friedland a defeat comparable to those he had dealt to the Austrians at Austerlitz and the Prussians at Jena.

At Tilsit, on a raft moored in the Niemen River, which formed the border between Prussia and Russia, the Emperor of the French and the Autocrat of All the Russias met to conclude a treaty of peace. During the conversations, the hapless Prussian king sat disconsolately on the bank. Napoleon, with unexpected magnanimity, asked for no Russian territory, but exacted a promise from Alexander I to abandon his British alliance and cooperate in excluding British trade from the Continent. The result of the talks was the Treaty of Tilsit, July 7, 1807. Alexander accepted Napoleon's supremacy in Western Europe. The Russian tsar was led to believe that he was to have a free hand in Finland and in Turkey, excluding Constantinople.

The French conqueror had favored the Russians with an easy peace, but he was more drastic in his treatment of the Prussians. At first he considered eradicating Prussia entirely, but finally decided to leave it in existence as a kind of buffer state between himself and Alexander. He reduced Prussia to half her former size. He took her recent annexations in Poland and incorporated them with those of Austria into the grand duchy of Warsaw under his German ally, the elector of Saxony. He appropriated all Prussian territory west of the Elbe and combined it with land taken from Hanover to form the new kingdom of Westphalia, a part of his new Confederation of the Rhine. He reduced Prussia's standing army to 42,000 men, imposed a large indemnity, and left a French army of occupation to be maintained at Prussian expense until the reparations were paid. Such was the price Prussia had to pay for venturing to declare war against the vengeful Corsican.

Tilsit marked the apex of Napoleon's career. The mighty conqueror had vanquished Central Europe and had transformed Prussia from enemy to ally. He was now the dictator of the European Continent, the equal of any emperor in history. Intoxicated by victory, he could not imagine that he was destined to an equally dizzy decline.

Napoleonic Nepotism. As triumphant conqueror, Napoleon placed his immediate relatives over the vassal kingdoms he had at his disposal, undoubtedly reasoning that they were to be more trusted than strangers. When he established the Kingdom of Italy, embracing Venice and the valley of the Po, he chose as viceroy his stepson (Josephine's son) and heir-apparent, Eugène de Beauharnais. He made his brother Louis the king of Holland. He deposed the Bourbon ruler of Naples and made his eldest brother, Joseph Bonaparte, king of Naples and Sicily, and later (1808) king of Spain. He made still another brother, Jérôme Bonaparte, king of the new state of Westphalia, established by the Treaty of Tilsit in 1807. He made Joachim Murat, his brother-in-law—married to Napoleon's youngest sister, Marie Armonciade Caroline—and one of his more distinguished generals, king of Naples in 1808. To make the family even happier he made another sister, Elise, princess of the diminutive state of Lucca. He saw to it that his "Uncle Joseph," his mother's brother, became Cardinal Fesch. He installed his mother in the Imperial court as Madame Mère. "If only it lasts!" said the old woman. Big Brother had done exceedingly well for an appreciative, if greedy, family.

Egoism: Psychological Fixation. Napoleon appealed to Frenchmen to modernize France and Europe by helping him to eliminate the half-overthrown relics of medievalism. At the same time he sought to revive the trappings and grandeur of ancient Rome. His very term "Grand Empire" was a tribute to the Roman tradition. His Cisalpine Republic, his Legion of Honor, his consuls, prefects, sub-prefects, tribunate, and Senate, all reflected the Roman experience. In Paris he converted the unfinished Church of St. Mary Magdalene on the Place de la Madeleine, begun in 1764, into a classical Roman "Temple of Glory." Inspired by the Roman example of erecting triumphal arches to celebrate the victorious return of generals, he adorned Paris with structures dedicated to his glory. In 1806 he began the celebrated Arc de Triomphe which was completed thirty years later.

Reorganization of the Germanies. The Napoleonic touch was especially effective in the Germanies. Before Napoleon the Germanies, a geographical expression, consisted of a conglomeration of states of varied size: some 30 medium-sized states, such as Bavaria, Württemburg, Saxony, and Baden, each with its ruling dynasty and court; nearly 150 petty states ruled by princes or prince-bishops; and the lands of at least 1,500 Knights of the Empire, each controlling a few square miles of land and a few hundred subjects. Every ruler regarded himself as sovereign in his own realm, presided over as brilliant a court as his funds allowed, made his own laws, collected his own tolls and tariffs, and looked with feudal disdain on his neighbors.

Napoleon showed a preference for the four medium-sized states, which he used as a balance against Austria and Prussia. All four states assisted him in the war against the Third Coalition in 1805, and each one was rewarded: he recognized Bavaria, Württemberg, and Saxony as kingdoms, and Baden as a grand duchy. A few months before the conquest of Prussia, the rulers of these four states, together with the Grand Dukes of Hesse-Darmstadt and Berg, the Archbishop of Mainz, and nine minor princes, at Napoleon's instigation, virtually seceded from the Holy Roman Empire and formed a new Confederation of the Rhine. To it was added the synthetic state of Westphalia, consisting of Hanover and parts of Prussia, Brunswick, and Hesse, all under Napoleon's younger brother, Jérôme. With Napoleon's approval the rulers divided among themselves the territories of the petty princes, the Knights of the Empire, and the towns. They were allowed to retain control of their own domestic affairs, but were required to accept Napoleon's domination of their foreign policies and pledge themselves to support the French emperor with 63,000 troops. This consolidation of the

Germanies, which survived Napoleon's fall, paved the way for the nineteenth-century national unification of Germany.

Napoleon declined to recognize the continued existence of the Holy Roman Empire. In 1806 Francis II, Hapsburg head of the Empire, laid down the venerable German imperial crown and had to content himself with his new title of Francis I, Hereditary Emperor of Austria. The old Holy Roman Empire, the traditional link between the Germanies for more than eight centuries since the coronation of Otto I in 962, was thus dissolved.

4. Decline and Fall of the Empire, 1808–1815

Road to Disaster. From that day in 1799 when the young officer overthrew the Directory to 1808, the story had been one of magnificent triumph after triumph. But after 1808 the drift to debacle can be traced to six basic causes: (1) fissures in the Napoleonic military framework; (2) failure of the Continental System; (3) the attempted annexation of Spain; (4) the crucial invasion of Russia; (5) the uprising in the Germanies; and (6) the final clash with Great Britain. In combination these factors thrust the French conqueror from his high pedestal to ignominious exile.

The Military Structure: From Fissures to Jagged Cracks. In his early campaigns Napoleon was a self-confident, ambitious, all-conquering general, the apotheosis of concentrated energy. But as he grew older, more corpulent, and slowed down by wealth and ease, he lost the magic touch. Every new conquest confirmed his belief in his own invincibility until he was overwhelmed by egomania. Equally significant was the change in the morale of his troops. Napoleon had taken the military machine initiated by Carnot and fellow Jacobins and had molded it into a fantastically loyal army which asked nothing more than to help the conqueror succeed in his "mission." Gradually, as the bloodletting increased and the deadly campaigns kept repeating themselves, the soldiers lost their zest for fighting. It was one thing to help the conqueror win a vital victory, but it was another to have to fight the battle all over again. As the number of volunteers steadily declined, Napoleon was forced more and more to resort to conscription. French families became increasingly reluctant to offer more sons to the altar of Napoleonic ambition. The dictator had to resort more and more to the practice of including foreigners in his forces. Thus diluted, the Grand Army lost the *esprit de corps* that had carried it triumphantly into the major capitals of the European mainland.

The Continental System. By 1808, with the victories of Marengo, Austerlitz, Jena, and Friedland behind him, Napoleon was master of the Continent. At the same time the British, in the battles of the Nile, Copenhagen, and Trafalgar, had solidified their mastery of the seas. The French conqueror had not been able to cross the Channel to destroy England on land, nor were the British strong enough to invade the Continent and meet the French armies head on. With the military-naval issue at a temporary stalemate, the struggle for power became primarily economic.

To kill off French commerce and shipping in both the Revolutionary and Napoleonic eras, the British declared France and her allies in a state of blockade. The British hoped thus to undermine the position of France in world markets and thereby weaken her war-making potential. To Napoleon this was a challenge from a contemptible nation of shopkeepers. He, too, would seek to choke his enemy in its one vulnerable spot. He established a tariff policy known as the Continental System, designed to close all European ports to British commerce. His purpose, similar to that of the British blockade, was to attack the enemy's trade, credit, and revenues by destroying his exports while building up markets for himself. Cut off from Continental trade, Britain would be brought to economic ruin and made ripe for invasion.

In the Berlin Decree, November 21, 1806, Napoleon proclaimed a paper blockade against the British Isles and ordered French and allied ports closed to ships coming from Great Britain or her colonies. The British retaliated with

Orders in Council, January–November 1807, which decreed that all ships trading with France or her allies were liable to capture and, further, that neutral vessels had to touch at British ports to be loaded with British goods before proceeding to Napoleonic ports. The British hoped in this way to move their exports into enemy territory through neutral ships; but this Napoleon was determined to prevent. In the Milan Decree, December 17, 1807, Napoleon announced that any neutral ship that stopped at a British port, or permitted itself to be searched at sea by a British warship, would be confiscated as soon as it entered a Continental harbor. The British vigorously applied the Orders in Council against American shipping; the resultant ill-feeling led eventually to the War of 1812 between Great Britain and the United States.

Napoleon's Continental System was more than a device for destroying Great Britain's export trade; it was also a scheme for developing the economy of Europe around France as a focal center. One after another virtually every major nation on the Continent, with the exception of Turkey, was herded into the Napoleonic commercial system. But the Continental System failed. It was responsible for widespread antagonism to the Napoleonic regime. Napoleon's dream of a united Europe under French rule was not attractive enough to warrant the necessary sacrifices by European peoples who preferred rather to deal with the British than do without them. During this economic contest Great Britain actually prospered. Smugglers of British goods to the Continent reaped a harvest, while Continental businessmen and workers, hard hit by the cessation of trade, faced ruin. Napoleon never ceased working at the tremendous task of bringing all Europe into the economic campaign against Great Britain. But he was not able to prevent the flow of British goods into Europe and on occasion even had to issue licences for the importation of British products. Even he could not produce overnight for his army 50,000 overcoats which, by devious means, came from British factories to the backs of French troops.

The Peninsular War, 1808–1814. Meanwhile, Napoleon turned his attention to Portugal, which for more than a century had been linked in close trade relations with Great Britain. He formally demanded that Portugal adhere to his Continental System and called for seizure of all British subjects and confiscation of all British property in the small kingdom. On the approach in 1807 of a Franco-Spanish army sent to force compliance with Napoleon's demands, the Portuguese royal family fled to Brazil.

On the throne of Spain sat the aging Charles IV (r. 1788–1808), father of Prince Ferdinand, an egotistical weakling. Realizing that he could not control Portugal without holding Spain, he decided to acquire the entire Iberian peninsula. French troops, continuing to cross the Pyrenees, eventually took it over. On a pretext Napoleon lured Charles IV and Ferdinand to Bayonne on the French frontier; by threats and promises he persuaded both to renounce all claims to the throne. The emperor then promoted his elder brother Joseph to the throne of Spain, while his brother-in-law, Joachim Murat, supplanted Joseph as king of Naples. In July 1808, under the bayonets of French troops, Joseph Bonaparte was crowned at Madrid.

The Spanish people, resenting these high-handed tactics, which made of their country a kind of commodity, rose in revolt. Napoleon found it easy to supplant the Spanish Bourbons, but he and his brother were not prepared for the angry insurrection which followed. Invigorated by patriotism, Spaniards denounced as a traitor their late king, who had been retired to Rome on a pension by Napoleon, and labeled their new king a foreign upstart. Using guerrilla tactics, they harried the French occupation troops and forced Napoleon to send more and more men and supplies into Spain.

Napoleon's difficulty in Spain was opportunity for the British. George Canning, the foreign minister, announced that any nation which opposed Napoleon, the common enemy of all, "becomes instantly our ally." A British army, under command of Sir Arthur Wellesley, later the duke of Wellington, landed in Portugal on August 21, 1808, and within three weeks overran the country. Angered, Napoleon assumed command of the French forces. By December 1808 he had driven the main British army out of Spain and reinstated Joseph on the throne. But it was only a temporary success. Called away to meet other European problems, Napoleon left behind him a pack of quarreling generals. Thanks to divisions in the French leadership, the harsh terrain with its steep mountain ranges, and British persistence, the British gradually wore down resistance until in 1814 the Napoleonic armies were finally driven from Spain.

Austrian War of Liberation, 1809. Inspired by the Spanish example, the Austrians, who had borne the brunt of Continental warfare against Napoleon, took heart and began to prepare for liberation. Utilizing the French principle of the "nation in arms," Emperor Francis I of Austria decided it was time to avenge the disasters and humiliations of the past. In April 1809, while Napoleon was occupied in Spain, Austria declared war on France and advanced into Bavaria. The French emperor immediately transferred his main armies from Spain to Austria. The German princes, firmly controlled in the Confederation of the Rhine, declined to join the Austrians. Alexander I, advised by Napoleon's foreign minister, Talleyrand, that Napoleon was overreaching himself, stayed on the sidelines. Napoleon, striking hard with lightning marches, was back in Vienna by the middle of May. On July 5-6 he defeated the Austrians at Wagram. By the Treaty of Schönbrunn (October 14, 1809), a part of Austrian Poland was taken to enlarge Napoleon's Grand Duchy of Warsaw; areas of Dalmatia, Slovenia, and Croatia were welded into a new state called the Illyrian Provinces; and the Tyrol, together with a part of Upper Austria, was ceded to Bavaria. The Russian tsar was highly displeased with a treaty which brought Napoleon to the edges of the Balkans.

Marriage to Marie Louise. Napoleon's terms for Austria were relatively lenient, partly because he wanted her support in the event of a future war with Russia, and partly because he wanted to marry the young Austrian archduchess, Marie Louise, daughter of Emperor Francis I. He had long considered the idea of making a spectacular marriage that would give him recognition in Europe's highest circles. He

debated between Romanovs and Hapsburgs, between a grand duchess and an archduchess, but St. Petersburg was not helpful on the availability of the tsar's sister. Using the cold argument that the aging Josephine had failed to present him with an heir to continue the Bonaparte dynasty, in December 1809 he obtained an annulment of his marriage on the ground that it had not been solemnized by a parish priest. Josephine, who had had two children by a previous husband, protested that her childlessness was not her fault. In April 1810, Napoleon married Marie Louise. He was now by marriage the nephew of Louis XVI, a remarkable promotion for a once poverty-stricken Corsican army officer. In the following year he joyously greeted the birth of a son, on whom he bestowed the high-sounding title "King of Rome". The son was later known as the duke of Reichstadt, or Napoleon II.

Napoleon at His Peak, 1810. Napoleon in 1810 was forty-one years of age and at the apogee of his power, lord of a domain stretching from Paris to Rome to Hamburg. To the north and the east were the allied states of Prussia, Austria, and Russia (all at war with Great Britain), and Denmark and Sweden.

In the French Empire, successor to the French Republic, were Belgium, Holland, and German territory to the Rhine and eastward to Hamburg; coastal areas of Italy down to Rome; Corsica; and the Illyrian Provinces. The heart of Napoleon's domain was surrounded by layers of satellite states which, together with the French Empire, formed the Grand Empire: the Confederation of the Rhine, and Grand Duchy of Warsaw, the Kingdom of Naples, Switzerland, and Spain.

But there were ever-widening cracks in this edifice. Napoleon had been unable to subjugate his main enemy, Great Britain. The Continental System was working badly. All his alliances, particularly that with Russia, were insecure. There was danger from a regenerated Prussia. The increasingly restless peoples of Europe awaited the chance to fight for national independence. Moreover, the dictator had lost the support of Catholicism in 1809, when he accused Pope Pius VII of admitting English goods to papal territory. He ended the argument by incorporating the Papal States into the French Empire and taking the venerable pontiff prisoner.

Russian Disaster, 1812. The Franco-Russian alliance, formed in 1807 at Tilsit, evaporated quickly after 1810. Tsar Alexander I was alienated by a complexity of grievances: Napoleon's refusal to allow him to take Constantinople; the Continental System, which he believed was reacting to his own disadvantage; Napoleon's Austrian marriage, which made it impossible for Russia to rectify her frontiers at the expense of Austria; the existence of a French-oriented Poland at his doorstep; Napoleon's hint to the Poles that they might recover their independence; and the choice of a Napoleonic marshal, Jean Baptiste Jules Bernadotte, as heir to the throne of Sweden. All Alexander had to show for his French alliance was the annexation of Finland in 1809. From all over Europe anti-Bonapartists came to St. Petersburg to tell the tsar that a Europe in chains looked to him for salvation.

Clearly there had to be an end to conquest, but the Emperor of the French, slave of his own system, could not stop. In 1811 he decided that he would no longer endure Russia's flouting of the Continental System. Collecting an army of 600,000 men from "20 nations," he set out in the spring of 1812 to punish the tsar and force his submission. So confident was he of success that he ignored the fate of the

Swedish king, Charles XII, who had led his armies to Moscow a century earlier and met disaster.

The invading French host, with the Russian armies vanishing before them, was led farther and farther into the heart of the country. Not until the French neared Moscow did they win the battle of Borodino (September 7, 1812). The invaders occupied Moscow but found the city abandoned and blackened by fire. Hoping that the tsar would surrender, Napoleon lingered on amidst the ruins for more than a month. On October 19 he finally gave the order for the homeward march. It was too late. The French were overtaken by the Russian winter, an enemy far more devastating than Russian troops. Attacked by bitter cold, disease, and starvation, harried by white waves of Cossack cavalry, leaving mounds of corpses behind, the *Grande Armée* melted away in the great retreat, a nightmare of horror. On December 12 only about a fifth of the original army staggered across the German frontier. A huge force had been sacrificed to the conqueror's mania for more power. Napoleon's strategy had been to force British capitulation by achieving mastery of the East, but his grandiose plan was frustrated by this tragic blunder.

War of Liberation, 1813. The disaster in Russia ended the myth of Napoleonic invincibility. Those peoples still under the Corsican's yoke took heart. Frederick William III, launching a program "to regenerate the state and bolster national defense under dynastic leadership," prepared Prussia for battle. Prussians and Austrians, with Russian aid, joined in a mighty War of Liberation. Thus challenged to defend himself in the Germanies, Napoleon hastily organized a conscripted army in exhausted France. He would show the world that his defeat in Russia was only an accident. He quickly won modest victories at Lützen (May 2, 1813), Bautzen (May 20, 1813), and Dresden (August 26–27, 1813). But the powerful allies cornered him at Leipzig, where he tried desperately to prevent a junction of his three opponents. At the "Battle of the Nations" (October 16–19, 1813) he was decisively beaten and forced to retire westward across the Rhine. The Grand Empire now began to collapse. Sensing the end, the vassal states, one by one, hastened to desert the conqueror.

Negotiations for peace began almost immediately. The coalition, still respecting Napoleon's military genius, offered him a favorable peace, including confirmation of the natural boundaries of France at the Rhine, the Alps, and the Pyrenees. But with the instinct of a gambler still convinced of his luck, Napoleon refused. Austrians, Prussians, and Russians were all pouring into France while Wellington, having driven the French from Spain, approached from the south. On March 31, 1814, the victorious allies entered Paris.

Abdication, 1814. On April 11, 1814, Napoleon abdicated and renounced unconditionally all of his claims to the throne of France. The allies granted him a pension of 2,000,000 francs a year, to be paid by France, and sovereignty over the small island of Elba near Corsica in the Mediterranean Sea off the coast of Italy. The French Senate, goaded by the triumphant allies, then took up the matter of reorganizing the government of France. It was decided to restore the Bourbon line in a limited monarchy headed by Louis XVIII (r. 1814–1824), brother of Louis XVI who had been guillotined in 1793. (Louis XVI's son, the dauphin, had been called Louis XVII, but he died in prison in 1795.)

The peace settlement allowed France to retain her boundaries of 1792. There was no war indemnity nor was there any army of occupation. Louis XVIII, urged not to undo the work of the Revolution, granted his subjects a charter confirming the liberties of the citizens.

The Hundred Days. The name of Napoleon still held great appeal in France. The nobility was delighted by the return of the Bourbons, but the middle class and peasantry were not altogether reconciled to the change. There was fear that returning *émigrés* and ecclesiastics would regain the privileges they had enjoyed before 1789. Frenchmen had grown tired of the bloodshed associated with the name of Napoleon, but they soon forgot that weariness. After nine months they began to show signs of dissatisfaction with the colorless Bourbon who had been brought to Paris in "the baggage wagons of the Allied armies."

Meanwhile, the exiled emperor, in his tiny island kingdom, grew impatient. While the Allies quarreled among themselves at Vienna on problems of European reconstruction, Napoleon slipped away from Elba and landed at Cannes on the southern coast of France on March 1, 1815. He was enthusiastically received by peasants and former soldiers. Officers sent to arrest him went over to his side. On March 20, after a triumphal journey, Napoleon was back in Paris. Louis XVIII, who had sworn to die in defense of his regime, fled to Belgium. Thus began the short rule generally called the Hundred Days (March 20 to June 29, 1815). Napoleon drew up a new constitution and solemnly promised to respect it.

The diplomats at Vienna, shocked by the news, hastily reconciled their differences. Once again war was declared on Napoleon as "the habitual disturber of the peace of Europe." But this time only Prussia and Britain were prepared to meet him. Napoleon decided once more to strike quickly by separating his enemies and defeating them one by one. But the coalition worked with even greater speed. Allowing Napoleon no time to prepare another gigantic army, they struck with overwhelming force. Napoleon defeated Blücher at Ligny (June 16, 1815), but the latter had a preconceived plan with Wellington. While Wellington fell back on Waterloo, Blücher rushed to join him as soon as possible. The strategy worked. Wellington held the field at Waterloo until the arrival of the Prussians. On June 18, 1815, the French were swept into headlong rout at Waterloo.

Despairing, with all hope lost, Napoleon returned to Paris. He thought of escaping to America, but, finding this impossible, he surrendered to the British on June 22, 1815, and abdicated a second time. He was banished to the volcanic island of St. Helena in the South Atlantic. Six years later, on May 5, 1821, in his fifty-second year, Napoleon died, a lonely, sick, embittered exile. As testimony to his greatness, only the words "Here lies" were engraved on his tombstone.

5. *Napoleon as Historical Phenomenon*

Historical Controversy: Hero—or Monstrous Man of Violence? Few men have been so variedly judged by historians as Napoleon. Some regard him as a source of inspiration, a superman who brought honor, glory, and prestige to France, while to others he was a vile, bloodthirsty creature who represented barbarism at its lowest point. Some describe him as one of the great military geniuses of all time, as one who understood all the amazing complexities of war. To others he was the villain who must bear the stigma of costing France a million casualties between 1799 and 1815. On the one side he is depicted as a leader whose incessant energy, psychological insight, and unbounded confidence were responsible for carrying the principles of 1789 to all Europe. On the other side he is shown as the man who, by rejecting all moral considerations in his conduct, brought dishonor and shame to a great nation. There are few commonly accepted conclusions on the personality, character, goals, and achievements of this many-faceted man.

French historians have long been fascinated by the protean figure of Napoleon, but they too have come to diverse conclusions in estimating him. On the favorable side there is admiration for an incomparably great man, both as ruler and commander, a good and attractive man. This was the view of Louis Adolphe Thiers, statesman and historian, who believed in the real goodness of Napoleon, in the purity of his motives, and in the sincerity of his conversion to liberalism and love of peace. To Thiers, Napoleon's despotism and lust for conquest were only "subsidiary faults"; the true Napoleon, the benefactor of the people and of mankind, had been purified by disaster.

This view was echoed by such admirers as Henri Houssaye, Fréderic Masson, and Albert Vandal, all of whom admired the great conqueror. To defend Napoleon's memory, they believed, was to serve France. The glory of Napoleon was a national possession; whoever touched it defaced the nation itself. At times the picture of Napoleon became mawkish: if he had a fault it was that of excessive kindness. How gentle he was in his relationships with his mother and brothers, with Josephine, even with the Hapsburg archduchess! Henri Houssaye represented this school with such writing as: "The broad masses with their common sense, realized that the Emperor, even though he might be the occasion or the pretext of the war, had by no means promoted its outbreak. . . . The peril of a new invasion ranged all hearts on Napoleon's side, for in him men still saw the sword of France."

Against this panegyric view was another which denounced Napoleon as an evil influence. In a pamphlet published in 1814 the great literary figure François René de Chateaubriand wrote of Napoleon as a destroyer, a despiser of men, a Corsican careless of French blood, a devourer of youth, a suppressor of all free opinion—in a word, a tyrant. In 1867 Pierre Lanfrey attacked the notion of the great Napoleon coined by Thiers. To Lanfry, Napoleon was not the leader who consolidated the Revolution, but a man of violence and trickery who suppressed liberty, who gave France nothing but misery, who eliminated free speech, enslaved parliament and the press, and who created a new vulgar aristocracy from among his sword-rattlers and bootlickers. "Napoleon is always on the stage, always concerned about the impression he is making. . . . He is lacking in that final human greatness which consists in estimating one's self at its true value, and as a result of his incurable self-conceit he remains on the level of small minds."

A. L. Guérard saw Napoleon as a man of no scruples, of limited culture, and boundless contempt for "ideology." Charles Seignobos judged him as "restrained by no inner curb" and added the devastating touch: "Napoleon never managed to feel a real Frenchman."

Against eulogies on the one side and polemics on the other is the more balanced view of the Dutch historian, Pieter Geyl, that Napoleon did not embody in their purity the principles of 1789 but became dictator and conqueror. This attitude recognizes both destructive and constructive facets of the many-sided Napoleon, but refuses to join either venerators or detractors. According to Geyl, Napoleon was a conqueror with whom it was impossible to live; a man who could not help turning allies into vassals or at least using such allies for his own exclusive advantage; and a man who decorated his lust for conquest with the fine-sounding phrases of progress and civilization. This is a fair judgment.

Character and Personality. Napoleon himself understood the meaning of his life when he said at St. Helena: "Centuries will pass before the unique combination of events which led to my career will recur in the case of another." At exactly the right moment he appeared on the scene, gave France two decades of glory, and then the humiliation of a decisive defeat. His fierce family loyalty, revealed in excessive nepotism in his years of power, reflected the clannishness of his background. He allowed nothing to stand in the way of his ambition—not his love for Josephine nor the lives of thousands of Frenchmen. Selfish, cynical, unscrupulous, he had a blind faith in his star of destiny. Of prodigious energy, he could work for twenty hours at a stretch, and then quickly regain his strength with a few hours of sleep. He bestrode the world like a colossus until he himself was struck down.

Certainly Napoleon was one of the great military geniuses of history. War was to him the highest of the arts, and few understood its complexities as well as he. Most of his campaigns were models of military strategy. Planning his defenses with painstaking care, he would lead his enemies to give battle under the most unfavorable circumstances for them, confuse them with rapid action, and then destroy them in decisive attack. He left nothing to chance—not the size and quality of his enemy, or its wealth, range of weapons, terrain, supplies, even its psychology.

This aptitude in war Napoleon matched by skill in administration. In domestic affairs he showed the same qualities that marked his behavior on the battlefield: unbounded confidence, incessant energy, and psychological insight. He inspired among his subordinates a profound devotion, though he worked them

to exhaustion. He was in truth a most uncommon man.

Benefits. To France, Napoleon bequeathed a legacy of benefits designed to enhance his name for posterity. Most of these reforms had already been inaugurated during the Revolution. The *Code Napoléon* gave all Frenchmen equality before the law without regard to rank or wealth. All classes in France had reason to thank Napoleon's regime for substantial gains. The clergy was grateful for his formula of religious peace. The old nobility, while annoyed by Napoleon's freezing of revolutionary gains, was pleased by his deference to aristocracy. Middle-class businessmen could thank Napoleon for the abolition of customs barriers, improvements in communications, encouragement of commerce and industry, and the uniform system of weights and measures. The peasants were happy about the abolition of the iniquitous feudal dues and for the new system of order in the countryside. The urban workers thanked Napoleon for substantial gains as well as for the privilege of dying gloriously in his armies. For the youth of France Napoleon gave a *mystique* which it could understand: service in the conqueror's armies, victory and glory, careers open to talent.

Debit Side of the Ledger. Politically, the work of Napoleon was reactionary. Not only did he put an end to the French Republic, but he also introduced anew the concept of hereditary monarchy as well as some of the worst features of Bourbon rule. His own Council of State was merely the rejected Royal Council of the Bourbons. The revolutionary era had brought the abolition of the *intendants,* but Napoleon revived exactly the same idea with his system of prefects. Frenchmen who had gone to the barricades for the right to think and write as they pleased found themselves caught in a strait jacket by the secret police. With his fanatical army, highly efficient bureaucracy, controlled educational system, and subservient clergy, Napoleon in fact introduced that absolutism against which Frenchmen had poured out their lives during frenzied times. It should be added that the defeat of Napoleon was more than the collapse of an aggressive, ambition-drunk military machine; it meant added strength for reaction, feudalism, tyranny. For another century the liberal forces of Europe had to face further struggle and repeated defeat in the battle to destroy the old feudal structures.

Psychology of Napoleonic Success. How was it possible for a people who had striven so hard in pursuit of independence and freedom to submit to Napoleon? An answer to this question requires assistance from the neighboring discipline of psychology. In Napoleon the citizens unused to reasoning saw a combination of attractive but conflicting elements. Napoleon answered the psychological needs of the French people. For the millions who were trapped in political chaos and years of revolutionary strife he provided an escape to order and what they believed to be security.

He was a glamorous response to the simple need for hero-worship: this was the man of the people who had brought *la gloire* to a great nation. He appealed to a craving for the miraculous.

Above all he catered to a rising national self-conceit. French vanity was delighted by the sense of superiority which their conquering dictator gave them. Had he not defended the sacred soil of France from her enemies, and had he not vanquished them in foreign campaigns? To those Frenchmen who enjoyed the methods and fruits of militarism the Napoleonic image was enormously satisfying.

Equally pleasing to French pride was the leveling process which Napoleon inaugurated. A proletarian emperor, Napoleon humiliated kings and noblemen. The masses saw a poverty-stricken young officer who had lifted himself until he could look down even on kings and nobles. This self-made aristocrat, who really had only contempt for the masses,

This rather romantic drawing of Napoleon at St. Helena captures the pensive, lonely quality of his final years.

paradoxically enjoyed tremendous popularity among them.

The Napoleonic Legend. Napoleon in exile on St. Helena carefully set about the task of shaping his reputation for posterity. In conversations noted by the Comte de Las Cases in a book that became a popular classic in France, Napoleon depicted himself as the Son of the Revolution, the man who eliminated the relics of feudalism in France, who restored order, and who forced peace upon the monarchs who hated France and the Revolution. He was a man of great genius, upon whom fate smiled, but, nevertheless, "a man of the people." Always he was devoted to the cause of emancipating mankind from the chains of monarchical absolutism. He took credit for consolidating the possession of liberty and equality. He told of his desire for a closely welded United States of Europe. (*See below.*) This had been his ultimate aim; all the wars he had fought had been forced upon him to shatter that dream. If it were possible for him

to return from the lonely rock of St. Helena, he at least would prepare the way for one of his family. Had not his final defeat led to the restoration of the Bourbons? He warned that all the longings of the French for liberty and glory would never be satisfied unless his own dynasty were to prevail.

Such was the Napoleonic apologia. Read by a generation of men who had never forgotten the glory which he brought to France, by those who were now faced with Bourbon reaction and the returned *emigrés,* by those intoxicated with the new romanticism, this made sense. It became the fashion of the day to magnify Napoleon's victories and to look back with regret to the good old days of glory and enthusiasm for liberty. Many Frenchmen forgot the cries of anguish, the long casualty lists, the death sentences, the suffering and misery associated with the conqueror's battles. The "perfidious" English had seized the great Emperor and nailed him to a rock in the ocean. "*Vive Napoléon,* the people's and soldier's father!"

❧ KEY DOCUMENT ❧

NAPOLEON BONAPARTE: ON THE UNITY OF EUROPEAN PEOPLES

Comte de Las Cases, *Memoirs of the Life, Exile, and Conversations of the Emperor Napoleon* (London, 1836), IV, 100–107.

NAPOLEON WAS ready and willing to use the aspirations of European peoples, but only so far as they fitted into his own system. He encouraged nationalistic aims in the Italies and Poland, but always considered what were to him the higher values of his dynasty and empire. In his own estimation, he was the new Caesar or the new Charlemagne. In a conversation with the Comte de Las Cases, officer and historian who shared his exile at St. Helena, Napoleon told how he had planned to further the nationalism of European peoples and how he intended to promote the unity of Europe.

The conversations of the day were diffuse and interesting, for the Emperor was exceedingly chatty. He discussed numerous subjects, perfectly heterogeneous in their nature, though they were naturally introduced one by another. His conversation abounded with ideas and facts totally new to me. But the number and importance of the Emperor's remarks rendered it impossible for me to seize them all. My eagerness

to note down the past observation sometimes occasioned the present one to escape me; but, for this very reason, I can, with the greater confidence, vouch for the accuracy of what I have preserved.

Speaking of the elements of society, the Emperor said: "Democracy may be furious; but it has some heart, it may be moved. As to aristocracy, it is always cold and unforgiving. . . .

"My enemies always spoke of my love of war; but was I not constantly engaged in self-defence? After every victory I gained, did I not immediately make proposals for peace?

"The truth is that I never was master of my own actions. I never was entirely myself. I might have conceived many plans; but I never had it in my power to execute any. I held the helm with a vigorous hand; but the fury of the waves was greater than any force that I could exert in resisting them; and I prudently yielded, rather than incur the risk of sinking through stubborn opposition. I never was truly my own master; but was always controlled by circumstances. Thus, as the commencement of my rise, during the Consulate, my sincere friends and warm partisans frequently asked me, with the best intentions, and as a guide for their own conduct, *what point I was driving at?* and I always answered that I did not know. They were surprised, probably dissatisfied, and yet I spoke the truth." . . .

After alluding to some other subjects, the Emperor said, "One of my great plans was the re-uniting, the concentration, of those same geographical nations which have been separated and parcelled out by revolution and policy. There are in Europe, dispersed, it is true, upward of thirty millions of French, fifteen millions of Spaniards, fifteen millions of Italians, and thirty millions of Germans; and it was my intention to incorporate these people each into one nation. It would have been a noble thing to have advanced into posterity with such a train, and attended by the blessings of future ages. I felt myself worthy of this glory!

"After this summary simplification, it would have been possible to indulge the chimera of the *beau idéal* of civilization. In this state of things, there would have been some chance of establishing, in every country, a unity of codes, principles, opinions, sentiments, views, and interests. Then, perhaps, by the help of the universal diffusion of knowledge, one might have thought of attempting, in the great European family, the application of the American Congress, or the Amphictyons of Greece; and then what a perspective of power, greatness, happiness, and prosperity! What a grand, what a magnificent, spectacle!

"The concentration of the thirty or forty millions of Frenchmen was completed and perfected; and that of the fifteen millions of Spaniards was nearly accomplished; for nothing is more common than to convert accident into principle. Because I did not subdue the Spaniards, it will henceforth be argued that they were invincible. But the fact is that they were actually conquered, and at the very moment when they escaped me, the Cortes of Cadiz were secretly in treaty with me. . . . Three or four years would have restored the Spaniards to profound peace and brilliant prosperity: they would have become a compact nation, and I should have well deserved their gratitude; for I should have saved them from the tyranny by which they are now oppressed, and the terrible agitations that await them.

"With regard to the fifteen millions of Italians, their concentration was already far advanced: it only wanted maturity. The people were daily becoming more firmly established in the unity of principles and legislation; and also in the unity of thought and feeling, that certain and infallible cement of human concentration. The union of Piedmont with France, and the junction of Parma, Tuscany and Rome, were, in my mind, but temporary measures, intended merely to guarantee and promote the national education of the Italians. You may judge of the correctness of my views, and of the influence of common laws. The portions of Italy that had been united to France, though that union might have been regarded as the insult of conquest on our part, were, in spite of their Italian patriotism, the very parts that continued by far the most attached to us. Now that they are restored to themselves, they conceive that they have been invaded and disinherited; and they certainly have been!

"All the South of Europe, therefore, would soon have rendered compact in point of locality, views, opinions, sentiments, and interests. In this state of things, what would have been the weight of all the nations of the north? What human efforts could have broken through so strong a barrier?

"The concentration of the Germans must have been effected more gradually; and, therefore, I had done no more than simplify their monstrous complication. Not that they were unprepared for centralization; on the contrary, they were too well prepared for it, and they might have blindly risen in reaction against us, before they had comprehended our designs. How happens it that no German Prince has yet formed a just notion of the spirit of his nation, and turned it to good account? Certainly, if heaven had made me a Prince of Germany, amidst the many critical events of our times, I should, infallibly, have governed the thirty millions of Germans united; and, from what I know of them, I think I may venture to affirm that, if they had once elected and proclaimed me, they would not have forsaken me, and I should never have been at St. Helena."

⟨ HISTORICAL INTERPRETATION ⟩

HANS KOHN ON NAPOLEON AND THE AGE OF NATIONALISM

Hans Kohn, "Napoleon and the Age of Nationalism," *The Journal of Modern History*, Vol. XXII (1950), pp. 22–23, 36–37. By permission of The University of Chicago Press and Hans Kohn.

NAPOLEON KNEW patriotic sentiment in his youth, when he was a Corsican, but it was a patriotism directed against France. Later, he abandoned this sense of localism, embraced the cause of the Revolution, and then sought to extend what he conceived to be its ideals to the rest of the Continent. He was responsible for distributing the seeds of nationalism throughout Europe. The French liberalism of 1789 persisted inside France, but outside France the traits of Napoleonic despotism were revived. The German "spirit of 1914" and Lenin's revolution, both opposed to the principles of 1789, were closer to Napoleonic conquest than to the principles of the French Revolution. In the following passage, Hans Kohn treats Napoleon as a "violent anachronism" in the age of nationalism.

For the French people the Revolution meant a full awakening to nationalism; for Napoleon its influence was different. He abandoned his Corsican patriotism to embrace the Revolutionary cause. Was he swayed by the promise of liberty it held out to French and Corsicans alike? Political liberty soon came to have as little meaning for him as did nationalism, but he sensed the dynamic possibilities in this enthusiastic upsurge of a great people. Edmund Burke had wrongly believed that the Revolution dealt a mortal blow to French strength, leaving the country a great void. Mirabeau, in a memorandum which he sent in September 1790 by Comte de La Marck to Emperor Leopold II, remarked that Burke "has said something very stupid, for this void is a volcano, the subterranean agitations and approaching eruptions of which no one could neglect for a moment without imprudence." He predicted incalculable earthquakes and innumerable grave consequences from the streams of lava that were to pour down on neighboring countries. Even more clearly than Mirabeau, Napoleon understood the dynamism of the French Revolution, this immense release of energy, this gateway to ceaseless activity and boundless ambition. His personality was admirably suited to his time. In a period which exalted the individual and his opportunities, Napoleon, as Friedrich Nietzsche so clearly sensed, was an extreme individualist, for whom France and Europe, nation and mankind, were but instruments of his destiny.

The same quest for an efficient government that brought about the Revolution in 1789 helped Napoleon to power ten years later. The French longed for a strong man who would safegard the main achievements of the Revolution in orderly security and stabilize the new frontiers and glorious conquests in peace. Of all the institutions of the young republic, the army alone possessed the prestige and the power to achieve this. Of its young generals, Bonaparte appeared the most promising. He did not disappoint the country's expectations. A man of rare vitality and capacity for work, of penetrating intelligence and prodigious memory, he proved a great administrator and organizer, continuing the line of enlightened monarchs of the eighteenth century and surpassing them by far, the last and the greatest of them. Like them, he did not understand and had no use for nationalism and the new popular forces. Like them, he believed in the state, in direction from above, in efficiency and rational order. But unlike the greatest of them, he did regard himself less the first servant of the state than its master. The state was the vehicle and instrument of his personal destiny. His primary end was not the welfare of his subjects or the *raison d'état* of France and not, except for brief moments, the perpetuation and glory of his dynasty. All these limited goals he accepted and from time to time promoted each one or all of them, but they did not satisfy or contain him. His ambitions knew no definite limits; his activities had no fixed and stable directions. He felt his will was strong enough to triumph over the nature of man and the nature of things alike. To him, the impossible was only "a phantom of the timid soul and the refuge of the coward."

Despite his youthful Rousseauan nationalism, he was an eighteenth century cosmopolitan for whom civilization was one and the world the stage; in other respects he anticipated the twentieth century. He set the earliest and greatest example in modern times for the potentialities of the cult of force that found so many adherents in the extreme movements of socialism and nationalism a hundred years after his death. The words of this eigthteenth-century man of genius sound sometimes like pronouncements of our times: "There is only one secret for world leadership, namely, to be strong, because in strength there is neither error nor illusion: it is naked truth." "Succeed! I judge men only by the results of their acts." He was a dynamic force, for whom "the world is but an occasion to act dangerously." Though his daring had ultimately to fail, it built much that lasted. . . .

Napoleon appeared as a "violent anachronism" in the age of nationalism; at its beginning, for the protection of their liberty, tranquillity, and diversity, the other peoples united against him and overthrew his new order of conquest and uniformity. Their resistance sealed his fate. In the first war of nationalities he perished. But his violence aroused dark passions hostile to the Enlightenment, which had formed the background of his own ideas. Napoleon was still a rational classicist whom Goethe and Hegel greeted as an embodiment of the world spirit, but the superman in him broke the bounds of the human and the humane. Romantically, a man alone against the world, he rose above the common law in the certainty of his historical mission. What would happen if a whole people followed his lead and—without the safeguards of respect for reason and the essential oneness of men of all classes and nations—also rose above the common law, ready to stand alone against the world, and bear this burden in equal certainty of historical mission?

❦[TEN BASIC BOOKS]❧

NAPOLEON AND THE GRAND EMPIRE, 1795–1815

1. Bruun, Geoffrey, *Europe and the French Imperium, 1799–1814* (New York, 1938).†

2. Deutsch, Harold C., *The Genesis of Napoleonic Imperialism* (Cambridge, Mass., 1938).

3. Geyl, Pieter, *Napoleon For and Against* (New Haven, Conn., 1949).†

4. Lanfrey, Pierre, *History of Napoleon the First,* 23rd ed., 4 vols. (London and New York, 1894).

5. Lefebvre, Georges, *Napoléon,* 3rd ed., (Paris, 1947).

6. Madelin, Louis, *The Consulate and the Empire* (New York, 1936).

7. Mowat, Robert, *The Diplomacy of Napoleon* (New York, 1924).
8. Rose, J. Holland, *The Life of Napoleon,* 11th ed., 2 vols. (London, 1934).
9. Tarlé, Eugene, *Napoleon's Invasion of Russia, 1812* (New York, 1942).
10. Thompson, James, *Napoleon Bonaparte, His Rise and Fall* (New York, 1952).

PART V

THE REVOLUTIONS RENEWED

1815–1871

THE CONCEPT OF LIBERTY[1]

John Stuart Mill

THE OBJECT of this Essay is to assert one very simple principle, as entitled to govern absolutely the dealings of society with the individual in the way of compulsion and control, whether the means used be physical force in the form of legal penalties, or the moral coercion of public opinion. That principle is, that the sole end for which mankind are warranted, individually or collectively, in interfering with the liberty of action of any of their number, is self-protection. That the only purpose for which power can be rightfully exercised over any member of a civilized community, against his will, is to prevent harm to others. His own good, either physical or moral, is not a sufficient warrant. He cannot rightfully be compelled to do or forbear because, it will be better for him to do so, because it will make him happier, because in the opinions of others, to do so would be wise, or even right. These are good reasons for remonstrating with him, or reasoning with him, or persuading him, or entreating him, but not for compelling him, or visiting him with any evil in case he do otherwise. To justify that, the conduct from which it is desired to deter him must be calculated to produce evil to some one else. The only part of the conduct of any one, for which he is amenable to society, is that which concerns others. In the part which merely concerns himself, his independence is, of right, absolute. Over himself, over his own body and mind, the individual is sovereign.

It is, perhaps, hardly necessary to say that this doctrine is meant to apply [only] to human beings in the maturity of their faculties. We are not speaking of children, or of young persons below the age which the law may fix as that of manhood or womanhood. Those who are still in a state to require being taken care of by others, must be protected against their own actions as well as against external injury. For the same reason, we may leave out of consideration those backward states of society in which the race itself may be considered as in its nonage. The early difficulties in the way of spontaneous progress are so great, that there is seldom any choice of means for overcoming them; and a ruler full of the spirit of improvement is warranted in the use of any expedients that will attain an end, perhaps otherwise unattainable. Despotism is a legitimate mode of government in dealing with barbarians, provided the end be their improvement, and the means justified by actually effecting that end. Liberty, as a principle, has no application to any state of things anterior to the time when mankind have become capable of being improved by free and equal discussion. Until then, there is nothing for them but implicit obedience to an Akbar or a Charlemagne, if they are so fortunate as to find one. But as soon as mankind have attained the capacity of being guided to their own improvement by conviction

[1] John Stuart Mill, *On Liberty* (London, n.d.), pp. 17–26.

or persuasion (a period long since reached in all nations with whom we need here concern ourselves), compulsion, either in the direct form or in that of pains and penalties for non-compliance, is no longer admissible as a means to their own good, and justifiable only for the security of others.

It is proper to state that I forego any advantages which could be derived to my argument from the idea of abstract right, as a thing independent of utility. I regard utility as the ultimate appeal on all ethical questions; but it must be utility in the largest sense, grounded on the permanent interests of man as a progressive being. Those interests, I contend, authorise the subjection of individual spontaneity to external control, only in respect to those actions of each, which concern the interest of other people. If any one does an act hurtful to others, there is a *prima facie* case for punishing him, by law, or, where legal penalties are not safely applicable, by general disapprobation. . . .

. . . There is a sphere of action in which society, as distinguished from the individual, has, if any, only an indirect interest; comprehending all that portion of a person's life and conduct which affects only himself, or if it also affects others, only with their free, voluntary, and undeceived consent and participation. When I say only himself, I mean directly, and in the first instance: for whatever affects himself, may affect others *through* himself; and the objection which may be grounded on this contingency will receive consideration in the sequel. This, then, is the appropriate region of human liberty. It comprises, first, the inward domain of consciousness; demanding liberty of conscience, in the most comprehensive sense; liberty of thought and feeling; absolute freedom of opinion and sentiment on all subjects, practical or speculative, scientific, moral, or theological. The liberty of expressing and publishing opinions may seem to fall under a different principle, since it belongs to that part of the conduct of an individual which concerns other people; but, being almost of as much importance as the liberty of thought itself, and resting in part on the same reasons, is practically inseparable from it. Secondly, the principle requires liberty of tastes and pursuits; of framing the plan of our life to suit our own character; of doing as we like, subject to such consequences as may follow: without impediment from our fellow-creatures, so long as what we do does not harm them, even though they should think our conduct foolish, perverse, or wrong. Thirdly, from this liberty of each individual, follows the liberty, within the same limits, of combination among individuals; freedom to unite, for any purpose not involving harm to others: the persons combining being supposed to be of full age, and not forced or deceived.

No society in which these liberties are not, on the whole, respected, is free, whatever may be its form of government, and none is completely free in which they do not exist absolute and unqualified. The only freedom which deserves the name, is that of pursuing our own good in our own way, so long as we do not attempt to deprive others of theirs, or impede their efforts to obtain it. Each is the proper guardian of his own health, whether bodily, or mental and spiritual. Mankind are greater gainers by suffering each other to live as seems good to themselves, than by compelling each to live as seems good to the rest. . . .

In the modern world, the greater size of political communities, and above all, the separation between spiritual and temporal authority (which placed the direction of men's consciences, in other hands than those which controlled their worldly affairs), prevented so great an interference by law in the details of private life; but the engines of moral repression have been wielded more strenuously against divergence from the reigning opinion in self-regarding, than even in social matters; religion, the most powerful of the elements which have entered into the formation of moral feeling, having almost always been governed either by the ambition of a hierarchy, seeking control over every department of human conduct, or by the spirit of Puritanism. And some of those modern reformers who have placed themselves in strongest opposition to the religions of the past, have been noway behind either churches or sects in their assertion of the right of spiritual domination: M. Comte, in particular, whose social system, as unfolded in his *Sytème de politique positive*, aims at establishing (though by moral more than by legal appliances) a despotism of society over the individual, surpassing anything contemplated in the political ideal of the most rigid disciplinarian among the ancient philosophers.

Apart from the peculiar tenets of individual thinkers, there is also in the world at large an increasing inclination to stretch unduly the powers of society over the individual, both by the force of opinion and even by that of legislation: and as the tendency of all the changes taking place in the world is to strengthen society, and diminish the power of the individual, this encroachment is not one of the evils which tend spontaneously to disappear, but, on the contrary, to grow more formidable. The disposition of mankind, whether as rulers or as fellow-citizens, to impose their own opinions and inclinations as a rule of conduct on others, is so energetically supported by some of the best and by some of the worst feelings incident to human nature, that it is hardly ever kept under restraint by anything but want of power; and as the power is not declining, but growing, unless a strong barrier of moral conviction can be raised against the mischief, we must expect, in the present circumstances of the world, to see it increase.

20

Restoration and Reaction, 1815-1830

WHEN THE Napoleonic adventure was at an end and that extraordinary despot had disappeared from the stage where he had reigned supreme; while his conquerors were agreeing or trying to agree among themselves so that they could unite in giving to Europe, by the restoration of old regimes and the timely manipulation of frontiers, a stable organization to replace the strongly held yet always precarious empire of the French nation—then among all peoples hopes were flaming up and demands were being made for independence and liberty. These demands grew louder and more insistent the more they met repulse and repression; and in disappointment and defeat, hopes went on springing up afresh, purposes were strengthened.

—BENEDETTO CROCE

1. The Vienna Peace Settlement, 1815

Congress of Vienna. A great international congress of European diplomats met from September 1814 to June 1815 at Vienna to settle conflicting claims to the Napoleonic Empire. Decisions were made by delegates of the Big Four that had overthrown Napoleon —Great Britain, Russia, Prussia, and Austria. Great Britain was represented by the quiet but practical foreign minister, Lord Castlereagh, and later by the Duke of Wellington. The liberal-minded Tsar Alexander I directed his own diplomacy but utilized the services of such foreign diplomats as Baron vom Stein. Frederick William III of Prussia sent as his plenipotentiary Karl August von Hardenberg and a group of hard-working civil servants. Prince Klemens Wenzel von Metternich (1773–1859), chief minister of Austria, master of dynastic diplomacy, and delegate for Emperor Francis I, was the outstanding statesman at the Congress. The astute, unscrupulous Charles Maurice de Talleyrand-Périgord (1754–1838) was present to obtain maximum concessions for defeated France. These leading personages, with a host of courtiers and secretaries, mixed business with pleasure. The Congress danced until Napoleon's return from Elba in March 1815 shocked it into action.

Principle of "Legitimacy." The diplomats at Vienna, intent upon restoring the map of 1789 as completely as possible, paid more attention to dynastic than to national or colonial claims. Talleyrand provided a *modus operandi* with a cunning invention—the principle of "legitimacy," by which the rulers of Europe who had lost their thrones projected a theoretical right to their former royal position. In the name of legitimacy Louis XVIII was restored to the throne of France. Similarly, the Bourbons were returned to their thrones in Spain (Ferdinand VII) and in Naples; an Austrian archduke of the house of Hapsburg was given Tuscany and Modena; German princes recovered their sovereign powers; the house of Orange in the Netherlands and the house of Piedmont and Sardinia were recognized; and the Papal States in central Italy were returned to the papacy. Each "legitimate" ruler was given his old territory or a reasonable approximation of it with the understanding that he would reverse all major changes made during the revolutionary era. Only one Napoleonic monarch, Sweden's Bernadotte, was permitted to retain his throne: he had aided the allies against Napoleon.

Principle of "Compensations." In remaking the map of Europe the statesmen of Vienna showed little regard for national sentiment. Considered more important in distributing the spoils of war was the necessity of strengthening the Great Powers at the expense of the weaker by awarding territorial "compensations." The Congress also worked out a plan to repay one nation for the loss of territory for some reason given to another nation.

Russia obtained most of the Grand Duchy of Warsaw. A new kingdom of Poland was created and joined to Russia in a personal union. Sweden gave up Finland to Russia. As compensation Sweden was given Norway, which was taken from Denmark because of the latter's protracted alliance with Napoleon. Russia's western border now was thrust almost into Central Europe.

To compensate Austria for the surrender of her claims on the southern Netherlands, she was given Lombardy, Venetia, most of the Tyrol, and virtual control over Parma, Tuscany, and Modena, and she shared in the redivision of Poland. Austria's population now became more heterogeneous than ever.

To compensate the Dutch and to set up a strong buffer state on the northern frontier of France, the southern (Austrian) Netherlands were joined to the northern (Dutch) Netherlands under the restored Dutch Prince, William I of Orange as King of the United Netherlands.

Prussia was awarded German territories taken by Napoleon. Moreover, she acquired Swedish Pomerania on the Baltic, about two-fifths of Saxony, all of Westphalia, and several lower Rhineland provinces. The smaller German states were organized into the German Confederation (*Bund*) under Austrian domination. Prussia emerged from the treaty strong enough to rival Austria for control of the Germanies.

Great Britain, in conformance with her traditional policy, expected and received the valuable colonies and naval outposts which she had already captured from the French and Dutch. She acquired Cape Colony, Ceylon, and a part of Honduras from the Netherlands, the island of Heligoland from Denmark, and Malta, Mauritius, Trinidad, Santa Lucia, and a protectorate over the Ionian Islands (*Heptanesus* or "Seven Islands").

Violations of Nationalism. There was little consistency in the work of the statesmen at Vienna. They recognized dynastic claims in some cases but not in others. They had two aims—to secure the victors against France and to destroy the remnants of republicanism. They sought to construct a rough balance of power among the larger nations, but in doing this they disregarded the growing sentiment of nationalism. They united Norway and Sweden against the wishes of the inhabitants; they joined Holland and Belgium, which differed in language, traditions, customs, and religion; they incorporated patriotic Poles into a hostile Russia; they combined the Germanies into a loose, obsolescent confederation unsatisfactory to Germans; and they denied the Italies a federal organization. The only concession they made to nationalism was to create a new kingdom of Poland and give it a new constitution—and then award it to Russia. They regarded nationalism as tinged with the spirit of the French Revolution, and they wanted to eliminate any vestiges of that unpleasant event. But without desiring it they unintentionally hastened the expression of a rising nationalism.

Violations of Democracy. Equally shortsighted was the attitude of the peacemakers of Vienna to democracy. By restoring the old dynasties in France, Spain, the Netherlands, and the Italies, they directly attacked popular desires. They disregarded such democratic principles as constitutionalism, equality before the law, and equitable taxation, because these had been too closely associated with revolution. They erected barriers against further democratic development and imagined that the issue had been settled. They underestimated the strength of the popular will for democracy and did not realize the potential power of the bourgeoisie, who were opponents of conservative reaction. At the same time they showed little respect for religious and intellectual liberty. They were to learn the bitter lesson that revolutions can be renewed.

Achievements of the Congress. There were some accomplishments on the credit side of the ledger. The Congress of Vienna brought Europe what it most needed—peace. By working out the rough principles of a balance of

power it enabled Europe to avoid a general war for a century until 1914. Its neutralization of Switzerland became a tenet of European international law and survived the two World Wars of the twentieth century. It provided for freedom of navigation on such international rivers as the Rhine and the Danube. It established principles of diplomatic preference, although it made no attempt to create a mechanism by which customs governing international relations could be adapted to the new trends of the nineteenth century. It

In the years 1814–1815, an imposing assemblage—kings, generals, celebrated diplomats, and even representatives of great banking houses—convened in Vienna to decide how Europe should best be settled into peace. A rather informal drawing-room atmosphere is usually associated with the gathering, as in this lithograph after an official painting of the Congress of Vienna by Jean Baptiste Isabey.

abolished the maritime traffic in slaves as contrary to the principles of civilization and humanity.

Failure of the Restoration. Because the statesmen of Vienna paid scant attention to the most powerful forces of the time they doomed their structure to disintegration. Since

many of the changes made during the revolutionary era could not be altered without endangering the entire social structure, they were allowed to remain. Little could be done about the decline of such traditional structures as the Holy Roman Empire, the Church, and feudalism-manorialism. Absolutism, in theory and practice, persisted, but its moral authority was gone. Instead of showing loyal obedience to absolute monarchs, the people were sullen and restive.

The political settlement was not lasting. Belgium rebelled against Dutch domination in 1830 and became an independent state. The union of Norway and Sweden lasted ninety years until 1905. Austria was to lose the territories she had acquired in 1815—Lombardy to united Italy in 1859 and Venetia to Italy in 1866. In the Revolution of 1830 in France the restored Bourbon, Charles X, had to flee for his life. The German Confederation lasted only until 1866; the settlement in the Italies was nullified by Italian unification.

2. The Concert of Europe

Holy Alliance, 1815. Along with the overthrow of Napoleon as heir of the Revolution occurred a reaction against the antireligious rationalism of the eighteenth-century Enlightenment. This religious revival was expressed in the formation of the Holy Alliance. The deeply pious, mystical Tsar Alexander I of Russia saw in the revolutionary era the work of God who had smitten down kings unwilling to rule in the spirit of Christianity. He regarded the fall of Napoleon, too, as the work of Providence. Alexander prevailed upon his fellow rulers to sign a document guaranteeing that from this time on the relations between nations would be based on "the sublime truth of the Holy Religion," and that "the precepts of Justice, Christian Charity, and Peace" must be utilized by princes in their work. Kings would be fathers to their subjects, who were advised "to strengthen themselves every day more and more in the principles and exercise of the duties which the Divine Saviour taught to Mankind."

Emperor Francis I of Austria and Frederick William III of Prussia subscribed to the pact signed on September 26, 1815. Nearly every ruler in Europe added his signature, with three notable exceptions: the prince regent of Great Britain (George III had been incapacitated by insanity); the sultan of Turkey, who as a Muslim was not impressed by Christian sentiments; and the pope, who refused to place his signature on a manifesto signed by "heretics." It was in truth a strange document. Liberals denounced it as the work of despots plotting to further autocracy by suppressing democracy under the cloak of religion. Conservatives were unimpressed: Metternich dismissed it as "loud-sounding verbiage," and Castlereagh called it "a piece of sublime mysticism and nonsense." It was said that when Emperor Francis signed it he remarked that he did not know what it meant: "If it is a question of politics, I must refer it to my chancellor; if of religion, to my confessor." The Holy Alliance was less a treaty than a vague, innocuous expression of a state of mind.

Quadruple Alliance, 1815. The critical problem faced by the statesmen of the Restoration was how to prevent the outbreak of any revolution or the return of Napoleon. The members of the final coalition against France had pledged themselves to remain united after victory. Accordingly, the Big Four—Russia, Prussia, Austria, and Great Britain—formally signed the Quadruple Alliance on November 20, 1815, pledging each member to maintain the settlement of Vienna by force, to guarantee the peace of Europe, and to meet at stated intervals to discuss matters of common interest and "to examine those measures judged most salutary for the repose and prosperity of the peoples." Though at first directed against the revival of revolution or Napoleonic militarism, the alliance became an instrument dedicated to the preservation of the *status quo* against liberal-democratic elements. The only way to fight revolutionary movements, the Big Four agreed, was to become international and support one another in the event of rebellion. At its base was the theory that if revolution could be international, then repression also should be international.

Diplomatic methods underwent a drastic change. The Big Four would act as the Concert of Europe, a loose organization based upon "a just equilibrium of strength." It would settle international disputes, formulate international policies, and above all prevent France from arising again to disturb the peace of Europe. A throttled France would not be able again to spread the virus of revolution from one corner of Europe to another. However, by the Congress of Aix-la-Chapelle (September 1818), France was admitted to the newly constituted Quintuple Alliance (although the old Quadruple Alliance remained in existence).

Role of Metternich. For a generation the most important political figure in Europe was Prince Metternich. Born to a noble family, he attended Strasbourg University, where he was alienated by the mob violence he observed in the early days of the Revolution. Frightened by the fury of the Terror, he confused democracy with panic and anarchy. In 1795 he married the granddaughter of the Austrian chancellor and diplomat, Prince Wenzel Anton von Kaunitz, and thus assured himself a prominent position at court. Named Austrian ambassador to France in 1806, he managed to remain on good terms with Napoleon. In 1809 he was made chancellor and foreign minister of Austria, in which capacity he played off Napoleon and Alexander I of Russia against each other. He negotiated the marriage between Napoleon and Marie Louise in 1810. His acute diplomacy obtained for Austria a dominating position in the overthrow of Napoleon and the negotiations which followed. Metternich was suave and cultured, impressively handsome, shrewd and witty, convinced of his own destiny.

Metternich's aims were (1) to consolidate Europe under Austrian hegemony and (2) to maintain a European balance of power. He advocated a philosophy of equilibrium both in relationship of the classes and in the interactions of the Great Powers. Because both had been disturbed by the French Revolution and Napoleon, he believed it essential to restore the balance and maintain it. Contemptuous of liberalism, he regarded it as an ideal invented and pursued by fools. He mistrusted the masses and demanded that they be ruled with an iron hand. His one great fear was nationalism, which would mean destruction of an Austria composed of conglomerate nationalities. He always sought to maintain the peace of Europe; it was his restraining hand that prevented further wars and enabled Europe to

Prince Klemens Wenzel von Metternich, determined and masterful manipulator of governments.

recover from the Napoleonic wars. The most astute statesman of his age, he was named a hereditary prince of the Austrian Empire.

Historical Controversy: Conservative Statesman or Reactionary Evil Genius? Few historians have challenged Metternich's talents as a technician of diplomacy, but there have been varying interpretations of the content of his diplomacy and the objectives toward which he worked. The difference in attitude appears in the conclusions of two professors of history at the University of Vienna. To Heinrich von Srbik, Metternich was the champion of historical order, a statesman of unusual talents, one of the greatest of all masters of international politics. "He deserves the title of political conqueror of Napoleon. It was because of him that Europe enjoyed comparative peace for 30 years. . . . His historical significance in the deepest sense was the constant and consistent opposition throughout the world of European civilization to the leveling nature of democracy and the mass rule which threatened the historical order of states, society, individual culture."

Victor Bibl, on the other hand, condemned Metternich as "truly the evil genius of Austria," a cunning and adroit manipulator who adopted a policy of reaction merely to stay in office and who by artificially suppressing nationalism and liberalism, the twin new vital forces of the day, eventually brought on the Revolution of 1848. "Everywhere Metternich acted as a disintegrative force on the authority of the state, enhanced mistrust between prince and people, prince and ministers. . . . He was not the preserver of European peace: everywhere he caused unrest. . . . The forces he repressed eventually burst on Europe with devastating effect."

On the one side Metternich is regarded as an infallible master of heroic proportions, on the other as the incarnation of evil. Between these two extremes appears the figure of a man of remarkable diplomatic talents, passionate likes and dislikes, strong egoism, and obstinate will. To him the sum of all evil was revolution, "a hydra with open jaws to swallow the social order." He regarded parliamentary government as a "perpetual somersault," which did no good for either ruler or ruled. A servant of despots, a master of secret intrigue, Metternich cleverly manipulated government in the interests of the aristocratic class to which he belonged. He rode the crest of the reactionary wave, and when it subsided he was forced to flee for his life.

3. Conservatism and Romanticism

Defense of Conservatism. At first the stirring events of the French Revolution sent a wave of optimism surging throughout Europe. Was not the new freedom at hand? Had there not been fulfilled at long last the great promise envisioned by the rationalists? But persistent mob violence, the Reign of Terror, and the long-drawn-out revolutionary wars brought in their wake a reaction against the entire movement. By contrast, the old order seemed more stable and more peaceful. Many people, yearning for the good old days, welcomed the settlement made at Vienna. To them it meant order instead of interminable conflict.

One of the most eloquent voices against the developments in France was that of Edmund Burke (1729–1797), whose *Reflections on the Revolution in France* (1790) saw nothing but evil in the outbreak of disorderly mobs against the rule of law. He could not reconcile the behavior of "the swinish multitudes" with his love of order, in which alone he saw the fruits of liberty. He wrote of certain vital but intangible forces which preserve a civilization. Burke believed that all rights of man were gradually established in accordance with a historically evolving and extremely complicated social structure. Because this social structure developed differently in every society, and because no group of men in a single lifetime could fully understand the intricacies of a given society, any attempt at social change should proceed slowly and with the greatest caution. The radical rationalist who struck right and left in a desire for progress actually tended to destroy this delicate fabric of the rights of man. Revolutionaries were wrong in regarding man as he might be or ought to be: they were unrealistic ideologists who expected human nature to fit their formulas. The best heritage of the past must be preserved, not remodeled or destroyed. "We ought to venerate what we are unable presently to comprehend." Burke was issuing a cold warning against the excesses of the Age of Reason.

Burke's arguments were convincing to European conservatives of the Restoration era. Even if the promises of the Revolution were substantial, was it not true that the sacrifices outweighed whatever gains had been made? What was the good of Liberty, Equality, and Fraternity, if, in achieving anything approaching what those terms meant, all society were plunged into chaos? From the conservative point of view, the *philosophes* had used their brains in an attempt to create a better world, only to make it a more dangerous place. And further, it was charged, the enlightened despots had been willing to experiment with reform, only to open the doors to political abuse and social disorder.

Gradually, there grew up around this opposition a conservative credo. (1) All aristocracies are stable, democracies fickle and unstable. (2) The ruling class has a higher capacity: what is good for the upper order is good for the general welfare. (3) The important things are honor, *esprit de famille*, *noblesse qui oblige*. (4) Always oppose radical experimentation. (5) Bring religion back to its proper place in society.

The conservatives reacted against the decay of organized religion that had taken place in the revolutionary era. Anti-clericalism was one thing, they felt, but skepticism, agnosticism, and atheism were undermining the new generation. In practical terms the attitude was expressed at the Congress of Vienna when the Papal States were restored to Pope Pius VII. At the same time there emerged a movement known as ultramontanism to "look beyond the mountains," across the Alps to the pope at Rome as head of the Catholic world.

The word *conservative* itself was orginated by Chateaubriand who, with Lamennais, established in Paris a newspaper, *Le conservateur,* designed to promote the struggle against revolutionary forces. In England a group of Tories began to call themselves conservatives about 1833. At roughly the same time the conservative faction in Prussia began as the Junker party. In the post-1815 period the conservative position was interchangeable with that of reaction. Later, the word conservative was widely used to denote a party intent upon "conserving" the best of the past.

Reaction Against Reason: Romanticism. The conservative mind reacted against "the self-evident dictates of pure reason," as well as to the excesses of the French Revolution. The movement known as romanticism emphasized the emotional rather than the rational side of human nature. It exalted faith and intuition instead of the intellect. The romantics saw their organic-genetic conception of culture as an expression of the national soul. They issued a plea for the claims of the imagination, of emotion and feeling, of individualism, and above all, for a synthetic expression of the national genius in all its aspects by philosophy, religion, politics, literature, and art. In interpreting life, nature, and history, they abandoned the rationalists' emphasis upon reason. Traditional and sentimental thinkers developed a fundamental philosophical defense of their position. Romanticism in philosophy turned into a type of metaphysics known as transcendental idealism, which stressed the emotions—ideals, spirit, and faith—with the same confidence that the rationalists had bestowed upon the intellectual faculties.

Romanticism had a development of its own. By the end of the eighteenth century the terms "imaginative," "extraordinary," and "visionary" were becoming more and more familiar. Rousseau presented the conception of the "noble savage," praised primitivism and sentimentalism, and insisted that happiness and salvation could be captured only by a return to natural freedom and innocence. In the Germanies in the 1770's, a youthful cult called *Sturm und Drang* ("Storm and Stress") represented a combination of tendencies: intuition and mysticism, return to nature as advocated by Rousseau, and love for the vague and mysterious; at the same time it denounced sterile rationalism (*Vernünftelei*) and the "pygmy French." In the early nineteenth century all these tendencies were popularized in a dogma composed of a multiplicity of attitudes. Romanticism, never an organized sect, revealed itself in many disguises, from mystic symbolism to openhearted humanitarianism.

Politically, romanticism merged into the reaction against that democratic rationalism that had been responsible for the tragic excesses of the Revolution. Romantics of all kinds looked back to the great past—days of order and security and legitimacy. They longed for the integration associated with the old Holy Roman Empire. There had been too much social change, too much bloodshed, too much revolution: Romantics deemed it best to return to the political and social ideals of a more complacent past.

Political romanticism outlasted its cultural counterpart. In its more blatant form it eventually became the dominant element of Fascism, particularly Adolf Hitler's National Socialism, with its perverted idea of the Nietzschean superman, its romantic myth of a nonexistent "pure" Aryanism, its anti-rationalistic emphasis on "thinking with the blood," its naive anti-intellectualism, and its glorification of military strength.

Romanticism and Nationalism. Politically, romantic interest in the past soon linked up with the rising sense of nationalism. Scholars began to turn to the study of national laws, institutions, and languages to prove that their own national culture was deeply rooted in history. Many aspects of romanticism—its enthusiasm for the past, its appeal to the emotions instead of reason, its dynamic accent upon the familiar and the marvelous, its stress upon the dignity of the common man, its accent on bourgeois social aspirations—all these harmonized with the tenets of the rising nationalism. The consciousness of national genius stimulated by romanticism inevitably led to claims of superiority. German romanticism described the German as valiant, truthful, pure, courageous, and blond, a kind of fantastic idealization of views presented by Tacitus. Fichte's Germanism, Herder's divine mission of the German nation, the Frenchman Gobineau's Aryanism, and Wagner's barbarian heroism—all romantic concepts—served to popularize German nationalism. Similarly, other nations underwent the same process of romantic sentimentalization ending in quickened nationalism.

Religious Aspects. The emotional outburst took the form of religious self-consciousness, an intensification of faith, a return to traditionalism, and the revival of supernaturalism and mysticism. Intellectual leaders who were appalled by the assault on the fundamental doctrines of Christianity, especially during the French Revolution, when "Reason" reigned, turned back to the impregnable foundation of faith. In the Germanies this movement was known as Pietism.

Cultural Romanticism. Classicism had remained relatively stable during the revolutionary and Napoleonic eras. Indeed, French revolutionaries, many of them classical scholars, thought of themselves as modern exponents of the democratic virtues of ancient Greece. Napoleon, too, had a weakness for the styles and forms of antiquity. Culturally, romanticism represented a reaction against the long-dominant classicism. In rebelling against classical restraint and formalism, the romantics turned away from purity of expression and exchanged it for a rich imagery. They sought beauty in

nature, in the mountains, lakes, and forests, instead of in artificial domes and columns. They stressed feelings and emotions. There were many shades of cultural romanticism, varying all the way from Wordsworth's praise of rural England's peasant diction, to the sentimental *Lieder* of Schubert, the restless anger of Delacroix, and the crashing symbolism of Richard Wagner.

English Romanticism. English romanticism was a reaction against the polished writing of such eighteenth-century classicists as Swift, Pope, Addison, Steele, and Samuel Johnson. William Wordsworth (1770–1850), producing delicate, emotional poetry, attacked the old formalized approach and replaced it with a simple style tinged with mysticism. Samuel Taylor Coleridge (1772–1834) wrote hauntingly of seas, ships, and phantoms. Sir Walter Scott (1771–1832) reconstructed Scottish and English legend and history with a touch of heather and magic. The sensitive poet, Lord Byron (1788–1824), typical romanticist and man of action, worked to free the fettered nations of Europe. Percy Bysshe Shelley (1792–1822) created "luminous images of mist and light and running water." John Keats (1795–1821), looking back to the Greeks for inspiration, worshiped at the shrine of pure beauty.

German Romanticism. The war against Napoleon for liberation turned German literature from the path of classicism to romantic exaltation of the imagination and medieval mysticism. German romantics revived many popular native traditions and sought refuge in folk stories and fairy tales. Poets of the War of Liberation—including Max von Schenkendorf (1783–1817), Theodor Körner (1791–1813), and Ernst Moritz Arndt (1769–1860) —composed passionate verses designed to awaken Germans to the necessity for driving Napoleon from their land. A new slant to philosophical speculation was given by a trio of German idealists—Immanuel Kant (1724–1804), who emphasized the moral duties of man; Johann Fichte (1762–1814), who devoted himself to the practical side of idealism by denouncing Napoleon; and Georg Wilhelm Hegel (1770–1831), at once idealist and mystic, proponent of both a world spirit and a national German sentiment. The Grimm brothers (Jakob [1785–1863] and Wilhelm [1786–1859]) devoted scholarly attention to German folklore and antiquity, and gathered the *Fairy Tales* well known to all children. Heinrich Heine (1797–1856), brilliant satirist and iconoclast, became the most popular German poet of his time.

French Romanticism. French romanticism reached full expression later in the nineteenth century. In the vanguard was Victor Hugo (1802–1885), master of rich and robust narrative. Other romanticists were Madame de Staël (1766–1817), opponent of French classicism and admirer of German romanticism; François René de Chateaubriand (1768–1848), pious, sentimental, melancholy; Alfred de Vigny (1797–1863), lyrical poet of uncommon range and sensibility; Alfred de Musset (1810–1857), brilliant and emotional spoiled child of romanticism; Alphonse de Lamartine (1790–1869), pessimistic lyricist of nature and religion; Théophile Gautier (1811–1872), emotional lyricist; and Alexandre Dumas (1802–1870), writer of vivid historical novels.

Romanticism in Painting. Painting, like literature, was influenced by the new mood of romanticism. The Frenchman Eugène Delacroix (1798–1863) sought inspiration in the historical themes of his country. Two English nature painters, John Constable (1776–1837) and J. M. W. Turner (1775–1851), were essentially romantic in their themes. The Spaniard Francisco Goya (1746–1828) appealed to the emotions of his countrymen by depicting the terrible atrocities of Napoleon's troops.

The romantic quality of this pastoral scene is enhanced by the nostalgic suggestiveness of the ruins of Kirkstall Abbey. After a water-color drawing by J. M. W. Turner.

Romanticism in Music. The mood of romanticism was even deeper in musical art. The great genius of the era was Ludwig von Beethoven (1770–1827), whose marvelous symphonies, concertos, sonatas, string quartets, and chamber music employed romantic themes. Other great German composers turned from classicism to romanticism: Karl Maria von Weber (1786–1826), creator of brilliant operas; Franz Schubert (1797–1828), master of pure melody; and Felix Mendelssohn (1809–1847), distinguished for his warm, descriptive melodies and gentle rhythms. At the head of the new movement were several Italian composers: Vincenzo Bellini (1801–1835), master of flowing melody; Gaetano Donizetti (1797–1848), distinguished for facility, vigor, and humor; and Gioacchino Rossini (1792–1868), composer of thirty-eight sparkling operas.

4. The Mainstream of International Repression

Liberal Opposition. No sooner were the monarchs restored to their thrones than they were faced with new revolts by the liberals. The vicious circle began when repression made open opposition impossible and forced the liberals into conspiracy. In southern Italy there arose a secret organization called the *Carbonari* (charcoal-burners) which, sworn to establish constitutional government, waged a terroristic campaign against reactionary officials. So successful were these conspirators that similar societies were founded in Spain, Portugal, and France.

The first tests of international control took place after uprisings led by the *Carbonari* in Spain, Portugal, Naples, and Piedmont. As soon as Ferdinand VII was restored to the throne of Spain he refused to recognize the constitution. Supported by army, nobility, and Church, he governed despotically. Determined to reconquer his American colonies, he began sending large contingents of soldiers to South America. In January 1820 two regiments about to embark at Cadiz, mutinied. Dismayed and frightened when the revolt spread, Ferdinand hastened to approve the Constitution of 1812

and promised his people an enlightened administration.

Heartened by events in Spain, the Neapolitans forced Ferdinand I of the Kingdom of the Two Sicilies, a cousin and reactionary counterpart of Ferdinand of Spain, to take an oath and grant a constitution and political rights. When their ruler Dom John was slow to return after the overthrow of Napoleon, the Portuguese people summoned a constituent assembly to draft a democratic constitution. In Piedmont the liberals forced King Victor Emmanuel I of Sardinia to vacate the throne in favor of his brother, Charles Felix.

Congress of Troppau, 1820. Alarmed by these developments, Alexander I of Russia proposed a meeting to mount a counteroffensive. This conference met at Troppau, Austria, in 1820. The issue at hand was the situation in Naples where the *Carbonari* were in control, but the monarchs of the Great Powers, apprehensive about the spread of revolutionary movements, wanted something more. Delegates of Russia, Prussia, and Austria, encouraged by Metternich, drew up a protocol announcing that "states which have undergone a change of government due to revolution, *ipso facto* cease to be members of the European Alliance, and remain excluded from it until their situation gives guarantees for legal order and stability." Russia and Austria proposed that the Powers intervene in Naples, but Great Britain refused to support intervention. The Quadruple Alliance was not working as well as expected. There were sour notes in the Concert of Europe.

Congress of Laibach, 1821. The following year another meeting of the Great Powers was held at Laibach, Austria, near the Italian border, to consider the situation in Naples. Ferdinand of Naples appeared before the assembly, repudiated his oath to grant a constitution, and asked for assistance against his people. British delegates held that the Neapolitan affair was solely Austria's problem, but the representatives of Austria, Prussia, and Russia insisted that all the Powers should unite against revolution wherever it appeared. For the moment the French supported the British stand. Finally, the Austrian government being commissioned to suppress the Neapolitan liberals, Metternich sent his troops into Naples and put down the rebellion. Restored to absolute power, Ferdinand took savage revenge upon those who had opposed him. Meanwhile, another Austrian army, now dubbed "Europe's fire brigade," helped overthrow the revolutionists in Piedmont. Metternich's system of international repression seemed to be working for the time being.

Congress of Verona, 1822. The last of the series of international congresses based on the principle of united action was held at Verona, the episcopal see of Venetia, in 1822. This time it was the turn of France to maintain the concept of international intervention. In 1818, at the Congress of Aix-la-Chapelle (Aachen) in Rhenish Prussia, France had been admitted to the councils of the Quadruple Alliance because Louis XVIII had demonstrated his loyalty to its principles. At Verona the French king, more anxious than ever to prove that his people repented of their revolutionary excesses, withdrew his support from Great Britain and cast his lot with the eastern powers. The argument was bitter. Alexander I of Russia offered to dispatch 150,000 troops through the Germanies to Piedmont, where they would be held in readiness to act against revolution anywhere; the suggestion was graciously but firmly declined. The British refused to support the idea of intervention in Spain, suspecting that this was only a pretext for reviving Bourbon ambitions in the Iberian peninsula. George Canning, successor to Castlereagh as foreign secretary, informed the French ambassador who had urged the British to intervene in Spain: "Be yours the glory of a victory by disaster and ruin; be ours the inglorious traffic of industry and ever-increasing prosperity."

In 1823, with the blessing of the Great Powers excepting Great Britain, Louis XVIII sent an army across the Pyrenees. Assisted by a working fifth column, the French invaders undermined the already weak structure of Spanish liberalism. After the capture of Cadiz, the *Cortes* fled, taking the king with it, and released him only when he promised a general amnesty. Restored to his throne by French intervention, Ferdinand VII forgot his promises and ordered imprisonment, exile, or execution for his liberal opponents. Again in power, Ferdinand requested the Great Powers to aid him further by helping him obtain the return of those American colonies which had broken from Spain during the Napoleonic Wars.

Monroe Doctrine, 1823. When in 1823 the French army invaded Spain and restored Ferdinand VII, Canning informed the French that Great Britain was not inclined to tolerate the subjugation of the Spanish colonies by force. His added proposal that a joint Anglo-American declaration oppose any interference in South America was rejected by the United States. But in December 1823 President James Monroe issued a paper which has since become famous as the Monroe Doctrine: "The American Continents, by the free and independent condition which they have assumed and maintained, are henceforth not to be considered as subjects for future colonization by any European powers." Monroe thus served notice on European nations that any interference would be regarded as the manifestation of an unfriendly disposition toward the United States. This proclamation might not have gone unchallenged had not Great Britain, which had important commercial interests in South America, supported the American position by recognizing the independence of several of the revolting colonies. The absolutist governments abandoned any intention of restoring Spanish control in Latin America. Metternich's system was blocked in the New World.

Greek Independence, 1821–1829. Angered by centuries of oppression and inspired by revolutionary sentiment throughout Europe, the Greeks were determined to seek independence from their Turkish masters. After they failed to obtain support from other Balkan nations, who were crippled by quarrels among themselves, the Greeks on their own opened the war. In Europe and the United States, lovers of the classical Hellenic civilization regarded the modern Greeks as worthy descendants of the Athenians and Spartans and sympathized with their move for independence. To Metternich the Greeks were rebels against their legitimate ruler, the sultan of Turkey, but he saw that the Holy Alliance could not very well intervene in favor of a Mohammedan ruler against Christian Greeks.

Attacking suddenly in 1821, the Greeks cleared the Turks from most of southern and central Greece. The next year the sultan sent a well-equipped army to Greece, whereupon the rebels resorted to guerrilla warfare. All the world was horrified by stories of atrocities coming from Greece, where both sides used ferocious tactics. Numerous volunteers went to Greece to join the struggle against "the abominable Turk." Lord Byron, the English poet, died in 1824 while aiding the Greek cause.

In 1825 an Egyptian army under Ibrahim Pasha came to the aid of the Turks, and with such success that the cause of the Greeks seemed lost. The Great Powers now decided to intervene: Russia because she saw in the Greek uprising an opportunity to attack Turkey, her traditional enemy; Great Britain through fear that the Russians might succeed in breaking through to Constantinople; France because she wanted leadership in Mediterranean affairs; and all three of them because each distrusted the others. On October 20, 1827, the combined fleets of the Great Powers reduced the Turco-Egyptian navy to a mass of wreckage in the harbor of Navarino. When a Russian army reached Adrianople, the Turks called an end to the war. By the Treaty of Adrianople (1829) with Russia, and by the Protocol of London (1830) with the other Powers, the sultan was compelled to recognize the independence of Greece.

Intervention by three reactionary Powers on behalf of a revolution was an extraordinary spectacle. It meant virtually the end of that Metternichian system which called for joint action against any people trying to change its government by revolutionary means. Something was saved from the wreckage of prin-

ciple by refusing to allow the Greeks to set up a republic. Instead, a Bavarian prince was awarded the throne as Otto I of Greece. But the despots had good cause to remain uneasy.

5. Reprise: The Revolutions of 1830

Interruption of Reaction. Metternich's policy of repression made more enemies for his system. Although the Holy Alliance had prevailed during the revolutionary movement of 1820, it could not eliminate the agitation for reforms and for constitutional government. A decade later came another uprising against the system of reaction. Royal and aristocratic power had received a setback in the French Revolution in 1789, but it had recovered after the fall of Napoleon. Now, once again, rebellion originated in Paris. Its sudden success sent another revolutionary tremor throughout Europe.

Second French Revolution, 1830. France, since the Congress of Vienna, had been committed to a compromise between conservatism and liberalism. Louis XVIII carried out his promise to grant a constitution guaranteeing liberties won during the Revolution. With freedom of speech allowed, a war of words took place among monarchists, Bonapartists, republicans, ultramontanes ("beyond the mountains" —clericals looking to Rome for leadership), and anticlericals. At first the king opposed the reactionaries, but gradually, alienated by the growth of radical sentiment and the assassination in 1820 of the duc de Berri, he leaned more and more in their direction. His successor, his brother Charles X, who mounted the throne in 1824, turned all the way to reaction, thereby arousing the enmity of middle-class businessmen, Napoleonic veterans, and old-line Jacobins. Charles forced parliament to vote a bill of indemnification for the aristocracy, and issued the July Ordinances which curbed the civil liberties of the people. In July 1830 armed insurrection resulted in three days of street-fighting. Charles X abdicated in favor of his ten-year-old grandson, the comte de Chambord, and fled to England. The July Days put an end to reaction in France.

Citizens attacking the militia during the July Revolution in France, 1830. Drawing by Bodem.

Revolt of the Belgian Netherlands. The quick success of the Parisian revolt inspired other uprisings. The first immediate impact was in Belgium. Friction between Belgians and Dutch had been acute since the Congress of Vienna set up the Kingdom of the Netherlands. The forced amalgamation was unwise: the Protestant Dutch, with a dominantly agricultural economy, were fused with the highly industrialized Catholic Belgians. The Dutch were influenced by German culture; the Belgians, who spoke French or Flemish, looked to France for inspiration. King William I of Orange, Dutch and Calvinist, was determined to subordinate the Belgian Catholics. The latter, in turn, overtly protested against all Dutch efforts to place education under state control, and strongly opposed the imposition of

the Dutch language as that officially sanctioned as the national language.

When news came from Paris in July 1830
about an uprising there, barricades went up
in Brussels. After a bloody riot, a national
assembly proclaimed the independence of Belgium, deposed the House of Orange, and
established a limited, hereditary monarchy
under Prince Leopold of Saxe-Coburg as Leopold I, King of the Belgians. When King
William refused to accept this settlement, he
was met by a French army and an English
fleet which forced the Dutch to acknowledge
Belgian independence. In 1839 the Great
Powers signed a treaty guaranteeing the frontiers and neutrality of Belgium (the famous
"scrap of paper" torn up by Germany when
she invaded Belgium in 1914). Once again
the Powers had to sacrifice the principle of
legitimacy in favor of emerging nationalism.

Revolutionary Movements Elsewhere. The
July sun penetrated as far as Poland, which
in 1815 had been joined to Russia in a personal union. The Poles enjoyed a considerable
amount of self-government, but they longed for
independence. In 1830–1831 they rebelled
against the Russians, but were overwhelmed
and deprived of concessions already granted.
In the Italies, insurrections in Modena, Parma,
Bologna, and the Romagna were quickly suppressed by Austrian intervention. In the

Germanies, several small states, including
Hesse-Cassel, Brunswick, and Hanover, were
forced to grant constitutions, but in Prussia
liberal forces were suppressed. In Austria, Metternich's secret police punished liberal or revolutionary movements. In Switzerland, growing
unrest led to the promulgation of a constitution and the introduction of liberal government
in twelve cantons. Absolutism persisted in
Spain and Portugal. In England, the conservative Wellington ministry was overthrown in
November 1830 to be followed by an era of
liberal reform in representation and franchise.

Significance of the Revolutions of 1830. The
Metternich system emerged from the Revolutions of 1830 scarred and battered. Despite its
professed aims, the Holy Alliance had not
been successful in forestalling new uprisings.
Europe was now split into two camps: one led
by France and England, constitutional monarchies which had made progress in democracy;
and the other by Austria, Prussia, and Russia,
all citadels of reaction and as yet undisturbed
by severe revolutionary storms. Each side
forced its image on smaller states: England
and France assisted the Belgians; Russia
crushed the Poles; Austria sent armies into
the Italian states to restore order. Notwithstanding the strong rally and triumphs of the
reactionary Powers, the revolutionary cause
was still alive.

⁅ KEY DOCUMENT ⁆

THE HOLY ALLIANCE, SEPTEMBER 14-26, 1815

Edward Hertslet, ed., The Map of Europe by Treaty (London, 1875), I, 317–19.

AFTER THE defeat of Napoleon at Waterloo, Great Britain, Russia, Austria, and Prussia
were motivated by one commanding thought—to prevent France from rising again as a
disturber of the peace of Europe. For a quarter of a century these countries had made
war on the French Republic and the French Empire. Tsar Alexander I urged the
formation of an alliance between Christian monarchs to maintain peace. Frederick
William III, King of Prussia, and Francis I, Emperor of Austria, subscribed to the pact,
which was formally signed on September 26, 1815.

In the name of the Most Holy and Indivisible
Trinity. Their Majesties the Emperor of Austria,

the King of Prussia, and the Emperor of Russia,
having, in consequence of the great events which

have marked the course of the last three years in Europe, and especially of the blessings which it has pleased Divine Providence to shower down upon those States which place their confidence and their hope on it alone, acquired the intimate conviction of the necessity of settling the steps to be observed by the Powers, in their reciprocal relations, upon the sublime truths which the Holy Religion of our Saviour teaches;

They solemnly declare that the present Act has no other object than to publish, in the face of the whole world, their fixed resolution, both in the administration of their respective States, and in their political relations with every other Government, to take for their sole guide the precepts of that Holy Religion, namely, the precepts of Justice, Christian Charity, and Peace, which, far from being applicable only to private concerns, must have an immediate influence on the councils of Princes, and guide all their steps, as being the only means of consolidating human institutions and remedying their imperfections. In consequence, their Majesties have agreed upon the following Articles:—

ARTICLE 1. Conformably to the words of the Holy Scriptures, which command all men to consider each other as brethren, the Three contracting Monarchs will remain united by the bonds of a true and indissoluble fraternity, and considering each other as fellow countrymen, they will, on all occasions and in all places, lend each other aid and assistance; and, regarding themselves towards their subjects and armies as fathers of families, they will lead them, in the same spirit of fraternity with which they are animated, to protect Religion, Peace, and Justice.

ARTICLE 2. In consequence, the sole principle of force, whether between the said Governments or between their subjects, shall be that of doing each other reciprocal service, and of testifying by unalterable good will the mutual affection with which they ought to be animated, to consider themselves all as members of one and the same Christian nation; the three allied Princes looking on themselves as merely delegated by Providence to govern three branches of the One family, Austria, Prussia, and Russia, thus confessing that the Christian world, of which they and their people form a part, has in reality no other Sovereign than Him to whom alone power really belongs, because in Him alone are found the treasures of love, science, and infinite wisdom, that is to say, God, our Divine Saviour, the Word of the Most High, the Word of Life. Their Majesties consequently recommend to their people, with the most tender solicitude, as the sole means of enjoying that Peace which arises from a good conscience, and which alone is durable, to strengthen themselves every day more and more in the principles and exercise of the duties which the Divine Saviour has taught to mankind.

ARTICLE 3. All the Powers who shall choose solemnly to avow the sacred principles which have dictated the present Act, and shall acknowledge how important it is for the happiness of nations, too long agitated, that these truths should henceforth exercise over the destinies of mankind all the influence which belongs to them, will be received with equal ardour and affection into this Holy Alliance.

Done in triplicate, and signed at Paris, the year of Grace 1815, 14-26 September.

(L.S.) FRANCIS

(L.S.) FREDERICK WILLIAM

(L.S.) ALEXANDER

⊰ HISTORICAL INTERPRETATION ⊱

CHARLES SEIGNOBOS ON THE RESTORATION

Charles Seignobos, *A History of the French People*, trans. by Catherine Alison Philips (London, 1933), pp. 315–317. By permission of Alfred A. Knopf, Inc.

ACCORDING TO the French historian, Charles Seignobos, professor of modern history at the University of Paris, France was left with a Napoleonic legend which disturbed its internal peace and led to profound distrust of the French as a bellicose people. His treatment of the opening of the Restoration era, written for French students, is reprinted here.

The defeat of Napoleon rendered a change of government necessary. The Allies were unwilling to leave France in his power and restored the old royal family for lack of another solution; but they made no attempt to restore the *ancien régime*. France therefore remained what it had been made by the Revolution and the partial restoration carried out under the Consulate by the men of the Revolution. National unity had been established once and for all by uniform territorial divisions, the unification of the system of measurements, and a common system of institutions and private law. The nation continued to enjoy the new social system based upon equality before the law and individual freedom of worship, labour, trade, and residence. It remained subject to a centralized administration, formed of a body of professional officials who performed their functions according to uniform rules for the whole country, under the direction of a central staff, the whole of which was established in Paris.

What it still lacked was a stable political system, and it had to pass through a series of revolutions before it could succeed in founding one. For sixty years France continued to pass through such frequent changes of constitution that they became a laughing stock. During this period the French acquired the reputation abroad of being a fickle people, incapable of settling down under any kind of government.

The restoration of the "legitimate" monarchy had taken place with the concurrence of the Imperial officials, whose chief desire was to keep their positions; it had been accepted without resistance by a people weary of wars, which was now permitted to abolish the two unpopular institutions of conscription and the *droits réunis* (administration of indirect taxation). The brother and heir of Louis XVI, who now returned from England, rejected the Constitution proposed by the Senate, but caused another to be hastily drawn up under the name of *Charte constitutionnelle* (Constitutional Charter), which gave the Government its organization, establishing a compromise between two sets of officials and two systems of government. The Imperial officials, who were revolutionary and bourgeois in origin, remained in possession of their functions and military rank, while those who had returned to France after the emigration received positions about the court, which was now restored, together with the ancient titles and ceremonial.

The survivals of the revolutionary order of things included all innovations based upon the principles of the Revolution: equality of personal rights, the territorial divisions, the unified system of government, the National Guard, the system of taxation, the judicial organization, and the Codes. The Imperial institutions that were preserved were the Concordat, the Legion of Honour, and the University. All acquisitions of property were respected, even those made by purchasers of *biens nationaux* ("nationalized" or confiscated property) as well as the titles of the Imperial nobility. Paris, which had brought about the Revolution, continued to be the residence of the king and the centre of the Government. Even such unpopular institutions as the *droits réunis* were soon to be restored, under the name of *contributions indirectes* (indirect taxation), and conscription, under the name of "recruiting." In theory the army was supposed to be composed only of those enlisting voluntarily, but since these were insufficient to furnish the necessary contingent, they were supplemented by means of compulsory service, the recruits being chosen by drawing lots, though it was permissible to provide substitutes, which as a matter of fact amounted to exempting the bourgeois from military service.

The only features of the *ancien régime* to be restored, beyond the royal family, were the principle of hereditary monarchy and the court, minus Versailles. The sale of the legal offices known as *offices ministériels* (those of notaries, greffiers, huissiers, avoués, etc.) and those of commission agents (*courtiers de commerce*) and stockbrokers (*agents de change*) had been revived in practice, and survives, indeed, to the present day, but this benefited none but the bourgeoisie.

In accordance with the principle established at the Revolution, the organization of the government was laid down by a written Constitution expressly limiting the power of the king and enumerating the rights of Frenchmen. It was formed on the model of England, which at that time possessed the only constitutional monarchy, and consisted of a council of ministers nominated by the king, a hereditary Chamber of Peers nominated by the king, and a Chamber of Deputies of the departments, elected by the larger taxpayers. No member of the assemblies received any emoluments. The English system was copied even in the details of nomenclature and procedure: the king had the right to summon, adjourn, and dissolve the elected Chamber; the ministers submitted proposed laws and taxation to the Chamber and could be impeached by the Chamber of Deputies and tried by the Peers. The King was allotted a "civil list" and made a 'speech from the throne' to which the Chamber replied by an "address."

The shares allotted to the old and new regime were very unequal. The new regime remained intact in all practical essentials, with all its institutions and officials and the maintenance of all that had been gained by the Revolution. Even the two Imperial governing bodies remained as they were: the senators were nominated as peers, and the *Corps législatif* was transformed into the Chamber of Deputies without election. Nothing was restored of the *ancien régime* but names and symbols. The King, the successor of Louis XVI, took the name of Louis XVIII and revived the style "by the grace of God, King of France and Navarre"; he started dating his official acts from the eighteenth year of his reign and declared that he had "granted" (*octroyé*) the Charter, with the object of indicating that he did not recognize either the sovereign right of the people of the revolutionary systems of government. He replaced the tricolour flag by the white flag, which was regarded as the ancient royal standard.

❧ TEN BASIC BOOKS ❧

RESTORATION AND REACTION, 1815–1830

1. Artz, Frederick, *Reaction and Revolution, 1814–1832* (New York, 1934).†
2. Grant, Arthur J., and Harold W. V. Temperley, *Europe in the Nineteenth and Twentieth Centuries (1789–1950)*, 6th ed. (London, 1952).
3. Hudson, Nora E., *Ultra-royalism and the French Restoration* (Cambridge, 1936).
4. May, Arthur, *The Age of Metternich, 1814–1848* (New York, 1933, R. 1963).†
5. Nicolson, Harold, *The Congress of Vienna: A Study in Allied Unity, 1812–1822* (New York, 1946, R. 1961).†
6. Perkins, Dexter, *The Monroe Doctrine, 1823–1826* (Cambridge, Mass., 1927, R. 1965).†
7. Phillips, W. Alison, *The Confederation of Europe: A Study of the European Alliance, 1813–1823*, 2nd ed. (London and New York, 1920).
8. Pirenne, Jacques H., *La Sainte-Alliance*, 2 vols. (Neuchâtel, 1946–1949).
9. Viereck, Peter *Conservatism Revisited: The Revolt Against Revolt, 1815–1849* new ed., Collier Book (New York, 1962).†
10. Webster, Charles K., *The Congress of Vienna, 1814–1815*, 2nd ed. (London, 1934, R. 1963).

21

The Emergence of Nationalism

POLITICAL NATIONALISM has become, for the European of our age, the most important thing in the world, more important than civilization, humanity, decency, kindness, pity; more important than life itself.

—SIR NORMAN ANGELL

By nationalism I mean first of all the habit of assuming that human beings can be classified like insects and that whole blocks of millions or tens of millions of people can be confidently labelled "good" or "bad." But secondly—and this is much more important—I mean the habit of identifying oneself with a single nation or other unit, placing it beyond good or evil and recognizing no other duty than that of advancing its own interests.

—GEORGE ORWELL

1. The Meaning of Nationalism

Growth of Nationalism and Liberalism. The revolutionary era bequeathed to Europe a new sentiment of nationalism and a rising faith in liberalism. There was a nexus between the two. Bourgeois liberalism defended man's right to freedom of speech, press, assembly, and religion. In political life these rights were to be assured through constitutionalism, parliamentarianism, and the franchise, in economic activity through *laissez-faire*. In the revolutionary period the rights of the individual gradually were extended to nationalities as a whole. Peoples began to demand self-determination, the right to name their own national governments. Earlier, the Europeans had shown attachments to a dynasty, the Church, a feudal lord, a guild, or a local community, but these loyalties had been weakened when industrialism disrupted the fabric of the old society and drew people from the rural areas to the cities. Allegiance was given now to the *nation*, to *la patrie*. Men began to accept and recognize

identity as Englishmen, Frenchmen, Germans, Italians, and Russians. Everywhere scholars ransacked historical archives to find evidence of national glory. The process was stimulated by the Industrial Revolution with which each nation's hitherto scattered economic interests now concentrated. The older agricultural nation, with its absolute monarch, landed aristocracy, and unprivileged commoners, gave way to the industrial nation, controlled by the new industrial classes and by parliaments, and distinguished by uniform laws for all citizens.

What Is Nationalism? Nationalism admits of no simple definition. It is a complex phenomenon, often vague and mysterious in character. Its most perplexing feature is that it differs in form according to the specific historical conditions and the special social structure of any given country. In various epochs of history there were different groups to which supreme loyalty was given. Today the term "nationalism" is used in so many different senses that such figures as Mazzini, Bolivar, and Woodrow Wilson are described as apostles of nationalism along with Mussolini, Hitler, and Stalin.

Scholars of nationalism approach the problem of definition from differing points of view. Attempting to construct a more precise definition, historians are turning to other social sciences for assistance. Anthropologists, political scientists, sociologists, psychologists, psychiatrists, and psychoanalysts have all been enlisted in the continuing effort to isolate the meaning of an elusive term.

Carlton J. H. Hayes described four shades of meaning:

Nationalism is an actual historical process. Here nationalism stands for the actual historical process of establishing nationalities as political units, of building out of tribes and empires the modern institution of the national state.

Nationalism is a theory. From this point of view, nationalism indicates the theory, principle, or ideal implicit in the actual historical process.

Nationalism concerns political activities. Nationalism may mean the activities of a particular political party, combining the historical process and a political theory (French nationalism; Chinese nationalism).

Nationalism is a sentiment. Nationalism may describe a condition of mind among members of a nationality, in which loyalty to the ideal or to the fact of one's national state becomes superior to all other loyalties, and in which pride is exhibited in the intrinsic excellence and in the mission of one's national state.

Hans Kohn titled his major work on the subject *The Idea of Nationalism.* He feels that nationalism is "first and foremost a state of mind, an act of consciousness, . . . the individual's identification of himself with the 'we group' to which he gives supreme loyalty." Boyd C. Shafer points out that men tend to seek realization of their dearest dreams, whatever they may be, within their nations. Everywhere they erect their nations into bulwarks, no matter how weak, against adversity. This devotion to their nation we call nationalism. Karl W. Deutsch approaches the problem with the help of communications theory and cybernetics. In place of the conventional political, economic, and cultural factors, one or more of which seems always to be missing, Deutsch proposes that the test of nationality (a term he prefers to nationalism) be the ability of a people to communicate more effectively with their fellow members than with outsiders.

Students of intellectual history are gradually beginning to use the phraseology of social psychology in defining nationalism. Thus, Crane Brinton says that "nationalism is at bottom no more than the important form [that] the sense of belonging to an in-group has taken in our modern Western culture." He describes it as one of the facts of life, one of the observed facts no scientist can neglect. It is most usefully studied, he says, by the social psychologist, who is as yet no more than at the beginning of his scientific work of building cumulative knowledge. Nationalism becomes a form of consciousness by which the individual proclaims his supreme loyalty to the nation.

Although most historians are in accord that nationalism is primarily a state of mind and that it is a psychological and social fact, they are aware that it is an ideal superimposed upon the natural order and endowed with a questionable personality. "Each state," says Edward Krehbiel, "is supposed to stand for something *sui generis;* to have a personality and qualities peculiar to it and not attainable by other peoples; and its ideas for *Kultur* are supposed to be incompatible with others and to lead to conflict." Nationalism is not chiefly a product of physical geography, but rests on traditions of politics, religion, language, war, invasion, conquests, economics, and society, which have been fashioned by peculiar and often fortuitous circumstances and which have been preserved and synthesized by great writers and other intellectuals. The motivating desire is always to increase as far as possible the consciousness of power of the dominating nationality.

The following is a workable definition: Nationalism is a condition of mind, feeling, or sentiment of a group of people living in a well-defined geographical area, speaking a common language, possessing a literature in which the aspirations of the nation have been expressed, being attached to common traditions, and, in some cases, having a common religion. (There are, of course, exceptions to every part of this definition.)

Classification: Types of Nationalism. The best-known classifications of nationalism is the formula of Carlton J. H. Hayes, which strikes a mean between chronology and description:

(1) *Humanitarian Nationalism:* The first systematic doctrine of modern nationalism was expounded in the eighteenth century during the Era of Enlightenment. Humanitarian nationalism, as the name implies, had strictly humanitarian objects: tolerance and regard for the rights of other nationalities. Its chief advocates were Henry St. John Bolingbroke (1678–1751), conservative English politician, who conceived of an aristocratic form of nationalism tinged with humanitarianism; Jean-Jacques Rousseau (1712–1778), the French *philosophe*, who advocated a democratic form of nationalism, humanitarian in spirit; and Johann Gottfried von Herder (1744–1803), a German philosopher who, unlike Bolingbroke and Rousseau, saw nationalism as a cultural rather than a political phenomenon. The humanitarian nationalists held that every nationality was entitled to its own development consonant with its own peculiar genius.

(2) *Jacobin Nationalism:* Under the impact of the French Revolution, the earlier nationalism, which had not crystallized into a dogma, separated into several distinct types. The democratic, humanitarian nationalism of Rousseau became known as Jacobin nationalism, after the revolutionary political club dedicated to the achievement of republicanism and democracy. Jacobin nationalism sought to "safeguard and extend the liberty, equality, and the fraternity which had been asserted and partially established under humanitarian auspices in the early days of the Revolution." The Jacobin nationalists, intolerant of opposition, relying upon force to achieve their ends, fanatical in their determination to succeed, and characterized by missionary zeal, gave to the present form of nationalism many of its basic qualities.

(3) *Traditional Nationalism:* The aristocratic, humanitarian nationalism of Bolingbroke emerged after the revolutionary period as traditional nationalism. The conservative and reactionary critics of the Jacobins were quite certain that "the quiet happiness of humanity could be assured less by the masses than by the classes." Being opposed to "revolution" and "reason" as factors in national development, they turned to "history" and "tradition." In effect, this type of nationalism was a counter-movement to the forces set in motion by the French Revolution; nevertheless, it claimed the same humanitarian motives as the Jacobins. Among the traditional nationalists may be included the Englishman Edmund Burke (1729–1797), the German Friedrich von Schlegel (1772–1829), and the Frenchman Louis Gabriel Ambroise (1754–1840).

(4) *Liberal Nationalism:* Midway between Jacobin and traditional nationalism was liberal nationalism, a type neither democratic or aristocratic, but with some of the characteristics of each. Mainly the creation of an English lawyer, Jeremy Bentham (1748-1832), liberal nationalism arose in England, the country of perpetual compromise, and later spread to the Continent. It emphasized the absolute sovereignty of the national state, but at the same time stressed the principle of individual liberty. It held all national states responsible for the establishment and maintenance of international peace. Liberal nationalists looked to the day when all nations would enjoy opportunities for independent development.

(5) *Integral Nationalism:* Liberal nationalism persisted throughout the greater part of the nineteenth century. However, with the sharpening of rivalries among national states, with the rise of imperialism, nationalism assumed a form decidedly hostile to liberalism and humanitarianism. Integral nationalism rejected sympathy for and cooperation with other nations, promoted jingoism, militarism, and imperialism, and opposed all personal liberties when they interfered with the aims of the State. Loyalty to the national state was elevated above all other loyalties, and all social, cultural, economic, and even religious considerations were subordinated to the ends of nationalism. Included in the general cate-

gory of integral nationalists are Barrès and Maurras in France; Kipling, Rhodes, and Balfour in England; D'Annunzio, Crispi, and Mussolini in Italy; Houston Stewart Chamberlain, Treitschke, Bernhardi, Stöcker, and Hitler in Germany; and Pobiedonostsev and Plehve in Russia.

(6) *Economic Nationalism:* Whereas previously only political considerations lay behind nationalism, a recent tendency has been to regard the state as an economic as well as a political unit. The desire of modern states to achieve economic self-sufficiency has led to the erection of tariff barriers between nations, and to an intensified struggle for control of markets, raw materials, and fields for capital investment. Economic nationalism thus merges with imperialism as one of the most powerful factors in contemporary civilization.

Nationalism and Patriotism. Although the terms nationalism and patriotism do not mean the same thing, there is a tendency to consider them equivalent. Nationalism is concerned primarily with the independence and unity of the nation (*natio*), while patriotism is more specifically that passion which influences the individual to serve the object of his devotion—his country (*patria*), whether in defending it from invasion, in protecting its rights, or in maintaining its laws and institutions in vigor and purity. Patriotism is the conviction that individual and group welfare depends on the preservation or expansion of a country's power. Patriotism becomes nationalism when this conviction is accompanied by a demand for action. Patriotism in some form has been present throughout the course of history; nationalism is a relatively new phenomenon.

Even though it has a distinct meaning, patriotism has come to be associated closely with nationalism. Patriotism in its exaggerated forms, known as chauvinism and jingoism, has much in common with nationalism in its integral, aggressive configuration.

Historical Controversy: Problem of National Character. Scholars differ on whether or not national character exists. According to Friedrich Hertz, British sociologist, national character is the totality of traditions, interests, and ideals which are so widespread and influential in a nation that they mold its image, both in the mind of the nation concerned and in that of others. Salvador de Madariaga y Rojo, Spanish literary critic, insists that there is such a thing as national character. "The fact is there and stares us in the face. History, geography, religion, even the common will are not enough to define a nation. A nation is a fact of psychology. It is that which is *natural* or *native* in it which gives its force to the word *nation*. A nation is a character."

This point of view is also held by Ernest Barker, British historian: national character, in its formation and manifestation, has its analogies with the character of the individual man. National character, in Barker's view, is a reality, "a sum of acquired tendencies." "We can experience the character of a nation, as we can experience the personality of an individual."

Exactly the opposite point of view is taken by Francis Delaisi in his *Political Myths and Economic Realities,* in which he deprecates the concept of national genius. Even a glance at history, he declares, will show that there are between nations no watertight compartments in matters of the mind. He points out that it would be hard to find a scientist, a philosopher, or an artist who would claim to be indebted only to his own national heritage, regardless of foreign contribution. Hamilton Fyfe, a British scholar, went even further and denounced the concept of national character as an illusion that is doing great harm to the world. The commonly held view that national characters are distinct, homogeneous, and well-defined, he said, is the most potent and dangerous of the elements making for war. Fyfe denounced the entire idea as a popular error, a superstition that has confused and injured mankind.

Midway between these two extremes is the view that national character has a limited validity, since its existence cannot be denied. Leopold von Ranke, German historian, voiced this reserved attitude when he stated that the national spirit could only be felt but not understood. It is "a spiritual air, permeating everything."

The beliefs which a nation holds concerning its own character and that of other nations are ordinarily a mixture of some truth with exaggeration and distortions. But even these illusions (such stereotypes that all Scotsmen are frugal, all Frenchmen amorous, all Germans warlike, all Swedes cold, all Americans aggressive and naïve) help to produce national solidarity and national rivalries. There may be only a small grain of truth in each illusion, but it may be of sufficient importance to have historical meaning.

Most scholars today reject the notion that national character persists *permanently*. In the eighteenth century the Germans were reputed to be a musically gifted, peaceful people; in the nineteenth and twentieth centuries they were regarded throughout the world as a warlike community bent on conquest or ruin. The English were once thought to be unruly and revolutionary, only to appear later as a solid people who prided themselves on the stability of their institutions. The French, at one time proud of their loyalty to the monarchy, executed Louis XVI and fashioned the revolutionary snowball that eventually covered all Europe. The character of a people apparently changes in response to varying historical stimuli.

2. Origins of Nationalism

Beginnings. Nationalism in its modern form is by no means a completely new phenomenon, but rather a revival and fusion of older trends. It existed in cruder form in the tribalism of primitive peoples. Throughout recorded history to the eighteenth century, tribal nationalism was submerged in metropolitanism (attachment to a city-state or cultural center) or localism (loyalty to the local village or region, akin to modern ruralism or regionalism). The peoples of the ancient world were faithful to their city—Athens, Sparta, or Corinth. Rome ruled a huge empire; the city itself was the focal point of a patriotic impulse. Some elements of nationalism existed in the medieval period among peoples with kindred languages, customs, and traditions, but this sort of group cohesion was more closely related to primitive localism than to modern nationalism.

Modern nationalism was the sequel to the emergence of the nation-state out of feudalism, manorialism, and the medieval concept of sovereignty. The feudal lords gave their allegiance to king, not country. Nationalism received a most potent early stimulus in mid-seventeenth-century England, the first modern nation where linguistic, political, economic, and religious factors merged to unite the people. The next great landmarks were the American and French Revolutions. The American Revolution proclaimed the principle of sovereignty as residing essentially in the nation. Nationalism penetrated from England to the Continent as a revolutionary force, attaining impetus among a people who had enjoyed no political freedom. Thus, popular nationalism may be dated from 1688, 1776, and 1789.

3. Development of Nationalism

The Historical Course. Almost all the important innovations of the early modern period favored the development of nationalism. Among them were such factors as disruption of the medieval Church and the establishment of national churches, the appearance of vernacular literatures, the rise of national armies, the emergence of the middle class, the development of mercantilism, and the revolutionary growth of capitalism. When the middle class began to feel that the nation belonged to the property owners, not merely to the king, modern nationalism assumed much of its character. The king, too, looked upon emerging nationalism as a means of perpetuating his dynasty. By this time Latin was being replaced, and vernacular languages were elevated to the position of national languages: in England the Anglo-Saxon, in France the *langue d'oïl* of northern France, in Spain the Castilian, in the Italies the Tuscan, and in the Germanies the Saxon.

The process was accelerated not only by the French Revolution but also by Napoleon. People throughout Europe—Englishmen, Frenchmen, Germans, Spaniards, and Italians—all thought themselves to be threatened from outside. They feared and hated foreigners (xenophobia). They used their national armies in holy wars against other peoples. Fear led to intensified national hatreds as well as to greater reliance upon the national government. People became united by strong bonds of community interests; flags symbolized national glory and prestige.

A Force for Unification (1815–1871): In this era nationalism was a unifying force: it helped to consolidate the states that had outgrown feudal division, and also to unify others that had long been split into hostile factions. This was the inspiration that motivated Simón Bolívar to free South America from colonial Spain. Both the Germanies and the Italies, for centuries merely "geographical expressions," were molded into national states, Germany under Bismarck, Italy under Cavour.

A Force for Disruption (1871–1900): The success of nationalism in forging German and Italian unity aroused the enthusiasm of subject nationalities in other countries. Minorities in Austria-Hungary, the Ottoman Empire, and other conglomerate states called for independence based on geographical unity, common language, interests, culture, traditions, customs, and sometimes on a nonexistent "race." Under the banners of nationalism Irishmen and Poles and Hungarians called for nationhood or death.

A Force for Aggression (1900–1918): Toward the end of the nineteenth century, as international rivalries rose, nationalism became virtually identical with imperialism. Superpatriots claimed it as their "mission" to "bring civilization" to the "backward peoples" of the earth. The collision of opposing national interests came with explosive impact in the First World War.

The New Nationalism (1918 on): The factors making for nationalism were present in a great degree during the Long Armistice from 1919 to 1939. After the Second World War, nationalism emerged somewhat tamed in the West, as Britain, France, and the Netherlands relinquished their overseas colonies. Added to this factor was the threat of Communist expansion, against which the Western nations formed regional federations. But nationalism persisted in the Soviet Union and emerged in imitative form in Africa, Asia, and the Near and Middle East. The New Nationalism retained many of the unattractive features of its earlier Western forms.

4. Nationalism in Major Countries and Areas

English Nationalism. Modern nationalism received its initial impetus in England, a country already territorially unified, a nation whose classes were distinguished by a healthy patriotism that had withstood even the ravages of revolution. Battered by civil strife in conflict between king and Parliament, the English, nevertheless, tended to become even more nationalistic. Both sides—Royal England and Puritan England—were thoroughly saturated with patriotism. Charles I died as an honorable Englishman. Cromwell described the English as a Chosen People—"to God as the apple of his eye."

As popular loyalty passed from the king to the national state, English nationalism took on a cloak of libertarianism. The idea of liberty received potent expression in the writings of John Milton, especially in the *Areopagitica* ("Give me the liberty to know . . ."). The new popular nationalism was promoted from several directions: both Lord Bolingbroke, Tory, and John Locke, Whig, helped engineer it to triumph.

In the eighteenth century, English nationalism took on the humanitarian tinge characteristic of the Age of Enlightenment. By this time England was a wealthy world power, admired and envied everywhere as a unified, free, and proud national state. With its long history and tradition, English nationalism became more stable, more tolerant, less vocal than other nationalisms. This concept of nationalism within a framework of historic liberties was studied and emulated throughout the world.

French Nationalism. French nationalism was born in 1789 in an explosive outburst. The intellectual way for the French Revolution, one of the great landmarks of history, was prepared in the Enlightenment. The idea of a French nation on which the individual could focus his loyalty was harder to grasp than the idea of loyalty to a king or a provincial noble family. The French of the revolutionary period were able to develop and adhere to this new idea because of the rise in the general cultural level in their homeland. In this atmosphere came the new nationalism with its exaltation of the secular, or national, state. Here, as elsewhere in Europe, nationalism was stimulated by Pietism, a reaction against religious skepticism. The Pietists retained belief in Christianity but disregarded any elaborate formalities associated with it. In placing emphasis upon emotionalism and individualism, they helped prepare the soil for the growth of nationalism.

When the Estates-General was convened in 1789 for the first time since 1614, it was soon transformed into the *National* Assembly. The name was significant: the National Assembly represented not the three Estates but the entire nation. In the revolution that followed, there was a distinct leveling procedure with a nationalistic tinge. Slowly the vestiges of feudalism, manorialism, and class privileges were abolished. Geographic and class barriers vanished. Old governmental institutions were replaced by a uniform, centralized, *national* administrative system. New *départements* replaced the old provinces. Church property was confiscated. Whereas before there had been disintegration, division, localism, and provincialism, now there came unity, nationalization, and federation. Nationalization was above all the desired goal. The Church became a national church. National fêtes were introduced. The armed forces were nationalized. Children were taught to use the national language.

The Declaration of the Rights of Man and Citizen made of France a new nation composed of free individuals protected by law. While the individual was shielded from the abuses of government, at the same time he was expected to maintain a feeling of loyalty to his country. He was expected "to be born, live, and die for the Fatherland." "This delightful land which we inhabit," intoned Robespierre, "and which nature caresses with love is made to be the domain of liberty and happiness."

French nationalism was soon suffused with a crusading zeal for converts. "What is good for France is good for Europe." The wealthy Girondins (the moderate Republicans), with a passion for prestige and power, began to see ghostly opponents in foreign lands. They demanded foreign wars as a means of forcing the fruits of liberty on other peoples. Nationalism thus not only motivated the consolidation and reconstruction of France in the revolutionary period, but it also inspired the French revolutionaries with the doctrine of national self-determination. The patriots of Paris felt that it was natural for any people who wished to be regarded as "French" to be incorporated into France. Once the process gathered momentum, good intentions were supplanted by power politics. Frenchmen in Belgium and the Italian peninsula turned out to be more nationalists than liberators.

Napoleon carried on this policy of revolutionary nationalism but tempered it with a strong dose of personal and family ambitions. He erased one-third of the familiar slogan by supporting equality and fraternity, but denying liberty. Since his time, French nationalism on the whole has retained its faith in the Declaration of the Rights of Man and Citizen. Reverence for this document prevented France from descending into that type of authoritarianism and totalitarianism that was to plague Germany, Italy, and Russia.

Spread of Nationalism. Undoubtedly, the example of Great Britain and France, unified nations, stimulated the ambitions of other peoples to emulate them. In the Germanies after 1815 there was a surge of sentiment on the national question; in the Italies there was a similar movement, the *Risorgimento*, or resurgence; and in eastern Europe there was a Slavic revival which stressed an equally deliberate and conscious program. The process was much the same everywhere. Usually, it began with application of Herder's conception of the *Volksgeist*, or national spirit, a cultural nationalism holding that each people must perfect its own language, history, and world view. This almost invariably passed into political nationalism, emphasizing the national sovereign state as necessary to preserve the heritage of national culture. To the divided and frustrated Germans and Italians the new nationalism became almost an obsession.

German Nationalism. German nationalism was born in the darkness of Napoleonic despotism. The attempt of the Corsican to spread the ideas of the French Revolution as he interpreted them into the Germanies by military force provided the exterior spark which ignited the fires of nationalism. Napoleon abolished vestiges of medieval rule and laid the foundation for modern government. The Germanies had been a medieval hodgepodge, the classic example of particularism at its worst, until Napoleon gave them a boost toward unity by wiping out most of the small principalities.

To forget their humiliation and despair, Germans turned in relief to their past, when the glorious German Empire had been a fulcrum of European power. Attracted by romanticism, they sought for an organic folk community wrapped in the old cloak of tradition. Romanticism took on a special form in the Germanies. Here the people sought to mobilize their heroic past as a bulwark against the principles of 1789 and the machinations of Napoleon. They would go back to the glorious Middle Ages with its folk songs, fairy tales, sagas, and poetry, with its accent on imagination instead of reason. There they would find the "medieval freedom" which had little in common with the French and English rationalistic concept of liberty. They would think with the blood, and give free rein to all that was German.

German apostles of romanticism were loud and correspondingly vague. Among them were the Schlegel brothers, the Grimm brothers, Schleiermacher, Görres, Adam Müller, Fichte, Arndt, and Jahn. The tone was set by Fichte in his ultrapatriotic *Addresses to the German Nation.* Friedrich von Schlegel, surcharged with emotionalism, expressed the sentiment precisely: "Awaken, Germans, from stupor and shame and ignominy! Awaken and act for the sake of German honor!" An anti-French spirit, combined with romanticism, culminated in the War of Liberation against Napoleon. National enthusiasm was promoted vigorously in the *Freikorps* (patriotic volunteers), Jahn's *Turnerschaften* (gymnastic societies), and the *Burschenschaften* (student fraternities). The germs of nationalism multiplied geometrically.

Italian Nationalism. Factors ordinarily making for national unification—excellent natural boundaries, common historical traditions and language—existed in the Italies. But other elements militated against unity—the persistent struggle between pope and Holy Roman emperor; the multiplicity of sovereignties; seemingly insurmountable social differences between North and South; and the unwillingness of Rome, Milan, Venice, Florence, and Naples to sacrifice their glorious past for the sake of national unity.

The French Revolution aroused Italian longings for national unification. Here, too, Napoleon stimulated a sense of national sentiment. His agent, Joachim Murat, to whom he gave the crown of Naples, became a champion of Italian unity. After Napoleon's fall, Austrian dominance in Italian affairs was restored. The Treaty of Vienna gave no satisfaction to Italians. The illiberal Metternichian system, turning the clock back, led Italians to call not only for political freedom but also for national independence.

At first Italian national sentiment was limited to a small minority of poets and dramatists. The playwright Vittorio Alfieri (1749–1803), who disliked the French Revolution, reacted violently against the French invasion of his homeland. Italians, he cried, must unite in a common hatred of France. The poet Ugo Foscolo (1778–1827) called upon the dead from Italy's past to rise from their tombs and fight against the hated Austrians. The nationalist movement gathered momentum as students, noblemen, and the middle class rallied to it.

Russian Nationalism. Absolutism in eighteenth- and nineteenth-century Russia recognized few elements of nationalism. The dynasty, the court, the army, and the bureaucracy were often more German than Russian. The highest court circle took pride in its ability to speak French. The intelligentsia substituted the Orthodox Creed for nationality. The mass of the people neither knew nor cared about nationality or nationalism.

Napoleon contributed a powerful impulse to the rise of Russian nationalism. To Russians he became an anti-Christ who sought to lead the Roman Catholic West against Moscow, citadel of the true faith. The Russian intelligentsia rejected rationalism and the liberal cosmopolitanism of the West, and in their place substituted a rigid nationalism based on uncompromising love for Mother Russia.

During the reactionary reign of Nicholas I (r. 1825–1855), Russian nationalism assumed a blind, ugly form. The glory of Russia became a new trinity of dynasty, Orthodox Church, and the village commune. Poets sang about the ordinary Russian as "the most perfect citizen on earth," and "Holy Russia, the first state in the world." "Europe is pagan, Russia is holy Christian." They often used the term nationalism interchangeably with Slavophilism. The past, they said, belonged to a West already decadent and senile, the future was the property of a great, young, and vigorous "race of Slavs." This new feeling was stimulated by the rise of the middle class. Along with it came a ruthless Russification of minorities, especially the Ukrainians and the Jews, both of whom were brutally persecuted.

American Nationalism. From its beginning American nationalism took a different course from that on the European Continent. In its early stages European nationalism was based partly upon common descent and common religion. Neither element was present in the emergence of the American form. The idea of a "melting pot," which appeared early in American history, was retained as a desirable characteristic of American society.

The new nation was born in the Age of Reason with its accent upon liberty, equality, fraternity, constitutionalism, and parliamentarianism. Americans had little use for medieval feudal, manorial, or ecclesiastical strictures. Above all they valued the concept of individual liberty—the inalienable right of every individual to life, liberty, and the pursuit of happiness. The poorer classes of Europe, burdened by political and religious restrictions, flocked to the New World. Here, infused with a spirit of sturdy individualism, they entered enthusiastically into the rough frontier life. Similar to the simple, natural man praised by Rousseau, they abolished monarchy and aristocracy, separated Church and State, and forged a national union based on individual liberty. American nationalism reflected their interests, desires, and ambitions.

Americans were blessed with great leaders, who demanded a clean break from the tangled threads of European politics. Like the *philosophes* they were optimistic men who delighted in projecting the vision of a wonderful future. Their view was epitomized by John Adams in a letter to Thomas Jefferson in 1813: "Our sure, virtuous, public-spirited federative republic will last forever, govern the globe, and introduce the perfection of man."

Consciousness of nationality was strengthened in America by the War of 1812 against Britain. Then came the era of westward expansion. The problem of national unity now became critical. Would there be one people, or many? Would there be the unity of federation or the disintegration of particularism? The answer, sealed in blood, came in the conflict between the industrial North and the agricultural South. The South was defeated not so much by force of arms as by its persistence in holding onto the outmoded vestiges of feudalism. The idea of a unified nation based on individual liberty and tolerance prevailed over strong sectional differences. After 1865 the unity of the American nation was never seriously threatened again.

Latin-American Nationalism. The countries of Spanish-America, unlike those of Anglo-America, received no training in self-government and democracy. Nevertheless, Americans of Spanish descent, under the leadership of such nationalists as Simón Bolívar (1783–1830), a Venezuelan, and José de San Martín (1778–1850), an Argentinian, fought for independence from Spain and attained this goal by the end of the first quarter of the nineteenth century. For the rest of the century, most of the Latin-American republics oscillated between dictatorship and anarchy. Strong military leaders vied for power and then set up dictatorships to maintain it. The indigenous Indian populations were kept in an inferior status.

⚡{ KEY DOCUMENT }⚡

ERNST MORITZ ARNDT: THE WAR OF LIBERATION, 1813

Ernst Moritz Arndt, *Das preussische Volk und Heer* (1813), quoted in *Geschichte für Mittelschulen*, ed. by P. Jennrich, K. Krause, and A. Viernow (Halle on Saale, 1941), pp. 111–112. Translated by the editor.

ERNST MORITZ ARNDT (1769–1860), apostle of nationalism during the Napoleonic wars, was one of the creators of modern German consciousness. Although not a great poet, Arndt represented those romantic scholars and publicists who saw in German culture the real expression of the German soul. In pamphlets, poems, and songs, expressed in Biblical language and images, Arndt sought to arouse a Germanic crusading spirit against Napoleon and the French. He was forced to flee to Sweden to avoid Napoleon's agents, but from exile he sent a steady stream of pamphlets and poems to his countrymen. The following passage, in which Arndt described the uprising of the Prussians against Napoleon, was used again and again in German textbooks as a means of training the child in love of country. Similar expressions of national sentiment, though perhaps not as warlike, may be found in the school textbooks of all countries.

The War of Liberation

Fired with enthusiasm the people rose "with God for King and Fatherland." Among the Prussians there was only one voice, one feeling, one anger, and one love, to save the Fatherland and to free Germany. The Prussians wanted war; war and death they wanted; peace they feared because they could hope for no honorable peace from Napoleon. War, war, sounded the cry from the Carpathians to the Baltic, from the Niemen to the Elbe. War! cried the nobleman and landed proprietor who had become impoverished. War! the peasant who was driving his last horse to death. . . . War! the citizen who was growing exhausted from quartering soldiers and paying taxes. War! the widow who was sending her only son to the front. War! the young girl who, with tears of pride and pain, was leaving her betrothed. Youths who were hardly able to bear arms, men with gray hair, officers who on account of wounds and mutilations had long ago been honorably discharged, rich landed proprietors and officials, fathers of large families and managers of extensive businesses—all were unwilling to remain behind. Even young women, under all sorts of disguises, rushed to arms; all wanted to drill, arm themselves, and fight and die for the Fatherland. . . .

The most beautiful thing about all this holy zeal and happy confusion was that all differences of position, class, and age were forgotten . . . that the one great feeling for the Fatherland, its freedom and honor, swallowed all other feelings, caused all other considerations and relationships to be forgotten.

⚡{ HISTORICAL INTERPRETATION }⚡

CARLTON J. H. HAYES ON NATIONALISM—CURSE OR BLESSING?

Carlton J. H. Hayes, *Essays on Nationalism* (New York, 1926), pp. 245–260. By permission of The Macmillan Company.

THE DUAL nature of nationalism—as a force for good or a force for evil—was set forth in this passage by Carlton J. H. Hayes. In Hayes' view, nationalism, when it becomes synonymous with the purest patriotism, is a unique blessing to humanity and the world. At the same time, he recognized that nationalism could be a mania, a kind of extended and exaggerated egotism, indicative of the delusions of grandeur from which it suffers.

It may appear to some . . . that nationalism is to the human race a curse, and nothing but a curse. On the other hand, it may seem to some critically minded persons that the nationalism hereby cursed is merely a fanciful caricature of a true and real nationalism which to humanity in its present stage of development is not a curse but a blessing. . . .

Whether nationalism *as a process* is a curse or a blessing, we have no stomach to declare. We have read enough history to make us timid, if not humble, about passing moral judgment or basing philosophic speculation on great and long continued historic processes. Nationalism as an historic process has been great and long continued, and to regret and condemn it would be for us purely academic diversions; we couldn't undo it if we would; we certainly couldn't refashion all those multitudinous factors, personal and social, economic and political, religious and cultural, which during many centuries now past recall have transformed city-states and feudal states and imperial states into national states. Nationalism of this sort is not a proper subject of praise or blame; it is simply a fact, and a fact as little deserving of benediction or anathema as the fact that man has two legs or the fact that the earth revolves about the sun.

But nationalism *as a belief* belongs to another category. To every thoughtful person, save only the unqualified fatalist, it is as fitting to criticise nationalism of this kind as to criticize any other popular creed, say Christianity or Socialism or Liberalism; it is important for our generation and for that which follows us that we should judge all living growing trees by their fruit, and that if to our taste any tree brings forth evil fruit we should attempt to cut down or at least engraft good fruit upon that tree. It is nationalism as a popular contemporary belief concerning which we would put the question, is it curse or is it blessing? . . .

It is possible, of course, to use the word nationalism, as some writers have used it, to indicate "wholesome national patriotism" and to describe certain precepts and practices of national life which do not incite to war or militarism or intolerance. But let us not dodge the issue by verbal quibbling. Grant that there is a rampant, blatant nationalism which produces evil fruitage and which is a curse, and it will gladly be conceded that there may be a sweet amiable nationalism which will bring forth good fruit in abundance and will be to all men a solace and a blessing. . . .

Nationalism—the combination of nationality, the national state, and national patriotism, as effected in our age—is the indivisible source of grave abuses and evils.

What, in summary, are these grave evils and abuses? First is the spirit of exclusiveness and narrowness. The national state, through education in national school, national army, and national journalism, through the social pressure of national patriotism, inculcates in its citizens the fancy that they are a world by themselves, sufficient unto themselves; it teaches them that they are a chosen people, a peculiar people, and that they should prize far more what is theirs as a nationality than what is theirs as human beings. It is this spirit of exclusiveness and narrowness which thrives on, and in turn nurses, a smugness that is laughable, an ignorance that is dangerous, and an uncritical pride that can be reduced, if at all, only by a beating.

Secondly, nationalism places a premium on unformity. It prescribes national models of art, national standards of thought, and national norms of conduct, and to these it expects all the inhabitants of each national state to conform. Individual differences, class differences, religious differences, are alike deemed unfortunate; and the individual of genius is suspect, especially if his genius displays itself in criticism of national uniformity. . . .

Thirdly, nationalism increases the docility of the masses. As a result of their national upbringing and their life-long nationalist education, they are seldom inclined to question the providential character of their nationality, of their state, of their government, or of the economic circumstances in which they live. If only a leader appeals to them in the cause of national patriotism, they are prepared to follow that leader unquestioningly and unhesitatingly into any undertaking upon which he has set his heart. In the name of national rights, national interests, and national honour, they will forego their own individual rights, sacrifice their own individual interests, and even forswear their own individual honour. . . .

Fourthly, nationalism in its present form focuses popular attention upon war and preparedness for war. War is that historic tradition of a nationality which the national state, under present conditions, does most to keep alive and active in the minds and hearts of its citizens. Military heroes outrank in national pantheons the heroes of science and art and learning. . . . It is notorious how quickly a popular interest in some educational or economic problem evaporates when confronted by the fierce heat of nationalist passion for military "defense." . . .

An intolerant attitude and behaviour towards one's fellows; a belief in the imperial mission of one's own nationality at the expense of other, particularly at the expense of backward, peoples; a habit of carrying a chip on one's national shoulder and defying another nationality to knock it off; a fond dwelling on the memory of past wars and a feverish preparing for future wars, to the neglect of present civil problems; a willingness to be led and guided by self-styled patriots; a diffidence, almost a panic, about thinking or acting differently from one's fellows; a spirit of exclusiveness and narrowness which feeds on gross ignorance of others and on inordinate pride in one's self and one's nationality: these are all too prevalent aspects of contemporary nationalism. If in these respects nationalism is not mitigated it will be an unqualified curse to future generations.

❧ TEN BASIC BOOKS ❧

THE EMERGENCE OF NATIONALISM

1. Barker, Ernest, *National Character and the Factors in its Formation* (New York and London, 1927).
2. Deutsch, Karl W., *Nationalism and Social Communication* (Cambridge, Mass., 1953).†
3. Hayes, Carlton J. H., *The Historical Evolution of Modern Nationalism* (New York, 1931).
4. Hertz, Friedrich, *Nationality in History and Politics: A Psychology and Sociology of National Sentiment and Nationalism* (London, 1951).
5. Kohn, Hans, *The Idea of Nationalism: A Study of Its Origin and Background* (New York, 1944, R. 1961).†
6. Royal Institute of International Affairs, *Nationalism: A Report by a Study Group* (London, 1939).
7. Shafer, Boyd C., *Nationalism: Myth and Reality* (New York, 1955).†
8. Snyder, Louis L., *The Meaning of Nationalism* (New Brunswick, N. J., 1954).
9. Whitaker, Arthur P., *Nationalism in Latin America: Past and Present* (Gainesville, Fla., 1962).
10. Znaniecki, Florian, *Modern Nationalities: A Sociological Study* (Urbana, Ill., 1952).

22

The Evolution of Liberalism

LIBERALISM IS the belief that society can safely be founded on this self-directing power of personality, that it is only on this foundation that a true community can be built, and that so established its foundations are so deep and so wide that there is no limit that we can place to the extent of the building. Liberty then becomes not so much a right of the individual as a necessity of society. . . . The rule of liberty is just the application of the rational method. It is the opening of the door to the appeal of reason, of imagination, of social feeling; and except through the response to this appeal there is no assured progress of society.

—L. T. HOBHOUSE

1. The Meaning of Liberalism

Meaning: General. Liberalism may be defined in a broad sense as an attitude or temper which seeks to place all the varied activities of man on a high plane of spiritual freedom. Looking upon history as the story of liberty, liberalism as a philosophy rejects any restraint upon the freedom of the individual—political, social, economic, religious, cultural, or moral. It repudiates the tyranny of emperors, kings, or any authority that would interfere with freedom of conscience or social and intellectual liberty. It excludes coercion, spiritual oppression, ignorance, and superstition. It seeks to achieve a higher spiritual life in the present world. It always accents individual freedom and free initiative.

Liberalism is closely allied with democracy in that both oppose absolutism and advocate popular sovereignty, political liberty, and civil equality. The two terms, liberalism and democracy, are sometimes used interchangeably, but there is a difference. In democracy, individuals are *centers of equal forces* to which it is necessary to attribute an equal field; in liberalism, individuals are *persons,* their equality being only that of their humanity. This is the

view of Benedetto Croce: "The democrats in their political ideal postulated a religion of quantity, of mechanics, of calculating reason or of nature, like that of the eighteenth century; the liberals, a religion of quality, of activity, of spirituality, such as that which had risen in the beginning of the nineteenth century."

Meaning: Specific. In its specific sense, liberalism refers to a political movement that arose in the early nineteenth century to implement spiritual ideals through political action. Groups holding the tenets of liberalism worked politically to limit the interference of government in private affairs, and to utilize the state as an organism designed to promote freedom of the individual. The term *liberal* came to be used in opposition to the term *conservative;* the liberal worked for progressive political policies, the conservative sought to maintain the *status quo.*

Psychology of Liberalism. Like nationalism, liberalism has psychological undertones expressing an attitude toward life. Whereas the nationalist seeks security by union with the crowd, the liberal represents the urge toward freedom. It would be unreasonable to say that men are born with a desire for an open society, for ideologies are shaped largely by environmental factors. But it seems rational to conclude that men fight passionately to retain those habits in which their privileges are involved. Throughout the course of history people have rebelled almost automatically against coercion, tyranny, absolutism, slavery, and serfdom. From Socrates to John Stuart Mill, from Erasmus to Mazzini, thinkers have made a deliberate effort to shape a mental climate conducive to freedom. This conscious, rational call for liberty, plus the unconscious impact of events, led eventually to a habit of mind and to that body of coherent doctrine which we call liberalism. It was a new kind of philosophy evolved as a response to a new kind of world.

Psychologically, liberalism as a way of life had strong emotional implications. It appealed to the dignity of the individual, to his sense of well-being, to his belief that he was something more than a cipher or automaton, to the sense of his right to shape his own destiny. This drive for recognition gave liberalism a powerful political motivation.

2. The Rise of Liberalism

Background. The way for European liberalism was prepared in the sixteenth century when the medieval world was in process of disintegration. It was a century which saw the emergence of a utilitarian, self-conscious middle class, and the rise of the modern state. Liberalism as an ideology was adapted to the needs of a new society with different foundations. Feudal economic relations had broken down, to be succeeded by capitalism with its call for a free hand in the pursuit of wealth. This sense of individuality came of age in the Renaissance and during the immense colonizing efforts of Spain, Portugal, France, and England. When this secular spirit encountered the theological movement of the Reformation, the result was the breakdown of religious uniformity and the nationalization of organized religion. Protestantism helped the growth of the liberal spirit by dealing a blow at

Carrying of the Cross (detail) by the highly individualistic Hieronymus Bosch (*c.* 1450–1516), who preferred to present his subjects in a grotesque, fantastic, or satirical form.

authority and loosening the hold of tradition. Both in doctrine and social results the Reformation was emancipating for the individual.

Liberalism in the Seventeenth Century. In the sixteenth century the battle against tradition had not yet been won; in the seventeenth the scales turned. Accumulating historical forces had become so powerful that together they prepared the soil for the growth of liberalism. Liberalism as a way of life and as a theory of the state was largely fashioned by the experience of England. In this pioneer land of revolution there emerged the basic principle of political liberalism in outline form. The British inaugurated a system of government which retained the monarchy but committed the constitutional government to protect the "liberty of the subject." Political parties, vital for the working of the liberal state, appeared, and the right of opposition was recognized as a legal right instead of treason. In the long run, liberalism won its way primarily because businessmen revolted against interference with their economic opportunities. Dryden expressed it accurately:

. . . and the springs of property were bent
And wound so high they cracked the government.

Liberalism in the Eighteenth Century. The
next great advance came with the American
Revolution. The Declaration of Independence
(1776) proclaimed the right of a people to
overthrow a despotic government, and the
Constitution of the United States was the first
written constitution adopted by a convention
chosen specifically for that purpose. The American Bill of Rights, the first ten amendments
to the Constitution, went even further than
the English Bill of Rights by *guaranteeing*
freedom of speech, press, assembly, and religion.

In eighteenth-century France, a society fermenting under the pressure of ideas, great
strides were made on the road to political
liberalism. As in the England of the Puritan
Revolution, the French discovered that traditional institutions could not be uprooted without an explosion. The French Declaration of
the Rights of Man and Citizen announced the
liberal credo: life, liberty, property, security;
popular sovereignty; equality before the law.
There was a temporary setback. Liberalism
almost vanished after 1791, when the revolutionary nation became enmeshed in civil and
foreign wars. As an ideology it was thrust
underground during the Reign of Terror, the
Directory, and the dictatorship of Napoleon.

3. The Development of Liberalism

Liberalism in the Nineteenth Century. Such
was the vitality of liberalism that it outlived
the dark days of 1791 to 1815 and went on
to become one of the great ideologies of the
nineteenth and twentieth centuries. Its stages
may be traced as follows:

(1) The Restoration (1815–1830): During
the decade and a half following the fall of
Napoleon, reactionary absolutism did what it
could to destroy the liberal movement. It was
impossible, however, permanently to throttle
continued demands for liberty—in both political theory and action. All efforts of reactionary governments, secret police, and national

armies to defend the old order were fruitless.
Absolutism was morally bankrupt, but liberalism gathered strength. The July Revolution of
1830, an open conflict between liberalism and
reaction, spread from Paris over all the world.

(2) Advance of Liberalism (1830–1848):
During the next two decades, the liberal movement went from the defensive to the offensive.
The winning of Belgian independence and the
acceleration of English electoral reform revealed a growing liberal power. Before its
triumph over absolutism, however, the liberal
movement found a new opponent in democracy in its extreme form—social democracy. A
struggle began between liberalism, spiritual
in essence, and social democracy, materialistic
in character.

*(3) Liberal-National Organization of Europe
(1848–1871):* Vestiges of absolutism and conservatism led in 1848 to a series of revolutions
in France, the Italies, the Germanies, Austria,
and Hungary. The revolts were crushed, and
autocratic regimes were reestablished, but it
became obvious that those rulers who refused
to make concessions to the liberal spirit would
eventually lose their thrones. During this
period Europe was reorganized along liberal-
national lines, as in the movements for unification in the Germanies and the Italies. By this
time, however, the dynamic force of nationalism was clearly in the ascendant.

(4) The National-Liberal Age (1871–1919):
The closing three decades of the nineteenth
century and the opening two decades of the
twentieth saw an intensification of national
rivalries and the crystallization of nationalism
as the dominant political force in modern society. Yet liberalism remained a powerful factor. Despite setbacks, it triumphed over its
old enemy—absolutism. For a long time there
were no more revivals of the old absolute
monarchies or explosions of new Caesarisms.
Kings now asserted themselves to be custo-
dians of the liberties of the people. Liberal
institutions were introduced in one country
after another. There seemed to be promise of
a new society in which the human spirit might
be free and unhampered, the essence of the
liberal creed.

(5) Challenge: The rise of dictatorship in

Europe from 1919 to 1939 brought with it a powerful threat to the further advance of liberalism. The fanatical activism of Germany, Italy, and Japan rejected the thesis that the individual deserves the blessings of liberty. Whole nations were transformed into huge concentration camps. But the outcome of World War II gave further life to liberalism.

4. National Patterns of Liberalism

Triumph of Liberalism in Great Britan. The progress of liberalism is most clearly visible in Great Britain. It was born there and its growth was continuous. All elements of the liberal pattern appear in the British experience. Economically, the state became the handmaiden of commerce. Politically, the victory was for constitutional government. Socially, there was generous recognition of the capacity of the lower classes to rise to higher standards. In religion there was a call for toleration. Psychologically, the British people assumed a critical attitude toward authority, whether secular or religious. They regarded their liberalism as a valuable complex of rights and privileges won over a long period of time, a bond of unity, a national heritage to be passed from generation to generation.

Substantial gains were made between the time of the Magna Carta (1215) and the seventeenth century, but there still remained traces of past illiberal traditions. The British liberal pattern assumed its shape in the nineteenth century with a victory for utilitarianism (the greatest happiness for the greatest number), promoted by Jeremy Bentham (1748–1832); philosophical radicalism, a program for political reform led by James Mill (1773–1836); and a movement for economic reform known as the Manchester School, under the guidance of Richard Cobden (1804–1865) and John Bright (1811–1889).

From Waterloo to the end of the nineteenth century, liberalism in Great Britain spoke with great authority as a way of life. As prophet of industrialism, exponent of free trade, advocate of religious toleration, champion of universal suffrage and parliamentarianism, the British liberal set a standard for the whole world.

Fluctuation: Liberalism in France. French liberalism developed along quite different lines from that in Great Britain. Unlike the British form, French liberalism had no deep historic roots. The liberal ideas of the *philosophes*, who prepared the way for the Revolution, were devised first of all to break down the existing order. The principles of Liberty, Equality, Fraternity were conceived as abstract ideals of worldwide significance; it was for this reason that the revolutionary leaders looked beyond the borders of France to spread their beliefs.

In nineteenth-century Great Britain, liberalism progressed steadily in influence: even the conservatives made it a point to hold on to liberal reforms. But liberalism in nineteenth-century France was forced to fight for its life against attacks from both Right and Left and, therefore, became hesitant and unsure of itself. At times it burst forth in savage militancy, at others it faded reluctantly into the background. This variation of pattern continued throughout the century. While the British fought their political battles in parliamentary debate, the French, to achieve political or social reform, rushed to the barricades.

Incomplete Pattern: Liberalism in the Germanies. While liberalism flourished in Great Britain and France, its growth was choked off in the Germanies. Authoritarianism, the opposite of liberalism, was the way of life in the German states. There was no liberal revolution there—no 1688, no 1776, no 1789. In the eighteenth and early nineteenth centuries the Germanies remained a combination of many loosely divided states whose people retained local rather than national loyalties. Political disunity, economic weakness, and social backwardness provided poor soil for the growth of liberalism. Especially significant was the lack of an energetic middle class that could undermine the authority of absolutism. The ideas of the Age of Reason and the revolutionary period reached only the small educated stratum of the population, not the broad masses. German intellectuals understood the meaning and implications of the liberal temper, but they were not successful in transplanting it into the Germanies. At first the liberal movement seemed to be headed for success, but it collapsed in the Revolution of 1848. In the minds of the German people this unfulfilled liberal revolution was stained thereafter with the odium of defeat, weakness, inefficiency, anarchism. When national unity was achieved it came not with a liberal coating but with the armor of Bismarck's iron-and-blood.

Liberal Nationalism in the Italies. The Italies, like the Germanies divided into many states, were also slow to adopt liberalism as a way of life. In the secular, individualistic spirit of the Renaissance there had been early evidences of liberal sentiment. But the progress of the middle class, standard-bearers of liberalism, had been slow and uncertain. True, a middle class existed, but it was small and uninfluential in comparison with British and French experience. The problem faced by Italians, as well as Germans, was to unify the national state before they could hope to establish a liberal government. Among both peoples the strands of nationalism and liberalism became inextricably interwoven. The unification of a free Italy was the work of a trio of

Although the young nation's founding fathers were deeply influenced by liberal ideology, a civil war was required to resolve the question of slavery in the United States.

liberal nationalists, Mazzini, Cavour, and Garibaldi.

United States: World Showcase for Liberalism. The United States, conceived in freedom, was dedicated to the libertarian formula. The Founding Fathers, intellectual stars of the Enlightenment, accepted the idea of individual freedom as the basic tradition of American life. They had specific political beliefs, but whatever their differences they always accepted the egalitarian formula, the historic root of liberalism. The written Constitution, the constitutional convention, the Bill of Rights, religious liberty, all were liberal concepts. The new nation was built in the liberal image. Jeffersonian democracy, with its rallying cry of equal rights for all, was succeeded by Jacksonian democracy, with its triumph of bourgeois initiative and ambition. American liberalism was strengthened when the new country became the Melting Pot for Europeans seeking a better life. But there was one dark stain on the fabric—slavery. The problem of Negro status was not resolved.

Worldwide Pattern. The value of liberalism in preserving and enlarging human freedom has been amply demonstrated in the major Western states. Throughout the world the smaller states tended to model their political life on the English, French, or American experience. These states, each afflicted with its own problems, learned that liberalism, with an accent on compromise, provides an effective machinery for reconciling conflicting interests. They also recognized the toughness of liberalism: neither two World Wars in the twentieth century nor the totalitarianism of fascism or communism have been able to erase the liberal state or the liberal ideal. As a motivating ideology, liberalism has demonstrated lasting values.

In the narrow political sense, liberalism has not yet fulfilled its promise. Politically, it was a by-product of the effort of the middle class to win a place in the sun. To the bourgeoisie the concept of freedom was necessary to escape from tyranny. According to negative critics, after its victory the middle class saw liberalism as a means of protecting itself from invasion from below or as a means of distributing charity to those who demanded social justice.

In the broader sense, however, liberalism holds fast to its fundamental principle of government by consent of the governed and of individual freedom under the law. The older form of liberalism concerned itself mainly with the protection of the individual against the arbitrary acts of the government. The new liberalism, seeks to protect him against arbitrary acts of private organizations as well. This ideal of social liberalism was proclaimed for all mankind in the Universal Declaration of Human Rights adopted by the United Nations in 1948. This set up "a common standard of achievement for all peoples and all nations."

❊ KEY DOCUMENT ❊

LORD BYRON EXTOLS GREEK LIBERTY

George Gordon, Lord Byron, Childe Harold's Pilgrimage, canto II, stanzas LXXIII–LXXVI.

LORD BYRON (1788–1824), English poet and internationally the most famous of the English romantic writers, was a zealous advocate of freedom for all countries. Conscious of Western civilization's debt to Greece, he, like other liberals, actively supported Greece in its war of independence against the Ottoman Turks (1821–1829). In the following stanzas of *Childe Harold's Pilgrimage,* Byron urged the Greeks to throw off the Turkish yoke.

. . . .

Fair Greece! sad relic of departed Worth!
Immortal, though no more; though fallen,
   great;
Who now shall lead thy scattered children forth,
And long accustomed bondage uncreate?
Not such thy sons who whilome did await,
The helpless warrior of a willing doom,
In bleak Thermopylae's sepulchral strait—
Oh! who that gallant spirit shall resume,
Leap from Eurotas' banks, and call thee from
   the tomb?

Spirit of Freedom! when on Phyle's brow
Thou sat'st with Trasybulus and his train,
Couldst thou forebode the dismal hour which
   now
Dims the green beauties of thine Attic plain?
Not thirty tyrants now enforce the chain,
But every carle can lord it o'er thy land;
Nor rise thy sons, but idly rail in vain,
Trembling beneath the scourge of Turkish hand,
From birth till death enslaved; in word, in deed,
   unmanned.

In all save form alone, how changed! and who
That marks the fire still sparkling in each eye.
Who but would deem their bosoms burned anew
With thy unquenchèd beam, lost Liberty!
And many dream withal the hour is nigh
That gives them back their father's heritage:
For foreign arms and aid they fondly sigh,
Nor solely dare encounter hostile rage,
Or tear their name defiled from Slavery's mourn-
   ful page.

Hereditary bondsmen! know ye not
Who would be free *themselves* must strike the
   blow?
By their right arms the conquest must be
   wrought?
Will Gaul or Muscovite redress ye? no!
True—they may lay your proud despoilers low,
But not for you will Freedom's Altars flame.
Shades of the Helots! triumph o'er your foe:
Greece! change thy lords, thy state is still the
   same;
Thy glorious day is o'er, but not thine years of
   shame.

{ HISTORICAL INTERPRETATION }

J. SALWYN SCHAPIRO ON THE WAY OF LIBERALISM

J. Salwyn Schapiro, *Liberalism: Its Meaning and History*, Anvil Book No. 21 (Princeton,
N. J., 1958), pp. 9–13.

LIBERALISM, by its very nature, exerts a strong appeal to the modern historian in that it
favors the free as opposed to the closed mind. The fundamental ideas of liberalism were
described by J. Salwyn Schapiro in these passages.

Liberalism, the Way of Freedom. What has characterized liberalism at all times is its unshaken belief in the necessity of freedom to achieve every desirable aim. A deep concern for the freedom of the individual inspired its opposition to absolute authority, be it that of the state, of the church, or of a political party. The fundamental postulate of liberalism has been the moral worth, the absolute value, and the essential dignity of the human personality. Every individual is therefore to be treated as an end in himself, not as a means to advance the interests of others. The political liberty of the individual

consists, according to the French Declaration of the Rights of Man, "in the power of doing whatever does not injure another . . . limits are determinable only by law." Liberals are deeply convinced that without liberty life is not worth living. Hence, they have ever sought to free the individual from unjust and hampering restraints imposed upon him by governments, institutions, and traditions. An autonomous individual would be free to choose his occupation, and to assert his opinions, to change his nationality, and to move from place to place.

Closely linked to the freedom of the individual

is that of association. Liberalism has advocated the right to form associations of all kinds—political, social, economic, religious, and cultural—that have as their objective the advancement of the legitimate interests of their members. Without freedom of association the individual would be helpless in opposing the restraints imposed by the established order. With it the power of numbers, arising from a cohesive group of like-minded individuals, can be asserted against injustice and tyranny.

Liberalism and Equal Rights. Equality is another fundamental liberal principle. Liberalism has proclaimed the principle of equality for all human beings everywhere. It must be borne in mind, however, that equality does not mean that all have equal ability, or equal moral perception, or equal personal attraction. What it means is that all have equal rights before the law, and that all are entitled to civil liberty. No law should confer special privileges on some, and impose special discriminations on others; it must be the same for all whether it aids, protects, or punishes. Liberalism has waged unceasing war against privilege, whether that of birth, wealth, race, creed, or sex, as an artificial hindrance to individual development. . . .

Liberalism and Government. The main impact of liberalism has been on government, as the institution with supreme power in the community. In the liberal view the chief end of government is to uphold the liberty, equality, and security of all citizens. For this reason, a liberal government, whether in form monarchical or republican, rests on the rule of law emanating from a law-making body freely elected by the people. No government is, therefore, legitimate, according to liberalism, unless it is based on the consent of the governed. In order to protect the rights of individuals and of minorities, liberalism has placed highly important limitations on the power of government. The liberal state is not the god-state of the Roman emperors, or the absolute state of the divine right monarchs, or the garrison state of the military dictators, or the totalitarian state of the communists and fascists. It is a government of laws, not of men.

Liberalism and Intellectual Freedom. Of all civil liberties, the most prized has been liberty of thought and expression. Liberals came to the deep conviction that all opinions, even erroneous ones, should have freedom of expression. Not infrequently have opinions, commonly held to be false, proved to be true. Furthermore, in the conflict between opinions even error serves a useful purpose in that it stimulates truth to clarify and fortify itself. For these reasons liberals have been in the forefront of movements to abolish censorships, whether official or non-official, as the chief hindrances to the peaceful progress of mankind . . .

Liberalism and Progress. Because of its secular attitude liberalism adopted a dynamic view of life, envisaging progress for mankind. It has therefore exerted every effort to make this world a better place in which to live. Man, according to liberalism, is born ignorant, not wicked; and throughout his life he is conditioned by a social environment that in many ways has been the product of the errors and injustices of the past. To rectify this situation it is necessary, therefore, to increase the sum of knowledge, to strive for enlightenment, and to create a society that will promote peace, prosperity, and good will. These views of the nature of man and of society were derived from the idea of progress, an idea both modern and characteristically liberal. Vaguely conceived in the seventeenth century, boldly proclaimed in the eighteenth the idea of progress became an article of faith in the nineteenth. According to the liberal view progress, slow at one time and rapid at another, results in transforming one system of society which is bad but not too bad, to another which is good but not too good. . . .

Way of Liberalism. The liberal temper blends idealism with practical considerations. Ideals are to serve as guides to ultimate ends. These are to be attained, not all at once but one by one, cautiously, moderately, yet continuously. Hence, the liberal is neither a romantic dreaming of an imaginary past wherein all was idyllic; nor is he a utopian dreaming of an imaginary future when a perfect society will be established once and for all. Time, place, and history determine the pace as well as the method of progress. The liberal way is the way of the "inevitability of gradualness" in the progress of mankind.

❦{ TEN BASIC BOOKS }❧

THE EVOLUTION OF LIBERALISM

1. Bullock, Alan L. C. and Maurice Shock, eds., *The Liberal Tradition* (New York, 1956).

2. Croce, Benedetto, *History of Europe in the Nineteenth Century*, trans. by Henry Furst (New York, 1933).†

3. Dewey, John, *Liberalism and Social Action* (New York, 1935, R. 1963).†

4. Hobhouse, Leonard T., *Liberalism* (London, 1911, R. 1964).†

5. Laski, Harold J., *The Rise of European Liberalism* (London, 1936). American ed. (New York, 1962).†

6. Neill, T. P., *The Rise and Decline of Liberalism* (Milwaukee, Wisc., 1953).

7. Ruggiero, Guido de, *The History of European Liberalism* (London, 1927, R. 1959).†

8. Schapiro, J. Salwyn, *Liberalism: Its Meaning and History*, Anvil Book No. 21 (Princeton, N. J., 1958).†

9. Stearns, Harold, ed., *Liberalism in America* (New York, 1919).

10. Woodward, Ernest, *The Age of Reform, 1815–1870*, 2nd ed. (New York, 1962).

23

Constitutional Reform in Nineteenth-Century England, 1815-1867

AN OLD, mad, blind, despised, and dying king,—
Princes, the dregs of their dull race, who flow
Through public scorn,—mud from a muddy spring,—
Rulers who neither see, nor feel, nor know,
But leech-like to their fainting country cling,
Till they drop, blind in blood, without a blow,—
A people starved and stabbed in the untilled field,—
An army, which liberticide and prey
Makes as a two-edged sword to all who wield
Golden and sanguine laws which tempt and slay;
Religion Christless, Godless—a book sealed;
A Senate,—Time's worst statute unrepealed,—
Are graves, from which a glorious Phantom may
Burst, to illumine our tempestuous day.

—PERCY BYSSHE SHELLEY, "England in 1819"

1. Recoil: The Era of Reaction, 1815–1822

England in 1815. The defeat of Napoleon brought peace but not prosperity to England. New lands of strategic importance had been added to an already mighty world-empire. The British navy was the most powerful on the seas. But these gains had been made at great expense. Thousands of soldiers who had fought against Bonaparte, more than 400,000 demobilized men, were thrown upon an already satiated labor market. Businessmen were ruined by competition from the Continent. The government was in debt, the people burdened by taxation and rising prices.

England in 1815, less of a democracy than an oligarchy, was a country ruled by a small but powerful group of landlords. The Tory ministers, who had saved England from the French Revolution and Napoleon, had been too fully occupied with foreign affairs to undertake urgently needed reforms. Now they were faced with a dissatisfied bourgeoisie and a rebellious working class. Parliament, having established its supremacy over the king, was controlled by a plutocracy. Popular government existed in theory, but in practice about 70 interrelated families ran the country. The House of Lords, an assembly of aristocrats, included several hundred hereditary peers, 30 bishops of the Anglican Church, and elective peers of Scotland and Ireland. The Lords, holding a potential veto on all legislation, suppressed significant reforms. The House of Commons, with 640 members, represented the English governing classes rather than the people.

Corn Law of 1815. During the last five years of the Napoleonic Wars, from 1810 to 1815, the landholding aristocracy accumulated

Bread riot at the entrance of the House of Commons, 1815.

huge profits from the sale of wheat. Peace brought a drop in prices. In 1815 Parliament passed the Corn Law, which placed heavy protective duties on breadstuffs. Members of Parliament were convinced that every encouragement should be given to the nation to produce its own food, that agriculture gave employment, and that rural life produced a healthy population. But the effect of the Corn Law was catastrophic. It raised the price of wheat beyond the means of the workers, thus intensifying the already acute economic distress. Failure of the grain crop in 1816 added to the discontent. Meanwhile, unemployed workers sought to destroy the new machinery, which they believed was the cause of their idleness. The Luddite Riots (1811–1816) by despairing, unorganized workers, were suppressed by factory owners acting in concert with the Tory government.

Agitation for Reform. Widespread discontent quickened the demand for change. The intellectual father of reform in England was Jeremy Bentham (1748-1832), philosopher,

jurist, and Utilitarian, who warned that the object of all legislation must be the greatest happiness of the greatest number, and that every law, tradition, and custom should be abolished unless it was useful. Bentham inspired a group of radicals who became champions of democracy. William Cobbett (1763–1835), fiery pamphleteer, denounced oligarchic rule as the real cause of working-class misery. Hard times, he thundered, were due not to new machinery, as many workers believed, but to the paralyzing grip of the upper class and to wasteful government, an extravagant court, corruption in high office, unfair representation, and limited franchise. Francis Place (1771–1854), self-educated master tailor, called for a campaign to repeal the Combination Acts which forbade trade unions, and demanded extension of the franchise to the workers. The radical reformers called for universal manhood suffrage, the secret ballot, and equal electoral districts.

Agitation came to a head on December 2, 1816, when a crowd assembled at Spa Fields, near London, to hear an address on parliamentary reform. The meeting was dispersed by troops. Frightened by the incident, the government in March 1817 suspended the Habeas Corpus Act for the first time in English history, enacted legislation prohibiting public assembly, and banned "blasphemous and seditious pamphlets" (Coercion Acts).

There was trouble in the English air. On August 16, 1819, a popular mass meeting of 60,000 persons was held at St. Peter's Fields in Manchester, to demand universal suffrage, parliamentary reform, and repeal of the Corn Laws. Because the meeting had been prohibited by the authorities, the yeomanry (cavalry militia organized on an aristocratic basis) charged the crowd, killed a dozen people, and wounded several hundred who were unable to escape the sabers and the horses' hoofs (Peterloo Massacre). The government thanked the yeomanry for "its magnificent performance."

The Six Acts, 1819. Following the Peterloo Massacre, Parliament passed the Six Acts, a collection of gag laws limiting freedom of speech, press, and assembly. These measures were: (1) prohibition of military exercises by persons not authorized to perform them; (2) quick trials for offenders against the law; (3) legalization of issue of search warrants for arms; (4) suppression of seditious publications and banishment of the authors; (5) prohibition of public meetings held without official permission; and (6) heavy stamp duties on newspapers. As an instrument of reaction the Six Acts matched Metternich's system of repression on the Continent. The radicals reacted violently. In February 1820 a plot (the Cato Street conspiracy) was hatched to massacre the whole Tory cabinet, set fire to London, and proclaim a provisional government. The plan was revealed to the police by one of the conspirators. The ringleaders were arrested, several hanged, and the others transported for life.

2. The Reform Bill of 1832

Background: Moderate Tory Reform. On the death of the insane George III in 1820, he was succeeded by his son, George IV, who was opposed to the notion of parliamentary reform. But the tone for his regime was set by a group of moderate Tories who had supplanted the old guard. Among them were George Canning (1770–1827) who became foreign minister on the suicide of Castlereagh; Sir Robert Peel (1788–1850), home secretary; and William Huskisson (1770–1830), president of the Board of Trade. These influential leaders understood that the new industrialism had rendered the old political system obsolete. Peel was the champion of prison reform. He put through Parliament in 1823 a bill abolishing the death penalty for about a hundred offenses. Shocked by conditions in British prisons, he obtained passage of the Gaol Act of 1823–1824, which provided for better sanitation in prisons. Peel founded the Metropolitan Police (hence nicknamed "Peelers" or "Bobbies").

Meanwhile, Huskisson, a disciple of Adam Smith, made a breach in the mercantile system. Although not a free trader, he was opposed to artificial restrictions on trade. He believed that if other countries used the same type of protective tariffs that had made Britain prosperous, they would ruin British industry. He induced Parliament in 1823 to modify the Navigation Acts and reduce duties on such imports as silk, wool, iron, wines, coffee, sugar, and cottons. In 1824, after a fiery campaign by Francis Place, Parliament repealed the Combination Laws of 1799 and 1800. But a resultant outbreak of strikes brought a demand from manufacturers to restrict the rights of unions. In 1825 a new law permitted the unions to organize, but forbade them to strike —thus virtually restoring the Combination Laws.

Progress was made under Tory leadership in religious freedom. On May 9, 1828, Parliament repealed the Corporation and Test Acts, thereby removing civil restrictions on nonconformists. The emancipation of Catholics was a considerably more difficult problem, as most Catholics were Irish, a subject nationality. The elder Pitt had promised that he would abrogate all legal disabilities for Catholics, but he was unable to carry out his pledge.

Pitt's pupil, Canning, who became prime minister in 1827, decided to redeem the promise. But to many Englishmen the very thought of Catholic Emancipation meant the end of liberty and empire. Canning was not successful, but in March–April 1829, under the Wellington ministry, Parliament finally abolished Catholic disabilities. Now, after taking an oath especially framed for them, Catholics had the right to sit and vote in Parliament. In Ireland, however, a new electoral law raising property qualifications disfranchised many Catholics.

Necessity for Electoral Reform. The haphazard, obsolete system of representation in Parliament had been retained despite the fact that the center of population had shifted from the Channel ports to the Midlands and the coal and iron regions of the north and west. Each of 40 counties, large or small, sent two representatives to Parliament. In addition, nearly 250 boroughs sent two members each. Scotland, with a population of 2,000,000, had only 45 members in the House, as against 44 members for Cornwall, with only one-eighth the population of Scotland. The landed aristocracy controlled both houses of Parliament. In 1793, fewer than 15,000 voters elected most of the members in the House of Commons. In 1800 just 197 patrons controlled a majority in the House; in 1827, some 276 seats were controlled by the privileged landowners.

There was much discontent with the scandalous borough system. To control Parliament the Tudor monarchs had depended on representatives from little villages dominated by friendly nobles. Later, the aristocracy maintained control of these pocket boroughs, which took their name from the saying that a particular borough was "carried in the pocket" of a political leader. The assumption was that once a borough had demonstrated its right to send burgesses to Parliament, it retained that right forever. Even worse were the "rotten boroughs," which had so few voters that they ceased to be boroughs, but still sent their traditional two representatives. In Old Sarum, a cathedral town, the entire electorate had long since been moved a few miles away to New Sarum, or Salisbury. Old Sarum, now a deserted hill with no voters, still sent its two "representatives" to Parliament. The village of Bute in Scotland had only one remaining inhabitant qualified to vote; on election day he moved and seconded his own nomination, voted, and was unanimously elected to a seat in the House of Commons. Bosseney in Cornwall, a hamlet of three cottages, had only nine electors, eight in one family, but it also sent two burgesses to London. Similarly, islands which had disappeared, ruined castles, cemetery plots, stone walls, and other dead areas returned two members each. At the same time, many large, flourishing towns in north England, humming with trade and activity, had no representatives at all in Parliament.

The Oscillating Political Situation. The Tories were not opposed to moderate concessions. Fearing, however, that democratic government would end their privileges, they united unanimously against parliamentary reform. The Whigs were also opposed to radical changes, but because they had been out of power for a generation, they saw it as politically expedient to favor a popular cause if they could keep it under their own direction. The radicals, few in number but influential, were zealous champions of reform. The most enthusiastic proponents of change, however, were the masses of industrial laborers in the factory towns. The cause of reform was stimulated when the unpopular George IV died on June 26, 1830. His brother, William IV (r. 1830–1837), the homely sailor king, was more amenable to change. Moreover, Englishmen were impressed by the moderate July Revolution in France.

Wellington Guesses Wrong. At the general election held in September 1830 a majority favorable to reform was returned to Parliament. But the ministry, headed by the duke of Wellington, hero of Waterloo, was not in a reforming mood. Wellington, a soldier accustomed to sharp orders and instant obedience, spoke vigorously at the first meeting of Parliament against a Whig motion for electoral reform. Existing laws, said Wellington, "answered all purposes of good legislation to a greater degree than . . . in any other country, at any time." This shortsighted conclusion cost Wellington not only his popularity but also his ministry. A wave of indignation swept over the country. Wellington was driven from office by a combination of Whigs with the moderate Tories, called Canningites. Thus ended a continuous Tory rule, with one short interval, of nearly half a century. The new Whig ministry, which came to power in 1831, with Earl Grey as prime minister, was pledged to parliamentary reform.

Struggle in Parliament. In March 1831 Lord John Russell brought in a reform bill to redistribute representation and extend the suffrage. A great debate took place not only on the bill itself but also on the fundamental principles expressed in it. Russell urged the House of Commons to redeem its pledge to sovereign, Parliament, and country: "Mr. Speaker: I rise, sir, with feelings of deep anxiety and interest, to bring forward a question, which, unparalleled as it is in importance, is likewise unparalleled in difficulty." The Tories denounced the bill as unnecessary and pointed out that the existing system had made possible the careers of such great statesmen as the Pitts, Burke, and Fox, all of whom represented rotten boroughs. After a fierce debate the act was passed by a majority of one vote in the House of Commons, but it was apparent that it could not be saved from amendments designed to emasculate it. Prime Minister Earl Grey then called for a general election to discover the wishes of the electorate. The Whigs obtained an overwhelming majority, but a second bill, passed in September 1831, was rejected by the House of Lords.

Again Lord Russell introduced the reform act. It was passed by the Commons but once more the Lords rejected it. By this time all England, angered by repeated frustration of the people's will, was on the verge of revolt. To rescue the bill, Grey demanded that King William IV pack the House of Lords with a sufficient number of peers to pass the measure. When the king hesitated, Grey resigned in protest. The stubborn monarch then called on the duke of Wellington to take office. The resultant outburst of public indignation was so frightening that King William recalled Grey and assented to the plan to create "such a number of peers as will insure passage of the Reform Bill." The Lords, realizing that further opposition was useless, ended the struggle. The Reform Bill became law on June 4, 1832.

Provisions of the Bill. The Reform Bill of 1832 was designed to change the system of representation and extend the franchise.

Redistribution of Seats: The act deprived 56 pocket and rotten boroughs with fewer than 2,000 votes of their 111 seats; 32 small boroughs with fewer than 4,000 voters lost one seat each. Of the 143 seats left free for redistribution, 65 were awarded to counties in England and Wales, 44 to the larger industrial cities, 21 to the smaller towns, 8 to the Scots, and 5 to the Irish. No attempt was made to create equal electoral districts, nor was any provision made for periodic redistribution of seats.

Qualifications for Suffrage: The ballot was given in all boroughs to all householders who owned or rented a building worth £10 (about $50) a year. In the counties the vote was given to all copyholders (farmers) and leaseholders (tenants) of land at a rent of £10 a year. In addition, the measure gave the vote to all short-term leaseholders and tenants-at-will paying an annual rental of £50. Lodgers still did not have the right to vote.

Significance. The Reform Bill of 1832 was a moderate measure. It increased the number of voters from 435,000 to about 656,000, nearly all of whom belonged to the prosperous middle class. Only about 15 per cent of males were now entitled to vote. Farm and industrial workers, as well as members of the lower bourgeoisie, were still disfranchised.

Yet this bill accomplished reform by constitutional means. The idea that great reforms could take place without revolution took deep root in British political life. The power of the old regime was broken. The measure was mild enough, although to irreconcilable Tories it seemed a blow at the very foundation of society, the end of the political world. A breach was made in the wall of aristocracy. The bill, a victory for the middle class, elevated the industrialists to the level of the older landed aristocracy and divided control of the government between them. It also meant the triumph of industrial interests over the agricultural. The disgusted workers, who had supported the measure during the struggle for its adoption, believed that they had been cheated out of the vote by the Whigs. The House of Lords came out of the struggle with shattered prestige and lessened powers. The precedent was now established that, in the event of disagreement between the two houses, the Lords must yield if a popular election tested the issue in favor of the Commons.

3. Regeneration: The Era of Reform

The Reform-Minded Middle Class. The Reform Bill of 1832 meant that the English middle class had come of age. Money was added to family as a key to social status. There was a new aristocracy composed of manufacturers, businessmen, bankers, and stockbrokers, some of whom were elevated to the peerage. Members of this new middle class were reform-minded, although whatever change they advocated coincided closely with their own interests. Reform in the franchise gave them political supremacy in Parliament; reform in tariff policies gave them control of worldwide markets; reform in religion gave them, as nonconformists, equality with the Anglicans. On the other hand, they were reluctant to grant reforms to the "lower order," because such changes brought the danger of higher taxes.

Abolition of Slavery. The slave trade in the British colonies was ended by the Abolition of the Slave Trade Act of 1807. In the meantime, a voluntary organization, the Anti-Slavery Society, led by the philanthropist William Wilberforce (1759–1833), stimulated public opinion to demand parliamentary action. Parliament in 1833 abolished slavery itself in the colonies.

Municipal Reform. Parliamentary reform stimulated similar reform in the municipalities. For centuries local governments had been burdened by inefficiency and corruption. Municipal governments, or corporations, were controlled by a small oligarchy consisting of mayor and town council, both of whom perpetuated themselves in office and used public funds for their own benefit. On occasion they might be elected to office by a limited number of privileged freemen. The Municipal Corporations Act (1835) provided for municipal councils elected by all who paid rates, or local taxes. Although the House of Lords sought unsuccessfully to block this innovation, the reform was immediately successful. Able citizens were attracted to local office, and British municipal government became a model for all the world.

Additional Reforms. Parliament made a thorough revision of the laws on pauperism. The Poor Law Amendment Act of 1834 provided for a new system which limited outdoor relief to the sick, aged, and indigent, and established workshops where the able-bodied were put to work. In "terminating the intolerable misuse of ratepayers' money," the measure ended the practice of giving charity to workers to compensate them for low wages. The country was divided into districts. Boards of guardians were elected in each district to administer the new law.

In 1833 came the first of a long series of measures to promote education. Parliament voted an annual grant of £20,000 for the use of elementary schools, most of which were still run by religious societies. Appropriations increased each year, even though the Anglican Church opposed any system of secular education. In 1836 the duty of registering births, deaths, and marriages was transferred from the Anglican Church to civil officials.

Industrialism had a cruel effect on workers, especially women and children. Aristocrats, notably Lord Shaftesbury (1801–1885), advocated factory reform. The first important Factory Law (1833) prohibited the employment of children under 9 years of age in the textile factories, and restricted the work of those between 9 and 13 to forty-eight hours a week. Factory inspectors were appointed to see that the law was carried out. From this time on, a series of factory acts gradually bettered the position of the workers who, as a class, had not received an adequate share of the new prosperity.

Jews, who were debarred from Parliament because of an oath required "on the true faith of a Christian," continued to suffer political discrimination even after the emancipation of the Catholics. On July 23, 1858, Parliament, in the Jewish Relief Act, prescribed a special oath for Jewish members.

4. Years of Glory: The Victorian Age

Constitutional Structure. The Reform Bill of 1832 was the signal for political consolidation. The British governmental structure, resting on custom and tradition rather than on a written constitution, became the prototype and model of liberal governments elsewhere. The British constitution, broadening "from precedent to precedent," consisted of a series of charters won from reluctant monarchs, acts of parliamentary reform, judicial decisions, and traditional practices. These were never combined into one basic document: the British constitution remains unwritten.

The British monarch, a symbol of national unity, had no authority or power but only influence. Although he could summon and dissolve Parliament, appoint and dismiss ministers, grant charters, declare war, make peace, and sign treaties, these were only legal and theoretical rights. In practice, such constitutional functions were delegated to ministers responsible to the House of Commons, which, in turn, was responsible to the voters.

Executive authority rested in the cabinet, composed of the prime minister and other ministers. Appointed by the king, the prime minister was chief of the currently dominant political party; he chose his colleagues and continued in office as long as he commanded the confidence of the House of Commons. Cabinet members were responsible to the House of Commons and presented their policies in person to it. They formulated the legislative program, introduced all important bills, and resigned in a body when the prime minister relinquished his office.

Parliament consisted of two chambers, the House of Lords and the House of Commons. In the House of Lords sat several hundred ecclesiastical and temporal peers, including royal princes, Anglican prelates, Scottish and Irish peers, dukes, earls, viscounts, and barons. Many members did not attend meetings. The Lords possessed judicial power as the supreme Court of Appeals. Gradually the House of Lords became inferior in power to the House of Commons. The House of Commons, elected by increasingly universal suffrage, was the more important legislative body. Its members served for five years, and met at least once each year to provide funds for the army and the Crown. By its control of the power of the sword and the power of the purse the House of Commons maintained political supremacy.

Conservatives and Liberals. The Reform Bill of 1832 brought a new image to the two main political parties. Both assumed new names. The Conservatives dropped the discredited name of Tories. Consisting of a right wing of wealthy landlords and a left wing of industrial capitalists, the Conservatives were still committed to aristocratic ideals, but at the same time were willing to accommodate themselves to new political conditions. The Liberals had a right wing of liberal aristocrats (the old Whigs), a center group of industrialists, and a left wing of radicals. They called for further reform of the suffrage, free trade, social reform, and Home Rule for Ireland. Both major parties regarded the Reform Bill of 1832 as a compromise, as "representative without being democratic, substantial and evolutionary without being revolutionary or demagogic."

Accession of Queen Victoria, 1837. When William IV died in 1837, he was succeeded by his niece, Victoria, only eighteen years of age, whose reign of nearly sixty-four years was one of the great epochs of British history. Trained in her early years by the Whig minister, Lord Melbourne (ministry, 1834, 1835–

1841), and assisted later by her husband, Prince Albert of Saxe-Coburg (1819–1861), Victoria became a highly successful ruler. Intelligent rather than brilliant, she revealed a strict regard for constitutional limits, a great capacity for work, and a regal, maternal dignity. The Victorian era, free from internal revolution, saw a rapid increase in population, growth of democracy stimulated by the consolidation of cabinet government, further reform in representation and suffrage, and intensified trade and industry. By 1900 the British could boast that one square mile in every four on earth was under the British flag, and one person of every five was a subject of the British queen.

Agitation: Chartism. The Reform Bill of 1832 was a bitter disappointment to the workers, who had expected the establishment of universal suffrage. But in 1837, the year of

Victoria's accession, the House of Commons voted 500 to 22 to entertain no further motions for electoral reform. Sir Robert Peel, Conservative leader in the early Victorian period, saw the Reform Bill as "a final and irrevocable settlement of a great constitutional question." Angered radicals organized popular meetings and processions to demand further political and social reform. On May 13, 1839, a giant petition, or charter (hence the name Chartism), was presented to Parliament. The People's Charter demanded six points: (1) universal manhood suffrage; (2) equal electoral districts; (3) salaries for members of Parliament; (4) abolition of property qualifications for members of Parliament; (5) secret ballot; and (6) annual elections of Parliament.

Gigantic petitions, each embodying the demands of the Chartists, were presented to Parliament in 1839, again in 1842, when labor

The Chartists on a protest march to Kensington, a wealthy residential borough of London.

trouble reached a serious stage, and in 1848, stimulated by the current revolutionary movement on the Continent. Each of these petitions was rejected. Neither monster processions nor the threat of rebellion succeeded in moving the predominantly bourgeois Parliament. Both Conservatives and Liberals opposed further

extension of the suffrage. Working-class leaders demanded that "all labor shall cease until the People's Charter becomes the law of the land," but they were unsuccessful in arousing the British people to revolt. The Chartist movement was further weakened by division among its leaders. Without effective leadership or organization, Chartism seemed to make little progress. Yet all its demands, with the exception of annual elections of Parliament, eventually became a part of the British constitution.

1815–

Repeal of the Corn Laws, 1846. The Conservative aristocrats were willing to make concessions on other customs duties, but not on corn (i.e., grain) tariffs, from which they profited directly. But the Conservative manufacturers wanted an end to the Corn Laws so that cheap foreign foodstuffs could be imported for the workers. The industrialists were not altogether altruistic: a reduction in living costs for the workers would enable the employers to pay lower wages and thus in the long run to reap higher profits. The working class opposed tariffs of any kind on the ground that they were at the root of high prices and rents.

In 1838–1839 a group of manufacturers in Manchester organized the Anti-Corn-Law League to work for repeal of protective duties on grain. Led by Richard Cobden (1804–1865), a cotton merchant, and John Bright (1811–1889), orator of the movement, the League called protest meetings and showered Parliament with petitions. While the House of Commons was mired in debate on the issue, the English harvest of 1845 was destroyed by rain. At the same time a terrible potato blight ruined the Irish crop. The government had to act quickly. The liberal-minded Conservative Prime Minister Peel, won over, carried through Parliament on June 6, 1846 the repeal of the Corn Laws and established free trade in grain. Disgruntled agrarian followers immediately overthrew him, repudiated his leadership, and cast him out of their ranks. However, a blow had been administered to the system of protection. Free trade was finally established in 1867, when the last of the protective duties was removed.

Foreign Affairs: Lord Palmerston. After the fall of Napoleon, Britain enjoyed a long period of peace. Her major enemy, France, was compelled to devote her attention to other prob-

lems. Both Castlereagh and Canning, suspicious of the Holy Alliance, kept Britain aloof from Continental affairs. Their successor, Henry Temple, Viscount Palmerston (1784–1865), as foreign minister, home secretary, and prime minister, guided Britain's foreign policy almost continuously from 1830 to 1865. An Englishman by birth but an Irish peer by virtue of large holdings in Ireland, affectionately called "Old Pam" by the people, Palmerston was an advocate of a strong foreign policy. Originally a Tory, he drifted to the side of the Liberals. His interest lay chiefly in foreign affairs. Militant and pugnacious, he called for a great navy and an effective army and vigorously supported the rights of British subjects in foreign countries. While opposed to the Chartists at home, he supported revolutionary movements in Spain, Portugal, Belgium, Hungary, the Germanies, and the Italies. His foreign policy had two specific aims: (1) to maintain a balance of power on the Continent and thereby prevent the rise of another Napoleon; and (2) vigorously to oppose Russia in its quest for an outlet to the sea.

Near Eastern Question: Crimean War, 1853–1856. Palmerston was particularly effective in the Near East, where he upheld Britain's traditional policy of supporting the sultan of Turkey against Russian maneuvers to break through to the Mediterranean. When Tsar Nicholas I built a great fortress and naval port at Sevastopol on the Crimean peninsula, he aroused Palmerston into action. The immediate cause of the Crimean War was a quarrel over custody of Christian shrines in the Holy Land. Napoleon III appealed to the sultan of Turkey to restore the shrines to Roman Catholic monks; Nicholas I demanded that Greek Orthodox monks be left undisturbed. When the Russian tsar claimed a protectorate over all Christians in the Turkish Empire, he was rebuffed by the sultan for interference in Turkish internal affairs. Nicholas thereupon dispatched troops to the Turkish principalities of Moldavia and Wallachia. (*See page 451.*)

Turkey, after declaring war on Russia on

October 4, 1853, was joined by England, France, and Sardinia. British and French fleets moved into the Gulf of Finland and forced the Russian navy to retire to Kronstadt. Russian armies fought stubbornly, especially at the Sevastopol fortification, but eventually they had to capitulate. The Treaty of Paris (March 30, 1856) opened the Black Sea to general commerce, declared the Danube River open to navigation by all nations, and required Russia to respect the integrity of the Turkish Empire. Palmerston's militant policies had achieved a resounding success.

Palmerstonian Diplomacy. The British obtained a foothold in China in the Opium War (1841–1842), forcing China to cede the port of Hong Kong and to open several ports, including Canton and Shanghai, to trade under consular supervision. Another war in 1856 helped open the Celestial Empire to penetration by the Western Powers. In India, British troops suppressed the Sepoy Mutiny of 1857, but Palmerston ended the power of the British East India Company and set up a new British administration with the Better Government of India Act of 1858. During the American Civil War, Palmerston supported the South. When Union vessels blockaded the South, the result was a cotton shortage in Britain: many factories were closed down, proprietors went bankrupt, and laborers were thrown out of work. Although Britain made sharp protests, the danger of war was averted by the prudence and ability of William H. Seward, the American secretary of state, and Charles Francis Adams.

Golden Age of British Economic Supremacy. With tariffs eliminated, Navigation Laws repealed, and free trade favored, British industry and commerce entered an era of prosperity. Britons were many times blessed with favorable advantages over other countries in the race for economic supremacy: they possessed abundant coal and iron, a large merchant marine and navy, a long coast line, fine ports, capital to invest, inventive genius, and the means and will to build railways and to

progress in steam navigation. England was the workshop of the world. "Made in England" became a world-known slogan. British ships roamed the seven seas. British textile, iron, and steel factories set standards for industry everywhere. London was the emporium of the world's commerce, the broker and banker for world trade. All this was reflected in the Great Exhibition of 1851, held May 1–October 15 in the Crystal Palace in Hyde Park. It was a magnificent international exposition displaying Britain's industrial and commercial might. *Prosperity* was the note sounded, and it was confidently expected that the exhibit would inaugurate a new era of world peace. Queen Victoria and her consort, Prince Albert, were present to add glamor to the spectacle. Visitors streamed to London from all over the world to gaze upon evidences of Britain's industrial genius and to seek to emulate it.

Victorian Compromise. Victoria's regime was regarded by both upper and middle classes as having achieved a happy adjustment of conflicting interests. The two classes—the aristocratic landlords and the industrial capitalists—found that it was to their mutual interest to work together. Landlords and country gentlemen represented the agricultural and rural areas; the prosperous industrialists and businessmen represented the urban districts. Dismayed at first by the repeal of the Corn Laws, the landlords were delighted to find that increased demand for agricultural products actually resulted in increased profits. Landlords and manufacturers, a sober and optimistic oligarchy—stern in morals, precisely correct in manners, reasonably humanitarian in outlook, traditionally business-minded—set the standard for Victorian life.

Reform Bill of 1867. Although Chartism had been suppressed, its ideas had made a deep impression on the British people. In the 1860's the issue of electoral reform again became sharpened. Something had to be done, and quickly, to relieve the discontent among unemployed British workers. This time the question of reform was not between political parties but between proponents and opponents within the parties. After the Liberal Russell—Gladstone ministry of 1865–1866 failed to put through a reform bill, it was succeeded by the Conservative Derby—Disraeli ministry of 1866–1868. To show the workers that Conservatives offered them greater concessions than Liberals, Lord Derby, leader of the Lords, and Disraeli, leader of the Commons, introduced a new suffrage bill.

The Reform Bill of 1867 gave the vote for the first time to all householders in the boroughs, and to lodgers who paid not less than £10 a year rent for unfurnished rooms. In the counties the franchise was given to tenants-at-will of property worth a rental of £12 a year and to leaseholders or copyholders of land worth a rental of £5 a year. Again there was a redistribution of seats: the remaining rotten boroughs were abolished and additional boroughs were reduced from two seats to one in the House of Commons.

This was the second installment of British democracy. The activities of the Chartists had been energetically suppressed, but in the usual British way substantial concessions were made to their demands. The suffrage was still far from universal. Under the Reform Bill of 1867, and two identical acts passed in 1868 for Scotland and Ireland, the electorate was increased from roughly 1,000,000 to 2,000,000. The agricultural laborers and miners were still deprived of suffrage.

⤙ KEY DOCUMENT ⤚

THE ENGLISH REFORM BILLS OF 1832 AND 1867

EARLY NINETEENTH-CENTURY England was burdened by an archaic electoral and representative system. The Reform Act of 1832, passed only after a fierce struggle, eliminated rotten boroughs or made them smaller, gave the franchise to tenant farmers and merchants, and provided representation for the larger cities of northern England. The Representation of the People Act of 1867, "the second installment of democracy" gave the vote to the artisans in the boroughs and abolished the remaining rotten boroughs. Following are the key provisions of the two major English Reform Acts of the nineteenth century.

A. The Reform Act of 1832 [1]

An act to amend the representation of the people in England and Wales. Whereas it is expedient to take effectual measures for correcting divers abuses that have long prevailed in the choice of members to serve in the commons house of parliament; to deprive many inconsiderable places of the right of returning members; to grant such privilege to large, populous, and wealthy towns; to increase the number of knights of the shire; to extend the elective franchise to many of his majesty's subjects who have not heretofore enjoyed the same; and to diminish

[1] *Statutes of the United Kingdom*, LXII, 154 ff., 2 William IV, ch. 45.

the expense of elections: be it therefore enacted that each of the boroughs enumerated in the schedule marked A to this act annexed [56 boroughs] shall, from and after the end of this present parliament, cease to return any member or members to serve in parliament.

And be it enacted that each of the boroughs enumerated in the schedule marked B [30 boroughs] shall return one member and no more to serve in parliament.

And be it enacted that each of the places named in the schedule marked C [22 places] shall for the purpose of this act be a borough, and shall return two members to serve in parliament.

And be it enacted that each of the places named in the schedule marked D [20 places] shall for the purpose of this act be a borough, and shall return one member to serve in parliament. . . .

And be it enacted that every male person of full age and not subject to any legal incapacity, who shall be seised at law or in equity of any lands or tenements of copyhold, or any other tenure whatever except freehold, for his own life or for the life of another or for any lives whatsoever . . . , of the clear yearly value of not less than £10 . . . shall be entitled to vote in the election of a knight or knights of the shire. . . .

And be it enacted, that every male person of full age, and not subject to any legal incapacity, who shall be entitled, either as lessee or assignee, to any lands or tenements . . . for the unexpired residue . . . of any term originally created for a period of not less than sixty years . . . of the clear yearly value of not less than £10 . . . , or for the unexpired residue . . . of any term originally created for a period of not less than twenty years . . . of the clear yearly value of not less than £50, or who shall occupy as tenant any lands or tenements for which he shall be *bonâ fide* liable to a yearly rent of not less than £50, shall be entitled to vote in the election of a knight or knights of the shire. . . .

And be it enacted, that in every city or borough which shall return a member or members to serve in any future parliament, every male person of full age, and not subject to any legal incapacity, who shall occupy within such city or borough . . . , as owner or tenant, any house, . . . or other building, . . . of the clear yearly value of not less than £10 shall, if duly registered . . . , be entitled to vote in the election of a member or members to serve in any future parliament for such city or borough. . . .

And be it enacted that . . . all booths erected for the convenience to taking polls shall be erected at the joint and equal expense of the several candidates. . . .

. . . Nothing in this act contained shall . . . in any wise affect the election of members to serve in parliament for the universities of Oxford or Cambridge.

B. *The Reform Act of 1867*
Representation of the People Act, 1867[2]

Every man shall, in and after the year 1868, be entitled to be registered as a voter and, when registered, to vote for a member or members to serve in parliament for a borough, who is qualified as follows: that is to say, (1) is of full age, and not subject to any legal incapacity; and (2) is on the last day of July in any year and has during the preceding twelve calendar months been an inhabitant occupier, as owner or tenant, of any dwelling-house within the borough; and (3) has during the time of such occupation been rated as an ordinary occupier in respect of the premises so occupied by him within the borough to all rates, if any, made for the relief of the poor in respect of such premises; and (4) has, on or before the twentieth day of July in the same year, *bonâ fide* paid an equal amount in the pound to that payable by other ordinary occupiers in respect of all poor rates that have become payable by him in respect of the said premises up to the preceding fifth day of January. Provided, that no man shall under this section be entitled to be registered as a voter by reason of his being a joint occupier of any dwelling-house.

Every man shall, in and after the year 1868, be entitled to be registered as a voter and, when registered, to vote for a member or members to serve in parliament for a borough, who is qualified as follows: that is to say, (1) is of full age and not subject to any legal incapacity; and (2) as a lodger has occupied in the same borough separately and as sole tenant for the twelve months preceding the last day of July in any year the same lodgings, such lodgings being part of one and the same dwelling-house, and of a clear yearly value, if let unfurnished, of £10 or upwards; and (3) has resided in such lodgings during the twelve months immediately preceding the last day of July, and has claimed to be registered as a voter at the next ensuing registration of voters. . . .

From and after the end of present parliament, no borough which had a population less than 10,000 at the census of 1861 shall return more than one member to serve in parliament. . . .

[2] *Public General Statutes*, II, 1082 ff., 30–31 Victoria, ch. 102.

❧ HISTORICAL INTERPRETATION ❧

GEORGE MACAULAY TREVELYAN ON THE REFORM BILL OF 1832

George Macaulay Trevelyan, *British History in the Nineteenth Century and After: 1782-1919*, 2nd ed. (New York and London, 1937), pp. 235–239. By permission of David McKay Company, Inc., and Longmans, Green and Co., Ltd.

THE FOLLOWING selection, written by George Macaulay Trevelyan (1876–1962), presents an explanation of how the Reform Bill of 1832 was passed. This passage reveals the constitutional method used in England in bringing about political change.

The Whigs had made a bad start. But when on March 1, 1831, Lord John Russell introduced the Reform Bill into Commons, and revealed the well-kept secret that all the "nomination" boroughs were to be abolished, without compensation to the borough-owners, Ministers sprang to the summit of popularity at a single bound. The Tories were dumbfounded. They had confidently expected a weak measure, buying up a few of the rotten borough seats to give them to a few great cities: such a Bill would have left the nation cold and the reformers divided; lacking support from outside, it could pass the House only by agreement, after being further whittled down. . . .

The anger and amazement of Opposition were shared in a less degree by many of the Government's supporters in the Commons, who relished their position as privileged senators of the modern Rome, and had no wish to become mere elected persons in a paradise of Benthamite utility. If, as soon as Russell had sat down, Peel had moved the rejection of the "revolutionary measure" on first reading, it was believed that the Bill would have been lost. But the Opposition, having come to the House expecting something very different, had no plan ready, and Peel's genius did not lie in dramatic moves and light-ning decisions. The opportunity was let slip. As the second reading debate dragged on night after night, many who had at first been doubtful or hostile, were converted by the unmistakable evi-dences of the national will. Three weeks after its introduction the Bill passed its second reading by one vote, in the most exciting division since the Grand Remonstrance.

A defeat in Committee soon narrowed the issue to a choice between a new Ministry with a much modified Bill, or a General Election to save Bill and Ministry together. . . .

The General Election was almost as onesided and enthusiastic, so far as popular opinion was concerned, as the elections for the Restoration Parliament. The Reformers carried almost all the open constituencies, including 74 English county seats out of 80. But no amount of popular in-timidation could shake the hold of the proprietors on the nomination seats. In their last Parliament the rotten borough members voted two to one against the Bill, in much the same numbers as before the election.

But there was now a majority of 136 for the Bill. It passed through the Commons that summer under Lord Althorp's patient management in Committee, and went up to the Lords, where it was thrown out on second reading by a majority of 41 votes.

Under the old system of government, the aver-age Englishman had had so little to do with politics that he was taken by surprise at this perfectly inevitable event, which had been long anticipated in Parliamentary circles. The popular enthusiasm, suddenly brought up against an ob-stacle which it had not expected and could at first see no legal way to remove, exploded in out-rages against bishops and peers who had voted against the Bill. A single false step by the Ministers might have precipitated anarchy. The Army, smaller than at any other period in our modern annals, was insufficient to keep order in England and Scotland, in addition to its usual task in Ireland. Peel's police as yet only existed in London. It was impossible to raise volunteer forces to put down Reform mobs. The workmen in the North were drilling and arming to fight the Lords. In the South the ricks were blazing night after night. Unemployment and starvation urged desperate deeds. The first visitation of cholera added to the gloom and terror of the winter of 1831–1832.

Employers and City men clamoured more loudly every week for a creation of peers to pass the Bill and save social order. The working classes, if it came to blows, would fight not for this Bill of the Ten Pound householders, but for a Bill that enfranchised their own class, and for much else besides. Civil strife, if it came, might easily degenerate into a war between "haves" and "have nots." The Bill seemed the sheet-anchor of society. . . .

Grey kept his head. He neither resigned nor, as the King urged, whittled down the Bill. On the other hand he refused, in spite of the remonstrance of the leading members of his Cabinet, to force the King to a premature decision about peer-making, before the time came when circumstances would be too strong for William's reluctance.

Before Christmas a new Bill was introduced, modified in detail to meet some reasonable criticisms and to save the face of the "waverers" among the peers, but not weakened as a democratic measure. It quickly passed the Commons, and was accepted by nine votes on the second reading in the Lords.

The final crisis, known as the "Days of May," was provoked by an attempt of the Lords to take the Bill out of the hands of the Ministers in charge, and amend it in their own way. This was countered by the resignation of the Cabinet. Resignation in the previous autumn, when the Lords had thrown the Bill right out, would have produced anarchy. Now it secured and hastened the last stages of a journey of which the goal was already in sight. . . .

Grey had resigned because the King refused to create peers. But William was now prepared to do anything short of that to get the Bill through intact. He appealed to Wellington to form a Tory Ministry for the purpose of carrying "the Bill, the whole Bill, and nothing but the Bill" through the House of Lords—on the precedent of Catholic Emancipation three years before. The most fearless, if not always the wisest, of public servants accepted this extraordinary commission, the nature of which was not understood in the country, where people naturally supposed that the victor of Waterloo, who had pronounced against all Reform, was coming back to rule them by the sword. If Wellington had succeeded in forming a Ministry, the Political Unions would have led resistance, with what result it is impossible to say. But the actual cause of the Duke's abandoning the task was not his fear of popular resistance, but the refusal of Peel and the Tories in the House of Commons to take part in a scheme so absurd and dangerous, no longer with a hope of modifying the Bill, but solely to save the face of the Lords. The King was obliged to come to terms with Grey, and could only get him back by a written promise to create any number of peers necessary to carry the Bill. The threat, when known in the Upper House sufficed, and the Reform Bill became law.

❧ TEN BASIC BOOKS ❧

CONSTITUTIONAL REFORM IN NINETEENTH-CENTURY ENGLAND, 1815–1867

1. Bagehot, Walter, *The English Constitution,* The World's Classics (London, 1952, R. 1966).†

2. Chrimes, Stanley B., *English Constitutional History,* 3rd ed. (New York, 1965).

3. Halévy, Élie, *History of the English People in the Nineteenth Century,* 2nd rev. ed., 6 vols. (London, 1949–1952).†

4. Hammond, John, and Barbara Hammond, *The Age of the Chartists, 1832–1854: A Study of Discontent* (London, 1930).

5. Keir, David, *The Constitutional History of Modern Britain, 1485–1951* (London, 1955).

6. Kitson-Clark, George, *The Making of Victorian England* (Cambridge, Mass., 1962).

7. Thomson, David, *England in the Nineteenth Century*, Penguin Book (Baltimore, 1950).†

8. Trevelyan, George Macaulay, *British History in the Nineteenth Century and After: 1782–1919*, 2nd ed. (New York and London, 1937).†

9. Woodward, Ernest L., *The Age of Reform, 1815–1870*, 2nd ed. (New York, 1962).

10. Young, George Malcolm, *Victorian England: Portrait of an Age*, 2nd ed. (New York, 1953).

24

France: From Monarchy to Empire, 1815-1870

HIS RUTHLESS host is bought with plunder'd gold,
By lying priests the peasants' votes controll'd;
    All freedom vanish'd
    The true men banish'd,
He triumphs; maybe, we shall stand alone.
    Britons, guard your own. . . .

We hate not France, but France has lost her voice,
This man is France, the man they call her choice.
    By tricks and spying,
    By craft and lying,
And murder was her freedom overthrown.
    Britons, guard your own.

'*Vive l'Empereur*' may follow bye and bye;
'God save the Queen' is here a truer cry.
    God save the Nation,
    The toleration,
And the free speech that makes a Briton known.
    Britons, guard your own.

—ALFRED, LORD TENNYSON, British Poet Laureate, "Denunciation of Napoleon III," published anonymously two months after the *coup d'état* of December 2, 1851

1. Reaction: Restoration of the Bourbons, 1815–1830

Inner Political Spirit of Nineteenth-Century France. Britain's Victorian Compromise, with its keynote of moderation, gave her comparative freedom from domestic political turmoil. But all during the nineteenth century two Frances were gripped in bitter conflict—the Left and Right. The struggle was between those who accepted and those who rejected the Revolution. There was no sense of compromise between these two intransigent and mutually hostile parties—between, on the one side, radical republicans and Bonapartists who sought to perpetuate revolutionary ideas, and, on the other side, reactionary ultraroyalists craving revenge for the excesses of the Revolution.

The story of France since 1815 is a history of change and revolutions in which the mass of people had little or no interest. It is a story of governments without popular support maintaining themselves in power only because their opponents could not agree on any common policy. It is a history in which change was brought about not by the give-and-take of parliamentary discussion but by the repeated cry of ambitious leaders: "To the barricades!" The White Terror of 1815, the Revolution of 1830, the June Days of 1848 with a new Reign of Terror, the *coup d'état* of 1851, the bloody Paris Commune of 1871, all reveal a national inability to resist sudden political change.

The Restoration. The cleft between Left and Right revealed itself clearly during the Restoration era from 1815 to 1830 in the form of a struggle between the Bourbon dynasty, seeking to revive Old Regime absolutism, and the bourgeois liberals, who wanted to keep the revolutionary gains. Louis XVIII (r. 1814–1824), easy-going brother of the guillotined Louis XVI, was restored to the throne within three weeks after Waterloo. A rare Bourbon, who had learned something from the past, Louis XVIII tried to bring about an orderly transition from absolutism to constitutional monarchy. He was determined to rule as a liberal sovereign. In his view the new *charte*, establishing constitutional government, was his own free gift to the people, not a charter of liberties extracted from the Crown. He would give the constitution a fair trial. He supported many political and social measures of the revolutionary era, including the Concordat, the Code Napoléon, the Imperial University, and the Legion of Honor. He agreed with those substantial concessions to civil liberty made in the *charte*—equality of all before the law irrespective of rank, freedom of speech, press, and religion, and protection against arbitrary arrest. This was liberal Bourbonism in action: the reasonable king understood well that he had been awarded the throne not by the will of his own people but by the Allied armies. He would be discreet enough to maintain the position of the Crown.

Revanche: **The White Terror.** Louis XVIII was unable to satisfy his closest followers—the Ultras, the royalist *émigrés* who had flocked back from exile on news of the restoration. Their thirst for revenge against democratic enemies was insatiable. At their head was the king's brother, the Count of Artois, the kind of Bourbon who never learned anything from the past and never forgot anything.

Encouraged by the elections of August 22, 1815, in which royalists and clericals won an overwhelming victory, the Ultras stepped up the campaign against all those who had been prominent in the revolutionary era. The White Terror, an orgy of legalized murder, began in Paris and then spread throughout France. Marshal Michel Ney (1769–1815), who had deserted Louis XVIII and turned to Napoleon during the Hundred Days after Elba, was executed in the midst of this new blood bath.

Louis XVIII was appalled by the excesses of the Ultras, but unwilling after a long exile to "go on his travels" again, he drifted with the tide. He dissolved the Chamber in September 1816, called for new elections, and happily noted the return of a majority of moderate royalists. But the issue was not settled. On February 13, 1820, the duc de Berri, second in direct line of succession to the throne, was assassinated by an obscure fanatic. Shocked and angered, Louis became reconciled to the counter-revolutionary movement. Returned to power, the Ultras, without any strong opposition from the king, suspended individual liberties, began a vigorous press censorship, revised the electoral laws to favor the rich, and surrendered control of education to the clergy. This was the beginning of the reaction that was to end only with the Revolution of 1830.

Search for Prestige: Spanish Expedition, 1823. Despite political unrest, France recovered slowly from the exhaustion of the Napoleonic wars. Meanwhile, the old irrepressible urge to promote French aims beyond the borders of France emerged again. Not content with the restoration of a Bourbon to the throne, a secret clerical society, the Congregation, urged French armed support for the Bourbon Ferdinand VII, who had been exiled from Spain. With support from the Holy Alliance, a French army invaded Spain, restored Ferdinand as monarch, and watched as he abolished the constitution and revived absolutism in its Spanish form. The success of the Spanish expedition insured the loyalty of the army to the Bourbon monarchy, but it enraged French liberals and radicals.

Hiatus: Reign of Charles X. When Louis XVIII died in 1824, he was succeeded by his brother, the Count of Artois, as Charles X (r. 1824–1830). Charles believed with utter sincerity that divine-right monarchy was the greatest form of government ever conceived and that the aristocracy was the only class worthy of ruling society. Hastily and efficiently, he restored ancient privileges to nobility and clergy. A Law of Indemnity (1826), which he sponsored, compensated the *émigrés* for their lost property with a billion francs, thus arousing the enmity of the bourgeoisie. He pleased the nobility by calling for a return of primogeniture. He delighted clericals by sponsoring a law against sacrilege. Favoring the "priest-party" in politics, he set off a bitter struggle between royalist clericalism and republican anticlericalism. Catholic support of the monarchy was so strong that the words Catholic and royalist became almost synonymous.

The return to reaction antagonized not only businessmen but also intellectuals and workers. The upper bourgeoisie was represented by a new political group, the *doctrinaires,* dedicated to the task of wresting political control from the aristocrats. Led by Pierre Paul Royer-Collard (1763–1845), philosopher-statesman, and François Guizot (1787–1874), historian-statesman, the *doctrinaires* were liberal monarchists and champions of constitutional government who wanted a moderate compromise between Revolution and Restoration.

2. Conflict: The Revolution of 1830

July Ordinances. Charles X revealed a peculiar inability to satisfy anyone other than the Ultras. The *doctrinaires* preferred the mechanism of constitutional government as it operated in Britain. Bourgeois bondholders objected to the king's financial concern for the *émigrés.* Anticlericals were angered by his efforts to restore a unified Church. Intellectuals demanded an end to Charles' favoritism for the old feudal aristocracy. Workers demanded relief from the system of iron repression. Even the Chamber of Deputies challenged the king's right to suppress it. It was

"France is tranquil." A satirical cartoon depicts the restraint of the press, one of the conditions that led to the Revolution of 1830.

obvious that Charles intended to disregard the *charte* altogether and that he was headed straight back to the old absolutism. On July 26, 1830, he issued a series of arbitrary decrees known as the July Ordinances which (1) suspended freedom of the press; (2) dissolved the newly elected Chamber of Deputies; (3) established a new electoral system disfranchising three-fourths of the voters, including the liberal bourgeoisie; and (4) called for new elections in September.

To the Barricades: The July Days. These ordinances stirred Parisians into action. Liberal printers and journalists demanded immediate action. Cries resounded through Paris: "Up with the Charter!" "Down with the government!" "To the barricades!" The Chamber of Deputies protested that the July Ordinances were "directly contrary to the constitutional rights of the Chamber of Peers, to the public law of the French, to the prerogatives and decrees of the tribunals, and calculated to throw the whole state into a confusion which would compromise both present peace and future security." Liberal owners closed their factories and shops and sent their workers to the streets. The workers, wearing the tricolor and singing the *Marseillaise*, rushed to the barricades made of paving stones, old furniture, wagons, and debris. Royal troops, ill-prepared, feebly led, and sympathizing with the rioters, found it impossible to advance through the narrow, crooked streets. The rebellion lasted three days, with only slight bloodshed. But Charles X abdicated in favor of his young grandson, the comte de Chambord, and fled to England bearing the white Bourbon flag with him into exile.

Significance of the Revolution. The abdication of Charles X meant the end of divine-right monarchy and feudal aristocracy in France. Liberalism had defeated reaction. But almost at once a heated debate arose on the nature of the political system to take the place of the old. Once again a revolutionary struggle had been won by a combination of bourgeoisie and proletariat. The workers had done the fighting in the streets, but again they were to see the better-organized middle class monopolize the fruits of victory. The proletariat wanted a democratic republic, the bourgeoisie favored a constitutional monarchy. The bourgeois liberals were quite content to accept another king provided that he recognized their right to rule the country.

Louis Philippe, Citizen King. The choice of the middle-class liberals for the throne was Louis Philippe, duke of Orléans, from the younger branch of the Bourbon dynasty, the son of that Philippe Égalité who had voted for the execution of Louis XVI. Louis Philippe's credentials were good. He had been present at the burning of the Bastille, he had been a member of the Jacobin Club, and he had held military office under the republic. He was supported by the aged Lafayette, hero of France, who had assumed leadership of democratic republican forces. On August 7, 1830, a rump parliament proclaimed Louis Philippe King of the French. The title was significant: by accepting this designation, instead of "King of France," Louis Philippe acknowledged the sovereignty of the people. He would be the champion of constitutional monarchy.

Happy with this unexpected appointment, Louis Philippe decided to become the model of a modern "bourgeois king," or "citizen king." He had already adopted such middle-class customs as sending his sons to public schools, and he had endorsed the writings of Voltaire and Rousseau. Now he restored the tricolor red, white, and blue cockade, symbol of revolution, and declared the people to be "citizens not subjects." He appeared in public with his famous green umbrella. But behind this mask of bourgeois respectability he hid a determination to restore the authority of the Crown. He carefully reminded the people of the past glory of France. He declared Napoleon "a great Frenchman" and ordered that the conqueror's bones be brought back to Paris. He covered the walls of the palace at Versailles with paintings commemorating the great battles of France. Both Bonapartists and Ultras were encouraged by these evidences of a kindred spirit.

Constitution of 1830. The new constitution, accepted willingly by Louis Philippe, was a modification of the Charter of 1814. The liberal bourgeois monarchy was modeled upon that of Britain. The king reigned but did not rule. The cabinet was responsible to parliament. Parliament in theory represented the nation but actually was chosen by a small minority of the people. Property qualifications were lowered and the number of voters was raised from 94,000 to 188,000 (in a population of approximately 30,000,000). Political power passed from the landed aristocracy to the upper bourgeoisie. Essentially a middle-class creation, the constitution virtually excluded the workingmen from the suffrage. But personal liberty, equality before the law, and freedom of press, assembly, and religion were guaranteed, and conscription was abolished.

Political Activism in the Bourgeois Monarchy. From its beginning Louis Philippe's regime was beset by political chaos. Bourgeois leaders, although determined to maintain the monarchy, found it difficult to work together. They disagreed on the extent of royal power and on the problem of liberalizing legislative procedures. On the Extreme Right were the Ultras, demanding a return to the era of feudal privilege. In the Right Center, a party of resistance supported the right of the king to share in governing, and stubbornly resisted all efforts at reform. In the Left Center, a party of action held that the king should reign but not rule, and demanded electoral and legislative reform. On the Extreme Left were the Utopian Socialists, who urged that the political structure be altered to give the working class a rightful share in government. Louis Philippe took advantage of these sharp political differences not only to consolidate his own position but also to extend his personal power.

Historians as Politicians. The period of the bourgeois monarchy was remarkable for the number of historians who played key roles in its development. The main spokesman of bourgeois liberalism, the party of resistance, was the historian-statesman, François Guizot (1787–1874), author of a well-known history of civilization. He served as minister of public instruction from 1832 to 1839, and as premier from 1840 to 1848. A devout Huguenot Calvinist, critical of the kind of popular movement that had put his father to death, he was convinced that the bourgeoisie was not simply a class but the people at its best. He opposed clerical reform on the ground that it would give political power to the economically unfit. Personally honest, he nevertheless countenanced graft and corruption to maintain his own power. His political line was a moderate course between reaction and revolution. Reformers were unable to pierce the hard rock of his ministry, dedicated to "peace and no reform."

Louis Adolphe Thiers (1797–1877), who wrote extensively on the French Revolution and, the Napoleonic era, was an ambitious, self-made liberal who distrusted the masses from which he had risen. He had a romantic attitude toward great men in history, especially Napoleon Bonaparte. Leader of the party of action, he held several positions in the cabinet, and became premier in 1840.

Spokesman for the democratic liberals was Alexis de Tocqueville (1805–1859), author of a classic analysis of American democracy. Opposed not only to absolute monarchy but also to capitalist oligarchy, Tocqueville supported manhood suffrage as the only legitimate source of political power. He was elected vice-president of the Assembly in 1849, but was dismissed when Louis Napoleon became emperor.

Louis Philippe's Foreign Policy. Louis Philippe dreamed of a France restored to a dominant position as arbiter of European affairs. He vacillated between an urge to promote peace in Europe and the more traditional aim of upholding the national glory and honor of France. He was careful to follow the British in such policies as establishing the independent kingdom of Belgium, and maintaining the *status quo* in the Near East by taking a position supporting the Russian tsar on the one side and the pasha of Egypt on the other. Some Frenchmen accused Louis Philippe of being a weak vassal of Great Britain. It was partly to answer this criticism that the king encouraged French intervention in North Africa. He sent French troops to repress Abd-el-Kader and to conquer Algeria, the opening step in creating a new French colonial empire.

Bourgeois Monarchy and Industrial Revolution. Louis Philippe encouraged industry by importing machinery from England and establishing new factories and foundries. Beginning in 1842, he stimulated the construction of a national system of railways administered by chartered companies with generous governmental subsidies. Industry did not develop in France as fast as in England because of several factors: insufficient coal; the small urban population; lack of a supply of cheap labor; and persistence in accenting such luxury industries as silks, wines, laces, tapestries, porcelains, and women's fashions. In 1846–1847 a severe agricultural and industrial depression led to widespread unemployment and misery among the farmers and workers. Louis Philippe paid more attention to men of means: like Henry IV before him, Louis Philippe created a new *noblesse de la robe* by awarding titles of nobility to rich merchants, manufacturers, and speculators.

Crystallization of Opposition. Louis Philippe's liberal monarchy had slight popular support and, unlike that of Britain, little stability. Nearly all parties in the country eventually came to oppose the king. The Ultras, still attached to the Old Regime, regarded Louis Philippe as "king of the barricades" and "usurper of the Crown," and proposed Charles X's grandson, the comte de Chambord, as the legitimate king. Catholics were angered by the king's attachment to the anticlerical University and by his refusal to support Catholic education. Republicans criticized him for his preference for the moneyed upper bourgeoisie and his distaste for popular government. Intellectuals accused him of not understanding the need for social reform. Socialists, disappointed by his unwillingness to recognize the rights of labor, urged his abdication. Finally,

Bonapartists, recalling the glorious memory of Napoleon, denounced the king for his "peace at any price" policy and demanded the restoration of the Napoleonic dynasty in the person of Louis Napoleon, nephew of the emperor. All this combined hostility led eventually to the political explosion of 1848.

3. Watershed: The Revolution of 1848

The February Revolution in Paris. Discontent with Louis Philippe's regime came to a head early in 1848. Republicans and Socialists, equally critical of the do-nothing government and impatient for reform, began to work together. Agitators drew up petitions and organized mass meetings. Guizot's opponents in the Assembly planned, in the English fashion, a series of public banquets to call attention to their demands. These banquets were but thinly disguised political rallies. One was scheduled for February 22, 1848. Fearful of the effects emotional oratory might have on the people, Guizot forbade the meeting. Protesting crowds marched and shouted in the streets. The next

Student demonstrators are shown passing the Madeleine on their way to the Chamber of Deputies, February 22, 1848. This picture appeared four days later in the *Illustrated London News*.

day Louis Philippe dismissed Guizot, which satisfied the middle class but not the workers. Then came the spark that set off the explosion: someone fired a shot which was returned by a volley from nervous troops of the National Guard. Sixteen people were killed. What started out as a riot changed into a revolution. Huge crowds carried the bodies through Paris in a torchlight parade. On February 24, like Charles X before him, Louis Philippe abdicated. Disguised as a Mr. Smith, he fled to England, traditional refuge of discredited French royalty.

Provisional Government. Republicans and Socialists now joined to proclaim France a republic. A Provisional Government included representatives of both Republicans and Socialists, working in uneasy partnership. The Moderate Republicans, the right wing, led by the poet-historian and politician Alphonse de Lamartine (1790–1869), favored a bourgeois republic. The Radical Republicans, under Alexandre Ledru-Rollin (1807–1874), were extreme democrats who called for a return of the Terror. The left-wing Socialists, led by the theorist Louis Blanc (1811–1882), demanded abolition of private property and a new social order.

The Provisional Government, intimidated by armed Parisian workers, issued one decree after another. Its first proclamation denounced the late government which had "left behind it trails of blood, which will forever forbid its return." Other declarations, ground out at top speed, guaranteed work to all citizens, established universal suffrage, opened the ranks of the National Guard to all citizens, eliminated the Chamber of Peers, voided all titles of nobility, and abolished slavery in all the colonies "as an outrage against human dignity."

Louis Blanc and the National Workshops. Louis Blanc, Socialist author of *The Organization of Labor* (1839), hoped to establish an industrial republic. He would organize the unemployed of Paris into socialized workshops, complete with companies and squads, to construct railway stations, improve navigation facilities and, in general, be busy with public projects. The product of the workshops

would be divided among the workers on the principle of "from each according to his capacity and to each according to his need." But the Provisional Government entrusted the Ministry of Public Works to Pierre Thomas Marie, a personal and political enemy of Blanc. The appointment was obviously intended to discredit the whole idea. Instead of socialist workshops (*ateliers sociaux*), state-supported cooperative productive societies, which Blanc favored, Marie proposed national workshops (*ateliers nationaux*). The plan was doomed to failure from the start. Marie regarded the experiment merely as a temporary measure to distribute relief to the masses and to humor the workers during a time of severe unemployment.

The June Days, 1848. Two months after the proclamation of the Second Republic, Frenchmen went to the polls to elect a National Constituent Assembly. The results revealed that provincial voters were little impressed by the events in Paris: the Assembly was about one-half republican, one-third royalist, and only one-tenth socialist, clearly no mandate for radicalism. When the Moderate Republicans and the royalists in combination voted to dissolve the national workshops, infuriated Parisian radicals, shouting that they had been betrayed, thronged to the barricades. For the first time since 1789 a popular uprising was confronted with a government strong enough to defend itself. In the bloody street fighting, which lasted for three days (June 23 to 26), General Louis Cavaignac (1802–1857), acting as republican dictator *pro tempore*, and leading a well-equipped National Guard, reduced the workshop army at the barricades. The victory cost 5,000 lives in some of the bloodiest street fighting Europe had ever seen. Workers were killed, executed, or deported to the colonies. As a political factor of importance, socialism disappeared for a generation.

Constitution of 1848. The new constitution, returning to the ideals of the early Revolution, declared France a democratic republic dedicated to protection of "family, labor, property, and public order." Executive power was vested in a president directly elected by universal manhood suffrage to serve for not more than one term of four years. Legislative power was placed in a single body of 750 members elected for three years. In separating executive and legislative powers, the constitution opened the way to differences between both. Unfortunately, the first president turned out to be more for himself than for the republic. The Legislative Assembly, by omitting to make the scions of all former ruling dynasties ineligible for office, opened the way for Bonapartists to come to political power.

Historical Controversy: The Second French Republic—Liberal, or Democratic-Social? In the France of 1848 the revolutionists agreed that a republic was necessary, but they disagreed on whether it was to be a "liberal republic" or a "democratic-social republic." De Lamartine was considered "the man of France" in the February revolution. As a leader of the Moderate Republicans, he had a glorified view of the earlier First French Republic. By the "people" he meant all Frenchmen, and he begged Frenchmen to become unified in one Fatherland. On the other hand, Louis Blanc demanded the creation of a democratic-social republic, meaning that the socialists were to take over the revolution and make the red flag the new official emblem. He criticized Lamartine's attempt to achieve general reconciliation: "In the long run, Lamartine is afraid of socialism, that great reality, as children are afraid of phantoms." Because the forces of liberalism were divided over political and social questions, they were unable to resist Louis Napoleon's attack from the Extreme Right or the assaults from the revolutionary radicals on the Extreme Left.

4. Mark Time: Louis Napoleon Bonaparte and the Second French Republic, 1848–1852

Louis Napoleon Bonaparte. Prince Louis Napoleon (1808–1873), son of Louis Bonaparte, brother of Napoleon I, was related to the great emperor by ties of blood. After the collapse of the Empire, he had an adventurous career abroad, first with the *Carbonari* in Italy and then in England as a special constable to suppress the Chartist rioters. In a series of writings he described his own political doctrines, which praised the Napoleonic Empire as the perfect realization of the principles of 1789, as a government solidified by ingenious leadership, and as a state resting upon a foundation of national sovereignty. Several times during the regime of Louis Philippe he sought to organize growing Bonapartist sentiment; in 1836 he was arrested and exiled to America, and in 1840 he was taken into custody and condemned to life imprisonment in Ham Fortress. In 1846 he escaped from prison in the guise of a workingman and made his way to England. The stirring February Days of 1848 made possible his return to France.

The people of France were ready for a new champion of "nationalism, law, and order." The aristocracy saw in Louis Napoleon its best chance for survival. The bourgeoisie, frightened by the specter of socialism, looked to the Napoleonic name as a symbol of order and security. The peasantry, alienated by the revolutionary workmen of Paris, yearned for a return to the good old days. Even the Parisian workmen were willing to have a president who would control all classes, reduce privileges for the rich, and treat the dispossessed with greater fairness. Added to these were the veterans who remembered the days of glory. "Why should I not vote for Louis Napoleon?" asked one, "I, whose nose was frozen at Moscow?"

Historical Plagiarism. Louis Napoleon, proud of his heritage, was a strange combination of egoist and politician, of realist and mystic. He had faith in his own destiny. "I believe," he said, "that from time to time men are created whom I call providential, in whose hands the destinies of their countries are placed. I believe myself to be one of those men." The first Napoleon had prescribed the pattern of "Caesarism" in its modern form. The First French Republic set up in 1792 had ended in dictatorship, with Bonaparte making himself

Emperor of the French. The question now was whether or not his nephew, heir of the Napoleonic tradition, would seek to re-create the earlier experiment. His uncle, said Louis Napoleon, had been a faithful servant of the Revolution, but "tyrant kings" had combined against him and thwarted his real aim of solidifying revolutionary principles. Much work remained to be accomplished. "I represent for you," Louis Napoleon told the French people, "a principle, a cause, a defeat. The principle

1848: Daumier caricatures the arrival in France of Louis Napoleon, riding to power on his uncle's legendary fame.

is the sovereignty of the people; the cause is that of the Empire; the defeat is Waterloo." Some denounced Louis Napoleon as a dangerous adventurer. Louis Blanc prophesied a new "despotism without the glory." Victor Hugo dubbed him "Napoleon the Little."

President of the Second French Republic, 1848–1851. In June 1848 Louis Napoleon was elected to the National Constituent Assembly. In the presidential elections of December 10, 1848 he received 5,327,345 votes; his opponents, including General Cavaignac, 1,879,345. Frenchmen of all opinions—liberals and democrats, radicals and reactionaries, patriots all—had raised the nephew of the great Napoleon to power in the Second Republic. His success surprised France and startled all Europe.

With his foot on the ladder, Napoleon began to climb while playing one political faction against the other. He appointed a cabinet dominated by Orléanists even though most members of the National Assembly were re-

publicans. With consummate shrewdness he allowed the members of the Assembly to bear the responsibility for disputed measures. When the Radical Republicans, led by Ledru-Rollin, revolted in 1849, the Assembly enacted a measure disfranchising a third of the population. When the deputies of the Right were asked by the president, posing as defender of the people, to restore the vote to the workers, they fell into the trap and refused. The country was now literally a republic without republicans. While pretending to establish freedom of education, Louis Napoleon, by the Falloux Law of 1850, encouraged the Assembly to hand control of schools to the Catholic Church. He also saw to it that radical journals were muzzled, and required all editors to deposit "caution-money" as a guarantee of good behavior.

Coup d'État of December 2, 1851. Conspirator by preference and vocation, Louis Napoleon secretly prepared the way to greater power. The constitution provided that no president could succeed himself; thus, to continue in power he had a choice of two moves: (1) to change the constitution, which was not likely, or (2) to resort to a coup. Through bribery he obtained control of the army by selecting his minister of war, commander of the National Guard, commander of the Paris garrison, and the prefect of police. He got funds from secret loans, largely from foreign sources. Making semi-royal excursions through the country, he spoke about vague Socialist plots and discreetly praised "my great uncle." The Assembly, unimpressed by his secrecy, and aware of what Louis Napoleon wanted, refused to abrogate the article of the constitution banning his re-election.

In November 1851, still posing as the champion of the people, Louis Napoleon issued an ultimatum to the Assembly calling upon it to establish universal suffrage at once. The Assembly refused. Then Louis Napoleon struck with his well-prepared plan. On the night of December 1, 1851, he arrested his political opponents and seized the printing shops. The next day, December 2, 1851, anniversary of the victory of Napoleon I at the Battle of Austerlitz, Louis Napoleon issued a manifesto pro-claiming a temporary dictatorship, dissolution of the Assembly, restoration of universal man-hood suffrage, and a popular referendum. The people of Paris read incredulously: "The Assembly . . . forges weapons for civil war; it makes an attack upon the authority which I hold directly from the people; it encourages all the evil passions; it puts in jeopardy the repose of France. I have dissolved it, and I will make the whole people judge between them and me."

Massacre of the Boulevards. The people of Paris, indifferent, bored, and tired, showed little enthusiasm. Louis Napoleon had guessed correctly: most Frenchmen would agree to his *coup*. The next day, on December 3, a few barricades were set up. An unlucky accident intervened when nervous patrolling troops heard a shot and started firing on the crowds. This time about 400 Parisians lost their lives in the wholly unnecessary "Massacre of the Boulevards." Louis Napoleon was appalled by the bloodshed, but he was relieved when it was not followed by a general uprising. The army controlled Paris and the country re-mained quiet.

5. *The Second Napoleonic Empire, 1852–1870*

Another Napoleon Proclaimed Emperor. Louis Napoleon was now virtually master of France. He ordered a plebiscite on this state-ment: "The French people desire the main-tenance of the authority of Louis Napoleon Bonaparte, and delegate to him the necessary powers to make a constitution." The result of this "free plebiscite" (in some rural areas the voters were marched to the polls in military fashion) was a seal of approval by 7,500,000 votes against 640,000.

Thus empowered, Louis Napoleon fashioned a new constitution, a travesty of republicanism. In reality it reproduced the imperial constitu-tion of the first Napoleon, though it retained the name of Republic. Louis Napoleon was "responsible to the nation" but he was given "free and unfettered authority." He would

serve as president for ten years, thus restoring the consulate idea, with full power to appoint and dismiss the cabinet. As president, he could appoint the Senate and Council of State, both of which, in the pattern set by his uncle, turned out to be subservient to him. The Legislative Assembly (*Corps législatif*) was to be elected by universal suffrage, but by carefully select-ing candidates Louis Napoleon was able to get a chamber of which fewer than 3 per cent of the members were radicals. In any event, its power was negligible, because all its legis-lation was subject to veto by the Council of State, which was responsible only to the president.

The next step was easy to predict. Louis Napoleon, still President of the Second Re-public, restored the Napoleonic insignia, and toured the provinces to obtain popular sup-port. There were cries of *"Vive l'Empereur!"* Another tricky and decisive plebiscite, this time by a vote of 7,824,000 to 253,000, made it official. On December 2, 1852, Louis Napoleon became in name what he already was in fact: Napoleon III, Emperor of the French. (Al-though he had never reigned and was never crowned, the son of Napoleon I, *"L'Aiglon"* (The Eaglet), was regarded as Napoleon II. He had died in Vienna in 1832 at the age of twenty-one.)

Significance of the New Napoleonic Experi-ment. Fortune had favored the new Napo-leonic adventurer who had pushed his way from exile and ridicule to the throne. Na-poleon III proclaimed to the world that he was the "final flower of the French Revolu-tion." The Bourbon restoration (1815–1830), he said, had been a government of the land-holding aristocracy; the bourgeois monarchy (1830–1848) had represented the middle class; his own Second Empire was "a govern-ment of the people." He, himself, would be the "beneficent motivator of the whole social order." French citizens, torn by strife and hungry for law and order, were willing to entrust him with power because they believed that under his rule France would return to stability and again take a dominant role in European affairs. Twice within half a century

they had experimented with republican democracy and then abandoned it in favor of a
dictatorship. Now, in another Napoleon, they
saw the right man, a strong executive, to fill
the vacuum of power.

Not the least important lesson of the French
experience was the end of the notion that the
common people, if given the vote, would automatically gravitate to Socialist candidates. The
French peasants, each holding his small unit
of property, made it plain that they preferred
a leader to a parliament. Many workers also
made the same choice.

**Despotism: The Autocratic Empire, 1852–
1860.** For eighteen years, from 1852 to 1870,
Louis Napoleon remained the fulcrum of
political force in France, and France again
became the leading power on the Continent.
For eight years, from 1852 to 1860, the Second
Empire was a paralyzing despotism. The
dreamy, generous-minded emperor turned out
to be an unscrupulous autocrat. He controlled
the Assembly by a vote-getting machine; muzzled the press; throttled liberalism in the universities; drove the opposition underground;
jailed or exiled his enemies; distributed patronage to his supporters; did little to root out
graft and corruption; and encouraged political
espionage. He obtained the support of the
clergy by favorable laws. He reestablished the
brilliant imperial court and filled it with loyal
friends. He was the new emperor-boss, the
strong hand in Paris who watched every aspect
of political life to see that his power remained
unchallenged. He gave France the shadow but
not the substance of self-government.

To compensate the people for their lost
liberties, Napoleon III offered them order,
prosperity, and freedom from revolution. He
encouraged trade, industry, and agriculture,
thereby winning the enthusiastic support of
the wealthy, who regarded him as the custodian of their bank balances. At the same
time, he did what he could to improve the lot
of the hitherto neglected working class. He
encouraged charitable foundations, established
hospitals, asylums, and pawnshops, and made
modest beginnings in social legislation. He
sought to arbitrate disputes between capital
and labor. He began a system of great public
works, thus at one blow giving work to the
unemployed Parisian workers whom he feared,
and rebuilding Paris with magnificent buildings, boulevards, and public squares. The
Universal Exhibition of 1855, the first Paris
exposition, proclaimed to the world French
technological and economic progress under
Napoleon III.

Napoleon III described his foreign policy
as *"L'Empire, c'est la paix!"* ("The Empire
means peace.") This was mere boasting. Personally timid, he was not anxious to undertake
dangerous adventures, but he was driven to it
by the Napoleonic name. To insure the support
of people and army, he had to seek military
glory. He encouraged the Crimean War (1853–
1856) even though there was little cause or justification for it. He was angered at Nicholas I,
who had refused to greet him as "my brother"
when he became Emperor of the French, and
he was anxious to ingratiate himself with
French clericals by claiming the right to protect Catholics in the Ottoman Empire. By
taking part in the Crimean War he raised
France once more to a leading role in European politics.

On January 14, 1858, an impatient Italian
named Felice Orsini attempted to assassinate
Napoleon III and the empress. Two persons
were killed and a hundred wounded in the
attentat. The episode initiated Napoleon's interest in Italian affairs. Seeking to emulate his
uncle, he led a French army into Italy to expel
the Austrians.

The Liberal Empire, 1860–1870. By 1860
there was compounding opposition to Napoleon III inside France. Bourgeois industrialists
were angered when, as a concession to Britain,
he began a free-trade policy which exposed
French industry to foreign competition. He
had already forfeited Catholic support by declining to aid the papacy against Italian revolutionaries. He now began to feel that leaning
toward liberalism might bring his dynasty
great rewards. Gradually, he began to grant
concessions to the liberals. He proclaimed an
amnesty for political offenders, and removed
gags from parliament, press, and education. To
obtain working-class support, he encouraged
the formation of trade unions and consumers'

cooperative societies. Discontented opponents, especially industrialists, Catholics, and monarchists, were alienated by these concessions. The election of 1869 brought in a *Corps législatif* in which the opposition was almost as strong as the emperor's party. It was a moral defeat for Napoleon.

The second half of Napoleon III's reign brought a series of humiliating disasters. His meddling in Italian affairs alienated both French and Italian Catholics. He sought to establish a French empire in Mexico, with Archduke Maximilian of Austria, a son of the Archduke Francis Charles, as puppet ruler. This ill-starred adventure ended in 1867 with the execution of Maximilian. Napoleon's defiance of the Monroe Doctrine incurred the hostility of the United States. His relations with Prussia became increasingly strained. The Napoleonic name became tarnished by one diplomatic defeat after another.

Franco-Prussian War and the End of the Empire, 1870. Old and ailing, lashed by aroused opponents, distrusted by the electorate, Napoleon III saw possible salvation in a foreign war. "Unless there is a war," he complained, "my son will never be emperor." Without making adequate preparations, he drifted into a conflict with energetic Prussia. Operating on a collision course with the shrewd and able Bismarck, Napoleon rushed straight into

catastrophe. Taken prisoner at Sedan, he lost both his nerve and his empire. After his release, he fled to England, where he died in 1873.

Historical Controversy: Napoleon III: Caesarian Democrat, or Fascist Dictator? Like his illustrious uncle, Louis Napoleon stimulated diametrically opposed opinions among historians. In 1943 Albert Guérard, in his *Napoleon III,* presented a favorable picture, depicting Louis Napoleon as a true romantic humanitarian of his times, in the spirit of Mazzini, Michelet, and Proudhon. "On the throne and to the great scandal of his fellow sovereigns, he remained attached to the faith he had professed when he was a conspirator and a Utopian publicist. It is not for us to sneer: his ideal was essentially the same as Woodrow Wilson's principle of self-determination." In Guérard's estimate, Napoleon III was a proponent of "Caesarian democracy."

Precisely the opposite point of view was taken by J. Salwyn Schapiro. The organization and policies of the Second Empire bore startling resemblances to the Fascist dictatorships of our time. It was a dictatorship based on popular support as expressed in plebiscites and in "elections." Louis Napoleon conceived the idea of having the entire press used as the mouthpiece of the government, an idea later applied in Fascist dictatorships. His industrial

Bismarck accepts the surrender of Napoleon III at Sedan on September 2, 1870.

councils suggested the Nazi Labor Front; he controlled the workers through the *livret,* or industrial passport; he did little to promote social reform; he ruthlessly suppressed all expressions of opinion hostile to himself. His great aim was to establish a political system based on unity of all classes. Schapiro concludes that Louis Napoleon first created the new type of state in the form of authoritarian plebiscitarian leadership.

ᴏᴄ KEY DOCUMENT ᴄᴏ

FIRST PROCLAMATION OF THE PROVISIONAL GOVERNMENT, FEBRUARY 24, 1848

Annual Register, 1848 (London, 1849), pp. 239–240.

ON FEBRUARY 22, 1848, angry crowds went to the barricades and called for the dismissal of the reactionary Guizot ministry. When the government called out the National Guard, the latter joined the insurgents in their march on the Tuileries. On February 24, 1848, the day of Louis Philippe's abdication, the Provisional Government issued its first proclamation, reprinted below. It was followed by many others defining the new government, providing for electoral reforms, and inaugurating radical social measures.

IN THE NAME OF THE FRENCH PEOPLE!

A retrograde Government has been overturned by the heroism of the people of Paris. This Government has fled, leaving behind it trails of blood, which will for ever forbid its return.

The blood of the people has flowed, as in July; but, happily, it has not been shed in vain. It has secured a national and popular Government, in accordance with the rights, the progress, and the will of this great and generous people.

A Provisional Government, at the call of the people and some Deputies in the sitting of the 24th of February, is for the moment invested with the care of organizing and securing the national victory. It is composed of MM. Dupont (de l'Eure), Lamartine, Crémieux, Arago, Ledru-Rollin, and Garnier Pagès. The Secretaries to this Government are MM. Armand Marrast, Louis Blanc, and Ferdinand Flocon. These citizens have not hesitated for an instant to accept the patriotic mission which has been imposed upon them by the urgency of the occasion.

Frenchmen, give to the world the example Paris has given to France. Prepare yourselves, by order and confidence in yourselves, for the constitutions which are about to be given to you.

The Provisional Government desires a Republic, pending the ratification of the French people, who are to be immediately consulted. Neither the people of France nor the Provisional Government desire to substitute their opinion for the opinions of the citizens at large, upon the definite form of government which the national sovereignty shall proclaim.

L'unité de la nation," formed henceforth of all classes of the people which compose it;

The government of the nation by itself;

Liberty, equality, and fraternity for its principles;

The people to devise and maintain order.

Such is the Democratic Government which France owes to herself, and which our efforts will assure to her.

Such are the first acts of the Provisional Government.

(Signed)

DUPONT (DE L'EURE)	ARAGO
LAMARTINE	BETHMONT MARIE
LEDRU-ROLLIN	CARNOT
BÉDEAU	CAVAIGNAC
MICHEL GOUDCHAUX	GARNIER PAGÈS

The Municipal Guard is disbanded.

The protection of the city of Paris is confided to the National Guard, under the orders of M. Courtais.

❧{ HISTORICAL INTERPRETATION }❧

TOCQUEVILLE ON THE CAUSES OF THE FEBRUARY 1848 REVOLUTION

Alexis de Tocqueville, *The Recollections of Alexis de Tocqueville*, trans. by Alexander
Teixeira de Mattos, ed. by J. P. Mayer (New York, 1896), pp. 79–81. Courtesy of The
Macmillan Company.

ALEXIS DE TOCQUEVILLE (1805–1859), the celebrated author of *Democracy in America,*
sought in his *Recollections* to analyze the causes of the Revolution of 1848. He was
depressed by the new revolution, which he feared would plunge France into an era of
intermittent anarchy instead of standing as a champion of "balanced liberty."

I have come across men of letters, who have written history without taking part in public affairs, and politicians, who have only concerned themselves with producing events without thinking of describing them. I have observed that the first are always inclined to find general causes, whereas the others, living in the midst of disconnected daily facts, are prone to imagine that everything is attributable to particular incidents, and that the wires which they pull are the same that move the world. It is to be presumed that both are equally deceived.

For my part, I detest these absolute systems, which represent all the events of history as depending upon great first causes linked by the chain of fatality, and which, as it were, suppress men from the history of the human race. They seem narrow, to my mind, under their pretence of broadness, and false beneath their air of mathematical exactness. I believe . . . that many important historical facts can only be explained by accidental circumstances, and that many others remain totally inexplicable. Moreover, chance, or rather that tangle of secondary causes which we call chance, for want of the knowledge how to unravel it, plays a great part in all that happens on the world's stage; although I firmly believe that chance does nothing that has not been prepared beforehand. Antecedent facts, the nature of institutions, the cast of minds and the state of morals are the materials of which are composed those impromptus which astonish and alarm us.

The Revolution of February, in common with all other great events of this class, sprang from general causes, impregnated, if I am permitted the expression, by accidents; and it would be as superficial a judgment to ascribe it necessarily to the former or exclusively to the latter.

The Industrial Revolution which, during the past thirty years, had turned Paris into the principal manufacturing city of France and attracted within its walls an entire new population of workmen (to whom the works of the fortifications had added another population of labourers at present deprived of work) tended more and more to inflame this multitude. Add to this the democratic disease of envy, which was silently permeating it; the economical and political theories which were beginning to make their way and which strove to prove that human misery was the work of laws and not of Providence, and that poverty could be suppressed by changing the conditions of society; the contempt into which the governing class, and especially the men who led it, had fallen, a contempt so general and so profound that it paralysed the resistance even of those who were most interested in maintaining the power that was being overthrown; the centralization which reduced the whole revolutionary movement to the overmastering of Paris and the seizing of the machinery of government; and lastly, the mobility of all this, institutions, ideas, men and customs, in a fluctuating state of society which had, in less than sixty years, undergone the shock of seven great revolutions, without numbering a multitude of smaller, secondary upheavals. These were the general causes without which the Revolution of February would have been impossible. The principal accidents which led to it were the passions of the dynastic Opposition, which brought about a riot in proposing a reform; the suppression of this riot, first over-violent and then abondoned; the sudden disappearance of the old Ministry, unexpectedly snapping the threads of power, which the new ministers, in their confusion, were unable either to seize upon or to reunite; the mistakes and disorder of mind of these ministers, so powerless to re-establish that which they had been strong enough to overthrow; the vacillation of the generals; the absence of the only princes who possessed either personal energy or popularity; and above all, the senile imbecility of King Louis Philippe, his weakness, which no one could have foreseen and which still remains almost incredible, after the event has proved it.

ⅼ TEN BASIC BOOKS ⅼ

FRANCE: FROM MONARCHY TO EMPIRE, 1815–1870

1. Artz, Frederick B., *France Under the Bourbon Restoration* (Cambridge, Mass., 1931, R. 1963).
2. Binkley, Robert C., *Realism and Nationalism, 1852–1871* (New York, 1935).†
3. Bruun, Geoffrey, *Revolution and Reaction—1848–1852: A Mid-Century Watershed,* Anvil Book No. 31 (Princeton, N. J., 1958).†
4. Guérard, Albert, *Napoleon III* (Cambridge, Mass., 1943, R. 1955).
5. Hudson, Nora E., *Ultra-Royalism and the French Restoration* (Cambridge, 1936).
6. McKay, Donald C., *The National Workshops: A Study of the French Revolution of 1848* (Cambridge, Mass., 1933).
7. Schapiro, J. Salwyn, *Liberalism and the Challenge of Fascism, 1815–1870* (New York, 1949, R. 1964).
8. Simpson, Frederick A., *Louis Napoleon and the Recovery of France, 1848–1856,* 3rd ed. (New York, 1951).
9. Thompson, James M., *Louis Napoleon and the Second Empire* (New York, 1955).
10. Wright, Gordon, *France in Modern Times* (Chicago, 1960).

25

Iron and Blood: The Unification of Germany, 1815-1871

GERMANY LOOKS not to Prussia's liberalism but to her power. Bavaria, Württemberg, and Baden may indulge in liberalism, but no person will because
of that reason assign Prussia's role to them. Prussia must gather up her
strength and maintain it in readiness for the opportune moment, which already
has passed by several times. Since the Treaty of Vienna, Prussia's borders
have not been favorable for a healthy state life. Not by parliamentary speeches
and majority votes are the great questions of the day determined—that was
the great mistake of 1848 and 1849—but by iron and blood.

—OTTO VON BISMARCK, to the Budget Commission of the Lower House
of the Prussian Parliament, September 30, 1862

1. Restoration: Austro-Prussian Partnership, 1815–1848

The German Confederation. Established at the Congress of Vienna in 1815, the German Confederation was a loose union of thirty-eight sovereign states, including the Austrian Empire, the kingdoms of Prussia, Bavaria, Saxony, Württemburg, and Hanover; the grand duchies of Baden, Hesse-Darmstadt, Mecklenberg-Schwerin and Strelitz, Saxe-Weimar, and Oldenburg; the electorate of Hesse-Cassel; the duchies of Brunswick, Nassau, Saxe-Coburg-Gotha, Meiningen and Hildburghausen, Anhalt-Dessau, Bernburg, and Cöthen; Denmark (since the king of Denmark was duke of Holstein); the Netherlands (since the king of the Netherlands was grand duke of Luxemburg); the four free cities of Lübeck, Bremen, Hamburg, and Frankfort-on-Main; and several small principalities. The *Bundestag*, or Diet, the legislative body of the Confederation (actually a congress of ambassadors), met at Frankfort to decide questions common to all the states. No member could declare war against any other member, or form any alliance with a foreign power that would be injurious to any one of the states. The army of the Confederation was composed of troops furnished on the basis of the population of each member and was commanded by officers appointed by the Diet.

The fact that the architects of reaction at Vienna gave Prussia a subordinate role in the German Confederation was a source of deep disappointment to Prussian patriots. The dualism between Austria and Prussia was retained, thus evading the problem of German unity. The problem of individual liberty was left to the states. In North Germany the pre-Napoleonic princes, once restored, promptly rescinded constitutional reforms. The South German states maintained the Napoleonic system of autocratic centralized power. The statesmen of Vienna, in the name of legitimacy, restored the boundaries of the old Reich, and paid no attention to the rising spirit of nationalism. Pursuing a policy of supranational cooperation, forced from above, they sought to turn the clock backward.

Actually, they set up a loose confederation (*Staatenbund*) to protect German monarchs against foreign enemies (France and Russia) and against their domestic foe (liberalism).

Repression in the Germanies. Prince Metternich, state chancellor of Austria, not only established a system of repression in Austria but also extended his measures to include Prussia. German patriots, announcing that they had not been permitted to reap the fruits of their sacrifices, reacted as they had earlier against Napoleon. The demand for union and freedom was especially strong in the German universities. "The *Bund* seemed to us," said a contemporary youth, "only a police organization dedicated to the suppression of all national life." Brotherhoods of young men, called *Burschenschaften*, pledged themselves to destroy all tyrants at home and to end what they called Metternich's meddling from Vienna.

On October 18, 1817, during the jubilee year of Luther's revolt, and the anniversary date of the Battle of Leipzig, students held a great celebration at the Wartburg, during which they consigned symbols of tyranny to the flames. On March 23, 1819, a fanatical student murdered August von Kotzebue, a well-known reactionary journalist suspected of being a spy in the pay of the Russian tsar. Annoyed by these "insurrections," Metternich drew up the Carlsbad Decrees (July 1819), providing for special officials in the German universities to supervise the conduct of students and teachers, for the establishment of a rigid press censorship, and for the arrest and imprisonment of vociferous German patriots. These decrees, sanctioned by the Diet of the German Confederation, throttled opinion for a generation.

Metternich, who considered himself the model of an enlightened rationalist, understood little of the twin forces of nationalism and liberalism. A cosmopolitan, he thought in terms of a European system, in which a great Austria would counterbalance France and Russia. Above all, he wanted to frustrate any German desires for freedom and unity that might lead to revolution. He would cooperate with Prussia so long as Prussia was kept in an inferior position; German nationalism, on the other hand, was a force to be rigidly suppressed because it would upset the nice balance of power in Europe.

2. German Economic and Social Life After 1815

The Germanies in 1815. The German Confederation in 1815 was almost entirely an agricultural area, poverty-stricken and underpopulated (with only 26,000,000 people). Most of the Germans lived in villages and small towns. In Prussia, only Berlin, Breslau, Königsberg numbered more than 50,000 inhabitants. Communications throughout the Confederation were primitive; many roads were merely paths through the forests.

The social structure in 1815 was divided into three main classes: the nobility, the educated middle class, and "the people" (the last including all those whom the middle class regarded as its inferiors—peasants, artisans, shopkeepers, domestic servants, and the proletariat). Economic life pivoted on the status of the *Bauerntum*, or peasantry. The Stein-Hardenberg reforms in Prussia in 1807, followed by other German states, gave the peasants personal freedom, but manorial jurisdiction of the landowners remained. The laws of 1811 and 1816 required the peasants to give up as much as half their land to the nobility; in one Pomeranian village alone these laws drove 49 of 61 peasants from the land. Many landless peasants, in an effort to survive, migrated from eastern Germany to the western industrial towns. The feud between big landowners and peasantry in the west and in the south was equally bitter.

Trade and industry were still regulated by medieval guild laws. Some traditional handicrafts remained—weaving in Silesia, toy-making in the Black Forest—but other crafts became obsolete. Journeymen began to lose their status in the guild system. Grouped indistinguishably with vagabonds and casual workers, the poor journeyman became the nucleus of the new proletariat. The Germanies at this time had no modern industries, no factories, no steam engines.

Dawn of Industrialism, 1815–1850. After 1815 the economic picture changed significantly. The whole German area swung around on its own axis and dragged itself out of apathy to create a thriving economic system. Influenced by economic liberalism and the Western form of capitalism, German entrepreneurs sought to break up the medieval inheritance and to accelerate the material recovery of their country. In 1835 the first German railroad was laid between Nürnberg and Fürth; by 1840 there were 282 miles of track; by 1850, 5,134; and by 1860, over 6,600 miles. Locomotive factories were constructed in Essen, great steel plants in Solingen, textile factories in Silesia. In 1850, the Germanies produced only 208,000 tons of iron; by 1860, the output had risen to 1,391,555 tons. Agricultural experts, notably Justus von Liebig (1803–1873), helped German agriculture make giant strides. The German postal system became one of the most efficient in the world.

Shifting Social Structure. These economic changes were accompanied by shifts in the social order. The monarchies of the Confederation, in conformance with traditional practice, had excluded the middle class as well as workers and peasants from public life. But now the spurt in industry resulted in antagonisms between the classes. The feudal aristocracy turned to large-scale agriculture. The middle class, composed of businessmen, manufacturers, and professionals, began to promote industrial expansion. Opposed to these two classes was an essentially new proletariat, consisting of landless peasants who had flocked to the towns after being dispossessed.

The subsequent development of the class system was to play a vital role in German history. The nobility lost some of its privileges in 1848. Some turned to industry where, together with the most successful middle-class capitalists, they formed a moneyed aristocracy, an oligarchy that was to control Prussia-Germany. The middle-class liberals either lost status or were forced out of the country by the events of 1848. Nineteenth-century Germany under Bismarck and William II was to have no responsible middle-class leadership and no firmly rooted peasantry.

Economic Impulse to Unification: *Zollverein.* The economy of the German states after 1815 was burdened by a bewildering variety of water, inland, and provincial tolls. Some 2,775 articles were subject to duties collected by an army of 8,000 officials. In the German Confederation, thirty-eight customs boundaries produced much the same effect as ligatures preventing the free circulation of blood. The merchant who traded between Hamburg and Austria, or Berlin and Switzerland, had to traverse 10 states, be familiar with 10 customs-tariffs, and pay 10 successive tariff dues. Prussia alone had 67 tariffs, which could be paid in 119 different currencies.

The *Zollverein* (customs union), founded by degrees between 1818 and 1834, forged the bonds of economic unity in the direction of national unification. The idea was originally promulgated by Friedrich List (1789–1846), a Württemberg economist, but leadership in the *Zollverein* movement was gradually appropri-

Friedrich List, political economist, pioneer of railways in the Germanies, and inaugurator of the *Zollverein.* Never fully appreciated during his lifetime, List's efforts played a major part in paving the way toward ultimate German unification.

ated by Prussia. Prussia had little consideration for the welfare of other German states and no desire to see a customs union worked out by common consent. Instead, Prussian administrators began an economic amalgamation of their own territories, which lay scattered throughout the Germanies. Economic pressure forced other German states one by one into the Prussian system. Both the South German and the Central German states, which desired customs unions of their own, were eventually drawn into the Prussian orbit. The *Zollverein,* completed on January 1, 1834, included eighteen German states, in an area of 162,870 square miles.

Friedrich List, the moving spirit in the formation of the *Zollverein,* was a battered and bruised soul during his lifetime, the target of unappreciative German industrialists and the prey of the Austrian secret police. His countrymen hurled such epithets at him as "revolutionary," "Jacobin," and "demagogue." To Metternich he was "an heroic swindler," and "the tool of squealing German manufacturers." After List's death, when it became obvious that his idea of national economy was in reality designed as a service to his country, he was placed on a pedestal as one of Germany's outstanding patriot-heroes. He was now hailed as "a great German without Germany," "Germany's Colbert," an economic genius who embodied the finest thinking of Cromwell, Canning, Dr. Quesnay, Robert Peel, even Aristotle. List was, indeed, a powerful factor in the unification of Germany. His concept of the *Zollverein,* his promotion of the German railway system, merchant marine, navy, and colonialism, and his theories of political economy—protective tariffs, Greater Germany, and *Mitteleuropa*—paved the way for Germany's political and industrial greatness. That List's ideal of a "practical, diligent, thrifty, enlightened, orderly, patriotic, and freedom-loving democracy" was not achieved in Germany may be attributed in part to the fact that subsequent German political leaders confused national greatness with national aggression and used List's ideas as a basis for extremist thinking and policies.

3. *The Revolution of 1848: Collapse of German Liberalism*

Metternich's System Disintegrates. The system of Metternich began to totter in 1830 after revolutions in France, Belgium, and Poland, with reverberations in the Germanies, where some of the minor princes felt themselves impelled to grant constitutions. At a meeting of some 25,000 persons at Hambach in the Palatinate in May 27, 1832, there were calls for a German union based on sovereignty of the people and for a European confederation of free republics. Metternich thereupon intensified his opposition to democrats and liberals. When, in 1848, another revolution began in France, it spread quickly to the Germanies, beginning in Baden and Württemberg and then running through the German states, until the whole country was aflame. In Prussia, Frederick William IV (r. 1840–

"Metternich on the run." Ironically, the first political caricature published in Vienna satirized the 1848 flight into exile of the man who had so rigidly restricted the press.

1861) at first promised reform, but when assured of the support of the army, he crushed the rebellion. Metternich's system, however, had already collapsed, and its author fled ignominiously to England.

Promise of the Frankfort Assembly. The German liberals issued a call for a *Vorparlament* (Preliminary Parliament), which met and ordered general elections for a National Assembly to give Germany a constitution. The

National Assembly (*Nationalversammlung*) convened on May 18, 1848, in St. Paul's Church in Frankfort-on-Main, established a provisional representative government, and chose the Archduke John of Austria as imperial regent (*Reichsverweser*). Several months later, the Assembly adopted a declaration of rights modeled on the American Bill of Rights and the French Declaration of Rights of Man and Citizen. On the matter of the territorial problem the Assembly was hampered by both the wishes of the multinational Austrian monarchy and by the Prussian urge for German leadership. Was there to be a "Big German" (*grossdeutsch*) solution, which would include the Germans of Austria, or a "Little German" (*kleindeutsch*) settlement which would leave out the Austrian Germans in favor of Prussian hegemony? When the Prussian king, Frederick William IV, was offered the crown of a united Germany by the Assembly, he refused to accept it because the offer "came from the gutter." As a royalist, he would not accept "a dog-collar chaining him to the revolution." Bitter inner dissensions, complicated by differences between conservatives, liberals, and radicals, were too much for the Assembly. Gradually, disgruntled members withdrew, and a last-ditch rump parliament, meeting at Stuttgart, was dispersed by force.

The German Revolution Breaks Down. The once-humiliated princes, now confident of their ability to stem the tide of revolt, turned viciously on the revolutionists. The liberals, especially, caught between the reviving autocracy and revolutionary radicalism, felt the wrath of the victors. Hundreds fled from the vengeance of the reactionaries. Heinrich Heine and Karl Marx remained in exile; Carl Schurz, Franz Sigel, and others emigrated to the United States, where they played an important role in the American Civil War; Richard Wagner and Theodor Mommsen returned, reconciled to an authoritarian Germany. As the liberal gladiators retired from the political arena, the poet Ernst Moritz Arndt penned a remarkable prophecy:

Away! Our heroes' arms grow tired,
  And stricken sore the strongest fall.
A truce of life no more desired!
  Away! The death-knell tolls for all.

On February 4, 1850, the king of Prussia took the oath to a conservative constitution providing for a three-class system of voting that insured the political domination of the propertied class and gave the king an absolute veto on all legislation.

Causes of the Failure of 1848. Historians have ascribed various reasons for the failure of the Revolution of 1848 in the Germanies. Lewis B. Namier stated that the movement was unsuccessful because the great majority of the members of the Frankfort Assembly were not true liberals, but nationalists and imperialists. "The professorial lambs at Frankfort, bitten by the Pan-German dog, caught rabies." The Germans, Namier said further, managed to make other nations believe that there was something especially noble and liberal-minded about the collectivity of Germans at that time and about their performance—"one of the legends of history." To Peter Viereck, the Revolution was "a pathetic muddle": "The liberal university professors, Metternich's fiercest foes and now so prominent in 1848, were often far from the cloudy idealists pictured in our textbooks. . . . The majority . . . was more Bismarckian than Bismarck ever realized."

Koppel S. Pinson attributed the failure to "the enormous disparity between the political aspirations of the German liberals and the mass support and actual power and influence they commanded." Erich Brandenburg laid the blame not on the Frankfort Assembly, but on "the power and self-assertion of the larger individual states, above all the two great powers [Austria and Prussia]." Edmond Vermeil saw the cause of failure not so much in external factors as in the mentality of the German people, molded and developed by peculiar German romanticism. German liberalism, he asserted, was extraordinarily weak, bowing before the work and will of pure power politics. A. J. P. Taylor considered it barren speculation to discuss the causes for the failure: "There was no successful revolution in Germany; and therefore nothing to fail. There was merely a vacuum in which the liberals postured until the vacuum was filled." And Taylor again: "For the first time since 1521, the German people stepped on to the center of the German stage only to miss their cues once more. German history reached its turning point and failed to turn. That was the fateful essence of 1848."

Meaning of the Revolution of 1848. The German Revolution of 1848 was something more than an ideological stage in German history. In his early career, Friedrich Meinecke explained the Revolution of 1848 in terms of pure idea. He was criticized by Erich Brandenburg, who said: "I remain of the opinion that for the masses elemental experiences affecting and disturbing them in their daily, personal lives, are more powerful than doctrines and theories which are handed down to them from above. Only through the former are slumbering impulses and needs aroused or forced into the foreground of their consciousness."

No doubt too much stress has been placed on the constitutional and national strivings of the liberal middle class. Somewhat more attention should be accorded to the economic and social conditions that made the masses ripe for revolution. Theodore S. Hamerow pointed to the necessity for an understanding of the social and economic implications of 1848. Franz Schnabel wrote about the close connection between the constitutional movement and industrial development during this vital period. Oscar J. Hammen observed that "economic and social factors helped to precipitate and to determine the course of the German Revolution of 1848." Hans Rosenberg described the events of 1848 as lending a powerful stimulus to the creation of economic conditions essential to an industrial state. Meinecke himself later recognized the importance of economic factors: "The German Revolution of 1848, admittedly, shows not only an all-pervading spirit of idealism, which often outstripped reality and became ideological. It also brought to bear what in actual effect was more powerful—the reality itself, the massive and elemental interests of individuals and social groups."

A Tragic Year. The year 1848 was a tragic one in German history. On the surface, it seemed that the streams of rationalism—liberalism, democracy, social contract, egalitarianism, tolerance, constitutionalism—were converging at long last in a common stream. For the first time in their history the German people seemed to have an opportunity to determine their own destiny. Critical decisions were for a while out of the hands of autocratic princes and in the possession of men who understood the currents of Western liberalism. German intellectuals suddenly found themselves, at a critical moment, the spokesmen for their people. Predominantly middle-class (there was not a single working-class representative at Frankfort; the Assembly believed that nothing good could come from intrusion of the masses into politics), the intellectuals sought unity through persuasion, progress through moderation, and a better world through the practice of tolerance and goodwill. They failed.

When the wave of revolution receded, liberalism had been submerged in the stronger movement of nationalism, and the people were left with Prussian discipline, authority, and efficiency. The aim of the Revolution had been "through unity to freedom," but the events showed that unity was to be achieved through power. German unification was thereafter to depend upon cohesion through force, and force through cohesion. Strength went out of the liberal idea. For the rest of the nineteenth century, in both intellectual and political spheres, the ethical concept of liberty as a postulate of the human spirit fought a losing battle in Germany. The tragedy affected not only Germany but the entire world.

4. Forge of Iron: Bismarck Unifies Germany, 1864–1871

Background: Austrian Hegemony, 1849–1866. The failure of the Revolution of 1848 left the Germanies confused and divided.

Frederick William IV (r. 1840–1861), and his chief minister, Joseph von Radowitz, recognizing the desire for unity, proposed a friendly arrangement between Protestant Prussia and Catholic Austria, by which the two countries would control a common policy for all Germany. Radowitz organized the Erfurt Union (also called the Prussian Union), an association of princes under Prussia's protection, and urged that this smaller *Bund* be placed on an equal basis with the old *Bund*. Prince Felix von Schwarzenberg, the Austrian chancellor and successor to Metternich, opposed the Prussian plan and insisted that only the Austrian sword could rule Germany. On September 1, 1850, Schwarzenberg officially announced the renewal of the old German Confederation.

There were now two German *Bunds* in existence, and the dispute soon turned into open conflict. The Elector of Hesse-Cassel, a member of the Erfurt Union, finding himself in constitutional difficulties with his parliament, called on the Frankfort Diet for assistance. When both confederations prepared to send troops into the country, war seemed inevitable. Schwarzenberg probably preferred an immediate settling of accounts with Prussia, but Francis Joseph I was reluctant to make war on his fellow monarch. Frederick William IV, faced with insubordination by the jealous princes in his Union and uncertain of support by the reactionary Junkers, decided to retreat. When Tsar Nicholas I, opposed to German unification of any kind, intervened in favor of Austria, the Prussian king gave up altogether. He dismissed Radowitz and sent the more yielding Otto Theodor von Manteuffel as successor to deal with the Austrians. By the Agreement of Olmütz, signed on November 29, 1850, Prussia renounced the Erfurt Union and recognized the revival of the German Confederation. Austria was once more the power in German affairs. Prussian patriots felt the "humiliation of Olmütz" to be a low point in their history, and resolved to seek revenge against Austria at the earliest opportunity.

The reestablished German Confederation, striking at once against liberalism and nationalism, renewed old feudal and absolutist policies. Each German state competed with others

in wiping out the vestiges of 1848. Despite her humiliation, Prussia in the 1850's began to emerge as an industrial power. Coal, iron, and steel poured in growing quantities from the Ruhr valley; increasing urbanization accompanied the development of the factory system; a network of railways was constructed. The coronation of William I on October 16, 1861, gave hope to depressed German nationalists who had been dissatisfied with the diplomatic confusion of Frederick William IV. Meanwhile, the Prussian general staff, appalled by the 1850 failure, began to reorganize the army for another confrontation with Austria. The railways in Prussia were constructed in conformity with a strategic plan worked out by military leaders. Prussia was more than ever determined first to make a moral conquest of Germany and then dominate her by the sword.

Otto von Bismarck's Role in German Unification. "I am a Junker and mean to profit from it." These were the words of Otto von Bismarck (1815–1898), outstanding political figure in the history not only of Germany but of all Europe in the second half of the nineteenth century. Jules Favre, the French foreign minister in 1870, called him "a statesman who surpasses everything that I can imagine." A. J. P. Taylor described Bismarck as "the greatest of all political Germans, [who] assembled in his own person all the countradictions of German dualism." Erich Eyck attributed not only the unification of the German nation but also all the great landmarks of European history from 1860 to the First World War to Bismarck: "Everybody sees that; what is not so apparent, but not less important and far-reaching, is the transformation of the spirit and mentality of the German people, for which he is also responsible."

Aristocratic, conservative, militaristic, monarchistic, Lutheran in religion, Bismarck had no use for "phrase-making and constitutions." He made it plain that he intended to obtain by "iron and blood" what he believed could not be achieved by the honeyed words of liberals. The reactionary genius of Europe, he defended all that was traditional in German history, including its feudal, monarchical features. A *Realpolitiker* (realist politician) he was firmly convinced that Germany's destiny demanded guidance by the firm hands of the Hohenzollern dynasty. Originally a Pomeranian patriot, he saw that Prussia was destined for leadership in a united Germany; therefore his local patriotism changed into a broader Prussian loyalty. Keeping only attainable ends in view, he led Prussia toward a new, powerful position. The man who once thought exclusively in terms of Prussia welded the Germans into a united nation.

Bismarck as Nationalist. Bismarck's conception of the nation was a narrow one, more in line with the reason of state (*Staatsräson*) than with other forms of the national idea. He was neither jingoistic, chauvinistic, nor racialist, nor was he a totalitarian. Yet, as pointed out by Otto Pflanze, Bismarck fostered the tradition of the *Tatmensch*, the man of deeds who manipulates the reins of power and is responsible only to his conscience for the results.

Nationalism meant to Bismarck that Germany was to be dominated by Prussia. "Never," he said, "did I doubt that the key to German politics was to be found in princes and dynasties, not in publicists, whether in parliament and the press or on the barricades. The opinion of the cultivated public as uttered in parliament and the press might promote and sustain the determination of the dynasties, but perhaps provoked their resistance more frequently than it urged them forward in the direction of national unity. The weaker dynasties leaned for shelter upon the national cause; rulers and houses that felt themselves more capable of resistance mistrusted the movement. . . . The Prussian dynasty might anticipate that the hegemony in the future empire would eventually fall to it, with an increase of consideration and power." Nothing was to stand in the way of Prussia's drive to hegemony in Germany. "If I have an enemy in my power," warned Bismarck, "I must destroy him." His goal was to achieve a unified Germany, but this had to be attained along with two corollary aims: (1) the preservation of his own social class and (2) the destruction of the political philos-

ophy of liberalism. "I am no democrat," he told Carl Schurz, "and cannot be one. I was born and raised an aristocrat."

Beginning of Bismarck's Political Career. In March 1848, when the existence of the Prussian monarchy was at stake, Bismarck, newly married and comfortably living at Schönhausen, gathered fowling pieces, gunpowder, and peasants, and rushed off to offer his services to the king. Not only was he angry at the revolution, but he did not understand it. Bismarck began his political career on May 11, 1851, as Prussian representative to the Federal Diet at Frankfort. Although resurrected by Austria, the *Bund* was in reality moribund. Bismarck's mission to Frankfort (1851–1859) opened a new epoch in German and European history—he planted the seeds of destruction in the *Bund* from the very first day he appeared at Frankfort. His stay there added to his contempt for Austria and at the same time transformed him from Prussian patriot into German nationalist. As ambassador in St. Petersburg from 1859 to 1862 he became acquainted with one of the Great Powers that was to play an important role in his future policies. In 1862 he was ambassador at Paris for a few months. Disraeli, who met him at this time, was impressed by the blunt Junker; "Take care of that man," said the Englishman; "he means what he says."

Bismarck as Minister-President of Prussia. Bismarck was forty-seven years old when he was named minister-president of Prussia. His appointment came at a time when Prussia was undergoing one of the most crucial constitutional conflicts in her history. The new king of Prussia, William I (r. 1861–1888), wanted to reorganize his military forces by increasing the power of the standing army at the expense of the militia. The Prussian *Landtag*, the House of Representatives, refused to grant the necessary funds, and accused him of wanting a large army in order to stifle democracy. When the new Progressive party, opposed to the king, increased its representation in the elections of May 6, 1862, William seriously considered abdicating. In this crisis General Albrecht von Roon (1803–1879), minister of war, prevailed upon the monarch to call the fiery Junker to Berlin. Twenty-four years earlier, as a youth of twenty-three, Bismarck had said: "I want to make only that music which I myself like, or no music at all." Prussia, Germany, and the whole of Europe were to hear Bismarck's music for the next three decades.

Bismarck began his ministry by withdrawing the budget for the next year. Before a committee of the House he made a sensational speech describing his future course: it was essential, he said, that Germany should look not to liberalism but to her own power. The great questions of the day could not be solved by speeches and majority votes—that was the great mistake of 1848 and 1849—but by iron and blood. This was the policy that Bismarck was to pursue until the unification of Germany in 1871. His solution for the conflict between king and parliament was simple: he dissolved the assembly. From 1862 to 1866, he ruled arbitrarily without legislative consent, collecting funds and invigorating the military without sanction of the *Landtag* and the voters. So successful was he in his foreign policy that the House, at its meeting in 1866, voted him a bill of indemnity legalizing all his acts during its absence.

Bismarck's course in his relations with Austria was clear: he was determined that Germany be unified under Prussian leadership, and that Austria be excluded from German affairs. He was blunt in his warnings. He urged the Austrians to move the center of Hapsburg gravity eastward to Hungary, which would have meant the relinquishing of Austria's position in Germany. He held out an enticing bait—Prussia then would become Austria's faithful ally.

Stage I: War Against Denmark, 1864. Bismarck's first major step toward national unity was to use a quarrel with Denmark to test the Prussian army and to mold public opinion. His opportunity came with the death, on November 15, 1863, of King Frederick VII of Denmark. The question of Schleswig-Holstein had disturbed European diplomats for some time. Lord Palmerston described the complicated problem: "Only three men have ever understood it. One was Prince Albert, who is dead. The second was a German professor, who became mad. I am the third, and I have forgotten all about it." After the Treaty of

THE UNIFICATION OF GERMANY, 1864-71

STEP 1

DENMARK

SCHLESWIG-HOLSTEIN

KINGDOM OF PRUSSIA

NETH.

o Berlin

RUSSIA

1864 War Against Denmark

BELG.

LUX.

o Paris

BADEN WURTT.

BAVARIA

AUSTRIA

o Vienna

FRANCE   SWITZ.

STEP 2

DENMARK

KINGDOM OF PRUSSIA

NETH.

o Berlin

RUSSIA

1866 Austro-Prussian War

BELG.

LUX.

o Paris

BADEN WURTT.

BAVARIA

o Vienna

FRANCE   SWITZ.

AUSTRIA

STEP 3

DENMARK

GERMAN EMPIRE

NETH.

o Berlin

RUSSIA

1870-71 Franco-Prussian War

BELG.

Sedan o   LUX.

o Paris

ALSACE-LORRAINE

o Vienna

FRANCE   SWITZ.

AUSTRIA

Vienna in 1815, the two duchies of Schleswig and Holstein, both of which had large German populations, were united with Denmark in a personal-union. Holstein was a part of the German Confederation, and the king of Denmark, as duke of Holstein, was a member of the Confederation and was represented in the Diet at Frankfort. During the Revolution of 1848, the Germans in Schleswig and Holstein rebelled against the "Danish foreigners," but their insurrection collapsed when Prussia withdrew her support.

From the beginning of his ministry Bismarck intended to annex the provinces to Prussia. "I have not the smallest doubt," he said, "that the Danish business can be settled in a way desirable for us only by war." All that was necessary was a favorable opportunity. It came on November 13, 1863, when the Danish *Rigsraad* passed a new constitution which Bismarck interpreted as incorporating Schleswig into Denmark and as a violation of the promise that the Danish king had given to Austria and Prussia in the Protocol of London in 1852. The death of Frederick VII brought the matter to a head.

Bismarck concluded an alliance with Austria (January 16, 1864), probably reasoning that he could eventually pick a quarrel with her over the spoils. On February 1, 1864, Prussian and Austrian armies crossed the frontiers of Schleswig. The Danes electing to fight, hoped desperately that England would come to their aid. Bismarck selected his moment shrewdly, for the British asked only that the integrity of the Danish monarchy not be violated. By April 18 the whole of Schleswig was in the hands of the invaders. Abandoned by the Great Powers, Denmark was forced to sue for peace. By the Peace of Vienna, August 1864, Denmark gave up the duchies to Austria and Prussia. By the Convention of Gastein, August 14, 1865, the Austro-Prussian condominium of the duchies was ended by dividing them. Austria was given control over Holstein and Prussia over Schleswig. The Austrians made the mistake of insisting that this partition be *provisional*, a shortsighted proposal that played directly into Bismarck's hands.

The result of the Danish war was received by Germans with jubilation. In the face of Austrian pretensions and the hostile Great Powers. Bismarck had engineered, boldly and almost recklessly, the most important territorial coup since the days of Frederick the Great. The victory also gave Bismarck further ammunition in his continuing battle with parliament.

Stage II: The Austro-Prussian War, 1866. Bismarck, who had never forgotten the humiliation at Olmütz and who never wavered in his plan to remove Austria as an obstacle to German unification, carefully isolated the Hapsburgs from foreign help. On April 8, 1866, he concluded with Italy an alliance which promised Venetia to the Italians as a reward in the event of a Prusso-Austrian war. This alliance was in direct defiance of the constitution of the German Confederation, which forbade any member to make a pact with a foreign power against any other member. Living in dreams of Napoleonic splendor, Napoleon III was unable to adopt any hard and fast policy to thwart Bismarck's designs. Bismarck, on the other hand, was certain of his policy—he must goad Austria into aggression.

The issue again revolved around Schleswig-Holstein. On June 1, 1866, Austria challenged Prussia by submitting the problem of Schleswig-Holstein to the Federal Diet at Frankfort. On June 12 the Austrian ambassador at Berlin and the Prussian envoy at Vienna asked for their passports. When, two days later, the Federal Diet passed an Austrian motion to mobilize the non-Prussian armies, Prussia declared the German Confederation ended and invited the German states to join a union under Prussian leadership. Bismarck now had his war with Austria. "If we are beaten," he said, "I shall not return. I can die only once, and it befits the vanquished to die."

The superbly organized Prussian army demonstrated its superiority over the Austrians within seven weeks. On July 3, 1866, the Prussians inflicted a decisive defeat on the Austrians at Königgrätz (Sadowa). To the dismay of William I and the Prussian Junkers, Bismarck at once insisted upon moderate peace terms. The Treaty of Prague (August 23, 1866) required Austria to recognize the end of the German Confederation, the incorporation of Schleswig-Holstein with Prussia, and the annexation of Venetia by Italy. Austria was to pay a small indemnity of 20,000,000 *thalers*, but she lost no territory. Bismarck, desiring Austrian neutrality in the event of a war with France, regarded these magnanimous terms as insurance. "We shall need Austria's strength in the future for ourselves." Once again Bismarck had taken a victorious path, and had won a war against what had seemed to be insuperable odds. He was now placed on a pedestal as the diplomatic genius of Prussia.

Historical Controversy: Bismarck as Instigator of War Against Austria? Historians differ as to whether it was Bismarck's intention from the beginning to make war on Austria. There have been voluminous and not altogether convincing dissertations on both sides of the question. The conclusion of Erich Eyck may be summarized as follows: Bismarck never had any scruples about a war of this kind, which he regarded as a kind of "fraternal" conflict. But it is another question as to whether he *wanted* the war. Eyck believes that he would have been willing to do without war if he had been able to achieve his aims by normal diplomatic means. While Bismarck was not from the beginning bent on war with Austria, he was engaged in a policy which made war unavoidable. The Austrian statesmen did not see in time that war was inevitable, and that military and political preparations were necessary. In a similar approach, Otto Pflanze described the twists and turns of Bismarckian diplomacy in the conquest of Schleswig-Holstein. It was a performance of incredible dexterity. Most historians today accept the view that Bismarck carefully prepared the ground for the war against Austria.

Bismarck's Actions Legalized: The Indemnity Bill. Before embarking on the war against Austria, Bismarck had once again dissolved the Prussian *Landtag*. After the general elections of July 3, 1866, the new House was faced with the problem of indemnity for the government's infringements of the constitution. An indemnity bill was introduced to acknowledge that the illegal expenditures of recent years had to obtain a constitutional basis through subsequent vote. According to the bill, the House would approve the budgets of 1862–1864, and the acts of the government during those years would not be considered unconstitutional. The act was passed on September 8, 1866 by a vote of 230 to 75, a triumph for Bismarck. With this decision, the strength of German parliamentary life ebbed away. The irrepressible Bismarck, after the vote was announced, stated that, if similar conditions rose again, he would repeat the same unconstitutional procedure. The shadow of 1862, when Bismarck showed his contempt for parliamentary institutions by ruling without parliament, fell over subsequent constitutional development.

Formation of North German Confederation, 1867. As a result of the Prussian triumph over Austria, the Prussian Hohenzollerns replaced the Austrian Hapsburgs as the reigning dynasty in the German state. In 1867 Bismarck consolidated Prussia's position by creating the North German Confederation, a union of twenty-two states and the principalities of North and Central Germany. A North German *Reichstag* was called on the basis of the universal suffrage law of 1849. The constitution of the Confederation, written largely by Bismarck, was similar to the one later adopted by the German Reich in 1871. It made the *Bundeskanzler* the responsible minister of the Confederation and the political and administrative head of the government, which was precisely Bismarck's aim. Although there was a coating of democratic suffrage, the people were in fact deprived of real political power. This was in conformity with Bismarck's aim to kill parliamentarianism through parliament. Instead of a democratic government, Germany got a veiled absolutism. "Let us put Germany in the saddle," said Bismarck; "she will know how to ride."

Stage III: The Franco-Prussian War, 1870–1871. The final step in the creation of the Second German Reich was the Franco-Prussian War of 1870–1871. Bismarck's brilliant successes of 1864 and 1866, together with the emergence of Italian nationalism, aroused the fears of Napoleon III. Aware that Germany and Italy as strong and unified national states would challenge French supremacy on the Continent, and determined to preserve the Napoleonic legend of military invincibility, Napoleon III tried at any cost to hinder German unification. He had mixed feelings on the subject. In a speech from the throne on November 18, 1867, he said: "We must frankly accept the changes which have been introduced across the Rhine and let it be known that so long as our interests and our dignity are not threatened we shall not interfere with changes that have been evoked by the German nation." But to others he confided that, if Bismarck were to draw the South German states into the North German Confederation, "our guns will go off by themselves." Napoleon's confused diplomatic meddling gave Bismarck a chance to strike the final blow for German unity. The Prussian chancellor was not at all averse to a war with France, for he believed that the outbreak of conflict would swing the South German states into line, thereby completing German unification.

With diplomatic cunning, the Prussian isolated the Frenchman, making certain that Italy, Russia, Austria, and England would not assist Napoleon. The Prussian army, under General Helmuth von Moltke (1800–1891), was in a high state of efficiency. Bismarck awaited his opportunity, which came with the conflict over the projected Hohenzollern candidacy for the throne of Spain. In 1868 Queen Isabella of Spain was dethroned by a military coup. The monarchists, regarding it as an opportunity, proposed as a candidate Prince Leopold von Hohenzollern-Sigmarin, a member of the Swabian branch of the Hohenzollern family, and a distant relative of both King William of Prussia and Napoleon III. The specter of a revived empire of Charles V to threaten France on both sides of her borders was one to haunt the nervous French emperor.

King William at Bad Ems was approached by Count Benedetti, the French ambassador, and was requested to abandon once and for all time any claims to the throne of Spain. An account of this meeting was telegraphed to Bismarck in Berlin. Unscrupulously editing the dispatch, Bismarck released it the next day, July 14, 1870. In its abbreviated form, the telegram gave the impression of an ultimatum. (*See page 433.*)

France declared war almost immediately (July 19, 1870). The South German states, to Napoleon III's consternation, joined Prussia. In less than two months the French armies were soundly defeated, and Napoleon was taken prisoner at Sedan. After the siege and capitulation of Paris the war was terminated finally by the Treaty of Frankfort, May 10, 1871. A humiliated France was required to cede Alsace and a part of Lorraine, including the fortresses of Metz and Didenhofen, to Germany and to pay an indemnity of 5 billion francs (approximately 1 billion dollars) within three years. Pending payment, the eastern departments of France were to be occupied. This time there was no generosity in the German terms.

German unification was now completed, based on Bismarck's policy of iron and blood.

As the crowning act of his three successful wars, Count von Bismarck reads the document proclaiming William I emperor.

The historian Heinrich von Sybel wrote passionately: "Tears run down my cheeks. By what have we deserved the grace of God, that we are allowed to live to see such great and mighty deeds? What for twenty years was the substance of all our wishes and efforts, is now fulfilled in such an immeasurably magnificent way." On January 18, 1871, King William of Prussia was proclaimed William I, German Emperor, at the Hall of Mirrors in Versailles. The North German Confederation was abolished, to be succeeded by the new Second German Empire consisting of Prussia and the North and South German states.

Historical Controversy: The Bismarck Problem. Bismarck's success in achieving German unification in just a few years after he became minister-president of Prussia in 1862 aroused conflicting views among historians. Heinrich von Sybel and the patriotic Prussian professor-prophets, awed by Bismarck's career, lauded him in sugary panegyrics. But after Germany's defeat in World War I revealed the impermanency of his Second Reich, there was a reappraisal of Bismarck's *Realpolitik*. In 1941–1944 appeared Erich Eyck's three-volume biography of Bismarck which, from a liberal point of view, appraised his work. According to

Eyck, Bismarck knew exactly what he was going to do in any given political situation and always kept the initiative by knowing beforehand how others would react to his moves. Eyck delegated to Bismarck the responsibility for initiating the three years of national unification.

Another school, represented by Franz Schnabel and Werner Richter among others, reject what they call the "legend" in school textbooks representing Bismarck as building day by day and brick by brick the edifice which came into being in 1871. These historians say that Bismarck never at any time had more than a general idea of what he sought ultimately to achieve. Thus, he did not manipulate history, but as a diplomatic genius took full advantage of the situations he faced and utilized them to achieve his goals. He used nationalism, took it into custody, and subordinated it to the needs of his people.

It is most difficult to describe this highly complex figure by a simple formula: good or bad, realist or idealist, wise statesman or rigid authoritarian, nationalist or European? Historians clash on all these interpretations: they present evidence to prove Bismarck both a destroyer of liberty and a compromiser with liberalism.

❑ KEY DOCUMENT ❑

THE EMS DISPATCH, JULY 13, 1870

Propyläen Weltgeschichte (Berlin, 1930), VIII, 248.

REPRODUCED BELOW are the texts of the original Ems dispatch as sent by Heinrich Abeken, German Councillor of Legation at Paris, to Bismarck on July 13, 1870, and the edited version which the latter submitted to the press. In its abbreviated form the dispatch gave the impression of an ultimatum. Both the French and German people interpreted it as an insult when it was published the next day, July 14th, Bastille Day in France.

The Abeken Text

EMS, JULY 13, 1870
TO THE FEDERAL CHANCELLOR, COUNT BISMARCK, No. 27, No. 61 EOD. 3:10 P.M. (STATION EMS: RUSH!)
His Majesty the King writes to me:
"M. Benedetti intercepted me on the Promenade

in order to demand of me most insistently that I should authorize him to telegraph immediately to Paris that I shall obligate myself for all future time never again to give my approval to the candidacy of the Hohenzollerns should it be renewed. I refused to agree to this, the last time somewhat severely, informing him that one dare not and cannot assume such obligations *à tout jamais.* Naturally, I informed him that I had received no news as yet, and since he had been informed earlier than I by way of Paris and Madrid he could easily understand that my Government was once again out of the matter."

Since then His Majesty has received a dispatch from the Prince [Charles Anthony]. As His Majesty informed Count Benedetti that he was expecting news from the Prince, His Majesty himself, in view of the above-mentioned demand and in consonance wih the advice of Count Eulenburg and myself, decided not to receive the French envoy again but to inform him through an adjutant that His Majesty had now received from the Prince confirmation of the news which Benedetti had already received from Paris, and that he had nothing further to say to the Ambassador. His Majesty leaves it to the judgment of Your Excellency whether or not to communi-

cate at once the new demand by Benedetti and its rejection to our ambassadors and to the press.

[Signed]

A[beken] 13.7.70

Bismarck's Edited Version

After the reports of the renunciation by the hereditary Prince of Hohenzollern had been officially transmitted by the Royal Government of Spain to the Imperial Government of France, the French Ambassador presented to His Majesty the King at Ems the demand to authorize him to telegraph to Paris that His Majesty the King would obligate himself for all future time never again to give his approval to the candidacy of the Hohenzollerns should it be renewed.

His Majesty the King thereupon refused to receive the French envoy again and informed him through an adjutant that His Majesty has nothing further to say to the Ambassador.

⋺{ HISTORICAL INTERPRETATION }⋵

HEINRICH VON SYBEL ON "THE GREAT COMPROMISE" OF 1866

Heinrich von Sybel, *The Founding of the German Empire by William I* (New York, 1890–1898), V, 390, 487–491.

HEINRICH VON SYBEL (1817–1895) was appointed director of the Prussian Archives in 1875. Thus having access to material not available to others, he wrote an account of the foundation of the German Empire. It was a strongly partisan narrative, in which Sybel attributed responsibility for the three wars of national unification to Denmark, Austria, and France. He judged Bismarck's policies as honorable, just, and correct, even including the editing of the Ems dispatch. The historiographer George P. Gooch described Sybel's work: "He went through life waving the Prussian banner and waging truceless war against France, Austria, and the Roman Church." Sybel's account of the bill of indemnity, which Bismarck sought in 1866 after ruling unconstitutionally, portrays Bismarck as the apotheosis of moderation and compromise. This passage treats the political consequences of the defeat of Austria in 1866.

The 3d of July had bought the Prussian Government, not only the overwhelming victory over Austria, but also a telling success against the Opposition at home. At the same time that the Prussian battalions were annihilating the Austrian army, the Opposition suffered such losses in the elections to the Parliament that the Government, whose party in the years of the constitutional struggle had at times melted away to ten or twelve members, carried through their candidates

for nearly half of the Lower House. With such a combination of political and military triumphs how many of the great conquerors of ancient or modern times would have resisted the temptation to break in pieces the hostile empire without, and to propose to themselves the overthrow of all constitutional restraints within.

But Bismarck was made of other stuff. He was not striving for world-dominion nor for boundless power, but for the means to secure and strengthen his Prussian Fatherland. So much acquisition of power and of territory as was necessary for this he laid hold of with iron grasp —so much and no more. The intoxication of victory never disordered his judgment, nor got the mastery over his fixed principles of moderation. . . .

The opening of the Parliament was fixed for Sunday noon, August 5th, in the celebrated White Hall of the royal palace; and it can easily be imagined with what intense suspense the appearance of the King was awaited. Every one said to himself that the old struggle over the organization of the army had been ended upon the battlefields of Bohemia: whoever might still have wished to dispute the intrinsic value of that creation of King William's would have exposed himself to everlasting ridicule. But who knew what further use the King would make of this triumph? The men of the *Kreuzzeitung* Party threatened, and those of the Party of Progress feared, that now a budgetless rule would be proclaimed to be the only proper system, and any further opposition would be put down by a dictatorship that had become all-powerful. The whole existence of the Constitution seemed to tremble in the balance. . . .

The Government had already, on the 14th of August, sent to the House the draft of an indemnity-bill, containing the motion to grant to the Ministry of State indemnity for the expenses incurred during the years 1862–1865, a general outline of which was appended; while for the year 1866, since the state of things was no longer adapted to the establishment of a regular budget, the Government desired a loan of 154 million thalers. In the budget-committee, to whose consideration the matter was referred, it was very soon evident that a large majority favored the acceptance of the bill.

The only determined opposition came from the members of the Party of Progress, who were not able to find in the draft of the bill the necessary security for the re-establishment of constitutional rights. These, therefore, approved the loan for 1866, but wished to decline for the present the proposal about the indemnity and to leave it with the Government to make the request again after the budget for 1867 should have been fixed upon.

To this the reply was made that if the present promise of the Government to adopt the budget for 1867 were not to be trusted, then the passage and adoption of this latter could not be looked upon as a sure guaranty for the acceptance of a regular budget for 1868. The main thing, it was asserted, was the serious intention of the Government to return to the basis of the Constitution; and this determination was believed to be sufficiently indicated in the bill. The whole dispute arose, it was said, from a difference of opinion about the new organization of the army, and who could at this late day think of undertaking any essential changes in the same? For, indeed, it was very probable that if it had been possible to foresee the last war and its consequences, the House would not have thought of refusing its approval to the new military constitution. The matter of the organization of the army must be settled anew, it was argued, by a definite law; but such a law would not under the existing state of things have to be passed by the Prussian Lower House but by the North German Parliament. The report revised by the deputy Twesten in accordance with these sentiments was adopted by the committee by a vote of twenty-five to eight.

In the House the discussion was, as ever, more lively, and the views more sharply opposed to one another. The whole Party of Progress set themselves determinedly against the bill. Waldeck considered that nothing whatever had been offered that justified any expectation of more constitutional conduct on the part of the Government. Schultze-Delitzsch declared that the whole war had been carried on not only without the consent, but even against the will, of the Prussian people; and he was *naïve* enough to refer to those melancholy addresses of peace of May and June as a brilliant proof of Prussia's careful prudence compared with the tumult of war which prevailed then at Vienna.

Virchow explained that he and his friends had known of a better way leading to German Unity than Bismarck's, namely, the way of Freedom. But as things now stood, he said, they were willing to sacrifice their wishes to Bismarck, and were willing to support his foreign policy, but must so much the more energetically defend constitutional rights. As if Benedek in June would have allowed himself to be deterred from marching upon Berlin by the fiery enthusiasm of the Party of Progress for Freedom! or as if there could have been at this time any worse foe to Bismarck's German policy conceivable than the continuance of the internal quarrel! The Professor of Catholic theology, Michelis, supplemented these remarks by the brilliant observation that Tetzel in 1517 was accused unjustly for having sold indulgences for future sins, but that this bill did indeed involve a pardon for all the future sins of the Ministry.

The Conservative party, delighted at the favorable sentiments, declared with great ardor that it would vote for the indemnity-bill in accordance with the wishes of the Government, although strictly speaking, something entirely different would be more properly in order, namely, a hearty vote of thanks to the Government for not having taken account of the foolish behavior of the House. The mediatory position held by Bismarck and Von der Heydt also received eloquent support from the parties of the Centre. Lasker and Georg Vincke, at other times seldom to be found on the same side, and also, at the close of the discussion, Twesten, who had made the report, demonstrated with convincing force the impor-

tance of the present situation, the consequence of a continued quarrel with the Government, and the power of Public Opinion which demanded unity of action.

The final vote on the report resulted in 230 in favor and 75 against, the latter including the Party of Progress, some few members of the Left Centre, and the Catholic fraction. The Upper House followed this example on the 8th of September, after Herr von Kleist-Retzow had given vent to his regrets at the injurious compliance on the part of the Government. The vote of the Upper House resulted in the unanimous acceptance of the bill as drawn up by the House of Deputies.

Internal peace was thus secured and the four years contest over the Constitution was ended. . . .

Since then more than twenty years have passed. Often enough have the representatives of the people refused to pass bills presented by the Government; but they have never found any reason to doubt the loyalty of the Ministers to the Constitution. It has not happened again.

❧ TEN BASIC BOOKS ❧

IRON AND BLOOD: THE UNIFICATION OF GERMANY, 1815–1871

1. Ergang, Robert R., *Herder and the Foundations of German Nationalism* (New York, 1931).

2. Eyck, Erich, *Bismarck and the German Empire* (New York, 1964).†

3. Hamerow, Theodore S., *Restoration, Revolution, Reaction: Economics and Politics in Germany, 1815–1871* (Princeton, N. J., 1958).†

4. Namier, Lewis B., *1848: The Revolution of the Intellectuals* (London, 1944, R. 1964).†

5. Pflanze, Otto, *Bismarck and the Development of Germany: The Period of Unification, 1815–1871* (Princeton, N. J., 1963).

6. Pinson, Koppel S., *Modern Germany: Its History and Civilization*, 2nd ed. (New York, 1966).

7. Snyder, Louis L., *Basic History of Modern Germany*, Anvil Book No. 23 (Princeton, N. J., 1957).†

8. Steefel, Lawrence D., *Bismarck, the Hohenzollern Candidacy, and the Origins of the Franco-Prussian War* (Cambridge, Mass., 1962).

9. Taylor, Alan J. P., *The Struggle for Mastery in Europe, 1848–1918* (Oxford, 1954).

10. Valentin, Veit, *1848: Chapters of German History* (London, 1940).

26

From Geographical Expression to National State: The Unification of Italy, 1815-1870

ITALY! O LOVELY LAND! O temple of Venus and of the Muses! How thou art portrayed by travellers who make a show of honouring thee! How thou art humiliated by foreigners who have the presumption to seek to master thee! But who can depict thee better than he who is destined to see thy beauty all his life long? Who can address to thee a more fervent and sincere exhortation than whoever is only honoured in honouring thee, only beloved in loving thee? Neither the barbarity of the Goths, nor the internal civil struggles, the devastation of many campaigns, the denunciations of theologians, nor the monopoly of learning by the clergy, could suffice to quench the immortal fire that animated the Etruscans and the Latins, that fired Dante's immortal spirit amidst the sufferings of his exile, Machiavelli in the anguish of his torture, Galileo among the terrors of the Inquisition, and Tasso in his wandering life. . . . Prostrate upon their tombs, ask the secret of their greatness and misfortune, and how their love of Fatherland, of glory and of truth increased their constancy of heart, their strength of mind and the benefits they have conferred upon us.

—UGO FOSCOLO, Inaugural Address, University of Pavia, 1809

1. Background: The Awakening

The Italian States in 1815. Factors ordinarily making for national unification—natural boundaries, historical traditions, and common language—existed in the Italian states. But other elements militated against unity: the persistent struggle between pope and emperor; the multiplicity of sovereignties; seemingly insurmountable social differences between North and South; and unwillingness of such cities as Rome, Milan, Venice, Florence, and Naples to sacrifice their glorious past for the sake of national unity. The French Revolution aroused longings in the Italies, as elsewhere, for national unification. Here, too, Napoleon stimulated a sense of nationalism. His agent, Joachim Murat, installed as king of Naples, became a champion of Italian unity.

In 1815, however, in the name of legitimacy, the Congress of Vienna restored the Italies to their former state of confused disunity; like Germany, Italy was, in effect, a geographical expression. The former Papal States in central Italy were returned to the papacy; the kingdom of the Two Sicilies (Sicily and Naples) was reestablished in the south; the kingdom of Sardinia (Sardinia and Piedmont), to which Genoa was added, was restored; large and small duchies were given back to their former rulers; and Lombardy and Venetia were awarded to Austria. The new states were nine in number: kingdom of Sardinia, Modena, Parma, Lucca, Tuscany, Papal States, kingdom of Naples, the republic of San Marino, and Monaco. Petty princes, vengeful nobility, and reactionary clergy, emulating Metternich, set out to repress revolutionary sentiment. Any vestiges of liberty, equality, and fraternity were wiped out by triumphant reactionaries.

The tyranny of the Restoration in the Italies met with opposition in the form of a rising nationalism. At first Italian national sentiment was limited to a small minority of poets and dramatists. The playwright Vittorio Alfieri (1749–1803), who disliked the French Revolution, reacted against the subsequent French invasion of the Italies. Italians, he cried, must unite in a common hatred of France. The poet Ugo Foscolo (1778–1827) called upon the dead from the Italian past to rise from their tombs and fight against the hated Austrians. The nationalist movement gathered momentum as students, noblemen, and the middle class rallied to the cause.

The Political Milieu. Most Italians were traditionalists, devoted to the past, opposed to revolutionary innovation, loyal to the absolute state, and convinced that authoritarianism was the best guarantee of order and security. Clericalism influenced not only intellectual but also political life. Most of the people, especially the peasantry, were convinced that the old world was best and that the privilege of class established by God was to be upheld. They attributed to the hated French such ideas as liberty, equality, and fraternity, and freedom of conscience and thought. The masses greeted the Austrians in Milan and the pope in Rome as guarantors of law and order.

The liberals, or anti-traditionalists, came almost exclusively from the small minority of the middle class which, unlike its counterpart in Britain and France, possessed neither drive nor power. The mass of the nation consisted of two groups: poor, illiterate peasants, indifferent to politics; and poverty-stricken, discontented workers seeking solace in dreams of social revolution. Liberalism had no deep roots in the country.

The history of the *Risorgimento* (revival, or rebirth) of 1815 to 1870 in the Italies is the story of the struggle of a progressive minority against domestic traditionalism and foreign domination. At first moderates and democrats contended for power. After 1849 there rose a new liberal movement composed of the more progressive moderates and the less doctrinaire democrats. In the process the national and liberal movements were bound together. Nationalism was the driving force, liberalism the cement. The makers of United Italy—Mazzini, Cavour, King Victor Emmanuel II, and Garibaldi—were all liberals who sought to unite the nation in freedom.

Role of the *Carbonari*. The *Carbonari* (charcoal-burners) played an important part in the emerging nationalism. Organized in the latter days of the Napoleonic Empire and carried over after 1815 into the period of Austrian domination, the political secret society aimed at freeing the country from foreign rule and obtaining constitutional liberties. Its members included army officers, nobles, landlords, government officials, workers, peasants, and even priests. The movement spread through southern Italy. Among the foreigners who joined it was Lord Byron, and Louis Napoleon was implicated in it in his early years.

The *Carbonari* used Christian and liberal phraseology in their constitutions: "Carbonarism teaches the true end of moral existence, and gives rules of conduct for social life. It is to the sacred rights of equality that the Good Cousins (*buon cugini*) must especially attach themselves." A fantastic and mysterious symbolism was designed to appeal to the masses. The members used a secret and impenetrable correspondence, by means of a dictionary of various words, referable to others of real meaning. Members were initiated by a complex ritual intended to impress them with the dire effects of betraying secrets. The societies, circulating forbidden literature, maintained a revolutionary ferment designed to assure Italian unity. Though harried by the Austrian police, the *Carbonari* carried on. Many members were executed, imprisoned, or exiled.

Insurrections. The revolutionary technique of the *Carbonari* was simple: they occupied the public buildings of an important city and then issued a manifesto calling on the people to support them. The difficulty was that the people usually remained apathetic and indifferent. In 1820 the *Carbonari* led a revolt in the Two Sicilies which was quickly suppressed. The next year they started a revolutionary movement in Piedmont, but the insurrection collapsed on the arrival of Austrian troops. They laid plans for an uprising in Lombardy, but it never took place. In February 1831, in the wake of the July Revolution of 1830 in France, the *Carbonari* organized a rebellion in the duchy of Modena and in Bologna. Once again, the Austrians crossed the Po and shattered the revolt. Guerrilla bands kept fighting in the mountains until they were crushed in early 1832. Meanwhile, Austrians and French occupied parts of the Papal States. By this time the *Carbonari* had spent itself; the survivors were old, tired, and disillusioned. Although they had failed as insurrectionists, they had strengthened an idea. They had done their share in preparing the way for the expulsion of Austrians from Italian affairs.

2. *Mazzini, Republicanism, and Revolution, 1831–1848*

Giuseppe Mazzini: Liberal Nationalist. Young Italian patriots were not discouraged by the repeated failures of the *Carbonari*. Among them was the twenty-five-year-old Giuseppe Mazzini (1805–1872), a native of Genoa, who joined the *Carbonari* in 1830, and within a few months was banished from his country. While living at Marseilles, he organized a new league, Young Italy, which included well-educated young men of liberal leanings for whom national unification was a holy cause. Organizing, agitating, educating, Mazzini worked to awaken his countrymen to the need for unity. A sentence of death was recorded against him in Sardinian courts. In 1837 he left for London, where he continued his labors. Nothing mattered to him except the cause; he never married. His entire life from 1831 to his death was motivated by one deeply-felt passion. He worked day and night meeting people, working with the revolutionaries, collecting money, making speeches, all for the cause. His writings were distinguished

by honesty, generosity, and determination. He loved Italy above all earthly things. "A nation," he said, "which has been enslaved for centuries can regenerate itself through virtue and self-sacrifice." He urged youth to take the lead: "Place the youth of the nation at the head of the insurgent masses; there are latent strength and magic in these young men."

Mazzini was the embodiment of the nineteenth-century concept of republicanism and nationalism. In his ideal state he saw no factions or parties. For him republicanism was the organization of the general will. His special contribution to the unification of Italy was the manner in which by his idealism he vitalized the struggling aspirations of the Italians. But his solution, a republic to be achieved without any foreign assistance, was apparently not in accordance with the political realities. The future of unification lay not with the republican idealist Mazzini but with the Piedmontese monarchy and its greatest statesman, Cavour.

Revolution of 1848 in the Italies. On March 4, 1848, King Charles Albert voluntarily promulgated a liberal constitution for Sardinia— the *Statuto*, granting a parliament elected by property owners, ministerial responsibility, and freedom of speech, press, and assembly. His son and successor, Victor Emmanuel II, maintained this constitution. The news of Metternich's flight from Vienna on March 13 gave impetus to the revolution throughout the Italies. In "five glorious days" (March 18–22, 1848) the people of Milan liberated their city from the Austrians, who were forced to fall back nearly 100 miles. Retreat of the hated "whitecoats" fired the Italians' imagination; they would drive the Austrians out of the Italies altogether.

On March 22 the Venetians proclaimed a republic, and on the same day Sardinia declared war on Austria. Volunteers rushed to join the war of liberation. The revolutionaries expected assistance from the new pontiff, Pius IX, who, since his accession in 1846, had revealed both liberal and anti-Austrian sentiments. But at the critical moment, Pius, fearing loss of Church control over the Papal States in the event of a successful nationalist revolution, withdrew his support. In addition, many Italians, including the Sardinian king, Charles Albert, distrusted the extravagant enthusiasm of the people and their radical leaders. One by one, Milan, Palermo, Rome, and Venice fell victim to the forces of reaction.

The war for Italian liberation thus far had failed because of lack of popular support, the attachment of Italians to traditionalism, and the inability of the liberals to act together. The Austrians again dominated the north; the princes returned to their thrones; the Italies were still fragmented. Mazzini had dreamed that the Italian people would rise in their might and bring his ideal republic into existence. It was a mirage. Mazzini became an exiled leader without a party.

3. Cavour's Plan for Unity, 1849–1861

The House of Savoy. Since 1815 every plan to unite the Italies had failed. Neither the *Carbonari* with its conspiracies, nor Young Italy with its dramatic call to arms, nor the general bitterness against Austria had been strong enough. Both the republicans and the papal party had shown themselves to be unequal to the task. Disappointed Italian patriots, grieved by the failure of every revolutionary movement, turned to Victor Emmanuel II of Sardinia and the house of Savoy for relief. Perhaps a kingdom of Italy could be achieved by uniting the other Italian states to Piedmont-Sardinia. Perhaps the Savoy house and Sardinia could play the same role in Italian history as the Hohenzollern dynasty and Prussia in the Germanies.

Victor Emmanuel of Savoy, King of Sardinia from 1849 to 1861, has been described as both hero and fool, as both an intelligent ruler of high principles and as a stupid, disloyal monarch. Whatever his character and personality may actually have been, he became, even more than Mazzini or Cavour, the symbol of Italian aspirations. Only Pius IX enjoyed as much prestige. "*Italia è Vittorio Emmanuele*" became the slogan of the struggle which led to the unification of Italy.

Cavour, Architect of United Italy. Count

Camillo Benso di Cavour (1810–1861) represented a new phase in the drive for unification. Descended from a noble Piedmontese family, he early became a fervent nationalist. Although he eventually became one of the nineteenth-century's greatest statesmen, he scarcely looked the part. Short and stocky, wearing small, steel-rimmed glasses, he ap-

Count Camillo Cavour, true champion of the cause of Italian unification. 1849–1861

peared to be a hard-working, conscientious clerk. In 1847 he helped found the newspaper, *Il Risorgimento*, in which he called for a representative system of government similar to that of England. He opposed absolutism as well as the use of military force to suppress political opposition. Cool, practical, he possessed, like Bismarck, an ability to discern the possible. He commanded more respect than affection. Mazzini, Garibaldi, and their followers either ridiculed or ignored him. To reactionaries and traditionalists he seemed a kind of modern devil.

But Victor Emmanuel II made Cavour his prime minister in 1852. Just as William I of

Prussia relied almost completely on his minister Bismarck, so did Victor Emmanuel allow Cavour a free hand to pursue his policies. Perhaps the king felt little personal sympathy for "that pestiferous little man," as he called him, but he was shrewd enough to recognize a remarkable ability and supported Cavour faithfully in one crisis after another.

Historical Controversy: Mazzini's Radicalism Versus Cavour's Moderation. Historians take opposing views on the efficacy of the approaches to unity by Mazzini and Cavour. While both leaders were nationalists, they differed in their attitude toward liberalism. Mazzini's radical vision of a united Italy was republican, democratic, and social; it was a liberalism derived from the democratic rather than the bourgeois school. He was opposed to *laissez-faire* policies and to the system of propertied suffrage or bourgeois liberalism. The British historian William Clarke praised his "lofty idealism, religious spirit, and his constant insistence on duty rather than rights."

Other historians are not impressed by Mazzini's approach to Italian unification. They see Mazzini's aims as idealistic dreaming and point to Cavour as the more able proponent of unity. They describe Cavour as more statesman than thinker, more man of affairs than idealist. Cavour, they say, saw his guide lines in British bourgeois liberalism. He derived his economic views from the Manchester school, his political views from the Whigs. His united Italy was to be a constitutional monarchy, liberal, but controlled by the propertied bourgeoisie. In the view of the Italian historian, Adolfo Omodeo, Cavour provided one of those rare cases in which the man of moderate views opposed extremism and won a magnificent political victory. Cavour, with his clear program, well-defined aims and ideals, was able to achieve what was necessary for national unity. Unlike Mazzini, he avoided mixing the national problem with the democratic and social, and was careful not to paralyze the only classes that could contribute to the Italian awakening.

"In the work of Cavour," wrote the Italian historian, Guido de Ruggiero, "we feel for the first time in Italian history the living spirit of the modern liberal state; the state which feeds upon mighty conflicts, which reconciles violent passions any one of which in isolation would be destructive and disastrous, while each, in its union with the others, is an element of life and progress."

Reform in Sardinia. As a preliminary step toward his goal, Cavour fashioned in Sardinia a smoothly working liberal bourgeois government. Expecting little from either selfish nobility or poverty-ridden peasantry, he favored policies designed to develop his little kingdom industrially and thereby enlarge the influence of the middle class. He reorganized the budget, improved the system of taxation, expanded credit, introduced free trade, and stimulated trade and industry. He broke the ecclesiastical hold, for which he was excommunicated, but he eliminated traditionalism as a major factor in Sardinian life. The State was now supreme over the Church in civil matters. He signed commercial treaties with the major countries of Western Europe, built highways and railroads, improved ports, rivers, and canals. All this led in a short time to an almost miraculous economic revival. Now there was money to create the military strength Cavour knew to be essential for the completion of Italian unity.

Preparing the Diplomatic Road. An unrelenting realist, Cavour had little use for popular uprisings, which he thought doomed to failure. He regarded Mazzini as an impractical visionary, as an emotional fanatic who, lacking common sense, would ruin the cause of unity. Cavour's plans were carefully precise: first he would block Austrian intervention, then eliminate the petty princes, and finally, submit the question of unity to the people in a plebiscite. Sardinia, he said, must be the champion of unity—the Italian people must rally to her in the struggle against both domestic and foreign despotisms.

Cavour would allow Europe to unite Italy. European powers had traditionally interfered in Italian affairs for their own interests. Italian patriots had to fight external as well as inter-

THE UNIFICATION OF ITALY, 1859-1870

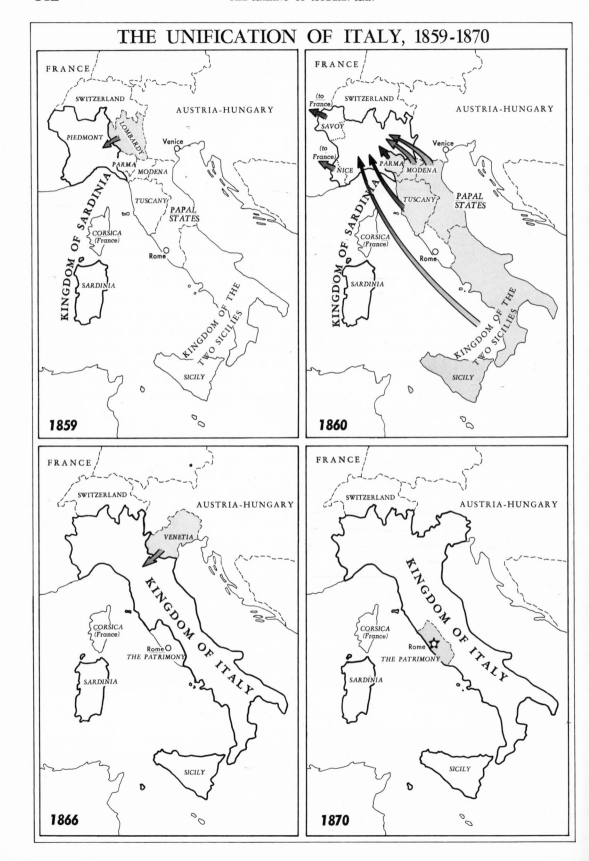

nal enemies. Why not induce one major power to intervene for the good of the Italians and help drive out the hated Austrians? Cavour's choice fell on France and her ambitious Louis Napoleon. Had not Napoleon III, himself partly of Italian origin, joined the *Carbonari* in his early days? And would not the French be attracted by war with Austria, their old enemy? To make it even more attractive, Cavour held out some enticing bait to France —the French-speaking district of Savoy and the city of Nice.

Cavour planned slowly but well. It was through his influence that Sardinia joined France and England in the Crimean War (1853–1856). As a result of that conflict Cavour was able to bring the case for Italian unity before the Great Powers at Paris in 1856. Two years later, in 1858, Napoleon III signed an alliance with Sardinia. Cavour had won the opening rounds. Sardinia now had the support of one of the strong powers of Western Europe.

Austro-Sardinian War, 1859. To make Austria appear the aggressor, Cavour instigated disturbances in Sardinia against Austrian rule. The Austrians, infuriated, threatened war. The British intervened by proposing a conference, which the Austrians refused. Then, in a major blunder, the Austrians on April 23, 1859, sent an ultimatum to Sardinia demanding that she disarm within three days. Cavour and Victor Emmanuel II, confident that Napoleon III would honor his word, rejected the ultimatum. Austrian troops invaded Sardinian territory on April 27, Napoleon III declared war, promising that he would "free Italy from the Alps to the Adriatic." Cavour's plan was working to perfection.

Like most European campaigns of the day, the 1859 war was brief, lasting a little over two months. At Magenta and Solferino the French and Sardinian forces were victorious. The Austrians were forced to abandon Lombardy. Solferino was costly: 1,600 officers and 40,000 men were killed on both sides. Depressed by the bloodshed and without preliminary understanding with Victor Emmanuel, Napoleon III deserted his ally and made a separate peace at Villafranca on July 11, 1859. Napoleon III was moved by various considerations: French Catholics had denounced him for his intervention in the Italies as "the modern Judas Iscariot," French losses were heavy, and Prussian armies were mobilizing along the Rhine. To join the Papal States into a united Italy was more than he had wanted; consequently, he stopped short without informing Cavour. Napoleon III and Francis Joseph I agreed that Austria would abandon Lombardy but keep Venetia, and that no changes would be made in the rest of the Italies. Austrian archdukes would continue to rule Tuscany and Modena, and the Papal States would remain intact. Cavour, driven to the point of fury by Napoleon's act of faithlessness, counseled Victor Emmanuel to continue the war alone, but the latter was wise enough to decline the advice of his angered minister. Sardinia, forced to make peace at Zürich, obtained Lombardy as her share of the spoils. In a rage, crying that Napoleon had betrayed him, Cavour resigned the Sardinian premiership.

Progress of Italian Unity. Napoleon III's intervention in Italian affairs stimulated the cause of Italian unity. At long last the Austrians had been beaten on Italian soil, and petty Italian tyrants could no longer rely on help from Vienna. Sardinia's role had earned for her the emotional support of Italians from every party—monarchists, federalists, republicans. In 1860, plebiscites were held in Parma, Modena, Tuscany, and the Romagna, as a result of which all these decided, virtually unanimously, to join Sardinia. Annexations followed. Napoleon III received his reward: plebiscites were also held in Nice and Savoy, both of which voted to join France. It was a double victory: Napoleon III had his taste of glory, and Italians had their road to unity.

4. Developments in the South

Garibaldi as Leader of the *Risorgimento*. The next step in Italian unification revolved about the romantic figure of Giuseppe Garibaldi (1807–1882), another hero of the *Risor-*

gimento. Through his participation in the earlier Italian revolts and in the Austro-Sardinian War of 1859, he became convinced that the destiny of Italy was linked with that of the house of Savoy. While Cavour worked in the north of Italy on his major objective of driving Austria from Italian affairs, Garibaldi was determined to settle accounts with the reactionary Neapolitan monarchy in the south. Assembling a motley force of 1,062 Italians and five Hungarians, wearing bright red woolen shirts and red hats, the fiery ex-candlestick maker set sail from Genoa on the night of May 5, 1860, to invade the southern kingdom, then under the despotic rule of Francis II. Luckily escaping Neapolitan cruisers, the ragged band, after a month of forced marches,

Patriot-leader Garibaldi fits the boot of Italy on Victor Immanuel II of Sardinia. Excellent likeness are presented in this contemporary cartoon.

sleepless nights, and exposure to mountain rains and semitropical sun, entered Palermo in triumph. Taking Sicily, Garibaldi sailed to Naples, and at Volturno on October 26, 1860 defeated an army twice the size of his own. He now assumed the dictatorship of Naples.

Kingdom of Italy. Cavour, who had swallowed his pride and returned to power, looked with alarm on the adventure of Garibaldi and the Thousand. He feared the hotheaded patriot might march on Rome, where French troops were stationed, a move that would bring him into an unwanted conflict with the French. Victor Emmanuel II crossed with his army into the Papal States, carefully avoiding Rome, and entered Naples. His parliament then voted for the annexation of the conquered territory, dependent on a favorable plebiscite. The vote was overwhelming for joining Sardinia. Victor Emmanuel and Garibaldi were both hailed in the streets of Naples. In November 1860 Garibaldi, refusing all honors, titles, and pensions, went back to his farm on Caprera "with a large bag of seed corn and a small handful of lira notes." It was the moment of his greatest statesmanship, although subsequently he felt himself to be slighted by those he had helped to power.

5. The Annexation of Rome, 1870

Death of Cavour. The pope had only Rome, garrisoned by French troops. With the exception of Rome, Venetia, and several smaller districts, all Italy, a country of 100,000 square miles and 22,000,000 inhabitants, was now united. The constitutional kingdom of Italy was proclaimed on March 17, 1861, at a meeting in Turin of the first Italian parliament. Thus ended Italian particularism, regionalism, and separatism.

Cavour died at the age of 51 soon after the proclamation of unity, leaving others to solve the difficult Venetian and Roman problems. Pope Pius IX declined to recognize the new kingdom, which he denounced as tainted with revolution. He excoriated Victor Emmanuel II as "a usurper innocent of every religious principle, despising every right, trampling upon every law." Rome itself was defended by a French army, as well as a volunteer Catholic army composed of Irish, Austrians, and Belgians dedicated to defense of the papacy.

Garibaldi Moves on Rome. Impatient at governmental delay, Garibaldi, in the spring of 1862, believing that he had the support of the king, organized volunteers for an attack on Venice. When his men were arrested, he went to Sicily where he raised the cry "Rome or death!" This time he was stopped by Italian troops at Aspromonte. Complaining loudly that he had been wounded "by an Italian bullet," Garibaldi again retired from the scene, this time in disgust.

Annexation of Venetia and Rome. The annexation of Venice and Rome took place in the wake of upheavals caused by the dynamism of Bismarck's foreign policy. In the Seven Weeks' War between Prussia and Austria in 1866, Italy joined forces with the Prus-

sian minister. Although the Austrians defeated the Italians in several battles, Prussia's overwhelming victory compelled Austria to cede Venetia to Italy. A plebiscite resulted in a call for annexation.

The next step came in the Franco-Prussian war of 1870–1871. Napoleon III fell into Bismarck's trap and quickly lost the war. Since he desperately needed troops to fight the Prussians, Napoleon withdrew the French garrison from Rome. On September 20, 1870, an Italian force entered the city. Papal mercenaries put up only a token resistance. By plebiscite, 134,000 to 1,500, the Romans voted to join Italy. The temporal power of the papacy in the Italies thus came to an end, and Rome became the capital of united Italy. Sardinia's *Statuto* became the new constitution. At long last the fragmented Italian states were consolidated into a united nation ready to take its place as one of the Great Powers of Europe.

⊰{ KEY DOCUMENT }⊱

GARIBALDI'S PROCLAMATION TO THE ITALIANS, MAY 5, 1860

Annual Register, 1860 (London, 1861), "History," p. 221.

ON THE NIGHT of May 5, 1860, Giuseppe Garibaldi set sail from Genoa with his Expedition of the Thousand to make war on the king of Naples. On that occasion the hero of the *Risorgimento* issued the following call to arms. What seemed to be a foolhardy attempt succeeded and brought fame to Garibaldi and his Red Shirts.

Italians!

The Sicilians are fighting against the enemies of Italy and for Italy. To help them with money, arms, and especially men, is the duty of every Italian.

Let the Marches, Umbria, Sabine, the Roman Campagna, and the Neapolitan territory rise, so as to divide the enemy's forces.

If the cities do not offer a sufficient basis for insurrection, let the more resolute throw themselves into the open country.

A brave man can always find a weapon. In the name of Heaven, hearken not to the voice of those who cram themselves at well-served tables.

Let us arm. Let us fight for our brothers;

tomorrow we can fight for ourselves.

A handful of brave men, who have followed me in battles for our country, are advancing with me to the rescue, Italy knows them; they always appear at the hour of danger. Brave and generous companions, they have devoted their lives to their country; they will shed their last drop of blood for it, seeking no other reward than that of a pure conscience.

"Italy and Victor Emmanuel!"—that was our battle-cry when we crossed the Ticino; it will resound into the very depths of Aetna.

As this prophetic battle-cry re-echoes from the hills of Italy to the Tarpeian Mount, the tottering throne of tyranny will fall to pieces, and the whole country will rise like one man.

❧{ HISTORICAL INTERPRETATION }❧

WILLIAM ROSCOE THAYER'S PORTRAIT OF CAVOUR

William Roscoe Thayer, *The Life and Times of Cavour*, (Boston, 1911), II, 500–507, *passim*. By permission of Houghton, Mifflin Company.

COUNT CAMILLO BENSO DI CAVOUR has been praised as the purposeful architect of Italian unity and has also been criticized as a reluctant politician who was equivocal in policies and actions. The following portrait was written by William Roscoe Thayer, an American historian best known for his works on Italian history. His *Life and Times of Cavour,* published in 1911, is probably the best biography of the Italian leader in any language.

To Italians, Cavour will stand for all time as the builder of their state. Many quarried: he took the blocks, of every size and shape and quality, and made United Italy out of them. He used the material at hand, as the true architect does, uncomplaining, in default of better: and though he died before the edifice was completed, yet the walls were up, the roof was on and the general plan finished. Like Michael Angelo, he left to others to add the façade and details. If only later Italians do not spoil Cavour's Doric design or hide it beneath a baroque exterior! . . .

It used to be contended that Cavour died opportunely for his fame. How he would have met the prosaic decades of financial and economic difficulties, how he would have warded off the undue pressure of France and opened the gates of Rome to the Italians, how he would have dealt with organized brigandage in the South or overcome the incessant feuds of the Party of Action, no one can say. But surely our best guide in such speculations is the statesman's record. To argue that Pericles, or Lincoln, or Cavour, who up to the moment of death commanded their situations, would have been unequal to cope with the confusion and panic caused by their death, is to employ a false logic.

Anyone can brandish the magician's wand; only the magician himself can conjure with it. Slowly the world has come to see that Cavour's achievement was not due to a succession of dazzling dexterities, but to the genius of the man— genius in which we must reckon temperament and natural aptitude, character, training, and an almost infallible eye for opportunity. He was a lifelong pupil of experience. He knew his time

and his people through and through. Having accepted certain principles, he never betrayed them. He devoted himself to Liberty, as a divine guide against which, until mankind shall cease to advance, the blasts of tyrannies and of hierarchies cannot prevail. He understood that progress is a growth and not a manufacture; that the harvest shall be according to the seed sown; that evolution, which is a mechanical process in the brute creation, can be assisted and even hastened by man's forethought for his kind. . . .

That in his statecraft he employed the accepted methods of diplomacy, many pages of this history have frankly shown. He could no more dispense with them than a general who hoped to win could abandon modern artillery and revert to arquebuses. No one recognized more clearly than he the conflict between private and public morals. "If we were to do for ourselves what we are doing for Italy," he remarked of the intrigues in the Two Sicilies in 1860, "we should be great rogues." He would be the first to welcome a happier era in which diplomacy as well as business and social life had the habit of perfect straightforwardness and crystalline candor.

But neither Cavour's scientific detachment, nor his readiness to sacrifice everyone, including himself, for his ideal, would have enabled him to make Italy, if he had not also possessed a vivid appreciation of the concrete. For him, persons were not abstractions, though in respect to the great design they must consent to be used or discarded as the need of the hour required. He saw which the partisans of the Old feared and hated but could not annihilate, must be grappled with. Democracy had arisen to make an end of

Feudalism, which, however transformed and wearing many names and strange disguises, was still, after a thousand years, the accepted principle of official Europe. Democracy was no longer a theory, but the ideal of multitudes whose numbers swelled every day.

In such a conflict between two mutually destructive systems, the consummate statesman is he who, averting the brute shock of a bloody revolution,—which often settles nothing,—leads out of the Old into the New by steps so gradual that the clash of readjustment may be minimized. This was Cavour's method. He did not destroy the Old, merely because it was old; nor did he rush fanatically to the New, merely because it was new. But perceiving that Liberty, the ideal which underlies Democracy, is a universal principle, by properly obeying which society may be organized on a higher level than the opposing principle of Authority can ever attain, he dedicated his genius to promoting Liberty in all fields. No one knew better than he how much Liberty presupposes, and how little hitherto mankind in the mass has possessed the qualifications required for working Democracy on a high plane; but he held that it

is better to fall short or to fail in striving for the highest, than to be content with the corroding prosperity of a system admittedly inferior. "Better the worst of Chambers," he said, "than the best of antechambers": and he set up reverence for Liberty as the test of man's moral nature. . . .

It is because Cavour, by the rare blending of Reason and disciplined Emotion, guided to victory the most marvelous and difficult struggle for freedom recorded in modern times, that his name will be cherished by generations yet unborn and by races yet uncivilized. Whoever fights for liberty anywhere, fights for the uplifting of mankind everywhere. All creeds agree in making absolute freedom an attribute of the Almighty: and finite man has in no way shown his kinship with the Infinite more clearly than by his incessant craving to be free. Without Liberty, the best loses for him its savor, and even religion becomes an anodyne instead of an inspiration. Among the champions of Liberty, since the beginning, none had a nobler vision of her beauty, none confided in her more loyally, none served her more wisely than Camillo di Cavour.

❧ TEN BASIC BOOKS ❧

FROM GEOGRAPHICAL EXPRESSION TO NATIONAL STATE:

THE UNIFICATION OF ITALY, 1815–1870

1. Albrecht-Carrié, René, *Italy from Napoleon to Mussolini* (New York, 1950, R. 1960).†
2. Berkeley, George F., and Joan Berkeley, *Italy in the Making, 1815–1848*, 3 vols. (Cambridge, 1932, 1935, 1940).
3. Greenfield, Kent R., *Economics and Liberalism in the* Risorgimento: *A Study of Nationalism in Lombardy, 1818–1848*, rev. ed. (Baltimore, Md., rev. ed. 1965).
4. King, Bolton, *The Life of Mazzini* (New York, 1929).
5. Mack Smith, Denis, *Cavour and Garibaldi* (Cambridge, 1954).
6. Orsi, Pietro, *Cavour and the Making of Modern Italy, 1810–1861* (London, 1914).
7. Salvadori, Massimo, *Cavour and the Unification of Italy*, Anvil Book No. 26 (Princeton, N. J., 1961).†
8. Taylor, A. J. P., *The Hapsburg Monarchy, 1809–1918* (London, 1949).†
9. Thayer, William R., *The Life and Times of Cavour*, 2 vols. (Boston, 1911).
10. Whyte, A. J., *The Evolution of Modern Italy* (Oxford, 1944, R. 1965).†

27

Autocracy, Orthodoxy, Agitation: Russia in the Nineteenth Century

IN THE year 1837 two Jews were condemned to death in Odessa because, from fear of the plague, they had attempted to escape across the frontier. Nicholas commuted the death penalty as follows: "The convicts are to run the gauntlet—a thousand men—twelve times. God be thanked, with us the death penalty has been abolished, and I will not reintroduce it." This was but one among numerous instances of the theocratic sovereign's power of self-deception and of his cruelty—for who had proposed that the Decembrists should be quartered, and who had commuted their punishment to hanging? In the year 1838 a student named Socinskii gave the director of the surgical academy a box on the ear. He was sentenced to run the gauntlet—five hundred men—three times. Nicholas revised the sentence thus: "To be carried out in the presence of all the students of the academy. Subsequently the offender, instead of being sent to Siberia, is to spend ten years, wearing fetters, in the disciplinary battalion at Kronstadt." It is hardly necessary to add that though there was no capital punishment, the men thus sentenced died under the blows of the soldiers.

—THOMAS G. MASARYK

1. From Liberalism to Reaction: Alexander I

Tsar Alexander I's Early Liberalism. Alexander I (r. 1801–1825), grandson of the despotic tsarina, Catherine the Great, was a handsome, gregarious monarch who dreamed of raising the level of his backward country. The first half of his reign was marked by such internal reforms as liberation of the serfs (without land) in the Baltic provinces and grant of permission to squires elsewhere to free their serfs with land. This was the first move of the government toward abolition of serfdom. The tsar also reorganized the universities, placed parish and normal schools in an extensive state educational system, and abolished torture of political prisoners. Alex-

ander soon turned his attention from domestic affairs to the long-range duel with Napoleon. The main event of his reign was the patriotic war in 1812 against France, in which the tsar regarded himself as an instrument of the Divine Will in the drama of Napoleon's downfall.

Alexander I's early liberalism was apparent in his handling of foreign affairs. He confirmed the traditional national liberties of Finland which he had annexed in 1809. He acquired Bessarabia in 1812. He reestablished a Polish national state with a constitutional government and named himself as king. He advised the restored Bourbon king of France to grant a constitutional charter. The Holy Alliance, which he was instrumental in forming in 1815, was viewed by many as a conspiracy of tyrants, but originally at least, it revealed a sincere effort on Alexander's part to inject a humane spirit into political relations between nations.

Russia in 1815. The empire of the tsars was a huge, sprawling state, lying half in Europe and half in Asia, and covering one-sixth of the land surface of the globe. Russia had the smallest navigable coastline of any great nation: in Europe her only free outlets to the sea were the Baltic port of St. Petersburg, and Archangel, a White Sea harbor frozen half the year. This vast semi-Oriental state, partly feudal, partly monarchical, lagged far behind the rest of Europe in political experience. Touched only slightly by the Renaissance, Reformation, Enlightenment, and Industrial Revolution, even by the French Revolution, Russia for the greater part of the nineteenth century was almost isolated from the mainstream of Western development. While Western Europe was shaping constitutional governments, Russia remained an absolute state under a tyrannical tsar. The Romanovs sat firmly on the throne, even more securely in control than the Hapsburgs and the Hohenzollerns. A small group of nobles became rich at the expense of the rest of the people. In the countryside were masses of illiterate peasants not yet infected with the germs of revolution. As late as 1855, nine-tenths of all Russian land was owned by the imperial family and about 100,000 noble families. Except for several small areas controlled by free peasants, the vast majority of serfs tilled the soil and served in the households of the nobility.

Conversion of Alexander I to Autocracy. Alexander I, his tendency toward morbid dreaming becoming more pronounced, fell under the influence of a religious mystic, Baroness von Krüdener. After 1815 his zeal for liberalism began to cool perceptibly, because several shocking events aroused his fears. In 1818 he was appalled by the discovery of a revolutionary conspiracy among officers of his own bodyguard. In 1819 a fanatical German student murdered the tsar's former agent August von Kotzebue. The Poles, ungrateful to the tsar for the constitution he

had granted them, began to agitate for independence. This was too much for Alexander who, at the Congress of Troppau in 1820, confessed to Metternich: "I deplore all that I said and did between the years 1815 and 1818. I regret the waste of time. You are right. Tell me what you want me to do, and I shall do it." From this time on, Alexander I became even more active than Metternich in opposing liberal movements.

Modern history has known few more tragic figures than Alexander I. The brilliant promise of his early years was frustrated. He left Russia a legacy of tyranny, a ruined economy, a political system rotten with graft and corruption, and a festering educational system.

2. *Autocracy: The Reign of Nicholas I, 1825–1855*

Decembrist Revolt, 1825. Alexander I died on December 13, 1825, in the Crimea. Since he had no children, the succession would normally have passed to his brother Constantine, but the latter, in 1822, had renounced his claims in favor of the younger brother, Nicholas. Nicholas, however, refused to accept the arrangement until he had obtained a further renunciation from Constantine. In the general uncertainty a military revolt was started by the Northern Society, a revolutionary group composed mostly of officers inspired by the *Carbonari*. The conspirators obtained the support of about 2,000 soldiers who, on December 26, 1825, revolted with the cry "Constantine and the Constitution!" (The troops were so ignorant of what free government meant that they actually believed "Constitution" to be Constantine's wife.) A few volleys of grapeshot from loyal troops ended the mutiny. Nicholas I personally led the examination of the conspirators and ordered severe sentences for the ringleaders. Five were hanged and more than a hundred others were deported to Siberia for penal servitude.

Although the Decembrist revolt was a trivial fiasco, at the same time it was the beginning of a series of explosions which, in the long run, led to the overthrow of the Romanov dynasty. For the time being, reactionary conservatism was triumphant, but there was growing resentment against the ruthlessness of the government. Though the masses remained comparatively untouched, members of the educated upper classes, victims of harsh treatment at the hands of Nicholas I, became leaders of the revolutionary movement.

The Nicholas System. The memory of the Decembrist revolt made Nicholas I an enemy of liberalism and a harsh, unbending autocrat. A man of magnificent physique, he had little aptitude for learning, but took great pleasure in parade ground and battlefield. He displayed faith only in matters of discipline and obedience and rarely rose above the standards of a narrow-minded bureaucrat. In his thirty-year reign he succeeded in stamping out all opposition inside Russia and made himself the most reactionary sovereign on the Continent. His regime was predominantly military in character. He appointed loyal officers to head most departments of state, including ecclesiastical affairs. His secret police, organized as Section III, or the Third Section, in the imperial chancery, controlled all aspects of life so thoroughly, and left so great an imprint on Russian affairs, that not even the Soviet Union after 1917 could afford to dispense with it. He made it a point to construct "mental dikes for the struggle with destructive notions." He sealed off Russia from what he regarded as the pestilential air of Western Europe: he ordered that every foreign visitor be examined at the borders for forbidden ideas, and every non-Russian book be searched for evidence of contraband thought. Any citizen who made the slightest dangerous remark soon found himself on the way to Siberia. So severe was Nicholas' rule that no school, hospital, or newspaper could be founded without his approval; the construction of a private dwelling with five windows or more required a special royal permit. The Nicholas System, which advocated an iron rule, was envied by every European autocrat.

Domestic Affairs. Nicholas I made a show of improving the administration, especially by reforming the financial system and codifying

Russian law (1832), but he was careful to keep his own powers intact. With Michael Speranski (1772–1839) as editor, the *Complete Collection of the Laws of the Empire of Russia* appeared in fifteen volumes in 1833. This codification remained definitive until 1917. Nicholas built railroads, but slowly and most often for military purposes. A loyal adherent of the established Orthodox Church, he regarded Church and State as one and inseparable. At the same time he vigorously persecuted all other groups, such as Roman Catholics, Jews, and dissenters.

To Nicholas I, the most irritating opposition came not from Russians but from Poles. Although parceled out among three powers in the three partitions in the late eighteenth century, the Poles, especially those in Russia, retained a lively sense of nationalism. Inspired by the French revolutionary movement, they rose in revolt, expelled a Russian garrison, and proclaimed their independence in 1831. Infuriated, Nicholas revoked the Polish constitution, suppressed the Diet, and sent an avenging army to Warsaw. He annexed Poland outright, outlawed the Polish language, and exiled families as refugees to all corners of Europe. This marked the beginning of the policy of Russification of Poland.

Foreign Policy: The Gendarme of Europe. Nicholas I was as much opposed to revolutionists outside Russia as to those inside his empire. He meddled in the affairs of Central Europe by sending armies to help the 1848 uprisings in Austria. He regarded himself as a kind of international policeman; indeed, during the mid-century popular rebellions, he was urged by other autocrats to halt the spread of European democracy. Nicholas's second aim was to destroy the Ottoman Empire in Europe. His eyes turned to Constantinople, key to Russian foreign policy since the regime of Peter the Great. Moreover, he would liberate his "little Slav brothers" in the Balkans from the rule of the hated Ottoman Turks. To the Russian tsar it was a matter of conscience and a new crusade to supplant the Muslim crescent with the cross on the dome of Saint Sophia in Constantinople.

RUSSIA'S DRIVE TO THE WEST
1: Crimean War, 1853-56
2: Attack on the Ottoman Empire, 1877-78
3: World War I, 1914-18
4: World War II and the Cold War, 1939-

Territory annexed by the U.S.S.R. since 1939

Satellite countries of Eastern Europe

Exercise in Futility: Crimean War, 1853–1856. Under the rule of Nicholas I, Russia was outwardly a great, powerful state. But the Crimean War, in the midst of which he died, revealed the weakness of autocratic Russia. In 1840 Nicholas had suggested that Great Britain join Russia to dismember European Turkey, but the wary British refused. The war between the Russian and Ottoman Empires began in 1853. To the annoyance of Nicholas, the Turks were joined by Great Britain and France in 1854 and by Sardinia in 1855. Britain had become the watchdog of the Mediterranean: it was a cornerstone of British policy to deny Russian claims to Constantinople and access to warm water. Nicholas expected assistance from the Austrians, especially in return for the service that he had rendered the Hapsburgs in 1848, but to his surprise and resentment they announced a policy of benevolent neutrality.

The struggle was confined mainly to military operations on the peninsula of the Crimea. Strong Allied armies laid siege to Sevastopol, which the Russians had fortified to dominate the Black Sea. The entire campaign, on both sides, was notorious for its incompetence and recklessness. An example was the charge of the Light Brigade, a troop of 600 British soldiers who won fame by a desperately valiant but fatal charge through the North Valley, an exploit immortalized in a popular poem by Tennyson. The Russian military machine was corrupt and weak, the Allies equally inefficient in providing arms, food, and sanitation. Both sides were unprepared to endure the snows and bitter cold. Sickness and starvation caused more havoc than bullets. An English nurse, Florence Nightingale, "the angel with the lamp," did what she could to alleviate the acute sufferings and deprivations of the soldiers, and set up some standards for future military health and sanitation.

Sevastopol, although desperately defended, fell after an eleven-month siege. Russia sued for peace in 1856. At Paris, a treaty was signed which (1) neutralized the Black Sea; (2) opened navigation on the Danube; and (3) gave Moldavia and Wallachia local autonomy under Turkish suzerainty. Russia recovered Sevastopol. The Great Powers assumed the responsibility for seeing that Turkey fulfilled her guarantees to Christians.

The Crimean War, which cost half a million lives and two billion dollars, checked Russian ambitions, but otherwise it did nothing to solve the vexing Near Eastern Question. Turkey emerged from the war with her territorial integrity guaranteed, and by being invited to Paris, was recognized as a member of the European family of nations.

Golden Age of Russian Literature. The era of Nicholas I was not altogether without glory in that, despite reactionary censorship, intellectual currents could not be restrained. Russian writers, escaping from the influence of French and German models, blossomed forth as creators of brilliant works which may be placed on a plane equal with the other great literatures of Western Europe. The pattern was distinctly national. Alexander Pushkin (1799–1837), greatest Russian poet and one of the outstanding figures of world literature, wrote such emotional poems as *Ode to Liberty*, and used his literary genius to attack the social standards of his day. Nicholas I exempted Pushkin from ordinary censorship and was himself Pushkin's only censor. A target for intrigues, Pushkin was led into a duel in which he was mortally wounded. Nikolai Gogol (1809–1852), father of Russian realism, described the desolate, drab, and mediocre life of noble, bureaucrat, and peasant, but at the same time he pointed to Russia's great future. A tortured soul, Gogol died at the age of forty-three, starved to death by religious fasting.

Later Russian novelists were influenced by Gogol's interest in character and attention to detail. Toward the end of Nicholas I's reign,

the Russian novel was dominated by a remarkable trio who portrayed a society in transformation under the impact of Western ideas for which it was historically ill-prepared. Ivan Turgenev (1818–1883) skillfully described the Russian life of his day while urging the necessity for reform. Feodor Dostoevsky (1821–1881), hostile to both reaction and radicalism, revealed his concept of a democratic, Christian nationalism while proclaiming Russian messianism. In a series of psychological novels Dostoevsky tried to explain the struggle of men and women for redemption through suffering. Leo Tolstoy (1828–1910) depicted the Russian scene while calling for renunciation of violence and wealth, inner self-improvement, and love of all living things. All three literary giants were interested mainly in the study of Russian character, but they dealt with personalities and situations that were not exclusively Russian but characteristic of humanity in general. In throwing light on the inner recesses of the human soul, these novelists faithfully recorded the dilemma of modern man.

The Great Debate: Westernization Versus Slavophilism. Russian intellectuals were engulfed in interminable discussions and philosophical ferment regarding the role of their country in civilization. Two great schools of thought emerged: Westernization and Slavophilism. The Westernizers, liberals impressed by the Enlightenment, the French Revolution, and Western experience in general, wanted Russia to join the mainstream of Western development. They denied that there were any discrepancies between Russia and the West. If Russia were to follow the lead of the West, then she could lift herself bodily from the level of backwardness and weakness. They urged that the Westernization policies of Peter the Great be extended. Among the leaders of the Westernizers was the exiled nobleman, Alexander Herzen (1812–1870), who from 1847 lived in exile, mostly in London, where he published *The Bell*, the first Russian *émigré* journal to be circulated clandestinely in Russia. Inside Russia was Vissarion Belinsky (1811–1848), the first important Russian literary critic with a passion for improving social conditions.

Belinsky was convinced that Russia's malady was "lack of personal independence." He warned that there must be reform along the lines achieved in the West. "Russia's future," he said, "will be a great danger to Europe and full of misfortune to herself if we do not have an emancipation of individual rights."

The second school, the Slavophiles, were distressed by the Hegelian hierarchy of great civilizations—first, the Greeks; second, the Romans; third and on top, the Germans. Where did that leave the Russians? Accordingly, Slavophiles began to glorify the Russian past and to praise its virtues as superior to those of the decadent West. This was nationalist romanticism in all its glory. There was also implicit in it a religious bias: the Russian Orthodox form of Christianity was considered superior to the religions of Western Europe because it had not been diluted by the weak wine of Protestantism and the strong liquor of atheistic science. The Slavophiles stimulated Pan-Slavism—the idea that all Slavic peoples, including those in the Austrian and Turkish empires, could count on the support of their Russian Slavic brothers. Leaders of this movement were the theologian Alexei Khomyakov (1804–1860), and later the publicist Ivan Aksakov (1823–1886), both of whom insisted that Russians could rely on their own national character and had no need to learn from the West. They were sure that Western destructive rationalism had led to violence, putrefaction, and chaos, while Slavophilism meant true spiritual life, justice, and charity.

3. From Reform to Repression: Alexander II, 1855–1881

The Tsar-Liberator. Their defeat in the Crimean War made it clear to Russians that reform was necessary. Nicholas I's son and successor, Alexander II (r. 1855–1881), was faced with the twin tasks of negotiating a humiliating peace with France and Britain and allaying domestic unrest. A sensitive, understanding monarch, Alexander, under the impulse of the Westernizers, occupied himself for the better part of a decade with the details of reform. Though the reforms were of funda-

"Tsar-Liberator" Alexander II, whose enthusiasm for reform waned as his efforts failed either to satisfy the liberal Westernizers or to sway the conservative Slavophiles.

mental importance, they remained but half-hearted concessions: autocracy, orthodoxy, and nationalism remained the goals of the reforming tsar. The regime which started with great expectations fell short of the aims and aspirations of even the moderate liberals.

Emancipation of the Serfs, 1861. Alexander II turned first to the problem of internal social reform, the lot of the peasants. Serfdom, characteristic of the social order of the Middle Ages, had by this time been abolished in Western Europe. But in the Russia of 1859 some 23,000,000 serfs were still bound to the soil by such proprietors as the imperial family, the state, the Orthodox Church, and individual masters. "The present position," said Alexander II, "cannot last, and it is better to abolish serfdom from above than to wait until it begins to be abolished from below." A committee of officials and nobles, acting under the inspiration of the tsar, drew up an Emancipation Law, which was issued as a ukase, or imperial decree, on February 19 (March 3), 1861. By this decree the peasant became *personally free* at once without any payment, and the proprietor was obliged to grant him his plot of land at a fixed rent, with the eventual possibility of redeeming it at a price to be agreed upon later. Lands were assigned to self-governing village communes called *mirs*. Each *mir* was to pay an annual rent, fixed by the tsar's agents, as indemnity, or to pay for the land outright. The members of the *mir* were held jointly responsible for the redemption payments. As a means of assuring equality of treatment, the land was to be redistributed every ten or twelve years.

Although the emancipation was a giant social step forward, it had many defects. The problems of allocating the land and sharing payment were not solved; consequently, the peasantry continued in a state of semi-starvation. The peasants still had too little to support their families. When land was divided between nobles and freedmen, the former usually got the best areas. Peasants indebted to their lords had to perform extra services. Yet the proclamation of emancipation was undoubtedly the most important event in the history of nineteenth-century Russia. It paved the way for other reforms as well as for the revolutionary movement that finally led to the destruction of tsarism.

Extension of the Reform Program. The Tsar-Liberator did not confine his reforming activities to freeing the serfs. For centuries the Russian courts had been notorious for their lack of experienced officials and for widespread corruption. Nicholas I had recodified Russian law, but there were still weaknesses in the entire legal system, such as secret testimony, and punishment guided by social status. In 1862 Alexander II decreed a judicial system modeled on that of the West: justices of the peace were to be elected locally; there would be district and circuit judges; and a senate would act as a court of appeal. The accused now had the right of trial by jury, and proceedings in the courts were opened to the public. Alexander hoped to eliminate the graft and corruption of the old days by establishing an independent judiciary, but he did not succeed in this goal.

In 1864 Alexander II decreed that each district of the thirty-four administrative provinces, or governments, into which Russia had been divided since the eighteenth century, was to have a local council, or *zemstvo*. The nobility, townsmen, and peasants, with no one class having a majority of the seats, served on these local boards. The *zemstvos* were empowered to maintain roads, schools, churches, and jails of the district, levy local taxes, establish savings banks, improve farming methods, and in general, exercise local authority. The theory was good, but the practice was disappointing. The *zemstvos* provided a training ground for liberals, but the local councils were often overruled by imperial officials still influenced by the tradition of a centralized bureaucracy.

Zealous for still further reform, Alexander II in 1864 also set up a secondary school system modeled on the German *Gymnasium* (classics) and *Realschule* (sciences). He allowed academic freedom in the university classrooms (as a result of which the institutions of higher learning became centers of revolutionary activity). He also accorded a measure of liberty to the press by simplifying the system of censorship. In 1874 he enacted a compulsory military-service law which required all Russian males to serve in the army for six years and for nine additional years in the reserve.

Alexander II pursued his program for a decade, but the reforms he decreed were actually an impulsive recognition of the demand by Westernizers for change. The tsar was caught in the middle: conservatives denounced him for what they called dangerous appeasement of the radicals, and the liberals criticized him for lukewarm reforms. His liberalism became weak and diluted; his enthusiasm for reform did not survive the increasing pressures.

Polish Revolt in 1863. Alexander II's urge for reform lessened considerably with the Polish rebellion of 1863. This discredited the

Westernizers and led him into the arms of the reactionary Slavophiles. For some time Polish patriots had been organizing secret conspiracies dedicated to independence. Though badly armed, they arose once more in rebellion. There was little help from Western Europe: Napoleon III, although sympathetic, remained aloof, while Bismarck offered Alexander the armed assistance of Prussia. The Russian government crushed the rebellion, executed or exiled its leaders, and appropriated their land. The Slavophiles lost no time in convincing the tsar that the Polish rebellion was the fruit of his concessions to the Westernizers.

A fanatic's attempt in 1866 to assassinate him wiped out the last vestiges of Alexander II's liberalism. From this time on he became as reactionary as his predecessor.

Revolutionary Movement: Populism. In its early phases the revolutionary movement was inspired by liberals recruited from the lower gentry, middle-class professionals, and conscience-stricken aristocrats. More extreme demands came from the radicals—students, writers, and professional men disturbed by the slowness of reform. During the decade after 1876 there began a branch of the radical movement, known as Populism, or the *Narod* (*Going among the People*) movement. The idea was to go directly to the peasants and teach them to demand "Land and Freedom." Leader of the Populists was Peter Lavrov (1823–1900), a professor of mathematics, whose *Historical Letters* (1868–1869) projected a philosophy of history which dominated subsequent Populist thought. More than a thousand students went to the countryside to train peasant leaders and spread the gospel of freedom. Many were arrested and sent to prison or exile. The movement had little success: the suspicious peasants, angered by the students' denunciations of the "Little Father," distrusted their would-be liberators and even handed them over to the police.

Iconoclastic Nihilism. The Russian intelligentsia formed a curiously unconventional group of malcontents. Isolated from the peasantry, unable to take part in governmental af-

fairs, harried by the secret police, they turned their energies to interminable discussion. The Nihilists, extreme wing of the radical movement, believed in nothing (Latin *nihil,* nothing) and demanded that "nothing must remain unchanged." They poured ridicule on idealism, but they exalted science. "Life is a workshop," said the Nihilists, "and to the rubbish heap with art, poetry, and music!" The currency of Nihilism owed much to Turgenev's novel, *Fathers and Sons* (1861), in which the chief protagonist of the creed, Bazarov, recognizes no authority, doubts all principles and values, and asserts the freedom of the sovereign individual. Some Nihilists joined the anarchists and adopted the tactics of terrorism, but the great bulk, taking no part in the political struggle, were content to make known their ideals through literature.

Activist Anarchism. The term *anarchism* was popularized by the writer Joseph Proudhon (1809–1865), who believed that all government was based on physical force and that people should live without compulsion of any kind. In 1846 a Russian nobleman, Michael Bakunin (1814–1876), met Proudhon in Paris and became a passionate proponent of anarchism. Bakunin, expelled from France in 1848, was handed over to the Russian authorities, who exiled him to Siberia in 1855. He escaped in 1861 and spent the remainder of his life in Switzerland. A combination of gentle intellectual and violent fanatic, Bakunin was a childlike man who was ready at any moment to embark on desperate revolutionary enterprises. He dedicated himself to a career of "pan-destructionism," the elimination of any institutions which restricted freedom, including government, religion, and marriage. Man, he said, must repudiate God, the State, and the family. Urged on by pity for suffering humanity, he demanded "terrible, total, inexorable destruction" of existing institutions, leaving the reconstruction of society to the future.

Propaganda of Deed: The Terrorists: Included among the extremists were the terrorists, who were convinced that no legal cure for the evils of the tsarist government was possible. Disappointed by the indifference of the peasants and angered by police persecution, young Russians in 1879 organized a "People's Will" movement, consisting of the most radical wing of the older Populist group. In a stirring manifesto they declared war on tsar and government, and turned to bomb, pistol, and dagger as instruments of their will. A new type of professional revolutionist appeared, who assumed aliases, lived in the underground, forged passports, published illegal journals, smuggled arms, and manufactured bombs. Terrorists tried to blow up the tsar's train and with a bomb destroyed a part of the Winter Palace. To Alexander II, the prime target, this was civil war. He redoubled his

efforts to crush the malcontents, but at the same time tried to win support by political concessions. On March 3, 1881, the terrorists finally achieved their main aim: Alexander was killed by a bomb on the very day that he had signed a decree approving a constitution for Russia. The Tsar-Liberator paid with his life for the sins of his father.

4. Reassertation of Autocracy: Alexander III, 1881–1894

Alexander III and Preservation of Autocracy. Alexander III, who succeeded to the throne in 1881, was determined to avenge his father's death and put an end to revolutionary

A convoy of prisoners bound for Siberia. Contemporary print shows Asian ruin in the background.

activities. He was certain that his father's appeasement of liberals and radicals had been responsible for the assassination. "The voice of God," he said, "orders us to stand firm at the helm of government." Accordingly, he restored the Nicholas System, hunted down opponents of his government, tried them in special courts, and sentenced them to death or exile. The unfortunate ones ended up in Siberia; the lucky ones fled to Switzer-

land, France, and America. Russia was once again frozen into a monolithic state under the old watchwords of autocracy, orthodoxy, nationalism.

Power Behind the Throne: Pobiedonostsev. To head the state police Alexander III selected Viacheslav Plehve (1846–1904), who directed the force with such efficiency that for several years revolutionary activities almost ceased. The tsar placed the over-all administration of reaction in the hands of his tutor, Constantine Pobiedonostsev (1827–1907), procurator of the Holy Synod and director of the Russian Orthodox Church. A puritanical professor of Russian law at the University of Moscow, Pobiedonostsev believed that the institutions of Western Europe and America should serve not as a model but as a warning for Russia. He rejected democracy, freedom of the press, and independence of the judiciary. Russian problems, he said, should be handled "in a Russian way." For a quarter of a century Pobiedonostsev was the most influential man in Russia. Under his reactionary drive the feeble trend toward liberal reform that had appeared in the early part of Alexander II's reign was not only abandoned but reversed. He ordered the secret police to watch students, muzzled the press, and denied citizens the right of assembly. On the excuse that the *zemtsvos* had become centers of poisonous liberalism, he curtailed their powers by means of new elective procedures designed to favor the aristocracy. By discouraging the development of public schools, he maintained an llliterate populace, the vast majority of whom could not read or write.

Policy of Russification. Pobiedonostsev did his best to combine the closely integrated twin forces of Russian nationalism and the Orthodox Church. "One Church, One Russia, One Tsar" was his motto. More than one-half of the population was non-Russian and many professed the Roman Catholic, Protestant Islamic, or Jewish faith. Pobiedonostsev, supported by the tsar in whose name he acted, began a systematic Russification of all subject peoples. He forbade the use of the Ukrainian, Byelorussian, and Lithuanian languages in either schools or books. He decreed that all teaching in Poland and in the Baltic provinces must be in Russian and no longer in Polish or German. He used violent, often brutal, means to convert all the subject peoples to Russian Orthodoxy.

Pogroms: Persecution of Jews. The heaviest blows fell upon Russia's 5,000,000 Jews, half the world's Jewish population. Many had come to Russia as a result of the partitions of Poland. Bigots and hooligans murdered Jews and stole their property. Pobiedonostsev legalized the process: he was said to have remarked that he would force one-third of the Jews to emigrate, convert another third to the Orthodox Church, and harry the remaining third to destruction. In 1881, especially in the southwest, a wave of pogroms (the Russian word for devastation) swept through the empire. The massacres lasted until nearly 1882, when the government introduced legislation to prevent the "exploitation" of the Russian people by Jews. Already in the early nineteenth century the Jews had been segregated in a Pale of Settlement, consisting of Poland, Lithuania, and the Ukraine. Regulations on residence, occupation, and education of Jews were now made more severe. They were allowed to live only in the western and southwestern provinces of the empire, in towns and not in rural areas, •were forbidden to acquire land, and were subjected to a *numerus clausus* (quota system) in high schools and universities. They were forced out of governmental positions, and the professions. Harassed by pogroms and new restrictive laws, Russian Jews began a mass emigration to Western Europe, the United States, and Latin America. Some among those who chose to remain in Russia became volunteers for the revolutionary cause.

Industrialization. In contrast to Alexander III's revived semi-Oriental autocracy was the economic development of his reign. The Russian giant began to awaken from centuries of slumber. Although the introduction of power-driven machinery and the factory system came to Russia much later than to Western Europe, once begun it progressed rapidly. Capitalism and a modern industrial economy were favored largely for the purpose of improving the military establishment. It was necessary to superimpose an advanced economy upon a backward agrarian state, but it was done. There was notable progress in the mining of coal, and the production of pig iron. By 1900 Russia was mining one-tenth as much coal as Great Britain, and ranked fourth among the world's nations in the manufacture of cotton cloth. Progress was also made in railroad construction. Alexander III, using as bait Russia's vast natural resources and tremendously large domestic market, welcomed foreign capital to invest in Russian industries.

The most important figure in the industrialization of Russia was Count Sergei Witte (1849–1915), minister of finance from 1892 to 1903 and a specialist in railway transportation. A disciple of the economic theory

preached by the German, Friedrich List, in his *National System of Political Economy,* Witte expanded the railway system, promoted the building of the Trans-Siberian Railway to link the West with Vladivostok, encouraged industry by subsidies and protective tariffs, drew foreign capital into Russia, and in 1897 placed the country on the gold standard. Aside from his work in economic moderniza-

Witte

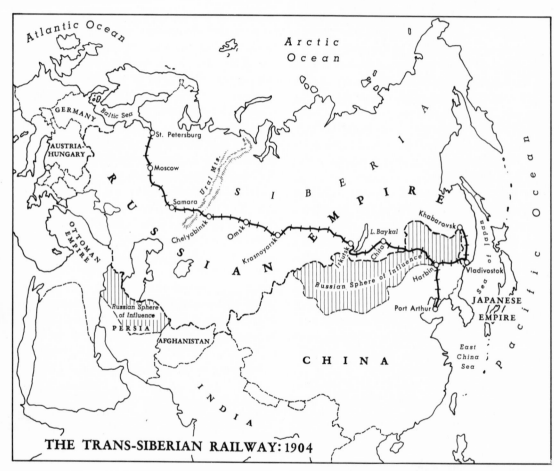

THE TRANS-SIBERIAN RAILWAY: 1904

tion, Witte was a reactionary and a proponent of autocracy. To encourage industry, he increased taxes, thereby shifting the burden most heavily to the peasants and workers. The impoverishment of the lower classes was worsened by repeated famines. The nobility still could receive loans on easy terms, but the peasants had to pay high interest rates. Such shortsighted economic practices produced growing dissatisfaction.

5. Revolutionary Ferment: The Reign of Nicholas II, 1894–1917

Nicholas II and Continued Autocracy. On his deathbed, Alexander III implored his son to retain the instruments of autocracy. Nicholas II (r. 1894–1917) faithfully carried on the familiar policies: repression, orthodoxy, Russification, anti-Semitism, Pan-Slavism, and industrial paternalism. The new tsar, weak and vacillating, with neither the will nor the mind to become a true autocrat, easily fell under the influence of stronger personalities. At first Nicholas was greeted with public expectation that another liberal era was at hand, but that hope was dashed when he informed the representatives of the *zemstvos* that they could not participate in the administration of national affairs.

Party Alignments: The Liberals. An important added factor in Russian politics was the formation of new parties with specific programs. Had all the discontented groups organized in one overpowering unified party at this time, the autocratic regime could not have long survived. But the agitators, moved by divergent ideals, were never able to reconcile their differences. By taking advantage of these divisions, Nicholas II was able to maintain the old reactionary regime.

The liberal elements, led by men who had gained political experience in the *zemstvos,* and such professional leaders as the noted historian, Paul Milyukov (1859–1943), broke into two groups. The left wing, called Constitutional Democrats, or Cadets, favored a democratic constitution, universal suffrage, and a constitutional monarchy something like that of England, with the tsar's powers severely curtailed. The moderate right-wing liberals, later called Octobrists, wanted a constitutional government subordinate to the tsar.

Revolutionary Drive: The Socialists. The father of Russian Marxism was Georgi Plekhanov (1857–1918) who believed that Russian social democracy should not provoke a revolution prematurely, but should educate the proletariat to be ready to assume power after Russia had passed through the stage of middle-class revolution. Early in the regime of Nicholas II, Plekhanov's disciples began to carry Marxist propaganda into factories and workshops. The Russian (Marxist) Social Democratic Labor Party, or "S.D." party, was founded at a congress held at Minsk in 1898. Factional divisions came to a head at the second party congress held in 1903 in London.

The Social Democrats split into two factions: the Bolsheviks (majority), who called for dictatorship of the proletariat at the earliest possible moment, and the Mensheviks (minority), who desired to reach the same goal through evolution and education. The Bolsheviks, led by Nikolai Lenin (Vladimir Ulyanov, 1870–1924), in the tradition of revolutionary conspiracy, preferred a small and select party consisting of tried conspirators under a strict authoritarian leadership. For the immediate present, the Mensheviks were willing to collaborate with nonsocialist parties, such as the bourgeois liberals, to sweep away autocracy and prepare the masses for socialism.

Social Revolutionary Party. Neither of the Social Democratic parties succeeded in obtaining the support of the peasants, who were interested primarily and almost exclusively in the land question. Their hopes went with the Social Revolutionaries, or "S.R." party, which took its inspiration from the earlier Populist movement of the 1870's. The S.R. demanded destruction of the monarchy, seizure of landed estates from the nobility, and distribution of a free farm to each peasant family. This was convincing language which every peasant could understand. The Social Revolutionaries hoped to win the help of discontented liberals and workingmen in the towns. Until the 1917 revolutions, they attracted more followers than either wing of the Social Democratic Party.

Russo-Japanese War, 1904–1905. Defeated in the Russo-Turkish War, the Russians turned eastward, aiming to control Manchuria, the Liao-tung peninsula, and Korea as steps to the warm waters of the Pacific. In order to extend the Trans-Siberian Railway (begun in 1891) across Manchuria, Russia in 1898 obtained a lease from China on the Liao-tung peninsula. With Port Arthur in her possession she at last had an ice-free port. The Japanese were alarmed by this penetration into their best area of raw materials and markets. In 1902 they found a Western ally in Great Britain; this was Japan's first alliance with a European power.

Without bothering to declare war, the Japanese attacked a Russian squadron off Port Arthur on the night of February 8–9, 1904. The entire world agreed that the Japanese did not have a chance against the Russian colossus. The Japanese army was small, only about 250,000 first-line troops, but it was superbly trained. Strategically, the problem for the Japanese was to get their troops across to the mainland and crush the tsar's Far Eastern armies before he could bring his tremendous reserves into the conflict. On the other hand, the Russians had to bring their reserves at least 3,000 miles across the single-track Trans-Siberian Railway despite a service supply riddled by corruption.

The Japanese laid siege to Port Arthur and after eleven months the fortress was forced to surrender. At the great battle of Mukden (February 23–March 10, 1905) with about 300,000 men on each side, the Russians lost a third of their troops, the Japanese less than half as many. It was a resounding victory for the Japanese and a humiliating defeat for the Russians. Meanwhile, the Russians tried to gain control of the sea by sending their Baltic fleet all the way around Africa, only to be annihilated by Admiral Heihachiro Togo (1847–1934) in the battle of Tsushima on May 27–28, 1905. The Russians lost 40,000 men killed, nearly 8,000 captured, and almost their whole fleet. This was the decisive battle of the war.

Revolution of 1905. The defeat by Japan revealed Russia to be a colossus with feet of clay. Such a disaster the decaying imperial structure was scarcely able to endure. Criticism, complaint, and disorder swept through the country, and the revolutionary movement was intensified. There were more illegal meetings, demonstration, strikes, multiplied assassinations. All Russia flared up in revolt after a peaceful procession of petitioners, led by Father Gapon, an Orthodox priest, was fired upon by government troops on Bloody Sunday, January 22, 1905. Some 70 persons were killed,

The beginning of the Revolution of 1905. A contemporary painting of "Bloody Sunday," the day on which Cossack guards fired on a peaceful procession of workers and their families led by Father Gapon.

and 240 wounded in a massacre which horrified the world. The Great General Strike, October 20–30, 1905, an uprising of discontented subject nationalities and factory workers, brought the entire country to a standstill.

October Manifesto. Alarmed, Nicholas II issued a manifesto (October 30, 1905) which promised to extend the suffrage, summon a *Duma* (parliament), and grant freedom of speech. These concessions did not satisfy the extreme radicals, who rebelled in December 1905 at Moscow. After a week of desperate fighting, the government quelled the uprising and executed its leaders or sent them to Siberia. The first *Duma* (May 10, 1906), the first

representative assembly in Russian history, demanded political amnesty, investigation of charges of corruption, autonomy for Poland and Finland, universal suffrage, a responsible ministry, and abolition of martial law. Nicholas II, appalled by these demands, responded by dissolving the assembly. The *Duma*, he said, was meddling in affairs with which it was not concerned. The revolutionaries replied by assassinating at least fifty governmental officials in a week. The Second *Duma* (1907), the Third *Duma* (1907–1912), and the Fourth *Duma* (1912–1916) all challenged the autocracy with equal lack of success. The voice of revolution seemed to be choked by reaction.

⟊ KEY DOCUMENT ⟊

TSAR ALEXANDER II'S DECREE EMANCIPATING THE SERFS, MARCH 3, 1861

Annual Register, 1861 (London, 1862), "History," pp. 207–212.

THE DISASTERS of the Crimean War revealed to Russians the weakness of their governmental and socioeconomic structure. The new tsar, Alexander II, undertook a series of reforms, including one which freed the serfs on the imperial estates. The nobility resisted, but Alexander nevertheless issued an emancipation decree on March 3, 1861, which gave the serfs civil freedom but at the same time left them in economic bondage.

By the grace of God, we, Alexander II, Emperor and Autocrat of all the Russias, King of Poland, Grand Duke of Finland, etc., to all our faithful subjects make known: . . .

In considering the various classes and conditions of which the State is composed we came to the conviction that the legislation of the empire having wisely provided for the organization of the upper and middle classes and having defined with precision their obligations, their rights, and their privileges, has not attained the same degree of efficiency as regards the peasants attached to the soil, thus designated because either from ancient laws or from custom they have been hereditarily subjected to the authority of the proprietors, on whom it was incumbent at the same time to provide for their welfare. . . .

Having invoked the Divine assistance, we have resolved to carry this work into execution. . . .

. . . the peasants attached to the soil will be invested within a term fixed by the law with all the rights of free cultivators.

The proprietors retaining their rights of property on all the land belonging to them, grant to the peasants for a fixed regulated rental the full enjoyment of their close; and, moreover, to assure their livelihood and to guarantee the fulfilment of their obligations towards the Government, the quantity of arable land is fixed by the said dispositions, as well as other rural appurtenances.

But, in the enjoyment of these territorial allotments, the peasants are obliged, in return, to acquit the rentals fixed by the same dispositions to the profit of the proprietors. In this state, which must be a transitory one, the peasants shall be designated as "temporarily bound."

At the same time, they are granted the right of purchasing their close, and, with the consent of the proprietors, they may acquire in full property the arable lands and other appurtenances which are allotted to them as a permanent holding. By the acquisition in full property of the quantity of land fixed, the peasants are free from their obligations toward the proprietors for land thus purchased, and they enter definitively into the condition of free peasants—landholders. . . .

For which end, we have deemed it advisable to ordain—

1. To establish in each district a special Court for the question of the peasants; it will have to investigate the affairs of the rural communes established on the land of the lords of the soil.

2. To appoint in each district justices of the peace to investigate on the spot all misunderstandings and disputes which may arise on the occasion of the introduction of the new regulation, and to form district assemblies with these justices of the peace.

3. To organize in the seigneurial properties communal administrations, and to this end to leave the rural communes in their actual composition, and to open in the large villages district administrations (provincial boards) by uniting the small communes under one of these district administrations.

4. To formulate, verify, and confirm in each rural district or estate a charter of rules in which shall be enumerated . . . the amount of land reserved to the peasants in permanent enjoyment, and the extent of the charges which may be exacted from them for the benefit of the proprietor as well for the land as for other advantages granted by him.

5. To put these charters of rules into execution . . . within the term of two years. . . .

6. Up to the expiration of this term, the peasants and domestics are to remain in the same obedience towards their proprietors, and to fulfil their former obligations without scruple. . . .

To render the transactions between the proprietors and the peasants more easy, in virtue of which the latter may acquire in full property their close (homestead) and the land they occupy, the Government will advance assistance, according to a special regulation, by means of loans or a transfer of debts encumbering an estate. . . .

Given at St. Petersburg, the 19th day of February (March 3), of the year of Grace 1861, and the seventh of our reign.

—ALEXANDER.

❧ HISTORICAL INTERPRETATION ❧

GEORGE KENNAN ON THE SYSTEM OF ADMINISTRATIVE ARREST IN TSARIST RUSSIA

George Kennan, *Siberia and the Exile System* (New York, 1891), I, 242–243, 245, 270–271.

IN LATE nineteenth-century tsarist Russia the number of political exiles to Siberia numbered nearly 20,000 each year. During the reign of Alexander III (1881–1894), an American engineer, George Kennan, made an extensive trip through Siberia and visited prisons and exile groups. His description of the system of arrest and Siberian exile of political offenders made a deep impression in Western Europe and America.

Exile by administrative process means the banishment of an obnoxious person from one part of the empire to another without the observance of any of the legal formalities that, in most civilized countries, precede the deprivation of rights and the restriction of personal liberty. The obnoxious person may not be guilty of any crime, and may not have rendered himself amenable in

any way to the laws of the state, but if, in the opinion of the local authorities, his presence in a particular place is "prejudicial to public order," or "incompatible with public tranquillity," he may be arrested without a warrant, may be held from two weeks to two years in prison, and may then be removed by force to any other place within the limits of the empire and there be put under police surveillance for a period of from one year to ten years. He may or may not be informed of the reasons for this summary proceeding, but in either case he is perfectly helpless. He cannot examine the witnesses upon whose testimony his presence is declared to be "prejudicial to public order." He cannot summon friends to prove his loyalty and good character, without great risk of bringing upon them the same calamity that has befallen him. He has no right to demand a trial, or even a hearing. He cannot sue out a writ of *habeas corpus.* He cannot appeal to his fellow-citizens through the press. His communications with the world are so suddenly severed that sometimes even his own relatives do not know what has happened to him. He is literally and absolutely without any means whatever of self-defense. . . .

In the year 1880 the well-known and gifted Russian novelist Vladimir Korolenko, two of whose books have recently been translated into English . . . , was exiled to Eastern Siberia as a result of what the Government itself finally admitted to be an official mistake. Through the influence of Prince Imeretinski, Mr. Korolenko succeeded in getting this mistake corrected before he reached his ultimate destination and was released in the West Siberian city of Tomsk. Hardly had he returned, however, to European Russia, when he was called upon to take the oath of allegiance to Alexander III, and to swear that he would betray every one of his friends or acquaintances whom he knew to be engaged in revolutionary or anti-Government work. No honorable and self-respecting man could take such an oath as that, and of course Mr. Korolenko declined to do so. He was thereupon exiled by ad-ministrative process to the East Siberian territory of Yakutsk, where, in a wretched native *ulus,* he lived for about three years. . . .

The grotesque injustice, the heedless cruelty, and the preposterous "mistakes" and "misunderstandings" that make the history of administrative exile in Russia seem to an American like the recital of a wild nightmare, are due to the complete absence, in the Russian form of government, of checks upon the executive power, and the almost equally complete absence of official responsibility for unjust or illegal action. The Minister of the Interior, in dealing with politicals, is almost wholly unrestrained by law; and as it is utterly impossible for him personally to examine all of the immense number of political cases that come to him for final decision, he is virtually forced to delegate a part of his irresponsible power to chiefs of police, chiefs of gendarmes, governors of provinces, and subordinates in his own ministry. They in turn are compelled, for similar reasons, to intrust a part of their authority and discretion to officers of still lower grade; and the latter, who often are stupid, ignorant, or unscrupulous men, are the persons who really make the investigations, the searches, and the examinations upon which the life or liberty of an accused citizen may depend. Theoretically, the Minister of the Interior, aided by a council composed of three of his own subordinates and two officers from the Ministry of Justice, reviews and re-examines the cases of all political offenders who are dealt with by administrative process; but practically he does nothing of the kind, and it is impossible that he should do anything of the kind for the very simple reason that he has not the time.

❧ TEN BASIC BOOKS ❧

AUTOCRACY, ORTHODOXY, AGITATION: RUSSIA IN THE NINETEENTH CENTURY

1. Florinsky, Michael T., *Russia, a History and an Interpretation,* 2 vols. (New York, 1953).
2. Karpovich, Michael, *Imperial Russia, 1801–1917* (New York, 1932).†
3. Kohn, Hans, *Basic History of Modern Russia,* Anvil Book No. 24 (Princeton, N. J., 1957).†
4. Mazour, Anatole G., *Russia: Tsarist and Communist,* 2nd ed. (Princeton, N. J., 1962).

5. Pares, Bernard, *A History of Russia,* rev. ed. (London, 1955).†

6. Robinson, Geroid T., *Rural Russia Under the Old Regime,* rev. ed. (New York, 1949).

7. Seton-Watson, Hugh, *The Decline of Imperial Russia, 1855–1914* (New York, 1952).†

8. Sumner, Benedict H., *A Short History of Russia,* rev. ed. (New York, 1949, R. 1962).†

9. Vernadsky, George, *A History of Russia,* rev. ed. (New Haven, Conn., 1961).†

10. Walsh, Warren B., *Readings in Russian History,* 4th ed. (Syracuse, N. Y., 1963).†

Polish patriots leave Paris to fight for freedom in their homeland. The revolutionary spirit of these tumultuous decades inspired the oppressed throughout Europe—a wave of patriotic resistance and armed revolt spread across the continent. This lithograph by Arnout and Adam shows representatives of the 4800 exiled Polish families in Paris as they take up arms and prepare to depart for Poland. The Provisional Government guaranteed the Poles safe-conduct to the German border.

28

The Secondary States of Europe

THE YEARS of slavery are past,
   The Belgian rejoices once more;
Courage restores to him at last
   The rights he held of yore!
Strong and firm his clasp will be,
   Keeping the ancient flag unfurl'd
   To fling its message on the watchful world:
For King, for Right, and Liberty!

For thee, dear country, cherished motherland,
   Our songs and our valor we give;
Never from thee our hearts are banned,
   For thee alone we live!
And thy years shall glorious be,
   Circled in Unity's embrace,
   Thy sons shall cherish thee in ev'ry place
For King, for Right, and Liberty.
      —"La Brabançonne," Belgian National Song

1. The Scandinavian Countries: Norway, Sweden, Denmark, and Finland

Role of the Lesser States. Small states, by their very existence, often influence the history of larger states; their role in the balance of power is often of great importance. In the ebb and flow of historical currents, the status of countries as first- and second-rate powers changes perceptibly. Portugal, Spain, Austria, and Sweden, all at one time or another placed in the category of great states, gradually sank to the level of "lesser" countries. On the other hand, some small states made their way to prominence. The emphasis historians give to the major states, with comparatively little attention to others, is naturally resented by the peoples who inhabit the smaller ones. But giving equal attention to Germany and Switzerland would distort historical meaning. Several countries discussed in this chapter played important roles in earlier times, only to lose their dominant position in the last hundred years.

Scandinavia: Area Characteristics. Scandinavia, composed of Sweden, Denmark, Norway, and Finland, is a vast region in northern Europe reaching from Russia west to the Atlantic, from the Baltic coast northward to the Arctic Circle. Most of Scandinavia is a hard world of trees and water, broken by a multitude of rivers, lakes, and islands. For centuries its peoples have worked laboriously to draw sustenance from rocky, grudging soil and the sea. Only about 3 per cent of mountainous Norway is arable. Finland's 60,000 lakes take up more space than its farms. Many of Sweden's 173,423 square miles are covered by forest and wilderness.

Separated by formidable physical barriers, as well as by historic rivalries and enmities, the Scandinavian peoples have developed distinctive national characteristics. Some observers regard these as exaggerated sterotypes, others see in them the results of differing environments and traditions. The Swedes, influenced in the last century by the Germans, are said to be stiff, thorough, and neurotic. The Norwegians are reputed to be simple, rough, and courageous. The Danes, closer to Western Europe, are considered to be jolly, friendly, and sophisticated. The Finns, non-Aryan-speaking and of Magyar origin, are close to Russia and are often described as introverted, dour, and melancholy.

Nevertheless, these diverse Nordic peoples have developed along similar lines in recent times and have produced egalitarian states unhampered by poverty, unemployment, and illiteracy. They have been more successful than most other peoples in distributing affluence equitably. They possess similar parliamentary, legal, and educational systems. They have developed what seems close to common citizenship, because today all citizens of the Nordic bloc may live, work, and draw welfare benefits anywhere in Scandinavia. In this respect the Scandinavians have presented an object lesson to contemporary peoples divided by national rivalries.

Scandinavia is one of the few areas of the world permeated with a psychology of peace. Scandinavians place war in the same category as cannibalism. They see war as producing pessimism, despair, and hopelessness, as an unnatural state not inherent in man. Sweden's part in the power struggles in the late seventeenth and eighteenth centuries came to an end with the Great Northern War of 1700–1721. Thereafter, although they did become involved in several conflicts with other nations, the Scandinavian countries remained at peace with each other. Moreover, they managed to avoid revolution and insurrections as well as the misery of poverty.

Scandinavians at one time relied primarily on working the land and sailing the seas for the major part of their income, but eventually they entered wholeheartedly into the Industrial Revolution. Scandinavian intelligence produced achievements in social reform. In capital-labor relationships, both sides were willing to respect the dignity of the other. In many ways Scandinavian experience and experiments have had a strong influence on the rest of mankind.

Seafaring Norway. The Norwegians, like the Danes and Swedes of Teutonic origin, are one of the great seafaring peoples. United to the Danish crown from 1397 on, Norway, contrary to the wishes of its people, was awarded in 1814 to Sweden. This union of Norway, inhabited by fishermen, merchants, and peasants, and Sweden, an aristocratic country of large estates and tenant farmers, was not a happy one, but it lasted for nearly a century. On June 7, 1905, the Norwegian Parliament, the *Storting*, declared the union with Sweden dissolved; the decision was ratified by a popular plebiscite on August 13, 1905. The Swedish *Riksdag* acquiesced, whereupon the Norwegian parliament invited a Danish prince to the Norwegian throne as King Haakon VII. A treaty with Sweden provided that all disputes were to be settled by arbitration, and that no fortifications be erected on the common frontier. The Great Powers recognized and guaranteed Norwegian independence. Since this peaceful separation, a rare accomplishment in European politics, Norway and Sweden have lived amicably as neighbors.

Norway is a constitutional, hereditary monarchy with a Parliament composed of 150 members. It has the distinction of being the first state in Europe to establish woman suffrage on equal terms with men (1913). The country has suffered heavy losses in population by emigration: at the end of the nineteenth century there were only about 2,500,000 people in the country. But Norway's merchant marine ranks as the third largest in the world.

Industrialized Sweden. From the Napoleonic wars Sweden emerged with the gain of Norway from Denmark and with a new royal dynasty stemming from Marshal Bernadotte of France, who became King Charles XIV (r. 1818–1844). The Bernadotte dynasty, despite its French and revolutionary origin, was stubbornly reactionary. Political reform was hindered at first by the monarch, a privileged upper class, and a cumbersome parliamentary system. The king played nobility, clergy, middle class, and peasants against one another. Long a people of aristocratic traditions, the Swedes in the nineteenth century continued to accept the domination of the great landowners. With the development of mining and manufacturing, Sweden became, in contrast to Norway, highly industrialized. A powerful bourgeoisie emerged to stand beside the old landed aristocracy. Discontent with the ruling oligarchy led to the growth of socialism as well as to an extraordinary rate of emigration. Between 1870 and 1914 Sweden lost 1,500,000 citizens, most of whom settled permanently in the United States. Swedish emigrants played an important role in the construction of American culture.

Progressive Denmark. The smallest of the Scandinavian countries, Denmark made the mistake of cooperating with Napoleon, as a result of which she was attacked twice by British fleets (1801 and 1807). In the year 1814 Denmark was forced to cede Norway to Sweden. In 1864 Bismarck, together with the Austrians, made war on the little country as an initial step in the unification of Germany. Denmark lost the provinces of Schleswig and Holstein.

Some 90 per cent of Denmark is productive and nearly three-quarters of the land is farmed. The main sources of the nation's wealth are dairy and meat products, most of which are widely exported. The Danish merchant marine, on a per capita basis, is one of the largest in the world. In the late nineteenth century, Christian IX (r. 1863–1906) stubbornly opposed any extension of political democracy, but eventually suffrage was given to both men and women over the age of twenty-three. Like her Scandinavian neighbors, Denmark promoted large-scale public assistance programs, health insurance, and disability and old-age pensions. There is also, as in the other Scandinavian countries, an effective cooperative movement.

Scandinavian Culture. Although the Scandinavian countries could not compete with the Great Powers in political, economic, and military affairs, they did achieve a cultural importance far greater than indicated by their size. World literature was enhanced by the charming fairy tales of the Dane Hans Christian Andersen (1805–1875); the sophisticated dramas of the Norwegian playwright Henrik Ibsen (1828–1906); the pessimistic plays of the Swede Johan August Strindberg (1849–1912); the early existentialism of the Danish philosopher Sören Kierkegaard (1813–1855); and the essays of Demark's literary critic Georg Brandes (1842–1927). Added to these was the national lyrical music of the Norwegian composer Edvard Grieg (1843–1907). The contributions of these and others reflected the high standards of intelligence and education.

2. The Netherlands, Belgium, and Switzerland

The Netherlands (Holland). Dutch enterprise in the sixteenth and seventeenth centuries had resulted in the construction of an imposing empire, including Java, Sumatra, Dutch Borneo, and Dutch New Guinea in the East Indies, Curaçao in the West Indies, and Dutch Guiana in South America. Like Spain and France, Holland eventually lost her status as a leading colonial power, but she still retained control of an immense volume of trade flowing into northern Europe through the ports of Rotterdam and Amsterdam. Napoleon forced the Dutch into his Continental System, whereupon the British struck back by annexing the Cape of Good Hope and Ceylon. In 1815, at the Congress of Vienna, the Austrian Netherlands (Belgium), against their will, were joined with Holland to form a bulwark against possible French aggression and also to compensate the Dutch for their loss of South Africa and Ceylon. This union lasted only until 1830.

Thereafter, Holland enjoyed a relatively tranquil internal development. A new constitution in 1848 established a limited monarchy and representative government. The administration was reorganized, popular education promoted, and modern industry encouraged. The Dutch remained loyally devoted to their dynasty. After William II (r. 1840–1849) and William III (r. 1849–1890) the male line of the House of Nassau became extinct. With her mother as Queen Regent, Princess Wilhelmina succeeded to the throne, and in 1898, on her eighteenth birthday, assumed the reins of government.

Belgium: Constitutional Monarchy. After the fall of Napoleon, the Congress of Vienna in 1815 joined the French Catholic Walloons of Belgium with the German Protestant Flemings of Holland (United Provinces) to form the Kingdom of the Netherlands. Dissatisfied Belgians, supported by Great Britain, rose in 1830 and declared their independence. The hostile Dutch refused until 1839 to acknowledge the division. The Belgians called a German prince, Leopold of Coburg, to the throne as Leopold I (r. 1831–1865). Under enlightened leadership and a constitutional government, Belgium rapidly forged her way to the front of the minor states of Europe. Industry and commerce prospered, and the condition of

Uprising in Brussels, 1830. (After a painting by Wappers.) Belgium was united with Holland in 1815, but it was an unfortunate union. When revolution broke out in Paris in 1830, the Belgians went to the barricades with the cry, "Imitons les Parisiens!" Such incidents were a favorite subject of contemporary painters who were moved to portray the revolutionary sentiments of the times.

the working class was improved through advanced social legislation.

International Guarantee of Belgian Neutrality, 1839. At London, on April 19, 1839, a treaty was signed between Great Britain, Austria, France, Prussia, and Russia, on the one part, and the Netherlands, on the other, in which the union between Holland and Belgium, established at Vienna in 1815, was formally dissolved. A similar treaty was signed with Belgium. In the annex to the first treaty, and repeated in the second, was an article guaranteeing Belgian independence and neutrality. (*See page 478.*) This guarantee was restated in a treaty between Great Britain and Prussia signed at London on August 9, 1870. The 1839 treaty was to have momentous consequences in 1914. After German troops crossed the Belgian border on the morning of August 4, 1914, Sir Edward Goschen, the British ambassador at Berlin, called on Chancellor von Bethmann-Hollweg for a final interview. "I found the Chancellor very agitated," Goschen reported. "His Excellency at once began a harangue, which lasted for about twenty minutes. He said that the step taken by His Majesty's Government was terrible to a degree; just for a word—'neutrality,' a word which in war time had so often been disregarded—just for a scrap of paper Great Britain was going to make war on a kindred nation who desired nothing better than to be friends with her."

Belgian Imperialism. In 1876, after the opening up of Africa, Leopold II (r. 1865–1909), King of the Belgians, formed the *Association Internationale Africaine* to exploit as his private property the almost unexplored regions of the Congo. The world was subsequently shocked by reports of cruel repression and exploitation of the indigenous population in Leopold's African domain. A commission of inquiry in 1905 revealed serious maladministration and abuses. In 1908 the Congo ceased to be Leopold's private company and was annexed to Belgium under his sovereignty as the Belgian Congo.

Switzerland: From Agglomeration to Federal State. Until the mid-nineteenth century the Swiss Confederation was politically a loose union of virtually autonomous cantons. With each canton enjoying a large measure of self-government, Switzerland was able to avoid the difficulties experienced by the Balkan states. The people spoke German, French, and Italian, all officially recognized as national languages in 1874. Romansch, a dialect of the Alpine regions, was added as a fourth national (but not official) language in 1937. The population varied around these figures: the German Swiss approximately 71.9 per cent; the French Swiss 20.4 per cent; and the Italian Swiss 6 per cent. To linguistic barriers were added religious differences, with Protestants dominant in more than half the cantons, and Catholics in the others.

In 1798, French revolutionary troops occupied Switzerland and named it the Helvetic Republic, "one and indivisible," but Napoleon in 1803 restored its federal government. At that time and again in 1815 the French- and Italian-speaking peoples of Switzerland were raised to political equality. In 1815 the Congress of Vienna neutralized Switzerland and recognized its independence. In 1847, seven Roman Catholic cantons seceded and organized a separate union called the *Sonderbund*. In 1848 the new Swiss constitution established a federal state modeled upon that of the United States, with powers shared between central government and individual cantons. The revised Federal Constitution of 1874 established a strong central government but still retained large powers of local control in each canton. Switzerland was the first European nation to make such experiments in political democracy as the *referendum* (the referral of proposed laws or constitutional amendments to the electorate before final passage), and the *initiative* (the direct popular introduction or enactment of a law or constitutional amendment).

Protected from invasion by her mountainous terrain, possessing little in the way of natural resources, Switzerland made certain to maintain neutrality in European conflicts. By mutual agreement her neutrality was respected by the Great Powers. Unable to compete in the Industrial Revolution, the Swiss turned to pursuits in which they could excel. Primarily an agricultural and pastoral people, the Swiss made their cheese products, milk, chocolate, and condensed milk world famous. They exported watches, machines, and precision instruments. They encouraged tourist traffic as another source of income. Above all, they became bankers to the world, drawing funds from nearly every country, including flight capital of deposed dictators, into their banks. The economic and social well-being of the Swiss aroused the envy of most other small nations.

3. Integration and Disintegration: Austria and Austria-Hungary

Austria, 1812–1867. Austria in 1812 was an ally of Napoleon, but in the year 1813 joined the Grand Alliance against him in the battle of Leipzig. She emerged from the Congress of Vienna in 1815 as one of the dominant powers on the Continent. Metternich managed, by a divide-and-rule policy, to hold together the numerous ethnic groups in the Austrian Empire. Denouncing nationalism, liberalism, and democracy as revolutionary ideas, he maintained an iron grip. At the same time he sent Austrian armies to stamp out revolution in other European countries. Internal discontent grew, as Magyars, Italians, and Bohemians demanded the right to govern themselves.

In the 1848 crisis Metternich was forced to flee for his life to England. The Austrian emperor, Ferdinand I, who had shown little ability during the crisis, promised a liberal constitution and social reform. Meanwhile, the rebellion was checked by Prince Ferdinand zu Windischgrätz, who crushed a revolt by the Slavs in Prague. Previous concessions were revoked. For the next ten years the revived policy of bureaucratic government only helped to increase the nationalistic fervor of minority peoples. The defeat of Austria by France and Sardinia in 1859 stirred the rebellious groups into action once more. In the meantime, Prus-

sia became increasingly influential in Austrian affairs.

The *Ausgleich*: The Dual Monarchy, 1867. In the revolution of 1848 the Hungarian Magyars, led by Louis Kossuth (1802–1894), revolted and established an independent state, only to fall to the reaction. After Austria's defeat by Prussia in the Seven Weeks' War (1866), the Hungarians again pressed their claim to be recognized as a separate country. Francis Joseph I (r. 1848–1916), the Austrian emperor, and Francis Deák (1803–1876), the Hungarian leader, in 1867 agreed upon a Dual Monarchy, or *Ausgleich*, by which the Aus-

Emperor Francis Joseph I, whose reign lasted for sixty-eight years.

trian empire and the Hungarian kingdom were united. Austria and Hungary each obtained separate constitutions, but were linked by the Crown, the Hapsburg emperor becoming emperor of Austria and king of Hungary. The task of Francis Joseph was to make the dualist system work. He ruled through responsible ministries in both Austria and Hungary, but he was able to impress his will in most matters of common concern. In effect, the *Ausgleich* was a combination of Germanic Austrians and Hungarian Magyars against the Slavs.

After 1867 various measures liberalized political life throughout the Austro-Hungarian Empire. The presence within its borders, however, of many different nationalities ("a museum of ethnic curiosities") made the task of settling all claims most difficult. With some justification, the Slavic element in the population, which outnumbered the Germans, regarded itself as being less favorably treated than the Austrians and Magyars. Demanding the same degree of independence as that enjoyed by the Hungarians, the Slavs called for formation of a trialism to be called Austria-Hungary-Bohemia instead of the dualism of Austria-Hungary. The Dual Monarchy made Hungary the most loyal of Hapsburg possessions, but having obtained what they wanted, the Magyars blocked the efforts of other groups to obtain similar rights. The political policy of almost complete separation between Austria and Hungary in the *Ausgleich* was modified in 1907 when economic ties were made much closer.

Austro-Hungarian foreign policy after 1867 was based on the desire to reach an understanding with Germany and Russia, but there was a perceptible drift to the German side. In 1879 an informal agreement was reached after Bismarck visited Vienna and arranged a treaty by which Germany agreed to support Austria-Hungary against Russia, and the latter promised to assist Germany against a combined attack by France and Russia. This Austro-German Dual Alliance of 1879 was the keystone of Bismarck's treaty system.

4. Spain and Portugal

Reduced Status of Spain. In the era of exploration, discovery, and colonization, Spain had won tremendous wealth and a vast colonial empire. The conquest of Peru by Pizarro (1531–1535) and of Mexico by Cortés (1519–1521) brought great prosperity to the mother-land. The Spanish Hapsburg dynasty, through a series of wars, diplomatic negotiations, and marriages, became for a time the most powerful in the world. But after the destruction of Philip II's Armada in 1588, Spain sank rapidly to the rank of a second-rate power and never again played a major role in European politics.

Chaos, Economic Backwardness, and Times of Trouble. The history of Spain in the nineteenth century is a story of political chaos, economic regression, clashes, and psychological troubles. The autocratic government was weakened by corruption and inefficiency, while military cliques competed for power. Feudal land tenure persisted in the Iberian peninsula, a semi-arid plateau with infertile soil. There was no independent class of peasant proprietors as in France. Industry, despite large deposits of iron and coal, lagged far behind that in other Western countries. The conservative masses, illiterate, poverty-stricken, and without initiative, were sealed off from European progress. Throughout the nineteenth century Spain staggered on the verge of insolvency.

The Spanish people, recognizing only their chosen king, Ferdinand VII, in 1813, drove out Joseph Bonaparte, whom Napoleon had placed on the throne in 1808. In the midst of the war for independence, the Liberal members of the national *Cortes* drew up the Constitution of 1812 at Cadiz. Ferdinand promised to be faithful to it. When he returned to Spain in 1814, however, he repudiated the constitution and, after armed intervention by the Holy Alliance in 1823, restored the old, traditional autocracy. Ferdinand decided to set aside the Salic law and transmitted the throne to his daughter Isabella II (r. 1833–1868). This act led to the Carlist Wars (1833–1840), in which the ultra-reactionary supporters of Ferdinand's brother, Don Carlos (1788–1855), sought unsuccessfully to establish their leader's claim to the throne. From 1833 to 1873 there was ferocious and lasting warfare between Carlists and Constitutionalists. Governmental changes were effected through *coup d'état*, never through constitutional elections. The administration became increasingly corrupt. In 1868 the despotic queen was driven from the throne.

From 1868 to 1870 a provisional government was set up. Monarchists, Carlists, and Republicans contended for control. The only immediate result of this battle for power was to supply France and Prussia with a *casus belli* for the war of 1870. When Napoleon III refused to admit the candidature of Prince Leopold of Hohenzollern-Sigmaringen for the throne of Spain, he impelled a diplomatic crisis and precipitated the Franco-Prussian War. Prince Amadeo I of Savoy, younger son of Victor Emmanuel II of Piedmont, was finally selected; he remained in the country for three years only to resign in disgust and discouragement. For a year Spain became a republic, and then the old Bourbon dynasty was reinstated in the person of Alfonso XII (r. 1875–1885). Alfonso restored peace and introduced a moderately liberal constitution, but the country was still far from free of its host of troubles. After the early death of Alfonso XII in 1885, the throne passed to a posthumous son, Alfonso XIII, who was recognized as king while his mother, Queen Maria Christina, acted as regent.

Colonial Decline. The secession of Spain's South and Central American colonies in the 1820's deprived the Spanish government of an important source of revenue. When Ferdinand VII appealed to the Holy Alliance for help in recovering his colonies, he was warned by the United States, with British support, that no imperialistic pretensions would be tolerated on American soil (Monroe Doctrine). The traditionally shortsighted Spanish colonial policy later precipitated a colonial revolt in Cuba, which led to a war with the United States. The immediate cause was the blowing up of the United States warship *Maine* in Havana harbor. Spain was decisively defeated and her navy destroyed. She surrendered not only Cuba, but Puerto Rico, the Philippine Islands, and Guam in the Pacific. As compensation, the United States paid her $20,000,000. This ignominious defeat, which lost Spain the last fragments of her empire, wounded Spanish national pride, already suffering from a long heritage of defeat, poverty, and misery. With the loss of her empire, Spain turned to North Africa to subjugate the Arab-Berber tribes of Spanish Morocco.

Portugal: Strife and Confusion. The history of Portugal in the nineteenth century, filled with dynastic quarrels and civil strife, was similar to that of Spain. In 1816 John VI succeeded to the throne but remained in Brazil. Discontented, the Portuguese rose in rebellion in 1820 and established a democratic government. This was too much for John, who hastened back to Lisbon, and gave his word to obey the Constitution of 1822. Meanwhile, Brazil obtained independence with the young prince-regent, Pedro I, as constitutional emperor. In 1823 a state treaty between Portugal and Brazil provided that the two crowns should never be united. On the death of John VI in 1826, Pedro, now Pedro IV of Portugal, abdicated in favor of his seven-year-old daughter, and returned to Brazil.

Queen Maria II (r. 1826–1853) was succeeded by her two sons, Peter V (r. 1853–1861) and Louis I (r. 1861–1889). At this time the parliamentary system was working, as in Spain, on the basis of rotativism, by which conflicting political factions succeeded one another in office. During this era of misrule and confusion, of excessive taxation and delay in critically needed reform, many thousands of Portuguese emigrated. There was a marked growth in anticlericalism, anarchism, socialism, and communism, all in counteraction to the chaotic political situation. Portugal entered the twentieth century with a largely illiterate population and a government blind to the need for reform.

Increasing protests against governmental inefficiency, incompetence, and corruption led to a revolt, and a republic was proclaimed on October 5, 1910. Both a royalist counterrevolution and an extremist Red revolution were suppressed, whereupon Portugal set up a government closely resembling that of the Third French Republic. Like the latter, it separated Church and State, reduced clerical influence, and introduced a state school system.

Portuguese Colonialism. Like Spain, Portugal lost her American possessions, notably Brazil, early in the nineteenth century. But, unlike Spain, she managed to retain an extensive colonial empire elsewhere: the Cape Verde Islands, the Azores, Angola, Portuguese Guinea, and Mozambique in Africa, Goa in India, and Macao in China. The cost of administering an empire strained the resources of the small country. She was obliged to release some of her territory in West and East Africa after a British ultimatum in 1890.

5. The Crumbling Ottoman Empire, 1815–1878

Near Eastern Question. After capturing Constantinople in 1453, the Ottoman Turks overran the Balkan Peninsula and for several centuries threatened Christian Europe. Their attempt to penetrate Western Europe in 1683 was repulsed at Vienna. The Muslim Turkish government, called the Sublime Porte, controlled a conglomeration of ethnic groups in a large empire. In Asiatic Turkey the vast majority of the inhabitants were Muslims, while in European Turkey most of the people under Ottoman control were Slavic Christians. The Near Eastern Question concerned primarily the peoples of the Balkan peninsula. Here dwelled the Slavic Serbs of Serbia, Montenegro, Bosnia, and Herzegovina; the Slavic Bulgars of Bulgaria; the Hellenes of Greece; Rumanians in Moldavia and Wallachia; the nomadic Albanians; and Armenians and Jews scattered all over the peninsula. The Christian inhabitants wanted freedom from the ruling Turks, whom they accused of barbaric cruelties.

Decline: "The Sick Man of Europe." Turkish decline had been continuous since the late eighteenth century. In the nineteenth century the Great Powers turned willingly to the task of partitioning the sultan's domain. Outraged by Turkish oppression of Christian subjects, but motivated also by an interest in strategic Ottoman lands, they began to scheme for shares of the disintegrating empire. Each was concerned lest a rival obtain a better portion of the spoils. One after another the suppressed nationalities in the Ottoman Empire demanded independence. Weakened by internal conflicts, by corruption and inefficiency in government, the Turks could not resist the squeezing-out process of dismemberment. The European powers sat at the bedside of "the sick man of Europe," like greedy relatives waiting for the death of a wealthy uncle. Each time a generous slice of Turkey was removed the European diplomats piously proclaimed to the world their anxiety to maintain the integrity of the Ottoman Empire. It was a classic example of hypocrisy in nineteenth-century diplomacy.

Dismemberment: Independence of Greece. In 1821 the Greeks rose in revolt against their Turkish masters. The sultan replied with a massacre of Greeks in Constantinople. For years a war raged with almost barbaric fury on both sides. European volunteers, among them the poet Byron, went to Greece to help its people in their struggle for independence. A joint Anglo-French-Russian naval intervention destroyed the Turkish fleet at Navarino Bay in 1827. The Russian tsar, Nicholas I, timed his invasion of Turkey so as to profit from the sultan's embarrassment during the Greek insurrection. French armies joined in the war against the Turks. The sultan was forced to sign the Treaty of Adrianople (September 14, 1829), which granted independence to Greece. The Russians were given a protectorate over the supposedly autonomous provinces of Moldavia and Wallachia as well as the territory of Georgia in the Caucasus. At the same time the Serbs, who had for years been rebelling against their Turkish masters, won autonomy. The Greeks and Serbs were the first people to win their freedom in these revolts. The Russians would have assumed protectorates over both had not the Western powers intervened to check Russian ambitions.

Crimean War, 1853–1856. The unfortunate status of the sultan's remaining Christian subjects led to increasing foreign intervention. The Crimean War of 1853–1856 grew out of Tsar Nicholas I's ambition to cut down the Turkish empire and obtain the major share of the Balkans for himself. There was supposedly a religious motive: members of the Greek Orthodox Church in Turkey looked to Russia for protection, while Roman Catholics sought help from France. Great Britain and France, annoyed more by Russia's increasing appetite than by the plight of Christians in Constantinople, supported Turkey. As already described (*see page 451*), Great Britain and France attacked Russia in the Crimea. The Treaty of Paris, which ended the Crimean War in 1856, solemnly maintained the integrity of the Ottoman Empire, and placed its Christian subjects under the aegis of the Great Powers instead of Russia. Russian designs were momentarily frustrated. The grateful sultan magnanimously made promises of reform —which he forgot almost immediately.

By 1870 the Christian peoples of the Ottoman Empire, inspired by German and Italian national unification, were demanding independence from Turkish rule. By 1878 the independent Balkan states became pawns in the game of Near Eastern international diplomacy.

Russo-Turkish War, 1877–1878. Abdul Hamid II (r. 1876–1909) described by an acidulous critic as "a creature half fox, half rat," ascended the Turkish throne in 1876. Faced with an uprising by the Bulgarians, who had assassinated Turkish officials, Abdul Hamid turned upon them his ferocious Bashi-Bazouks, savage bands of irregulars. The merciless slaughter roused all Europe against "the unspeakable Turk." Tsar Alexander II, at this time leader of the Pan-Slavic movement, stepped forward again as defender of Christians. The Big Slav would save his Little Slav brothers. In 1877 Russia declared war on Turkey. Russian armies poured through the Balkans, captured Adrianople, and prepared to march on Constantinople.

Once again the Near Eastern question precipitated a European crisis and once again foreign intervention alone halted the Russian drive toward Constantinople. Great Britain sent a fleet to the Bosporus and Austria mobilized an army to meet the Russians in the Balkans. The tsar hastily signed with the sultan the Treaty of San Stefano (March 3, 1878), which recognized the independence of Serbia,

Rumania, and Montenegro, and established a new Greater Bulgaria, consisting of Bulgaria, Rumelia, and Macedonia. The sultan was permitted to keep only Constantinople and its vicinity, and Albania. But the attentive Great Powers, especially Great Britain and Austria, were not willing to accept this solution, especially the creation of a Greater Bulgaria under Russian influence. They threatened war unless the tsar would consent to an international congress called to revise the Treaty of San Stefano. The Russians reluctantly agreed.

Congress of Berlin, 1878. The international convention gathered at Berlin. Otto von Bismarck, the German chancellor, announcing that Germany had no direct stake in the Near Eastern Question, proposed to take the part of an *ehrlicher Mäkler,* an honest broker, determined to reconcile the interests of his clients. To Bismarck the whole Near Eastern Question was not worth "the bones of a Pomeranian grenadier," but he nevertheless recognized its capacity to cause trouble for Europe. At Berlin the Treaty of San Stefano was disregarded. Once again, as at Vienna in 1815, an international assembly concerned itself not with satisfying legitimate national interests but with rectifying frontiers in favor of the strongest powers.

The Treaty of Berlin formally recognized the independence of Serbia, Rumania, and Montenegro. Greater Bulgaria was divided into three parts: Bulgaria proper was made an autonomous principality under the suzerainty of the sultan; Eastern Rumelia was given an "administrative autonomy" under a Christian ruler; and Macedonia was awarded to Turkey. The provinces of Bosnia and Herzegovina, although legally still a part of Turkey, were to be occupied by Austria-Hungary on notification to the Great Powers. Cyprus was handed over to British control. The Russians were allowed to retain several conquered towns in the Caucasus, as well as a strip of Bessarabia in Rumania. The Turks were permitted to retain Albania, Macedonia, and Thrace in Europe, all of which remained a constant bait for covetous neighbors.

After this use of its giant carving knife, the

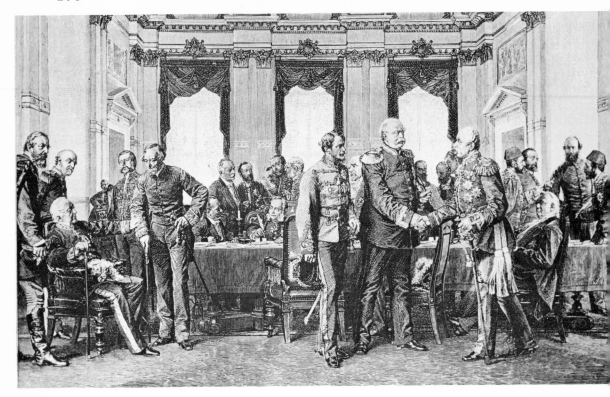

The Congress of Berlin, 1878. Bismarck and Disraeli were prominent among the representatives of the great powers of Europe who convened in twenty sessions to modify the treaty of San Stefano. As a result of this conference, Russia's aggressive policy was at least temporarily checked.

Congress solemnly guaranteed the "integrity of the Ottoman Empire." This was not, however, a satisfactory solution of the Near Eastern Question. The Balkan peoples, those most concerned with the settlement, received little consideration. Those freed from Turkish control were angered because they were not given the frontiers they wanted. There were now five Christian states in the Balkans, but the Congress had failed to safeguard the rights of Christian minorities still under Turkish rule. Moreover, the Congress evaded the problem of ensuring necessary reforms. Irredentist movements began almost immediately after the settlement. The entire Balkan region, the powder keg of Europe, seethed with intrigues, conspiracies, and disorders which helped generate World War I.

Greece, 1829–1912. After achieving independence in 1829, the Greeks were faced with the dual problems of reorganizing their political system and economy and rescuing the Greek-inhabited islands still under Ottoman control. With the crown awarded to Otto, son of Ludwig I of Bavaria, many Greeks complained that they had freed themselves from Turkish control only to succumb to Bavarian rule. Throughout Otto's reign there was much discontent, leading to an insurrection in 1862 which ended with the deposition of the king. George, second son of the king of Denmark, was then chosen king. In 1863 the Ionian Islands, under British protection, were ceded unconditionally to the kingdom. The Congress of Berlin in 1878 promised Greece modification of her frontiers. In 1881 she acquired Thessaly from Turkey. Insisting that the allocation was not sufficient, the Greeks demanded Crete. Their war with Turkey, begun in 1896, was short-lived and disastrous.

By the Treaty of Constantinople (August 25, 1897), Greece was required to pay an indemnity, submit to a readjustment of her frontiers, and accept control by the Great Powers of her financial affairs. Crete was granted autonomy under a Greek prince, and, as a result of the Balkan Wars (1912–1913), was ceded to Greece by the Treaty of London. Under George I (r. 1863–1913) and Eleutherios Venizelos (1864–1936), prime minister in 1910, the Greeks then sought to project for the world a new image of themselves as heirs of the Hellenic civilization.

Autonomy and Atrocity: Bulgaria, 1878–1912. The Treaty of Berlin in 1878 set up an autonomous though tributary Bulgaria in the north Balkans, while to the dominantly Bulgarian province in the south, known as East Rumelia, it granted administrative autonomy. Alexander of Battenberg, made prince of Bulgaria in 1879 at the suggestion of the tsar, ruled under a liberal constitution. But most of the higher administrative officials were Russians, who acted with the assurance that Bulgaria owed her existence to Russia. Nationalist Bulgarians demanded freedom from Russian influence. In 1885 East Rumelia was incorporated into the Bulgarian state, despite the bitter opposition of Tsar Alexander III. In 1886 Prince Alexander abdicated and was succeeded by Ferdinand of Saxe-Coburg, an opponent of Russian influence. Ferdinand's minister-president from 1887 to 1894, Stefan Stambouloff (1854–1895), leader of the anti-Russian national-liberals, was assassinated in 1895 by Macedonian revolutionaries. In 1908, taking advantage of the Young Turk revolution and Austria's annexation of Bosnia and Herzegovina, Ferdinand repudiated the last shreds of Turkish suzerainty and declared Bulgaria's independence. Bulgaria became a kingdom and Prince Ferdinand took the title of tsar.

From Home Rule to Independence: Rumania, 1878–1912. The Rumanian people were a mixture of Vlachs, Slavs, and descendants of the ancient Romans who had settled north of the Danube in Wallachia and Moldavia. They spoke a language derived from Latin. Their leaders called for national unity and independence from the Ottoman Empire. Following the Crimean War, the Treaty of Paris (1856) made provisions for home rule of the two Rumanian provinces in the Ottoman Empire. Two years later Moldavia and Wallachia were permitted to elect their own parliaments and choose their own reigning princes. Both assemblies unanimously chose Prince Alexander John Cuza, thereby accomplishing an important step toward the creation of a united Rumanian nation. Cuza's radical reforms alienated the nobility and clergy, who forced him to abdicate in 1866. Prince Charles of Hohenzollern-Sigmaringen, elected in his place, governed under a new and liberal constitution. When the Russo-Turkish War of 1877 broke out, Rumania sided with Russia. Her reward at the Congress of Berlin in 1878 was independence. In 1881 she was elevated to the position of a kingdom. Although King Carol I (r. 1881–1914) was a popular ruler, domestic policies continued to be disturbed by religious disputes, persecution of the Jews, and peasant grievances. Discontented peasants who rebelled against the *boyars* (wealthy proprietors) were rapidly suppressed by the government.

Militancy Rewarded: Serbia and Montenegro, 1878–1912. A land of tough Slavic herdsmen, Serbia began her struggle for independence as early as 1804, when Kara George ("Black George"), a swineherd, led an unsuccessful rebellion against Turkish rule. In 1815 another move for independence was made under the leadership of Milosh Obrenovitch, sworn enemy of Kara George. The Serbs obtained a measure of independence in 1830, when the sultan gave them local autonomy with Milosh as their hereditary prince. From then on, Serbian history was a confused story of bitter struggles between the Obrenovitch dynasty and the Karageorgevitches, descendants of Kara George. Intrigues, murders, assassinations, and civil war became common for the rest of the century as the Crown wavered between the two dynasties. In the Russo-Turkish War of 1877 Serbia cooperated with Russia. The Congress of Berlin formally recognized the independence of Serbia, though Bosnia and Herzegovina were ceded to Austria. The first king, Milan Obrenovitch, was an unpopular absolute monarch who abdicated in 1889 in favor of his son Alexander. Even more autocratic than his father, Alexander I was assassinated in 1903 in Belgrade, and was succeeded by a Karageorgevitch, Peter I.

The other Serb nation in the western Balkans, Montenegro, or "Black Mountain," had never been completely subjected by the Turks. Its prince-bishop (*vladika*) had received annual subsidies from Russia since the time of Peter the Great. In 1851 Danilo I succeeded to the throne, declared the line of prince-bishops at an end, and ruled as a secular prince (*gospodar*). The Turks invaded Montenegro in 1853, but were halted by the intervention of the Great Powers. In 1910 Nicholas, prince of Montenegro, assumed the title of king.

Rise of Turkish Nationalism, 1878–1912. Turkey emerged from the Congress of Berlin reduced in size, embittered, and humiliated by what she regarded as unfair treatment. Defeated but unrepentant, Abdul Hamil II continued the game of playing off one Christian nation against another, grandiloquently promising reform inside his corruption-ridden empire but doing little or nothing to change the *status quo.* Plots were hatched by discontented groups in Constantinople. In 1894–1896 occurred a terrible massacre of Armenians, who were suspected of being implicated in the anti-government plots. The atrocities earned Abdul Hamid II the titles of "Great Assassin" (Gladstone) and "Abdul the Damned" (poem by William Watson).

Meanwhile, a strong nationalist movement rose. The Young Turks, dissatisfied with Abdul Hamid's rule, and angered by the speedy disintegration of the empire, began to agitate for radical reform. They would introduce Western ideas and institutions, and eliminate the traditional incompetence, graft, corruption, and disorder. A Committee of Union and Progress, supported by army officers, struck in 1909, deposed the sultan, and proclaimed his brother Mohammed V a constitutional monarch. The terror which hung like a pall over the entire Turkish empire vanished with the fall of the hated sultan.

The Young Turks announced that a new era had opened. They declared themselves believers in the watchwords of the French Revolution—liberty, equality, and fraternity—and proclaimed freedom of religion. They centralized the administration, removed privileges from the wealthy, and demanded fair treatment for minority groups in the empire. By abrogating capitulations, special privileges for foreigners in the empire, they incurred the hostility of foreign powers which had long enjoyed such privileges. But this era of goodwill was brief. While the Young Turks were busy remaking their country, Bulgaria repudiated Turkish sovereignty, Austria seized Bosnia and Herzegovina, and Italy took Tripoli. Appalled by what they regarded as further dismemberment, the Young Turks turned about-face, purged themselves of their liberalism, and stepped back to the autocratic methods of Abdul Hamid II. They would force the minority peoples of the empire to be Ottomanized.

❧[KEY DOCUMENT]❧

INTERNATIONAL TREATY GUARANTEEING THE NEUTRALITY OF BELGIUM, 1839

Edward Hertslet, ed., *The Map of Europe by Treaty* (London, 1875), II, 982–985.

ON APRIL 19, 1839, a treaty was signed by the European Powers guaranteeing the independence and neutrality of Belgium. This was the famous agreement which the German chancellor, von Bethmann-Hollweg, called a "scrap of paper" in August 1914, on the outbreak of World War I.

Annex to the Treaty signed at London, on the 19th of April, 1839, between Great Britain, *Austria, France, Prussia, and Russia, on the one part, and the Netherlands, on the other part.*

ARTICLE 1. The Belgian Territory shall be composed of the Provinces of: South Brabant; Liège; Namur; Hainault; West Flanders; East Flanders; Antwerp; and Limburg; such as they formed part of the United Kingdom of the Netherlands in 1815, with the exception of those districts of the Province of Limburg which are designated in Article 4.

The Belgian Territory shall, moreover, comprise that part of the Grand Duchy of Luxemburg which is specified in Article 2.

ARTICLE 2. In the Grand Duchy of Luxemburg, the limits of the Belgian Territory shall be such as will hereinafter be described. . . .

ARTICLE 4. In execution of that part of Article 1 which relates to the Province of Limburg, and in consequence of the cessions which His Majesty the King of the Netherlands, Grand Duke of Luxemburg, make in Article 2, His said Majesty shall possess, either to be held by him in his character of Grand Duke of Luxemburg, or for the purpose of being united to Holland, those Territories, the limits of which are hereinafter described. . . .

ARTICLE 7. Belgium, within the limits specified in Articles 1, 2, and 4, shall form an Independent and perpetually Neutral State. It shall be bound to observe such Neutrality towards all other States. . . .

❦{ HISTORICAL INTERPRETATION }❧

JOHN LINDBERG ON THE SPECIAL CHARACTER OF SWEDISH NATIONALISM

John Lindberg, "The Long Sleep," *American-Swedish Historical Museum Yearbook, 1944* (Philadelphia, 1944), pp. 36–38. By permission of the American Swedish Historical Foundation.

THE SWEDISH scholar, Gustaf Sundbärg, said: "We Swedes . . . slept through the age of nationalism. All our efforts during this period give an impression of having been carried out in our sleep." This view of the special attitude of Sweden to nationalism was examined by John Lindberg, former teacher at the University of Stockholm and active in the work of the League of Nations. It is a classic statement on the nature of nationalism.

Returning to Sundbärg's ideas of nationalism . . . , the truly dominating movement of the nineteenth century was not nationalism, in the modern sense; in fact, . . . nationalism arose largely as a reaction to economic internationalism. Sweden was in the midstream of this great economic movement, as is shown, among other things, by its liberal emigration policy consistent only with such a viewpoint. Nationalism, in fact, was during the nineteenth century still in the position of a contender, for it did not rise to dominance or full growth until the twentieth century. As a matter of fact, it is only in our century that Sweden might be said to have been forsaken by the dominant "spirit of the age."

But the matter is more complicated than this, even according to Sundbärg. In spite of his amiable weakness for the "spirit of the age" and for national revival he parted company with German nationalists who, since Hegel, conceived of nationalism as a manifestation of absolute reason and the highest form of human life. "Nationalism," he writes, "obviously has approached a new phase in its development. It will no longer be enthroned in the history of mankind as the dominant idea of the age. . . . The new power which probably will dominate the next period is the social idea." This was written on the very eve of the feverish outbreak of nationalism in which we now live. Yet, as we have seen, instead of being supplanted by the social idea, nationalism married it. Sandbärg's contention, however, may perhaps be taken as implying an understanding that unless nationalism is supplanted the realization of the social idea will perish with it.

If this is a fair interpretation it is rather puzzling that Sundbärg's generation of Swedish patriots viewed the absence of nationalism, in its essentially German form, as a dark misfortune. They were blind to the vital developments taking place at their very doorsteps, for this "long sleep" gave Sweden the chance, spared by the devitalizing passions of nationalism, to devote herself to a solution of the great problem of social and economic balance in the Western tradition and outside, as it were, of the old Europe which was gradually turning into a spiritual slum.

The absence of nationalism in the absolute sense explains much of Swedish economic prosperity, built largely on the maintenance of her foreign trade on a relatively free basis. But above all, Sweden experienced great spontaneous movements on a broad democratic basis, without which the renaissance during the interwar period would have been inconceivable. Without assistance or sympathy from above, the common people originated the temperance movement and caused it to prosper. The country was swept by waves of popular revivals, often in close interdependence with Anglo-Saxon pietistic movements. The people created trade unions, cooperatives, and a wide-spread adult education system. They learned to apply their own standards. Their loyalties became both differentiated and firmly rooted, and the state became to them an instrument to be used and not an end in itself. Therefore, at the same time as Sweden integrated herself economically in the world, she prepared herself on a broad popular front for an era of social adjustment to the newly created economic universe.

It is fitting, then, that both from the practical and the symbolical point of view the slogan of social reform became that of making Sweden the "home of the people," of all of the people. This slogan implied the idea of unity and of building a harmonious whole. By a fortunate turn of history, Sweden could approach the basic problem of creating a balance between economic and social development in what may be termed an objective spirit. Her inspiration, if we may use this expression, was not Swedish but universal, in the sense that justice is universal. On a small scale and naturally colored by Swedish conditions, her internal experimentation represents, as we have explained, an experiment of universal significance. Few Swedes, even when they believed themselves to be nationalists, conceived of Sweden as the essence of all things. Rather they believed with Hjärne that nations have their ultimate justification in their service to a world community. The times have not been kind to this ideal, but so much the worse for the times, one might say. Sweden realized even before many of the belligerents did, that abundance and security alike can be hoped for only on a world plane, and that owing to circumstances beyond the control of any one country the time of isolation has passed.

While in most countries nationalism has taken up social reform, social reformers in Sweden have gradually turned patriots. In this there may be a danger of nationalism, if the pride of and love for Sweden is not tempered with the belief in the priority of the whole over the part, and if the country tries to profit rather than to serve. It is significant, therefore, that perhaps the most deeply felt need in Sweden at the present time is whole-hearted participation in post-war reconstruction, a feeling that has already received concrete expression in action.

❧ TEN BASIC BOOKS ❧

THE SECONDARY STATES OF EUROPE

1. Arneson, Ben, *Democratic Monarchies of Scandinavia* (New York, 1949).

2. Cammaerts, Émile, *The Keystone of Europe: History of the Belgian Dynasty, 1830–1939* (London, 1939).

3. Eyck, F. Gunther, *The Benelux Countries,* Anvil Book No. 44 (Princeton, N. J., 1959).†

4. Gewehr, Wesley, *The Rise of Nationalism in the Balkans, 1800–1930* (New York, 1931).

5. Kohn, Hans, *The Hapsburg Empire, 1804–1918,* Anvil Book No. 52 (Princeton, N. J., 1961).†

6. Madariaga, Salvador de, *Spain,* rev. ed. (New York, 1958).

7. Marriott, Sir John, *The Eastern Question,* 4th ed. (Oxford, 1940).

8. Rappard, William, *The Government of Switzerland* (New York, 1936).

9. Seton-Watson, Robert, *The Rise of Nationality in the Balkans* (London, 1917).

10. Vlekke, Bernard H. M., *Evolution of the Dutch Nation* (New York, 1945).

PART VI

ROAD TO WAR:

THE NEW INDUSTRIALISM AND IMPERIALISM

THE NEW IDEAL OF ACTIVISM[1]

Benedetto Croce

A FTER 1870, in Europe, the active meditation of moral and political matters had
...A diminished, as well as the faith that it alone produces and renews, and the warmth
and enthusiasm that follow upon faith. . . . This languor and this kind of spiritual empti-
ness [were dangerous], and . . . the danger did not diminish but indeed grew graver when
materialism, naturalism, and positivism were shaken off, a more cultivated philosophy was
taken up, and the insidious paths of mysticism and irrationalism were willingly preferred.
This danger was that of the formation and elevation of a false ideal. The conditions
favourable to it already lay in the very forces of the modern world, in its indefatigable
activity in commercial and industrial enterprises, in its technical discoveries, its ever
more powerful machines, its geographical explorations, its colonization and economic
exploitation, its tendency to confer primary importance on scientific and practical rather
than on speculative and humanistic studies. . . .

Warfare, bloodshed, slaughter, harshness, cruelty, were no longer objects of deprecation
and repugnance and opprobrium, but were regarded as necessities for the ends to be
achieved, and as acceptable and desirable. They were clothed with a certain poetic attraction, and even afforded a certain thrill like that of religious mystery, so that one spoke
of the beauty that lies in war and bloodshed, and of the heroic intoxication that in this way
alone man can extol and enjoy. This ideal may be designated by the word, which has
already been uttered here and there, "activism": a generic term, which gathers together
all its particular forms and therefore seems to be the most suitable. And although it has
been called imperialism, we must point out that this name, which arose in England about
1890, did not in itself mean anything but a better, stronger, and more coherent development to be given to the British colonial policy, and that activism alone imprinted another
character on it. And although it has also been called, and more commonly, nationalism,
we must remember that this second name arose in France at the time of anti-Dreyfusism,
and bore a connotation of anti-Semitism and at the same time of reaction or monarchical
absolutism, but that the national idea in itself, and in the classical form that it received
from Mazzini, was humanitarian and cosmopolitan, and therefore the contrary of this
nationalism which became activism and ran through the parabola already divined by
Grillparzer in the formula: "Humanity, through nationality, returns to bestiality."

What was, in its innermost nature, this ideal of activism which was taking form and
consistency in the soul of Europe? Notwithstanding that above everything it fought and

[1] Benedetto Croce, *History of Europe in the Nineteenth Century*, trans. from the Italian
by Henry Furst (New York, 1933), pp. 339–345, *passim*. Courtesy of Agenzia Letteria
Internazionale.

loathed liberalism, the only element that—ready as it was to receive all other elements and to enter into every alliance, including that with Catholicism and the Church—it never received, and with which it never allied itself; notwithstanding this, and indeed because of this, its original impulse was nothing other than the principle of liberty, so intrinsic in the modern world that it is not in any way possible to do without it. . . .

Such is the moral and religious or (which amounts to the same thing) the irreligious and immoral nature of activism. . . . Its deepest genesis still lies in morbid romanticism, which was never completely vanquished, although put to sleep for a while in the life of Europe (and to vanquish it altogether and eradicate it forever is certainly impossible, because it too is a perpetually recurring crisis of the human soul), that romanticism which had already put in a new appearance after 1860 under the form of aloofness from practice and politics and as "decadence," and which now, stripped of all the ideal and noble elements of its primitive epoch, was overflowing—and this was what counted— into the practical and political field. The result was the plethora of "dilettanti" of these things who were seen and heard and who filled old and expert statesmen with irritation and distrust. Literature, which was already feeding on erotic and pathological images, soon became imbued with this new romantic, pseudo-heroic, brutal, and sanguinary tendency and confirmed it and introduced it into people's minds. Admiration for Napoleon started afresh, not as it had been in the *grognards,* in the surviving soldiers and officers of the *Grande Armée* and in the young men who listened to the narratives of that epic age, but rather in the form that Stendhal had given to it and that his contemporaries had neither understood nor felt, but which now found its right time (just as its author had foretold in 1880, specifying more or less the exact date when his fortunes would begin to mend). And a sort of *imitatio* was conceived of that man of action, audacious, resolute, clear-sighted, who cherished no hesitation or scruples, who took fortune by storm and conquered the world, and of other personages who resembled him in various ways or who were interpreted in the same fashion. A philosopher, too, who was more of a poet and who bore in his heart the yearning for purity and greatness, Nietzsche, was interpreted materially and turned into the prophet of activism. Men like D'Annunzio in Italy, Barrès in France, and many others libidinous and sadist like them turned, out of sensual delight or from the caprices of new stimuli and emotions, to this new romanticism. This, not content with inspiring the activistic ideal, after having on various occasions tried the hermetic style, lost even that modesty of style and became activistic or "dynamic" even in the artistic form itself, and called itself futurism.

The young men, naturally, were carried away by images of such grandiose appearance, and were stimulated by this instigation to throw away the past and with it all prudence and precaution, and in great numbers became "nationalists," "imperialists," "dynamists," "sportists," and "futurists," or all these things at once. And this happened in every part of Europe, and even outside of Europe; and not in Germany alone, which in this respect was neither more nor less morbidly affected than any other country, and cultivated no thoughts of this kind that were not cultivated elsewhere.

29

Nineteenth-Century Enlightenment: The New World of Industry and Science

NEVER PERHAPS in history did people live so improvidently, so carelessly as to the inevitable results of their behavior, as the industrial peoples of Europe in the second half of the nineteenth century. The undreamed-of progress in all technical matters so completely overthrew former conceptions of what was possible that even the very conditions of human physical existence seemed to have altered. . . .

As a result of these various conditions, the luxuries of life became cheaper, and modern comforts due to invention and technical progress came within the reach of every one; but the ordinary necessaries of life became dearer and more difficult to secure.

—EDUARD FUETER

1. The New Industrialization, 1850–1900

Industrial Expansion. During the first phase of industrialization, commencing in the mid-eighteenth century, Great Britain had been the original manufacturing country. The Industrial Revolution then spread to the Continent, developing along similar lines as in Great Britain. The textile industry was the first to be affected; changes followed in the production of clothing and foodstuffs; then came new methods in the extraction and use of iron and steel; and finally the manufacture of machines. Instead of importing British goods, Continental nations used British industrial methods. They fostered and protected home industries, and began to value machines, factories, and mines more than land. Industrial progress became synonymous with national wealth and status.

Midway in the nineteenth century there began a new phase of industrialization, with revolutionary changes in production and distribution. The old textile, steel, and coal industries were transformed and, simultaneously, industries emerged to provide the consumer with new kinds of goods. Machines quickly became outmoded, to be scrapped and replaced by more powerful machines.

American and German Challenge. During this new phase of industrialization, Great Britain had to face the competition of the United States and Germany. The United States, with its seemingly limitless supplies of raw materials, immigrant labor, and ready capital, with its enterprising citizens and ingenious inventors, made tremendous economic progress. The main American pursuit had been agriculture and commerce until after the Civil War, when accelerated industrialization began. Americans adapted and improved upon European techniques, while adding procedures of their own. The special American contribution was the introduction of mass production, or the manufacture of standardized articles in great quantities by means of specially designed machines and by application of a planned division of labor. To American competition was added the rapid industrialization of Germany after her unification in 1871, especially in

The Krupp Works, 1885. The celebrated iron and steel works at Essen were founded in 1848 by Alfred Krupp (1812–1887). Krupp armaments made the new Germany the leading military power in the world.

chemistry and allied industries. Thoroughness in research, skill and discipline in factories, and painstaking organization of distribution enabled the Germans quickly to take a place as one of the leading industrialized nations.

Age of Super-power. Industrialization was strengthened by discovery of new sources of power. Coal, the basic fuel of power in the early stage, gave way to oil, and steam was largely replaced eventually by electricity. On August 28, 1859, E. L. Drake, an American, drilling a well near Titusville, Pennsylvania, struck mineral oil, or petroleum. Soon drilling for oil began all over the world. Crude petroleum could be converted into many useful products by fractional distillation, each fraction being further purified by chemical treat-

ment. The fractions recovered, in order of importance, were: crude benzine, the final product of which was used as gasoline in internal-combustion engines; kerosene, serving as a fuel in stoves and as a solvent; lubricating oils, used for reducing friction in machinery; and such by-products as paraffin wax.

A series of related discoveries had already laid the groundwork for use of electricity: the Frenchman André-Marie Ampère (1775–1836) first demonstrated the relationship between magnetism and electricity; an Italian, Alessandro Volta (1745–1827), devised the earliest electric battery; the Italian Luigi Galvani (1737–1798) discovered the principle of galvanic action, the union of negative charges with positive electricity; and the German Georg Simon Ohm (1787–1854) discovered a basic law—the strength or intensity of an un-varying electrical current is directly propor-tional to the electromotive force and inversely proportional to the resistance of the circuit. Because of its high efficiency of transmission and its great flexibility, electricity was an ideal source of power. For steam, gasoline, and diesel engines, fuel had to be carried to the machine, a process involving high costs. Elec-tricity, on the other hand, was a cheap means of transmitting power. It could be generated in a variety of ways—by steam, gasoline, oil, or water—and could be transmitted over wires to any point desired.

A deluge of inventions followed, including Michael Faraday's discovery of the process of electroplating in 1830; Werner von Siemen's working dynamo in 1867; and Thomas Edi-son's incandescent light in 1879.

Primacy of Steel. Steel, the essential ma-terial for the new machines, was the name given to various alloys of iron with small quantities of carbon, manganese, silicon, sul-phur, and phosphorus. The strength of steel was 20 times that of wood, 10 times that of stone, and 5 times that of cast iron. Moreover, it had the virtue of resisting corrosion and could be produced cheaply. The Bessemer process, perfected in 1855 by an English in-ventor and engineer, Henry Bessemer (1813–1898), used an air blast to oxidize and remove impurities from molten pig iron in order to convert it into steel. The open hearth process, invented in 1856 by William (Karl Wilhelm) Siemens (1823–1883), an Anglicized German, used a coal- or gas-fired reverberatory furnace, arranged in such a manner that air and fuel gas could enter at one end and burn over the hearth, while the hot waste gases escaped at the other end. Later, both Bessemer and open-hearth processes were combined in the Duplex operation to produce a finer steel. These inven-tions resulted in a tremendous increase in steel production and brought the price tumbling down. By the end of the century, steelmaking was one of the great industries.

Invention to Order. The earlier inventors worked in their own shops or attics. On occa-sion they were suddenly elevated to positions of wealth and prominence. The new era of industrialization could not wait for inventions to come by chance. Great industrial firms invested large sums in research laboratories, and hired staffs of inventors, chemists, and physicists, gave them specific problems, and called for machines and implements of special types. One of the most revolutionary steps in the new industrialization was invention to order.

The New Factory System and Mass Pro-duction. About the middle of the nineteenth century the factory, using more complex ma-chinery, tended to become larger and larger. The manufacturer of one product under con-trolled conditions involved the highest degree of specialization. Mass production eliminated waste due to inefficiency and duplication of effort, and by introducing standardized and interchangeable parts, made possible the man-ufacture of vast quantities of finished goods at low prices. At the same time, the development of large-scale production, with a consequent greater volume of goods to be marketed, called for new methods of distribution. Scientific management in distribution as well as produc-tion made for increased efficiency and for lower prices.

Under the new factory system, production was concentrated in such large units that most entrepreneurs found it difficult if not impos-sible to finanace their industries independently. Henry Ford (1863–1947), the genius of mass production in the United States in the early twentieth century, was an exception who was able to establish and maintain a family cor-poration during his lifetime. But most others satisfied the demand for heavy investment of capital by turning to joint-stock companies. This trend brought the transformation of the older form of industrial capitalism to finance or corporate capitalism. As a result ownership was divorced from management.

Mechanization of Transport. The mid-cen-tury saw a spectacular increase in railroad construction; there was a veritable railroad mania. More powerful locomotives, more ca-pacious freight cars, and more comfortable passenger coaches were built. Grades and curves were eliminated. The railroad became the nerve center of the world's economy. In England in 1825 there were only 26 miles of railways; by 1900 the mileage had risen to 21,855. In 1840 there were only 1,808 miles of track completed for all railroads in Europe; by 1900 there were 176,179 miles, an hundredfold increase. In the United States a boom period of railroad construction began after the Civil War. The first transcontinental line, comprising the *Union Pacific* and the *Central Pacific*, from the Missouri River to San Francisco, was opened in 1869, the two lines meeting near Salt Lake City. During the decade from 1880 to 1890, some 70,000 miles of track were laid in the United States. The Trans-Siberian Railway (1891–1903) which connected Moscow and Vladivostok, gave Russia her desired outlet to the Pacific. Germany's Berlin-to-Baghdad Railway, planned to link

Continental Europe with Asia, became an important factor in Anglo-German rivalry in the era just preceding World War I.

Similarly, shipping between 1850 and 1900 increased on a comparable scale. The beautiful clipper ship was replaced by the steamship. Luxurious passenger ships were built. All major and some smaller countries constructed merchant fleets to care for commerce, to import food and export manufactured products, to provide communication with colonies, and to serve as troop and auxiliary vessels in time of war. Although unprofitable at first, transatlantic shipping was encouraged by governmental help.

Inland waterways had long been used to facilitate domestic commerce. Now interoceanic canals were constructed to speed international trade. The Suez Canal, joining the Mediterranean and Red Seas, was built be-

The *Great Eastern*. Completed in 1857, this 680-foot steamship was the largest of its day. In 1860 she made the trip from England to New York in eleven days. In 1866 she was used to lay the Atlantic telegraph cable.

tween 1856 and 1869 at a cost of $80,000,000. This great waterway, 87 statute miles long (66 miles of actual canal and 21 miles of lakes), became an important link between Europe and Asia. The Kiel Canal (Kaiser Wilhelm Canal), 61 miles long and connecting the Baltic with the North Sea, was opened by William II in 1895. The Panama Canal in Central America, connecting the Atlantic with the Pacific Ocean, was begun by a French company in 1881 and completed in 1914 by the United States.

Still another revolutionary achievement was the invention of automotive transportation. The United States assumed a commanding position in the production of automobiles. In 1900 there were only 4,000 passenger cars in the United States; in 1962, 6,933,000 were sold in one year. The production of heavy trucks to carry freight over a vastly improved highway system meant new competition for the railroads.

Added to this development was the achievement of Wilbur and Orville Wright, who on December 17, 1903, made the world's first airplane flight over barren sand dunes at Kitty Hawk, North Carolina. The rapid development of the aircraft industry further revolutionized transportation.

2. Aspects of a Changing Civilization

Delaisi's Zones of Civilization.* Nineteenth-century Europeans regarded their own continent as the center of civilization. European civilization, they were certain, had become synonymous with material progress. In 1929 a French publicist, Francis Delaisi, in his *Les deux Europes: Europe industrielle et Europe agricole*, described three "zones of civilization" that had arisen since 1870: (1) the inner zone; (2) the outer zone; and (3) the Afro-Asian zone. The inner zone, the "Europe of steam," was in a radius of approximately 700 miles from Frankfort-on-Main, in western Germany, and passed through Glasgow, Stockholm, Danzig, Trieste, Florence, and Barcelona—an area including Great Britain, Belgium, Germany, France, northern Italy, and western Austria.

*I am indebted to Richard M. Brace for calling attention to Delaisi's classification.

This zone contained virtually all European heavy industry. Here science was most advanced, the natural resources of the world most exploited. Here, in the home of constitutional government, were the highest living standard in the world and the greatest contributions in art, literature, and music. Important areas outside the periphery, such as the northeastern United States, were actually part of the inner zone; the United States would one day become the heart of this advanced zone.

Delaisi's outer zone included most of Ireland, most of the Italian and Iberian peninsulas, all of Europe east of Germany, Bohemia, and Austria. This zone was primarily agricultural, although the productivity per farm worker per acre was actually far less than that of the inner zone. Here there were sharp differentiations between the wealthy aristocracy and the poor, illiterate peasantry. The middle class was weak and comparatively ineffectual. The zone lived mostly by selling grain, livestock, wool, or lumber to the more industrialized inner zone, but it was too poor to buy manufactured products. It borrowed its capital from the inner zone. Its standard of living, and also its production in the realm of ideas, were considerably lower than those of the inner zone.

Beyond the European world lay the third zone, the vast continents of Asia and Africa called "backward" by European standards. An exception was Europeanized Japan, which was in the outer zone in the late nineteenth century but which, in the twentieth century, advanced to the inner zone. China and India had contributed to world civilization with magnificent old and traditional cultures, but they had remained "uncivilized" by European standards, because they lacked the essential prerequisites of an advanced material civilization—industrialization and scientific knowledge.

Demographic Trends. A marked increase in population occurred at first only in the industrial centers of Great Britain, but in the nineteenth century this phenomenon appeared in similar proportions in other equally industrialized countries. This was part of a worldwide increase, as shown in the following approximate table:

World Population

	1869	1891	1900
Europe	276,000,000	357,000,000	403,000,000
Asia	755,000,000	826,000,000	875,000,000
Africa	200,000,000	164,000,000	170,000,000
America	68,000,000	122,000,000	146,000,000
Australia	1,400,000	3,200,000	4,200,000
Polynesia	1,500,000	1,400,000	1,500,000
TOTAL	1,302,000,000	1,474,000,000	1,600,000,000

Europe's Population

	1800	1900
Great Britain	16,200,000	41,600,000
Italy	18,100,000	32,400,000
Germany	21,000,000	56,300,000
Austria-Hungary	23,100,000	45,400,000
European Russia	38,000,000	111,300,000

Of even greater impact was the population increase in Asia, where the population made up more than half the world's total and where the rate of population growth was more than double that of Europe.

Motivating Factors. Behind the remarkable spurt in population was a variety of contributory factors. Progress in medicine and sanitation led to longer human survival as well as an increased birth rate. With the rise of national states, people received more protection and could live longer. The plagues and famines of the Middle Ages were cut down. The industrialization of Europe meant the production and distribution of great quantities of cheap food. This growth in population, stimulated by the new industry and science, was one of the outstanding facts of modern history. It continued well on into the twentieth century, at such a rate that experts have begun to fear the effects of what they call a population explosion.

Migration of Europeans Abroad. With the age of industrialization came a transfer of population to regions outside the Continent in what amounted to a mass movement. Emigrants went to every corner of the earth. It is estimated that between 1837 and 1891 at least 30,000,000 Europeans emigrated to other lands, the bulk to English-speaking countries. Emigration from Europe helped to swell the population of the United States from 5,300,000 in 1800 to an accumulated 77,100,000 in 1900. Some of these migrants, perhaps as many as

25 per cent, later returned to their original homes, but the great majority put down roots in the New World. Emigration across the Atlantic was partly spurred by agricultural conditions, among them the 1846 failure of the potato crop in Ireland and the European-wide depression of 1873. But there were also such factors as political discontent, the demand for workers in an increasingly prosperous United States, the possibility of acquiring riches in an expanding economy, and easier means of transportation. Emigrants came from densely populated European countries as well as from such smaller countries as Sweden, Norway, and Switzerland. The American Melting Pot, a mixture of "energetic mongrels" from all over Europe, was a result of this Atlantic migration.

Impact of Urbanization. Almost as striking as the rise in population was the gravitation of the rural populace to towns and the consequent rapid rise of densely populated cities. Population everywhere began to shift to industrial towns, a development already observable in England at the close of the eighteenth century. Nearly every phase of the new industrial and technological revolution favored the growth of cities at the expense of country districts. The significance of this trend may be judged by the fact that only about a century ago the peoples of Europe lived mostly on the land, supporting themselves by some kind of agricultural labor. But cities soon began to outnumber villages. In 1800 there were only about a dozen cities in Europe with a population of more than 200,000; by 1900 there were several hundred. Villages grew into towns and towns into cities.

The great increase in production and wealth was accompanied by urban congestion of homes and factories; living conditions became deplorable. There were new problems: policing the towns, providing local government, insuring an adequate water supply, and disposing of refuse. The transformation was so swift that there was no adequate planning, with the result that masses of unfit and crowded dwellings remained in city centers while the spacious surroundings of suburban life were offset by long journeys between home and work. The problems of urbanization in an industrialized society led to battles between capital and labor and a loud demand for social justice.

Rise of Feminism. The nineteenth century saw the rise of a revolutionary movement known as feminism. For centuries women had been regarded as an inferior sex, whose main function was child-bearing and whose main occupation was housekeeping. A pioneer in changing this status was Mary Wollstonecraft Godwin (1759–1797), an Englishwoman of Irish descent, whose *Vindication of the Rights of Women* (1792) called for complete and full equality for women and led to her denunciation as a "hyena in petticoats." Industrialization played an important part in changing women's status: the machine, making no distinctions between male and female, drew both into the factories. Laws for woman suffrage in England were defeated in 1867 (Second Reform Bill) and 1884 (Third Reform Bill), but the demand for an equal franchise did not abate. At the end of the nineteenth century, women became more and more insistent upon the right to vote. For several years before 1914 all England was in political turmoil as militant suffragettes heckled political speakers and organized violence by setting buildings on fire or handcuffing themselves to public buildings as a means of bringing attention to the justice of their demands. The patriotic service of women in World War I led to the triumph of woman suffrage in the English Reform Bill of 1918. In the United States, the Nineteenth Amendment to the Constitution provided for woman suffrage (August 26, 1920).

3. The Expansion of Science

Forerunners: Theory of Biological Evolution. The theory of biological evolution was an epoch-making contribution to nineteenth-century thought. The idea that all life might have developed from a simple cell was projected early by pre-Socratic Greek cosmologists, but not until the nineteenth century did anyone formulate the theory of the evolution of both universe and man with any degree of scientific accuracy. As early as 1802 the French naturalist Jean Baptiste Lamarck (1744–1829) had worked out a theory of organic evolution but had mistakenly based his concept on the idea of transmission of acquired characteristics through heredity. In 1830–1833 the British geologist Sir Charles Lyell (1797–1875) had called attention to the long evolution of the earth.

Darwinian Theory. The idea that the multiplication of life forms and the survival of the fittest might have been the result of natural forces occurred independently to two English naturalists, Alfred Russell Wallace (1823–1913) and Charles Darwin (1809–1882). The absence of jealousy between the two naturalists and the harmony in which they conducted their researches was something rare in the annals of scientific progress. In 1859 Darwin published his book, originally titled *On the Origin of Species by Means of Natural Selection, or the Preservation of Favoured Races in the Struggle for Life,* in which he expounded the doctrine now known as Darwinism. In this famous work Darwin presented five main theses: (1) Nature tends to give birth to more individuals of every species than can possibly survive. (2) Hence, within every species, among the various species, and between the individual and the conditions of its life, there is a constant struggle for existence. (3) Variation, or differences between members of the same species, results in some individuals being better adapted to their environment than others, and thus better fitted to survive. (4) This leads to the law of natural selection between the more and the less adaptable individuals. (5) The final result is the survival of the fittest. (*See page 500.*)

Darwin's second major work, *The Descent of Man* (1871), was an application to man of the principles expounded in the *Origin of Species*—to consider "firstly, whether man, like every other species, is descended from some pre-existing form; secondly, the manner of his development; and thirdly, the value of the differences between the so-called races of man." In this book Darwin collected evidence to show the descent of man from some lower form. From the evidence provided by embryological development, he inferred that man and the anthropomorphous apes had a common ancestor.

The concepts presented by Darwin were in general already familiar, but he explained the causes of evolution so clearly and so convincingly that he performed the valuable task of removing it from the abstract sphere of philosophical speculation. In gathering evidence and systematizing his doctrine, Darwin explained the struggle for existence (necessary because organisms tend to increase faster than their means of subsistence), the survival of the fittest, and natural selection (continuation of the unconscious selecting process in the struggle for existence).

Controversy on Darwinism: Defense and Attack. The theories of Darwin led to a violent intellectual battle. Bourgeois industrialists welcomed Darwin's ideas as compatible with the principle of free competition. Herbert Spencer correlated Darwinism and *laissez-faire*, to the unrestrained satisfaction of capitalists. The idea of the survival of the fittest was attractive to those who had outlived the fierceness of competition. Radicals saw in evolution convenient support for their attacks on the existing social order. Most scientists rushed to Darwin's defense.

To theologians and the devout, Darwin's theory was the product of a devilish mentality and a direct assault on the most sacred of religious ideas. Some denounced it as "scientific atheism." Above all, they decried the theory of any direct relationship between man and the higher primates. Fundamentalists pointed to the account of Creation in the first book of the *Old Testament* and asked how that could be reconciled with Darwinian theory. The attacks on Darwin were bitter, harsh, and unending.

Social Darwinism. Starting from the Darwinian theory, social science took a new turn. From a mechanistic concept of the world and society, social scientists turned now to biological evolution for new ideas and new analogies. Darwinism was applied to society. Some political leaders used this social Darwinism as

a justification for a policy of blood and iron, which was simply another way of saying that because the fittest survive, nations must arm and win wars in the struggle for existence. Darwinism was also used to bolster the argument that human beings should be permitted to struggle freely in the social and economic environment, assured that by natural selection the fittest would survive. (*See page 502.*)

The New Sciences: Physics and Chemistry. The methods which Darwin used to describe the life sciences were utilized by physicists in new explanations of the physical world. We have already seen how great discoveries were made in electricity by Ampère, Volta, Galvani, and Ohm. Other physicists investigated heat, light, and sound, and the nature of color. Benjamin Thompson (1753–1814), an American, demonstrated the nature of heat, showing how it was generated in proportion to energy expended. Hermann von Helmholtz (1821–1894), a German, published studies on the perception of tone and on physiological optics. Others worked in the field of thermodynamics, investigated the nature of sound and light, and developed spectrum analysis.

Dmitri Mendeleyev, whose predictions of elements yet to be discovered proved remarkably accurate.

Equally significant was the work of nineteenth-century chemists. The German Justus von Liebig (1803–1873), father of scientific agriculture, investigated the life processes of animals and plants and made many valuable discoveries. The Russian Dmitri Ivanovitch Mendeleyev (1834–1907) projected the periodic law of atomic weights (every eighth element in the series possesses similar characteristics) which enabled scientists to predict the existence of hitherto unknown elements. The German Friedrich August Kekulé von Stradonitz (1829–1896) proposed laws of synthesis which made possible the construction of numerous compounds from several elements. This work led to the invaluable use of carbon compounds in synthetic chemistry.

Scientific Medicine. One of the crowning glories of the nineteenth century was progress in scientific medicine. Darwinian theories led to more intensive study of comparative anatomy and painstaking classifications of all forms of organic life. Louis Pasteur (1822–1895), French chemist, using improved microscopes, examined the diseases of beer, wine, and vinegar, and discovered the microorganism of fermentation. By proving the presence of bacteria, he eliminated the old theory of spontaneous generation. He demonstrated that dangerous bacteria, disease germs, could be killed simply by elevating the temperature of their environment (pasteurization). Isolating the bacilli of such diseases as anthrax, diphtheria, and rabies, he prepared vaccines to provide immunity for the higher animals and man. On July 16, 1885, he inoculated Joseph Meister, an Alsatian boy who had been bitten by a rabid dog, and the boy did not develop rabies. It was an epoch-making event in the conquest of disease.

In 1882 a Prussian physician, Robert Koch (1843–1910), raised bacteriology into a science by isolating the bacillus of tuberculosis. Within a decade the bacteria of such diseases as cholera and bubonic plague were identified. There was hope that the world would at last see the end of the great plagues that had crippled mankind for centuries.

The germ theory was equally important in surgery. New knowledge made it possible to combat infection with antiseptics and sterilization of instruments (asepsis). The introduction of anesthetics made possible the great progress of modern surgery. William Thomas Green Morton (1819–1868), an American dentist, introduced the use of ether as an anesthetic for surgical operations (1842). The anesthetic properties of ether were first studied by Dr. Crawford W. Long (1815–1878), but he failed to induce many physicians to make use of his discovery.

4. The New Philosophy and Religion

Philosophical Controversy: Idealism Versus Realism. The nineteenth century saw an intensive and continuing discussion between two older philosophical concepts, idealism and realism. Idealism was a system of thinking which denied the objective reality of the material world, and regarded it rather as a manifestation of "ideas" or "spirit." This conception that ideas are the only things known had developed along varying lines from the time of Plato; later systems were projected along different lines by Locke, Descartes, Spinoza, Leibnitz, Kant, and Hegel. Georg Wilhelm Friedrich Hegel (1770–1831), last of the four great German idealist philosophers of the early nineteenth century (Kant, Fichte, Schelling), agreed with Kant that it is impossible to consider life philosophically as a purely material existence apart from essential ideas. Matter, he said, is nonexistent except as a perception, i.e., an expression to an individual mind of some essential idea. He therefore recommended that the idea, not the form, of thought be examined, since what is true of a perception is true of the object. Hegelianism maintained that there is no reality beyond the comprehension of man.

Directly opposed to Hegelian idealism was realism, or the belief that time, space, and their attributes are real (transcendental realism); that phenomena exist apart from our consciousness or conception (empirical realism); and that our perception is always motivated by direct intuitive cognition, not by the intermediate process of representative ideas.

This point of view also had figured in philosophy from the time of Socrates, Plato, and Aristotle. Among the many nineteenth-century realists was Herbert Spencer (1820–1903), who saw the universe completely outside himself as a separate entity.

Both idealism and realism were used to describe certain types of literature and art in the nineteenth century. For example, idealism has taken another meaning in a pure literary sense—the expression of beautiful or optimistic temperament. This we observe in the writings of Lessing, Shelley, and Maeterlinck. Anti-idealistic realism, claiming to show life as it really is, in both joy and sorrow, beauty and ugliness, was presented in the works of Zola, Dostoevsky, and Thomas Hardy.

Darwinism in Philosophy: Huxley and Haeckel.

Darwin himself was careful not to seek philosophical implications of his theories, but others did. A new group of philosophical materialists appeared, supporting materialism and attacking spiritual values as products of ignorance and superstition. Among them was Thomas Henry Huxley (1825–1895), British scientist who became an enthusiastic champion of Darwin's theory of natural selection. An agnostic, Huxley claimed that there was no evidence for the existence of a personal God. Advocating a philosophy of pessimistic materialism, he attacked Hegelian idealism, especially its acceptance of a First Cause. Similarly, the German biologist Ernst Heinrich Haeckel (1834–1919) sought to reconcile the theory of evolution with a philosophical concept of the universe. In importing his evolutionary theories into philosophy, morals, and religion, he expressed a materialist philosophy which led him to atheism.

Pessimism: Schopenhauer and Nietzsche.

The leading German exponent of the philosophy of pessimism was Arthur Schopenhauer (1788–1860), who believed that the final solution of the problem of life is to be found in ethics, asceticism, and purely disinterested contemplation, as in science. He introduced the idea of will, the universal blind instinct of individuals and species to survive. The will

is independent of time and space: it is *das Ding an Sich* ("the thing in itself"), a compelling force, without reason, manifesting itself as the will to live. The subconscious will, always seeking an independent existence, is invariably frustrated; hence pain and sorrow arise. Schopenhauer called for a world of non-pain or non-being, very close to such Eastern philosophies as Buddhism. It was a philosophy of passive resignation leading to utter pessimism.

Friedrich Nietzsche (1844–1900) began his career as an apostle of Schopenhauer but eventually broke with him and introduced his own special concept of the meaning of the will. Instead of Schopenhauer's passive will to survive, Nietzsche transformed it into a "will to power," the will pushed to its ultimate positive point. Humanity, said Nietzsche, was composed of two fundamentally opposed types: the weak and the strong, slaves and masters, the masses and the aristocratic few. Each side sought to depreciate the other and to impose its will on the other. The weak commend meekness, compassion, poverty, and renunciation (Christianity). But what was strong was good. Nietzsche recommended the morality of the strong, the more dominant race (*Uebermensch*, or Superman). Nietzsche was rarely read or respected by his contemporaries, many of whom dismissed him as either neurotic or insane. Nietzschean philosophy was perverted in the later nineteenth and the early twentieth centuries as a justification for German nationalism, although Nietzsche himself had envisioned the Superman as a cosmopolitan concept and as a European-wide phenomenon.

Religion in the Modern Age.

The impact of the new culture-patterns on religion was critical. Although nearly a century had passed since the separation of Church and State in the French Revolution, religion was now attacked more than ever. The whole tenor of a materialistic society worked against religion and kept people away from churches. Darwinian evolution and its implications challenged the very basis of Christian belief. The scientific method was now applied to Biblical or textual criticism. The attack upon both Old and New Testaments, and especially upon such dogmas as the Resurrection and the Virgin Birth, helped to undermine faith in religion. The emphasis upon materialism in a secular age left spiritual activity in a subordinate role. Institutional Christianity was challenged by a German theologian, David Friedrich Strauss (1808–1874), whose *Life of Jesus* (1835) discussed Christianity as a pseudo-mythological religion and Christ as a kind of Socrates. The storm which greeted this work was surpassed by an explosive controversy set off by the French historian Ernest Renan (1823–1892), whose *Life of Jesus* (1863) portrayed Christ as an inspired but human philosophic teacher. No fewer than 1,500 books and pamphlets were published to refute or defend Renan.

Reaction of the Roman Catholic Church.
The Roman Catholic Church, already experienced in combating medieval heresy and the shock of the Reformation, resisted the challenge of materialism and science. Pope Pius IX (1846–1878) started his pontificate with reforms of a liberal nature. In the Revolution of 1848 he proclaimed his neutrality, with the result that he was forced to leave Rome. By 1850, when the aid of foreign arms enabled him to return, he was purged of liberal sentiment. He began a vigorous campaign against what he called "the errors of modern society and thought." His series of criticisms of the influence of modernism on ecclesiastical life culminated in the famous encyclical *Quanta cura* and the accompanying *Syllabus of Errors,* published on December 8, 1864. The encyclical condemned liberalism, individualism, and secularism, and upheld the earlier ideal of the Christian state. The *Syllabus* included all the doctrines that had received papal condemnation and specifically castigated freethinkers, agnostics, materialists, naturalists, anticlericals, nationalists, liberals, Freemasons, and "indifferent" persons. Pius claimed for the Church the control of culture, science, and education and rejected liberty of faith, conscience, and worship for other creeds. In effect, the *Syllabus* declared war on some aspects of modern society and committed the papacy to the prin-

ciples of ultramontanism (papal supremacy). It was strongly criticized by Protestants. Catholic circles belittled the significance of the manifesto and pointed out that it was issued not as ecclesiastical dogma (it was compiled by a committee of cardinals and was not signed by the pope personally), but rather as counsel against the "abuses" of modern liberalism. However, its English translator, Cardinal Manning, archbishop of Westminster, declared it to be an emanation from the highest doctrinal authority in the Church.

At the Vatican Council of 1869–1870, the first such council since that of Trent three centuries before, the traditional teaching of the Church on the relationship between faith and reason was reaffirmed. In a sensational pronouncement, the council proclaimed the infallibility of the pope and the universality of his episcopate. It was announced as "a dogma divinely revealed" that, when the pope speaks *ex cathedra*—that is, when in discharge of the office of pastor and doctor of all Christians—on any matter of faith and morals, he possesses infallibility. Catholics insisted that papal infallibility referred only to matters of dogma, faith, and morals. Protestants attacked the concept on the grounds that there is no established or accepted definition of the phrase *ex cathedra,* and that all departments and functions of human life fall within the domain of morals. A storm raged over the doctrine: Catholics defended it as merely an ecclesiastical dogma, while Protestants condemned it as a scheme to elevate the papacy above secular governments and to enable it to interfere in national politics. Papal infallibility was denounced by Bismarck and Gladstone by anticlericals in France, by revolutionists in Spain, and by liberals in Italy and Austria. Pius IX defended it as the consistent tradition of Catholic Christianity.

Pope Leo XIII (1878–1903), successor to Pius IX, was concerned with introducing a doctrine of social Catholicism. The problems of the Industrial Revolution had led to the formation of a Catholic "social" movement designed to combat economic liberalism on the one hand and Marxian socialism on the other, while simultaneously aiming at the Christianizing of modern industrial society. On May 15, 1891, Leo XIII issued a famous encyclical, the *Rerum novarum,* which won for him the title of "the workingman's Pope." The document denounced Marxian socialism as violating the natural right to property and as inciting to class hatred, stressed the importance of the family, protested against exaltation of the State, and condemned the doctrine of economic determinism. The solution to the social problem, said the pope, was to be found in harmonious relations between capital and labor. He urged workmen to be peaceful and loyal to their employers, and at the same time, advised the latter to treat their workers as Christian freemen and not to exploit them as slaves. The pontiff called for a wider distribution of private property, the fostering of industrial trade unions, and the restriction of working hours, especially for women and children. He emphasized, above all, the place of the Church in bringing about a better social order. The *Rerum novarum* stimulated the formation throughout Europe of Catholic trade unions, which won a following second only to those of the Socialists.

Pius X (1903–1914), faced with anticlericalism in Catholic countries and modernism inside the Church itself, opposed the new trends in Catholic life. He reaffirmed the traditional Church doctrines but urged that they be made consistent with modern science.

Protestantism and Materialism. Protestantism was less successful than Catholicism in opposing the materialistic trends. As doubts accumulated about the literal truth of the Bible, Protestants tended to turn away from church attendance. Those Protestants who kept the faith despite the challenge of the new science often turned to fundamentalism (an insistence upon a literal interpretation of the Scriptures). Rural people tended to stay with the old-time religion. Another group of Protestants, the modernists, lost faith in the Bible but continued to go through the motions of worship and church attendance. Most Protestant churches were slow to meet the challenging social problems of the day, preferring to leave the care of orphans, the aged, sick,

and insane to the civil governments. Not until the twentieth century was there a Protestant movement aimed at reasserting basic doctrines and unifying the divergent Protestant churches.

Judaism. Orthodox Judaism, too, reflecting the changing standards of the age, underwent the dissolving effects of science and secularism. Reformed Judaism appeared as the Jewish counterpart to modernism in the Christian faiths. The new political liberalism allowed the Jews to act as citizens and enter business or the professions, thus freeing them from centuries of legal discrimination. At the end of the nineteenth century, Jewish nationalism was expressed in Zionism as the first international Zionist Congress met at Basle (1897). Meanwhile, a steady rise of anti-Semitism culminated in barbaric pogroms, or massacres, in Russia, and the notorious Dreyfus case (1894–1906) in France.

5. Trends in Literature

Impact of Naturalism. Both literature and the fine arts, in works of creative imagination, followed intellectual and institutional changes, such as rapid industrialization, social determinism, and irrationalism. The literary romanticism which had appeared in the early decades of the century as a rebellion against classical restraint and formalism continued in England and on the Continent at mid-century. The romantics had not shared the classicists' respect for purity of expression or for esthetic conventions, and had turned to unbridled emotionalism and rich imagery. Influenced by the new industrialization and the great strides in science, a new kind of writing, known as naturalism, emphasized scientific methods of observation and experiment in the treatment of character. Writers everywhere turned to the portrayal of social problems, dealing with such social evils as industrial strife, strikes, divorce, prostitution, and insanity. The high-flown, fantastic imagery of romanticism gave way to simple exposition with almost scientific concern for factual detail.

The phenomenon was not only European but worldwide. In England romanticism persisted, although its greatest era had already passed. Victorian literature revealed the impact of growing industrialization, bourgeois moral righteousness, social unrest, and the clash between science and faith. New writers turned to fidelity of expression, and freedom from prejudice and convention. Appalled by the social effects of industrialization, naturalistic writers eloquently presented the need for social reform. Among them were Charles Dickens (1812–1870), who sympathized with the victims of the machine and made public opinion aware of their plight, and William Makepeace Thackeray (1811–1863), who exposed the hypocrisy of his contemporary society in highly satirical novels. Among other Victorian novelists, George Eliot (1819–1880) presented a strong sense of moral purpose. George Meredith (1828–1909) provided masterly character analysis. Benjamin Disraeli (1804–1881) wrote brilliant political satires which prefaced his great career in English politics. Thomas Hardy (1840–1928) published masterpieces of naturalistic fiction.

French novelists, too, denounced the sordidness of contemporary life. Honoré de Balzac (1799–1850), disgusted with the misery induced by industrialization, exposed the bourgeoisie's ruthless struggle for material success behind a mask of hypocrisy. The work of Guy de Maupassant (1850–1893), a masterful technician of the short story, was suffused with disillusionment. Émile Zola (1840–1902), novelistic social commentator and crusader for social justice, wrote *J'Accuse* (*see page 523*) and took a leading role in the Dreyfus affair. Anatole France (1844–1924), poet, essayist, and novelist, wrote highly polished works notable for a caustic, Voltairean wit and irony and a satirical skepticism.

Russian literature, morbid, gloomy, and melancholy, reflected the misery and discontent of the masses. After Alexander Pushkin (1799–1837), a romantic-nationalist poet, established Russian as a literary language, a school of novelists with similar naturalistic characteristics emerged. Feodor Dostoevsky (1821–1881), master of psychological insight, described the

Leo Tolstoy on the ploughfield (1887). Painting by Ilya Repin.

lives of the downtrodden masses. Ivan Turgeniev (1818–1883) revealed the reaction of the Russian mind against an oppressive environment. Leo Tolstoy (1828–1910), humanist and humanitarian, called for a return to Christian ideals: brotherhood of man, peace, and goodwill. Anton Chekhov (1860–1904) described the misery of Russians under the iron heel of tsarism. Throughout the Russian novel was a deep and brooding concern with human destiny and the importance of the soul.

Scandinavian writers also made important contributions to the literature of naturalism. Henrik Ibsen (1828–1906) wrote scathing dramas on the effete Puritanism and social prejudices of Norwegian provincial life. European critics were stung into fury by his biting satire. August Strindberg (1849–1912), Swedish novelist and dramatist, criticized the social order of his day in introspective, pessimistic but penetrating observations on humanity. The Danish critic, Georg M. C. Brandes (1842–1927), aroused violent discussion by his acute interpretations of the whole range of European literature.

6. The Fine Arts: Painting, Sculpture, Architecture, Music

Trends in Art. New thinking in the physical sciences and in the political and social spheres was also revealed in novel techniques and forms in the arts. Artists were impelled by a fresh spirit of experimentation to find approaches free from the traditions of earlier epochs. They took into account a multitude of trends: the dominance of the middle class and its institutions, the conflict between democracy and reaction, the urbanization and secularization of society, and the new scientific discoveries. Although the degree of change varied, in general the pattern shifted from eighteenth-century classicism to romanticism, then to realism and naturalism. A motivating factor was that evolution and its implications had deprived artists of the support of religion without giving them a suitable replacement. Artists accepted faith in science as their watchword in the new Enlightenment, but many

refused to use it as a satisfactory substitute for faith in God. The new art forms produced heated controversy, for the tradition-minded academicians were slow to recognize the need or desirability for change.

Painting: Break With Early Standards. In the post-Napoleonic era of reaction, painters had turned from restrained classicism to emotional mysticism. There developed a new style of interpretation called impressionism—an attempt to bring the viewer's participation into the work of the delineator. This loose but vibrant form of art, in which design and the use of striking color were stressed, brought a revolution in painting. Led by Claude Monet (1840–1926), Edouard Manet (1832–1883), Pierre Auguste Renoir (1841–1919), Edgar Degas (1834–1917), and Camille Pissarro (1830–1903), the impressionists introduced new techniques in handling color and light. Art critics of the day, arguing that "drawing is everything, color is nothing," outdid one another in attacking impressionism as "a frightening spectacle of human vanity gone astray to the point of madness." By the mid-1880's, however, despite recurrent attacks, impressionism had won its recognition. A further step was taken by such leading post-impressionists as Paul Cézanne (1839–1906), who reduced nature to almost geometrical forms; Vincent van Gogh (1853–1890), whose emotional personality triumphed over structure; and Paul Gauguin (1848–1903), who combined a bold color technique with symbolism.

In the early twentieth century Henri Matisse (1869–1954) and a group who called themselves *fauves*, or wild beasts, influenced by van Gogh, began to use colors instead of perspective to suggest depth. Pablo Picasso (1881–   ), a Spaniard living in France, and Georges Braque (1881–1963), a Frenchman, began to present human figures in their essential geometric angles and planes, retaining just enough of the form to suggest the original model. Abstract cubism also underwent—and survived—savage critical attack.

In Central Europe, meanwhile, an art form called expressionism also moved away from realism. The German Emil Nolde (1867–1956) and the Austrian Oskar Kokoschka (1886–) used a bold, almost savage, expressionistic style to express their emotions in color and line.

Sculpture. New techniques in sculpture were also appropriate to the changing social order. By far the greatest sculptor of the century was the Frenchman François Auguste Rodin (1840–1917), a master in depicting the rhythmic movement of human forms and a keen student of contours. On their appearance, his works were hotly denounced, but eventually were accepted as masterpieces.

Architecture. Only in architecture was there some resistance to economic and social transformation. Bourgeois governments hewed to such older styles as classic and Gothic in constructing public buildings. One of the few architectural innovations was the skyscraper in the United States. In general the new architecture was functional in character, designed to serve social needs in the mass age.

Music. Music during the last decades of the nineteenth century continued to be dominated by the romantic masters. The German composer, Richard Wagner (1813–1883), combined music and dramatic poetry in a mighty torrent of musical color. His famous *Ring* cycle, which blended the old Germanic *Nibelungenlied* epic with Christian mysticism, was a grandiose expression of nationalism in music. Giuseppe Verdi (1813–1901), a prolific composer of dramatic melodies (*Aïda, Rigoletto*), represented national Italian opera. Verdi's operas became popular throughout the world. Johannes Brahms (1833–1897), a German liv-

An imaginative representation of Wagner's famous *Ring of the Nibelungen*. From the title page of a popular narrative translation published in America.

ing in Vienna and composing in all forms except that of opera, considered himself an apostle of German nationalism. The Russian composer, Peter Ilyich Tchaikovsky (1840–1893) put together melodious symphonic and ballet music in the traditional romantic and national framework. Richard Strauss (1864–1949), at first a follower of Wagner, later introduced the use of dissonance in his symphonic tone poems, thereby making a profound break with the romantic past. Claude Debussy (1862–1918) and Igor Stravinsky (1882–) also reflected the intellectual freedom of the new scientific and social thought by breaking with past forms and experimenting with impressionism and symbolism. Like literature and other arts, music sought to evolve new theories, ideas, and forms by breaking from earlier standards.

❧ KEY DOCUMENT ❧

CHARLES DARWIN ON THE THEORY OF EVOLUTION, 1859

Charles Darwin, *On the Origin of Species by Means of Natural Selection*, rev. ed. (London, 1860), *passim*.

THE MOST momentous event in the intellectual history of the nineteenth century was the publication on September 24, 1859, of *On the Origin of Species by Means of Natural*

Selection by Charles Darwin (1809–1882). The first edition of this book, 1,250 copies, was a first-day sell-out, an extraordinary publishing event at the time. In this book Darwin held that, because offspring can vary from parents and because nature tolerates only the survival of the fittest, the principle of natural selection can explain the evolution of a higher species from a low one. This theory was of great historical importance. Following are extracts from Darwin's *The Origin of Species*.

A. Extracts from the Introduction, The Origin of Species (*1859*)

When on board H.M.S. *Beagle*, as naturalist, I was much struck with certain facts in the distribution of the organic beings inhabiting South America, and in the geological relations of the present to the past inhabitants of that continent. These facts . . . seemed to throw some light on the origin of species—that mystery of mysteries, as it has been called by one of our greatest philosophers. On my return home, it occurred to me, in 1837, that something might perhaps be made out on this question by patiently accumulating and reflecting on all sorts of facts which could possibly have any bearing on it. After five years' work I allowed myself to speculate on the subject, and drew up some short notes; these I enlarged in 1844 into a sketch of the conclusions, which then seemed to me probable: from that period to the present day I have steadily pursued the same object. . . .

My work is now (1859) nearly finished; but it will take me many more years to complete it, and as my health is far from strong, I have been urged to publish this Abstract. . . . This . . . must necessarily be imperfect. I cannot here give references and authorities for my several statements; and I must trust to the reader reposing some confidence in my accuracy. No doubt errors may have crept in, though I hope I have always been cautious in trusting to good authorities alone. . . .

In considering the Origin of Species, it is quite conceivable that a naturalist, reflecting on the mutual affinities of organic beings, on their embryological relations, their geographical distribution, geological succession, and other such facts, might come to the conclusion that species had not been independently created, but had descended, like varieties, from other species. Nevertheless, such a conclusion, even if well founded, would be unsatisfactory, until it could be shown how the innumerable species inhabiting this world have been modified, so as to acquire that perfection of structure and coadaptation which justly excites our admiration.

It is . . . of the highest importance to gain a clear insight into the means of modification and coadaptation. . . .

. . . I shall devote the first chapter of this Abstract to Variation under Domestication. We shall thus see that a large amount of hereditary modification is at least possible; and, what is equally or more important, we shall see how great is the power of man in accumulating by his Selection successive slight variations. . . . In the next chapter the Struggle for Existence amongst all organic beings throughout the world, which inevitably follows from the high geometrical ratio of their increase, will be considered. This is the doctrine of Malthus, applied to the whole animal and vegetable kingdoms. As many more individuals of each species are born than can possibly survive; and as, consequently, there is a frequently recurring struggle for existence, it follows that any being, if it vary however slightly in any manner profitable to itself, under the complex and sometimes varying conditions of life, will have a better chance of surviving, and thus be *naturally selected*. From the strong principle of inheritance, any selected variety will tend to propagate its new and modified form.

This fundamental subject of Natural Selection will be treated at some length in the fourth chapter; and we shall then see how Natural Selection almost inevitably causes much Extinction of the less improved forms of life, and leads to what I have called Divergence of Character. In the next chapter I shall discuss the complex and little known laws of variation. In the five succeeding chapters, the most apparent and gravest difficulties in accepting the theory will be given:

namely, first, the difficulties of transitions, or how a simple being or a simple organ can be changed and perfected into a highly developed being or into an elaborately constructed organ; secondly, the subject of Instinct, or the mental powers of animals; thirdly, Hybridism, or the infertility of species and the fertility of varieties when intercrossed; and fourthly, the imperfection of the Geological Record. In the next chapter I shall consider the geological succession of organic beings throughout time; in the twelfth and thirteenth, their geographical distribution throughout space; in the fourteenth, their classification or mutual affinities, both when mature and in an embryonic condition. In the last chapter I shall give a brief recapitulation of the whole work, and a few concluding remarks.

B. Extracts from the Recapitulation and Conclusion, The Origin of Species (1859)

I see no good reasons why the views given in this volume should shock the religious feelings of any one. It is satisfactory, as showing how transient such impressions are, to remember that the greatest discovery ever made by man, namely, the law of the attraction of gravity, was also attacked by Leibnitz, "as subversive of natural, and inferentially of revealed, religion." A celebrated author and divine has written to me that "he has gradually learnt to see that it is just as noble a conception of the Deity to believe that He created a few original forms capable of self-development into other and needful forms, as to believe that He required a fresh act of creation to supply the voids caused by the action of His laws." . . .

Authors of the highest eminence seem to be fully satisfied with the view that each species has been independently created. To my mind it ac-

cords better with what we know of the laws impressed on matter by the Creator, that the production and extinction of the past and present inhabitants of the world should have been due to secondary causes, like those determining the birth and death of the individual. When I view all beings not as special creations, but as the lineal descendants of some few beings which lived long before the first bed of the Cambrian system was deposited, they seem to me to become ennobled. . . .

It is interesting to contemplate a tangled bank, clothed with many plants of many kinds, with birds singing on the bushes, with various insects flitting about, and with worms crawling through the damp earth, and to reflect that these elaborately constructed forms, so different from each other, and dependent upon each other in so complex a manner, have all been produced by laws acting around us. These laws, taken in the largest sense, being Growth with Reproduction; Inheritance which is almost implied by reproduction; Variability from the indirect and direct action of the conditions of life, and from use and disuse: a Ratio of Increase so high as to lead to a Struggle for Life, and as a consequence to Natural Selection, entailing Divergence of Character and the Extinction of less-improved forms. Thus, from the war of nature, from famine and death, the most exalted object which we are capable of conceiving, namely, the production of the higher animals, directly follows. There is grandeur in this view of life, with its several powers, having been originally breathed by the Creator into a few forms or into one; and that, whilst this planet has gone cycling on according to the fixed law of gravity, from so simple a beginning endless forms most beautiful and most wonderful have been, and are being evolved.

❧ HISTORICAL INTERPRETATION ❧

WALTER BAGEHOT ON SOCIAL DARWINISM

Walter Bagehot, *Physics and Politics* (New York, 1873), pp. 41–46, 49, 78–80.

AN IMPORTANT corollary of Darwinism in the nineteenth century was Social Darwinism, which held that the doctrine of natural selection in physical science should be utilized not only for animal history, but also, with a change of form and an identical essence, should be applied to human history. Thus, a scientific idea was presented that those nations which are strongest should prevail over others. This point of view was presented by the British critic Walter Bagehot (1826–1877) in his *Physics and Politics, or Thoughts on the Application of the Principles of "Natural Selection" and "Inheritance" to Political Society* (1873).

. . . .

"The difference between progression and stationary inaction," says one of our greatest living writers, "is one of the great secrets which science has yet to penetrate." I am sure I do not pretend that I can completely penetrate it; but it undoubtedly seems to me that the problem is on the verge of solution, and that scientific successes in kindred fields by analogy suggest some principles which wholly remove many of its difficulties, and indicate the sort of way in which those which remain may hereafter be removed too.

But what is the problem? Common English, I might perhaps say common civilised thought, ignores it. Our habitual instructors, our ordinary conversation, our inevitable and ineradicable prejudices tend to make us think that "Progress" is the normal fact in human society, the fact which we should expect to see, the fact which we should be surprised if we did not see. But history refutes this. . . . Only a few nations, and those of European origin, advance; and yet these think —seem irresistibly compelled to think—such advance to be inevitable, natural, and eternal. Why then is this great contrast? . . .

In solving, or trying to solve, the question, we must take notice of this remarkable difference, and explain it, too, or else we may be sure our principles are utterly incomplete, and perhaps altogether unsound. But what then is that solution, or what are the principles which tend towards it? Three laws, or approximate laws, may, I think, be laid down, with only one of which I can deal in this paper, but all three of which it will be best to state, that it may be seen what I am aiming at.

First. In every particular state of the world, those nations which are strongest tend to prevail over the others; and in certain marked peculiarities the strongest tend to be the best.

Secondly. Within every particular nation the type or types of character then and there most attractive tend to prevail; and the most attrac-

tive, though with exceptions, is what we call the best character.

Thirdly. Neither of these competitions is in most historic conditions intensified by extrinsic forces, but in some conditions, such as those now prevailing in the most influential part of the world, both are so intensified.

These are the sort of doctrines with which, under the name of "natural selection" in physical science, we have become familiar; and as every great scientific conception tends to advance its boundaries and to be of use in solving problems not thought of when it was started, so here, what was put forward for mere animal history may, with a change of form, but an identical essence, be applied to human history. . . .

The progress of the military art is the most conspicuous, I was about to say the most *showy*, fact in human history. Ancient civilisation may be compared with modern in many respects, and plausible arguments constructed to show that it is better; but you cannot compare the two in military power. Napoleon could indisputably have conquered Alexander; our Indian army would not think much of the Retreat of the Ten Thousand. . . . Taken as a whole, and allowing for possible exceptions, the aggregate fighting power of mankind has grown immensely, and has been growing continuously since we knew anything about it. . . .

The cause of this military growth is very plain. The strongest nation has always been conquering the weaker; sometimes even subduing it, but always prevailing over it. Every intellectual gain, so to speak, that a nation possessed was in the earliest times made use of—was *invested* and taken out—in war; all else perished. Each nation tried constantly to be the stronger, and so made or copied the best weapons; by conscious and unconscious imitation each nation formed a type of character suitable to war and conquest. Conquest improved mankind by the intermixture of strengths; the armed truce, which was then called peace, improved them by the competition of training and the consequent creation of new power. Since the long-headed men first drove the short-headed men out of the best land in Europe, all European history has been the history of the superposition of the more military races over the less military —of the efforts, sometimes successful, sometimes unsuccessful, of each race to get more military; and so the art of war has constantly improved. . . .

But how far are the strongest nations really the best nations? How far is excellence in war a criterion of other excellence? . . . War, as I have said, nourishes the "preliminary" virtues [of valor, veracity, the spirit of obedience, and the habit of discipline], and this is almost as much as to say that there are virtues which it does not nourish. All which may be called "grace" as well as virtue it does not nourish;

humanity, charity, a nice sense of the rights of others, it certainly does not foster. The insensibility to human suffering, which is so striking a fact in the world as it stood when history first reveals it, is doubtless due to the warlike origin of the old civilisation. Bred in war, and nursed in war, it could not revolt from the things of war, and one of the principal of these is human pain. Since war has ceased to be the moving force in the world, men have become more tender one to another, and shrink from what they used to inflict without caring; and this not so much because men are improved (which may or may not be in various cases), but because they have no longer the daily habit of war—have no longer formed their notions upon war, and therefore are guided by thoughts and feelings which soldiers as such—soldiers educated simply by their trade—are too hard to understand.

❧ TEN BASIC BOOKS ☙

NINETEENTH-CENTURY ENLIGHTENMENT: THE NEW WORLD OF INDUSTRY AND SCIENCE

1. Barzun, Jacques, *Darwin, Marx, Wagner: Critique of a Heritage*, Anchor Book (New York, 1958).†
2. Brandes, Georg M. C., *Main Currents in Nineteenth-Century Literature*, 6 vols. (New York, 1901–1905).
3. Brinton, Crane, *A History of Western Morals* (New York, 1959).
4. Clarke, George N., *The Idea of the Industrial Revolution* (Glasgow, 1953).
5. Dampier, William C., *A History of Science and Its Relations with Philosophy and Religion*, 4th ed. (Cambridge, 1961).†
6. Faure, Élie, *History of Art*, 5 vols. (New York, 1937), vols. IV and V.
7. Friedell, Egon, *A Cultural History of the Modern Age*, 3 vols. (New York, 1932), vol. III.
8. Métraux, Guy S., and François Crouzet, eds., *The Nineteenth Century World*, Mentor Book (New York, 1963).†
9. Russell, Bertrand, *A History of Western Philosophy* (New York, 1945).†
10. Usher, Abbott P., *A History of Mechanical Inventions*, rev. ed. (Cambridge, Mass., 1954).†

30

The British Constitutional Monarchy from 1867 TO 1914

AND NOW, Sir, let us for a moment consider the enormous and silent changes which have been going forward among the labouring population. May I use the words to hon. and right hon. gentlemen once used by exhortation by Sir Robert Peel to his opponents, "elevate your vision"? Let us try and raise our views above the fears, the suspicions, the jealousies, the reproaches, and the recriminations of this place and this occasion. Let us look onward to the time of our children and of our children's children. Let us know what preparation it behooves us should be made for that coming time. Is there or is there not, I ask, a steady movement of the labouring classes, and is or is not that movement a movement onwards and upwards? I do not say that it falls beneath the eye, for, like all great processes, it is unobservable in detail, but as solid and undeniable as it is resistless in its essential character.

—WILLIAM EWART GLADSTONE, in the House of Commons,
April 27, 1866

1. The March of Democracy in Britain

Britain's Golden Age. Great Britain's era of greatness continued through the last years of the nineteenth century and the opening decade of the twentieth. For more than sixty years, spanning two-thirds of the nineteenth century, Queen Victoria reigned in an era of political stability and material prosperity. The British Empire was the most powerful empire on earth. The constitutional monarchy was the great example of rational and orderly self-government through peaceful and parliamentary means. "Made in Britain" was the lodestar of the industrial world. Britain's magnificent literary tradition was respected throughout the world. Inside Britain, two great political parties, Liberal and Conservative, heirs of the Whigs and Tories, in the 1850's crystallized into a new pattern and produced two great leaders in Gladstone and Disraeli.

Gladstone, Apostle of Liberalism. William Ewart Gladstone (1809–1898), son of a Liverpool merchant of Scottish descent, began his political career as an able representative of the stern, unbending Conservative faction. Under the influence of Sir Robert Peel, he turned to the cause of liberalism. He served as Liberal prime minister four times between 1868 and 1894. Representing the commercial rather than the landed aristocracy, Gladstone supported free trade, political and economic liberalism, and retrenchment in governmental expenditures. His main interest was in domestic affairs. A man of deeply religious feeling, he was robustly humanitarian and unwavering in his sense of public duty. His efforts to make political life "truly Christian" prompted Queen Victoria to refer to him as "that half-mad firebrand." A spellbinding orator (Disraeli once described him as "intoxicated with the exuberance of his own verbosity"), he could hold the attention of the House of Commons even when reciting a list of figures. One of the leading statesmen of his century, he regarded it as his major duty to understand the will of the people and to act in their name. In finance, he was one of Britain's best chancellors of the exchequer. Gladstone was one of those great British statesmen who enhanced the reputation of Parliament.

Disraeli, Apostle of Conservatism. Benjamin Disraeli, earl of Beaconsfield (1804–1881), Gladstone's rival, was twice prime minister between 1868 and 1880. Descendant of a family of Levantine Jews, he was baptized as a Christian in 1817. In his early years he was notorious for extreme foppery in dress, admired for his witty, paradoxical speech, and famous for brilliant novels and satires. A political opportunist, he entered the House of Commons in 1837. As he made his first speech he was howled down by hecklers, but he warned the mockers that the day would come when they *would* hear him. Within a decade he was leader of the Conservative party. For more than a quarter of a century he led the Conservatives, educating them in the need for social reform and insisting that, for their own good, they ally themselves with the masses. They reluctantly submitted to his dominance. Queen Victoria, fascinated by his charm and flattery, affectionately dubbed him "Dizzy." The British people were delighted by his success in foreign affairs. Thomas Carlyle expressed amazement that "this superlative Hebrew conjurer could spellbind all the great lords, great parties, great interests, and lead them by the nose like helpless, mesmerized, somnambulant cattle."

It would be difficult to find two political leaders more different in background and temperament than Gladstone and Disraeli. Gladstone was conservative in temperament and liberal in opinion, Disraeli was radical in temperament and conservative in action. These two statesmen, alternating in power, led Great Britain through some of her most productive and prosperous years.

Reform of the Suffrage, 1867. British reformers were not satisfied with the First Reform Bill of 1832, which had given the vote to only one Englishman in thirty, or about one-eighth of the entire adult male population. The overwhelming majority still had no vote. Both major parties, Conservatives as well as Liberals, favored an extension of suffrage, and both wanted credit for what they regarded as an inevitable change. The matter was closely related to the serious economic situation. The Civil War in the United States (1861–1865) and the era of reconstruction there had cut off the supply of cotton, thus closing many English factories. Something had to be done quickly to relieve discontent among the workers. Perhaps extension of the suffrage might help. There followed some complex political maneuvering. The Liberal Russell-Gladstone ministry of 1865–1866 proposed to add about 400,000 voters to the lists, but the bill was rejected and the ministry resigned. Then Disraeli, who headed a new ministry, decided that the Conservatives, to remain in power, would have to make concessions. Lord Derby, Conservative leader of the House of Lords, and Disraeli, then Conservative leader of the House of Commons, introduced the Reform Bill of 1867, (*see page 402*), a giant step forward in extension of suffrage.

The Conservatives took credit for the maneuver. Disraeli said that he had "dished the Whigs" (stolen the thunder of the Liberals). However, the right to vote was still far from universal. Only about 2,000,000 out of a population of 32,000,000 in the United Kingdom could vote, while the agricultural laborers and miners were still disenfranchised. Reactionaries, however, believed that the propertied class was the only one with sufficient intelligence to vote and regarded the new bill as a step on the road to perdition. Even Lord Derby described it as "a leap in the dark."

Pendulum of British Politics. British politics in the era of Gladstone and Disraeli was distinguished by a kind of productive rivalry. The two parties, Conservative and Liberal, alternated in power, each making it a point to retain and extend the policies of its predecessor in office. There was a profitable equilibrium during the alternate ministries: Derby-

Disraeli, 1866–1868; Disraeli, 1874–1880; and Gladstone, 1868–1874, 1880–1885, 1886, and 1892–1894. Both parties sought support wherever they could find it, the Conservatives from the landed aristocracy, the Liberals from the industrial and commercial interests. The Liberal platform was peace, retrenchment, and domestic reform, and that party was more willing to take pioneer steps in government. The Conservatives departed from these aims: their program did not entail peace because they wanted consolidation and expansion of the empire, which meant war; it did not mean retrenchment, because they demanded ever greater appropriations for the armed forces; it advocated reform not merely for Britain but for the whole empire.

2. Victorian Rivals: Gladstone and Disraeli

Gladstone's First Reform Ministry, 1868–1874. Gladstone's first ministry after the Reform Act of 1867 was pledged to reform. To meet the perplexing Irish problem ("My mission is to pacify Ireland"), he disestablished the Irish (Episcopal) State Church in 1869 and enacted the Irish Land Act in 1870. For part of the nineteenth century, elementary education in England was much inferior to that on the Continent. In 1870 there were accommodations in inspected day schools for about 2,000,000 children; the average attendance was about 1,168,000. There were, with the exception of the well-to-do class, some 1,500,000 children who attended no school at all or schools not under inspection. Under the stimulus of William Edward Forster (1818–1886), the Gladstone administration in 1870 undertook a comprehensive measure of educational reform. The Elementary Education Act, introduced on February 17, 1870, provided the framework for a system of national education. By eliminating religious tests in 1871 Gladstone enabled non-members of the Church of England to study at and be graduated from Oxford and Cambridge (University Tests Act). He also supported a measure designed to allow labor unions to incorporate, and also repealed the old conspiracy laws designed to intimidate unions, thereby legalizing labor unions. He abolished the system of purchasing commissions in the army, placed promotion on a merit basis, and reduced the term of service from 12 years to 6 with the colors and 6 in the reserves. He introduced the secret ballot (Australian ballot) in 1872 for parliamentary elections. He improved the civil service by abolishing the outmoded system of rewarding political favorites and substituted instead competitive examinations.

Each reform was won only against bitter opposition: both British Conservatives and the Irish opposed Gladstone's measures designed to help Ireland; Nonconformists objected to the elementary education act; labor unions, while grateful for the right to strike, opposed a law making criminal any show of intimidation; the military clique denounced army reforms; and Liberals opposed the secret ballot on the ground that no man should fear to announce his vote publicly. Disgusted with what he believed to be political stupidity, Gladstone astounded the country in 1874 by announcing that he would retire and devote himself to "Homeric and ecclesiastical studies."

Disraeli's Imperial Administration, 1874–1880. Gladstone could not match his domestic policies with an aggressive foreign policy. He had little influence on the course of the Franco-Prussian War of 1870–1871. He did not succeed in preventing the Russians from rebuilding the fortress of Sevastopol. The British public resented his weakness in handling the Alabama Claims of the United States. During the American Civil War the *Alabama,* a Southern privateer equipped in British waters, had preyed on Northern commerce. When the United States later demanded compensation, Gladstone referred the entire matter to an international tribunal and then paid the damages awarded. To the British public this was inexcusable timidity.

Disraeli's Conservative government of 1874, to counter Gladstone's weakness, turned to a crusading imperialism. For the next six years proud Britons saw a vigorous foreign policy. At its root was a traditional aloofness from Continental affairs and the protection of Tur-

"New Crowns for Old." An 1877 caricature by Tenniel suggests that magician Disraeli may be exchanging the crown of India for Queen Victoria's old one.

key against Russian designs. Disraeli in 1875 acquired control of the Suez Canal by purchasing 176,000 shares owned by Khedive Ismail of Egypt. Great Britain now commanded a vital part of her system of imperial communications. The next year, in 1876, he won the lasting gratitude of his queen by sponsoring her coronation, in a splendid ceremony, as Empress of India. Victoria never forgot that Disraeli had made her the successor of the Mogul emperors. Some Englishmen opposed the title as "un-English" and in disrepute through the fall of Emperor Napoleon III, but the opposition was appeased by the promise that Victoria would not use the title in England.

In 1878 Disraeli compelled Russia to yield the Near Eastern question to a European conference at Berlin. He then loosened the Russian grip on Turkey, forcing Russia to relinquish the gains she had made in the Russo-Turkish War of 1877. He returned to London bearing "Peace with Honor" as well as a British right to occupy the island of Cyprus. In

1878 he dispatched a British army to Afghanistan, forcing the Russians to withdraw, and placed a friendly ruler on the throne. After the annexation of the Transvaal in 1877, he brought a war against the neighboring Zulus to a successful conclusion and thereby laid the groundwork for future British expansion in South Africa. Not since the days of Lord Chatham had British foreign policy been promoted as vigorously as it was by the flamboyant Disraeli.

Third Reform Bill, 1884. After the fall of Disraeli's ministry in 1880, he was succeeded by Gladstone, who decided to redeem a previous pledge to extend the suffrage. The third reform bill, Representation of the People Act of 1884, gave the vote to self-supporting unskilled laborers and servants in both the boroughs and the counties. Some 2,000,000 new voters were added to the rolls. England thus finally became a democracy, in the sense that all self-supporting males—three out of four adult males—now had the right to vote. Some thirty-four years later, in 1918, universal suffrage became law, and the vote was given to all women over the age of 30. In 1928 the franchise was extended to all women over 21, thereby giving women the same voting rights as men. In slightly less than a century, from 1832 to 1928, Britain had changed from a state controlled by the vote of propertied squires and merchants to one in which all, men and women alike, could vote. This revolutionary constitutional change was accomplished without violence and bloodshed.

The pace of suffrage reform and reapportionment quickened. The Redistribution Bill of 1885 reallocated 160 seats in the House of Commons. All boroughs and districts with fewer than 15,000 voters were deprived of their seats, and the larger towns and counties were divided into districts represented in Parliament according to their size. For the first time in British history, the individual (rather than the county or borough) became the responsible unit of representation in the House of Commons. The principle now was "one vote, one value."

The County Council Bill of 1888 provided for the popular election by local voters of a council for each county, while the Parish Councils Bill of 1894 democratized the governments of local parishes by setting up popularly elected assemblies and councils in parishes and districts.

3. The Irish Problem

Land, Religion, Politics. The old antagonism between England and Ireland, conqueror and conquered, began as early as 1172 when Henry II landed in Ireland, organized the country after the Norman fashion, reduced the population to serfdom, and granted lands to his favorite barons. The ensuing long struggle between England and Ireland had three aspects: economic, religious, and political.

By the early nineteenth century, at least six-sevenths of Irish lands had been acquired by English absentee landlords. Irish peasants, miserable and wretched, were often evicted unjustly from their lands. In 1846 came a terrible potato famine, which caused widespread starvation and led to mass emigration to the United States. The first major attempt to ease the lot of the Irish peasantry came with Gladstone's Irish Reform Bill of 1870, which protected tenants from eviction as long as they paid rent, and provided for loans to tenants. Between 1864 and 1914 Ireland changed from a land of tillage to one of pasturage. In 1879 Michael Davitt (1846–1906), son of an evicted tenant, organized the Irish Land League to work for the "three F's"—fair rent, fixed holdings, and freedom of sale. Varied means were used to obtain concessions from landlords, including the boycott, or refraining by concerted action from purchasing (used for the first time in 1880 against a Captain Boycott, agent for a British landlord in Mayo). Irish members of Parliament, using obstructionist tactics, bargained expertly with both Liberals and Conservatives, and in 1881 obtained a Land Act virtually conceding the three F's. The Land Purchase Act of 1903 (the Wyndham Act) set up a fund to enable Irish peasants to purchase farms from absentee English landlords.

The religious factor in the Irish question hinged on the rivalry of Catholicism and Anglicanism. The population of Ireland was mostly Catholic, except in the six northern counties known as Ulster. In the early nineteenth century no Irish Catholic could vote or hold office. This situation was changed in 1829, when Daniel O'Connell (1775–1847) was elected to a seat in Parliament under the Catholic Emancipation Act. Catholic Irish, resenting the forced payment of tithes to the Anglican Church, revolted in the Tithe Wars (1831–1838). In 1869 Parliament disestablished the Irish Church, thus relieving the Irish of paying tithes to support Anglicanism.

Equally difficult were Anglo-Irish political relations. A great rebellion had broken out in Ireland in 1641. The execution of Charles I in 1649 released parliamentary troops for service in Ireland. Cromwell's Irish campaign, with the massacres of Drogheda and Waterford, degenerated into savage butchery, which the Irish never forgot. After suppression of an Irish rebellion in 1789, Parliament passed an Act of Union abolishing the Irish legislature and joining Great Britain and Ireland. The Irish were to be represented in the House of Lords by 28 Irish peers and 4 bishops elected for life by the whole of the Irish peerage. One hundred members were supposed to represent Ireland in the House of Commons. Pitt intended that the Act of Union be accompanied by a measure of Catholic emancipation, but George III insisted that his coronation oath forbad it. Rather than break what he regarded as a pledge, Pitt resigned (1801). Roman Catholics could not sit in the House of Commons until 1829, when the Roman Catholic Emancipation Act allowed them to take seats in that body.

Home Rule Bills, 1886, 1893, 1914. Throughout the nineteenth century, patriotic Irishmen sought for independence and self-government. Robert Emmet (1778–1803), who planned an insurrection to seize Dublin Castle, was captured, tried, found guilty, and hanged. Fanatical patriots who called themselves Young Ireland agitated for independence, only to see their leaders imprisoned or exiled. Irish emigrants in the United States organized the Fenian Brotherhood, or *Sinn Fein* ("We Ourselves") nationalist movement, which spread to Ireland, where it was suppressed. Charles

THE NON-STOP CAR.

Erin. "COME ON OUT O' THAT NOW, DARLINT, OR YE'LL BE KILT INTIRELY."

Stewart Parnell (1846–1891), by a policy of obstructive legislation (fillibustering) in Parliament, drew attention to the political aspects of the Irish question. Gladstone brought forward two Home Rule Bills, one in 1886 and one in 1893, but both were rejected. Conservatives sought to "kill Home Rule by kindness" by such agrarian measures as the Wyndham Act. A third Home Rule Bill was introduced in the House of Commons in 1912. This act received royal assent in 1914 but, because of the outbreak of World War I, its operation was suspended.

4. The Quest for Social Justice

Conservatives in Power, 1895–1906. When Disraeli died in 1881, he left behind him a strong Conservative Party which was in part his own creation. In 1886 the Liberals joined the Irish Nationalists in calling for Irish Home Rule, whereupon a minority of Liberals, calling

themselves Liberal Unionists, joined with the Conservatives in rejecting Home Rule. More nationalist and imperialist than liberal, the Liberal Unionists thereafter supported the Conservative cause. A coalition of Conservatives and Liberals assumed political power from 1895 to 1906 in the ministries of the marquis of Salisbury (1895–1902) and Arthur James Balfour (1902–1905). Traditionally, conservative emphasis was more on imperial affairs and protectionism than on social legislation and domestic reform. The party pushed the Boer War (1899–1902), which led to the incorporation of South Africa into the empire, and promoted British interests in India, China, Persia, Australia, and Egypt. A magnificent Jubilee in 1897 celebrated the sixtieth anniversary of Victoria's accession. On the queen's death in 1901, the throne went to Edward VII (r. 1901–1910), to whose title, "King of Great Britain and Ireland, Emperor of India, and Defender of the Faith" was added "Sovereign of the Dominions beyond the Seas."

In 1903 Joseph Chamberlain (1836–1914), aggressive businessman and shrewd statesman, stated his belief in an imperial preference tariff (giving priority to imports from any part of the empire). He also supported an empire-wide share in military matters (imperial defense), and regular consultation on common problems (imperial conference). He spent the years 1903–1906 traveling through the country advocating his system of tariff reform. The policy of protectionism split both major parties: free trade had won the support of the middle class, the masses, and even of some Conservatives.

The New Liberalism, 1906–1916. The elections of 1906 gave a landslide victory to the Liberals. The new Labour Party won 29 seats. Liberal Britain, with its stress on political freedom and religious toleration, gave way to a "radical" Britain concerned with social legislation and improvement of the condition of the masses. The old liberalism representing industry was succeeded by a new liberalism more sensitive to the needs of the common man. The new Liberals won a mass following by turning their attention to domestic matters concerning the working class. Chief among the apostles of a social Britain was David Lloyd George (1863–1945), son of a poor Welsh schoolmaster, who became the voice of radical Britain. A fighting statesman equally effective in debate in the House of Commons and on the public platform, Lloyd George was determined to reconstruct the social system to give the poor a better chance. Britons turned to him as a popular idol-leader in the struggle for reform.

The Labour Party. The passage of the Second Reform Bill of 1867 gave voice to the organized labor vote. The first general trade-union congress was held at London in 1899; in the next year it organized the Labour Representative Committee, with J. Ramsay MacDonald (1866–1937) as secretary. When formed in 1900, its membership was 375,000, and it succeeded in returning two members to the House of Commons in that year. At the outbreak of World War I in 1914 it had 1,500,000 votes and 40 members in the House. The Labour Representation Committee was supported by several groups: the Fabians, intellectual socialists such as George Bernard Shaw and Sidney and Beatrice Webb, who called for gradual socialization; the Social Democratic Federation, an organization with a strictly Marxian program; and the Independent Labour Party, a faction organized in 1893 by Keir Hardie, an ex-miner. In 1906 the Labour Representation Committee became known as the Labour Party. By 1914 the Labourites had consolidated and increased their forces until they formed a compact group.

Development of Trade Unionism. Trade unions began to win a position of greater and greater importance. Deprived of the right to strike, workers turned to revolutionary agitation, which developed into Chartism and the

The Great Strike of 1889. The major industrial upheaval of the nineteenth century lasted from August 13 to September 16. The Port of London was brought to a standstill as the dockers struck for better working conditions and higher pay. A contemporary drawing shows strikers dramatizing their protest in a strike parade.

working-class movement of Utopian Socialism. By 1870 legislation was being enacted to repeal the Combination Laws and allow workers to perform acts in combination which they could do legally as individuals. The Dockers' Strike of 1889 led to expansion of trade unions among the hitherto unorganized semi-skilled and un-skilled workers. The Taff Vale decision of 1901 —issued by the House of Lords acting as the supreme court of England, holding any union responsible for illegal acts of its members— endangered the entire trade-union movement. To conciliate aroused workers, Parliament in 1906 passed the Trade Disputes Act which nullified the Taff Vale decision. The House of Lords in 1909 rendered the Osborne Judgment prohibiting the use of trade-union funds for political purposes, but this act halted neither the rise of trade unionism nor that of the Labour Party.

Accelerated Social Legislation. Meanwhile, the Liberal Party, with a mandate from the people, pushed its program of social legislation. The Workingman's Compensation Act, which at first had been applied only to a few industries, was extended in 1906 to all industries. In that same year an Education Act provided for free meals for undernourished children. Three important pieces of social legislation were enacted in 1908–1909: the Children's Act, providing for free medical attention, recreation facilities, and schooling; the Coal Mines Act, which set up on eight-hour day for miners; and the Old Age Pension Act, which granted state pensions to needy elderly persons. The Labour Exchanges Act of 1909 set up a system of free public employment bureaus. These and similar measures were denounced by critics as radical and irresponsible. Although such acts did not succeed in abolishing poverty, they did ameliorate the condition of those workers close to starvation, who were numerous enough to be matters of concern.

Lloyd George's Budget of 1909. The expensive program of social reform, together with mounting military and naval costs, painfully strained the treasury. Lloyd George, chancellor of the exchequer in 1909, proposed that the greater share of taxation should be borne by "the broadest shoulders," an indelicate hint to wealthy British citizens. He asked for heavy inheritance taxes, levies on undeveloped land, a tax on unearned increment of land values, and a graduated income tax. Lloyd George could not have shocked the Conservatives more had he brought the devil to earth. The House of Lords promptly defeated his bill. But, with widespread popular support for the measures, the budget was finally passed.

Parliament Bill of 1911. In 1910 a coalition of Liberals, Labourites, and Irish Nationalists, convinced that something had to be done to remove the House of Lords as a barrier to social reform, introduced a bill proposing: (1) that financial measures passed by the House of Commons should become law one month after presentation to the Lords even if the latter disapproved them; (2) that all other bills should become law if passed by the Commons in three successive sessions, or if two years elapsed between the first consideration of any bill and its final enactment; and (3) that elections for the Commons be held at least every fifth instead of every seventh year. (*See page 513.*) This act, which would have destroyed the legislative powers of the House of Lords, was bitterly opposed. In ensuing debates Liberals attacked "reactionaries, plutocrats, and aristocrats," and the Conservatives accused their political opponents of "revolutionary socialism." Liberal leaders finally persuaded the new king, George V (r. 1910–1936), to agree to "pack" the House of Lords with enough Liberal peers to outvote opponents of the bill. The battle was won when the Lords passed the bill emasculating its own powers. From this time on the House of Lords was little more than a debating society.

Shifts in Economic Wealth and Prosperity. Great Britain grew in wealth and prosperity in the 1870's. British mills sent enormous quantities of cotton and woolen goods to all parts of the world. British mines produced nearly half the world's coal supply. British ships carried domestic and foreign goods across the seas. Yet Britain had an unfavorable balance of trade. Able to produce only a quarter of her needed food supply, she was forced to import foodstuffs. The resultant imbalance was more than amply compensated for by tremendous invisible earnings (income from foreign investments). As industrialization increased rapidly on the Continent and in the United States, Britain's virtual monopoly of worldwide commerce was broken. Among her competitors, Germany was pressing hard. This rivalry would carry over into the blood bath of World War I.

⌐ KEY DOCUMENT ⌐

THE PARLIAMENT ACT OF 1911

1 and 2 George 5, ch. 13 (extracts).

THE PARLIAMENT ACT of 1911 brought about as great a change in the British system of government as the First Reform Bill of 1832. By giving almost unchecked political power to the House of Commons and merely a suspensive veto to the House of Lords, it actually established a single-chamber government. From this time on, the House of Lords, stripped of power, became an appendage instead of a powerful factor in British government.

An Act to make provision with respect to the powers of the House of Lords in relation to those of the House of Commons, and to limit the duration of Parliament. (18th August 1911.)

Whereas it is expedient that provision should be made for regulating the relations between the two Houses of Parliament:

And whereas it is intended to substitute for the House of Lords as it at present exists a Second Chamber constituted on a popular instead of an hereditary basis, but such substitution cannot be immediately brought into operation:

And whereas provision will require hereafter to be made by Parliament in a measure effecting such substitution for limiting and defining the powers of the new Second Chamber, but it is expedient to make such provision as in this Act appears for restricting the existing powers of the House of Lords:

Be it therefore enacted by the King's most Excellent Majesty, by and with the advice and consent of the Lords Spiritual and Temporal, and Commons, in this present Parliament assembled and by the authority of the same, as follows:

1. Power of House of Lords as to Money Bills

(1) If a Money Bill, having been passed by the House of Commons, and sent up to the House of Lords at least one month before the end of the session, is not passed by the House of Lords without amendment within one month after it is so sent up to that House, the Bill shall, unless the House of Commons direct to the contrary, be presented to His Majesty and become an Act of Parliament on the Royal Assent being signified, notwithstanding that the House of Lords have not consented to the Bill.

(2) A Money Bill means a Public Bill which in the opinion of the Speaker of the House of Commons contains only provisions dealing with all or any of the following subjects, namely, the imposition, repeal, remission, alteration, or regulation of taxation; the imposition for the payment of debt or other financial purposes of charges on the Consolidated Fund, or on money provided by Parliament, or the variation or repeal of any such charges; supply; the appropriation, receipt, custody, issue or audit of accounts of public money; the raising or guarantee of any loan or the repayment thereof; or subordinate matters incidental to those subjects or any of them. . . .

2. Restriction of Powers of House of Lords as to Bills other than Money Bills

(1) If any Public Bill (other than a Money Bill or a Bill containing any provision to extend the maximum duration of Parliament beyond

five years) is passed by the House of Commons in three successive sessions (whether of the same Parliament or not), and, having been sent up to the House of Lords at least one month before the end of the session, is rejected by the House of Lords in each of those sessions, that Bill shall, on its rejection for the third time by the House of Lords, unless the House of Commons direct to the contrary, be presented to His Majesty and become an Act of Parliament on the Royal Assent being signified thereto, notwithstanding that the House of Lords have not consented to the Bill:

Provided that this provision shall not take effect unless two years have elapsed between the date of the second reading in the first of those sessions of the Bill in the House of Commons and the date on which it passes the House of Commons in the third of those sessions. . . .

7. Duration of Parliament

Five years shall be substituted for seven years as the time fixed for the maximum duration of Parliament under the Septennial Act, 1715.

❧ HISTORICAL INTERPRETATION ❧

WALTER BAGEHOT ON CABINET GOVERNMENT

The Works of Walter Bagehot, ed. by Forrest Morgan (Hartford, Conn., 1889), IV, 59–63.

IN HIS FAMOUS book, *The English Constitution* (1867), Walter Bagehot described the English constitutional system as it was actually working in his day. He refuted the dogma that the legislative and executive powers are entrusted to separate sets of persons, each independent of the other, and asserted that the peculiar excellence of the unwritten Constitution is the practical fusion of the executive and legislative powers through the cabinet. Following is Bagehot's description of the cabinet system.

The efficient secret of the English Constitution may be described as the close union, the nearly complete fusion, of the executive and legislative powers. No doubt by the traditional theory, as it exists in all the books, the goodness of our Constitution consists in the entire separation of the legislative and executive authorities; but in truth its merit consists in their singular approximation. The connecting link is *the Cabinet.* By that new word we mean a committee of the legislative body selected to be the executive body. The legislature has many committees, but this is its greatest. It chooses for this, its main committee, the men in whom it has most confidence. It does not, it is true, choose them directly; but it is nearly omnipotent in choosing them indirectly. . . . as a rule, the nominal Prime Minister is chosen by the legislature, and the real Prime Minister for most purposes—the leader of the House of Commons—almost without exception is so. There is nearly always some one man plainly selected by the voice of the predominant party in the predominant House of the

legislature to head that party, and consequently to rule the nation. We have in England an elective first magistrate as truly as the Americans have an elective first magistrate. The Queen is only at the head of the dignified part of the Constitution; the Prime Minister is at the head of the efficient part. . . .

The leading minister so selected has to choose his associates, but he only chooses among a charmed circle. The position of most men in Parliament forbids their being invited to the Cabinet; the position of a few men insures their being invited. Between the compulsory list whom he must take, and the impossible list whom he cannot take, a Prime Minister's independent choice in the formation of a Cabinet is not very large; it extends rather to the division of the Cabinet offices than to the choice of Cabinet ministers. Parliament and the nation have pretty well settled who shall have the first places; but they have not discriminated with the same accuracy which man shall have which place. . . .

The Cabinet, in a word, is a board of control

chosen by the legislature, out of persons whom it trusts and knows, to rule the nation. The particular mode in which the English ministers are selected; the fiction that they are, in any political sense, the Queen's servants; the rule which limits the choice of the Cabinet to the members of the legislature,—are accidents unessential to its definition, historical incidents separable from its nature. Its characteristic is, that it should be chosen by the legislature out of persons agreeable to and trusted by the legislature. Naturally, these are principally its own members; but they need not be exclusively so. A Cabinet which included persons not members of the legislative assembly might still perform all useful duties. Indeed, the peers, who constitute a large element in modern Cabinets, are members nowadays only of a subordinate assembly. The House of Lords still exercises several useful functions; but the ruling influence, the deciding faculty, has passed to what, using the language of old times, we still call the "lower House,"—to an assembly which, though inferior as a dignified institution, is superior as an efficient institution. . . .

But the detail of the composition of a Cabinet, and the precise method of its choice, are not to the purpose now; the first and cardinal consideration is the definition of a Cabinet. We must not bewilder ourselves with the separable accidents until we know the necessary essence. A Cabinet is a combining committee,—a *hyphen* which joins, a *buckle* which fastens, the legislative part of the state to the executive part of the state. In its origin it belongs to the one, in its functions it belongs to the other.

The most curious point about the Cabinet is, that so very little is known about it. The meetings are not only secret in theory, but secret in reality. By the present practice, no official minute in all ordinary cases is kept of them; even a private note is discouraged and disliked. The House of Commons, even in its most inquisitive and turbulent moments, would scarcely permit a note of a Cabinet meeting to be read; no minister who respected the fundamental usages of political practice would attempt to read such a note. . . .

But a Cabinet, though it is a committee of the legislative assembly, is a committee with a power which no assembly would—unless for historical accidents, and after happy experience—have been persuaded to intrust to any committee. It is a committee which can dissolve the assembly which appointed it; it is a committee with a suspensive veto, a committee with a power of appeal. Though appointed by one Parliament, it can appeal if it chooses to the next. Theoretically, indeed, the power to dissolve Parliament is intrusted to the sovereign only, and there are vestiges of doubt whether in *all* cases a sovereign is bound to dissolve Parliament when the Cabinet asks him to do so; but neglecting such small and dubious exceptions, the Cabinet which was chosen by one House of Commons has an appeal to the next House of Commons. The chief committee of the legislature has the power of dissolving the predominant part of that legislature,—that which at a crisis is the supreme legislature. The English system, therefore, is not an absorption of the executive power by the legislative power: it is a fusion of the two. Either the Cabinet legislates and acts, or else it can dissolve. It is a creature, but it has the power of destroying its creators. It is an executive which can annihilate the legislature, as well as an executive which is the nominee of the legislature. It *was* made, but it *can* unmake; it was derivative in its origin, but it is destructive in its action.

❦[TEN BASIC BOOKS]❧

THE BRITISH CONSTITUTIONAL MONARCHY
FROM 1867 TO 1914

1. Ausubel, Herman, *The Late Victorians: A Short History,* Anvil Book No. 3 (Princeton, N. J., 1955.)†
2. Brinton, Crane, *English Political Thought in the Nineteenth Century,* 2nd ed. (Cambridge, Mass., 1949, R. 1962).†

3. Cole, George D. H., *Short History of the English Working Class Movement, 1789–1947*, rev. ed., 3 vols. (London, 1960).

4. Ensor, Robert C. K., *England, 1870–1914*, rev. ed. (Oxford, 1949).

5. Laski, Harold J., *Parliamentary Government in England* (New York, 1938).

6. Lynd, Helen M., *England in the Eighteen-Eighties* (Oxford, 1945).

7. Pelling, Henry, *The Origins of the Labour Party, 1880–1900*, 2nd ed. (New York, 1964).

8. Schuyler, Robert Livingston, and Corinne Comstock Weston, *British Constitutional History Since 1832*, Anvil Book No. 18 (Princeton, N. J., 1957).†

9. Utley, T. E., and J. Stuart Maclure, eds., *Documents of Modern Political Thought* (Cambridge, 1958).

10. Young, George M., ed., *Victorian England: Portrait of an Age*, 2nd ed. (Oxford, 1953).†

31

Triumph of Republicanism: The Third French Republic, 1871-1914

YEA, HAPPY they who serve our France,
And neither pain nor danger fly;
But in the front of war's advance
Still deem it but a glorious chance,
To be among the brave who die!

No splendid war do we begin,
No glory waits us when 'tis past;
But marching through the fiery din,
We see our serried ranks grow thin,
And blood of Frenchmen welling fast.

French blood!—a treasure so august,
And hoarded with such jealous care,
To crush oppression's strength unjust,
With all the force of right robust,
And buy us back our honor fair. . . .

Good fighting! and God be your shield,
Our pride's avengers, brave and true!
France watches you upon the field.
Who wear her colors never yield,
For 'tis her heart ye bear with you!

—PAUL DÉROULÈDE, "Good Fighting,"
in *Poèmes Militaires*, 1872

1. Establishment of the Third French Republic

L'Année Terrible. When, in September 1870, Napoleon III revealed his helplessness against Bismarck and Prussia, revolutionaries in Paris, as in 1792 and 1848, again proclaimed a republic. They set up a Provisional Government of National Defense led by the fiery Léon Gambetta (1838–1882), who demanded continued resistance against the Germans. With the German armies already surrounding Paris, Gambetta escaped in a balloon, organized armies in the provinces, and tried to raise the siege. He struggled on, sternly and bitterly opposed to surrender, until finally repudiated by the revolutionary government, he fled to Spain. After four months of resistance, during which the people of Paris suffered the horrors of famine and disease, Paris capitulated on January 28, 1871. Bismarck, who had made it plain that he would discuss peace terms only with a constitutionally elected government, permitted the election of a National Assembly. Voting on February 8, 1871, the French people, revealed their distrust of republicanism by returning the monarchists to power. In the popular mind, monarchism was equated with peace, while republicanism of the radical variety was suspected of wanting to continue the war to a finish. Therefore, the vote was rather a mandate for peace than for monarchy. The new National Assembly contained only about 200 republicans among more than 600 deputies.

The National Assembly, with its royalist majority, convened on February 13, 1871, and established a Provisional Government. But the Paris republicans, annoyed by the election results, which they attributed to the provincial and rural vote, refused to recognize the au-

Street vendor during "L'Année Terrible." While the Germans held Paris under siege in 1870, starvation and pestilence threatened the city from within. This drawing grotesquely characterizes the horrors of the siege.

thority of the Assembly. There followed a civil war between the National Assembly, sitting in Versailles, and the radical republicans in the city of Paris.

Disaster: The Paris Commune. Inside Paris the republicans set up a revolutionary municipal council or Commune, adopted the red flag, and called for revolution. Attempts to create other Communes in France failed. The civil war was confined to Paris. The Paris Commune, which lasted from March to May 1871, appeared on the surface to be an explosion of communism, but that view is historically incorrect. True, toward its end, a small faction of radicals gained control of the movement, but it consisted of many groups of varying kinds generally opposed to the war with Prus-

sia and disgusted with the strongly centralized, incompetent government. Actually, the Commune was a revival of the Jacobinism of 1793, fiercely republican, patriotic, anti-Prussian, and opposed to privileged bourgeoisie, aristocrats, and clergy. Although it supported government control of economic life, it was still not socialist or communist. The Commune meant different things to different people: to the bourgeois middle class it was a savage destroyer of nineteenth-century civilization; to Karl Marx and the Marxists it was a sword wielded to cut down the bourgeoisie and bring the proletariat to victory.

The National Assembly, using troops returned from German prisons, decided to strike down the Commune before it attained too much power. On April 2, 1871, Paris, just recently assaulted by Prussian armies, was attacked now by Frenchmen. There ensued two months of brutality and carnage. The Communards seized bourgeois and clerical hostages. In the final days an undisciplined mob burned public buildings (Tuileries and *Hôtel de Ville*) and executed several hostages, including Archbishop Darboy of Paris. Government troops, under Marshal Marie Edmé de MacMahon (1808–1893), bombarded Paris, cleared the streets, and on May 28, 1871, set up a national government in Paris. The government, taking frightful vengeance on the Communards, matched and even surpassed them in ferocity. It was an exercise in cruelty and viciousness. More than a quarter of a million persons were denounced, 38,000 arrested, 17,000 executed, and many thousands deported. Others fled the country to evade the fury of the Assembly. Thus, in an atmosphere of pain, terror, and hatred, was born the Third French Republic.

Victory of Republicanism. Meanwhile, on May 10, 1871, the Treaty of Frankfort ended the war with Prussia. France was required to cede Alsace and a part of Lorraine, including the fortresses of Metz and Strasbourg, to Prussia, and to pay what was then a harsh indemnity of one billion dollars. With peace restored, the National Assembly turned to the business of giving France a workable system of government. By the Rivet Law it conferred upon Louis Adolphe Thiers (1797–1877), historian, statesman, and liberal royalist, the title of Head of the Executive Power in the French Republic. But, wishing to avoid being made the instrument of monarchist intrigue, Thiers voluntarily resigned in 1873.

The monarchist majority in the Assembly was evenly divided between Bourbonist and Orléanist factions; this split enabled the republicans to consolidate their power. A struggle took place between the republicans, led by Gambetta, and the monarchists, supporting Marshal MacMahon. The latter was elected president on the resignation of Thiers. The Bourbon pretender, the Comte de Chambord, alienated virtually everyone by insisting that the Assembly abolish the tricolor flag, symbol of the revolution, and restore the white *fleur-de-lys*, symbol of reaction. Once again a Bourbon proved that he had forgotten nothing and learned nothing.

Constitution of 1875. After heated discussion of various possibilities, the Assembly adopted in 1875 not a constitution but a set of organic laws providing for a president, a Chamber of Deputies elected by universal manhood suffrage, and a Senate elected by local bodies. The new Chamber was republican, the Senate strongly royalist. On May 16, 1877, the famous *Seize Mai*, President MacMahon dismissed the republican ministry which had the backing of the Chamber, and appointed a royalist ministry which had his confidence but not that of the Chamber. He then dissolved the Chamber and held new elections. The public, however, remembering vividly Napoleon III's transformation of the Second Republic into a dictatorship, was not impressed. The sovereign voice of the people gave a decisive victory to the republicans, thereby again vindicating the principle of parliamentary primacy. MacMahon resigned in 1879 and was succeeded by a republican, Jules Grévy.

System of Government. The Third French Republic was highly centralized, with a president, a bicameral legislative body, and a responsible ministry. The country was divided into provinces (*départements*) presided over by prefects appointed from Paris. The president was elected for a seven-year term by the Chamber of Deputies and the Senate meeting in joint session. He had little actual power and could act in vital matters only with the consent of the ministry and the Assembly. The true executive was the premier. The Chamber of Deputies, elected by universal manhood suffrage for four-year terms, initiated and enacted all legislation. The Senate consisted of 300 members, 75 appointed for life by the National Assembly, and the remaining 225 chosen for nine-year terms by electoral colleges in the *départements*. Holding only limited powers, the Senate could merely revise or amend bills introduced in the Chamber. The cabinet, appointed by the president at the recommendation of the Chamber, was composed of representatives of various groups —not, as in Britain, of a major party. Government by bloc or coalition was a flexible arrangement by which governments were changed relatively frequently. Such changes of ministry were balanced by the steadying force of the entrenched bureaucracy. The many political parties were divided into Right (monarchists, clericals, and militarists); Center (republicans and liberals); and Left (radical socialists, socialists, and communists).

Problem of Reconstruction. Despite the humiliating military defeat, France recovered rapidly. A careful plan of reconstruction was adopted. Thrifty French peasants contributed from their savings to help pay the harsh indemnity imposed by Bismarck. The government saw to it that reform followed reform. A military law, passed in 1872, reorganized the French army along Prussian lines, on the understandable assumption that defeated France could learn from triumphant Prussia. Conscription was introduced and strong fortresses were built along the Franco-German frontier. Again, in the belief that "the Prussian schoolmaster had triumphed at Sedan," the entire French school system was revised. The Ferry Laws (1882) established for the first time a national system of free, obligatory, and nonclerical education. Meanwhile, the government pursued a vigorous colonial policy which quickly brought France to a level second only to Great Britain as a colonial power.

2. Trials of the Third Republic

Man on Horseback: Boulanger Affair. The bankruptcy in 1888 of a company organized by Ferdinand de Lesseps to construct the Panama Canal caused thousands of Frenchmen to lose their savings. Monarchists were quick to attribute the scandal to republican graft, in-

General Boulanger's "dangerous" aspirations are clearly exposed in this anti-Boulangist print which appeared in 1888, a year before his hesitation or loss of nerve impaired a *coup d'état* and the would-be Bonaparte fled to Brussels.

efficiency, and corruption. At the same time they denounced the peaceful policy of the Third Republic as cowardly and shouted for *revanche* against Germany. Meanwhile, General Georges Boulanger (1837–1891), a demagogue who had been appointed minister of war in 1886, was selected by monarchist conspirators to lead a *coup d'état* against the hated republic. For a time the most popular man in France, Boulanger obviously aimed to establish a dictatorship. In self-defense the government called Boulanger to be tried for treason, but in April 1889, when a warrant was issued for his arrest, he fled the country. He was convicted in his absence and condemned for treason. In 1891 he committed suicide in Brussels on the grave of his mistress. The monarchist conspiracy collapsed with his death.

"J'Accuse": Dreyfus Case, 1894–1906. On the surface the Dreyfus affair appeared to be an imbroglio of what Thomas Carlyle would have called "despicable personalities," but actually it was a significant chapter in the history of France. In the fall of 1894 Alfred Dreyfus, a captain of artillery attached to the French General Staff, was arrested and accused of having sold military secrets to the Germans. On being found guilty by court-martial, he was stripped of his commission in a public ceremony and condemned to solitary confinement on Devil's Island, a notorious convict settlement near French Guiana. Dreyfus was a Jew. Bigoted French nationalists, seeking a scapegoat for their country's troubles, derived considerable satisfaction from the conviction of the Jewish officer. The real issue, it appeared, was the maintenance of a caste system, not only in the army, but also in French society. Various political factions rallied to one side or the other. Monarchists, clericals, and anti-Semites joined hands to contend that Dreyfus was guilty, Republicans, including an intellectual fringe, defended him. The struggle between Dreyfusards and anti-Dreyfusards became world news. Millions followed closely this detective story on a national scale.

The complicating and disturbing fact was that Dreyfus was innocent. A saving factor in an incredibly nasty situation—the railroading of an innocent man—was the behavior of a group of distinguished Frenchmen—Émile Zola, Jean Jaurès, Georges Clemenceau, and Anatole France—who had a zealous regard for their country's honor. Zola, a highly successful novelist, was fascinated by the case of the Jewish captain that was convulsing French politics and social life. Several days after the acquittal of the real culprit, a debauched nobleman, Major Count Walsin-Esterhazy, Zola published in the newspaper *L'Aurore* an impassioned letter headed *"J'Accuse,"* addressed to the President of the Republic. (*See page 523.*) "It was a breast bared," wrote one observer, "an indignant conscience calling other consciences to its aid." To Anatole France it was "a moment in the conscience of mankind."

An American view of the degrading implications of the Dreyfus Affair.

For his pains Zola was convicted of libel, his name was struck from the rolls of the Legion of Honor, and he was forced to leave France and live in exile in England for more than a year. Eventually, in 1906, Dreyfus was fully exonerated, restored to the army, and promoted in rank. Zola died before the affair ended; his remains were buried with great pomp in the Pantheon. The honor of France was vindicated by the dismissal of officers who had testified falsely against Dreyfus. The affair turned out to be not a "great Jewish conspiracy" to deliver France to the enemy, but a momentous political battle in which republican and democratic ideas won a major victory against the forces of reaction.

Revival of French Nationalism. An outcome of the conflict over Dreyfus was the emergence of a new integral nationalism in sophisticated form in the writings of Charles Maurras (1868–1952) and Léon Daudet (1867–1942). In the newspaper *Action Française* founded in 1899, these nationalists called for the restoration of the monarchy and the enhancement of French power and prestige. Added to these was Augustus Maurice Barrés (1862–1923), a politician and famous novelist who, although unsympathetic to the restoration of the monarchy, nevertheless demanded the promotion of national unity. He turned to nation, soil, and ancestors as repositories of such traditional elements as the army and the monarchy. He identified the individual spirit with the national past. Asking for harmonization of the forces of nationalism and socialism, Barrés projected an ideology foreshadowing that of Mussolini and Hitler.

3. Social and Economic Development

Anticlerical Legislation. Another result of the Dreyfus affair was the revival of differences between Church and State. In 1901, exactly a century after the Concordat of 1801, an Associations Law suppressed unauthorized religious orders and ordered their property confiscated. In 1905 parliament passed, by a large majority, a Separation Law which abrogated the Concordat of 1801, formally separated Church and State, and also prohibited financial aid to any religious institutions. From this time on the Catholic Church, as well as all other churches which had received subsidies, were to be self-supporting and self-governing. There was purpose behind anticlerical legislation: by reducing the power of the Church in governmental affairs, the republicans hoped to discourage monarchists in their aim to restore the old order. There was bitter opposition. Pius X, declaring the law null and void, urged French Catholics not to obey it. But despite difficulties the separation of Church and State was accomplished. Many Catholics abandoned the monarchists, whom they blamed for making the hostile anticlerical legislation possible.

Progress of Social Legislation. After weathering the storm of the Dreyfus affair, the government gave belated attention to social problems. Republicans now found it convenient as well as necessary to ally themselves with socialists on the path of social reform. A law passed in 1892 set the stage for factory reform by limiting minors' work in factories to ten hours a day. A series of successive factory laws further reduced working hours until in 1907 an eight-hour law was established for minors. The initial Workmen's Compensation Law, providing for payment to workers injured in industrial accidents, was passed in 1898. After a commission studied the subject and recommended legislation, a law of 1905 provided for old-age pensions for the indigent over seventy years of age. The Pensions Law of 1910 was compulsory for wage-earners: at the age of sixty-five all employees were entitled to a pension.

The Labor Movement. The Law of Coalitions, passed in 1791, abolished guilds and corporations, made trade unions illegal, and forbade even the meeting of workers to discuss grievances. Despite the policy of suppression, workers, inspired by the socialist theories of Louis Blanc, organized trade unions; these were responsible for the June Days of 1848. Labor unions continued to work for the right to strike. In 1884, after increasing pressure, the old Law of Coalition was repealed in a law which gave workers full freedom to organize and to strike. This came to be known as a "charter of liberties" for French labor.

From this time on trade unionism made great strides. In 1895 all French trade unions organized the General Confederation of Labor (C.G.T.—*Confédération Générale du Travail*) to protect their interests and to struggle for emancipation. In 1902 the Confedera-

tion, allied with the Chambers of Labor (*Bourses du Travail*), adopted a syndicalist policy advocating direct action to achieve their aims. (Syndicalism is the French word for trade-unionism—*syndicat*, a union. It demanded that the workers' unions become the supreme authoritative institution in society, replacing property as well as government.) Through the use of strikes, notably the General Strike of 1906 and the Railway Strike of 1910, syndicalists tried to undermine the capitalistic order. The government, which had survived attacks from the Right, now suppressed outbreaks from the Left. Syndicalism, however, gradually disappeared as a political factor as workers came to acknowledge the objective role of the government as arbiter between labor and capital.

Pace of Industrialism. Under the Third Republic, France maintained a nice balance between industry and agriculture. Unlike Great Britain and Germany, she was not highly industrialized; neither did she have a small, powerful class of industrial capitalists nor a large working class. The majority of Frenchmen lived on small farms or in small towns. Possessing insufficient coal, France sent her vast supplies of iron ore to Germany, where it was converted into steel and returned to France. More important in the French economy than heavy industry were such luxury products as wine, silks, and perfumes. A large part of French national income came from tourists who flocked to the City of Light from all parts of the earth. The Third Republic abandoned the free-trade policy instituted by its predecessor, the Second Empire, and with the tariff law of 1892 set high protective duties on imported products. Foreign trade increased steadily until imports rose above exports. An unfavorable balance of trade was compensated for by investment of capital in foreign countries and by the flow of gold from the tourist trade.

Self-sustaining in food production, agriculturally healthy, commercially busy, France was a prosperous country. Her division of wealth was probably greater than in any other European country: there were but few wealthy industrialists and few poverty-stricken common people. Frenchmen worked hard and lived well, but carefully saved their money.

The Republic: Positive Factors. The Third French Republic came into existence as a result of Napoleon III's disastrous foreign policy and critical domestic difficulties. Born unwanted and unloved at the outset, it had managed to survive attacks from both Right and Left and had earned the loyalty of the overwhelming majority of the people. Republicanism had been tried in France and had been shown to be compatible with law and order, with parliamentary government and economic prosperity. Bourgeois France had earned its way to acceptance. Frenchmen were sick and tired of bloody barricades: they had butchered one another in 1789, 1792, 1830, 1848, and 1871, and now they wanted peace and security. Economically, the country was prosperous, despite the fact that she lagged behind Germany in industrial and technical development. Her role in the new industrialization was minor, yet she shared in the economic health of Western Europe.

The Republic: Weaknesses. These favorable factors were offset by serious weaknesses. Po-

litically, France was burdened by the fragmentation of political parties. Instead of compact, well-organized major parties, there were many loosely organized groups with varying shades of opinion—royalist, moderate, radical, or socialist. Parliamentary coalitions were hard to keep together because of loose party ties, and consequently there were frequent cabinet crises. From the French point of view these were merely democratic reflections of divided public opinion. Moreover, it was said, administrative stability was retained by a continuing bureaucracy in the permanent civil service.

Another source of weakness was the disaffection of French labor. Dissatisfied with the slow pace of labor legislation, workers called for a "social republic" more to their liking. The Radical Socialists belied their name; actually, they represented small shopowners and petty bourgeoisie and were not inclined to support the kind of social legislation demanded by labor. When the Third Republic came into existence, its political leaders had to hew a straight line between royalists, Church, and army on the Right, and socialists on the Left. At the end of the nineteenth century socialism reached a point where it seriously challenged the bourgeois republic.

⚬{ KEY DOCUMENT }⚬

ZOLA'S "J'ACCUSE," JANUARY 13, 1898

L'Aurore, January 13, 1898. Translated by Ida Mae Snyder.

THE MOST sensational incident in the Dreyfus affair was the publication on January 13, 1898, of an open letter to the president of the Third Republic by the novelist, Émile Zola. Zola charged that members of the general staff and their tools in the army were working with forgers and conspirators to find Dreyfus guilty. Prosecuted for defamation, Zola fled from France to evade imprisonment. This famous letter, with its passionate zeal for justice, played an important role in the history of the Dreyfus case.

A court-martial has dared, by command, to acquit a man like Esterhazy, thus dealing a supremely insolent blow to all truth and justice. It has been done. France bears this stain upon her cheek. . . . Since they have dared, I shall dare

also. . . . It is my duty to speak out. I do not wish to be an accessory. My dreams would be haunted by the spectre of an innocent man who is suffering the most frightful agonies for a crime that he did not commit. . . .

Ah! The feebleness of this indictment! It is a monstrous thing that a man should be found guilty on such a charge. I defy any man of honesty to read it without being overcome with indignation and crying out in horror at the thought of the unlimited suffering there on Devil's Island. Dreyfus knows several languages; this is a crime. No compromising papers were found at his house; this is a crime. On occasion he pays a visit to the country of his birth; this is a crime. He is industrious, he wants to know about everything; this is a crime; He is not nervous, a crime; he is nervous, a crime. . . .

They have spoken to us of the honor of the army, that we should respect and love it. Ah, yes, indeed, that army that is ready to rise at the first danger, that would defend the soil of France, that army which is the people itself, and we have nothing but respect and tenderness for it. However, it is not merely a question of that army, the dignity of which we seek to maintain, when we demand justice. It is a matter of the sword, the master who might possibly be our ruler tomorrow. Shall we devoutly kiss the hilt of the sword, the God? No! . . .

It is a crime, while impudently plotting to fool the whole world, to bring an accusation of disturbing France against those who desire to recognise her as a noble leader of free and righteous nations. It is a crime to mislead public opinion, to make murderous use of that opinion, after having perverted it to a delirium. It is a crime to poison the minds of the obscure and humble, to awaken the passions of intolerance and reaction, while hiding behind the vile anti-Semitism of which the great liberal France of the Rights of Man will surely die, if she is not cured of it. It is a crime to exploit patriotism in the cause of hatred. And, finally, it is a crime to make a modern God of the sword, when all human science works in the growing cause of justice and truth. . . .

When truth is driven underground, it grows and gathers so great an explosive force that, when it finally does explode, it carries everyone before it. Indeed, we shall see whether there has not already been prepared—possibly for some future time—the most shocking of disasters.

But this letter has become too long, Mr. President, and it is time to conclude it.

I accuse Lieutenant-Colonel du Paty de Clam of having been the devilish author of this judicial miscarriage of justice—unconsciously, I am ready to believe—and then for three years of having defended his vile work by the most absurd and guilty machinations.

I accuse General Mercier of having made himself the accomplice, certainly by his lack of firmness, of one of the greatest injustices of the century.

I accuse General Billot of having had in his hands certain proofs of the innocence of Dreyfus, and of having kept them quiet, of having made himself guilty of the crime of *lèse-humanité* and *lèse-justice* because of political aims and in order to protect the compromised General Staff. . . .

I accuse the three handwriting experts, *Sieurs* Belhomme, Varinard, and Couard, of having made false and fraudulent report, unless it be found by medical examination that they have been suffering from defective vision and diseased judgment.

I accuse the War Office of having carried on in the press, especially in *Éclair* and *Écho de Paris*, a rotten campaign to hide its mistakes and to mislead the public.

Finally, I accuse the first court-martial of having violated the law by condemning an accused man on the basis of a secret document. In addition, I accuse the second court-martial of having, in obedience to orders from above, hidden that illegality by committing in its turn the legal crime of knowingly acquitting a guilty man.

In making these charges, I am well aware that I am bringing myself under Articles 30 and 31 of the Press Law of July 29, 1881, which decrees punishment for libel. I do so voluntarily.

I do not know the men I accuse. I have never seen them. I have no resentment nor enmity toward them. For me they are merely entities, spirits of social evil. And what I am doing here is only a revolutionary means of hastening the revelation of truth and justice.

My only passion is—light. I crave it for the sake of humanity, which has suffered so much and which is entitled to happiness. My passionate protest is just the outcry of my soul. I dare them to bring me before the Court of Assize and make an inquiry in broad daylight!

I wait.

❧ HISTORICAL INTERPRETATION ❧

JONATHAN SCOTT ON THE INCULCATION OF NATIONALISM IN FRENCH SCHOOLS AFTER 1871

Jonathan Scott, *Patriots in the Making* (New York, 1916), pp. 244–251. Copyright by D. Appleton and Co. By permission of Appleton-Century.

AFTER THE defeat in the war against Prussia in 1870–1871, French schools were required to place great emphasis upon the teaching of loyalty to the Republic and to the principles of the French Revolution—liberty, equality, and fraternity. Legislation made education in France free, compulsory, and secular.

As the battle of Jena awoke the slumbering nationalism of Prussia, so Sedan aroused from the comfortable lethargy of the Second Empire the patriotism of France. Like Fichte before him, Gambetta set his hopes for the future of his country on the development of a truly national system of education. . . .

The work of French patriotism was, first, to develop an adequate national defense and rehabilitate national prestige. Secondly, it was to place on a firm foundation the insecure structure of the Republican form of government. The strength and glory associated with the ancient monarchy were to be revived by a democracy imbedded in the hearts of the people. The school was to sustain the state in its efforts to solve the problems which the Franco-German war had ushered in.

The educational renaissance of France may be divided into four periods. During the first of these—lasting for more than a decade from the founding of the Third Republic—Republicanism engaged with clericalism in a struggle to control the public school. However lofty the teachings of the Church—and what doctrines could be nobler than the fundamental tenets of Catholicism?—ardent republican patriots did not believe the clerical interpretation of them to be sufficiently adapted to the pressing needs of the time. The Church might indeed teach love of France, but logically this love must be subordinated to devotion to Catholic principles. Patriotism could at best be only the second virtues; republicans would place it first. . . .

In the early eighties the *école laïque* was established; and the second period of the educational renaissance began. The religion of the Fatherland held the field without a rival. The education of

patriotism and loyalty was placed on a sound basis by the government, by devoted textbook writers, by zealous teachers. Children were trained to the belief that love of country was the first of duties, and that the first element of that duty was to defend France from her enemies in time of war. Above all thought of self, the Fatherland must be enshrined in the hearts of her citizens. Hence her future defenders must learn courage. . . .

At the same time the school was used to intrench the Republican form of government. Instead of learning to look forward to the re-establishment of monarchy as had the children of the seventies, the pupils of the *école laïque* were taught to shun the very thought of a royalist restoration, of imperialism, of dictatorship. Nor was the Church treated with that complete justice which the ideal of toleration demanded and which the government proclaimed would be realized. The religious beliefs of many little hearts were wounded; many were turned against the Church of their forefathers. . . .

From the time of its establishment the lay school has continuously inculcated patriotism and loyalty. Toward the close of the nineteenth century, however, began a period of reaction against the intense nationalism of earlier years. Disciples of various intellectual, political and social creeds clamored for recognition in the school, and attempted to undermine certain tenets of the religion of *La Patrie*. Thus a group of scientific historians demanded that unswerving devotion to truth alone should characterize the writing and teaching of their subject. They insisted also that the attention given to military campaigns and exploits should be diminished, while the history of civilization should be brought to the foreground.

Their efforts were crystallized in the programs of 1902; the glow of patriotic history seemed to pale before the cold, white light of science and the doctrine of evolution. . . .

But the movement lacked depth. It probably weakened but little the carefully fostered psychology of national defense, though it must have curbed chauvinism and modified the teaching of *revanche*. Furthermore, its influence was brief. While the wild cries of anti-patriotism were resounding through the air, alarming those who held their country's good dearer than aught else, suddenly the German menace loomed darkly along the horizon of peace and prosperity. As the cloud grew blacker and blacker, the frightened onlookers ceased their petty squabbles and prepared to face unitedly the coming storm. Thus the years immediately preceeding the present war constituted the fourth and last period of the educational revival. Not that revolutionary socialism died a sudden death; men sang the "Internationale" on the very eve of the great conflict. But the crisis was passed. New school manuals appeared, intensely patriotic in character. The *jeunesse intellectuelle* showed new vigor, was more athletic, and above all responded more fervently than ever to the loudly voiced appeal for devotion to the Fatherland. France was herself again.

The greatest immediate result of the education of patriotism and loyalty has been to lay a psychological foundation for a determined resistance to attack. In this respect the patriotism taught in the French schools is perhaps superior to that taught in Germany, since it is more discerning, more critical of national errors. In France are inculcated the misfortunes as well as the triumphs of the Fatherland; in Germany it is chiefly the triumphs.

❧ TEN BASIC BOOKS ❧

TRIUMPH OF REPUBLICANISM:

THE THIRD FRENCH REPUBLIC, 1871–1914

1. Brabant, Frank, *The Beginning of the Third Republic in France* (London, 1940).
2. Brogan, Denis, *France Under the Republic: The Development of Modern France, 1870–1939* (New York, 1940).†
3. Bury, John P. T., *Gambetta and the National Defence: A Republican Dictatorship in France* (London, 1936).
4. Chapman, Guy, *The Dreyfus Case* (London, 1955).
5. Derfler, Leslie W., *The Third French Republic, 1870–1940*, Anvil Book No. 87 (Princeton, N. J., 1966).†
6. Halasz, Nicholas, *Captain Dreyfus: The Story of a Mass Hysteria* (New York, 1955).
7. Hanotaux, Gabriel, *Contemporary France*, 4 vols. (London and New York, 1903–1909).
8. Kranzberg, Melvin, *The Siege of Paris, 1870–1871* (Ithaca, N. Y., 1950).
9. Scott, John A., *Republican Ideas and the Liberal Tradition in France, 1870–1914* (New York, 1951, R. 1966).
10. Thomson, David, *Democracy in France: The Third and Fourth Republics,* 2nd ed. (New York, 1952).

32

United Germany: From Bismarck to William II, 1871-1914

Where is the German's Fatherland?
Name me at length that mighty land!
"Where'er resounds the German tongue,
Where'er its hymns to God are sung."
Be this the land,
Brave German, this thy Fatherland!

There is the German's Fatherland,
Where oaths are sworn by clasp of hand,
Where faith and truth beam in the eyes,
And in the heart affection lies.
Be this the land,
Brave German, this thy Fatherland!

There is the German's Fatherland,
Where wrath the Southron's guile doth brand,
Where all are foes whose deeds offend,
Where every noble soul's a friend.
Be this the land,
All Germany shall be the land!

All Germany that land shall be,
Watch o'er it, God, and grant that we,
With German hearts, in deed and thought,
May love it truly as we ought.
Be this the land,
All Germany shall be the land!

—Ernst Moritz Arndt, "The German's Fatherland"

1. The Era of Bismarck, 1871–1890

The New German Empire. The German Empire, founded in January 1871, was a federal union of 25 states, each of which, though enjoying a measure of local autonomy, was responsible to the central government at Berlin. The German emperor, as president of the federal union, was commander-in-chief of the army and navy; with the consent of the *Bundesrat* he could declare war and make peace. As king of Prussia, he exercised what amounted to dictatorial control over German affairs. The *Bundesrat,* representing the states, was composed of 61 personal agents of the 25 states (Prussia, 17; Bavaria, 6; Saxony, 4; Württemberg, 4; Baden, 3; Hesse, 3; Mecklenburg-Schwerin, 2; Brunswick, 2; all others, 1 each). Alsace-Lorraine, annexed as a result of the Franco-Prussian War, was designated a *Reichsland* under an imperial governor called a *Statthalter,* and made the common property of all German states.

Because the representatives to the *Bundesrat* had to vote as a unit on instructions from their monarch, and since only 14 votes were enough to defeat any amendment to the constitution, Prussia, with her 17 votes, dominated the body. The *Bundesrat* had power to pass on all legislation, to accept treaties, to assent to the emperor's dissolution of the *Reichstag,* and to confirm all appointments of federal officials. The *Reichstag,* elected by universal manhood suffrage, was a mere debating society, which could not initiate legislation or overthrow the chancellor. The chancellor, appointed by the emperor and responsible only to him, appointed administrative officials, directed foreign policy, and played an important part in shaping all legislation.

Role of Prussia. The Prussian *Landtag* (legislative body) was composed of two houses, the upper body consisting of the landed aristocracy, and the lower body representing the property-holding bourgeoisie. The lower house was elected by a three-class system of voting—the electorate was divided into three groups according to the amount of taxes each voter paid. Each class elected one-third of the members. As a result the small class of wealthy taxpayers had as many votes as the considerably larger number of poor taxpayers. Even so, the Prussian *Landtag* had limited powers, and the German emperor, as king of Prussia, exercised autocratic control. In practice the Prussian prime minister, who was at the same time the German chancellor, became the real legislative power. Since the executive had no parliamentary responsibility, it was difficult if not impossible for the parliamentary leaders to represent the people.

Bismarck as Imperial Chancellor. The period of nearly two decades from the foundation of the German Empire in January 1871 to Bismarck's dismissal in March 1890 is often called the Age of Bismarck. During this time Bismarck was the fulcrum not only of German but also of European politics. With a powerful army, an efficient bureaucracy, and a loyal bourgeoisie, he was able to prevent revolutionary outbreaks. His domestic policy was to consolidate a powerful, centralized union under Prussian domination and to promote the prosperity of the new German Empire. As a means of maintaining German military supremacy he required all male citizens to be conscripted for training. He proposed new civil and criminal laws, organized an imperial bank, unified the railroad system, and introduced a national system of coinage. Though at first a proponent of free trade, in 1879 he favored a policy of protection for home industries.

At first the only support Bismarck received in the *Reichstag* came from the National Liberal Party. To the left the Progressive Party cooperated in matters of unity, but in other affairs was less willing to compromise with the government. The Center Party, founded in 1871, was designed to give political representation to Catholics. Conservatives opposed Bismarck on the ground that the events of 1866 and 1871 had diluted Prussian strength. The conservatives split into two groups, one of

which, the *Reich* Party, for a time supported Bismarck. In general, however, Bismarck was firmly against any internal rivals and insisted that all opposition to the Prussian conception of the state be crushed.

Bismarck's foreign policy was to consolidate the position he had won for Germany. In the first period of his administration, from 1862 to 1871, he had waged three wars, enhanced Prussia, and unified Germany under Prussia. Now that Germany was *saturiert*, or satiated, Bismarck regarded it as his vital task to maintain what Germany had acquired. He sought to solidify Germany's position in Europe by constructing a system of military alliances. Expecting France to seek revenge, he worked to isolate her from any possible allies. In order to turn French eyes from the lost provinces of Alsace and Lorraine, he offered France a free hand "within reasonable limits" in North Africa. Meanwhile, he tried to conciliate Britain by opposing German colonial expansion and by discouraging the construction of a large German navy.

Kulturkampf, 1871–1883. Bismarck was less successful on the domestic scene. No sooner was the German Empire established than he embarked on a battle against what he described as "the enemies of the empire." In 1864 Pope Pius IX had issued his *Syllabus of Modern Errors,* including among these civil marriage and secular education. In 1870 the Vatican Council announced that the pope was "infallible" when speaking on matters of faith or morals. Both these proclamations angered Bismarck, but since he needed Catholic support at the time, he decided to await a more propitious moment to meet the "challenge." The struggle against the Catholic Church began in 1871. The Liberals, who joined the conflict, called it a "fight for civilization" (*Kulturkampf*). Bismarck himself was concerned only with its political aspects. In 1872 he obtained an imperial law expelling the Jesuits from Germany. He promulgated in the Prussian *Landtag* the May Laws (1873–1874), by which he gave the state complete control over marriage and education, muzzled the Catholic press, confiscated Church property, and persecuted recalcitrant priests, monks, and

Ludwig Windthorst, Bismarck's opponent in the *Kulturkampf* and leader of the Catholic Center Party. Bismarck once said, "Hate is just as great an incentive to life as love. My life is preserved and made pleasant by two things—my wife and Windthorst. One exists for love, the other for hate."

nuns. An inevitable result was the emergence of the Catholic Center Party as a vital political power. Bismarck boasted that *he* would not go to Canossa, as Henry IV had done in 1077, and submit to the papacy. But the concurrent rapid growth of the Socialists in Germany convinced him that the "red international" was a considerably more dangerous enemy than the old "black international." The accession of the

moderate Pope Leo XIII (1878) facilitated Bismarck's change of heart. The chancellor abandoned the *Kulturkampf*. By 1887 virtually all the anti-Catholic laws were repealed as Bismarck sought clerical support in his battle against the Socialists.

Antisocialist Campaign, 1878–1890. Bismarck had only contempt for the Socialists, whom he regarded as dangerous republicans, pacifists, internationalists, and irreconcilable enemies of capitalism. The Socialists, gathered at Gotha in 1875, united the followers of Ferdinand Lassalle and Karl Marx, a warning Bismarck did not intend to ignore. The number of Socialist voters rose from 124,000 in 1871 to 493,000 in 1877. Two attempts on the life of William I in May and June 1878 gave Bismarck his pretext for striking a blow against his political enemies despite the fact that neither of the assassins was a member of the Socialist Party. In 1878 Bismarck had the *Reichstag* enact a series of Exceptional Laws, forbidding freedom of the press and initiating a campaign of persecution against "Socialist machinations dangerous to the common weal." These measures were directed against the Socialists, but it was apparent that Bismarck in a subtle way was also pointing his fire toward the Liberals.

Once again repression proved to be a stimulus to revolutionary agitation. The Socialists went underground, and despite all efforts to eliminate them as a political factor, they thrived and grew in numbers. The Exceptional Laws, originally enacted for two and a half years and thereafter renewed, were allowed to expire in 1890, the year of Bismarck's retirement.

2. *Economic, Social, and Intellectual Currents, 1871–1914*

Germany in the New Industrial Revolution. The transformation of Germany in the second half of the nineteenth century from a predominantly agrarian to a modern, industrialized nation is one of the most striking and spectacular phenomena of recent European history. Several factors were responsible for the pace of German economic expansion. With the achievement of national unification in 1871, Germany plunged wholeheartedly into the New Industrial Revolution. She was centrally located in Europe which was to her advantage economically. Her industries were equipped with the most modern machinery. Thoroughness in research, skill and discipline in production and distribution enabled Germany to take

a place as one of the world's great industrial nations and to challenge British and American supremacy in the markets of the world. The speed of Germany's economic development nearly equaled that of the United States.

Increase in Population. Along with industrialization occurred a radical change in population, both in numbers and distribution. At the opening of the nineteenth century the area of Germany later equivalent to the Bismarckian *Reich* housed a population of about 24,000,000. By 1914, despite an annual average of some 70,000 emigrants, the population of William II's Germany had risen to 67,790,000, with a density of population of about 125 inhabitants per square kilometer. To some extent this increase may be attributed to a falling death rate, innovations in medicine, and sanitary improvements. There was a rapid shift of population from the rural areas to the towns and cities. In 1850, only 2.8 per cent of the population lived in cities of more than 100,000 population; by 1910 this percentage had increased tenfold. Berlin, which in 1820 had only 200,000 inhabitants, in 1910 had a population of 2,071,907—the fifth largest city in the world.

Industrial Expansion. German industrial expansion during the late decades of the nineteenth century and the early twentieth century presents an imposing picture. Of special significance was the expansion of the state-controlled railways: in 1860 there were 11,026 kilometers of railway lines in Germany; by 1910 they had increased to 59,031 kilometers. German coal production, centered chiefly in the Ruhr and the Saar regions, increased from 29,398,000 tons in 1871 to 191,500,000 in 1913; Germany thus became the greatest producer of coal after the United States and Britain. From the early 1880's onward Britain gradually lost the industrial leadership she had enjoyed during most of the century:

IRON EXTRACTION (*in tons*)

	1850	1900	1902
Great Britain	2,300,000	8,959,691	8,839,124
Germany	350,000	8,381,373	17,586,521

The German iron and steel industries expanded rapidly. During the period from 1882 to 1892, German exports of iron and steel rose by 11 per cent, while English exports of the same products dropped by 37 per cent. Huge iron and steel empires were created by the Krupps, Thyssens, and Stumm-Halbergs.

Germany also became Britain's rival in shipping. Germany's tonnage was steadily augmented until by 1913 her merchant marine, which consisted almost entirely of new vessels using steam, reached a net tonnage of more than 3,000,000. Two great shipping companies, the Hamburg-America Line and the North German Lloyd of Bremen, together made up one of the most powerful merchant fleets in the world. German agents established business connections in all continents.

The United States had originated the idea of mass production in the New Industrial Revolution; Germany's special contribution to that revolution was innovation in the chemical industry. German scientists took advantage of the rich salt and potash beds in Saxony, Thuringia, and Alsace. The most valuable developments were in synthetic dyes, drugs, oil, nitrates, and *ersatz* (substitute) rubber. German leadership in chemistry was important in World War I, when Germany was cut off from South American supplies for manufacturing explosives. Fritz Haber developed a process of extracting nitrates from air, an epoch-making discovery that enabled blockaded Germany to hold out for four years.

Another factor in German economic prosperity was the development of the electrical industry. At the opening of the twentieth century Germany was using a greater variety of electrical products than any other country in the world. Two giant firms—Siemens and Halske, controlled by Werner von Siemens, and the Allgemeine Elektrizitäts Gesellschaft (AEG), directed by Emil Rathenau—competed with each other in constructing power transmission systems and a network of electric railways.

The Armaments Industry. The German armaments industry was regarded not only as one of the major causes for industrial prosperity but also as an indispensable corollary of national interests. During the Franco-Prussian War of 1870–1871 the Krupp works at Essen supplied the Prussian army with highly effective artillery. The worldwide reputation of Krupp armaments brought orders to Essen from all continents; this foreign demand, added to that of the German military machine, resulted in a tremendous increase in Krupp business. German performance in the armaments industry was a powerful factor in the snowballing arms race that preceded World War I.

Banking and Industrial Concentration. Germany's rapid industrial and commercial expansion was aided by a banking system geared closely to the promotion of economic life. The new banks worked closely with industrial corporations, providing credits for expansion and participating directly in management. This procedure ran counter to British experience, for British banks were not able to meet the heavy demands of new industries. So successful was the German practice that by the end of the nineteenth century Germany's strong banking system was exporting capital along with industrial enterprise.

One result of large-scale industrialism in Germany was the trend toward huge enterprises, called cartels, which were used to protect invested capital, eliminate competition, stabilize profits, and avoid business cycles. There were different types of cartels—to fix prices, limit production or supply, centralize certain markets, or regulate foreign trade—but in all cases the tendency was characteristically monopolistic. There were some flaws: small industry was submerged or kept at a disadvantage; prices were maintained at a high level; and the mercantile class was reduced to little more than a figurehead. But the Germans felt that this was a small price to pay for escape from the economic anarchy characteristic of countries where cartels had not been developed. The vast I. G. Farben Trust, whose amalgamation was completed in 1925, became the world's most powerful industrial combination. It controlled more than 380 firms scattered over Germany, along with some 500 enterprises in foreign countries, in a closely interlocking relationship. Party to 2,000 cartel agreements, it manufactured 43 major products, which it distributed throughout the world. It directed an army of scientists, industrialists, statesmen, even spies. A huge economic octopus, it used its restrictive power of patent tie-ups with foreign industrialists to slow-up production of strategic war materials in countries that the Germans considered potential enemies.

Education for Industry. Germany's industrial battles were won in her institutes of technology, trade schools, and industrial continuation schools. The development of these scientific and technical institutions after 1871 helped Germany's rise as an industrial power. The *Technische Hochschule*, or polytechnic schools and institutes of technology, modeled upon the French *école polytechnique*, were oriented in the interests of higher science, with attention to practical uses of electricity, motors and machinery, shipbuilding, construction of all kinds, and the application of science to industry. Special commercial institutions, called *Handelshochschule*, supported by city governments or by chambers of commerce, were devoted to scientific investigation of production and consumption in relation to the world's markets. Of university caliber, these schools sent a stream of experts into commerce and government service. Trade schools, financed by the state, specialized in different occupations such as building, machine-making, metalwork, and weaving. The most important institutions in industrial training were the continuation schools, some compulsory and some voluntary, whose purpose was to get the children after they had left elementary school and train them as citizens and workers. In Prussia in 1912 there were 2,637 continuation schools, with 455,478 scholars.

From *Laissez-faire* to Protection. Until the late 1870's Germany's economic policy was moderate *laissez-faire*. The interests of the landed classes were identical with those of the free traders, and the growth of population contributed much to the new prosperity. Up to this time Germany was exporting more

grain than she was importing. The building of railways in both the United States and Russia brought the competition of cheaper grain. Bismarck was converted to a policy of protection in agriculture for several reasons: he did not want to see his country transformed into a purely industrial nation; he believed that a flourishing agriculture was necessary for self-sufficiency in war; a strong rural life was needed to preserve traditional conservatism; and tariff duties would provide a new source of revenue.

Protection of iron was just as important as protection of grain. After the financial panic of 1873, the German iron and steel makers for the first time began demanding a protective tariff, on the ground that free trade and liberalism had resulted in German markets being flooded by manufactures from England and France. After the elections of 1878 brought a protectionist majority, the *Reichstag* enacted a protective tariff law which took effect on July 12, 1879. Protectionism was an important step in the creation of a powerful Greater Germany. Politically, it represented another blow to liberalism, democracy, and constitutionalism by the agrarian and industrial interests combined with the Crown.

German Colonialism. Closely associated with the rising industrialization was the emergence of German colonialism. Before 1871 Bismarck had had neither thoughts of nor the possibility of acquiring colonies for Germany; from 1871 to 1881 he adopted a course of watchful waiting for the desired opportunity; after 1881 he inaugurated a cautious but definite colonial policy. His attitude in 1871 was expressed in a typical Bismarckian aphorism: "A colonial policy for us would be like the silk and sables of Polish families who have no shirts." In conformity with the then current anti-imperialist sentiment, he looked upon colonies only as a means of providing sinecures for officials and concluded that they were too costly a luxury for Germany. In the middle 1870's he regarded as obstacles to a German colonial policy the *Kulturkampf*, the jealousy of France, the acute irritability of Britain, and Germany's own modest position in world affairs. But in the

1880's the *Kulturkampf* was at an end, the *revanche* policy of France had been softened, and Germany's position in Europe had been strengthened in 1882 by the Triple Alliance. Impatient at British delays and aware of German strength, he assumed an aggressive stand and successfully inaugurated the creation of a colonial empire by taking Angra Pequena in South-West Africa.

Germany had all the motivating factors for colonial expansion—need for raw materials, for food supplies, and for outlets for capital. A late starter in the African hunt, she nevertheless obtained several areas: the Cameroons, Togoland, German South-West Africa, and German East Africa. Although it was large in size, her share of Africa was comparatively poor in natural resources. Later, she was checked in North Africa by Britain and France, in the Balkans by Russia, and in the Near East and Far East by Great Britain and other powers. On June 1, 1914, William II sent a message to President Wilson complaining that "all the nations of the world are directing the points of their bayonets at Germany."

Social Consequences of the Industrial Age. The rapid industrialization of Germany brought with it all the social problems generally associated with the industrial age. But where social reform was slow and painful in Britain and the United States, it was rapidly promoted in Germany. A highly organized system of social legislation, designed to undermine Socialist agitation, was introduced by Bismarck, starting in 1881, with a thoroughness that aroused the interest and admiration of the world. He asked the *Reichstag* to "heal social evils by means of legislation based on the moral foundations of Christianity." Important social reforms were enacted: sickness insurance (1883), accident insurance (1884), and old-age insurance (1889). The working class was not appeased by these concessions, which it regarded as politically inspired conciliatory bribes. However, the success of the system was due largely to the fact that the tradition of paternalism worked to destroy the resistance of those who opposed social reform. Bismarck was certain that reform was the business of the state, not of the Socialists. After Bismarck's anti-Socialist legislation, Socialist efforts increased steadily. Despite opposition by industrialists, there was a marked growth of trade-union membership.

Militarism. Militarism infected all modern countries in varying degrees. But there arose, especially among Prusso-German intellectuals, an enthusiasm for war itself as an ennobling experience. Heinrich von Treitschke recognized the Prussian army as "the embodiment of national characteristics and virtues" and extolled the proud military instinct of the army as "an indispensable blessing." (*See page 538.*) Bismarck was certain that "it was not the wolf's fault that God created him the way he was." The educational system was reformed so as to become adjunct to the military machine, on the assumption that "national school-time keeps body and soul together in strength and vigor." The military way of life penetrated into government, bureaucracy, and business. It conditioned the masses, who were told that Germany could reach the heights of national and world power only through the sword. Even so level headed an intellectual as Thomas Mann (who later revised his beliefs) was engulfed by the military spirit in 1914: "German militarism is the manifestation of German morality. . . . The militarism inherent in the German soul, its ethical conservatism, its soldier-like morality—an element of demonism and heroism: this is what refuses to recognize the civilian spirit as a final ideal of mankind."

The Great General Staff. Closely allied with militarism was the expert professional leadership of the Prussian—and later the German—Great General Staff. At the beginning of the industrial age, war was taken out of the hands of monarchs and aristocrats and placed under the direction of highly specialized, anonymous technicians. In Germany, in particular, the General Staff developed a set of rigid traditions: anonymity in planning and command, complete divorcement of military from political affairs, strict moral and intellectual standards, and an inflexible caste system. It was led by a succession of officer-aristocrats: Scharnhorst, Boyen, Gneisenau, Clausewitz, the two Moltkes, Waldersee, Schlieffen, Hindenburg, Ludendorff, Seeckt, Schleicher, Beck, Keitel, and Jodl. The long and involved history of the General Staff in Germany was to some extent responsible for the aggravation of an expansionist, adventurous, and militaristic national temperament. Despite its insistence upon a strict divorcement of military policy from political affairs, the General Staff has functioned as a powerful factor in the historical development of Germany. It provided firm leadership in the German drives for world power in the twentieth century. It was not eliminated by the Treaty of Versailles, although its leadership of German militarism was known by the Allied authorities.

3. Wilhelmian Germany, 1888–1918

The Ninety-nine Days of Frederick III. Emperor William I, who had passed the age of ninety, died in March 1888. His son, the fifty-six-year-old crown prince, ascended the throne as Frederick III. Unfortunately, this tragic figure of the Hohenzollern dynasty was suffering from a fatal disease, cancer of the throat; his reign lasted just ninety-nine days. Frederick III, who was married to the eldest daughter of Queen Victoria of Great Britain, had been deeply impressed by British constitutional institutions. The great hope of German liberals died with him.

William II. Frederick III's son and successor, William II (r. 1888–1918), who ascended the throne at the age of twenty-nine, presented a sharp contrast to his liberal father. The young emperor was an extraordinary individual whose character embraced a world of contradictions. Although definitely talented and cultivated, he was inclined to act at times in a highly erratic manner. On occasion, he could be a most engaging person, but he could easily change into an impatient, fickle, and clumsy boor. Although aware of the responsibilities of his position, he was susceptible to the flattery of courtiers. Both as prince and as ruler he tried to study and command all the

William II (1859–1941), Emperor of Germany until two days before the World War I armistice, lived to see the beginning of the Second World War.

problems of business, art, science, and government. Possessing a remarkable memory and a willingness to learn, he surrounded himself with leading scholars, industrialists, and artists. At the same time, his impulsive nature kept him from penetrating deeply into any of the problems he studied.

A sincere patriot, William II was convinced beyond doubt that his high position was entrusted to him by God. He believed it to be his duty to maintain the monarchy that had been bestowed on him by Divine Providence. "I regard my whole position," he said, "as given to me direct from heaven and I have been called by the Highest to do His work, by One to whom I must one day render an account." In another speech he proclaimed: "Remember that the German people are chosen by God. On me, as the German Emperor, the spirit of God has descended. I am His weapon, His sword, and His Vice-Regent." To his friend "Nicky" (Nicholas II, tsar of Russia), he wrote: "A sacred duty is imposed by Heaven on us Christian Kings and Emperors— to uphold the doctrine of the Divine Right of Kings." William II's nationalistic, warlike utterances were probably compensatory gestures for what was in reality a weak, uncertain personality. The German people regarded him as a symbol of national greatness who was to lead them in the vital task of counteracting the diabolical *Einkreisungspolitik* (encirclement policy) of the European Powers. If now and then he struck a discordant note in the Concert of Europe by ill-advised diplomatic action, he was forgiven by his people on the ground that he was Germany's leader in her march to "a place in the sun."

Bismarck's Dismissal, 1890. Disagreement was unavoidable between the elderly chancellor, "who had seen three kings naked," and the impulsive young ruler. The chief cause of difference between the two arose regarding prolongation of the law against the Socialists. The bill expired in 1890, whereupon Bismarck proposed to make it permanent, but William II was opposed on the ground that the disaffection of labor could be removed by remedial measures. Bismarck also hoped to renew the Reinsurance Treaty with Russia (*see page 591*), which was due to expire in 1890, but William would not agree. Moreover, the latter feared that Bismarck intended to create a "Bismarck dynasty" in the person of his son, Herbert, whom the chancellor hoped to have as his successor in important political posts. The issue came to a head on a constitutional matter concerning a Cabinet Order of 1852. Bismarck regarded his treatment by William II as a degradation of his position. (*See page 537.*) He was forced to resign in 1890. The captain of the German ship of state dropped his experienced pilot.

The "New Course." William II's New Course called for an intensified colonialism and the construction of a powerful navy. In speech after speech the flamboyant emperor

Kaiser Wilhelm (William II) dropping the pilot. Cartoon depicting the dismissal of Bismarck.

announced that "our future lies on the seas" and "the trident must pass into our hands." There were many reasons for the rise of German navalism. German merchants, economists, and militarists were convinced that a powerful navy was the surest protection for foreign commerce and capital investment. The German Navy League molded public opinion to demand a large navy. The importance of sea power had been demonstrated to the German people by the American victory in the Spanish-American War and by the British conquest of the Boer republics in South Africa. But above all was the tremendous personal enthusiasm of the emperor, who was determined to make the German navy the finest in the world. "Our navy," he said, "will grow and flourish during peaceful times to promote the peaceable interests of the Fatherland, and in war times to destroy the enemy, if God helps us." The British, dominant on the high seas, were annoyed by these and similar remarks.

Era of Inept Diplomacy. During his long tenure of office Bismarck had made foreign affairs his exclusive domain and had carefully kept the monarch in the background. William II, anxious to maintain his personal rule, appointed a series of weak chancellors: General Georg Leo von Caprivi (1890–1894), an old soldier; Prince Chlodwig zu Hohenlohe (1894–1900), aged uncle of the emperor; Prince Bernhard von Bülow (1900–1909), a vain courtier whose main efforts were spent on explaining his master's impulsive actions; and Theobald von Bethmann-Hollweg (1909–1917), a weak statesman. For many years the most important director of German policy was the eccentric Fritz von Holstein, councilor at the Foreign Office, who, in the words of S. H. Steinberg, "wove William [II's] inconsistencies into a supersophisticated pattern, the only recognizable *leitmotif* of which was that the more waters Germany troubled the more fish she might catch."

A few examples among many reveal William II's awkward sense of diplomacy. When, in January 1896, the Jameson Raid in South Africa collapsed, he dispatched a telegram offering his sincere congratulations to President Kruger of the Transvaal Republic. William II's action was applauded in Germany, but in England it aroused a storm of resentment. Lord Salisbury later (1899) said: "The raid was folly, but the telegram was even more foolish."

Even more irresponsible was the notorious *Daily Telegraph* interview. On October 28, 1908, that London newspaper published an account of a meeting between William II and an unnamed British subject. Although he sought to present himself as a sincere lover of peace, William, through his own words, showed himself to be an advocate of the iron fist in international relations. Seeking to allay British anxiety over Germany's big-navy plans, he used arguments that, characteristically, blended distorted historical fact with offensive flattery. This incredible *faux pas* was protested in both Britain and Germany and nearly led to the Kaiser's abdication.

William II's chaotic foreign policy gradually led to a union of Germany's opponents. France, Russia, and Britain, settling their long-standing differences in the face of the German threat, evolved a series of coalitions which culminated in the Triple Entente of 1907. By providing for mutual assistance by the three partners in the event of war with any of the Central Powers, the Triple Entente served as a counteracting force to the Triple Alliance. Europe was now divided into two armed camps, each seeking to maintain the delicate balance of power. Both coalitions feverishly began to arm.

⊰ KEY DOCUMENT ⊱

BISMARCK'S LETTER OF RESIGNATION, MARCH 18, 1890

Otto von Bismarck, *Gedanken und Erinnerungen* (Stuttgart and Berlin, 1898–1919), III, 650–654, *passim.*

THE ARROGANT young monarch, William II, and the elder statesman, Bismarck, found it difficult to work together in harmony. The differences between emperor and chancellor came to a head on a constitutional issue. Bismarck, annoyed by the fact that the emperor was discussing problems of administration with colleagues without informing him, reminded William of the Cabinet Order of 1852. This decree had been enacted as a means of giving the then minister-president the complete control that was necessary if he were to be responsible for the whole policy of the government. William ordered Bismarck to reverse the decree of 1852. Bismarck refused, on the ground that his position would be degraded by such an action. The emperor then forced Bismarck's dismissal, although he sought to give it the tone of a resignation. The following document contains excerpts from Bismarck's letter of resignation.

At my respectful audience on the 15th of this month, Your Majesty commanded me to draw up a decree annulling the All-Highest Order of September 8, 1852, which regulated the position of the Minister-President *vis-à-vis* colleagues.

May I, your humble and most obedient servant, make the following statement on the genesis and importance of this order:

There was no need at that time of absolute monarchy for the position of a "President of the State Ministry." For the first time, in the United Landtag of 1847, the efforts of the liberal delegate (Mevissen) led to the designation, based on the constitutional needs of that day, of a "Premier-President," whose task it would be to supervise uniform policies of the responsible ministers and to take over responsibility for the combined political actions of the cabinet. With the year 1848 came constitutional customs into our daily life, and a "President of the State Ministry" was named. . . . The relationship of the State Ministry and its individual members to the new institution of the Minister-President very quickly required a new constitutional regulation, which was effected with approval of the then State Ministry by the order of September 8, 1852. Since then, this order has been decisive in regulating the relationship of the Minister-President and the State Ministry, and it alone gave the Minister-President the authority which enabled him to take over responsibility for the policies of the cabinet, a responsibility demanded by the Landtag as well as public opinion. If each individual minister must receive instructions from the monarch, without previous understandings with his colleagues, it becomes impossible in the cabinet to sustain uniform policies, for which each member can be responsible. There remains for none of the ministers and, especially, for the Minister-President any possibility of bearing constitutional responsibility for the whole policy of the cabinet. . . .

To this time I have never felt the need, in my relationships with my colleagues, to draw upon the order of 1852. Its very existence and the knowledge that I possessed the confidence of their late Majesties, William and Frederick, were enough to assure my authority on my staff. This knowledge exists today neither for my colleagues nor for myself. I have been compelled, therefore, to turn back to the order of 1852, in order to assure the necessary uniformity in the service of Your Majesty.

On the aforementioned grounds, I am not in a position to carry out Your Majesty's demand, which would require me to initiate and counter-sign the suspension of the order of 1852 recently brought up by me, and despite that, at the same time carry on the presidency of the Ministry of State. . . .

Considering my attachment to service for the monarchy and for Your Majesty and the long-established relationship which I had believed would exist forever, it is very painful for me to terminate my accustomed relationship to the All

The "Iron and Blood Chancellor" in his final years.

Highest and to the political life of the Reich and Prussia; but, after conscientious consideration of the All Highest's intentions, to whose implementation I must always be ready to act, if I am to remain in service, I cannot do other than most humbly request Your Majesty *to grant me an*

honorable discharge with legal pension from the posts of Reich Chancellor, Minister-President, and Prussian Minister for Foreign Affairs. . . .

VON BISMARCK

To His Majesty the Emperor and King

⤜{ HISTORICAL INTERPRETATION }⤛

HEINRICH VON TREITSCHKE ON WAR AS THE GREAT MOLDER OF NATIONS, 1895

Heinrich von Treitschke, *Germany, France, Russia, and Islam* (London, 1915), pp. 198–201, 210–213, 220–223.

THE THREE great masters of the Prussian School of historiography, the professor-prophets who sought to work politically through history (*"durch die Geschichte politisch zu wirken"*), were Johann Gustav Droysen (1808–1884), a fervent champion of the Hohenzollern dynasty; Heinrich von Sybel (1817–1895), quasi-official Prussian historian; and Heinrich von Treitschke (1834–1896). Treitschke, the youngest, most enthusiastic, and most influential of the three, more publicist than historian, lashed out indiscriminately against socialism, Jews, parliamentarianism, England, France, and pacifism. He believed every fiber of his body to be German, and he loved Prussia ("This weapon-proud eagle land of the North—the real State-forming force in German history"). He expressed his views with clarity and with little room for misunderstanding. On July 19, 1895, Treitschke delivered an address at the Festival of the Commemoration of the Great War of Liberation from Napoleon at the Frederick William University in Berlin. The following excerpts from this speech reveal the quality of Treitschke's nationalism.

Dear Colleagues and Fellow-Soldiers,

Today's festival recalls to us of the older generation the golden days of our life—the days when the grace of God after battle and tribulation and mourning gloriously fulfilled beyond all our expectations all the longings of our youth. And yet, as I begin to speak, I feel keenly how profoundly the world has changed in this quarter of a century. It is not given to every period to do great deeds nor to understand them rightly. After the great crises of history there generally follows a generation which hears the iron voice of war, the great moulder of nations, still vibrating in its own heart, and rejoices with youthful enthusiasm over what has been gained. But without the constant work of self-recollection and self-testing progress is impossible. . . .

We had been for centuries hampered and impeded in the simple task of national policy by the world-wide power of our Holy Roman Empire, just as the Italians were through their Papacy; in our Confederation of States we were obliged to let many foreign powers co-operate, and saw ourselves at the same time linked on to a half-German Power, a disguised foreign one whose insincerity a great part of the nation, misled by old, fond recollections, would never recognize. . . . At the same time there grew and grew in the nation the consciousness of an immeasurable strength, a living indestructible union of both intellectual and political life. A nation in a position of such unexampled difficulty, so strong in its justifiable self-esteem, and so weak through its wretched federal constitution, must necessarily fall into confused and aimless party struggles, and pass through all the infant ailments of political life.

Among the millions abroad there was only one, our faithful friend Thomas Carlyle, who, in spite of the confusion of our party divisions, recognized the nobility of the soul of the German nation. All others were unanimous in the belief that we would come to nothing, and that this central part of the Continent, on whose weakness the old society of States had so long rested, would never become strong. In the eyes of foreigners we were only comic-looking, jovial members of singing and shooting clubs, and the German word *"Vaterland"* was, in England, simply a term of contempt. . . . Was this state of things to continue?

What we needed was a complete, incontestable victory, won solely by German strength, which would compel our neighbors to acknowledge at last respectfully that we, as a nation, had attained our majority. . . . The Empire stands upright, stronger than we ever expected; every German discerns its mighty influence in the ordinary occurrences of every day, in the current exchange of the market-place. None of us could live without the Empire, and how strongly the thought of it glows in our hearts is shown by the grateful affection which seeks to console the first Imperial Chancellor for the bitter experiences of his old age. In my youth it was often said, "If the Germans become German, they will found the kingdom on earth which will bring peace to the world." We are not so inoffensive any longer. For a long time past we have known that the sword must maintain what the sword won. . . .

The happy success you must hold fast in memory, my dear comrades, when your heads grow dizzy with the frenzy of party-spirit. Our festival to-day has especial significance for you.

It is the privilege and happiness of youth to look up, to trust the future in good spirits, not to despise the deeds of their fathers, nor to become submerged in the controversies of the day. . . . You have obtained it, without any merit on your part, this united Fatherland, which for the good of mankind mounted ever higher, from Fehrbellin to Leuthen, from Belle Alliance to Sedan. It can provide scope for every virile force, and the best is hardly good enough for it. If the call of the war lord should ever summon you under the banners of the eagle, you will not wish to be weaker in courage and faithfulness, in the fear of God and devotion, than the old Berlin students, whose honoured names we preserve in marble in our University hall. Whether Germany demands from you the toils of peace or the deeds of war, cherish ever the vow which once the poet, looking down on the corpse-strewn field around Metz, made in all our names:

Think not that the blood you shed
Flowed in vain, O honoured dead,
Or shall ever be forgot!

And now, gentlemen, as we do in all national festivals of our University, let us remember, reverentially, with loyal fidelity, the ruler who guards our Empire with his sceptre. God bless his Majesty, Our Emperor and King. God grant him to exercise a wise, righteous, and firm rule, and grant us all strength to guard and to increase the precious inheritance of those glorious times. Come, good Germans, everywhere! join with me in the cry, "Long live Emperor and Empire!"

❧ TEN BASIC BOOKS ❧

UNITED GERMANY: FROM BISMARCK TO WILLIAM II, 1871–1914

1. Brandenburg, Erich, *From Bismarck to the World War: A History of German Foreign Policy, 1870–1914* (London, 1927).
2. Dawson, William H., *The German Empire, 1867–1914, and the Unity Movement,* 2 vols. (London, 1919, R. 1966).
3. Eyck, Erich, *Bismarck and the German Empire, 1867–1914* (London, 1950, R. 1964).†
4. Flenley, Ralph, *Modern German History,* 2nd rev. ed. (New York, 1964).

5. Pinson, Koppel S., *Modern Germany: Its History and Civilization,* 2nd ed. (New York, 1966).

6. Snyder, Louis L., *Documents of German History* (New Brunswick, N. J., 1958).

7. Taylor, A. J. P., *The Course of German History* (London, 1945, R. 1962).†

8. Townsend, Mary Evelyn, *The Rise and Fall of Germany's Colonial Empire, 1884–1918* (New York, 1930).

9. Valentin, Veit, *The German People* (New York, 1946).

10. Wertheimer, Mildred S., *The Pan-German League, 1890–1914* (New York, 1924).

33

Imperialism: The White Man Assumes a Burden

TAKE UP the White Man's burden—
Send forth the best ye breed—
Go bind your sons to exile
To serve your captives' need;
To wait in heavy harness,
On fluttered folk and wild—
Your new-caught, sullen peoples,
Half devil and half child.

Take up the White Man's burden—
In patience to abide,
To veil the threat of terror
And check the show of pride;
By open speech and simple,
An hundred times made plain,
To seek another's profit,
And work another's gain.

—RUDYARD KIPLING, "The White Man's Burden"

1. Characteristics of the New Imperialism

Nature: Reaction and Revival. The urge toward expansion has often been present in European civilization. In the modern era there emerged the old imperialism of the seventeenth and eighteenth centuries, which arose concomitantly with the Commercial Revolution and with the discovery of the New World. Motivating influences were the three G's—Gold, Glory, God. Spain, Holland, Portugal, France, and England founded colonial empires and Europeanized the Americas. During this wave of imperialism the interests of the colonies were regarded as subservient to those of the mother country—an accurate reflection of the mercantilism of the day.

Enthusiasm for acquiring colonies abated with the end of the first French colonial empire in 1763, the decline of the first British empire in 1783, and the loss of South America by Spain and Portugal in the early 1820's. Many decried the quest for colonies as wasted effort. In any case, the energies of European peoples were spent in the French Revolution, the Napoleonic Wars, and the subsequent struggles between reaction and liberalism. After the defeat of Napoleon only two strong colonial empires remained—the British and the Dutch. The period from 1815 to 1875 was comparatively free of colonial ventures and rivalries.

The decade after 1870 saw a revival of imperialism, a new era of overseas expansion. On the pretext of Europeanizing backward

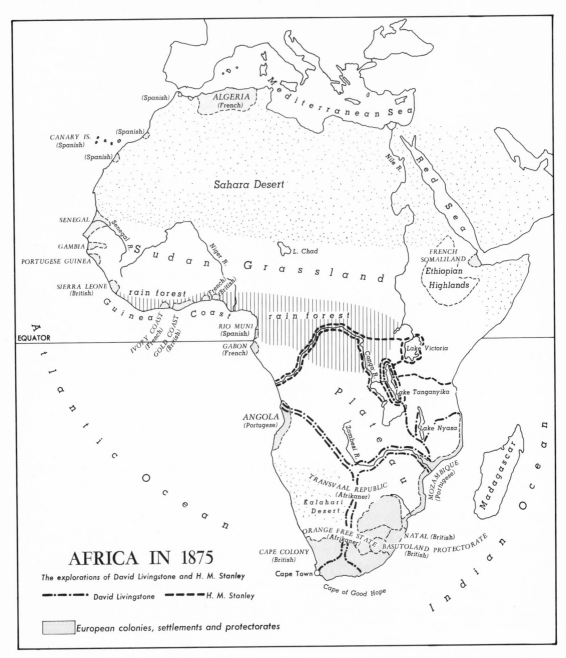

AFRICA IN 1875

The explorations of David Livingstone and H. M. Stanley

—·—·—·— David Livingstone ———— H. M. Stanley

European colonies, settlements and protectorates

peoples, the imperialist nations scrambled for rich territories in Asia, Africa, and the Near and Middle East. This renewed outburst of imperialism had both zealous defenders and bitter critics.

Motivation. Behind the new aggressive movement were many motives, a primary one being economic. The New Industrial Revolu-

tion pushed country after country into the machine age of the late nineteenth century. Growing industrialization called for the discovery of new markets, new sources of raw materials to feed the insatiable machines, more food to satisfy the hunger of increased populations, and new fields for investing excess capital. European life required many products which only tropical regions could supply. The desire of industrial countries to sell their own products in new markets was essentially a revival of eighteenth-century mercantilism. Entrepreneurs found that money invested in "backward" areas would bring a higher rate of return than if used at home.

A second basic motive for the new expansion was psychological. By the last quarter of the nineteenth century, exaggerated national self-consciousness had entered an acute stage. Poets and historians began to talk about "historic mission." Nationalism merged into imperialism; both were saturated with the same romanticism and mysticism. There was talk about "a place in the sun," "the white man's burden," "manifest destiny," "the lamp of life." Germany and Italy, now unified, envied British and French colonial successes and began to look for new worlds to conquer. Colonies were valuable, it was said, as a field for the transplantation of "excess population" from Europe —even if, ironically, comparatively few Europeans migrated to the colonies.

Mary Evelyn Townsend described a union of two drives: "Nationalistic romanticism united with industrial materialism to demand colonial expansion: the former to satisfy its urge for power, prestige, adventure, a sense of superiority, a religious humanitarianism; the latter to translate these idealistic terms into the realism of increased business and trade, which in an industrial age is the only language that defines a 'first-class' power."

Not the least significant motive was the urge to spread Christianity. Both Catholic and Protestant missionaries were sent to convert nonbelievers. It was true enough that the missionaries themselves were motivated by religious, humanitarian ideals; but these altruistic individuals were used by imperialists bent on gaining entry to new and valuable regions. When an overzealous missionary violated native customs and as a result paid with his life, a handy pretext was created for aggression. Imperialism was sparked by other ideals than mere justice.

Pioneers and Agents. The new imperial pioneers were a variegated lot. Each country joining the scramble had its own combination of explorers, promoters, traders, diplomats, soldiers, engineers, and missionaries. The explorers were adventurous men-of-fortune who started out on their own initiative and ended as agents of the imperialist powers, such men as Savorgnan de Brazza, founder of the French Congo, and Dr. Karl Peters, the German patriot-explorer in East Africa. Capitalist promoters, of whom the Englishman Cecil Rhodes was the best example, were masters of manipulation who, with governmental influence, became the great empire builders of the day. Merchants and traders, such as F. A. E. Lüderitz of Bremen, founder of German South-West Africa, were pioneers who established footholds in rich colonial areas. Among the more important agents of the movement were the diplomats, mainly consuls charged with the task of protecting the interests of their nationals in the states designed for acquisition. To this group should be added the soldier-administrators (Gordon and Kitchener in Egypt, Lyautey in Morocco), who spent their military service in the cause of empire. Engineers, too, flocked to backward countries to construct roads and bridges and to ease the way for the white man.

Variety in Methods. Imperialists used a variety of methods and pretexts. In most cases they did not seek outright annexation of colonies, but preferred the more subtle process of peaceful penetration. Where the local government was strong—as, for example, in Turkey—it was prevailed upon to grant concessions, either for the construction of railroads, or for trade. Where the native government was weak, as in China, the country was divided into spheres of influence, in which the representatives of one foreign power or another had the right to exploit markets and natural resources. Each imperial power holding a sphere of influence had a monopoly of the economic resources of its area, and enforced an elaborate system of special laws protecting its own citizens. Wherever too obvious economic penetration seemed inadvisable, the imperialist power could establish a protectorate, maintaining the current ruler on his throne, but reserving actual political and economic control for itself

A German view of British techniques for colonial exploitation in Africa.

(as in Tunis, Morocco, Egypt, or Haiti). A variation of the protectorate was the leasehold, in which an imperialist power took a "lease" on a backward region for a definite number of years (Port Arthur and Kiao-chau in China). The ultimate stage in the process was annexation of a backward region (Ceylon, Algeria, or Togoland), the acquired area becoming a new colony of the motherland. After World War I, a new type of politico-economic control was devised in the form of mandates, which gave to the victorious countries the right to administer certain regions as agents for the League of Nations.

Effects of Imperialism. The imposition of European civilization on underdeveloped peoples, the out-thrust of the white man's civilization, had some beneficial results. This was evident specifically in promotion of education, improvement of living conditions, and development of local commerce and industry. But sometimes the living conditions of the indigenous people were depressed rather than improved. Individual entrepreneurs in the colonizing countries often made enormous profits, but the average citizen gained little more than the pleasure of pointing to colored splotches on the map as "our colonies." Imperialist policies needed strong military and naval forces, which meant higher and higher taxes.

The populations of Asia and Africa, awakened from ancient lethargy, learned to protest against exploitation and oppression. For the first time the peoples in exploited areas became influenced by the spirit of nationalism.

The development of modern imperialism is a story of a most impressive achievement as well as the creation of a momentous world-problem. It is a story of material interests, but it is also a story of ideas. Parker Thomas Moon put it this way: "Altruism, national honor, economic nationalism, surplus population, self-protection—such are the principles or ideas which nerve nations to valiant feats of empire-building. The initiative, to be sure, is taken by interests; but the support is given by ideas .... Imperialism, nay, all history, is made by the dynamic alliance of interests and ideas."

Historical Controversy: Pros and Cons of Empire. A great debate has centered on whether imperialism has been a blessing or curse. On the one side, it was contended that imperialism pays off handsomely in terms of national wealth while bestowing incalculable benefits on the inhabitants of the areas involved. All the major countries had advocates of imperialism. In Britain, Joseph Chamberlain (1836–1914), an aggressive Birmingham manufacturer, held that British workingmen could have employment only if there were a market for products they made; the British colonies would afford that market then and for posterity. Jules Ferry (1832–1893), who as premier presided over the building of the new French colonial empire, defended colonial expansion as "international manifestation of the eternal laws of competition." Friedrich List (1789–1846), a German economist, regarded the acquisition and exploitation of overseas possessions as the certain and best means for any country to attain a commanding economic position. O. P. Austin (1848–1933), chief of the United States Bureau of Statistics in 1900, saw it as a tribute to Western nations that they could give the blessings of civilization to those peoples who had not had the facilities for creating modern societies.

Against this view was the contention of anti-imperialists that the movement is beset by fallacies and evils, that empire-building is carried on at public expense, that huge profits accrue to relatively few entrepreneurs, and that nations as a whole gain but little profit from imperialism. In 1902 appeared a classic indictment by John A. Hobson (1858–1940), a British economist, who stated that imperialism is clearly condemned as a business policy because "at enormous expense, it has procured a small, bad, unsafe increase of markets and has jeopardized the entire wealth of a nation in rousing the strong resentments of other nations." (*See page 557.*) Grover Clark (1891–1938), an American economist, examined and found fallacious the three main arguments of expansionists: (1) that colonies yield huge commercial profits; (2) that colonies provide outlets for surplus population; and (3) that colonies furnish sources for essential raw materials. In 1901 Samuel Clemens (Mark Twain) (1835–1910), novelist and humorist, denounced "The Blessings-of-Civilization Trust": "There is more money in it, more territory, more sovereignty, and other kinds of emolument, than there is in any other game that is played."

The debate continues to the present day as imperialists insist that without their work Africans would still be living in a primitive wilderness with little hope for civilized government. Anti-imperialists continue to condemn the movement as an unmitigated evil, unreasonable, unprofitable, unfair, and outmoded.

2. Conquest and Exploitation of Africa

Opening the Dark Continent. There are five Africas, not one. The northern coastline, bordering the Mediterranean, is a temperate area that historically has been an adjunct of European civilization. Just south of this area is the belt of the Sahara, Libyan, and Nubian deserts, where the white and Negro strains begin to blend. The next belt stretches across the continent from Guinea to the Sudan, the so-called "land of the blacks." Next is Central, or Equatorial, Africa, a land of dense jungles inhabited by Negroes. At the southern tip of the continent is again a temperate zone in the area around South Africa.

For most of the nineteenth century, European nations had only small footholds on this great continent. The French, British, and Portuguese had coastal trading posts, but none had penetrated the interior. Then, in the last quarter of the century, came a hot scramble for control of Africa. In March 1866 David Livingstone (1813–1873), a Scottish Protestant missionary, landed on the shore of East Africa in his final expedition "to blaze a trail for the gospel." Without knowing it, he prepared the trail for partition of the African continent. When the outside world lost contact with Livingstone, James Gordon Bennett, owner of the New York *Herald,* sent Henry Morton Stanley (1841–1904), a British journalist, to find the missionary-turned-explorer. Stanley found Livingstone on November 10, 1871. The effect was extraordinary. Fired with enthusiasm, hundreds of explorers hit the African trails. The sources of the Nile were explored by Burton, Speke, Baker, Schweinfurth, and Grant; the Sahara and Sudan by Nachtigal, Barth, Laing, and Denham; the Niger by Caillé, Clapperton, and Lander; the Zambesi

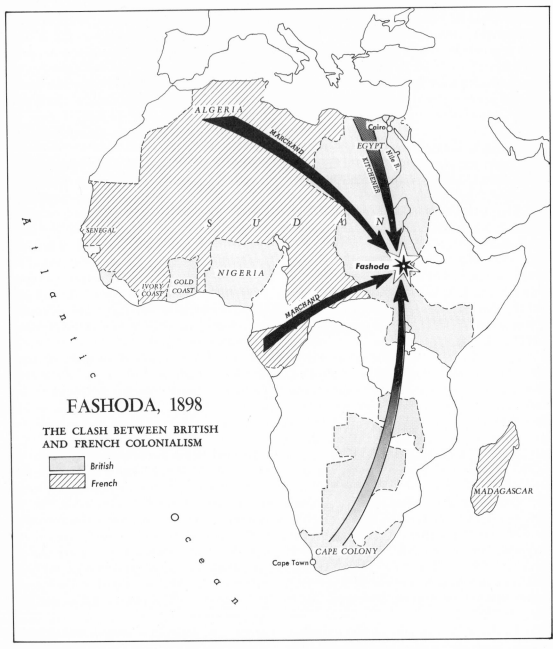

FASHODA, 1898

THE CLASH BETWEEN BRITISH
AND FRENCH COLONIALISM

British
French

valley by Livingstone; the Congo by Stanley and de Brazza. Europe turned its eyes not only to scientific aspects of the explorations but also to possibilities for commerce, for missionary work, and for expressing national ideas of expansionism.

In 1876 Leopold II (r. 1865–1909), King of the Belgians, organized a commercial company to exploit Central Africa. The Great Powers somewhat reluctantly consented to the formation of Leopold's Congo Free State, a private empire, from which the Belgian ruler acquired an enormous fortune (rubber and ivory). But Leopold's unscrupulous treatment of the natives aroused such universal indignation that his private domain was abolished in 1908 and the region was annexed to Belgium as the Belgian Congo.

The major European powers, while assuring the world that their object was merely to "Christianize and civilize" the Africans, rushed in to acquire the natural resources of Africa. The Africans, too weak to protest, exchanged their lands and their freedom for work, taxes, and exploitation. It was not long before most of the continent was partitioned among the powers.

The British, working quietly, efficiently, and with tone, tact, and taste, obtained the lion's share. Already holding Cape Colony, the British seized Egypt in 1882, and in 1889 established virtual sovereignty over Anglo-Egyptian Sudan. In South Africa the British and the pastoral-minded Dutch settlers went to war (Boer War, 1899–1902). Eventually Britain won the whole of South Africa. In the west she acquired the Gold Coast, Nigeria, Sierra Leone, and the lower Gambian region. In East Africa she annexed Uganda, Kenya, and a part of Somaliland.

France got a foothold in Algeria as early as 1830, then gradually extended her control into Morocco and Tunisia along the Mediterranean coast, and annexed most of northwest Africa from Algeria south to the Congo River. In East Africa she acquired a part of Somaliland and the island of Madagascar (1896).

The expansion of French colonial interests in the west and east, and that of the British in the north and south resulted in a confrontation between the two powers. In March 1898 the British general Sir Herbert Kitchener led an Egyptian force up the Nile. On September 19 he reached the small town of Fashoda, which had been occupied on July 10 by the French under Major Jean Baptiste Marchand. Kitchener invited Marchand to withdraw, but Marchand declined to move without authorization from the French government. The Fashoda problem brought Anglo-French relations to the point of crisis. The British would not even begin negotiations until Marchand had evacuated. The French, not in a position to risk war over the question, yielded to the British demands and on November 4 ordered Marchand to withdraw. The affair was finally settled in March 1899: The French were forced to give up their claims to land along the Nile,

and in return the British recognized French possession of territories in the Sahara Desert.

Germany was a late starter in the African hunt. She was able to obtain a number of vacant areas, such as Togoland (1884), German East Africa (1884–1889), German Southwest Africa (1884–1890), and the Cameroons (1884–1911). Although good-sized areas on the map, they were poor in natural resources, leftovers in the scramble. To that disappointment was added German resentment at accusations of brutality in handling the natives.

Italy, following her unification, sought new prestige as well as economic enhancement by annexing Eritrea and Italian Somaliland, both coastal districts in East Africa. When she sought to acquire Abyssinia (Ethiopia), Italy was halted with a crushing defeat at Adowa (1896). She managed to wrest Tripoli and Cyrenaica from the Turks. Population pressure was used as an additional motivation for Italian expansion.

Portugal, as her share of the spoils, obtained Angola, Portuguese Guinea, and Portuguese East Africa. Spain took Rio de Oro on the extreme west coast, the northern coast of Morocco, and a few small offshore islands.

Ground Rules: Berlin Act, 1885. From November 15, 1884 to February 26, 1885 the Berlin Conference on African Affairs met to lay down rules for occupation of Africa. The signatories promised "to protect the natives in their moral and material well-being, to cooperate in the suppression of slavery and the slave-trade, to further the education and civilization of the natives, to protect missionaries and explorers." The powers also agreed that occupation of African lands must not be on paper only, and that a country with holdings on the coast had prior claims to the back country. Intentions were good, but the opportunity was lost to prevent greedy aggression and land-grabbing. Profits came first, the well-being of the people a poor second. Within fifteen years after the Berlin Conference the only non-colonial lands remaining in Africa were Ethiopia and Liberia, the latter founded in 1822 as a colony for emancipated American slaves.

Business Versus Altruism. By this time the process was familiar. A small group of white men—explorers, traders, promoters—would appear in the wilderness, bringing with them a handful of treaties, sometimes merely printed forms. They would seek out a willing chief who appeared to have some influence over his people and bestow upon him powers which he ordinarily did not possess—such as the right to

convey sovereignty, sell land, or grant concessions. (*See page 556.*) Thus, control was gained indirectly through tribal chieftains. Then came what amounted to forced labor and exploitation of the area.

The imperialist powers squeezed Africa of its wealth, but at the same time announced to the world that they were suppressing slavery, tribal warfare, superstition, and disease. Col-

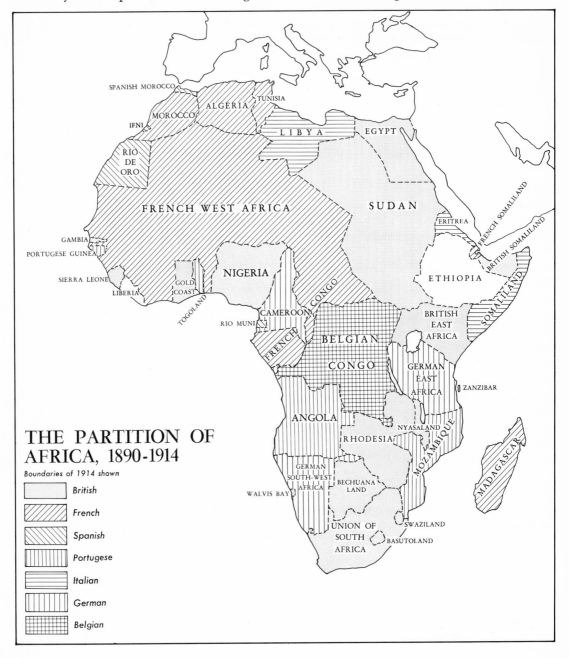

THE PARTITION OF
AFRICA, 1890-1914

Boundaries of 1914 shown

British
French
Spanish
Portugese
Italian
German
Belgian

onizers spoke in terms of altruism—education for the native, bringing him the benefits of civilization, playing light on the Dark Continent. Actually, many were more interested in such indigenous treasures as gold, rubber, diamonds, ivory, ebony, copra, cocoa, palm oil, sisal, coffee, cotton, and nuts. The Africans knew it. Resenting both paternalism and exploitation, they later would turn the tools of nationalism on their occupiers. There were, of course, some obvious secondary effects of imperialistic exploitation: the new nations emerging in Africa showed intense interest in Western technology and administrative techniques.

3. The Spoliation of China

China in the Nineteenth Century. The initial attempt by a great power to "open" China to the West was made by the British in the Opium War (1841–1842). When the Chinese government tried to stop the opium trade (European merchants gathered the opium poppy in India and sold it in the huge Chinese market), the British intervened. China was promptly defeated. By the Treaty of Nanking (1842), China was forced to pay a heavy indemnity, cede Hong Kong to Britain, and open five ports (Canton, Ningpo, Foochow, Shanghai, and Amoy) to British trade. China was also required to recognize the principle of extraterritoriality, granting foreign residents in China the rights they had enjoyed at home, exempting them from the jurisdiction of native courts (capitulations). Convinced that they had made concessions only under extreme pressure, the Chinese tried to discourage trade with the West and avoided diplomatic contact with Westerners. In 1856 England and France made war on China. The Treaties of Tientsin (1858) required China to pay an indemnity, open additional ports to foreign trade, protect Christian missionaries, and guarantee foreigners the right of travel in China.

Western imperialists, assisted by Chinese corruption and inefficiency, carved out large "spheres of influence" and acquired rich concessions in China. The principal European nations were interested in Chinese "treaty ports." There was much to attract the Westerners: large supplies of coal and iron, a huge supply of cheap labor, an enormous market, and many opportunities for investment.

The Japanese Turn to China. The process of spoliation continued when Japan, aroused from feudal slumber, turned her eyes to the mainland. The Sino-Japanese War (1894–1895), the outcome of a decade of rivalry in Korea, resulted, to the astonishment of the world, in triumph for the Japanese. By the Treaty of Shimonoseki (1895) China was forced to pay Japan a large indemnity, to recognize the independence of Korea, and to relinquish the island of Formosa and the Liaotung Peninsula (including the naval base of Port Arthur) to Japan. The Great Powers, regarding the annexation of Liaotung as an "encroachment" on China proper, forced Japan to return the peninsula and accept instead an increased indemnity. The Japanese resented this interference, and filed away their resentment for future reference.

Japanese success promoted a new scramble for influence in China. In 1898, as compensation for the murder of two missionaries, Germany extracted a ninety-nine-year lease on the harbor of Kiao-chau as well as the right to exploit coal mines in the province of Shantung. In the same year France "leased" Kwang-chau Wan, England the port of Wei-hai-wei, and Russia the southern part of the Liaotung Peninsula and Port Arthur. Russia also obtained the right to construct the Chinese Eastern Railway across Manchuria, thus cutting the distance to Vladivostok by several hundred miles.

The United States and the Open-Door Policy. American activity in China was closely bound with that of the British. American-Chinese trade commenced in 1785 at Canton under the auspices of the British East India Company. The United States received most-favored-nation status in the Treaty of Wanghsia (1844), modeled on the British Treaty of Nanking. The settlement of Tientsin (1858) included the United States. In 1899 the United States enunciated the Open Door policy for trade, a doctrine formulated chiefly by Englishmen. This policy gave Britain support in maintaining the position of trading nations territorially remote from China. In its origins, at least, the Open Door was an Anglo-American defensive measure, and not, as it pretended to be, a policy designed to maintain the interests of the Chinese state. John King Fairbank expressed this point of view on the Open Door policy: "Since 1900 we have stood for the territorial integrity of China, usually without any reliance upon British diplomacy. The fact remains that our traditional policy began as an inheritance from the British who, as a trading nation at a great distance from China, wished to preserve China as an open market. The contradictory elements in our China policy can be understood only if we remember that until the early 1920's our in-

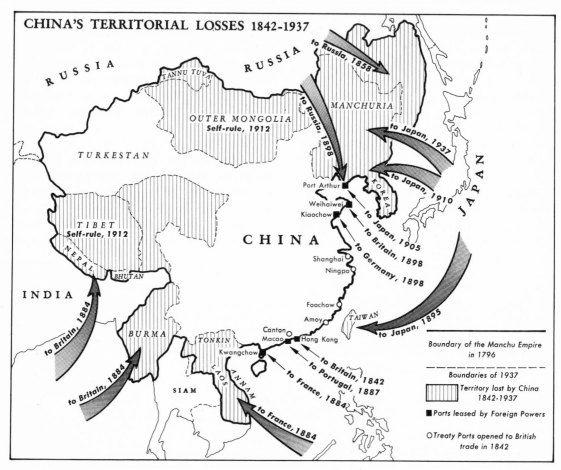

CHINA'S TERRITORIAL LOSSES 1842-1937

Boundary of the Manchu Empire in 1796

Boundaries of 1937

Territory lost by China 1842-1937

■ Ports leased by Foreign Powers

O Treaty Ports opened to British trade in 1842

terests in China were junior to those of Britain, under whose leadership they had grown up. This allowed us the luxury of constantly denouncing British imperialism while steadily participating in its benefits."

Drive for Independence. Continued imperialism in China aroused grave discontent among the Chinese people. The young emperor, Kwang-su, convinced that only rapid Westernization could solve China's troubles, in 1898 promulgated several decrees providing for reforms in army, civil service, and education. Chinese reactionaries, who hated the "foreign devils," vigorously opposed this attempt to Europeanize China and deposed the emperor. The Boxers (Society of Harmonious Fists), a patriotic society, in a campaign of terrorism, killed missionaries and other foreign civilians in China and Manchuria. When they murdered the German minister, Baron von Ketteler, in Peking on June 20, 1900, and besieged foreigners who sought refuge in legations, an international army of British, Russian, German, French, Japanese, and American troops invaded China, relieved the legations, and took steps to eliminate the Boxers. The empress dowager, through the decade after 1902, announced a new reform campaign based on the earlier projected reforms. But it was too late. In 1911, revolutionaries led by Dr. Sun Yat-sen overthrew the ancient Manchu dynasty, and in 1912 established a republic. In 1928 Chiang Kai-shek, the Kuomintang leader, became head of the Nationalist government at Nanking and generalissimo of all Chinese Nationalist forces. China had suffered decades of terrible civil war and apparently was still unready for free democratic government on the Western model.

4. Westernization of Japan

Opening-up of Japan. In the sixteenth century Portuguese navigators and Jesuit missionaries sought to establish a foothold in Japan, but once their influence became apparent they were expelled. For centuries the Japanese remained isolated from the West. In 1850 the island-empire, eastern neighbor of China, was a feudal state controlled by a class of fighting nobility called *samurai*. The emperor (*mikado*) was considered too sacred to mingle in ordinary affairs; the executive power was vested in a hereditary prime minister, the *shogun*. In 1853 Commodore Matthew Calbraith Perry, an American naval officer, visited Japan and, aided by several impressive battleships, ultimately negotiated a treaty opening Japanese ports to American commerce. In 1858 Townsend Harris, the first American representative to Japan, negotiated a commercial treaty. The European Powers quickly sought treaties and extraterritorial privileges. When the conservative Japanese protested against foreign penetration, they were taught a lesson in Western diplomacy by the bombardment of the town of Shimonoseki (1864). The Japanese concluded that Western military, political, and economic methods were far more effective and desirable than their own. Thereafter, being both adaptable and fanatically nationalistic,

Commodore Perry meeting the Japanese Imperial Commissioners at Yokohama, March 8, 1854. Perry led the expedition to the Far East which opened communication and trade between Japan and the rest of the world after centuries of isolation.

in contrast to the disunited Chinese, they resisted Western imperialism, but used Western methods to develop an imperialism of their own.

Transformation of Japan. The rapid Westernization of Japan is one of the most remarkable phenomena of modern times. Virtually overnight the whole structure of Japanese society was transformed from top to bottom. In 1867 a vigorous young ruler, Mutsuhito, wrested power from the *shogun*, and 700 years of military government came to an end. During the rest of his reign (1867–1912) he inaugurated reforms that changed feudal Japan into a modern constitutional state, an industrial nation, and a world power. In 1871 an imperial decree abolished the fiefs and the land was divided among independent farmers. The year 1872 saw the opening of the first railroad in Japan and the introduction of compulsory elementary education. Universal military service under German direction, and the construction, under British guidance, of a modern navy, followed. Reform succeeded reform: students were sent abroad to study Western culture and science; new codes of civil and criminal law were drafted; religious liberty was established; and trade and industry were promoted by the government, so effectively that Japan quickly became a dynamic industrial power. In 1889 the *mikado* promulgated a constitution. The emperor's powers were carefully guarded. A bicameral diet consisted of an upper house of peers (363 members) and a lower house elected through limited suffrage (463 members). Compared with the transformation of Japan, the industrialization of England had been snail-like. Western nations were astonished to find in Japan a strong commercial rival, one able to compete successfully with them in the markets of the world.

Japanese Expansion. Japan, like European countries, insisted that she required colonies, markets, raw materials, areas in which to invest surplus capital, and an outlet for her surplus population. Regarding herself as the protector and guardian of Oriental civilization, she turned to China—an impotent giant already

in process of dismemberment. In 1876 Japan recognized Korea as an independent kingdom. Her subsequent attempts to control Korea led to the Sino-Japanese War (1894–1895), which resulted in a quick Japanese victory.

Meanwhile, Russia became Japan's rival in the Far East. The Japanese were infuriated by a series of Russian coups: Russia interfered in Chinese diplomatic affairs, established a Russo-Chinese bank (1896) to pay the Chinese indemnity to Japan, obtained a concession for the Chinese Eastern Railway to Vladivostok, leased the Liaotung Peninsula and Port Arthur, and penetrated Korea and Manchuria. Japan, after obtaining a Western ally (Anglo-Japanese Alliance of 1902), in 1904 demanded that Russia withdraw from Manchuria and Korea. When the Russians refused, Japan went to war. The Russo-Japanese War (1904–1905), to the further amazement of the world, ended in the rout of the Russian armies at Mukden, and the annihilation of the Russian fleet at Tsushima. At the suggestion of the American president, Theodore Roosevelt, the peace concluded in the Treaty of Portsmouth (New Hampshire) in 1905 required both belligerents to evacuate Manchuria, but recognized their spheres of influence there. In addition, it awarded Port Arthur, a lease on the Liaotung Peninsula and the southern half of the island of Sakhalin to Japan. It recognized Japanese influence in Korea, later (1910) annexed by Japan. Russia paid no indemnity.

5. *British Imperialism in India*

British Penetration. India, with its teeming population, had been valuable to the British not only as a rich source of raw materials, but also as a market for British products and as a lucrative field for investment. British penetration of the huge peninsula had begun in the early seventeenth century under the auspices of the East India Company. The rival French were defeated in the Seven Years' War (1756–1763), chiefly through the efforts of Robert Clive and Warren Hastings. Gradually, by a combination of treaty-making and conquest, the East India Company extended its control to the borders of Afghanistan and China, over a territory of some 2,000,000 square miles. British mastery of the vast area was facilitated by political, cultural, and religious rivalries (Hindus versus Muslims) among the hundreds of petty states.

The India Act of 1784 gave a measure of local autonomy, but actual control remained in the hands of British officials, named by Parliament to succeed the often corrupt East India Company officials. The peoples of India resented attempts to change their religious and social customs. The issue came to a head in 1857, when the Sepoys, or local soldiers in British service, protested against the use of their weapons. At this time the cartridges used in rifles were greased with animal fat. Pious Muslims, forbidden to touch any product of the pig, refused to hold the cartridges with their teeth. Moreover, religious Hindus, believing that the grease contained the fat of cows—sacred animals—declined to bite the cartridges. The mutiny spread quickly, but was, with great difficulty, finally suppressed.

Queen Victoria was crowned Empress of India in 1877. This made little difference to Indian nationalists who wanted to emancipate the country economically as well as politically. Indian leaders accused the British of failing to solve the problems of the caste system, infanticide, illiteracy, poverty, famine, and disease. In defense, the British pointed to the construction of roads and railways, the establishment of schools and universities, and improvements in the codification of laws and the administration of justice.

Indian demands for an end to British control persisted. The British countered with a series of reports. The Montague-Chelmsford Report (1918) proclaimed a greater degree of self-government for India. The Rowlatt Acts (1919), as a response to riots, restricted the liberties of the people. The Simon Report (1930) again recommended a gradual increase in self-government, but stressed the necessity for continued British control.

Mohandas Karamchand Gandhi, born in 1869, an enigmatic little man, toothless and bald, was the key figure in India's drive for independence. For thirty years this fabulous saint and mystic, his frail body emaciated by fasting and asceticism, worked for a free India. "One of that unbroken line of saints and seers, running like the stitches of a golden thread through the tangled pattern of human affairs, who have insisted that man, like God,

In 1858 a private company was formed to finance a Suez Canal (in spite of British objections to the "foolhardy" venture); 56% of the shares were purchased by numerous private investors, mostly French, and the remainder by Khedive Ismail of Egypt. In 1875 the more international-minded Benjamin Disraeli recognized that the canal offered a vital trade route between Europe and Asia. He negotiated his government's purchase of the Khedive's shares, thereby making Great Britain the largest single shareholder in the company.

is spirit, and can achieve his ends, and thus fulfill his life," said John Haynes Holmes in tribute. Gandhi once said that he had "learned from Christ passive resistance and nonviolence, from Tolstoy non-cooperation, from Thoreau civil disobedience." Gandhi began and popularized a policy of non-cooperation and passive resistance which eventually led to independence for India in 1947.

6. Imperialism in the Near and Middle East

Attraction of a Strategic Area. The ancient Near East—Asia Minor and the city of Constantinople, which together form a natural bridge to Asia—was strategically important to Western imperialists. For centuries Russia had sought to obtain an outlet to the Mediterranean through the Near East. On two occasions in the nineteenth century—the Crimean War (1853–1856) and the Russo-Turkish War (1877–1878)

—Britain intervened to frustrate Russian hopes of expansion. The imperialist impulse in the Near East was a response to the vacuum left by the steady dissolution of the Ottoman Empire. For two centuries the Ottoman Empire had been in a continuing process of disintegration. The regions lost in the eighteenth century were annexed either by Austria or Russia. Those European territories lost in the nineteenth century ultimately emerged as independent states. In the twentieth century the attraction for Western powers, in addition to economic and strategic interests, was oil. Rivalry for the spoils of the Ottoman Empire was one of the motivating causes for World War I.

Germany, unsuccessful elsewhere, turned to the Near East as a field for economic penetration. After several visits to the Turkish sultan, William II obtained concessions for German capitalists to construct a railway linking Berlin to Baghdad and the Persian Gulf. This railway, if completed, would have given Germany

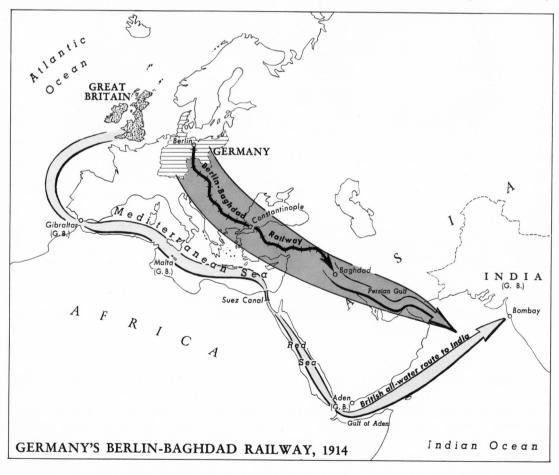

GERMANY'S BERLIN-BAGHDAD RAILWAY, 1914

access not only to the Near East, but also to the rich areas of central and eastern Asia. Britain resolutely opposed the project, which would have provided a shorter and cheaper route to India for non-British products, would have been a threat to the Suez Canal, and would have forced a wedge between England and India. British agents put economic pressure on local rulers to prevent completion of the railway. This issue was one of the factors leading to World War I.

Britain and Russia were also rivals in the Middle East (Persia, Baluchistan, Afghanistan). Although thinly populated, the area was strategically valuable to both Russia and Britain. While Russia penetrated southward, England pushed her Indian frontiers north in Baluchistan. Russia reached the northern boundaries of Afghanistan in 1895. Both Russian and British agents sought concessions for the construction of railways and mines in Persia. The Persians graciously accepted "loans" from both sides. Alarmed by the "peaceful penetration" of their country by foreigners, Persians rose in revolt in 1905 and demanded parliamentary control of finances. The country plunged into civil war. In 1907 Britain and Russia concluded a treaty: Persia was divided into three spheres—a Russian sphere of influence in the north, a British sphere in the

THE HARMLESS NECESSARY CAT.

British Lion (to Russian Bear). "LOOK HERE! *YOU* CAN PLAY WITH HIS HEAD, AND *I* CAN PLAY WITH HIS TAIL, AND WE CAN *BOTH* STROKE THE SMALL OF HIS BACK."
Persian Cat. "I DON'T REMEMBER HAVING BEEN CONSULTED ABOUT THIS!"

The British Lion and Russian Bear covetously fondle the Persian Cat. This famous *Punch* cartoon comments on the Convention of 1907 concerning disposition of Persia.

south, and a neutral area in the center. Here, too, the issue of oil was paramount.

7. United States Imperialism in the 1890's

Manifest Destiny. The last decade of the nineteenth century saw an intensification of imperialism both in Europe and in the United States. In 1895 President Grover Cleveland reaffirmed the principles of the Monroe Doctrine and denied the British the right to deal directly with Venezuela in a boundary dispute with British Guiana. The British were forced to bow to international arbitration. But when revolutionists in the Isthmus of Panama rebelled against Colombia, Washington recognized Panama as an independent republic (1903). Soon the United States leased the Canal Zone and began to build the Panama

Canal. Some Europeans called Panama a protectorate of the United States.

Meanwhile, revolutionary activity broke out in the vestiges of the old Spanish American empire—in Cuba and Puerto Rico. Cuba, particularly, was important for American strategic interests in the Caribbean, especially because of the soon-to-be-built Panama Canal. Moreover, Americans had $50,000,000 invested in Cuba. The new "yellow" press began to attack the barbarism of the Spanish authorities in dealing with the Cuban rebels and whipped the American public into a fury of moral fervor. The Spanish-American War of 1898 began when an American warship, the *Maine,* was sunk in Havana harbor. The United States easily won the war. Puerto Rico was annexed, as were the Philippine Islands in the Pacific. Cuba was set up as an independent republic, but subject to the right of the United States to intervene in matters of "life, property, and individual liberty." Critics spoke of another American protectorate in the Caribbean.

The Spanish-American War and its outcome marked the emergence of the United States upon the international scene as one of the Great Powers. The settlement made after that war meant a sharp divergence from earlier American traditions. For the first time in its history the United States went beyond its continental limits to annex lands which lay close to Asia. There were now new strategic, political, and economic outposts in the Far East, which called for the protection of a growing navy. President Theodore Roosevelt proclaimed the greatness of the United States to the world. In 1904 he announced that weakness or misbehavior "which results in a general loosening of ties of civilized society may . . . require intervention by some civilized nation." He was denounced by anti-imperialists who demanded to know whether a republic like the United States could afford to cast aside its old traditions by assuming control over peoples who were not to be citizens but subjects.

❧ KEY DOCUMENT ❦

A TYPICAL AFRICAN BLANK TREATY, 1880's

Edward Hertslet, ed., *The Map of Africa by Treaty* (London, 1894), I, 467 ff.

IMPERIALIST TREATY-MAKING in Africa followed a preconceived pattern. Agents bearing supplies of liquors and tinseled ornaments together with blank treaty forms set out on expeditions. Below is the blank treaty used by the Royal Niger Company in its drive to obtain sovereign rights in the valley of the Niger. The advantage, of course, lay with those who offered the treaties.

We, the undersigned Chiefs of   , with the view of bettering the condition of our country and people, do this day cede to the Royal Niger Company (Chartered and Limited), for ever, the whole of our territory extending from

We also give to the said Royal Niger Company (Chartered and Limited) full power to settle all native disputes arising from any cause whatever, and we pledge ourselves not to enter into any war with other tribes without the sanction of the said Royal Niger Company (Chartered and Limited).

We understand that the said Royal Niger Company (Chartered and Limited) have full power to mine, farm, and build in any portion of our country.

We bind ourselves not to have any intercourse with any strangers or foreigners except through the said Royal Niger Company (Chartered and Limited).

In consideration of the foregoing, the said Royal Niger Company (Chartered and Limited) bind themselves not to interfere with any of the native laws or customs of the country, consistently with the maintenance of order and good government.

The said Royal Niger Company (Chartered and Limited) agree to pay native owners of land a reasonable amount for any portion they may require.

The said Royal Niger Company (Chartered

and Limited) bind themselves to protect the said Chiefs from the attacks of any neighbouring aggressive tribes.

The said Royal Niger Company (Chartered and Limited) also agree to pay the said Chiefs measures native value.

We, the undersigned witnesses, do hereby solemnly declare that the   Chiefs whose names are placed opposite their respective crosses have in our presence affixed their crosses of their own free will and consent, and that the said,

has in our presence affixed his signature.

Done in triplicate at   , this   day of   188 .

Declaration by Interpreter

I,   , of   , do hereby solemnly declare that I am well acquainted with the language of the   country, and that on the   day of   , 188 . I truly and faithfully explained the above Agreement to all the Chiefs present, and that they understood its meaning.

❧ HISTORICAL INTERPRETATION ❧

JOHN A. HOBSON'S CLASSIC ASSAULT ON IMPERIALISM, 1902

John A. Hobson, *Imperialism, A Study* (London, 1902), 3rd rev. ed., 1938, pp. 55–56, 59–61. By permission of George Allen & Unwin, Ltd.

AN IMPORTANT study of imperialism was published by John A. Hobson (1858–1940), an English economist, more than a half-century ago. Hobson traced the origins of imperialism, discussed its theory and practice, evaluated its effects upon "lower" or alien peoples, and described its moral reactions upon the Western nations. He found a common "taproot" for imperialism in the aim of capitalists to obtain profitable investments overseas. Hobson's attack was used by Lenin in his analysis of imperialism as the final stage of a collapsing capitalism.

Aggressive Imperialism, which costs the taxpayer so dear, which is of so little value to the manufacturer and trader, which is fraught with such grave incalculable peril to the citizen, is a source of great gain to the investor who cannot find at home the profitable uses he seeks for his capital, and insists that his Government should help him to profitable and secure investments abroad.

If, contemplating the enormous expenditure on armaments, the ruinous wars, the diplomatic audacity or knavery by which modern Governments seek to extend their territorial power, we put the plain, practical question, *Cui bono?* the first and most obvious answer is, the investor.

The annual income Great Britain derives from commissions on her whole foreign and colonial trade, import and export, was estimated by Sir R. Giffen at £18,000,000 for 1899, taken at 2½ per cent, upon a turnover of £800,000,000. This is the whole that we are entitled to regard as profits on external trade. Considerable as this sum

is, it cannot serve to yield an economic motive-power adequate to explain the dominance which business considerations exercise over our imperial policy. Only when we set beside it some £90,000,000 or £100,000,000, representing pure profit upon investments, do we understand whence the economic impulse to Imperialism is derived.

Investors who have put their money in foreign lands, upon terms which take full account of risks connected with the political conditions of the country, desire to use the resources of their Government to minimise these risks, and so to enhance the capital value and the interest of their private investments. The investing and speculative classes in general have also desired that Great Britain should take other foreign areas under her flag in order to secure new areas for profitable investments and speculation.

If the special interest of the investor is liable to clash with the public interest and to induce a wrecking policy, still more dangerous is the special interest of the financier, the general dealer in investments. In large measure the rank and file of the investors are, both for business and for politics, the cat's paw of the great financial houses, who use stocks and shares not so much as investments to yield them interest, but as material for speculation in the money market. . . .

The wealth of these houses, the scale of their operations, and their cosmopolitan organization make them the prime determinants of imperial policy. They have the largest definite stake in the business of Imperialism, and the amplest means of forcing their will upon the policy of nations.

In view of the part which the non-economic factors of patriotism, adventure, military enterprise, political ambition, and philanthropy play in imperial expansion, it may appear that to impute to financiers so much power is to take a too narrowly economic view of history. And it is true that the motor-power of Imperialism is not chiefly financial: finance is rather the governor of the imperial engine, directing the energy and determining its work: it does not constitute the fuel of the engine, nor does it directly generate the power. Finance manipulates the patriotic forces which politicians, soldiers, philanthropists, and traders generate; the enthusiasm for expansion which issues from these sources, though strong and genuine, is irregular and blind; the financial interest has those qualities of concentration and clear-sighted calculation which are needed to set Imperialism to work. An ambitious stateman, a frontier soldier, an overzealous missionary, a pushing trader, may suggest or even initiate a step of imperial expansion, may assist in educating patriotic public opinion to the urgent need of some fresh advance, but the final determination rests with the financial power. The direct influence exercised by great financial houses in "high politics" is supported by the control which they exercise over the body of public opinion through the Press, which, in every "civilized" country, is becoming more and more their obedient instrument. . . . Add to this the natural sympathy with a sensational policy which a cheap Press always manifests, and it becomes evident that the Press has been strongly biased towards Imperialism, and has lent itself with great facility to the suggestion of financial or political Imperialists who have desired to work up patriotism for some new piece of expansion.

Such is the array of distinctively economic forces making for Imperialism, a large loose group of trades and professsions seeking profitable business and lucrative employment from the expansion of military and civil services, and from the expenditure on military operations, the opening up of new tracts of territory and trade with the same, and the provision of new capital which these operations require, all these findings their central guiding and directing force in the power of the general financier.

The play of these forces does not openly appear. They are essentially parasites upon patriotism, and they adapt themselves to its protecting colours. In the mouth of their representatives are noble phrases, expressive of their desire to extend the area of civilization, to establish good government, promote Christianity, extirpate slavery, and elevate the lower races. Some of the business men who hold such language may entertain a genuine, though usually a vague, desire to accomplish these ends, they are primarily engaged in business, and they are not unaware of the utility of the more unselfish forces in furthering their ends. Their true attitude of mind was expressed by Mr. Rhodes in his famous description of "Her Majesty's Flag" as "the greatest commercial asset in the world."

❧ TEN BASIC BOOKS ❧

IMPERIALISM: THE WHITE MAN ASSUMES A BURDEN

1. Clark, Grover, *A Place in the Sun* (New York, 1936).
2. Hobson, John A., *Imperialism, A Study,* 3rd rev. ed. (London, 1938, R. 1965).†
3. Langer, William L., *The Diplomacy of Imperialism, 1890–1902,* 2 vols. (New York, 1935).

4. Moon, Parker Thomas, *Imperialism and World Politics* (New York, 1926).

5. Rudin, Harry, *The Germans in the Cameroons, 1884–1914: A Case Study in Modern Imperialism* (New Haven, Conn., 1938).

6. Schumpeter, Joseph, *Imperialism and Social Classes* (Village Station, N. Y., 1951).†

7. Snyder, Louis L., *The Imperialism Reader: Documents and Readings on Modern Expansionism* (Princeton, N. J., 1962).†

8. Strausz-Hupé, Robert, and Henry W. Hazard, eds. *The Idea of Colonialism* (New York, 1958).

9. Townsend, Mary Evelyn, *European Colonial Expansion Since 1871* (Philadelphia, 1941).

10. Winslow, Earle M., *The Pattern of Imperialism: A Study in the Theories of Power* (New York, 1948).

34

Socialism and Other Dissenting Movements

RISE UP, ye victims of privation,
Rise up, all ye who are forlorn;
For there's an end to degradation,
For now a new world's being born.
Right close at hand emancipation
Will loose the chains that held you fast;
The time is near for your salvation,
A better day has dawned at last.
> O comrades, assemble from afar to face the fight;
> The Internationale bids all the world unite.
> O comrades, assemble from afar to face the fight;
> The Internationale bids all the world unite!

Come, workers of the world, as brothers
To wrest the wealth from land and sea;
Your rights demand, and for all others,
Crush the foes of Liberty.
Too long the rich our lives are taking,
Trampling Freedom to the ground;
O now arise, from sleep awaking,
Land to land our tocsin sound.
(Refrain)

—"The Internationale," 1888

1. Emergence of Socialism: Political Doctrine and Movement

Bourgeoisie and Proletariat. The immediate beneficiary of industrialization in the late eighteenth and nineteenth centuries was the bourgeoisie, or middle class, which assumed economic power by accumulating and controlling production and capital. Guided by the principle of *laissez-faire*, it called for and obtained freedom to pursue its economic ends without restriction by the state. It demanded free competition, free economic enterprise, and the right to hold private property, but it denied workers the right to interfere with economic organization. This energetic class won political dominance in England in the late seventeenth century, in France in the late eighteenth, and maintained it throughout the nineteenth, the century of bourgeois power.

For the proletariat, or lower class of peasants and workers who possessed nothing beyond their ability to work, the promise of liberty and equality had not been fulfilled. Typical of its experience was that of French workers who, allied with the bourgeoisie in the revolt against the landed aristocracy, had gone to the barricades, helped overthrow the Old Regime, and then received no satisfactory economic or social reward for their pains. Without property, without franchise, dependent upon the bourgeoisie for its existence, the proletariat had no sense of security in the new order. Little wonder, then, that the masses tended to regard the Declaration of the Rights of Man and Citizen as in effect a "Declaration of the Rights of the Bourgeoisie."

Development of Trade Unionism. Trade unionism, or the organized activity of wage earners to better their condition, appeared in all industrialized nations. It was a weapon of the proletariat in its struggle with the bourgeoisie, at once a reaction and a protest against subjugation by a more powerful class. Its origins may be traced to the medieval guild system when journeymen, denied membership in craft guilds by masters, organized crude secret societies to protect their interests. The unprivileged medieval peasants revolted repeatedly against intolerable conditions, only to be suppressed. Without leadership, without cohesion, unaware of their latent strength, they had to endure centuries of oppression. The urban proletarians also suffered the misery of an oppressed class. At first they struck out blindly against the new machines, but such sporadic destruction and the burning of a few factories could neither provide any solution for workers' problems nor prevent the march of industrialization. Gradually, there arose among peasants and workers consciousness of a shared class, a feeling that they were united by common economic and social aspirations. This sense of potential power in class unity produced new demands for a share in human dignity. There were many trial-and-error efforts to develop new social movements: fraternal orders, savings banks, insurance companies, and cooperative producing and purchasing societies. But by far the most significant innovations were trade unions and socialism.

With the concentration of population in the cities, workers could discuss their wrongs and plan collectively for redress of grievances. Convinced that casual uprisings were ineffective and realizing that strength lay in numbers, they saw organization as the logical solution of their problems. The first trade unions, organized along occupational lines, included only skilled craftsmen and artisans. A later form was the industrial union, including unskilled and semi-skilled as well as skilled workers. Once the workers found that they could obtain real immediate gains through organi-

zation, they flocked to the unions in great numbers.

The development of trade unionism was conditioned by national or regional differences in social and economic organization. Britain, the first country to become industrialized, was also the first to create a labor movement. When the process of industrialization gathered momentum in the late eighteenth century, workers' societies appeared among urban craftsmen, factory workers, and miners. Parliament, frightened by the implications of the French Revolution, passed the Combination Acts (1799 and 1800), which forbad political agitation among industrial workers to obtain higher wages or shorter hours. Urban craftsmen for the most part were left undisturbed, but factory workers and miners were forbidden to organize. Yet, despite legal persecution, trade unions flourished. Agitation in support of unions led, in 1824, to a comprehensive act repealing the prohibitions of combination and, in 1825, to an act recognizing the right of combination. From then on trade unionism developed rapidly, especially after the Reform Bill of 1832, which raised labor's hopes of political gains. New unions were established, especially among the coal miners, while others were amalgamated. The progress of unionism was closely allied with the struggle for the extension of the franchise. After the economic depressions of the 1870's and 1880's, trade unionism advanced rapidly.

Trade unionism on the Continent lagged behind that in Britain. The spread of trade unions in Germany was deferred until the middle 1860's, when the acceleration of German industrial growth first became apparent. But development thereafter was relatively slow, in part because of the persistence of the guild system. In France, trade-union activity was restricted by the Le Chapelier Law of 1791, which was not finally revoked until 1884. Nevertheless, workers' organizations were tolerated, and appeared in most industries. The slow development of trade unionism in France may be explained by the facts that the French maintained an approximate balance between industrial and agricultural pursuits, that wage earners were scattered in small workshops, and that many workers were employed in government-controlled industries. In Belgium, Austria, Switzerland, and the Netherlands, trade-union activity paralleled the development of industrialization. In Russia, Spain, and Portugal, which remained mostly agricultural, there was no active unionism comparable to that in Britain and the more highly industrialized countries on the Continent.

Trade unions were used by workers primarily to bargain with the owners of the means of production. Later, a movement appeared for the elimination of capitalism through revolutionary political activity. Socialism progressed rapidly in periods of economic crises and unemployment. The weapon of revolution, appearing on the Continent, was used to the greatest extent there. In Britain the labor movement proceeded along evolutionary, or reformist, lines.

Meaning of Socialism. Socialism is a political doctrine and movement which advocates the partial or complete abolition of private property and the establishment of society upon a common ownership of some or all of the means of production, distribution, and exchange. It aims to replace competition by cooperation, and profit-seeking by social service, and to distribute income and social opportunity more equitably. Oscar Jászi summarizes socialist theory as follows: first, a condemnation of the existing social and political order as unjust (that is, that the worker is not rewarded with food and goods in proportion to his merits, indeed is often deprived of them); second, support of a "new order consistent with moral values"; third, a belief that the ideal may be realized; fourth, a conviction that the difficulties of the present economic order may be traced to corrupt institutions; fifth, a program of action leading toward the successful institution of a new order; and sixth, a revolutionary will to carry out this program.

Communism, the more radical variation of socialism, contends that revolution must precede good order, and that a dictatorship is essential to obtain national equality. Communists openly repudiate socialist notions of gradual change and proclaim that the existing capitalist system must be torn down, no mat-

ter how great the immediate cost, before a new one can be devised. Russian communism, successful in revolution and the establishment of a dictatorship, used education and propaganda to achieve its end, but apparently there was no lessening of the need for dictatorship. Communism throughout the world is promoted by those who find socialist teachings not sufficiently forceful.

Socialist Objections to Capitalism. While socialists differ among themselves on proper methods of realizing their social ideal, they agree on what is wrong with capitalist society. Capitalism, they say, is a system based upon the law of the jungle, in which the individual works for himself without any regard for the welfare of the vast majority of his fellows. By its very nature, they argue, capitalism leads to waste in production, incompetence and corruption in government, and maldistribution of the products of labor. Free competition and unregulated production result, they further believe, in a chaotic economic system that provides no security for the masses. They hold that the worker, who has a major share in production, receives much less for his work than he deserves; the "iron law of wages," a principle of capitalistic production, keeps labor at a subsistence level. Moreover, they point out, the conflicting interests of capitalists in various countries lead to imperialistic wars. To combat what they call an unreasonable, illogical, and inequitable system, socialists call for elimination of capitalism and the creation of an international socialist state.

Defense of Capitalism. Defenders of the capitalist order reject these arguments as fallacious. To the charge that capitalism is based on the law of the jungle, they reply that nothing satisfactory has yet been devised to take the place of competition as a regulator of production. To the contention that capitalism is wasteful and that it results in an unequal distribution of wealth, they answer that, nevertheless, it has been responsible for a generally higher standard of living, and that all classes have been benefited by the availability of large supplies of machine-made articles. They reject the accusation of incompetent leadership, and bring the countercharge that any form of collectivism is burdened by even greater inefficiency. Finally, answering the argument that capitalism breeds wars, they point to the constant warfare that occurred in such noncapitalistic forms of society as feudalism.

2. Socialism Before Marx

Pre-Marxian Socialism. The idea of socialism was not new. Precursors of Marx wrote of socialism in metaphysical and religious rather than economic terms. In his *Republic,* Plato described an ideal society which, although essentially aristocratic, was based on communal ownership of wealth. In his *Utopia* (1516), Thomas More, distressed by the misery of the peasantry, projected an ideal society with a community of goods, work for all, and a philosophy placing the welfare of the community above that of the individual. The pre-Reformation Albigensians and Lollards preached a kind of socialism, while the Anabaptists founded communist societies on a Christian basis. But these movements were essentially religious in character, not economic.

Utopian Socialism. With the Industrial Revolution came unsanitary factory conditions, wretched housing, and mass misery. Utopian socialism arose to meet these new problems. Claude Henri de Saint-Simon (1760–1825) recommended a social system in which each man would be placed according to his capacity and rewarded according to his works. He denounced exploitation of the masses by industrial lords, demanded abolition of the law of inheritance, and called for transfer of property rights from the family to the State. Economic forces, he said, should be harnessed for the welfare of all the people.

Another Frenchman, François Fourier (1772–1837), urged the formation of social units for an improved society. Describing free competition and individualism as immoral, he recommended collective effort. All society would be divided into departments, or phalanges, each numbering about 1,600 persons, each having common occupations, and each dividing its common produce among the workers.

François Fourier, Utopian Socialist whose theories were responsible for the founding of a number of cooperative communities, both in Europe and in America. This painting by E. Gigoux is in the *Louvre.*

Fourier was responsible for about forty short-lived semi-socialistic communities, most in Europe and some in America. All his life he waited in vain for a wealthy benefactor to step forward and support a test of his theories.

Robert Owen (1771–1858), an English businessman and philanthropist, tried to organize cooperative communities along socialistic lines. There would be unlimited prosperity, he said, if disorderly competition were eliminated. His cotton mills at New Lanark, Scotland, were showplaces of cleanliness, in contrast to the demoralizing conditions of most factories. Social reformers, statesmen, even royal personages made pilgrimages to New Lanark to observe the wonders there. Owen recommended the foundations of communities from 500 to 3,000 persons, mostly agricultural, but possessing the best machinery. Members would work and live according to communal principles. He hoped that such communities would branch into federations, until the whole world was included in a new Utopian society.

In 1825 Owen transferred his activities to America. He founded a cooperative colony at New Harmony, Indiana, as a model for a rational system of society. Beset by jealousies among its members and by factional disputes, the experiment was abandoned after four years. Owen, with most of his fortune lost, returned to England.

Utopian socialism did not appeal to either capitalists or workers. The former dreaded radical change, the latter were confused by an idea they understood imperfectly. Utopian socialists were ridiculed as impractical visionaries whose humanitarianism was granted but whose common sense was questioned. They failed in their goal of superimposing a new social structure on the older one. Though it practically ceased to exist after the mid-nineteenth century, Utopian socialism left behind it a heritage of ideas that strongly influenced social reform. It gave substance to the formation of a social conscience by supporting a new right—the right to work. Utopian socialist schemes failed, but they nevertheless set into motion the socialist movement.

Christian Socialism. In England of the 1830's and 1840's a type of social dissent known as Christian socialism won followers among both Catholics and Protestants. Appalled by the evils that followed in the wake of industrialism, the Christian socialists were imbued with two ideals: (1) to eliminate the evils of capitalism; and (2) to bring the workers back to religion and away from the anti-Christian movements of the day. They found it impossible to reconcile capitalism "based on selfishness" with the Christian principle of brotherly love. They felt that because capitalism regarded labor as a commodity instead of an activity, it violated the Christian principle of human dignity. An economic system based on fraternity, said the Christian socialists, would be more in harmony with the ideals of Christianity.

In England the recognized leaders of Christian socialism were Frederick Denison Maurice (1805–1872), a cleric, and Charles Kingsley (1819–1875), also a clergyman and novelist. Among Catholics the movement came to be called Social Catholicism, which began in Germany during the late nineteenth century and then spread to other parts of Europe. One of its pioneers was Wilhelm Emmanuel von Ketteler (1811–1877), who urged that the Christian principles of justice, charity, and the common good could solve the social problem. In 1891 Pope Leo XIII, in his encyclical, *Rerum novarum,* officially committed the Church to policies designed to advance the welfare of the working class.

Another version of Christian socialism appeared in Germany under the auspices of a fiery demagogue, the court chaplain Adolf Stoecker (1835–1909). Stoecker's Christian socialism had little in common with that of Kingsley and the English form. Stoecker, a fanatical and unbending German nationalist, wanted to inculcate the worker with Christian ideals and love for the Fatherland, which had been undermined, he said, by the Social Democrats. Stoecker's movement was rigidly anti-Semitic.

3. *Karl Marx and Scientific Socialism*

The Marxian Synthesis. Although Greek and Roman thinkers and the early Christian Fathers criticized private property and advocated common ownership, modern socialism derives more directly from the eighteenth-century Enlightenment. Socialist thought in the pre-Marxian era was essentially moral or religious in nature; it now became "scientific." The founders of scientific socialism were Karl Marx (1818–1883) and Friedrich Engels (1820–1895), German publicists who jointly composed the *Communist Manifesto* (1848). The manifesto traced the history of the working-class movement, surveyed existing socialist literature, and explained the outlines of communism. It denounced all existing socialist movements as bourgeois, and gave to the Marxian movement the name *communism.* (See page 571.)

The elements of Marxian theory were presented in Marx's *Das Kapital*, the first volume of which was published in 1867, the second, third, and fourth appearing posthumously in 1885. Some elements of scientific socialism existed before Marx and Engels, but generally independently of one another. Plato spoke of the class struggle; Turgot described surplus value. Utopian socialists wrote about the growing misery of the proletariat, the concentration of capital, and business crises, Marx and Engels synthesized and completed these ideas and fashioned them into a revolutionary ideology.

Economic Interpretation of History. The first principle of the Marxian synthesis was a materialist conception of historical forces. Economic forces are basic; all major changes in history result from changes in the mode of production of life's necessities, and the resultant changes in men's relations to each other in production—that is, in the class composition of society. Social, political, religious, and cultural institutions make up merely a superstructure on the economic foundation. In other words, man's spiritual life is dependent upon and derivative from his material life. Social, political, religious, and cultural forces may hasten, retard, or modify the development of the means and methods of production and human relations in production, and thus strongly influence the course of history. When the economic structure changes, the superstructure must also change. But since the class structure of society is highly resistant to modification, political and social developments lag behind economic change. The resultant disharmony, being contrary to natural law, forces a drastic readjustment, usually through revolution. Then the old superstructure of society crashes in ruins, and a new one, "more in harmony with economic conditions," comes into existence.

Class Struggle. Marx saw the process by which this readjustment is accomplished as the class struggle. The philosophical basis was Hegelian dialectic. Hegel conceived of history as a continuous conflict of ideas: each idea (thesis) has its negation (antithesis), and out of the resulting struggle between them arises a new and higher idea (synthesis), which then

becomes a new thesis, to do battle in its turn. The history of civilization, said Hegel, is the story of this conflict of ideas, from the time of the oriental despots to that of "the highest form of society—the Prussian monarchy." Marx accepted the general form of Hegelian dialectic, but for the battle of ideas he substituted the struggle of economic forces and classes. Marx "stood Hegel on his head." One class, elevated to power by economic forces, automatically brings into existence an antagonistic class. History, according to Marx, is a conflict between opposing classes, between master and slave, lord and peasant, and capitalist and worker. With power concentrated in the capitalists' hands, the proletariat becomes consolidated, develops a will of its own opposing that of its master, turns upon its oppressors, and finally overthrows them. Then, said Marx, the workers form a new sociopolitical superstructure more in harmony with the forces of production.

Inevitability of Socialism. This revolutionary change, Marx insisted, was inevitable, as surely as night follows day. It is useless in the long run to attempt to prevent the creation of a new society which is already developing in the body of the old. Either the new class, representing new economic forces, triumphs, or society itself crashes in ruins after fratricidal strife. The rationalists of the late eighteenth century had applied the idea of natural law to nature, religion, government, and society; Marx claimed to go one step further by applying it to history. History thus becomes a science; the broad trends of the future, according to Marx, can be predicted. In his view, the predictable approaching revolution will be final: it will emancipate the last class in history and create a classless society. Man's primitive period will end, and he "will make the final leap from the realm of necessity into the realm of freedom."

Concept of Surplus Value. The theory of surplus value, the fourth main tenet of Marxian socialism, was the principal theme of *Das Kapital*. In Marx's view, a commodity produced under capitalistic enterprise is "a mass of congealed labor-time." The value of a commodity is determined primarily by the amount of socially necessary labor required to manufacture it. The modern worker produces more than enough to provide for himself a decent standard of living, but he is paid only a subsistence wage, the current market price for the labor power consumed. The capitalist keeps for himself the greater share of the proceeds. The residue left after the worker is paid his small pittance, Marx termed surplus value; from this the capitalist draws his interest, rents, and profit. If the laborer works 10 hours a day, and only 5 hours' labor are needed to pay for his subsistence, he creates surplus value for his employer in the amount of 5 hours' labor. The worker must perform this extra work for the capitalist, who owns and controls the means of production, or else give up his job to another worker from the growing industrial reserve army of the unemployed.

Internationalism. Marx saw his theory in terms of internationalism. He believed that all the workers of the world are comrades, members of that class that have "the historic mission of bringing about a better social order." Their interests, he said, transcend the limits of national loyalties. The national interests of workers are identical with their international interests. He urged a new battle-cry: "The proletarians have nothing to lose but their chains. They have a world to win. Workingmen of all countries, unite!"

Historical Controversy: Critique of Marxism. The Marxian analysis of the nature of history and society, and the Marxian prognostications, were attacked by critics as incorrect. Anti-Marxists declare that the economic interpretation of history is exaggerated, since political, social, cultural, and religious factors are often much more than mere "ideological veils" for the fundamental economic factors. Moreover, they say, the concept of materialism fails to take into consideration the spiritual elements in human nature.

Critics of Marxism further argue that upon close examination the concept of the class struggle falls down, because the stratification of society into classes has never been complete. There are not two general classes, but many,

and the interests of some social groups merge imperceptibly with those of the others. To the Marxian contention that socialism is inevitable, critics maintain that nothing in historical development is absolutely certain. They say that the thesis of inevitability makes of history an exact science, which they believe it never has been and cannot possibly be. Moreover, the concept of inevitability fails to take into account the highly accidental factors whose nature is difficult to prophesy.

Critics also reject the theory of surplus value on the ground that it does not take into consideration the important part played by capital in creating value. The capitalists deserve the greater share of profits, they claim, because they give leadership and direction to enterprise. Finally, critics deny that the worker's first obligation is to his international class. On the contrary, they say, his first concern generally has been, and should be, the country of his birth. In times of crisis, they contend (for example, in 1914), the workers invariably rally to the defense of their own countries. (*See page 573.*)

4. *Diffusion: The Development of Socialism*

Segmentation Among Socialists: Revisionist Marxism. The course of Marxism was rough and uneven. The emergence of hostile factions may be explained in part by varying degrees of class consciousness in different countries and in part by differences in national cultures. German socialists, precise, thorough, and disciplined, were impressed by the rigid architecture of the Marxian synthesis, while the British and French, more deeply grounded in the principles of freedom and individual rights, were slow to accept a system in which individualism was discarded in favor of collectivism.

Toward the end of the nineteenth century came a dissent from Marxian precepts when a movement arose among socialists to reconcile the principles and methods of the socialist movement in the light of historical changes that had taken place. Arising in Germany, it was known as Revisionism because it sought to revise the doctrines of Karl Marx. Its leading protagonist was Eduard Bernstein (1850–1932), who believed that the class struggle was diminishing, that Marx's theories, therefore, must be revised to meet existing conditions, and that the socialist parties should work for the gradual transformation of capitalism rather than support a revolutionary program. Bernstein and Jean Jaurès in France were economic determinists who believed that capitalism, with alterations, might provide adequately for the working class. Bernstein emphasized the lasting value of liberalism and urged the Social Democratic Party to emancipate itself from outworn dogma. His revisionism was the German version of English Fabian socialism.

Marxism in Germany. Marxism took deep root in Germany, homeland of its initiator. In 1863 Ferdinand Lassalle (1825–1864) founded the General Workmen's Union with a simple program: a demand for universal suffrage. In 1869, Marx's followers, August Bebel (1840–1913) and Wilhelm Liebknecht (1826–1900), organized the Social Democratic Labor Party at Eisenach and announced its support for Marx's International. Division among the two groups continued until 1875, when they were joined together at Gotha to form the German Social Democratic Party. Bismarck's Anti-Socialist Law, promulgated in 1878, although it continued in force until his resignation in 1890, failed to prevent the growth of socialism. The Erfurt Program, adopted in 1891, was wholly Marxist in character.

Marxism in France. French Utopian socialism was succeeded by experiments in insurrectionary organization. Louis Blanc (1811–1882), who recommended a system of national workshops, and Pierre Joseph Proudhon (1809–

The "Sideshow of Socialist Ideas," a caricature by Bertall, pokes fun at Fourier, Proudhon, Louis Blanc, and a variety of other socialist thinkers and their ideas in general.

1865), who favored trade unions and coopera-tives without suppressing capitalism, set the stage for the French Revolution of 1848. After the publication of the first volume of Marx's *Das Kapital* (1867), it was not certain whether the international organization of socialists would become Proudhonist or Marxist. The suppression of the Paris Commune in 1871 led to a weakening of the French socialist move-ment, but it recovered from the debacle despite conflicting ideologies. Proudhonism was revived at the end of the nineteenth cen-tury in the form of syndicalism.

Marxism in England: Fabian Socialism and Guild Socialism. Marxism never won enthusi-astic support among the British working class. British trade unionism preferred cautious prog-ress to revolutionary tactics. In 1884, with the formation of the Fabian Society by Sidney Webb (1858–1947) and his wife, Beatrice Pot-ter Webb (1858–1943), British socialism took on a moderate evolutionary character. The word *Fabian* was derived from the Roman general Fabius, who refused to meet Hannibal in battle and preferred to weaken him through delaying tactics. The Webbs, together with the dramatist George Bernard Shaw (1856–1950), were dissatisfied with both the policies of liberalism and Marxian socialism. They re-jected the ideas of revolution and class conflict. They refused to accept the Marxian concept of surplus value, and held instead that value is determined by utility. The socialist state, they said, would come whenever the prole-tariat was sufficiently educated to vote it into power.

Fabianism converted British socialism from propaganda for social revolution to a realiz-able program for the the working-class move-ment. English socialism became synonymous with Fabianism. In the 1900's, Fabians founded the Labour Party, whose first platform was distinctly Fabian in character. This platform had four basic measures, known as the "Four Pillars of the House": (1) universal enforce-ment of a national minimum; (2) the demo-cratic control of industry; (3) a revolution in national finance; and (4) the surplus for the common good. Fabianism became an outlet for radical social ideas not only for the Labour Party but also for its opponent, the Conserva-tive Party. The great success of Fabianism came with the establishment of the Welfare State during the ministry (1945–1951) of a Fabian, Clement Attlee. This guaranteed a minimum level of subsistence from cradle to grave.

Another characteristically British variation of socialism was Guild socialism, which flour-ished during the first quarter of the twentieth century. One of its early leaders, G. D. H. Cole (1889–1959), was leader of the Fabian So-ciety from 1939–1946. Guild socialism had three major beliefs: (1) it was opposed to the Marxian concept of the dictatorship of the proletariat; (2) labor was not a commodity; and (3) workers should try to advance their cause within capitalism and through trade unions. The wage system, said the Guild social-ists, was worse than slavery because it was responsible for the economic evil of insecurity. The working class could be emancipated only through abolition of the wage system. The transition to the new order would be both gradual and peaceful. There would be no di-rect action as advocated by syndicalists, no revolutionary uprisings as suggested by Marx-ists. Instead, there would be "encroaching control," by which labor would wrest power bit by bit from the capitalists.

Guild socialists advised labor to negotiate collective bargaining agreements which would allow them to participate in the organization of production, in choosing supervisors, and in hiring and firing workers. Meanwhile, the gov-ernment would levy heavy taxes on the wealthy classes. Inevitably, the capitalists would be forced out of business. Labor unions would then take over in the form of "National Guilds." These democratic guilds would carry on the affairs of industry.

Few British workers responded to Guild socialism. It lasted only for about a genera-tion. To social thought it contributed the idea that freedom and equality can be won only when economic power is not concentrated in any one class or in the government.

Marxism in Russia. Marxism in Russia had to contend with the popularity of anarchism, which was opposed to formal government of any kind. Early in the twentieth century the Social Democratic movement in Russia split into two hostile groups: the Mensheviks (minority), who favored a loose organization and opposed the peasantry as a "reactionary mass," and the Bolsheviks (majority), who wanted a closely-knit party and called the peasantry the logical ally of the urban proletariat. The Bolsheviks, under Lenin, formed the Communist Party, which advocated a quick and direct shift to the proletarian state. The Mensheviks, after the fall of tsardom in 1917, favored collaboration with the bourgeoisie in setting up a constitutional republic. The first practical experimentation in applied Marxism began in November 1917, when the Soviet of Workers' and Soldiers' Deputies, under Communist leadership, seized power.

An anti-communist cartoon in the United States, 1874. This drawing by Thomas Nast reveals a deadly communist "Emancipator of Labor" trying to fool honest working-people.

Socialist Organization. The First International, or the International Working Men's Association, was founded by Karl Marx in London in 1864. In the next decade branches of the First International were established in one country after another. These organizations consisted of a conglomeration of radicals of all kinds, including anarchists. The First International, unable to survive the fall of the Paris Commune in 1871, quietly expired in 1876. After its dissolution, the history of the socialist movement became one of separate national movements. In 1889 the Second International, an organization of national socialist parties, was founded on the principle that each country must be educated separately in the ideals of socialism before an international state could be constructed. With the outbreak of World War I in 1914, the parties of the Second International split over the question of support for their respective governments in the war. In all countries except Russia, the factions favoring support of their national governments gained control. The Second International crumbled. In 1919, after the Bolshevik Revolution, the Third, or Communist International, was founded on the principles of international communism. The Communist parties of all countries were considered to be members of the Third International, with its headquarters in Moscow.

After the triumph of Stalin over Leon Trotsky and the expulsion of the latter from Russia, Trotsky proclaimed the birth of the Fourth International. He charged that Stalin had reverted to a system of national communism, and asserted that he himself advocated the only true internationalism. The relatively weak Trotskyist movement was dealt a crippling blow by the assassination of its leader in Mexico in 1940.

5. Other Movements of Social Dissent

Anarchism: From Godwin to Kropotkin. Anarchism went beyond Marxism in a spirit of total dissent. Its basic idea was the doctrine of the sovereignty of the individual, the complete liberty of every individual to do as he pleased. It was opposed to any institutions holding coercive authority. Such institutions, whether they were the state, property, or family were to be destroyed. Worst of all, in the anarchist view, was the state, which was the complete expression of coercion. In a free society the social order would permit the complete development of the individual. Religion, considered to be the handmaiden of the state, was to be abolished. The system of private property, according to anarchism, was another source of despotism which should be eliminated. In addition, anarchism denounced the marriage system as authoritarian, because it made the husband a master, the wife a slave, and the unhappy child a victim of both.

Various schools of anarchism emerged with different ideas on how to establish anarchism. These ranged all the way from peaceful to violent. The philosophical anarchists believed that the system was to be established slowly and through persuasion. Another school favored social revolution with resultant confiscation of property and abolition of the state. The most extreme group called for terror and violence against rulers, statesmen, and capitalists, especially by assassination.

Anarchistic tendencies were revealed in the writings of William Godwin (1756–1836), an Englishman who began his career as a Presbyterian minister. Sympathizing with English radicalism and with the French Revolution, Godwin taught that government is not an end in itself and that man's true growth should be toward emancipation from authority. His repudiation of the state became the starting point of anarchist agitation, though he never used the word "anarchism." The first self-styled anarchist was Pierre Joseph Proudhon (1809–1865). In his famous work *What Is Property?*, Proudhon denounced the state as "that fictitious being, without intelligence, without morality." Democracy, he said, was merely "the idea of the state indefinitely extended." Property, he said, was "robbery." When men became just, free, and equal, there would no longer be a need for government. In the future he saw a classless, libertarian social order which he called "mutualism": property would be abolished, and rent, profit, and interest would disappear.

In the early nineteenth century, anarchism was a vague, ideological concept represented by isolated thinkers. But in the second half of the century it developed into an organized movement due mainly to two Russian intellectuals, Michael Bakunin (1814–1876) and Peter Kropotkin (1842–1921). Bakunin advocated the destruction of any institutions which discouraged the operation of natural law. Born in an aristocratic family, he became active in revolutionary movements. Although personally opposed to violence, he was convinced, nevertheless, that anarchism could not be established without a baptism of blood. To his followers he became known as the "apostle of universal destruction." Kropotkin, another aristocrat turned revolutionist, held similar views, but without Bakunin's passion and belief in violence. Kropotkin recommended the village community as the ideal unit of society. He was venerated by British and French intellectuals for his noble character and personal integrity.

The negative quality of anarchism discouraged support of its doctrines. Moreover, many were alienated by its outbursts of violence. In 1894 the Italian anarchist Caserio assassinated the French President, Marie François Sadi Carnot (1837–1894), at Lyons. In 1900 another Italian anarchist, named Bresci, killed King Humbert I of Italy (1844–1900), at Monza. In 1901, in Buffalo, New York, a Polish anarchist, Leon Czolgosz, shot William McKinley (1843–1901), twenty-fifth president of the United States. These and other outrages led to the decline of anarchism at the beginning of the twentieth century.

Syndicalism: The Idea of Direct Action. The main tenet of anarchism—the repudiation of the state—became the heritage of syndicalism, a revolutionary labor movement beginning in the first decade of the twentieth century. The founders of syndicalism were dissatisfied French anarchists who believed that anarchism had only limited appeal for the working class. Like socialism, syndicalism sought to destroy the capitalist system and replace it by a cooperative social order. The word "syndicalism" itself was derived from the French word, *syndicat*, meaning labor union. From Marxism, syndicalism took the doctrine of the class struggle. The key role in this struggle was assigned to the labor union, created by the workers for their own interest. The union would wage class warfare through "direct action." This would emancipate the working class and fulfill its function by forming the "cells of the future society." Syndicalists would work within the realm of the possible: they considered capture of the shop as more important than the anarchist goal of capturing the state.

According to the syndicalist view, the strike—direct action—was the most powerful weapon in the war against capitalism. This would demonstrate the unity and power of organized workers. Strikes in the coal, steel, or railway industries could paralyze an entire nation. Even if the strike were lost, it would be a success in that invariably and inevitably it would promote the cause of workers' emancipation. When workers were not on strike, they could substitute for direct action any form of sabotage (from the French word, *sabot,* a wooden shoe; during a strike, a worker would throw a *sabot* into a machine to ruin it).

The most influential advocate of syndicalism was Georges Sorel (1847–1922), a French social philosopher. Influenced by the anarchist philosophy of Proudhon and Bakunin, Sorel denied the belief in progress and advocated instead "a heroic conception of life." In his *Reflections on Violence* (1908) Sorel described the great conflict of the twentieth century as that between a decadent bourgeoisie and a virile proletariat. He was certain that capitalism could be destroyed only through decisive force. Violence in class war, he said, was as legitimate as in a national war.

Syndicalist philosophy permeated the French General Confederation of Labor (*Confédération Générale du Travail,* abbreviated as C.G.T.), founded in 1895. In 1906 the C.G.T. created a national panic when it called a general strike. In the United States in 1905 a syndicalist body, the Industrial Workers of the World (I.W.W.) was organized in opposition to the American Federation of Labor.

Syndicalism never had more than limited support. It collapsed in the period following World War I. Its leaders turned either to communism or fascism.

⟩{ KEY DOCUMENT }⟨

THE COMMUNIST MANIFESTO, 1848

Karl Marx and Friedrich Engels, *Manifesto of the Communist Party,* authorized English translation, edited and annotated by Friedrich Engels (Charles S. Kerr and Company, Chicago, n.d.), pp. 1–59, *passim.*

THE ESSENTIALS of Marxian theory were set forth in the *Communist Manifesto* issued in 1848 by an organization known as the Communist League. It was drawn up by Karl Marx (1818–1883) and Friedrich Engels (1820–1895) as a kind of party platform for an international gathering of workingmen in London. The pamphlet traced the history of the working-class movement, surveyed critically the existing socialist literature, and explained the outlines of communism. Starting with the materialistic interpretation of history and using Mill's labor theory of value, Marx and Engels spoke of an inescapable class struggle, the inevitable triumph of the proletariat, and the establishment of the Communist state. Further elaboration of the main elements of Marxian theory was made in Marx's monumental work, *Das Kapital* (1867–1894). Following are extracts from the *Communist Manifesto.*

A spectre is haunting Europe—the spectre of Communism. All the powers of old Europe have entered into a holy alliance to exorcize this spectre; Pope and Czar, Metternich and Guizot, French Radicals and German police-spies.

Where is the party in opposition that has not been decried as communistic by its opponents in power? Where the Opposition that has not hurled back the branding reproach of Communism, against the more advanced opposition parties, as well as against its reactionary adversaries?

Two things result from this fact.

I. Communism is already acknowledged by all European Powers to be itself a Power.

II. It is high time that Communists should openly, in the face of the whole world, publish their views, their aims, their tendencies, and meet this nursery tale of the spectre of Communism with a Manifesto of the party itself.

To this end, Communists of various nationalities have assembled in London, and sketched the following manifesto, to be published in the English, French, German, Italian, Flemish and Danish languages. . . .

Bourgeois and Proletarians

The history of all hitherto existing society is the history of class struggles.

Freeman and slave, patrician and plebeian, lord and serf, guild-master and journeyman, in a word, oppressor and oppressed, stood in constant opposition to one another, carried on an uninterrupted, now hidden, now open fight, a fight that each time ended, either in a revolutionary reconstitution of society at large, or in the common ruin of the contending classes. . . .

The modern bourgeois society that has sprouted from the ruins of feudal society, has not done away with class antagonisms. It has but established new classes, new conditions of oppression, new forms of struggle in place of the old ones.

Our epoch, the epoch of the bourgeoisie, possesses this distinctive feature: it has simplified the class antagonisms. Society as a whole is more and more splitting up into two great classes directly facing each other: Bourgeoisie and Proletariat. . . .

The bourgeoisie, wherever it has got the upper hand, has put an end to all feudal, patriarchal, idyllic relations. It has pitilessly torn asunder the motley feudal ties that bound man to his "natural superiors," and has left remaining no other nexus between man and man than naked self-interest, than callous "cash payment." It has drowned the most heavenly ecstasies of religious fervor, of chivalrous enthusiasm, of philistine sentimentalism, in the icy water of egotistical calculation. . . .

But not only has the bourgeoisie forged the weapons that bring death to itself; it has also called into existence the men who are to wield those weapons—the modern working class—the proletarians.

In proportion as the bourgeoisie, i.e., capital, is developed, in the same proportion is the proletariat, the modern working class, developed, a class of laborers, who live only so long as they find work, and who find work only so long as their labor increases capital. These laborers, who must sell themselves piecemeal, are a commodity, like every other article of commerce, and are consequently exposed to all the vicissitudes of competition, to all the fluctuations of the market. . . .

But with the development of industry the proletariat not only increases in number, it becomes concentrated in greater masses, its strength grows, and it feels that strength more. The various interests and conditions of life within the ranks of the proletariat are more and more equalized, in proportion as machinery obliterates all distinctions of labor, and nearly everywhere reduces wages to the same low level. The growing competition among the bourgeois, and the resulting commercial crisis, make the wages of the workers ever more fluctuating. . . .

Proletarians and Communists

In what relation do the Communists stand to the proletarians as a whole?

The Communists do not form a separate party opposed to other working-class parties.

They have no interests separate and apart from those of the proletariat as a whole.

They do not set up any sectarian principles of their own, by which to shape and mould the proletarian movement.

The Communists are distinguished from the other working class parties by this only: 1. In the national struggles of the proletarians of the different countries, they point out and bring to the front the common interests of the entire proletariat independently of all nationality. 2. In the various stages of development which the struggle of the working class against the bourgeoisie has to pass through, they always and everywhere represent the interests of the movement as a whole. . . .

Of course, in the beginning, this cannot be effected except by means of despotic inroads on the rights of property, and on the conditions of bourgeois production; by means of measures, therefore, which appear economically insufficient and untenable, but which, in the course of the movement, outstrip themselves, necessitate further inroads upon the old social order, and are unavoidable as a means of entirely revolutionizing the mode of production.

These measures will of course be different in different countries. . . .

In place of the old bourgeois society, with its classes and class antagonisms, we shall have an association, in which the free development of each is the condition for the free development of all. . . .

Position of the Communist in Relation to the Various Existing Communist Parties

The Communists everywhere support every revolutionary movement against the existing social and political order of things.

In all these movements they bring to the front, as the leading question in each, the property question, no matter what its degree of development at the time.

Finally, they labor everywhere for the union and agreement of the democratic parties of all countries.

The Communists disdain to conceal their views and aims. They openly declare that their ends can be attained only by the forcible overthrow of all existing social conditions. Let the ruling classes tremble at a Communist revolution. The proletarians have nothing to loose but their chains. They have a world to win.

Workingmen of all countries, unite!

⤷ HISTORICAL INTERPRETATION ⤶

BERTRAND RUSSELL ON THE FLAWS IN KARL MARX'S THEORIES

Bertrand Russell, *Proposed Roads to Freedom: Socialism, Anarchism and Syndicalism* (New York, 1919), pp. 25–27. By permission of George Allen & Unwin, Ltd.

THE BRITISH philosopher, Bertrand Russell (1872–   ), was one among many who was not convinced that Karl Marx's laws of historical development are correct. In his *Proposed Roads to Freedom,* Russell pointed out the many flaws in Marx's theories.

In actual fact, time has shown many flaws in Marx's theories. The development of the world has been sufficiently like his prophecy to prove him a man of very unusual penetration, but has not been sufficiently like to make either political or economic history exactly such as he predicted that it would be. Nationalism, so far from diminishing, has increased, and has failed to be conquered by the cosmopolitan tendencies which Marx rightly discerned in finance. Although big businesses have grown bigger and have over a great area reached the stage of monopoly, yet the number of shareholders in such enterprises is so large that the actual number of individuals interested in the capitalist system has continually increased. Moreover, though large firms have grown larger, there has been a simultaneous increase in firms of medium size. Meanwhile the wage-earners, who were, according to Marx, to have remained at the bare level of subsistence at which they were in the England of the first half of the nineteenth century, have instead profited by the general increase of wealth, though in a lesser degree than the capitalists. The supposed iron law of wages has been proven untrue, so far as labor in civilized countries is concerned. If we wish now to find examples of capitalist cruelty analogous to those with which Marx's book is filled, we shall have to go for most of our material to the Tropics, or at any rate to regions where there are men of inferior races to exploit. Again: the skilled worker of the present day is an aristocrat in the world of labor. It is a question with him whether he shall ally himself with the unskilled worker against the capitalist, or with the capitalist against the unskilled worker. Very often he is himself a capitalist in a small way, and if he is not so individually, his trade union or his friendly society is pretty sure to be so. Hence the sharpness of the class war has not been maintained. There are gradations, intermediate ranks between rich and poor, instead of the clear-cut logical antithesis between the workers who have nothing and the capitalists who have all.

❧{ TEN BASIC BOOKS }❧

SOCIALISM AND OTHER DISSENTING MOVEMENTS

1. Barzun, Jacques, *Darwin, Marx, Wagner: Critique of a Heritage,* 2nd rev. ed. (New York, 1958).†

2. Carew Hunt, Robert N., *The Theory and Practice of Communism* (London, 1950).

3. Cole, George D. H., *A History of Socialist Thought,* 4 vols. (London, 1953–1956).

4. Hayek, Friedrich, *The Road to Serfdom* (Chicago, 1944, R. 1955).†

5. Hook, Sidney, *Marx and the Marxists: The Ambiguous Legacy,* Anvil Book No. 7 (Princeton, N. J., 1955).†

6. Laski, Harold, *The Communist Manifesto, Socialist Landmark* (London, 1948).

7. Mehring, Franz, *Karl Marx* (New York, 1936).†

8. Plamenatz, John P., *German Marxism and Russian Communism* (New York, 1954).†

9. Schumpeter, Joseph, *Capitalism, Socialism, and Democracy,* 3rd ed. (New York, 1950).†

10. Strachey, John, *Theory and Practice of Socialism* (London, 1936).

PART VII

THE TWENTIETH CENTURY:

WAR—LONG ARMISTICE—WAR

THE REVOLT OF THE MASSES[1]

José Ortega y Gasset

THE KEY TO this analysis is found when . . . we ask ourselves: "Whence have come all these multitudes which nowadays fill to overflowing the stage of history?" Some years ago the eminent economist, Werner Sombart, laid stress on a very simple fact, which I am surprised is not present to every mind which meditates on contemporary events. This very simple fact is sufficient of itself to clarify our vision of the Europe of today, or if not sufficient, puts us on the road to enlightenment. The fact is this: from the time European history begins in the sixth century up to the year 1800—that is, through the course of twelve centuries—Europe does not succeed in reaching a total population greater than 180 million inhabitants. Now, from 1800 to 1914—little more than a century—the population of Europe mounts from 180 to 460 millions. I take it that the contrast between these figures leaves no doubt as to the prolific qualities of the last century. In three generations it produces a gigantic mass of humanity which, launched like a torrent over the historic area, has inundated it. . . .

To the last century, then, falls the glory and the responsibility of having let loose upon the area of history the great multitudes. And this fact affords the most suitable viewpoint in order to judge that century with equity. There must have been something extraordinary, incomparable, in it when such harvests of human fruit were produced in its climate. Any preference for the principles which inspired other past ages is frivolous and ridiculous if one does not previously show proof of having realised this magnificent fact and attempted to digest it. The whole of history stands out as a gigantic laboratory in which all possible experiments have been made to obtain a formula of public life most favourable to the plant "man." And beyond all possible explaining away, we find ourselves face to face with the fact that, by submitting the seed of humanity to the treatment of two principles, liberal democracy and technical knowledge, in a single century the species in Europe has been triplicated.

Such an overwhelming fact forces us, unless we prefer not to use our reason, to draw these conclusions: first, that liberal democracy based on technical knowledge is the highest type of public life hitherto known; secondly, that that type may not be the best imaginable, but the one we imagine as superior to it must preserve the essence of those two principles; and thirdly, that to return to any forms of existence inferior to that of the nineteenth century is suicidal.

Once we recognize this with all the clearness that the clearness of the fact itself demands, we must then rise up against the nineteenth century. If it is evident that there was in it

[1] José Ortega y Gasset, *The Revolt of the Masses* (New York, 1932), pp. 53–63, *passim*. By permission of W. W. Norton & Company.

something extraordinary and incomparable, it is no less so that it must have suffered from certain radical vices, certain constitutional defects, when it brought into being a caste of men—the mass-man in revolt—who are placing in imminent danger those very principles to which they owe their existence. . . .

What is he like, this mass-man who today dominates public life, political and non-political, and why is he like it, that is, how has he been produced?

It will be well to answer both questions together, for they throw light on one another. The man who today is attempting to take the lead in European existence is very different from the man who directed the nineteenth century, but he was produced and prepared by the nineteenth century. Any keen mind of the years 1820, 1850, and 1880 could by simple *a priori* reasoning, foresee the gravity of the present historical situation, and in fact nothing is happening now which was not foreseen a hundred years ago. "The masses are advancing," said Hegel in apocalyptic fashion. "Without some new spiritual influence, our age, which is a revolutionary age, will produce a catastrophe," was the pronouncement of Comte. "I see the flood-tide of nihilism rising," shrieked Nietzsche from a crag of the Engadine. . . .

What appearance did life present to that multitudinous man who in ever increasing abundance the nineteenth century kept producing? To start with, an appearance of universal material ease. Never had the average man been able to solve his economic problem with greater facility. Whilst there was a proportionate decrease of great fortunes and life became harder for the individual worker, the middle classes found their economic horizon widened every day. Every day added a new luxury to their standard of life. Every day their position was more secure and more independent of another's will. What before would have been considered one of fortune's gifts, inspiring humble gratitude towards destiny, was converted into a right, not to be grateful for, but to be insisted on.

From 1900 on, the worker likewise begins to extend and assure his existence. Nevertheless, he has to struggle to obtain his end. He does not, like the middle class, find the benefit attentively served up to him by a society and a state which are a marvel of organisation. To this ease and security of economic conditions are to be added the physical ones, comfort and public order. Life runs on smooth rails, and there is no likelihood of anything violent or dangerous breaking in on it. Such a free, untrammelled situation was bound to instill into the depths of such souls an idea of existence which might be expressed in the witty and penetrating phrase of an old country like ours: "Wide is Castile." That is to say, in all its primary and decisive aspects, life presented itself to the new man as *exempt from restrictions*. The realisation of this fact and of its importance becomes immediate when we remember that such a freedom of existence was entirely lacking to the common men of the past. On the contrary, for them life was a burdensome destiny, economically and physically. From birth, existence meant to them an accumulation of impediments which they were obliged to suffer, without possible solution other than to adapt themselves to them, to settle down in the narrow space they left available.

But still more evident is the contrast of situations, if we pass from the material to the civil and moral. The average man, from the second half of the nineteenth century on, finds no social barriers raised against him. That is to say, that as regards the forms of public life he no longer finds himself from birth confronted with obstacles and limitations. There is nothing to force him to limit his existence. Here again, "Wide is Castile." There are no "estates" or "castes." There are no civil privileges. The ordinary man learns that all men are equal before the law.

Never in the course of history had man been placed in vital surroundings even remotely familiar to those set up by the conditions just mentioned. We are, in fact, confronted with a radical innovation in human destiny, implanted by the nineteenth century. A new stage has been mounted for human existence, new both in the physical and the social aspects. Three principles have made possible this new world: liberal democracy, scientific experiment, and industrialism. The two latter may be summed-up in one word: technicism. Not one of those principles was invented by the nineteenth century; they proceed from the two previous centuries. The glory of the nineteenth century lies not in their discovery, but in their implantation. No one but recognises that fact. But it is not sufficient to recognise it in the abstract, it is necessary to realise its inevitable consequences. . . .

35

The Pattern of the Twentieth Century

22ND DEC.—The old century is very nearly out and leaves the world in a pretty pass, and the British Empire is playing the devil in it as never an empire before on so large a scale. We may live to see its fall. All the nations of Europe are making the same hell upon earth in China, massacring and pillaging and raping in the captured cities as outrageously as in the Middle Ages. The Emperor of Germany gives the word for slaughter and the Pope looks on and approves. In South Africa our troops are burning farms under Kitchener's command, and the Queen and the two Houses of Parliament, and the bench of bishops thank God publicly and vote money for the work. The Americans are spending fifty millions a year on slaughtering the Filipinos; the King of the Belgians has invested his whole fortune on the Congo, where he is brutalizing the Negroes to fill his pockets. The French and Italians for the moment are playing a less prominent part in the slaughter, but their inactivity grieves them. The whole white race is revelling openly in violence, as though it had never pretended to be Christian. God's equal curse be on them all! So ends the famous nineteenth century into which we were so proud to have been born. . . .

31st Dec.—I bid good-bye to the old century, may it rest in peace as it has lived in war.

—WILFRID SCAWEN BLUNT

1. Background: Character of the New Century

The World in 1900. Concurrent with the accelerated tempo of the New Industrial Revolution and the New Imperialism in the closing decade of the nineteenth century came an epidemic of minor imperialistic wars in Africa and Asia. Hitherto, the international struggle for supremacy had been an exclusively European phenomenon, but now the United States and Japan had the status of global powers.

The world entered the twentieth century fearful and divided against itself. The most critical unsolved problem was the threat of war. There was little sense of moral power among the nations, nor was there any international organization capable of settling recurrent disputes between nations. The cumulative achievements of science had brought swift changes in living but also terrible and more destructive weapons. Perfecting the techniques of science went on with vigor, but it was a vitality of fever, not health. There was as yet no adequate answer to the crucial question of how to utilize these techniques. Man had learned to control nearly everything except the savageries of his own nature and the confusions of his governments. The nations of the world competed to make applied science serve as an instrument of national policy.

Added to the threat of war were such unsolved issues as problems of class conflict, poverty, and social justice. The world's wealth had increased immeasurably, but there remained a sizable gap between production and distribution of wealth. In addition to the hazard of international conflicts there was the danger of class warfare inside industrialized nations.

These were the twin challenges of the new century—how to resolve burning animosities on both international and domestic scenes. The world of 1900, seemingly progressive and rich in accomplishment, was on the verge of a series of gigantic struggles. "Everybody's nerves are tense," said Colonel E. M. House, special advisor to President Wilson, in the spring of 1914. "It only needs a spark to set the whole thing off." On the class issue, J. B. Bury, British historian, uttered a solemn warning in 1913: "If a revolutionary movement prevailed, led by men inspired by faith in formulas (like the men of the French Revolution) and resolved to impose their creed, experience shows that coercion would almost inevitably be resorted to." Both predictions were accurate.

The Historical Milieu. The twentieth century has been variously called the Age of Technology, the Age of Nationalism, the Age of Democracy versus Dictatorship, the Age of World Wars, the Age of the Common Man, and the Age of Freud. Each term describes one strand in a historical pattern. Economically, the century saw a broadening of the new Industrial Revolution and rapid developments in communication and transportation. Politically, the period was distinguished by intensification of nationalism and by a struggle between democracy and dictatorship. Militarily, the century saw two gigantic World Wars, whose casualties were considerably greater than the 18,000,000 men lost from the end of eleventh century to the twentieth. Socially, the nineteenth century was preeminently the Age of the Bourgeoisie; the twentieth saw an advance in the status of the proletariat. Psychologically, the twentieth century, under the impulse of Sigmund Freud, marked the beginnings of a scientific investigation of the human psyche, human behavior, and the psychopathology of everyday life. The history of the twentieth century is a combination of all these developments.

Monistic interpretations of history, by their very nature, fit the twentieth century into their particular patterns of causation and motivation. Marxists see the century as fulfilling Karl Marx's prediction of the inevitability of socialism. Arnold J. Toynbee regards it as another phase of his theory of challenge-and-response. Others, notably Pareto, Bergson, and Croce, discuss the century in terms of the rise, maturity, and decay of cultures that have no redeeming faith. Oswald Spengler in his *Decline of the West* saw the present age as one of disillusionment about the past and despair for the future. We are on the downward curve, he said, of another historical cycle such as that which involved the ruin of the ancient Roman Empire and its civilization; cosmos turns to chaos and civilization reverts to barbarism. These monistic views are condemned by the pluralistic school of historical causation on the ground that there are several acceptable concepts of history rather than a single correct one.

Specialists in the history of the twentieth century place emphasis upon different basic developments. J. Salwyn Schapiro sees the twentieth century as not just another century, but as a new era in civilization, like its predecessors, the thirteenth and eighteenth centuries. He feels that more than any previous period the twentieth century is a century of "one world," created by the almost miraculous advance of science and its offspring technology. Hans Kohn finds the central development to be a dichotomy between the spirit of the West (tolerance, compromise, self-criticism, fair-minded objectivity, reasonableness, and individualism) and the spirit of the East (authoritarianism, the cult of force, the dethronement of reason, fanatical faith in the state, infallible leaders, ruthlessness, barbarism, and slavery). This concept is stated also by Sir Harold Butler, who regards the current cold war not as just a conflict between communism and democracy, but as a struggle between the free ideals of Western civilization and the authoritarian ideas of the East—a struggle between peace and power. To Hajo Holborn the collapse of the traditional European system is an irrevocable fact of the twentieth century. What is commonly called the "historic" Europe, he says, is dead and beyond resurrection. Carlton J. H. Hayes saw the world of the twentieth century becoming more unified and contracted in some respects, more fragmented and complex in others. He warned of the central historical (and physical) fact that change always appears much greater at close range than from a distance. "In all probability, the present age of world war, dictatorship, and chaotic art and science will seem to later generations progressively less revolutionary than it appears to us."

The World Situation. The decisive changes of the twentieth century were the decline of Western European supremacy; the deterioration of the British Empire; the new order in Asia; and the rise of the United States and the Soviet Union as leading world powers. Weakened by wars and revolutions and enclosed between the Atlantic and the natural frontiers of Soviet Russia, Europe lost her traditional dominance. In the words of a French historian, Edmond Vermeil: "Uncertain of herself after a shattering war; with little support from an Africa seething with revolt; squeezed between America and Russia, . . . a divided and Balkanized Europe has to struggle to defend herself . . ., but without being able to choose or create a new order strong enough to maintain the balance between the great forces engaged in conflict." Western Europe may recover and resume its position as the fulcrum of world civilization, but at present this seems a remote possibility.

The United States emerged in the twentieth century as the most wealthy and powerful nation on earth. After contributing to final victory in 1918 in World War I, the nation, unfortunately, did not undertake the task of rebuilding a world damaged by four years of war. She had given tremendous material and military aid to her Allies in Europe, but now she withheld the moral support so desperately needed. Rejecting the Wilsonian gospel of a world order, she took refuge in protective isolation. Four years of prosperity were followed by the cataclysmic economic crisis of 1929. The nation recovered under Roosevelt's New Deal, but, in the meantime, an unrepentant Germany was given a second, this time unhoped-for,

chance to drive for world power. Overcoming another wave of isolationism, the American people supported Roosevelt in his resistance to Hitler. Once again, just when she felt herself to be on the verge of victory, Germany, after advancing deep into the Soviet Union, crashed in ruins. After 1945, the phenomenally prosperous United States assumed the mantle of world leadership once held by Great Britain.

Challenge to American dominance came from the Soviet Union. After the Revolution of 1917, the Bolsheviks liquidated all internal opposition and survived foreign intervention. The new political structure of the Soviet Union was rigidly oriented around despotism, mass discipline, fanaticism, terror, and propaganda, all distinguished by a bitter, implacable hatred for the capitalist world. Leninist-Stalinist ideology erased the slate of the past, introduced a new idea of man and society, and denounced the cultural humanism of the West as an outmoded expression of a decadent bourgeois world. Once the Revolution was solidified, world-revolutionary communism was fused with Russian messianic nationalism. Bolshevik totalitarianism sought to convert the entire world—a concept for which Trotsky had been rewarded by an assassin's blows. Russian expansionism was something more than the old Pan-Slavism in a new dress. Stepping into the power vacuum after World War II, the Kremlin spread its tentacles in all directions as its drive for power took on global dimensions. European states were engulfed in a new system of satellites. Soviet ideological influence extended to the Near and Middle East and Southeast Asia.

2. *The New Economic Design*

Age of Technology. The New Industrial Revolution of the late nineteenth century opened great resources of power, expanded production, and enhanced the wealth of the world. The new century saw an almost miraculous advance of science and technology. Time and space were annihilated by new inventions. For the first time in history all parts of the world came into communication with one another. Vast stretches of the earth were telescoped into neighborhoods, and no nation could remain untouched by events on other continents. It seemed that the *humanitas* of the Hellenistic philosophers and the "humanity" of the eighteenth-century rationalists were at last to be realized by the inventions of modern science.

New forms of power appeared in the Age of Technology. A century of steam had been followed by what seemed to be at first a century of petroleum, but very soon after 1900 it became evident that the new era was to be an age of electricity. Cheap electric power unlocked the energy of coal and utilized water to drive an amazing variety of machines. New sources of power stimulated the development of the factory-plant system and the mass production of goods. As man became more and more dependent upon his machines, he had to find the raw materials they required. If he could not find them at home, he had to look abroad. Those nations geared to an agrarian economy were at a disadvantage in this race for natural resources. World equilibrium was unbalanced as dynamic, industrialized states began to compete with one another to satisfy their technological appetites. The appearance of new industrial giants—the United States, Germany, and Japan—was a threat to the prosperity of the older industrialized nations.

The New Capitalism. The twentieth century saw changes in the capitalistic system of production, distribution, and exchange. The new technology called for industrial reorganization in more advanced nations, particularly in Western Europe and the United States. Giant national corporations were transformed into international cartels. Industrial plants were run by a new managerial class. Concurrent with these changes came the rise of large craft and industrial unions. No longer able to stand aside, governments now became supervisors and regulators of economic activities. The older form of liberal capitalism changed to economic planning. Governments, holding strategic positions in economic affairs, stepped in to guide taxing and spending, contracted or expanded bank credit, controlled the issuing of securities, set maximum and minimum pro-

duction schedules, and took measures to conserve natural resources. Whereas the old capitalism had functioned for private interest, the new economic planning was conceived to be in the public's interest.

Twilight of Imperialism. Nineteenth-century imperialism continued into the twentieth century. The insatiable demand of the machines for raw materials made it imperative for the industrial nations to obtain ready access to raw-material sources. The older imperialism of Great Britain and France came into head-on conflict with the new imperialism of Germany, Italy, and Japan. These latter "Have-not" nations were not impressed with the argument that the backward areas of the earth had already been appropriated; they intended to create new colonial empires even at the risk of conflict. The bitterness engendered by these colonial ambitions was one of the primary causes for the two World Wars.

3. *Kaleidoscope: A Changing World*

Political Heritage. The twentieth century inherited from the nineteenth the concept of democracy, with its accent upon human rights and fundamental freedoms, as well as constitutional and representative government. In Western Europe, particularly in Britain and France, and in North America, the functioning of democracy was marked by extension of the franchise and the supremacy of representative institutions. Imperial Russia, however, remained an absolute monarchy based on divine right and run by an inefficient and corrupt bureaucracy. Bismarckian Germany, despite its constitution, was in fact a semi-autocracy. Democracy was virtually unknown in Asia, Africa, and Latin America. Nationalism, in the nineteenth century almost inseparable from democracy, gradually lost its liberal character and became more and more integral in nature as dissatisfied nationalities sought to implement their national yearnings. The problems of national self-determination remained unsolved, especially in Europe, where subject peoples demanded freedom from the Russian, Austrian, and Ottoman empires. As the century opened, stirrings of nationalist movements began in India, China, Egypt, and Africa. A remarkable nationalistic transformation had already taken place in Japan, where a backward, feudal people, within two decades after 1868, became a sovereign, national state on the Western model. National minorities all over the world demanded independence in the age of nationalism.

Coalitions and Balance of Power. From the nineteenth century the twentieth inherited a system of international relations based on balance of power. The nations of the world were divided into three ranks—the great powers, the middle-sized powers, and the small powers. If any attempt were made to disturb this balance, the other nations would combine in coalition to prevent aggrandizement. This system was successful in preventing a great world war, but it was not strong enough to stop a multitude of civil and national wars. Burning international animosities were churned up for a hundred years before 1914. Except for the weak Hague Court of Arbitration founded in 1899, there was no effective international organization. The world atmosphere was embittered and international confidence was undermined by rapidly expanding competition in the building up of military forces. Militarism thrived in an atmosphere of sword rattling as all the major nations entered the armament race. French nationalists sought *revanche* for 1871; Russian nationalists, disgusted with a series of diplomatic defeats, attempted to restore their prestige by supporting Pan-Slavism in the Balkans; German nationalists demanded a place in the sun and angered the British by insisting upon the construction of a great navy; and British nationalists supported the *status quo* in the face of growing threats from abroad.

Social Impact of Industrialism. The new industrialism stimulated growth of population, concentration of people in urban areas, rise of metropolitan problems, decline of illiteracy, and the mass-circulation press. The early nineteenth-century class conflict between nobility and bourgeoisie was now succeeded by a strug-gle between the middle class and the proletariat. Once the workers became enfranchised and politically literate, they formed parties to further their interests. Socialism became a militant workers' movement aiming to use political power to advance economic interests. The socialist movement, worldwide in scope, was strongest in those areas which retained a rigid class system, the heritage of feudalism. Trade unions emerged as instruments of collective strength to bargain for the interests of the working class. The pattern of the social fabric, always reflecting the economic status of individual classes, began to change in the era of rising industrialism.

Religion. The idea of religious freedom fashioned in the nineteenth century continued in the twentieth. The American system of separation of Church and State was extended elsewhere, but there were still large areas of the world where there was no religious toleration. The Orthodox religion in Russia discouraged dissenters, and Jews were savagely persecuted. Non-Catholics were subjected to rigid restrictions in Spain, Portugal, and the Latin-American countries. There was mutual hostility among Hindus and Muslims in India.

Intellectual Patterns. The tremendous progress in technical discoveries and the cumulative achievements of science brought about a profound revolution in thought. The intellectual life of the twentieth century was saturated with the new technology. Like the *philosophe* of the Age of Reason, the average man of the early twentieth century was an optimist, certain that civilization was progressing toward higher and higher planes. The next generation would certainly be wiser and better than his own. Many believed that in time liberal ideas would encompass the whole world; they considered progress as inevitable as the growth of a tree. Herbert Spencer had already proclaimed the new age: "Progress is not an accident but a necessity. What we call evil and immorality must disappear. It is certain that man must become perfect." Men of goodwill saw a new world in process of formation. The fact that there had been no *general war* for a century was regarded as indicative of a great future for mankind. Others were less optimistic, warning that new systems of coercion would negate the gains of democratic self-government, national self-determination, religious toleration, and freedom of thought. The explosive Marxian doctrines, emphasizing historical materialism and the inevitability of socialism, provided a new force that was to challenge the optimism of those who foresaw a peaceful world.

Psychological Implications. A well-rounded picture of historical development must include something more than a study of man's economic needs. Modern man attained his intellectual maturity through attempts to think for himself. The magnificent achievements of the Enlightenment were due directly to man's faith in himself and in his own reason. Out of this grew freedom of thought, recognition of the right to disagree, and the rational settlement of arguments and disputes by discussion and compromise.

Gradually over the course of the nineteenth century there arose a growing distrust in reason. Romanticism, at first a protest against rationalism, merged with nationalism. Instead of praising reason and the intellect, the romantic nationalists turned to the heart, and soul, and the blood for inspiration. As a necessary step in national expression, they glorified the past. They were convinced that reason was powerless against such biological forces as instincts. The best chance for survival, they declared, existed in the warmth and friendliness of the homogeneous group in the nation. Stimulated by this type of thinking, masses of men turned to leaders, witch doctors, and demagogues who urged them to "think with the blood" or adopt a perverted "science of history." Human beings accepted the ideas of worshiping the hero and tolerating war. On occasion, they became victims of new forces far more uncompromising in opposition to democracy than had ever been the absolute monarchs of the past.

The twentieth century witnessed a high-water mark in this dethronement of reason and the appeal to myths. This development can be understood better by applying the tools of psychological diagnosis, in terms of moral and intellectual decay. A new scholarly trend may be noted in the emergence of a multi-disciplinary approach to the study of history, by which historians, social psychologists, anthropologists, and sociologists work together to clarify such historical phenomena as national character.

The Decline and Rise of Europe. Europe had become the center of world power. The European Continent, really a peninsula of Asia, reached a dominating position in the nineteenth century. European nations ruled almost all of Africa, Asia, and Australia. People of European background controlled the two great continents in America.

The decay and fall of the Roman Empire was a long drawn out process that took the better part of three centuries before it succumbed to outside forces. But the decline of Europe in the twentieth century was seemingly precipitous and catastrophic. It took only about twenty-five years, and was the result of two world wars. Both World War I and World War II were fought primarily on the European Continent. The nations of Europe were so weakened by the blood-letting that their colonial empires melted away. A large part of Europe lay in ruins. Straight through its heart ran the Iron Curtain, which divided the Continent into a Western and Eastern Europe as in the days before the nineteenth century.

Then came a miraculous recovery. Stimulated by the American Marshall plan, and protected by the shield of NATO (North Atlantic Treaty Organization) against Russian expansion westward, the Continent rose from the ashes. There had been predictions that West Germany, which had been bombed heavily in the late days of World War II, would not recover for generations. But, with her economic pump primed with American money, and with a carefully controlled capitalism in operation, she astonished the world by the success of her revival in slightly more than a decade. Other major Western European countries—Britain, France, and Italy—also regained economic health. It was a grievous disappointment to those theorists who had predicted the inevitability of capitalist collapse after the shattering blow of World War II.

The European Coal and Steel Community, ESC (1951); the European Atomic Energy Community, or Euratom (1956); the European Economic Community, EEC or Common Market (1957); European Free Trade Association, EFTA (1959); all these gave striking evidence of the overwhelming push toward *economic* unity. "Eurocrats," advocates of a political integration of Europe, called for an extension of economic unity into a "United States of Europe." However, although there were many attempts to organize European ideological energy for Continental solidarity, fissiparous nationalism, with its emphasis on fragmentation, persisted. Under the New Nationalism, as under the older form, European nations seemed to be unwilling to relinquish even a small portion of their national sovereignty in favor of an integrated European parliament.

⊰{ KEY DOCUMENT }⊱

PRESIDENT WOODROW WILSON'S PLEA FOR A WORLD ORDER, 1919

In H. W. V. Temperley, ed., *A History of the Peace Conference*, 6 vols. (London, 1920–1924), III, 62–65. By permission of Oxford University Press under the auspices of the Royal Institute of International Affairs.

As CHAIRMAN of a committee to draft a covenant or constitution for a society of nations, President Woodrow Wilson reported back to a plenary session of the Paris Peace Conference on February 14, 1919. The following selection from his speech in presenting the draft reflected the desire of a war-weary world for peace.

Fourteen nations were represented, among them all of those Powers which for convenience we have called the Great Powers, and among the rest a representation of the greatest variety of circumstances and interests. So that I think we are justified in saying that the significance of the result, therefore, had the deepest of all meanings, the union of wills in a common purpose, a union of wills which cannot be resisted, and which, I dare say, no nation will run the risk of attempting to resist.

Now as to the character of the document. While it has consumed some time to read this document, I think you will see at once that it is very simple, and in nothing so simple as in the structure which it suggests for a League of Nations—a body of delegates, an executive council, and a permanent secretariat. . . .

A living thing is born, and we must see to it what clothes we put on it. It is not a vehicle of power, but a vehicle in which power may be varied at the discretion of those who exercise it and in accordance with the changing circumstances of the time. And yet, while it is elastic, while it is general in its terms, it is definite in the one thing that we are called upon to make definite. It is a definite guarantee of peace. It is a definite guarantee by word against aggression. It is a definite guarantee against the things which have just come near bringing the whole structure of civilization to ruin.

Its purposes do not for a moment lie vague. Its purposes are declared, and its powers are unmistakable. It is not in contemplation that this should be merely a League to secure the peace of the world. It is a League which can be used for co-operation in any international matter. . . .

. . . I think I can say of this document that it is at one and the same time a practical document and a human document. There is a pulse of sympathy in it. There is a compulsion of conscience throughout it. It is practical, and yet it is indeed to purify, to rectify, to elevate. And I want to say that, so far as my observation instructs me, this is in one sense a belated document. I believe that the conscience of the world has long been prepared to express itself in some such way. We are not just now discovering our sympathy for these people and our interest in them. We are simply expressing it, for it has long been felt, and in the administration of the affairs of more than one of the great States represented here—so far as I know, all of the great States that are represented here—that humane impulse has already expressed itself in their dealings with their colonies, whose peoples were yet at a low stage of civilization.

We have had many instances of colonies lifted into the sphere of complete self-government. This is not the discovery of a principle. It is the universal application of a principle. It is the agreement of the great nations which have tried to live by these standards in their separate administrations to unite in seeing that their common force and their common thought and intelligence are lent to this great and humane enterprise. I think

it is an occasion, therefore, for the most profound satisfaction that this humane decision should have been reached in a matter for which the world has long been waiting, and until a very recent period thought that it was still too early to hope.

Many terrible things have come out of this war, gentlemen, but some very beautiful things have come out of it. Wrong has been defeated, but the rest of the world has been more conscious than it ever was before of the majority of right. People that were suspicious of one another can now live as friends and comrades in a single family, and desire to do so. The miasma of distrust, of intrigue, is cleared away. Men are looking eye to eye and saying: "We are brothers and have a common purpose. We did not realize it before, but now we do realize it, and this is our covenant of friendship."

❧ HISTORICAL INTERPRETATION ❧

SIMONDS AND EMENY ON THE "HAVES" VERSUS THE "HAVE-NOTS"

Frank H. Simonds and Brooks Emeny, *The Great Powers in World Politics, International Relations and Economic Nationalism,* rev. ed. (New York, 1937), pp. 33–37, *passim.* By permission of American Book Company.

THE NEW CENTURY saw a strong spirit of economic nationalism in most countries of the world. The Great Powers, those who already held control of vital areas, were reluctant to agree to territorial demands of such emerging states as Germany, Italy, and Japan. The idea of "Haves" versus "Have-nots" was popularized by Frank H. Simonds and Brooks Emeny, specialists in international relations, in a standard work.

By reason of their physical circumstances, the Great Powers may be divided into two classes, the "Haves" and the "Have-nots." Of these, the first class, to which the British Empire, France, Russia, and the United States belong, is composed of the nations whose territories are large and rich and whose ethnic unity has been achieved. The second class of Great Powers, which are characterized by lands that are relatively exiguous and poor in material resources, include Japan, Italy, and Germany. In the case of Germany, moreover, the situation is further aggravated by lack of ethnic unity, because of the inclusion of important German minorities within the boundaries of some of Germany's immediate neighbors.

For the first group of states, the Haves which are sated and therefore satisfied, security through

the maintenance of the status quo is the sole objective of national policy. Having, their chief purpose is to hold. For the group of Have-nots, on the other hand, their present situation being precarious, through deprivation of many of the essentials of security and power, the acquisition of what they lack assumes primary consideration.

In theory the existing disparity between the "Have" and "Have-not" Powers might be abolished in one of two ways: the sated states might consent to sacrificing a portion of their territory or that of some smaller nations as a means of restoring the balance of material wealth; or they might share with the "Have-nots" equal rights and security in investment and trade in their own resources. In practice, however, no relief by such means is discoverable for the less fortunate states;

for both solutions run counter to the basic principles of sovereignty, which holds the national territory and the control of its resources to be inalienable. Faithful to that principle, states are rarely willing to cede their land voluntarily to others, and never to surrender any part of their right to the privileged exploitation of their national wealth.

The fact that forty-two millions of French not merely possess a homeland area large and rich enough to satisfy their needs and their aspirations, but also control a vast colonial empire, while a large number of Italians are crowded into a narrow peninsula and were, up to the conquest of Ethiopia, extremely poor in colonial territories, has appeared to Italian thought clearly the consequence of accidents of history and not of the operation of divine law.

In the same way, the fact that the sixty-five millions who constitute the white population of the British Commonwealth own and exploit the well-nigh inexhaustible resources of an empire on which the sun never sets, while the same number of Germans are cooped up in a relatively insignificant and economically insufficient region of Central Europe, is explicable to the German mind only in terms of luck, of the good fortune which enabled Great Britain to achieve national unity centuries before Germany.

It is customary to think of the territory of a state in the same fashion as of the private property of an individual; but it is evident that there is here a double contrast. Within states, courts and police uphold titles and maintain lawful owners in possession of their land, which was acquired by the lawful processes of inheritance, purchase, or barter. By contrast, in the matter of national territory not only is there lacking any international authority to maintain the present owner in possession, but also that nation's title almost invariably derives from war.

In Europe, at least, all present frontiers are derived from former conquests. As a consequence, states which were anciently possessors of provinces, until their eviction through defeat in war, still regard the present tenure as based upon neither legal nor moral warrant. Furthermore, such states are entitled to believe that the present tenure may also prove transitory like the past.

The student of international affairs, then, is confronted with two mutually exclusive conceptions of national policy, the first static, and the second dynamic. Here, too, he also touches the very heart of the problem of peace in the contemporary world, which is posed by the demand of one group of peoples for security based upon the status quo, and of another for a prosperity, prestige, or ethnic unity obtainable only by a modification of that status quo. And the collision between these conceptions is as old as history and has obviously been hitherto, an inescapable concomitant of the nation-states system.

Today, as always in the past, the static theory is naturally embraced by those states which already have prosperity and now seek security. . . . Thus it is found to be the familiar thesis of the peoples of such states that mankind has, at last, reached the point where the territorial division of the earth's surface has become immutable because the title of the present possessors is both legally and morally imprescriptible; morally, because it can be assailed only by war—and war has now been adjudged a crime.

❧ TEN BASIC BOOKS ❧

THE PATTERN OF THE TWENTIETH CENTURY

1. Black, Cyril E. and Ernst C. Helmreich, *Twentieth Century Europe,* 2nd rev. ed. (New York, 1959).
2. Bruun, Geoffrey, *The World in the Twentieth Century* (Boston, 1952).
3. Chambers, Frank P., Christina Phelps Harris, and Charles C. Bayley, *This Age of Conflict* (New York, 1950).
4. Ergang, Robert R., *Europe in Our Time,* 3rd ed. (Boston, 1958).

5. Hayes, Carlton J. H., *Nationalism: A Religion* (New York, 1960).

6. Holborn, Hajo, *The Political Collapse of Europe* (New York, 1951).

7. Kohn, Hans, *The Twentieth Century: Midway Account of the Western World* (New York, 1949).

8. Langsam, Walter C., *The World Since 1870* (New York, 1963).

9. Schapiro, J. Salwyn, *The World in Crisis* (New York, 1950).

10. Swain, Joseph W., *Beginning the Twentieth Century* (New York, 1938).

36

Armageddon: World War I, 1914-1918

THE SONG OF HATE, 1914

FRENCH AND Russian they matter not,
A blow for a blow and a shot for a shot;
We love them not, we hate them not,
We hold the Weichsel and Vosges-gate,
We have but one and only hate,
We love as one, we hate as one.
We have one foe and one alone.

He is known to you all, he is known to you all,
He crouches behind the dark grey flood,
Full of envy, of rage, of craft, of gall,
Cut off by waves that are thicker than blood.
Come, let us stand at the Judgment place,
An oath to swear to, face to face,
An oath of bronze no wind can shake,
An oath for our sons and their sons to take.
Come, hear the word, repeat the word,
Throughout the Fatherland make it heard.

We will never forego our hate,
We have but one single hate,
We love as one, we hate as one,
We have one foe, and one alone—
      ENGLAND!

—ERNST LISSAUER, "Hasslied," (*Jugend*, 1914)

1. Diplomatic Background of the War

La Belle Epoch. Europe in 1914 breathed easily in an aura of ordered stability. There had been no major wars on the Continent since 1871—those forty-three years were the longest period of peace in European history, thanks to a balance of power maintained by two sets of alliances. From the capitals of the Continent, Europeans governed most of Asia, Africa, and the Near and Middle East. Even such small countries as Belgium and the Netherlands possessed colonies many times the size of the mother country. European fleets roamed the seas to protect lifelines to the colonies. It was an age of European grandeur.

Life was good on the edge of the abyss. There were few travel restrictions in Europe west of the Russian Empire. There was poverty everywhere, but people looked the other way.

The spirit of the day was epitomized in Strauss waltzes in Vienna and in the can-can danced in Parisian music halls. This was an era of wealth, of discipline, of order.

Few people were aware of the explosive mixture behind the façade of peace and prosperity. Beneath its outer tinseled coating, the world of 1914 suffered from a terrible ignorance. Neither statesmen nor military leaders understood the tremendous potentialities for destruction at their command. Weak, inept, they could not cope with the avalanche once it started.

Two shots fired by a nineteen-year-old revolutionary in the Balkan town of Sarajevo set the world on fire and led to two global blood-lettings in one generation. A half-century of turmoil saw two world wars that took many millions of lives, the Russian Revolutions that shook the world, a decade of Hitler's bestiality, the dismantling of Europe's great overseas empires, the spread of nationalism to Asia, Africa, and the Middle East, the cold war between the United States and the Soviet Union, the space race, and the threat of nuclear destruction.

System of Secret Alliances. "You can explain most wars very simply," said President Woodrow Wilson in 1917, "but the explanation of this war is not simple. Its roots run deep into all the obscure soils of history." Conflicting national and economic conditions caused deep suspicion and distrust throughout Europe. The quest for safety took the form of secret agreements among nations which considered themselves threatened by the same enemies. The outcome was a war which marked a turning point in modern history—the first stage in the temporary decline of Europe, a continent that in the previous four centuries had conquered and begun to industrialize the rest of the world.

During the four decades before 1914 the European nations were gripped by an overpowering sense of insecurity. Because it was believed that national alliances could offer some stability, the nations gradually aligned themselves into two rival groups, culminating in the Triple Alliance on the one hand, and the Triple Entente on the other. As long as this system of alliances—some open, some secret— remained in balance, peace could be maintained. But there was always the danger that a political explosion could result in a *casus belli,* an event which is a cause of war.

Dual Alliance Between Germany and Austria-Hungary, 1879. After the three wars for national unification, Bismarck organized an involved system of alliances designed to maintain Germany's hegemony on the European scene. His purposes were to isolate France, conciliate Great Britain, and keep Russia as a friendly power.

There was an outburst of indignation in Russia after the Congress of Berlin in 1878, for the results of which the Russians held Bismarck responsible. For the time being, it seemed impossible to maintain the cooperative spirit between Russia and Germany, inaugurated by the Three Emperors' Conference of 1872–1873. Bismarck decided to choose between Russia and Austria-Hungary. Although Russia was obviously the stronger, she was not Bismarck's choice when the option had to be made. He chose Austria for a number of reasons: (1) He calculated that it was always best to choose a weak partner in an alliance, since two strong partners might well come to blows; (2) there was a community of interest and "blood" between Germans and Austrians; (3) any difficulties with Austria would reopen the wounds of 1866 and throw her into the arms of France; (4) an alliance with Russia would preclude the possibility of an alliance with England; and (5) Austria and Russia might conclude an alliance to the exclusion of Germany. The Dual Alliance of 1879 was one of the most important diplomatic steps of Bismarck's later career. For the next three decades it was to remain the pivot of the European-state system.

Three Emperors' League, 1881. The second major step in the formation of the Bismarckian treaty system leading to the Triple Alliance was the Three Emperors' League (*Dreikaiserbund*), signed on June 18, 1881. With this alliance Bismarck hoped to prevent an Austro-

Russian war or a Franco-Russian coalition. The German chancellor regarded this agreement as so secret that he refused to entrust the negotiations to his assistants and wrote out the documents with his own hand. The Three Emperors' League was renewed in 1884 and terminated in 1887.

Triple Alliance, 1882. In 1882 Bismarck further amplified his system of treaties by drawing Germany, Austria-Hungary, and Italy into a Triple Alliance. The initiative by which the Dual Alliance became the Triple Alliance came from Italy. After 1871 Bismarck encouraged France in her colonial ambitions, seeking by this means to distract her from thoughts of *revanche*. In 1881 France seized Tunisia, which contained a hundred Italians to one Frenchman. Without support, Italy was in no position to challenge French claims. To achieve her ambitions in North Africa and the Adriatic, Italy was determined to have a powerful ally at her back. Moreover, she desired assistance in the event of a possible attempt by France to restore the temporal power of the papacy. Under the circumstances Bismarck was not at all averse to the overtures. A solid block of Central European powers would make France consider carefully before she engaged in a war of revenge. Austria's motive was to achieve security against an attack by Russia; for this security she was willing to come to terms even with the Italians. Driven out of both Germany and Italy, the Austrians might well find compensation by expansion in the Balkans. Bismarck was now close to his aim of keeping France, potentially his strongest enemy, in isolation. In an amazing display of diplomatic ingenuity, the Germain chancellor, an expert juggler, succeeded in "keeping five balls in the air at once."

Reinsurance Treaty, 1887. In 1887 the Three Emperors' League came to an end when Alexander III, annoyed by Austrian opposition to Russian interests in the Balkans, refused to renew the treaty. Bismarck, aware of Germany's strategic weakness on her eastern frontier, was determined, nevertheless, "to keep the wires to St. Petersburg open." Conve-

niently forgetting to inform his ally, Austria-Hungary, of his intentions, he negotiated with Russia, the Reinsurance Treaty, by which he recognized Russian interests in the eastern Balkans. This was standard operational procedure for the German chancellor: already allied with Austria-Hungary by secret treaty, he now negotiated a secret treaty with Russia against Austria-Hungary. William II allowed the treaty to lapse in 1890. Only after his forced resignation in that year did Bismarck reveal the existence of the Reinsurance Treaty.

Triple Entente. The Triple Entente—France, Russia, and England—was formed as a counterpoise to German hegemony in Europe. European powers outside the Bismarckian treaty system began to forget their differences and joined one another to form a balance against it. Isolated France gradually managed to free herself from the net the Iron Chancellor had woven around her. Bismarck's anti-Russia policy at the Congress of Berlin (1878) was a factor in turning Russian eyes toward an alliance with France.

Franco-Russian Military Convention, 1892. Germany's position as the strongest power on the Continent was maintained by the Bismarckian treaty system. Meanwhile, France, Russia, and England settled their differences and concluded a series of alliances. The first step was an alliance between republican France and absolutist Russia. The general understanding took definite form in the Military Convention of August 1892 signed by the French and Russian chiefs of staff. It was given binding effect in January 1894 by an exchange of diplomatic notes, thereby attaining the force of a treaty. This Military Convention was not made public until 1918.

Entente Cordiale Between Britain and France, 1904. Great Britain, which for many years had pursued a policy of holding herself in "splendid isolation" from the Continent, was disturbed by William II's new *Weltpolitik*, a policy taking into consideration the political situation of the whole world. By her aggressive nationalism, her new imperialism, her military and naval strength, and her sympathy for the Boers during the South African war at the turn of the century, Germany forfeited Britain's goodwill. Britain and France, despite centuries of hostility, now began to draw together. British and French colonial interests had clashed at Fashoda in Africa (1898), but the crisis was safely passed. On April 8, 1904, was signed the "Declaration between the United Kingdom and France Respecting Egypt and Morocco, Together with the Secret Articles Signed at the Same Time." Although not an outright treaty or alliance, the agreement amounted in effect to the same thing. Unlike the alliances of the Central Powers, the Entente did not provide definitely for military cooperation.

Anglo-Russian Entente, 1907. The Anglo-Russian Entente of 1907 marked the establishment of the Triple Entente. For a century Britain had been fearful of Russian designs in the Near East. After the conclusion of the Entente Cordiale between Britain and France, the latter had worked to reconcile Britain and Russia. In 1907 Britain and Russia finally agreed upon adjusting their differences in the Near East. In providing for mutual assistance by the three partners in the event of war with any of the Central Powers, the Triple Entente served as a counteracting force to the Triple Alliance.

Europe was now divided into two armed camps, each seeking to maintain the delicate balance of power. Germany, which had initiated the system of alliances, complained of *Einkreisung* (encirclement) by the Entente powers, thus tacitly admitting that she had been defeated in the game of international diplomacy. Uncertain of Italian loyalty, Germany and Austria began to arm rapidly, whereupon the Entente coalition entered the armament race with great energy.

2. Fundamental Origins of the War

Anglo-German Economic Rivalry. The diplomatic maneuvers in the pre-1914 era were surface manifestations of serious economic and political rivalries, the underlying causes of the war. The rapid industrialization of Europe in the late nineteenth century caused a fierce struggle for markets, raw materials (especially coal, iron, and oil), food supplies, and fields for investment. From 1860 to 1880 Great Britain was economically the strongest power in the world. Her colonial empire was first in size and importance, her industry was highly advanced, and her navy was dominant on the seas. From the early 1880's onward she gradually lost the industrial and commercial monopoly which she had enjoyed throughout most of the century. Germany's rise as a powerful rival in the markets of the world was a real challenge to British supremacy. German economic expansion had been efficient and rapid. The unification of Germany had bolstered her economic as well as political power. Her strategic location in Central Europe made her the logical leader in Continental trade. Her great coastal cities, notably Hamburg and Bremen, were excellent ports for handling exports as well as imports. German efficiency and scientific genius, and the paternalism of the government, were additional advantages.

Once entered into the race for colonies the Germans found themselves checked in North Africa by Great Britain and France, in the Balkans by Russia, and in the Near and Far East by Great Britain and other powers. On June 1, 1914, William II sent a message to President Wilson complaining that "all the nations of the world are directing the points of their bayonets at Germany."

Role of Nationalism. A vital contributory cause to World War I was the repression of nationalities. There were many national grievances which became sources of friction. Among the national sore spots was Alsace-Lorraine, the object of Franco-German rivalry for more than a thousand years. Germany annexed Alsace and most of Lorraine by the Treaty of Frankfort (1871) although the majority of the inhabitants were French. For Germany the provinces were important economically because of the Alsatian plain, the city of Strasbourg, and the Lorraine iron mines, politically as the first conquest by the new empire (*Reichsland*), and strategically as protection for the Rhine. French patriots demanded the restoration of Alsace-Lorraine, but Germans maintained that the district had originally been stolen by Louis XIV from the Holy Roman Empire.

Equally critical sore spots were the Austrian-held, but dominantly Italian, district of Trentino, and the cities of Trieste and Fiume. Although Italy and Austria were treaty partners (Triple Alliance, 1882), they were at odds on the question of *Italia Irredenta* ("Italy Unredeemed"). As in France, emotional patriots angrily demanded the return of the "lost provinces."

Poland, destroyed as a nation in the Three Partitions (1772, 1793, and 1795), was reborn during the Napoleonic Wars as the Grand Duchy of Warsaw, only to be dismembered again in 1815, and divided among Russia, Austria, and Prussia. But the flame of national patriotism had not been extinguished. Polish nationalists welcomed war as a means toward building up a new Poland.

Suppressed national groups under the Hapsburg Dual Monarchy, dominated by a minority of Austrians and Hungarians, called for national self-determination and independence. The government of Austria-Hungary, which never had any kind of national cohesion, attempted to hold the lid down on the submerged nationalities—Slovaks and Slovenes, Czechs and Serbians, Ruthenes and Rumanians. The Czechs were particularly insistent in their demand that the old dualism be abolished, and a trialism or a triple union of Austrians, Hungarians, and Slavs, be established in its place. The two Serbian provinces of Bosnia and Herzegovina, administered by Austria-Hungary since the Treaty of Berlin (1878), were annexed by Austria-Hungary in 1908 to prevent the formation of a great Slavic state in the Balkans. The predominantly Slavic population of Bosnia-Herzegovina resented Austrian control, and demanded reunion with independent Serbia.

The Balkans, "the powder keg of Europe," seethed with discontent in 1914. Greece, Serbia, Bulgaria, and Rumania, the Balkan heirs of Turkey, wanted a greater share of the spoils of the disintegrating Ottoman Empire. Greece demanded southern Albania, Thrace, Constantinople, and parts of Asia Minor; Rumania hoped to annex Transylvania, Bukovina, and Bessarabia; and Serbia wanted to fashion a Greater Serbia embracing all the Balkan Slavs. In conflict with these frustrated national ambitions were Austro-German Pan-Germanism (union of all Germans in a Great *Reich*), the German *Drang nach Osten* ("Advance to the East"), and Russian Pan-Slavism (union of all Slavs). Pan-Germanism and Pan-Slavism collided head-on in the Balkans.

Militarism and International Anarchy. Europe on the eve of World War I was a camp of potential belligerents, each heavily armed and each feverishly preparing for the coming struggle. The introduction of military con-

THE TUG OF PEACE.

EVERYBODY *(to everybody else)*. "AFTER YOU, SIR!"

Failure of the Second Hague Peace Conference, 1907. In this *Punch* cartoon, each of the great powers bids another to be the first to move toward disarmament.

scription and the development of new instruments of warfare revealed the expansive mutual distrust of the European states. Military and naval expenditures of both large and small nations increased enormously between 1872 and 1912. In Germany there was an increase of 335 per cent; in Russia, 214 per cent; in France, 133 per cent; and in England, 180 per cent. This state of armed peace imposed a staggering burden on all the countries.

In 1926 the British essayist G. Lowes Dickinson (1862–1932) published a significant book titled *International Anarchy, 1904–1914* which was concerned with the series of events and situations leading up to World War I. His theme was that the general situation of international anarchy, resulting from the juxtaposition of independent and armed states, was the basic cause of the catastrophe. He described the selfish secret intrigues of all the Powers which caused the international anarchy culminating in the war. Without any effective supranational authority to curb aggressor states, he said, world war was inevitable.

Although each nation maintained the peace within its own borders by constitutional and legal provisions, the family of European nations had no restraining international organization. International relations, based on the principle of national autonomy, permitted each power to act as it thought best in all matters. International law, a body of rules and regulations supposedly governing relations among nations, existed in theory, but in the absence of any international authority, offenders were subject only to the judgment of mankind. Diplomacy became a labyrinth of trickery, sworn allies were not necessarily loyal friends; and in some cases, nations made secret agreements with the enemies of their allies.

3. From Diplomatic Crises to Outbreak of War

Diplomatic Crises, 1905–1913. The most critical spots were in Morocco and the Balkans. William II, protesting against French economic domination of Morocco and demanding recognition for Germany's influence in world affairs, landed at Tangier on March 31, 1905,

and ostentatiously recognized the Sultan of Morocco as an independent monarch. It was agreed, however, at the German-instigated Algeciras Conference of 1906 that an open-door policy in Morocco would be maintained under some French supervision. This result convinced Germany that she had nothing to gain at international conferences. In 1911 she again protested French domination of Morocco. Similarly, a series of crises in the Balkans in 1908, 1912, and 1913 aggravated what was already a tense situation. It had been agreed at the Congress of Berlin in 1878 that Austria-Hungary was to have only a protectorate over the Serbian provinces of Bosnia-Herzegovina. But in 1908, in defiance of Russia's pretensions in the area, Austria-Hungary formally annexed them. Russia's protests went unheeded. In 1911 Italy seized the Turkish province of Tripoli. In the Balkan Wars of 1912–1913, Serbia, Montenegro, Bulgaria, and Greece jointly made war on Turkey, and then went to war with one another over the spoils. Austrians and Serbians, Teutons and Slavs, now became deadly enemies in the Balkans.

Immediate Causes. By 1914 it had become clear that peace was at the mercy of an accident. The peoples of Europe, lulled into a false sense of security by four decades of peace, went about their every-day affairs in happy ignorance of the gathering storm clouds. Each year there was one or another serious diplomatic crisis threatening to bring the interlocking alliances into war, but each time the foreign ministers maneuvered their way out of the trap, and the crisis passed. Without a long-range policy to maintain the peace, the harassed diplomats improvised temporary solutions, suspecting that the hour was approaching when nothing could be done to prevent a frightful clash of arms.

On June 28, 1914, Archduke Francis Ferdinand, heir to the throne of Austria-Hungary, and his wife were assassinated at Sarajevo, the capital of Bosnia. The assassin was Gavrilo Princip, a young Bosnian youth acting on behalf of the Serbian Union or Death (the Black Hand) Society, a terrorist organization agitating against Austria. Austria-Hungary, through her foreign minister, Count Leopold von Berchtold, seized the opportunity to reassert Austrian supremacy in the Balkans by dispatching, on July 23, 1914, a severe ultimatum demanding, among other things, that Serbia submit to Austrian control of her police and law courts. William II had already pledged that he would support Austria in whatever demands she made (the so-called "Blank Check"). Within the 48 hours allowed them, the Serbs submitted a conciliatory reply, accepting most of the demands except that calling for collaboration with Austrian officials in suppressing anti-Austrian propaganda. The Serbs also offered to submit the entire matter to the Hague Permanent Court of Arbitration, but simultaneously they began to mobilize.

For this new crisis no peaceful solution was improvised. All efforts to localize the conflict were futile. When Austria-Hungary began mobilization, Russia threatened a similar step the moment the Austrians invaded Serbia. In the dangerous climate of 1914, mobilization could mean war. When Germany inquired what England would do if war were to begin, Sir Edward Grey, the British foreign minister, replied that England would do that which best served her interests. The oracle at Delphi could not have delivered a more dangerously ambiguous response. Grey further proposed a European conference to settle the crisis, but Germany declined on the ground that the quarrel could be localized. Austria, refusing to accept the Serbian reply, declared war on Serbia on July 28, 1914. Russia mobilized the next day. On August 1, after demanding in vain that the Russians disarm, Germany declared war on Russia. Two days later, on August 3, Germany declared war on France. Italy and Rumania, asserting that they would not take part in an offensive war, announced their neutrality.

On the evening of August 3, with Great Britain on the verge of war, Sir Edward Grey stood at a window of the Foreign Office in London, watching the lamps being lit in the dusk, and said: "The lamps are going out all over Europe; we shall not see them lit again in our lifetime."

Historical Controversy: Problem of War Guilt. There is a difference of opinion among historians on the question of responsibility for World War I. One group (notably Bernadotte Schmitt and H. R. Trevor-Roper) believed that the war was the result of a policy of German aggression. It was stated that the German General Staff wanted war and prepared carefully for it, and that some forty years of planning lay behind the conflict. It was admitted that errors were made by non-German as well as by German statesmen, but these errors were ultimately irrelevant when compared with the German drive to war.

A group of revisionist historians (Harry Elmer Barnes, Frederick Bausman) presented the explanation that, although Germany made some moves that contributed to a war situation, she could not be accused of deliberately plotting to bring the war about. It was false, they said, to paint Germany's prewar record as uniquely black, since her statesmen worked more effectively than others to avert the war, and they knew that war might place German progress, already attained by peaceful means, in jeopardy. Some revisionists set the order of guilt for direct and immediate responsibility upon Serbia, France, and Russia, with the guilt equally divided; next, far below, Austria; and finally England and Germany, in the order named. This point of view was most acceptable, of course, to German historians then in the midst of an organized campaign to combat what they called the *"Kriegsschuldlüge"* ("war-guilt lie").

A third approach holds that responsibility for the war of 1914 was equally distributed, and that the war was the fatal result of unresolved economic clashes, the morass of diplomatic squabbles and intrigues, national rivalries, sword rattling, and a psychologically unsound conception of security. Those who take this attitude do not have in mind only the crisis of 1914, but rather the general cultural and institutional situation back of the July clash. Serious mistakes of judgment were made on all sides during the critical weeks. While explanations may differ as to which individuals were responsible for casting the final die in the tragedy of errors of 1914, most historians agree that the milieu was dangerously receptive to war. Lloyd George explained the catastrophe in these words: "The more one reads of the memoirs and books written in the various countries of what happened before August 1, 1914, the more one realizes that no one at the head of affairs quite meant war. It was something into which they glided, or rather staggered and stumbled."

4. Course of the War

The Great War. World War I was the most terrible conflict so far in all history. It was the first war fought with huge guns and airplanes, with flame throwers and poison gas. It was the first war in which the civilian population was attacked by submarines and Zeppelins (rigid airships). It was the first war in which blockade and counter-blockade became major struggles. There were so many casualties in this great blood bath that they had to be memorialized by tombs of the Unknown Soldier, another innovation in modern civilization.

Schlieffen Plan. After the Franco-Prussian War of 1870–1871, the Great General Staff of the Imperial German Army agreed that in a future war Germany would have to fight on two fronts, against France and Russia. In 1871 it was decided that, in the event of such a war, Germany would immediately attack France while holding off Russia. In 1879 General Helmuth von Moltke reversed the plan to an offensive against Russia while fighting a defensive war against France. In 1905 Count Alfred von Schlieffen, who became Chief of the Great General Staff in 1891, submitted a plan under which the Austrians would be relied upon to hold Russia in check while Germany hurled the bulk of her forces against France. Then, after the annihilation of the

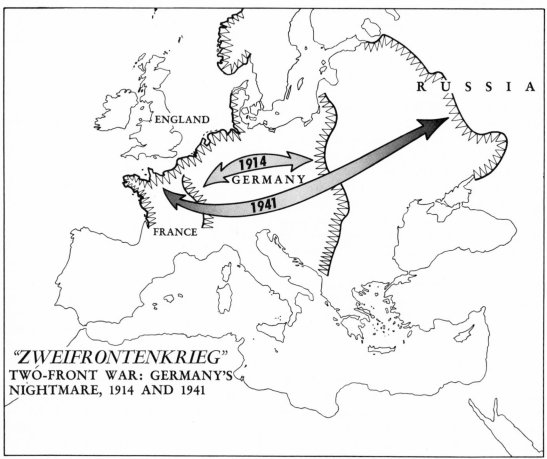

"ZWEIFRONTENKRIEG"
TWO-FRONT WAR: GERMANY'S
NIGHTMARE, 1914 AND 1941

French armies, Germany, at her leisure, would defeat Russia. Count von Schlieffen was dismissed in 1906, but his plan, in slightly modified form, was adopted in 1914.

On August 2, 1914, the German ambassador at Brussels, Herr von Below Saleske, delivered a note to M. Davignon, Belgian minister for foreign affairs, asking the Belgian government to permit an army to march through Belgium, promising to respect Belgian territory, to evacuate it on conclusion of peace, and to pay an indemnity for any damage caused by German troops. The Belgians refused. The German armies then invaded Belgium and Luxemburg with the object of swinging like a hammer in a wide arc on Paris. Speedily mobilized, the Germans streamed into Belgium. On August 4, 1914, shortly after invasion, Theobald von Bethmann-Hollweg, the German imperial chancellor, appeared before the *Reichstag* to define Germany's position in the war. He admitted the unjust violation of Belgian neutrality but promised that the injustices would be made good as soon as the necessary military goal was attained. The neutrality of Belgium had been guaranteed in 1839 by the European powers; its violation brought England into the war. Italy, claiming that she was not bound under the terms of the Triple Alliance to assist in an offensive war, declared her neutrality.

War on the Western Front, 1914. The Allied nations outnumbered the Central Powers in military strength in 1914 by some 30,000,000 to 22,000,000 combatants. The German army, carefully organized and equipped, was superbly trained. The British navy dominated the seas everywhere. The tiny Belgian army was eliminated within two weeks. At the First Battle of the Marne (September 5–12, 1914), the Germans were defeated when a French force, led by General Joseph Joffre, attacked their right wing, and another French army, commanded by General Ferdinand Foch, struck at the center. The Schlieffen plan was rendered ineffective when the German general, Helmuth von Moltke, nephew of the great Moltke, became alarmed by the unexpected speed of Russian mobilization. Despite the heroic Belgian resistance and the prompt

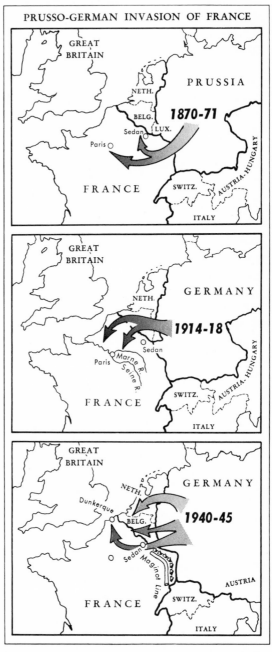

PRUSSO-GERMAN INVASION OF FRANCE

aid of England, Moltke detached several divisions from his right wing to be sent to the east, thereby weakening the striking power of his seven colossal armies in the west. Retreating to the Aisne River, the Germans then tried to extend their lines as far west as possible, to gain access to the English Channel. The Allies sought to thwart this maneuver at the First Battle of Ypres (October 30–November 24,

1914), which cost a quarter of a million lives. The Allies, winners in the race to the sea, held Calais, Boulogne, and Dunkirk, thereby insuring communication between Britain and France for the duration of the war. The German dream of a quick and decisive victory, recalling those of Bismarck's three wars of national unification, vanished.

War on the Eastern Front, 1914. Meanwhile, vast Russian armies poured into East Prussia and Galicia and turned like a giant steamroller toward Berlin. Led by Generals Paul Rennenkampf and Alexander Samsonov, two separate armies operating without liaison went to one of the most dramatic defeats in history. The Germans, under Generals Paul von Hindenburg and Erich Ludendorff, drove a wedge between the two armies and annihilated one at Tannenberg (August 26–30, 1914) and defeated the other at the Masurian Lakes (September 5–15, 1914). The Russians lost a quarter of a million men as well as an enormous quantity of supplies. Stunned by these defeats, Russia, nevertheless, attacked Austria and took many thousands of prisoners. In the meantime, Hindenburg failed in an attempt to take Warsaw.

As 1914 ended Germany was in a favorable military situation. Her territory was intact; her resources were abundant; she had taken important enemy positions; and Turkey was fighting at her side.

Battle for Control of the Seas. As soon as war was declared, the British fleet swept German commerce from the seas, bottled up the German battle fleet at Kiel, and began the task of eliminating German submarines, destroyers of commerce. German U-boats took a grave toll of Allied merchant shipping. They nearly won the war for Germany until the Allies began using the convoy system of grouping ships under naval escort. Britain's superior navy enabled her to establish a naval blockade of Germany, to protect the British Isles, to safeguard Allied commerce, to transport troops, and to conquer the German colonies. This naval supremacy contributed much to the ultimate defeat of Germany and her allies.

Battle of Propaganda. From the outset there was a battle of propaganda, which strongly influenced the course of the war. Every belligerent government organized its propaganda experts not only to educate its own citizens on the necessity for the war but also to destroy the morale of the enemy, In Britain there was the Crewe House; in France *La Maison de la Presse;* in Germany the *Kriegspresseamt;* and later in the United States the Committee on Public Information. Eventually, an inter-Allied board was created under the direction of Lord Northcliffe. German propaganda was heavy-handed and relatively ineffective; that of the Allies, especially the British, was subtle and more convincing.

The War in 1915. In late 1914 the conflict on the Western front settled into a war of attrition. Whole armies burrowed into the ground like moles. Terrible weapons—machine guns and howitzers—were used by both sides. In May 1915 Italy, after making a secret agreement with the Allies on her territorial demands, declared war on Austria. At the bloody Second Battle of Ypres (April 22–May 25, 1915), the British suffered a serious defeat. On April 22, 1915, the Germans discharged chlorine gas from cylinders across the Allied lines. To the unprotected troops, this attack came as a staggering surprise. The German press boasted of this "triumph of chemistry." Why the Germans did not immediately seize the opportunity offered by the use of poison gas to launch a decisive all-out attack along the various war fronts remains one of the great mysteries of the war. Within a few days the Allies were equipped with a crude, elementary respirator, thus disposing of the danger of a knockout blow. Then came retaliatory attacks.

In early 1915 Hindenburg led a drive through Poland, capturing Courland and Lithuania. The exhausted Russians retreated from Galicia and Poland by October 1915. After a year of invasions and counterinvasions, fighting on the Eastern Front came to a standstill. On October 14, 1915, Bulgaria declared war on Serbia because of the latter's leadership against her in the Second Balkan War. A German army, supported by Bulgarian troops, conquered Serbia. The Central Powers thus controlled the entire line from Berlin to Constantinople to Baghdad.

The Allies decided to attack Constantinople in order to hit the enemy from the "soft underbelly of Europe." Capture of the Bosporus Straits would enable the Allies to comunicate with Russia through the Black Sea. It would also isolate Turkey from the Central Powers, encourage the neutral Balkan states to join the Allies, and permit an Allied drive on Austria from the south. Though brilliantly conceived by Winston Churchill, then First Lord of the Admiralty, the execution of the Dardanelles campaign was a failure. A Franco-British fleet, striking in early 1915, was driven from the narrow Straits by Turkish land batteries. A land attack on Gallipoli by British, Australian, and New Zealand troops was ineffective. The venture was abandoned in late 1915.

Stalemate: The Year 1916. Early in 1916 the Germans sought to end the conflict by a tremendous offensive at Verdun. Striking again and again at the French ring of fortresses, the Germans lost at least half a million lives, but the Allies also suffered huge losses. In the second half of 1916 the Allies began a counteroffensive at the Battle of the Somme, July–November, 1916, designed to relieve the pressure on Verdun. In March 1917 the Germans retired to the Hindenburg Line after evacuating a thousand square miles of French territory. Once again the Western front degenerated into a stalemate.

In the East the Russians, recovering from defeat, began an offensive in June 1916 and reconquered parts of eastern Galicia. Meanwhile, the Italians, who had been fighting the Austrians since the middle of 1915, drove the enemy into the Austrian Trentino. Allied successes in the East, and a secret treaty with the Allies promising territorial gains, led Rumania to declare war on Austria-Hungary on August 27, 1916. Patching up the Galician front, German Generals August von Mackensen and Erich von Falkenhayn turned to Rumania, struck forcefully, and conquered virtually all of that country. The Treaty of Bucharest

(March 1918) gave economic privileges and territories to the Central Powers, including all Dobrudja and the Carpathian passes.

The most important naval battle of the war, the Battle of Jutland (May 31–June 1, 1916), was between the British fleet, commanded by Admirals David Beatty and John Jellicoe, and the German High Seas Fleet, led by Admiral Reinhard Scheer. Although both sides claimed victory, the German fleet had to retire to Kiel and remain there for the duration of the war. Great Britain maintained her control of the seas.

The War in 1917. The Western Front was deadlocked throughout 1917. The British victory at Arras (April 9–May 4, 1917) was inconclusive, and another battle at Ypres (July 31–November 10, 1917) had no immediate effects. The Germans, occupying most of Belgium and northern France, as well as the Balkans, seemed to have the advantage. Having conquered Serbia and Rumania, the Central Powers turned to Italy, and decisively defeated her at Caporetto (October 24, 1917). The demoralized Italians lost thousands as prisoners. This defeat was a disaster to Allied hopes, but British and French reinforcements prevented the complete collapse of Italy.

The war in the Near East at first went badly for the Allies. Added to the Dardanelles fiasco (1915) was the campaign in Mesopotamia: an Anglo-Indian army advancing up the Tigris River was surrounded in September 1915 at Kut-el-Amara and was forced to capitulate. In addition, an Anglo-Egyptian army was just barely strong enough to hold the Suez Canal. Early in 1917, however, a British force invaded Mesopotamia, defeated the Turks, and took Baghdad. Later, another British army, commanded by General Edmund Allenby, invaded Palestine and captured Jerusalem. Allied prestige in the Near East rose again.

A combination of military reverses, incompetent leadership, and popular disaffection led in March 1917 to a revolution in Russia, and her eventual retirement from the war. After the abdication of Tsar Nicholas II on March 15, 1917, the Provisional Government, led by Prince Lvov and Alexander Kerensky, tried to continue the war. But the masses, tired of military blundering and heavy losses at the front, gradually drifted to the left. After the November Revolution of 1917, which brought the Bolsheviks to power, the Russians signed the Treaty of Brest-Litovsk (March 1918), by which Russia ceded to Germany nearly all the European territory which she had acquired since the time of Peter the Great.

The United States Enters the War, 1917. Public opinion in the United States in 1914 was hesitant and confused. The Irish-Americans were anti-English; the German-Americans pro-German, the Italian-Americans pro-Italian, and the Jews anti-Russian. President Woodrow Wilson declared America's neutrality. He protested against British interference with neutral trade and confiscation of American mail, and the use of American flags on British ships. There was much resentment against British policies, but there was even more against Germany's submarine campaign.

The sinking of the Cunard liner *Lusitania* by a German submarine on May 7, 1915, with a loss of more than 1,100 passengers and crew, including 124 Americans, aroused great indignation in the United States. Germany modified her submarine campaign in response to repeated American notes. On January 19, 1917, the German foreign secretary, Alfred Zimmermann, sent a note to the German ambassador in Mexico proposing to Mexico an alliance providing for a joint war against the United States. Interception and publication of the note in the United States strengthened the demand for war, especially in the hitherto lukewarm Southwest, which Germany proposed to cede to Mexico. When Germany resumed unrestricted submarine warfare (February 1, 1917), the United States severed diplomatic relations and declared war (April 6, 1917).

The United States joined in the war as the result of several interrelated factors: her economic stake in an Allied victory; the triumph of British over German propaganda; a series of German diplomatic blunders; the resumption of the unrestricted submarine campaign; and the popular conception that the United

States was fighting a war to "make the world safe for democracy." Americans believed that with the collapse of the autocratic tsarist regime in Russia, the war had resolved into a struggle between autocracy, represented by the Central Powers, and democracy, represented by the Allies. The vast manpower and resources of the United States, thrown into the conflict with unexpected speed, tipped the scales in favor of the Allies.

Moves for Peace. Proposals for peace had been made as early as 1916 by the Central Powers (December 12, 1916) and by President Wilson (December 18, 1916). On August 1, 1917, Pope Benedict XV, grieved by the horrors of the conflict, urged a just and honorable peace, but he was ignored by both sides. In May 1917 an international conference of labor to discuss peace was called at Stockholm by the Russian Council of Workers' and Soldiers' Delegates, but several of the belligerent governments refused to permit Socialist delegates from their countries to attend. There seemed to be no end in sight. On both sides there was war-weariness as well as pessimism.

On January 8, 1918, President Wilson issued a statement, the Fourteen Points, of what he believed to be Allied war aims, until then not expressed. (*See page 605.*) The morale of the German people, already weakened by the tightening of the blockade and the waning effectiveness of their submarine campaign, was still further undermined by the prospect of peace based on the Fourteen Points.

1918: The End of the War. The beginning of 1918 seemed favorable to Germany. German troops were still entrenched on the Western front. Russia, Serbia, Rumania, and Italy had been eliminated as military factors. In France and England defeatism was widespread. In March 1918 the Germans launched an offensive to deliver a knockout blow in the West before the Americans could arrive in overwhelming numbers. The Allies held on tenaciously. For the first time in the war, they agreed upon the appointment of one man, General Ferdinand Foch, to supreme command of the Allied forces. A German attack against the French (May 27, 1918) carried the Germans once more to the Marne. The Allies now had their backs to the wall.

The Allied counteroffensive was crowned with success. At the Second Battle of the Marne (July 15–August 7, 1918) the Germans were decisively defeated—by the British at the Somme, by the French from Amiens to Rheims, and by the Americans in the Saint-Mihiel salient and in the Meuse-Argonne campaign. The German armies began a general retreat from France and Belgium. The Central Powers began to disintegrate. The Serbians, Greeks, Rumanians, and Italians launched offensives on other fronts. Bulgaria was the first to surrender (September 30, 1918). Her capitulation was followed by the collapse of Turkey (October 31) and the surrender of Austria (November 3).

Meanwhile, the German home front was shattered. The German people, appalled by the collapse of the Hindenburg Line, were distressed by the news that the triumphant Allies were approaching the German frontier in the West. On October 4, 1918, Germany sued for peace on the basis of Wilson's Fourteen Points. On November 11, 1918, an armistice was signed in a railway car at Compiègne. The terms called for the evacuation of France, Belgium, Alsace-Lorraine, and the west bank of the Rhine; abrogation of the Treaties of Brest-Litovsk and Bucharest; surrender of German warships, submarines, guns, locomotives, and railway cars to the Allies; freedom for all Allied prisoners; occupation of the Rhineland by the Allies until the conclusion of the peace; and continuation of the blockade of Germany.

5. The Paris Peace Conference, 1919

Organization and Procedure. Representatives and experts of twenty-seven victor nations met at Versailles on January 18, 1919, to mend a shattered world by making a new map and reducing the territorial chaos. The problem was to effect a reasonable peace settlement in the presence of conflicting ambi-

GHOSTS AT VERSAILLES.

In this *Punch cartoon,* the spectral forms of Bismarck, William I, and Moltke look on with contempt as a defeated Germany accepts the bitter terms of peace.

tions, imperialistic aims, demands of military leaders for strategic frontiers, after-war bitterness, the Bolshevik threat, and the popular desire for reparations. Germany, Austria-Hungary, Turkey, and Bulgaria were not represented at the conference sessions.

The Council of Ten, consisting of the premiers and foreign ministers of the major victor powers, was abruptly reduced to the Big Three—the United States, Great Britain and France—when it proved to be too unwieldy. (Originally, Italy was included among the Big Four, but when Vittorio Orlando, the Italian representative, walked out in an emotional outburst, he was not called back.) The dominating personality at the conference was the American president, Woodrow Wilson

(1856–1924), who, as spokesman for the masses, had received an extraordinary enthusiastic welcome in Europe. Wilson was denounced by his enemies as an impractical idealist and an indifferent diplomat. Believing that the people shared his hatred of war, militarism, and the old diplomacy, he was determined to see the world purged of war by the creation of a League of Nations. Georges Clemenceau (1841–1929), the French spokesman, demanded gruffly that once and for all time France must be made safe from German attack. He expressed his contemptuous attitude toward Wilson in a fiery statement: "God Almighty had only Ten Points; Wilson has to have Fourteen!" David Lloyd George (1863–1945), the British delegate, had promised the British people in the elections of December 14, 1918, that he would work to "hang the Kaiser" and collect from Germany the costs of the war "shilling for shilling and ton for ton." The routine commissions and the plenary sessions discussed a host of problems, including the League of Nations, the security of France, reparations, disposition of the Saar Basin, the Polish question, Fiume, and the German colonies. In practice the opinions of the Big Three governed the solution of all major problems.

At Versailles, Wilson's Fourteen Points came into head-on conflict with the Secret Treaties, by which the Allied powers had agreed that Russia was to get Constantinople and the Straits, Italy was to obtain sections of *Italia Irredenta,* and France was to be awarded Alsace-Lorraine. In 1917, after the November Revolution, the Bolsheviks had published the Secret Treaties found in the Russian archives, thereby exposing the deals that had been made and embarrassing the Allies in their peace-making activities.

Territorial Provisions. By the Treaty of Versailles, Germany lost an eighth of her land area, some 6,500,000 people, and all her colonies. She was required to relinquish Alsace-Lorraine to France; Eupen, Malmédy, and Moresnet to Belgium; some parts of Upper Silesia to Czechoslovakia and Poland by plebiscite;

northern and central Schleswig to Denmark by plebiscite; much of West Prussia (the Polish Corridor) and Posen to Poland; Danzig to the League of Nations under mandate; Memel to the Allies and later (1924) to Lithuania; Kiaochau to Japan; and her remaining colonies to the major powers as mandates of the League of Nations.

Military and Naval Clauses. Germany was required to submit to Allied occupation of the Rhineland with provisions for gradual retirement. The German army was limited to 100,-000 men, and conscription was abolished. The German navy was limited to 6 battleships, 6 light cruisers, 12 destroyers, and 12 torpedo boats, and no submarines. The German air force was eliminated. German manufacture of munitions was restricted, German use of poison gas was prohibited, and German fortifications along the North and Baltic Seas were ordered demolished. The German General Staff was abolished. William II and other leaders were to be tried before Allied tribunals as criminals against international peace.

Signing of the Treaty. On May 7, 1919, the peace treaty was presented to the German delegates assembled in the Hall of Mirrors at the Trianon Palace at Versailles, where, in 1871, the German Empire had been proclaimed by Bismarck. The Germans were given three weeks to reply. On May 29, the German delegation submitted 443 pages in reply to the 230-page draft of the treaty, listing their objections to what they called a Carthaginian peace. They protested that the terms were not in keeping with the conditions on which Germany had laid down her arms and that many of the clauses could not possibly be fulfilled. The Allies, rejecting the German reply, gave Germany seven days, under threat of invasion, to accept the slightly modified treaty. On June 28, 1919, the Germans reluctantly signed.

Parallel Treaties. In the meantime, work went ahead on a series of more than a dozen treaties to liquidate the war. The Treaties of

Saint-Germain and Trianon effected the partition of the Austro-Hungarian dual monarchy and led to the Balkanization of Central Europe. The Treaty of Neuilly with Bulgaria and the Treaty of Trianon with Hungary followed the general lines of that at Versailles. Turkey repudiated the Treaty of Sèvres and, under Mustapha Kemal and his Turkish Nationalists, went to war against the Greeks, who had British aid. Victorious, the Turks in 1923 negotiated the Treaty of Lausanne, by which they maintained their ethnic frontiers, freedom from international bondage, and national independence.

Minority Treaties. Aware that all national aspirations could not be satisfied, the Allied statesmen sought to protect the rights of minority ethnic and religious groups. Although they declined to follow the same policies in their own countries, they compelled Poland, Yugoslavia, Czechoslovakia, and Greece to sign treaties guaranteeing equal rights to all citizens, regardless of race, religion, or language. The supervision over minority rights was left to the League of Nations; only by a majority vote of the League Council could these rights be modified in any way. Several countries, notably Poland, complained that these treaties were subversive of their national sovereignty, since the pacts were said to encourage separatist movements.

Effect on Germany. By the Treaty of Versailles, Germany lost her colonies, virtually all her investments abroad, 15.5 per cent of her arable land, 12 per cent of her livestock, nearly 10 per cent of her manufacturing plants, two-fifths of her coal reserves, almost two-thirds of her iron ore, and more than half of her lead. Her navy was almost wiped out, and her merchant marine was reduced from 5,700,000 tons to fewer than 500,000 tons. The surrender of colonies meant the loss of access to rubber and oil supplies. During the postwar period, every political party in Germany from right to left denounced the treaty as the *Versaillesdiktat*, as a peace designed to destroy Germany. The Germans preferred to ignore the fact that only

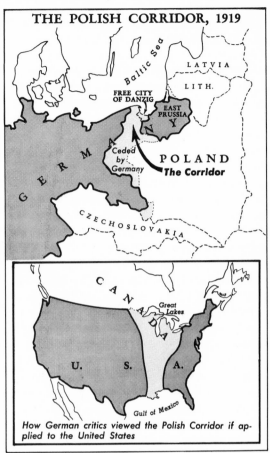

THE POLISH CORRIDOR, 1919

How German critics viewed the Polish Corridor if applied to the United States

slightly more than a year earlier they had imposed still harsher terms on the Russians at the Treaty of Brest-Litovsk (March 3, 1918).

Estimates of the Treaties. Although the treaty was attacked in its day, the peacemakers at Versailles succeeded in signing a treaty with the principle enemy within six months and with the lesser enemies within eight. This result should be contrasted with the lack of treaties more than two decades after World War II. The conference at Versailles drew up, in thirty hours of committee meetings and two plenary sessions, a covenant for a world peace agency. A similar effort, after World War II, required a special conference of over a thousand delegates meeting for two months at San Francisco. The delegates at Versailles were handicapped by the fact that many new states had come into existence before the armistice, and had already set their frontiers and consolidated their positions. Any significant change in this pattern could be made only through the use of force.

Historical Controversy: Carthaginian Peace?

German historians, almost without exception, argued that the Treaty of Versailles was a dictated peace, a harsh and vindictive symbol of all that was wrong in the postwar world. Historians in the Allied countries took the opposite point of view, holding that the treaty was a just one, punishing Germany for her crimes. In 1919 the German case was bolstered by the appearance in London of John Maynard Keynes' *The Economic Consequences of the Peace,* which presented the views that the treaty was clothed with insincerity, with an apparatus of self-deception, "with a web of Jesuitical exegesis," elements which were to distinguish it from all its historical predecessors. Its provisions, said Keynes, were "dishonourable," "ridiculous and injurious," "abhorrent and detestable"; they revealed "imbecile greed," "oppression and rapine." This treaty, said Keynes, "reduced Germany to servitude." (*See page 617.*)

There were immediate angered reactions to Keynes, culminating in 1944 when a young French scholar, Étienne Mantoux, proposed an answer. The Keynes interpretation, he said, was pessimistic, unreasonable, unfair. The major problems of the postwar era, he argued, were the outcome of the war itself, not of the treaty. The peace terms were proper, he asserted and could have been carried out had the West had the will to do so, and had the Germans had the desire to live in peace with their neighbors. The chief weapon in Hitler's arsenal of ideas, he charged, was his loud fulminations against the so-called iniquities of Versailles. Moreover, said Mantoux, the political effects of the treaty were far more significant than the economic. Far from being a Carthaginian peace, the Treaty of Versailles, in Mantoux's view, was as intelligent a treaty as could be devised in an explosive situation.

Costs of World War I.

The human and material losses of World War I, which lasted 1,565 days, were staggering. Some 65,000,000 men

were mobilized during the course of the conflict, out of which about 9,000,000—one in seven—died in action or of wounds. At least 22,000,000—one in three—were disabled; 7,-000,000 were permanently disabled. More than 5,000,000 men were reported missing. The following chart gives the approximate figures in round numbers:

	Dead	Wounded	Prisoner
Great Britain	947,000	2,122,000	192,000
France	1,385,000	3,044,000	446,000
Russia	1,700,000	4,950,000	2,500,000
Italy	460,000	947,000	530,000
United States	115,000	206,000	4,300
Germany	1,808,000	4,247,000	618,000
Austria-Hungary	1,200,000	3,620,000	2,200,000
Turkey	325,000	400,000	

The estimated number of civilian deaths was in excess of the military casualties. The total real economic cost was nearly $400,000,-000,000. (This and the following figures represent pre-1945 dollars. The total cost, if figured at the present dollar value, would be much greater.) According to the Carnegie Endowment for International Peace, this sum would have been sufficient to:

1. Provide every family in England, Ireland, Scotland, Belgium, Russia, the United States, Germany, Canada, and Australia with a $2,500 house on a $500 five-acre lot and furnish it with $1,000 worth of furniture;

2. Provide a $5,000,000 library and a $10,-000,000 university for every community possessing a population of 20,000 or over;

3. Create a fund which, at 5 per cent interest, would yield enough to pay $1,000 a year to 125,000 teachers and 125,000 nurses; and

4. Leave a surplus enough to purchase every piece of property and all the wealth of both France and England.

These figures do not take into account the disruption of the European economy, the wholesale crippling of soldiers and civilians, or the vast sums to be appropriated for generations in the form of pensions and interest on war debts. Added to this were the irreconcilable hatreds engendered by the conflict.

Results of the War. Four great empires were broken by the events of 1914–1918. The Russian, Austro-Hungarian, and Turkish Empires, all belonging essentially to Eastern Europe, and the German Empire, with one foot in Eastern and the other in Western Europe, crashed in ruins. The Europe that had dominated the world of 1900 was now a shambles, and there seemed to be no possibility of reviving its prewar power. The Continent was temporarily swept as bare as if a swarm of locusts had descended upon it. Crowns rolled in the gutter, ancient tyrannies were broken, the economic system was in general bankruptcy, and the people were exhausted and insecure. Human ethics and morality had taken a vicious beating.

Two world messiahs emerged from this era of decay. Leadership from a battered Europe seemed to be out of the question. On the day the Armistice was signed, President Wilson announced: "It will now be our fortunate duty to assist by example, by sober, friendly coun-sel, and by material aid in the establishment of a just democracy throughout the world." Woodrow Wilson gave new hope to despairing Europe and urged his people to assume the unaccustomed role of leadership in the attempt to rebuild the world on a democratic basis. From Soviet Russia came the voice of Nikolai Lenin, foremost of Bolshevik revolutionaries, proclaiming the International World Revolution and urging his followers to organize the whole world in one single community dominated by the proletariat. The Wilsonian ideal envisioned a world reorganized on a democratic basis; the Leninist faith called for all power to the proletariat class or, in the words of a popular song, "All or nothing at all!" Between these two points of view, which became solidified in the following decades, there was no compromise possible. These were destined to be frustrating decades, witnessing the paradox of a drift toward world utopias and the concurrent intensification of nationalism.

{ KEY DOCUMENT }

THE FOURTEEN POINTS, 1918

United States Serial 7443. Document No. 765, January 8, 1918.

ON JANUARY 8, 1918, President Woodrow Wilson put into definite form the conditions of peace that had been left vague by other Allied statesmen. After the Bolshevik Revolution, Communist leaders began to publish the Allied treaties discovered in the Russian archives. As a countermove the American president came forward with the famous Fourteen Points, delivered at a joint session of the two houses of Congress and accepted by war-weary Germans. Germans later denounced this statement as a trick deliberately designed to destroy their morale. Other Allied leaders maintained that the Fourteen Points represented an American and not necessarily an Allied viewpoint.

We entered this war because violations of right had occurred which touched us to the quick and made the life of our own people impossible unless they were corrected and the world secured once for all against their recurrence. What we demand in this war, therefore, is nothing peculiar to ourselves. It is that the world be made fit and safe to live in. . . . The programme of the world's peace . . . is our programme; and that programme, the only possible programme, as we see it, is this:

I. Open covenants of peace, openly arrived at, after which there shall be no private international understandings of any kind but diplomacy shall proceed always frankly and in the public view.

II. Absolute freedom of navigation upon the seas, outside territorial waters, alike in peace and in war, except as the seas may be closed in whole or in part by international action for the enforcement of international covenants.

III. The removal, so far as possible, of all economic barriers and the establishment of an equality of trade conditions among all the nations consenting to the peace and associating themselves for its maintenance.

IV. Adequate guarantees given and taken that national armaments will be reduced to the lowest point consistent with domestic safety.

V. A free, open-minded, and absolutely impartial adjustment of all colonial claims, based upon a strict observance of the principle that in determining all such questions of sovereignty the interests of the populations concerned must have equal weight with the equitable claims of the government whose title is to be determined.

VI. The evacuation of all Russian territory and such a settlement of all questions affecting Russia as will secure the best and freest coöperation of the other nations of the world in obtaining for her an unhampered and unembarrassed opportunity for the independent determination of her own political development and national policy and assure her of a sincere welcome into the society of free nations under institutions of her own choosing; and, more than a welcome, assistance also of every kind that she may need and may herself desire. The treatment accorded Russia by her sister nations in the months to come will be the acid test of their good will, of their comprehension of her needs as distinguished from their own interests, and of their intelligent and unselfish sympathy.

VII. Belgium, the whole world will agree, must be evacuated and restored, without any attempt to limit the sovereignty which she enjoys in common with all other free nations. No other single act will serve as this will serve to restore confidence among the nations in the laws which they have themselves set and determined for the government of their relations with one another. Without this healing act, the whole structure and validity of international law is forever impaired.

VIII. All French territory should be freed and the invaded portions restored, and the wrong done to France by Prussia in 1871 in the matter of Alsace-Lorraine, which has unsettled the peace of the world for nearly fifty years, should be righted, in order that peace may once more be made secure in the interest of all.

IX. A readjustment of the frontiers of Italy should be effected along clearly recognizable lines of nationality.

X. The peoples of Austria-Hungary, whose place among the nations we wish to see safeguarded and assured, should be accorded the freest opportunity of autonomous development.

XI. Rumania, Serbia, and Montenegro should be evacuated; occupied territories restored; Serbia accorded free and secure access to the sea; and the relations of the several Balkan states to one another determined by friendly counsel along historically established lines of allegiance and nationality; and international guarantees of the political and economic independence of territorial integrity of the several Balkan states should be entered into.

XII. The Turkish portions of the present Ottoman Empire should be assured a secure sovereignty, but the other nationalities which are now under Turkish rule should be assured an undoubted security of life and an absolutely unmolested opportunity of autonomous development, and the Dardanelles should be permanently opened as a free passage to the ships and commerce of all nations under international guarantees.

XIII. An independent Polish state should be erected which should include the territories inhabited by indisputably Polish populations, which should be assured a free and secure access to the sea, and whose political and economic independence and territorial integrity should be guaranteed by international covenant.

XIV. A general association of nations must be formed under specific covenants for the purpose of affording mutual guarantees of political independence and territorial integrity to great and small states alike.

In regard to these essential rectifications of wrong and assertions of right we feel ourselves to be intimate partners of all the governments and peoples associated together against the Imperialists. We cannot be separated in interest or divided in purpose. We stand together until the end.

⤙ HISTORICAL INTERPRETATION ⤚

BERNADOTTE E. SCHMITT ON THE ORIGINS OF WORLD WAR I

Bernadotte E. Schmitt, *The Origins of the First World War*, Pamphlet No. 39, The Historical Association (London, 1958), pp. 6–7. By permission of The Historical Association.

AMONG THE most respected interpreters of World War I is Bernadotte E. Schmitt, Andrew MacLeish Distinguished Service Professor Emeritus of Modern History at the University of Chicago, and sometime United States Editor-in-Chief of *Documents of Foreign Policy, 1918–1945*. Professor Schmitt was unimpressed with the popular explanation that the war had grown out of economic jealousies and rival imperialism. While admitting the existence of such rivalries, he saw the more important factor in political conflict.

The primary cause of war was the conflict between political frontiers and the distribution of peoples, the denial of what is commonly called the right of self-determination (although this term was not ordinarily used before 1914). In 1914, from the Rhine eastwards, political frontiers, as determined by the Congress of Vienna a century before and by the wars of the nineteenth century, everywhere cut across well recognized lines of nationality. To begin with, Germany held Alsace-Lorraine, taken from France in 1871, where the majority of the population resented having been annexed to Germany, disliked German rule, and wished to return to France. Austria-Hungary contained eleven different racial groups, nine of which were kept in greater or less submission by a ruling clique of the other two (Germans, Magyars). In the Balkans, racial and political frontiers rarely coincided. Finally, the western portion of the Russian Empire was made up of non-Russian regions represented today by Finland, the Baltic States, and Poland. Poland was the most notorious case, for it was still divided between the Austrian, German and Russian empires which had partitioned it in the eighteenth century. So Germany was faced with the problem of French, Danish and Polish minorities, and Austria-Hungary consisted chiefly of minorities. Some minorities were treated more harshly than others, but everywhere they were growing increasingly restless and demanding change. In some cases minorities were able to look across their own frontiers to free kinsmen who, it was hoped, would one day free them from the oppression (as they saw it) under

which they suffered. The Yugoslavs in both Austria and Hungary, denied relief by their Habsburg rulers, turned for help to Siberia under King Peter Karageorgevich, and the Romanians of Transylvania, in south-eastern Hungary, gazed longingly across the Carpathians at independent Romania under its Hohenzollern king. Neither Yugoslavs nor Romanians had in the past been united, but if the nineteenth century had seen the unification of Italians and Germans, why should not the twentieth century witness the joining together of Yugoslavs or Romanians? The Poles, too, dreamed of reunion, even if before 1914 there seemed no prospect of it.

More than any other circumstance, this conflict between existing governments and their unhappy minorities was responsible for the catastrophe of 1914. Germany understood perfectly well that the annexation of Alsace-Lorraine could be maintained only by the sword, and France knew equally well that the provinces could be regained only by the sword. The multi-national Habsburg state depended more and more on force, less and less on the loyalty of its peoples. The partition of Poland was maintained only by force. Since the astonishing victories of Prussia in the wars against Denmark, Austria and France were attributed to its conscript armies, it was not surprising that the new German Empire established in 1871 continued to recruit its armies by universal service. Inevitably, Germany's neighbours adopted the same system. Not only that, but every increase in strength, every improvement in the weapons of war made by one country, had to be met by all. From 1872 to 1913, this rigorous competition in the building up of armies went on, every government spending as much money as it could persuade its people to pay or its national economy would support (Germany bore this cost easily, but for Italy the burden was ruinous), without, however, any corresponding increase in security being felt. In fact, the proportionate strength of the various armies was not greatly different in 1914 from what it had been in 1872, but the feeling of insecurity was much greater than it had been forty years earlier. The memoirs of General Ludendorff, the most famous German soldier of the war, are eloquent on this point.

Of course, disputed and unstable frontiers were not the exclusive reason for great armies. From time immemorial European governments had maintained armies, partly to keep order at home, partly for use in diplomatic bargaining, and sometimes for aggression and conquest; but certainly the determination of monarchs and governments to preserve their territories intact in the face of growing dissatisfaction with the *status quo*, made the competition in armaments more deadly than it had been in earlier generations.

It was because of the increasing feeling of insecurity that European governments, one after another, sought to strenghten their respective positions by concluding alliances with other governments having similar interests.

❧ TEN BASIC BOOKS ❧

ARMAGEDDON: WORLD WAR I, 1914–1918

1. Albertini, Luigi, *The Origins of the War of 1914,* 3 vols. (New York, 1952–1957).

2. Buchan, John, *A History of the Great War,* 4 vols. (New York, 1921–1922).

3. Churchill, Winston S., *The World Crisis, 1911–1918,* 6 vols. (New York, 1923–1929).

4. Edmonds, James E., *A Short History of World War I* (New York, 1951).

5. Falls, Cyril, *The Great War* (New York, 1959).†

6. Fay, Sidney B., *The Origin of the War,* 2 vols., 2nd ed. (New York, 1943, R. 1966).†

7. Liddell Hart, Basil H., *A History of the Great War, 1914–1918* (London and Boston, 1934).

8. Montgelas, Maximilian von, *The Case for the Central Powers* (New York, 1925).

9. Schmitt, Bernadotte E., *The Coming of the War, 1914,* 2 vols. (New York, 1930).

10. Tuchman, Barbara, *The Guns of August* (New York, 1962).†

37

The Long Armistice, 1919-1939

GENTLEMEN, PLENIPOTENTIARIES OF THE GERMAN EMPIRE,

THIS IS neither the time nor the place for superfluous words. You have before you the accredited plenipotentiaries of the great and lesser Powers, both Allied and Associated, that for four years have carried on without respite the merciless war which has been imposed upon them. The time has now come for a heavy reckoning of accounts. You have asked for peace. We are prepared to offer you peace. . . .

There will be no verbal discussion, and observations must be submitted in writing. The plenipotentiaries of Germany will be given fifteen days in which to put into French and English their written observations on the entire treaty. . . .

—GEORGES CLEMENCEAU to the German delegation at Versailles, May 7, 1919

1. World Order: The League of Nations

The League of Nations. The critical task in the postwar world of 1919 was to achieve international order in a milieu marked by the discontent of the defeated powers, the disillusionment of the victors, and the retreat of the United States into isolation. The League of Nations was devised as an attempt to achieve the centuries-old dream of humanitarians—that a warless world was a possibility. "The Covenant we offer," said Wilson, "must be based primarily upon moral sanctions with resort to force only as a last necessity."

The League of Nations, suggested by the South African soldier and statesman Jan Smuts (1870–1950), was designed as an agency for handling affairs of common concern to all nations. The fourteenth of Wilson's famous points had suggested the formation of such a general association. The first twenty-six articles of the Treaty of Versailles embraced the Covenant or written constitution of the League of Nations. The Preamble revealed the aims of

the new world organization: "The High Contracting Parties, in order to promote international cooperation and to achieve international peace and security by the acceptance of obligations not to resort to war, by the prescription of open, just, and honorable relations between nations, by the firm establishment of the understandings of international law as the actual rule of conduct among Governments, and by the maintenance of justice and a scrupulous respect for all treaty obligations in the dealings of organized peoples with one another, agree to this Covenant of the League of Nations."

Membership in the League was reserved for the victor powers (Germany was accepted as a member in 1926, Russia in 1934). The League organization consisted of: (1) an Assembly, representing all the members, in which each member was entitled to three delegates but only one vote, and which conferred, advised, and deliberated, but did not legislate; (2) a Council, composed at first of nine members (five permanent, representing the Great Powers, and four nonpermanent, chosen by the

Assembly), with authority to formulate plans for the reduction of armaments and mediate in international disputes; and (3) a permanent Secretariat, composed of a staff of civil servants to collect data, register treaties, and perform the secretarial work of the League. Supplementary organizations, such as the technical organization of the Economic and Financial Organization, and advisory committees, such as the Committee on Mandates, worked hand-in-hand with the League.

Functions of the League. Article 10 of the League Covenant provided for an agreement among the member nations "to respect and preserve as against external aggression the territorial integrity and existing political independence of all Members of the League." The key article of the Covenant was Article 16, calling for the application of economic sanctions (penalties) against any nation resorting to armed hostilities. Many observers attributed the weakness of the League to the fact that this clause lacked military teeth:

ARTICLE 16. Should any Member of the League resort to war in disregard of its covenants under Articles 12, 13 or 15, it shall *ipso facto* be deemed to have committed an act of war against all other Members of the League, which hereby undertake immediately to subject it to the severance of all trade or financial relations, the prohibition of all intercourse between their nationals and the nationals of the covenant-breaking State, and the prevention of all financial, commercial or personal intercourse between the nationals of the covenant-breaking State and the nationals of any other State, whether a Member of the League or not.

Handling of Political Disputes. The League handled more than thirty serious political dis-

European boundary changes after 1919.

putes, most of them legacies of the war. Differences over the Aaland Islands in the Gulf of Bothnia between Finland and Sweden were settled by awarding the islands to Finland with the provision that she was to respect Swedish rights. The Mosul Boundary dispute was ended by fixing the boundary between Turkey and Iraq. The Corfu dispute between Italy and Greece was resolved by ordering Greece to pay an indemnity to Italy for the assassination of Italian diplomats on Greek soil. Similarly, disputes over Vilna, Memel, Upper Silesia, Albania, Chaco, and Leticia were arbitrated with more or less success. While settling relatively minor differences, the League failed to deal effectively with such major disputes as those arising over Japan's actions in Manchuria in 1931, the Italo-Ethiopian War, and the Spanish Civil War.

Administrative Work. The League sought to alleviate economic distress in Austria, Hungary, Greece, Bulgaria, Estonia, and Danzig, but without much success in an era of general worldwide economic insecurity. It supervised the plebiscite of January 13, 1935, by which the Saar Basin was awarded to Germany. It administered Danzig until the Nazis seized control of the city in 1939. Each year the League received reports on the mandates, the surrendered possessions of Germany and Turkey. (Class A mandates were lands which had reached a comparatively high stage of development—Syria, Lebanon, Palestine, Transjordania, and Iraq; Class B mandates, lands which were less advanced—the Cameroons, East Africa, Togoland, and Ruanda-Urundi; and Class C mandates, remote and backward areas—Western Samoa, Nauru, South-West Africa, and former German Pacific Islands). At the same time the League sought to guard the rights of some 30,000,000 people scattered throughout Europe under the special minority treaties. Little could be done, however, except protest against the more flagrant violations of minority rights.

Handicaps of the League. The importance of the League of Nations lay in the fact that it established a precedent for a world order.

It was handicapped by its failure to include the defeated powers in the original membership. A more severe difficulty was the abstention of the United States. In his history of World War II, Winston Churchill claimed that the League of Nations was ruined by the failure of the United States to take an active role in its affairs. Other contributing factors to the seeming failure of the League were the survival of power diplomacy, the unwillingness of the major powers to disarm, and the fact that the Peace Treaties were not adjusted to new conditions. Nevertheless, with the adoption of the Covenant, the governments as well as the peoples of the world, perhaps unconsciously, emerged from the chaos of unrestricted national sovereignty, and established a modest beachhead by providing world society with a formal constitution. Despite all its limitations, the League was the first important step in a system of organized international cooperation.

International Labor Organization and World Court. Article 23 of the League Covenant provided for an autonomous International Labor Organization dedicated to the maintenance of "fair and humane conditions of labor for men, women, and children in all countries." The I.L.O., an integral part of the League of Nations despite its autonomous position, made recommendations for the improvement of working conditions throughout the world, promoted progressive labor legislation, and supported research on labor problems. Although the United States refused to join the League of Nations, she became affiliated with the I.L.O. in 1935. A separate protocol provided for the formation of a Permanent Court of International Justice, or World Court, consisting of fifteen judges elected for a term of nine years. Its purpose was "to hear and determine any dispute of an international character which the parties thereto submit to it," as well as to issue advisory opinions upon any dispute referred to it by the Council or the Assembly of the League of Nations. A court of law (unlike the Hague Court, which was a court of arbitration), the World Court rendered decisions based upon international law. Presidents Warren G. Harding (1865–1923) and Calvin

Coolidge (1872–1933) vainly made efforts to have the United States become a member of the World Court.

2. Financial Chaos: Reparations and War Debts

Problems of Reparations. Article 231 of the Treaty of Versailles was the controversial war-guilt clause, to which the Germans objected. In effect, it placed moral responsibility on Germany and her allies for causing the war, the first time in history that the right of the conqueror was not considered as sufficient in itself. The controversy over war guilt was heated and embittered. On July 25, 1914, shortly before he was assassinated, Jean Jaurès, the French Socialist leader, said in his last speech: "In an hour so grave, so filled with perils for all of us, I am not going to look for responsibility. We have ours, and I testify before History, that we should have foreseen them. . . . The colonial politics of France, the political underhandedness of Russia, and the brutal will of Austria have contributed to create the horrible mess in which we find ourselves." Germans protested that they were not to blame for the war. Nevertheless, the victorious Allies insisted that Germany pay heavy reparations.

The Peace Conference at Versailles, while fixing categories of payment (pensions, allowances, etc.), did not set a total figure of reparations but called for a payment of approximately $5,000,000,000 on account. In July 1920, Allied statesmen at the Spa Conference fixed apportionment of the indemnity: France 52%; the British Empire 22%; Italy 10%; Belgium 8%; and others 8%. In January 1921 the Supreme Council fixed the total at $55,000,000,000. In April 1921 the Reparations Commission set the figure at $35,000,000,000. By the London Agreement of May 1921 the total was reduced to $16,000,000,000. The unwillingness, and indeed inability, of the Germans to meet the annual installments led to French occupation of the Ruhr in January 1923. Germany soon underwent a crippling inflation and economic collapse.

The Dawes Plan (1924) was devised to balance Germany's budget and stabilize the mark. The recommendations of the Dawes Committee included: (1) a sliding scale of German payments for five years from $250,000,000 to $625,000,000; (2) the funds were to be obtained from mortgages on German railways, industries, and a transport tax; (3) German currency was to be stabilized by means of a foreign loan; and (4) fiscal and economic unity was to be restored to Germany. The Dawes Plan failed because it did not set a total reparations bill and because Germany was still subjected to foreign international control.

In 1929 another attempt, the Young Plan, was made to solve the reparations problem. This plan provided for: (1) a fixed capital value of reparations at $8 billion payable in

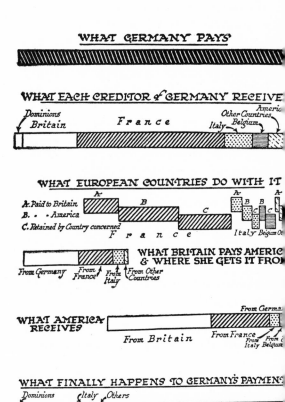

The Young Plan, 1929, was upset by the world depression.

fifty-eight annual installments; (2) identity of the number of installments with the number of interallied debt installments; and (3) provision for a Bank of International Settlements (B.I.S.) for handling all payments. The Young Plan was upset by the world depression of 1929. President Hoover in 1931 proposed a year's moratorium on war debts and reparations. The next year, by the Lausanne Settlement, Germany was required to make a final payment of $714,000,000 in bonds to the B.I.S., the bonds to be renegotiated at the end of three years, while a Gentlemen's Agreement made settlement contingent upon a satisfactory adjustment of war debts.

Issue of War Debts. The problem of reparations was closely linked with that of war debts. Debts owed to the United States totaled $10,000,000,000, to England $8,750,000,000, to France $2,000,000,000. American statesmen demanded the repayment of these debts as legitimate loans, while their European counterparts, pointing to America's augmented wealth during the war and the fact that she had entered the conflict late, urged cancellation. Funding agreements between the nations provided for cancellations varying from 18 to 75 per cent, a decrease in interest rates, and payment in annual installments over a period of sixty-two years. Even the generous reduction of debts failed to solve the bitter differences of opinion. The outbreak of World War II merely suspended the controversy over debts incurred in World War I.

3. International Relations: Quest for Security and Disarmament

The Diplomatic Climate. The system of diplomatic alliances and the armaments race before World War I did not succeed in forestalling global conflict. After 1919 the lessons of experience were largely forgotten as nations revived their past futile behavior in the quest for security and disarmament. The defeated powers, discontented with the peace settlements, did what they could to repudiate the agreements. Soviet Russia and the Western nations were mutually suspicious of one another, the French were depressed by a feeling of insecurity, and the British continued to think and act in terms of the old balance of power. The stage was being set for an even greater conflict.

The League's Security System. In this highly dangerous situation the League sought to improve the security system it had organized. The Draft Treaty of Mutual Assistance, unanimously adopted in September 1923, called for member nations to aid one another if attacked, and directed the League Council to determine the aggressor within four days after the outbreak of a dispute. This draft treaty was strongly criticized on the ground that the terms "aggressor" and "aggression" were not adequately defined. No nation signed it. Britain, especially, opposed the agreement because it called for global commitments that she was not prepared to undertake. In 1924 Eduard Herriot (1872–1957) and James Ramsay MacDonald (1866–1937) proposed the Geneva Protocol, or the Protocol for the Pacific Settlement of International Disputes, which defined an aggressor as a member nation which resorted to war before employing some peaceful method of settling a dispute. This, too, proved futile. The British Conservative ministry, under Prime Minister Stanley Baldwin (1867–1947), refused ratification, and the document never came into force.

Rival Alliances. Three systems of military alliances—French, Russian, and Italian—were set up almost at once after World War I. France, with a passion for security amounting almost to an obsession, proposed immediately after the peace negotiations an Anglo-American Treaty of Guarantee designed to preserve her from future attack by Germany, but the United States Senate refused to ratify the treaty and Britain was reluctant to give a unilateral guarantee. Unwilling to depend for security upon the League, the French concluded a series of alliances and alignments designed to assure their hegemony in Europe (Belgium, 1920; Poland, 1922; Czechoslovakia,

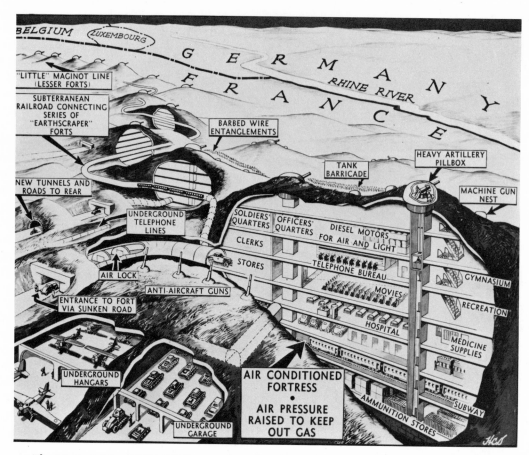

The Maginot Line (1929–1934) was planned and constructed along the eastern frontier of France as an impregnable defense against possible invasions. The line of fortifications discontinued along the French-Belgian border, partly due to Belgian objections but also because France anticipated no threat in this area. The very sense of security derived by the French from the Maginot Line was to some extent responsible for their rapid defeat by Nazi Germany in 1940.

1924; Rumania, 1926; Yugoslavia, 1927; Russia, 1933; and Britain, 1938). In the meantime France encouraged the formation, by Masaryk and Beneš in 1920 and 1921, of the Little Entente between Czechoslovakia, Yugoslavia, and Rumania, designed to prevent the restoration of Hapsburg dominions.

Fearing a combined international effort to destroy her communist experiment, Russia concluded a chain of nonaggression pacts and commercial treaties with her neighbors (Germany, 1922; Turkey, 1925–1933; Lithuania, 1926; Afghanistan, 1926; Persia, 1927; Finland, 1931; Latvia, 1933; France, 1933; Poland, 1933; and Rumania, 1934).

Italy, disappointed by the peace treaties and

eager to obtain Nice, Savoy, and areas of North Africa, similarly concluded a series of treaties of friendship and neutrality (Czechoslovakia, 1924; Yugoslavia, 1924; Rumania, 1926; Albania, 1927; Hungary, 1927; Turkey, 1928; Greece, 1928; and Germany, 1936).

These international agreements were expanded in a complicated maze of alignments. The Four Power Treaty (1933), between Italy, France, England, and Germany, was regarded by Soviet Russia as a new "Holy Alliance" directed against her. The Balkan Pact (1934), signed by Greece, Rumania, Turkey, and Yugoslavia, was designed to prevent Italian expansion in the Balkans. The Stresa Agreement (1935) sought to form a united front between

Great Britain, France, and Italy. The balance of power shifted once more in 1936 with the formation of the Rome-Berlin Axis and again in 1939 with the Berlin-Moscow Axis.

Locarno Treaties (1925). The Rhineland still remained one of the danger spots. When Germany proposed frontier guarantees to France, Gustav Stresemann (1878–1929) of Germany, Aristide Briand (1862–1932) of France, and Austen Chamberlain (1863–1937) of England met at the Locarno Conference in Switzerland (October 5–16, 1925) and drafted a series of seven treaties. The boundaries of Germany, France, and Belgium, as set by the peace treaties, were guaranteed; the signatories agreed to arbitrate all disputes; Germany renounced her claim to Alsace-Lorraine; France agreed to relinquish her efforts to establish a separatist republic in the Rhineland; and Germany was to be admitted to the League of Nations (her formal entry took place in 1926). There was much praise for the Spirit of Locarno, which it was believed, would lead to a new era of peace and goodwill.

Kellogg-Briand Peace Pact (1928). The spirit of conciliation was again demonstrated in 1928 when the French petitioned the United States to enter into a pact mutually outlawing war. The United States then proposed a multilateral treaty, the Kellogg-Briand Peace Pact, or the Paris Peace Pact (August 27, 1928), by which the signatories of fifteen nations agreed to renounce war as an instrument of national policy and subscribed to the principles of arbitration and conciliation to settle international disputes. By 1933, sixty-two nations had signed the pact, but its failure to settle the Manchurian controversy in 1931 showed that something more than an international agreement was required to prevent war. (*See page 616.*)

Problem of Disarmament. The desire of reasonable men to reduce or abolish the old competition in military and naval armaments was frustrated by the close link between security and disarmament. The Covenant of the League of Nations contained several provisions for disarmament, but they were never successfully implemented. In 1921–1922 President Warren G. Harding called the Washington Naval Conference which, by a Five-Power Treaty, provided for a ten-year capital-ship holiday and restricted the remaining ships to a ratio of United States, 5; Great Britain, 5; Japan, 3; France, 1.67; and Italy, 1.67. The Geneva Naval Parley, called in 1927 to limit the construction of smaller ships, broke up without any accomplishments. The London Naval Conference of 1930 decided on a six-year agreement limiting the tonnage of cruisers and submarines, but its effect was destroyed by including an escalator clause permitting any signatory to increase its naval tonnage should it feel that any other country endangered its security. The London Naval Parley of 1935–1936 was called when Japan demanded naval equality with Great Britain and the United States. The result of this conference was that the Great Powers terminated the capital-ship holiday and resumed unlimited construction.

Attempts to achieve land disarmament were similarly unsuccessful because of the lack of a common yardstick on which all nations could agree. The League strove to achieve a measure of disarmament but always without success. At the World Disarmament Conference, opened at Geneva in 1932, various plans were proposed to surmount the difficulties. President Herbert Hoover (1874–1964) suggested a one-third reduction in land forces and the total abolition of tanks, bombing planes, and large mobile guns. Germany insisted that she be permitted to arm to French parity; on failing to win this point, she left the Conference and resigned from the League (October 1933). Further meetings in 1934 resulted only in hopeless deadlock, whereupon the Conference adjourned. The conference having failed, all further efforts to limit armaments were abandoned. The diplomats of the major nations were becoming convinced that it would be foolhardy to disarm at a time when Adolf Hitler was building German military power and threatening vengeance for Versailles.

❧{ KEY DOCUMENT }❧

THE KELLOGG-BRIAND PACT FOR THE RENUNCIATION OF WAR, AUGUST 27, 1928

United States Department of State, *The General Pact for the Renunciation of War*, Text (Washington, 1928), pp. 1–3.

THE KELLOGG-BRIAND PACT, resulting from a correspondence between Aristide Briand, the French foreign minister, and Frank B. Kellogg, the American secretary of state, was a comprehensive plan to renounce war "as an instrument of national policy." The pact was accepted later by nearly all the nations of the world, including Germany, Italy, and Japan. It was widely believed that this pact would usher in an era of international understanding. But in fact international relations in Europe and the world deteriorated as the system of collective security was gradually undermined.

The President of the German Reich, the President of the United States of America, His Majesty the King of the Belgians, the President of the French Republic, His Majesty the King of Britain, Ireland and the British Dominions beyond the Seas, Emperor of India, His Majesty the King of Italy, His Majesty the Emperor of Japan, the President of the Republic of Poland, the President of the Czechoslovak Republic,

Deeply sensible of their solemn duty to promote the welfare of mankind;

Persuaded that the time has come when a frank renunciation of war as an instrument of national policy should be made to the end that the peaceful and friendly relations now existing between their peoples may be perpetuated;

Convinced that all changes in their relations with one another should be sought only by pacific means and be the result of a peaceful and orderly process, and that any signatory Power which shall hereafter seek to promote its national interests by resort to war should be denied the benefits furnished by this Treaty;

Hopeful that, encouraged by their example, all the other nations of the world will join in this humane endeavor and by adhering to the present Treaty as soon as it comes into force bring their peoples within the scope of its beneficent provisions, thus uniting the civilized nations of the world in a common renunciation of war as an instrument of their national policy;

Have decided to conclude a Treaty and . . . have agreed upon the following articles:

ARTICLE 1. The High Contracting Parties solemnly declare in the names of their respective peoples that they condemn recourse to war for the solution of international controversies, and renounce it as an instrument of national policy in their relations with one another.

ARTICLE 2. The High Contracting Parties agree that the settlement or solution of all disputes or conflicts of whatever nature or of whatever origin they may be, which may arise among them, shall never be sought except by pacific means.

ARTICLE 3. The present Treaty shall be ratified by the High Contracting Parties . . . in accordance with their respective constitutional requirements. . . .

This Treaty shall . . . remain open as long as may be necessary for adherence by all the other Powers of the world. Every instrument evidencing the adherence of a power shall be deposited at Washington. . . .

It shall be the duty of the . . . United States to furnish each Government named in the Preamble and every Government subsequently adhering to this Treaty with a certified copy of the Treaty and of every instrument of ratification or adherence.

⊰{ HISTORICAL INTERPRETATION }⊱

JOHN MAYNARD KEYNES ON THE ECONOMIC CONSEQUENCES OF THE PEACE, 1919

John Maynard Keynes, *The Economic Consequences of the Peace*, pp. 226–249, *passim*. Copyright, 1919, by Harcourt, Brace & World, Inc.; renewed, 1948, by Lydia Lopokova Keynes. Reprinted by permission of the publishers.

IN 1919 JOHN MAYNARD KEYNES presented the first non-German criticism of economic aspects of the Versailles Peace Conference. Believing the economic features of the peace unfair and unworkable, Keynes condemned Wilson, Clemenceau, and Lloyd George for their work at the conference. His book, a popular success, became almost at once the subject of a controversy that has not yet subsided. It reflected accurately the bitterness of the immediate post-World War I era.

This chapter must be one of the pessimism. The Treaty includes no provisions for the economic rehabilitation of Europe—nothing to make the defeated Central Empires into good neighbors, nothing to stabilize the new States of Europe, nothing to reclaim Russia; nor does it promote in any way a compact of economic solidarity amongst the Allies themselves; no arrangement was reached at Paris for restoring the disordered finances of France and Italy, or to adjust the systems of the Old World and the New.

The Council of Four paid no attention to these issues, being preoccupied with others—Clemenceau to crush the economic life of his enemy, Lloyd George to do a deal and bring home something which would pass muster for a week, the President to do nothing that was not just and right. It is an extraordinary fact that the fundamental economic problems of a Europe starving and disintegrating before their eyes, was the one question in which it was impossible to arouse the interest of the Four. Reparation was the main excursion into the economic field, and they settled it as a problem of theology, of politics, of electoral chicane, from every point of view except that of the economic future of the States whose destiny they were handling. . . .

The essential facts of the situation, as I see them, are expressed simply. Europe consists of the densest aggregation of population in the history of the world. This population is accustomed to a relatively high standard of life, in which, even now, some sections of it anticipate improvement rather than deterioration. In relation of

other continents Europe is not self-sufficient; in particular it cannot feed itself. Internally the population is not evenly distributed, but much of it is crowded into a relatively small number of dense industrial centers. This population secured for itself a livelihood before the war, without much margin of surplus, by means of a delicate and immensely complicated organization, of which the foundations were supported by coal, iron, transport, and an unbroken supply of imported food and raw materials from other continents. By the destruction of this organization and the interruption of the stream of supplies, a part of this population is deprived of its means of livelihood. Emigration is not open to the redundant surplus. For it would take years to transport them overseas, even, which is not the case, if countries could be found which were ready to receive them. The danger confronting us, therefore, is the rapid depression of the standard of life of the European populations to a point which will mean actual starvation for some (a point already reached in Russia and approximately reached in Austria). Men will not always die quietly. For starvation, which brings to some lethargy and a helpless despair, drives other temperaments to the nervous instability of hysteria and to a mad despair. . . .

The significant features of the immediate situation can be grouped under three heads: first, the absolute falling off, for the time being, in Europe's internal productivity; second, the breakdown of transport and exchange by means of which its products could be conveyed where they were most wanted; and third, the inability of Europe to purchase its usual supplies from overseas. . . .

What then is our picture of Europe? A country population able to support life on the fruits of its own agricultural production but without the accustomed surplus for the towns and also (as a result of the lack of imported materials and so of variety and amount in the saleable manufacture of the towns) without the usual incentives to market food in return for other wares; and an industrial population unable to keep its strength for lack of food, unable to earn a livelihood for lack of materials, and so unable to make good by imports from abroad the failure of productivity at home. . . .

Lenin was certainly right. There is no subtler, no surer means of overturning the existing basis of society than to debauch the currency. The process engages all the hidden forces of economic law on the side of destruction, and does it in a manner which not one man in a million is able to diagnose. . . .

We are faced in Europe with the spectacle of an extraordinary weakness on the part of the great capitalist class, which has emerged from the industrial triumphs of the nineteenth century, and seemed a very few years ago our all-powerful master. The terror and personal timidity of the individuals of this class is now so great, their confidence of their place in society and in their necessity to the social organism so diminished, that they are the easy victims of intimidation. . . .

The inflationism of the currency systems of Europe has proceeded to extraordinary lengths. The various belligerent Governments, unable, or too timid or too short-sighted to secure from loans or taxes the resources they required, have printed notes for the balance. In Russia and Austria-Hungary this process has reached a point where for the purposes of foreign trade the currency is practically valueless. The Polish mark can be bought for about three cents and the Austrian crown for less than two cents, but they cannot be sold at all. The German mark is worth less than four cents on the exchanges. In most of the other countries of Eastern and South-Eastern Europe the real position is nearly as bad. The currency of Italy has fallen to little more than a half of its nominal value in spite of its being still subject to some degree of regulation; French currency maintains an uncertain market; and even sterling is seriously diminished in present value and impaired in its future prospects. . . .

Thus the menace of inflationism described above is not merely a product of the war, of which peace begins the cure. It is a continuing phenomenon of which the end is not yet in sight.

All these influences combine not merely to prevent Europe from supplying immediately a sufficient stream of exports to pay for the goods she needs to import, but they impair her credit for securing the work capital required to re-start the circle of exchange and also, by swinging the forces of economic law yet further from equilibrium rather than towards it, they favor a continuance of the present conditions instead of a recovery from them. An inefficient, unemployed, disorganized Europe faces us, torn by internal strife and international hate, fighting, starving, pillaging, and lying.

❧ TEN BASIC BOOKS ❧

THE LONG ARMISTICE, 1919–1939

1. Bassett, John S., *The League of Nations* (New York, 1928).
2. Birdsall, Paul, *Versailles Twenty Years After* (Hamden, Conn., 1941).
3. Carr, Edward H., *International Relations Between the Two World Wars, 1919–1939*, rev. ed. (New York, 1948).†
4. Craig, Gordon A., and Felix Gilbert, eds. *The Diplomats, 1919–1939* (Princeton, N. J., 1953, R. 1963).†
5. Gathorne-Hardy, Geoffrey M., *A Short History of International Affairs, 1920–1939*, 4th ed. (London and New York, 1950).

6. Hogan, Willard N., *International Conflict and Collective Security* (Lexington, Ky., 1955).

7. Madariaga, Salvador de, *Disarmament* (New York, 1929).

8. Martin, Andrew, *Collective Security: A Progress Report* (Paris, 1952).

9. Walters, Francis P., *A History of the League of Nations*, 2 vols., rev. ed. (New York, 1960).

10. Zimmern, Sir Alfred E., *The League of Nations and the Rule of Law*, 2nd ed. (London, 1939).

38

The Democratic States on Trial, 1919-1939

IN THE future days, which we seek to make secure, we look forward to a world founded upon four essential human freedoms.

The first is freedom of speech and expression—everywhere in the world.

The second is freedom of every person to worship God in his own way—everywhere in the world.

The third is freedom from want—which, translated into world terms, means economic understandings which will secure to every nation a healthy peacetime life for its inhabitants—everywhere in the world.

The fourth is freedom from fear—which, translated into world terms, means a worldwide reduction of armaments to such a point and in such a thorough fashion that no nation will be in a position to commit an act of physical aggression against any neighbor—anywhere in the world.

That is no vision of a distant millennium. It is a definite basis for a kind of world attainable in our own time and generation. That kind of world is the very antithesis of the so-called new order of tyranny which the dictators seek to create with the crash of a bomb.

—PRESIDENT FRANKLIN D. ROOSEVELT, Four Freedoms Speech,
January 6, 1941

1. Great Britain and the Democratic Tradition

General Progress of Political Democracy. The great hope of the twentieth-century democratic world was to advance the gains in democracy initiated in the English Revolution of 1688, the American Revolution of 1776, and the French Revolution of 1789. At the opening of the new century, popular rule was neither complete nor unchallenged. Progress was rapid in those countries where democracy had taken root and where distrust of the common man as a potential revolutionary had begun to disappear. The franchise was extended, and the woman suffrage movement, though slow in getting started, was successful in Britain

(1918), in Germany (1919), and in the United States (1920). The democratic countries revised the bicameral system of legislation by stripping their upper houses of much legislative power. With the defeat of ruling dynasties in Germany, Austria-Hungary, Russia, and Turkey, most succession states became democratic republics. Monarchical Europe, with a thousand years of ruling dynasties, was transformed into republican Europe, with only eight monarchies left, among twenty-six states. In the Orient, despite relics of imperialism, democracy made a belated appearance, but its path was rugged. Gains in religious and educational equality were made in the democratic states throughout the world.

Political Developments in Great Britain.
Great Britain, although on the winning side in World War I, found herself beset in the postwar period with problems of chronic unemployment, declining foreign trade, and an unstable currency. The Lloyd George coalition (1916–1922) negotiated with the Irish, proposed reforms for India, and in 1921 concluded a trade treaty with Soviet Russia. The cabinet fell because of public dissatisfaction with its pro-Irish attitude, its weak foreign policy, and economic depression. The Conservative ministries of 1922–1924, promising "tranquility and stability," tried to solve financial difficulties by enacting higher protective tariffs and by lowering duties on British Empire merchandise (imperial preference). The first Labour ministry (January 1924–November 1924), headed by James Ramsay MacDonald (1866–1937), accepted the Dawes Plan, issued the Geneva Protocol, and recognized Soviet Russia, but it was defeated on the issue of Anglo-Soviet friendship. The Conservative ministry (1924–1929) accepted the Locarno Pact (1925), sponsored German membership in the League of Nations, and severed diplomatic relations with Russia. This ministry fell on the issue of unemployment. The second Labour ministry (1929–1931) agreed to the Young Plan, and renewed relations with the Soviet Union, but failed to solve the unemployment problem. The National Coalition (1931–1935) abandoned the gold standard, supported the Disarmament Conference of 1932–1933, and called the World Economic Conference (1933). The Conservative government forced the abdication of Edward VIII (December 10, 1936), attempted to neutralize the Rome-Berlin Axis by concluding defensive alliances, and declared war on Germany (September 3, 1939).

Economic Policies. The English depression became chronic after World War I because of the burden of the national war debt, economic rivalry with the United States and Japan, obsolete machinery, impoverishment of British customers, high tariffs, and British persistence in remaining on the gold standard until 1931. Many attempts were made to solve economic problems. The Lloyd George coalition ministry enacted the Unemployment Insurance Act of 1920, increased the dole, and passed the Safeguarding of Industries Act which established a protective tariff of 33⅓ per cent. The Conservative and Labour parties differed on the problem of free trade versus protection; the former favored higher protective tariffs, while the latter supported free trade. Both parties extended the system of unemployment insurance and advocated widows', orphans', and old-age insurance. The Labour Party proposed a capital levy on large fortunes and the nationalization of key industries, while the Conservatives saw a solution in higher income taxes and reduced salaries for government employees.

Religion and Education. The Anglican Church is the State Church of England, and the sovereign is by law the supreme head of the Church. Full religious liberty exists, and there are no civil disabilities because of religion. In 1919 the Church of England Assembly (Powers) Act was passed, designed to make the Church more self-governing, although Parliament still retained ultimate authority. In 1928 the new revised Prayer Book, intended to bring the doctrines of the Anglican Church closer to those of the Roman Catholic Church, was rejected by the House of Commons, mostly through the opposition of non-Anglican Protestants. In 1918 the Fisher Educational Act provided for a system of free, compulsory elementary education and scholarships for secondary education. The postwar years brought a great expansion of the British university system.

Irish Free State. For centuries most of the Irish people earnestly wanted their freedom from Britain. The British, regarding a free Ireland as a possible military base for their enemies, refused to grant independence. The twenty-six southern countries of Ireland, agricultural and Roman Catholic, demanded freedom, while the six northern counties of Ulster, industrial and Protestant, preferred to retain their bonds with the Empire. At the beginning of World War I the British Parliament enacted the Home Rule Bill of 1914, granting Ireland a large degree of autonomy, but its operation was suspended because of the war. Agitation was followed by rebellion in 1916. The Irish Home Rule Bill of 1920 set up two distinct governments, Northern Ireland and the Irish Free State. The Irish Constitution of 1937 made no mention of the king of England or the British Commonwealth. Eire continued to demand the return of the whole island, including the northern counties of Ulster.

The British Commonwealth of Nations. Since the great Imperial Conference of 1911, the slow political growth of dominion authority in Canada, Newfoundland, the Union of South Africa, Australia, and New Zealand had been sanctioned by Britain. In 1930 the Imperial Conference accepted the Balfour Report declaring Great Britain and her dominions to be autonomous communities within the British Empire, but that all were bound to the Crown by a common allegiance. These principles were expressed in the Statute of Westminster (1931), creating the British Commonwealth of Nations and binding the nations in a Commonwealth citizenship. (*See page 629.*)

2. *The United States as a World Power*

Postwar America. The United States emerged from World War I as a mighty political and economic power. Between 1790 and 1920 the population of the United States, a fusion of diverse peoples, increased more than twenty-six times, rising from 3,929,214 to 105,710,620. On the domestic scene after World War I, the giant nation was absorbed with the problems of conserving natural resources and assuring social justice in a rapidly expanding economy. In foreign affairs, the nation had to face its new role of "manifest destiny" in world affairs, the pressing problem of relations with Asia, and the conflict of isolationism versus world-leadership.

Second Presidency of Wilson (1917–1921): Return to Isolationism. Woodrow Wilson (1856–1924) had been reelected in 1916 on the slogan, "He kept us out of war." Despite

the triumph of 1918, the American people quickly reverted to their traditional policy of keeping out of foreign entanglements. Although President Wilson tried to persuade the people of the United States to accept the Covenant of the League of Nations and the Versailles Treaty, he was unable to overcome the opposition of what he called "a little group of willful men" (including Senators Henry Cabot Lodge, W. E. Borah, and Hiram Johnson). The most serious objection to the League concerned Article 10 of the Covenant, which guaranteed the territorial integrity and political independence of all member nations, and which, the isolationists felt, would mean that American troops would have to be sent to adjust any further quarrels in Europe. In November 1919 and again in March 1920, the Senate rejected acceptance of the Covenant in any form, thereby, in effect, dooming the usefulness of the League.

Warren G. Harding (1921–1923): Return to Normalcy. In the election of 1920 the Democrats were thrown out of power on the issues of the League, the Peace Treaty, the high cost of living, and the economic dislocation caused by the closing of war industries. Under President Warren G. Harding (1865–1923), who called for a return to normalcy, the Republican Congress repealed the excess-profits tax and enacted higher protective tariff schedules. The Harding administration was blackened by exposure of graft and corruption in the Veterans Administration and in the leasing of government oil fields (Teapot Dome scandal). Harding's most important achievement in foreign affairs was the Washington Naval Conference (1921–1922), which attempted to limit naval armaments and to find solutions for problems in the Far East.

Calvin Coolidge (1923–1929): The Mad Twenties. Vice-President Calvin Coolidge (1872–1933), who succeeded to the presidency upon Harding's death in 1923, was reelected in 1924. The country now entered a period of prosperity, during which the national debt and personal income taxes were reduced. In foreign affairs the Coolidge ad-

The President marches in a Liberty Day Parade. Woodrow Wilson's idealistic hopes for the United States as part of the League of Nations were thwarted by the isolationist tendencies of a nation not accustomed to being a major world power.

ministration was faced with the perplexing problems of international war debts, confiscation of American investments in Mexican mines and oil fields, a revolution in Nicaragua that led Coolidge to send American marines there to protect treaty rights, furtherance of goodwill in the Latin-American states, and the issues of the World Court and the League of Nations. At the end of his second term Coolidge announced, "I do not choose to run."

Herbert Hoover (1929–1933): The Depression. In the election of 1928 Herbert Hoover (1874–1964), the Republican candidate, was elected to the presidency on a platform of farm relief, economy in government, better international relations, and enforcement of prohibition. It soon became apparent that the

greatest industrial nation in the world could not isolate itself economically. The short-lived postwar prosperity was followed by the stock-market crash of October 24, 1929, after which American trade and capital export declined precipitously. The Hoover administration attempted a series of moves to counteract the depression: The Federal Farm Board was created in 1929 to help the farmer by buying his surplus production; the Smoot-Hawley Tariff of 1930 further increased the rates on manufactured goods and agricultural products; the Glass-Steagel Act of 1932 sought to rehabilitate business by making it less difficult to obtain loans; and the Reconstruction Finance Corporation, created in 1932, made loans to distressed financial enterprises. In foreign affairs the Hoover administration took part in the

London Naval Conference of 1930 and the Disarmament Conference of 1932–1933. The Stimson Doctrine (1932), refusing to recognize any territorial changes brought about in violation of the Kellogg-Briand Peace Pact, was announced after Japan's invasion of Manchuria in 1931 and her establishment of the puppet state of Manchukuo.

Franklin D. Roosevelt (1933–1945): The New Deal. Franklin Delano Roosevelt (1882–1945), defeating Herbert Hoover for the presidency in 1932, took office during the gravest economic depression in American history. Roosevelt launched a "New Deal" for the "forgotten man" and an extensive program of social reform. His purpose, denounced by *laissez-faire* critics, was to bring all business enterprises under stricter federal control, on the ground that the stock-market collapse, the perilously accelerating rate of bank failures, and unemployment in millions had been brought about by bankers, promoters, and industrialists. Furthermore, Roosevelt sought to protect the little man from destitution as the business depression spread. The Democratic Congress passed legislation providing for relief for the unemployed, federal loans to banks, financial aid to farmers, a civil works program, a Social Security Act for the aged and indigent, and controlled inflation. The new acts came quickly: Emergency Bank Relief (March 9, 1933) provided for stringent bank control and the prohibition of exporting or hoarding gold; the Agricultural Adjustment Act (May 12, 1933) gave relief to the farmers by reducing the acreage of basic agricultural products; the Muscle Shoals-Tennessee Valley Act (May 18, 1933) provided for a great public works project; the National Industrial Recovery Act (June 13, 1933) brought codes of fair competition and the regulation of production; and the Railroad Relief Act (June 10, 1933) rescued the railroads from bankruptcy. Prohibition was repealed (In October 1919 Congress had passed the Volstead Act prohibiting the manufacture and selling of intoxicating liquors.) Immediate employment was offered to young men in the Civilian Conservation Corps. Small home-owners were helped. These relief measures rapidly increased the federal debt, whereupon new taxes were applied to corporation profits, income taxes, and amusements.

The swing was definitely toward governmental economic and social control. Employers and businessmen complained, but small farmers, city workers, and the middle class in general approved the New Deal, and reelected Roosevelt in 1936 and 1940 by imposing majorities. Roosevelt thus became the first American president to serve a third term. Roosevelt's unorthodox domestic policies were supplemented by a strong foreign policy stressing world cooperation, friendship with the Latin-American countries, and rigid opposition to aggressive nationalism. The world situation was so critical that the Roosevelt administration was forced to extend its efforts to bridge the economic gaps into a broad program of national defense.

3. Canada and Latin America

Dominion of Canada. Canada, bridge between Great Britain and the United States, was an autonomous self-governing Dominion in the British Commonwealth of Nations. Politically oriented toward Great Britain, Canada was geographically and to some extent economically tied with the United States. A vast and richly endowed country, Canada became one of the leaders of world trade. She maintained a restrictive immigration policy, accepting immigrants slowly. The two main national groups, British and French, remained loyal to their respective European cultural heritages, although politically they were tied to the British Crown.

Latin-American States. Economically retarded, Mexico was beset in the twentieth century with problems of land reform and with the desire to curb foreign economic infiltration. Government after government fell on the issue of altering the hacienda system (of large estates) introduced by the Spanish three centuries earlier. Attempts were made to resolve the issue of foreign economic control by confiscation, repudiation, or refunding.

LATIN AMERICA

Most of the population in Brazil, the fifth largest country in area in the world, was clustered along the narrow coastline, with the Brazilian hinterland forming the world's largest tropical forest. The country's progress was hindered by unsatisfactory transportation, lack of coal, a lack of electrification, an oppressive climate, and the prevalence of disease. Nevertheless, with thousands of immigrants coming from the distressed areas of Europe, Brazil made significant strides in education, transportation, and the exploitation of her natural resources. She maintained a traditional policy of friendship with the United States. The Argentine Republic, while retaining the outer forms of democracy, developed into a dictatorship in 1946 with the election of Juan Perón. The Argentine government took the lead among Latin-American countries in opposing the influence of the United States.

Latin-American nations in general had a similar pattern of problems: mixed populations, inadequate transportation, poverty, disease, bad climate, political instability, and economic vulnerability. While accepting the protection of the Monroe Doctrine, they resented North American "interference" in their affairs. Some twenty-one Latin-American republics remained economically dependent on the United States. A series of meetings between the Latin-American nations and the United States was designed to meet the problems of regional solidarity and hemispheric security. The Pan-American Union, established as early as 1890, and given its name in 1910, convened a series of inter-American conferences every four years in the capitals of member states. The Union also intervened whenever an armed conflict appeared imminent. The system functioned well: only one major war—the Chaco War between Bolivia and Paraguay in 1932–1935—occurred in Latin America in the twentieth century.

4. Dichotomy: Democratic France in the Twenties and Thirties

The Political Image Unfolds. Having suffered huge losses in manpower, money, and natural resources, France after World War I

set herself to the tasks of restoration, raising money to defray costs, and achieving a system of national security. The Third French Republic was a centralized state, with a weak executive, a bicameral legislature, and a cabinet. Whereas party government was the rule in England, coalition or bloc government was the order in France. The multiplicity of political parties and the constant cabinet reshuffling made for an unstable government, although the French believed that stability was maintained by a continuing bureaucracy and by consistent political principles among the various parties. The *Union Sacrée* (1914–1919) functioned as a coalition cabinet during the war years under the leadership of Georges Clemenceau (1841–1929). The Bloc National (1919–1924) upheld the Treaty of Versailles, demanded severe punishment for Germany, resumed diplomatic relations with the Vatican, strongly opposed socialism, restored the devastated areas of France, and organized the futile occupation of the Ruhr in 1923. The Left Bloc (1924–1926) introduced anticlerical measures, sponsored stability of the franc, accepted the Dawes Plan (1924), withdrew French troops from the Ruhr, and helped negotiate the Locarno Pact (1925). The National Union ministry (1926–1929) reformed the system of taxation, stabilized the franc, refunded the national debt, and continued the reconstruction of devastated areas.

From 1929 to 1935 there was continued ministerial instability, reflecting the economic distress of the period, fear of Germany, and internal unrest. The Popular Front (1936–1938), composed of a coalition of Radical Socialists, Socialists, and Communists, attempted reform by enacting legislation favorable to the workers, nationalizing the armament industry, reorganizing the Bank of France, and increasing taxes. In the meantime, it opposed such Fascist organizations as the *Croix de Feu* and the *Action Française*. The Daladier ministry (1938–1940) suspended much legislation of the Popular Front, sought to stimulate production for national defense, negotiated the Munich Pact with Germany (1938), and was responsible for the declaration of war on Germany (September 3, 1939).

Critical Economic Situation. Postwar France remained in chronic financial distress, with a huge war debt, heavy reconstruction costs, an ancient system of taxation, and an inflated franc. Ministries emerged and fell on the issue of inflation. The government was on the verge of bankruptcy and revolution as one ministry after another sought to balance the budget and restore some measure of national prosperity. The critical economic situation was aggravated by the world economic depression, loss of tourist trade, nonpayment of reparations by Germany, persistence of France in remaining on the gold standard, and a high-tariff policy. Added to these troubles was the attitude of many Frenchmen who failed to see any connection between payment of income taxes and national solvency.

The Religious Scene. In 1901 and 1905 a growing sense of secularization had led to reduction of religious orders in France, closing of monasteries and religious schools, and nationalization of Church property. In 1921, diplomatic relations were resumed with the Vatican, and the rightist political parties made efforts to effect a reconciliation with the Church.

Recurrent Thorn: Alsace and Lorraine. The cession of Alsace and Lorraine to France by the Treaty of Versailles was followed almost immediately by disputes there over religion, language, political rights, and economic policies. An effort to Gallicize the area by banning the German language was opposed in the provinces. A compromise solution allowed French to be taught exclusively in the first two years of a child's school life, with German instruction permitted as a choice thereafter. The German-speaking natives objected when they were ousted from positions in the civil service and the public utilities. An attempt by the Left Bloc in 1924 to disestablish the Church in Alsace and Lorraine was met with a strike. Again, a compromise solution called for attendance at the same lay schools, with religious instruction offered in separate religious schools. Then, in 1925, Alsace and Lorraine were incorporated into the governmental system of France and were governed from Paris until the Nazi invasion.

5. Other Democratic States

The New Truncated Austria. The Treaty of Saint-Germain dissolved the Dual Monarchy of Austria-Hungary which had been established by the *Ausgleich* (compromise) of 1867. When a constituent assembly, convening in February 1919, failed to achieve an Austro-German *Anschluss* (union) because of French protests, a federal republican constitution was promulgated, with a bicameral legislature and Dr. Michael Hainisch as first president. Reduced to one-quarter of her former size and with a population now of only 6,680,000, Austria found it almost impossible to maintain an independent economic existence except with financial aid arranged by the League of Nations. The League Council in 1924 guaranteed a loan of $131,690,000 for 20 years, subject to the supervision of a League Commissioner. Political dissension was unending as Pan-Germanists, Social Democrats, Christian Socialists, and Communists sought to obtain control. The country was split into two opposing forces, the Reds and Blacks. The *Schutzbund* (Defensive Alliance), dominantly socialist and worker, was opposed by the *Heimwehr* (Home Defense Force), representing the Pan-German, Fascist, agricultural, and religious interests. Engelbert Dollfuss (1892–1934), a Christian Socialist, became chancellor in May 1932.

The advent of Hitler to power in Germany in 1933 created a new menace for Austria, when the Nazis launched an aggressive program to bring about *Anschluss* between Austria and Germany. For the time being, the intervention of Mussolini saved Austria's political independence. On September 21, 1933, Dollfuss suspended the Austrian republican constitution and established a corporative state under authoritarian leadership. Nazi pressure, instigated from Germany, continued. In 1934 the Austrian Nazis, with the complicity of Nazi Germans, staged an unsuccessful revolt. On July 25, 1934, Dollfuss was assassinated by Austrian Nazis. In 1938, following a stormy

Austrian Chancellor Engelbert Dollfuss whose assassination in Vienna cleared the way for the ultimate union of Austria and Nazi Germany.

meeting with Hitler, Kurt Schuschnigg, the Austrian chancellor, was forced to appoint several pro-Nazi ministers to his cabinet. Fearing the outcome of a plebiscite ordered by Schuschnigg, Hitler invaded and annexed Austria on March 12–15, 1938. Following a Nazi-run plebiscite that obtained 99 per cent affirmative votes, Austria was formally incorporated into the German Reich.

Citadel of Democracy: Czechoslovakia. The Republic of Czechoslovakia was created out of the three former provinces of Bohemia, Moravia, and Austrian Silesia, and the two former Hungarian provinces of Slovakia and Ruthenia. Thomas Masaryk and Eduard Beneš were the fathers of what turned out to be, while it lasted, the most democratic state in

Central Europe. Its constitution provided for a confederated republic, a legislature consisting of a Senate and a Chamber of Deputies, and a president elected for seven years by both houses. From its birth the Czechoslovak Republic had such internal problems as differences with the Catholic Church because of its expropriation of Church lands; confiscation of land from royalty and nobility; and minority questions (in a population of 14,000,000 people there were, in addition to Czechs and Slovaks, some 3,300,000 Germans, 760,000 Magyars, and 480,000 Ruthenians, as well as Poles and Jews). The new republic was the most prosperous economically of the Succession States. Most old Austro-Hungarian industries were located in what became Czechoslovakia and, although landlocked, the new nation negotiated several fruitful commercial treaties with other countries. Since their absorption of Austria was only a prelude to further expansion in Central Europe, the Nazis intensified their propaganda among the German minority in the Sudeten area of Czechoslovakia. The Czech government vainly offered a series of concessions, but it was apparent that Hitler would settle for nothing less than union with Germany. German troops occupied the Sudeten area after the Munich Agreement of 1938. Although Britain and France guaranteed her new frontiers, Czechoslovakia did not survive her amputation. Beneš resigned under pressure from Germany, and the Czech government was reorganized along pro-Nazi lines. By March 1939 Germany occupied the entire republic.

The Smaller States. Belgium obtained valuable timber and zinc resources as a result of the acquisition of Eupen, Malmédy, and Moresnet at Versailles in 1919. King Albert I (r. 1909–1934), who had achieved great popularity in World War I, rebuilt his country and devalued the Belgian franc after having been given dictatorial powers in a severe financial crisis. The most persistent difficulty was the Flemish problem. The Flemish half of the population agitated for suffrage and linguistic reforms.

Queen Wilhelmina, who had begun her reign in the Netherlands as a ten-year-old girl in

1890, continued on the throne after World War I. The Dutch, traditionally friendly to political exiles, granted asylum to Germany's deposed emperor, William II. With a well-administered government, a large supply of skilled labor, effective union organizations, and a wealthy colonial empire, the Netherlands prospered. The foreign policy was to preserve strict neutrality in the quarrels among the Great Powers.

The Treaty of Versailles forbade Luxemburg to continue as a member of the German tariff union. A tiny nation, Luxemburg faced the world with an army consisting of one company of volunteers with 170 men and 6 officers. It remained industrially strong because of its great iron deposits. Its influence on the international scene was negligible.

Sharing similar historical backgrounds, the Scandinavian countries of Norway, Denmark, and Sweden were progresive democracies with paternalistic governments and advanced systems of social insurance. All three operated on the basis of a capitalistic economy, somewhat modified by the widespread devel-

opment of cooperatives. Educationally, the three countries remained at the head of the European states. Illiteracy was virtually unknown. All three states maintained a traditional neutrality and expressed their international-mindedness by strongly supporting the League of Nations.

Established in a small country about half the size of Maine, the Swiss developed a reputation as the one consistently neutral nation of Europe but, at the same time, imposed an obligation of personal military service on every male citizen from twenty to forty-eight years of age. Switzerland's system of democratic government was one of the most advanced in modern times. One of the most industrialized countries in Europe, Switzerland produced watches, precision instruments, laces, and pharmaceuticals. She became the most important financial center in the world. With an advanced educational system, full religious freedom, a tradition of political sanctuary, and a rigid policy of neutrality, Switzerland was among the most prosperous nations in Europe.

$\{$ KEY DOCUMENT $\}$

THE STATUTE OF WESTMINSTER, DECEMBER 11, 1931

The Public General Acts of Great Britain, 1932 (London, 1933), pp. 13–17, *passim.*

GREAT BRITAIN was the first of the Western democracies to realize that the days of centralized empire were past. In one of the most remarkable changes of modern times, the old empire disappeared and in its place there came one resting solely on voluntary cooperation. The Statute of Westminster, passed by the British Parliament in December 1931, made legal the new status of the British dominions. Following are the key paragraphs of the Statute.

. . . Whereas . . . inasmuch as the Crown is the symbol of the free association of the members of the British Commonwealth of Nations, and as they are united by a common allegiance to the Crown, it would be in accord with the established constitutional position of all the members of the Commonwealth in relation to one another that any alteration in the law touching the Succession to the Throne or the Royal Style and Titles shall hereafter require the assent as well of the Parliaments of the Dominions as of the Parliaments of the United Kingdom;

And whereas it is in accord with the established constitutional position that no law hereafter made by the Parliament of the United Kingdom shall exend to any of the said Dominions as part of the law of that Dominion otherwise than at the request and with the consent of that Dominion;

And whereas the Dominion of Canada, the Commonwealth of Australia, the Dominion of New Zealand, the Union of South Africa, the Irish Free State, and Newfoundland have severally requested and consented to the submission of a measure to the Parliament of the United

Kingdom for making such provision with regard to the matters aforesaid as is hereafter in this Act contained;

Now, therefore, be it enacted by the King's most excellent Majesty by and with consent of the Lords Spiritual and Temporal, and Commons, in this present Parliament assembled, and by the authority of the same, as follows:

. . . .

2. a. The Colonial Laws Validity Act, 1865, shall not apply to any law made after the commencement of this Act by the Parliament of a Dominion.

b. No law and no provision of any law made after the commencement of this Act by the Parliament of a Dominion shall be void or inoperative on the ground that it is repugnant to the law of England. . . .

3. It is hereby declared and enacted that the Parliament of a Dominion has full power to make laws having extraterritorial operation.

4. No Act of Parliament of the United Kingdom passed after the commencement of this Act shall extend or be deemed to extend, to a Dominion as part of the law of that Dominion, unless it is expressly declared in that Act that that Dominion has requested, and consented to, the enactment thereof. . . .

❦ HISTORICAL INTERPRETATION ❧

HELEN HILL ON THE SPIRIT OF MODERN FRANCE

Helen Hill, *The Spirit of Modern France*, World Affairs Pamphlet, No. 5, Foreign Policy Association (New York, 1934), pp. 14–17. Courtesy of the Foreign Policy Association, Inc.

FRANCE BETWEEN the two World Wars was beset by her traditional political instability, with a multiplicity of parties and frequent ministerial shifts. These political pecularities were explained by Helen Hill in a passage describing "the two Frances."

The French Revolution irrevocably divided the internal politics of France; since that time there have been twin Frances, mortal enemies. The residual bitterness of the American Civil War is still a measurable political factor, yet in America the geographic solidarity of the two sides has been an incomparably softening influence. The French Revolution was a Civil War in which, over large areas, the lines were drawn on a social rather than a geographic basis; when it was over, no softening distance mitigated the bitterness of the ex-combatants. As the completeness of the democratic victory, with the passage of time and the coming of reaction, became less complete, two Frances emerged to confront each other—authoritarian France, founded on the institutional trinity of monarchy, army and Church, in later years particularly the Church, and democratic France, founded on the ideological trinity of liberty, equality and fraternity between individual citizens. All through the nineteenth century these two were locked in an uncertain struggle for supremacy, with now one the victor, now the other. Since the Revolution, each has been four times dominant. The Third Republic has now lasted some sixty years, but its stability has more than once been highly doubtful. Certain recurrent issues have never exhausted their dynamite; a generation ago the Dreyfus case touched off a charge no less powerful than that of the Dred Scott decision; today the Stavisky affair is giving republican institutions a similar shock.

The ceaseless struggle between authoritarian and democratic France is the reality which renders French politics explicable. Three factors go to make it up—the political, the economic, the religious; and closely connected with all of them, since the French system of representation in this respect parallels the American, is that of geographic location.

The centralization of French life in Paris is all too apt to blind the foreigner to the diversity of provincial France, and to the way that diversity affects French politics.

Take the map of France as a study in political geography. Straight across the country, south of the Loire, lies the France of democracy. The

French Revolution swept all before it in the south; Toulouse has never ceased to be the capital of radicalism. The Breton peninsula of the west also has changed but little since the bloody days of La Vendée; it is a country of Celtic extremes, where the black conservatism of Church and château lowers over the red fringe of the fishing fleet. In the northeast is Alsace-Lorraine and the vulnerable frontier, the scene of past wars, present fortifications, future anxieties, where a strong government is held to be the best one. In the north-center is Paris, which exerts on these very diverse elements the unifying influence of a political capital.

Take the map of France as a study in economic geography. The south and east are the home of the French peasant proprietor, of most of the four and a half million Frenchmen with holdings of less than fifteen acres, of the million more with holdings of less than seventy-five. In the west are the large landed estates, little changed through a century. Eighty-five per cent of the industrial wealth of France lies in the north-north-east; the major part of the iron and steel industry is within a short gunshot of the frontier. In the cities—Paris, Lyons, Marseilles—are entrenched the class-conscious workers. . . .

Take the map of France as a study in religious geography. Thirty-six of the forty million French are adherents of the Roman Catholic Church, but in studying the political aspect of their religion it is important to discriminate between those who are Catholics by conviction and those who are Catholics by convention. There are some twelve million Catholics by conviction, the intensity of whose religious life causes them to be classified as *catholiques pratiquants*. There are twice as many others whose conventional Catholicism is directly comparable to the conventional Protestantism of the United States. They call the priest for weddings and funerals; they throng the churches for the principal services of Christman and Easter Day; and when a campaign contains a religious issue, they vote with a passion that exceeds their faith. The famous Frenchman who said *"Je suis athée, mais naturellement, je suis catholique"* adequately summarizes the nature of their conformity. A church so constituted tends to become a temporal institution. . . .

❧ TEN BASIC BOOKS ❧

THE DEMOCRATIC STATES ON TRIAL,
1919–1939

1. Brogan, Denis W., *The Development of Modern France, 1870–1939* (London, 1940).†
2. Bruun, Geoffrey and Victor S. Mamatey, *The World in the Twentieth Century* (Boston, 1962).
3. Clough, Shephard B., *France: A Study of National Economics, 1789–1939* (New York, 1939, R. 1964).
4. Kohn, Hans, *Force or Reason* (Cambridge, Mass., 1937).
5. Mansergh, Nicholas, *Survey of British Commonwealth Affairs: Problems of External Policy, 1931–1939* (London, 1952).
6. Marriott, John A. R., *Dictatorship and Democracy* (New York, 1935).
7. Mowat, Charles L., *Britain Between the Wars, 1918–1940* (Chicago, 1955).
8. Rappard, William E., *The Quest for Peace Since the World War* (Cambridge, Mass., 1940).
9. Rauch, Basil, *The History of the New Deal, 1933–1938* (New York, 1944, R. 1963).†
10. Schlesinger, Arthur M., Jr., *The Vital Center* (Boston, 1949).†

39

Reprise of Tyranny: The Totalitarian States, 1919-1939

COME, COMRADES in strong ranks,
Let us march toward the future.
Let us be bold and proud phalanxes,
Ready to dare, ready to venture.
Let the ideal for which we fought so much triumph
    at last:
The national brotherhood
Of Italian civilization.

Let not our people remain
Any longer craven or debased;
Let them reawaken to a new life
Of more powerful splendor.
Come, let us raise high the torch
To light us the way,
In toil and in peace
Let there be true freedom.

Refrain:
    Youth, youth!
    Springtime of beauty,
    In Fascism is the salvation
    Of our liberty.

        —"Giovinezza", Official anthem of Mussolini's
        Fascist Italy

1. The Rise of Totalitarianism

The Hard Legacy. World War I left in its wake an interrelated tangle of troublesome problems: unemployment, inflation, industrial dislocation, contracted markets, depression, and colonial unrest. The attempt by the Have-not powers to achieve economic self-sufficiency in age of economic dislocation led to their repudiation of liberal and democratic methods and the emergence of absolutist and intolerant ideologies. Bewildered by the complexities of government and the stresses and strains of economic troubles, and not vigilant in recognizing encroachments on their liberty, the peoples of these nations sought a quick solution of their problems by turning to the promises of dictators.

All the postwar dictatorships had certain common characteristics, regardless of their official titles: (1) one leader became the symbol of the state, with unchecked power to enforce his will; (2) propaganda, controlled by the government, was used to glorify the dictatorial regime, excoriate opponents, and mold the educational system to the whims of the leader; (3) all opposition was forcibly crushed, and failure to support the dominant party was considered equivalent to treason; (4) secret police and spies were utilized to cement the dictatorship; and (5) aggressive nationalism and militarism were promoted as a means of assuring the continued existence of the dictatorship.

Until World War I the term "revolution" had generally indicated an advance of democracy, a movement toward individual freedom. After the war there appeared a new kind of revolutionary movement dedicated to the elimination of democratic ideas and practices. This totalitarianism took two forms—fascism and communism—both of which denied the freedom of the individual and established a new order elevating the State to an exalted position. Despite its denial of the dignity of the individual, the new totalitarianism obtained the support of millions. It became the most powerful and uncompromising enemy that democracy had ever known. Economic dislocations resulting from the war hit both the working and the middle classes. In some countries helpless and despairing workers turned to communism as a solution for their misery. In others, the middle class, hard hit by inflation, depression, and burgeoning monopolistic combinations, accepted fascism because it promised to destroy communism and curb Big Business. Those democratic countries maintaining the tradition of individual freedom were able to resist totalitarianism by inaugurating economic reforms. Others—notably Soviet Russia, Italy, Germany, Hungary, and Spain—turned to communism or fascism as a solution for their ills.

Historical Controversy: The Nature of Totalitarianism. It is difficult to establish precise definitions of the current "-isms." This is especially true in ascertaining the nature of totalitarianism in the twentieth century. Is contemporary totalitarianism a unique phenomenon? Or is it a movement with antecedents both in thought and action? There is no general agreement among scholars. The term "totalitarianism" may be applied to two closely related but, nevertheless, distinct meanings. In one meaning it denotes a *type* of society characterized by such traits as concentration of power in the hands of one man or a few men, the absence of individual rights, and the equation of the state with society. In the second meaning it refers to one definite *trait*, the unlimited extension of state functions.

A further problem relates to the question as to whether Fascist and Communist totalitarianism were basically alike or not. Thus, Hans Kohn, in *Revolutions and Dictatorships* (1939), and Sigmund Neumann, in *Permanent Revolution* (1942), treated them as basically alike. On the other hand, Franz Neumann, in *Behemoth* (1942), dealt with the Nazi dictatorship as something distinctive, the creation of big business, bureaucracy, and army. Konrad Heiden, in *Hitler's Rise to Power* (1944), and Alan Bullock, in *Hitler—A Study in Tyranny* (1952), stressed the personal side of dictatorship, thereby tending to obscure the uniqueness of totalitarianism. Hannah Arendt, in *The Origins of Totalitarianism* (1951), argued that totalitarianism is an outgrowth of the establishment of dictatorship under modern conditions. She saw totalitarianism as the fruit of imperialism and "the organization of atomized men."

2. *Ideological Drive: The Union of Soviet Socialist Republics (U.S.S.R.)*

Prologue: March 1917 Revolution. At the outbreak of World War I the Russian nation was swept by a wave of patriotic fervor. Under the weight of prolonged struggle, however, the spirit of the people began to break. There was much dissatisfaction with the inefficient and corrupt government, incompetent military leaders, and a series of military disasters. Famine fanned the popular discontent; shops were looted; and strikes broke out among the transport and metal workers. In February 1917 Tsar Nicholas II tried to crush a factory strike in Petrograd, and on March 11, he dissolved the *Duma*. In the meantime, the workers had organized the Petrograd Soviet of Workers' and Soldiers' Deputies which, together with members of the dismissed *Duma*, led a revolution against the tsar and formed a Provisional Government headed by Prince Georgi Lvov (1865–1925), a moderate Constitutional Democrat (the *Cadet* party), and Alexander Kerensky (1881–   ), leader of the Social Revolutionary Party. The Romanov dynasty ended when the tsar recognized the new government and abdicated. The Allies promptly recognized the Provisional Government.

The Provisional Government on Trial. The Provisional Government granted full civil, political, and religious liberties, restored the constitution of Finland, granted self-government to Poland, and decided to continue the war against the Central Powers. But the Lvov cabinet and the Petrograd Soviet began quarreling over continuing the war. The liberals

were soon forced out of office, although Kerensky remained in the cabinet. Local governments fell into the hands of revolutionary councils, or soviets of workers', peasants', and soldiers' delegates who demanded immediate peace and the nationalization of all industries. The Bolsheviks (majority wing of the Social Democratic Party) opposed the Provisional Government as bourgeois and called for extending the revolution.

Explosion: November 1917 Revolution. At this critical moment the Germans, anxious to get Russia out of the war, sent exiled revolutionary Nikolai Lenin (1870–1924) across

Familiar scene during the Russian revolutions of 1917–1920. Innocent bystanders as well as revolutionaries were indiscriminately cut down by machine-gun fire.

Germany in a sealed train to Russia. Preaching the slogan of "Peace! Land! Bread!"—understandable to the Russian masses—Lenin organized a *coup d'état* which was executed on November 6 and 7, 1917, just preceding the proposed convocation of the second All-Russian Congress of Soviets. Lenin became chairman of the new Council of People's Commissars; Leon Trotsky (1879–1940), who had played a leading role in the revolution, commissar for foreign affairs; and Joseph Stalin (1879–1953), commissar for national minorities. The Bolshevik government announced a

program calling for immediate peace, suppression of all opposition, establishment of a dictatorship of the proletariat, and world revolution.

Historical Controversy: Fall of the Provisional Government. There is little agreement on the explanation of why the Bolsheviks were able to overthrow the Provisional Government in November 1917 and seize power. Alexander Kerensky, the leading figure in the coalition government set up in March 1917, claims that it was betrayed by both the Left and the Right. Adherents of a personal dictatorship, he said, impatiently awaited the overthrow of the Provisional Government in the mistaken belief that after three weeks of Bolshevik rule there would be a national authority established. This view was challenged by Leonid Strakhovsky, a Russian monarchist exile in Canada, who argued that Russia was betrayed by Kerensky himself. According to Strakhovsky, Kerensky was cowardly, irresponsible, and foolish enough to accuse General Kornilov, who might have saved Russia, of being a counter-revolutionary.

Bolshevik historians, without exception, hold that the Marxist-Leninist political philosophy guided the Communists to triumph and made victory under Lenin's leadership inevitable. The Bolshevik Party, they say, could not possibly have won in November 1917 if its leaders had not mastered the theory of Marxism and if they had not learned to regard this theory as a guide to action. Non-Communist historians prefer the explanation that the Bolsheviks won because they were the only well-organized, disciplined, and efficiently led political movement able to take advantage of a fluid situation. Bolshevik organization and strategy, thorough and shrewd, brought victory for what was not actually a majoritarian movement. The enemies of Bolshevism were weak, poorly organized, divided, and apathetic. Non-communist historians say that Lenin emphasized the divisions among his opponents and capitalized on their apathy.

A German Peace: Treaty of Brest-Litovsk. As a means of exposing "the capitalist imperialist powers" the Bolsheviks published the secret treaties of the Allies, to which the tsarist regime had subscribed. Trotsky suggested a peace based on self-determination, no annexations, and no indemnities, but he was ignored by the Allies. On March 3, 1918, the Bolsheviks signed a separate peace with Germany at Brest-Litovsk. Russia was obliged to abandon Poland, Lithuiania, the Ukraine, the Baltic provinces, Finland, and Transcaucasia, pay 6,000,000,000 gold marks in reparations, and grant Germany the status of most-favored nation in Russian markets. The Treaty of Brest-Litovsk, an indication of what was in store for the Allies had they lost the war, was later abrogated by the victors' peace.

Solidification: Consolidation of the Revolution. The Red Army, impelled by revolutionary fervor, was engaged from 1917 to 1920 in combating a series of counter-revolutionary movements led by former tsarist officers, adventurers, and representatives of the Allied nations. Aiming to revive the Eastern Front against Germany and to prevent the spread of Bolshevism, the Allies financed these counter-revolutionary attacks and blockaded Russia. The White (anti-Bolshevik) invaders were ultimately expelled (1920) by Trotsky's Red Army, and one by one the counter-revolutionary governments of Kolchak, Judenich, Denikin, and Wrangel collapsed. At the same time, opposition to the Bolsheviks inside Russia was crushed by the *Cheka,* the secret police, who operated on the basis of terror and sent thousands of opponents before revolutionary tribunals. Nicholas and his family were exterminated in a cellar. The old nobility and the bourgeoisie, many of whom sided with the counter-revoutionary leaders, were stripped of their power.

Political Structures: Hierarchy and Mass. The Union of Soviet Socialist Republics (U.S.S.R.) consisted originally of seven confederated socialist states, of which the Russian Socialist Federated Soviet Republic (R.S.F.S.R.) was the largest and most influential. These constituent republics were in turn divided into some 2,500 political units. The federal state was declared to be a "free socialist society of the working people of Russia." All the governments announced their belief in Communist ownership of the means of production, to be effected through dictatorship of the proletariat with "complete authority" vested in the local soviets. The ballot was given to both sexes over eighteen years of age, provided that the voters were productive workers. As representation was vocational rather than geographic, and indirect instead of direct, the upper authorities in the hierarchy were almost entirely removed from popular control.

Despite this outer democratic coating, the U.S.S.R. was in fact a dictatorship directed from above. Behind the elaborate and formal façade was the real power, the Communist Party, consisting of about 2,500,000 members (in a nation of more than 180,000,000), confined largely to the male population and the city workers. The head of the party, the secretary-general, exercised political dictatorship through supreme control of the All-Union Communist Party. The Constitution of 1936 raised the number of constituent republics from 7 to 11, abolished the All-Union Congress, simplified the structure of the state, established the Supreme Soviet, reformed the judiciary, issued a Soviet Bill of Rights, codified Marxist-Leninist-Stalinist principles, and retained the basic Soviet ideology and the one-party system.

Giant Leap: Era of War Communism. Between 1917 and 1921 the Bolsheviks, in a surge of revolutionary fervor, attempted to introduce "pure communism" throughout Russia. They abolished all private ownership of land without compensation; turned over estates of Crown, nobility, and Church to district Soviets of Peasants' Deputies; and seized all factories, mines, railways, banks, shipyards, and natural resources. They forbade the ownership of private property, canceled debts to foreign countries, and expropriated foreign investments in Russia. Chaos resulted as inexperienced party members attempted to run the factories and mines. The transportation system broke down and foreign trade almost disappeared. The peasants, resisting collectivization, hoarded their grain supplies. With production declining and a severe famine following a poor harvest, Russia was on the verge of complete breakdown.

Compromise: The New Economic Policy. In 1921 Lenin recommended a New Economic Policy (N.E.P.), actually a temporary compromise with capitalism. Private retail trade was permitted under government regulation, small factories and shops were restored to their former owners, graduated wage scales were introduced, and experts were imported from abroad to manage the factories. In order to obtain liquid capital for industrial development, concessions were offered to foreign capitalists for exploitation of mines and oil wells inside Russia. Finances were reorganized, inflation was halted, and the currency was stabilized on a gold basis. The system of requisitioning foodstuffs from the peasants was abandoned and a fixed tax on produce was substituted. The renewed opportunity to dispose of their surplus in the open market encouraged peasants to enlarge their cultivable acreage. The government organized cooperative farming to bring about an increase in agricultural output. The result of these measures, "taking one step backward in order to take two forward," as Lenin expressed it, was that industry, business, and agriculture were brought back to prewar standards.

Revolutionary Program: The Five-Year Plans. The First Five-Year Plan (1928–1933) aimed at the complete industrialization of Russia. Under a State Planning Commission (*Gosplan*), production quotas were fixed, and plans were inaugurated for the rapid construction of new plants, factories, and mills, for the faster operation of older enterprises, and for special efforts in the chemical, coal, oil, and similar industries. The goal was to increase manufacturing about 130 per cent and agriculture about 50 per cent. Although some objectives were achieved, the quality of the output remained poor, and inefficient transportation hindered the distribution of manufactured goods. Some three-fourths of the arable land was collectivized. The Second Five-Year Plan (1933–1938) sought to eliminate the "exploitation of man by man" by improving the quality of consumers' goods, promoting collective farming by liquidating the *kulaks* (landowning peasants) and *Nepmen* (small businessmen), and establishing new industrial centers. The Third Five-Year Plan (1938–1942) called for the complete socialization of industry and the full collectivization of farming. The Stakhanov movement, introduced at this time, attempted to substitute "Socialist competition" for capitalist initiative by rewarding workers who produced above the norm in their factory or mine work. The Third Five-Year Plan was converted into a munitions-production program when World War II began.

Social Life in Bolshevik Russia. The educational system of the Soviet Union attacked illiteracy, promoted experiments in progressive education, and emphasized the construction of technical schools. Great importance was attached to education, not only to combat the widespread ignorance among the masses but also to infuse the younger generation with loyalty to the Communist regime. In addition to the schools, every phase of national life was molded by propaganda to conform with Leninist-Stalinist ideology. On the assumption that organized religion was, as Marx had called it, an opiate of the people, the Russian Orthodox Church was disestablished, its property confiscated, and its churches converted to use as museums. "Godless societies" were encouraged, on the ground that religion and

counter-revolution went hand-in-hand. Marriage was removed from ecclesiastical supervision and placed under civil control. The legal system and criminal codes were reformed in accordance with Communist doctrine. Prostitution and crime were treated as illnesses. The death penalty was reserved for the "true criminals—the enemies of the State."

Deadly Rivalry: Stalin Versus Trotsky. After Lenin's death in 1924 a violent struggle for power took place between Stalin and Trotsky. Stalin advocated a policy of socialism in one country; Trotsky demanded a continuing, permanent world revolution. This battle for political supremacy was won by Stalin, who thereupon ruthlessly proceeded to consolidate his own power by removing any opponents or possible enemies from the scene. Stalin's regime became a stark tyranny. Exiled from Russia, Trotsky, who had proposed the organization of a Fourth International, was assassinated in Mexico in 1940.

Lenin Arrives in Petrograd, 1917. Trotsky is noticeably absent in this propagandistic drawing which was done in 1943, after he had been "discredited." Were the picture to be done today, Stalin would probably be left out also.

Foreign Policy of the U.S.S.R. The foreign policy of the Soviet Union was based on the premise that the entire world was in deadly opposition to Russia. When the global revolution failed to materialize, Russia entered upon more or less normal relations with the capitalist nations. In 1922 she won *de facto* recognition at the Conference of Genoa, and at the same time concluded the Treaty of Rapallo with Germany. When Britain recognized Soviet Russia in 1924, there ensued a worldwide movement to accept the new state as a member of the family of nations. Soviet Russia was admitted to the League of Nations in 1934. Between 1922 and 1938 she negotiated a series of trade, nonaggression, and neutrality treaties with her neighbors, while, at the same time, building a powerful army. Accusing Great Britain and the Western democracies of favoring Germany's drive to the East, Soviet Russia in 1939 concluded a pact with Germany. Russia abandoned her doctrine of collective security (full cooperation with the democracies against fascism) and adopted a policy of aggressive expansion in Finland, the Baltic states, and Poland.

The Red Colossus: Soviet Communism in Action. It is not easy to understand the Russian temperament and character. In Winston Churchill's words: "I cannot forecast to you the action of Russia. It is a riddle wrapped in a mystery inside an enigma." Lenin sought to create a monolithic world of one faith and one leadership. This was the only kind of society, he believed, that could bring security to itself as well as salvation for the whole of mankind. Only if the enemies of the true faith were liquidated could there be a safe and secure world. To achieve this aim Soviet Russia fashioned a closed society, in which there was to be no opposition to the regime. Western ideas of liberalism and democracy were scornfully cast aside as inadequate by men who were convinced that they were wielding the sword of history. The task of enforcing absolute obedience was entrusted to the dread OGPU (later the NKVD and the MVD), the secret police that held unlimited power over Soviet citizens. No one could be certain that his neighbor was not a member of the secret police. The result was a general spirit of distrust and suspicion.

Leaders of the Soviet Union contributed a novel kind of morality—anything was desirable if it was in the interest of the revolution. Thousands of peasants starved to death in the early twenties when Lenin's grain collectors took bread from them by force. In the thirties Stalin's agents took the land as well as the bread, exterminating those *kulaks* who resisted. When Winston Churchill later asked Stalin how many had been "blotted out or displaced forever," the latter replied, as recorded in Churchill's memoirs: "'Ten million,' he said, holding up his hands. 'It was fearful. For years it lasted. . . . It was all very bad and difficult —but necessary.'"

At the same time a novel Aesopian language was invented—the distinctly undemocratic society of Soviet Russia was termed "a people's democracy." The aim supposedly was to establish a democratic society by the path of a totalitarian dictatorship. Class rule was abolished in favor of a ruling *political* class, something unique in history. The state was made identical and coextensive with society. Everyone had to do what the government prescribed. This repudiation of democracy was termed by Bolshevik logic "the new democracy."

Perhaps the best way to judge the Soviet state is to compare promise with performance. Marx described the revolutionary period that would ensue between capitalist and Communist society as "nothing but the dictatorship of the proletariat." In reality, the Soviet Union was a dictatorship *over* the proletariat rather than *of* it. The Central Committee of the Communist Party comprising the "collective leadership" of the state is said to represent the best elements of the Soviet society; yet, not one of this group today is a member of the Soviet proletariat.

The leaders of the Soviet Union today maintain that the government must be strengthened ceaselessly as a means of defending socialism from foreign attack. Communist political theology speaks of the Soviet Union as a democracy for the proletariat, *i.e.*, democracy for all. In fact, no divergences of political opinion are permitted; the Communist Party is the only party allowed to exist and all candidates for office must have the approval of the party. In the police state there is little freedom for cultural expression. Lenin preached the doctrine of equality—equality of wages, equality of labor, equality of human beings—and visualized the day when the maxim could be applied: "From each according to his ability; to each according to his needs." His vision received little attention. Actually, a new privileged class arose, consisting of ruling government officials, successful authors and entertainers, and top members of the Communist Party. At the other end of the scale is a mass of peasants and unskilled workers, whose standard of living remains low. Though economic progress was made, it was purchased at high cost in terms of human suffering. Whether the success of forced industrialization was worth the price is still open to question.

3. Sawdust Caesar: Mussolini and Fascist Italy

Milieu: Postwar Italy. Italian patriots, grievously disappointed by the Treaty of Versailles, demanded that their claims to Dalmatia and Albania be recognized, and pleaded that possession of these areas was essential to the establishment of Italian control over the Adriatic. They condemned the government for its failure to acquire colonial spoils in the Near East and Africa. The domestic situation in postwar Italy was critical: a shortage of food and raw materials, a rapid increase in the cost of living, an unbalanced budget, and currency inflation. Revolutionary activities were encouraged by the desperate plight of the masses. Imitating the example of the Bolsheviks in Russia, Italian workingmen resorted to direct action by seizing factories and expelling the owners. An epidemic of strikes disorganized industry and essential public services. Serious disorders broke out in agricultural districts, where peasants seized the land, burned houses, and destroyed crops. Paralyzed by factional intrigues, the government seemed powerless. The country was ripe for revolution. It was at this juncture that the Fascist counter-revolution was set into motion.

Baited Trap: Origins of Fascism. In his early days Benito Mussolini (1883–1945) had been a zealous Socialist. During World War I he was ousted from the party when he demanded that Italy renounce her neutrality and join the Allies. Later, as editor of *Il Popolo d'Italia,* he advocated a program of violent nationalism designed to appeal to all his compatriots suffering from postwar discontent. Mussolini portrayed fascism as a politico-religious philosophy. "Fascism," he said, "is a religious conception in which man is seen in his immanent relationship with a superior law and with an objective Will that transcends the particular individual and raises him to conscious membership of a spiritual society. . . . Fascism besides being a system of government is also, and above all, a system of thought. . . . Fascism is opposed to all the individualistic abstractions of a materialistic nature like those of the eighteenth century; and it is opposed to all Jacobin utopias and innovations. . . . Against individualism, the Fascist conception is for the State; and it is for the individual in so far as he coincides with the State, which is the conscience and universal will of man in his historical existence. . . . Liberalism denied the State in the interests of the particular individual; Fascism reaffirms the State as the true reality of the individual."

Impressed with these ideas, dissatisfied ex-soldiers, the depressed middle class, patriotic youths, hungry farmers, and radical intellectuals joined together in a compact political party called the *Fascio di Combattimento,* or Union of Combat. The "Fascist" name was derived from the Latin *fasces,* a bundle of rods encircling an axe, used in ancient Rome as a symbol of authority. Fascism, portrayed as a unifying factor that would save Italy from Bolshevism, gradually pervaded the bureaucracy, the police, the courts, and the army. Semi-military bands of Black Shirts began breaking up Socialist headquarters, attacking Communist meetings, and compelling workers to return to their jobs. Guns, clubs, and castor oil were used to make converts. The Fascists were victorious in the savage warfare in the streets—a virtual civil war. The triumph of fascism became inevitable when wealthy businessmen and industrialists rallied to its support. On October 26, 1922, some 50,000 Fascists marched on Rome, while Mussolini went in the same direction in a *wagon-lit,* a railway sleeping car. He intimidated the Chamber of Deputies and forced the resignation of Premier Facta. Several days later King Victor Emmanuel III made Mussolini prime minister.

Mussolini Fashions a Dictatorship. Within a year Mussolini transformed the Italian government, which had been modeled upon that of England, into a dictatorship. Rejecting democratic institutions, he demanded and received permanent control over all the military, air, and naval forces as well as over the conduct of foreign affairs. He was given the authority to create legislation by decree. Declaring that there was no room in Italy for any opposition, he suspended civil rights and discouraged his political enemies by imprisoning or exiling their leaders. When Giacomo Matteotti (1885–1924), head of the Socialist Party, was found brutally murdered, the Socialists seceded from the Chamber in protest. Mussolini further silenced criticism by establishing a rigid censorship, suppressing opposition newspapers, forbidding public meetings, dismissing university professors, and establishing special military tribunals to try all opponents of the regime. The Acerbo Election Law, enacted in December 1923, provided that the party polling a plurality vote in a national election was to have two-thirds of the seats in the Chamber of Deputies. With this contemptuous rejection of popular sovereignty Mussolini solidified his dictatorship.

Role of the Fascist Party. The Fascist Party consisted of: (1) the Grand Council of 20 members, which drafted new legislation, filled its own vacancies, appointed the ministers, and named members of the National Directory; (2) the National Directory, composed of the secretary-general of the party and 9 members, with Mussolini at their head; and (3) such

A three-year old Fascist salutes. Indoctrinating the coming generations was a common goal of dictatorships.

auxiliary organizations as the *Balilla,* boys from 8 to 14; the *Avanguardisti,* boys from 14 to 18; the *Giovine Fascista,* boys from 18 to 21; and the Fascist Militia, or Black Shirts, for whom military service was compulsory. Mussolini sought to satisfy the Italian thirst for the theatrical and the spectacular by reintroducing use of the Roman salute, colorful parades, distinctive uniforms, and the Fascist hymn, *Giovinezza.*

Mussolini's Corporate State. In originating the ideology of fascism, Mussolini had been influenced by the views of the syndicalist Georges Sorel, who had repudiated the state, denounced capitalism, and demanded that the syndicalist state governed by trade unions be brought about by direct action and the general strike. In 1919 Edmondo Rossoni organized syndicates which defended private property, opposed class war, championed class collaboration, and supported integral nationalism. In 1926 Mussolini placed the vast organization of Fascist syndicates under his own control. There were to be no strikes, lockouts, or class warfare, but instead, class discipline, absolute obedience, and "the sacrifice of the individual for society." Wages, hours, and conditions of work were to be regulated by a National Council of Corporations. A Charter of Labor, enacted on April 21, 1927, proclaimed: (1) higher pay for night workers; (2) an annual paid vacation; (3) no labor on Sundays; (4) social services to be provided by the government; and (5) free vocational education. In 1928 Mussolini enacted a law which made Italy the first Western state to have a national legislature representing economic divisions of the people. Women were excluded from the national franchise.

The Home Front in Totalitarian Italy.

On the assumption that his people were apathetic and undisciplined, Mussolini introduced a series of reforms. He drastically revised the system of taxation and finance, re-funded foreign debts, and stabilized the currency. He enacted high tariffs, expanded the merchant marine, and concluded trade pacts with other countries. His extensive program of public works was designed to alleviate unemployment. He encouraged foreign capitalists to invest money in Italy, and began a campaign to attract tourists. In an effort to combat illiteracy, he reorganized the educational system. By means of bonuses and tax exemptions, he encouraged large families, on the assumption that the future of Italy depended upon an adequate supply of fighting men. He banned birth control, divorce, and emigration. The power-hungry dictator attempted to give his people everything except freedom.

Covenant: Solution of Roman Question.

After the unification of Italy in 1870, the Church persistently refused to recognize the loss of the Papal States. As a means of resolving the Roman Question, Mussolini, on February 11, 1929, concluded with Pope Pius XI a Treaty and Concordat, by which the absolute sovereignty of the pope in the small Vatican City State was recognized in exchange for papal recognition of the kingdom of Italy. Roman Catholicism was decreed to be the state religion. The papacy was reimbursed for its 1870 losses by a large indemnity, partly in cash and partly in state bonds. In July 1929, after fifty-eight years of "papal imprisonment," Pope Pius XI emerged into the square of St. Peter's as a signal of the settlement of the Roman Question.

Chest-Thumping Aggression: Fascist Foreign Policy.

Fervent exaltation of nationalism was a cardinal tenet of Mussolini's dictatorship. The goal of Italy's foreign policy was to expand the colonial empire to provide outlets for surplus population and to obtain raw materials. The Adriatic and eventually the entire Mediterranean were to become an Italian lake (*Mare Nostrum*). Mussolini concluded a series of nonaggression and friendship treaties with the Central and Eastern Powers. His designs on Corsica, Savoy, Nice, and Tunis angered the French. Seizing upon a boundary dispute between Ethiopia and Italian Somaliland, Fascist Italy, in October 1935, invaded Ethiopia and annexed it despite stubborn Ethiopian resistance and sanctions imposed upon Italy by the League of Nations. In 1936 the Italian dictator aligned himself with Hitler (Rome-Berlin Axis) in the belief that the future belonged to the Fascist have-not powers. Italian support for the insurgent cause in the Spanish Civil War was an important factor in Franco's victory. But in 1940–1941 the myth of Italian military strength, blown to enormous proportions by Mussolini's boasts, was shattered on the sands of Libya before British tanks and in Albania before Greek bayonets.

The Sorry Record of Italian Fascism.

Twenty-three years of Fascism demonstrated that Mussolini was operating in the wrong century. Italy's geographic position, the hard core of the old Roman Empire, was outdated in the twentieth century, when it became merely a peninsula locked in the Mediterranean. The Fascist philosophy in action had little to recommend it. The motto devised by Mussolini—"believe, obey, fight"—was not suited to the Italian temperament. Rejecting individualism and accepting the Hegelian dogma of the State as an ethical whole, Mussolini sought to mold an entire people in his own image. He denounced democracy as a "putrescent corpse," insisted that the masses were incapable of governing themselves, demanded the elevation of a new élite, and glorified war. The Italian people learned painfully about the effects of this philosophy. Instead of lifting Italy to new heights of glory, an egocentric dictator was responsible for her descent into defeat and misery.

4. Germany: From the Weimar Republic to Nazi Totalitarianism

The Hesitant Revolution. At the outbreak of World War I all political parties, including Social Democrats, convinced that Germany's opponents had plotted her destruction, sprang to defense of the Fatherland. As the war dragged on and the people suffered increasing hardships, distress and disillusionment began to undermine national unity. Workers went on strike, and the sailors at Kiel mutinied. A coalition government, headed by Prince Max of Baden, converted the German Empire into a weak, limited monarchy, but President Wilson refused to deal with any other than a popular government. On October 23, 1918, William II fled to Spa. On November 9, 1918, the imperial regime yielded as Friedrich Ebert and the Majority Socialists took over controlling power from Prince Max. The emperor abdicated and fled to Holland.

Although leaders rejected William II and twenty-five sovereigns of the German states and proclaimed the nation a republic, the country was still burdened by the old socioeconomic order. A federation of republican states, temporarily headed by a Council of Six People's Commissars (three Majority Socialists and three Independent Socialists), was set up under the joint chairmanship of Ebert and Hugo Haase. The Independent Socialists bolted, and the Majority Socialists took over. The Spartacists (the Communist party) sought to extend the revolution into a dictatorship of the proletariat, but the Social Democrats, with the assistance of Gustav Noske, crushed them. In the course of this struggle Spartacist leaders Karl Liebknecht and Rosa Luxemburg were killed.

Experiment in Democracy: The Weimar Constitution. The political system set up by the Weimar Constitution in 1919 was pieced together from the American, British, French, and Swiss forms of government. Germany was to be a democratic republic, with universal suffrage for all citizens over twenty years of age. The constitution provided for a president elected by direct vote of the people for a term of seven years, after which he was eligible for reelection. Actual executive authority was vested in a ministry headed by a chancellor, appointed by the president, but responsible to the *Reichstag*. The *Reichstag*, elected for a period of four years, had the power of initiating bills. The old *Reichsrat*, representing the states, was retained, but it was now only of secondary importance. A comprehensive bill of rights insured the legal equality of the sexes, established free and compulsory education up to the age of eighteen, and provided for a system of social legislation.

The Weimar Constitution of the German Republic was one of the most advanced democratic constitutions in history. However, the entire document could be invalidated in spirit by Article 48, which permitted the *Reich* president to suspend temporarily the Fundamental Rights guaranteed by the document:

ARTICLE 48. If a *Land* [state] fails to fulfill the duties incumbent upon it according to the Constitution or the laws of the *Reich*, the *Reich* President can force it to do so with the help of the armed forces.

The *Reich* President may, if the public safety and order of the German *Reich* are considerably disturbed or endangered, take such measures as are necessary to restore public safety and order. If necessary, he may intervene with the help of the armed forces. For this purpose he may temporarily suspend, either partially or wholly, the Fundamental Rights established in Articles 114, 115, 117, 118, 123, 124, and 153.

The *Reich* President shall inform the *Reichstag* without delay of all measures taken under Paragraph 1 or Paragraph 2 of this Article. On demand by the *Reichstag* the measures shall be repealed.

Trials of the Republic. The Weimar Republic was burdened from its very beginning with an overwhelming combination of problems: the bitter humiliation of defeat, the currency debacle, reparations, and acute economic distress. Not only were the German people ill-prepared for an advanced form of democracy, but the victor powers showed little sympathy or understanding for the fledgling republic.

The new German government had to fight for its existence against determined opposition from both Left and Right. In 1919 the Communists were held in check by ruthless suppression. On March 13–17, 1920, the Monarchists, including Junkers, Pan-Germanists, and militarists, organized the Steel Helmets (*Stahlhelm*) and the League of the Upright, and sought to overthrow the government by marching on Berlin (the Kapp *Putsch,* named after Dr. Wolfgang Kapp of Königsberg, one of its leaders). This drive to overthrow the government and establish a military dictatorship failed when a general strike was called. On November 8–11, 1923, Adolf Hitler and General Erich Ludendorff attempted a rebellion in Munich (the "beer-hall putsch"), but the movement was dissipated and Hitler was

sent to prison. A Rhineland Republic was established, but it was short-lived partly because of differences among the leaders and in part because of British opposition. The German currency inflation of 1923, one of the most spectacular the world has ever seen, reduced most of the middle class to poverty. The critical economic conditions made for political instability, as one coalition after another sought unsuccessfully to cope with the problems. Public sentiment gradually shifted from a lukewarm liberalism to extreme conservatism.

Adolf Hitler: Apotheosis of Germany's "Little Man." The pivot around which the revolutionary movement revolved was Adolf Hitler, who was born in the Austrian village of Braunau on April 20, 1889, the son of a minor customs official. Imbibing a passionate German nationalism from his teachers, he moved to Vienna in 1907, where he led a precarious existence by selling postcards and working at odd jobs such as bricklaying. "In Vienna," he later wrote, "I became a convinced anti-Semite, a mortal enemy of Marxian philosophy, and a Pan-German." Serving with the Bavarian army on the Western Front in World War I, he was twice wounded and was decorated with

Adolf Hitler, dramatic dictator of Nazi Germany.

the Iron Cross, first class. During the postwar political chaos, he organized a small group of malcontents, later reorganized as the National Socialist German Workers' Party.

Hitler was a character familiar in every German *Bierstube*. Shrewd, arrogant, and voluble, he held forth on every subject from food to world politics, from music to military tactics. Pompous and omniscient, he refused to discuss his ideas, but instead issued dicta and ukases. He mistook his intuitions for scientific fact and believed that he knew all the answers to the meaning of history. He lived in a curious dream world, dismissing as insane anyone who disagreed with his judgments and disconnected monologues. In *Mein Kampf*, written while he was confined in the fortress of Landsberg after the beer-hall putsch of 1923, and which later became the Nazi Bible, Hitler paraphrased some of the world's worst literature, including Arthur de Gobineau's *Essay on the Inequality of Human Races*, Houston Stewart Chamberlain's *Foundations of the Nineteenth Century*, the false document of a worldwide Jewish plot titled *Protocols of the Learned Elders of Zion*, and ill-digested interpretations of Nietzsche, Schopenhauer, Mackinder, Haushofer, Frederick the Great, and Carlyle. The British historian, H. R. Trevor-Roper, described Hitler's mind as "a terrible phenomenon, imposing indeed in its granite harshness and yet infinitely squalid in its miscellaneous cumber—like some huge barbarian monolith, the expression of giant strength and savage genius, surrounded by a festering heap of refuse—old tins and dead vermin, ashes and eggshells and ordure—the intellectual *detritus* of centuries." This was the psychopathic personality fated to become Germany's dictator. "May God help the German people," Goethe had once said, "if a Napoleon appears amongst them."

Regression to Primitivism: Emergence of National Socialism.

Adolf Hitler made political capital of Germany's misery. In the summer of 1919 he became the seventh member of the executive committee of the tiny German Worker's Party. Within two years he was in control of the movement, now called the National Socialist German Workers' Party, or the

N.S.D.A.P., after its German initials. The word Nazi came from the first two words of the German name—*NAtional SoZIalist*. To this party flocked such discontented elements as disgruntled war veterans, impoverished students, ambitious monarchists, struggling shopkeepers, dissatisfied workers, frightened industrialists, anti-Semites, anti-Catholics, anti-liberals, anti-socialists, anti-communists, and unreconciled nationalists. A hypnotic orator, Hitler promised his followers the abrogation of the Treaty of Versailles, an end to the "war-guilt lie," the restriction of citizenship rights to those of "Aryan" racial origin, expulsion of aliens from Germany, nationalization of industries, land reforms, a highly centralized government, restoration of German colonies, anti-Semitism, economic prosperity, and a mighty, invincible army. Nazi political strength gradually increased until in the *Reichstag* elections of July 1932 the Hitler party received 230 seats, against 133 for the Social Democrats and 97 for the Catholic Centrists. When the Social Democrats and the Communists, irreconcilable opponents, refused to join forces against the Nazi threat, they sealed the republic's doom. On January 30, 1933, President Paul von Hindenburg appointed Hitler as chancellor.

Once installed in office, Hitler set about obliterating democracy and fashioning a totalitarian state. He destroyed all opposing political parties; dissolved the trade unions and confiscated their property and funds; abrogated all individual rights guaranteed by the Weimar Constitution; and coordinated every phase of national life, including Church, press, education, industry, and army. A shocked world witnessed a barbarous campaign "to protect German honor" against the Jews—who numbered about one per cent of the population. Hitler himself assumed executive, legislative, and judicial powers, while passionately proclaiming the legality of all his actions. Abolishing all other political parties, he decreed that there was to be only one party in Germany, the National Socialist. In a sweeping program of centralization, he placed federal, state, and local governments under his absolute authority. On June 30, 1934, in a barbaric blood-purge, he liquidated several hundred of his followers who had attempted to extend the revolution.

War on Religion: Coordination of Churches. Hitler sought to subordinate religion to the state by throwing pastors and priests alike into concentration camps. He further tried to split Protestantism by organizing a German-Christian Church which, as a new form of "positive Christianity," was to be subjected to state control. He violated a concordat with the Catholic Church, made in July 1933, by which he had promised that Catholics would not be molested as long as they remained aloof from politics. In the meantime, he sought to win the German public to a neopagan movement which denied Christianity and re-created the old Teutonic mythology. The churches did not submit as quietly as had German citizens. There were spirited, if unsuccessful, protests from all corners of the Nazi Third Reich.

Planned Chaos: The Nazi Economy. The Nazi *Fuehrer* (Leader) aimed to bring the national economy into line with the declared principle of self-sufficiency. He solved the problem of unemployment by dismissing enemies of the state, decreeing compulsory military service, providing for extensive public works, and organizing labor camps. He obtained funds for the remilitarization of Germany by a system of forced loans from banks, industries, and insurance companies, and by suspending payments on foreign debts. In 1936 he launched a four-year plan to make the nation economically independent and self-sufficient. Lacking an adequate gold supply, he adopted a barter system to compete with other countries for world markets.

Throwback to Barbarism: Nazi Culture. The Third Reich subordinated cultural activities to Nazi ideology. Schools were transformed into propaganda agencies, and women were returned to the kitchen. All cultural activities were required to imbue citizens with the ideas of glorification of the Leader, fanatical worship for the Fatherland, intolerant racial prejudices, hatred for enemies of the Third Reich, blind obedience, and zest for war. Dr. Paul Joseph Goebbels (1897-1945), Hitler's minis-ter of propaganda and public enlightenment, was assigned the task to coordinate all cultural activities.

Typical of the tone and taste of Nazi culture was the "Horst Wessel Song," the Nazi anthem, written by a young street-fighter, who was made a national hero after his violent death:

Hold high the banner! Close the hard ranks serried!
S. A. marches on with sturdy stride.
Comrades, by Red Front and Reaction killed, are buried,
But march with us in image at our side.

Gangway! Gangway! now for the Brown battalions!
For the Storm Trooper clear roads o'er the land!
The Swastika gives hope to our entranced millions,
The day for freedom and for bread's at hand.

The trumpet blows its shrill and final blast!
Prepared for war and battle here we stand.
Soon Hitler's banners will wave unchecked at last,
The end of German slav'ry in our land!

The Tiger Complex: Nazi Aggression. Hitler's foreign policy was to regain Germany's prestige as a world power, bring about the restoration of her colonies, promote Pan-Germanism ("One Reich, One People, *One Fuehrer*"), and revive the *Drang nach Osten* ("Drive to the East"). To free Germany from what he called the shackles of Versailles, in March 1935 Hitler announced the rearmament of Germany, reintroduced conscription, enlarged the army and navy, and launched a formidable air force. The next year German troops, in violation of the Locarno Treaties, marched—unopposed and unquestioned—into the Rhineland. Now emboldened, Hitler officially repudiated Article 231, the war-guilt clause, of the Treaty of Versailles. On March 15, 1938, in order "to preserve Austria," he formally incorporated that state into the Third Reich. After signing the Munich Pact in September 1938 Hitler piously announced that his territorial aims in Europe were satisfied. But his invasion of Poland in 1939 brought on World War II.

Nationalism Gone Berserk. The Nazi regime in power represented a descent into vulgarization and bestiality such as the world had seldom witnessed. How was it possible for a highly civilized people such as the Germans to allow themselves to be imprisoned in this cunningly devised straitjacket? The complete mastery of Germany by the Nazis was due only in part to ruthless suppression of all opposition. More important, it was the result of a national tradition of discipline and obedience, grounded in the Germans by a combination of Hegelian worship of the state, Prussian intransigence, and militarism. The contention that Nazi extremism was a bolt out of the heavens, a "catastrophe" that was suddenly visited upon the German people, is inaccurate. German extremist nationalism did not occur in a vacuum; its roots lay deep in a century and a half of German history. Behind it was a pattern of thinking, tempered by romanticism and historicism (the use of history for political purposes). The Germans who later professed to be shocked and amazed by the excesses of Hitlerism never understood that the political regime that had led them almost to destruction was the logical outcome of a long and dangerous intellectual tradition. Despite its claims of historical novelty in seeking to combine the waves of nationalism and socialism, the Nazi movement in reality was stale and unoriginal. Little in Nazism was new except the fanatical and ferocious methods used to implement its ideology.

Germans respect for power (*die Obrigkeit*), for the uniform, the title, and the office is not, as apologists have often maintained, a trivial and unimportant stereotype, but on the contrary, a characteristic deeply rooted in German history. Traditional German respect for authority resulted in an undiscriminating loyalty to the individual or party in power, with no questions asked about the decency or indecency of the ruler or party. As a consequence of this slavish obedience and respect for authority, most Germans appeared to have only contempt for democracy as a way of life. The contention that the German national character is *congenitally* authoritarian is, of course, invalid, but there is much historical evidence to show that the environmentally produced traditions of authoritarianism, discipline, and servility led the Germans to accept dictatorship more willingly than most other peoples. Added to this was a strong predilection for abstract ideas and cosmopolitan dreams. This preference for philosophic systems, accompanied by a self-righteous rejection of the actual forces at work in the world, resulted in a dangerous political immaturity.

Hitler, the supposedly omniscient *Fuehrer*, promised the German people a way out of their misery and the path to world power. Originally a bit skeptical about this strange Austrian, the Germans became more and more convinced of his infallibility as he delivered one crippling blow after another at the system of Versailles. As the unquestioned focal point of authority in Germany, he made sense to the Germans when he spoke of a Thousand-Year Reich. Politically illiterate Germans had little understanding of what was happening to them before the bar of humanity. It was necessary to invent a new name—genocide—for a totally new and stupendous crime against humanity— the slaughtering of millions of Jews by asphyxiation in gas ovens. The massacre of other millions, the devitalization of nations, the inhuman atrocities, and particularly the condoning of these horrors, led the world to believe that the German nation had taken leave of its senses. There has been little to compare with it in the entire history of civilization. It took a worldwide coalition to bring Nazi Germany down to earth and to smash its monomaniacal *Fuehrer*.

5. Spain and the New, Enlarged States of Central Europe

Spain: From Frustration to Tragedy. The Spain of 1919 was still in a semi-feudal stage. Much of the land was owned by absentee landlords (*grandees*); industrial development was backward; political power was concentrated in the hands of the king; and three privileged classes—*grandees,* clergy, and *juntos,* or officers' councils—monopolized social and economic power. There were strong movements for local autonomy in the provinces, especially in Catalonia, resulting mainly from the mountain barriers and poor transportation. Such outbreaks were sternly suppressed. The nation was miserable and discontented. The government was weakened by its failure to quell an uprising in Spanish Morocco led by the chieftain Abd-el-Krim. In 1923 General Primo de Rivera (1870–1930) established himself as military dictator, ended civil liberties, and ruled by court martial. Attracting but little popular success, he suddenly resigned in 1930. King Alfonso XIII (1886–1941) abdicated in 1931. A Spanish Republic was established under Niceto Alcala Zamorá (1877–1949), who separated Church and State, nationalized ecclesiastical property, confiscated the land of the *grandees*, granted Catalonia local autonomy, and introduced sweeping social and economic reforms. In the elections of February 1936 the parties of the Left—including Republicans, Socialists, Communists, and Anarchists, united in a Popular Front—won an overwhelming victory, and soon called for more land reform, nationalization of industries, and improvement of conditions for the peasants. Supported by the propertied elements, the

THE VICTIM.

SPAIN. "WHICHEVER WINS, MY AGONY ENDURES!"

The bitter Spanish Civil War is satirized in this *Punch* cartoon.

Fascist opposition, under command of General Francisco Franco (1892–   ) rebelled against the regime. The Spanish Civil War, started on July 18, 1936, was a bloody, fratricidal struggle marked by mass executions, air raids on the civilian population, and wanton destruction of lives and property. What started out as a domestic struggle was soon transformed into a dress rehearsal for World War II: Italy and Germany sided with the rebels and Soviet Russia supported the Loyalists. The relentless conflict came to an end on March 28, 1939, with the victory of Franco. Announcing himself as *El Caudillo* (The Leader), Franco liquidated all opposition and established a dictatorship in Spain.

Maimed Hungary. By the Treaty of Trianon, Hungary lost two-thirds of her land and three-fifths of her population. Shortly after the Armistice, Emperor Charles I of Austria, who was also King Charles IV of Hungary, abdicated, and a Hungarian liberal republic was established under the prompting of a wealthy nobleman, Count Michael Károlyi (1875–1955). In June 1919 the republic was overthrown by Bela Kun, an officer in the Austro-Hungarian army who had been associated with Lenin and Trostky in the Russian Revolution of November 1917. The short-lived Hungarian Soviet Republic fell to the dictatorship of Hungarian Whites under Admiral Nicholas Horthy (1868–1957). Efforts to solve the desperate economic situation were fruitless. The most discontented of the Balkan Succession States, Hungary waged an unceasing agitation for revision of the peace settlement.

Development of Other States. The Polish state had been abolished by the Three Partitions of 1772, 1793, and 1795, but Polish nationalism still existed. Poland was re-created by the Treaty of Versailles as a result of the efforts of two national heroes, Joseph Pilsudski (1863–1935) and Ignace Paderewski (1860–1941), and the sympathetic attitude of President Wilson. The early history of the Polish Republic, founded in 1921, was marked by political quarrels, legislative chaos, and assassinations. Pilsudski came out of retirement in 1926, overthrew the government, and established a dictatorship, or what he called an "authoritarian democracy." Polish domestic affairs were complicated by economic distress, the necessity for land reform, the treatment of such minorities as Jews, Ukrainians, and Germans, and the persistent problems of the Polish Corridor, Danzig, and Vilna. Caught in the middle between rival great powers, Poland's foreign policy gravitated first to one side and then the other. The problem of her continued existence as a sovereign state played a major role in precipitating World War II.

Doubled in size as a result of World War I, Rumania had a perplexing problem in handling her minorities of Transylvanian Magyars, Bessarabians, Ukrainians, Germans, Jews, and Bulgarians. Although she signed minority treaties, Rumania was accused of maltreatment of her minority groups. Attempts were made to solve the land problem by confiscating the nobles' land and distributing it among the peasants. The Magyar landowners in Transylvania, objecting strenuously, obtained the support of Hungary in their appeals to the League of Nations. Rumania's government remained unstable. King Carol II (r. 1930–1940) set up a dictatorship in February 1938.

Yugoslavia—the kingdom of Serbs, Croats, and Slovenes—came into existence in 1919 under the rule of King Peter I of Serbia (r. 1919–1931). The new kingdom was split into two major warring factions: the Serbs, Greek Catholic in religion and Levantine in culture,

comprising 45 per cent of the population, and the Croatians, Roman Catholic and Westernized, forming 37 per cent of the population. The political history of postwar Yugoslavia, like that of the Balkans in general, was a story of riots, assassinations, and civil war. In November 1928 King Alexander I set up a dictatorship; he was assassinated six years later on October 9, 1934, while on a goodwill tour of France. Yugoslavia sought to maintain her independence by joining the Little Entente, but she fell to German aggression in 1941.

After successfully resisting Communist infiltration, the Finns in 1919 established a republican government and joined the League of Nations the next year. The great problem of the Finns was to maintain their existence as a neighbor of Russia. Finland fought with the Third Reich against Russia in World War II.

Estonia, Latvia, and Lithuania came into existence as Baltic Succession States after World War I. All three nations set up republican forms of government united loosely by a common fear of Russia. In 1934 a Baltic Union was formed to frustrate Hitler's Germany. The three states were occupied by the Russians in 1939 and annexed outright the following year. From 1940 to 1944 they were occupied by German troops and then were recaptured by the Russians. Western nations, including the United States, have refused to recognize the Russian annexation of the three little Baltic states.

⁌ KEY DOCUMENT ⁊

THE ENABLING ACT, MARCH 24, 1933: CONSOLIDATION OF HITLER'S DICTATORSHIP

Department of State, *National Socialism: Basic Principles*, prepared by Raymond E. Murphy, F. B. Stevens, Howard Trivers, and Joseph M. Roland (Washington, 1943), pp. 217–218. Courtesy of United States Government Printing Office.

A CLASSIC EXAMPLE of how dictators consolidate their powers was revealed by Adolf Hitler when, on March 24, 1933, he forced a reluctant German *Reichstag* to promulgate an Enabling Act legalizing his Nazi revolution. Hitler never officially repudiated the Weimar Constitution: he acted formally and legally under that document while actually violating its spirit and meaning.

Law to Remove the Distress of People and State: The Enabling Act, March 24, 1933

The *Reichstag* has resolved the following law, which is, with the approval of the National Council, herewith promulgated, after it has been established that the requirements have been satisfied for legislation altering the Constitution.

ARTICLE 1. National laws can be enacted by the National Cabinet as well as in accordance with the procedure established in the Constitution. This applies also to the laws referred to in article 85, paragraph 2, and in article 87 of the Constitution.

ARTICLE 2. The national laws enacted by the National Cabinet may deviate from the Constitution so far as they do not affect the position of the *Reichstag* and National Council. The powers of the President remain undisturbed.

ARTICLE 3. The national laws enacted by the National Cabinet are prepared by the Chancellor and published in the *Reichsgesetzblatt*. They come into effect, unless otherwise specified, upon the day following their publication. Articles 68 to 77 of the Constitution do not apply to the laws enacted by the National Cabinet.

ARTICLE 4. Treaties of the *Reich* with foreign states which concern matters of national legislation do not require the consent of the bodies participating in legislation. The National Cabinet is empowered to issue the necessary provisions for the execution of these treaties.

ARTICLE 5. This law becomes effective on the day of publication. It becomes invalid on April 1, 1937; it further becomes invalid when the present National Cabinet is replaced by another.

Berlin, March 24, 1933

> *Reich President* VON HINDENBURG
> *Reich Chancellor* ADOLF HITLER
> *Reich Minister of the Interior* FRICK
> *Reich Minister for Foreign Affairs*
> BARON VON NEURATH
> *Reich Minister of Finances*
> COUNT SCHWERIN VON KROSIGK

❦ HISTORICAL INTERPRETATION ❧

WILHELM ROEPKE ON FASCISM AND COMMUNISM AS MODERN TYRANNIES

Wilhelm Roepke, *The Solution of the German Problems*, trans. by E. W. Dickes (New York, 1947), pp. 6–18, *passim*. By permission of G. P. Putnam's Sons, Inc.

TO WILHELM ROEPKE, German economist deprived of his position as a professor by Hitler in 1933, Fascism and Communism were similar collectivist and totalitarian movements which were in essence twentieth-century mechanized revivals of ancient tyrannies. He saw the Western democracies as bearing a share of responsibility for the destruction wrought by these latter-day tyrannies because they approved the new tyrannies until they themselves were attacked. Western observers and scholars are not inclined to accept this point of view which seeks to shift the blame for home-grown evils to others abroad.

It did indeed call for no exceptional clarity of vision to recognize Nazism as a frightful barbarian invasion of the laboriously hedged garden of civilization. But why was there general blindness to this in Germany, as later in the rest of the world, and why, in both cases, were men's eyes opened only when it was too late, when Germany had suffered the catastrophe of tyranny, and the world the catastrophe of war? The main reason lay in the *weakening of the moral reflexes*. That was what prevented so many people, faced with a barbarism that in the preceding generation would have made its perpetrators utterly impossible in the civilized world, from taking up the only proper attitude of flaming and uncompromising indignation, and nipping the evil in the bud. People were blind because they were determined to be blind. But that determination in face of unprecedented barbarism proved the serious weakening of the moral sense, of which the world had already given a first sign in the case of Fascist Italy when men praised the punctuality of the trains and the improvement of tourist travel, but forgot what that regime meant for the Italians.

Thus the failure to recognize the true features of Nazism was in the last resort a moral failure, which men sought to cover up with all sorts of theories by way of excuse, euphemism, or even justification, and with stale witticisms. *But this is a responsibility the world must share in full with the Germans.* There was certainly a good deal in the National Socialism that was anything but edifying, and certainly its victims deserved sympathy and assistance. But on the other hand, had not Germany been given order and discipline? Were not the *Autobahnen*, the motor roads, perfect? Was not the economic and social policy of the Third Reich a thoroughly interesting experiment, perhaps worth emulating?

One of these questions of ours has reference to the fact that one ground for coming to terms with Nazism was the idea that it was an efficient bulwark against Bolshevism, or at least was, in comparison with Bolshevism, the lesser evil. In this belief there was all too ready acceptance of the Nazi propaganda claim that the *coup d'état* of 1933 saved Germany from a Communist revolution. That theory was indeed one of the trump cards played by National Socialism against unfavorable world opinion—we know with what success. At the outset and for a long time very few realized that this was no more than casting out devils through Beelzebub, and that the differences between the Red collectivism and the Brown totalitarianism could not remove from the world the essential similarity of their principles of structure. . . .

It remains a serious fault that the world should have allowed itself to be so led astray in its judgment and its moral susceptibilities by this playing off of Communism against National Socialism. How grave is this fault and how ready our times show themselves to submit to this mental and emotional confusion is shown by the fact that today we see the same unsureness and denseness in regard to Communism. Nobody who actively defends Communism or even finds excuses for it has any right to be indignant with the people for its seduction by the Brown collectivism, and a world that today shows the same attitude to Communism that it showed in the past to National Socialism, an attitude of palliation and of appeasement, if not of actual encouragement, proves to us that it is in a moral and mental condition that might have made it an accomplice in Nazism.

This play between Fascism (National Socialism) and Communism was facilitated by a certain interpretation of National Socialism. We refer to the idea that National Socialism, like Fascism, was fundamentally simply a spurious and insincere collectivism, with the aid of which "capitalism" was trying to maintain its position in a last desperate struggle against genuine collectivism, without troubling too much about the methods of government or the ideologies to be worked off on the masses who were to be fooled. Such a theory was well adapted to make the fundamental opponnets of collectivism more ready to come to terms with National Socialism, if it did not actually throw them into its arms, while winning the allegiance of the others for "true" collectivism. One side was persuaded in this way to see in National Socialism an ally in the struggle against collectivism, and the other to see in collectivism an ally against Nazism. One side thus became partisans or promoters of Nazism and the other of Communism. . . .

Intellectual confusion and moral obtuseness united to clear away the obstacles in the path of the Nazis—obstacles that otherwise would soon have made an end of their dominance. We who knew what Nazism meant had assumed in those critical years after the *coup d'état* of 1933 that the conclusions we had drawn must force themselves upon the whole world. We took it for granted that at the very outset the Third Reich must come to grief through the resistance of the outer world, after the internal resistance had proved inadequate. We imagined the world's reactions and power of decision to be still more or less normal, so that we could not believe that the Nazi regime would last long. We thought the object lesson the Nazis had given in Germany would be sufficient to open the eyes of the rest of the world; the failure in Germany would increase the resolution abroad; since the battle had been lost in Germany, in the international field the determination not to lose it could not, we thought, but increase accordingly. . . .

During the first years of the regime it would have been child's play to make an end of the monstrous thing, and in all probability even in 1936 the simple mobilization of France would have sufficed to turn the treaty-breaking reoccupation of the Rhineland from a triumph into an annihilating political defeat of Hitler. When in 1938 Austria was violated, nobody stirred, and when in the autumn of that same year the same game of extortion and menace was played against Czechoslovakia in the Munich capitulation, world policy in regard to the Third Reich descended to the uttermost extreme of weakness. During the whole period countless Germans had set their last desperate hopes on a firm attitude on the part of the great powers, but again and again they had to witness the triumph of their hated tyrants over a spineless world. Finally, Russia too made concessions to Hitler in the Molotov-Ribbentrop

agreement, enabling Hitler at last to let loose war and, with the support of Russian deliveries, to carry it on successfully for a considerable time. The dismal picture is completed by the sudden chorus of praise from the Communists of all countries of the coalition of Nazism and Communism against the "imperialist and capitalist world."

If we consider all this soberly and with scientific objectivity, we can no longer doubt that the *world-wide catastrophe of today is the gigantic price the world has to pay for its deafness to all the warning signals that prophesied with ever increasing shrillness from 1930 to 1939 the hell the satanic forces of National Socialism were to let loose, first against Germany herself and then against the rest of the world. The horrors of the war correspond exactly with those that the world permitted Germany to suffer, while it actually maintained normal relations with the Nazis and organized with them international festivals and congress.* . . .

❧ TEN BASIC BOOKS ❧

REPRISE OF TYRANNY: THE TOTALITARIAN STATES, 1919–1939

1. Borgese, Giuseppe A., *Goliath: The March of Fascism* (New York, 1938).
2. Carr, Edward H., *A History of Soviet Russia*, 7 vols. (London, 1950–1960).
3. Ebenstein, William, *The Nazi State* (New York, 1943).
4. Halperin, S. William, *Mussolini and Fascist Italy*, Anvil Book No. 67 (Princeton, N. J., 1964).†
5. Heiden, Konrad, *A History of National Socialism* (New York, 1935).
6. Neumann, Franz L., *Behemoth: The Structure and Practice of National Socialism, 1933–1942*, 2nd ed. (New York, 1944, R. 1963).
7. Rauch, G. von, *A History of Soviet Russia*, 4th ed. (New York, 1964).†
8. Salvemini, Gaetano, *The Fascist Dictatorship in Italy* (New York, 1927).
9. Seton-Watson, Hugh, *From Lenin to Khrushchev: A History of World Communism* (New York, 1960).†
10. Shirer, William L., *The Rise and Fall of the Third Reich* (New York, 1960).†

40

Impact: Revolution in Asia

WE HAVE no quarrel with the English people much less with the English worker. Like us he has himself been the victim of imperialism and it is against this imperialism that we fight. With it there can be no compromise. To this imperialism or to England, we owe no allegiance, and the flag of England in India is an insult to every Indian. . . .

The end of our struggle approaches and the British Empire will soon go the way of all the Empires of the old. The strangling and the degradation of India have gone on long enough. It will be tolerated no longer, and let England and the world take notice that the people of India are prepared to be friends with all who meet them frankly as equals and do not interfere with their freedom. But they will be no friends with such as seek to interfere with their liberties or to exploit the peasant or the worker. Nor will they tolerate in the future the humbug and hypocrisy which has been doled out to them in such ample measures by England. . . .

Long Live Free India!

—JAWAHARLAL NEHRU, Central Prison, Maini, October 24, 1930

1. The Transformation of the Orient

Dynamic Change in Eastern Asia. The vast land mass of Asia contains some of the highest mountains, some of the most inhospitable deserts, and some of the most intensively cultivated lowlands on earth. This is the homeland of nearly one-third of the human race. The coastal areas are packed with a teeming population. No region on earth has undergone such striking changes and is so wracked with conflict as Eastern Asia. For a century some of its nations have been struggling to modernize their ancient cultures and to win independence and positions of world leadership.

In the nineteenth century the accessible areas of Eastern Asia either became colonies of European powers or submitted to "the unequal treaty system." The fact that imperialism stems from human and societal use of power, that it was not a European monopoly, is evi-

dent from Japan's later participation in such practices. European civilization penetrated deeply into Asian societies and progressively transformed them. Indians, Chinese, and Japanese felt the impact of Western industrialism and capitalism and learned about European politics, technology, and power. Eventually, they rebelled against European imperialism and demanded self-government and a place of equality among the world powers. Western imperialism had threatened Chinese sovereignty with its extra-territorial rights and leaseholds, and had invaded the large areas of India, Indochina, the Philippine Islands, and the Netherlands East Indies. The people of Asia wanted freedom, but at the same time they remained dependent upon the West for scientific and technical education, as well as capital, without which they could not modernize and regain cultural and political initiative. At the basis of revolt were several related factors: (1) a rising nationalism geared to resentment against European domination; (2) dissatisfaction with the Westernization of Asia; and (3) a growing belief in communism as a liberating force.

The process of rebellion was hastened by World War I. Asians grew even more critical of a civilization which produced overwhelming catastrophe and often involved their own countries against their wills. After the war, defeated European powers lost their territories, their leased positions, and special treaty rights in Asia and Oceania. "Asia for the Asiatics" became a growing demand. There was little satisfaction with the halfhearted attempts of the European powers to award a greater degree of self-government to their Asian possessions. Asian nationalists, encouraged by President Wilson's ideal of self-determination, asked for more than half-measures. They would be satisfied with nothing less than full independence from Western impositions. In the wake of the war, discontent kept flaring up throughout the vast subcontinent of India. The Chinese, who entered the war against Germany in 1917, were angered after the conflict when Japan was permitted to retain the former German leasehold of Shantung. Later, the Japanese returned the area but kept the former German concessions and privileges. While the Western nations were preoccupied in their theaters of war, Japan avoided exhaustive actions, instead expanding her trade and industries and becoming an important exporter of capital, chiefly to her colonies and spheres of influence on the nearby continent.

The Russian Revolution gave additional impetus for revolt in Asia. Lenin's denunciation of capitalism and imperialism, especially his thesis that imperialism was but one aspect of capitalism, made a deep impression throughout the Far East. The colonial peoples of Asia had already identified the hated imperialists with capitalism because virtually all the large industrial and business enterprises were in foreign hands, and now they saw how the Marxist-Leninist ideology linked the two. It was precisely what they wanted. As a result, throughout Asia the new moves for independence merged into socialism. National libera-tion leaders, demanding equality, independence, and freedom from "white imperialists," turned to socialism in one of its forms, all the way from democratic to Bolshevik varieties.

The socialist motivation worked two ways. When it became obvious that the expected great Revolution had not penetrated into the highly industrialized countries of Western Europe as predicted by Marx, Russian activists turned to Asia as a kind of ready-made substitute. Perhaps capitalism might be outflanked in a vast pincer movement with its pivot point in the Far East. There began an intensive two-way traffic of ideologists and activists from Moscow to Asia. Liberation leaders went to Soviet Russia to learn firsthand the techniques of revolution that might be used by the masses at home. Communists were sent from Moscow to strategic points in Asia to stir up discontent among an already dissatisfied people. This was favorable soil for Communist growth.

While communism was an important factor in the revolt, nationalism was by far the more motivating sentiment in an explosive situation. At first, nationalists resorted to economic boycotts, to counter Western or Japanese measures. In the early stages only a shallow elite was involved in movements for independence, but after 1919, peasants and workers gradually became organized for broader participation. The entire process was further stimulated by the fast-moving events of World War II. Efforts to form a Pan-Asian movement were unsuccessful because of the vast differences between cultures in the area. Each major country of Asia sought change in its own pattern.

2. The Emergence of Nationalism in India

British Rule in India. The huge and populous triangle of India, jutting southward out of Asia, for centuries had exerted influence in South and Southeast Asia. The size of the Indian subcontinent is 1,581,000 square miles, about half the area of the United States. Its population has increased enormously: from an estimated 140,000,000 in 1750 to 330,000,000 in 1900, and to nearly 500,000,000 in 1964—

almost three times the population of the United States. India's growth resulted chiefly from the degree of administrative effectiveness, economic unity and development, expanded irrigation and transportation, and improved health services built under British leadership.

British influence in India increased from the seventeenth to the twentieth century. The British East India Company, chartered in 1600, controlled key positions and provinces in the subcontinent until 1784, when Pitt's India Act created a board of control and placed political, financial, and military control in the hands of the government. In 1857, following the disaster of the Sepoy mutiny, the administration of India passed into the hands of the Crown. In 1876 Queen Victoria assumed the title of "Empress of India," and it became customary to look upon the Indian empire as "the brightest jewel in the British Crown." Most Englishmen regarded the subjugation of India not as conquest or oppression but as a civilizing mission.

The task of modernizing India was not easy. About three-fifths of the subcontinent was ruled directly by the British. The other two-fifths, the 562 Indian states, were controlled by petty or major princes with varying degrees of autonomy under British protection. Some states, Kashmir for example, were larger in area than some European countries. The British retained control of foreign affairs, defense, and currency in the princely states of India.

The British tried to meet the problem of population growth, but the subcontinent was constantly overpopulated in relation to its food supply. They managed to reclaim some 56,-000,000 acres through irrigation: they built the great Ganges and Jumna canals with 1,200 miles of main channels and 6,500 miles of distributaries. However, the industrialization of India was painfully slow. The British held the traditional view that colonies were to provide raw materials for the mother country. Despite comprehensive measures to combat epidemics and food shortages, local famines occasionally were severe. The ravages from poverty continued to be immense.

One cause of the almost universal poverty was the ancient system of landholding. Indian rulers had farmed out the collection of taxes to agents called *zamindari*. Eventually, the agents became landlords, while the peasants became sharecroppers. The *zamindari* flourished, while the peasants grew increasingly poverty-stricken. A slightly better system was the *ryotwari*, by which the government leased the land directly to the farmers. But both systems favored the rich over the poor. Before the later land reforms in independent India, one-quarter of the landowners held nearly three-quarters of the arable fields.

The Awakening of India. Before the English came, India had been a huge battlefield for clashing rulers and tribes. The British brought with them the real advantages of peace and order. But to Indian nationalists British rule meant only a progressive exploitation and manipulated division of their country. They insisted that India in the seventeenth century had been Asia's leading agricultural country and the industrial workshop for much of the world, and that British conquest had reduced Indian prosperity. They began to call for complete independence. Taxes and tariffs, they said, should be adjusted to benefit India, not Britain.

In World War I the Indian people and the princes remained loyal to Britain. They furnished money and 1,200,000 fighting men for the British war effort. In 1919 the British Parliament passed the Government of India Act, partly in recognition of India's loyalty during the war and partly as a concession to growing nationalist demands. The preamble stated that it was the policy of Britain "to provide for the increasing association of Indians in every branch of administration and the gradual development of self-governing institutions with a view to the progressive realization of responsible government in India as an integral part of the British Empire." Offices in administration were opened to Indian civil servants. The people received a greater share in local government. Most important of all was the establishment of a national parliament, with a Legislative Assembly and a Council of State, meeting at Delhi. But only a million people in India's vast population were allowed to vote.

Indian Nationalists were not satisfied with this act. They wanted more responsible government both at the center and at provincial levels. Agitation continued for more basic reforms. In 1927 the British government appointed a royal commission under Sir John Simon to examine the situation. This commission, after two visits to India, presented its report in 1930, calling for greater Indian responsibility in administration, enlargement of the suffrage, and a decentralized government. Indian Nationalists condemned it as "a cup of milk for the hungry lion." More than 30,000 Indian patriots complained so loudly that they were jailed by the British. The Muslim League, which had been organized in 1906, for some years cooperated with the multi-communal National Congress of India in opposition to British domination.

Gandhi. Mohandas Karamchand Gandhi (1869–1948) became known to the world as a frail little man who, bowed down by the weight of years and the sorrows of mankind, worked for a free, united India. In 1888 he arrived in England, studied at University College, London, and was called to the bar at Inner Temple. He returned to India in 1891, and later went to Pretoria on business. He decided to remain in South Africa to support the cause of Asiatic immigrants. After a stay of twenty-one years in South Africa, he returned to India in 1914. Now he began to apply the methods he had learned in South Africa to the Indian home-rule movement. He called for resistance to British imperialism by "soul force" and "non-cooperation." This later developed into a general campaign of civil disobedience or non-violent non-cooperation. "In the application of *satyagraha* [soul force], I discovered in the earliest stages that pursuit of truth did not admit of violence being inflicted on one's opponent; he must be weaned from error by patience and sympathy." The little Hindu lawyer captured the imagination of the Indian people who, impressed by his ideals and ascetic habits, revered him as a

Nationalist leader Nehru proudly welcomes Gandhi back from a prolonged fast undertaken in the cause of Indian independence.

mahatma, a "great-souled" or saintly man. The new nationalist movement for the first time reached India's more than half a million villages, penetrated to the urban factories and slums, and became truly a mass movement. The people followed Gandhi's admonition to boycott all foreign-made goods and buy only those produced in India. Only in this way, Gandhi said, could *swaraj* (self-determination) be obtained.

Gandhi's policy of civil disobedience and boycott, repeatedly and contrary to his insistence, led to rioting and disorder for which he and others were jailed. The nationalist movement was headed by Gandhi's leading follower, Jawaharlal Nehru (1889–1964), who had been educated at Harrow and Trinity College, Cambridge. The Independence League, formed in 1930, called for severance of British ties and freedom.

In the drive for independence a crucial role was played by the India Congress, a national body formed as early as 1885. In August 1942, in the midst of World War II, the Congress launched what was virtually an India-wide rebellion against British rule. The British refused to yield and jailed the leaders of the Congress for the rest of the war. Meanwhile, the Muslim League demanded that those parts of India where the Muslim population was most heavily concentrated should become a separate state when independence was won.

To this the India Congress was violently opposed. The failure of the government to overcome the friction between the India Congress and the Muslim League convinced the British that no solution to the problem could be found without partition.

Independence and Partition. In 1935 the British approved another Government of India Act. The new instrument of government followed along the lines of the Simon Report: it added to the federal structure of British India; gave the eleven provincial legislatures competence in certain less sensitive fields such as education and health; provided for more elected delegates to the central legislature at Delhi; and sought to protect such minorities as the Muslims and Untouchables by providing for electoral districts based partly on communal representation and partly on population. Suffrage was extended to about 35 million

voters. The new India Act went part way in meeting the demands of Congress and other Indian leaders, but it still provided safeguards for the viceroy's powers and for British control of military and foreign affairs, transportation, and finance. The Nationalists, led by Nehru, refused to accept the new framework, arguing that the legislatures at both levels should have complete responsibility and authority. The problem of Anglo-India relations was not then solved, though the Congress did present candidates in the elections of 1937, winning majorities—hence forming cabinets—in five provinces and forming parts of coalitions in three others. The Muslim League was supported by Muslim majorities in only two provinces; elsewhere Muslims who were either pro-Congress or independents filled most of the seats reserved for legislators of their faith. This situation began to change in favor of the League in and. after 1939.

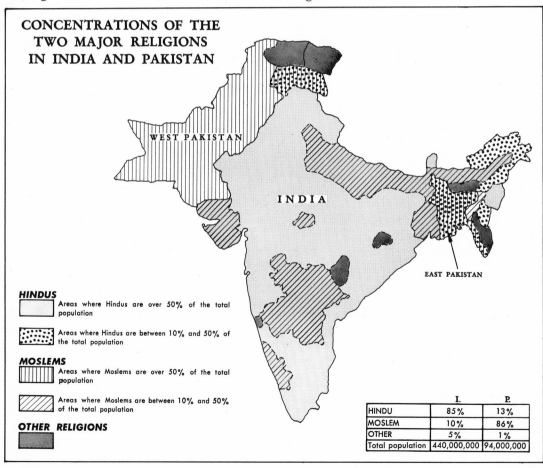

CONCENTRATIONS OF THE TWO MAJOR RELIGIONS IN INDIA AND PAKISTAN

WEST PAKISTAN

INDIA

EAST PAKISTAN

HINDUS

Areas where Hindus are over 50% of the total population

Areas where Hindus are between 10% and 50% of the total population

MOSLEMS

Areas where Moslems are over 50% of the total population

Areas where Moslems are between 10% and 50% of the total population

OTHER RELIGIONS

	I.	P.
HINDU	85%	13%
MOSLEM	10%	86%
OTHER	5%	1%
Total population	440,000,000	94,000,000

When World War II broke out, the Indian National Congress immediately offered to assist Britain, provided that India be granted dominion status at once. The British replied that this was impossible during the war when they were fighting for their lives. They did offer to extend the Indianization of the viceroy's Council and to permit an elected constituent assembly which could complete self-rule after the war. Congress leaders—but not the Muslim League or the Indian Communist Party—refused to cooperate. Congress provincial cabinets resigned; the British were called upon to "quit India"; civil disobedience again was launched and once more broke into violence. Some 14,000 Congress leaders were jailed for the remainder of the war, while their political rivals gained strength.

After the war there was continued rivalry between the Indian Congress and the Muslim League. In 1946 both agreed to a long-term plan for a constitution, but the Muslim League soon reverted to its position of unconditional partition. In February 1947 Britain announced that it was ready to transfer power to responsible Indian hands by June 1948. By June 1947 agreement was reached to partition India along religious lines and to divide the provinces of Bengal and the Punjab, which the Muslims had previously claimed. The Indian Independence Act was passed in July 1948. On August 15, 1948, the Indian Empire, which had existed under British rule for nearly a century, was split into the Republic of India (1,261,416 square miles, 1964 population, 471,627,000), and the new Republic of Pakistan (365,529 square miles, 1964 population, 100,762,000). Pakistan was divided into two unequal parts separated by a thousand-mile expanse of India. Retaining membership in the Commonwealth of Nations, India became leader of the neutralist bloc in the cold war. The country was still beset by the problems of expanding population and mass poverty.

3. Southeast Asia

Crossroads of the East. Across the Bay of Bengal, to the east of India, is a second peninsula with a jagged coastline and a somewhat smaller population. On the mainland today are seven continental states (Thailand, Burma, Malaya, North Vietnam, South Vietnam, Cambodia, and Laos), which are separated from the rest of Asia by mountain barriers. Added to this peninsula to form Southeast Asia are the two archipelagos of the Philippines and Indonesia. These tropical lands, situated on the crossroads between Asia and Australia, control the passages between the Indian Ocean and the Pacific Ocean. The population in this area is greater than that of the United States. Among the varieties of ethnic strains are Indians and Chinese, but several thousand years have produced intermingled stocks.

During the nineteenth century all the Southeast Asia area except Siam (Thailand) came under colonial control of the Europeans. The British annexed Malaya and Burma, the French obtained Indochina, and the United States acquired the Philippines from Spain. The peoples of Southeast Asia are tractable and industrious, and are united only in their attitude toward colonial exploitation: they regard Western imperialism as insufferable oppression. Each country is inflamed with an intense spirit of nationalism, and each took a separate course to nationhood without much cooperation from its neighbors.

Burma, Malaya, and Thailand. Burma, with an area of 261,789 square miles, and a coastline of 1,200 miles, is bounded on the west by the Bay of Bengal and India. To safeguard their Indian frontier, the British fought three wars in Burma (1824–1826, 1852, and 1885), and formally annexed it to the British Empire in 1885. British administration, as in India, brought the quarreling states of the ancient kingdom under the rule of a governor and district commissioners. In 1937 the British separated Burma from India and established it as a Crown colony. Invaded by the Japanese in World War II, Burma became an important battlefield. In 1942 the Japanese set up a puppet government. The Allied forces liberated the country in 1945; and it was declared an independent nation in 1948.

British Malaya, at one time consisting of the Straits Settlements (Singapore, Penang, and

Malacca), the Federated Malay States, the Unfederated Malay States, and several islands, covered about 50,000 square miles with a population of nearly five million. In 1511 the Portuguese established a base at Malacca, which was taken by the Dutch in 1614, and acquired by the British during the Napoleonic Wars. The British obtained a foothold in Penang in 1786, and in 1819 took Singapore, located at one of the few vital bottlenecks in the world's ocean trade, and built it into a strong bastion. The Straits Settlements colony was administered by a British governor who was also high commissioner for British North Borneo, Sarawak, and the Federated and Unfederated Malay States. In 1946 Singapore was made a separate colony; Penang, Malacca, and the Malay States were united as the Malayian Union, which became the Federation of Malaya in 1948. The Federation gained its independence in 1957, retaining its membership in the Commonwealth of Nations. In 1963 Malaya, Singapore, Sabah (North Borneo), and Sarawak joined to form the Federation of Malaysia. Singapore, finding insoluble the tension between its large Chinese population and the Malays who controlled the government, withdrew from the Federation and became an independent state in 1965.

Thailand (Siam), comprises an area of 198,455 square miles with a population of 26,257,916. Occupied in the sixth century A.D. by invaders who came from their homeland in northern Asia, Siam fought sporadically with Cambodia and Burma for several centuries. The Siamese were able to survive the march of rival imperialisms because neither the British nor the French would allow the other to annex the country. The British managed to obtain recognition of their paramount interests in Siam in 1824. In 1896 British and French interests in Siam were recognized in a treaty which guaranteed Siamese independence. Siam, yielding to Japanese occupation during World War II, became one of the most valuable bases for Japan in its efforts to establish control of the entire Far East. After the Japanese surrender, Siam repudiated its declaration of war on the Allies. After 1945 it pursued a consistently pro-Western course.

The Netherlands East Indies. The Netherlands East Indies, or what was later named Indonesia, consisted of an area of 735,000 square miles and a population of approximately 70,000,000, two-thirds of whom were concentrated in the islands of Java and Sumatra. One of the world's richest areas, with great wealth in tin, rubber, spices, oil, quinine, and copra, the East Indies became a battleground for Christian, Hindu, and Muslim religions. Muslim invasions began in the thirteenth century; most of the area was Muslim by the fifteenth century. The Portuguese traders who arrived in the sixteenth century were ousted by the Dutch. In the early seventeenth century the Dutch extended their influence, and in 1798 the Netherlands government took over the Dutch East India Company. Dutch power continued to expand until in 1922 the islands became an integral part of the Netherlands kingdom. The Dutch were most reluctant to give self-government to this carefully guarded society.

It was not easy for the peoples of the Netherlands East Indies to combine for any collective action, especially because they inhabited more than 3,000 islands stretching across nearly 2,800 miles of ocean. But, like the inhabitants of India, the people of the Indies began to demand independence. Added to the desire for self-government was a strong economic factor—the Netherlands had tried to supply all the manufactured goods required in the Indies from factories in the home country. Indonesian patriots regarded this pressure as unfair, and pointed to the difference in standards of living in Holland and in the Indies. There was further discrimination in education and the social order in general. The Dutch colonizers were primarily interested in maintaining the old social system rather than improving it. In favoring the dominantly Chinese class of businessmen, in protecting the plantation-owners of European origin, and in leaving the Indonesian population largely in subservient status, the Dutch played directly into the hands of the National Indonesian Party which agitated for independence.

In World War II the Netherlands East Indies were occupied by the Japanese, who evacuated the area in August 1945. At this time Dr. Achmed Sukarno, a Nationalist leader, announced the formation of the Indonesian Republic and took over control of parts of Sumatra and Java. The Dutch resorted to force to retain their rich colony. Difficulties continued until 1948 when the United Nations intervened. Gradually, ties between the new country of Indonesia and the Netherlands were broken. The transfer of sovereignty took place at Amsterdam on December 27, 1949.

The dilemma of the Indonesians was not solved by independence. They believed, like other African and Asian peoples, that freedom from colonial control would automatically bring prosperity. With foreign investments confiscated, foreign loans halted, unbalanced budgets, and ruinous inflation, Indonesia embarked on a rocky road.

Indochina: From French Control to Partition. French Indochina before 1939 consisted of the colony of Cochin-China, with four protectorates: Annam, Cambodia, Tonkin, and Laos. This area of 281,174 square miles, one fourth larger than France itself, and housing a population of 25,000,000, had been conquered and organized by the French. Behind its conquest was a long history of French expansion in the area. In 1787 the king of Hue ceded to France a base in Tourane and Poulo Condore. After assuming the throne of Annam, he asked for Chinese assistance and expelled the French. The French, resenting this treatment, struck back until all Indochina came under their rule.

Demands for independence became stronger with each passing year in the twentieth century. French colonial rule received a critical blow when the Japanese occupied Indochina in 1941. The French hoped to maintain their control of the area after the war. General de Gaulle, leader of the Free French, promised Indochina a new political status within the French Community, but his plans were frustrated by opposition from President Roosevelt. At the Potsdam conference, the Big Three— the United States, Russia, and Great Britain— agreed that French Indochina would be occupied by Chinese Nationalist troops in the north and by the British in the south.

Meanwhile, a Communist group called the Vietminh, led by Ho Chi Minh, a Moscow-trained Communist, proclaimed the Republic of Vietnam at Hanoi after forcing the abdication of the Emperor Bao Dai. Unable to come to terms with the French, Ho Chi Minh decided on revolt. Thus began the Indochinese war, which lasted eight years. The struggle took on the character of guerrilla warfare, with the French controlling the cities and the Vietminh the countryside. The French set up a counter-government at Saigon and brought back the former Emperor Bao Dai. When the Communists took over the Chinese mainland, they recognized Ho Chi Minh's government and began to give him military support.

In 1954 the weakness of the French position in Indochina was revealed by the Vietminh victory at Dienbienphu, a fortified camp on the Laotian border. A conference of foreign ministers held at Geneva was attended by representatives of France, Britain, Russia, and Communist China. It was decided (July 21, 1954) to put an end to the war and to partition Vietnam along the 17th parallel between the Communist government at Hanoi in the north and the pro-West government at Saigon in the south. The conference also confirmed the independence of Laos and Cambodia. This effectively shattered French influence in Indochina.

For the United States this entire area was vital in the arc set in the Far East to contain Communist expansion. Washington had remained aloof from the Geneva agreement. The United States now stepped in to fill the gap left by French defeat in Southeast Asia. The Southeast Asia Treaty Organization (SEATO) was organized as a collective security agreement to halt Communist aggression. Increasingly chaotic conditions in South Vietnam led to gradual American involvement in Southeast Asia.

The Philippines. In 1521 the people of the Philippines welcomed the Portuguese navigator Fernando Magellan with fruit, rice, and chickens. Two decades later the islands were appropriated by a Spanish exploration party and named in honor of Prince Philip, later

Philip II of Spain. Spain held possession of the islands for the next 350 years. In 1898, after the Spanish-American War, the seven thousand islands which make up the archipelago of 115,707 square miles were formally acquired by the United States. At first the Filipino people accepted American rule, but gradually, under the leadership of Emilio Aguinaldo and other nationalists, they began to demand independence. In 1934 the Tydings-McDuffie Act provided for Philippine independence in 1946. Under a constitution approved by the people in 1935, the Commonwealth of the Philippines was established under the presidency of Manuel Quezon y Molina.

The Philippines were invaded by Japanese troops on December 8, 1941, a day after the attack on Pearl Harbor. The independence promised by Congress in 1934 was therefore delayed. After the war, the Republic of the Philippines was inaugurated on July 4, 1946, with a Senate and House of Representatives and suffrage for citizens over twenty-one. Communist guerrillas sought to continue and extend chaotic conditions with a view to overthrowing the republic, but their resistance was suppressed. The Philippine economy was strongly supported by the United States, which also sent military aid to the republic and maintained air and naval bases in the islands. In 1947 the United States and the Republic of the Philippines concluded a ninety-nine year mutual defense pact. Despite some friction, American-Philippine relations remained close.

4. The Chinese Struggle for Unity

The "Time of Troubles." At the end of the nineteenth century, the Manchu dynasty, which had ruled China since 1644, was in crisis. During the two generations between the first Anglo-Chinese War (1839–1842) and the Boxer Uprising (1899–1901), there had been only a few, inadequate efforts to modernize China. After a series of great rebellions in middle decades of that century, as part of an imperial restoration, a group of orthodox Confucian "self-strengtheners" tried to introduce modern engines of power within the traditional system of values and institutions. Un-

like the experience of modernizers in Meiji Japan (1867–1912), most of the Chinese officially-sponsored efforts failed. The Manchus came to be regarded by republican and more revolutionary Chinese as foreign usurpers. Especially after defeat by "upstart" Japan (1894–1895), the imperial regime became bankrupt and more vulnerable. In October 1911 discontent flared into open revolt. General Yuan Shih-kai, a dedicated supporter of the Manchu dynasty, was made premier of the imperial government in December 1911, but shortly thereafter abandoned the imperial cause. Negotiations between the revolutionary leader Dr. Sun Yat-sen and General Yuan resulted in the abdication of the infant emperor.

Sun Yat-sen. On January 1, 1912, a revolutionary assembly at Nanking elected Dr. Sun Yat-sen (1866–1925) president of a provisional republican government. A physician turned patriotic plotter who had been forced to spend much time in exile, Dr. Sun was a founder of a party which had several earlier names but finally came to be called the *Kuomintang* (Nationalist Party). He had a fervent belief in the future of his country, which he felt would one day play a leading role in world affairs. He organized Chinese youth and others, including anti-Manchu secret societies, into a movement designed to arouse the Chinese people from lethargy. Hoping to unite the country, Dr. Sun relinquished the presidency of the new Republic to his northern rival, General Yuan. Yuan, however, proceeded to create a dictatorship which culminated in his vain attempt to found a new Chinese dynasty. Regionalism had been gaining in China for many decades; as this belated traditional effort collapsed, the country broke into warlord regimes which were not fully centralized until the Communist conquest was completed in 1949.

Sun and his adherents tried to revolt against subversion of the Republic but were defeated and took refuge again in Japan. When they returned to the continent it was to renew their party movement in the region around Canton. Dr. Sun sought funds and munitions from Japan and from the United States, but when

Communist Mao Tse-tung and Nationalist Chiang Kai-shek in the days before they became bitter enemies in the civil war that began in 1927.

these overtures were rebuffed, he turned to the Soviet Union. The Chinese Nationalists were ardent about anti-imperialism and an end to the Unequal Treaty provisions, but they were divided about the nature and pace of socioeconomic revolution. Sun's basic political ideas had been evolved in the first years of the century. In the early 1920's they were enunciated in a series of lectures and became part of the Nationalist credo under the title of "The Three Principles of the People"—nationalism, democracy, and a vaguely defined principle of livelihood.

Despite Sun's efforts, much of China's history for a decade continued to be a confused struggle between competing warlord factions. In the disorders, trade was crippled, and China's agrarian crisis deepened. Dr. Sun and his for the most part southern associates found it almost impossible to bring order to the dis-

traught country. The *Kuomintang's* entente with the Soviet Union entailed a united front with the new and still tiny Chinese Communist Party which became a disciplined "bloc within." Its factions exercised disproportionate influence, and together with the Soviet advisers, helped to broaden the social base of the Nationalist movement. Labor and peasant unions for the first time became significant in China. On a fruitless mission to the north to persuade contenders to reunite the country under the Republic, Sun died of cancer on March 12, 1925.

Chiang Kai-shek. In 1926 the Nationalists, pressing two military columns northward from Canton, defeated warlord opponents and spread the revolution to the middle Yangtze Valley. The Soviet advisers and revolutionary organizers prevailed in the wing which established a new capital at Hankow, while General Chiang (1886–   ) commanded the more easterly and conservative contingents. He allied with certain warlords in eastern China and with conservative business and underworld elements in Shanghai and the Lower Yangtze. There ensued a race for control of the lower Valley. This was won by Chiang's forces and allies, who suppressed the armed labor unions and carried out a "white terror."

Stalin through the Comintern belatedly ordered the Communists and their military units to make a bid for power. Their putsches came too late, and they were expelled from the cities and from contact with their favored proletariats. Instead, Mao Tse-tung and others were obliged to retreat to mountain hideouts, at first in part of Mao's native Hunan Province; later his units moved eastward to straddle the borderland of Kiangsi and Fukien Provinces. It was there that they founded the first Chinese "Soviet Republic" in which programs such as redistribution of land were instituted. This regime was surrounded by Nationalist and allied warlord forces. Even with German advisors, however, it required six campaigns before Chiang's divisions were able to defeat Communist guerrilla armies and impel the exodus which, known as the "Long March," became the Chinese Communist Party's epic of endurance. In several columns the pursued Communists trekked westward, later northeastward, deciding to form a new border government in China's near northwest.

After that fateful split in the Nationalist movement during 1927–1928, China's dominant, militarized parties—both modelled on the Communist Party of the Soviet Union—tended increasingly to polarize politics. The Nationalists under Chiang lost much of their reformist zeal. Confucianism re-emerged as their basic philosophy, even though Sun Yat-senism became a regimented doctrine, and during the civil war, an abortive "New Life Movement" had been attempted.

However, a stronger Nationalist government was established at Nanking and quickly gained recognition by the relieved treaty powers. In 1928 with warlord allies from the northwest, it defeated a coalition which had controlled the northeastern plain and its centers, Peking and Tientsin. Chang Tso-lin, the "Old Marshal" of Manchuria, retreating from the Nationalist forces toward his capital, Mukden, was assassinated by the Japanese who hoped to create an excuse for taking over Manchuria where since 1905 they had heavily invested in economic development. (*See page 552.*) The warlord's son and heir, Chang Hsueh-liang, against Japanese advice raised the Nationalist flag over Mukden, but continued to play the regime in Nanking and the Japanese against each other.

Chiang and certain others in the Nationalist factions were trying desperately to unify China and build power from above without wide-ranging social and economic reforms. Some significant gains, such as unification of currency and freedom from tariff controls set by conventions, were made; but in general the Chinese economy stagnated and failed to break through to self-generating momentum. The Nationalists wanted to crush the Communists first, then face Japanese aggression, and perhaps later come to the increasingly demanded reforms. After the occupation of North China and the formal adherence of Manchuria, the regime in Nanking declared the military phase of the revolution, as envisaged by Dr. Sun, to be ended and the era of party tutelage to have begun. As suffering continued and the Japanese encroached, Chiang and the *Kuomintang* found themselves increasingly caught between two millstones: Japanese imperialism and the internal Communist demand for a "revolutionary war of popular resistance." Even many erstwhile supporters of the *Kuomintang* became alarmed at appeasement and susceptible to Communist calls for a new united front, formal abatement of its own revolutionary programs, and institution of democratic reforms along with national resistance against aggression. These trends lay behind the kidnapping of Generalissimo Chiang at Christmas time in 1936 by young officers who had been expelled from Manchuria by the Japanese. Perhaps it was on orders from Stalin that the Chinese Communist Party sent a delegation to work toward a verbal formula which led to Chiang's release and, painfully over the following year, to an imperfect second united front.

The Rise of Communist China. The emergence of Communist China was one of the most significant events of the post-World War II era. The civil war had been going on between the Nationalists and the Communists since 1927. During World War II the Nationalists and Communists united against the common enemy, but they had little trust in each other. In theory the Communist army was under the nominal command of Chiang Kai-shek and the *Kuomintang*, but despite Chiang's efforts, Communist power began to spread in northern and central China. Mao Tse-tung sent his guerrillas deep into Japanese zones, where they won wide support among the peasants. ("The soldiers are fish and the people water".)

As the Communists gathered support at the grass roots, the Nationalist position began to deteriorate. Expelled from the cities of eastern China, the Nationalists lost popular support while the Communists were gaining it. To meet growing Communist strength, the Nationalists began a policy of repression that soon took on the tones of dictatorship.

When the Japanese surrendered in September 1945, the stage was ready for another clash between Nationalists and Communists. The critical confrontation came in Manchuria in the late days of World War II. The invading Russians had signed a treaty with Nationalist China pledging support, but they violated it as soon as it was made. Instead of encouraging the Nationalists to take control in Manchuria, Moscow permitted the Chinese Communists to appropriate huge stores of Japanese arms. Then the Russians evacuated Manchuria, taking with them to Siberia as many of the Japanese industrial plants as they could conveniently carry.

China was now split between Nationalists and Communists. The United States, concerned about possible Communist control of China, made a final effort to resolve the dispute. In 1945 President Harry S. Truman sent General George C. Marshall, just retired as chief of staff of the United States Army, to China on a peace mission. General Marshall's task was to arrange a truce and to persuade both sides to agree to a coalition government. Then the United States would give China massive economic aid to rebuild the shattered country. The Marshall mission was unsuccessful. Neither side was ready for a compromise. The Nationalists were convinced that they had the strongest army and would easily win the civil war. The Communists, enthusiastic in their cause and skilled in guerrilla warfare, were equally unwilling to negotiate for peace.

By the end of 1946 the country was engaged in full civil war. General Marshall, blaming hard-headed Nationalists and recalcitrant Communists alike for opposition to genuine coalition government, returned in disgust to Washington. The Nationalists at this time seemed to be the stronger of the rivals. With three million troops they held the cities, while about a million Communist guerrillas occupied the countryside. In approved guerrilla fashion, the Communists avoided battle with their better-armed opponents and waited for the Nationalists to make mistakes. The reasoning was correct. The Nationalist government, weakened by graft, corruption, and inefficiency, made no effort to improve the lot of the peasantry, a critical mistake which worked to the advantage of the Communists. Although Washington poured several billion dollars' worth of military and economic aid into China, it could not prevent the growing disorganization of the reactionary government.

The Communists ingeniously exploited the weaknesses of the *Kuomintang* regime. They renamed their guerrillas the "People's Liberation Army" and won peasant support by proposing and instituting land reforms. They attracted intellectuals and students who were disgusted by Nationalist inefficiency and corruption and who as yet had no idea of the nature of Communist rule. Meanwhile, the Communists were winning in the field. By 1948 they were laying siege to Nationalist garrisons in the cities and cutting off communications between them. One city after another in Manchuria fell to the Chinese Reds. Then the Communists turned south, and in January 1949 marched into Peiping.

The year 1949 saw the rapid disintegration of Nationalist China. In April the Communists crossed the Yangtze River and captured Nanking, the capital. The fall of Shanghai followed. In October 1949 Mao Tse-tung proclaimed the People's Republic of China in Peiping. The city became the capital of Red China, and was renamed Peking.

Nationalist resistance collapsed on the Chinese mainland by the end of 1949. The defeated government fled to the island of Formosa, or Taiwan. On this island, just one hundred miles off the coast of south China, Chiang Kai-shek continued to rule the remnants (about 200,000 men) of the Nationalist army. Several million Chinese followed him there. Supported by American aid, Chiang awaited the day of vengeance. The United States was disturbed by the loss of mainland China to the Communists. A 1949 State Department "White Paper" blamed Nationalist weakness for the calamity.

After 1949 there were two Chinas, the Communist People's Republic of China on the mainland, and the National Republic of China on Formosa.

The Development of Communist China. Mao Tse-tung, the son of a rich peasant, became chairman of the Chinese Communist Party. With his lieutenants, Chou En-lai, Chu Teh, and Liu Shao-chi, Mao took a firm grip on government in the new nation. In theory a "people's democratic state," Communist China was actually under totalitarian rule. The Communist Party was the propagandizing element. Here, as in many other organizational respects, the Chinese leaned on Russian experience. Secret police, mass arrests, executions, forced labor, brainwashing—all the familiar practices

of Stalin's Russia—were introduced into Red China. Every part of society was communized according to the gospel of Mao, The Young Pioneer Corps, for example, was inculcated with the "five loves"—Fatherland, people, labor, science, and public property.

As in Soviet Russia, Soviet China was mobilized into a great effort to transform the country from agricultural economy to industrial power. The first Five-Year Plan (1949–1952) was designed to restore and rehabilitate the economy and at the same time redistribute the land. According to Communist sources, usually unreliable, about 45 per cent of the land under cultivation—some 110 million acres —was taken from landlords and distributed to about 300 million peasants. The task was pursued with extreme ruthlessness. Landlords were publicly humiliated and then executed. The land distribution program was completed in late 1952. Meanwhile, there were substantial advances in industrialization, especially in the output of coal, iron ore, and steel.

In 1958 came a second Plan, the "great leap forward." Because industry was outstripping agriculture, the planners in Peking decided to revolutionize agriculture by a great collectivization drive. The land but recently given to the farmers was taken away. In stages, the peasants were forced to join cooperatives, which paid them for the use of their land and labor. Millions of peasants were herded into 24,000 communes. Each commune contained about 5,000 families and was supposed to cultivate about 10,000 acres. The work was organized along military lines with squads of peasants marching to and from work each day. The entire life of the peasant was organized from cradle to grave. Babies were sent to nurseries, older people to "happy homes for the aged." By 1961 "the great leap forward" had collapsed ignominiously. Communist leaders blamed the failure on flood and drought, but a still more important reason was the rebellion of peasants against the impossibly high goals set for the communes and the terribly exhausting work loads.

The leaders of Communist China, although preaching peace, adopted an aggressive foreign policy. In 1951 Communist China occupied Tibet on the ground of old claims to Chinese suzerainty. When the Tibetans broke into revolt in 1959, the Chinese put down the rebellion. Border disputes with India nearly led to war on several occasions. Chinese Communists intervened in the Korean War in late 1950. China supported Communist North Vietnam in its struggle with South Vietnam. Again and again Peking proclaimed that it would "liberate" Formosa from Chiang Kai-shek's Nationalist government. Here, as in Korea and Vietnam, the United States stepped in to prevent Chinese Communist expansion. Aware of her growing strength, Communist China has sought to increase her influence in Asia, Africa, and Latin America. Communist China was denied membership in the United Nations.

The existence of a second major power turned out to be a threat to the leadership of the Soviet Union in the Communist world. In 1950 Soviet Russia and Communist China signed a thirty-year treaty of friendship and mutual aid. For the next several years Moscow played a determining role in the industrialization of Soviet China. Gradually the two Communist giants began to pull apart. After the death of Stalin, Peking began to assert her independence of Russian control. When Khrushchev announced that there were "different roads to socialism," Mao replied with the aphorism: "Let a hundred flowers bloom, let a hundred schools of thought contend." Soon Mao regarded himself the spokesman for orthodox Marxism-Leninism. Both sides began to criticize each other in increasingly bitter terms. Peking accused Moscow of revisionism and retreat from orthodoxy; Moscow denounced Peking for reckless aggression. It became increasingly obvious that Soviet Russia and Communist China were moving on a collision course.

Nationalist China. Taipei, the capital of Formosa, became the capital of the Republic of China on December 7, 1949. At first the United States appeared to have abandoned the Nationalists, but a change in American policy came at the time of the Korean War

(1950–1953). The Nationalists, bolstered by massive aid from the United States, created a prosperous economy. Governmental efficiency was increased by ruthless reform; the armed forces were reorganized; education was expanded. Just as a prosperous West Berlin remained a showcase for Western capitalism alongside a bare East Berlin, so Formosa remained a thorn in the side of the Communist leaders. Nationalist China became an outpost of the free world in the Pacific. The Nationalist government proclaimed that it had every intention of one day invading the mainland. The Chinese civil war thus continued in theory, although by the 1960's there was little actual fighting.

5. *Japanese Expansion*

Course of Aggression. At the time of crisis in 1937, when the second modern Sino-Japanese war broke out, the outcome was by no means an entirely foregone conclusion. The Japanese hoped to carve out a new puppet state without a decisive military showdown. But as war developed and the *Kuomintang* was expelled from those few provinces that it had completely controlled and from the urban bastions of its strength, vast countrysides became politically fluid. The Japanese were able to clamp down their grid of control and create several puppet regimes, but actually a triangular struggle was in progress between the Japanese, the Communists, and the Nationalists. Several times during the war, the Japanese tried unsuccessfully to heal the break with the conservative Nationalists and restore the anti-Communist front on possibly attractive but pro-Japanese terms. During the gruelling strife, the second Nationalist-Communist united front deteriorated, then broke down, and the Communists expanded until at war's end they held nineteen so-called "liberated areas" containing about 93 million people. President Roosevelt hoped that China would become a great, stabilizing power, but the China of 1945 was far from being united. Aside from *Kuomintang* conservatism, the factors most responsible for the continuing disunity were Communist-developed programs which won peasant support, and Japanese encroachments which were often masked as opposition to communism.

Japanese expansion did not follow a long-laid master plan inexorably pursued. There were always Japanese super-patriots and imperial aggrandizers, but there were also moderates who preferred commercial expansion and peace, and Japanese Pan-Asian champions who wanted Japan to lead non-Western modernization. But nationalism, the norms of power politics, and crises such as wars, depressions, and tariff reprisals more often played into the hands of militarists and their civilian allies. There were also tensions within Japanese society which sought release through overseas adventures.

The train of events which at last led to the outbreak of war at Marco Polo Bridge in 1937 began at least two generations earlier when Japan first showed its interest in acquiring Formosa and began to wean Korea away from its Chinese suzerain. In 1894–1895, Japan inflicted a decisive defeat on China, becoming one of the creditor and treaty powers, its nationals able thenceforth to build factories in treaty ports to compete for Chinese markets. Formosa was placed under Japanese naval governors. Within another decade, Japan had defeated Tsarist Russia, cleared the way to dominance in—and, by 1910, annexation of—Korea, and succeeded the vanquished in control of the Liaotung peninsular tip with its naval base at Port Arthur and its prime port of Dairen. The seventeen-mile swath along what came to be the South Manchuria Railway became the channel for Japanese economic penetration of that region.

During World War I, the Japanese seized German interests in the northeastern province of Shantung and, in treaties which incorporated four groups of the Twenty-One Demands (1915), made further inroads into South Manchuria, Eastern Inner Mongolia, and even into the main heavy industrial complex in China's middle Yangtze "Chicagoland." Japanese financiers also lent large amounts through unstable, warlord-pressured regimes in the northeast. Such credits sometimes permitted Japanese control over certain rail lines as well as mineral and timber resources for stipulated periods. (*See page 668.*)

After the war and the general settlements, Japan was an important member of the League of Nations. The renewed ability of other powers —chiefly Great Britain, the United States, and France—to restrain Japan was felt. At the Washington Conference (1921–1922), the Anglo-Japanese Alliance of twenty years' standing was superseded by the Four-Power Pact, and the Nine-Power Pact by which Japan with China and seven other powers subscribed to upholding the territorial and administrative integrity of China. Moderates were in ascendance in Tokyo; they favored friendly relations with their huge neighbor as Chinese nationalism was rising. However, others in Japan and some officers in the Japanese army in South Manchuria were alarmed by the prospect of a militantly unified China. When the status quo attempted through the treaties of the Washington Conference produced no machinery and little by way of cooperative diplomacy, each of the powers began bilateral negotiations with China. Social tensions were aggravated, when the international depression struck Japan and its trade. Devaluation of the yen in preparation for trade offensives led to tariff and quota reprisals by other governments. Military extremists promised the Japanese continental lands for resettlement, control of Asian raw materials and markets, and control of exploitative economic interests at home.

The first successful step in a new sequence of expansion was taken by young Japanese military conspirators in South Manchuria in September 1931 in defiance of their own government and of the League of Nations. In the following May, and again in February 1936, coups were attempted by military-rightist groups in Tokyo. These and quieter pressures gradually increased the Army's role in Japanese politics, and each "incident," in which Japanese prestige and interests seemed to be at stake before a critical world majority, roused Japanese nationalism to a higher pitch. Neutralism and pacifism were then almost as strong in the United States as they were in Japan after 1945; and both Britain and the United States tended to appease Japanese expansion (or to pursue an ineffective non-recognition policy), hoping to assist Japan's moderate elements and regarding her as a needed counterpoise against the Soviet Union. Japan's expansionists were able to exploit this situation by assuming an anti-Communist stance.

Their course was rather decisively set from the occupation of Manchuria and establishment of a puppet state there in 1931–1932. At that time the Chinese offered little resistance; a boycott of Japanese goods precipitated a limited invasion by Imperial marines in the vicinity of Shanghai. British and American influence patched up that affair, but in the following year, the Japanese Army from Manchuria occupied the adjacent province of Jehol and imposed an agreement which left Japanese garrisons in a wedge-shaped sector inside the Great Wall, including Peking and Tientsin, but required the withdrawal of Nationalist forces. Next the Japanese military and their civilian spokesmen in Tokyo sought to create a puppet state in the five northeastern provinces of China Proper but found it necessary for a time to settle for an East Hopei-Chahar Political Council. It was while Japanese units were maneuvering for control of the rail approach to Peking from the south that a local Chinese commander decided to resist, and the clash occurred at Marco Polo Bridge. Fortunately this happened when a new Chinese united front was in the making. In the months of bitter losses and migrations which ensued, Chinese morale held; Chiang's prestige had seldom been so high, nor was it again to be. The Nationalist government ordered scorching of the earth and retreated westward, first to Hankow, then farther up river to Chungking.

In her expansionist course, Japan had developed common revisionist interests with the European Fascist Axis, and began to time her actions with them. In 1936 this enlarged alliance was pointed against the Soviet Union; in 1940 a reconstituted Axis was designed chiefly to counter the United States. By that time, Japanese expansionists were particularly eyeing the Southeast Asian colonies orphaned by the Nazi conquest of the Netherlands and France and the direct threat to the United Kingdom. Aware of oil and other riches to be controlled in what the Japanese were soon calling the "Southern Resources Area," they sent Foreign Minister Yosuke Matsuoka to Moscow where, in April 1941 he signed a non-aggression pact. This served to protect the Japanese rear. Soon they pressed into southern Indochina, which precipitated the oil embargo by the American, British, and Dutch governments. That, in turn, led to Japan's attack on Pearl Harbor. Greater changes were yet in store for Asia.

{ KEY DOCUMENT }

THE TWENTY-ONE DEMANDS, 1915

Foreign Relations of the United States: 1915 (Washington, 1924), pp. 99–103.

IN AUGUST 1914 the Japanese declared war on Germany, and in November violated the neutrality of China. Determined to take advantage of the situation, the Japanese on January 18, 1915, secretly presented twenty-one demands to the Chinese government "to settle outstanding questions." The demands would have reduced China to a Japanese puppet. The Japanese tried to keep the negotiations secret, but by March 1915 the United States minister Paul Reinsch was able to send a reasonably accurate summary of the demands to the State Department in Washington. The United States managed to obtain an adjournment of Japanese demands on China, but had to recognize their "special interests" in China.

I

The Japanese Government and the Chinese Government being desirous of maintaining the general peace in Eastern Asia and further strengthening the friendly relations and good neighborhood existing between the two nations, agree to the following articles:

ARTICLE I. The Chinese Government engages to give full assent to all matters upon which the Japanese Government may hereafter agree with the German Government relating to the disposition of all rights, interests and concessions which, by virtue of treaties or otherwise, Germany possesses in relation to the Province of Shantung.

ARTICLE II. The Chinese Government engages that within the Province of Shantung and along its coast no territory or island will be ceded or leased to a third power under any pretext.

ARTICLE III. The Chinese Government consents to Japan's building a railway from Chefoo or Lungkou to join the Kiaochou-Chinanfu Railway.

ARTICLE IV. The Chinese Government engages, in the interest of trade and for the residence of foreigners, to open by herself as soon as possible certain important cities and towns in the Province of Shantung as commercial ports. What places shall be opened are to be jointly decided upon by the two Governments in a separate agreement.

II

The Japanese Government and the Chinese Government, since the Chinese Government has always acknowledged the special position enjoyed by Japan in South Manchuria and Eastern Inner Mongolia, agree to the following articles:

ARTICLE I. The two contracting parties mutually agree that the term of lease of Port Arthur and Dalny and the term of lease of the South Manchurian Railway and the Antung-Mukden Railway shall be extended to the period of 99 years.

ARTICLE II. Japanese subjects (literally, Japanese officials or common people) in South Manchuria and Eastern Inner Mongolia shall have the right to lease or own land required either for erecting suitable buildings for trade and manufacture or for farming.

ARTICLE III. Japanese subjects (literally, Japanese officials or common people) shall be free to reside and travel in South Manchuria and Eastern Inner Mongolia and to engage in business and in manufacture of any kind whatsoever.

ARTICLE IV. The Chinese Government agrees to grant to Japanese subjects (literally, Japanese officials or common people) the mining rights of all the mines in South Manchuria and Eastern Inner Mongolia. As regards what mines are to be opened they shall be decided upon by the two Governments jointly.

ARTICLE V. The Chinese Government agrees that, in respect of the (two) cases mentioned herein below, the Japanese Government's consent shall be first obtained before action is taken:

(a) Whenever permission is granted to the subject of a third Power to build a railway or to make a loan with a third Power for the purpose of building a railway in South Manchuria and Eastern Inner Mongolia.

(b) Whenever a loan is to be made with a third Power pledging the local taxes of South Manchuria and Eastern Inner Mongolia as security.

ARTICLE VI. The Chinese Government agrees that if the Chinese Government employs political, financial or military advisers or instructors in South Manchuria or Eastern Inner Mongolia, the Japanese Government shall first be consulted.

ARTICLE VII. The Chinese Government agrees that the control and management of the Kirin-Changchun Railway shall be handed over to the Japanese Government for a term of 99 years dating from the signing of this agreement.

III

The Japanese Government and the Chinese Government, seeing that Japanese financiers and the Han-yeh-ping Company have close relations with each other at present and desiring that common interests of the two nations shall be advanced, agree to the following articles:

ARTICLE I. The two contracting parties mutually agree that when the opportune moment arrives the Han-yeh-ping Company shall be made a joint concern of the two nations; and they further agree that, without the previous consent of Japan, China shall not by her own act dispose of the rights and property of whatsoever nature of the said company nor cause the said company to dispose freely of the same.

ARTICLE II. The Chinese Government agrees that all mines in the neighborhood of those owned by the Han-yeh-ping Company shall not be permitted, without the consent of the said company, to be worked by other persons outside of the said company; and further agrees that if it is desired to carry out any undertaking which it is apprehended may directly or indirectly affect the interests of the said company, the consent of the said company shall first be obtained.

IV

The Japanese Government and the Chinese Government, with the object of effectively preserving the territorial integrity of China, agree to the following special article:

The Chinese Government engages not to cede or lease to a third Power any harbor or bay or island along the coast of China.

V

ARTICLE I. The Chinese Central Government shall employ influential Japanese (literally, Japanese who have strength, power, or influence) as advisers in political, financial and military affairs.

ARTICLE II. Japanese hospitals, churches and schools in the interior of China shall be granted the right of owning land.

ARTICLE III. Inasmuch as the Japanese Government and the Chinese Government have had many cases of dispute between Japanese and Chinese police to settle, cases which caused no little misunderstanding, it is for this reason necessary that the police departments of the important places (in China) shall be jointly administered by Japanese and Chinese or that the police departments of these places shall employ numerous Japanese, so that they may at the same time help to plan for the improvement of the Chinese police service.

ARTICLE IV. China shall purchase from Japan a fixed amount of munitions of war (say 50 percent or more of what is needed by the Chinese Government) or that there shall be established in China a Sino-Japanese jointly worked arsenal. Japanese technic-experts are to be employed and Japanese material to be purchased.

ARTICLE V. China agrees to grant to Japan with the right of constructing a railway connecting

Wuchang with Kiukiang and Nanchang, another line between Nanchang and Hanchou, and another between Nanchang and Chaochou.

ARTICLE VI. If China needs foreign capital to work mines, build railways and construct harbor-works (including dock-yards) in the Province of Fukien, Japan shall be first consulted.

ARTICLE VII. China agrees that Japanese subjects shall have the right to propagate Buddhism (in Chinese text, reference is to religion and not especially to Buddhism) in China.

❧ HISTORICAL INTERPRETATION ❧

RUPERT EMERSON ON THE END OF WESTERN DOMINATION OVER MANKIND

Rupert Emerson, *From Empire to Nation* (Cambridge, Mass., 1960), pp. 5–7. Copyright 1960 by the President and Fellows of Harvard College. Reprinted by permission of Harvard University Press.

IMPERIALISM WAS the prime source of the vehement Asian and African nationalism. The reaction of colonized peoples' to imperialism was described in Rupert Emerson's *From Empire to Nation,* with the significant subtitle: *The Rise to Self-Assertion of Asian and African Peoples.* Emerson's summation of the end of Western supremacy follows.

A great era of human history has come to a close—the era of Western domination over the rest of mankind. In many respects that era is too near to us, too much a part of our daily lives, whether we be of the West or of the East, to make possible the kind of objective and dispassionate evaluation which would be desirable. To undertake to be the historian of several hundred years hence or that always shrewd and penetrating visitor from Mars is a risky business. A plausible case can, however, be made for the proposition that the future will look back upon the overseas imperialism of recent centuries, less in terms of its sins of oppression, exploitation, and discrimination, than as the instrument by which the spiritual, scientific, and material revolution which began in Western Europe with the Renaissance was spread to the rest of the world. To broaden this proposition as widely as does a recent analyst of British rule in India who contends that imperialism throughout the ages has been "the main process by which civilization has been diffused" is to leap unduly far. The importance of more peaceful and egalitarian processes of cultural diffusion need not be minimized in order to identify the positive role which imperialism has played.

To assert that imperialism has served through the ages as a great diffuser of civilization is not to imply that every imperialism played the role of bringing a higher civilization to a people at a lower level. Imperialism, by definition, involves the domination of one people over another, of a stronger over a weaker community; yet it would be grossly improper to assume a universal identification of greater strength with loftier culture. Few today would back the optimistic claim of Walter Bagehot in the first flush of evolutionary doctrine, not only that the strongest nations tend to prevail over the others, but also that "in certain marked pecularities the strongest tend to be the best," and his further, more elaborate, claim that: "Conquest is the premium given by nature to those national characters which their natural customs have made most fit to win in war, and in many most material respects those winning characters are really the best characters. The characters which do win in war are the characters which we should wish to win in war." The general superiority of Roman civilization to that of the bulk of the peoples whom Rome overran would not be open to much question, but Rome also overran Greece and was itself later overrun by the barbarians from the north, and the Mongol hordes imposed themselves on China. The diffusion of civilization through imperialism is by no means always a one-way affair. In the contemporary scene, Nazi imperialism would find few supporters as the vehicle for the advance of civilization.

In the case of the overseas imperialism of modern times, the peoples of Western Europe have carried with them the civilization of the revolution which they were experiencing, driven or inspired by the force of the revolution itself and increasingly endowed by it with the necessary greater strength. This is, of course, in no way to suggest that it was the deliberate intent of the builders of empire to fulfill the *mission civilisatrice* of which they occasionally boasted and by which their apologists justified their actions. Only in the rarest instances, if ever, do states or statesmen, embarking on imperial expansion, appear to have been swayed by the desire to do good for their fellow, but alien, man. Missionary zeal of one stamp or another has rarely been wholly absent, but the desire for power and profit, the rivalry of states and peoples, and perhaps even a sense of insecurity, have all been more constant factors in imperialism. The question of intent is, however, in the long run of less consequence than the actual impact of what was done. Even the resolution to hold back the peoples who were overrun by denying them access to the languages and instrumentalities of European civilization could do more than delay the impact. It was only by staying firmly at home that the Europeans could fail to spread their new outlooks and techniques, and staying at home was the one thing which seemed quite impossible. The imperialist explicitly out for the profit, strategic advantage, or glory of his own people was likely to be as radical a transformer of the native society on which he impinged as the avowed missionary or modernizer.

❧ TEN BASIC BOOKS ❧

IMPACT: REVOLUTION IN ASIA

1. Buss, Claude A., *The People's Republic of China,* Anvil Book No. 61 (Princeton, N. J., 1962).†
2. Clubb, O. Edmund, *Twentieth Century China* (New York, 1964).†
3. Fairbank, John K., *The United States and China.* 2nd rev. ed. (Cambridge, Mass., 1961).†
4. Fairbank, John K., Edwin O. Reischauer, and A. M. Craig, *A History of East Asian Civilization,* Vol. II, *East Asia: The Modern Transformation* (Boston, 1965).
5. Lamb, Beatrice P., *India, A World in Transition* (New York, 1965).†
6. MacNair, H. F., and D. F. Lach, *Modern Far Eastern International Relations,* 2nd ed. (New York, 1955).
7. Nehru, Jawaharlal, *Toward Freedom: The Autobiography of Jawaharlal Nehru* (New York, 1941).†
8. Reischauer, Edwin O., *Japan Past and Present.* 3rd ed. (New York, 1964).
9. Reischauer, Edwin O., *Wanted: An Asian Policy* (New York, 1955).
10. Ward, Barbara, *The Interplay of East and West* (New York, 1957).†

41

World War II, 1939-1945

YESTERDAY, DECEMBER 7, 1941—a date which will live in infamy—the United States of America was suddenly and deliberately attacked by naval and air forces of the Empire of Japan.

The United States was at peace with that nation and, at the solicitation of Japan, was still in conversation with its Government and its Emperor looking toward the maintenance of peace in the Pacific. . . .

No matter how long it may take us to overcome this premeditated invasion, the American people in their righteous might will win through to absolute victory.

I believe I interpret the will of the Congress and of the people when I assert that we will not only defend ourselves to the uttermost but will make very certain that this form of treachery shall never endanger us again.

Hostilities exist. There is no blinking at the fact that our people, our territory and our interests are in grave danger. With confidence in our armed forces—with the unbound determination of our people—we will gain the inevitable triumph—so help us God.

I ask that the Congress declare that since the unprovoked and dastardly attack by Japan on Sunday, December 7, a state of war has existed between the United States and the Japanese Empire.

—FRANKLIN D. ROOSEVELT, War Message to Congress, December 8, 1941

1. Fundamental Causes of World War II

Tinderbox: Underlying Issues. Bidding farewell to the Allied Armistice Commission in 1919, a German representative made a skeptical remark: "See you again in twenty years." The accuracy of his prophecy is not so striking as the fact that it represented a climate of opinion that seemed to make war inevitable. The period between 1919 and 1939, called appropriately the Long Armistice, saw an extension of all the motivating factors that had led to the outbreak of World War I. It became increasingly obvious that the blood-bath of 1914–1918 had brought neither peace, security, nor democracy, and that the European system was undergoing further social and moral disintegration. The same conditions, with some variation, that had led to the outbreak of World War I continued to exist in even more aggravated form.

Economic Time-Fuses. The failure of the victorious democracies to achieve politico-economic stability, together with the effects of the world depression, caused havoc and panic among the nations of the world. Three dissatisfied powers—Germany, Italy and Japan—regarding themselves as "Have-not nations," complained that they had not been given a fair share of the world's raw materials, markets, and capital-investment areas. The democracies, although disunited and unprepared, sought to retain economic advantages in the world. For a time they were willing to make concessions to the clamoring Have-not nations in the hope that appeasement would avert war, but their efforts to maintain peace were fruitless when it became apparent that the Axis would not be satisfied with anything less than global domination. In a world in which all nations wanted a favorable balance of trade and economic self-sufficiency, each country resorted to economic warfare, including protective tariffs, managed currencies, subsidized trade, and cutthroat competition. The next logical step seemed to be the battlefield.

International Anarchy. The failure of the League of Nations to establish a system of collective security led individual members to revert to the traditional device of diplomatic alliances and alignments. Nationalism, far from retreating, became much stronger. Even the friends of the League admitted that it was unable to assure security. Others, for varying reasons, denounced it. An Italo-American historian at Harvard, Gaetano Salvemini, later expressed a widely held view: "The history of the League of Nations between World War I and World War II was the history of the devices, ruses, deceptions, frauds, tricks, and trappings by which the very diplomats who were pledged to operate the Covenant of the League managed to circumvent and stultify it. They were its most effective foes, since they were undermining it from within, while nationalists, militarists, and Fascists were attacking it openly from without in all lands." The Nazis ridiculed the League as "a joint-stock company for the preservation of the booty won in the war." And there was no world public opinion powerful enough to neutralize attacks on the League.

Militarism: The Race to Arms. Still another failure of the League of Nations was its inability to achieve any real progress toward disarmament. After the breakdown of peace machinery, the nations once again turned to an unchecked armament race. Each country, suspiciously eyeing the growing armed strength of its neighbors, strengthened its own military machine. The dictators saw rearmament as the means to power and glory; the democracies, overburdened with economic troubles, sought to stave off the expense of armaments until the last moment. In 1933, the last effective year of the League of Nations system, the world's armies numbered 7,000,000 men, its navies totaled 3,000,000 tons, its military planes numbered 14,000, and $4,000,000,000 went into armaments. In 1938, the year of Munich, the figures skyrocketed to 10,000,000 men, 8,000,000 naval tons, 50,000 military planes, and $17,000,000,000 in armament costs. The French army alone had 800,000 men, with a trained reserve of 5,500,000, in a total male population of 20,000,000. Men were afraid of war, but the fear of its outcome led them to prepare for it.

Impact: The Clash of Ideologies. A new challenge to the West arose in the global strategic goals and the tactical flexibility of Nazi Germany and Fascist Italy. "War is eternal, War is life." This was the philosophy, expressed in six words, of Adolf Hitler. Pouring vituperation upon democracy and self-righteously chiding it for its failure to solve the economic dilemma, the dictators pointed to their own totalitarianism as the logical order of society in the new world. "We are riding," they said, "the wave of the future." The democracies felt that this was nothing but a renascence of ancient tyranny. It was becoming clear that something more than the sweetness and light of Locarno was necessary to resolve the critical issues. Neither side was willing to accept the view of the other or to compromise with it. The choice lay between appeasement or armed force. Soviet Russia, considering the democracies the lesser of two evils, fought on their side against the Fascist threat, but promptly entered into a "cold war" with the West after Mussolini and Hitler had disappeared from the scene.

The Psychological Climate. Added to the powerful economic and political factors making for war was an important psychological fact. The sentiment of nationalism, which had dominated every phase of human conduct in the years before 1914, persisted afterward in more aggravated form. Men of goodwill hoped that the peoples of the world, disgusted with periodic descents into barbarism, would become converts to a spirit of international conciliation. The peace settlements of 1919 remade the map of the world along strictly national lines. What was lacking was a psychology directed toward the common interests of mankind as something precious.

Many who lived through the horrors of World War I had insisted that never again would they support war. But they soon forgot, just as men cease remembering the pains of illness and push annoying thoughts deep into the subconscious. The fatal flaw lay in the educational process. Impressionable youngsters were nourished on tales of war-comradeship, heroism under fire, the glory of victory, the inadmissibility of defeat. Veterans, forgetting the horrors and filth of war, boasted to their sons about feats on the battlefield.

Dedicated scholars worked hard to clear up the "mystery" of war. They showed how, in the past, spiritual limitations on war had been suggested by the teachings of Plato, by the Christian view of nature as corrupt and sinful, and by the application of moral imperatives in education and politics. Further, they revealed how these restraints had gradually broken down under the impact of material progress and the concomitant undermining of morals and ethics. The new science had created an economy of abundance and along with it overwhelmingly destructive weapons. Men were living, said the scholars, in an era of illusion, irrationalism, and aggression. The thing to do was to devote as much attention to the conquest of the war spirit as to any communicable disease, to relegate war to the status of cannibalism. The best possible way to achieve understanding of the blight of war was through the process of education. This was the conclusion of rational men, but it went unheeded.

There was no easy solution to the key question of the day: How could the world rid itself of the stench of Hitlerism without force?

2. *Immediate Causes*

Germany's Bid for World Dominion. The problem of war-guilt for World War I has never been satisfactorily resolved. Today historians are inclined generally to absolve Germany of exclusive responsibility for the outbreak of the war of 1914. The blame for *starting* World War II, however, rests solely and squarely on Germany. Admittedly, the general politico-economic and psychological climate of the world was such that war could be expected; but continual aggressions by Nazi Germany in a bid for world domination provided the immediate sparks for the conflagration. The very existence of Nazi Germany was a threat to world peace. It is clear from Hitler's writings, and especially from secret reports captured during the war, that Nazi Germany's immediate aim was to conquer Europe and that her ultimate goal was global power. Obsessed with the idea that the superior German "race" was destined to rule mankind, Hitler was ready to smash his way to domination or ruin. "For the good of the German people," Hitler said in his *Secret Conversations,* "we must wish for a war every fifteen or twenty years. An army whose sole purpose is to preserve peace leads only to playing at soldiers— compare Sweden and Switzerland." At the same time, the Nazi leader, master of the technique of the lie, was informing the world: "I am not crazy enough to want a war. The German people have but one wish—to be happy in their own way and to be left in peace."

Stages of Aggressive Strategy. A series of aggressive steps taken by Japan, Italy, and Germany led to the catastrophe. The initial stage came with the Manchurian dispute of 1931, when Japan seized Manchuria and established the puppet state of Manchukuo. The failure of the League of Nations to solve this dispute, followed by the withdrawal of Japan from the League in 1933, set a precedent for further aggression in defiance of world opinion. Italy's invasion of Ethiopia in 1935 and her annexation of that country in 1936 were the next steps. The League tried to halt aggression by imposing sanctions on Italy, but the Italians paid no attention. After the annexation of his country by Italy, Haile Selassie I, Emperor of Ethiopia, made a prophetic speech at Geneva on June 30, 1936. He stood patiently at the rostrum before the Assembly of the League of Nations, while his efforts to speak were drowned out by shouting pro-Mussolini newsmen:

> I, Haile Selassie, Emperor of Ethiopia, am here today to claim that justice which is due to my people, and the assistance promised it eight months ago, when fifty nations asserted that aggression had been committed. . . .

> It is my duty to inform the governments of the deadly peril which threatens them. . . . It is a question of trust in international treaties and of the value of promises to small states that their integrity shall be respected. In a word, it is international morality that is at stake. . . .

> Apart from the Kingdom of God, there is not on this earth any nation that is higher than any other. . . . God and history will remember your judgment.

The League rejected Haile Selassie's plea that sanctions be continued, and thereby opened the way to the era of appeasement. It lost additional prestige when Italy resigned in 1937. Italo-German cooperation with the insurgent General Franco in the Spanish Civil War of 1936–1939 was another stride toward World War II. When the Japanese in 1937 opened hostilities with China to establish a New Order in Asia, the League once again was unable to halt the aggressor. While this continual flouting of the League went on, the French extended their security system by signing a Franco-Russian Mutual Assistance Pact on May 2, 1935.

At the Seventh World Congress of the Communist International, meeting in Moscow in July 1935, the Russians passed resolutions condemning Japanese imperialism in the Far East, and Hitler's actions in the West. On November 25, 1936, Germany and Japan re-plied by concluding an Anti-Comintern Pact. Shortly before this, Germany and Italy laid the foundations for the Rome-Berlin Axis, an agreement transformed into a formal tripartite political and military treaty between Germany, Italy, and Japan on September 27, 1940 (Pact of Steel).

Keystone: German Foreign Policy. Although the statesmen of the Weimar Republic bitterly resented and criticized the Treaty of Versailles, they nevertheless adopted a program of reconciliation. They cooperated in the system of collective security, obtained several drastic reductions in reparations, accepted membership in the League of Nations, and effected evacuation of the Rhineland in 1930. This conciliatory attitude was abruptly reversed in 1933 with the accession of Hitler. Insisting that Germany had never been defeated on the battlefield in World War I, but that she had been stabbed in the back (*Dolchstoss*) by traitors at home (Jews and Social Democrats), the Nazi *Fuehrer* struck one crippling blow after another at the system of Versailles. On October 14, 1933, Germany resigned from the League. On July 25, 1934, Chancellor Engelbert Dollfuss of Austria was assassinated by Austrian conspirators in collaboration with German Nazis. In 1935 Hitler repudiated the military and naval clauses of the Treaty of Versailles. In 1936 he remilitarized the Rhineland, and denounced international control of the Rhine, Elbe, Oder, and Danube rivers. On March 12–15, 1938, he occupied and annexed Austria. Defenders of the system of Versailles, paralyzed into inaction, did not lift a hand to thwart the German dictator. Like a shrewd prizefighter, he danced and jabbed, seeking an opening to deliver the knockout punch.

Appeasement: Munich Pact, 1938. The Nazi policy of aggression was masked by use of the liberal slogan of national self-determination. Hitler's tactics, added to the Italian conquest of Ethiopia and Japan's war against China, made it clear to the Western Allies that a general war was imminent, despite the *Fuehrer's* promises. On September 26, 1938, Hitler

The diplomatic parley of the Big Four at Munich. In effect, Chamberlain of England and Daladier of France bartered Czechoslovakia for the precious time needed to increase the fighting strength of their respective countries.

delivered a speech at the *Sportpalast,* in Berlin, assuring British Prime Minister Neville Chamberlain that, if the Sudeten problem were solved, Germany would have no more territorial problems in Europe. The somewhat skeptical world was led to believe that the *Fuehrer's* ambitions were about to be fulfilled. "We now come to the last problem which has to be solved and will be solved. It is the last territorial demand I have to make in Europe. In 1919, 3,500,000 Germans were torn away from their compatriots by a company of mad statesmen. The Czech state originated in a huge lie and the name of the liar is Beneš."

Unprepared for a major conflict, England and France temporarily avoided war by signing the Munich Pact with Germany and Italy on September 29, 1938. The new democratic republic of Czechoslovakia, dating from 1918, was sold down the river and partially dismembered. The Sudetenland, scene of Nazi activity, was annexed to Germany. Soviet Russia, although not invited to Munich, offered to come to the assistance of Czechoslovakia, but her proposal was rejected by England and France. Chamberlain returned to London from Munich, waving a piece of paper and assuring his people that he had brought "peace in our time."

The betrayal of Czechoslovakia meant the end of collective security. After announcing, in March 1939, that all his territorial demands in Europe had been achieved, Hitler invaded and annexed the whole of Czechoslovakia—with the exception of the Carpatho-Ukraine (given to Hungary)—and seized Memel. It was finally clear that the policy of appeasing Hitler was fruitless and mistaken. Englishmen began digging slit trenches in London, and gas masks were issued to the people.

Prelude to War. The next month, in April 1939, Italy occupied and annexed Albania. At last awakened to the danger, Britain hastened to rearm, while France gave Premier Daladier dictatorial powers to prepare for the expected conflict. The British, in a reciprocal treaty of mutual assistance, guaranteed Poland, Greece, and Rumania against German aggression:

ARTICLE 1. Should one of the Contracting Parties become engaged in hostilities with a European Power in consequence of aggression by the latter against that Contracting Party, the other Contracting Party will at once give the Contracting Party engaged in hostilities all the support and assistance in its power.

Both Britain and France began negotiations with the Soviet Union. Apparently, both the Western democracies and the Soviet Union were anxious to turn the weight of Axis aggression to the other side. In the midst of these negotiations, despite the mutually hostile ideologies of the two dictators, the Stalin-Hitler Pact was signed on August 23, 1939. Hitler believed that the agreement would remove the danger of having to fight a war on two fronts, while Stalin suspected that Britain and France were primarily concerned with getting Soviet Russia and Germany involved in a war in which both would bleed to death. Although Britain and France had warned Germany that there was a point beyond which they could no longer tolerate German aggression, Hitler sent his armies crashing into Poland on September 1, 1939. Fifty hours later, on September 3, Britain declared war on Germany, thus initiating the Second World War of the twentieth century.

Historical Controversy: Responsibility for World War II. The acrid historical controversy over fixing responsibility for the outbreak of hostilities in World War I was repeated after World War II. The issue revolved not so much around the matter of fundamental causes (most historians agreed on basic causes), but on the immediate responsibility for lighting the fuse. Such historians as Sir Lewis Namier and John W. Wheeler-Bennett, two of Britain's most distinguished scholars, and the American histor-

ian, William Langer, saw the driving force in Hitler and Nazi Germany and criticized both for the holocaust.

Then came a new revisionism. The Oxford historian, A. J. P. Taylor, expressed cynicism about the 1938 foreign policy of all the major European nations. Revisionists came to the conclusion that equal if not more blame should be placed on British and French statesmen than on Hitler. Some went so far as to say that Lord Halifax, then Britain's foreign secretary, by careful scheming had brought about World War II against Hitler's intense desire for peace. These historians apparently took Hitler's public utterances at face value, discounted his private statements, and perhaps unconsciously, twisted the evidence to support the thesis of Allied guilt. The contention that Nazi Germany was innocent of starting World War II became the center of a sharp controversy, but it gained little credence in either scholarly or public circles.

The Hossbach Document. The record of Hitler's intentions may be found in the Hossbach document (although revisionists doubt its authenticity). At a secret meeting held on November 5, 1937, he outlined to his military leaders the practical steps for undertaking aggression against other countries. The minutes of the meeting, as recorded by Colonel-General Friedrich Hossbach, Hitler's adjutant for the *Wehrmacht* (National Defense Service), reveal how, two years before the outbreak of hostilities, Hitler planned to wage war:

The *Fuehrer* then stated: The aim of German policy is the security and the preservation of the *Volk* and its propagation. This is consequently a problem of space. . . . The question for Germany is where the greatest possible conquest can be made at lowest cost.

German politics must reckon with its two hateful enemies England and France, to whom a strong German colossus in the center of Europe would be intolerable. Both these states would oppose a further reinforcement of Germany, both in Europe and overseas, and in this opposition they would have the support of all parties. . . .

If the *Fuehrer* is still living, then it will be his irrevocable decision to solve the German space problem no later than 1943–1945. . . . For the improvement of our military political position it must be our first aim, in every case of entanglement by war, to conquer Czechoslovakia and Austria simultaneously, in order to remove any threat from the flanks in case of a possible advance westward. . . . Once Czechoslovakia is conquered—and a mutual frontier of Germany-Hungary is obtained—then a neutral attitude by Poland in a German-French conflict could be more easily relied upon. Our agreements with Poland remain valid only as long as Germany's strength remains unshakeable. . . .

The *Fuehrer* believes personally, that in all probability England and perhaps also France, have already silently written off Czechoslovakia. . . . Without England's support it would also not be necessary to take into consideration a march by France through Holland and Belgium. . . . Naturally, we should in every case have to secure our frontier during the operation of our attacks against Czechoslovakia and Austria. . . .

Military preparation by Russia must be countered by the speed of our operations; it is a question whether this needs to be taken into consideration at all, in view of Japan's attitude.

3. Unfolding of World War II: Era of Axis Domination

***Blitzkrieg* in Poland.** Using *Blitzkrieg* ("lightning-war") tactics, the formidable German military machine struck at Poland

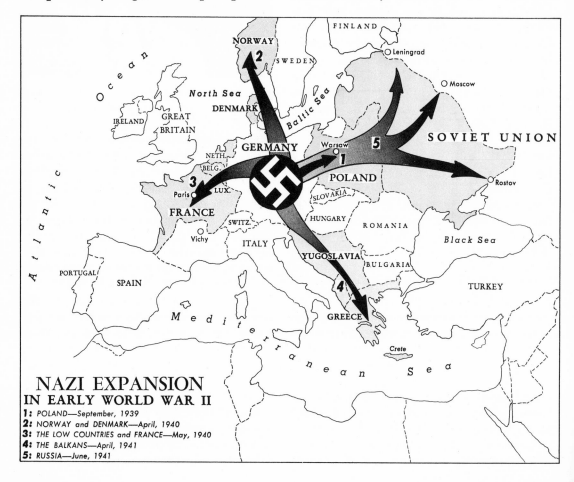

NAZI EXPANSION
IN EARLY WORLD WAR II
1: POLAND—September, 1939
2: NORWAY and DENMARK—April, 1940
3: THE LOW COUNTRIES and FRANCE—May, 1940
4: THE BALKANS—April, 1941
5: RUSSIA—June, 1941

with speed and fury. Coordinated aerial, tank, and infantry thrusts paralyzed the sadly under-armed defenders. Holes were blasted in the Polish lines, as foot soldiers poured through to hold the conquered ground and mop up any remaining resistance. German bombers destroyed communications behind the Polish troops and prevented reinforcements, supplies, and ammunition from being brought forward, and at the same time upset Polish plans for re-forming the armies. A horde of German secret police and spies poured into Poland and disrupted her war effort and will to resist. Poland was disastrously defeated within a few weeks.

As the German army rushed eastward, the Red troops in accordance with the Hitler-Stalin Pact, marched westward. The two invaders partitioned Poland between them, Soviet Russia occupying the eastern half, populated by Ukrainians and White Russians, and Germany taking the western half, containing Danzig and the Polish Corridor. Having been denied entrance to the Baltic by the democracies, Soviet Russia, as the partner of Germany, proceeded to annex Estonia, Latvia, and Lithuania (1940). Despite courageous resistance, the Finns were forced to relinquish strategic ports, naval bases, and airdromes to the U.S.S.R. What the British had denied Soviet Russia as the price of a military alliance against Germany, the Kremlin obtained with the consent of Hitler. The League of Nations condemned Soviet Russia and expelled her from membership. In June 1940 the Russians occupied both Bessarabia and Northern Bukovina.

Axis Aggression in the West. Thoroughly prepared and already placed on a war economy, the Germans launched a peace campaign, in the now naïve belief that the Allies would accept their demands for a redistribution of colonies, reduction of armaments, and a guaranteed peace. Britain and France, disgusted with appeasement and having no further reliance on Hitler's word, declined. Hitler replied with a series of thrusts at his weak neighbors. First, Denmark was occupied in April 1940; Norway, where a British expedi-

tionary force was overwhelmed despite fierce resistance, was conquered by June; then Holland, Belgium, and Luxemburg capitulated to the Nazi war machine.

The armies of Germany and France faced one another in what was called satirically the *Sitzkrieg* ("Sit-down War"). The world waited for the contest between the irresistible force—the Nazi army—and the supposedly immovable object—the French Maginot Line. Sud-

Paris, June 23, 1940. A Frenchman reacts to the bitterness of his country's defeat by the Germans.

denly, the Nazi armies struck at France, broke through the gateway at Sedan, outflanked the Maginot Line, drove the British forces from the Continent at Dunkirk, captured Paris, and forced France to sign an armistice on June 22, 1940. The conquering Hitler began the first step of a jig of joy, duly photographed for posterity, when news reached him of the fall of France. Occupying most of the country, the Nazis allowed the establishment of a friendly appeasement government at Vichy, 200 miles southeast of Paris, under the elderly Marshal Henri Pétain, hero of World War I. Disgruntled Frenchmen rallied around General Charles de Gaulle, who established a Free French headquarters in London.

Role of Italy. Italy remained neutral during the early months of the war. Then, observing that France was about to fall, Mussolini joined Hitler in June 1940 to help administer the final blow. President Roosevelt described this action as a "stab-in-the-back." In December 1940 the British forces in Libya and Ethiopia inflicted paralyzing blows on Mussolini's African empire. Envious of Hitler's successes, and perhaps fearing that Germany might get too large a proportion of the spoils, Mussolini, in the meantime, invaded Greece, where his armies were unexpectedly hurled back. In the next few months the vaunted Italian fleet was almost blasted out of the Mediterranean by the British navy. The master was now forced to genuflect to the pupil as Mussolini desperately called to Hitler for help.

Stone Wall: Battle of Britain. Immediately upon the outbreak of war the British navy drove the German commercial and naval fleets from the seas and began an intensive blockade. The Germans sought to break this by an unrestricted submarine campaign. Traditionally a slow starter, Britain managed to survive the initial blows. All the dominions, with the exception of Ireland, rallied to her cause. On his opening address to Parliament in May 1940, Winston Churchill offered his countrymen nothing but "blood, toil, tears, and sweat," and defined his policy as one "to wage war by sea, land, and air, with all our might and with all the strength that God can give us."

On June 18, 1940, the golden-voiced Churchill rallied his people in another extraordinary speech, one of the most dramatic and effective in the annals of mankind.

What General Weygand called the "Battle of France" is over. I expect that the battle of Britain is about to begin. Upon this battle depends the survival of Christian civilization. Upon it depends our own British life, and the long continuity of our institutions and our Empire. The whole fury and might of the enemy must very soon be turned on us. Hitler knows that he will have to break us in this island or lose the war. If we can stand up to him all Europe may be free and the life of the world may move forward into broad, sunlit uplands; but if we fall, then the whole world, including the United States, and all that we have known and cared for, will sink into the abyss of a new dark age made more sinister, and perhaps more prolonged, by the lights of a perverted science. Let us therefore brace ourselves to our duty and so bear ourselves that if the British Commonwealth and Empire last for a thousand years men will still say, "This was their finest hour."

On July 19, 1940, Hitler, flushed with victory on the Continent, offered to give the British a last chance to surrender before their complete annihilation. "I am not the vanquished seeking favors," he said, "but the victor speaking in the name of reason." The British maintained a contemptuous silence. Hitler countered with an all-out attack by the *Luftwaffe* on English ports, airfields, industrial centers, and London. This was the Battle of Britain, the first great air battle in history and the turning point of the war. Thousands of civilians were killed and wounded as Germans sought to demoralize and terrorize the population as a prelude to invasion. The small Royal Air Force held firm. ("Never in the field of human conflict was so much owed by so many to so few" was Churchill's reaction.) The mass attacks suddenly came to an end on May 10, 1941, when Rudolf Hess, Hitler's psychotic deputy *Fuehrer,* piloted a plane to Scotland and singlehandedly sought to end the war by convincing Churchill that the British were destined for destruction.

Clash in Africa. Italian troops, pressing across the Libyan border in 1940, established themselves about sixty miles inside Egypt. In December, British troops, in a surprise attack that carried them halfway across Libya, crushingly defeated the Fascist forces. Only by enlisting German aid was Italy able to recover some of the Libyan territory she had lost. The Fascist dream of empire, however, was shattered by the British in East Africa. British command of the Mediterranean was maintained by smashing a large part of the French fleet at Oran and the Italian fleet at Taranto.

War in the Balkans. After the defeat of France, Germany turned eastward. Weakened by fifth columnists, spies pretending to be tourists, and saboteurs, Rumania succumbed to German pressure, and King Carol fled as Nazi troops poured in. In March 1941 Bulgaria decided to join the Axis and permitted Nazi soldiers to enter her territory. Despite their own resistance and British aid, both Yugoslavia and Greece were overrun in April 1941. A German parachute force occupied Crete, and most of the islands in the Aegean Sea fell to the Nazis. The revised German strategy apparently aimed at a thrust through the Balkans and an eastward drive across North Africa to the Suez Canal.

War in the Near East. After having successfully resisted the German thrust at Suez from Libya, the British turned their attention to the task of removing Axis threats to their lifeline in the Near East. In a short campaign, the British ousted pro-Axis forces which had seized control of Iraq, the site of valuable oil fields. When the French Vichy government permitted Nazis to use Syria as a base, the British sent their own forces and Free French troops into the French mandate and in early 1941, forced it to ask for an armistice. The British, now assuming full control over Syria, promised her independence after the war. The position of Turkey changed with the fortunes of the war. Although when the war began they had an alliance with the British, the Turks modified their attitude toward the Germans as the latter marched through the Balkans. Then, when Germany invaded Soviet Russia and the British took the opportunity to strengthen their position in the Near East, Turkey found herself under pressure from both Britain and Russia for active support against the Nazis. In August 1941, British and Russian forces occupied Iran, which had refused to expel thousands of Nazi "tourists."

Lifeline Neptune: War at Sea. At the beginning of the war, German submarines, long-range bombers, and sea raiders took a heavy toll of British merchant shipping. With the aid of fifty over-age destroyers, exchanged by the United States for air bases in British possessions in the Western Hemisphere, the British were able to strengthen their convoy system. On May 24, 1941, the new 35,000-ton German battleship *Bismarck* engaged the 42,500-ton British battle cruiser *Hood* off Greenland, and sank the British ship after a five-minute engagement. Jubilantly announcing the end of British mastery of the seas, the German High Seas Command was appalled to learn within three days that the British navy had trailed the *Bismarck* and had sent her to the bottom. In the meantime, the British navy, in cooperation with its air arm, virtually demolished the Italian fleet at Taranto (November 11–12, 1940) and Matapan in the Ionian Sea (March 30, 1941). While the British lost an immense amount of tonnage as a result of submarine and air attacks, their navy managed to keep open the sea lanes to England. Shipping losses were critical, however; the problem of reducing sinkings became crucial.

Situation in Spring, 1941. Germany in the spring of 1941 was in a strong position, having increased her area from 180,976 to 323,360 square miles, plus 290,000 more in occupied but unannexed lands, and her population from 65,000,000 to 106,000,000. Hitler in April 1941 had at his disposal 40,000 airplanes, 180 submarines, 363,171 tons of surface navy, 214 infantry divisions, and 12 *Panzer* (armored and mechanized) divisions. Against this powerful force were pitted the might of the British Commonwealth, a worldwide public opinion opposed to Nazi aggression, and the resources of the United States. Hitler's strength had mounted rapidly but so had that of his opponents. Formerly he had been able to divide his opponents and then annihilate them one by one, but now the Nazi *Fuehrer* faced a world united in distrust.

Operation Barbarossa: Invasion of Russia. In August 1939 Germany and Soviet Russia signed a ten-year nonaggression pact. About two years later, on June 22, 1941, Hitler sent

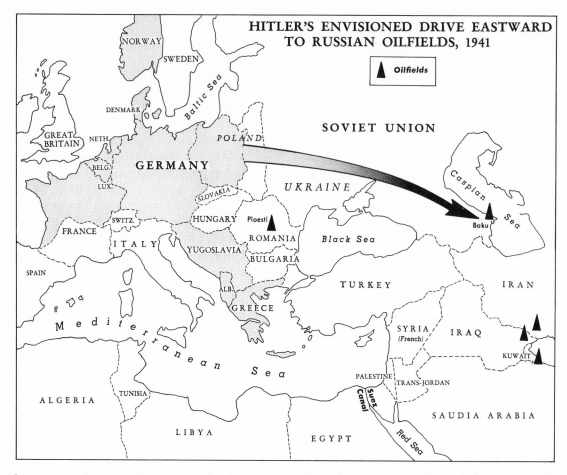

HITLER'S ENVISIONED DRIVE EASTWARD TO RUSSIAN OILFIELDS, 1941

his war machine crashing across the frontiers of the U.S.S.R., unleashing a furious *Blitzkrieg* on a 1,500-mile front extending from the Baltic Sea to the Black Sea, on land, at sea, and in the air. As pretext for the invasion, Hitler accused the Kremlin of treachery, of threatening the German frontiers, and of carrying on anti-German and Communist propaganda. Thus, at the choice of the Nazi leader, the German people were burdened once more with a dreaded two-front war. Describing his assault as a crusade against Bolshevism, Hitler, in reality, wanted to obtain wheat, oil, and mineral supplies in sufficient quantities to enable Germany to defy the British blockade. The strategy was obvious—a *Blitzkrieg* against three primary objectives: Leningrad in the north, Moscow in the center, and Kiev in the south.

Despite his aversion to Communism, Churchill promised the Russians economic and technical assistance. Italy and the Axis satellites—Rumania, Czechoslovakia, and Hungary —allied themselves with Germany. Vichy France gave her approval to the attack and broke diplomatic relations with Moscow. Britain severed relations with Finland, which the Germans were using as a base for their invasion of Russia. Sweden granted permission for Nazi troops to cross her territory. Turkey proclaimed her neutrality. Japan adopted a policy of watchful waiting. When the Japanese occupied naval and air bases in French Indochina, in agreement with the Vichy government, Britain, the United States, and the Netherlands East Indies retaliated by freezing Japanese funds.

Recovering from initial surprise, the Russians astonished the world by their fierce resistance. In the beginning of the invasion, thousands of Red troops surrendered to the Germans, but Hitler's policy of treating the vanquished populations as virtual slaves stimulated a stubborn reaction. Stalin called for a scorched-earth policy. The Nazis paid dearly for every mile of advance into Russian territory. On July 13, 1941, Soviet Russia signed a mutual-aid pact with Britain. The United States also promised help. With the Nazi campaign slowed to a crawl on the Russian plains, Hitler explained to his people that he had miscalculated the strength of the Red forces. "We made a mistake about one thing: we did not know how gigantic the preparations of this opponent against Germany had been, and how tremendous had been the danger which aimed at the destruction not only of Germany but of Europe."

Resistance: War Behind the Lines. Hitler found it increasingly impossible to pacify the 140,000,000 non-German European peoples who by this time had been subjugated by the Nazi war machine. The conquered peoples refused to stay conquered. Driven by dissatisfaction over food shortages and the excesses of the occupation forces, Czechs wrecked trains, blew up munition dumps, and destroyed factories supplying the German armies; Dutchmen killed Nazi officers and soldiers and threw their bodies into canals; and Norwegians organized a campaign of sabotage. A union of hate welded Frenchmen, Belgians, Yugoslavs, and others into a powerful counterforce. Meanwhile, the myth of Nazi invincibility was being destroyed on the plains of Russia. German occupation authorities sought to stem the tide of rebellion by ordering scores of natives to be executed for every German soldier harmed, by condemning hundreds to death for high treason, and by executing hostages.

Role of the United States. From the beginning of the conflict in Europe the sympathy of the American public was with the Allied cause. Isolationist sentiment, strong at the beginning, evaporated when the Nazi aim of global power stood clearly revealed. Before the war, American neutrality legislation forbade the selling of war supplies to belligerent nations. In 1939 a revised neutrality law permitted the sale of war supplies on a cash-and-carry basis, while forbidding American vessels and nationals from traveling in combat zones. This was obviously designed to prevent such incidents as the death of Americans in the sinking of the *Lusitania* on May 7, 1915, in World War I. In September 1940 the first peacetime draft law in the history of the United States provided for the registration of 17,000,000 men. The Alien Registration Act of 1940 aimed to curb any possible fifth-column activity. In 1941 Congress passed the Lend-Lease Act, empowering the President to take any necessary steps to insure the shipment of vital materials to Britain. Measures were taken to defend the Western Hemisphere by patrolling the Atlantic Ocean. American forces occupied Greenland and Iceland. In August and September 1941 the sinking of American-owned ships led to an order to the American navy to attack submarines on sight.

War Aims: The Atlantic Charter. On August 14, 1941, President Roosevelt and Prime Minister Churchill formulated plans for a new world based upon an end to Nazi tyranny, disarmament of aggressors, and the fullest cooperation between all nations for social and economic welfare. The dramatic meeting on a war vessel off Newfoundland was designed as a counterthrust to a possible new Hitler peace offensive, and at the same time, stated the aims of Churchill and Roosevelt for the postwar world. The joint declaration of the Atlantic Charter announced eight peace aims. (*See page 691.*)

Crisis in the Far East. Since the invasion of Manchuria in September 1931, Japanese militarists had consistently pushed an expansionist program. The outbreak of the European war in 1939 gave them further opportunity to pursue an even more aggressive policy. Japanese designs on the South Pacific, particularly on the Netherlands East Indies, the main source of America's rubber and tin, brought a sharp warning that any attempt to seize those islands would be regarded as a hostile act. Japan replied on September 27, 1940, by signing a military alliance with Germany and

Italy. The United States then embargoed the shipment of war materials to Japan and froze all Japanese credits in the United States. Japan's special envoy, Saburo Kurusu and her ambassador, Admiral Kichisaburo Nomura, held prolonged conversations in Washington with President Roosevelt and Secretary of State Cordell Hull, with the professed purpose of negotiating a peaceful settlement. The United States asked Japan to halt her aggressions, withdraw from China, respect the open-door policy, and break her tie with the Axis.

The Japanese, insisting that they would not deviate from their immutable policy of setting up a Greater East Asia, under Japanese domination, demanded an immediate lifting of the economic blockade.

While these discussions were still in progress, Japan made a sudden surprise air and sea attack on Pearl Harbor, the American naval base in Hawaii. It came on Sunday, December 7, 1941—"a date which will live in infamy," and it was followed by a formal declaration of war. The American public,

Pearl Harbor, December 7, 1941. Japan's surprise attack paralyzed U.S. naval and air power in the Hawaiian Islands, but it added great strength to the Allied cause by bringing the United States into the war as an active participant.

appalled by Japanese treachery, at once submerged all differences and united to repel the attack. On December 8, President Roosevelt asked for a declaration of war against Japan, which Congress immediately voted. On December 11, Japan's Axis partners declared war on the United States, which answered the challenge the same day.

Historical Controversy: Pearl Harbor, The Debate. The revisionists saw Pearl Harbor in an entirely different light. Detractors of President Roosevelt accused him of personal responsibility for plunging the United States into an unnecessary war. American historians Charles A. Beard and Charles C. Tansill, among others, charged the president and his advisors with leading the country into war while professing a policy of peace. They said further that the Democratic administration turned to war in an effort to cover up domestic failures. Roosevelt wanted to insure his own reelection, they said, and he even had grandiloquent ideas of world leadership. Misunderstanding the problem facing the Japanese, he and his advisers alienated Japan, forced her to look for support to the Axis, and actually "goaded the Japanese" to attack Pearl Harbor.

Roosevelt's supporters, including the historians William L. Langer, Dexter Perkins, and Arthur M. Schlesinger, Jr., accused the revisionists of historical hindsight and partisan differences. Some admitted that the charges against Roosevelt were partially correct—that is, that he had had to escort "the notoriously short-sighted masses" in the direction of defending their own interests. Others denied that he had any desire to lead the United States into war. They said that he took every possible measure, short of abandoning American principles altogether, to keep the United States out of war. What he did, they said, was to obtain precious time for preparedness in the face of isolationist obstructionism. They called an outrageous falsehood the allegation that Roosevelt consciously maneuvered Japan into the war. To shift the blame for the Pearl Harbor disaster to the United States, they said, was the last word in historical obtuseness.

4. Triumph of the Allies

The Great Coalition. With Japan's attack on the United States the war passed into a new global phase. On January 2, 1942, after a series of inter-Allied conferences in Washington, an anti-aggressor bloc of nations, led by the United States, Great Britain, the Soviet Union, and China, signed an agreement binding its signatories to fight the war through to victory and to make no separate peace. Subscribing to the principles of the Atlantic Charter, these nations affirmed their conviction that complete defeat of the enemy was essential to defend life, liberty, independence, and religious freedom. The Latin-American countries either declared war against the Axis, broke off diplomatic relation with the aggressors, or granted the United States access to their ports. A conference of foreign ministers of the twenty-one Latin-American republics, meeting in Brazil on January 21, 1942, adopted sweeping sanctions against the Axis, including the breaking off of financial, commercial, and economic relations.

United States at War. The United States went on a full war footing immediately after the first bombs fell on Pearl Harbor. All key industries were ordered to go on a 24-hour day and a 7-day week. In his annual message to Congress in January 1942 President Roosevelt outlined an arms production program such as the world had never known: for the year 1942 he called for 60,000 planes, 45,000 tanks, 20,000 anti-aircraft guns, and 8,000,000 tons of shipping. A War Production Board was organized to coordinate this vast war-procurement program. Government agencies conserved supplies, a rationing system was introduced, critical war industries were subsidized, and an Office of Price Administration was established to check rising prices. The stupendous cost of the war program, estimated at almost $59,000,000,000 for the fiscal year beginning July 1, 1942, was financed by raising taxes to the highest level in American history. Industry and labor agreed to ban strikes and lockouts for the duration of hostilities and accepted the view that all controversies should be settled by peaceful means. Selective Service was extended to enroll 25,000,000 men in the war effort. Congress conferred on President Roosevelt full war authority. The Office of Civilian Defense enrolled volunteer workers to protect civilian populations from the hazards of modern warfare.

The Japanese Smell Victory. The unexpectedness of the Japanese blow in the Pacific brought a serious setback to the United States. Severe losses were inflicted on the U.S. Navy, but much damage was repaired and the losses replaced. The Japanese capture of Guam, Midway, and Wake Islands severed direct American lines of communication to the Far East. The loss of Hong Kong, further impaired Allied naval action. Gaining a foothold in Thailand, the Japanese launched an offensive down the Malay Peninsula toward Singapore. The ultimate objective of the Japanese was the Netherlands East Indies, especially Sumatra and Java, with their untold wealth in rubber, oil, tin, and other essentials for modern war. The Japanese aimed further to prevent the flow of supplies from America and to obtain bases for a possible invasion of the Australian mainland. The long distances

and the dispersal of Anglo-American navies over all the oceans, as well as initial Japanese air superiority in the Far East, made the dispatch of Allied aid a hazardous venture.

Turn of the Tide, 1942–1943. In late 1942 and during 1943 great rivers of supplies began to move among the Allied Nations as they gained mastery of the sea lanes. Wartime research achieved sensational results, including radar, rockets, penicillin, and atomic energy. The great Japanese amphibious offen-

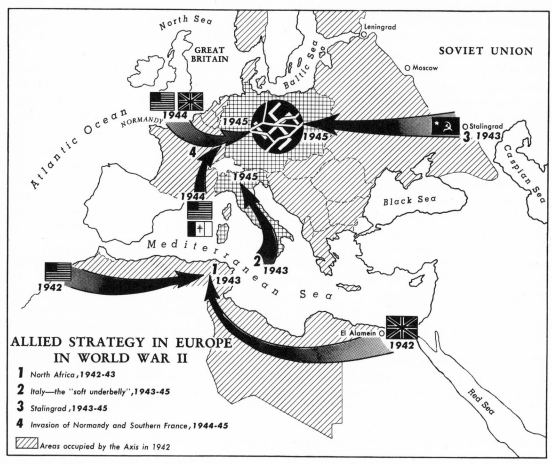

ALLIED STRATEGY IN EUROPE IN WORLD WAR II

1 North Africa, 1942-43
2 Italy—the "soft underbelly", 1943-45
3 Stalingrad, 1943-45
4 Invasion of Normandy and Southern France, 1944-45
Areas occupied by the Axis in 1942

sive in the Far East came to a halt on May 7–8, 1942, when one of its task forces, caught in the Coral Sea northeast of Australia, was severely battered by an Allied air and sea fleet. United States Marines landed on Guadalcanal in the Solomons on August 7, 1942. In the meantime, on April 18, 1942, the first air raid

on a surprised Tokyo was staged by Lt. Col. James H. Doolittle's sixteen medium bombers from the United States carrier *Hornet*. On June 4–7, 1942, the Japanese suffered a major naval defeat at Midway Island.

Despite appalling losses in the German invasion, the Red armies continued to offer stubborn resistance. The tide of German conquest had been stemmed following the arrival of fresh troops from Siberia and of British and American equipment, as well as by the good fortune of a remarkably severe winter. In late November 1941, Soviet forces wrested the initiative from the Germans as they began a steadily advancing counteroffensive, hurling back the Nazis along the entire 1,500-mile front. Having failed to destroy the Soviet armies, the Germans now attempted to reach Voronezh in the north, Stalingrad on the Volga, and Sevastopol in the south. The German Sixth Army of some 300,000 men under Field Marshal Friedrich Paulus reduced Stalingrad to rubble in November 1942 but was not successful in holding the city. In January 1943 Paulus and his staff were captured and his army almost annihilated. Hitler was now unable to isolate Moscow and Leningrad.

In the spring of 1942 General Erwin Rommel launched a drive across Libya and into Egypt. He was finally stopped on July 1 by General Bernard L. Montgomery at El Alamein, just seventy miles from Alexandria. The British counterattack reached Tripoli, 1,400 miles from its starting point, at the end of January 1943. In the meantime, on November 8, 1942, three Anglo-American landings were made at Casablanca, Oran, and Algiers.

From January 17–27, 1943, after the Allied landings in North Africa, Roosevelt and Churchill met at Casablanca in French Morocco in a wartime conference. Surveying the entire field of the conflict, theater by theater, they agreed that all resources were to be marshaled for more intense prosecution of the war by sea, land, and air. At the close of the conference, Roosevelt and Churchill, together with Generals Charles de Gaulle and Henri Giraud, convened on the lawn of the villa to meet thirty foreign correspondents. The official communiqué of the conference had not mentioned the words "unconditional surrender," which were used by Roosevelt in the press interview. This was the first reference about the Allied objective of the war—

a phrase that ruled out any negotiations with Germany through the channels of diplomacy. Critics later claimed that another less harsh phrase, such as "honorable capitulation," might have encouraged the Germans to surrender long before they did.

Pressed by Montgomery from the east and Eisenhower from the west, the Axis made a hard stand in Tunisia, where in April–May 1943, the German and Italian armies were forced into a general rout. The victory in North Africa was followed shortly by the invasion of Sicily and landings on the Italian mainland. Against stubborn German resistance, Anglo-American forces reached Naples on October 1, 1943, and Rome on June 4, 1944. At the same time, the Russians delivered sledge-hammer blows at the Germans, securing the center of the long front, freeing Leningrad and Novgorod in the north during the winter of 1943, and driving the Germans from Odessa and the Crimean Peninsula in the south in May 1944. Meanwhile, scores of German cities were reduced to rubble by British night bombing and American high-altitude daylight attacks. In more than five years of bombing, Germany suffered a toll of 305,000 civilians dead and 780,000 wounded.

Retribution: Invasion of France. "Overlord" was the code name for what was to be the supreme event of the year 1944 and one of the most remarkable expeditions in military history—the Anglo-American amphibious landings on the Normandy beaches of France. The June 1944 invasion on "D-Day" was a stupendous logistical undertaking. It was necessary to train a million and a half men in Britain and to construct two enormous artificial harbors to be placed along the invasion beaches. The storming of Hitler's Fortress Europa and the Atlantic Wall was made with complete initial surprise. The German system of defense in France was quickly smashed. By July 1944 the flow of troops from the United States reached 150,000 a month, and shipments of material approximately 150,000 tons a month. Over a million Allied troops pushed the Germans steadily eastward, bypassing

Paris and literally cutting the Germans to pieces in a *Blitzkrieg* unmatched by previous German drives in 1940. By September 1944

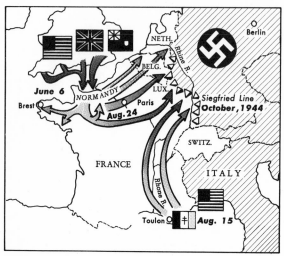

LIBERATION OF FRANCE, June-Nov., 1944

six of General Eisenhower's armies were drawn up against Germany's western borders.

Historical Controversy: The Yalta Conference. From February 7–12, 1945, President Roosevelt, Prime Minister Churchill, and Marshal Stalin conferred at Yalta in the Crimea, accompanied by members of their military and diplomatic staffs. An announcement declared that they had concerted plans for the final defeat of Germany, and for the occupation, control, and collection of reparations from the conquered nation. The three powers also pledged their joint efforts to assist the liberated countries of Europe.

The meeting at Yalta became one of the most controversial events of the twentieth century, a storm center of dispute. It was criticized violently by one group as an unfair bargain by which Stalin obtained the lion's share because of Roosevelt's naïveté and idealism. William Henry Chamberlin described "the Munich called Yalta" as the high point of Soviet diplomatic success and correspondingly the low point of American appeasement. "The whole historic basis of American foreign policy in the Far East was

upset by the virtual invitation to Stalin to take over Japan's former exclusive and dominant role in Manchuria." Chester Wilmot called it "Stalin's greatest victory," a grave miscalculation of Russia's political ambition, and an error of judgment which gave Stalin the opportunity of establishing the Soviet Union as the dominant power in Europe.

Roosevelt was defended on the ground that, at the time, the Yalta agreements did not seem to be an unfair bargain. The difficulty arose later when the Big Three tried to implement the Yalta Pact. Edward R. Stettinius, Jr., American secretary of state in 1945, defended the agreement as "on the whole, a diplomatic triumph for the United States." Henry Steele Commager did not consider Yalta a "calamity": "Aside from such things as the restoration of Russian sovereignty in Sakhalin and the Kuriles, the Western allies conceded nothing that Russia did not already have or could not have taken."

Steamroller: The Drive into Germany, 1944–1945. In December 1944 the Germans under Marshal Gerd von Runstedt attempted a desperate counteroffensive in the Ardennes sector, held mainly by United States troops. This "Battle of the Bulge," penetrating the American lines for about fifty miles, was finally stopped by December 25. In January 1945 the Russians opened a major offensive through Poland directly toward Berlin. The next month eight armies of the Allies began moving steadily eastward. Soon the Germans were deprived of most of their industrial areas. Disorganized and demoralized by powerful blows from both east and west, the German forces disintegrated as the Allies rushed almost unopposed across Germany. The Allied and Russian armies met at Torgau on April 26, 1945, splitting Germany in two.

Death Comes to Three Leaders. In April 1945, within eighteen days, death came to three top war leaders. One of the architects of victory, President Franklin D. Roosevelt, whose buoyant spirit had been strained to the breaking point, died suddenly on April 12,

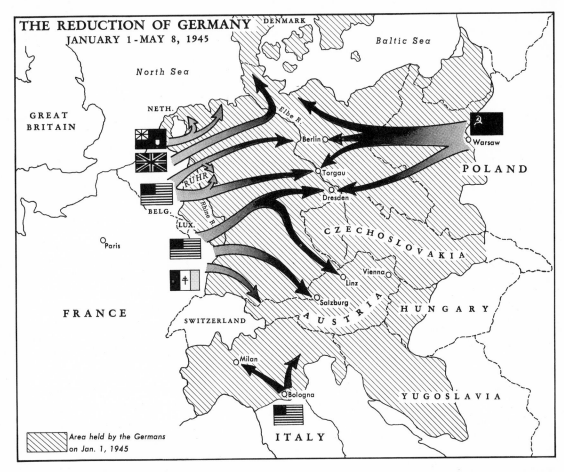

THE REDUCTION OF GERMANY
JANUARY 1 - MAY 8, 1945

Area held by the Germans
on Jan. 1, 1945

1945, fewer than three months after his fourth inaugural. The last words he wrote, in a draft for a Jefferson Day address, were a fitting epitaph to his own life: "The only limit to our realization of tomorrow will be our doubts of today. Let us move forward with strong and active faith." Roosevelt's death was reported in the American press on an "Army-Navy Casualty List." The nation mourned the passing of a vigorous president who had led it through a shattering economic crisis and the greatest war in its history.

Fewer than three weeks later, death came to the man who wanted to be Caesar and to the man who wanted to be Napoleon. Benito Mussolini, egocentric demagogue with Calvinistic determination and Cromwellian confidence, was the first dictator to go. Wandering in northern Italy as a Nazi puppet ruler, he was captured near Lake Como by anti-Fascist

Partisans and, together with his mistress, Claretta Petacci, was executed on April 28, 1945. "Let me save my life," Mussolini begged his captors, "and I will give you an empire!" The bullet-ridden corpses were strung up by the heels and then dumped like carrion on the public square in Milan where Fascism had begun its life. An eyewitness reported this "finish to tyranny as horrible as ever visited on a tyrant." Citizens of Milan kicked the body and spat upon the man who had promised them world grandeur and had brought them the odor of beastliness and the odium of defeat.

Within two days, Hitler followed Mussolini to the grave. On April 30, 1945, Hitler and his wife of a few hours, Eva Braun, died in a suicide pact in a besieged bunker under the Chancellery in Berlin. It was a Wagnerian death accompanied by crashes of Russian artillery. It had taken the combined might of three great world powers to bring Hitler and his lunatic structure to the ground.

The fighting in Italy ended on the day of Hitler's suicide. By May 4, more than a million Germans had surrendered in the north, bringing the war in Holland and northern Germany to its conclusion. On May 7 Admiral Karl Doenitz, who temporarily succeeded Hitler as *Fuehrer,* accepted the situation, and all hostilities ceased at 12:01 on May 9. With this unconditional surrender, the war in Europe was over.

Twilight: Offensive in the Pacific. The Japanese, with their supplies cut off by Allied submarines and naval aircraft, were now on the verge of defeat. The predicted revolt in Asia against European imperialism had not materialized, despite the fact that the Jap-

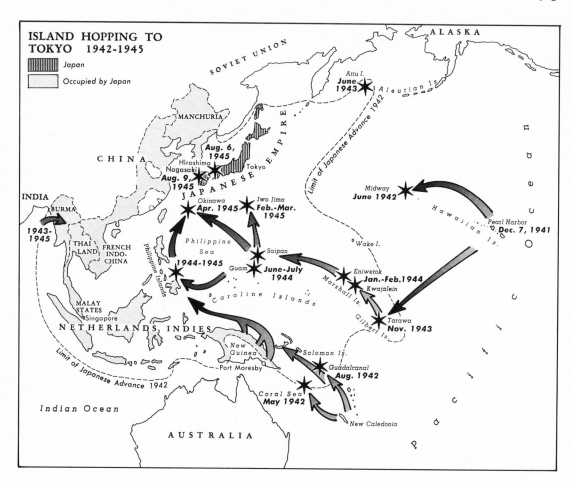

anese war machine had swiftly collected some 500,000,000 people, a quarter of the world's population. In November 1943, American troops captured the Gilbert Islands, and in February 1944 attacked the Marshall Islands. Kwajalein was taken on February 6 and the Marianas by June, in a series of island hops. General Douglas MacArthur, who had promised that he would return to the Philippines, landed at Leyte on October 19.

Japanese attempts to halt these landings were struck down. Operating from newly won bases in the Marianas, American airmen raided Japan. The Japanese highway of empire was now cut in two.

Despite these rapid Allied successes, President Harry S. Truman, feeling that conquest of the Japanese mainland might be a long and costly process, ordered use of the atomic bomb. The first A-bomb was dropped on

Hiroshima on August 6, 1945, with catastrophic results, destroying three-fourths of the city and causing the deaths of 78,150 people. Two days later, according to the terms of the Yalta Agreement (February 1945), Soviet Russia declared war on Japan and began a drive on the Manchurian frontier. A second A-bomb dropped on Nagasaki on August 9 convinced the Japanese that further resistance was useless. Accepting the Allied terms on August 14, the Japanese signed the surrender document in Tokyo Bay on board the U.S.S. *Missouri* on September 2, 1945. American occupation forces had already landed in Japan. The tragedy of World War II was thus brought to an end.

⊰ KEY DOCUMENT ⊱

THE ATLANTIC CHARTER, AUGUST 14, 1941

Congressional Record, LXXXVII (77th Congress, 1st Session), p. 7217.

PRESIDENT FRANKLIN D. ROOSEVELT and Prime Minister Winston Churchill met off the coast of Newfoundland in August 1941, in the first of their wartime conferences. The outcome of this conference, the Atlantic Charter, was a general statement of policy in which the two leaders pledged allegiance to democratic principles and promised to work for a world in which political and economic equality would prevail among nations "after the final destruction of the Nazi tyranny."

The President of the United States and the Prime Minister, Mr. Churchill, representing His Majesty's Government in the United Kingdom, have met at sea.

They have been accompanied by officials of their two governments, including high ranking officers of their military, naval and air services.

The whole problem of the supply of munitions of war, as provided by the Lease-Lend Act, for the armed forces of the United States and for those countries actively engaged in resisting aggression has been further examined.

Lord Beaverbrook, the Minister of Supply of the British Government, has joined in these conferences. He is going to proceed to Washington to discuss further details with appropriate officials of the United States Government. These conferences will also cover the supply problems of the Soviet Union.

The President and the Prime Minister have had several conferences. They have considered the dangers of world civilization arising from the policies of military domination by conquest upon which the Hitlerite government of Germany and other governments associated therewith have embarked, and have made clear the steps which their countries are respectively taking for their safety in the face of these dangers.

They have agreed upon the following joint declaration;

The President of the United States of America and the Prime Minister, Mr. Churchill, representing His Majesty's Government in the United Kingdom, being met together, deem it right to make known certain common principles in the national policies of their respective countries on which they base their hopes for a better future for the world.

First, their countries seek no aggrandizement, territorial or other;

Second, they desire to see no territorial changes that do not accord with the freely expressed wishes of the peoples concerned;

Third, they respect the right of all peoples to choose the form of government under which they will live; and they wish to see sovereign rights and self-government restored to those who have been forcibly deprived of them;

Fourth, they will endeavor, with due respect for their existing obligations, to further the enjoyment by all States, great or small, victor or vanquished, of access, on equal terms, to the trade and to the raw materials of the world which are needed for their economic prosperity;

Fifth, they desire to bring about the fullest collaboration between all nations in the economic field with the object of securing, for all, improved labor standards, economic adjustment and social security;

Sixth, after the final destruction of the Nazi tyranny, they hope to see established a peace which will afford all nations the means of dwelling in safety within their own boundaries, and which will afford assurance that all the men in all the lands may live out their lives in freedom from fear and want;

Seventh, such a peace should enable all men to traverse the high seas and oceans without hindrance;

Eighth, they believe that all of the nations of the world, for realistic as well as spiritual reasons, must come to the abandonment of the use of force. Since no further peace can be maintained if land, sea or air armaments continue to be employed by nations which threaten, or may threaten, aggression outside of their frontiers, they believe, pending the establishment of a wider and permanent system of general security, that the disarmament of such nations is essential. They will likewise aid and encourage all other practicable measures which will lighten for peace-loving peoples the crushing burden of armaments.

FRANKLIN D. ROOSEVELT
WINSTON S. CHURCHILL

❧ HISTORICAL INTERPRETATION ❧

WINSTON CHURCHILL ON THE BANKRUPTCY OF APPEASEMENT

Winston S. Churchill, *The Gathering Storm* (Boston, 1948). pp. 318–321. By permission of Houghton Mifflin Co., Inc.

CHARLES L. MOWAT characterized Munich as "the nadir of diplomacy—a personal deal between two men at the expense of a third party." That agreement gave the word "appeasement" a most disagreeable meaning, implying moral cowardice and an unwillingness to defend one's rights against aggression. Most vociferous among the critics of Munich was Winston Churchill who, in the passage reprinted here, asserted that had the West stood firm in 1938, Hitler might well have retreated from his determination to go to war, if necessary, to obtain the Sudetenland in Czechoslovakia. Churchill based his argument not only on military common sense but also on moral grounds.

We have now also Marshal Keitel's answer to the specific question put to him by the Czech representative at the Nuremberg Trials:

Colonel Eger, representing Czechoslovakia, asked Marshal Keitel: "Would the Reich have attacked Czechoslovakia in 1938 if the Western Powers had stood by Prague?" Marshal Keitel answered: "Certainly not. We were not strong enough militarily. The object of Munich [i.e., reaching an agreement at Munich] was to get Russia out of Europe, to gain time, and to complete the German armaments."

Hitler's judgment had been once more decisively vindicated. The German General Staff was utterly abashed. Once the *Fuehrer* had been right, after all. He with his genius and intuition alone had truly measured all the circumstances, military and political. Once again, as in the Rhineland, the *Fuehrer's* leadership had triumphed over the obstruction of the German military chiefs. All these generals were patriotic men. They longed to see the Fatherland regain its position in the world. They were devoting themselves night and day to every process that could strenghten the German forces. They, therefore, felt smitten in their hearts at having been found so much below the level of the event, and in many cases their dislike and their distrust of Hitler were overpowered by admiration for his commanding gifts and miraculous luck. Surely here was a star to follow, surely here was a guide to obey. Thus did Hitler finally become the undisputed master of Germany, and the path was clear for the great design. The conspirators lay low, and were not betrayed by their military comrades.

It may be well here to set down some principles of morals and action which may be a guide in the future. No case of this kind can be judged apart from its circumstances. The facts may be unknown at the time, and estimates of them must be largely guesswork, coloured by the general feelings and aims of whoever is trying to pronounce. Those who are prone by temperment and character to seek sharp and clear-cut solutions of diffcult and obscure problems, who are ready to fight whenever some challenge comes from a foreign Power, have not always been right. On the other hand, those whose inclination is to bow their heads, to seek patiently and faithfully for peaceful compromise, are not always wrong. On the contrary, in the majority of instances they may be right, not only morally but from a practical standpoint. How many wars have been averted by patience and persisting good will! Religion and virtue alike lend their sanctions to meekness and humility, not only between men but between nations. How many wars have been precipitated by firebrands! How many misunderstandings which led to wars could have been removed by temporising! How often have countries fought cruel wars and then after a few years of peace found themselves not only friends but allies!

The Sermon on the Mount is the last word in Christian ethics. Everyone respects the Quakers. Still, it is not these terms that Ministers assume their responsibilities of guiding states. Their duty is first so to deal with other nations as to avoid strife and war and to eschew aggression in all its forms, whether for nationalistic or ideological objects. But the safety of the State, the lives and freedom of their own fellow countrymen, to whom they owe their position, make it right and imperative in the last resort, or when a final and definite conviction has been reached, that the use of force should not be excluded. If the circumstances are such as to warrant it, force may be used. And if this be so, it should be used under the conditions which are most favorable. There is no merit in putting off a war for a year if, when it comes, it is a far worse war or one much harder to win. These are the tormenting dilemmas upon which mankind has throughout its history been so frequently impaled. Final judgment upon them can only be recorded by history in relation to the facts of the case as known to the parties at the time, and also as subsequently proved.

There is, however, one helpful guide, namely, for a nation to keep its word and to act in accordance with its treaty obligations to allies. This guide is called *honour*. It is baffling to reflect that what men call honour does not correspond always to Christian ethics. Honour is often influenced by that element of pride which plays so large a part in its inspiration. An exaggerated code of honour leading to the performance of utterly vain and unreasonable deeds could not be defended, however fine it might look. Here, however, the moment came when Honour pointed the path of Duty, and when also the right judgment of the facts at that time would have reinforced its dictates.

For the French Government to leave her faithful ally, Czechoslovakia, to her fate was a melancholy lapse from which flowed terrible consequences. Not only wise and fair policy, but chivalry, honour, and sympathy for a small threatened people made an overwhelming concentration. Great Britain, who would certainly have fought if bound by treaty obligations, was nevertheless now deeply involved, and it must be recorded with regret that the British Government not only acquiesced but encouraged the French Government in a fatal course.

❦ TEN BASIC BOOKS ❧

WORLD WAR II,
1939–1945

1. Bryant, Sir Arthur, *Triumph in the West* (New York, 1959).
2. Churchill, Winston S., *The Second World War,* 6 vols. (London, 1948–1953, R. 1962).†

3. Eisenhower, Dwight D., *Crusade in Europe* (New York, 1948).†

4. Falls, Cyril, *The Second World War* (London, 1948).

5. Feis, Herbert, *The Road to Pearl Harbor* (Princeton, N. J., 1950, R. 1962).†

6. Fuller, John F. C., *The Second World War, 1939–1945: A Strategical and Tactical History* (New York, 1949).

7. Langsam, Walter C., *Historic Documents of World War II*, Anvil Book No. 34 (Princeton, N. J., 1958).†

8. Millis, Walter, ed., *The War Reports of General George Marshall, General H. H. Arnold, Admiral Ernest J. King* (New York, 1947).

9. Morison, Samuel E., *History of the United States Naval Operations in World War II*, 15 vols. (Boston, 1947–1960).

10. Snyder, Louis L., *The War: A Concise History, 1939–1945* (New York, 1960).†

42

Aftermath: The Age of Political and Social Turmoil

WE THE PEOPLES OF THE UNITED NATIONS,
DETERMINED

TO SAVE succeeding generations from the scourge of war, which twice in our lifetime has brought untold sorrow to mankind, and

to reaffirm faith in fundamental human rights, in the dignity and worth of the human person, in the equal rights of men and women and of nations large and small, and

to establish conditions under which justice and respect for the obligations arising from treaties and other sources of international law can be maintained, and

to promote social progress and better standards of life in larger freedom,

AND FOR THESE ENDS

to practice tolerance and live together in peace with one another as good neighbors, and

to unite our strength to maintain international peace and security, and

to ensure, by the acceptance of principles and the institution of methods, that armed force shall not be used, save in the common interest, and

to employ international machinery for the promotion of the economic and social advancement of all peoples,

HAVE RESOLVED TO COMBINE OUR EFFORTS TO
ACCOMPLISH THESE AIMS.

—PREAMBLE TO THE CHARTER OF THE UNITED NATIONS,
June 26, 1945

1. The World in Flux

Basic Changes. World War II, one of the great tragedies of history, produced four fundamental changes in the international situation:

1. The old European states system, which had been dealt a shattering blow in World War I, was now further undermined. France lost her role as leading Continental power. Great Britain was no longer able to promote a policy of balance of power on the Continent.

2. The area of decisive global power shifted from its old European habitat to the United States and the Soviet Union, each of which became a possible nucleus of world hegemony.

3. The invention of new weapons altered old concepts of military geography. The industrial nations of the West became increasingly vulnerable in an age of atomic weapons.

4. Nationalism was extended to Asia and

Africa, where colonial peoples, demanding self-determination and an end to imperialism, upset the political and economic *status quo*.

Course of Peace Negotiations. Before World War II ended in August 1945, the diplomats of the Big Three—the United States, Great Britain, and Soviet Russia—had already laid a temporary groundwork for peace.

Roosevelt, Churchill, and Stalin met at Teheran, November 28–December 1, 1943, where plans were made for concluding the war, and where it was agreed that a general international organization should be established at the earliest practicable date. At the secret Yalta Conference of the Big Three, held on February 7-12, 1945, it was agreed that the liberated peoples of Europe should create

The Big Three at a secret peace-planning conference in the Crimea (Yalta). It was at this meeting in 1945 that Great Britain, Soviet Russia, and the United States planned and endorsed the projected first conference of the United Nations. The reassuring aura of unity and cooperation was soon dispelled as the Cold War developed between the realigned "Free World" and the "Iron Curtain" countries.

democratic institutions of their own choice and that they would have restored to them the sovereign rights and self-government of which they had been deprived by the aggressor nations. This declaration was violated later by the Soviet Union as it established satellite

states in Eastern Europe. Furthermore, it was decided at Yalta that defeated Germany was to be divided into occupation zones; Germany was to pay reparations; and Soviet Russia was to enter the war against Japan. At the final wartime conference, held at Potsdam, July 17–

August 2, 1945, the Allies fixed the terms for defeated Germany: disarmament and demilitarization; dissolution of the National Socialist party and its affiliates; elimination of militarism; democratization of Germany; trial of war criminals; and stiff reparations.

Beginning of the Cold War. Wartime unity quickly evaporated as Soviet Russia sought to expand her area of influence, and as the United States and Britain, which had deferred to Stalin's wishes at Yalta and Potsdam, refused to recognize further Soviet expansion. During the first postwar year, the Kremlin rapidly consolidated its power in Eastern Europe and then withdrew behind what Winston Churchill called an "Iron Curtain" stretching from Stettin to Trieste. Settlements for Germany, Austria, and Japan had to be postponed. The rift separating the Western Allies and the Soviet Union developed into what was called a Cold War, in effect a continuation of global conflict. On the one side was the Free World, on the other the Soviet Union and its vassal states. The aim of the West was to "contain" further Soviet expansion. (*See page 724.*)

The Cold War was fought on several fronts —political, economic, military, and propagandistic. On the political side, as the prospects of world collective security dimmed, the old system of power politics—checks and balances through alliances—was revived. Both West and East sought for German support by promising to aid German desires for unity. When the Kremlin sought to establish a permanent sphere of influence in Iran, the Security Council of the United Nations demanded and forced the withdrawal of Russian troops (May 6, 1946).

The United States returned to full participation in European affairs with the promulgation of the Truman Doctrine on March 12, 1947, preventing Soviet penetration into Greece and Turkey. Militarily, the American stockpile of atomic bombs and advances in nuclear armament gave the West a temporary tactical advantage. When the United States proposed the establishment of an International Atomic Development Authority to supervise commercial and scientific use of atomic energy

through a system of licensing and control, the Soviet Union killed it in June 1948 by veto in the United Nations. The Marshall Plan, announced on June 5, 1947, proposed full cooperation of the United States with the European states in a Continent-wide reconstruction program. Some $12,000,000,000 of Marshall Plan funds helped Western Europe to rebuild her shattered economy. The North Atlantic Treaty Organization was born in 1949 as a political and military alliance against the threat of Soviet expansion. On the propaganda front, both sides used every instrument of communication in the battle for men's minds.

The Cold War continued into the 1960's. Although Premier Nikita Khrushchev proclaimed his principle of "peaceful coexistence," he did not renounce Soviet faith in the ultimate triumph of Communism. He told the West, particularly the United States, "We will bury you," and added that "Your grandchildren will live under socialism." The Cold War continued under Khrushchev's successor, Aleksei N. Kosygin.

German and Austrian Treaties. The Council of Foreign Ministers, meeting in Paris in 1946, in Moscow in the spring of 1947, and in London in the winter of 1947, remained deadlocked on the issue of German and Austrian peace treaties. Soviet representatives, refusing to yield or to compromise, denounced the Western Powers as warmongers. When the latter gave West Germany a larger role in the European Recovery Program, the Russians replied on June 19, 1948, with a blockade of the Western sector of Berlin. A hastily improvised Anglo-American airlift supplied the residents of Berlin with the essentials of life, a strategy that could be met only by risking war. On May 12, 1949, the Kremlin lifted the blockade.

Japanese Settlement. Initial steps to demilitarize and democratize Japan had already been taken during the provisional occupation by American troops under General Douglas MacArthur. On September 5, 1951, six years after the end of the war, delegates of forty-nine nations assembled in San Francisco to settle the peace. The Soviet bloc attempted a filibuster by calling for a harsh treaty with Japan. Forty-eight nations and Japan signed the treaty, reestablishing the latter as a sovereign nation. The peace pact reduced Japan to her boundaries of 1854, handed over the Kuriles and the southern half of Sakhalin Island to Soviet Russia according to the terms of the Yalta agreement, gave the Bonins and the Ryukyu Islands to the United Nations under a trustee administration, and deprived Japan of Formosa and the former German islands—the Marianas, Marshalls, and Carolines. Japan thus lost her entire overseas empire. Provision was made for reparations by negotiation, but no specific restrictions were placed on Japanese rearmament. The Japanese monarchy was retained and provision was made for Japan's resumption of diplomatic relations with other nations. The Kremlin lodged a formal protest against the treaty.

2. The United Nations

Formation. The League of Nations, the post-World War I organization dedicated to the maintenance of world peace by international cooperation, was virtually moribund by the time World War II began. But the idea of an international authority did not die with the League. "The mere conquest of our enemies is not enough," said Franklin D. Roosevelt in 1945. "We must go on to do all in our power to conquer the doubts and fears, the ignorance and the greed, which make this horror possible." At a series of conferences during the war, including the Atlantic Charter meeting (1941), the Moscow Conference (1943), Dumbarton Oaks (1944), Yalta (1945), and San Francisco (1945), declarations and resolutions were formulated to provide a basis for a new world organization. The Charter of the United Nations, adopted at San Francisco on June 26, 1945, was the result of a compromise between big and little nations.

The United Nations was a general world parliament, whose principles and purposes were an extension of those of the League of Nations. The original membership comprised those fifty-two nations that had participated in the San Francisco conference. The Security Council consisted of eleven members, five of whom (United Kingdom, the Republic of China, France, the United States, and the Soviet Union) held permanent membership. In all matters except procedural, the Great Powers had the right of veto, desired at San Francisco by both the United States and Russia. The General Assembly, a kind of town meeting of the world, was composed of five representatives of each nation, each delegation casting a single vote. According to Article 10 of the Charter, the General Assembly "may discuss any questions or any matters within the scope of the present Charter or relating to' the powers and functions of any organs provided for in the present Charter." The third organ of the United Nations, the Economic and Social Council, was designed to promote economic stability and general welfare among all peoples. The fourth body, the International Court of Justice, adjudicated disputes among sovereign national states.

Major United Nations Actions. The first important United Nations case led to the withdrawal of Russian troops from Iran (1946). The Communist-led rebellion in Greece faded after United Nations intervention (1946). The General Assembly sent a commission to Korea to set up a free government (1947). United Nations efforts to set up controls over atomic energy were thwarted by Soviet-bloc opposition (1946–1948). The United Nations brought about a truce in Indonesia (1948), which led eventually to Indonesian independence from the Netherlands (1949). A commission obtained a truce in the India-Pakistan quarrel over Kashmir (1949 and 1965). A United Nations force was sent to Korea in 1950 to maintain the peace there. The United Nations denounced the U.S.S.R. for "violation of the Charter in depriving Hungary of its liberty and independence" (1956). In response to a United Nations demand, Britain, France, and Israel ceased an attack on Egypt and the Suez Canal; a United Nations Emergency Force was stationed in Egypt to preserve the peace (1956). The United Nations intervened in Lebanon to restore stability and facilitate withdrawal of

American and British troops (1958). To maintain order in the chaotic Congo, the United Nations sent a police force with troops from eighteen nations (1960). The United Nations Congo Force completed its pacification of dissident Katanga Province on January 21, 1963.

Evaluation of the United Nations. The United Nations, a new and streamlined continuation of the League of Nations, was more powerful in some respects and weaker in others. The fact that the United States played an important role in the formation and the activities of the new world organization made the United Nations inestimably stronger. The Charter of the League of Nations had been appended to the peace treaties at the conclusion of World War I, thereby tying it up with the real or imagined grievances associated with the settlements. The United Nations, on the other hand, was an independent organization. The desires of the smaller states were taken into consideration in both the planning and functioning of the United Nations. The most significant advance of the Charter of the United Nations over the League Covenant was the new Article 43, providing for an international police force to prevent aggression, a considerable improvement over the League's Article 16, which had been concerned primarily with economic sanctions. The United Nations, however, was burdened with cumbersome machinery for employing armed force against aggressors. The organization was weakened by Russian use of the veto power in the Security Council. Another blow was the death of the widely respected Secretary-General Dag Hammarskjöld in an airplane accident in the Congo on September 17, 1961.

Despite criticism, the United Nations demonstrated its capacity for flexible adjustment to emergencies. Perhaps its main contribution has been the prevention of a direct clash between the United States and the Soviet Union. By providing a forum for the discussion of grievances, the United Nations prevented the two giants from colliding in a nuclear holocaust that might destroy civilization. The hope of mankind for peace reposes in the United Nations.

3. The United States and Great Britain

United States as a World Power. The United States emerged from World War II the richest and most powerful nation on earth. Within five years after 1945 it doubled its industrial output, tripled the amount of money circulating within its borders, and quadrupled its savings. Fears that quick demobilization of its fighting machine would result in a massive wave of unemployment proved to be groundless. At the same time, the American economy was beset by rising prices, fear of inflation, and a rapidly increasing national debt. On the domestic scene there was a greater concentration of federal powers: the government stepped into social services, public education, and many other areas of national life. In foreign policy, the traditional preference of Americans for isolation gave way to an acceptance of the tasks shouldered by a great global power. The threat of Russian expansion led to a decision to recognize that world responsibilities of the United States had not ceased with the victory of 1945. The United States committed itself to the task of playing the principal role in the containment of Soviet Russia and defending all nations threatened by Communism. The Point-Four Program promised American help for the free peoples of the world. America's entry into World War I had marked the dawn of her world leadership; she was now thrust into a position of awesome power.

The Eisenhower administrations (1953–1961) denounced Soviet interpretations of wartime agreements and informed "captive" peoples behind the Iron Curtain that they could depend on American aid. On January 5, 1957, the Eisenhower Doctrine warned the Communist powers that the United States would allow no further Communist conquests in the Middle East. In 1957 and again in 1958, the United States sent the Sixth Fleet to the eastern Mediterranean to meet crises in Jordan and Lebanon. In his inaugural address on January 20, 1961, President John F. Kennedy, calling for a "grand and global alliance" to combat tyranny, poverty, disease, and war, served notice that the United States was ready "to pay any price to assure survival."

United States attitudes on issues of foreign policy began to stiffen. In April 1961 President Kennedy approved a plan for the invasion of Communist-subverted Cuba by an army of Cuban exiles and refugees trained in Florida and Guatemala. The plan, however, ended in disaster at the Bay of Pigs, and the image of the United States throughout Latin America was impaired. United States prestige was in large measure revived when, in October 1962, Kennedy instituted a naval blockade of Cuba to prevent Russia from supplying offensive weapons to that country. Premier Khrushchev, not prepared to risk a distant war, took alarm and promised to remove Soviet missiles and bombers from Cuban soil. Kennedy also took a strong position against the spread of Communism beyond its existing borders. He gave military and economic assistance to pro-Western regimes in Southeast Asia, notably in Laos and South Vietnam. He warned the Soviet Union that the United States would uphold its rights of access to West Berlin.

The United States suffered a grievous blow on November 22, 1963, when President Kennedy, while on a visit to Dallas, Texas, was assassinated by a sniper. The entire world was shocked and saddened by this senseless striking down of a brilliant young American leader at the height of his career. Kennedy's successor, Lyndon B. Johnson, elected again in 1964, faced an escalating war against Communists in Vietnam and continuing trouble in Santo Domingo (May 1965).

Recovery in Postwar Britain. With heavy war casualties, her cities bombed, and more than half of her 21,000,000 tons of merchant shipping destroyed, Great Britain emerged exhausted from the war. As she had little money to pay for imports, the nation was again in a serious economic plight. Foreign competitors had penetrated her overseas markets, British production methods were obsolete, and the coal, cotton, and steel industries acutely needed modernization. Although Churchill had led the British to victory, he was unable to convince the British people

that he was their proper leader in peacetime. At the general election of July 5, 1945, the Labour Party won 393 seats against the Conservatives' 198, thus achieving a clear majority in a 640-member House of Commons. The Conservatives, led by a disappointed Churchill, now formed "His Majesty's Loyal Opposition." The Labour government nationalized Britain's major industries, extended social services, and instead of removing wartime controls, maintained them in a policy of austerity. The pound was devalued, thereby forcing the British consumer to pay more for his essential needs, but also stimulating foreign trade by reducing export prices. Loans from the United States helped in this program of reconstruction. In the fall of 1951 the Conservatives, after six years of Labour rule, won a victory. Retaining the welfare gains of their predecessors, the Conservatives continued a program of drastic economies. On February 6, 1952, George VI died and was succeeded by his twenty-five-year-old daughter, Elizabeth II.

After the voluntary resignation of Churchill in 1955, Sir Anthony Eden became prime minister. Eden resigned on January 9, 1957, following the abortive Anglo-French-Israeli invasion of Egypt. Under Prime Minister Harold Macmillan there was a striking increase in prosperity. In Macmillan's words, "Most British people have never had it so good." The Welfare State, guaranteeing a livable minimum wage from cradle to grave, brought full employment. Since costs had to be met by increased exports, the new British slogan became "Export or die!" The Macmillan government tottered in 1963 when Conservative War Minister John Profumo was driven out of the cabinet in disgrace after a sex-espionage scandal involving prominent names. In October 1963 Macmillan, in hospital for an operation, resigned and was succeeded as prime minister by Alexander Frederick Douglas-Home. In November 1964 the new Labour government, with Harold Wilson as prime minister announced a program calling for renationalization of the country's steel industry, increases in retirement benefits, and restoration of rent control.

The Evolving British Commonwealth. "We British," said Churchill in 1946, "have our own commonwealth of nations. These do not weaken–on the contrary they strengthen–the world organization." The decentralized British Commonwealth was maintained after the war and bolstered with continued economic trade preferences but loose political ties. Britain withdrew as a mandatory power from Palestine in 1948. She tried to consolidate her position in the Sudan by encouraging an independence movement there. Burma was

Queen Elizabeth with the Prime Ministers of Commonwealth countries. Represented are Ceylon, Federation of Rhodesia and Nyasaland, New Zealand, India, Pakistan, Union of South Africa, Australia, Great Britain, and Canada.

granted independence in 1948 but remained within the British sphere of influence. Singapore once more became Britain's major Far Eastern naval base; Hong Kong was returned to British control. A most important change was British withdrawal from India in 1947 and the establishment of two Dominions –India and Pakistan. King George VI dropped the title of Emperor of India and a native Indian became governor-general. Mahatma Gandhi, who had done so much for India during his lifetime, was assassinated by a Hindu fanatic on January 30, 1948. The Irish Parliament repealed the External Relations Act in November 1948 and then broke Ireland's last ties with Britain. In 1948 Premier Jan Christian Smuts was defeated in South Africa, to be succeeded by Dr. Daniel François Malan, a fervent advocate of *apartheid,* or total segregation of races.

The Suez Expedition of November 1956 brought condemnation by the United Nations and the fall of Prime Minister Eden. The American alliance remained a cornerstone of British foreign policy, although there were differences of opinion, especially on the Suez attack (opposed by the United States).

4. France and Germany

From Fourth to Fifth French Republic. After their liberation from the Nazis, the French people threw out the collaborationist Vichy government which had ruled them from June 16, 1940, to the Allied invasion of 1944. Marshal Henri Pétain, who had collaborated with the Nazi leaders, was imprisoned on the Ile d'Yeu, where he died on July 23, 1951. Pierre Laval, his right-hand man, had been executed before a firing squad on October 14, 1945. The Provisional Government, headed by General Charles de Gaulle, who had organized the Free French movement during the war, lasted only from October 21, 1945, to January 20, 1946. In September 1946 a new constitution was promulgated for the Fourth French Republic, retaining the old form of government by bloc.

From January 1946 to July 1954 France had nineteen governments; none of them lasted for more than thirteen months, and one lasted for only four days. These frequent changes of government indicated that France was still plagued by her old political instability and indecisiveness. Contributing to the political tangle was the large number of parties, each with different interests. Heavy Communist strength reflected dissatisfaction with economic conditions rather than support of the Soviet Union.

France was beset by a multitude of economic woes, including loss of foreign trade, inflation, flight of capital, and national deficits. The industrial system remained inefficient, with much obsolete machinery and equipment. The treasury was depleted by the heavy cost of holding on to the French empire, as well as by the high price of rearmament. The

ineffectiveness of the outmoded French system of taxation added immeasurably to economic troubles. The tax burden fell mostly on industrial workers and consumers. Because tenants insisted upon rents fixed years in the past, there was little impetus to construct new dwellings to meet the acute housing shortage.

In May 1958 a coalition of nationalists and conservatives whose spearhead was the French Army of Algeria brought down the Fourth Republic. The newly established Fifth Republic, under the leadership of General de Gaulle, was a "presidential democracy" with a strong executive and balanced powers. De Gaulle believed his country's salvation lay in a kind of authoritarian democracy with himself as the power figure. "I do not think," he said, "that I could in all conscience serve the nation well . . . by presiding in impotence over an impotent state." His aim was to pull France up by her bootstraps to the position of a first-rate power. Many old problems (inflation, taxes) remained, but the French economy improved greatly. In April 1962 de Gaulle announced that the long, exhausting war in Algeria was at an end. While French relations with neighboring European countries became closer, French ties with Asian and African peoples slackened. De Gaulle's "grand design" for an independent Europe under French leadership clashed with the will of his allies and in 1966 provoked a crisis in the Atlantic alliance. He was suspicious of American influence: "Europe, the mother of modern civilization, must establish herself from the Atlantic to the Urals in harmony and cooperation, so as to play, in conjunction with America, her daughter, the role that falls to her in the progress of two billion men." This was de Gaulle's way of saying that he wanted less American influence in European affairs.

Enigma Renewed: The Federal Republic of Germany. The Third Reich, which Hitler boasted would live for a thousand years, went down to disastrous defeat after an existence of only twelve years. The Germans paid a heavy price for their devotion to this monomaniacal Austrian—10,500,000 killed and wounded, many missing in action or captured, more than 7,000,000 homeless, the rest of the population stunned and bewildered, and the cities in ruins. Hardened troops of the Allied occupation forces were sickened by the scenes they saw in the concentration camps at Belsen, Dachau, Buchenwald, and Nordhausen.

The Nuremberg Trials: Fair Trial or Victors' Justice? The Nuremberg trials took place between November 1945 and October 1946 at the scene of Nazi party rallies. A mass of documentary evidence, mostly from German sources, was presented before a tribunal consisting of an American, a British, a French, and a Soviet judge, under the presidency of the British Justice Sir Geoffrey Lawrence. The evidence filled forty-two bulky volumes. Twenty-one persons were tried. The verdicts condemned 12 to death (including Martin Bormann, tried *in absentia*), 3 to life imprisonment, 2 to twenty years, 1 to fifteen years, 1 to ten years, and 3 were acquitted. Also found guilty as criminal organizations were the Nazi Leadership Corps, the *Gestapo* (secret police), the S.A. (storm-troopers), and the S.S. (Hitler's elite corps). (*See page 722.*)

The debate on the trials was prolonged and impassioned. On the one side, advocates such as the lawyer Herman Phleger argued that there was no suitable alternative. The trials, he said, were the beginning of what could be, with good luck and good will, a valid and stable system of international law and justice. They were conducted with painstaking care and dignity and the evidence was overwhelming against the accused. On the other side, critics such as Lord Hankey, one of Great Britain's most prominent public servants, contended that the authority of an international court could not be based on a charter drawn up by the victors for the purpose of punishing defeated enemies. This was a "victors' trial," said Lord Hankey. "Would anybody, even if confident of innocence, if placed in the position of a defeated enemy, feel that a fair deal could be counted on from a similar Court created by an enemy after a victorious war?"

Development of West Germany. Under the Potsdam Agreement, the victor powers divided Germany into four zones of control—American, British, Russian, and French, cutting across the formerly established state and provincial boundaries. Greater Berlin was split into four sectors, thus forming a fifth zone. The occupying authorities began to purge Germany of Nazis and Nazism and to destroy the foundations of Hitler's shaky structure. After 1947, attempts to demilitarize, decartelize, and democratize Germany were weakened by increasing friction between the West and the Soviet Union.

In September 1949 Dr. Theodor Heuss was elected first president of the Federal Republic of Germany. The new republic embraced slightly more than half the area of prewar Germany but nearly three-quarters of its population. The capital was established at the old university city of Bonn, where a federal parliament functioned under a new constitution based upon that of the Weimar Republic. Great Britain, the United States, and France retained authority for the time being over demilitarization, reparations, decartelization, and foreign affairs. In 1951 Germany was invited to create a military force and to unite it with the armies of the West. On May 26, 1952, West Germany was indirectly integrated into the North Atlantic Alliance by signing with the Western powers a peace contract which included her in the community of free nations as an equal partner.

The Federal Republic was heavily subsidized by its Western sponsors, particularly the United States. Under the conservative chancellor, Konrad Adenauer, West Germany made a rapid economic recovery. German consumer goods began flowing in such quantities to world markets that some countries, notably Britain, began to fear a price competition that they could not meet. Many called it an economic miracle. The German automotive industry, starting with gutted factories and scattered labor forces, began to sell not just cars but complete assembly plants to Brazil, Australia, and Argentina. The real increase in West Germany's gross national product achieved a spectacular 8.8 per cent in 1960 and 4 per cent in 1962. Her industrial production in 1960 was 276 per cent above the level of 1936. She had sufficient surplus resources to give economic and technical aid to scores of underdeveloped nations. Chancellor Adenauer, aged eighty-seven, resigned on October 11, 1963, and was succeeded by Ludwig Erhard, the sixty-six-year-old economics minister, architect of West Germany's incredible prosperity. Chancellor Erhard denied that there was any such thing as a "German economic miracle." It was rather, he said, "the purposeful use of economic means and strict adherence to the market economy which brought success."

The enormity of Hitler's crimes had shocked and disgusted all mankind, but the German people apparently felt no profound sense of guilt. The very magnitude of the atrocities seemed to have a numbing effect on the nation. A kind of conspiracy of silence inside Germany tended to becloud the issue of atrocities. German crimes and acts of aggression were left out of or treated superficially in school textbooks in postwar Germany, thus leaving young and impressionable minds with little or no comprehension of what had happened in the Hitler era. When, in 1965, there was an attempt made in the Bonn parliament to bring in a statute of limitations for crimes committed under the Nazi regime, there was an outburst of resentment outside Germany. The parliament retreated before world opinion.

Even in its truncated condition West Germany by 1966 became again the foremost economic, military, and political factor on the European Continent. As kingpin of the Atlantic Alliance, she was wooed by both France and the United States. The Soviet Union and the nations of Eastern Europe feared the new power. American policy had to cope with the possibility of a new Rapallo, the eastward orientation of a united Germany.

Satellite East Germany. A few weeks after the formation of the Federal Republic, the Russians, who had ostentatiously avoided taking the first step in the splitting of Germany, formed the People's Republic of East Germany with East Berlin as the capital city. Controlled by the Kremlin, East Germany was converted into a Soviet satellite state. The East German Republic, containing 27 per cent of Germany's population and 31 per cent of its area, was ruled by its Communist Party under close Russian supervision. Non-Communist parties were permitted to have a nominal existence, but they were not allowed to oppose acts of the regime. A People's Police was set up as the possible nucleus of an army. Economic conditions sank to the level of those in Soviet Russia. Refugees by the thousands crossed the "green border" into West Germany. On August 12–13, 1961, East Germany closed the border between East and West Berlin to stop the exodus of East Germans to the West. The East Germans built

Destroyed upon discovery by Communist East Berlin security agents, this escape route was 450 feet long and 24 to 30 feet underground.

a wall dividing the city. The unpopularity of the Communist regime among East Germans was demonstrated in a serious uprising on June 17, 1953, in East Berlin—the first open revolt of the century by workers themselves against a government claiming that it represented the working masses. Economic programs, adopted in 1958 and continuing into the 1960's, called for a rise in industrial production for East Germany.

5. *The Communist World*

The Soviet Union. In World War II the Soviet Union suffered heavier casualties than all the other Allied nations combined—6,000,000 dead and more than $100,000,000,000 in property damage. After the war the Soviet government proposed successive five-year plans to promote economic recovery. The goal of the Fifth Five-Year Plan, announced in August 1952, was "to mechanize mining and labor-consuming operations, to automatize and intensify production processes, and considerably to extend and improve the utilization of the operating plants and to build new ones." The Sixth Five-Year Plan, integrated with corresponding blueprints for the satellite states, ran from 1956 through 1960. Politically, the Communist Party, reinforced by the secret police, continued its rigid supervision over the people. No concessions were made to political principles, but some deviations from the Marxian norm were permitted in matters of religion and family life. The Russian Orthodox Church was reestablished, divorce was made more difficult, and steps were taken to encourage large families.

Every form of activity in the Soviet Union was integrated to strengthen and perpetuate the Communist regime: art, education, literature, and labor were regimented as a means of maintaining the orthodox revolutionary spirit. In foreign affairs, Soviet leaders dropped their spirit of compromise with the Allies—the friendly sentiment that had existed during the war—and reverted to their traditional attitude of distrust and suspicion of capitalist nations.

Soviet Russia's Policy of Expansion. As soon as victory was won in World War II, Soviet Russia embarked upon a program of expansion. The Kremlin operated on the theory that the weakening of capitalism offered a great opportunity. The war had destroyed the old European balance of power, under which no nation had been able permanently to dominate Europe. Since 1939 Soviet Russia brought under her domination nine previously independent European nations and parts of Austria

and Germany. When the Polish republic was reconstituted after World War II, the U.S.S.R. retained almost 70,000 square miles of that country. Soviet armies occupied and incorporated the independent republics of Latvia, Lithuania, and Estonia, as well as the Petsamo region of Finland, adding some 6,000,000 people in the Baltic lands to the U.S.S.R. Additional acquisitions included Sub-Carpathian Ruthenia, Moldavia, most of Bessarabia, East Prussia, the Kurile Islands, and the southern half of Sakhalin (the latter two by the terms of the Yalta Pact).

Attracted by the softening of frontiers, Soviet Russia began to establish a large area of influence in Eastern Europe. Czechoslovakia, Hungary, Rumania, and Bulgaria were penetrated by Soviet agents. As satellite states, they were subjected first to united-front governments, and then placed under the supreme control of the Kremlin. In Yugoslavia, however, Marshal [Josip Broz] Tito was able not only to declare his country's independence but also to maintain it against verbal attacks of the Cominform (Communist Information Bureau, formed in 1947 to coordinate the moves of European Communist parties). Further Russian attempts to expand into Iran, Greece, Turkey, and Korea were discouraged by Western resistance.

By mid-century, Soviet Russia had become the hub of a Communist wheel that encompassed more than one-third of the population of the earth. About one-fifth of the world's land area was controlled by the U.S.S.R. in a Communist bloc extending over much of the Eurasian land mass. Soviet Russia alone possessed a formidable military power, with probably 175 divisions, 40,000 tanks, 20,000 planes, 300 submarines, and atomic weapons. But Communist influence was threatened in the 1960's by an ideological break between Moscow and Peking. At the same time, faced with increasing unrest in the satellites, Moscow hinted at a new principle of polycentrism, or a degree of satellite and foreign party independence.

Historical Controversy: Imperialists or Liberators? According to Lenin, imperialism

was the final stage of capitalism, which preceded and produced the eventual collapse of
capitalist society. In his thinking, imperialism
was not confined to direct political and territorial control. To him imperialism was linked
with all forms of foreign capitalistic investment. Thus, the direct politics of imperialism
were less significant than the economics of
imperialistic exploitation. Lenin would have
denied vociferously the possibility of any form
of Communist imperialism. Critics of Lenin
say that, if we regard imperialism in its simple
sense—the process by which peoples or nations
conquer, subdue, and then dominate other
peoples or nations—it follows that in recent
years, along with the steady decline of Western imperialism, there has indeed emerged
a new form—Communist imperialism. In the
years since 1945 some thirty-three countries
once subject to Western control have achieved
independence, and the process is not yet
ended. And during this same period a dozen
countries have fallen under Communist
domination.

There is a difference in form between
Western imperialism and the new Communist
variety. Whereas the Western powers went to
widely scattered areas of Africa, Asia, and the
Near and Middle East in search of land, raw
materials, markets, and investment areas,
Communist imperialism at first sought expansion through contiguous lands. Russia's
expansion eastward has been called "a continental movement of almost geological
irresistibility." Even more obvious was Soviet
expansion westward. Here again the Communists claimed that they were merely seeking
"buffer zones" for defensive purposes against
enemy attack. This was supposed to be a
natural cohesion of empire spread by land. But
the overtones and undertones of imperialism
were there. This was not the "white man's
burden," the control of the colored man by
the white man; it was a case of white men
oppressing other white men.

Once in control of its satellites (East
Germany, Poland, Czechoslovakia, Hungary,
Rumania, Bulgaria, Latvia, Estonia, and
Lithuania), the Kremlin moved to reshape
them in the Soviet image. Formal sovereignty

was left to the individual satellites, but power
was consolidated in the hands of a ruling
Communist Party. Party leaders in each state
were obviously dependent upon Moscow. The
economy of each state was transformed by
industrialization, collectivization, and planning on the Soviet model. All political opposition was eliminated. Meanwhile, Soviet propaganda machines played records of "people's
democracies" and "liberation" and "self-determination."

At the same time, Communist imperialism
called for the penetration of "underdeveloped"
countries. The strategy was to augment
Soviet influence in the former colonial and
semi-colonial countries and to advance Soviet
interests through diplomacy, propaganda, and
economic penetration. In the Near East as
well as in South and Southeast Asia, Moscow
granted loans and credits on favorable terms
and undertook to construct huge industrial
and welfare enterprises ranging from hospitals
to dams and steel mills. Meanwhile, any
Western evidence of similar economic enterprise was vigorously denounced as vestiges of
a decaying capitalistic imperialism.

The Kremlin now claimed that world Communism was considerably stronger than forces
of "Western imperialism." "The anticolonial
struggle," Moscow asserted, was successful in
areas containing 700,000,000 people. In the remaining colonial areas, with some 600,000,000
people, there was said to be a growing tide
against the West.

Critics charged that the issue was clouded
with Communist doubletalk. While pursuing
its own expansionist ends, the Soviet Union
posed as the protector of the small colonial
states in their common hostility to the West.
The Kremlin insisted that it was fighting
capitalistic encirclement and bourgeois imperialism while it reached outward for more
and more control of the earth's surface. The
jargon was easily recognizable: "unjust wars"
took place only between imperialist states; the
Communist states always fought "just wars."
Imperialism was a "facet" of capitalism. Communist imperialism was not imperialism at all,
but "liberation."

The Communist propaganda campaign met

with much success. In Africa, Asia, the Middle East, and in Latin America, Western imperialism was widely considered to be a continuing fact. Soviet Russia and Communist China did not seem to be regarded as imperialist powers, nor were they looked upon as systematic plotters for world domination. Few ex-colonial peoples were worried about Communist expansionism. Historically, they were still enmeshed in the psychology of the old imperialism of the West without being concerned about the new imperialism of the Communist variety. Their memories looked backward to Western intervention and control. The same views were common among the uncommitted peoples who did not share the West's attitude toward Communist imperialism.

From Stalin to Khrushchev to Kosygin. On March 6, 1953, the world was startled by a broadcast from Moscow: "The heart of the comrade and inspired continuer of Lenin's

Familiar faces may be recognized on the Presidium at Stalin's last Congress (1952). While Malenkov spoke for four hours, patiently sitting behind him on the platform were Molotov, Khrushchev, Beria, Bulganin, and other possible successors to Stalin.

will, the wise leader and teacher of the Communist Party and the Soviet people, has stopped beating." Joseph Stalin, Soviet dictator, had died on the previous day at the age of seventy-three after being in power twenty-nine years. Any attempt to catch the elusive personality of Stalin is an exercise in futility. He has been described as a combination of Ivan the Terrible, Peter the Great, Genghis Khan, and Adolf Hitler. His ruthless policies were responsible for the death of millions by forced collectivization; he sent other millions to enslavement in labor camps; he eliminated

possible rivals by a duplicity almost unique in history. In Soviet Russia, on the other hand, Stalin was honored as the glorious ruler who had transformed a backward nation into the second greatest industrial power on earth. Communists heaped saccharine adulation upon him, hanging his portrait not only in every museum, but in every room in every museum. On December 21, 1950, Stalin's birthday, the Prague radio broadcast this message:

Giant of the Revolution, Comrade Stalin,

you are the world's hope, the world's dream, the world's ambition. You are another name for immortality. Earth is grateful to you. Comrade Stalin; sunshine is grateful.

"Without Stalin," said the editor of *Izvestia,* "no one can understand or write anything of interest."

Following a bitter struggle for power among the eleven members of the *Politburo,* the successor of the "Great Stalin" was Georgi Malenkov. The loser, L. P. Beria, now denounced as a traitor, was executed, and his photograph and biography were removed from all Soviet textbooks and encyclopedias. After a military interlude, Nikita Khrushchev, first secretary of the Communist Party's Central Committee, gradually pushed his way to supreme power. On February 25, 1956, addressing the Twentieth Congress of the Communist Party, he exploded a bombshell by detailing the "crimes of the Stalin era." In the following years Khrushchev's policy wavered between ideological thaw, and following the Polish and Hungarian revolutions, a "re-freeze." This balance between rigor and leniency continued into the 1960's. Nevertheless, there was a notable relaxation of tension and terror. In foreign policy, Khrushchev called for coexistence with the capitalist world.

On October 15, 1964, shortly after midnight, the announcement came from Moscow of the resignation of Khrushchev as premier and first secretary of the Central Committee of the Communist Party after a decade in firm control of the Soviet scene. Ostensibly the resignation had been for "reasons of health," but Khrushchev was accused by *Pravda,* the party organ, of "harebrained scheming" and other wrongs. His pictures were removed from public display and his books ordered taken out of Moscow bookstores. The posts held by Khrushchev were taken by two men: the party secretaryship went to Leonid I. Brezhnev (1907–) and the premiership to Aleksei N. Kosygin (1904–). It was not evident at first which of these two held actual power in the country. The change provided a dilemma for Communist parties elsewhere. Less than

wholehearted approval came from Communist leaders in Poland, Hungary, and Yugoslavia, as well as from party chiefs in Italy, France, and the United States.

The most striking recent development in Soviet foreign policy was the gradual estrangement from Red China. According to Mao Tsetung, enigmatic ruler of Soviet China, the Russians had abandoned Marx and Lenin, while he, Mao, was the only new and noble architect of People's Socialism. The Chinese attacked Khrushchev not only as a "revisionist," but also as a "great power chauvinist" who was seeking to "wield a baton" over the entire Socialist world. In retaliation, Moscow employed against China the richly vituperative vocabulary built up in years of excoriating Trotskyites, revisionists, and "Fascist dogs." To the Russians, Mao was a "foul liar" who was "trying to destroy the unity of the Socialist camp." Soviet Russia was obviously fearful of an expanding China, which might cast envious eyes on near-by Russian territory. Chinese Communist leaders had made the removal of Khrushchev a pre-condition for any Chinese-Soviet settlement. The new Soviet government apparently wanted to heal the ideological rift with Peking, but at the same time, it assured the West, and especially the United States, that it would continue its policy of coexistence with the West—a policy condemned by the Chinese Communists.

6. The Smaller States

Post-Fascist Italy Redeemed. Following its armistice with the Allies on September 3, 1943, Italy joined the war against Germany as a co-belligerent. Postwar Italy was left in a precarious position, burdened by heavy losses, the end of her African empire, political chaos, and a shattered economy. In a referendum on June 2, 1946, the Italians voted to abolish the monarchy and set up a republic (12,718,641 for a republic, 10,718,502 for a monarchy). King Humbert II departed and Premier Alcide de Gasperi became head of the government. De Gasperi's most pressing aim was to restrain the Communists, who had obtained almost one-fifth of the popular vote in both national and communal elections. Economic reconstruction was helped considerably by American assistance under the Marshall Plan. The central problem was to increase the productivity of both industry and agriculture in a country that had some 2,000,000 unemployed in a working population of 21,000,000. Energetic efforts were made to close the gap between exports and imports. The new Italian government established a cordial relationship with the Vatican.

Remarkable progress in revitalizing economic life led to a boom—a rare occurrence in Italian history—in the early 1960's. The Christian Democrats maintained themselves in power, closing ranks with other democratic elements against threatening reactionary parties— the Monarchists and Neo-Fascists. The Italian Communist Party remained one of the largest in Western Europe. The Italian conquests in Africa—Libya, Eritrea, Italian Somaliland, and Ethiopia—became independent.

Small States of Western Europe. In 1947 Belgium, the Netherlands, and the Grand Duchy of Luxemburg united in the Benelux Customs Union for the purpose of maintaining joint tariffs on goods from other countries and of abolishing duties within the union itself. The Scandinavian countries, having escaped from the war with relatively little damage, rehabilitated their economies, but because of their delicate geographical position vis-à-vis Soviet Russia they were unable to negotiate a common defense pact. Switzerland came out of the war with her traditional neutrality preserved and with the most stable currency on the Continent. Portugal and Spain were among the European nations least affected by World War II. The government at Lisbon was in form a democratic republic, but actually it was a dictatorship. Franco's Spain, criticized in the West as Fascist in character, managed to consolidate her position in the postwar years. When the Cold War between East and West became intensified, the democratic nations began to regard ultra-conservative Spain as an unsinkable aircraft carrier in the struggle against Soviet expansion. In late May 1962 there were student riots in Portugal against the regime of Premier António Salazar, and in Spain there were walkouts in several industrial centers and student demonstrations against Franco. Typical of the problem of small states in Europe was the announcement in September 1963 of a new law creating a formal language barrier across Belgium—Flemish, the official tongue in the north, French in the Walloon-dominated south.

Rebirth of Israel. In 1933, Jews fleeing from Germany and the Nazi regime sought asylum in Palestine. In that year immigration rose to 30,327, of whom 5,392 were from Germany and 13,125 from Poland. In 1934 there were 42,359 "authorized" Jewish immigrants, and in 1935, 61,854. By 1939 the influx of Jewish settlers had raised the population of Palestine to 500,000. The Arab population refused to be reconciled to the admission of Jewish immigrants, and the resultant feud stained the Holy Land with both Jewish and Arab blood. The issue was further complicated when the British set up a quota system to restrict the entry of Jews just when the systematic Nazi persecution of European Jews made the Jewish desire for a national homeland more urgent than ever. On May 14, 1948, the British began to depart, leaving Jerusalem under the guardianship of the Red Cross, the entire Holy Land in war, and the United Nations Security Council with the problem of maintaining peace in Palestine. That same day witnessed the rebirth of Israel. Chaim Weizmann was elected president and David Ben-Gurion was named prime minister. The new state, a parliamentary democracy, became the fifty-ninth member of the United Nations in May 1949. The establishment of Israel stimulated the revival of Arab nationalism in the Near East. The League of Arab States—including Syria, Egypt, Iraq, Lebanon, Saudi Arabia, Transjordan, and Yemen—had been defeated in the war with Palestine in 1947–1948. Although torn by dynastic and political differences, the Arabs, nevertheless, continued their opposition to Israel. Gamal Abdel Nasser, Egypt's strong man, made it clear that he would one day seek to destroy Israel. The Israeli army, small but efficient, remained in a state of alert.

7. *Containment of Communism*

Organization in the Atlantic Area. From 1939 to 1947 the balance of power in Europe shifted drastically as the Soviet Union annexed 200,000 square miles of European territory with some 24,000,000 inhabitants and exerted its pressure on additional countries. To save the rest of Europe from Communist domination, the Western nations began to consolidate. In the immediate postwar years the United Nations Relief and Rehabilitation Administration (U.N.R.R.A.) reached into some European areas. In 1947 American Secretary of State George C. Marshall proposed further support to the nations of Europe to prevent any additional disintegration. Under the European Recovery Program (E.R.P.., or Marshall Plan) billions of dollars were sent to the participating countries. On April 4, 1949, Britain, France, Belgium, the Netherlands, Luxem-

burg, Norway, Denmark, Iceland, Italy, Portugal, Canada, and the United States became the original dozen members of the North Atlantic Treaty Organization (N.A.T.O.), which agreed that an armed attack on any one or more of them in Europe or North America would be considered an attack against them all. In the meantime, there were other movements for European Union. The various plans were combined in May 1948 in an International Committee of Movements for European Unity, which in August 1949 was organized into a Council of Europe. At long last an attempt had been made in the direction of establishing a single parliament for all the nations of Europe.

Added to these efforts for political consolidation was a series of regional economic agreements. The Benelux Customs Union (Belgium, the Netherlands, and Luxemburg), signed in 1947, was followed by the Brussels

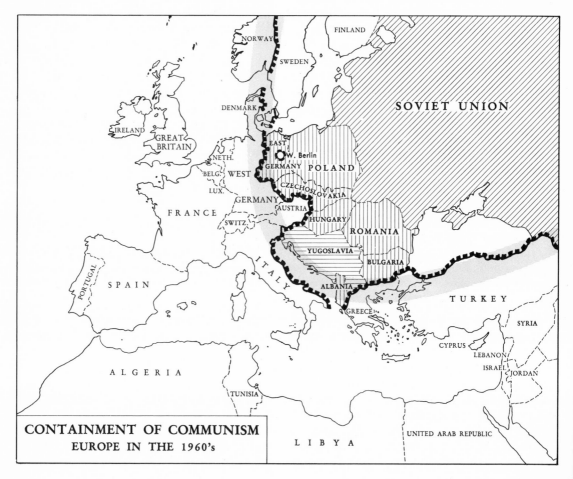

CONTAINMENT OF COMMUNISM
EUROPE IN THE 1960's

Pact of 1948, by which Great Britain, France, Belgium, Luxemburg, and the Netherlands agreed on a fifty-year treaty to collaborate in "economic, social and cultural matters and for collective defense." In 1950 the French minister for foreign affairs, Robert Schuman, proposed the Schuman Plan, which called for the union of French and German coal and steel industries under supranational control, as well as elimination of tariffs in the "core" nations of Western Europe—France, Italy, Western Germany, and the Low Countries ("Little Europe" or the "Inner Six" or the "Common Market").

The six states that entered into the Coal and Steel Community in 1952 were encouraged by the American and British governments to expand their cooperation into a military alliance. A new organization, to be called the European Defense Community (E.D.C.), would combine the armed forces of the member states for their mutual protection. Although carefully worked out with money and diplomacy, the E.D.C. was defeated mostly by rigid French opposition. The American policy of containment had to be pursued by different means.

The pressure for integration—looser than union but tighter than alliance—continued. In 1956 the Inner Six pooled their resources of nuclear energy in "Euratom." In November 1959 the seven nations of the European periphery—Britain, Norway, Sweden, Denmark, Switzerland, Austria, and Portugal—became the "Outer Seven," a counter-agreement for the reduction of trade barriers (E.F.T.A.).

The French President de Gaulle's objective was to protect the Continental economic and political community from what he saw as a threat of "domination" by the "Anglo-Saxons" —Britain and the United States. To this end, in January 1963, France vetoed Britain's application for membership in the Common Market, voiding sixteen months of painful negotiations. The Americans as well as the British were angered by de Gaulle's policy. Washington and London launched a major diplomatic effort to strengthen European opposition to de Gaulle. In late June 1966, pursuing his policy of restoring French prestige, de Gaulle

visited Moscow in a highly publicized effort at Franco-Russian *rapprochement*.

Counterbalance: Containment of Communism. The projects for military, political, and economic integration had two aims—to meet the challenge of the older system of power politics, separatism, and protectionism, and to contain Communism. When the North Atlantic Treaty was signed in 1949, the military weakness of Europe was matched by its political uncertainty and its economic instability. Western Europe lay open to a Soviet army which needed only marching orders to roll westward, almost totally unopposed, to the Atlantic Ocean. There were only fifteen under-strength army divisions from Norway to Italy. European production was approximately at the 1938 level, and the problem of trade deficits was grave. By 1954, fourteen N.A.T.O. nations (Greece and Turkey were added to the original twelve) had pooled their military and economic strength in a unique working partnership. With 48 active divisions in Europe, a powerful force of jet aircraft, and 350 jet airfields, the N.A.T.O. powers possessed a defensive shield deemed sufficient to deter aggression. On October 3, 1954, following the collapse of E.D.C., nine nations (the United States, Great Britain, Canada, France, West Germany, Italy, and the three Benelux countries) signed a pact moving toward closer Western European unity (Act of London).

8. *World in Ferment: The New Africa*

Decline of Western Imperialism. Western imperialism declined precipitously in the twentieth century. World War I, called an anti-imperialist war, put an end to Germany's inflated ambitions by depriving her of a colonial empire. The victors divided among themselves the colonial inheritance of the vanquished, only to find the imperialist system wavering all over the world. True, the holding of colonies and the theory of mandates—both maintaining the rule of advanced nations over backward populations—persisted, but the whole system of Western imperialism was collapsing. The colonial revolt reached flood tide in the years immediately after World War II and became one of the most important transformations in the history of civilization.

Nationalism and Turmoil in Africa. Africa, the second largest continent, had an area of 11,500,000 square miles. Three times the size of Europe and rich in natural resources, it had been carved into colonies and protectorates by European conquerors in the nineteenth century. Europeans had laid the foundation for the transformation of Africa by halting tribal wars, reducing the toll of disease, improving transportation and communication, and constructing roads, power plants, and many plantations. Yet, at mid-century, of the total population of 200,000,000 in Africa, only 6,000,000, or approximately 3 per cent, were of Euro-

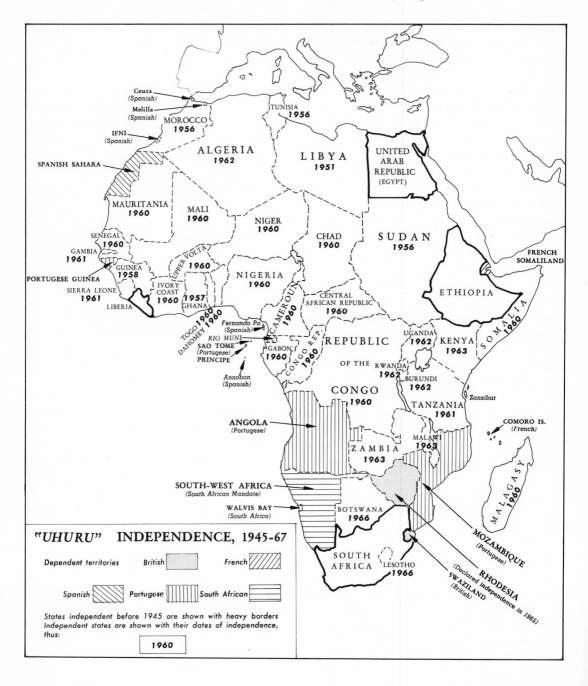

"UHURU" INDEPENDENCE, 1945-67

Dependent territories — British — French — Spanish — Portugese — South African

States independent before 1945 are shown with heavy borders
Independent states are shown with their dates of independence, thus:

1960

pean background. In 1945 there were only four independent states in Africa (Ethiopia, Liberia, Egypt, and South Africa).

In what has been called a "revolution of rising expectations," all Africa, from Cairo to the Cape of Good Hope, exploded in a drive for political emancipation. The process, far from being a smooth one, developed into a wild scramble. It began in the north in the relatively progressive Arab-Muslim states which, because of their geographical association with the Mediterranean world, were better prepared for self-rule. From there the cry for *Uhuru* ("freedom" in Swahili) was heard everywhere south of the Sahara. The white minority was overwhelmed in this rising tide.

The older map of Africa, with its colored outlines of British, French, Belgian, Italian, Portuguese, and Spanish possessions, lost all meaning, as a patchwork of independent states emerged. By the early 1960's there were some thirty-three independent states in Africa, surpassing Europe (thirty-one and Asia twenty-nine). The conquests of the European powers seemed irretrievably lost. In the three natural segments of the giant continent—North Africa, Tropical Africa, and South Africa—there were concurrent drives for independence. Between 1950 and 1960 most of the African peoples in the two upper segments had obtained their independence. In South Africa the white minority, comprising only about one-third of the population, continued to hold power.

Receding Colonialism: The British Pattern. The British presupposed the developments in Africa. From the beginning of their nineteenth-century expansion, the British foresaw the possibility of eventual self-rule for their colonies. They attempted with considerable success to train able Africans for the responsibilities of future self-government. They placed African chiefs in charge of local affairs under guidance of British officials in a kind of indirect rule. They made provision for steps to independence, encouraging mixed legislative councils, and delegated more and more power to local leaders. They gave voting privileges to an increasing number of people. Eventually, the British were able to withdraw from most

of Africa without the ignominy of being pushed out.

Typical of the British pattern in the New Africa was the case of Ghana, the former Gold Coast. About the size of Minnesota, with a population of 6,726,815, the country was given a legislative council in 1946, financial responsibility in 1948, an African president of the Council in 1949, and a new constitution in 1951. Ghana became a self-governing nation on March 6, 1957, and a republic in 1959, although it remained within the Commonwealth of Nations. Its charismatic leader,

Nigerian Ambassador Jaja Wachuku and Adlai Stevenson exchange views shortly before the opening of a session of the United Nations General Assembly.

Kwame Nkrumah, first prime minister and then president, began great engineering projects to electrify the country. Bearing the title *Osagyefo* ("Leader of Power") Nkrumah suppressed political opposition and exhibited a tendency toward dictatorial rule. Early in 1966 while on a state visit to Communist China, Nkrumah was overthrown by a group of high-ranking army officers and police officials who promised Ghanaians a return to more democratic practices.

Nigeria, the most populous country in Africa, with 55,000,000 people, living on 356,669 square miles, became independent on October 1, 1960, as the Federation of Nigeria. Carefully trained for self-government, the Nigerians under Nnamdi Azikiwee made the transition with little friction. The country became a republic on October 1, 1963.

On the east coast, Kenya, Uganda, and Tanganyika, with a combined population of 25,000,000 became newly independent states freed from British rule. Formerly a British colony and protectorate (British East Africa), Kenya had some 8,832,000 Africans, about 200,000 Asians and Arabs, and 60,000 Europeans. In 1953 the British went to war with the Mau Mau, a secret anti-white society that was determined to drive out all foreigners. For four years Kenya suffered under violent terror. After suppression of the uprising, Kenya was prepared for independence, which came in December 1963. Tanganyika was given responsible self-government in 1960, as the mainland part of the United Republic of Tanzania (Tanganyika and Zanzibar). Uganda became a fully independent member of the Commonwealth on October 9, 1962.

British withdrawal from Egypt was not easy. Here agitation against the British centered on control of the Suez Canal. In 1952 King Farouk I was overthrown in a military coup which later brought an army colonel, Gamal Abdel Nasser, to power. When Nasser seized the Suez Canal in 1955, British, French, and Israeli troops marched on Suez. The United Nations, supported by the United States, condemned the move in such strong terms that the British withdrew.

The French Pattern. For decades France had centralized in Paris the administration of her African colonies. The basic concept was "assimilation," that is, the colonies were to be assimilated into a national French framework. In 1944, at the Brazzaville Conference, the Free French changed the colonial policy to this extent—the word "colony" was rejected to be succeeded by "overseas territory of the French Union." By 1946 all French colonies were allowed to elect deputies to the French National Assembly. However, France still dominated her colonies.

War broke out in Algeria in 1954 when the Muslim majority, under the leadership of the National Liberation Front (FLN) went to war against the French. In this bitter struggle France spent billions of dollars and many thousands of lives. President de Gaulle, although sympathizing with the cause of the French *colons* in Algeria, nevertheless brought about a cease-fire in March 1962. France proclaimed Algerian independence on July 3, 1962, despite outbursts of terrorism by the Secret Army Organization (O.A.S.).

Between 1958 and 1960, some 12,000,000 people in the hinterland of the Sahara Desert were given their independence, although they remained loosely joined to France in the French Union. Five new states—Mauritania, Senegal, Mali, Niger, and Chad—appeared in North Africa. In addition, French Equatorial Africa, French Congo, Ivory Coast, Dahomey, Gabon, Upper Volta, and Madagascar (all in tropical Africa) became independent republics by 1958, remaining vaguely in the French Union.

The Belgian Pattern. The fever of independence reached the Belgian Congo in the late 1950's. After an uprising in January 1959, the Belgians on June 30, 1960, suddenly granted full independence to the Congo. The Congolese were totally unprepared for self-government by their colonial masters, who until the last moment thought that the people were contented with Belgian rule. Chaos followed the sudden granting of independence. United Nations troops, amid tribal fighting, were able to form a central government at Léopoldville. The rich province of Katanga, led by President Moise Tshombe, refused to join the Congo nation and insisted on independence. There was serious fighting between United Nations troops and Katanga warriors. The United Nations, in a rare intervention, defeated the province's troops. Its secession ended, Katanga was split up into three provinces. In 1964, after the withdrawal of United Nations troops, Tshombe returned to take over the office as the Congo's premier. Tribal rebellions remained to be put down.

The Italian Pattern. The Italians lost their African possessions in the upheaval of World War II, but retained the administration of

Somaliland through the United Nations. Ethiopia won her liberation early in the war; Libya was declared independent in 1951; Eritrea was joined to Ethiopia by the United Nations in 1952; and Italian Somaliland was declared independent in 1960. Italy, in effect, was pushed off the great continent.

The Spanish and Portuguese Pattern. Spain and Portugal were the first to come to Africa and the last to leave. They refused to go along with wholesale grants of independence. Both countries continued to designate their African possessions as "overseas provinces," in theory holding the same rights as metropolitan areas, but actually remaining under strict colonial control. There were few changes. Spain gave up her protectorate in Morocco but not in the rest of her Spanish colonies. Although Portuguese colonists in Angola on the Atlantic Coast and Mozambique on the Indian Ocean were outnumbered by the indigenous inhabitants about 50 to 1, Portugal refused to grant independence to these colonies. Both Iberian states tried to resist the pressures that had brought freedom to 150,000,000 Africans.

Problems in the New Africa. In one significant respect the new sub-Saharan African nationalism differed from the European variety. The old tribalism was succeeded by a sentiment more closely related to racialism than nationalism. After loyalty to the tribe, the next higher loyalty was not to "Ghana" or some such European legalism but to race—to the black man as opposed to the white man. For this the latter—with his "white man's burden"—was to a large extent responsible.

Black racialism was but one of the problems facing the New Africa. Africans had won liberation from European control, but not necessarily from European civilization. Almost overnight, Africans, for the most part totally untrained for democracy, were called upon to vote, form political parties, and decide issues of national policy. Clerks now became presidents, lived in palatial quarters, and rode in luxurious limousines. There was much political incompetence, much corruption in high quarters as white assets and jobs were Afrikanized.

Full-time demagogues found it impossible to work constructively.

Africans had mistakenly believed that liberation would be followed by economic well-being; they were deeply disappointed. Workers were angered by lower wages induced by falling profits. The few European experts left behind found themselves unable to carry out their assigned tasks without adequate assistance. The result was often economic chaos.

A special problem was the uncertain future of the European minorities. In some cases they could have chosen to leave or be expelled. The French *colons* in Algeria, for example, had nowhere to go. Disorders in Uganda, Kenya, and Tanganyika in 1964 made the lot of the remaining whites a difficult one, and in such cases there was a call for British troops. There were similar difficulties in Zanzibar in 1964. In Rhodesia the white minority proclaimed independence from Great Britain in late 1965. The Rhodesian whites tried to maintain their dominant position, while other African states were obtaining self-government.

The major problem appeared in most acute form in South Africa, occcupying the continent south of the Tropic of Capricorn. Here, in a total population of 16,000,000, there were 11,000,000 Africans, 3,000,000 whites, 1,500,000 "Coloreds," and 500,000 Asians from India. The most industrialized and most prosperous of all African nations, South Africa became a republic on May 31, 1961. The whites adopted a racial policy of *apartheid* (separateness), which in practice meant segregation of the races. To the rest of the world *apartheid* was morally and economically unsound, but with their economy dependent upon cheap labor, the white South Africans persisted in retaining a policy of inequality. The situation became increasingly explosive.

9. *Turbulence in the New Asia*

Twilight of Colonialism. Asia, a continent of ancient cultures and gigantic revolutions, housed a vast population of 1,783 million people, as contrasted to Europe (including the U.S.S.R.), 668 million; South America, 162 million; North America, 286 million; Africa,

304 million; and Oceania, 17.1 million. The critical problem of overpopulation was compounded by the white-oriented policy of excluding Asiatic immigrants from other sparsely settled areas of the world. The teeming, growing population of Asia was burdened by a primitive economy, poverty, pestilence, famine, and unending struggle for an uncertain existence. Years of exploitation by colonial powers left their mark on the vast area. To offset every altruistic missionary, doctor, or teacher who worked for the welfare of Asians, there were many promoters whose only desire was to build up a fortune at the expense of the inhabitants. Some great achievements of Western civilization were introduced into Asia, but Asians saw in the white man too much indifference and hostility.

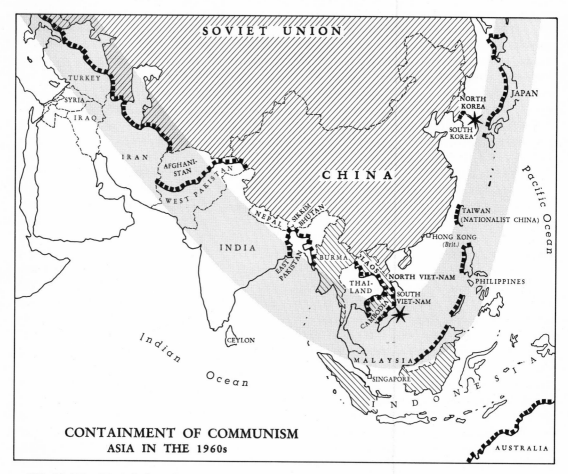

CONTAINMENT OF COMMUNISM
ASIA IN THE 1960s

World War II ended with most of Asia in chaos. By this time, however, the West had sown the seeds of freedom and nationalism. Admitting that their governments were inexperienced and their economies backward, the peoples of Asia nevertheless insisted upon becoming masters in their own houses. Everywhere there was resentment against Western intrusion; concomitant with it was a rise of national self-consciousness and nationalism. During World War II the colonial powers tried to halt the process by promising postwar constitutions and other reforms, but it was far too late. Japanese penetration of Indochina, Malaya, and the East Indies revealed to the people in these areas that the West was not as strong as had been feared. The old colonialism was on its way out.

The era of great Western empires in Asia came to an end. The transition from colonial status to nationhood took place within the framework of a struggle between the Free

World and the Communist bloc for strategic and economic dominance. In this great historical upheaval ancient cultures were reshaped.

Dissolution of the British Empire in Asia. The British were faced in Asia with a gigantic task similar to that in Africa—how to withdraw without friction and leave behind orderly governments and stable economic systems. The first major step came in 1947 with the division of the Indian subcontinent into India, Pakistan, and Ceylon. Both the Indian Nationalist movement under Mohandas Gandhi and the Muslim League for Pakistan demanded independence. Lord Louis Mountbatten, the last British viceroy of India, handed over freedom to India and Pakistan. Although both nations remained in the Commonwealth (no longer called the British Commonwealth), almost immediately strife between Hindus and Muslims began again over Kashmir.

With its 471,000,000 people, exceeded only by China's approximately 700,000,000, the Republic of India struggled with enormous political, economic, and educational problems. On January 30, 1948, Gandhi was assassinated by a Hindu extremist. Jawaharlal Nehru, a sensitive aristocrat with socialist leanings, succeeded to Gandhi's position as leader of the Indian people. The Indian constitution became effective on January 26, 1950. Pakistan, a new nation of 100,000,000 people, mostly Muslims, began its existence under handicaps of geographic division, backwardness, corruption, and lack of experienced administrators. Under Field-Marshal Muhammad Ayub Khan, president of the republic, reforms were inaugurated to improve the demoralized regime. In late 1965 India and Pakistan went to war but quickly came to terms after pressure from the United Nations and Western supporters of both countries.

The British also withdrew from the tropical island of Ceylon, source of the world's finest tea, and the third nation of the Indian subcontinent. The former British colony stayed in the Commonwealth and took advantage of independence to construct a parliamentary government basically pro-Western in orientation. Burma, too, won her freedom, but unlike Ceylon, withdrew from the Commonwealth. Because of strife between Communists and anti-Communists in Burma, the British decided to move slowly in Malaya. In 1963 the British created the Federation of Malaysia, a union of Malaya, Singapore, Sarawak (on Borneo), and Sabah (British North Borneo).

Finale of the Dutch Empire. At the close of hostilities in World War II, the Dutch moved to reoccupy their Far Eastern empire. It turned out to be an insurmountable task. Guerrillas armed with Japanese weapons called for independence. The Dutch tried at first to negotiate but without success. Nationalists, led by Dr. Achmed Sukarno, proclaimed a republic on August 17, 1945. There followed four years of intermittent warfare between the Netherlands and Indonesian liberation forces, terminated by an agreement signed on November 2, 1949, by which sovereignty over nearly all Indonesia was transferred to the United States of Indonesia. The Republic of Indonesia was proclaimed on August 16, 1950, and in September of that year became the sixtieth member of the United Nations. Nearly fifteen years later after an unsuccessful effort to block the seating of Malaysia as a nonpermanent member of the Security Council, Indonesia became the first nation to withdraw from the United Nations. Sukarno was named president for life on May 18, 1963. Promoting the cause of national expansion, he laid claim to the rest of New Guinea held by Australia. When the British relinquished North Borneo to Malaysia, Sukarno also claimed that area. He called for acquisition of the whole archipelago of the southeast coast of Asia. In late 1965, with what was interpreted by many as tacit support by the president, the Communists attempted to take control of the country; the coup was thwarted in a blood bath. By the spring of 1966 it appeared that Sukarno was having difficulty maintaining his position of absolute authority.

Resurgent Japan: Testing Ground of Democracy. Defeated Japan was occupied by American forces in August 1945. The symbol of American occupation became General

Douglas MacArthur, Supreme Commander for the Allied Powers. Under American sponsorship, democratic reforms were introduced in a new 1947 constitution, replacing the old "gift" of the Meiji emperor. Although it rejected the old emperor system, the new constitution allowed Emperor Hirohito to reign as a figurehead. Japan became a constitutional monarchy, much like England, with all citizens over twenty, including both men and women, holding the franchise. Military officers were made ineligible for cabinet posts. One article of the constitution expressly forbade Japan ever to wage aggressive war again.

Japanese economic recovery was phenomenal. A great land reform program was successful; today almost all farmers own their own land. Under American encouragement, the old monopolistic industrial combinations called *zaibatsu* were opened to public sale, although they were succeeded by new monopolies. Japanese industry quickly recovered from the damage of World War II. By the 1950's new factories began to spring up throughout the country. The economy developed at an extraordinary pace as coal, iron, and steel output rose to new heights. Industry made giant strides in shipping, machine tools, locomotives, and automobiles. Electronic devices from Japan such as radios, transistors, television sets, and computers, appeared in markets all over the world. The United States became Japan's most important customer and supplier of raw materials, although busy Japan traded with almost every nation on earth.

Dragon Awakened: Communist China. In 1949 the Chinese Communists overthrew Chiang Kai-shek and established a People's Republic, with Peking as its capital. For years ragged forces under the leadership of Mao Tse-tung had waged war against the government of Nationalist China. With weapons supplied mainly by Soviet Russia, the Chinese Communists conquered the mainland. Chiang Kai-shek retreated to the nearby island of Formosa (slightly larger than the state of Maryland), from which refuge he claimed to speak for the people of China. The 11,000,000

people of Formosa and the small Nationalist army were heavily dependent upon United States aid. The People's Republic of China remained a source of difficulty for the Western powers. The United States, regarding, either recognition or appeasement of Communist China as a loss to the balance of power in the world, refused to recognize the Peking regime.

Clash with the West: Korean War. At the end of World War II, Korea was occupied by Soviet and United States troops. The two occupying countries were unable to agree on the formation of an All-Korean provisional government. On May 1, 1948, a North Korean People's Republic was formed in the Soviet-controlled zone north of the 38th parallel. It claimed jurisdiction over all Korea. On June 25, 1950, the North Korean army attacked South Korea. The United Nations Security Council, in an emergency meeting, declared the invasion a breach of the peace, and agreed to send in a United Nations force. President Truman ordered General MacArthur to aid the South Koreans. The North Korean forces, with the initial advantage of surprise, overran South Korea within a few weeks. The United Nations counteroffensive drove them back to the line of the 38th parallel by October 1950. When General MacArthur crossed the dividing line and pushed toward the Manchurian border, he was met by Chinese troops. Apparently the war was being pursued beyond its minimum objective.

The conflict continued in 1951 until the front became stabilized roughly along the familiar 38th parallel. The fighting went on for another year while truce negotiators disputed over details and technicalities. An uneasy truce was finally achieved by the end of 1952. The United States forces suffered casualties of 22,209 dead, 91,730 wounded, and 10,815 missing; the total Communist casualties were much higher. By the Korean War the West served notice on the Communist bloc that the era of appeasement and do-nothingism was coming to an end.

Fall of French Indochina: War in Vietnam. In 1940 the Japanese surged into French Indochina and set up separate governments in Vietnam, Laos, and Cambodia. Vietnamese nationalists under Ho Chi Minh organized the Vietminh Independence League, a guerrilla organization, to fight the Japanese. The guerrillas then turned to face the French when they returned to Hanoi in 1945. The French responded by offering semi-independence, which was unacceptable to the nationalists. A full-scale conflict then began between France and the Vietminh, in which the French paid a tremendous cost in money and lives. The fall of Dienbienphu in May 1954 was a serious blow to the French. With French power broken, truce negotiations were opened at Geneva. The Geneva Conference of 1954 restored peace temporarily by dividing Vietnam into two parts (*see page 659*). The states of Laos and Cambodia remained in non-Communist hands.

For more than a decade thereafter, the United States sustained a show of strength and patience to save the freedom of Vietnam. The alliance to defend South Vietnam against guerrillas of the Communist Vietcong (meaning "red Viet") called for the presence of United States troops and a cost of several million dollars a day. In mid-1964 Communist guerrillas penetrated into Laos. The fate of the whole Indochina peninsula depended on the United States and its desire to contain Communism. In March 1965 the Vietnam crisis threatened to explode into a major war as Americans, goaded by Vietcong terror attacks, sent their planes to hit Communist bases in North Vietnam.

At first the United States, alarmed by the turn of events, had acted only to increase military, financial, and technical aid to South Vietnam. United States advisers and technicians were sent to train Vietnamese troops. American helicopters were used for surprise raids against Vietcong guerrillas. The Vietcong, confident that it could defeat the Americans as well as the French, began to step up terrorist activities. American foreign policy was predicated on the assumption that the Communists were to be contained at the mark of the 17th parallel. This was confrontation between the United States and the Communist bloc.

The war rapidly escalated until early in 1966 more than 200,000 American troops were in Vietnam fighting not only the Vietcong guerrillas but elements of the regular North Vietnam army. The United States tried a unilateral peace offensive in January 1966 to encourage negotiations, but resumed bombing of North Vietnam when the hiatus proved unsuccessful in bringing the Communists to the peace table. American opinion was divided on the excruciating problem which faced American President Lyndon B. Johnson. The "hawks" favored expansion of the war to crush the Communists, while the "doves" insisted that this was "the wrong war, in the wrong place, at the wrong time."

10. *Friction in the Middle East*

Crises at the Continental Crossroads. Europe, Asia, and Africa meet in the area lying to the east of the Mediterranean Sea. Some historians call it the Middle East, others recognize the designation "Near East," dating back to the time when Marco Polo passed through the area on his way to India and China. Here Judaic, Arabic, and European cultures have intermingled in such countries as Turkey, Iran, Iraq, Egypt, Syria, Lebanon, Israel, Jordan, Saudi Arabia, Yemen, and smaller countries. The great majority of its 90,000,000 people are Arabic-speaking.

In the mid-twentieth century the Middle East moved to the center of the world's stage. The discovery of great deposits of oil under the sandy soil of the Middle East made the region of supreme importance to the economies of Western Europe. While some individuals became enormously wealthy from oil profits, the vast majority of people remained poverty-stricken. The most important problem was the lack of water, as a result of which only 5 per cent of the land could be cultivated. Attempts were made through the building of dams and irrigation projects to solve this major difficulty. Added to this was a population explosion which intensified the all-pervading poverty.

After the two World Wars the nations of the Middle East threw off centuries of foreign

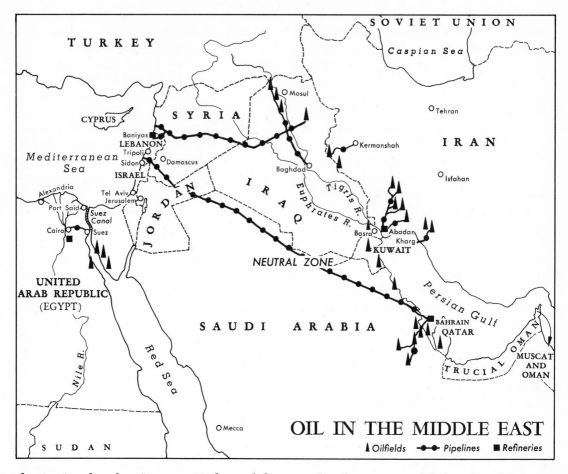

OIL IN THE MIDDLE EAST

▲ Oilfields   ●—● Pipelines   ■ Refineries

domination by the Ottoman Turks and by such colonial powers as Great Britain and France. Nationalist liberation movements appeared everywhere. After 1950 there were either rebellions or revolutions in every Middle East country with the exception of Israel. Democratic parliamentary institutions did not fare well in the area; the trend was toward military control. After World War II the Arab League, led by Egypt's Nasser and composed of Egypt, Syria, Iraq, Lebanon, Jordan, and Saudi Arabia, sought to unify all Arabs against both Israel and the Western powers, but the unity failed to function because of intense and apparently irreconcilable Arab rivalries. In the Cold War both Russia and the United States sought increased influence in the Middle East. The nationalist leaders there claimed a neutralist position.

One crisis after another appeared in the Middle East, some of which threatened to touch off war on a global scale. The United Nations devoted more of its time and effort to Middle East crises than to those in any other area of the world.

11. Tensions in the New Latin America

Struggle for a New World. The vast land of Latin America, like the rest of the world, underwent profound change. With every possible variety of geographical feature and climate, with abundant natural resources, with some of the finest agricultural lands on earth, twenty-two nations of Latin America experienced a great revolutionary transformation. There were varying developments, but some composite patterns may be recognized.

The destiny of Latin America was molded by Spain and Portugal, which for three centuries held vast areas of the Americas. In the nineteenth century the political influence of both Iberian countries receded and many republics came into existence. Politically, the tendency was toward weak democracies, recurrent revolutions, and the rise of dictators. In the new Latin America, although dictatorship remained a threat, there was growing democratic influence. There was less political instability, and military coups became less frequent.

Economically, Latin America lagged behind her northern neighbor. Despite rich natural resources, she had many underdeveloped areas. Some of the major countries depended on one major export product, such as Brazilian coffee, Bolivian tin, and Venezuelan oil. Alongside conspicuous wealth in the large cities there was extreme poverty. There were promising changes as Latin America surged forward in industrialization. The stranglehold of the old combination of landed aristocrats and military leaders was challenged by a new bourgeoisie and by a newly stimulated working class. Along with industrial expansion came better education, housing, and medical treatment. Although the pace varied, change was unquestionably taking place.

There were still many tensions. The road to political democracy, outside the traditional

mold, was a rough one. Military dictatorship under a professional officer class still persisted. Under Fidel Castro, Cuba became the first Communist country in the Americas and sought to introduce its revolution to the mainland. Throughout Latin America there remained much resentment against the United States and "Yankee imperialism." In the "Alliance for Progress" program, the United States tried to assist her southern neighbors in the struggles for monetary stability, industrial expansion, and social change.

12. World Trouble Spots

Areas of Friction. There was no magic formula for peace in the contemporary world. Trouble spots existed everywhere. The Cold War between Soviet Russia and the West continued. The Russians maintained pressure on West Berlin. East Berlin was divided from West Berlin by a wall constructed by the Communists to prevent defections to the West. In the Middle East tensions persisted between Arabs and Jews. Africa was torn by factional disputes in the Congo, and by lingering colonialism in Angola. Latin America, burdened by economic instability, saw a Communist bridgehead created by Fidel Castro in Cuba and the danger of dictatorship elsewhere. The Far East was troubled by divisions in Korea, by militant Communist Chinese pressure on Formosa and India, by the Pakistan-India dispute over Kashmir, and by the war between North and South Vietnam with United States involvement. Sore spots appeared all over the world in a kind of global political smallpox.

The Nuclear Race. On November 1, 1952, the United States solved the secret of the fusion process leading to the awesome hydrogen bomb. The first H-bomb explosion took place over Eniwetok Atoll in the South Pacific, raising a force 250 times more powerful than the atom bomb that killed nearly 80,000 in Hiroshima. In August 1953 the Soviet Union in turn exploded a hydrogen device, an indication of the speed of Russian nuclear progress. In November 1958 both sides

Cuban Premier Castro romps with Moscow children in a winter playground at the Kremlin (1964).

declared a test moratorium; it was now clear that thermonuclear weapons could be manufactured cheaply and that any nation with a small supply of A-bombs could use them as trigger devices for thermonuclear bombs. In September 1961 the Soviet Union unilaterally ended the moratorium with extensive new test series. The United States, reacting with shock and anger, resumed testing in April 1962. The position of the United States was that, by rejecting all suggested means of true inspection, the Soviet Union was responsible for the new nuclear escalation.

In the summer of 1963 came a glimmer of hope when a nuclear test ban treaty was negotiated in Moscow. "Yesterday," said President Kennedy on July 26, 1963, "a shaft of light cut into the darkness." Although the ban called only for a halt to testing in the atmosphere, it was a reflection of Moscow's professed desire to have better relations with the West.

The alternative was an epitaph to civilization in flame and smoke. On a moral level, some called for an end to the idea of atomic retaliation. This point of view was expressed by Lewis Mumford: "Let us cease all further experiments with even more horrifying weapons of destruction, lest our own self-induced fears further upset our mental balance. . . . Let us deal with our own massive sins and errors . . . and have the courage to speak up . . . against the methods of barbarism to which we are now committed." Others held with equal vehemence that American nuclear superiority was the only deterrent to further Communist aggressions. It was an unescapable and agonizing debate.

Peace or War? Some observers believe that the power in the hands of the two great antagonists—the United States and the U.S.S.R.— is so great that neither side will dare to use thermonuclear weapons. Thus, peace rests on a foundation of mutual terror. Quincy Wright reminds us that nations do not necessarily stop fighting as their knowledge of more devastating weapons increases. The European powers alone have fought seventy-four wars in the first thirty years of the twentieth century. The "most enlightened century" has a bad record in the shedding of human blood. The issue of peace or war now appears not only to be urgent, but final.

⊰ KEY DOCUMENT ⊱

EXTRACTS FROM THE NUREMBERG TRIAL JUDGMENTS, OCTOBER 1, 1946

Condensed from the official text in *Trial of the Major War Criminals before The International Military Tribunal* (Nurenberg, 1948), XXII, pp. 524–533, 539–541, 552–556, 556–571.

THE PUBLIC TRIAL of twenty-two Nazi leaders began at Nuremberg in November 1945. Although in the past special courts had sometimes been set up to judge political crimes by extraordinary authority, no such court had ever obtained such universal recognition. Here was the first significant step in the creation of an international court to judge crimes against peace, against humanity, and against defenseless minorities. The legality of the proceedings troubled many jurists, who were disturbed by the *ex post facto* implications of the trials.

"Tode durch den Strang!"—"Death by the rope!" This was the verdict for eleven of the defendants: Goering (age 52), Ribbentrop (53), Keitel (63), Kaltenbrunner (43), Rosenberg (53), Frank (46), Frick (69), Streicher (61), Sauckel (48), Jodl (56), and Seyss-Inquart (54). Bormann (45) was also sentenced *in absentia* to death. Three others were sent to prison for life—Hess (52), Funk (56), and Raeder (70).

Four were condemned to terms of imprisonment—Doenitz (55) to 10 years, Shirach (39) to 20 years, Neurath (72) to 15 years, and Speer (40) to 20 years. Three were acquitted—Schacht (69), von Papen (66) and Fritsche (46). Extracts from the verdicts follow.

The four counts of the indictment:

1. Conspiracy to commit crimes alleged in other counts;
2. Crimes against peace;
3. War crimes;
4. Crimes against humanity.

GOERING: From the moment he joined the party in 1922 and took command of the street-fighting organization, the S.A., Goering was the adviser, the active agent of Hitler and one of the prime leaders of the Nazi movement. As Hitler's political deputy he was largely instrumental in bringing the National Socialists to power in 1933, and was charged with consolidating this power and expanding German might. He developed the *Gestapo* and created the first concentration camps, relinquishing them to Himmler in 1934; conducted the Roehm purge in that year and engineered the sordid proceedings which resulted in the removal of von Blomberg and von Fritsch from the Army. . . .

Goering commanded the *Luftwaffe* in the attack on Poland and throughout the aggressive wars which followed. . . . The record is filled with Goering's admissions of his complicity in the use of slave labor. . . .

Goering persecuted the Jews, particularly after the November 1938 riots. . . .

There is nothing to be said in mitigation. . . . His guilt is unique in its enormity. The record discloses no excuse for this man.

VERDICT: GUILTY on all 4 counts.

SENTENCE: Death by hanging.

HESS: . . . As deputy to the *Fuehrer*, Hess was the top man in the Nazi party with responsibility for handling all party matters and authority to make decisions in Hitler's name on all questions of party leadership. . . . Hess was an informed and willing participant in German aggression against Austria, Czechoslovakia, and Poland. . . .

That Hess acts in an abnormal manner, suffers from loss of memory, and has mentally deterior-

ated during this trial, may be true. But there is nothing to show that he does not realize the nature of the charges against him, or is incapable of defending himself. He was ably represented at the trial by counsel, appointed for that purpose by the Tribunal. There is no suggestion that Hess was not completely sane when the acts charged against him were committed.

VERDICT: GUILTY on counts 1 and 2.

SENTENCE: Life imprisonment.

ROSENBERG: Recognized as the party's ideologist, he developed and spread Nazi doctrines in the newspapers *Völkischer Beobachter* and *N. S. Monatshefte*, which he edited, and in the numerous books he wrote. . . .

Rosenberg bears a major responsibility for the formulation and execution of occupation policies in the Occupied Eastern territories. . . . On July 17, 1941, Hitler appointed Rosenberg *Reich* Minister of the Eastern Occupied Territories, and publicly charged him with responsibility for civil administration. . . . He helped to formulate the policies of Germanization, exploitation, forced labor, extermination of Jews and opponents of Nazi rule, and he set up an administration which carried them out. . . . His subordinates engaged in mass killings of Jews, and his civil administrators considered that cleansing the Eastern Occupied Territories of Jews was necessary. . . . His signature of approval appears on the order of June 14, 1941, for the *Heu Aktion*, the apprehension of 40,000 to 50,000 youths, aged 10–14, for shipment to the Reich. . . .

VERDICT: GUILTY on all 4 counts.

SENTENCE: Death by hanging.

RIBBENTROP: Ribbentrop was not present at the Hossbach Conference held on November 5, 1937, but on January 2, 1938, while ambassador to England, he sent a memorandum to Hitler indicating his opinion that a change in the *status quo* in the East in the German sense could only be carried out by force and suggesting methods to prevent England and France from intervening in a European war fought to bring about such a change. . . . Ribbentrop participated in the aggressive plans against Czechoslovakia. . . .

Ribbentrop played a particularly significant role in the diplomatic activity which led up to the attack on Poland. He participated in a conference held on August 12, 1939, for the purpose of obtaining Italian support if the attack should lead to a general European war. . . .

He played an important part in Hitler's "final solution" of the Jewish question. In September 1942 he ordered the German diplomatic representatives accredited to various satellites to hasten deportation of the Jews to the East. . . . It was because Hitler's policy and plans coincided with his own ideas that Ribbentrop served him so willingly to the end.

VERDICT: GUILTY on all 4 counts.

SENTENCE: Death by hanging.

⟨ HISTORICAL INTERPRETATION ⟩

WINSTON CHURCHILL ON THE BEGINNING OF THE COLD WAR: "AN IRON CURTAIN HAS DESCENDED"

Winston S. Churchill, speech at Westminister College, Fulton, Mo., March 5, 1946.

POSTWAR OBJECTIVES of Soviet Russia were to consolidate her gains and to exploit any opportunity to extend her influence in any part of the world. These aims clashed head-on with the goal of the Western world to maintain the *status quo*. That the conflict had degenerated into a Cold War, a war in time of peace, was recognized first by Winston Churchill, statesman-historian, in a speech made at Fulton, Missouri, in 1946.

A shadow has fallen upon the scenes so lately lighted by the Allied victory. Nobody knows what Soviet Russia and its Communist international organization intends to do in the immediate future, or what are the limits, if any, to their expansive and proselytizing tendencies.

I have a strong admiration and regard for the valiant Russian people and for my wartime comrade, Marshal Stalin. There is deep sympathy and good-will in Britain—and I doubt not here also —toward the peoples of all the Russias and a resolve to preserve through many differences and rebuffs in establishing lasting friendships.

We understand the Russian need to be secure on her western frontiers by the removal of all possibility of German aggression. We welcome Russia to her rightful place among the leading nations of the world. We welcome her flag upon the seas. Above all, we welcome or should welcome constant, frequent, and growing contacts between the Russian people and our peoples on both sides of the Atlantic.

It is my duty, however, and I am sure you would not wish me not to state the facts as I see them to you, it is my duty to place before you certain facts about the present position in Europe.

From Stettin in the Baltic to Trieste in the Adriatic, an iron curtain has descended across the Continent. Behind that line lie all the capitals of the ancient states of central and eastern Europe —Warsaw, Berlin, Prague, Vienna, Budapest, Belgrade, Bucharest, and Sofia—all these famous cities and the populations around them lie in what I might call the Soviet sphere, and all are subject, in one form or another, not only to Soviet influence but to a very high and in some cases increasing measure of control from Moscow.

Police governments are pervading from Moscow. But Athens alone, with its immortal glories, is free to decide its future at an election under British, American, and French observation. . . .

The Communist parties, which were very small in all these eastern states of Europe, have been raised to pre-eminence and power far beyond their numbers, and are seeking everywhere to obtain totalitarian control.

Police governments are prevailing in nearly every case, and so far, except in Czechoslovakia, there is no true democracy. . . .

If now the Soviet government tries, by separate action, to build up a pro-Communist Germany in their areas this will cause new serious difficulties in the American and British zones, and will give the defeated Germans the power of putting themselves up to auction between the Soviets and the western democracies. Whatever conclusion may be drawn from these facts—and facts they are—this is certainly not the liberated Europe we fought to build up. Nor is it one which contains the essentials of permanent peace. . . .

I do not believe that Soviet Russia desires war. What they desire are the fruits of war and the indefinite expansion of their power and doctrines.

But what we have to consider here today while time remains, is the permanent prevention of war and the establishment of conditions of freedom and democracy as rapidly as possible in all countries. Our difficulties and dangers will not be removed by closing our eyes to them. They will not be removed by mere waiting to see what happens; nor will they be removed by a policy of appeasement.

What is needed is a settlement, and the longer this is delayed, the more difficult it will be and the greater our dangers will become.

From what I have seen of our Russian friends and allies during the war, I am convinced that there is nothing they admire so much as strength, and there is nothing for which they have less respect than for weakness, especially military weakness.

For that reason the old doctrine of a balance of power is unsound. We can not afford, if we can help it, to work on narrow margins, offering temptation to a trial of strength.

If the Western Democracies stand together in strict adherence to the principles of the United Nations Charter, their influence for furthering those principles will be immense and no one is likely to molest them. If, however, they become divided or falter in their duty, and if these all-important years are allowed to slip away, then indeed catastrophe may overwhelm us all.

Last time I saw it all coming, and cried aloud to my own fellow-countrymen and to the world, but no one paid any attention. Up till the year 1933 or even 1935, Germany might have been saved from the awful fate which has overtaken her and we might all have been spared the miseries Hitler let loose upon mankind.

There never was a war in history easier to prevent by timely action than the one which has just desolated such great areas of the globe. It could have been prevented, in my belief, without the firing of a single shot, and Germany might be powerful, prosperous and honored today, but no one would listen and one by one we were all sucked into the awful whirlpool.

We surely, ladies and gentlemen, I put to you, but surely we must not let that happen again. This can only be achieved by reaching now, in 1946, this year 1946, by reaching a good understanding on all points with Russia under the general authority of the United Nations Organization and by the maintenance of that good understanding through many peaceful years, by the world instrument, supported by the whole strength of the English-speaking world and all its connections.

❧ TEN BASIC BOOKS ❧

AFTERMATH: THE AGE OF POLITICAL AND SOCIAL TURMOIL

1. Bruun, Geoffrey, and Victor S. Mamatey, *The World in the Twentieth Century*, (Boston, 1962).
2. Cole, George D. H., *World in Transition* (New York, 1949).
3. Gatzke, Hans, *The Present in Perspective: A Look at the World Since 1945*, 3rd ed. (Chicago, 1961).
4. Graebner, Norman A., *Cold War Diplomacy, 1945–1960*, Anvil Book No. 58 (Princeton, N. J., 1962).†
5. Holborn, Hajo, *The Political Collapse of Europe* (New York, 1951).
6. Hook, Sidney, *World Communism*, Anvil Book No. 62 (Princeton, N. J., 1962).†

7. Kennan, George F., *Realities of American Foreign Policy* (Princeton, N. J., 1954, R. 1966).†

8. Lippmann, Walter, *The Communist World and Ours* (Boston, 1958).

9. Seton-Watson, Hugh, *Neither War Nor Peace: The Struggle for Power in the Postwar World* (New York, 1960).†

10. Wright, Gordon, and Arthur Mejia, Jr., *An Age of Controversy* (New York, 1963).†

43

The Mind of Contemporary Man

THE WESTERN world today is caught in an apparent dilemma between two conflicting modes of thought. The one thinks in terms of absolutes—the absoluteness of truth, beauty, justice, goodness, themselves all deriving from an Absolute of absolutes, which is God. The natural world is complemented by the supernatural, the body by the soul, the temporal by the eternal. This view gives an essentially static world-picture; the flux of events is merely change, in which the only progress is a spiritual one, toward the perfection of eternal values. Empiricism and the experimental method are alien to it. . . . Man's place in the universe is the place of an eternal soul, created by God, and working out its destiny in terms of eternal values.

The other is the scientific method. It subjects the conclusions of reason to the arbitrament of hard fact to build an increasing body of tested knowledge. It refuses to ask questions that cannot be answered, and rejects such answers as cannot be provided except by Revelation. . . . It introduces history into everything. Stars and scenery have their history, alike with plant species or human institutions, and nothing is intelligible without some knowledge of its past. . . .

These two ways of approaching and thinking about the universe are irreconcilable—as irreconcilable as is magic with scientific agriculture, witch-doctoring with preventive medicine, or number-mysticism with higher mathematics. Because our thinking still contains elements from both, it and we are confused.

—JULIAN S. HUXLEY, *On Living in a Revolution: A Biologist Looks at Man*

1. Main Currents in the New Age

Heritage of the Nineteenth Century. The flowering of the Industrial Revolution brought tremendous industrial and scientific achievements but also a corresponding series of material inequalities. "The nineteenth century," said Crane Brinton, "was a time of extraordinary diversity of thought, an age of multi-unanimity. Its extremes were great extremes, its tensions clearly marked—tradition against innovation, authority against liberty, faith in God against faith in the machine, loyalty to the nation against loyalty to humanity—the list could be very long indeed. Somehow the nineteenth century managed to keep these warring human aspirations, these basically conflicting ideals of the good life, in uneasy balance." The Victorian compromise attempted to hold conflicting forces in check by working toward the goal of moderation in political democracy, nationalism, and capitalism.

The twentieth century saw the greatest material achievements in the history of mankind. But the kind of balance sought for in the Victorian compromise was shattered by two great wars and a great depression. A new intellectual and emotional restlessness, as well as a new anxiety and insecurity, took the form of politico-economic experiments in Communism, Fascism, Nazism, and the welfare state, expressionism in the creative arts, and anti-intellectualism in thought. Conflicts at every level in the nineteenth century were succeeded by even greater tensions in the twentieth. Contemporary man finds himself in an era of inevitable transition. Scientific discovery and greater historical awareness cause his immediate world to get smaller as his knowledge of the universe expands. Increased knowledge is accompanied by increased perplexity as the complex of alternatives seems to hold forth both threat and promise for the future. Modern man is confronted with the necessity of finding some sort of new balance among the new dimensions of his age.

Material Progress: The New Physics. The achievements of science and technology excelled by far the successes of preceding centuries. Most striking of all was the rapid and revolutionary development of physics. At the end of the nineteenth century the fundamentals of physical science were believed to be the Newtonian laws of motion and the principles of the conservation of mass and the conservation of energy. These basic hypotheses were modified or shattered by a series of discoveries. The atomic theory of the composition of matter was abandoned in 1892, when Hendrik Anton Lorentz (1853–1928), a Dutch physicist, introduced the electron theory. In 1895 Wilhelm Konrad Roentgen (1845–1923), a German physicist, discovered X-rays and opened the field of radioactivity. In 1896 Antoine Henri Becquerel (1852–1908), a French engineer, discovered emanations from phosphorescent and fluorescent substances, subsequently known as Becquerel rays. Pierre Curie (1859–1906), Marie Curie (1867–1934), Ernest Rutherford (1871–1937), and other scientists demonstrated that certain forms of matter, high in the table of elements, were disintegrating, a portent for the future. In 1901 Max Planck (1858–1947), a German physicist, propounded the quantum theory, holding that energy was thrown from the atom in spurts rather than in a flow of uniform waves.

By the turn of the century it had become

Physicist-philosopher Albert Einstein put forth theories which, like those of Copernicus, Darwin, and Freud, have had major impact upon man's concept of his relation to the world around him.

obvious that the atom was not a solid, hard, impenetrable mass, but a tiny universe in itself, in which many of the previously accepted principles of physics failed to operate. Albert Einstein (1879–1955), a German-American theoretical physicist, published his special theory of relativity in 1905, projecting the idea that time and space were not absolute, as Newton had claimed, but were relative to the observer. Einstein's general theory of relativity (1917), and his unified field theory (1931), extended his generalizations to include gravitational phenomena and electromagnetism. His work led to the successful development of the atomic bomb in 1945. These discoveries made the scientist the magician and *enfant terrible* of modern society. "His modest guesses," said Geoffrey Bruun, "abolish a plague or overturn a school of philosophy; his prescriptions bring life or death, poverty or plenty to uncomprehending millions; his sibylline equations direct the course of destiny."

Aladdin's Lamp: The New Technology. The twentieth century also marked an extraordinary development of machinery and technology, revolutionizing not only transportation and communication but also the entire social order. Such servants of man as the locomotive, steamship, automobile, and airplane were improved and developed into mechanical marvels. Engines, generators, and electrons became obedient slaves to the needs of man. The list is long: diesel crude-oil engines, motion pictures, radio, talking pictures, television, nautical gyro-compass, gyro-pilot, petroleum cracking process, televox, radar, cellophane, synthetic nitrates, nylon, precision instruments, and a host of other inventions and mechanisms. Twentieth-century man came to accept without wonder this array of mechanical marvels. The new technology was a force for both good and evil; its peacetime potentialities were enormous, but unfortunately it was utilized by dictators in drives for world power. When controlled by ambitious men, it represented a force for evil.

Age of Super-power. The new industrial machine demanded ever larger quantities of nature's energy. A huge variety of power-hungry installations consumed energy as fast as it was turned out. After World War II, coal was dethroned as king of fuels, largely because of the inconvenience in obtaining it from the ground as well as the high costs of transportation. The coal industry was revolutionized, nevertheless, in much the same way as the harvester changed farming. Additional oil was obtained by drilling under water to tap off-shore supplies. The gas industry introduced big-bore pipelines to transport its yield to metropolitan centers. The energy of river waters, rushing to the seas, was harnessed by constructing giant tunnels and dams. Most significant of all was the arrival of the age of nuclear power. In the United States the Atomic Energy Commission prepared to use nuclear energy to run electric generating stations. Like coal-fueled power plants, the atomic plants generate electricity by making steam in boilers, using it to revolve turbines, which then turn the rotors of electric generators. Experiments were begun to run power stations on solar radiation.

Wonder World of Electronics. Equally promising was the technological progress in electronics. The transistor, a revolutionary substitute for the glass vacuum tube, was invented, a tiny device that radically reduced the size and increased the effectiveness of electronic equipment. Computing machines performed prodigious mathematical feats. Work-simplification devices were developed to produce vest-pocket-size radios, electronic cooking utensils, and machines for cancer therapy. Microwave relay systems improved communications.

The Race for Space. Another aspect of the rivalry between Communist and non-Communist worlds was the rush of brilliant scientists and engineers on both sides to probe the universe. The Russians sent the first two men into orbit—Major Yuri Alekseyevitch Gagarin, who made one orbit around the earth on April 12, 1961, and Major Gherman Titov, who circled the globe seventeen and a half times in twenty-five hours starting on August 6, 1961. The first manned United States space shot was that of Navy Commander Alan B. Shepherd, Jr., on May 5, 1961; the second, of Air Force Captain Virgil I. Grissom on July 21, 1961. Both these flights were suborbital. On February 20, 1962, Marine Colonel John H. Glenn, Jr., orbited the earth three times in a space capsule. On May 15–16, 1963, Major L. Gordon Cooper made twenty-two orbits. The American launchings of men into orbit took place in the full glare of publicity, while the Russians surrounded their space probes with an air of secrecy. In June 1963 the Russians launched Valentina Tereshkova while another cosmonaut, Major Valery Bykovsky, was already in orbit. The latter stayed up for four days, twenty-three hours and six minutes, while the first woman in space, Tereshkova, nicknamed "Seagull," logged forty-eight orbits —more than all the American astronauts put together. In March 1965, a thirty-year-old Russian cosmonaut, Aleksei Leonov, took earthman's first giant step—literally—into space. A sixteen-foot cable attached to his waist, he ventured from his *Voskkod* (Sunrise) *II* into the hostile environment 110 miles above earth for ten minutes. A few days later the United States sent its Gemini spaceship into orbit with astronauts Virgil I. Grissom and John W. Young maneuvering their craft in space for the first time. In late 1965, *Gemini VII* (Frank Borman and James A. Lovell, Jr.) and *Gemini VI* (Walter Schirra and Thomas Stafford) made

Cosmonaut Gagarin, first man into space, and proudly smiling Russian Premier Khrushchev are shown against a background of cheering crowds in Red Square, 1961. International political rivalry based on scientific accomplishment becomes a major dimension of modern world affairs.

an important rendevous in space. The spacemen brought their crafts within a few feet of each other and demonstrated the practicality of space docking, a *sine qua non* for travel to the moon.

Both the United States and the U.S.S.R. instituted programs to put men on the moon. On February 3, 1966, the Russians sent their *Luna 9* spacecraft to make a semi-hard landing on the moon. On June 9, 1966, the American black-and-silver spacecraft, *Surveyor,* weighing 620 pounds, settled down softly on the flat plain of the moon's Ocean of Storms. In response to a command signal sent across 234,-000 miles of space, *Surveyor's* 22-pound television camera began to transmit to earth a rich harvest of thousands of lunar photographs. *Surveyor* pictured a rubble-strewn but reason-

ably hard and dust-free lunar surface. Clearly, these were giant steps to the goal of placing men on the surface of the moon.

March of Medicine. One by one many of the most dreaded plagues of mankind were conquered. Diseases that once threatened to decimate the population of the earth were rendered harmless. Asepsis and antisepsis, and the cultivation of serums and vaccines, cut the death-rate and led to prolongation of human life. Among recent contributions of medical science were hormone and vitamin therapies, improved anesthesia, synthesizing of new drugs (insulin, penicillin, sulfonamides and derivatives), new understanding of body metabolism, public-health developments, and increasing attention to mental ills. Modern medical research scientists, working collectively, turned their attention to such unconquered diseases as cancer, high blood pressure, muscular dystrophy, and multiple sclerosis. Typical of medical advances was the near-conquest of poliomyelitis by use of the killed-virus Salk vaccine, which was injected, and the live-virus Sabin vaccine, taken by mouth.

2. New Patterns of Thought

Philosophies of History. Despite his achievements in science, technology, and medicine, twentieth-century man remained troubled in mind and spirit. The search for the meaning of history was now beset by a feeling of pessimism. Oswald Spengler (1880–1936) voiced a gloomy prediction in his *Decline of the West* (1918–1922), a deterministic view of history, warning that the urbanization and materialism of European society would soon lead to its decay. Arnold J. Toynbee (1889–   ), English historian and educator, sought an explanation for the ills of the West in his *A Study of History* (1934–1954), a comparative study of how earlier civilizations reacted in a rhythm of challenge-and-response. Pitirim Alexandrovich Sorokin (1889–   ), Russian-born American sociologist, in his *Social and Cultural Dynamics* (1937–1941), presented an interpretation of history recognizing only a series of fluctuations between spiritual and secular eras that modern man could not hope to change. These and other views raised more speculations than they resolved.

Philosophy: Positivism and Pragmatism. Philosophers, searching always for the eternal verities, saw the necessity for proposing a fusion of philosophy and science. Positivism, stemming from Auguste Comte (1798–1857) and oriented around natural science, strove for a unified view of the world of phenomena, both physical and human, through application of methods of natural science. Positivism excluded everything but the natural phenomena or properties of knowable things. Systematized by Herbert Spencer (1820–1903) and supported by Charles Darwin (1809–1882), positivism as a philosophy continued into the

twentieth century, keeping pace with revolutionary scientific discoveries. A variation of this belief in the positive, the concrete, and the workable was pragmatism, born in the mind of William James (1842–1910) and extended by John Dewey (1859–1952). Pragmatism stressed the primacy of change, movement, and activity, the desirability of novelty, and belief in immediate experience. It urged use of a practical formula: "It's true if it works."

Pioneer Sociology. The lag between material and social progress led to an attempt to translate sociology into an exact and natural science. The Marxian theory of economic determinism, appearing in the mid-nineteenth century, became the inspiration of millions in the twentieth, while Marxists, orthodox and reformed, wrangled with religious fervor over its interpretation. Georges Sorel (1847–1922), a French engineer and social theorist, preached the dynamic activism of direct action and the general strike as the best way for the militant proletariat to seize control of society. Vilfredo Pareto (1848–1923), Italian sociologist, put forward a vigorous argument for an objective social science, denuded of value judgments and resting on the experimental methods of the natural sciences.

Emergence of a New Anti-Intellectualism. The twentieth-century trend of thinking as portrayed in philosophical systems, interpretations of history, sociology, psychology, and psychoanalysis revealed a deepening urge toward introspection. The tremendous material achievements of man in recent times were not matched by his ability to live with himself and others. Some scholars called this passionate quest for man's inner self "anti-intellectualism," or the attempt to arrive rationally at a just appreciation of the roles of rationality and non-rationality in human affairs. Fundamentally, the new approach was a protest against the over-optimism of the eighteenth-century Age of Reason, when it was believed that the aims of order, happiness, and individual freedom could and would be achieved. Anti-intellectualism looked toward these same goals, but believed that they could be attained only imperfectly and very slowly on earth. The best way, it was said, was to work patiently at building up a true social science based on the long-tried methods of cumulative knowledge.

Religion and the Collapse of Morals. The conflict between science and religion left a wide split in the mind of twentieth-century man—material expansion and moral contraction, a schism potentially as dangerous as the atom bomb. It was an old story—men failed to see, said Pascal, that "it is the heart that senses God, and not the reason." The fierce rivalries of nations, the horrors and carnage of two World Wars, the fanaticism and brutality exhibited by human beings toward one another, all these caused contemporary man to wonder whether his moral and ethical life was in danger of collapsing. Some turned to religion, others became cynical, agnostic, or atheistic. State Churches were disestablished in Soviet Russia, Hungary, Czechoslovakia, and Mexico. Anticlericalism and increasing secularization became the rule rather than the exception in a period described by religious leaders as beset by moral nihilism.

The New Education. The war of the spirit between democracies and dictatorships was reflected in education. The twentieth century saw a decline of illiteracy throughout the world, but also sharply differing attitudes as to how the young were to be trained. In an age of persisting regard for national sovereignty, educational policy was subordinated to political ideals. The democratic nations struggled to preserve the integrity of the free mind and to permit individual development without indoctrination. Under dictatorships the educational system was centralized, subordinated drastically to governmental aims, and used to indoctrinate and regiment the young into obedient tools. Generally speaking, the new education followed the political philosophy prevalent in the country concerned.

3. Psychology in the Age of Anxiety

Psychology: The Role of Behaviorism. Modern psychology developed a unitary purpose and a consistent formulation, despite the crisscrosses of opinion and the conflicts in definition and method. Psychologists no longer consider anatomical heredity to be the primary or exclusive determinant of personality. In 1913 John B. Watson (1878–1958) founded the behaviorist school, stressing environment as the more important determinant of human behavior. Ivan Petrovich Pavlov (1849–1936), a Russian psychologist trained in physiology, further developed behaviorism by demonstrating that training (conditioning) could produce automatic responses in animals. For some social scientists this meant that the environment could be manipulated to give organisms new responses. Behaviorism and reflexology were used by Communists to implement the theory of materialism. Other psychologists, in an attempt to penetrate the psyche and see it whole, turned their attention to studies in motivation, mechanisms, and organization.

Psychoanalysis: The Freudian Revolution. The search for the real inner self of man became a dominating passion among twentieth-century psychologists. Outstanding in this new quest was a Viennese physiologist and psychologist, Sigmund Freud (1856–1939), father of psychoanalysis. Freud originally designated his theory as metapsychology, "a dynamic conception which reduces mental life to the interaction of reciprocally propelling and repelling forces." The great patriarch of psychoanalysis in its early days, Freud himself was no popularizer. His books, notably *The Interpretation of Dreams* (1900) and *Three Contributions to the Sexual Theory* (1905), were far too technical for public consumption.

The Freudian vocabulary, basic in psychology, began to be used more or less accurately, outside medical circles. The following brief schematic outline defines the major terms:

Id: The huge mass of unconscious impulses acquired by the human personality from birth. It is dominated by the pleasure principle and blind, impulsive thinking.

Ego: That organized part of the id, the force of self-preservation which has been modified by the direct influence of the external world. The ego is the umpire, the governor, the guardian of the interests of the organism as a whole. It acts as a kind of honest broker between the id and the outside world.

Superego: The instrument of conscience; that part of the mental apparatus that criticizes the ego and causes pain to it whenever it tends to accept impulses emanating from it. It is a sort of inner monitor synonymous with conscience.

Libido: The dynamic expression of the sexual instinct or the energy of that instinct which deals with all that is included in the word "love" (sexual love, self-love, filial love, friendship, love for humanity, attachment to concrete objects and abstract ideals). The libido is the constructive driving force in man.

In the mentally healthy individual, the id, the ego, and the superego cooperate to keep him aware of the realities of his environment. In the neurotic individual, desires balked by

Sigmund Freud, whose name is quite familiar to the average man even though his actual theories are not.

the negative of the ego or superego are driven back into the unconscious where they continue to live. Freud's approach to therapy was to teach the patient to know what he really wants through a long, elaborate, and expensive process of psychoanalysis, helping him to understand and become aware of his bundle of confused thoughts and desires. Feelings, events, and fantasies that had been put out of the mind because they were disagreeable were replaced with acts of judgment which might result either in the acceptance or rejection of what formerly had been repudiated. (*See page 740.*)

Psychoanalysis, a specialized part of psychiatric practice, soon became a battlefield of factions. The first to break from Freud was his former pupil, Alfred Adler (1870–1937), who projected a new individual psychology, an interpretation of the interaction of the individual with society, emphasizing such dynamic units as feelings of inferiority and compensation for such inferiorities. The next schismatic was another Freudian pupil, Carl Gustav Jung (1875–1961), whose analytical psychology held that the flow of the libido is the entire system of psychic energy of which the sexual is only a part. Jung placed less stress upon sexual conflicts and substituted a theory of religious instincts for Freud's ideas about unconscious sexual love.

Other variations of Freud's theoretical and practical postulates include the work of Otto Rank (the birth of individuality); Karen Horney (abandonment of the artificial and cumbersome *libido* theory and the search instead for an understanding of people in terms of social environment and the problems which it generates); Erich Fromm (logico-philosophical foundation for the explanation of man's nature and behavior); and Harry Stack Sullivan (interpersonal relations and emphasis upon the relationship of personality to the social order). All these deviating approaches of the post-Freudians admitted the value of Freud's researches into the subconscious mind and the part played by the subconscious impulses in human thought and conduct.

Psychoanalysis became both an object of intense faith and a subject of bitter controversy. Because its subject matter was the submerged part of the human psyche, it was often attacked as a cult instead of a science, as merely another form of religion. Some physicians denounced psychoanalysis because of its lack of statistical data in the "cure" of neurosis. Others insisted that it has earned its place as a valued branch of the medical sciences. Its defenders called it the most important and most comprehensive of recent contributions in abnormal psychology. They held that, in seeking motivations in intimate primal drives and tracing their issues to the most complex of cerebral functions, Freud took a giant step in the centuries-old quest for understanding the human mind.

Nexus of History and Psychology. Not the least significant development in historical study has been a new interest and attention by the historian to the relatively new social science of psychology. During the last fifty years the scope of historical study has been extended. The traditional attention to political and military history became more comprehensive, more analytical, and was enhanced by researches into economic, social, intellectual, and scientific aspects of past development. To this "horizontal expansion" of historical interest has been added new penetration in depth into the findings of modern psychology and psychoanalysis.

This point of view was expressed in an important presidential address to the American Historical Association on December 29, 1957, by William L. Langer, Coolidge Professor of History at Harvard University. Langer called the new interest in dynamic or depth psychology and psychoanalysis the historian's "next assignment." Modern psychology, he said, is bound to play an ever-greater role in historical interpretation. He did not plead for psychoanalytical techniques *per se,* but rather for awareness by the historian of the effect of famines, plagues, wars, overcrowding, and epidemics on mass psychology. Examples may be found in Thucydides's report on the great plague of Athens in 430 B.C. or in varied treatments of the effects of the Black Death in the middle of the fourteenth century. What was

needed, in Langer's view, was more analyses of the psychic content of mass phenomena such as imperialism, nationalism, and totalitarianism. One of the most stimulating non-Marxist interpretations of imperialism, that of Joseph Schumpeter, rested squarely on a psychological base. Similarly, scholarly work on nationalism stressed the importance of psychological factors.

Certainly the nexus of history and psychoanalysis did not settle all the perplexities of the historian. Historians remained very much aware that human motivations were complex and could not be explained always in simple terms. There were no final answers to many of the riddles and enigmas of man's development. But the new stress on psychological factors undoubtedly enriched an understanding of the past. It may well be that a student reading these lines will one day project a psychological interpretation of history which will match the significance of Marx's economic interpretation of historical development.

4. Literature and the Arts

Literature: Era of Disillusionment. A mirror of the development of world society can always be seen in concurrent trends of literature. In an age of increasing materialism, with its anxieties, fears, and frustrations the creative spirit was hampered by a confusing combination of social awareness, dissent, despair, and disillusionment. After the impact of each of the World Wars there appeared literary trends characterized by a sentiment of moody resignation. The feelings of the "lost generation" after World War I were expressed by Thomas Stearns Eliot (1888–1965), whose poems showed a repugnance toward the industrial and materialistic civilization of his century. A similar disillusionment may be noted in the young writers following World War II, the new lost generation that turned to existentialism, an unsystematic conception of philosophy developed in France by Jean-Paul Sartre, (1905–   ): "We and things in general exist, and that is all there is to this absurd business of life."

When the bourgeois-dominated nineteenth

century gave way to "the century of the common man," literary artists began to attack the middle-class pattern of society. Thomas Mann (1875–1955), German novelist, denounced the decadence of the bourgeois world and the sickness of an acquisitive society. John Galsworthy (1867–1933), British novelist, portrayed the slow disintegration of a British family gradually losing its bearings and sense of security. Henrik Ibsen (1828–1906), Norwegian dramatist, brilliantly satirized the artificiality and falsity of modern society, and in a series of plays that were at first denounced as immoral, urged social reform. George Bernard Shaw (1856–1950), Irish dramatist and critic, satirically attacked the social conventions of his times and boldly pronounced himself a socialist at a time when the word was

Modern set design for an Ibsen play. The single stage setting is used for all scenes in the play as area lighting directs the attention of the audience to the sections representing forest, mountain, desert, hut, and interiors.

anathema. Stefan Zweig (1881–1942), Henri Barbusse (1874–1935), Romain Rolland (1866–1944), and Bertrand Russell (1872–   ) attacked militarism and war as a reversion to barbarism and a disgrace to the human race.

The new psychology of Freud stimulated a school of writers to dissect the human soul and to probe into the mysteries of the human mind. Marcel Proust (1871–1922), French novelist, stripped the novel of its meaningless plots and sought for psychological penetration and introspective analysis. Henry James

(1843–1916), American novelist, similarly turned to realistic psychological penetration and analysis. An Irishman, James Joyce (1882 –1941), developed a stream-of-consciousness technique, through which he attempted to throw light upon the conflict between the worlds of the intellect and the emotions. Eugene O'Neill (1888–1953), American dramatist, wrote grim and pessimistic studies of the people of his time, occasionally with mystical and religious overtones. These writers and a host of others (including Hemingway, Faulkner, Wolfe, Conrad, Hardy, Aldous Huxley, Werfel, H. G. Wells, D. H. Lawrence, Sinclair Lewis) portrayed a society in a mood of indecision, confused and bewildered, shifting in its human relations, frightened and insecure. Where eighteenth-century rationalists never doubted the eventual perfectibility of man, twentieth-century intellectuals saw human beings as aimless driftwood in a sea of troubles. It was a formidable century, they admitted, but it was burdened by increases in power and peril, by crippling anxieties and unsolved problems.

Fine Arts: Painting. Until the twentieth century the underlying motive in painting had been portrayal. The new esthetic formula of the artist matched the ferment and confusion of his times. Torn by conflicting ideas, artists agreed among themselves only in rejecting the older method of faithfully depicting nature and in searching for new modes of expression. Novel methods of painting introduced an intentional lack of traditional depiction of forms, atmosphere, and color, as well as exaggerated means of awakening the emotions. Among the most gifted of these artists were Paul Cézanne (1839–1906), who broke away from the older techniques; Camille Pissarro (1830–1903), who introduced a deliberate distortion of form; Vincent van Gogh (1853–1890), who used prodigious splashes of color in an almost barbaric display of intense emotion; and Paul Gaugin (1848–1903), who was inspired by the primitivism of the Pacific Islanders.

The search for expression went far in the work of Henri Matisse (1869–1954), who painted distorted pictures of primitive scenes but with a profusion of bold images and color-drenched canvases. Pablo Picasso (1881–   ) sought for meaning in geometrical designs. In Mexico there was a significant renaissance of mural painting, especially in the work of Diego Rivera (1886–1957) and José Clemente Orozco (1883–1949), both of whom combined Mexican Indian art with the symbolism of the machine age. Deviations of expressionism appeared in dadaism, stressing artistic free-thinking rather than logic; constructionism, a mechanistic interpretation of the machine age; surrealism, a reaction against the precision of realists; and cubism and futurism, emphasizing motion, mechanics, and energy. In the meantime, painting in Persia, Arabia, India, China, and Japan, more decorative than in the West, maintained a conventional approach.

Architecture: The New Utilitarianism. Modern architecture, with a wealth of materials from which to draw—new types of glass, reinforced concrete, steels, and alloys—was mainly utilitarian in design. The new architects relied on simplicity of line but developed its approach to a point where it could suggest grandeur. The new railroad station in Florence, Italy, the *Bauhaus* in Dessau, Germany, and the Lever Brothers building in New York all used a streamlined effect with the utmost utilization of space and economy of area. Frank Lloyd Wright (1869–1959) was the leader in the United States of functionalism, a technique seeking to escape from the old stylism and to develop an architecture suitable to the needs of modern life. Rockefeller Center, the Empire State Building, the George Washington Bridge, and an extensive series of apartment-house buildings represented a fusion of mechanical needs and the age of power.

Experimentalism in Music. The experimentalism of the scientific age brought about new developments in music. Harmonic novelties, polytonality, fixed tonality, and dissonances were used to avoid emotional elements and to concentrate more fully upon the physical impression produced by musical sounds. Much

The Bridge. Oil painting, one of five panels entitled "New York Interpreted" by Joseph Stella.

of the new music reflected the hardness and disillusionment of modern life–it rejected old standards, and indulged in a constant, almost neurotic quest for new life. Russian composers, including Igor Stravinsky, Aram Khatchaturian, Dmitri Shostakovich, and Sergei Prokofiev, sought for new forms despite curbs on artistic expression in the Soviet Union. Arnold Schoenberg, Paul Hindemith, Béla Bartók, Jean Sibelius, Ralph Vaughan Williams, George Antheil, and others attempted new musical forms, although often some of them were responsive to the spirit of nationalism. In extreme cases, melody, polyphony, and structure were simply banished as worthless. In general, there was a lack of homogeneity in modernist schools of music, as composers

sought among Asian and African peoples for inspiration and used elaborate experimentation in multiple themes and strange rhythms. The popularity of jazz, rock-and-roll, and the rhythm of Beatles may be in part accounted for by the reckless spirit of youth searching for new modes of expression.

5. Into the Seventh Decade: Retrospect and Prospect

Promise of Progress. It seemed at the opening of the twentieth century that a decent world society was in process of formation. Tremendous strides in science, industry, and communication had been made. There was hope in the minds of men of goodwill that, at long last, human beings would become aware of their common humanity and would finally reject force as inappropriate to civilized society. War, the relic of barbarism, would be banished. To paraphrase the closing sentence of *The Education of Henry Adams:* "Perhaps some day . . . for the first time since man began his education among the carnivores, [we shall] find a world that sensitive and timid natures could regard without a shudder."

Shattering Force of Nationalism. In perspective it is now clear that this favorable prognosis was shattered by the continuing system of hostile sovereign national states. Some observers believe that the modern national state is scarcely the logical political unit for organizing the economy of an industrial age; others remain suspicious of any attempt to create a world order. The extension of political authority to continental or international spheres made it necessary for individual national states to rely upon their own power and that of military alliances. Rivalries between nations became more and more pronounced. Motivated by emotional interests surviving from the past, human beings tended to forget that all men are fundamentally alike as individuals. The necessities of integral nationalism made it imperative that other nations be defeated before one could live in peace. In theory, the competition between states and coalitions could remain peaceful in the realm of politics and economics, but, in practice, war seemed to be preferable to national "humiliation."

A World Society. The transference of political sovereignty from national states to larger political units provided enormous problems for twentieth-century man. His history conditioned him to associate his material welfare and his emotional satisfactions with his national state. After World War I the bold experiment of the League of Nations disintegrated, and the nations of the world drifted back to nationalism. The tragedy of World War II drove home the idea to some observers that nationalism could not solve the difficulties of the world and that it was becoming increasingly necessary to achieve some workable form of world government. The thorny path of the United Nations has seemed to indicate that no sudden shift from the national state to world

A new view of the modern world. Based on actual pictures sent to earth from satellites in space and from the lunar surface, this representation of our planet as seen from the moon parallels in many ways the first illustration in this book (*see page 10*). Both could be entitled "Dawn of a New Era."

sovereignty can be made. Efforts to achieve a tentative regionalism, as a first step to a peaceful world society, have been made. There is some hope that the old notions of rigid sovereignty and segregation will be outgrown, and that integral nationalism will be rejected in favor of cultural nationalism with an emphasis upon tolerance and understanding of other peoples. Men of vision point out the imperative necessity for submerging selfish national feelings in the interest of a common humanity.

The Fate of Man. In contrast to the pessimism of Spengler and his fellow prophets of doom, other historians have done their best to salvage what they could of the great democratic dream of the eighteenth-century Enlightenment. "Twentieth-century man," wrote Hans Kohn, "has become less confident than his nineteenth-century ancestor was. He has witnessed the dark powers of history in his own experience. Things which seemed to belong to the past have reappeared: fanatical faith, infallible leaders, slavery and massacres, the uprooting of whole populations, ruthlessness and barbarism. But against all expectations of the totalitarians, by the middle of the twentieth century, Western civilization has proved its power of resistance against fanatic ideologies."

A similar refusal to be overwhelmed by cynicism may be noted in the penetrating ideas of an able University of Chicago historian, William H. McNeill. In his book, *Past and Future,* McNeill traces a basic pattern in world history in two psychological tendencies among human beings—one toward intellectual innovation and the other toward habit, custom, and routine. There have been four critical innovations in human history, each accompanied by violent, revolutionary change—the pedestrian epoch, the equestrian epoch, the epoch of ocean shipping, and the epoch of mechanical transport. In the twentieth century man has been once again involved in revolutionary changes in transport and communication. The United States and the Soviet Union are both heads of transnational groups of states, each of which might eventually do for the whole world what Rome did for the Western world in the first century A.D. McNeill expresses the hope that this unifying power will be the United States of America, and that it will use its power to further democratic, liberal traditions stemming from the Enlightenment.

Let us hope, then, that despite the fears and anxieties of the present there may be a better future. It is possible that a new era of Western civilization, distinguished by close collaboration between Western Europe and North America, might emerge beyond the stage of xenophobic nationalism, with its irrational fear of the stranger. The intense faith of Western man in liberty can survive the unpleasant troubles of the present. In the words of Winston Churchill: "It may well be that the lively sense of universal brotherhood and of the bright hopes of the future may stir in humanity those qualities which will enable it to survive the dread agencies which have fallen into its as yet untutored hands."

⤙ KEY DOCUMENT ⤚

THE UNIVERSAL DECLARATION OF THE RIGHTS OF MAN, DECEMBER 1948

Courtesy of the United Nations.

THE GENERAL ASSEMBLY of the United Nations in December 1948, without a dissenting vote (48 voting, 8 abstaining), adopted a Universal Declaration of the Rights of Man, the first attempt in history to set down the minimum rights which every person should enjoy. The first ten of the thirty articles follow.

ARTICLE 1. All human beings are born free and equal in dignity and rights. They are endowed with reason and conscience and should act toward one another in a spirit of brotherhood.

ARTICLE 2. (1) Everyone is entitled to all rights and freedoms set forth in this declaration, without distinction of any kind, such as race, color, sex, language, religion, political or other opinion, national or social origin, property, birth or other status.

(2) Furthermore, no distinction shall be made on the basis of the political, jurisdictional or international status of the country or territory to which a person belongs, whether this territory be an independent, Trust, Non-Self-Governing territory, or under any other limitation of sovereignty.

ARTICLE 3. Everyone has the right to life, liberty, and security of the person.

ARTICLE 4. No one shall be held in slavery or servitude; slavery and the slave trade shall be prohibited in all their forms.

ARTICLE 5. No one shall be subjected to torture or to cruel inhuman or degrading treatment or punishment.

ARTICLE 6. Everyone has the right of recognition everywhere as a person before the law.

ARTICLE 7. All are equal before the law and are entitled without any discrimination to equal protection before the law. All are entitled to equal protection against any discrimination in violation of this Declaration and against any incitement to such discrimination.

ARTICLE 8. Everyone has the right to an effective remedy by the competent national tribunals for acts violating the fundamental rights granted to him by the constitution or by law.

ARTICLE 9. No one shall be subjected to arbitrary arrest, detention or exile.

ARTICLE 10. Everyone is entitled in full equality to a fair and public hearing by an independent and impartial tribunal in the determination of his rights and obligations and of any criminal charge against him.

❧{ HISTORICAL INTERPRETATION }❧

CRANE BRINTON ON FREUD AND HUMAN HISTORY

Crane Brinton, "Freud and Human History," in *The Saturday Review*, May 5, 1956, pp. 8–9, 35–36. By permission of Crane Brinton and *The Saturday Review*.

THE IMPACT of Sigmund Freud before 1914 was small, but after World War I came the full impression of his influence. Some historians even refer to current times as the Freudian Age, as past observers spoke of the Age of Socrates or the Age of Newton. Some praise him as one of the great thinkers of history, others see him as a disruptive thinker who believed man and society to be totally irreconcilable. In the following essay, Crane Brinton, distinguished professor of history at Harvard University, presents an assessment of Freud's place in modern intellectual history.

I should like to attempt a brief description of the world-view (there really is no substitute for that blessed German word *Weltanschuung*) most congruous with Freud's place in Western thought. Now in spite of the romanticists' attempt to unseat eighteenth-century Right Reason with appeals to the Oversoul, to *Vernunft*—the transcendental in us all—no one had yet really shown ordinary educated men in 1900 that conscious analytical thought is under many circumstances impossible. This Freud really did achieve, build-

ing on the work of his predecessors as a scientist must and summarizing the familiar sequence of purely hysterical symptoms, hypnosis, Charcot, Breuer, and so on to the famous tripartite map of the mind as id, ego, and superego. . . . Freud concluded that what really kept men from straight thinking was not, to use awkward but clear terms, the macro-environment of Church, State, Society but the micro-environment of nursery, family, peer-group, school, neighborhood. Reform of these last was clearly, even to the most convinced environmentalists, a formidable task.

It came to seem to Freud a very hard task indeed, an impossible one in terms of a human lifetime. But it did not seem an impossible task to free certain individuals from these deeply-rooted environmental evils. Freud was at bottom a good child of the eighteenth century. He was no optimist, but neither was that misplaced Jansenist the Marquis de Condorcet. Freud did believe that the individual under psychoanalysis and with due guidance could *think* his way out of a bad environment and into happiness here on earth. The process was longer, harder, and above all more expensive than Condorcet had dreamed. But the neurotic patient whose analysis has been successful has learned the truth, and the truth has made him free.

Freud is then at bottom one of ours. He is, to use Disraeli's famous phrase quite without irony, on the side of the angels—somewhat Unitarian if not actually positivist angels, it is true, but still angels. He does not urge us—nor did he urge his patients—to think with our blood, to follow our id, libido, or unconscious as the true guide, to kick over the traces. He was not even very romantic, as scientists go. His pessimism, which was very real and very profound, had a kind of folk background of common sense and even good humor. It was nothing like the pessimism of a Kierkegaard or a Kafka, both of which psychotics the good doctor would have thought of as almost too far gone for psychoanalytical saving. Freud wanted the decencies, the nineteenth-century decencies. . . .

For the pure orthodox of the tradition of the Enlightenment any attempt to question the dogma of the natural goodness and reasonableness of man is of course heresy. And, in a narrow way, the orthodox here is not without some logical justification. Anti-democrats and anti-parliamentarians have now for years been able to get ammunition from William James, Bergson, Graham Wallas, Walter Bagehot, who were basically "liberals," as well as from ambivalent thinkers like Nietzsche and Mosca and from firm anti-democrats like Carlyle, Wagner, Pareto—and Mussolini and Hitler themselves. In fact, one may risk the statement that some of their best ammunition came from some of the liberals. Freud, for whom the rationalist and associationist psychology of the Enlightenment was simply wrong, as Ptolemy was for Copernicus and Galileo simply wrong, has also provided ammunition to those who want to do away with democracy.

Yet I do not think that in the long run the purely orthodox democrat in the tradition of the Enlightenment has a leg to stand on here. If democracy cannot adapt itself to the implications of Freud's scientific achievements then by the standards of its own basic sources it has failed. This is the real paradox: that Freud the real scientist (this does not mean he was infallibly right), whose findings seem to challenge basic democratic beliefs in the nature of man, is a far better guide for us than, say, Marx the pseudo-scientist (this does not mean he was always wrong), whose life was honestly dedicated to an attempt to gain for all men the democratic decencies so far denied to so many.

For though the Freudian ways of the mind—id, ego, superego—may one day seem quite absurd, though much of the particulars of his science may be—indeed almost certainly will be—quite out of date quite quickly, what may with some exaggeration be called his "discovery" of the unconscious mind is a genuine scientific achievement on a par, say, with Harvey's discovery that the heart is a pump. We can never go back to mind as Descartes, the philosopher, or even Locke and Condillac, understood mind. We can of course always go back to mind as St. Thomas Aquinas or Descartes the theologian understood it, but that has nothing directly to do with the physiological and psychological sciences.

❧ TEN BASIC BOOKS ❧

THE MIND OF CONTEMPORARY MAN

1. Bell, Daniel, *The End of Anxiety* (Glencoe, Ill., 1960).
2. Berkner, L. V., and Hugh Odishaw, *Science in Space* (New York, 1961).

3. Cook, Robert C., *Human Fertility: The Modern Dilemma* (New York, 1951).

4. Herz, John H., *International Politics in the Atomic Age* (New York, 1959, R. 1962).†

5. Huxley, Julian, *On Living in a Revolution: A Biologist Looks at Man,* 3rd ed. (New York, 1944).

6. Kahn, Herman, *On Thermonuclear War* (Princeton, N. J., 1960).

7. LaPiere, Richard, *The Freudian Ethic* (New York, 1959).

8. Laves, Walter H. C., and Charles A. Thomson, *UNESCO: Purpose, Progress, Prospects* (Bloomington, Ind., 1957).

9. Myrdal, Gunnar, *Rich Lands and Poor* (New York, 1958).

10. Piel, Gerard, *Science in the Cause of Man* (New York, 1961).†

CHRONOLOGY

Chronology

1438–1918: The Hapsburg Emperors

c. 1450: Johann Gutenberg (1400?–1468) prints with movable type

1453: Fall of Constantinople to Turks

1485–1603: Tudor dynasty, England

1492: Discovery of America by Christopher Columbus (1451–1506)

1492: Expulsion of Jews and Moors from Spain

1495: "Last Supper," Leonardo da Vinci (1452–1519)

1497–1498: Voyage of Vasco da Gama (1469?–1524) to India around Cape of Good Hope

c. 1500: Beginning of "High Renaissance" in Italy

1508–1512: Sistine ceiling, Michelangelo Buonarotti (1475–1564)

1509: *In Praise of Folly*, Desiderius Erasmus (c. 1466–1536)

1511: "School of Athens," Raphael (1483–1520)

1513: *The Prince*, Niccolò Machiavelli (1469–1527)

1516: *Utopia*, Sir Thomas More (1478–1535)

1517: *95 Theses*, Martin Luther (1483–1546); beginning of Reformation

1519–1522: Circumnavigation of globe, Ferdinand Magellan (1480?–1521)

1521: Diet of Worms, Germany

1523: Huldreich Zwingli (1484–1531) establishes Reformation in Zurich

1524: Revolt of peasants, Germany

1526: "Four Apostles," Albrecht Durer (1471–1528)

1529: Siege of Vienna by Turks

c. 1530: *De Revolutionibus Orbium Coelestium* (published 1543), Nicholas Copernicus (1473–1543)

1533: *Pantagruel* and *Gargantua* (1535), François Rabelais (1494?–1553)

1534: Act of Supremacy, England

1534: Ignatius Loyola (1491–1556) founds Society of Jesus

c. 1536: Hans Holbein the Younger (1491?–1543) court painter to Henry VIII

1536: *Institutes*, John Calvin (1509–1564)

1543: *De Humani Corporis Fabrica*, Andreas Vesalius (1514–1564)

1545–1563: Council of Trent; the Counter-Reformation

1546–1547: Schmalkaldic War

1555: Religious Peace of Augsburg

1558: England loses last Continental possession (Calais)

1562–1598: Religious wars with Huguenots, France

1568–1648: The Netherlands battle Spanish occupation

1571: Battle of Lepanto

1572: Massacre of St. Bartholomew's Day, France

1576: Tycho Brahe (1546–1601) establishes observatory on island of Hven

1579: Union of Utrecht, Netherlands

1582: Gregorian calendar

1588: Defeat of Spanish Armada

1589–1792: Bourbon rulers, France

1597: *Essays*, Francis Bacon (1561–1626)

1598: Edict of Nantes, France

1600: East India Company established, England

c. 1603: *Hamlet*, William Shakespeare (1564–1616)

1604–1613: Time of Troubles, Russia

1605: *Don Quixote*, Miguel de Cervantes (1547–1616)

1607–1733: Thirteen English colonies
founded in North America

1611: King James' version of the Bible

1612: Last heretic burned, England

1616: Circulation of blood,
William Harvey (1578–1657)

1618–1648: Thirty Years' War

1619: *On the Harmony of the World,*
Johannes Kepler (1571–1630)

1620: Plymouth Colony in America

1624–1642: Cardinal Richelieu
(1585–1642) chief minister of France

1625: *On the Law of War and Peace,*
Hugo Grotius (1583–1645)

1628: Petition of Right, England

1632: *Dialogue Concerning the Two
Systems of the World,* Galileo
(1564–1642)

1636: Harvard College established,
America

1637: *Discourse on Method,*
René Descartes (1596–1650)

1640–1660: Long Parliament, England

1642: "The Night Watch," Rembrandt
(1606–1669)

1642–1648: Puritan rebellion and
Civil War, England

1643–1661: Cardinal Mazarin, France

1648: End of Thirty Years' War;
Peace of Westphalia

1649: Execution of Charles I

1649–1653: The Commonwealth, England

1650–1800: Age of Reason

1651: *Leviathan,* Thomas Hobbes
(1588–1679)

1653–1660: Protectorate, England

1660: Restoration of the Stuarts, England

1661–1715: Age of Louis XIV, France

1665: Plague in London

1666: Great Fire in London

1667: *Paradise Lost,* John Milton
(1608–1674)

1670's: Whigs and Tories firmly

established, England

1677: *Ethics,* Baruch Spinoza (1632–1677)

1679: Habeas Corpus Act, England

1685: Revocation of Edict of Nantes,
France

1687: *Principia,* Sir Isaac Newton
(1642–1727)

1688: Bloodless Revolution, England

1689: Bill of Rights, England

1690: *Essay Concerning Human
Understanding,* John Locke (1632–1704)

1697: Russia expands contacts with West

1700–1931: Spanish Bourbons

1700–1721: Great Northern War

1701–1714: War of Spanish Succession

1701–1918: Hohenzollern kings,
Prussia

1701: Act of Settlement, England

1705: Steam engine, Thomas Newcomen
(1663–1729)

1707: England and Scotland united

1713: End of War of Spanish Succession;
Treaty of Utrecht

1714: Beginning of Hanover dynasty,
England

1714: *Monadology,* Gottfried von Leibnitz
(1646–1716)

1719: South Sea Bubble

1729: *St. Matthew Passion,* J. S. Bach,
(1685–1750)

1733: Fly shuttle, John Kay (d. 1764)

1733–1738: War of Polish Succession

1738: End of War of Polish Succession;
Treaty of Vienna

1740–1748:War of Austrian Succession

1740–1790: Height of Age of
Enlightenment

1748: *Spirit of Laws,* Charles
Montesquieu (1689–1755)

1748: End of War of Austrian Succession;
Treaty of Aix-la-Chapelle

c. 1750: Beginning of Industrial
Revolution

1751–1772: *Encyclopedia,* Denis Diderot (1713–1784)

1756–1763: Seven Years' War

1762: *Contrat social,* Jean Jacques Rousseau (1712–1778)

1763: End of Seven Years' War; Peace of Paris

1764: *Philosophical Dictionary,* Voltaire (1694–1778)

1765: Stamp Act, Great Britain and America

1769: Steam engine, James Watt (1736–1819)

1772: First partition of Poland

1776: *Wealth of Nations,* Adam Smith (1723–1790)

1776: American Declaration of Independence

1779: Spinning "mule," Samuel Crompton (1753–1827)

1781: *Critique of Pure Reason,* Immanuel Kant (1724–1804)

c. 1784: "Oath of the Horatii," Jacques Louis David (1748–1825)

1787: *Don Giovanni,* Wolfgang Amadeus Mozart (1756–1791)

1788: First issue of *The Times* of London

1789: Beginning of the French Revolution; Fall of the Bastille

1789: Declaration of the Rights of Man and Citizen, France

1790: Civil Constitution of the Clergy, France

1790: First iron ship

1791–1792: Legislative Assembly, France

1792–1799: First French Republic (National Convention, 1792–1795; Directory, 1795–1799)

1793: Second partition of Poland

1793–1794: Reign of Terror, France

1793: Cotton gin, Eli Whitney (1765–1825)

1795: Third partition of Poland

1795: Stock-breeding experiments, Robert Blakewell (1725–1795)

1796: *Age of Reason,* Thomas Paine (1737–1809)

1798: *Essay on Population,* Thomas Malthus (1766–1834)

1798: *Lyrical Ballads,* Samuel Taylor Coleridge (1772–1834) and William Wordsworth (1770–1850)

1799–1804: Consulate, France

1801: Concordat between Napoleon I and Pope Pius VII

1802: Napoleon named consul for life

1804: Coronation of Napoleon I

1804: Third symphony (*Eroica*), Ludwig van Beethoven (1770–1827)

1804–1814: [First] Empire, France

1805: Atomic theory, John Dalton (1766–1844)

1806: End of Holy Roman Empire

1806–1812: Napoleon's Continental System

1806–1825: Independence movements in Latin America

1807: Peace of Tilsit (France, Russia, Prussia)

1808: *Faust,* Part I, Johann Wolfgang von Goethe (1749–1832)

1812–1814: War of 1812

1812–1816: *Logik,* Georg Wilhelm Friedrich Hegel (1770–1831)

1814: End of War of 1812; Treaty of Ghent

1815: End of the Napoleonic wars; Congress of Vienna

1815–1848: Era of Metternich

1815: Holy Alliance, signed by all European rulers except the English king, the Turkish sultan, and the pope

1815: Quadruple Alliance (England, Austria, Prussia, Russia)

1818: Congress of Aix-la-Chapelle

1819: "The Liberator," Simón Bolívar

(1783–1830), wins Colombian
independence

1819: Six Acts, Great Britain

1819: *The World as Will and Ideas,*
Arthur Schopenhauer (1788–1860)

1819: Carlsbad Decrees, Germany

1819–1871: *Zollverein* (German customs
union)

1820: Congress of Troppau

1821: Greek Revolution

1821: Congress of Laibach

1822: Congress of Verona

1823: Monroe Doctrine, United States

1825: World's first railway line, England

1828–1829: Catholic Emancipation Act,
England

1830: Revolutions of 1830

1830: *Hernani,* Victor Hugo (1802–1885)

1830: Separation of Belgium and Holland

1832: First English Reform Bill

1833: Abolition of slavery, British Empire

1834: Reaper, Cyrus Hall McCormick
(1809–1884)

c. 1840: "Entrance of the Crusaders into
Constantinople," Eugène Delacroix
(1798–1863)

1840: *Organization of Labor,* Louis Blanc
(1811–1882)

1841: *National System of Political
Economy,* Friedrich List (1789–1846)

1844: First telegraph message, Samuel
B. Morse (1791–1872)

1848: *Communist Manifesto,* Karl Marx
(1818–1883) and Friedrich Engels
(1820–1895)

1848: Frankfurt National Assembly,
Germany

1848: Revolutions of 1848

1848–1874: *Der Ring des Nibelungen,*
Richard Wagner (1813–1883)

1848–1852: Second Republic, France

1852–1870: Second Empire, France

1853–1856: Crimean War

1854–1868: Opening of Japan to West

1854–1871: Wars of national consolidation

1855: Steel process, Sir Henry Bessemer
(1813–1898)

1857: *Madame Bovary,* Gustave Flaubert
(1821–1880)

1859: *Origin of Species,* Charles Darwin
(1809–1882)

1859–1870: Unification of Italy

1861: Emancipation of serfs, Russia

1861–1865: United States Civil War

1862: Machine gun, Richard Gatling
(1818–1903)

1863: "Déjeuner sur l'herbe," Edouard
Manet (1832–1883)

1863: Emancipation of slaves, United
States

1864: Syllabus of Modern Errors,
Pope Pius IX

1864: War between Prussia and Denmark

1864–1871: Unification of Germany

1865: Law of heredity, Gregor Johann
Mendel (1822–1884)

1866: Seven Weeks' War

1866: *War and Peace,* Leo Tolstoy
(1828–1910)

1866: Transatlantic cable

1867: North German Confederation

1867: Second English Reform Bill

1867: *Ausgleich* (political and commercial
union of Austria and Hungary)

1867: *Das Kapital,* Karl Marx

1869: Opening of Suez Canal; shares
owned by private, mostly French,
investors (56%) and Khedive Ismail of
Egypt (44%) who sold his holdings to
British government (1875)

1870–1871: Franco-Prussian War

1870–1914: The Third Republic, France

1871: Periodic Table of Elements,
Dmitri Mendeleyev (1834–1907)

1871: Paris Commune

1871–1883: Bismarck's *Kulturkampf*

1871–1918: German Empire

1876: Telephone, Alexander Graham Bell (1847–1922)

1876–1886: Four symphonies, Johannes Brahms (1833–1897)

1877–1878: Russo-Turkish War

1878: End of Russo-Turkish War; Congress of Berlin

1879: *A Doll's House*, Henrik Ibsen (1828–1906)

1880–1914: Height of Imperialism

1881–1891: Irish Acts, Great Britain

1882: Triple Alliance, Italy, Germany, Austria

1883: *Also Sprach Zarathustra*, Friedrich Wilhelm Nietzsche (1844–1900)

1883: Fabian Society, England

1884: Third English Reform Bill

1884–1886: "The Burghers of Calais," Auguste Rodin (1840–1917)

1885: Vaccination against rabies, Louis Pasteur (1822–1895)

1885: *Germinal*, Emile Zola (1840–1902)

1886–1891: Boulanger Affair, France

1887: Reinsurance Treaty, Russia and Germany

1889: *Symphony No. 1*, Gustav Mahler (1860–1911)

1891: *Tess of the D'Urbervilles*, Thomas Hardy (1840–1928)

1894–1895: Sino-Japanese War

1894–1906: Dreyfus Affair, France

1895: Wireless telegraphy, Guglielmo Marconi (1874–1937)

1898: Isolation of radium, Pierre (1859–1906) and Marie (1867–1934) Curie

1899: (First) Hague Peace Conference

1900: Boxer Rebellion, China

1900: *The Interpretation of Dreams*, Sigmund Freud (1856–1939)

1901: Taff Vale decision, England

1902: Anglo-Japanese Alliance

1903: First successful airplane flight, Wilbur (1867–1912) and Orville (1871–1948) Wright

1904: *Entente cordiale*, England and France

1904–1905: Russo-Japanese War

1905: Revolution, Russia

1905: Theory of Relativity, Albert Einstein (1879–1955)

1906: Trade Disputes Bill, England

1907: Triple Entente, Russia, France, England

1907: Second Hague Peace Conference

1909: Budget of 1909, England

1909: *Elektra*, Richard Strauss (1864–1949)

1910: Formation of Union of South Africa

1910: *The Firebird*, Igor Stravinsky (1882–   )

1911: Parliamentary Act of 1911, England

1912–1913: Balkan Wars

1914–1918: World War I

1917: Bolshevik Revolution, Russia

1918–1920: Great Civil War, Russia

1918–1922: *Decline of the West*, Oswald Spengler (1880–1936)

1918: Woodrow Wilson's Fourteen Points

1919: Mahatma Gandhi (1869–1948) organizes Satyagraha (passive resistance), India

1919: End of World War I; Treaty of Versailles

1919: *Love for Three Oranges*, Serge Prokofief (1891–1953)

1919–1933: Weimar Republic, Germany

1919–1946: League of Nations

1922: *The Waste Land*, T. S. Eliot (1888–1966)

1922: *Ulysses*, James Joyce (1882–1941)

1922: Establishment of Irish Free State

1922: Establishment of U.S.S.R.

1924: *Mein Kampf*, Adolf Hitler (1889–1945)

1924: Dawes Plan for German reparation payments

1925: Locarno Treaties

1928: *A la recherche du temps perdu* (final volume published), Marcel Proust (1871–1922)

1929: Young Plan for German reparation payments

1929: Beginning of Great Depression

1931: "Persistence of Memory," Salvador Dali (1904–   )

1933: Hitler becomes chancellor in Germany

1934–1954: *A Study of History,* Arnold J. Toynbee (1889–   )

1936: Rhineland reoccupied by Germany

1936: Great purges, Russia

1936: *General Theory of Employment,* John Maynard Keynes (1883–1946)

1936: Civil War, Spain

1937: "Guernica," Pablo Picasso (1881–   )

1938: *Anschluss,* Germany and Austria

1938: Appeasement at Munich

1939: German invasion of Poland

1939: Atomic fission

1939–1945: World War II

1940: Fall of France

1940: Battle of Britain

1941: German invasion of Soviet Union

1941: Pearl Harbor

1943: German surrender at Stalingrad

1943: *Being and Nothingness,* Jean Paul Sartre (1905–   )

1944: D-Day; Allied landings in Normandy (June)

1945: *Peter Grimes,* Benjamin Britten (1913–   )

1945: Yalta Conference

1945: V-E Day (May)

1945: Atomic bomb on Hiroshima and Nagasaki (August); V-J Day (September)

1945: Formation of the United Nations

1946–1958: Fourth French Republic

1946: Winston Churchill makes "Iron Curtain" speech

1947: Division of Indian subcontinent to form dominions of India and Pakistan

1947: Truman Doctrine for containment of communism

1947: Marshall Plan for rebuilding European economies

1948: Republic of Ireland officially proclaimed

1948: Founding of Israel

1948–1949: Berlin blockade and airlift

1949: North Atlantic Treaty Organization

1949: Council for Mutual Economic Assistance (Comecon)

1949: Establishment of People's Republic of China

1950–1953: Korean War

1952: European Coal and Steel Community

1955: Salk Polio vaccine

1955: Warsaw Treaty Organization

1956: Hungarian and Polish uprisings

1956: Suez Canal crisis

1957: European Economic Community (Common Market)

1957: First earth satellite, U.S.S.R.

1957: *Doctor Zhivago,* Boris Pasternak (1890–1960)

1959: Cuban Revolution

1961: First man in space, U.S.S.R.

1961: Berlin Wall

1962: Opening of Twenty-first Ecumenical Council

1962: Beginning of Sino-Soviet rift

1963: Partial Nuclear Test Ban Treaty

1964: Atomic bomb, China

1966: Escalated war in Vietnam

1966: U.N. resolution barring weapons from moon and outer space

1967: Israeli-Arab War

APPENDICES

1. Rulers and Regimes in the Principal European Countries Since 1500

HOLY ROMAN EMPIRE

Date of Rule	Ruler	Lineage
1493–1519	Maximilian I	Hapsburg
1519–1556	Charles V	Hapsburg
1558–1564	Ferdinand I	Hapsburg
1564–1576	Maximilian II	Hapsburg
1576–1612	Rudolph II	Hapsburg
1612–1619	Matthias	Hapsburg
1619–1637	Ferdinand II	Hapsburg
1637–1657	Ferdinand III	Hapsburg
1658–1705	Leopold I	Hapsburg
1705–1711	Joseph I	Hapsburg
1711–1740	Charles VI	Hapsburg
1742–1745	Charles VII	Bavaria
1745–1765	Francis I	Lorraine
1765–1790	Joseph II	Hapsburg-Lorraine
1790–1792	Leopold II	Hapsburg-Lorraine
1792–1806	Francis II (Francis I, Emperor of Austria, after 1804	Hapsburg-Lorraine

AUSTRIA

Date of Rule	Ruler	Lineage
1276–1806	Part of Holy Roman Empire	
1804–1835	Francis I	Hapsburg-Lorraine
1835–1848	Ferdinand I	Hapsburg-Lorraine
1848–1916	Francis Joseph I (also King of Hungary after 1867)	Hapsburg-Lorraine
1916–1918	Charles I	Hapsburg-Lorraine
1918–1938	First Republic	
1938–1945	*Anschluss* with Germany	
1945–	Second Republic	

FRANCE

Date of Rule	Ruler	Lineage
1461–1483	Louis XI	Valois
1483–1498	Charles VIII	Valois
1498–1515	Louis XII	Valois

1515–1547	Francis I	Valois
1547–1559	Henry II	Valois
1559–1560	Francis II	Valois
1560–1574	Charles IX	Valois
1574–1589	Henry III	Valois
1589–1610	Henry IV	Bourbon
1610–1643	Louis XIII	Bourbon
1643–1715	Louis XIV	Bourbon
1715–1774	Louis XV	Bourbon
1774–1792	Louis XVI	Bourbon
1792–1799	First Republic	
1792–1795	National Convention	
1795–1799	The Directory	
1799–1804	The Consulate	
1804–1814	Napoleon I (First Empire)	Bonaparte
1814–1824	Louis XVIII	Bourbon
1824–1830	Charles X	Bourbon
1830–1848	Louis Philippe	Bourbon
1848–1852	Second Republic	
1852–1870	Napoleon III (Second Empire)	Bonaparte
1870–1940	Third Republic	
1940–1944	Vichy Regime	
1945–1946	Provisional Government	
1946–1958	Fourth Republic	
1959–	Fifth Republic	

ENGLAND (GREAT BRITAIN, from 1603)

Date of Rule	Ruler	Lineage
1485–1509	Henry VII	Tudor
1509–1547	Henry VIII	Tudor
1547–1553	Edward VI	Tudor
1553–1558	Mary I	Tudor
1558–1603	Elizabeth I	Tudor
1603–1625	James I	Stuart
1625–1649	Charles I	Stuart
1649–1653	The Commonwealth	
1653–1658	Oliver Cromwell (The Protectorate)	
1658–1659	Richard Cromwell (The Protectorate)	
1660–1685	Charles II	Stuart
1685–1688	James II	Stuart
1689–1702	William III and Mary II (d.1694)	Stuart
1702–1714	Anne	Stuart
1714–1727	George I	Hanover

1727–1760	George II	Hanover
1760–1820	George III	Hanover
1820–1830	George IV	Hanover
1830–1837	William IV	Hanover
1837–1901	Victoria	Hanover
1901–1910	Edward VII	Saxe-Coburg
1910–1936	George V	Windsor
1936	Edward VIII	Windsor
1936–1952	George VI	Windsor
1952–	Elizabeth II	Windsor

PRUSSIA

Date of Rule	Ruler	Lineage
1640–1688	Frederick William, the Great Elector of Brandenburg	Hohenzollern
1688–1713	Frederick I (Frederick III, Elector of Brandenburg until 1701)	Hohenzollern
1713–1740	Frederick William I	Hohenzollern
1740–1786	Frederick II, the Great	Hohenzollern
1786–1797	Frederick William II	Hohenzollern
1797–1840	Frederick William III	Hohenzollern
1840–1861	Frederick William IV	Hohenzollern

GERMANY

Date of Rule	Ruler	Lineage
881–1806	Part of Holy Roman Empire (The First Reich)	
1806–1813	Part of Confederation of the Rhine	
1815–1866	Part of German Confederation (*Bund*)	
1866–1871	Part of North German Confederation (*Bund*)	
1871–1919	The German Empire (The Second Reich)	
1871–1888	William I, Emperor (King of Prussia, 1861–1871)	Hohenzollern
1888	Frederick III	Hohenzollern
1888–1918	William II	Hohenzollern
1919–1933	Weimar Republic	
1933–1945	Adolf Hitler (The Third Reich)	
1945–1949	Allied Occupation	
1949–	Federal Republic of [West] Germany and [East] German Democratic Republic	

ITALY

Date of Rule	Ruler	Lineage
1861–1878	Victor Emmanuel II (King of Sardinia, 1849–1878)	Savoy
1878–1900	Humbert I	Savoy
1900–1946	Victor Emmanuel III	Savoy
1922–1943	Benito Mussolini, Premier	
1946	Humbert II	Savoy
1946–	Republic of Italy	

RUSSIA

Date of Rule	Ruler	Lineage
1462–1505	Ivan III, the Great	Rurik
1505–1533	Basil III	Rurik
1533–1584	Ivan IV, the Terrible	Rurik
1584–1598	Feodor I	Rurik
1598–1605	Boris Godunov	Rurik
1604–1613	Time of Troubles	
1605	Feodor II	Rurik
1605–1606	Dmitri	Rurik
1606–1610	Basil (IV) Shuiski	Rurik
1610–1613	Interregnum	
1613–1645	Michael	Romanov
1645–1676	Alexis	Romanov
1676–1682	Feodor III	Romanov
1682–1689	Ivan V and Peter I	Romanov
1689–1725	Peter I, the Great	Romanov
1725–1727	Catherine I	Romanov
1727–1730	Peter II	Romanov
1730–1740	Anna	Romanov
1740–1741	Ivan VI	Romanov
1741–1762	Elizabeth	Romanov
1762	Peter III	Romanov
1762–1796	Catherine II, the Great	Romanov
1796–1801	Paul I	Romanov
1801–1825	Alexander I	Romanov
1825–1855	Nicholas I	Romanov
1855–1881	Alexander II	Romanov
1881–1894	Alexander III	Romanov
1894–1917	Nicholas II	Romanov
1917–1922	Provisional Government and Communist Revolution	
1922–	Union of Soviet Socialist Republics	

SPAIN

Date of Rule	Ruler	Lineage
1474–1504	Ferdinand of Aragon (King of Castile as Ferdinand V, joint ruler with Isabella; King of Aragon as Ferdinand II, 1479–1516) and Isabella of Castile	
1504–1506	Castile: Philip I and Juana; Ferdinand II (of Aragon), Regent	Hapsburg
1506–1516	Castile: Charles I; Ferdinand II, Regent	Hapsburg
1516–1556	Charles I (Charles V, Holy Roman Emperor after 1519)	Hapsburg
1556–1598	Philip II	Hapsburg
1598–1621	Philip III	Hapsburg
1621–1665	Philip IV	Hapsburg
1665–1700	Charles II	Hapsburg
1700–1724	Philip V	Bourbon
1724	Louis I	Bourbon
1724–1746	Philip V	Bourbon
1746–1759	Ferdinand VI	Bourbon
1759–1788	Charles III	Bourbon
1788–1808	Charles IV	Bourbon
1808	Ferdinand VII	Bourbon
1808–1813	Joseph I	Bonaparte
1813–1833	Ferdinand VII (restored)	Bourbon
1833–1868	Isabella II	Bourbon
1868–1871	Provisional Government	
1871–1873	Amadeo I	Savoy
1873–1874	First Republic	
1874–1885	Alphonso XII	Bourbon
1886–1931	Alphonso XIII	Bourbon
1932–1939	Second Republic	
1939–	Franco Regime	

II. The Papacy Since 1458

Pius II (1458–1464)
Paul II (1464–1471)
Sixtus IV (1471–1484)
Innocent VIII (1484–1492)
Alexander VI (1492–1503)
Pius III (1503)
Julius II (1503–1513)
Leo X (1513–1521)
Adrian VI (1522–1523)
Clement VII (1523–1534)
Paul III (1534–1549)
Julius III (1550–1555)
Marcellus II (1555)
Paul IV (1555–1559)
Pius IV (1559–1565)
Pius V (1566–1572)
Gregory XIII (1572–1585)
Sixtus V (1585–1590)
Urban VII (1590)
Gregory XIV (1590–1591)
Innocent IX (1591)
Clement VIII (1592–1605)
Leo XI (1605)
Paul V (1605–1621)
Gregory XV (1621–1623)
Urban VIII (1623–1644)
Innocent X (1644–1655)

Alexander VII (1655–1667)
Clement IX (1667–1669)
Clement X (1670–1676)
Innocent XI (1676–1689)
Alexander VIII (1689–1691)
Innocent XII (1691–1700)
Clement XI (1700–1721)
Innocent XIII (1721–1724)
Benedict XIII (1724–1730)
Clement XII (1730–1740)
Benedict XIV (1740–1758)
Clement XIII (1758–1769)
Clement XIV (1769–1774)
Pius VI (1775–1799)
Pius VII (1800–1823)
Leo XII (1823–1829)
Pius VIII (1829–1830)
Gregory XVI (1831–1846)
Pius IX (1846–1878)
Leo XIII (1878–1903)
Pius X (1903–1914)
Benedict XV (1914–1922)
Pius XI (1922–1939)
Pius XII (1939–1958)
John XXIII (1958–1963)
Paul VI (1963–   )

III. Principal International Organizations and Agreements Since 1944

1944

BENELUX ECONOMIC UNION
Belgium
The Netherlands
Luxemburg

1945

UNITED NATIONS: The following European governments are not members:
German Federal Republic (Bonn Republic)
German Democratic Republic (East Germany)
Liechtenstein
San Marino
Switzerland

1948

BRUSSELS PACT: WEST EUROPEAN UNION
Belgium
France
German Federal Republic (1955)
Italy (1955)
Luxemburg
The Netherlands
United Kingdom

1949

NORTH ATLANTIC TREATY ORGANIZATION (NATO)
Belgium
Canada
Denmark
France
German Federal Republic (1955)
Greece (1952)
Iceland
Italy
Luxemburg
The Netherlands
Norway
Portugal
Turkey (1952)
United Kingdom
United States

1949

COUNCIL OF EUROPE
Austria (1956)
Belgium
Denmark
France
German Federal Republic (1951)
Greece
Iceland (1950)
Irish Republic
Italy
Luxemburg
The Netherlands
Norway
Portugal
Saar (1950–1956)
Sweden
Turkey
United Kingdom

1949

COUNCIL FOR MUTUAL ECONOMIC ASSISTANCE (COMECON)
Albania
Bulgaria
Czechoslovakia
German Democratic Republic
Hungary
Poland
Rumania
U.S.S.R.
Yugoslavia (Associate Member)

1951

EUROPEAN COAL AND STEEL COMMUNITY
(ECSC)
Belgium
France
German Federal Republic
Italy
Luxemburg
The Netherlands

1952

NORDIC COUNCIL
Denmark
Finland (1956)
Iceland
Norway
Sweden

1954

SOUTHEAST ASIA TREATY ORGANIZATION
(SEATO)
Australia
New Zealand
Pakistan
Philippines
Thailand
United Kingdom
United States

1955

WARSAW PACT: EASTERN SECURITY PACT
Albania
Bulgaria
Czechoslovakia
German Democratic Republic
Hungary
Poland
Rumania
U.S.S.R.
Yugoslavia (Associate Member)

1955

CENTRAL TREATY ORGANIZATION
(CENTO) (Formerly Baghdad Pact)
Iran
Iraq (withdrew 1959)
Pakistan
Turkey
United Kingdom
United States (Represented)

1958

EUROPEAN ECONOMIC COMMUNITY (EEC)
(Also called Inner Six, Common
Market)
Belgium
France
German Federal Republic
Greece (Associate Member)
Italy
Luxemburg
The Netherlands

1958

EUROPEAN ATOMIC ENERGY COMMUNITY
(EURATOM)
Belgium
France
German Federal Republic
Italy
Luxemburg
The Netherlands

1960

ORGANIZATION FOR ECONOMIC COOPERA-
TION AND DEVELOPMENT (OECD)
Austria
Belgium
Canada
Denmark
Finland (Associate Member)
France

German Federal Republic
Greece
Iceland
Irish Republic
Italy
Japan (Associate Member)
Luxemburg
The Netherlands
Norway
Portugal
Spain
Sweden
Switzerland
Turkey
United Kingdom
United States
Yugoslavia

1960

EUROPEAN FREE TRADE ASSOCIATION
   (EFTA) (Also called Outer Seven)
   Austria
   Denmark
   Finland (Associate Member)
   Norway
   Portugal
   Sweden
   Switzerland
   United Kingdom

1963

PARTIAL NUCLEAR TEST BAN
   United Kingdom
   United States
   U.S.S.R.

Illustration Acknowledgments

Grateful acknowledgment is extended to the kind owners of those private collections that were made available during the preparation of this work and to the following:

Archives Nationales, Musée de l'Histoire de France (AE II 1316): 311.

Archives Photographiques, Paris: 53.

The Bettmann Archive: 10, 18, 24, 34, 36, 54, 84, 87, 116, 125, 139, 143, 158, 169, 171, 173, 179, 186, 204, 214, 232, 241, 249, 261, 269, 282, 330, 332, 365, 392, 398, 408, 444, 487, 489, 508, 529, 544, 551.

Bibliothèque Nationale, Paris: 306.

British Information Service: 701.

British Museum, London: 236; Sloane Collection, 224.

Brown Brothers: 386, 634.

Charivari (1848): 414.

Firestone Library, Princeton University: 511, 520, 535, 569.

Galleria Degli Uffizi, Firenze: 50.

Ghent Cathedral, Belgium: 383.

Illustrated London News (1848): 411.

Le Journal pour rire (1848): 567.

Don Kurtis: 738.

Library of Congress: 38.

Musée Carnavalet, Paris: 465.

Musée Nationale du Louvre, Paris: 563.

By courtesy of the Trustees, the National Gallery, London: 67.

Collection of the Newark Museum: 737.

New York Public Library: 62, 264, 417, 423, 424, 521, 628.

The New York Times: 612.

Official U.S. Army Photograph: 696.

Official U.S. Navy Photograph: 684.

Reproduced by permission of the Proprietors of *Punch*: 510, 555, 593, 601, 647.

Alan W. Richards, Princeton, New Jersey: 728.

Royal Library, Windsor Castle, New Windsor: 65.

Sovfoto: 460, 498, 707.

United Nations: 713.

United Press International Newspictures: 655, 661.

War Department General Staff: 623.

Wide World Photos: 614, 640, 676, 679, 704, 721, 730, 733.

H. Van Zandt: 735.

INDEX

Index